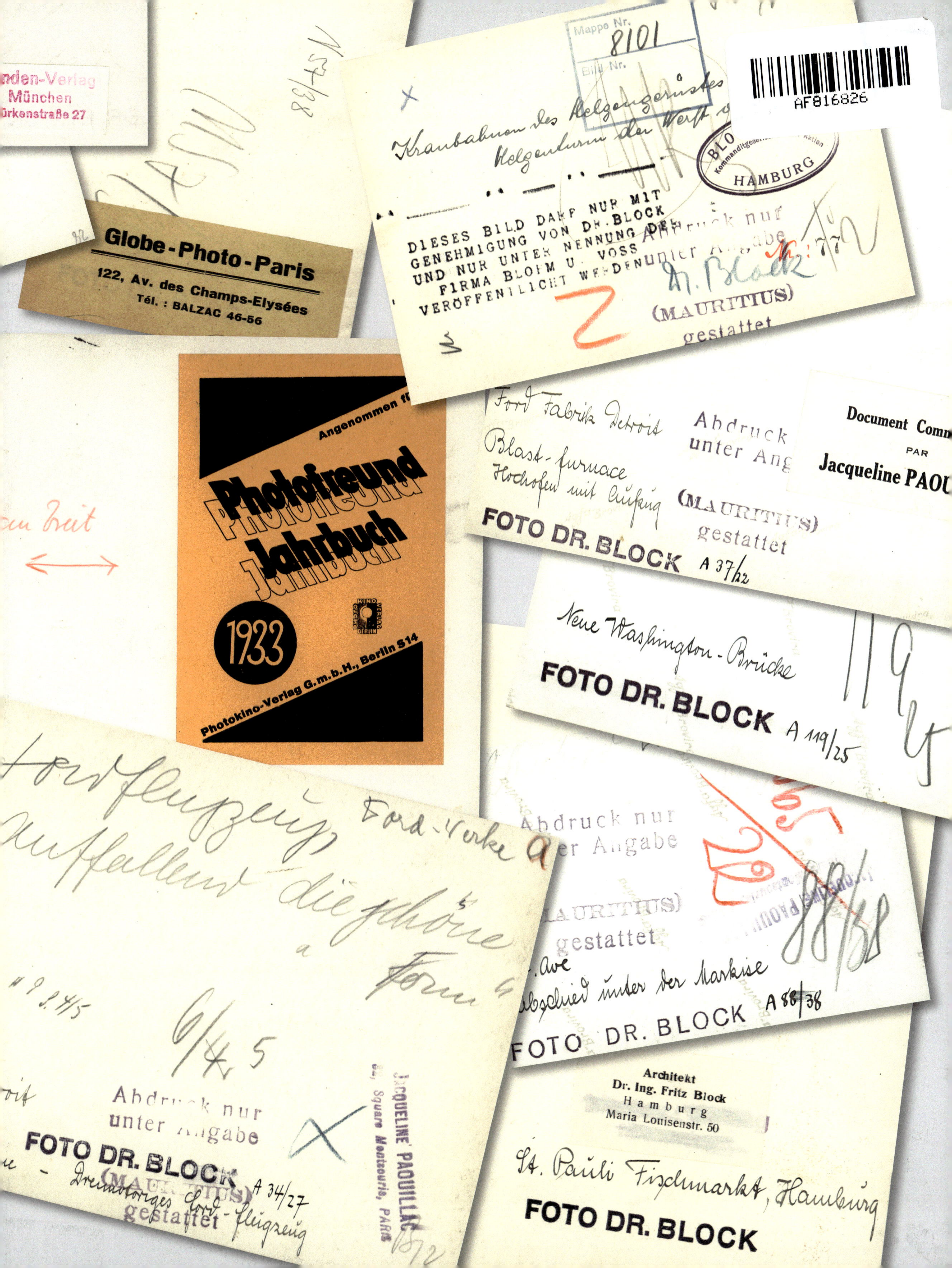

München
Globe-Photo-Paris
122, Av. des Champs-Elysées
Tél. : BALZAC 46-56
Mappe Nr.
8101
Bild Nr.
HAMBURG
DIESES BILD DARF NUR MIT
GENEHMIGUNG VON DR. BLOCK
UND NUR UNTER NENNUNG DER
FIRMA BLOHM U. VOSS
VERÖFFENTLICHT WERDEN
(MAURITIUS)
gestattet
Angenommen für
Photofreund Jahrbuch
1933
Photokino-Verlag G.m.b.H., Berlin S14
Ford Fabrik Detroit
Blast-furnace
Hochofen mit Aufzug
Abdruck nur
unter Angabe
(MAURITIUS)
gestattet
FOTO DR. BLOCK
A 37/22
Document Communiqué
PAR
Jacqueline PAOUILLAC
Neue Washington-Brücke
FOTO DR. BLOCK
A 119/25
Abdruck nur
unter Angabe
(MAURITIUS)
gestattet
Abschied unter der Markise
FOTO DR. BLOCK
A 88/38
Ford-Werke
Abdruck nur
unter Angabe
FOTO DR. BLOCK
(MAURITIUS)
gestattet
A 34/27
Dreimotoriges Ford-Flugzeug
JACQUELINE PAOUILLAC
64, Square Montsouris, PARIS
Architekt
Dr. Ing. Fritz Block
Hamburg
Maria Louisenstr. 50
St. Pauli Fischmarkt, Hamburg
FOTO DR. BLOCK

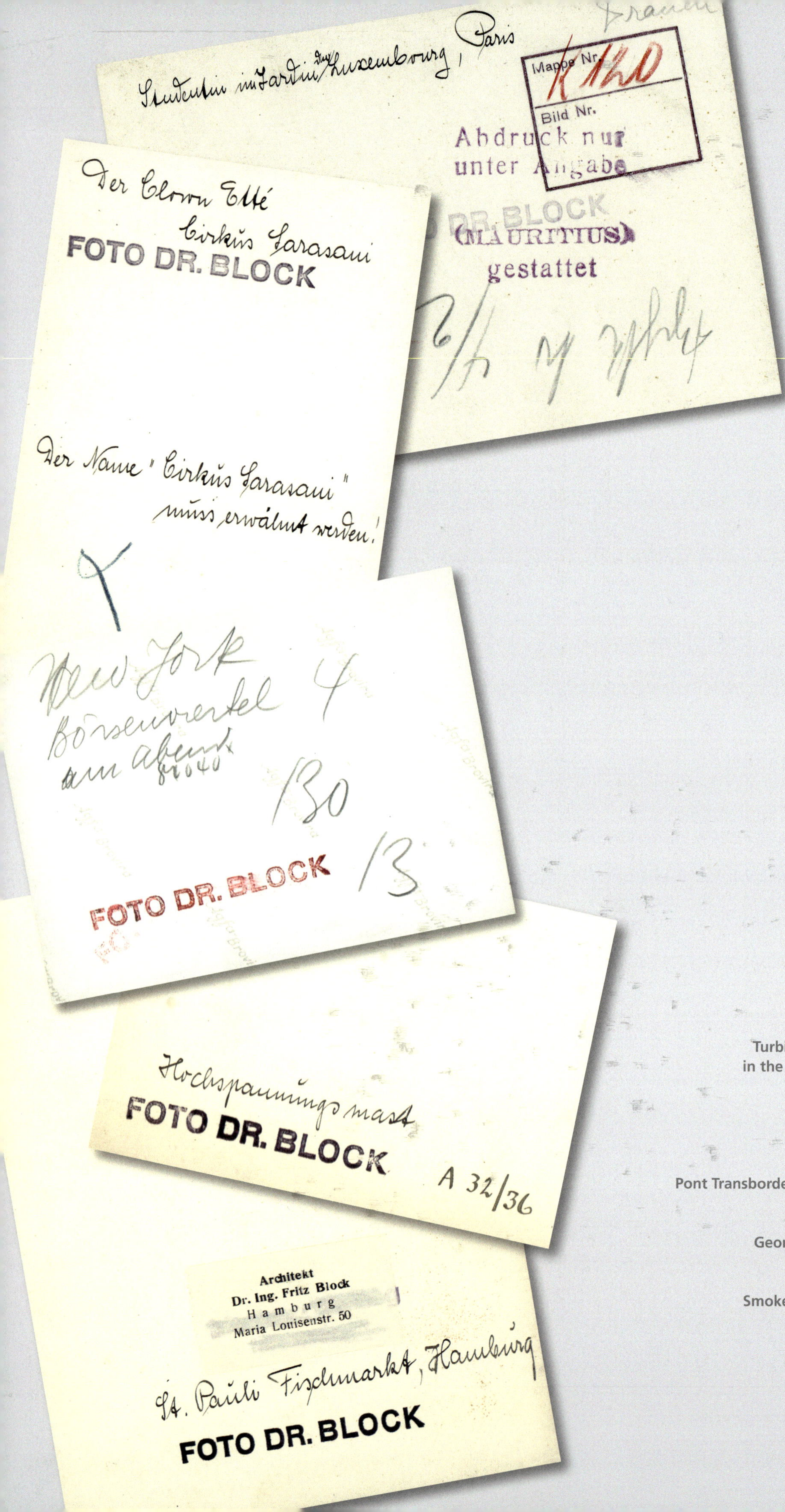

page 1
Turbine steamship *Europa* at a floating dock in the Blohm & Voss shipyard, Hamburg, 1929

page 2
New Elbe Bridge, Hamburg, 1929

page 3
Pont Transbordeur (Transporter Bridge), Marseille, 1931

page 4
George Washington Bridge, New York, 1931

page 5
Smokestacks of the Ford Factory in Dearborn, Detroit, 1931

page 6
Fritz Block, ca. 1932

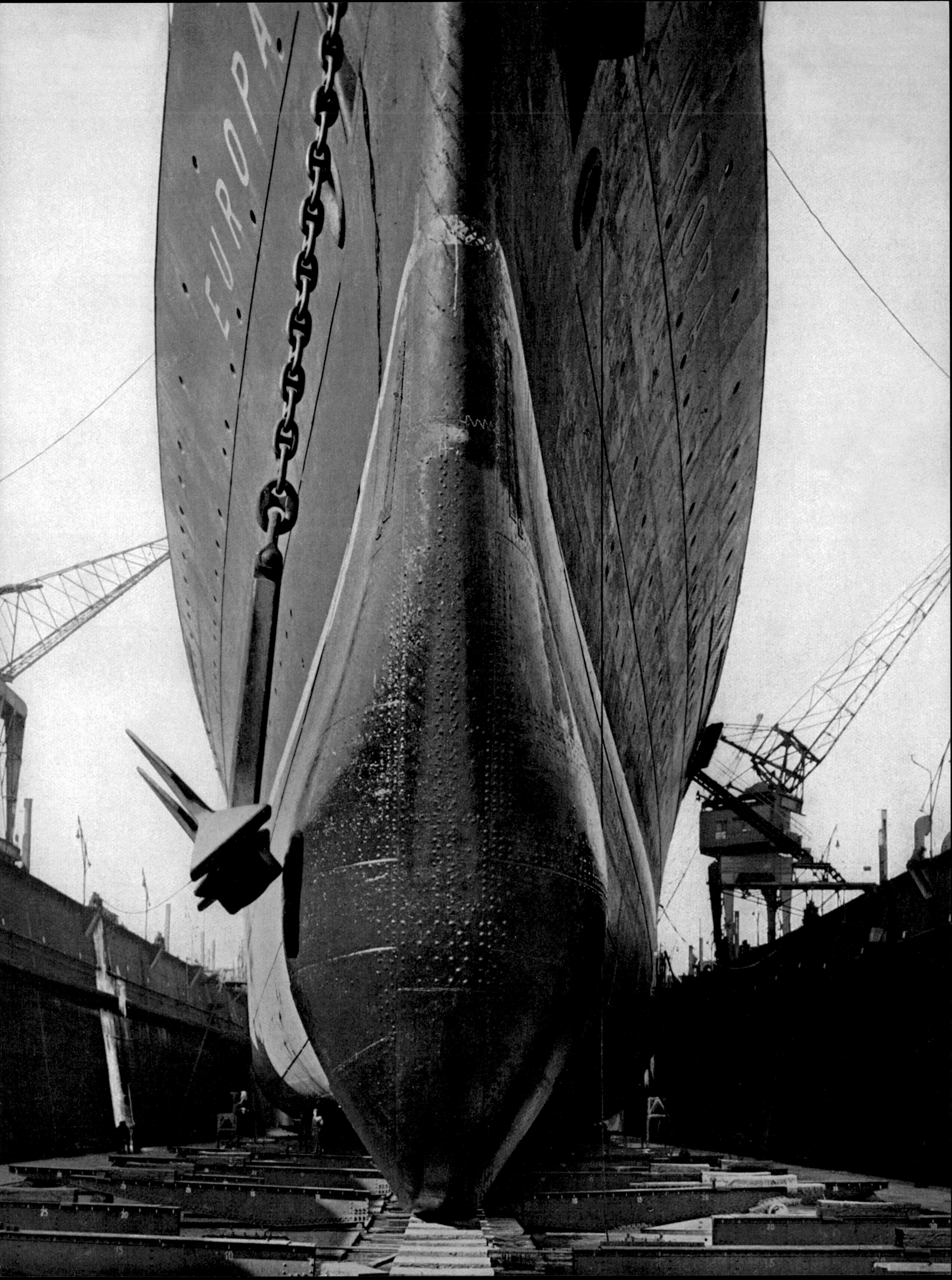
EUROPA

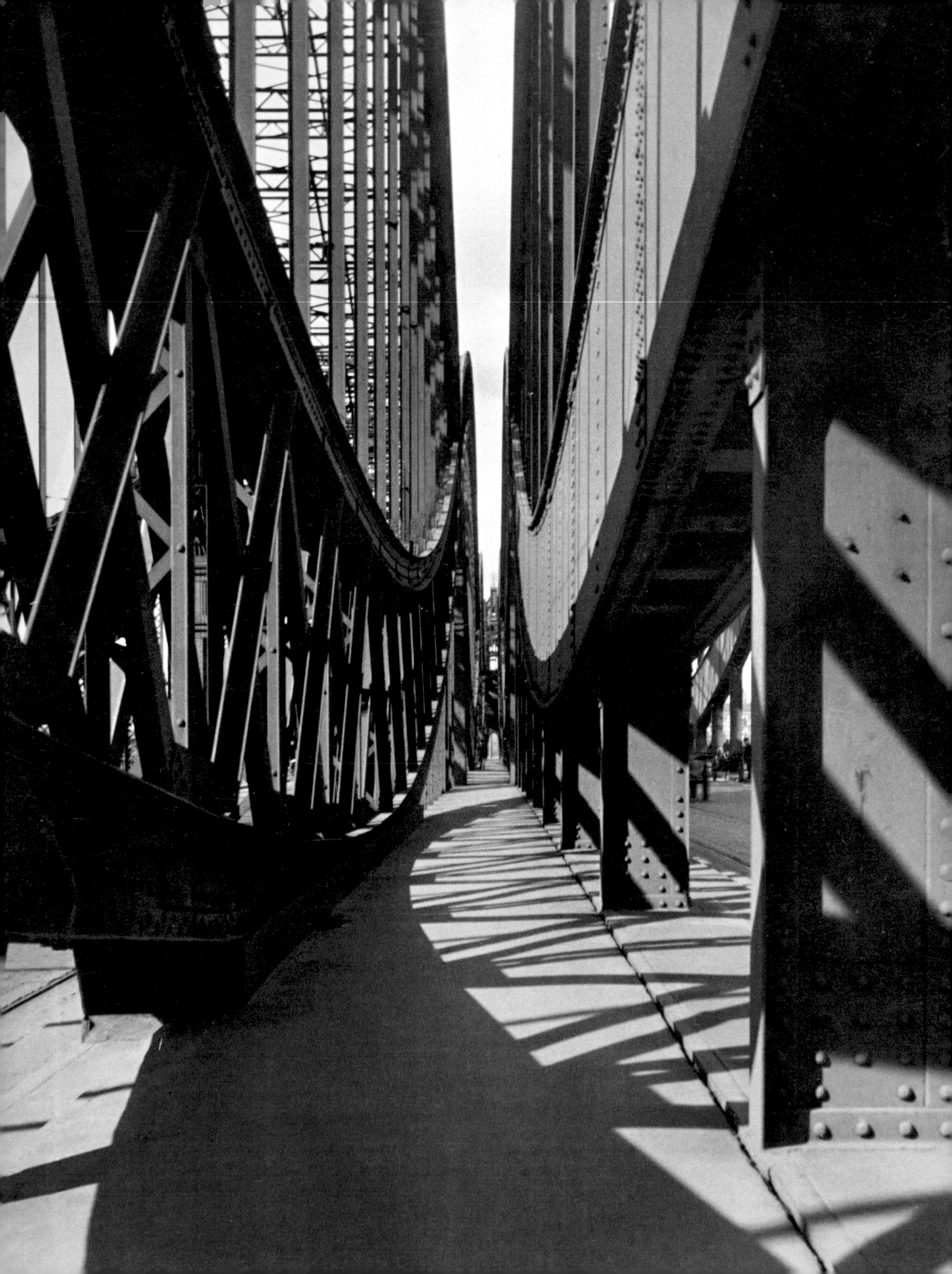

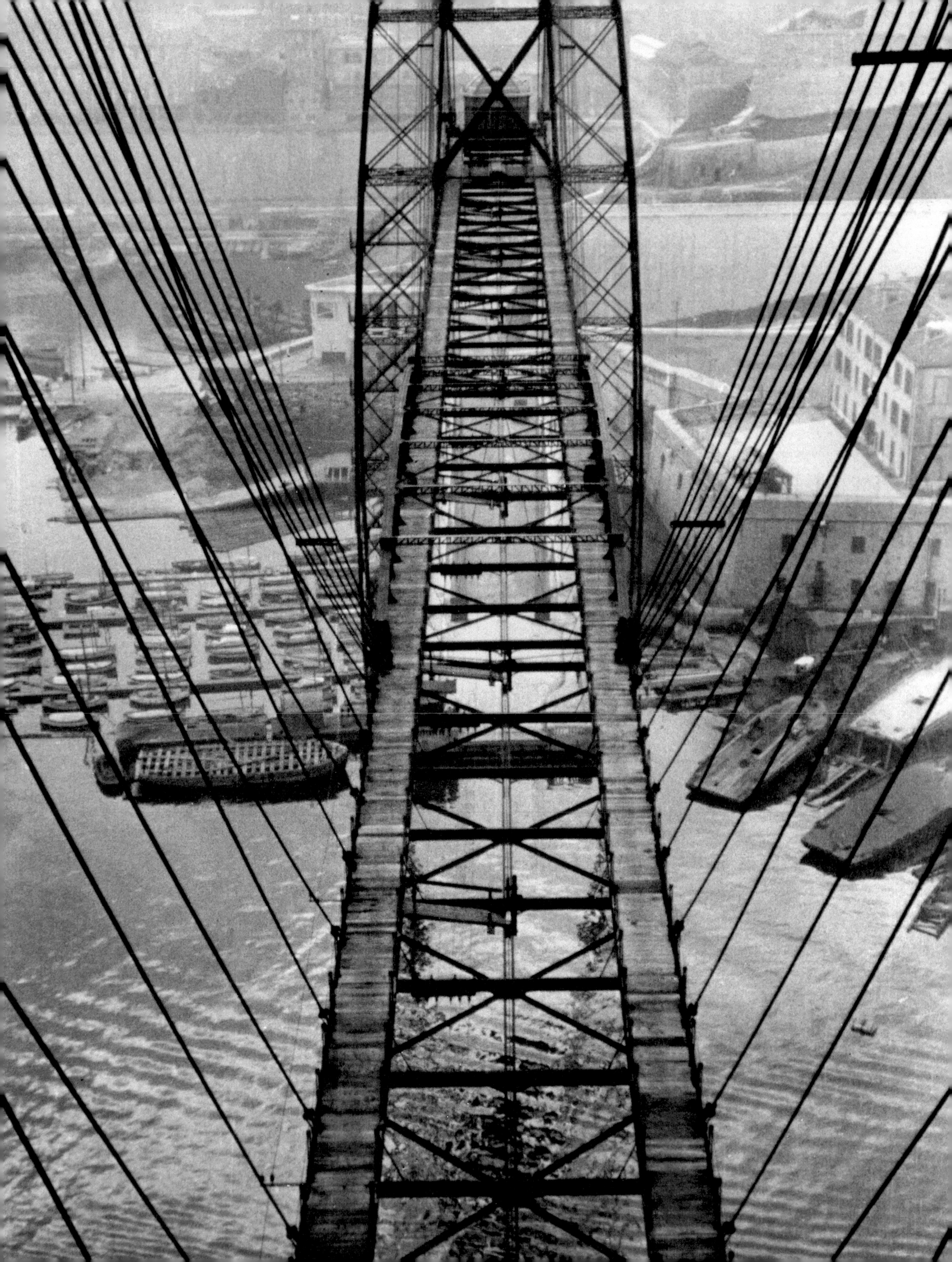

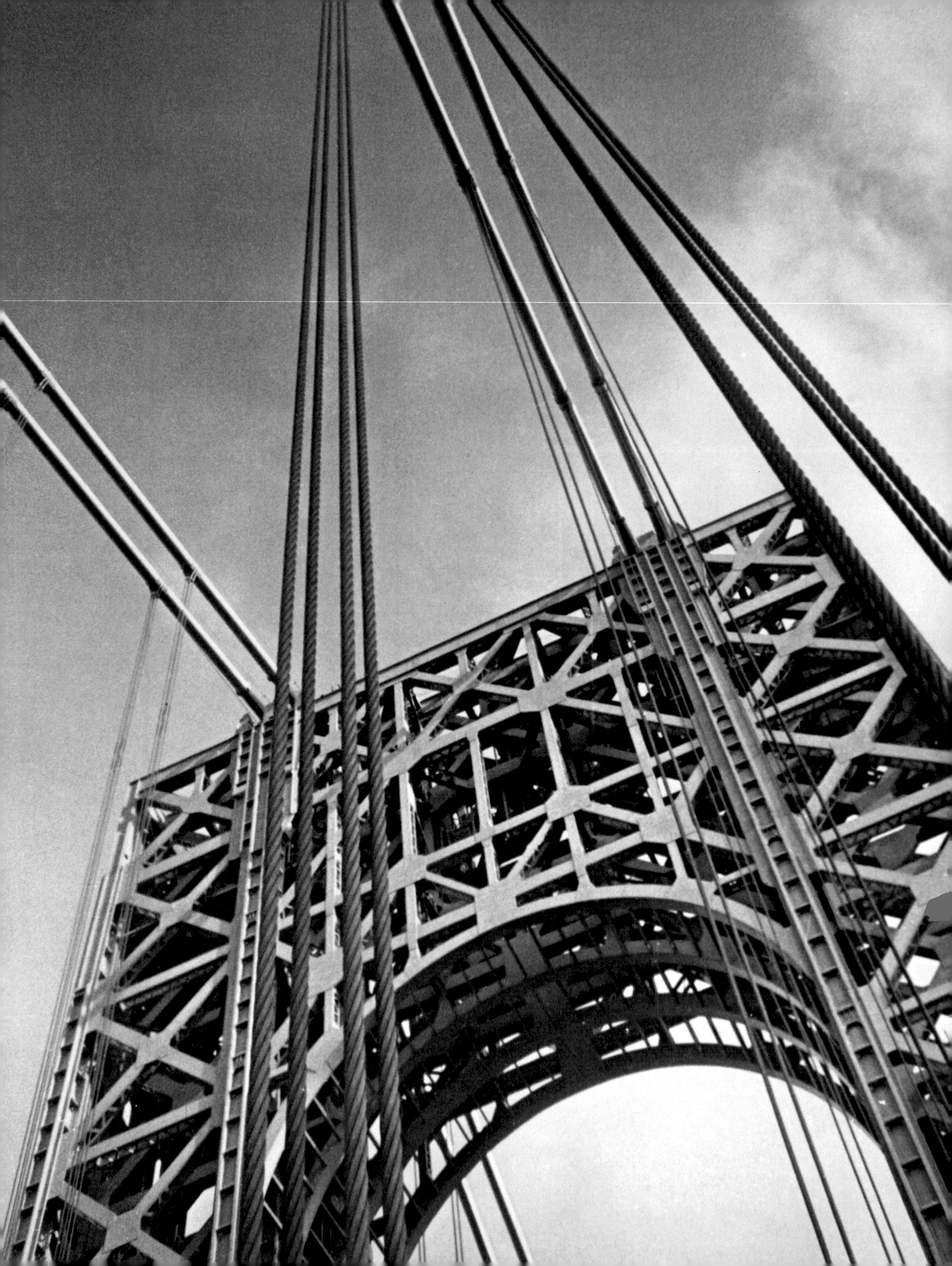

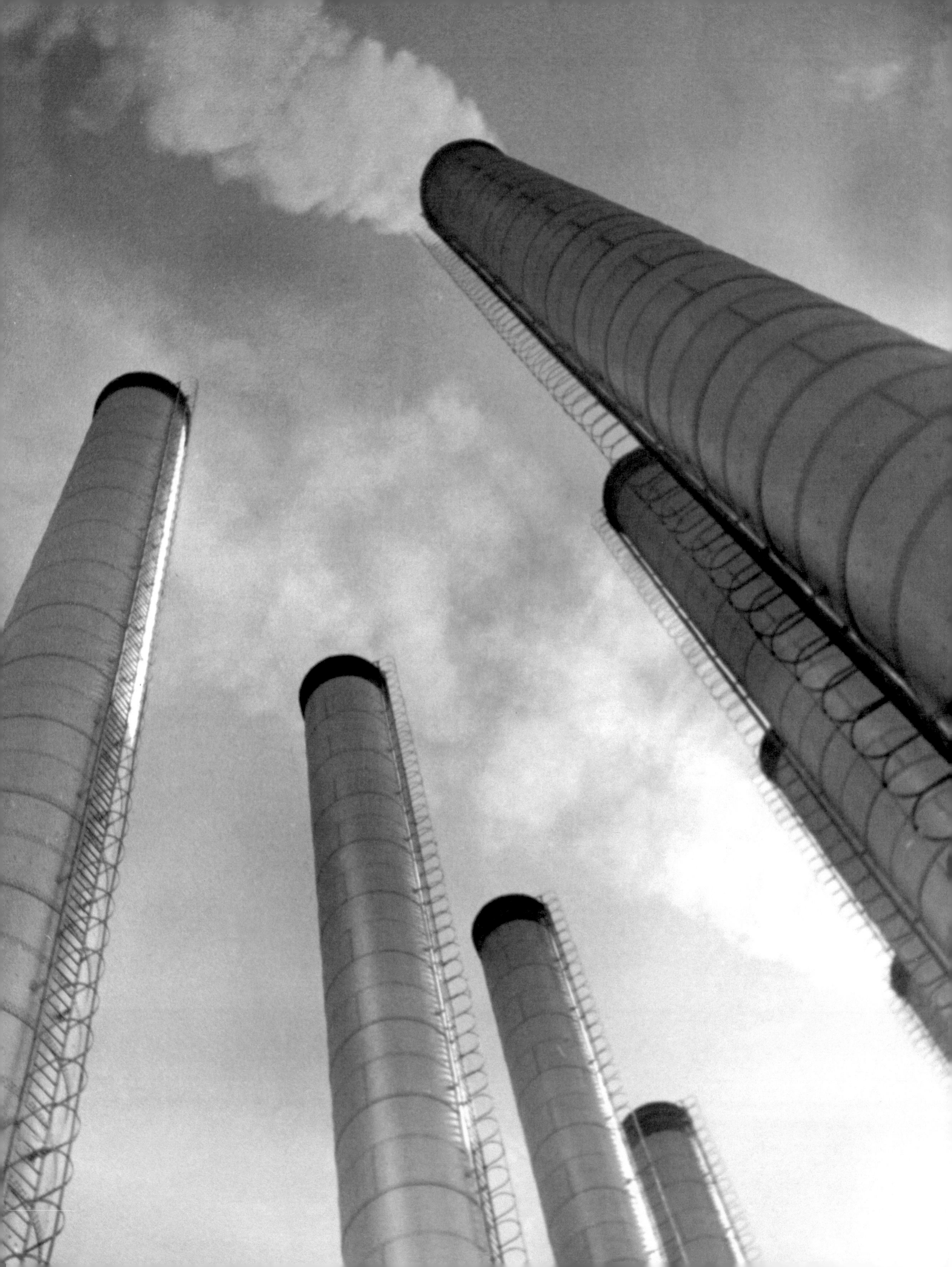

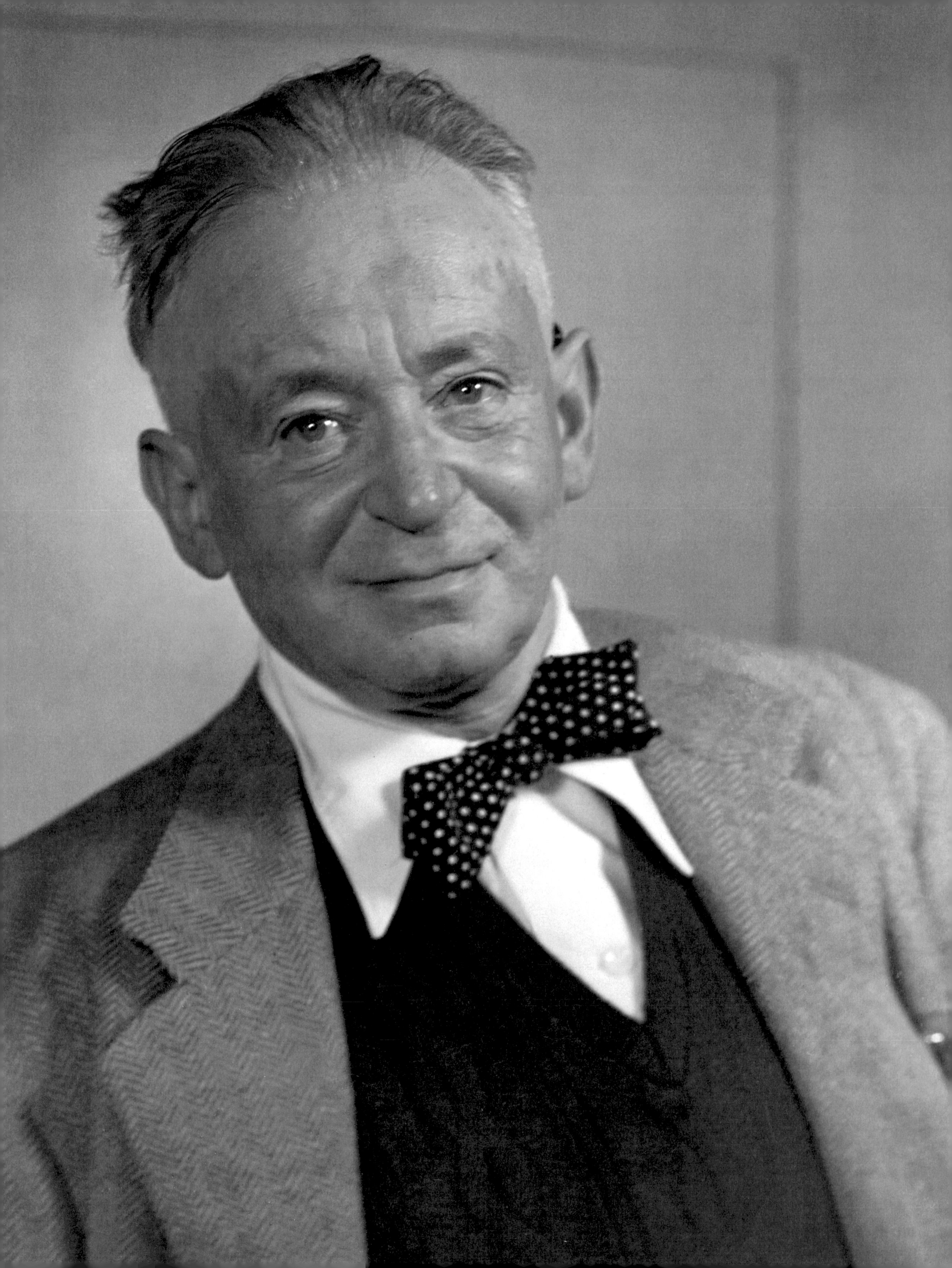

Roland Jaeger

PHOTO-EYE
FRITZ BLOCK
New Photography
Modern Color Slides

Scheidegger & Spiess

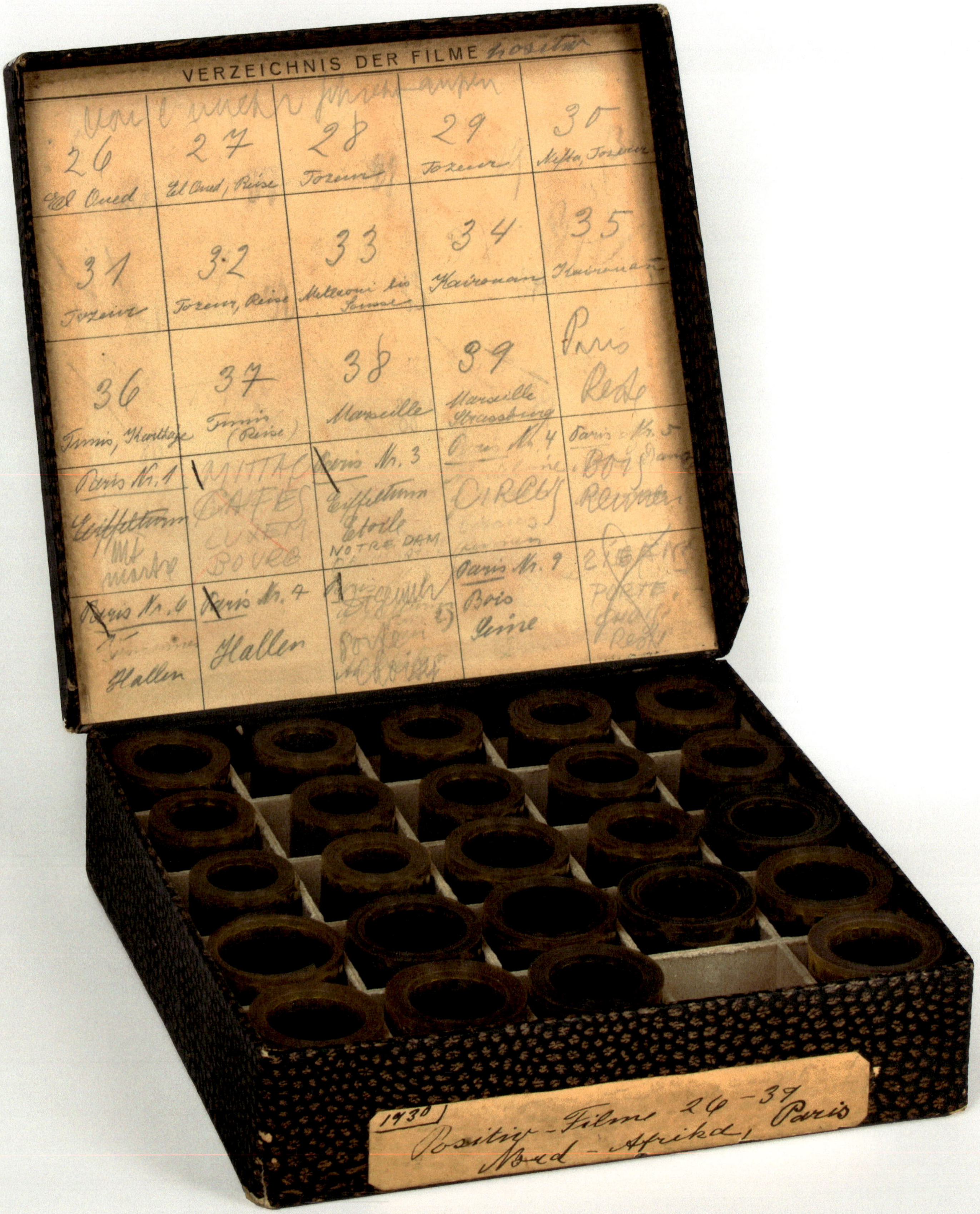
VERZEICHNIS DER FILME
26
El Oued
27
El Oued, Reise
28
Tozeur
29
Tozeur
30
Nefta, Tozeur
31
Tozeur
32
Tozeur, Reise
33
34
Kairouan
35
Kairouan
36
Tunis, Karthago
37
Tunis (Reise)
38
Marseille
39
Marseille Strassburg
Paris Rede
Paris Nr. 1
Paris Nr. 3
Paris Nr. 4
Paris Nr. 5
Paris Nr. 6
Paris Nr. 9
Hallen
1930
Positiv-Filme 26–39 Paris Nord-Afrika

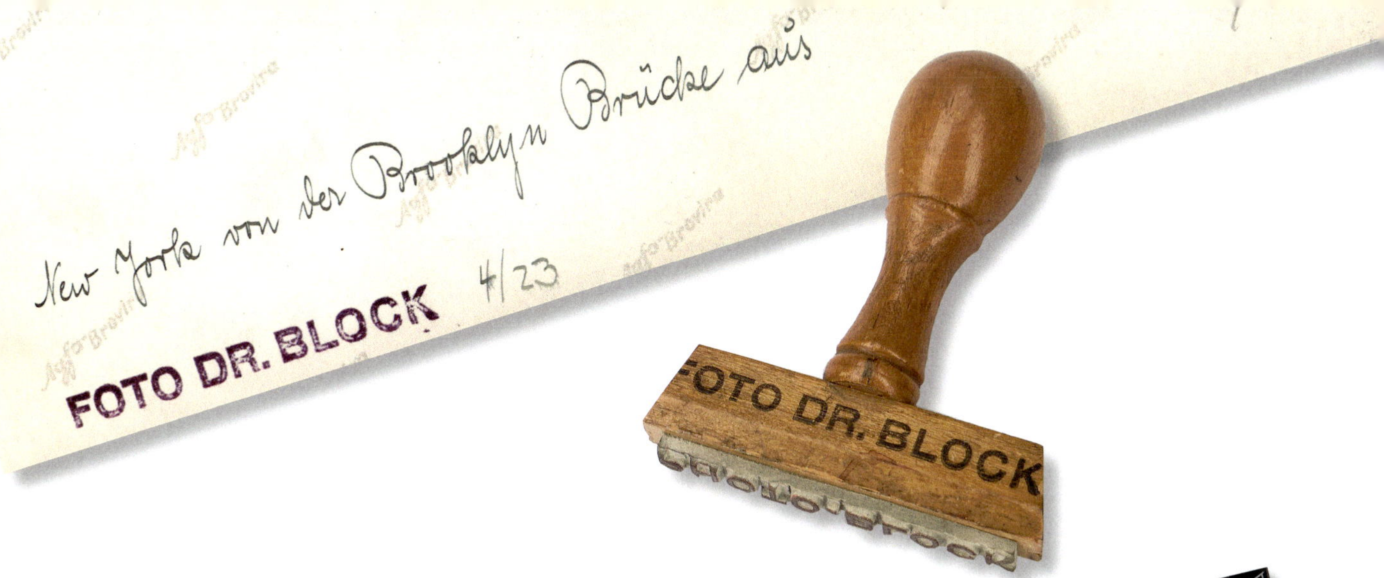
New York von der Brooklyn Brücke aus
4/23
FOTO DR. BLOCK
FOTO DR. BLOCK

AGFA ISOPAN F

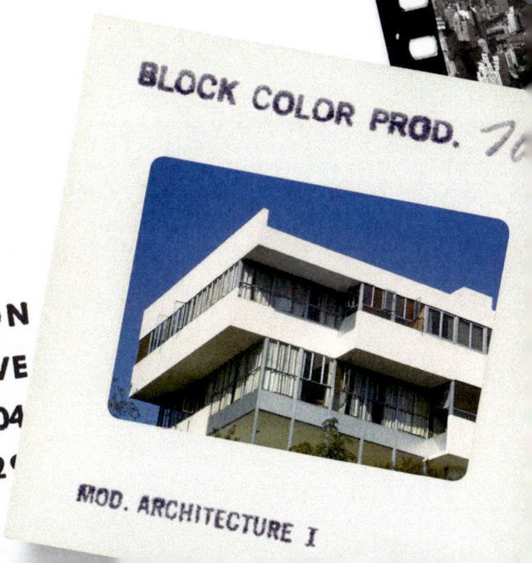
BLOCK COLOR PROD.
MOD. ARCHITECTURE I

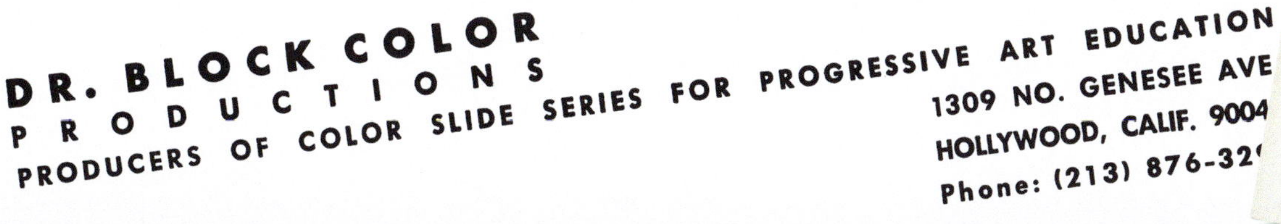
DR. BLOCK COLOR
PRODUCTIONS
PRODUCERS OF COLOR SLIDE SERIES FOR PROGRESSIVE ART EDUCATION
1309 NO. GENESEE AVE
HOLLYWOOD, CALIF. 9004
Phone: (213) 876-32

Finally Visible Again

A Figure in Modern Photography

Fritz Block? This is a name that does not appear in German or international histories of twentieth century photography. Nor can it be found in photographic lexicons. Block was a Jewish German photographer who began working in Hamburg in 1929, made photographs on a number of trips abroad, and continued his work in exile in the US as of 1939. Given the quality and range of works that he produced, gathered here for the first time in an extensive scope, this lack of recognition is astonishing—and calls for explanation.

One plausible reason is that Fritz Block (1889–1955) originally began his career as an architect, not as a photographer. In the 1920s in Germany he was among the enthusiastic adherents to Neues Bauen (New Architecture), the functionalist approach to modern architecture. In Hamburg he headed the architectural firm Dr. Block & Hochfeld with Ernst Hochfeld, a friend from his student days. Their main work was the Deutschlandhaus built in 1928/29 in Hamburg, a modern office building with a dynamic, rounded façade reminiscent of the style of Erich Mendelsohn, which included Europe's largest cinema at the time. Block was also an active member of the Deutscher Werkbund (German Association of Craftsmen) and the Bund Deutscher Architekten (Association of German Architects). He took part in exhibitions, held slide lectures, and published in architectural journals. In addition, he was the editor of an important book at the time in the debate surrounding housing, *Probleme des Bauens* (The Problems of Building, 1928, published in late 1927), which included contributions by well-known architects such as Walter Gropius, Richard J. Neutra, and others. For Block, the aims and mission of modernism did not merely apply to design but also to the promotion of ideas.

New Objectivity and New Vision

Not until 1929 did Block start working as a photographer. The initial impetus came from his desire to document the construction of the Deutschlandhaus in photographs. The architect not only approached the task with technical finesse and artistic talent, but he also possessed a highly developed visual sensibility—which compensated for his hereditary deafness—a veritable photographic eye. As a photographer, Block was self-taught, but he did not consider himself an amateur. Instead, he saw photography as a contemporary medium of artistic expression that corresponded with his concept of architecture. In contrast to professional photographers, he did not primarily pursue photography as a source of income. However, the decline in building activity as a result of the global economic crisis soon led to the architect having more time to take photographs and publish his photographs in illustrated magazines.

Block was not an avant-garde photographer, but his work was on par with the proponents of New Photography in the period around 1930. He used a small-format Leica, which, due to its light handling, was suited for the kind of travel and reportage photography that he preferred. He found inspiration in the works of like-minded photographers, the emerging genre of the photo book, and, not least, photographic reportages in the illustrated press. At first Block's photographs reflected the sensibility of New Objectivity, creating cropped compositions of objects and forms. He also shared his contemporaries' fascination for technology and the study of nature. In addition, his architect's eye for constructive shapes and structures characterizes many of his photographs. At the same time, Block possessed a good instinct for striking depictions of people in various everyday and working situations. In general he tended to focus more on series of thematically related images that form a photo reportage than individual motifs.

Clearly visible is Block's initial affinity for the works of Albert Renger-Patzsch, who also was active as a photographer in Hamburg in 1928/29. In a regional context, there are parallels between Block's work and that of the Hamburg photographers Arvid Gutschow and Ernst Scheel. At first, Block's attention was primarily captured by the technical visual world of Hamburg's harbor. However, he soon developed a broader spectrum of motifs. For example, his circus photographs recall similar works by Umbo and Sasha Stone, and his animal photographs bear similarity to the images of Dr. Paul Wolff. Furthermore, Block experimented with the vocabulary of New Vision, which included unusual perspectives, inverted negatives, and X-rays. Blocks photographic oeuvre is thus exemplary for the characteristic facets of New Photography in Germany.

"The modern photo is simply the most powerful expression of our time: clear, straightforward, and internationally intelligible."

Fritz Block, 1931

Urban and Travel Photography

His specialty, however, was the kind of urban and travel photography that typified the era and lent expression to his far-ranging cultural interests. This took Block to Paris, among other places, where, like Germaine Krull, he photographed the iron construction of the Eiffel Tower, and also to Marseille, where he climbed the Pont Transbordeur to obtain a view from above, as did László Moholy-Nagy, Herbert Bayer, and other photographers. His trip to the US in the fall of 1931 was particularly fruitful, during which he produced some 4,000 photographs. In New York he took photos of the recently finished George Washington Bridge, which recall images by Edward Steichen from the same period, and in Detroit he managed to take photographs of the Ford Factory that have parallels with motifs in Charles Sheeler's now iconic photographs. With his reportage-like photographs of everyday scenes in major cities like Paris or New York, Block also produced early examples of street photography.

During this time, Block published a number of photographs and photo reportages in German magazines, and his work was also distributed in France and Switzerland through photo agencies. Reproductions of his photographs were printed in the Deutsche Werkbund journal *Die Form*, the architectural journal *Baugilde,* the Ullstein-magazine *Der Querschnitt*, and the photographic yearbooks *Das Deutsche Lichtbild* and *Photofreund-Jahrbuch*. Block planed illustrated books on Hamburg and Paris, but due to the vicissitudes of the time, he was never able to publish a photo book. A volume planned in 1931 by art historian Franz Roh for his photo book series *Fototek*, in which Block was to represent modern photography from Hamburg (along with Arvid Gutschow and Ernst Scheel), never came to fruition.

Although Block did not take part in the exhibition *Film und Foto* of the Deutscher Werkbund—which was first mounted in Stuttgart in 1929 and played a seminal role in establishing New Photography—he was included in the 1930 *Internationale Ausstellung "Das Lichtbild"* (International Exhibition "The Photograph") in Munich that developed out of the first exhibition. He also participated in the *Internationale Foto-Ausstellung* (International Photo Exhibition) in Hamburg in 1932, which was based on the leading private collection of modern photography at the time, of Dresden industrialist Kurt Kirchbach. Subsequently a number of the Block's America photos that had been shown in Hamburg were acquired for the collection. Within three years the architect thus managed to be accepted into the circle of the international avant-garde as a photographer.

The fact that Block has gone unrecognized in the history of photography, despite his level of achievement at the time, is certainly due to the upheavals of the era. After the assumption of power by the National Socialists, as a "Jewish" photographer, from the spring of 1933 onward he was not allowed to publish anymore (and was also prohibited from working as a self-employed architect). In response, he only took photographs on his trips abroad, for example in 1933 on flight with a zeppelin to Rio de Janeiro (on board was also the photographer Alfred Eisenstaedt). After the technical and scientific motifs and photographic innovations of the 1920s had been exhausted, Block focused on photographing people in the 1930s. When he had the opportunity, he still managed to produce striking series of images, which include his photographs of Petticoat Lane Market in London from 1935, which recall similar photographs by Moholy-Nagy. During a world cruise in 1938, which given the threatening situation and racial persecutions in Germany also served the purpose of scouting out potential exile destinations, Block predominantly photographed the faces of the people in the countries he visited, creating portraits of the diversity within the "family of man."

Educational Color Photography in Exile

In November 1938 Block and his wife managed to emigrate to the US, and he was able to bring along a portion of his household belongings, library, and photographic archive. Living in exile in Los Angeles, he was not able to take up work again as an architect for a number of reasons. Instead, Block made photography, which he had previously pursued more as a hobby, into his main profession. However, he did not continue with black-and-white photography but soon turned to color photography, which had taken off in the late 1930s in the US with the introduction and popularization of small-format slide film (Kodachrome). At the age of

"I have not mentioned artistic skill, since for me this is a self-evident prerequisite that is better confirmed by achievement than words."

Fritz Block, 1932

fifty Block thus began a new phase of life as a "color photographer" Starting from a commission to produce visual aides for schools in Los Angeles, he established a one-person company, Dr. Block Color Productions, which produced the innovative format of color slide series, which focused on the topics of architecture, art, nature, technology, and design for modern art education at American universities, colleges, and schools. The Museum of Modern Art in New York was particularly supportive of his work and allowed his slides to be loaned.

Block's artistic focus thus shifted towards pedagogical aims, in which the individual image was less important than the impact and concept of the series, designed to convey a specific content. In addition, he studied theories of color perception and promoted the establishment of "educational color libraries" as a contemporary way of supplementing the visual offerings of a museum. Since Block maintained an interest in architecture, his images of exemplary buildings of modern architecture in the American West were a point of emphasis in his color slide production. Although these images are not as spectacular as those of professional architectural photographer Julius Shulman, who still primarily worked in black and white at the time, they present the buildings and interiors of Frank Lloyd Wright, Richard J. Neutra, and others in color for the first time—from an everyday perspective and with an architect's eye for functional details.

This phase of Block's work has been neglected in the history of photography, largely because his color photography was focused on the production and distribution of color slides. Also, he did not produce color prints, and due to a lack of opportunities to publish there are no printed versions of his images. However, in 1950 Block was included in the *Color Photography Exhibition,* the first exhibition of the Museum of Modern Art dealing with color photography, along with famous photographers ranging from Ansel Adams to Paul Outerbridge and Edward Weston. So here too, he achieved a level of recognition within the circle of the international avant-garde. However, his contribution was sufficiently lacking in terms of an explicit artistic intention or vocabulary to gain a lasting place in the history of color photography. At the same time, Block's Educational Color Photography represents a unique achievement within the field of photography in exile that hitherto has also not received appropriate attention.

Rediscovery and Reconstruction

Block became an American citizen in 1944, never once returned to his native country, and died in Los Angeles in 1955. In postwar Germany, he was forgotten as an architect and photographer. Since Block had never sold any prints, and because his estate remained in private hands, his works are not represented in any museums or private photography collections. This has also contributed to the lack of historical attention given to his achievement or exhibitions including his work. The same applies to the international photo market. One exception is the handful of prints from photographs taken during his America trip and stemming from the former Kirchbach Collection, which was auctioned in 1997 in London and in 2005 in Berlin. Although Block's color slides are part of institutional collections in the US, they were not archived as examples of his artistic activities. In addition, since the slides are always duplicates, they lack the character of a unique work of art. Finally, given the changes in the use of media, these slides are generally no longer in use.

The rediscovery of Fritz Block did not take place through his photography per se but due to a reawakened interest in the architecture of the 1920s in Germany during the 1970s. This was accompanied by a new look at cultural contributions made by German Jews to the Weimar Republic and research into their biographies of exile. At least a brief survey of Block's photographic activities was included in a monograph on the work of the architectural firm Dr. Block & Hochfeld published in 1996. On the occasion of the fiftieth anniversary of his death, the magazine *Leica Fotografie international* published a two-part portfolio, which showed a cross-section of his photographic oeuvre. Since then an increased interest in the history of photography from the 1920s to the 1940s, and certainly in photo books and illustrated magazines from this period, has provided more fertile ground for a better recognition and appreciation of Block's photographic work.

"A library of first-class color slides could take on an educational value equal to that of our museums."

Fritz Block, ca. 1950

This book has been conceived as a combination of a ››documentary‹‹ monograph and an "artistic" photo book. A conscious attempt has been made to diverge from the conventions of most illustrated photography books, which include an introductory essay followed by a section of illustrations with individual images centrally positioned on each page. The arrangement of the illustrations attempts to avoid foregrounding the aesthetic impact of individual images and instead shows the photographs in a larger context. The book's graphic design is also aimed to present the works in a way that is in keeping with the versatility of this photographer and the wide range of visual material that he produced. Following a biographical section tracing the development of Block's career from an architect to a photographer is a chronological representation of the various phases of his work, accompanied by texts that give a more detailed picture than the brief account presented here. These are illustrated with relevant series of images and examples of his photographs in print. Full-page images at the beginning of the book (black-and-white) and the end (color) mark the two poles of Block's oeuvre, both in biographical and photographic terms.

From an Estate Archive to a Photo Book

The materials in the photographer's estate formed the basis for the reconstructive survey of his work and thus also this monograph. Although these materials do not cover his entire production, they can offer a representative and meaningful overview. This is possible thanks to Block's wife Anna-Sophie, née Levy (1895–1986), who maintained his archive in Los Angeles until her death. It then passed to her niece, Ingrid Levy-Hüneberg of Stockholm, where it has been preserved in the ownership of the family. The architectural portion of the estate and a certain amount of Block's photographic materials were donated in 1986 to what is today known as the Architecture and Design Collection at the Art, Design & Architecture Museum of the University of California, Santa Barbara. These holdings were researched for this volume as well.

The visual material for the book was selected from several hundred prints—largely vintage prints by Block dating from around 1930 and some original prints from 1939, the beginning of his exile in Los Angeles. The prints almost all stem from small-format negatives and are 17 × 23 cm or smaller. Their quality and their condition are not always perfect. However, in favor of authenticity the decision was made not to radically optimize the digital versions of these images for printing. In cases in which prints did not exist, recourse was made to the small-format negatives, that is negative or positive rolls of film in the estate, which also clearly bear the marks of time. In contrast, Block's color slides, dating from 1940 onward, have been preserved in large numbers, both as originals and duplicates. In this case the challenge was to make a selection and decide how to accentuate motifs of photographic and architectural interest.

The date of the prints, which is not indicated on the photographs themselves, is largely taken from the details of Block's life, his travel documentation, and publications. In the case of the color slides, at least the date is known, when each individual series was produced. The image titles are taken from the notes made on the back of the prints by Block, or when these are lacking, the titles simply reflect what is shown. For the color slides, the titles are taken from the explanatory sheets accompanying each series. To a certain extent, publications including Block's work were preserved in the archive, but in some cases they were researched specially for this monograph. The ongoing digitalization of illustrated magazines may lead to more discoveries of Block's work in the future.

This compilation of Block's oeuvre demonstrates both to what extent his work was aligned with the photography of his era and also his unique contribution. It recounts the productive life's work of a Jewish German individual, which spanned modern photography in Germany and color photography in America. The reexamination enabled by this book highlights a remarkable figure in modern photography, making his work finally visible again and thus reclaiming his name for the history of photography: Fritz Block!

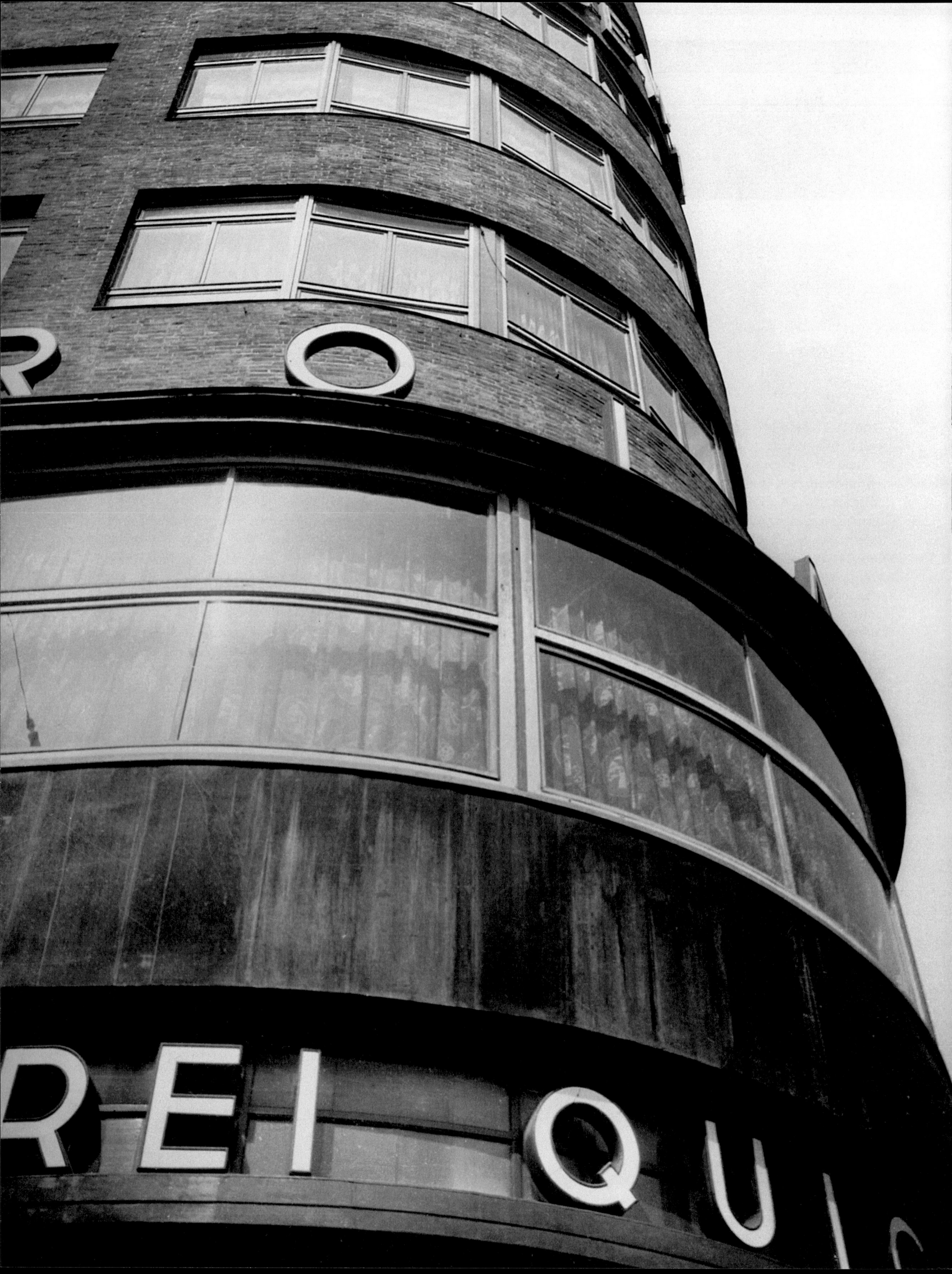
R O
REI QUI

Modern Architecture and New Photography

An Architect Turns Photographer

In the 1920s, a mutually productive relationship between architecture and photography evolved in Germany: Modern Architecture became an important subject for New Objectivity photographers, and architectural photography played a significant role in the growing genre of architectural journalism and publishing—and thus in the propagation of modern architectural concepts.[1] There were also similarities of both form and content in the design and dissemination of contemporary building and its principles. Swept up by the era's general enthusiasm for photography, a number of architects picked up their cameras to document the construction process of their buildings, or to capture architectural impressions while traveling. When they needed professional documentation—for example, for publications—they usually commissioned specialized architectural photographers.[2] In most cases, photography remained peripheral to architects' professional activity; that is, they did not harbor photo-artistic ambitions.

The best-known example of an architect fond of taking photos is Erich Mendelsohn, who used his own photographs to illustrate his books *Amerika* (1926; second edition, 1928) and *Russland – Europa – Amerika* (1929).[3] Nevertheless, photography remained for Mendelsohn an interlude. The pictures architect Walter Gropius made during his 1928 trip to America were not published at the time.[4] Richard J. Neutra, on the other hand, used his own photographs early on to illustrate his architectural reports from the United States.[5] Architect Konrad Wachsmann's photographs, reproduced in two 1934 brochures, about Salzburg and Berlin, were taken with photographic design in mind.[6] Fritz Block's photography was initially an extra-occupational hobby that began in 1929. He then engaged in it with increasing intensity and developed it into an independent form of artistic expression, alongside his architectural practice. Later, in American exile, Block adopted photography as his main profession—and architecture as one of his most important subjects. In terms of numbers, no architect of the twentieth century created such a large and varied photographic body of work as Fritz Block.

Life as an Architect

Fritz Block was born on January 13, 1889, in Warburg (Westphalia), son of a Jewish merchant family.[7] In 1908, he began architectural training at the technical universities of Karlsruhe, Munich, Darmstadt, and Dresden. He completed his studies in 1913, and then undertook a study trip to southern France; in 1915, he received a doctorate in engineering in Dresden. Although he illustrated his publications on architectural history with photographic images, it is questionable whether he took the photographs himself; at that time, freehand drawing was his preferred method of documentation.[8] At the outbreak of the First World War, Block was disqualified from military field service because of a hearing impairment; he thus initially served as a paramedic. Beginning in August 1916, he worked in the Department of Planning and Construction of Königsberg (then part of Prussia). In 1918, he was awarded the prestigious Staatspreis für Architektur (Schinkelpreis) (National Award for Architecture) by the Architekten-Verein zu Berlin (Berlin Association of Architects). In 1920, Block published his project for a Jewish hospital in Königsberg, which was never executed.

After Block's university friend Ernst Hochfeld won the competition for a veterans' memorial at the Jewish cemetery in Hamburg-Ohlsdorf, the two architects moved to the Hanseatic city, in 1921, and founded the architectural firm Dr. Block & Hochfeld.[9] In 1922, they became members of the Bund Deutscher Architekten (Association of German Architects) and, in 1924, of the Deutscher Werkbund (German Association of Craftsmen). In 1925, an overview of their architectural projects was published as a monographic issue of the magazine *Neue Baukunst*.[10] In the following years, Dr. Block & Hochfeld belonged to the exponents of the Neues Bauen (New Architecture) movement in Hamburg. They represented the concepts of contemporary objective-functional architecture—cubic structures, flat roofs, and rational floor plans. In 1928, they created a modern

Detail of the Deutschlandhaus façade, Hamburg, 1930

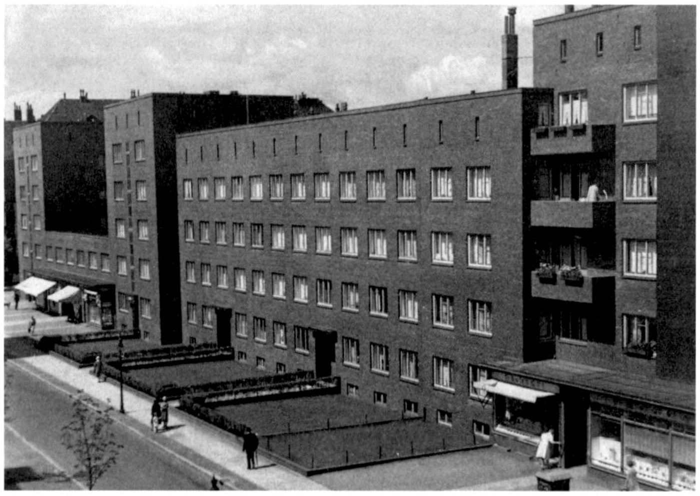
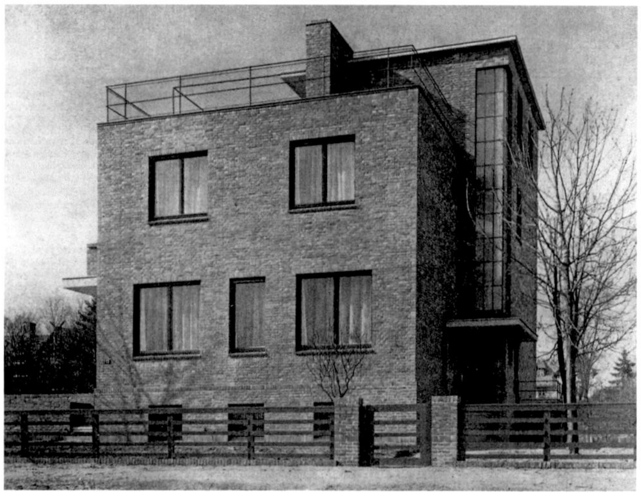

Dr. Block & Hochfeld, housing block (1928/29) and Philip Residence (1928, photo: Ernst Scheel), Hamburg

brickstone mansion, Haus Philip [p. 16]. That same year, with their contribution to the residential area Jarrestadt [p. 16], they took on one of the most important construction tasks in Germany: the building of small apartment complexes. In 1929–30, they executed rows of housing in Hamburg-Wandsbek [p. 17], the most advanced form of housing construction at the time.

Dr. Block & Hochfeld's major work of 1928/29—and simultaneously their largest commission—the Deutschlandhaus was a modern commercial building with offices and retail spaces and an innovative fast-food restaurant [pp. 17 and 20–25], located at the Gänsemarkt, a busy square in the center of Hamburg. The building became known for how it boldly integrated the courtyard Ufa-Palast, at the time one of largest cinemas in Europe. The Deutschlandhaus was a modern steel-skeleton construction overlaid with the brick cladding typical of Hamburg buildings. The dynamically rounded façade, rimmed with windows, was inspired by the traffic pattern on the streets below. Compared to the Hanseatic city's conventional merchant architecture, the Deutschlandhaus, reminiscent of buildings by Erich Mendelsohn, conveyed the seminal impression of metropolitan modernity. During the bombing of Hamburg in 1944, the cinema section was destroyed and the façades were damaged. After the war, the building was restored (without the theater) but was not granted the status of a historical landmark. Its original condition and appearance were further altered by a total renovation that took place from 1976 to 1982. A current, controversial plan proposes demolishing the Deutschlandhaus altogether and replacing it with a similar-looking new building.[11]

In addition to architectural design, Block committed himself in various ways to promoting Modern Architecture. In 1925, he delivered lectures on "Modern Living", about which the *Hamburger Anzeiger* enthusiastically reported: "Block has the experience of a practical architect and is inspired by a consistently modern attitude. [...] The kind of lectures delivered by Dr. Block are enormously important to any modern person. The architect today has the most important things to say about the design of modern life—from how a chair is built to how entire cities are organized [...]. Block had so much to say and to show (in beautiful slides) about what everyone is really interested in [...]. We are lucky to have such architects. It is in considering their work that we can see the dawn of better days."[12] In 1926, Block secured the Hamburg presentation of the traveling exhibition *Typen neuer Baukunst* (Types of Modern Architecture), organized by the Bund Deutscher Architekten. In preparation, he traveled to the Netherlands to choose examples of housing architecture, and, for the exhibition's event program, gave a slide lecture on "Social Housing."[13] In the fall of 1927, Block showed his architectural designs at the *Neues Wohnen* (New Living) exhibition,[14] which accompanied the annual meeting of the Bund Deutscher Architekten in Hamburg. In November 1927, he lectured on "Homes and Apartments of Modern Man" at the Hamburger Kunsthalle (Hamburg Art Museum).[15] From 1927–29, Block worked as an architecture and urban-planning editor for the Hamburg cultural magazine *Der Kreis*, a publication equivalent to the Berlin-based *Der Querschnitt*.[16]

Although Block's own construction projects were confined to the Hamburg area, his influence extended beyond this Hanseatic city. From 1925–33, for example, he served as executive secretary of the Studienausschuss des Bundes Deutscher Architekten für zeitgemäßes Bauen (Study Committee of the Association of German Architects for Contemporary Building). In this function, he published *Probleme des Bauens* (1928) (The Problems of Building), a collection of texts by renowned architects on aspects of rationalization in housing construction. In addition, from 1927–33 Block belonged to the committee for architecture at the Deutscher Werkbund.[17] From 1928–31, he was a member of the expert council of the Reichsforschungsgesellschaft für Wirtschaftlichkeit im Bau- und Wohnungswesen (Imperial Research Society for Economic Efficiency in Building and Housing). His articles in technical architecture magazines contributed to currents in architectural discourse, particularly in the area of small apartment complexes. Block's public lectures and journalistic activities underscore that his understanding of modernity included communicating concepts and goals to a broader audience.

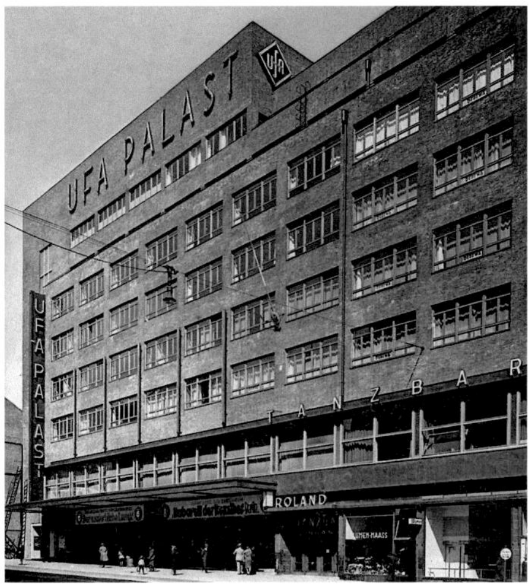

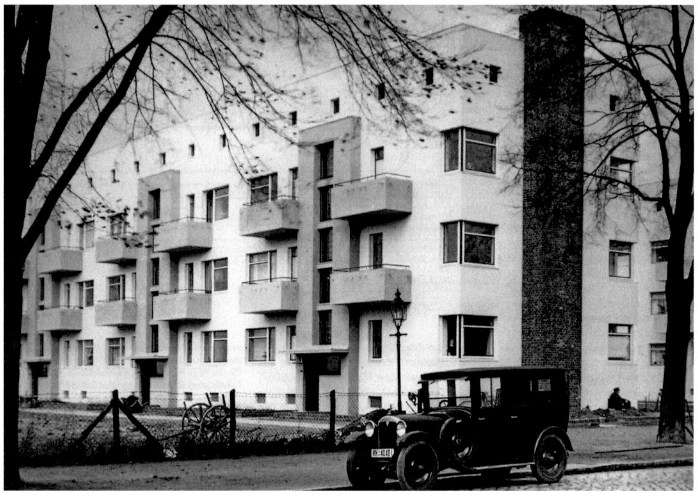

Dr. Block & Hochfeld, Deutschlandhaus with "Ufa-Palast" (1928/29) and row housing (1930), Hamburg

Fritz Block belonged to the liberal-minded citizens of Hamburg, one of the centers of Jewish assimilation in Germany. Within the Jewish German community, he was a liberal. But he felt more connected to German cultural tradition and cosmopolitanism than to a religiously inflected Judaism. He moved in educated circles, and was open to modern lifestyles that thrived in a metropolis. He was interested in art and music, and possessed an optimistic nature and positive attitude. Financially independent at an early age, he developed a passion for travel—a passion he maintained professionally and privately after the First World War. In 1925, he participated in the Deutscher Werkbund conference in Bremen. In 1926, he visited the Bauhaus in Dessau with a delegation of the Bund Deutscher Architekten. In 1927, Block reported in the cultural magazine *Der Kreis* on the Stuttgart Werkbund exhibition *Die Wohnung* and the Weissenhofsiedlung (Weissenhof Estate), built especially for the event.

In the spring of 1925, Block married Anna-Sophie Levy (1895–1986) [pp. 326–327], the daughter of a Hamburg realtor.[18] The couple moved into an upper-class home, owned by the Levys, at the Rondeelteich of the Outer Alster, one of Hamburg's most prestigious residential neighborhoods. Block collected artworks of various cultures and had an extensive library. He and his wife partook in Hamburg's cultural life, attended exhibitions, concerts, and other events, including artists' festivals that took place every year during Fasching, which he photographed in 1932.[19] Their economic situation enabled the childless Block couple a comfortable life. Their vacation and cultural journeys took them to various European countries and, at the beginning of 1928, to Egypt.[20]

Becoming a Photographer

Dr. Block & Hochfeld previously had their buildings documented by professional architectural photographers, including by leading Hamburg photographers Carl Dransfeld (1880–1941) and Ernst Scheel (1903–1986). The large-scale project Deutschlandhaus (1928/29) was the impetus for Block to begin taking architectural photographs himself, since he wanted to record the construction's progress. At the turn of the year 1928/29, Block first acquired a medium-format camera, with which he recorded the different stages of construction in spring 1929—from the foundation to the completion of the interior design [p. 21]. In addition to chronicling the construction's progress, Block was also interested in the reproduction of its structural details, in particular those of the new steel-skeleton construction. In 1929, he took a series of photographs of the Deutschlandhaus's completed building façade, which emphasize the rounded structure of the streetscape below [pp. 20, 22–23]. Block presented his Deutschlandhaus photographs at the 54. Deutscher Architekten- und Ingenieurtag (German Architects' and Engineers' Convention) in Hamburg in September 1929,[21] and published them several times in special interest journals between 1929 and 1931.[22]

Block quickly exchanged his unwieldy medium-format camera for a 35mm-Leica, launched in 1925 and promptly adored by professional photographers, particularly those in the press.[23] Block later wrote of the switch: "There remains the widespread opinion that the Leica is less suitable for architectural photography because it demands such image sharpness. And I must admit, I used to share this opinion. [...] Now [I shoot] all my buildings with a Leica, mainly with a wide-angle lens [...] I think the results are equally good."[24] Block also looked at the Deutschlandhaus artistically: extreme worm's-eye view shots of the distinctive rounded corner, and bird's-eye perspectives of the staircase. These mark his transition from being a photographer for documentary purposes to being one of the New Vision [pp. 14 and 24–25].

As a photographer, Block was an autodidact, so he lacked technical craftsmanship and experience. But he did not consider himself an amateur photographer and was not a member of the Hamburg Association of Amateur Photographers. He instead joined the more progressive Leica Club. Textbooks and illustrated volumes in Block's estate indicate that he was engaged in the new developments in photographic technology, and with the work of contemporary photographers. He knew the relevant books of avant-garde

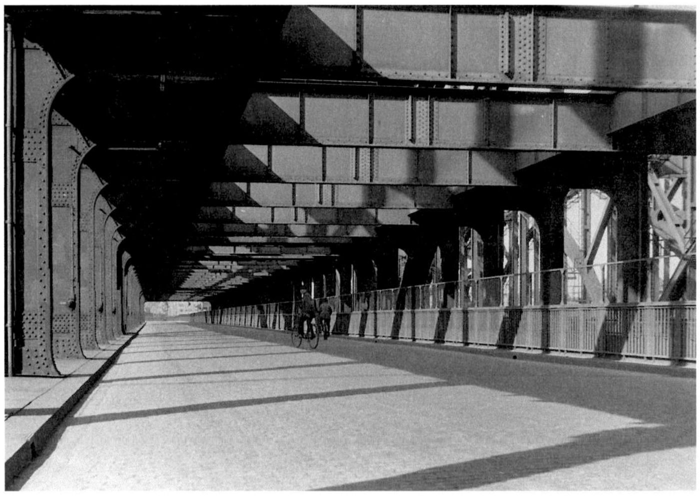

Freeport Elbe Bridge, Hamburg, 1929

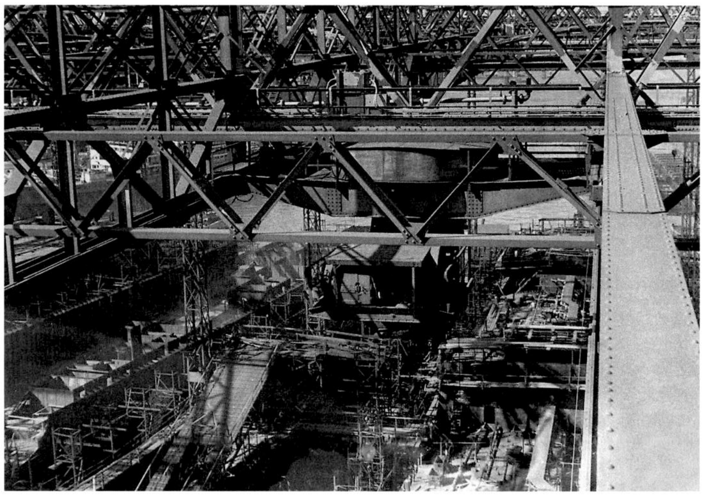

Gantry structure at the Blohm & Voss shipyard, Hamburg, 1930

photography, from László Moholy-Nagy's Bauhaus book *Malerei, Photographie, Film* (Painting, Photography, Film, 1925), to the photo book *Die Welt ist schön* (The World is Beautiful, 1928), by Albert Renger-Patzsch—which influenced Block greatly—to Hanns Günther's (aka. Walter de Haas) volume *Technische Schönheit* (Technical Beauty, 1929), from the series *Schaubücher*, which contains industrial photography mainly by Emil Otto Hoppé and Albert Renger-Patzsch. Block devoted himself to the aims of New Photography, especially photo reportage, but he saw his contribution less in terms of theory and more in terms of praxis: "I have not mentioned artistic skill, since for me this is a self-evident prerequisite that is better confirmed by achievement than words."[25]

From 1929 onward, Block took photos with an architect's eye for technology, first in Hamburg, especially in the harbor [p. 18], but also with a good eye for the working world of fishermen or scenes from the circus. He was also interested in motifs of natural history—various animals and plants; he even made X-rays of shells and snails. He was not interested in portrait and landscape photography. Although Block traveled a lot in Germany, he didn't take many pictures there. Extant from his stays in Berlin are only photographs of the radio tower—probably dating from 1929 [pp. 26–27]. With perspectives typical of the New Vision, these images recall similar photographs made in 1928 by László Moholy-Nagy.[26] Only typescripts—no photographs—are preserved from Block's photo reportages of a Krupp steel mill near Duisburg and from the Oktoberfest in Munich. But Block photographed extensively on his travels abroad, establishing urban and travel photography as his specialties.[27] Examples are photographs he took in North Africa, Paris and Marseille in 1930, and at the Côte d'Azur in 1931. A trip across the United States in the fall of 1931 led to his most comprehensive photographic output.

Publications and Exhibitions

Block initially photographed with no commercial intent. But the global economic crisis resulted in declining architectural commissions, beginning in 1930, offering him more time for the journalistic application of his travel photos. His wife, Anna-Sophie, wrote thematic accompanying texts. The illustrated press of the Weimar Republic was reaching an apex of modern photojournalism. In Hamburg, daily newspapers published supplements with photo reportages printed in gravure. Block published his images primarily in the weekly supplement of the bourgeois-liberal *Hamburger Anzeiger*, in the weekly supplement of the Social Democratic *Hamburger Echo*, in the *Bilderrundschau*, a supplement of the conservative *Hamburger Nachrichten*, and in the weekly magazine *Hamburger Illustrierte*. Other reproductions of his photos came about via photo agencies such as Mauritius, Berlin, and Linden-Verlag, in Munich, as well as the Paris-based Globe, Nord-Sud, Jacqueline Paouillac, and Laquert. This is how Block's photographs also reached the *Schweizer Illustrierte Zeitung* and the *Basler Illustrierte Zeitung*, as well as the French illustrated magazines *Photomonde* and *Miroir du Monde*.[28]

Block also published in special-interest magazines on photography. He worked for the magazine *Leica* and published photographs in brochures for the Ernst Leitz Company, manufacturer of the Leica camera, located in Wetzlar.[29] In 1931, he won a photo contest sponsored by the magazine *Photofreund*, and was also represented in the photographic yearbooks *Das Deutsche Lichtbild. Jahresschau 1931* (1930) and *Deutscher Kamera-Almanach 1932* (1931). In 1932, Block reported in detail on the photographic aspects of his North America trip in the *Photofreund-Jahrbuch 1933* and in the architecture magazine *Baugilde*—and on the Detroit Ford Factory, in the Werkbund magazine *Die Form*. Inspired by the photo-book form—a new genre of the time—he also began planning the publication of his Hamburg and Paris photographs as monographs. Although these projects were never realized, they do underscore Block's ambition as a photographer.

In addition to publishing his photos, Block also showed them in exhibitions. The first time he exhibited his photographs was in the fall of 1929, at the *Kunst-Ausstellung Altona* (Art Exhibition Altona), in then-Prussian Altona, a city near Hamburg.[30] Photography (including photomontage) had its own section—in addition to a high-level selection of modern painting and sculpture and a photographic series about Modern Architecture in Germany, by Ernst Scheel. Block, together with other Hamburg photographers (Arvid Gutschow, Ernst Scheel, Fritz Schleifer, and others) exhibited alongside nationally known photographers, among them Aenne Biermann, Hugo Erfurth, Andreas Feininger, the Leistikow siblings, Alice and Oskar Nerlinger, Albert Renger-Patzsch, and Sasha Stone. Block showed Hamburg-centric motifs, likely including shots of ships that appeared slightly later, in the magazine *Die Form* [pp. 54–55]. The *Hamburger Anzeiger*, however, judged his contribution rather critically: "The Hamburg subjects by Dr. Fritz Block are meticulously produced but show little originality, and are only moderately successful."[31] Block was not included in the more influential *Film und Foto* exhibition, put on by the Deutscher Werkbund. One assumes, however, that he did visit it—either in early summer 1929, in Stuttgart, or at its second presentation, in late fall of 1929, in Berlin. Block was indeed present at the 1930 *Internationale Ausstellung "Das Lichtbild"*, in Munich. He is listed in the catalogue, under the heading "In the Service of Science", subsection "Technology, Architecture, and Sculpture", with the areas "Urban photographic series, industrial plants, ports, and others; travel reportages".[32]

Finally, in 1932, Block participated in the *Internationale Foto-Ausstellung* at the Kunstverein Hamburg,[33] organized by the art historian and director of the Kunstverein, Hildebrand Gurlitt. Inspired by the exhibition *Film und Foto*, Gurlitt had built the most important private collection of contemporary photography of the time,[34] for his friend the Dresden-based industrialist Kurt Kirchbach. The Hamburg exhibition, based on this collection, included photographs by Karl Blossfeldt, László Moholy-Nagy, Hugo Erfurth, Umbo, Sasha Stone, Walter Peterhans, Andreas Feininger, Hans Finsler, and Albert Renger-Patzsch. Gurlitt supplemented works by Hamburg photographers Johannes Grubenbecher, Ernst Scheel, Arvid Gutschow and Fritz Block.[35] Block was represented by some twenty of his photographs from America, especially New York. As part of the exhibit program, he also gave lectures with slides he made from photos he had taken in New York and Paris. Following the exhibition, a selection of his America photographs was acquired for the Kirchbach Collection. And so entered architect Fritz Block into the circle of the photographic avant-garde.

1 See, among others, Andreas Haus, "Fotografische Polemik und Propaganda um das 'Neue Bauen' der 20er Jahre," *Marburger Jahrbuch für Kunstwissenschaft, Bd. 20* (1981), pp. 90–106. – Roland Jaeger, *Neue Werkkunst. Architektenmonographien der zwanziger Jahre* (Berlin, 1998). – Eds. Claudia Quiring, Andreas Rothaus, and Rainer Stamm, *Neue Baukunst! Architektur der Moderne in Bild und Buch* (Bielefeld, 2013). – Roland Jaeger, "Vom Neuen zum nationalsozialistischen Bauen. Fotoillustrierte Architekturbücher der Zwischenkriegszeit," in *Autopsie. Deutschsprachige Fotobücher 1918 bis 1945. vol. 2*, eds. Manfred Heiting and Roland Jaeger (Göttingen, 2014), pp. 378–409.

2 See, among others, Michael Stöneberg, *Arthur Köster. Architekturfotografie 1926–1933. Das Bild vom "Neuen Bauen"* (Berlin, 2009).

3 See Roland Jaeger, "Bilderbücher eines Architekten. Erich Mendelsohn im Rudolf Mosse Buchverlag," in Heiting/Jaeger, *Autopsie* (note 1), *vol. 1* (Göttingen, 2012), 174–187.

4 *Walter Gropius. Amerikareise 1928*, eds. Gerda Breuer and Annemarie Jaeggi (Berlin, 2009).

5 See "Richard Neutra. Photograph und Architekt," *Camera* 42, no. 5 (1963), 8–13.

6 Konrad Wachsmann, *Salzburg, die Altstadt* (Berlin, 1934) (Eidon, vol. 1). – Idem, *Berlin, Unter den Linden* (Berlin, 1934) (Eidon, vol. 2).

7 For biographical information, see, among others, Fritz Block, *Curriculum Vitae* (manuscript Los Angeles, c. 1950). – Anna-Sophie Block, *Antrag nach dem BEG (Bundesentschädigungsgesetz* (manuscript Los Angeles, 1955). – Anna-Sophie Block, *Oral History Interview* (Los Angeles, 1979) (all in the Fritz Block Estate Archive, Stockholm/Hamburg).

8 For Block's publications as an architect, see the list on page 326.

9 See Roland Jaeger, *Block & Hochfeld. Die Architekten des Deutschlandhauses. Bauten und Projekte in Hamburg 1921–1938. Exil in Los Angeles* (Berlin, 1996), 223–241, about Block as a photographer.

10 Adolf Goetz, "Dr.-Ing. Block, Dr.-Ing. Hochfeld, Architekten, B.D.A., D.W.B.," *Neue Baukunst* 1, no. 7/8 (1925).

11 See Roland Jaeger and Jörg Schilling, *Das Deutschlandhaus von Block & Hochfeld, 1929–2019* (Hamburg, 2018) (hamburger bauheft, no. 25).

12 [Hugo] Si.[eker], "Architekt Dr. Block [...]," *Hamburger Anzeiger*, no. 292, Dec. 15, 1925.

13 *Hamburger Anzeiger*, no. 113, May 5, 1926. – *Hamburger Nachrichten*, no. 229, May 20, 1926.

14 Fritz Block, "Neues Wohnen. Zur Ausstellung 'Neues Wohnen' in der Stadthalle," *Hamburger Nachrichten*, no. 433, Sept. 16, 1927. – Bernhard Gaber, "Vom Bundestag 1927 in Hamburg," *Die Baugilde*, 9, no. 18 (1927) 1093–1095, esp. 1094–1095.

15 *Hamburger Nachrichten*, no. 527, Nov. 10, 1927.

16 *Der Kreis* 4, no. 10 (1927), 590.

17 *Bau-Rundschau* 18, no. 9 (1927), 141.

18 The spelling of her first name varies; here 'Anna-Sophie' (with hyphen) is used.

19 "Hamburger Karneval," *Hamburger Illustrierte* 14, no. 6 (1932), 20–21, 24.

20 Block's travel journal marked with a roman "I" (Fritz Block Estate Archive, Stockholm/Hamburg) dates from 1914 and includes his travels until the beginning of 1929. It thus unfortunately does not cover his relevant photographic travels. A second travel diary has not been found.

21 Beginning in 1927, Block belonged to the Architekten- und Ingenieur-Verein zu Hamburg (Architects and Engineers Association of Hamburg); previously he was a member of its Berlin division.

22 Fritz Block (photos), "Bildbericht über einen Großbau," Deutsches Bauwesen 5, no. 9 (1929), 226–228. – Fritz Block (photos), "Der Bau des Deutschlandhauses in Hamburg," *Die Form* 5, no. 5 (1930) 118–120. – "Architekten Dr. Block u. Hochfeld, Hamburg. Deutschlandhaus in Hamburg," *Bauwelt* 21, no. 21 (1931), suppl. 1–8.

23 See Hans-Michael Koetzle, *Eyes wide open! 100 years of Leica photography* (Heidelberg/Berlin, 2015).

24 Fritz Block, "Photoreportage mit der Leica in Amerika," in *Photofreund-Jahrbuch 1933*, ed. Fr. Willy Frerk (Berlin 1932) 77–88; quotation, 84.

25 Ibid. 88.

26 See the exh. cat. *Berlin Metropolis 1919–1933* (München/London/New York, 2015) 208–211. – *Moholy Nagy: Future Present*, eds. Matthew S. Witkovsky, Carol S. Eliel, and Karole P. B. Vail (New Haven / New York, 2016), 131–137.

27 Roland Jaeger, "Fritz Block. Around the World with Leica, part. 1: Europe," *Leica Fotografie International*, no. 4 (2005), 6–17; " ... part 2: America," ibid., no. 5 (2005), 14–25.

28 For Block's photographic publications, see the list on pages 326–328.

29 See, among others, Ernst Leitz, Optische Werke, *Leica, die Kamera der Zeit* (Wetzlar 1933, list Photo No. 7325), 9 and back cover.

30 Exh. cat. *Kunst-Ausstellung Altona 1929* (Altona 1929). The catalogue lists the photographers' names but no captions of images and is not illustrated. – See *Der Ring. Illustrierte der Altonaer Nachrichten*, Sept. 28 and Oct. 5, 1929, with photos by Hans Finsler, Ernst Scheel, Ursula Wolff, Ehrhard Dörner, und Arvid Gutschow.

31 Sdt. [Pol Sackarndt], "Neue Lichtbildkunst?," *Hamburger Anzeiger*, no. 221, Sept. 21,1929.

32 Exh. cat. *Internationale Ausstellung "Das Lichtbild" München 1930* [Führer durch die Ausstellung] (München 1930), 18.

33 See Herbert Molderings, "Die internationale Foto-Sammlung Kurt Kirchbach, Dresden. Eine Pioniersammlung der modernen Fotografie," in idem, *Die Moderne der Fotografie* (Hamburg, 2008), 273–284. – Meike Hoffmann and Nicola Kuhn, *Hitlers Kunsthändler Hildebrand Gurlitt 1895–1956. Die Biographie* (München, 2016), 154–155.

34 Skr. [Hugo Sieker], "Photo-Sammlung Kurt Kirchbach," *Altonaer Nachrichten*, no. 19, Jan. 23, 1932.

35 See Roland Jaeger and Cornelius Steckner, *Zinnober. Kunstszene Hamburg 1919–1933* (Hamburg, 1983) 36–39. – Roland Jaeger, "Vom Lichtbild zum Großfoto. Kataloge zu Ausstellungen von und mit Fotografie," in Heiting/Jaeger 2014 (see note 1), 40–75, thereof 49.

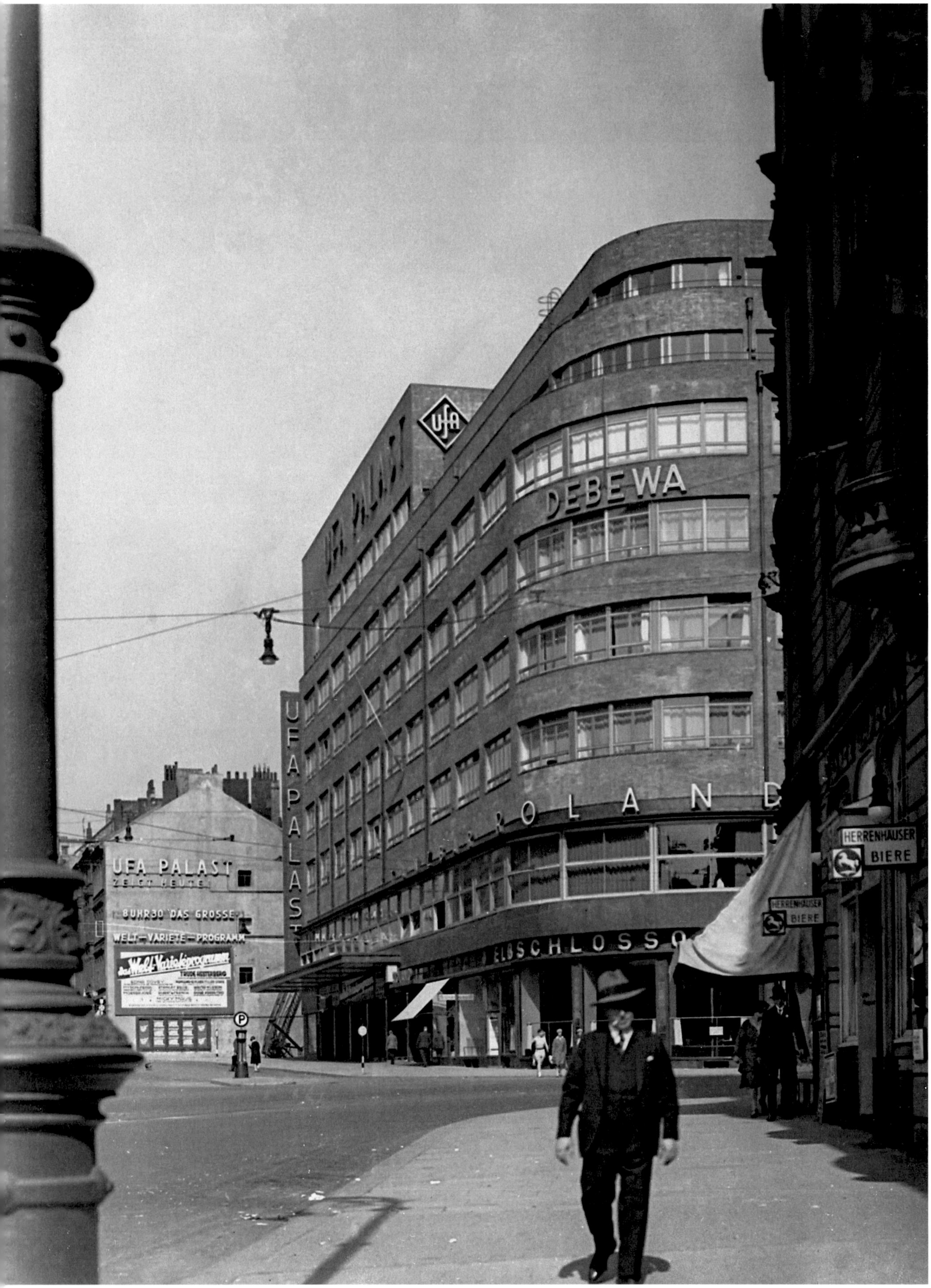

Fritz Block in front of the *Deutschlandhaus*, Hamburg, 1930

"Architects Dr. Block a.[nd] Hochfeld, Hamburg" (*Bauwelt* 21, no. 21, 1931)

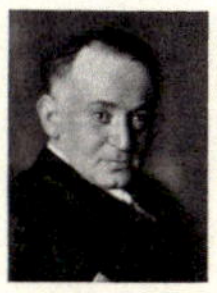

Architekten Dr. Block u. Hochfeld, Hamburg

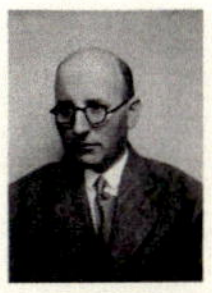

Deutschlandhaus in Hamburg

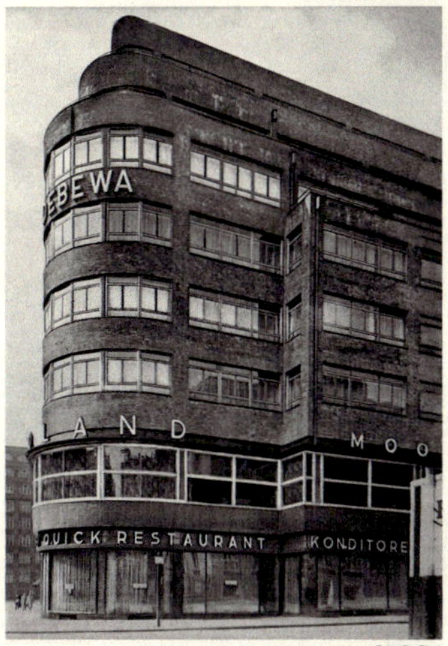

Ansicht Ecke Drehbahn-Dammtorstraße

Foto: Dr. Block

Das Bauprogramm

Im Mittelpunkt der Stadt war ein Lichtspieltheater zu errichten, an das in bezug auf Größe und Mannigfaltigkeit der Einrichtungen und des Gebrauchszweckes höchste Anforderungen gestellt waren. Zugleich sollte das Theater mit gewerblichen Räumen, Läden, Kaffee-, Büro- und Verkaufsräumen so nutzbringend wie möglich verbunden werden.

Städtebauliche Lösung

Die Erfüllung des Bauprogrammes wurde wesentlich beeinflußt durch die städtebauliche Lage. Der 5700 m² große Bauplatz liegt nahe einem Haupteinfallstor der City, dem Dammtor; er wird begrenzt von den Straßen: Drehbahn—Dammtorstraße—Valentinskamp.

Der Bau

Auf Grund zahlreicher Vorentwürfe entstand der Ausführungsplan: achtgeschossige Bürohausflügel an den 3 Straßen, im Innern des Grundstückes das Theater, durchgehend vom Valentinskamp bis zur Drehbahn. Das Grundstück ist außerordentlich stark ausgenutzt, bis auf einen Hof von 160 m² voll bebaut und vollständig unterkellert.

Die Bürohausflügel zeigen die übliche Anlage. Von den 3 Treppenhäusern wurde auf Wunsch des Bauherrn das Dammtorstraßen-Treppenhaus während des Baues von der Hofseite auf die Straßenseite verschoben. Da bereits die Eisenkonstruktion sehr weit vorgeschritten war, konnte die Schauseite nicht mehr geändert werden.

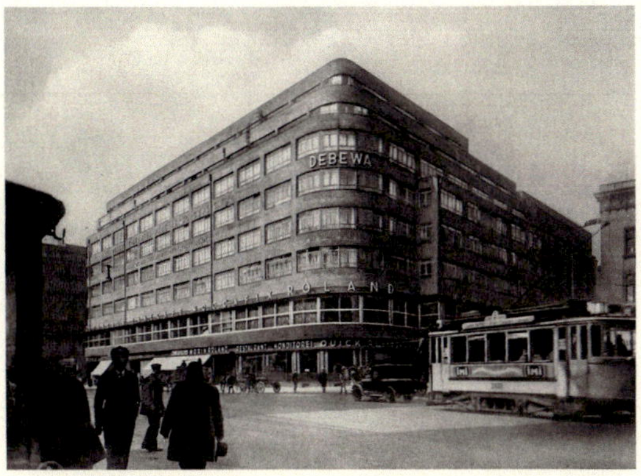

Ansicht Ecke Drehbahn-Dammtorstraße

Foto: Dr. Block

Block u. Hochfeld

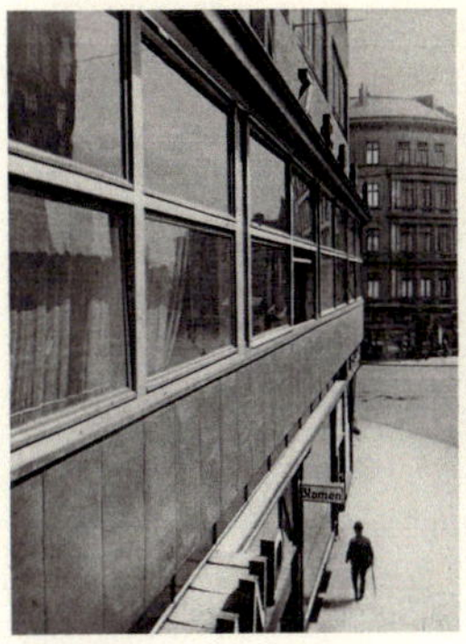

Erker Einzelheit

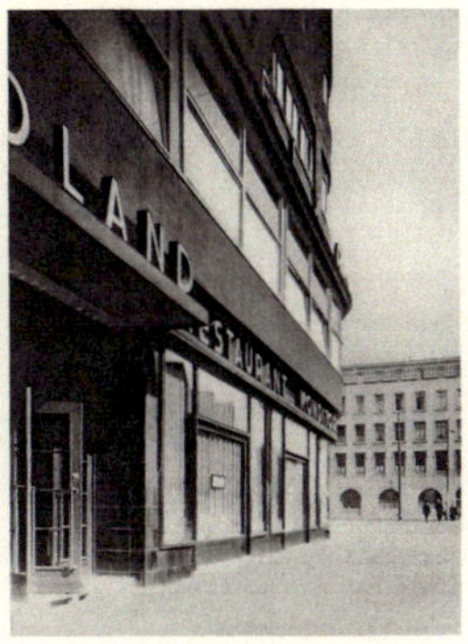

Einzelheit des Erdgeschosses

"Construction of the *Deutschlandhaus* in Hamburg" (*Die Form* 5, no. 5, 1930)

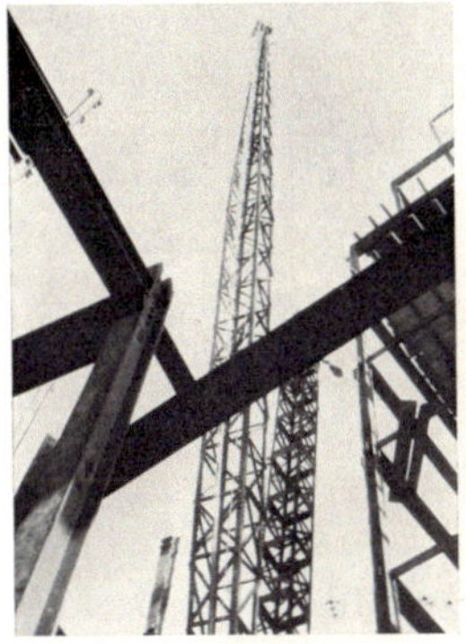

Eisenkrane

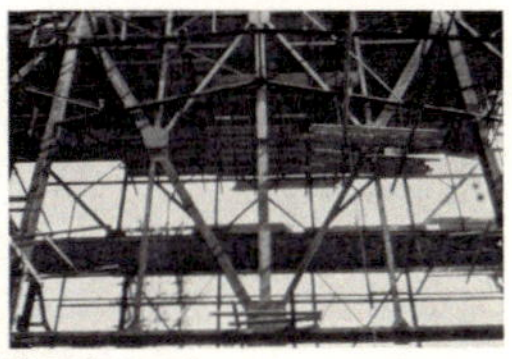

Bühnen-Innenwand

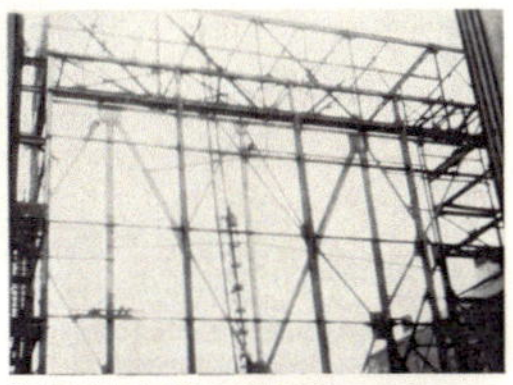

Stahlskelett des Bühnenhauses

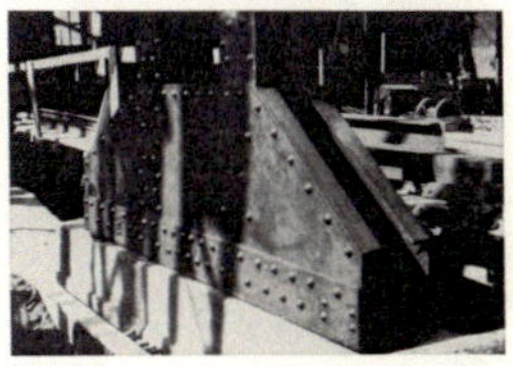

Säulenfuß

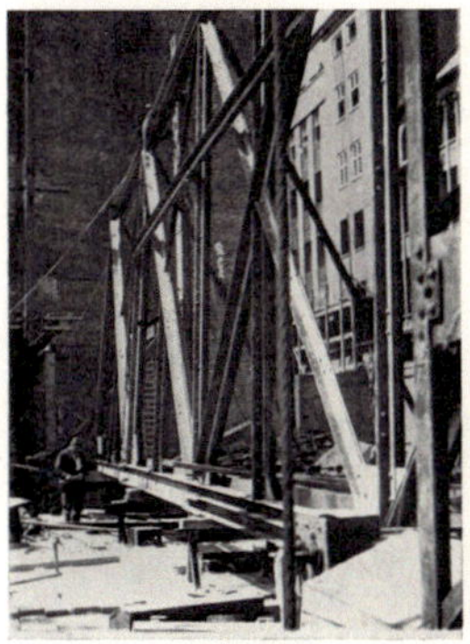

Gitterträger des Bühnendaches

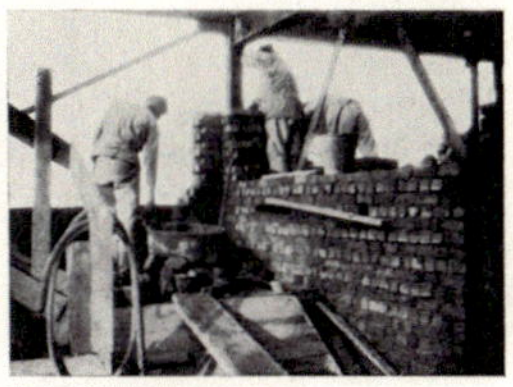

Fachwerkausmauerung

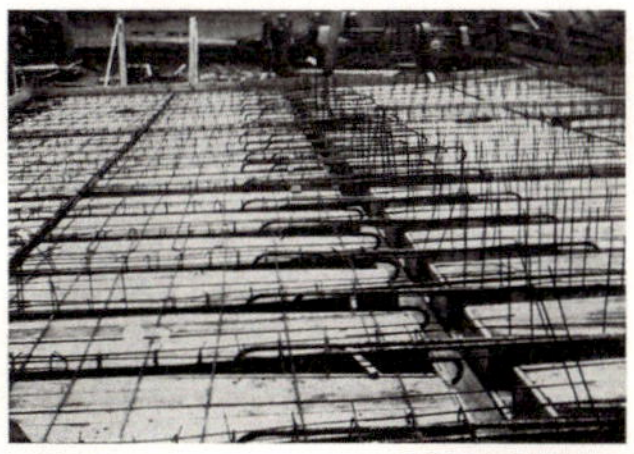

Pohlmanndecke vor der Einbringung des Betons

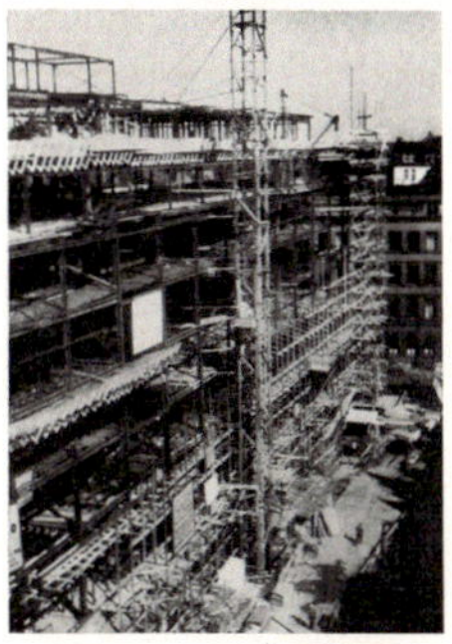

Front Dammtorstraße mit Deckeneinschalungen

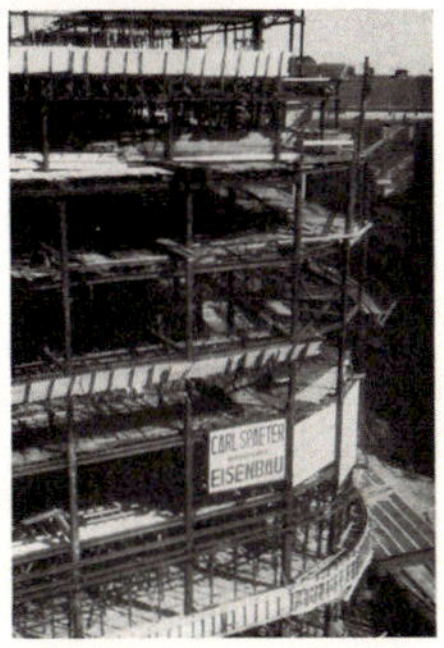

Ecke Valentinskamp u. Dammtorstr. bei der Herstellung der Decken

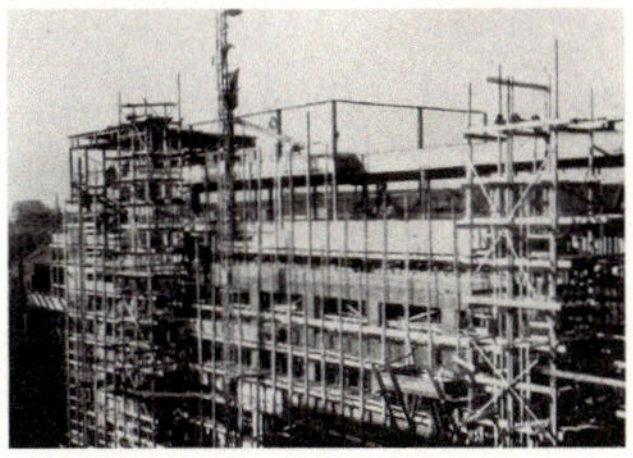

Einrüstung der Front Valentinskamp

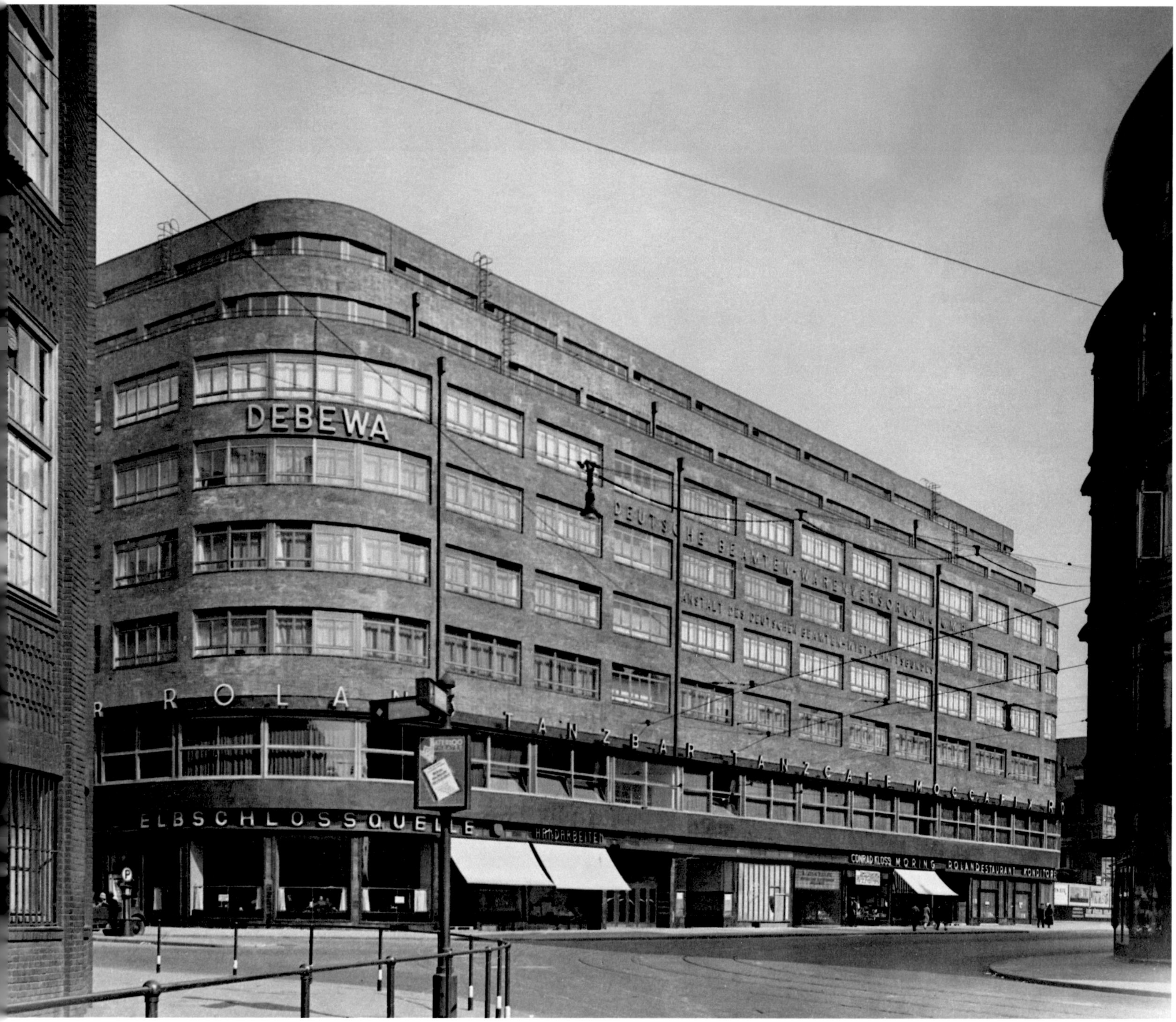

Façade of the *Deutschlandhaus*, Hamburg, 1930

Façade of the *Deutschlandhaus*, Hamburg, 1930

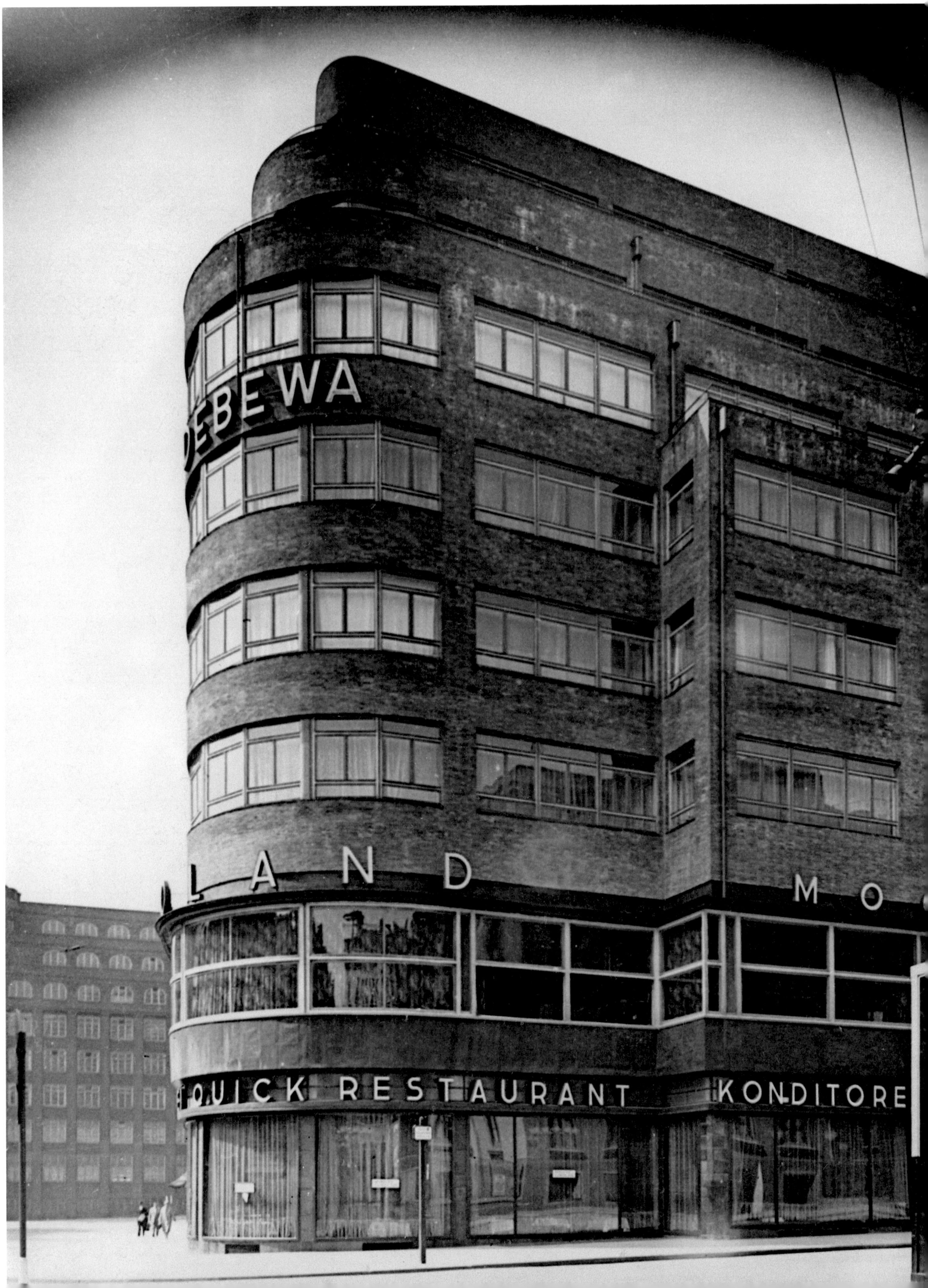
DEBEWA
LAND
MO
QUICK RESTAURANT
KONDITORE

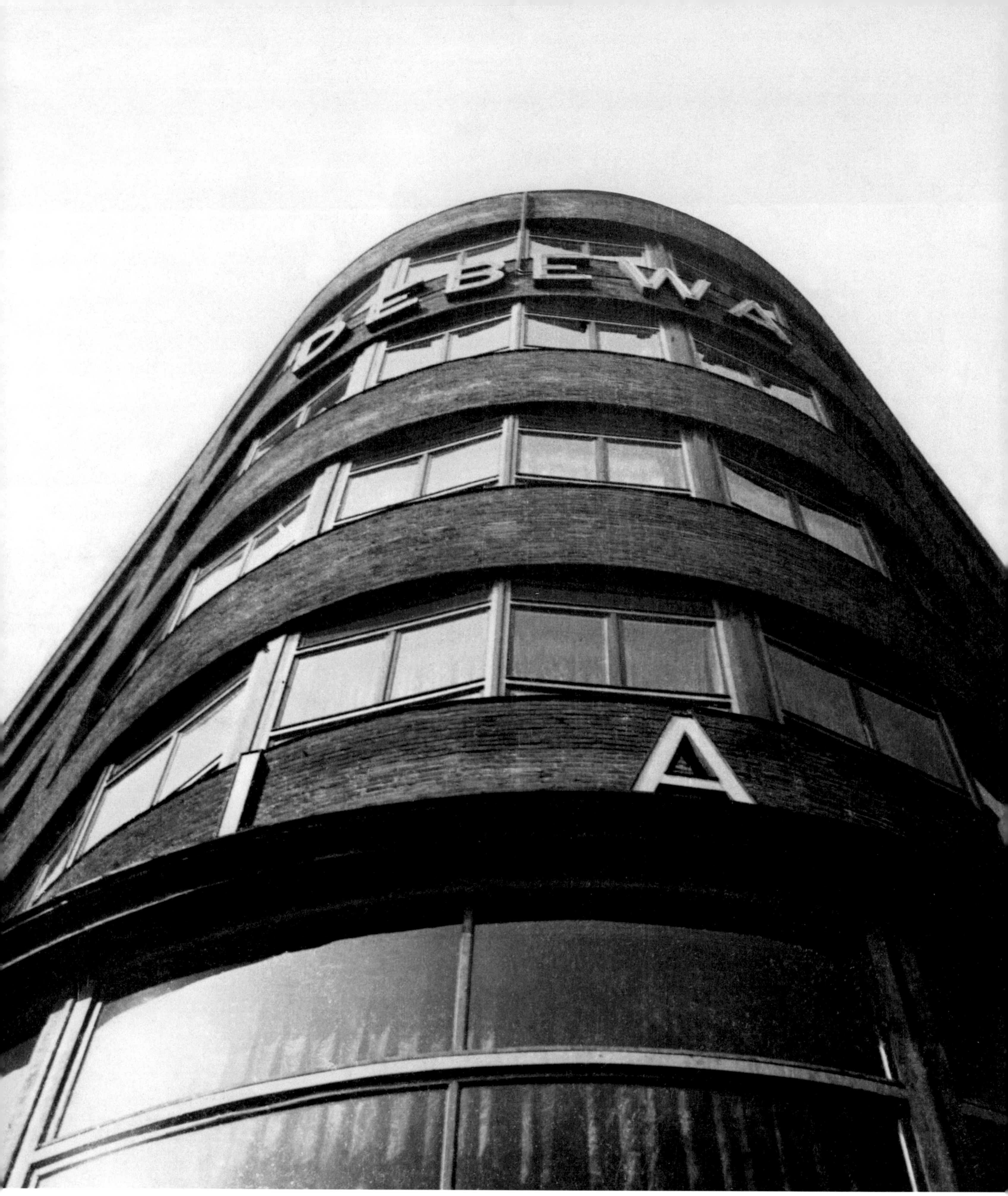

Detail of the *Deutschlandhaus* façade, Hamburg, 1930

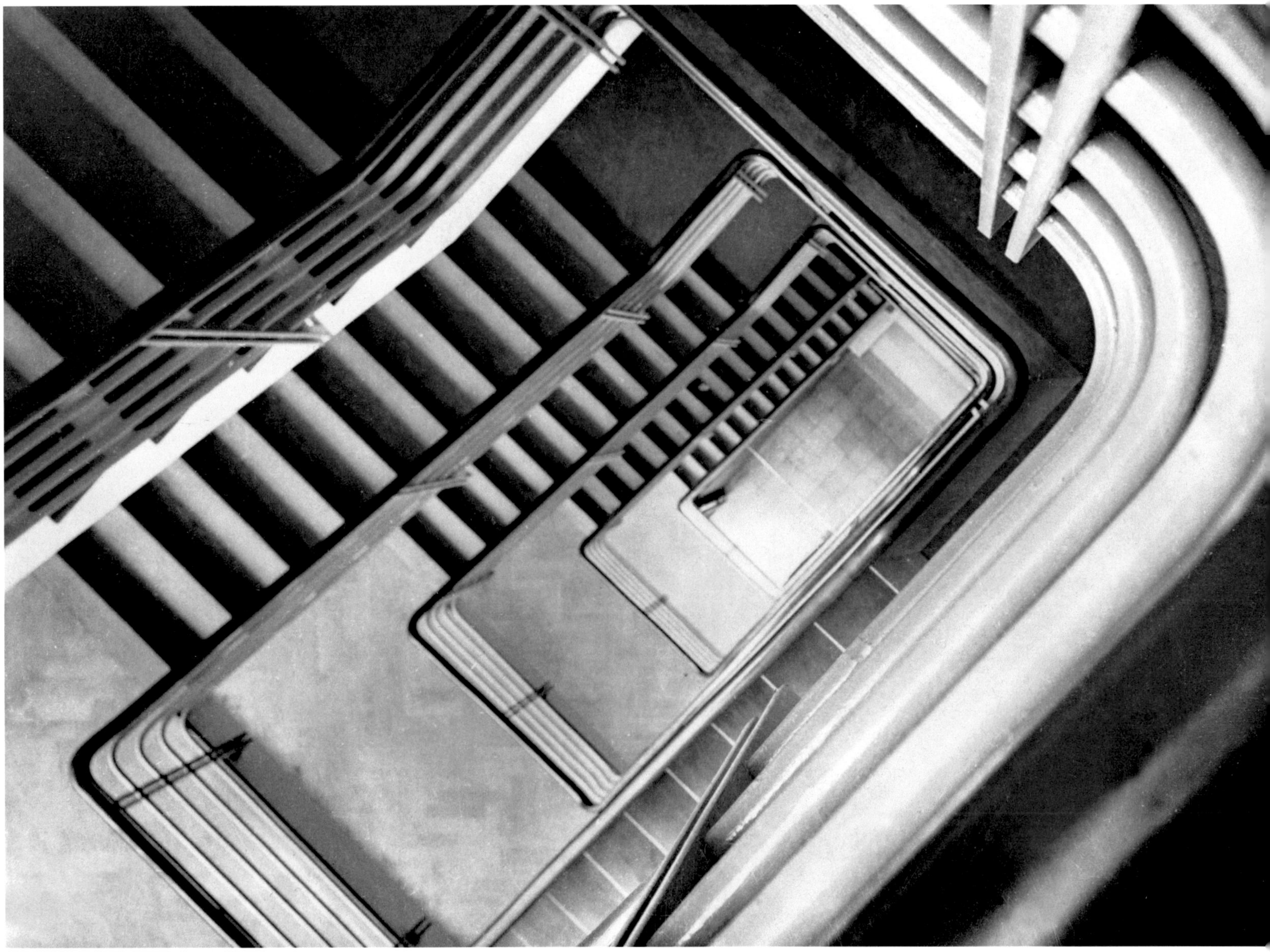

Staircase in the *Deutschlandhaus*, Hamburg, 1930

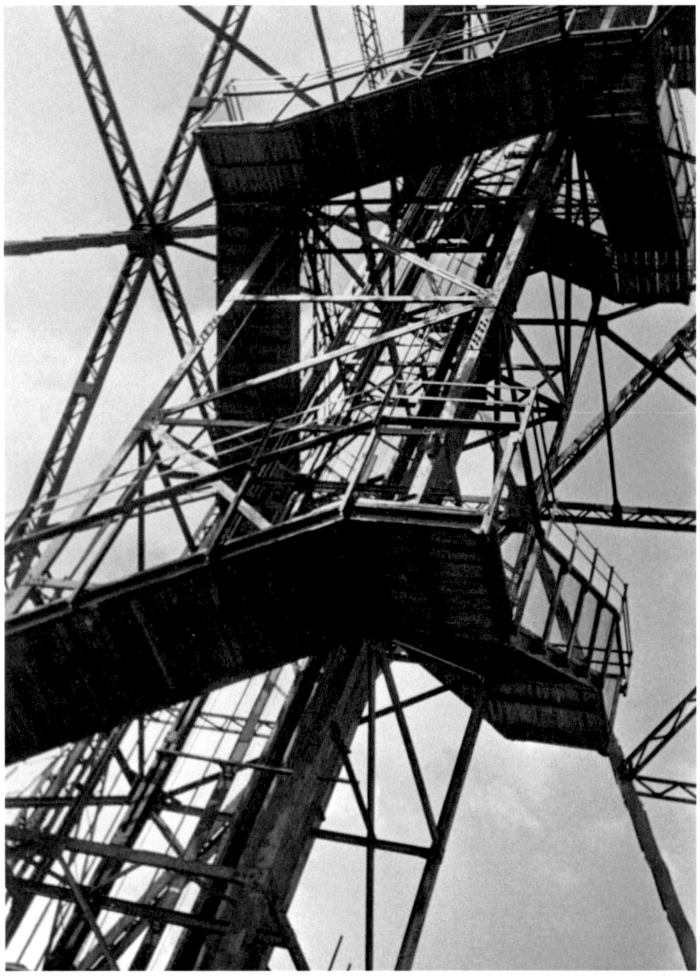

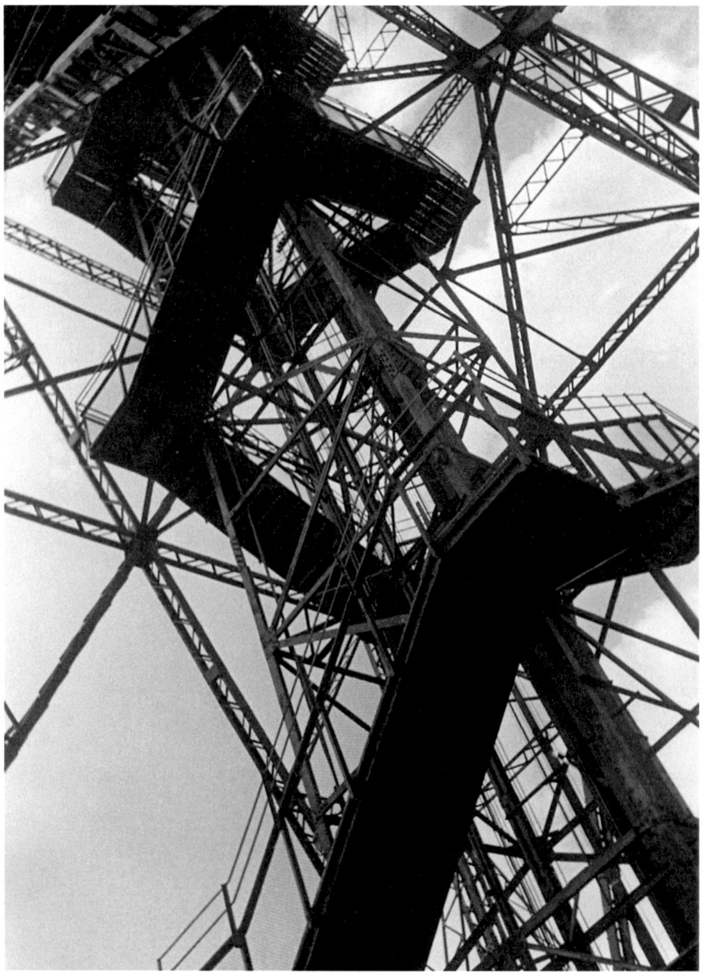

Upward view of the Berlin Radio Tower, 1929

Downward view from the Berlin Radio Tower, 1929

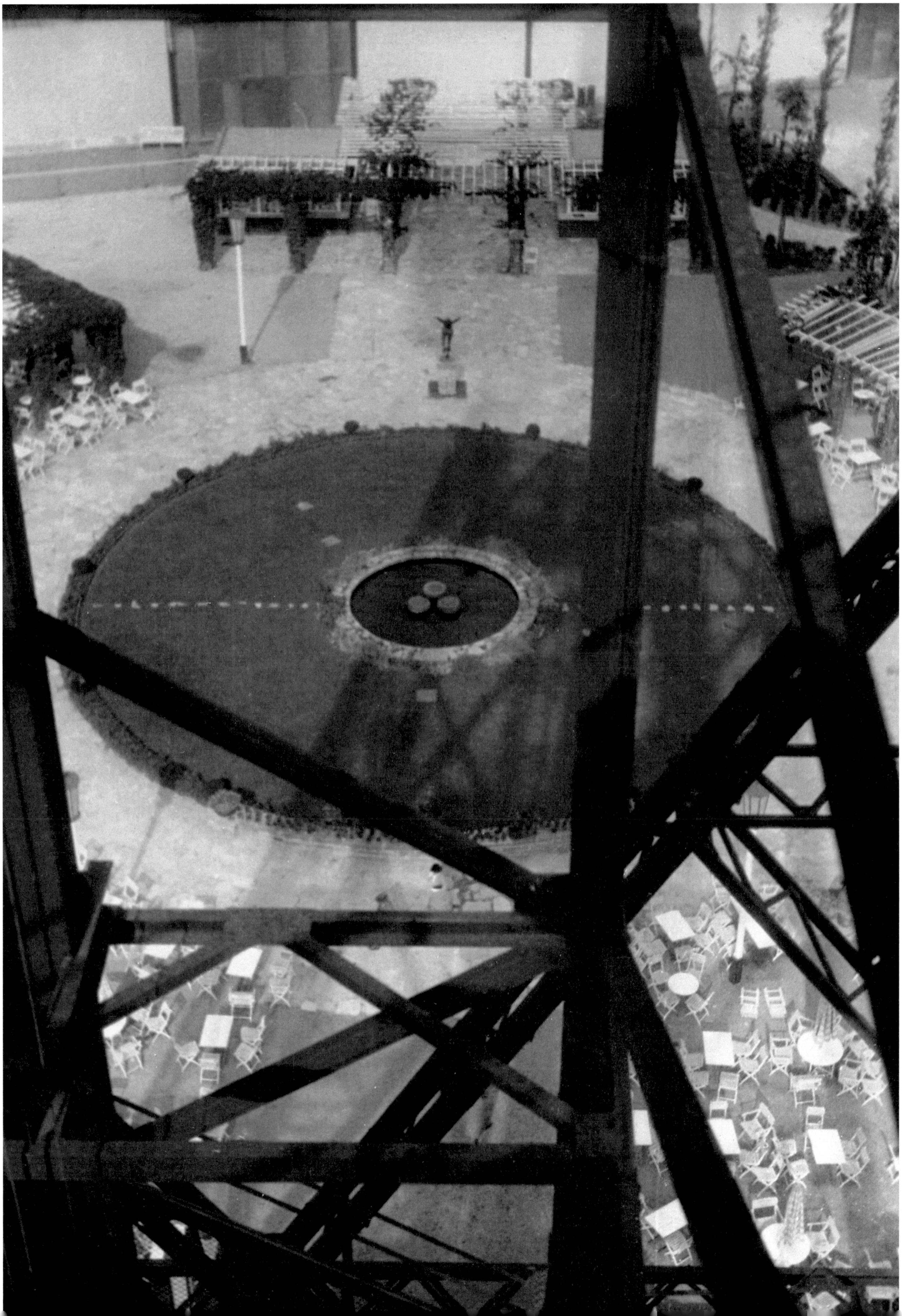

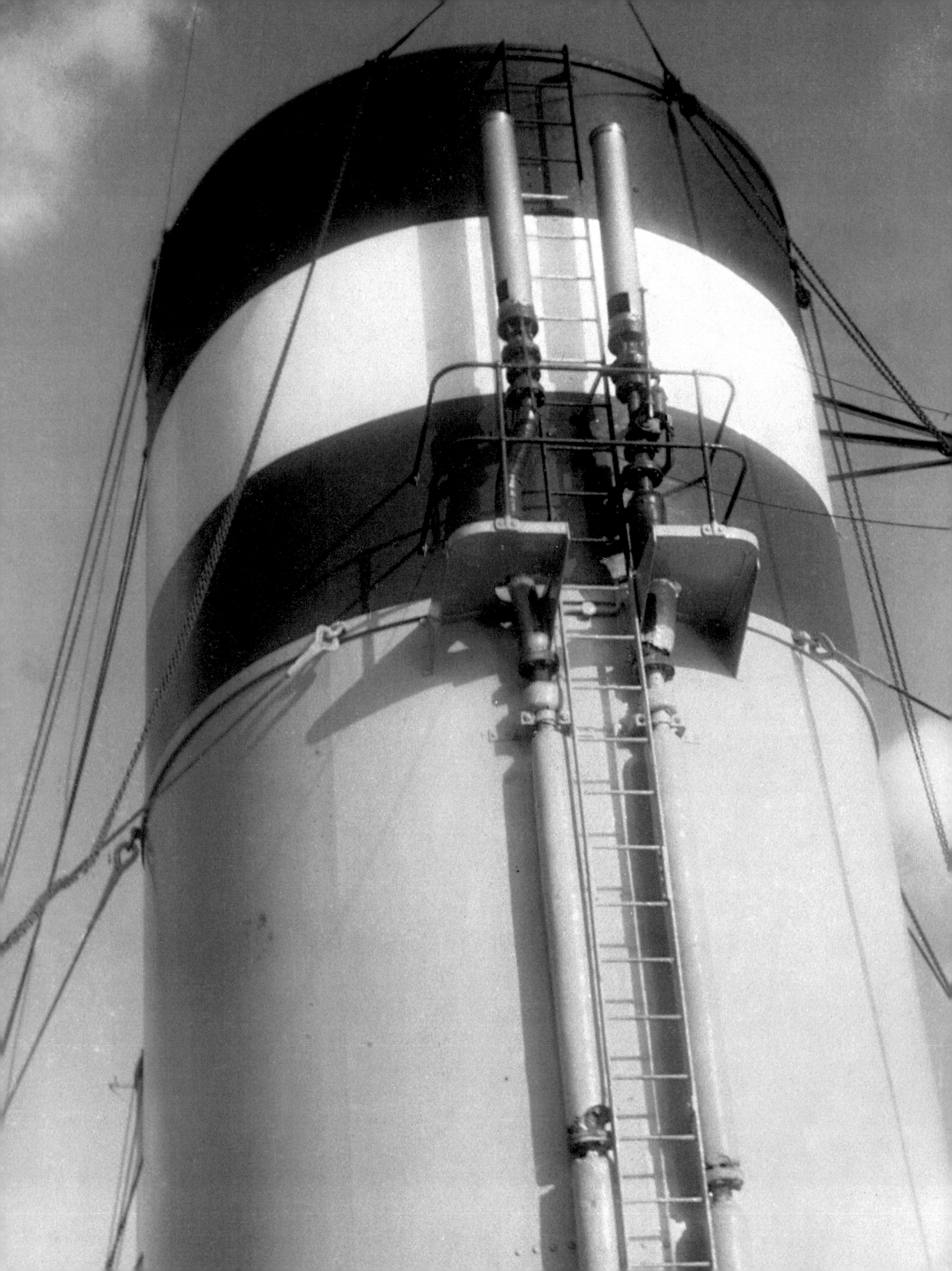

A Fresh View on Hamburg

Modern Images of the City and the Harbor

Since Fritz Block did not have formal training as a photographer, or a career working as one, he stayed literally close to Hamburg and the photographic opportunities it offered—including the documentation of his Deutschlandhaus—and he engaged with the work of the city's photographers. As a means of entry into the movement of New Photography, however, this was not altogether a bad start: the Hanseatic city offered not only a broad range of contemporary motifs, it also had a harbor full of technical and industrial equipment ready to pose for the camera. Moreover, well-known photographers of the New Objectivity were already working in the city.[1] Furthermore, the year 1929 was a good one for Block to open his eyes to novel photographic possibilities: the New Photography in Germany was prevailing as a modern movement. Block's photos taken in and of Hamburg are therefore to be seen less in a regional context and more as an exemplary contribution to this phase of German photographic history.[2]

Photos of Hamburg

Up until the mid-1920s, the photographic image of Hamburg was strongly influenced by photo-illustrated publications, in the lineage of albums featuring scenic views of the city. A late example is *Hamburg. 110 Ansichten von der Freien und Hansestadt und ihrer Umgebung* (1928) (Hamburg. 110 Views of the Free and Hanseatic City and Its Surroundings), which was also intended to advertise the city to potential tourists. It contains pictures in photogravure of the city's monuments and sights, as well as atmospheric impressions. The images are not aesthetically uniform; they come rather from various regional photographers, some of them from the era of art photography.

By the late 1920s, topographical scenic-view collections like this had seen their day. A new genre of photo books had emerged, one in which the photographer no longer merely served as one of several "image suppliers" but rather as the author of images that, through pursuing a subjective perspective, offered an individual style. This type evolved especially in the genre of illustrated travelogues. The photographer Kurt Hielscher (1881–1948), with his volumes in the *Orbis Terrarum* series, is considered an exemplary German pioneer in this field. He did not stand out for forward-looking photography or for his choice of modern motifs, but rather because he developed a unique and recognizable picturesque style. His photo book *Deutschland. Baukunst und Landschaft* (1924) (Germany. Architecture and Landscape), included atmospheric images of Hamburg, its harbor and canals.

The German-English photographer Emil Otto Hoppé (1878–1972) took pictures of Hamburg too, in 1925 and again in 1928.[3] Some of these images found their way into his photo book *Deutsche Arbeit* (1930) (German Work). Hoppé's photo of a Hamburg canal appears in *Orbis Terrarum's* new edition of *Deutschland. Baukunst und Landschaft* (1931). The concept of international cities as seen through the eyes of individual photographers was pursued, above all, in the photo book series Das *Gesicht der Städte* (The Face of the Cities).[4] It was not by chance that the first volume was *Hamburg* (1927)—preceding even Berlin, Paris, and other major cities. But the author of the book was actually not from Hamburg; he was August Rupp (1874-1958), a photographer living and working in Berlin. His images appear at the transition from the conventional city-portrait to the contemporary urban photo book.

Photographically illustrated special-interest books on harbor works and services were also being published. Among them was the volume *Der Hafen von Hamburg* (1928) (The Port of Hamburg), published by public authorities and available in an English edition as well. Similar photos could be found in the book *Der Hamburger Hafen* (1928) (The Hamburg Harbor), by John Fuhlberg-Horst, a technology writer. But the illustrations in these books were not photographs attributed to specific photographers; they were rather mostly anonymous works made by port authorities, shipping companies, shipyard firms, or harbor crane manufacturers. These photographs of technical port constructions served to

Funnel of the steamship *Hamburg*, Hamburg, 1929

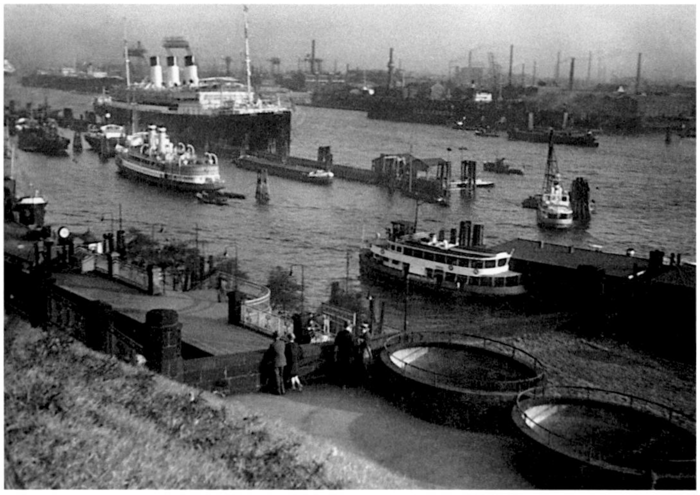

View of the cruise terminal and harbor, Hamburg, 1929

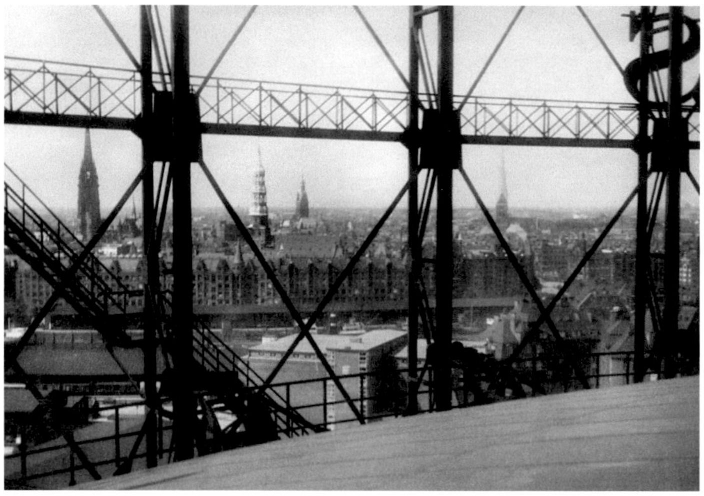

View from the gasometer of the inner city, Hamburg, 1929

illustrate their form and function, not to express an artistic vision.

One may assume that Block knew at least a few of these books. The city's illustrated press also had an impact on his conception of photography. Towards the end of the 1920s, the weekly photogravure supplements of Hamburg daily newspapers (see p. 18) featured increasing numbers of photo reports on contemporary topics, often in lively graphic arrangement. Furthermore, the weekly *Hamburger Illustrierte* featured press photographers in particular. One of them was Ursula Leidmann-Wolff (1906–1977), who later married the Hamburg architect Karl Schneider, who collaborated on construction projects with Dr. Block & Hochfeld.[5] Others include Cami (1898–1975) and Sasha Stone (1895–1940), who took photos in Hamburg at the end of 1927 and in 1929. However, most images of the harbor and the cityscape and many of the city's nightlife were made by Cami Stone.[6] Beginning in 1930, Block would also publish photos and photo reportages in these pages.

Renger-Patzsch, Scheel, and Gutschow

The pioneering representative of New Objectivity in German photography was Albert Renger-Patzsch (1897–1966). Block was inspired by his work, as were many photographers of the time—from Renger-Patzsch's view of the physical world to his selection of motifs. Block certainly knew his photo books *Lübeck* (1928) and *Die Welt ist schön* (The World is Beautiful, December 1928). As a reader of the Werkbund journal *Die Form*, Block came across Renger-Patzsch's photography early, in 1928, also in the North German culture-magazine *Der Kreis*. Block may also have seen his exhibitions at Hamburg's Kunstsalon Maria Kunde, in the early summer of 1928 and in April 1929, the latter already including Renger-Patzsch's Hamburg photos.[7]

Renger-Patzsch spent time in the Hanseatic city of Hamburg in 1928 and 1929, initially to complete a private commission for the Warburg banking family, and then to take photos for his book *Hamburg* (1930), published in December 1929.[8] Block would have certainly noticed this, since there were echoes of motif between Renger-Patzsch's photos and his own.[9] But that's not to say that Block copied Renger-Patzsch. For example, Block had published his own photos of ships in *Die Form* in December 1929. Immediate comparisons are, in any case, moot: on one hand, the general influence of Renger-Patzsch on Block is unquestionable, and, on the other hand, their shared, aesthetically modern way of seeing things led to similar pictorial solutions, as it did for many photographers of the time. There were also differences: Block only partially reiterated Renger-Patzsch's style of the detailed close-up. This was not only because his Leica was not as precise as Renger-Patzsch's plate camera, it was also because Block was less focused on mastering a single photo; he was more concerned with reportage-like series.

Block also drew his attention to two representatives of the New Photography in Hamburg, whose work corresponded to his objective concept of photography: Ernst Scheel (1903–1986) and Arvid Gutschow (1900–1984). Scheel was specialized in architectural photography, in particular of buildings by the architect Karl Schneider, but he also took artistic photos that were concerned with technology.[10] Block must have had personal contact with Scheel, since Scheel took photos of buildings that had been designed and constructed by the Dr. Block & Hochfeld architectural firm, including views of Haus Philip [p. 16]. Moreover, Block most certainly was familiar with Scheel's Hamburg photos in the illustrated press. The similarity of both their subjects and style is evident: Block's photographs of a ship's funnel [p. 28], mast [p. 59], and a wooden roller coaster [p. 38], are all similar to images made by Scheel.[11] One practical difference, however, was that Scheel worked with a tripod and plate camera, which is why his thoroughly prepared images are characterized by compositional rigor and graphic precision. Block, with his Leica, was more concerned with catching the ideal moment.

Block and Arvid Gutschow were similar in several ways: both were photography autodidacts, and both were not professional photographers; Gutschow was a civil servant.[12] And Gutschow also came to artistic photography through architectural photography.[13] In 1929, he had even taken and

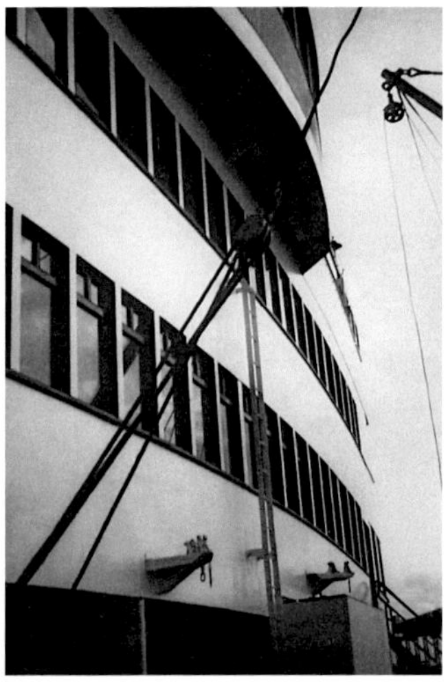

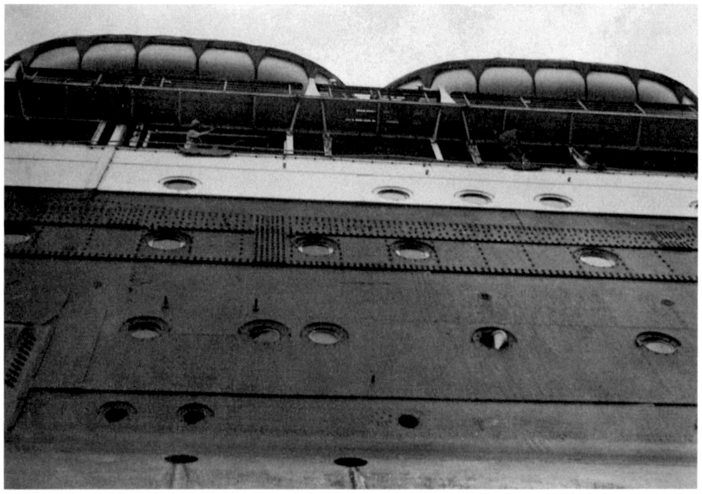

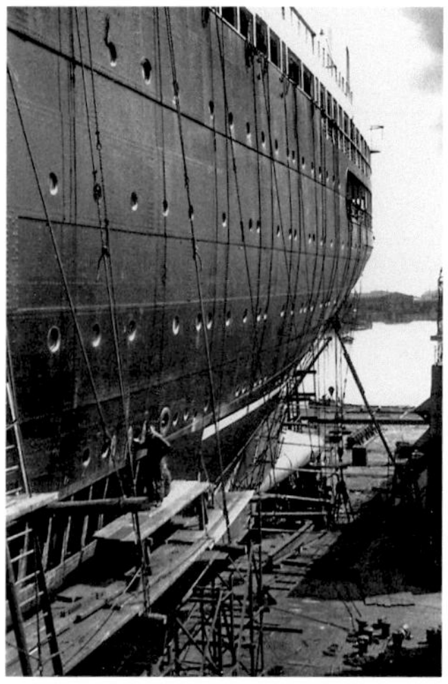

Details of the steamships *Hamburg* and *Columbus*, Hamburg, 1929

published photos of the construction site of the Deutschlandhaus.[14] Block would have met Gutschow in person, because, in 1929, the architect Konstanty Gutschow, Arvid's brother, moved into an office in the Deutschlandhaus next to Dr. Block & Hochfeld. Both photographers are similar in terms of their objective perspective, as well as in their Hamburg motifs. Gutschow made images of the Elbe bridges, which appeared in the illustrated press as of 1928.[15] He showed images of the Hamburg harbor at the 1929 Werkbund exhibition *Film und Foto*, and he published them in the photo book *Das Werk. Technische Lichtbildstudien* (1931) (The Work. Photographic Studies of Technology). Here, photos by Block could also have been published, were it not for the book's inclusion of similar images by Hamburg photographer Will (Wilhelm) Keiling, a journalist for the Hamburg-America Line (Hapag), whose oeuvre was, of course, replete with images of ships and cruises.[16]

Block is also missing from the ambitious Hamburg photo publication *Das Bild. Monatshefte für Kunst + Technik* (The Image. Monthly Journal of Art + Technology), which is based on *Das neue Frankfurt* and of which only a single issue was published, in March 1930. Included as representatives of Hamburg's modern photography were Ernst Scheel, Arvid Gutschow, and Fritz Schleifer (1903–1977).[17] In 1931, Block was supposed to represent the New Photography in Northern Germany, together with Scheel and Gutschow, in a book about Hamburg photographers planned by art historian Franz Roh, for his series *Fototek*.[18] Alas, the series was discontinued after only two titles, and the volume on Hamburg was never published. Its existence would have lastingly secured Block's place in photographic history.

Bridges, Cranes, and Shipyards

Within his Hamburg photographs, Block was interested neither in standard cityscapes, nor in modern architecture. Instead, he took a fresh look at the harbor, people, and nature, within the rubrics of specified motifs. Only a few of these photographs are preserved in Block's estate. One is a rather conventional view of the Stintfang [p. 30], a traditional scenic viewpoint over the Elbe River, where people watched passenger ships and the harbor. Significantly more creative was his panoramic view of the city from atop the Grasbrook gasometer [p. 30]. Block apparently also took photos of the Tiefstack gasometer, which was completed at the beginning of 1930 and was one the largest gasworks in Central Europe—but none of them survived. His photos either originated simultaneously or were inspired by similar photos by Scheel.[19]

Furthermore, Block made some detail shots of buildings in the city—not to depict them, but rather to try out perspectives of the New Vision. These images include photos of St. Michaelis church [p. 36], a city landmark, from below at a sharp angle, and of a mill that then stood on the edge of Heiligengeistfeld [p. 36], a large open space in the city. Block was less interested in closed structures, and more in technical constructions. Such objects, among the preferred ones of New Objectivity photographers, could be found all over Hamburg's harbor. A favorite was the dynamically curved New Elbe Bridge [pp. 2 and 37],[20] which offered Block the opportunity to contrast the static structure of the steel beams with a moment of "movement": the arch construction itself or the play of its shadows. In contrast, the Freeport Elbe Bridge was a more rigid structure. Block used a central perspective to effectively capture its skeletal steel frame [p. 39].

A special attraction for photographers was Hamburg's petroleum harbor, with its hulking oil tanks appearing as large technical sculptures. Block was familiar with the location: the architectural firm of Dr. Block & Hochfeld had built an administration building for an oil-storage company here in 1927. He captured views through the rows of oil tanks, the pipes connecting them, and of the oil barrels around them, dramatically cropping some of the images in final prints [p. 40–41]. Block highlighted the functionality and monumentality of technical equipment in his photographs of cranes, a traditionally popular motif in harbor photography.[21] He created details of different crane types [p. 43 and 46] and high-contrast backlit photographs, all to great graphic effect [p. 42–43 and 46].

The shipyards' docks and building slips offered an additional variety of harbor architecture. The largest shipyard in

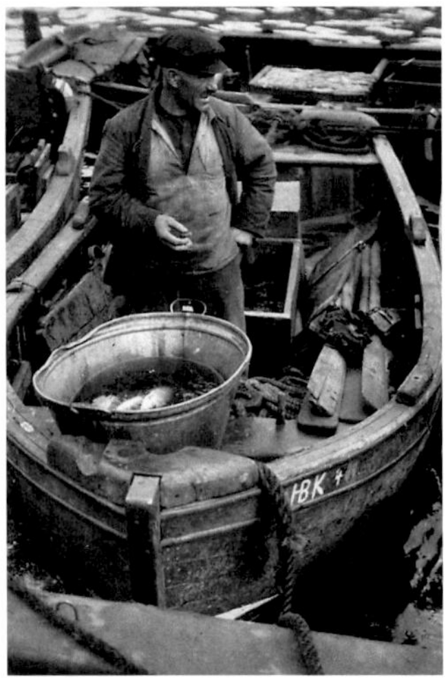
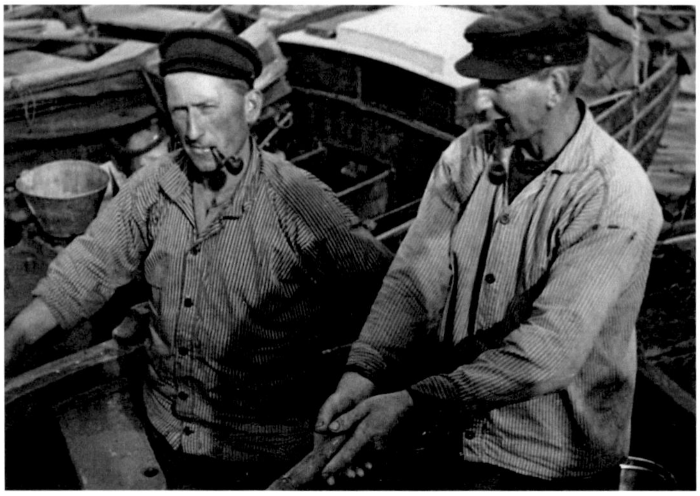
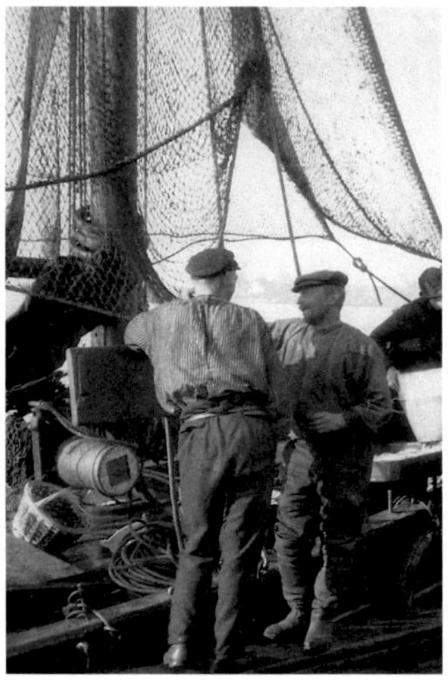

Fishermen at the St. Pauli Fish Market, Hamburg, 1931

Hamburg—in fact, in all of Germany—was Blohm & Voss. Located on the southern side of the Elbe River, directly opposite the city, it was an integral part of Hamburg's identity, not least as an employer. Their shipyard offered plentiful visual opportunities for both their own and external photographers alike. For the latter, publication of any photos required prior approval by Blohm & Voss, which was also permitted to use the images for its own presswork. In 1929–30, Block took nearly a hundred photos at Blohm & Voss, most exhibiting the shipyard's seemingly bizarre crossing steel structures [p. 18], or looking down from them as new ships were being built [p. 49].

A noteworthy event in German and Hamburg shipbuilding history was the construction of the turbine steamship *Europe,* for North German Lloyd, in 1928–30, at Blohm & Voss. This ship and its sister vessel, *Bremen* (built in the eponymous city), were the fastest and most elegant ships on the North Atlantic route. This prestige object received appropriate coverage in the illustrated press, and Scheel and Renger-Patzsch also documented the spectacle.[22] Attention was further enhanced by the circumstances surrounding its completion: after the water-launch of the *Europe*, in August 1928, a workers strike postponed further work aboard the vessel. In March 1929, a fire on the ship broke out while it was at the equipment quay, causing severe damage. The *Europe* had to be repaired in a floating dock, where photographers had the opportunity to take pictures of the entire hull. Block documented the hull and bow of the *Europa* in the floating dock—directly from the front, from the bottom, and together with cranes [pp. 1 and 48]. He also took a close-up of an entire propeller [p. 47].

At the same time, Block captured the work of dockyard laborers, particularly riveters, as part of shipbuilding as an undertaking made possible foremost by technology [p. 50]. While this motif was formed primarily by images of individual workers, Block also peered down from the building-slip's gantry structure, to the square in front of the shipyard's main building, as workers headed out on their lunch break [p. 51]. In February 1931, this photo was on the cover of the company magazine *B & V Werft-Zeitung*,[23] which, in another issue, also included a photo by Renger-Patzsch.[24] Scheel had taken a similar picture, from the same position, already in 1928, albeit less abstracting in the manner of the New Vision.[25] In January 1931, the illustrated supplement of the *Hamburger Anzeiger* published a double-page report on shipyard work, with photos by Block and other Hamburg photographers [pp. 52–53].

Ships, Nets, and Fishermen

The book *Schönheit der Technik* (1928) (Beauty of Technology), by Franz Kollmann, programmatically expressed a fascination with the aesthetic dimension of technical functionality, which was typical of the time. In December 1929, he published an "Essay on Technical Form Analysis" in the Werkbund journal *Die Form,* using the example of ship photos: "It is interesting to see how an architect photographically deals with a certain subject."[26] All of the images accompanying the essay, including the cover photo of the journal itself, were by Block [pp. 54–55]. The latter shows a row of three smokestacks of the *Cap Arcona,* of the shipping company Hamburg Süd. Additional pictures illustrate ship details, from the propeller to the hull and bridge to the superstructure, including, above all, funnels rising like modern sculptures [pp. 28, 31 and 56–57]. Kollmann wrote of Block's photos of the exhaust ducts of the Hamburg-America Line's steamship *Hamburg*: "Often, the effect of individual elements is reinforced by grouping and gradation. Identical or similar bodies gain the strongest effect when they are clustered together. The new photographer sees a lot here."[27] Incidentally, these comments contain repeated references to the (alleged) manner in which shipbuilding formed a model for modern architecture. Block's photographs were taken at the same time that Hans Finsler (1891–1972) took photos of the North German Lloyd's steamship *Bremen,* in July 1929.[28] Finsler's pictures also show the hull in great detail, and close-ups of various arrangements of geometric volumes.

In principle, Block tended more towards the direction of New Photography's new objectivity than he did towards the New Vision's technical experiments. For example, there is no evidence of Block making double exposures or photo-

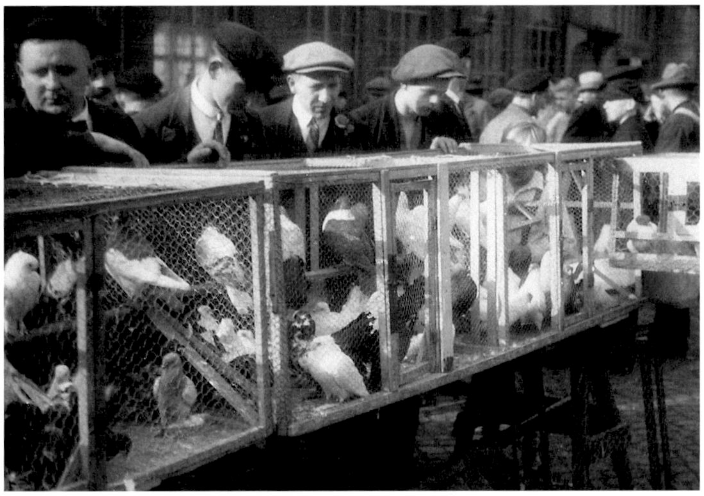

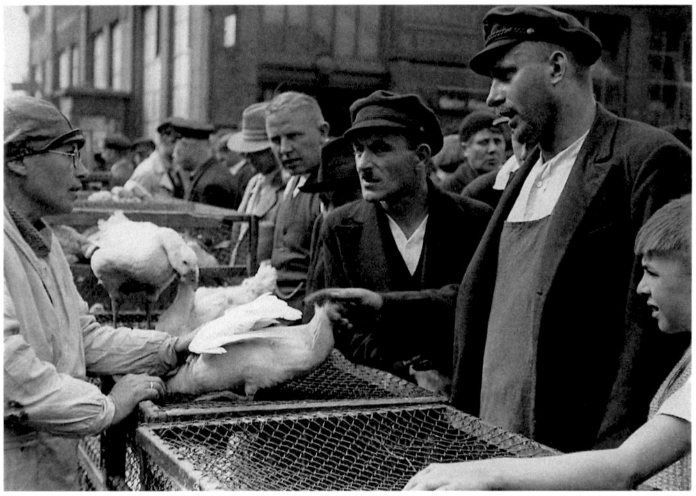

St. Pauli Fish Market (poultry section), Hamburg, 1931

grams. He did, however, create reversal photos on occasion—prints reproduced in negative. Werner Gräff noted of this procedure, in his book *Es kommt der neue Fotograf!* (1929) (Here Comes the New Photographer!): "The photographic distortion of tonal value is an artificial means of expanding the capacity of our eyes."[29] As examples, he offers motifs by Andreas Feininger (1906–1999), who, by the way, had also photographed in Hamburg in 1930–31.[30] Reversal photos were also shown at the *Film und Foto* exhibition in 1929, and examples were subsequently included in the book *foto-auge* (1929), by Franz Roh and Jan Tschichold. These examples may have inspired Block to create a negative print of his images of the steamer *Cap Arcona's* deck [p. 57].

While Block's photographs of ship superstructures focused on the objects' sculptural corporeality, photographs of masts, rigging, and loading-gear gave him the opportunity to emphasize linear patterns and structures [pp. 58–59]. Kollmann writes: "Single forms can become, in large units, body shapes (hulls), while body shapes can turn into skeletal forms under certain conditions. Masts, in small sections, can become massive tubes, which when joined to yards and ropes become a delimiting spatial framework. This limited space does not look flat; it merely replaces bodies with lines."[31]

Like Renger-Patzsch, Block tried to find motifs in the harbor, in addition to technical imagery, in which well-considered details not only created a compositional effect but also offered atmospheric impressions. Successful examples are his photographs of a mooring post [p. 60] and of fishing boats and their reflections in the water [p. 61]. Block's motivation had nothing to do with documenting local history but with photographic design, a fact evidenced also in his photographs of fishing-boat nets [p. 62]. Models for these photos can be found in Renger-Patzsch's books *Die Halligen* (1927) (The Halligen) and *Die Welt ist schön* (1928). Block's emulation of Renger-Patzsch is particularly evident in the image of a small boat's fishing nets [p. 63], which is almost identical to a motif in Renger-Patzsch's book *Hamburg* (plate 44).

Block more so shared a similar view of fishermen's everyday work with Arvid Gutschow.[32] In an entire photo series, Block documented fishing boats at the St. Pauli fish market, from which fresh catch was sold directly on the quay. His perspectives ranged from group pictures to views from above, to the individual portrait [pp. 32, 64–67], each of them seemingly authentic snapshots. The fish market included additional merchants, like poultry traders, who offered their goods in cages ogled by the passing crowds [p. 33]. Block had a special eye for such scenes of everyday life.

Circus, Animals, and Plants

Manifestations of popular culture, vaudeville and circus enjoyed great popularity in the 1920s, and thus were often pictorial themes in the illustrated press. Block shared this interest with other representatives of the New Photography, including Umbo (Otto Umbehr) and Sasha Stone. Hagenbeck's traveling circus, operating in the open air, offered Block a variety of motifs, from horse acts [p. 34] to audiences of children [pp. 70–71]. His photos of aerialists [pp. 72–73] perform their own feat of negating all spatial reference, and, as such, partake of the New Vision. Block's photos of clowns, in turn, confirm his talent for creating compelling studies of people [pp. 74–75]. This can also be seen in a series of clown portraits from the great Circus Sarrasani, which came to Hamburg frequently [p. 76]. One of these images landed on the cover of the North German radio magazine *Norag,* in 1932 [p. 77]. In 1931, Block photographed the Swedish clowns of the Bronett Brothers at their appearance at the Hamburger vaudeville house Flora [p. 75].

Circus Sarrasani's program featured not only animals and performers but also, in an anthropological display common for the times, representatives of various ethnic groups. Block took photographs of "Indians" (Native Americans) as well as actual Indians, both in local clothing (or costumes) [p. 78]. Among the circus artists portrayed was a French aerial acrobat [p. 79]. Block took humorous snapshots, too, like the one of a performer who allows her hair to be combed by a friendly chimpanzee [p. 34]. The popularity of such circus photographs is evidenced by various publications of Block's

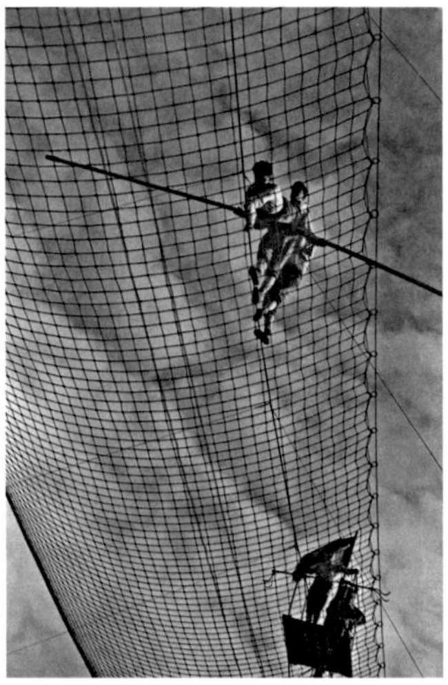
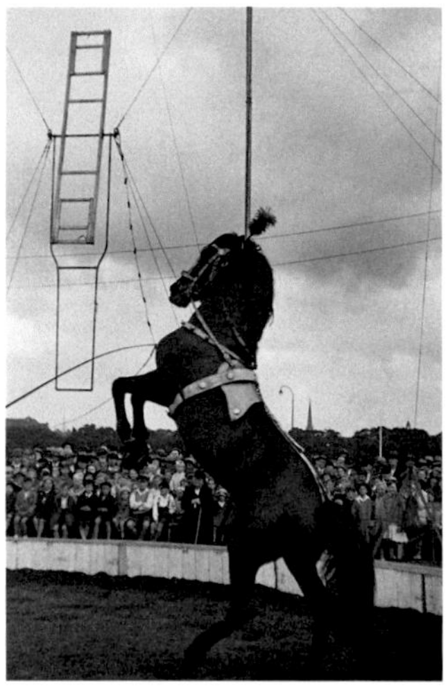

Open-air circus with aerialists and horse act, Hamburg, 1931

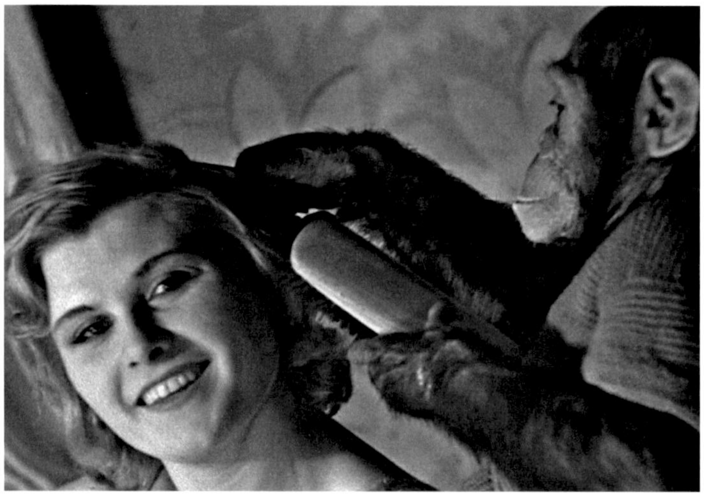

"Friendship between circus performers," Hamburg, 1932

images, including in *Das Echo der Woche*, an illustrated supplement from the *Hamburger Echo*, and the *Basler Illustrierte Zeitung,* from Switzerland [pp. 68–69].

In the 1920s, wildlife photography became popular for amateur as well as professional photographers.[33] Animals were no longer seen as exotic creatures or scientific objects, but were regarded and respected as beings with individuality. Motifs appropriate to this understanding found their way into the illustrated press and photo books. Particularly influential were animal photos by Hedda Walther (1894–1979), published together with texts by Paul Eipper, in books such as *Tiere sehen dich an* (1928) (Animals Looking at You). A copy of this book is preserved in Block's estate. The photographs herein were not taken in the wild, but rather in the zoos of major German cities, among them Berlin, Frankfurt, and Leipzig. With Hagenbeck's Zoo, Hamburg had a particularly traditional and nationally known zoo. It formed part of the identity of the city and was featured in tourist advertisement and in the illustrated press.

Renowned photographers of the time visited Hagenbeck's Zoo to take photos of animals. The most well known are by Renger-Patzsch, seen in his books *Die Welt ist schön* (1928) and *Hamburg* (1930). Dr. Paul Wolff also took photos here, for his book *Aus Zoologischen Gärten* (1929) (From the Zoos). Block turned his gaze less upon Hagenbeck's larger animals such as the hippopotamus [p. 80] and rather on lamas, ponies, and sheep or penguins, flamingos, and geese. He was especially fond of photographing baby animals, which the zoo took special pride in presenting to the public in early summer. Block's photographs include those of two young lions [p. 80]. He was inspired by the photo book *Tierkinder* (1929), by Hedda Walther, a copy of which he owned. Block composed his pictures for a photo reportage that appeared in July 1933, in the illustrated supplement of the *Hamburger Anzeiger* [p. 81]. This was the last time that Block, because he was Jewish, would be allowed to publish photos in Hamburg's local press.

A complementary photographic motif in the second half of the twenties, alongside technology, were forms of the plant world.[34] Based on the documentation of botanical samples, these photographs were mostly formal close-ups, characteristic of the New Objectivity. Examples include Renger-Patzsch's photographs as well as the photo books *Urformen der Kunst* (1928) (Art Forms in Nature), by Karl Blossfeldt, *Die Pflanze als Lebewesen* (1930) (Plants as Forms of Life), by Ernst Fuhrmann, and *Formen des Lebens. Botanische Lichtbildstudien* (1931) (Forms of Life. Botantical Photo Studies), by Dr. Paul Wolff. Block was likely familiar with all of these publications; a copy of Wolff's book is found in his estate. Of his own plant photos, only one survived: a close-up shot of a Sour Fig flower *(Mesembryanthemum acinaciforme)* [p. 82] from above. There are also negatives of Block's studies of backlit grasses and of tree roots. Above all, he was fascinated by leafless trees, which allowed him to explore the nature's principles of construction. He looked up the tree trunks into the treetops to take photographs of the sprawling tree branches [p. 83]. Block visualized the same ideas that concerned him as an architect: the analogies between architecture, technology, and nature.

Photo Book of Hamburg

Block had apparently planned to publish his 1929 Hamburg photos in book form: in his estate exists a book dummy labeled "Fotobuch Hamburg", with roughly sixty prints glued into it. But this is not simply a dummy for a photo book. It is rather an album that references his images and, at the same time, offers a sketch of a larger book concept. However, an accompanying text by Block has not been preserved. The motivation was likely his desire to see his work in the format of a photo book. But publishing it was unrealistic, because Block's pool of images was too limited for a portrait of Hamburg. For a pure photo book, the images did not yet evidence a consistent or sufficient level of technical or artistic quality. Moreover, Renger-Patzsch's photo book *Hamburg* was published at the end of 1929, preemptively filling the need for a modern photographic portrait of the city.

All things considered, it must be noted that Block photographed a remarkably broad spectrum of topics in Hamburg—from ports and ships to fishermen and circus clowns, to animals and plants—and all in a relatively short time. In terms of design and style, his body of work from Hamburg can also be regarded as exemplary of important trends in the New Photography in Germany around 1930. With his still lifes and X-rays of shells and snails, Block further honed his photographic eye. And with his travel photography, he expanded his breadth of motifs, and throughout he grew in artistic autonomy. In these respects, among the Hamburg photographers of his generation, and seen in light of his entire photographic output, Block was the most versatile.

1 Burcu Dogramaci, "Stadt der Fotografie. Hamburger Kamerakünstler zur Zeit der Weimarer Republik," in "*Himmel auf Zeit*". Die *Kultur der 1920er Jahre in Hamburg*," Dirk Hempel and Friederike Weimar, ed. (Neumünster, 2010) 259–290, for Block, see 271, 272 and 287–289.
2 Since an exact dating of Block's Hamburg photos is not always possible, those dated here are done so according to plausibility, not certainty.
3 See Katharina Heise, "'Von meinen fünf Sinnen ist mir die Gabe des Sehens am wichtigsten'. Hamburg in den Photographien von Albert Renger-Patzsch, E. O. Hoppé, Andreas Feininger, und Herbert List" in *Hamburger Ansichten. Maler sehen die Stadt*, Ulrich Luckhardt ed. (Köln, 2009) 37–61 (partly with incorrect dates).
4 Roland Jaeger, "Ein Bilderkompendium aller Weltstädte. Die Reihe *Das Gesicht der Städte* im Albertus-Verlag, Berlin," in *Autopsie. Deutschsprachige Fotobücher 1918 bis 1945*, Manfred Heiting and Roland Jaeger, eds. vol. 1 (Göttingen, 2012), 202–217, esp. 204–205.
5 See Martin Malte Blumenthal, *Ursula Wolff (1906–1977) – Fotografin für die illustrierte Presse. Leben und Werk einer modernen Fotojournalistin in der Weimarer Republik* (diss. Hamburg, 2007; 2012, 2nd edition).
6 See the auction catalog *Argenteuil. Maison de Vente, Cami et Sasha Stone* (Argenteuil, 2009), 78–83, no. 235–255. – Birgit Hammers, "Sasha Stone *sieht noch mehr*". *Ein Fotograf zwischen Kunst und Kommerz* (Petersberg, 2014).
7 For the early reception of Renger-Patzsch in Hamburg, see Roland Jaeger, "Moderne Stadtwerbung mit Photographie: Das 'Hamburg'-Buch von Albert Renger-Patzsch," in *Aus dem Antiquariat*, 2005, no. 3, 171–183.
8 See idem, "Optischer Eindruck und schöpferischer Blick. Fotobücher des Gebrüder Enoch Verlags, Hamburg," in Heiting/Jaeger (note 4), vol. 2 (Göttingen, 2014) 244–257, especially 247–251.
9 See, for example, *Alte Speicher am Fleet* (16), *Dampfer Cap Polonio* (32), *Kräne am Hafen* (34), *Die Europa im Bau* (40), *Gerät eines Kleinfischers* (44), *An Bord eines Überseedampfers* (46) and *Die Hamburger Elbbrücken* (88).
10 Roland Jaeger, "Architekt der Fläche: Der Fotograf Ernst Scheel," in *Architektur in Hamburg. Jahrbuch 2003,* Hamburgische Architektenkammer, ed. (Hamburg, 2003), 172–181. – *Ernst Scheel Fotograf 1903–1986*, Hans Bunge, ed. (München/Hamburg, 2015).
11 See Bunge 2015 (note 10), 75 (Schornstein), 73 (Schiffsmast) and 189 (Achterbahn).
12 See Roland Jaeger, "Arvid Gutschow gedruckt: Werkbelege des Fotografen in Buch und Presse," in *Aus dem Antiquariat*, NF 10, 2012, no. 6, 265–274. – *Arvid Gutschow*, Stefanie Odenthal, ed. (Ostfildern 2012).
13 Konstanty Gutschow, "Das technische Gesicht unserer Zeit," in *H.A. Illustrierte Zeitung. Wochenbeilage des Hannoverschen Anzeigers*, July 8, 1928 (with photos by Arvid Gutschow).
14 "Impressionen vom Bau. Photostudien von Arvid Gutschow," in *Illustrirte Zeitung*, vol. 173, no. 4414 (October 17, 1929), 542.
15 See, among others *Die Elbbrücke Hamburg-Harburg*, in *Der Querschnitt* 8, 1928, no. 1, facing 32. – *Elbbrücke zwischen Hamburg und Harburg*, in *Scherl's Magazin* 4, 1928, no. 8, 916.
16 In 1930, a volume announced as *Das Ozeanschiff. Gestalt und Aufgabe* in the *Schaubücher* series, was never published. See also Will Keiling, "Ozeanriesen," in *Atlantis* 3, 1931, no. 5, 268–272.
17 See Bunge 2015 (note 10), 176–183.
18 See Simone Förster, "'Der neue Fotograf packt die Dinge aus der Nähe'. Ernst Scheel und die Fotografie um 1930," in Bunge 2015 (note 10), 186–197, especially 195. – The author is greatful to Simone Förster, München, for this information.
19 See Bunge 2015 (note 10), 19, 178–179.
20 See Sven Bardua, *Brückenmetropole Hamburg. Baukunst – Technik – Geschichte bis 1945* (München/Hamburg, 2009), 101–108.
21 See Harry Braun, *Kräne im Hamburger Hafen. Eine Zeitreise* (Erfurt, 2014).
22 *Hamburger Illustrierte* 10, no. 33 (August 18, 1928) (cover photo by Scheel). – Albert Renger-Patzsch, *Hamburg* (Hamburg, 1930), 40–41.
23 *B & V Werft-Zeitung* 2, 1931, no. 5 (Feb. 27, 1931), 1. – Another photo by Block *ibid.*, no. 1 (Jan. 2, 1931), 1.
24 *Ibid.* 1, 1930, no. 10 (July 4, 1930), 1. – The photo archive of the shipyard Blohm & Voss is not yet accessible for conducting photo-historical research. Moreover, the archive is organized according to internal shipbuilding project numbers rather than the names of the photographers or chronologically.
25 *Hamburger Illustrierte* 10, no. 33 (August 18, 1928), 9.
26 Franz Kollmann, "Versuche zur technischen Formanalyse," in *Die Form* 4, 1929, no. 23, 625–630; quotation, 625.
27 *Ibid.*, 626.
28 See *Hans Finsler. Neue Wege der Photographie*, Klaus E. Göltz et al., eds. (Leipzig, 1991), 235–242. – The archive of the shipping company North German Lloyd (now Hapag-Lloyd) is not yet accessible for conducting photo-historical research.
29 Werner Gräff, *Es kommt der neue Fotograf!* (Berlin, 1929), 36.
30 See *Feiningers Hamburg. Die Hansestadt zu Beginn der 30er Jahre* (Düsseldorf/Wien, 1980).
31 Kollmann 1929 (note 26), 629–630.
32 "Vom Hamburg Altonaer Fischmarkt. Geschautes und Erlauschtes," in *Illustrirte Zeitung*, vol. 172, no. 4387 (April 11, 1929), 522.
33 See Eckhardt Köhn "'Rätsel der Tiernatur'. Aspekte der Zoo- und Zirkusfotografie in der Weimarer Republik," in *nützlich, süß und museal. Das fotografierte Tier*, Ute Eskildsen / Hans-Jürgen Lechtreck, eds. (Göttingen, 2005), 103–178.
34 See, among others, Rainer Stamm, *Die Welt der Pflanze. Photographien von Albert Renger-Patzsch und aus dem Auriga-Verlag* (Ostfildern-Ruit, 1998). – *Die Sprache der Pflanzen. Klassiker der Pflanzenfotografie im frühen 20. Jahrhundert,* Rainer Stamm and Kai Uwe Schierz, eds. (Erfurt, 2000).

St. Michaelis Church,
Hamburg, 1929

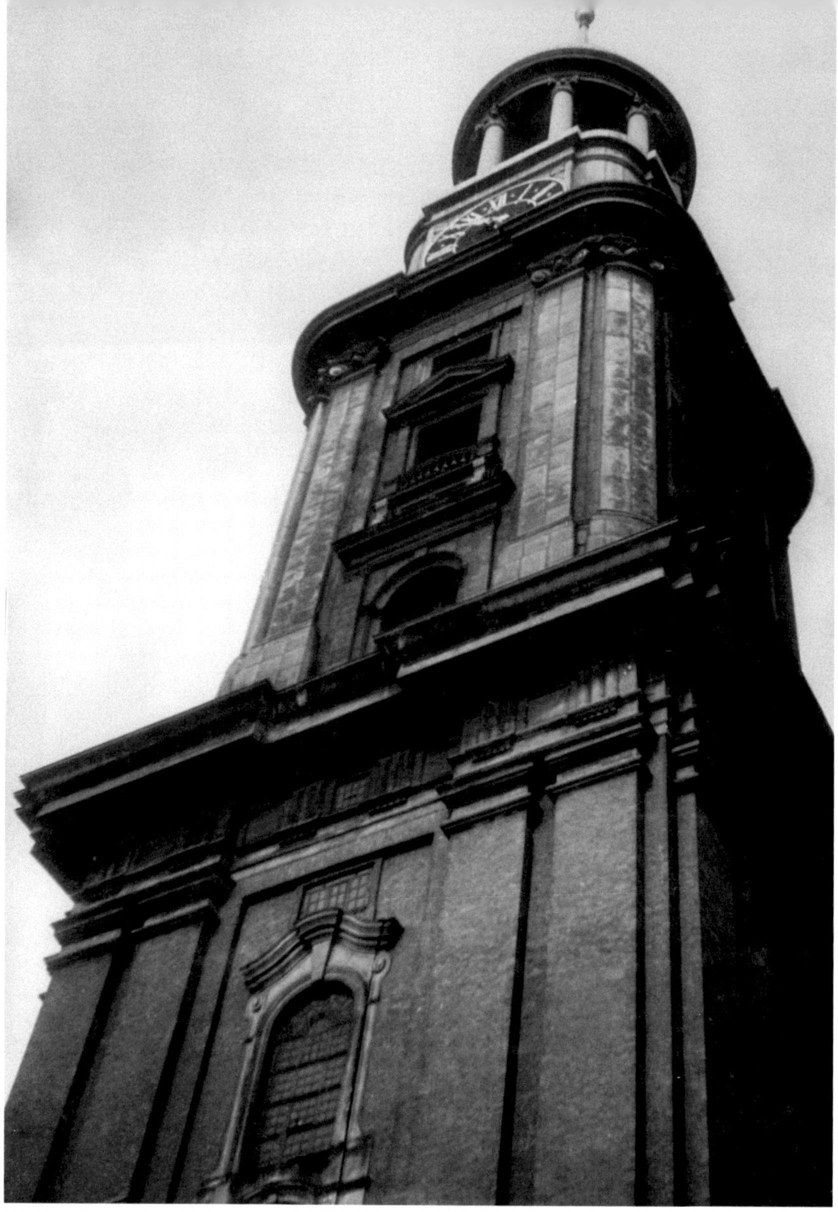

Windmill, Hamburg, 1929

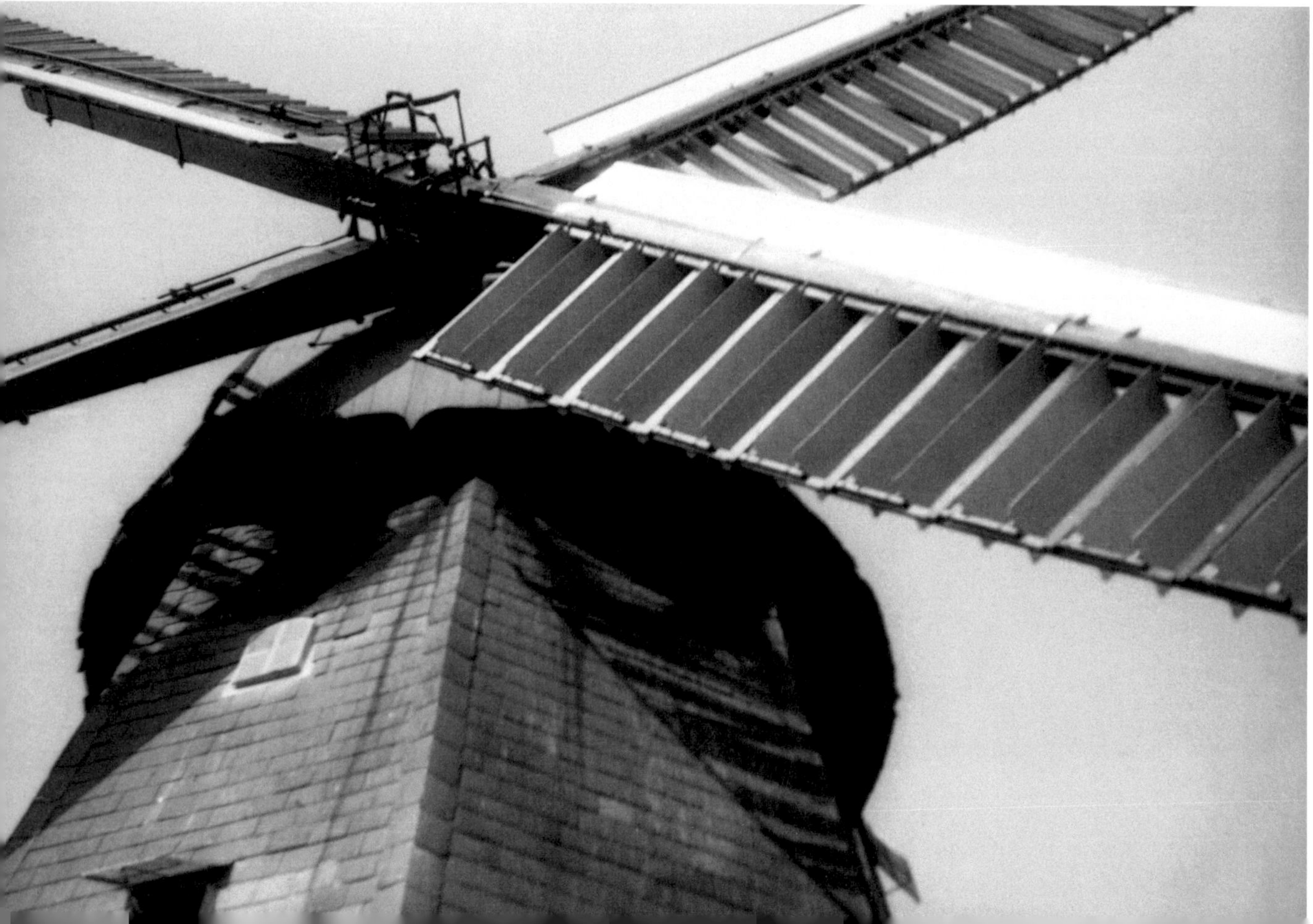

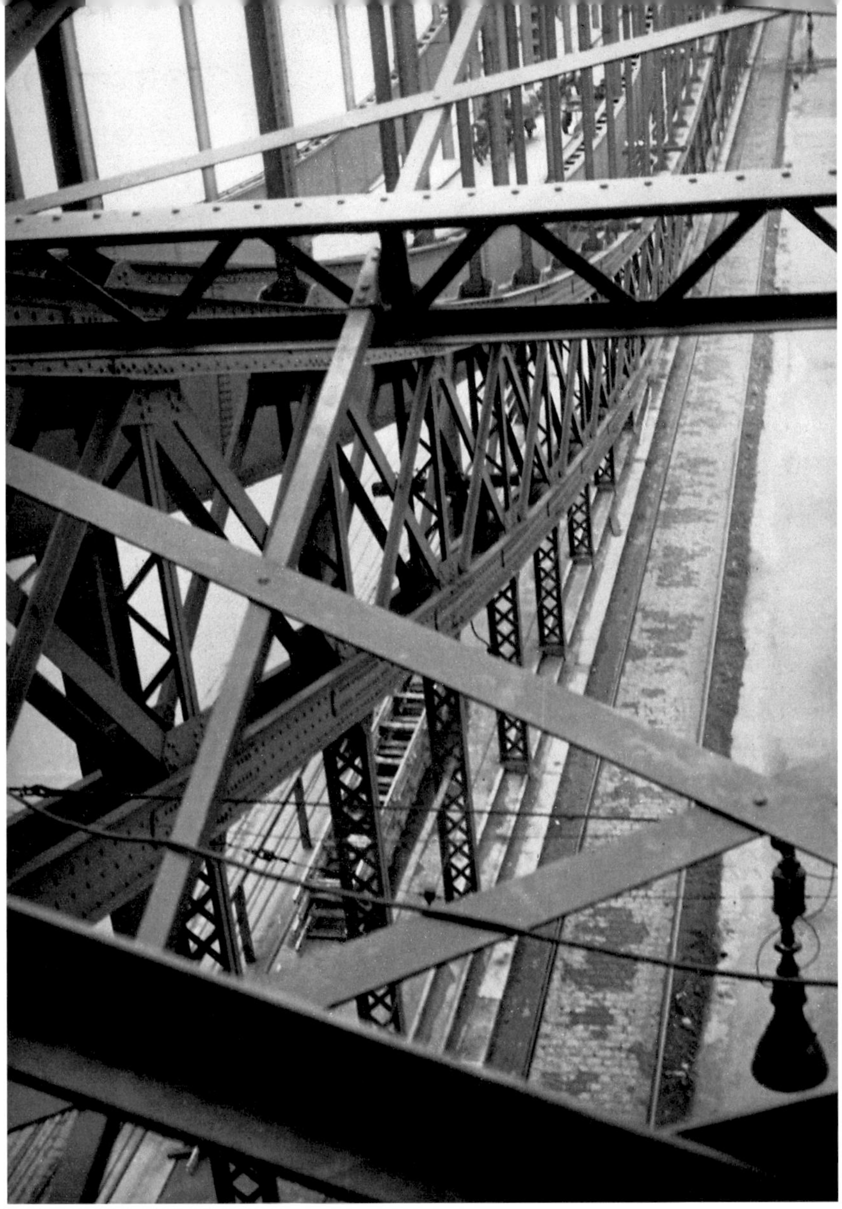

New Elbe Bridge,
Hamburg, 1929
(also see page 2)

New Elbe Bridge, Hamburg, 1929

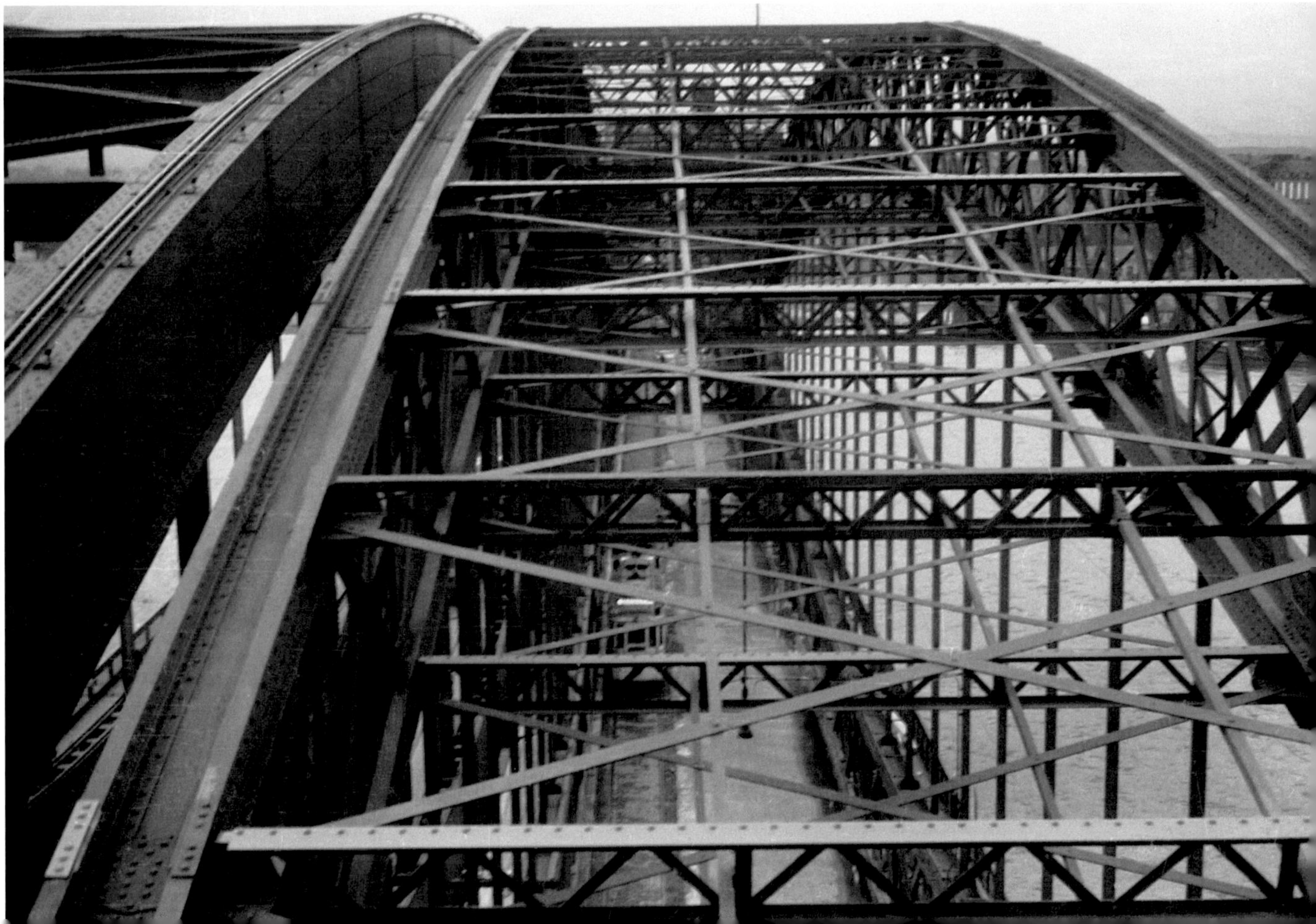

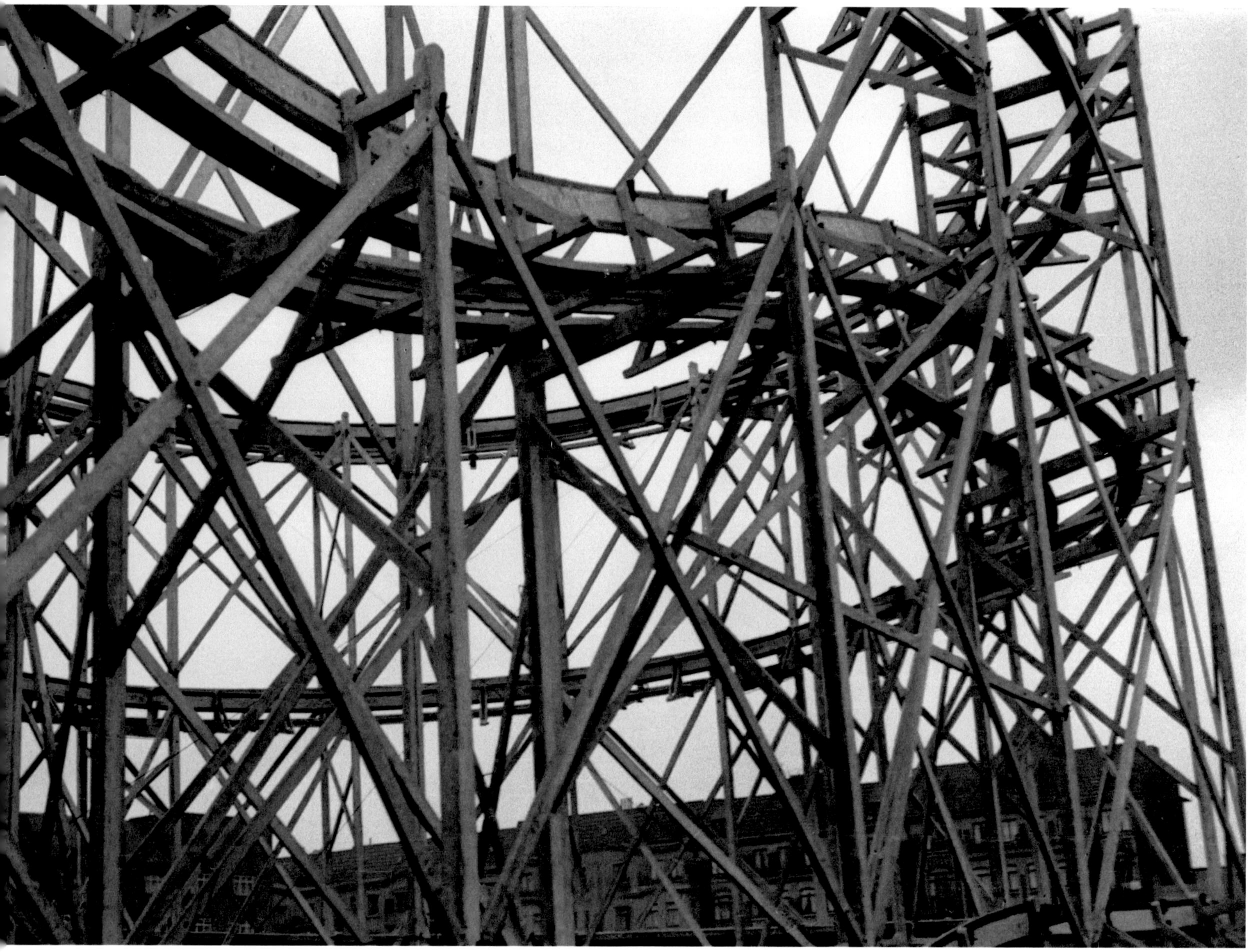

Wooden structure of a roller coaster, Hamburg, 1929

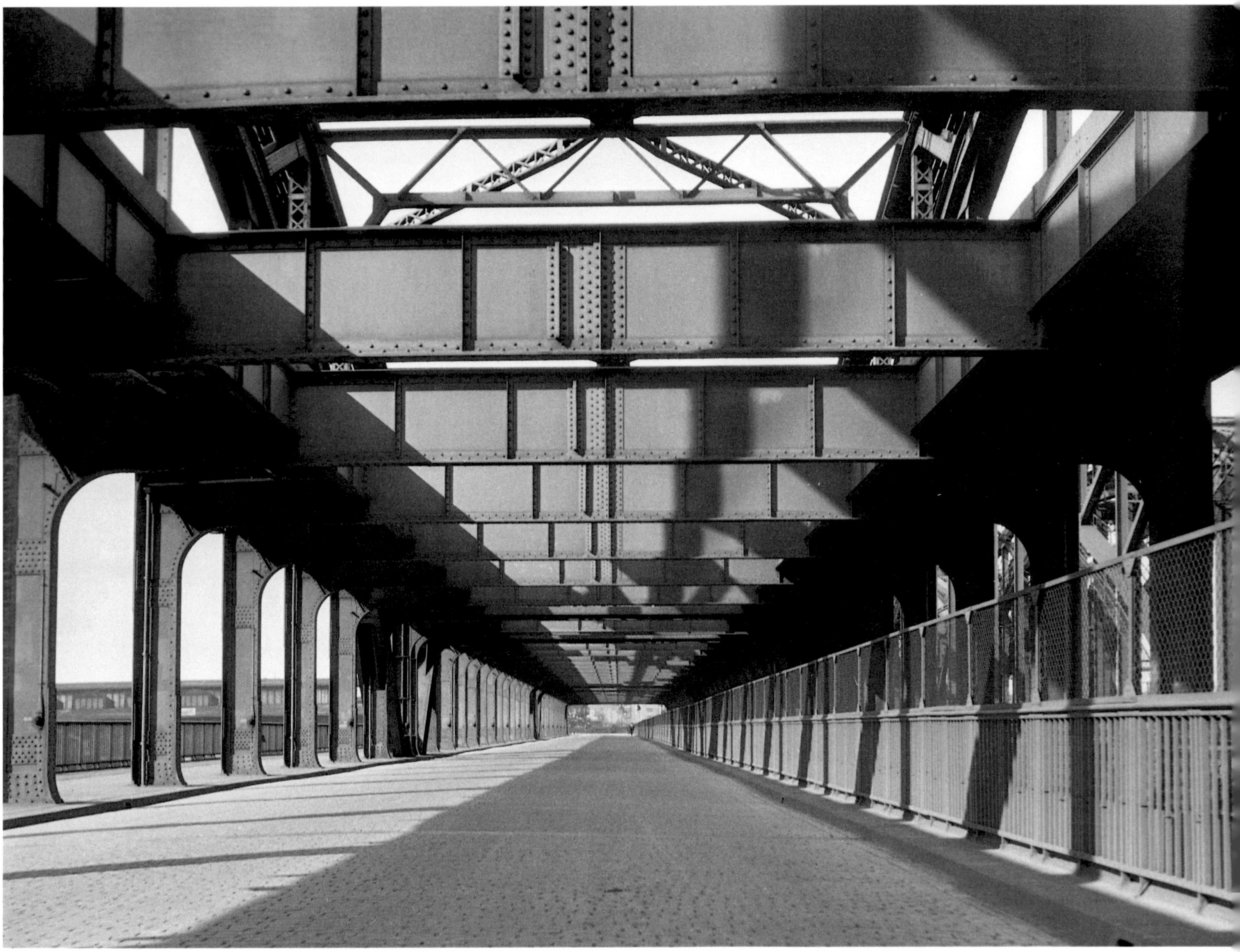

Freeport Elbe Bridge, Hamburg, 1929

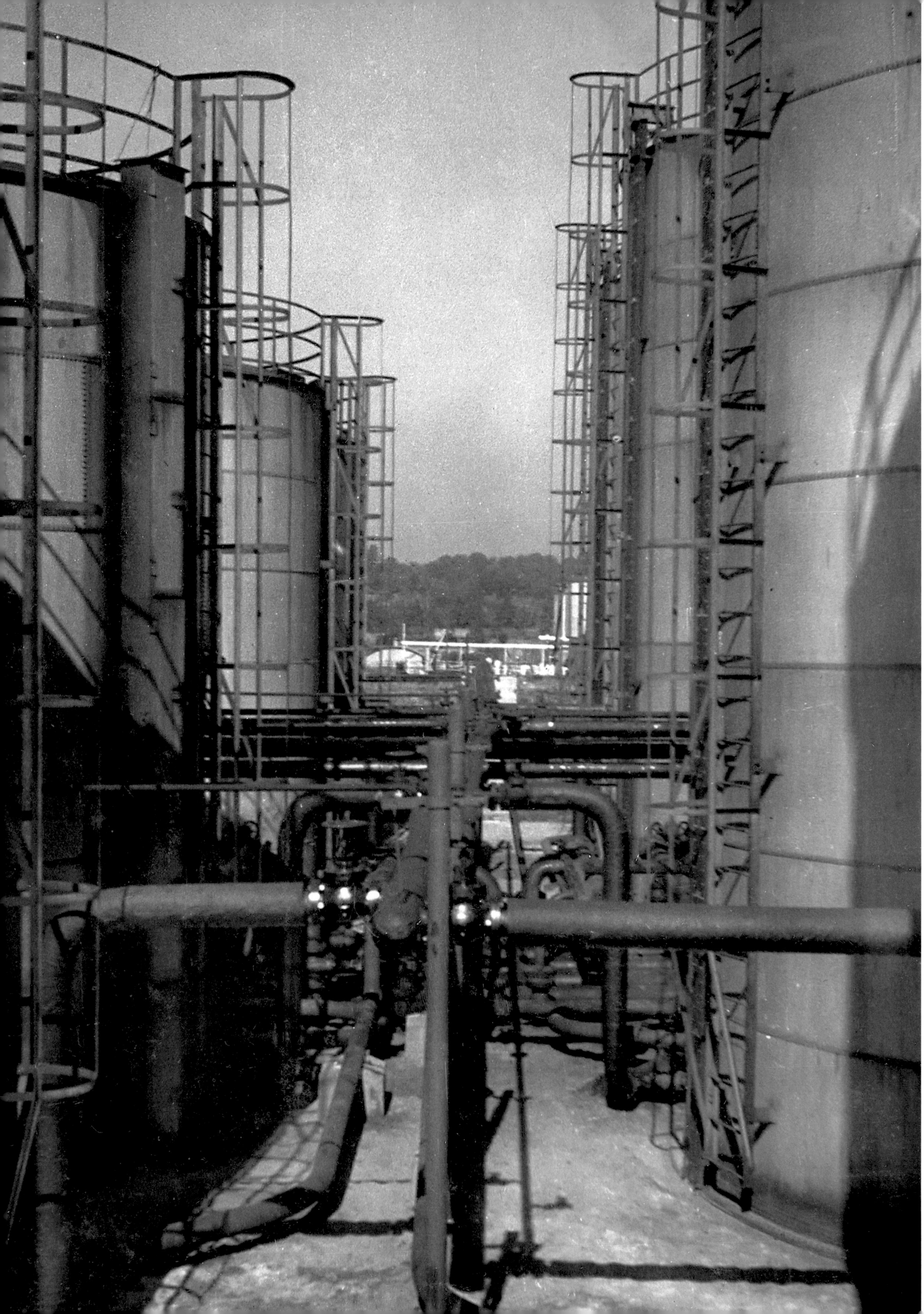

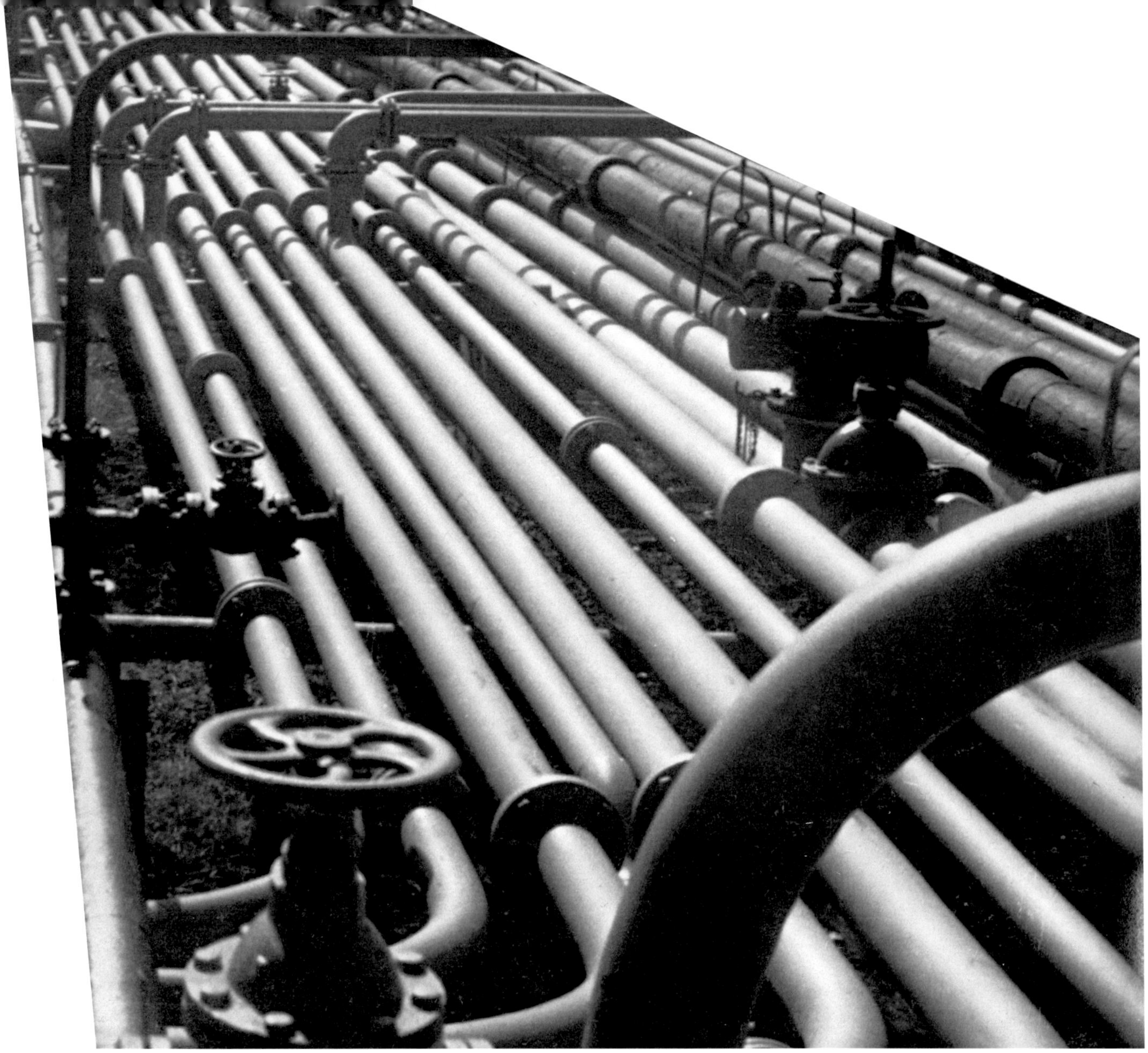

Oil tanks, pipes, and barrels in the Petroleumhafen, Hamburg, 1929

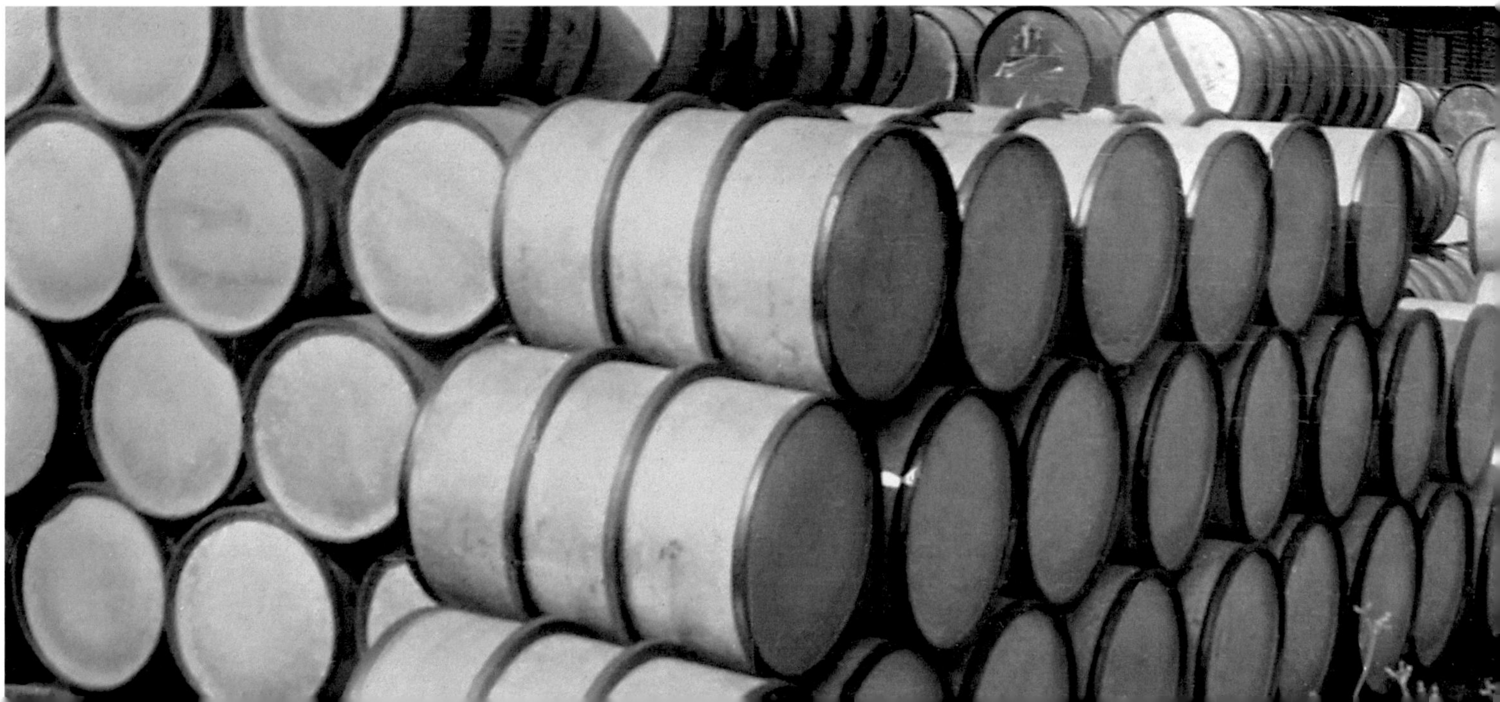

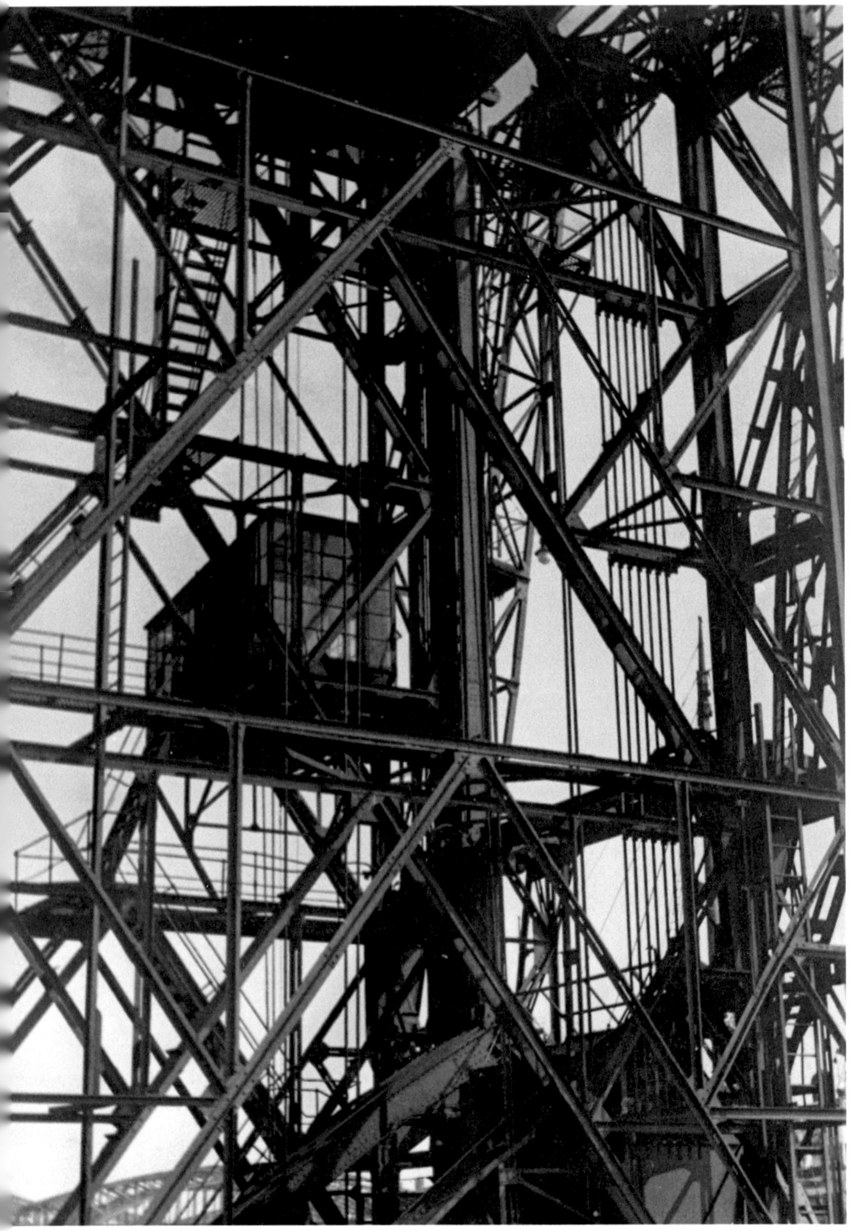

Coal hoist,
Hamburg, 1929

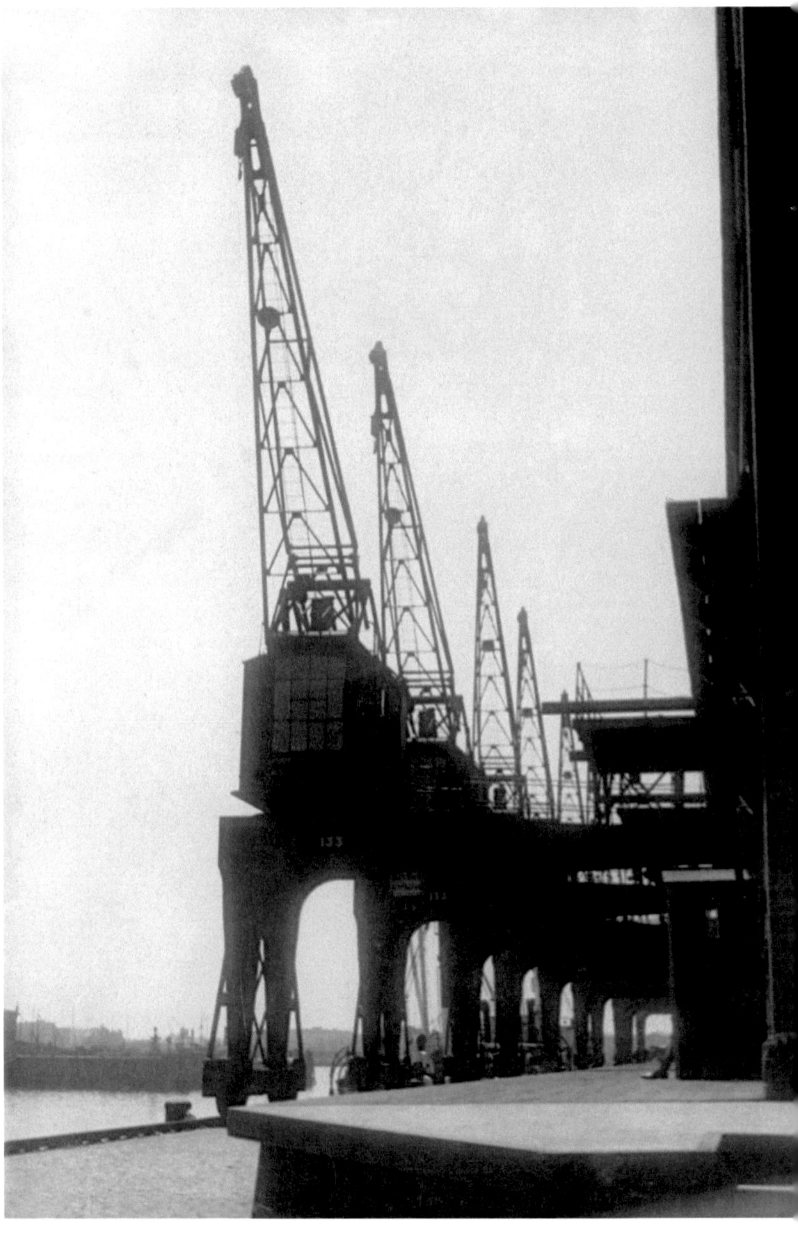

Semi-portal cranes, Hamburg, 1929

Harbor crane, Hamburg, 1929

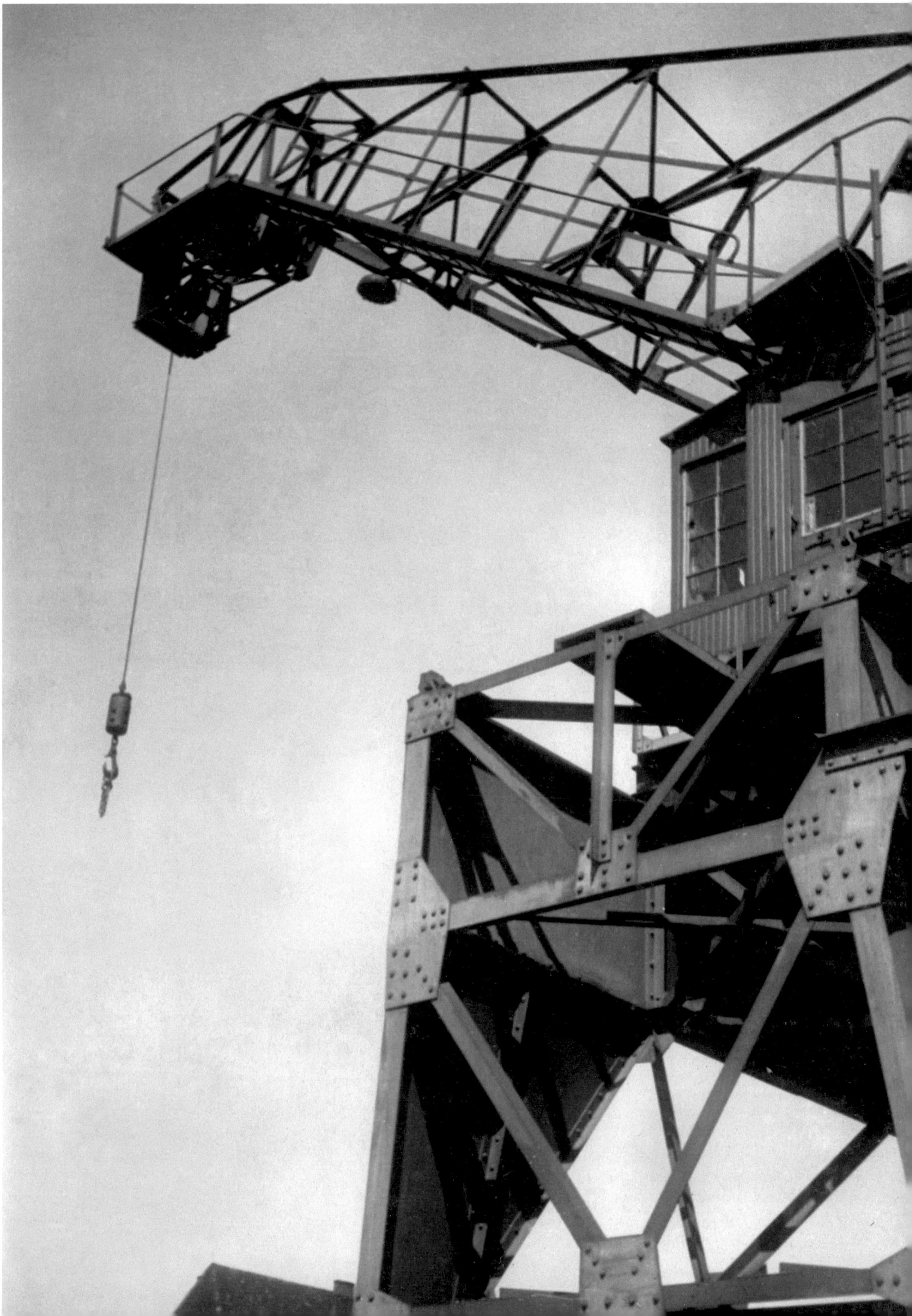

Ein Schiff wird gebaut

Sämtliche Bilder von Blohm & Voß, Hamburg (Fotos: Dr. Block)

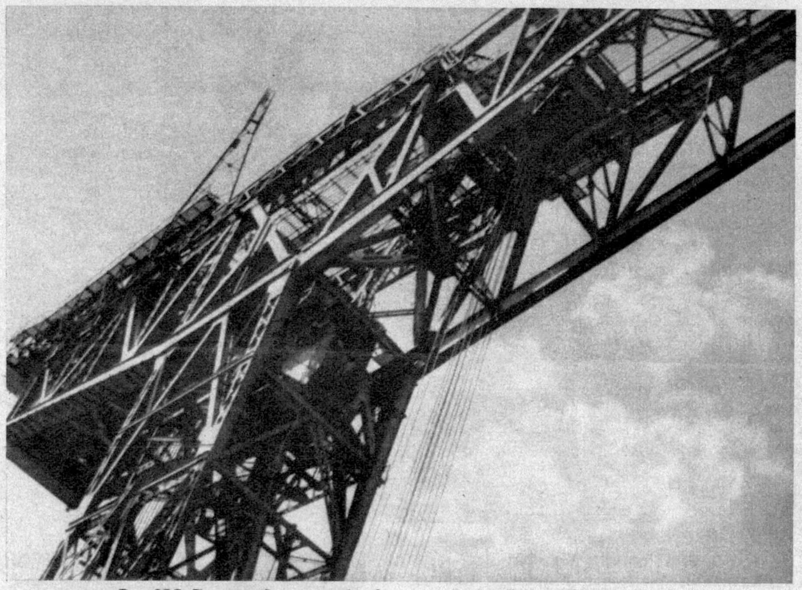

Der 250-Tonnen-Hammerwippkran am Steinwärder Ufer der Werft

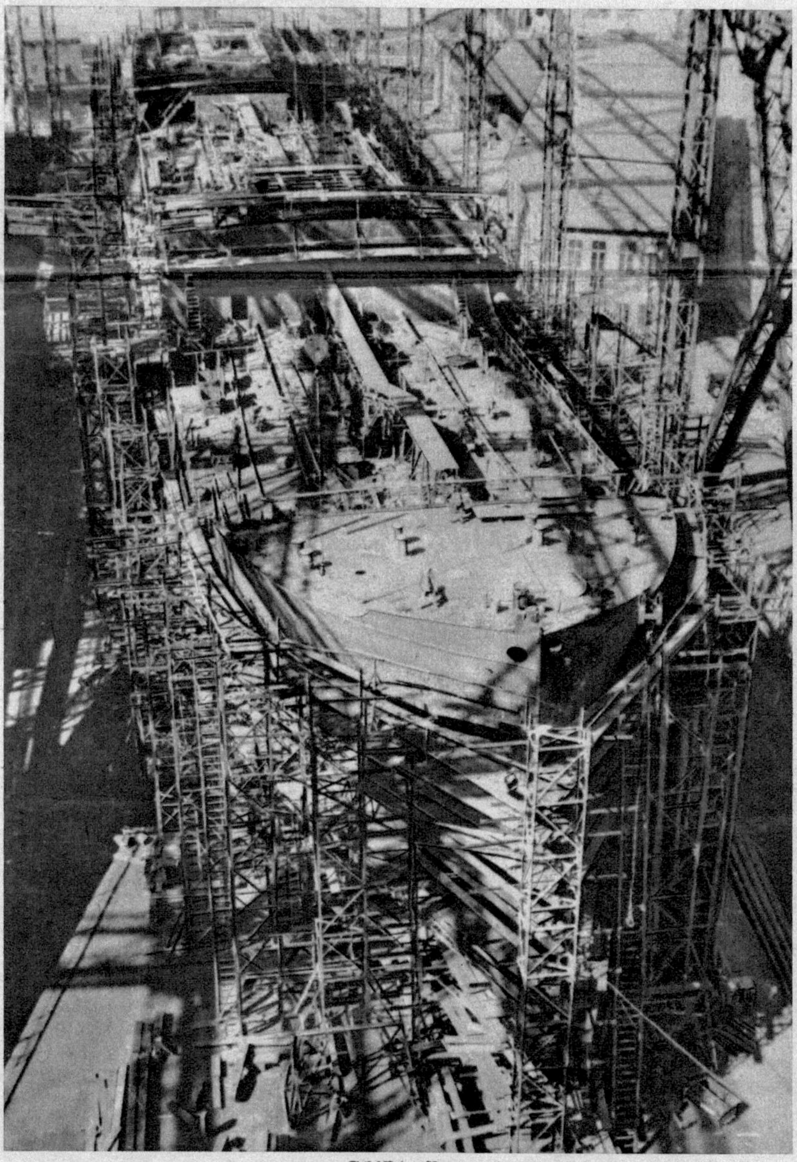

Schiff im Bau

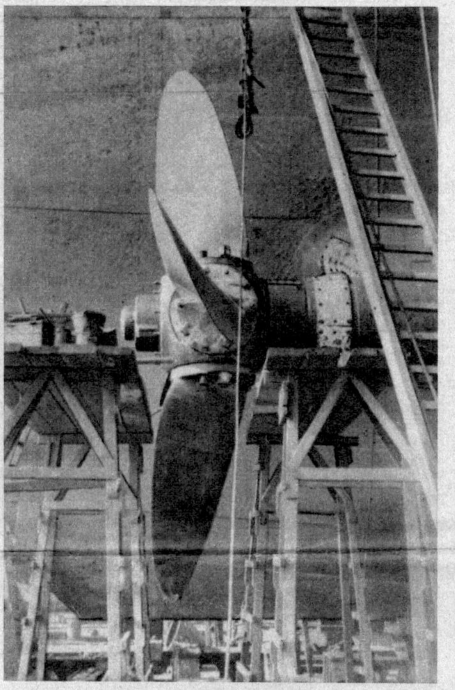

Propeller eines Schiffes
(Beachtenswert der Zinkschutz am Wellenbock)

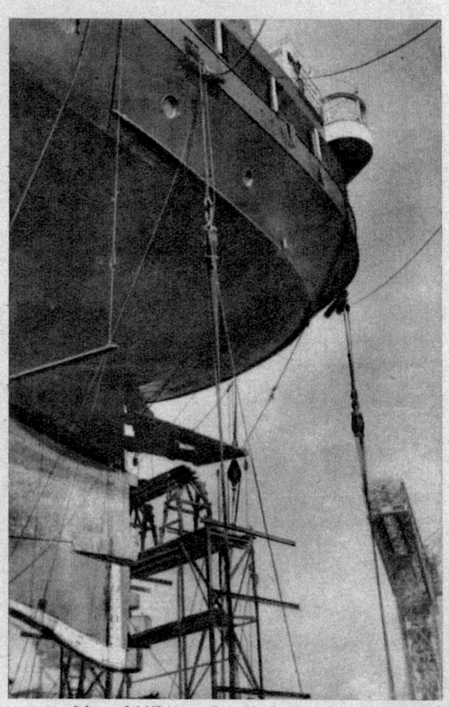

Hinterschiff der „Cap Polonio" im Dock

"A Ship under Construction," in an illustrated newspaper (not identified), 1933

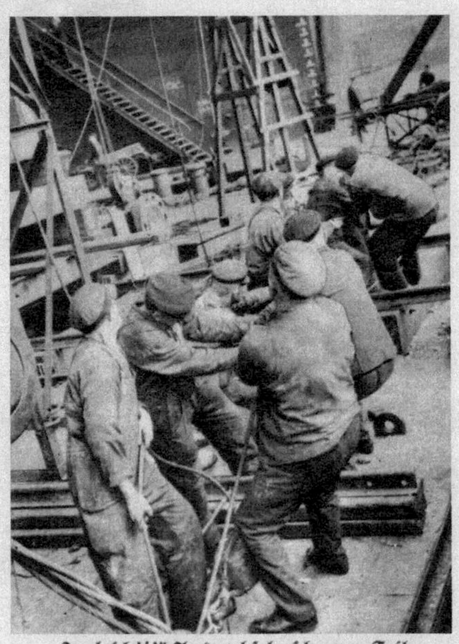

„Zugleich!!!" Auswechseln schwerer Teile

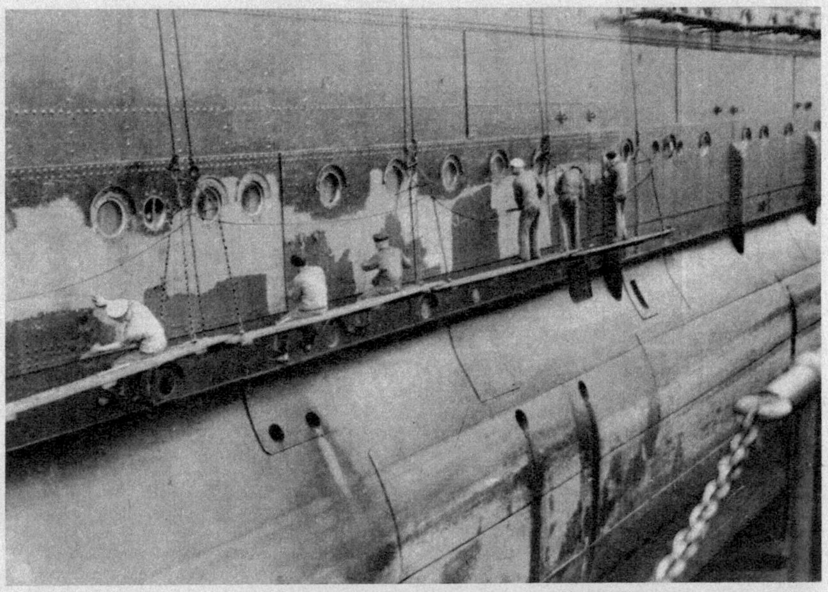

Farbeschraper auf der Hängestellage im Dock
Beachtenswert sind die Ausbauchungen der Schiffswand zur Erhöhung der Stabilität des Schiffes („Cap Polonio")

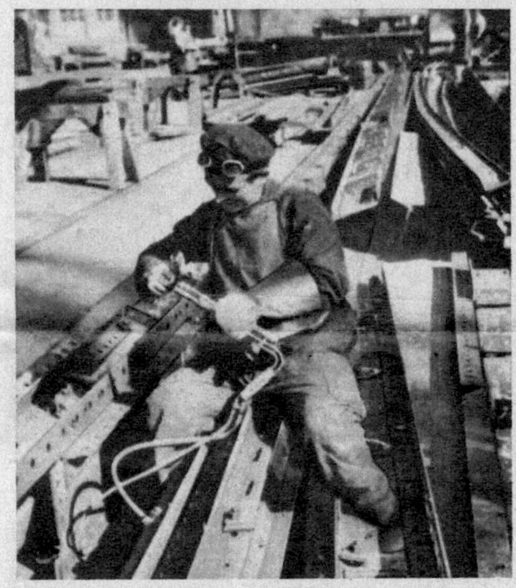

Der Schneidbrenner (Prüfung des Apparates)

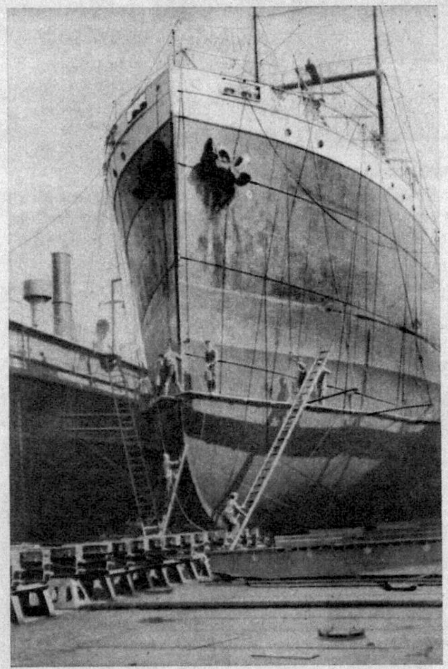

Schiff im Dock. Im Vordergrund Kielpallen

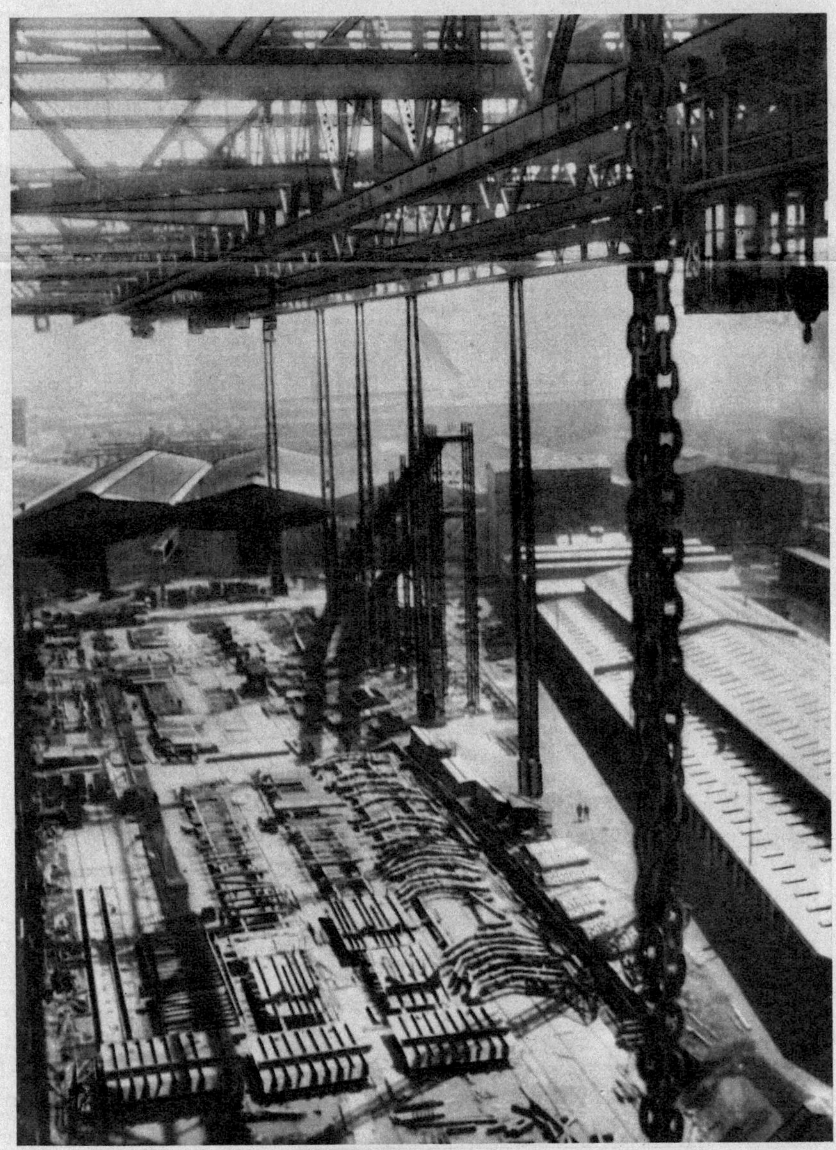

Schiffswerft Blohm & Voß, Hamburg

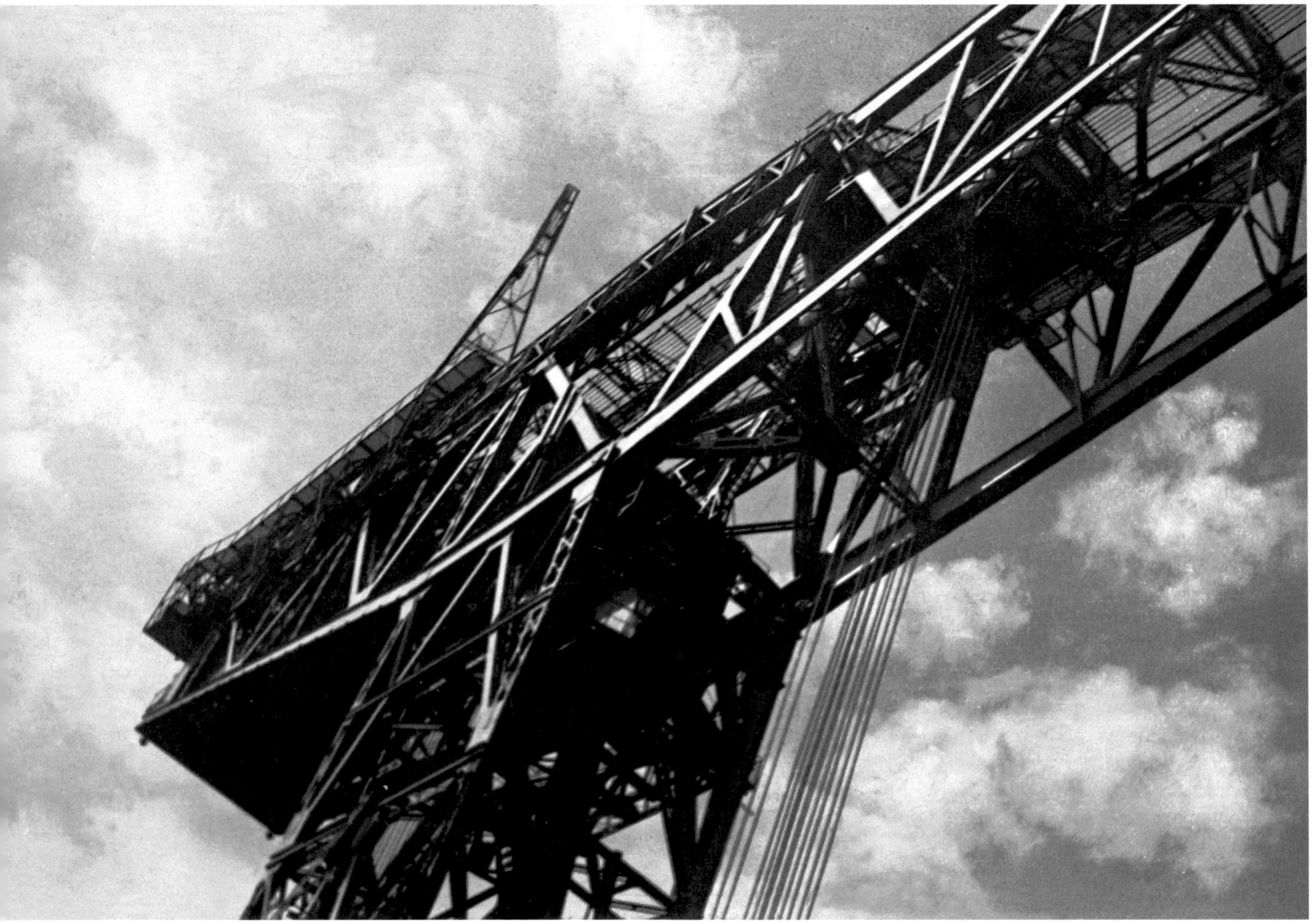

Hammer-headed dock crane in the Blohm & Voss shipyard, Hamburg, 1929

Ship's propeller at a floating dock in the Blohm & Voss shipyard, Hamburg, 1929

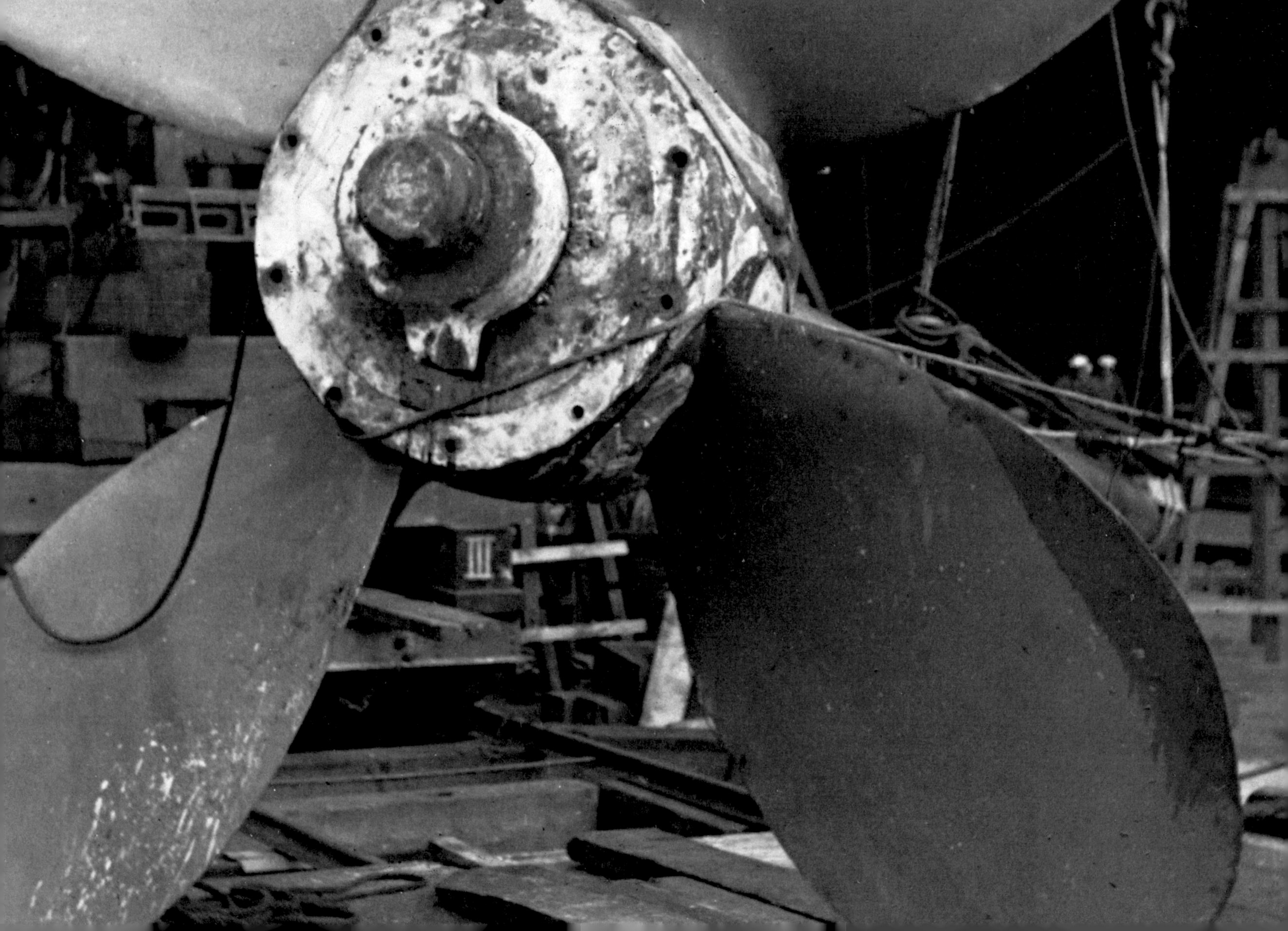

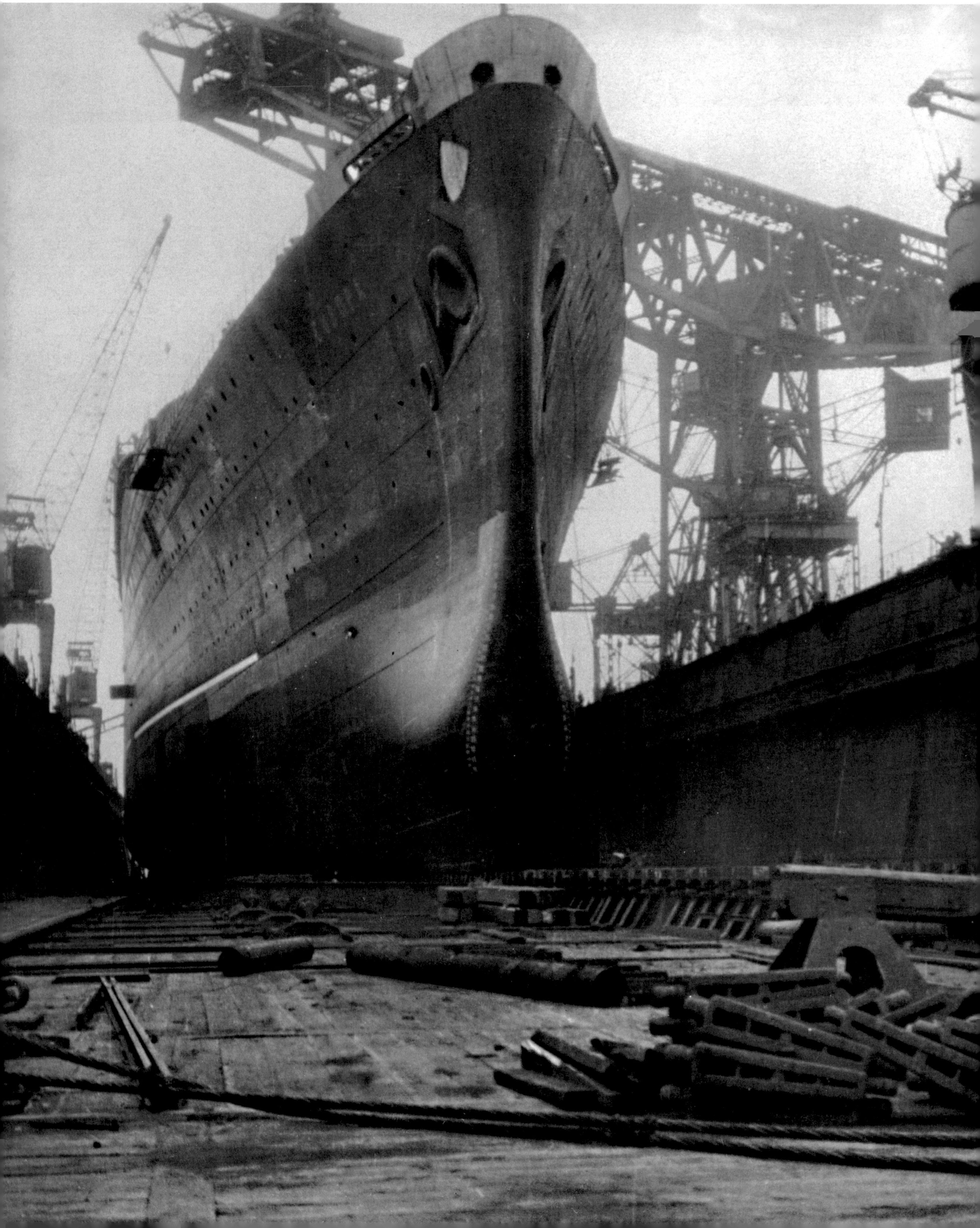

Ship under construction in
the Blohm & Voss shipyard,
Hamburg, 1930

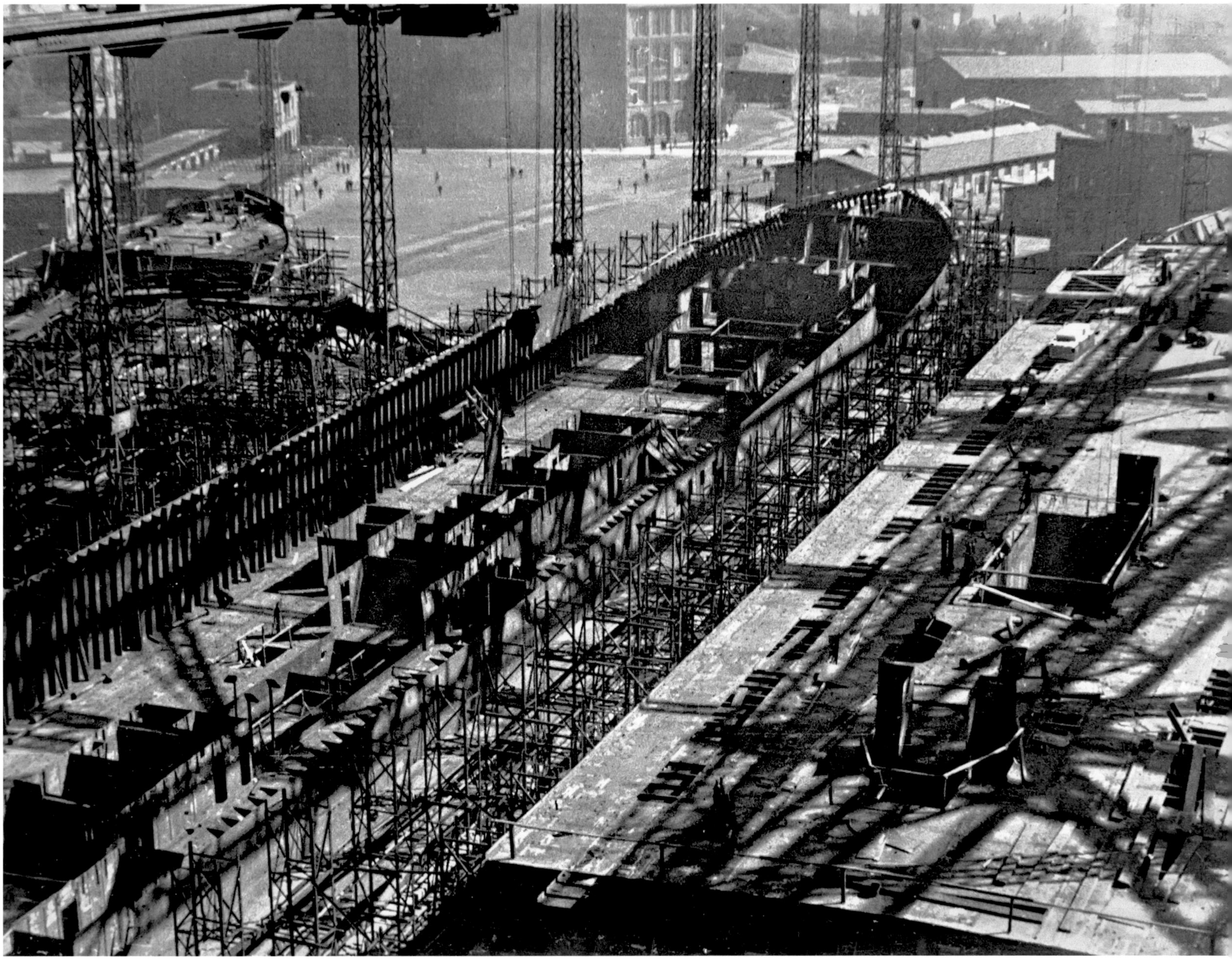

The turbine steamship *Europa*
at a floating dock in the Blohm &
Voss shipyard, Hamburg, 1929
(also see page 1)

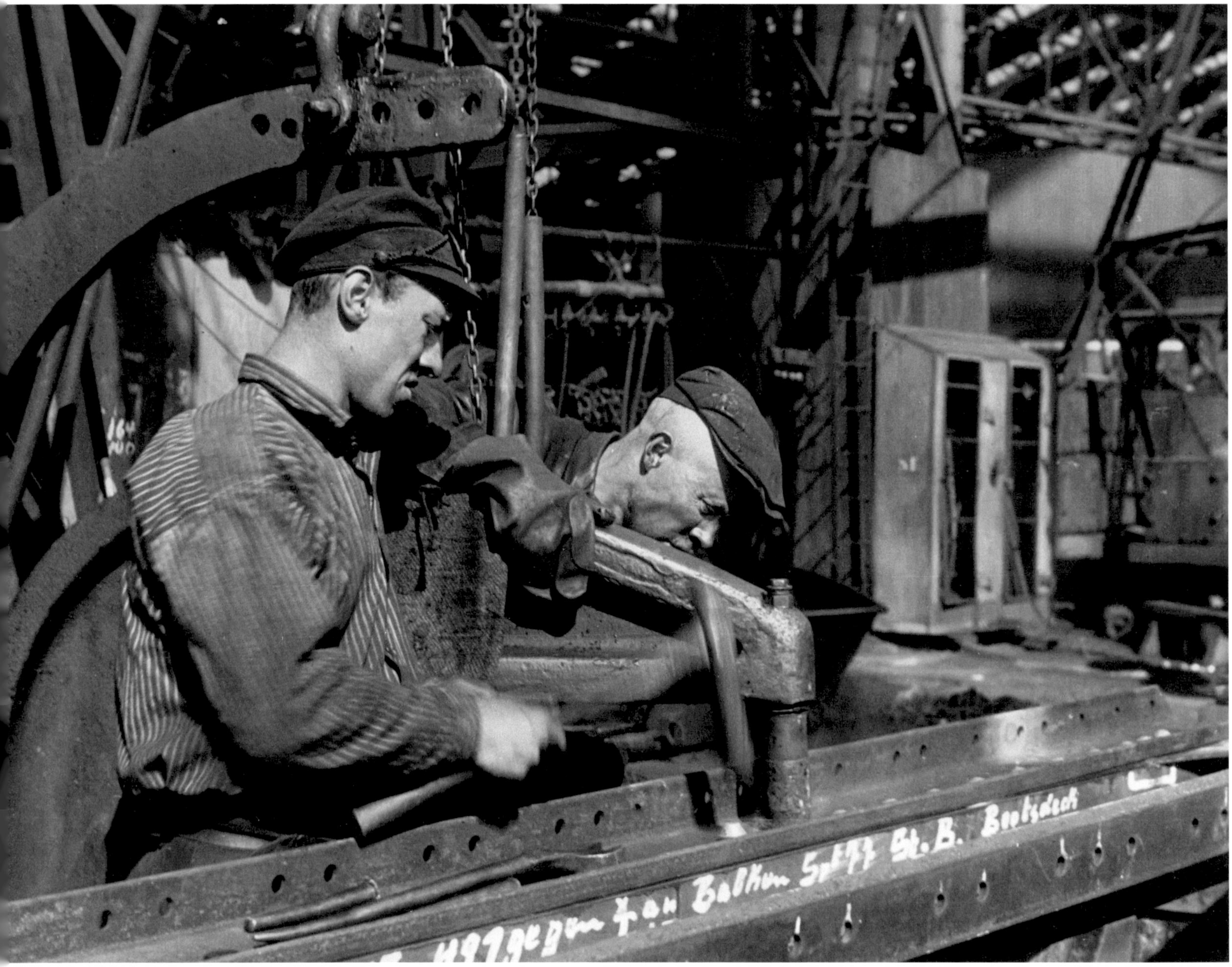

Riveters in the Blohm & Voss
shipyard, Hamburg, 1930

Lunch break in the Blohm &
Voss shipyard, Hamburg, 1930

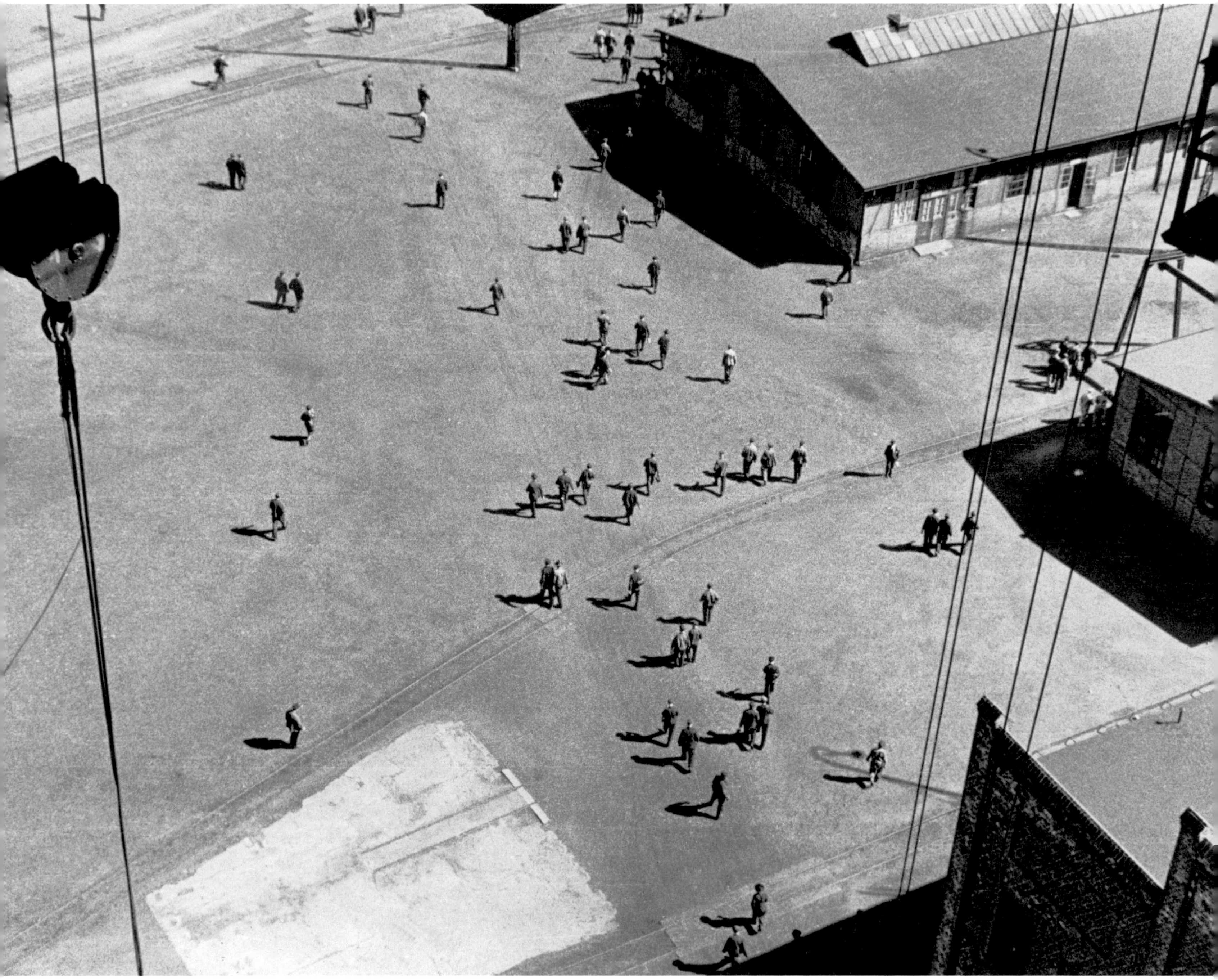

"Hamburg Shipyard Work" (*Hamburger Anzeiger. Illustrierte Wochenbeilage*, no. 5, 1931)

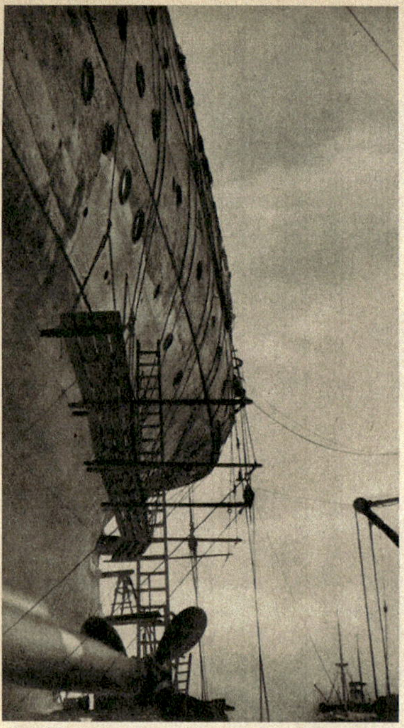

Dockarbeit am Heck, an Schrauben und Außenhaut

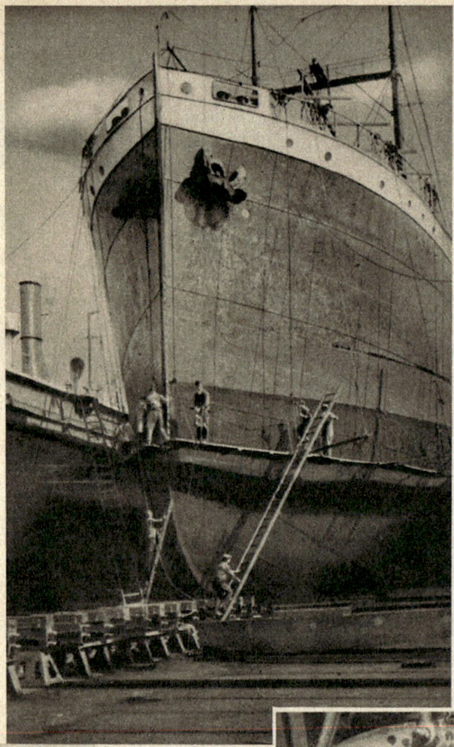

Hängegestellagen für das Konservieren der Außenhaut (Schiff im Dock)

Hamburg

Organisierte Zusammenarbeit an und mit naturgegebenen Dingen und Kräften schafft die Riesenschiffe, mit denen wir sicher und schnell die für uns Landbewohner scheinbar unzugänglichen, todbringenden Ozeane durchfurchen. Solche Zusammenarbeit macht das Unmögliche möglich, das Mythische zur Wirklichkeit. Und jede sogenannte Handarbeit, die an einem Stück Holz oder Eisen oder an der Erdscholle geleistet wird, ist zugleich geistige Arbeit: sie führt aus und gestaltet, was ein intellektuell geleiteter Wille befiehlt, und sie formt natürliche Dinge zweckmäßig um, die wiederum ausnahmslos beseelt sind. Wären sie das nicht, so könnten sie durch die Sinne auf unseren Geist überhaupt keine Wirkungen ausüben.

Mitnichten also sollte Handarbeit, Werkarbeit mit Hilfe von Werkzeugen und Maschinen, seelische Dürren und Wüsten schaffen; sie ist zweckmäßiges Wirken in beseelter Wirklichkeit und nur dem Grade nach verschieden vom Wirken des Wissenschaftlers, des Künstlers, des Organisators, des Ingenieurs, des Staatsmannes. Keine wie immer geartete Arbeit darf der Wirklichkeit widersprechen, wenn sie nicht zur Pfuscherei und Phantasterei werden soll. Unzählige Entdeckungen von Naturgesetzen, Erfindungen, die auf der richtigen Erkenntnis von Naturgesetzen beruhen, mußten gemacht werden, bevor der Bau von guten Seedampfern möglich war. In Reih und Glied arbeiten auf einer großen Schiffswerft zusammen die Organisatoren des ganzen Unternehmens, die Ingenieure, die Meister, die Handwerker und Arbeiter. Mit gleichem Stolz kann jeder Mitarbeiter auf das große Kulturwerk eines neuen vollendeten Schiffes blicken.

Unsere Bilder der Arbeit an großen Seeschiffen stammen von der Hamburger Werft Blohm & Voß. Von jeder anderen Schiffswerft ließen sich ähnliche Urkunden aus einem der lebenswichtigsten Gewerbe unserer Stadt beibringen. Jeder Schiffbauer spricht von dem großen Unternehmen am Südufer der Elbe als von einem technischen Musterbetriebe. Nicht nur die großen Seeschiffe, die dort gebaut werden, sind ein organisatorisches Wunder, die Werft selbst ist eine imposante schöpferische Leistung. Bis zu 14 000 Angestellte und Arbeiter fanden während der Hochblüte des Unternehmens Arbeit in den Werkstätten, auf den Helgen und den Docks dieser Schiffbauanstalt.

Ingeni
und M
und S
hier zu
delsfah
958 00
576 00
sowie
die W
größte
marck (
Lloyd
Schnel
Ozean
von B
See u
Ambr
und 6
keit vo
der M
44 Mi
Stok
burger
geheur
nunger
Höchstl
graues
seine K
zusamm
Zwe
Schiffs
Rollen
durchf
hat zu
die neu
schärfe
Salzfl
Tropfe
strömen
am St
Bei
Docks
Körper
Arbeits

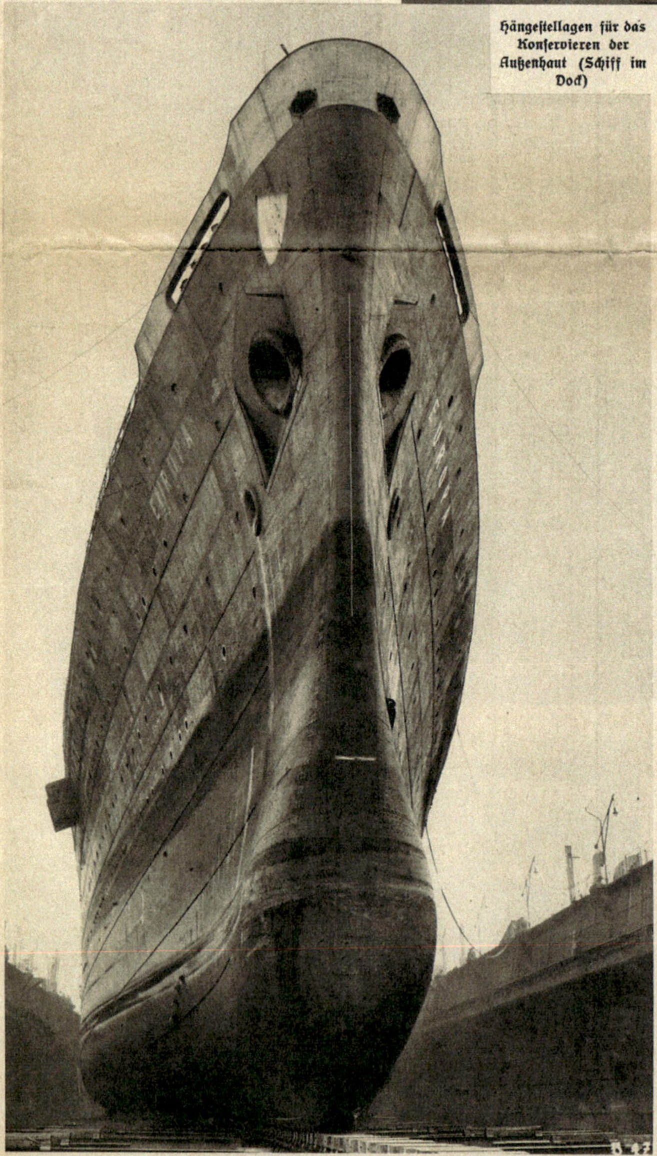

Der Bug der „Europa“
(Schiff im Dock von Blohm & Voß)

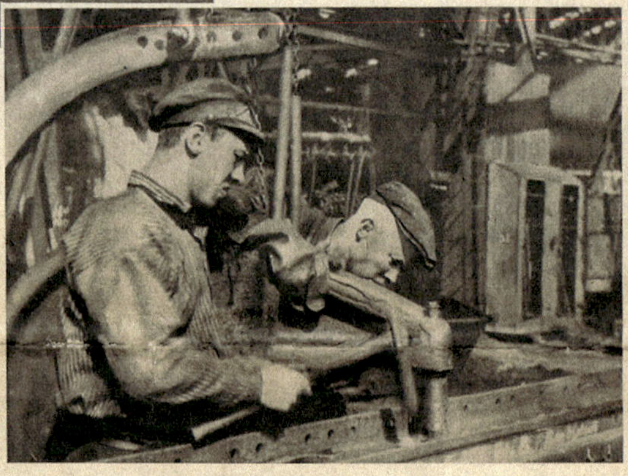

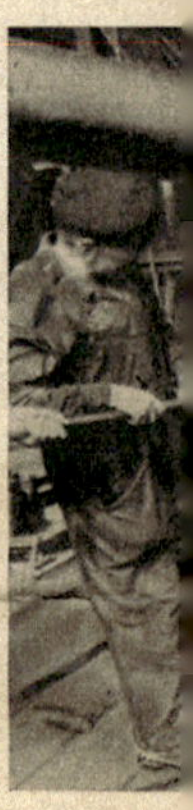

Hydraulische Nietung

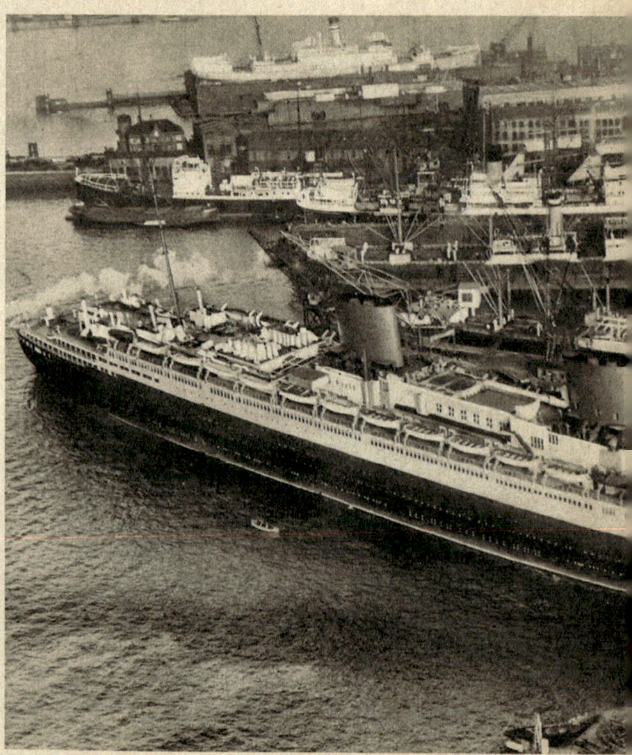

Die „Europa“ am Kai der Werft von Blohm

Werftarbeit

ltungsbeamte, Maschinenbauer
er und Tischler, Gießer, Nieter
: und Schirrmeister bildeten sich
n in ihrem Fach aus. 249 Han-
78 000 Br.-R.-T. mit rund
200 Kriegsfahrzeuge von rund
nd rund 1 621 000 Pferdekräften
on 280 000 t Hebefähigkeit hat
rnommen. Sie hat die bisher
elt, Vaterland (1914) und Bis-
hre beiden für den Norddeutschen
bauten Vierschrauben-Turbinen-
as Blaue Band des Atlantischen
gte auf der am 19. März 1930
ngetretenen Reise trotz grober
e klassische Strecke Cherbourg—
chiff in 4 Tagen 17 Stunden
einer Durchschnittsgeschwindig-
der Stunde zurück. (Der von
Rekord war 4 Tage, 22 Stunden,

Zusammenarbeit auf der Ham-
& Voß erzielt hat! Eine un-
ahrungen, von genauen Berech-
ewissenhaftigkeit steckt in solchen
en neun Helgen, deren riesiges
n Gesicht Hamburgs gehört wie
irme, werden die Schiffsrümpfe

s herrschende Prinzip bei der
ell, sicher, ohne Stampfen und
ende Körper die Meereswellen
ium des strömenden Fluidums
des Vorderstevens geführt, die
aufweisen. Nicht die alte Messer-
h am geeignetsten erwiesen, die
tandslos zu teilen, sondern die
hsam einschmiegt in das flüssige,
aß dessen Teilchen schmeichelnd
en.
Hallen und Werkstätten, auf den
ie Werftarbeiter beschäftigt; ihre
dert- und vertausendfacht durch
größte Kran bei Blohm & Voß

hebt mit seinem eisengegatterten Ausleger ein Gewicht von 250 000 Kilogramm, hebt es turmhoch und läßt es mit ruhigem Schwung sanft und gehorsam an der richtigen Stelle herunter. Er hebt den fertigen Riesenschornstein oder Stahlmast auf seinen Platz, er schwingt die gewaltigen Röhrenkessel in den Maschinenraum. Nicht mehr der Arbeiter ist der Sklave, sondern die Arbeitsmaschine, die er beherrscht mit einem Hebelzug oder einer Schraubendrehung. Nicht mehr der Arbeiter hämmert, sondern die Preßluft. Nicht mehr Menschenkraft biegt die Spanten, sondern die unwiderstehliche Stärke der hydraulischen Maschine.

Und neben der Werft liegen die acht Schwimmdocks, die zusammen eine Last von 170 000 t zu heben vermögen. Die größten Schiffe der Welt können hier gedockt, das heißt aus dem Wasser gehoben werden, damit man sie reinigen und reparieren kann. Sehr einfach: man läßt den ungeheuern schwimmenden Dockkasten mit den hohen hohlen Seitenwänden voll Wasser laufen, er versinkt, und das zu dockende Schiff fährt zwischen die Seitenwände wie in eine offene Schleuse. Dann läßt man die Hohlräume des Docks durch starke Pumpen entleeren, das Dock fängt wieder an zu schwimmen und hebt das große Seeschiff mit aus dem Wasser. Auch hier versteht die Werftarbeit, ungeheure Naturkräfte in ihren Dienst zu stellen.

Erschütternd muß auf jeden denkenden Menschen die wachsende Beschäftigungslosigkeit einer im höchsten Grade leistungsfähigen Arbeitsorganisation wirken. Hier wankt einer der Grundfesten der Volks- und Weltwirtschaft und damit des eigenen Staates und des internationalen Gedeihens. Wenn ein solches, dem friedlichen Weltverkehr dienendes Unternehmen seinen Betrieb stark einschränken muß, so weist das hin auf die schwersten wirtschaftspolitischen und politischen Fehler, deren Abstellung mit höchster Energie und Eile betrieben werden sollte. Nur ein schleuniges, verständnisvolles Zusammenwirken aller leitenden Faktoren im eigenen Staat und der Völker kann helfen. Politische Zusammenarbeit, die den realen Kräften und Verhältnissen ebenso genau Rechnung trägt, wie sie beim Bau großer Seeschiffe erforderlich ist, muß als das dringendste Gebot der Stunde bezeichnet werden.

Spectator.

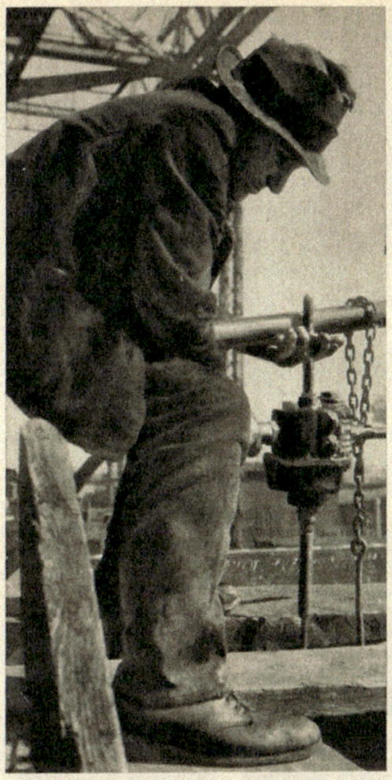

Preßluftbohrer mit den einfachsten Hilfsmitteln gehalten

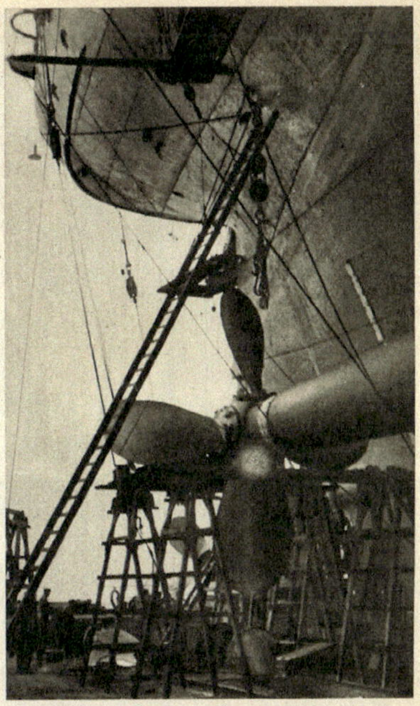

Arbeit an den Propellern im Dock von Blohm & Voß

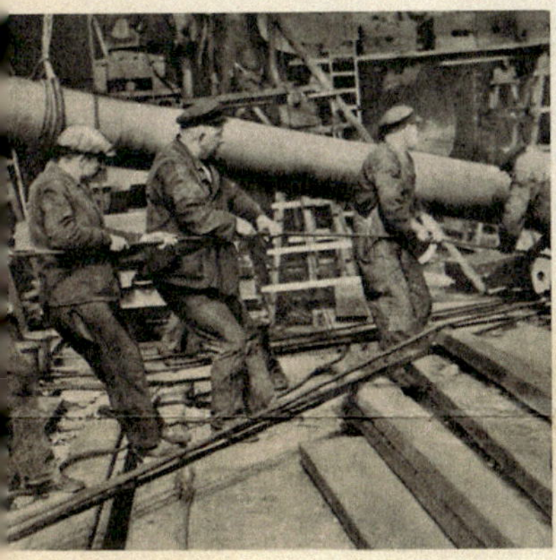

chwanzwelle im Dock von Blohm & Voß

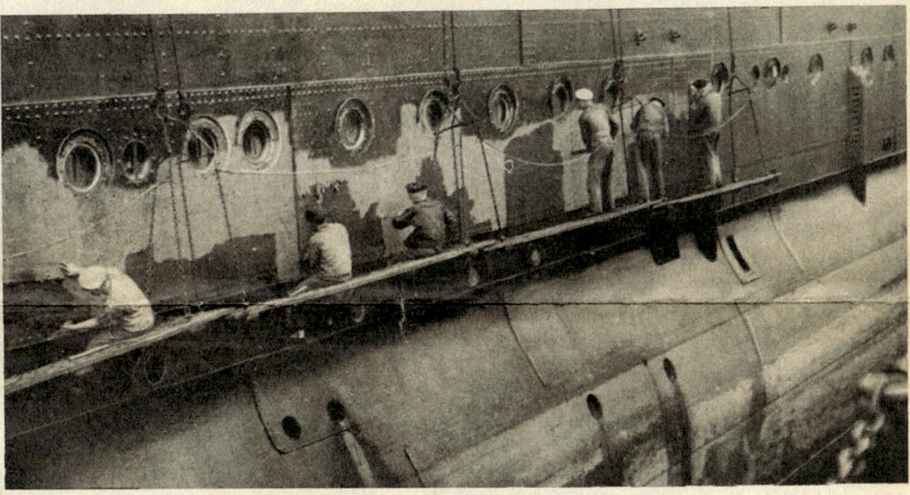

Abklopfen und Abkratzen der Außenhaut

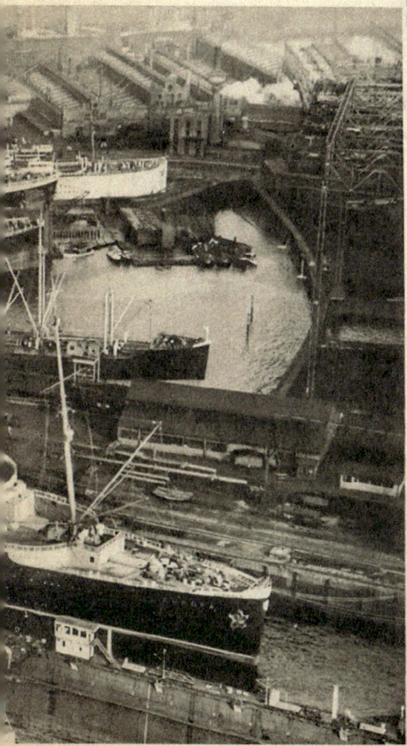

ember 1930

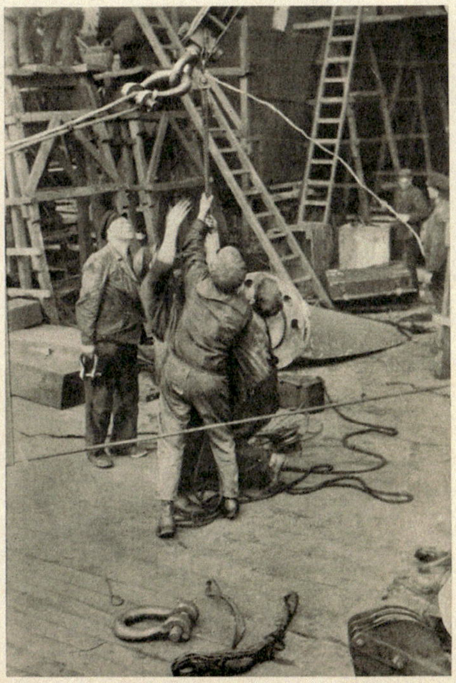

Klarmachen der Taljen für das Heben der Propeller

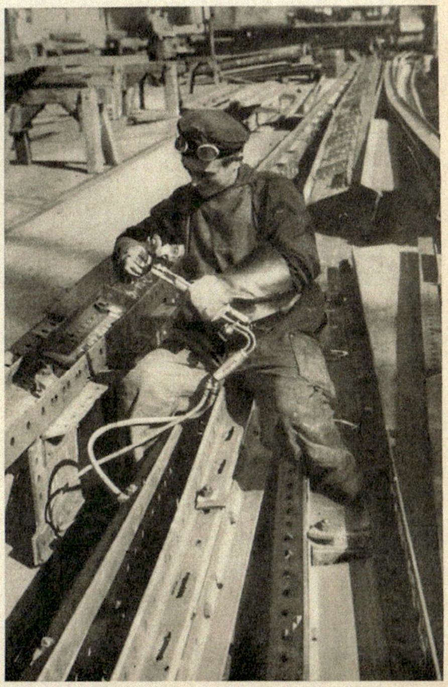

Der Mann untersucht (prüft) seinen Brenner

DIE FORM

ZEITSCHRIFT FÜR GESTALTENDE ARBEIT

4. JAHR

HEFT 23

1. DEZEMBER 1929

VERLAG HERMANN RECKENDORF G. M. B. H. BERLIN SW 48

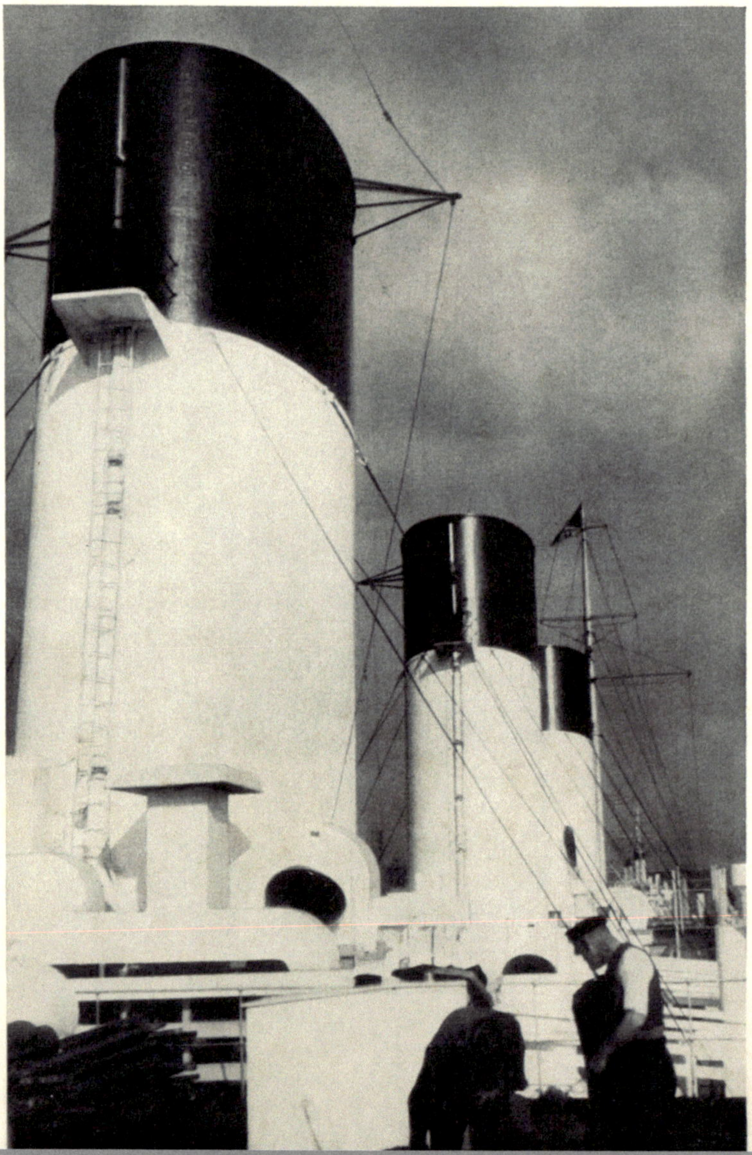

Die Form 4, no. 23, 1929

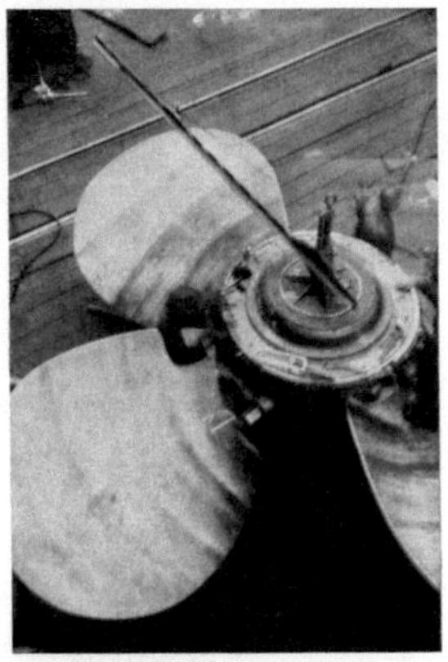

Schiffsschraube

Die Schiffsschraube als Treibmittel beweist eindringlich die Schönheit des wahrhaft Organischen. Sie ist Grenzfall, da bei ihrer Gestaltung auf jede ästhetische Absicht verzichtet wird. Wer ihre Reize nicht empfindet, kann über die Natur zum richtigen Sehen gelangen; freilich dürfen ihn nicht primitive Ähnlichkeitsvergleiche leiten (z. B. vierblättriges Kleeblatt), sondern er muß wesensverwandte, starre, drallbestimmte Gebilde suchen (z. B. Flugsamen).

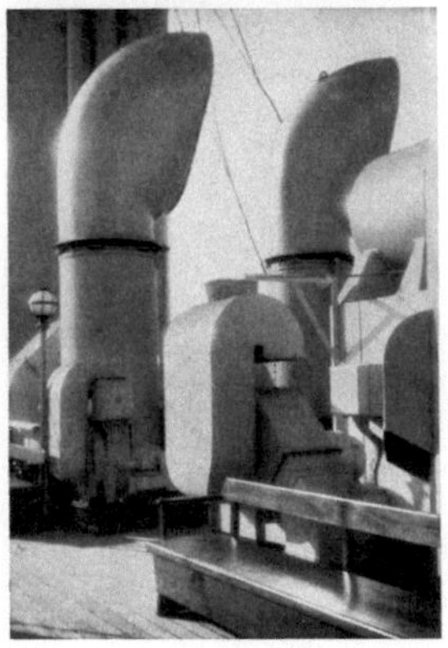

**Dampfer „Hamburg"
von der Hamburg-Amerika-Linie**

Häufig ist in der Technik die Wirkung einzelner Organe verstärkt durch Gruppen- und Stufenbildung. Untereinander gleiche oder ähnliche Körper erlangen in Mehrzahl kräftigste Wirkung. Der neue Fotograf sieht hier oft viel.

Dampfer „Columbus" vom Norddeutschen Lloyd

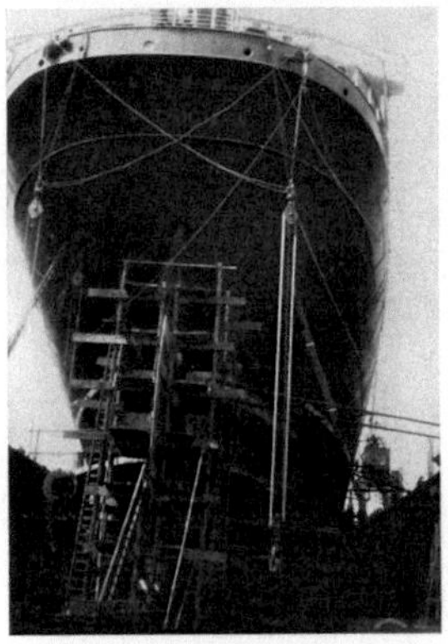

Leicht wird das Sehen dann, wenn die „Masse" den Blick fängt. Durch unsere Landarchitektur haben wir 10-m-Maßstäbe gewonnen, die wir plötzlich am Schiffsleib anlegen können. Hier haben wir große, gebaute Körper mit der Ausdehnung mehrerer Miethäuser, aber mit einer jenen meist fremden Einheitlichkeit. Man erkennt, daß auch der technische Großbau Organform hat. Die ausladende bewegte Wölbung des Heckes verrät Stabilität und Seefähigkeit. Der Ansatz des Ruders und der Übergang zum Rumpf bringen eine vollkommen geschlossene Wirkung, die beim aufgedockten Schiff durch das unorganische Wirrsal von Tauen und Gerüsten zu einem künstlerischen Erlebnis gesteigert wird.

Dampfer „Columbus" vom Norddeutschen Lloyd

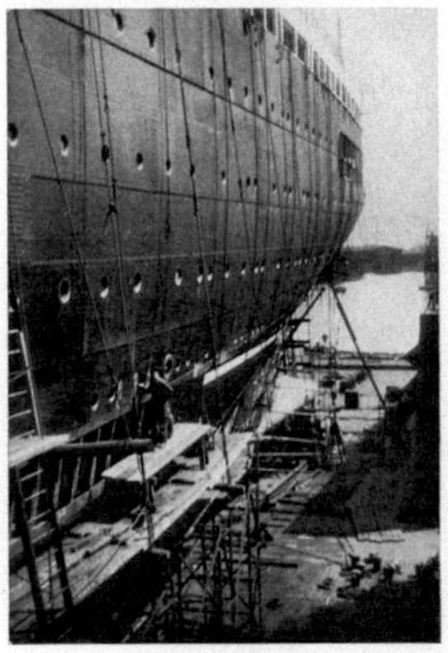

Gespannte Seile sind körpergewordene Kraftlinien und wie jede plastische Äußerung der Kraft voll eigentümlicher Schönheit. Man braucht dabei gar nicht an Hoppés Bilder von amerikanischen Hängebrücken zu denken, die oft romantischen Einschlag haben. Der Schiffsrumpf mit den an Reling befestigten Aufhängseilen von Arbeitsbühnen ist schön. Wenn man es nicht das erstemal spürt, dann Feuerbachs Rat zur Betrachtung eines Kunstwerks befolgen: immer wieder kommen bis der magnetische Rapport zu wirken anfängt.

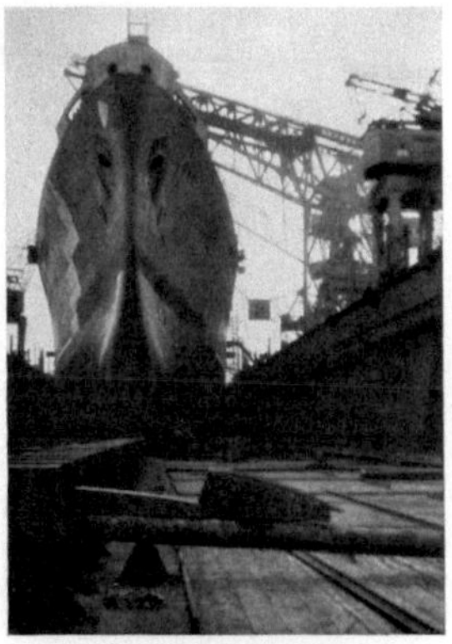

Dampfer „Europa" vom Norddeutschen Lloyd

Alle, die die Schönheit der Technik verleugnen oder verleumden, sollten einmal ein aufgedocktes Schiff von vorne betrachten. Der glockenförmige Querschnitt des Rumpfes fällt sofort auf, belehrt über die statische Sicherheit; wir sehen das Schiff schwimmen. Und also müssen beste Bauten wirken: gotische Türme wachsen, reißen einen schwindelnd empor, Barock versetzt in einen Kreis von irdisch-himmlischer Lust (die „Wies"), Fabrikbauten sollen fesseln durch den klaren Ausdruck der Arbeit in ihnen und Schiffe schwimmen eben. Schiffe brauchen dazu einen Körper mit wasserdichter Haut, Krane hingegen brauchen nur skelettartiges Fachwerk. Zweifache Dynamik hat die technische Form: eine den Stoff bejahende, in der Hülle erscheinende (Schiffsrumpf) und eine den Stoff verneinende, im Skelett wirksame.

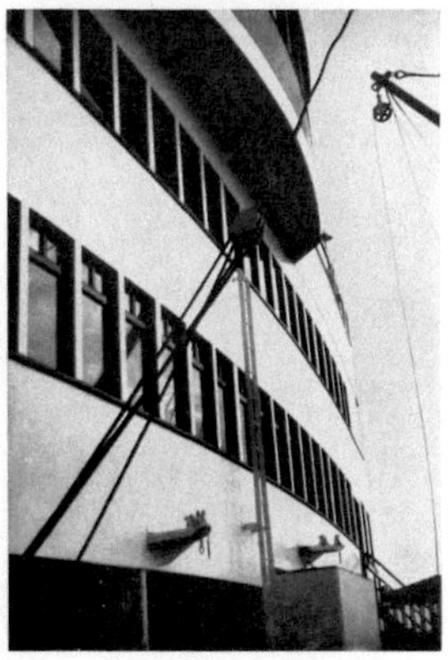

**Dampfer „Hamburg"
von der Hamburg-Amerika-Linie**

Wie bewegt und lebendig übrigens eine leicht geschwungene Front ist! Sie ergibt sich von selbst für die Fensterreihen der Decks. Schade, daß es bei Landbauten anders ist. Nur ganz selten findet man Fassaden mit organischer Kurvenschmiegung. Altes Beispiel: Markt in Landsberg am Lech, neues Beispiel: Chilehaus in Hamburg.

Schornstein des Dampfers „Hamburg"

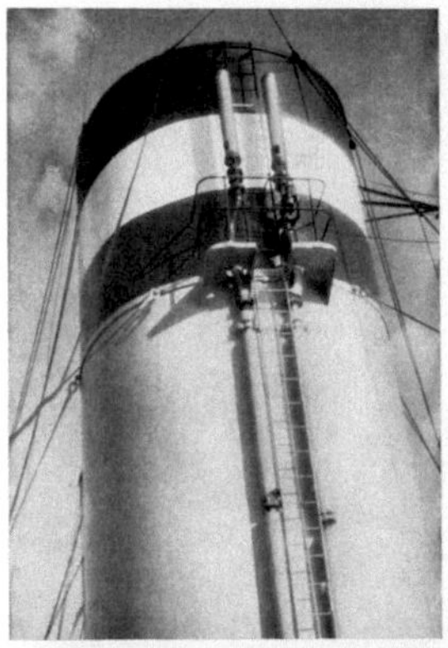

Auch die geometrischen Grundformen, die Le Corbusier — wiewohl ein wenig übertrieben — preist, stehen dem Ingenieur uneingeschränkter zu Gebote als dem Architekten. Schiffsschornsteine sind meist riesige elliptische Zylinder, freilich vor jeder Einförmigkeit durch Perspektive und technische Zutaten (Leiter, Sirenen, Plattform, Erkennungsringe, Verspannungen) gesichert. Einzureihen sind sie gemäß unseren einleitenden Definitionen unter die reinen Körperformen; denn es fehlt ihnen jene aktive Bestimmung, die das „Organ" stets hat; sie sind gebaut nach menschlichen Gesetzen (Saugzug, Luftwiderstand, Proportion zum Schiffsrumpf).

**Mast des Dampfers „Cap Arcona"
von der Hamburg-Südamerikanischen
Dampfschiffahrts-Gesellschaft**

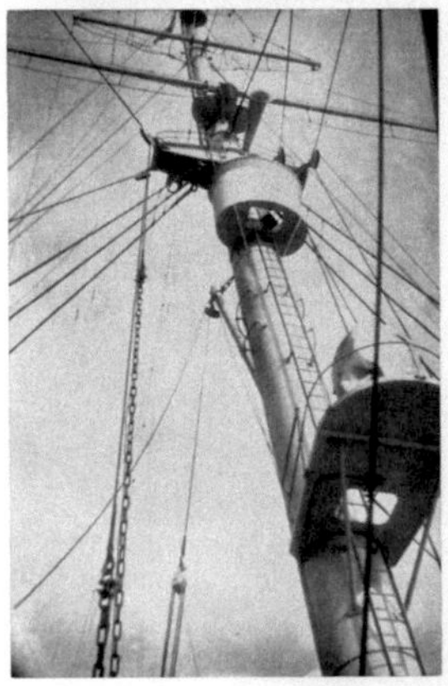

Organformen können bei gewissen großen Einheiten zu Körperformen (Schiffsrumpf), Körperformen ihrerseits unter bestimmten Voraussetzungen zu Skelettformen werden. Maste, in kleinem Ausschnitt gewaltige Röhren, werden in großem Gefüge mit Rahen und Tauen zu einem nur mehr beschränkt räumlichen Gerüst.

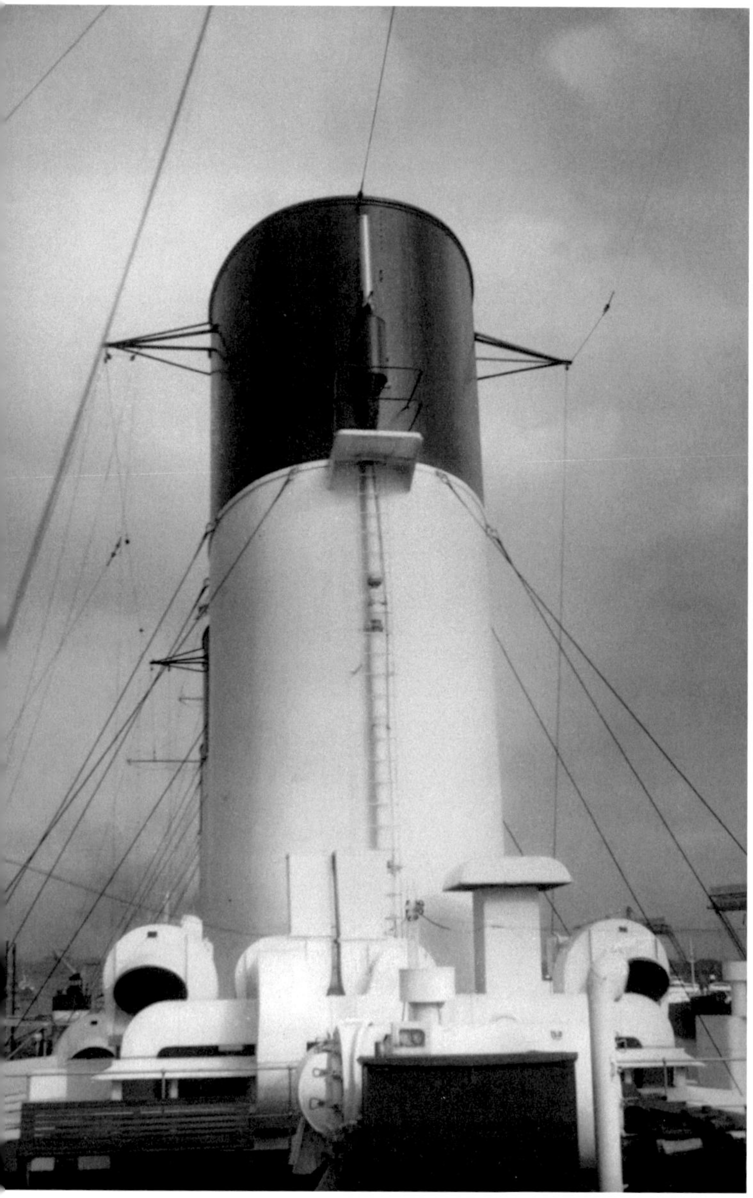

Funnel of the steamship *Cap Arcona*, Hamburg, 1929

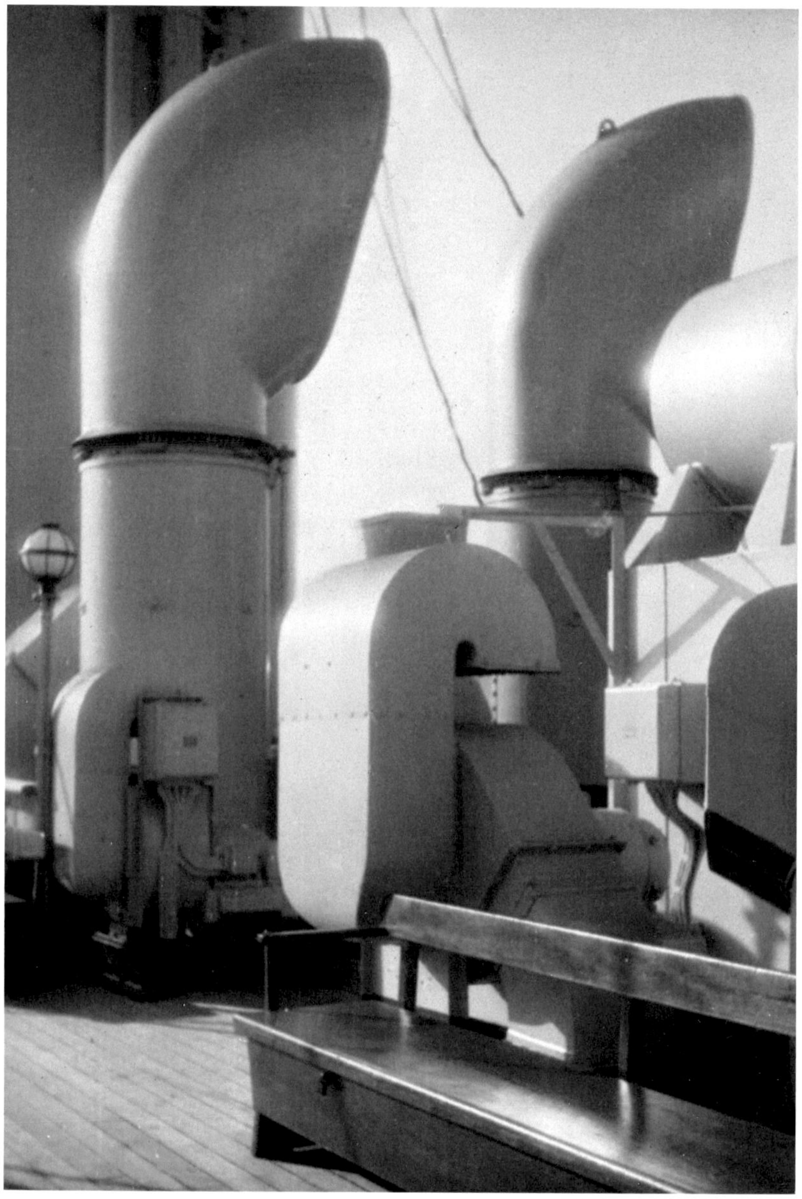

Exhaust ducts of the steamship *Hamburg*, Hamburg, 1929

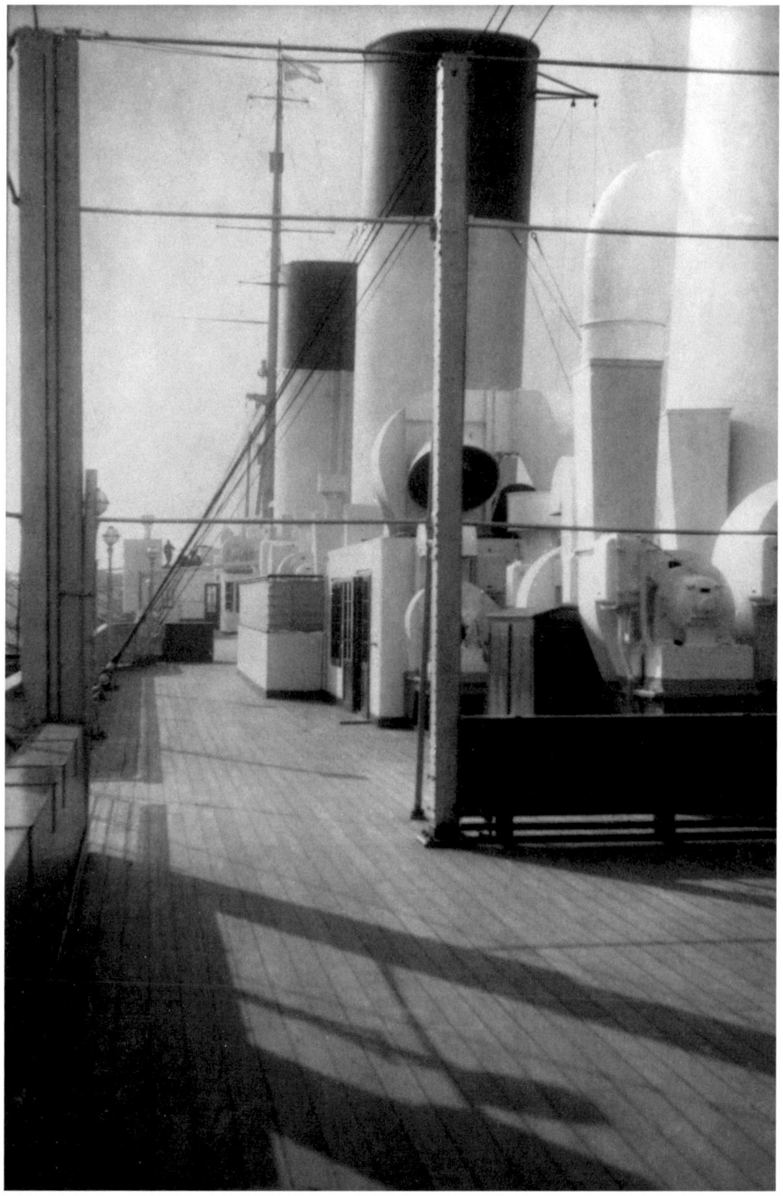

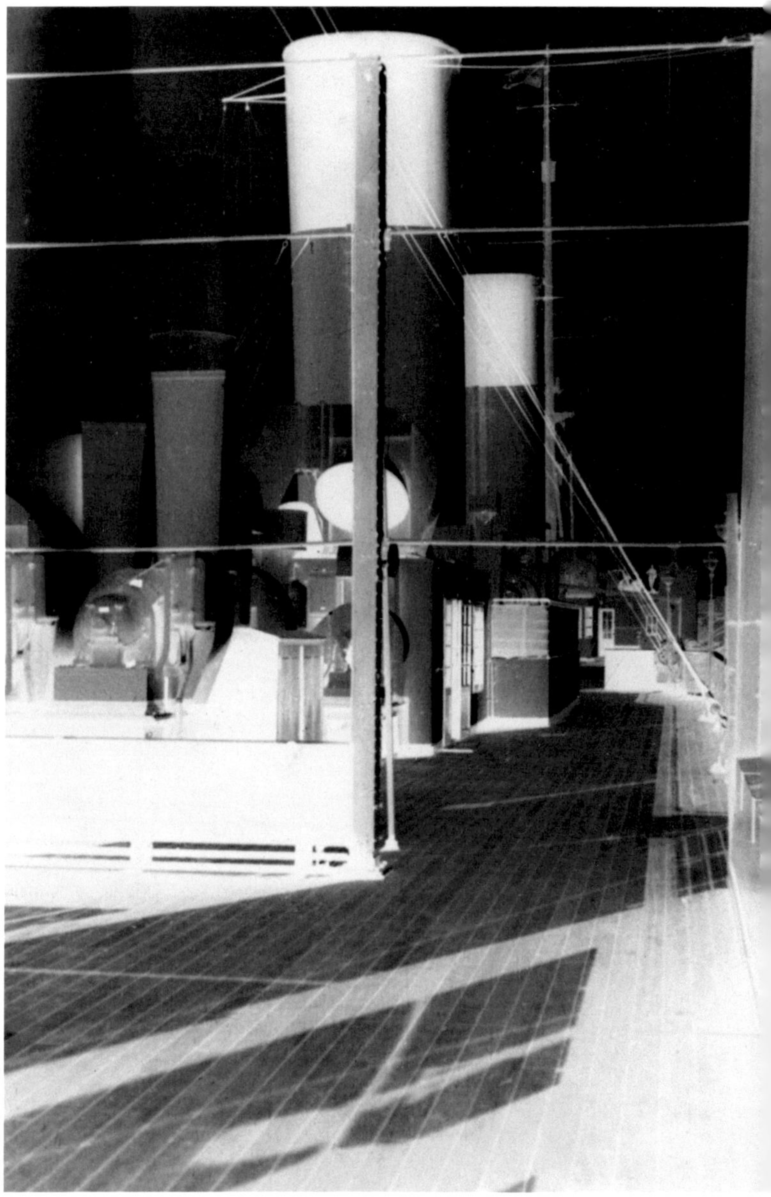

Deck of the steamship *Cap Arcona*, Hamburg, 1929 (positive and reverse)

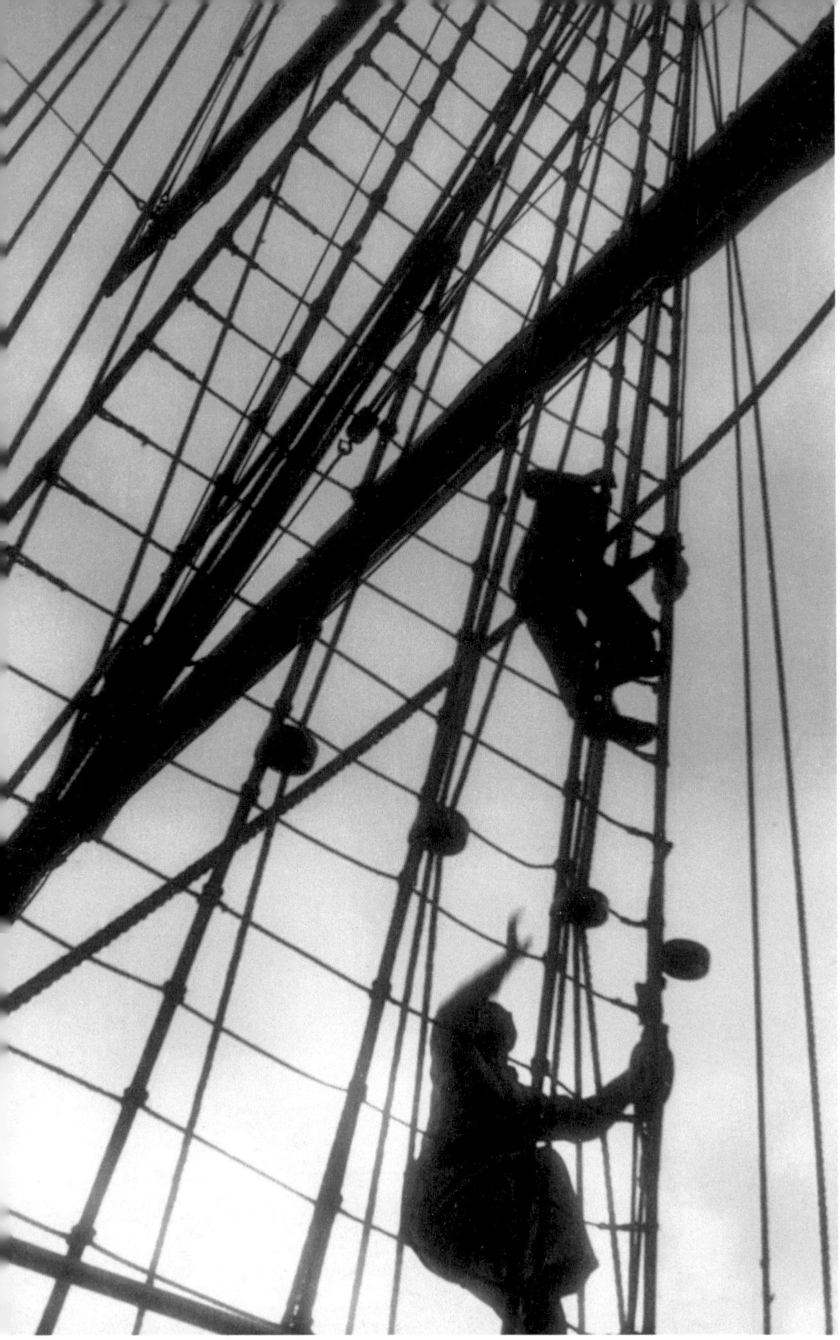

Training on the sailing school ship
Presidente Sarmiento, Hamburg, 1929

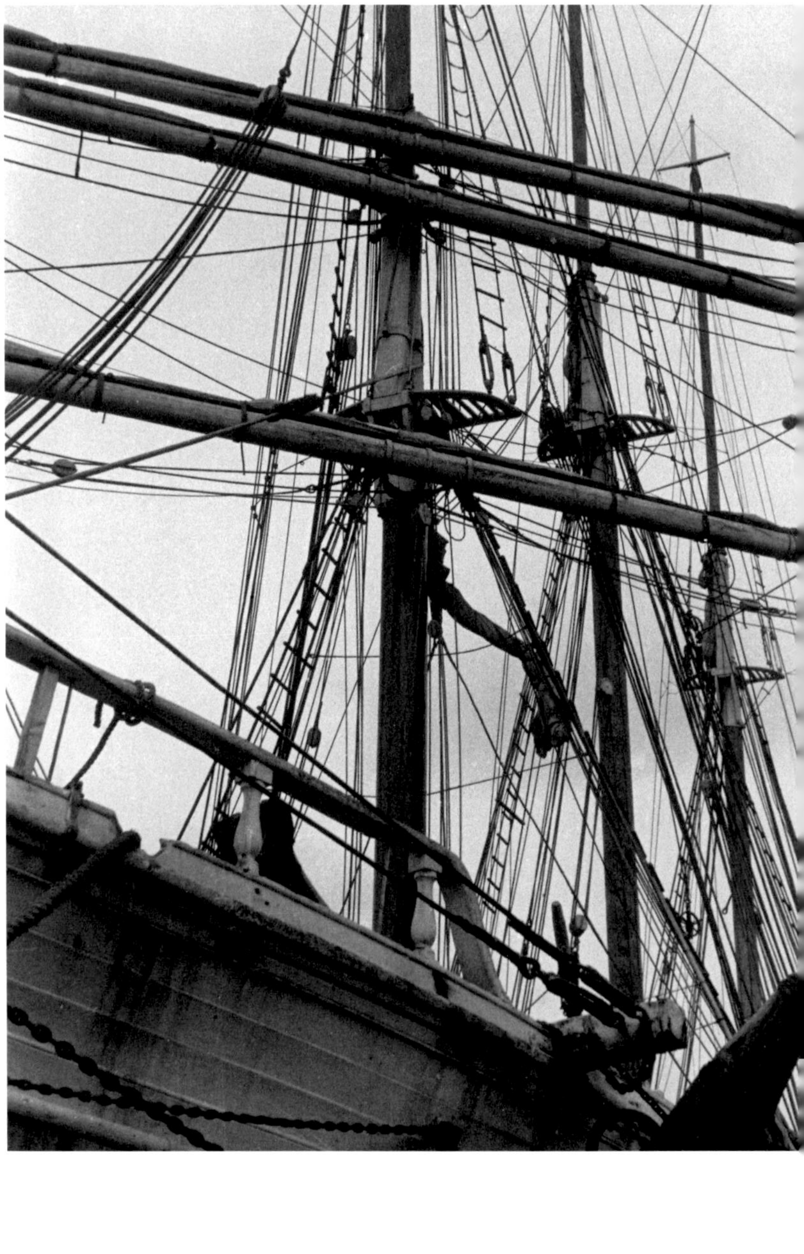

Rigging, Hamburg, 1929

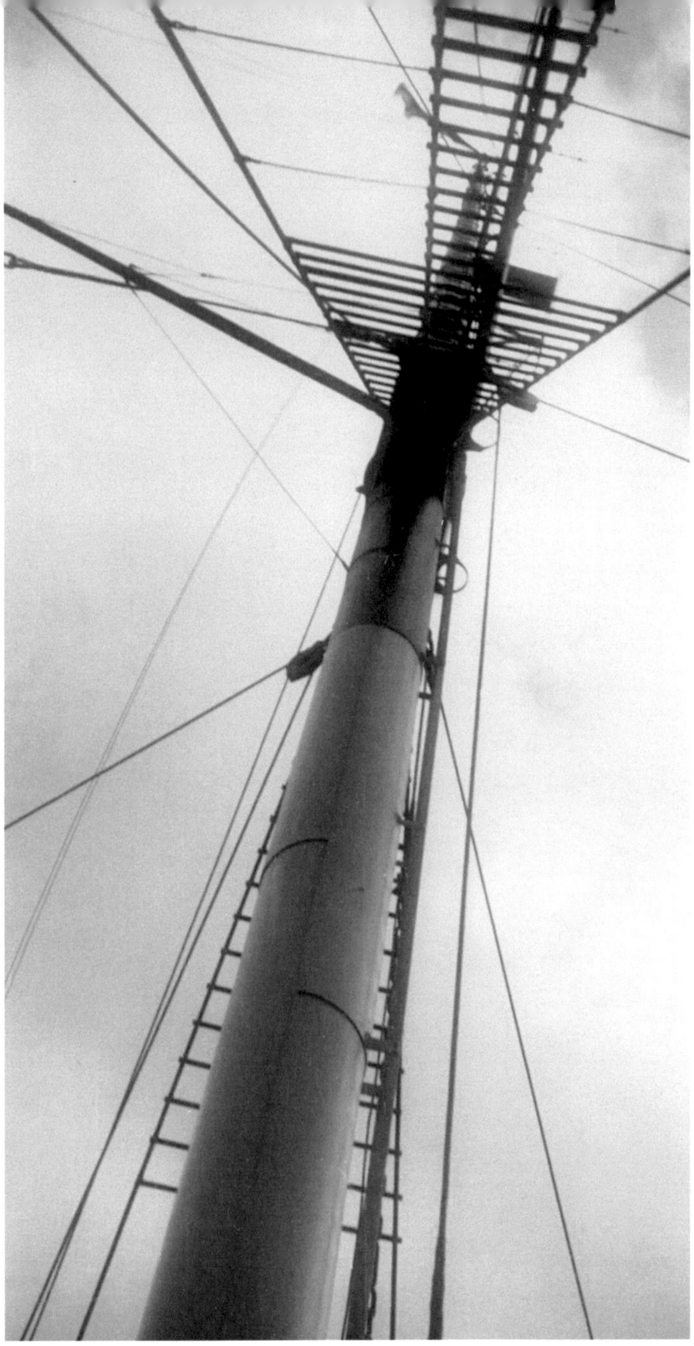

Ship's mast, Hamburg, 1929

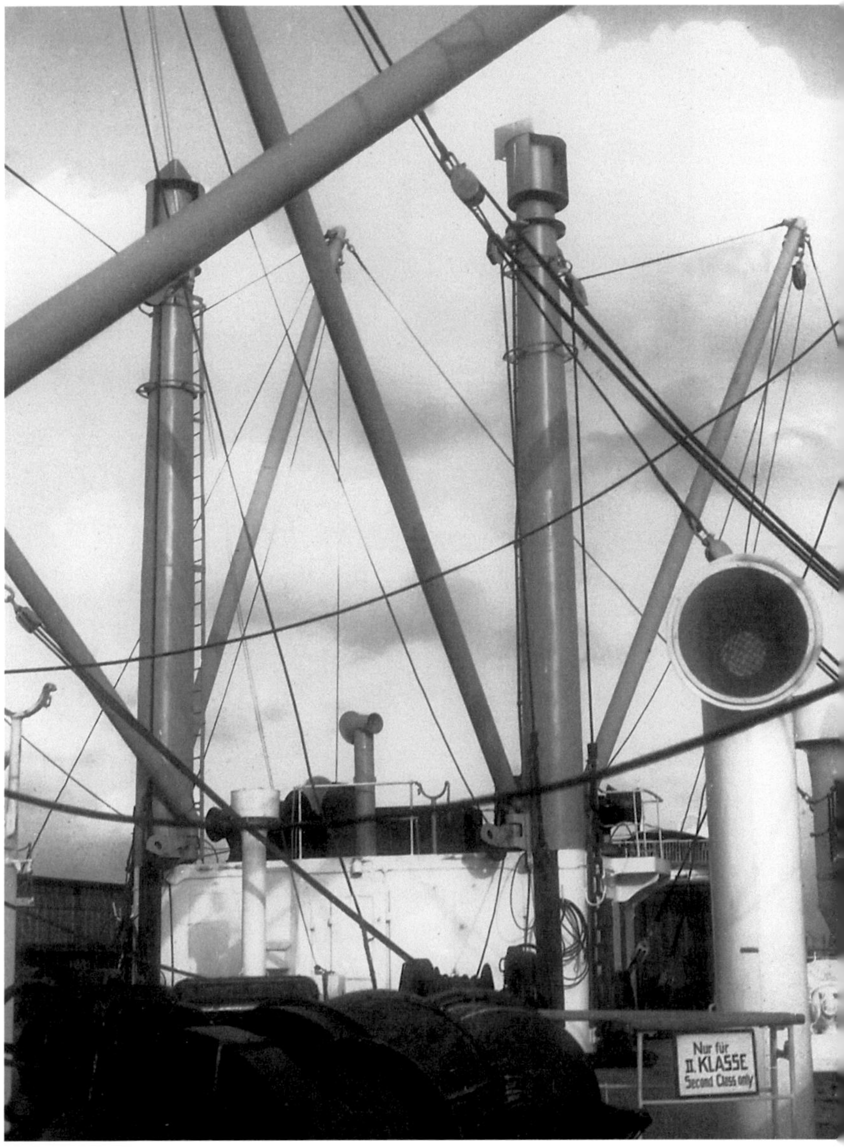

Cargo gear, Hamburg, 1929

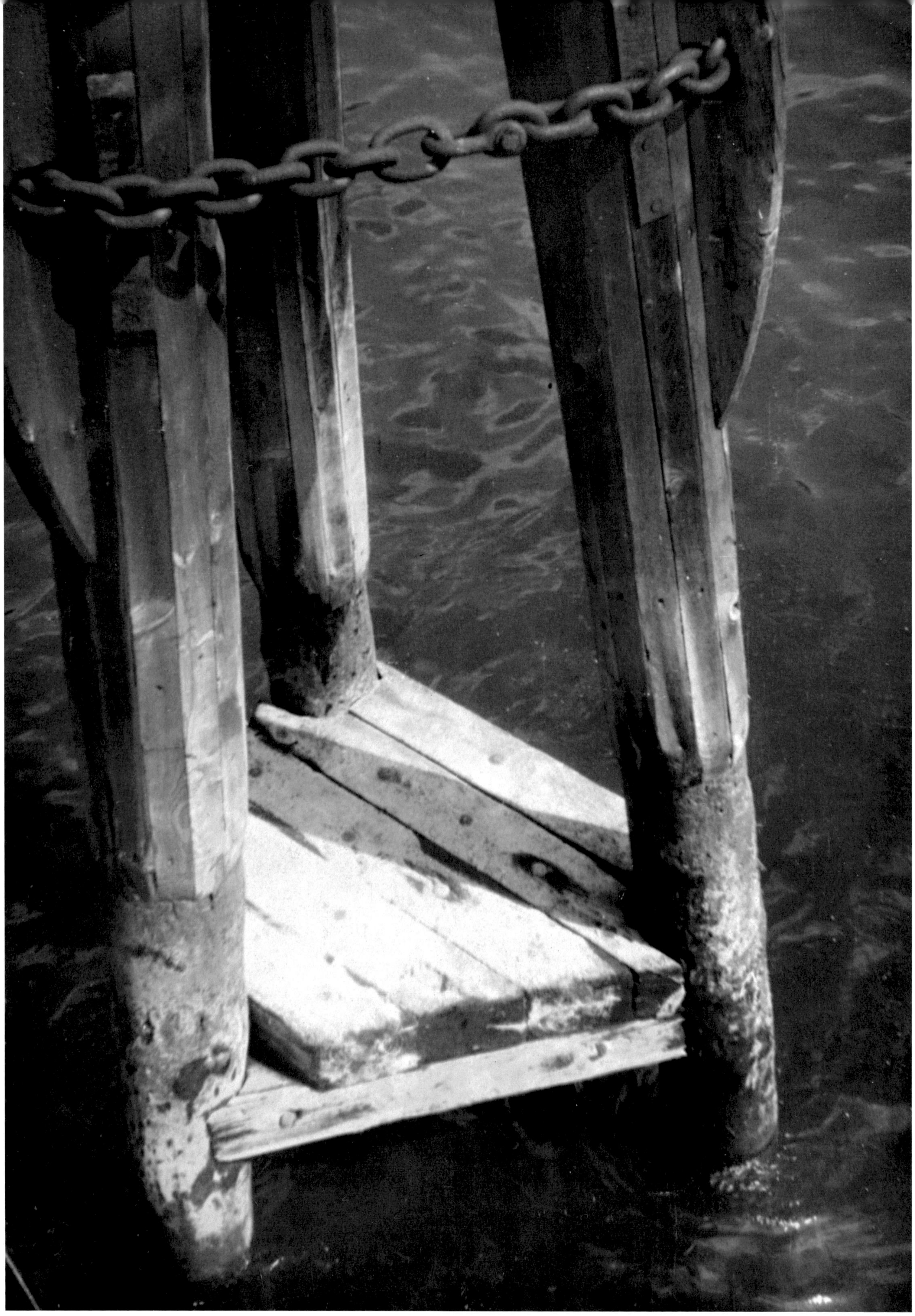

Mooring post, Hamburg, 1929

Fishing boats, Hamburg, 1929

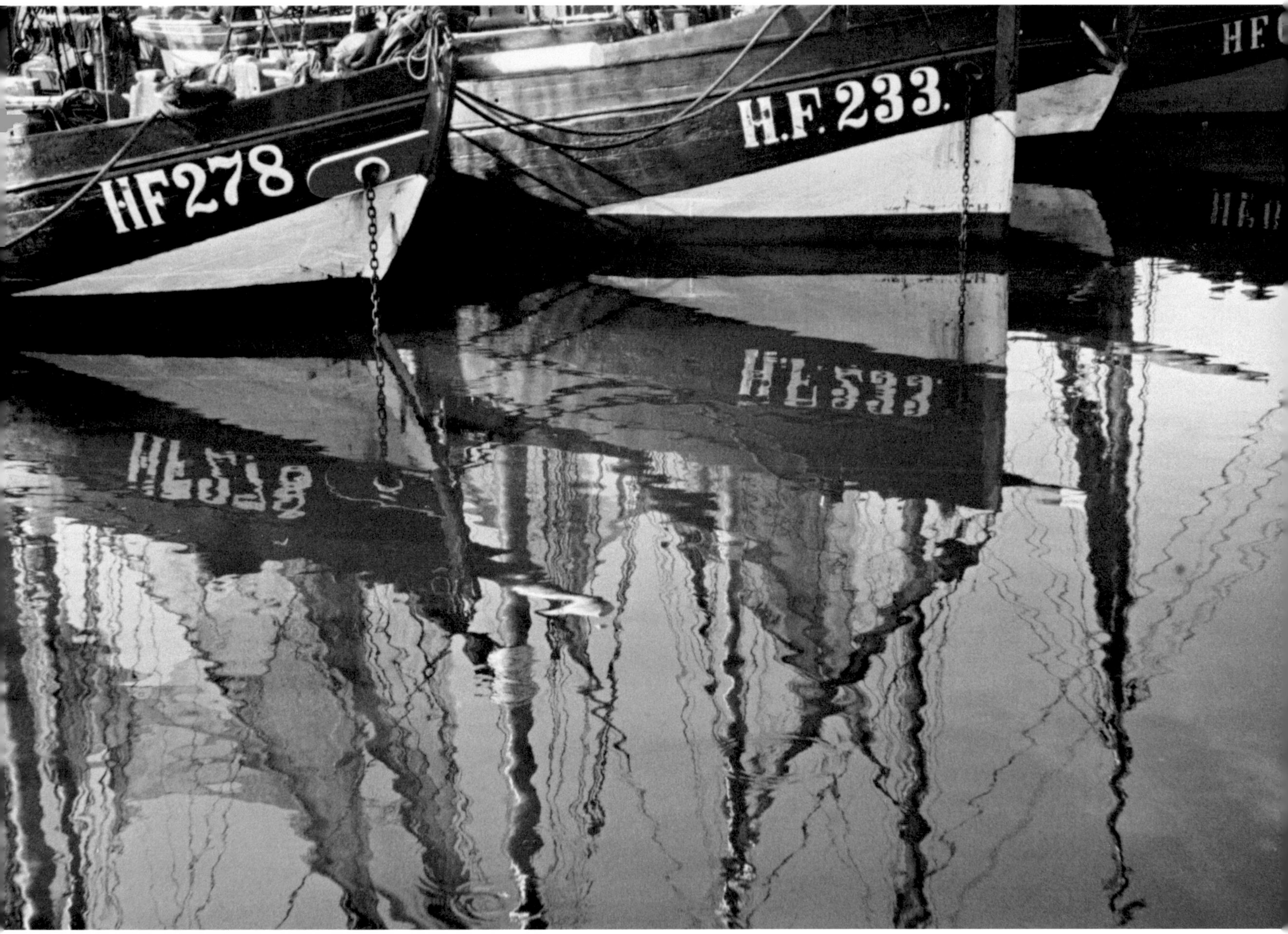

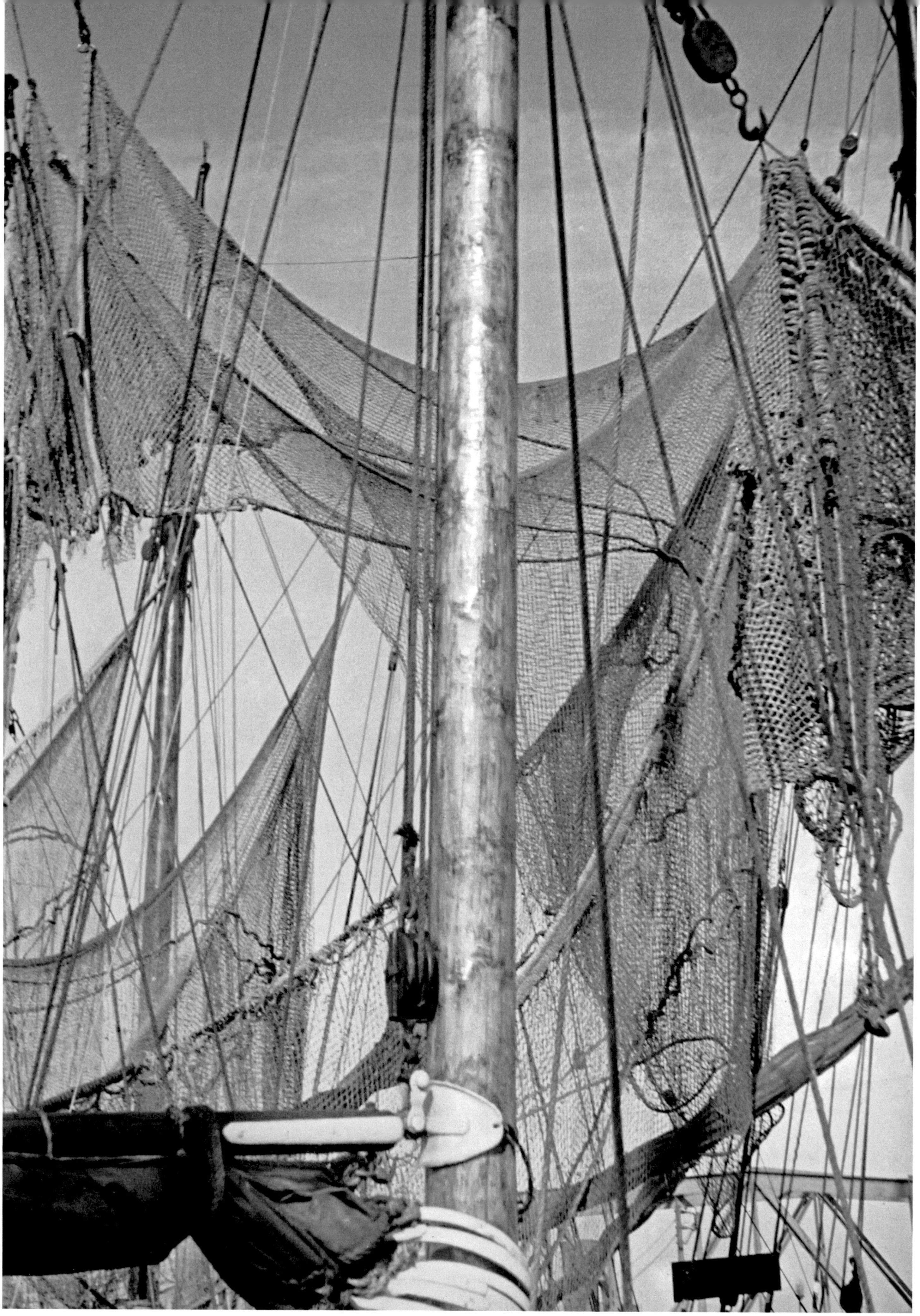

Nets of a fishing boat, Hamburg, 1929

Fishing nets, Hamburg, 1929

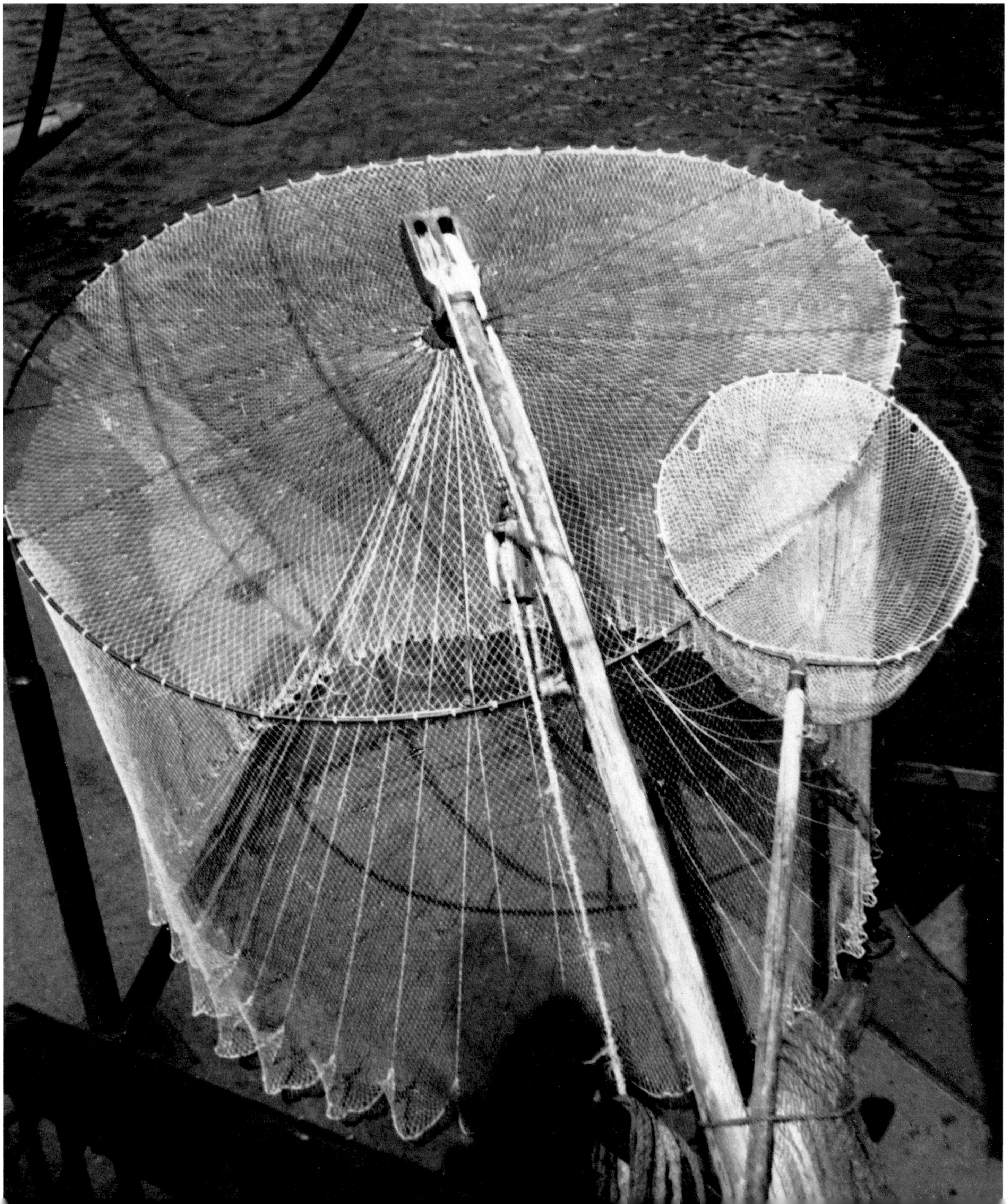

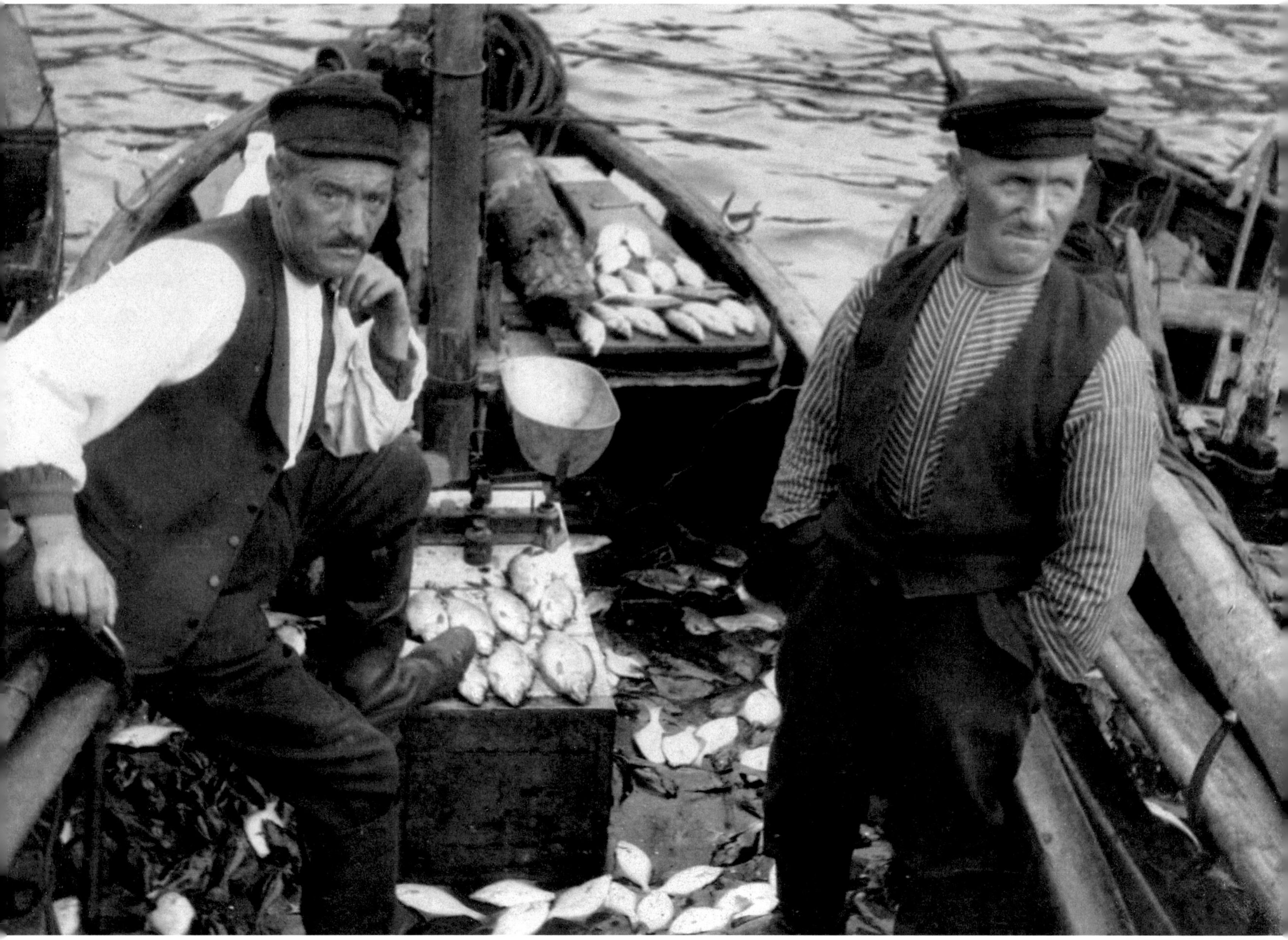

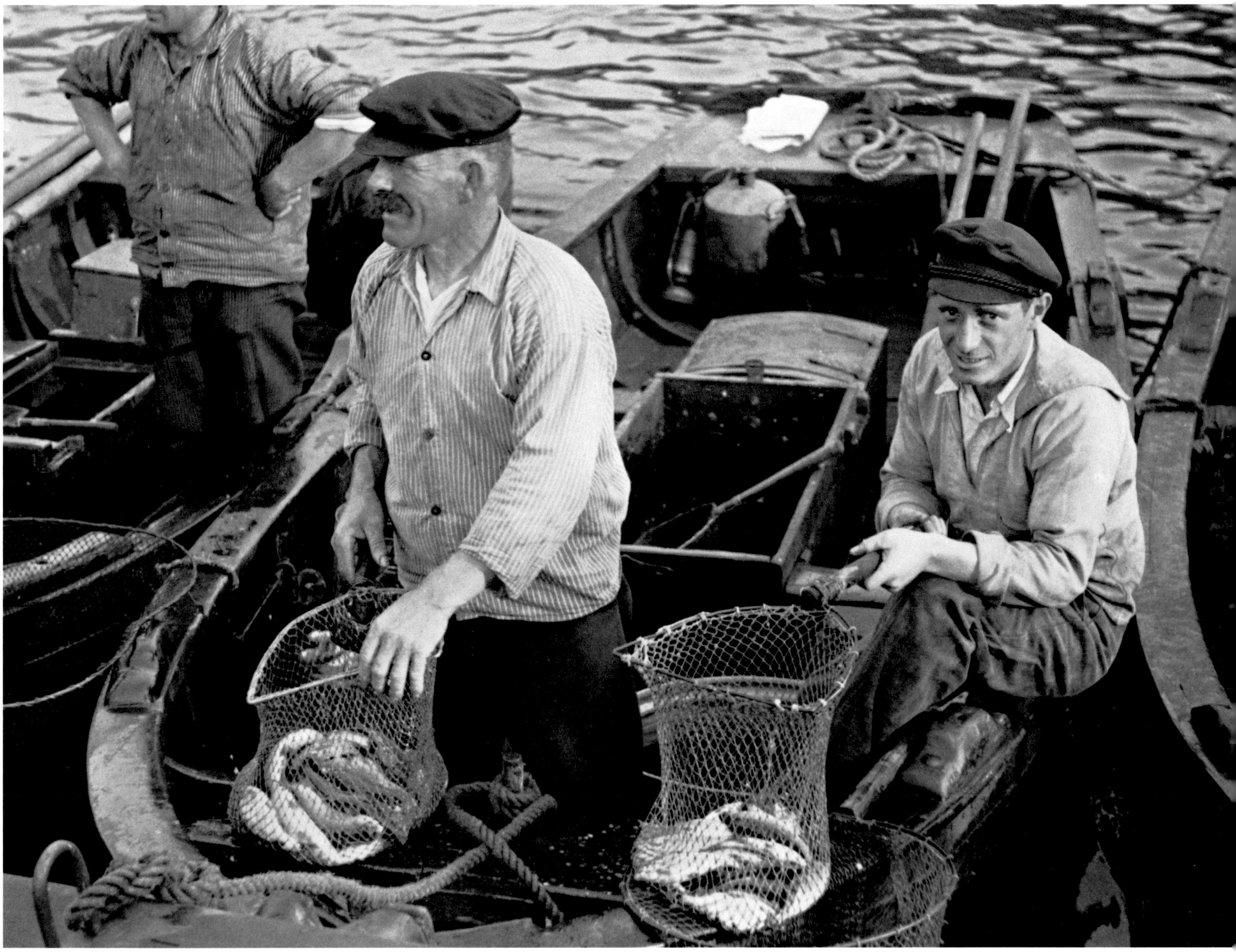

Fishermen at St. Pauli Fish Market, Hamburg, 1931

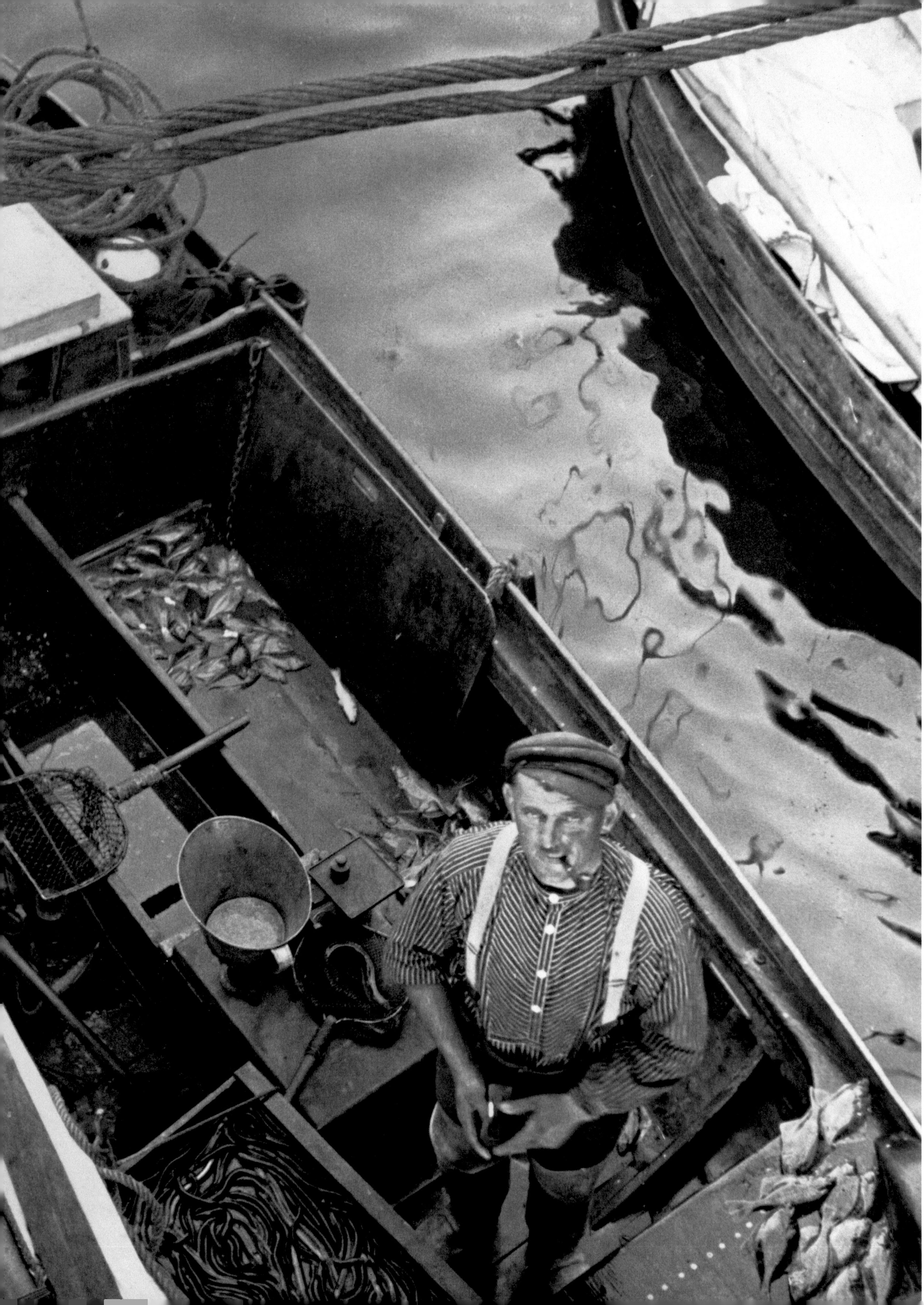

Fishermen at St. Pauli Fish Market, Hamburg, 1931

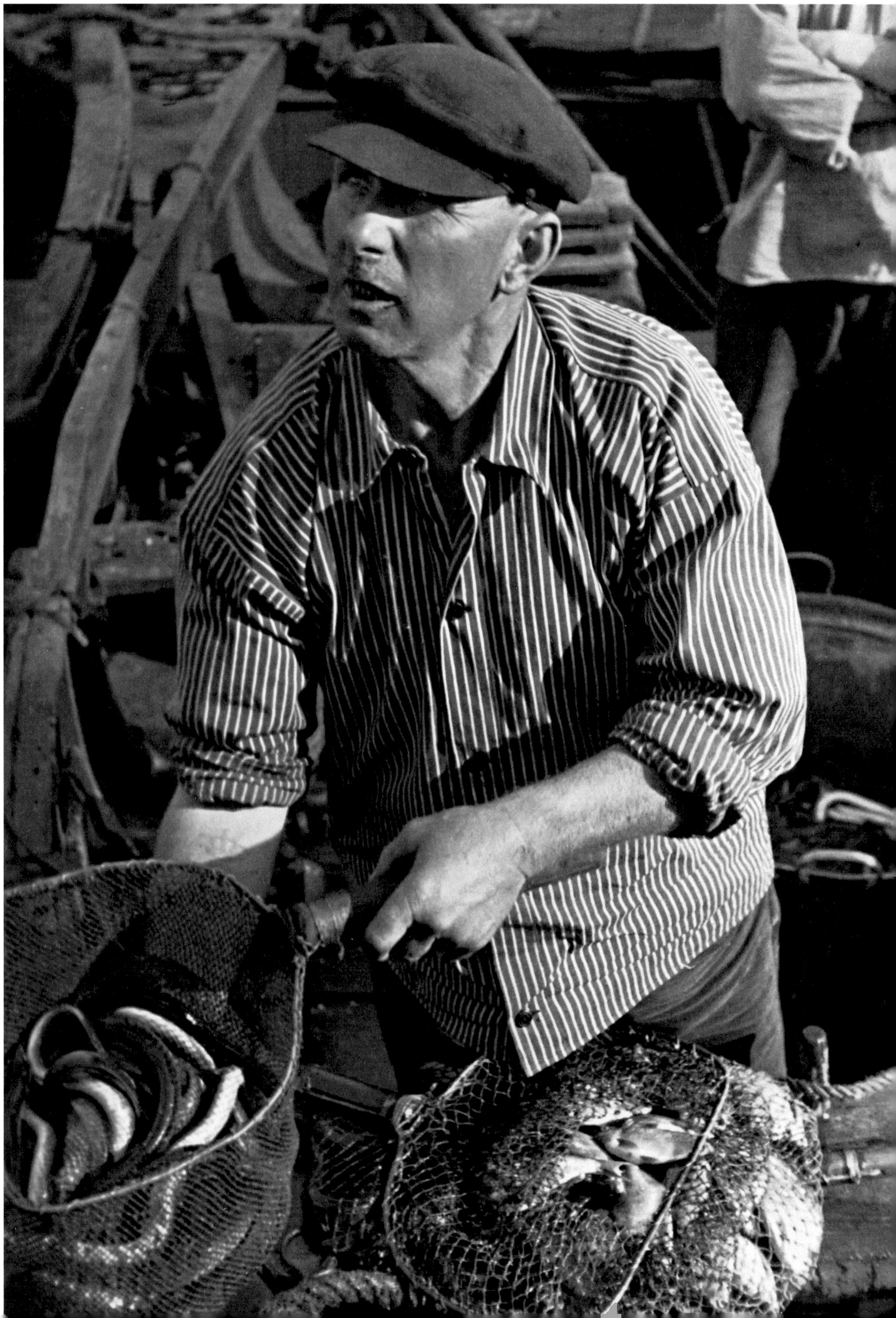

Der Zirkus kommt!

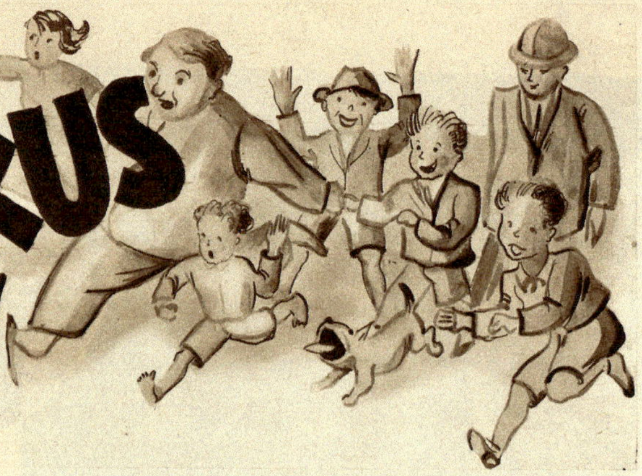

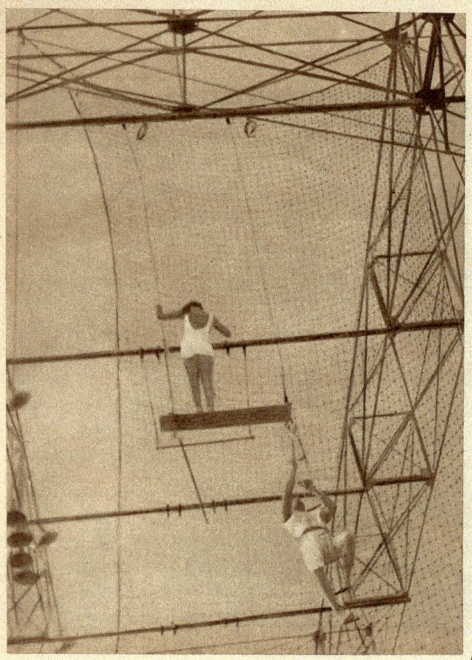

Klopfenden Herzens schauen Kinder und Erwachsene den tollkühnen Akrobaten zu. Über die Festigkeit des Fangnetzes wird diskutiert.

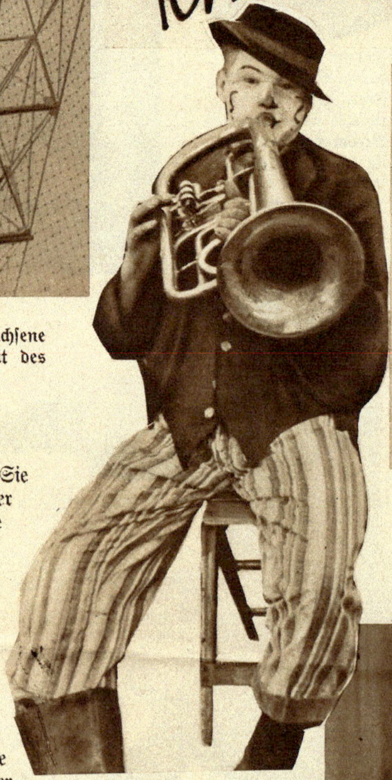

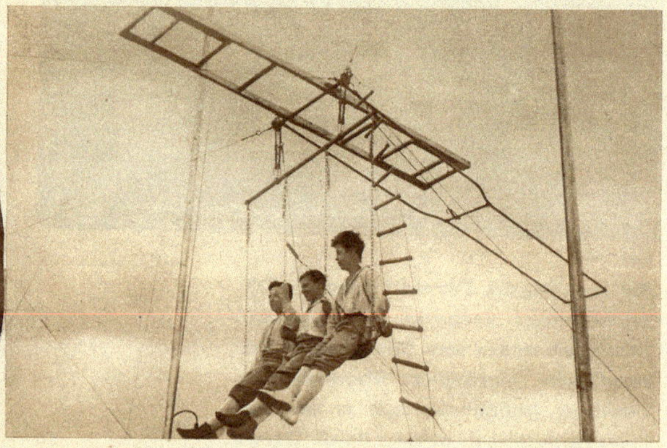

Kaltblütig und ihrer Sache absolut sicher blicken die waghalsigen Akrobaten auf die Dächer der umliegenden Häuser.

Schauderhafte Töne hallen über den sonst so stillen Dorfplatz.

Immer hereinspaziert meine Herrschaften! Sie werden sehen den Todessprung der Brüder ..., den weltberühmten Clown, — treten Sie näher, junger Herr ... Mit Tschingteräng und Bums der beiden Clowns tönt diese Einladung über den Dorfplatz. Und die jungen Herren und Damen, die ganze Dorfjugend strömt herbei, die Eltern gemessener hinterdrein, teils schmunzelnd, teils spöttisch verbergen sie die Erwartungen auf die bunte Welt.

Romantisch ragen die Geräte für die Akrobaten hoch über die Dächer der nächstgelegenen Häuser empor. Die waghalsigen Spiele, Streiche und Scherze, im Alltagsleben der Jugend verstreut, hier sind sie Aufgabe, Beruf, das tägliche Brot. Trapezkünstler hängen und wirbeln in der Luft, Clowns purzeln herum, schneiden Grimassen — man kommt nicht zu Atem vor lauter Überraschung, Staunen, ängstlicher Bewunderung und Lachen. Das sind andere, fremde Menschen, sie kennen kein Heim, besitzen keine Wiesen, Tiere. Die Kinder brauchen nicht in die Schule zu gehen. Ein rollendes Haus führt sie in die weite Welt, von einem Ort zum andern. Kein dankbareres Publikum findet das fahrende Volk, nirgendwo wirkt der Flitter und die tausend Posen, die Gefahr stärker, niemand genießt dies uneingeschränkter als die Menschen auf den stillen Dörfern, wo jeder Tag seine geregelte klare und harte Arbeit verlangt.

Aufnahmen Dr. Block

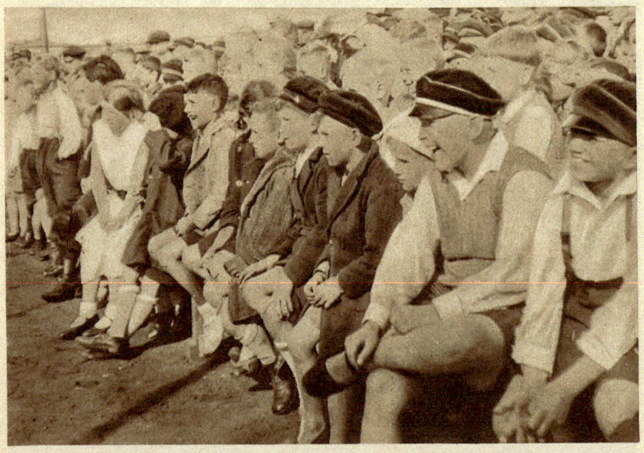

Am meisten Freude an dem ganzen Rummel haben natürlich die Schulkinder, die den Nachmittag für die Schülervorstellung frei bekamen.

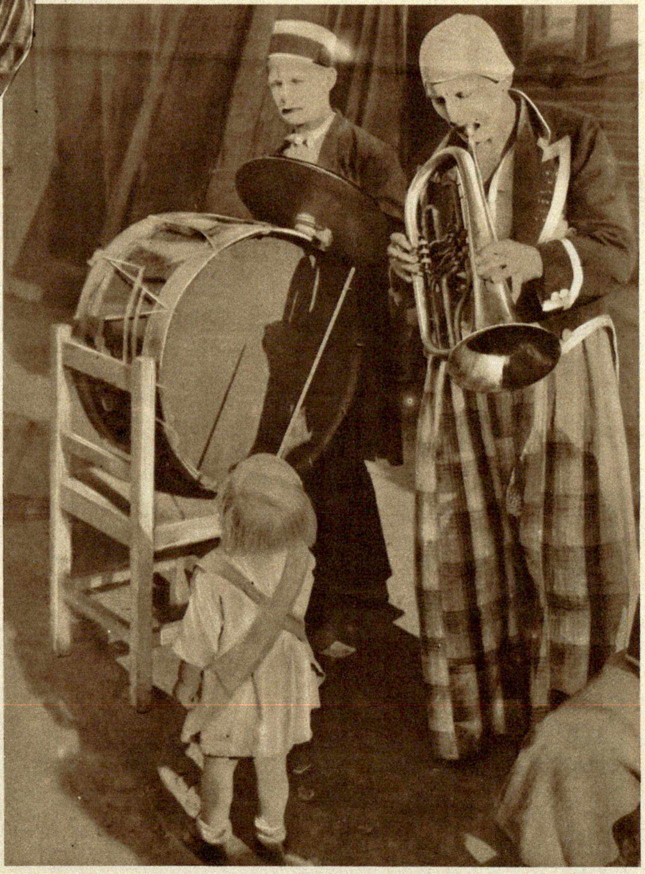

Darf ich auch mal?

"The Circus is Coming!" (*Basler Illustrierte Zeitung* 1, no. 42, 1932)

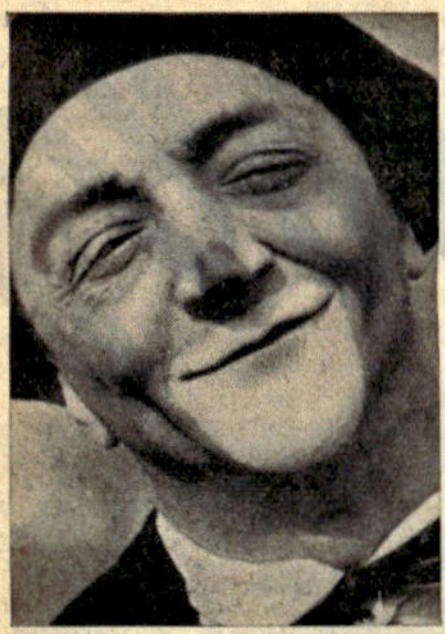

Der Clown Etté

Menschen im Zirkus

Das große Sterben im Zirkusgewerbe scheint ein weiteres Opfer zu fordern: Zirkus Sarrasani hat zum Ende dieses Monats seine sämtlichen Angestellten, Artisten und Arbeiter gekündigt. Von 48 deutschen Zirkussen haben in den letzten Jahren bereits 39 ihre Zelte für immer abbauen müssen.

Selbst in unserer an Kummer aller Art gewöhnten Zeit läßt eine solche Nachricht aufhorchen. Erschien das Leben hinter der leichten Zeltwand unserer Wanderzirkusse nicht losgelöst zu sein von allen schweren Bedingungen des Lebenskampfes? Mußte nicht die Tänzerin auf dem Drahtseil, der Artist am fliegenden Trapez, die Schulreiterin und wie die Vertreter der leichtgeschürzten Muse alle heißen, mußte ihnen nicht die Welt auch dann noch offen stehen, wenn zufällig einmal das Unternehmen verkrachte, mit dem sie durch einen Vertrag für eine Spielzeit verbunden waren?

Wer einmal hinter die Kulissen eines Zirkus geschaut hat, wußte längst, daß das Artistenvölkchen auch nichts anderes ist als eine Gruppe hart ums Brot ringender Proletarier.

Oder warum sonst reitet heute noch, mit mehr als 70 Jahren, die Trägerin eines weltumspannenden Namens noch Abend für Abend die hohe Schule in der Manege? Nicht um uns zu demonstrieren, daß die Zirkuskunst jung erhält, sondern ganz einfach, weil trotz aller „Erfolge" nicht so viel zu verdienen gewesen ist, daß sich die Reiterin mit 70 Jahren zur Ruhe setzen konnte und weil die Artisten durch die Sozialversicherung nur teilweise erfaßt werden.

Oder betrachten wir die Helden des dreifachen Saltos. Hundert vielleicht waren es, die den Versuch gemacht haben, durch den dreifachen Salto eine besondere Sensation zu schaffen, die ihnen die in der ganzen Welt knapp gewordenen Brotstätten öffnen sollte. Von allen, die das Kunststück versucht haben, ist es einer einzigen Truppe gelungen. Alle andern hat der Tod bei der Probe erwischt. Aber immer wieder finden sich die Artisten, die den Dreifachen versuchen, weil ganz einfach mit dem Doppelsalto kaum noch etwas zu verdienen ist.

Viele Artisten lassen ihre Kinder einen „bürgerlichen" Beruf erlernen. Freilich holt das im Lichterglanz so verführerisch strahlende Chapiteau diese Artistenkinder meist wieder zurück. Gewiß, es ist ein Ammenmärchen, daß den Artisten in frühester Jugend die Knochen gebrochen werden, um die Körper geschmeidig zu machen. Aber die Peitschenschläge, die nicht für das Pferd, sondern für die jugendliche Schulreiterin bestimmt sind, die an der Longe in der Luft schwebt und noch nicht gewandt genug ist um im eleganten, spielerisch aussehenden Sprung auf dem Rücken des in der Manege umherlaufenden Pferdes zu landen, diese Peitschenschläge hat nie jemand gezählt und registriert.

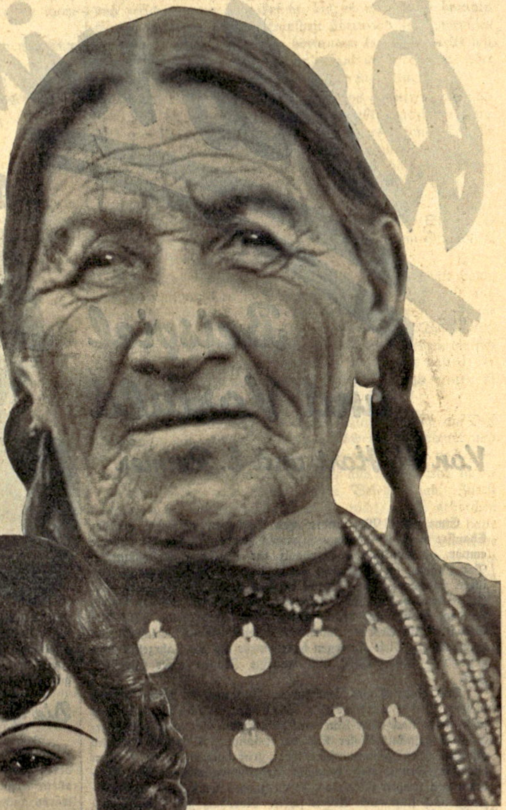

Die alte Indianerin

Vier Generationen Artisten

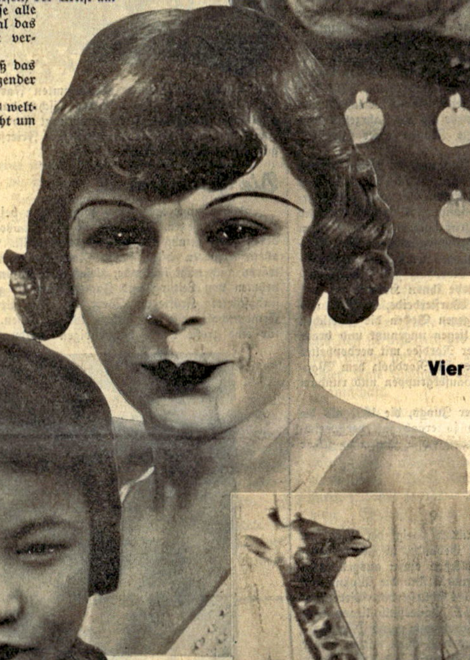

Die französische Luftakrobatin

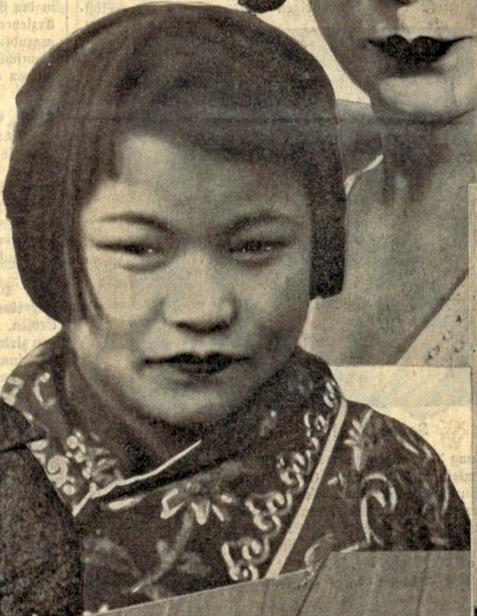

Die chinesische Zauberkünstlerin

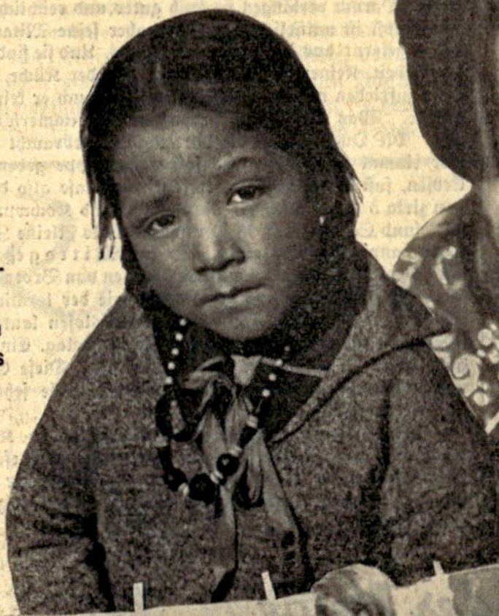

Das Indianerkind, geboren im Zirkus

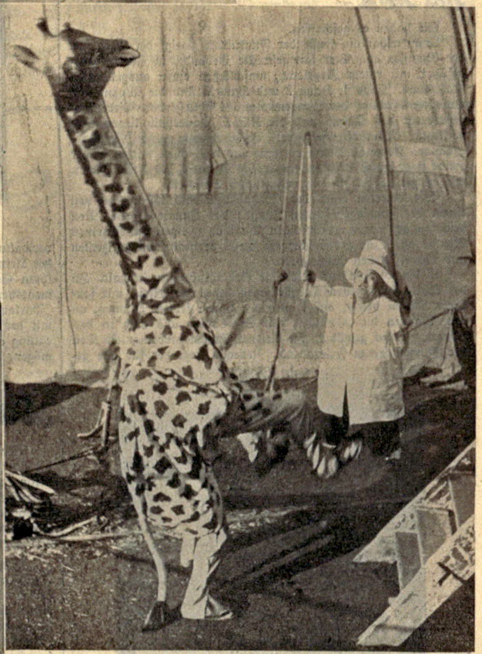

Unermüdlich proben die Clowns ihre neue Lachattraktion

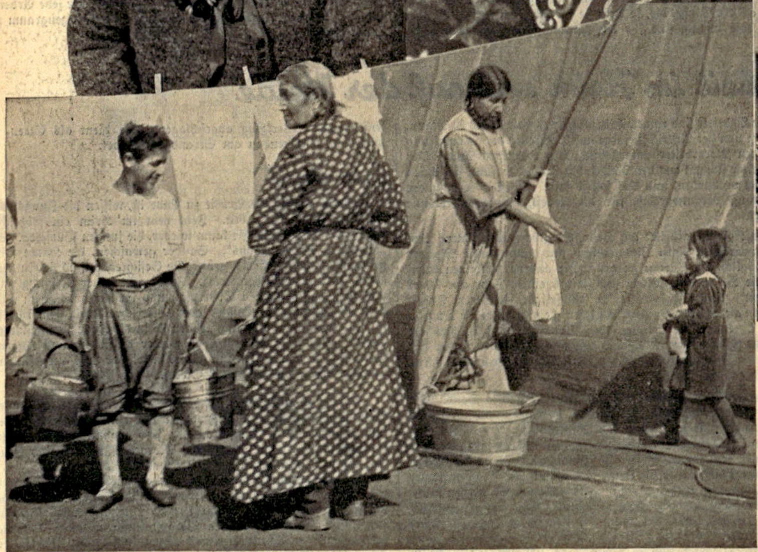

Zwischen den Zelten spielt sich der Alltag ab wie zwischen den Häusermauern der Straßen

Und das Zirkusballett. Es sieht so schön aus. Aber: 12 Mädel wohnen und schlafen in einem kleinen Wohnwagen. Vor der Vorstellung muß geprobt werden und die Kostüme sind auch in Ordnung zu halten.

Einmal hat es einen Tierclown gegeben, der wollte sich für den sozialen Aufstieg der Artisten einsetzen. Er gründete zusammen mit einigen Gleichgesinnten die freigewerkschaftliche Internationale Artistenloge. Der Tierclown, obwohl vorher eine gesuchte und hochbezahlte Attraktion, bekam plötzlich keine Engagements mehr. Er spielte dann zuerst auf Teilung mit einigen Kollegen, dann gründete er sich einen eignen kleinen Zirkus. Der Zirkus wuchs und wuchs, bereiste die ganze Welt, jedes Kind in Deutschland kennt den Namen des Zirkus. Es ist Hans Stosch-Sarrasani, den jetzt trotz seines geradezu sagenhaften Aufstiegs auch das Schicksal packen will.

Erro.

"People of the Circus" (*Das Echo der Woche*, no. 21, 1932)

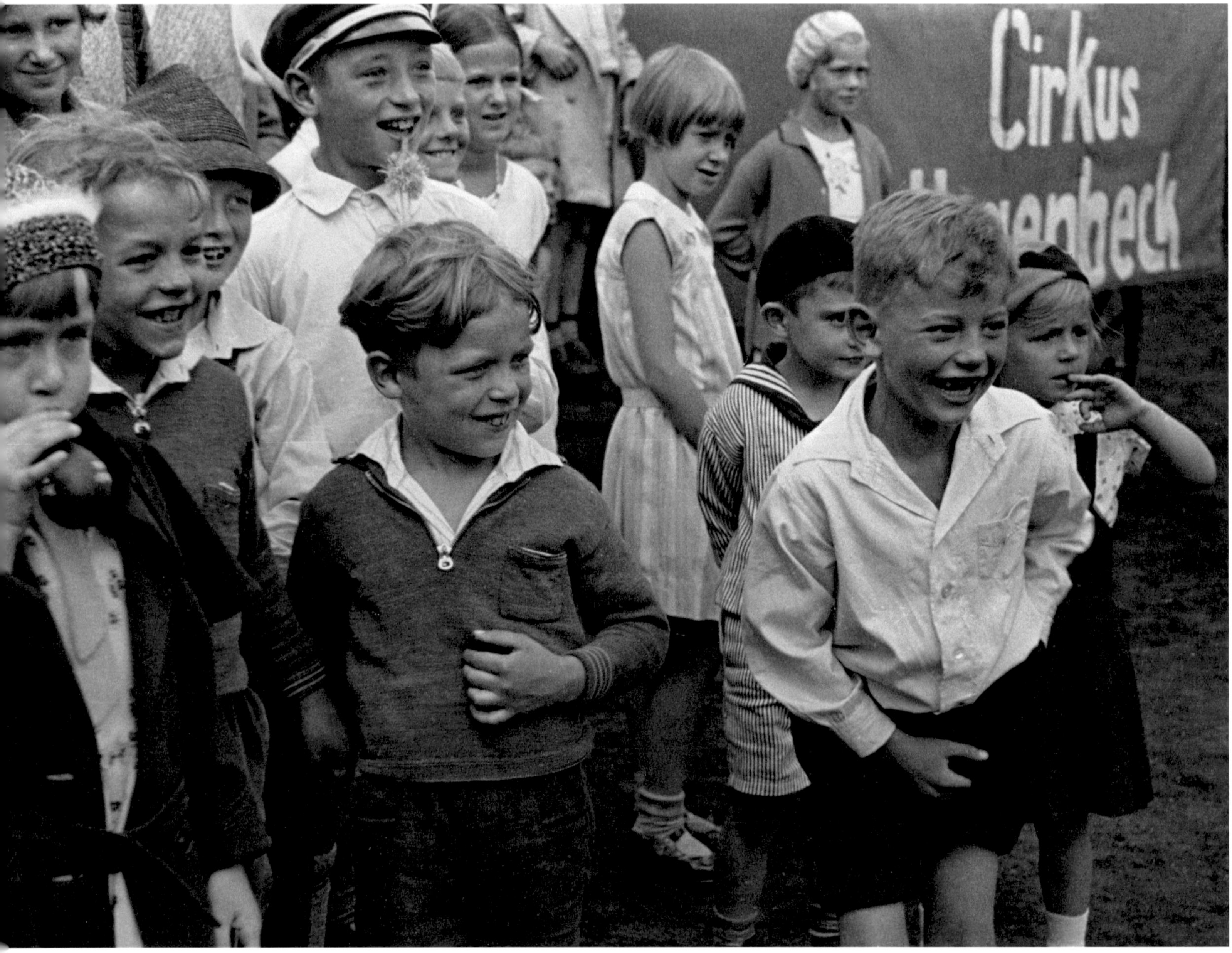
Cirkus

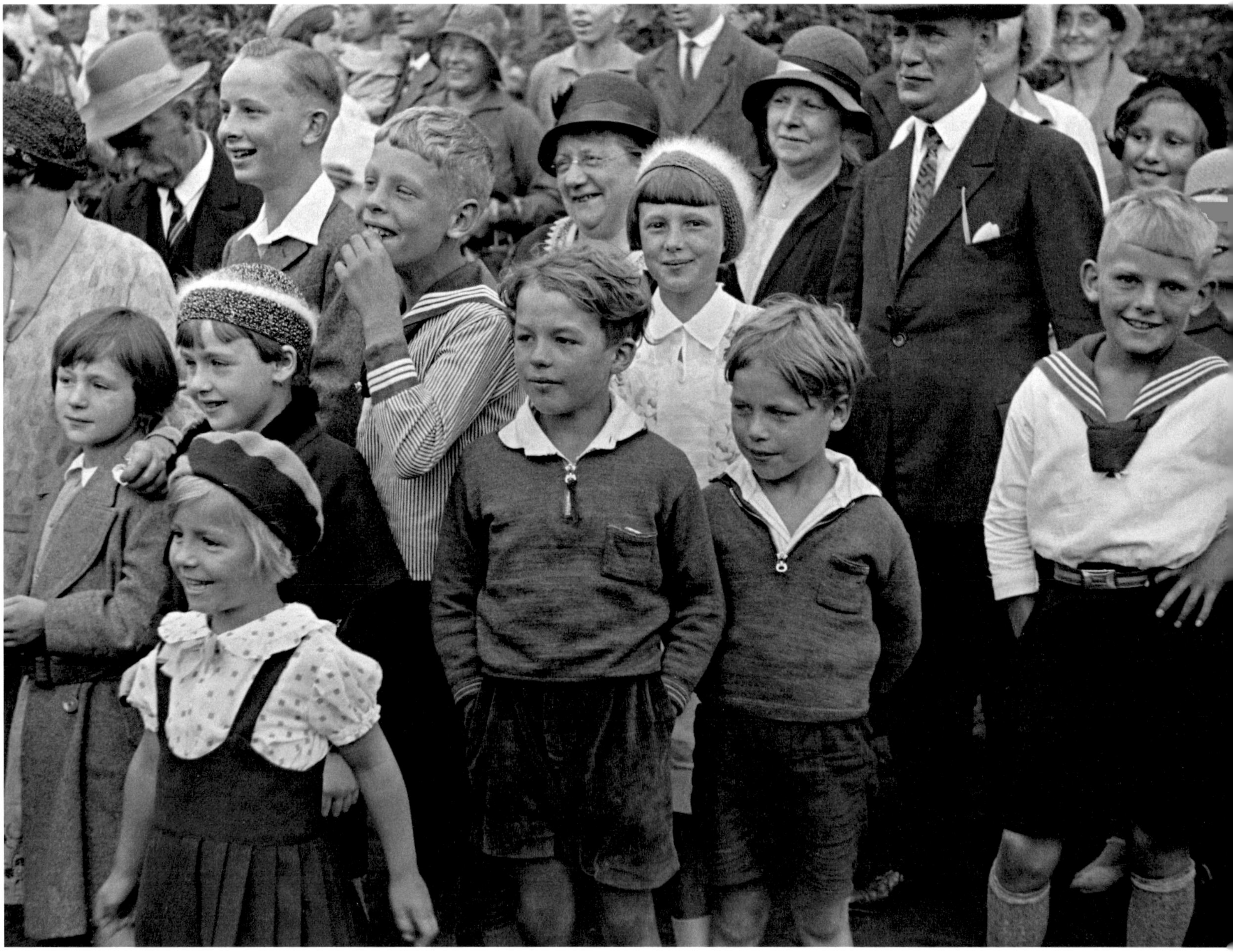

Children at Circus Hagenbeck, Hamburg, 1931

Aerialists, Hamburg, 1931

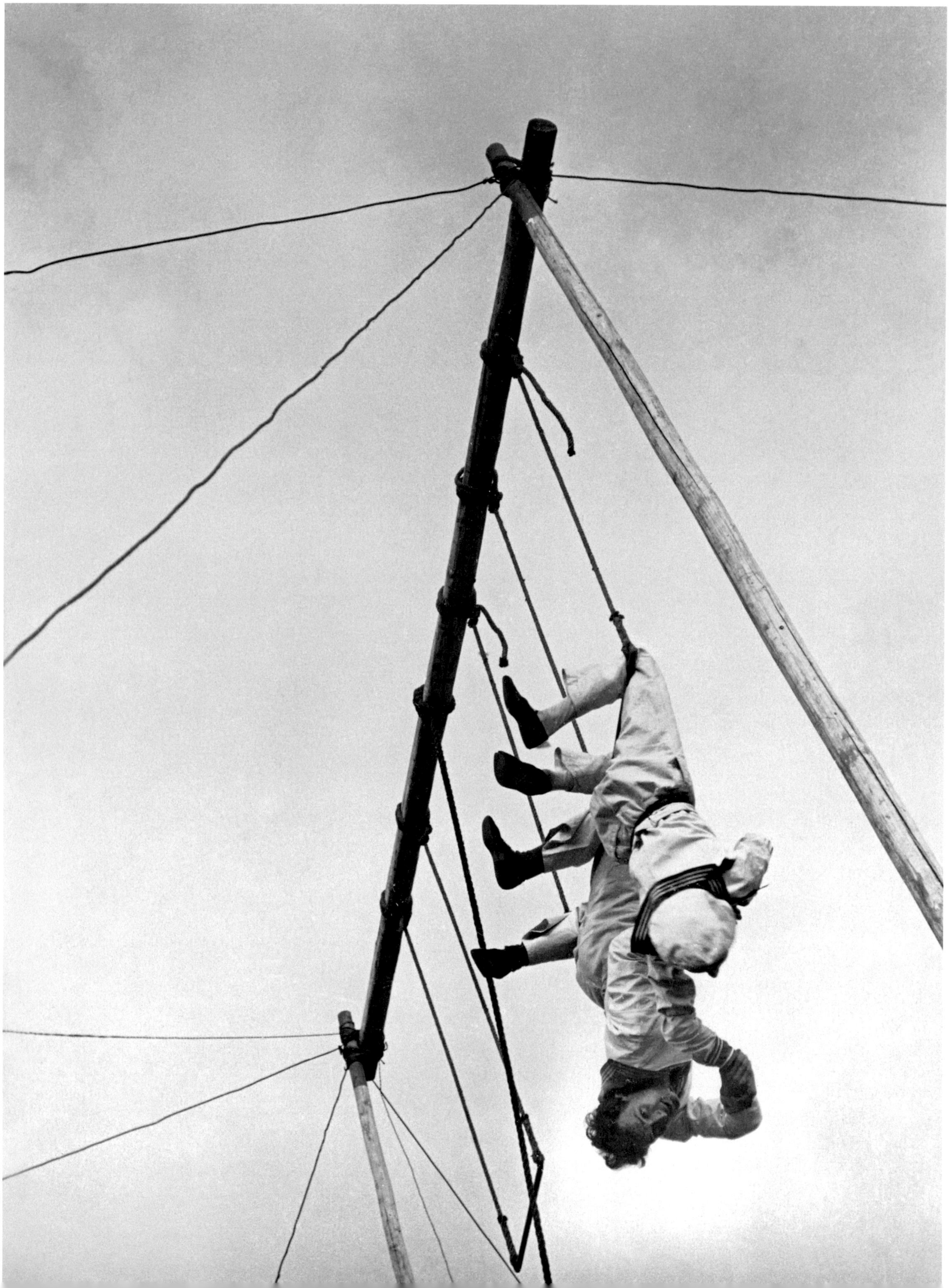

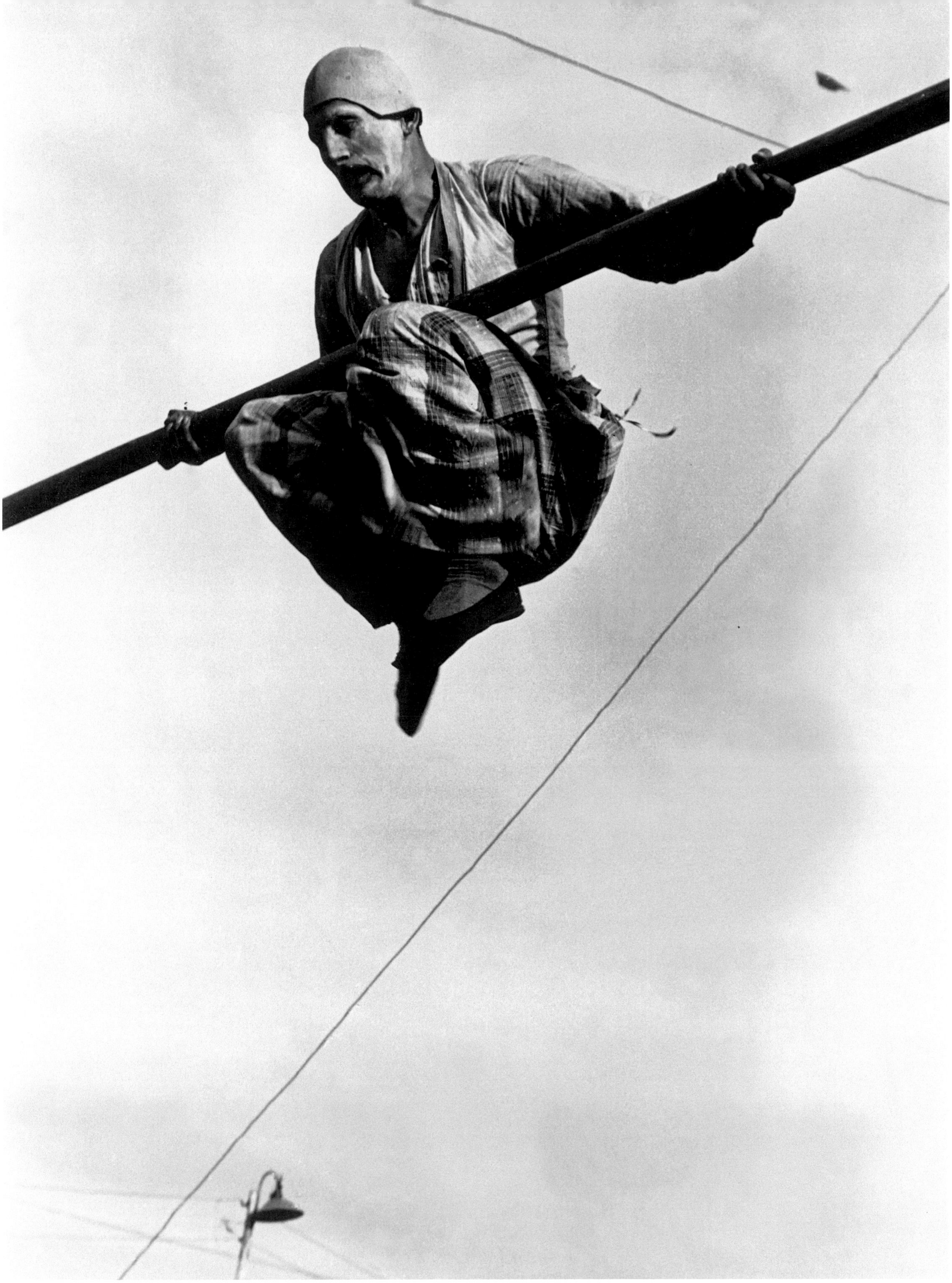

Aerialist clown, Hamburg, 1931

Clown, Hamburg, 1931

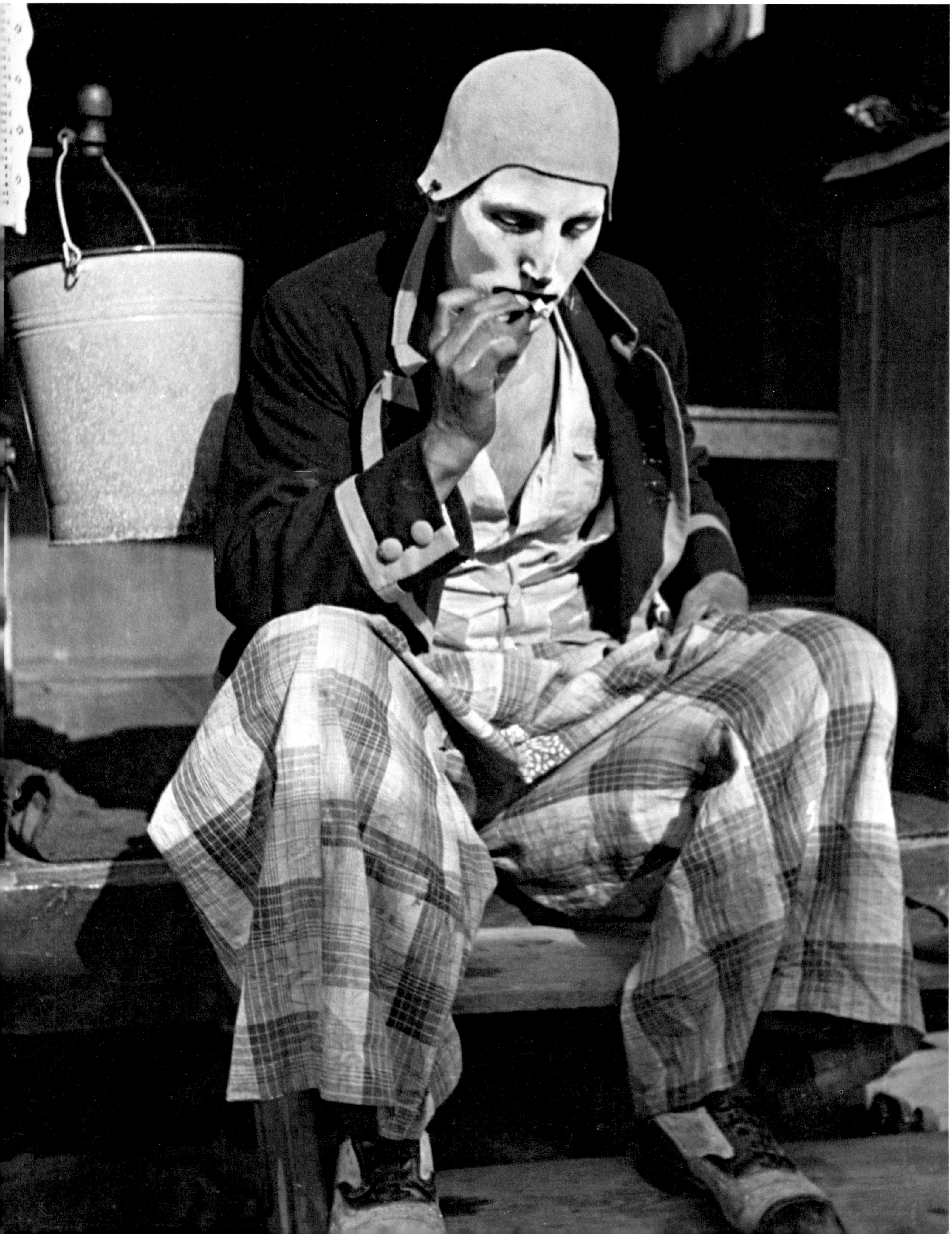

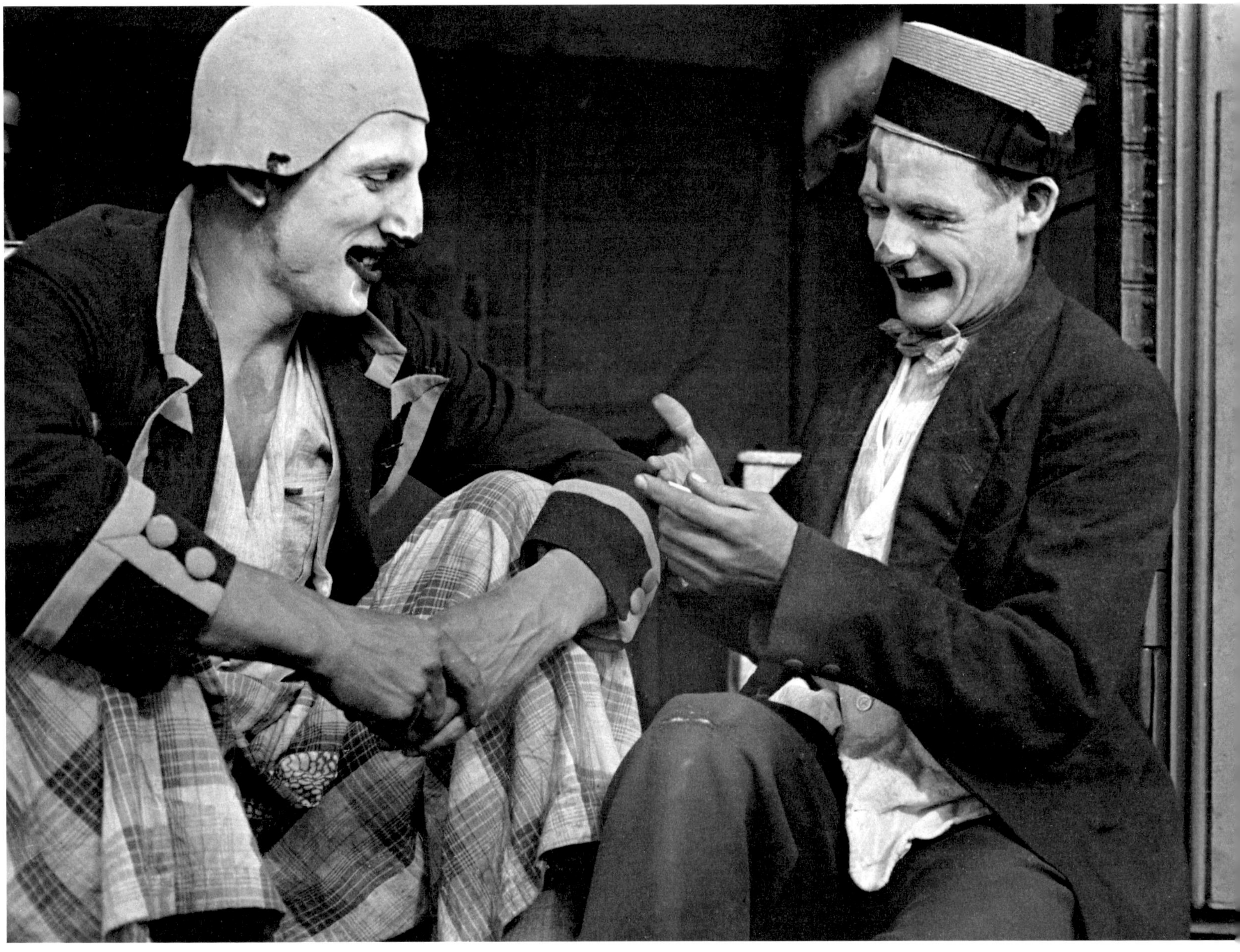

Clowns, Hamburg, 1931

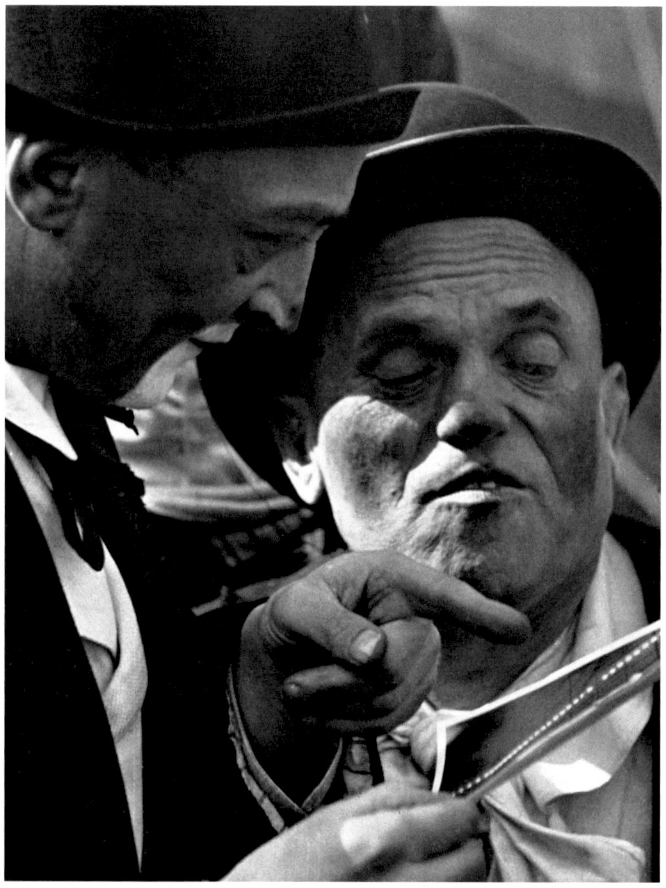

Clowns Etté and François, Circus Sarrasani, Hamburg, 1932

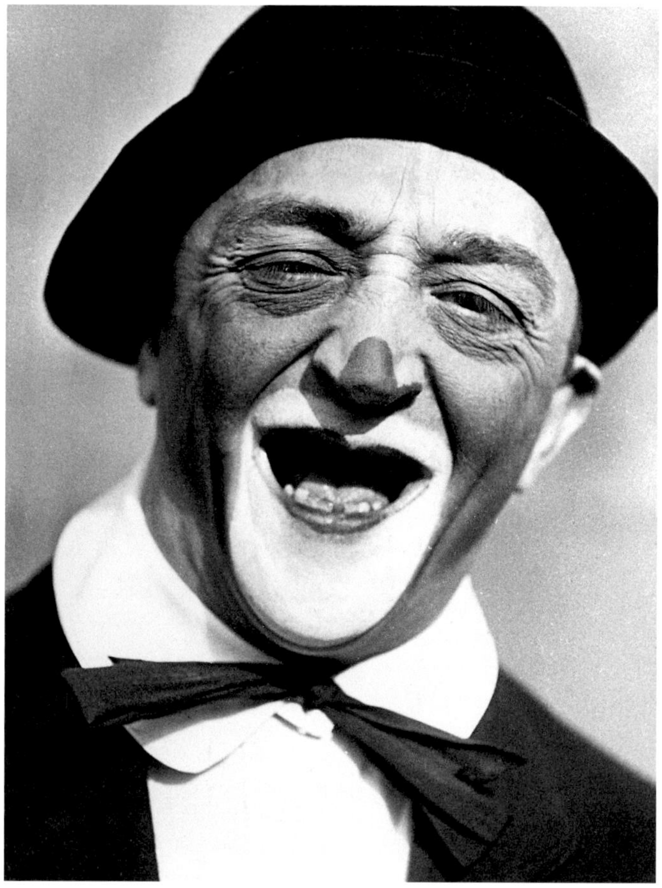

Clown Etté, Circus Sarrasani, Hamburg, 1932

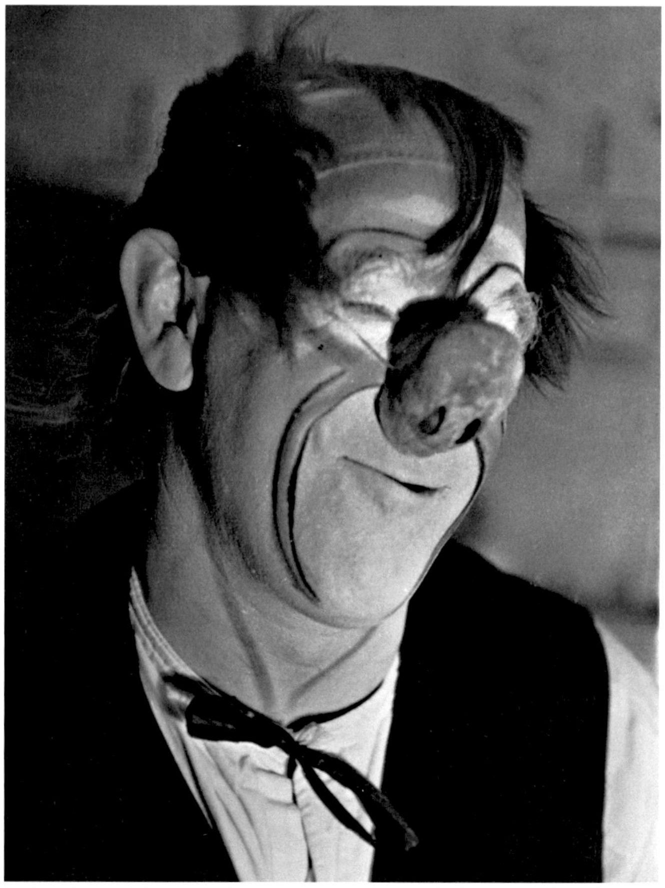

Clown, Circus Sarrasani, Hamburg, 1932

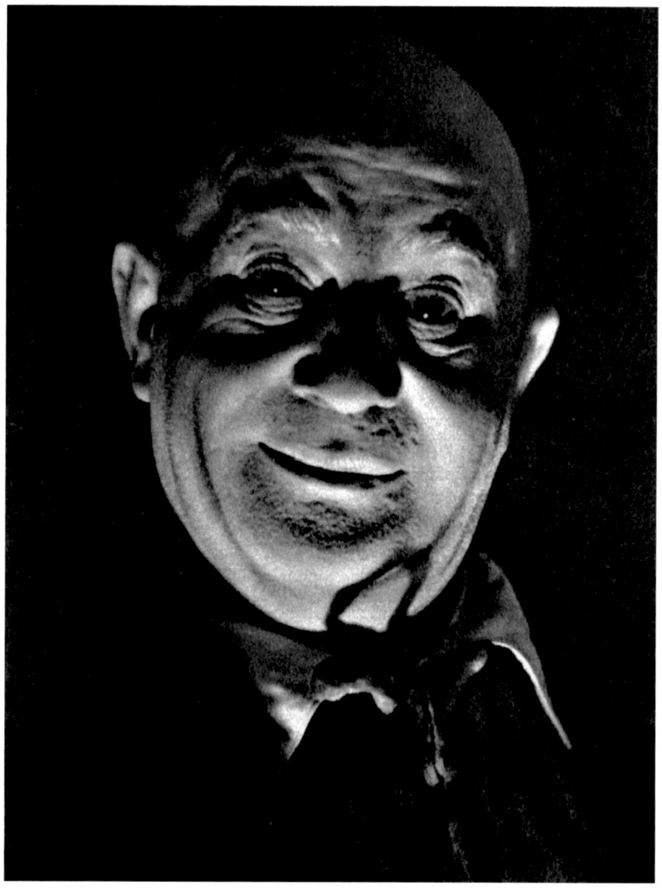

Clown (Kalle Bronett), Hamburg, 1932

NORAG

DAS OFFIZIELLE ORGAN DER NORDISCHEN RUNDFUNK A.G.

Ausgabe **B***

NR. 28

HAMBURG
9. JAHRGANG
10. JULI 1932

MIT GERÄTE-
VERSICHERUNG

Programmfolge:

Kostenlose Probenummer

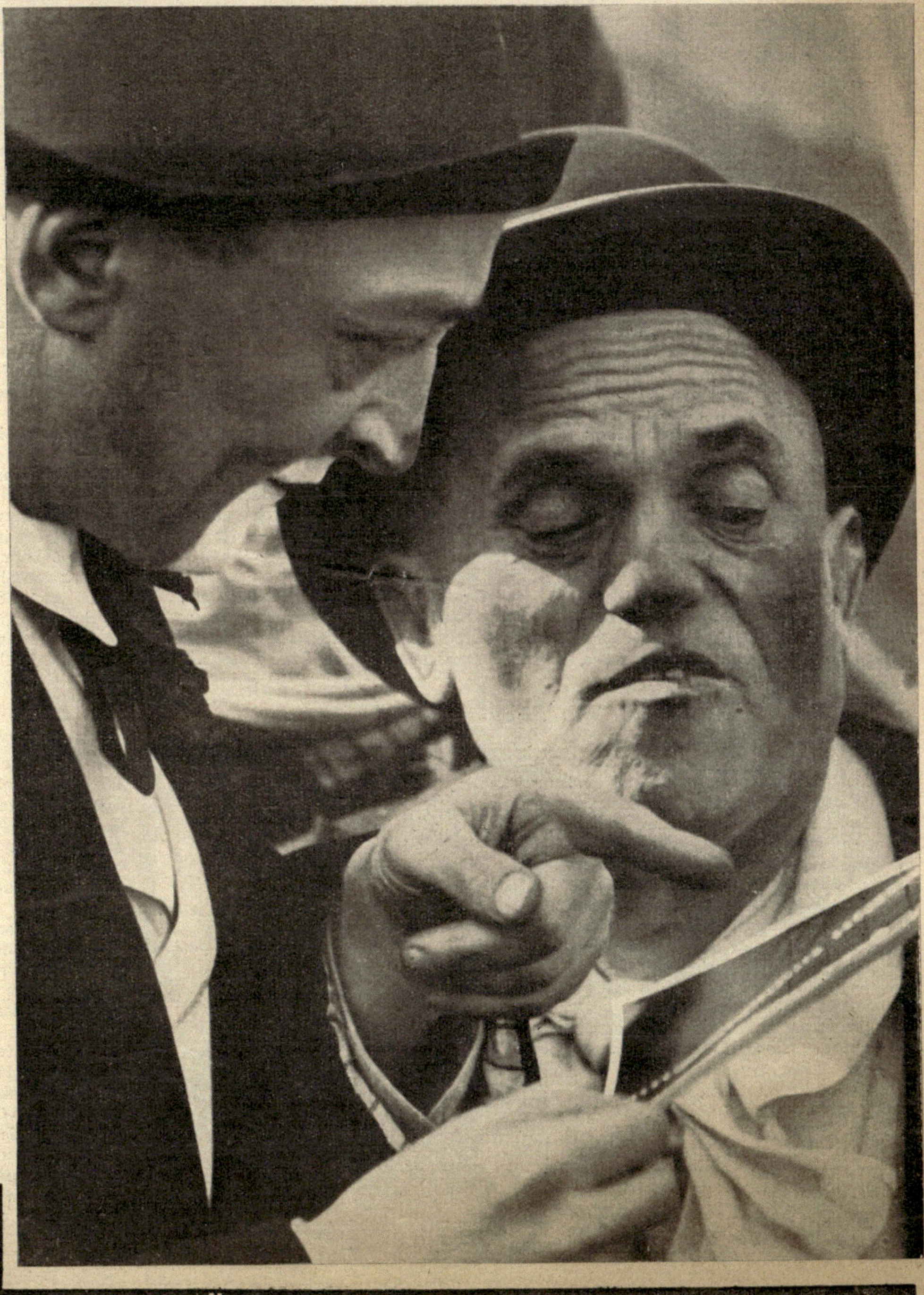

Die Clowns Francois und Etté (Zirkus Sarrasani) zur bunten Stunde der Internationalen Artistenloge Sonntag, 20 Uhr

Aufn.: Dr. Block

15 PF. MIT AUSFÜHRLICHEM NORAG-PROGRAMM

NORAG 9, no. 28, 1932

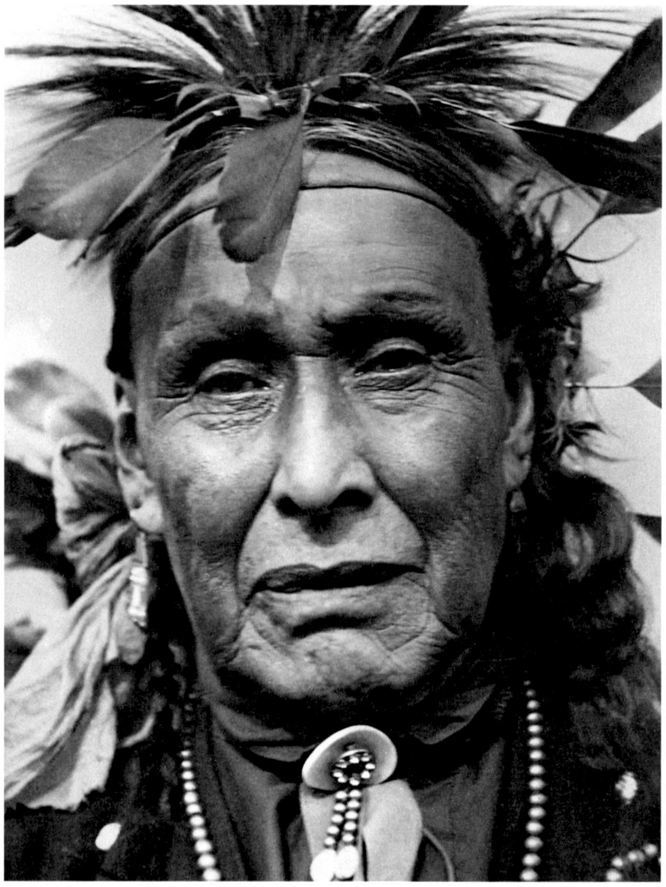
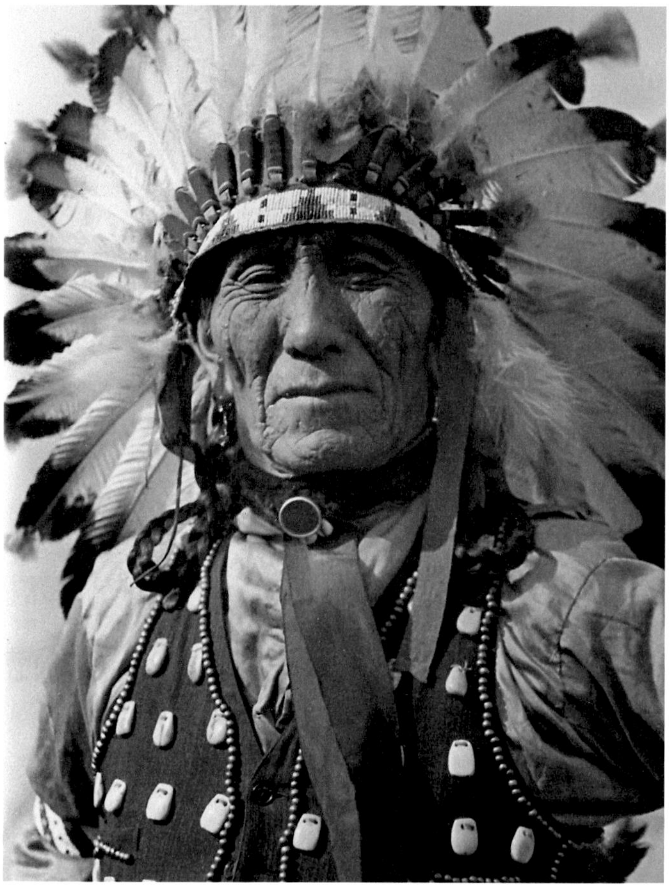

Sioux Indians of Circus Sarrasani, Hamburg, 1932

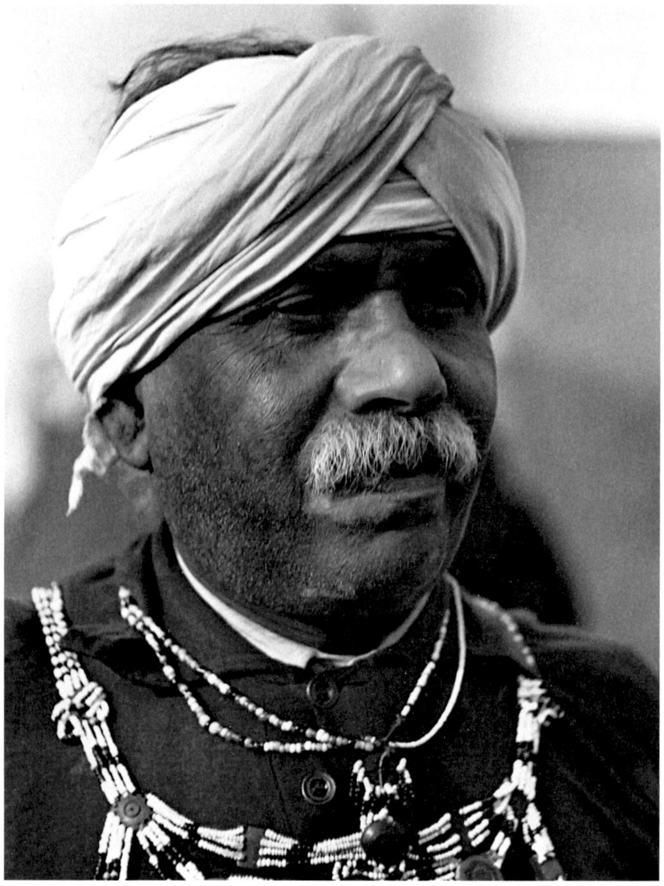
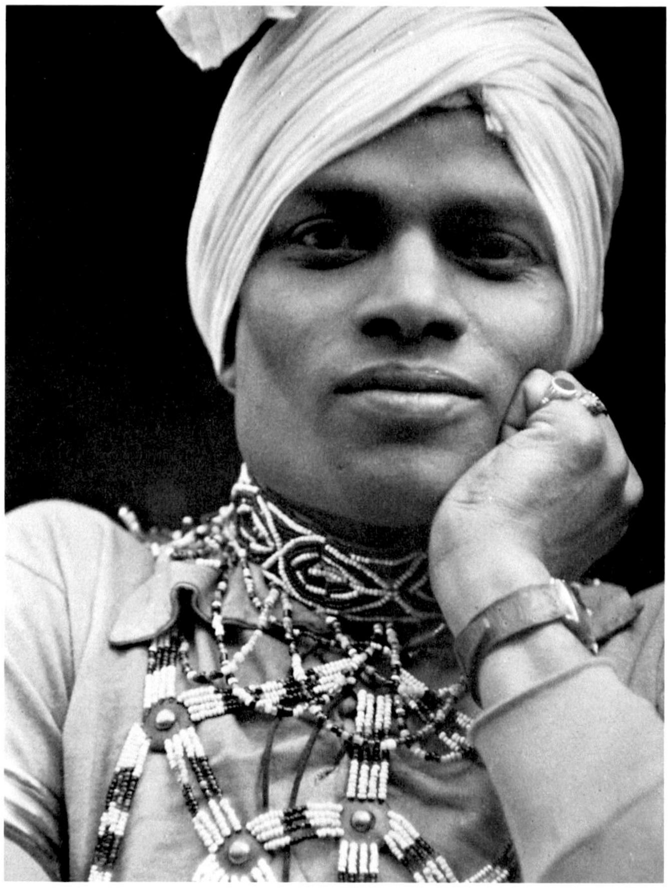

Indian temple dancers of Circus Sarrasani, Hamburg, 1932

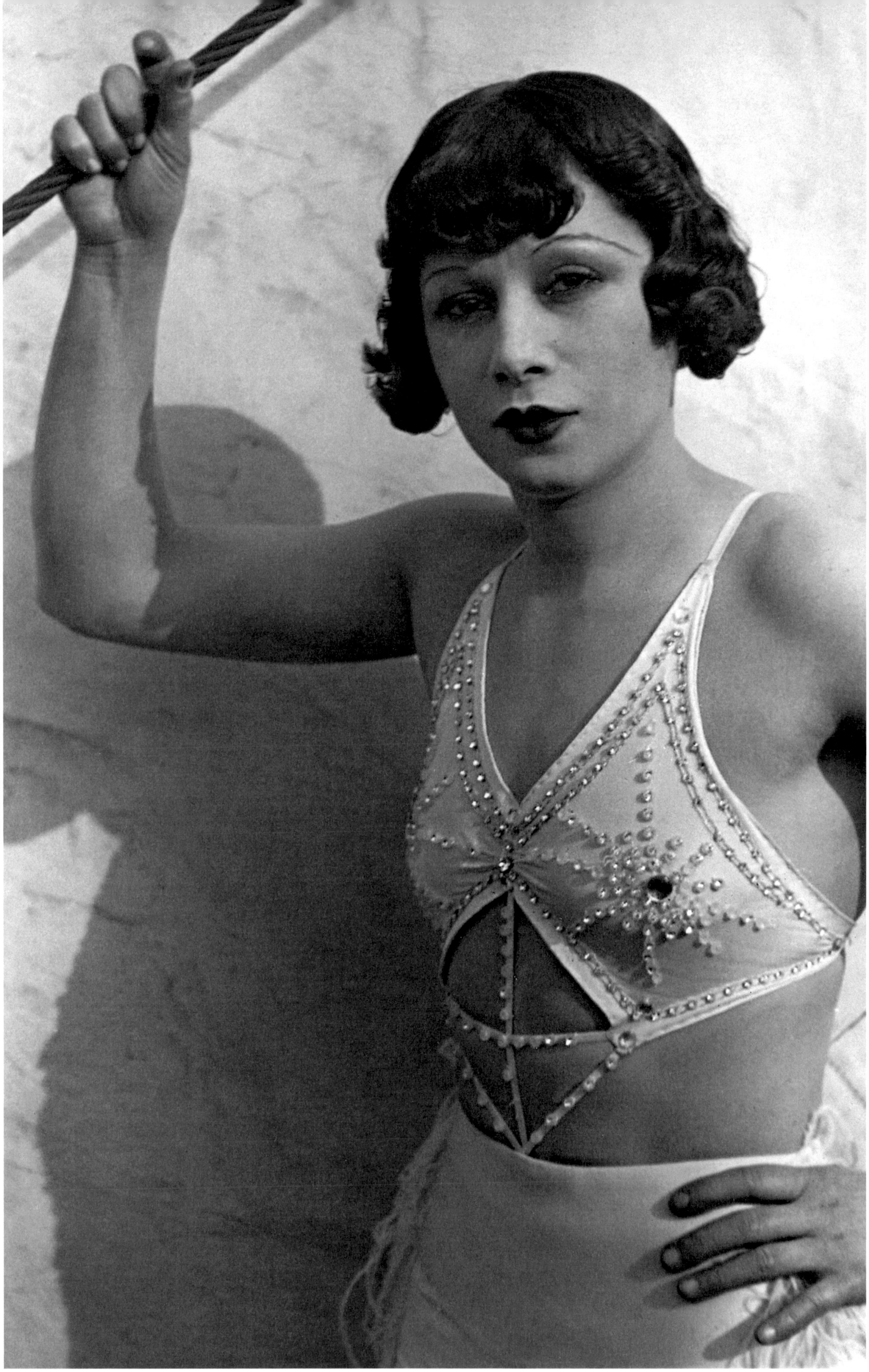

Aerialist of Circus Sarrasani, Hamburg, 1932

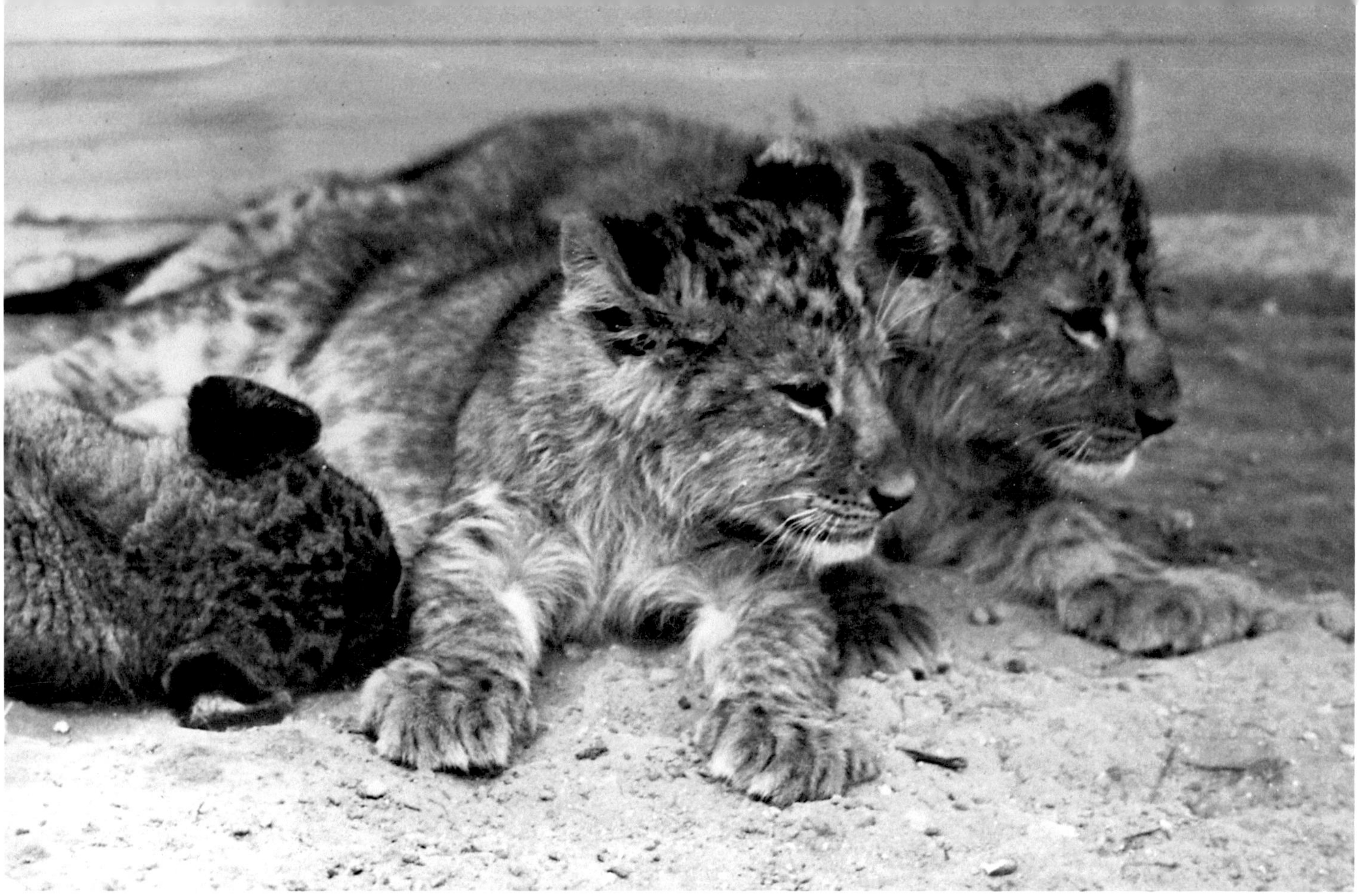

Young lions and a hippo at Hagenbeck Zoo, Hamburg, 1933

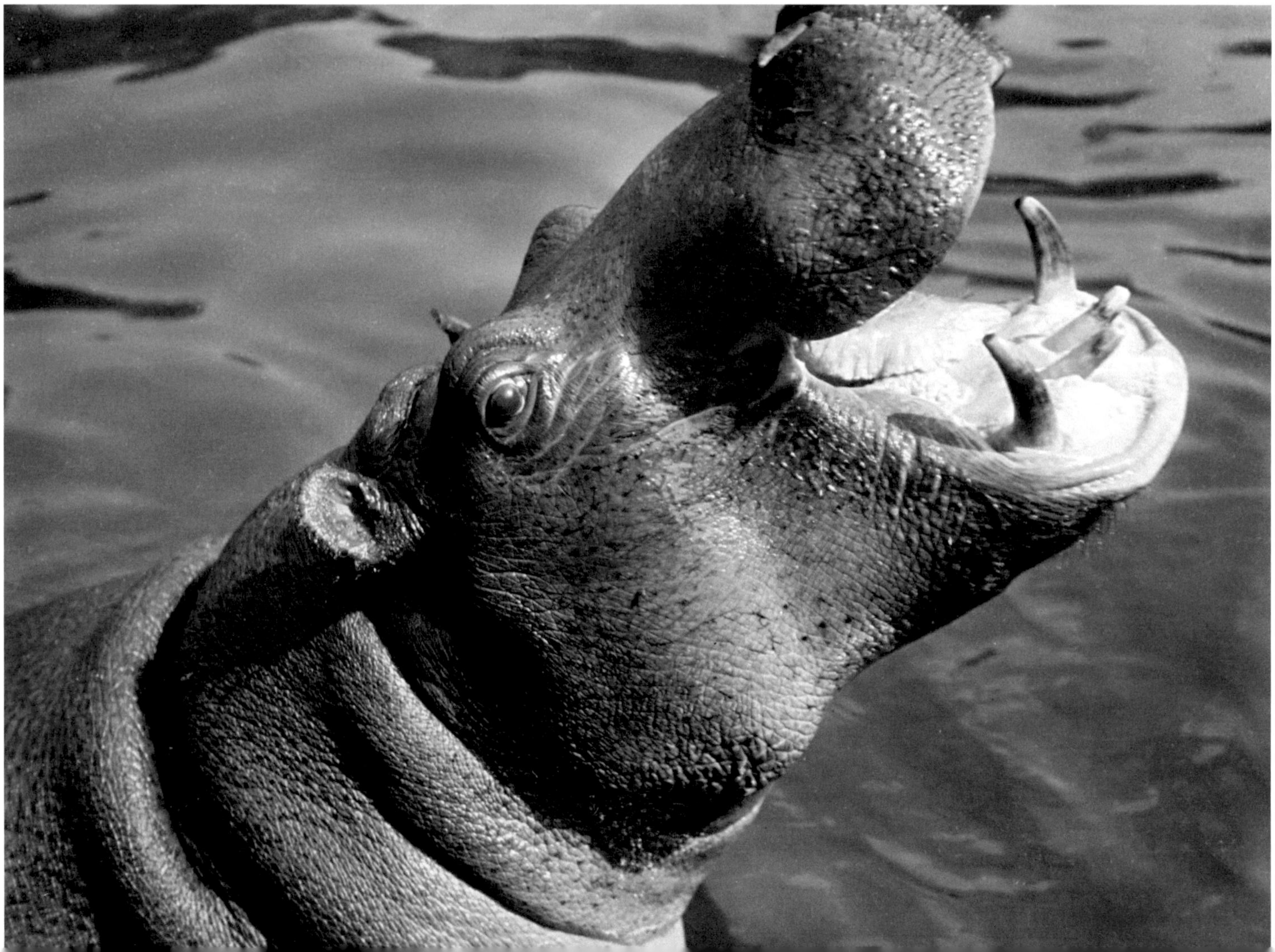

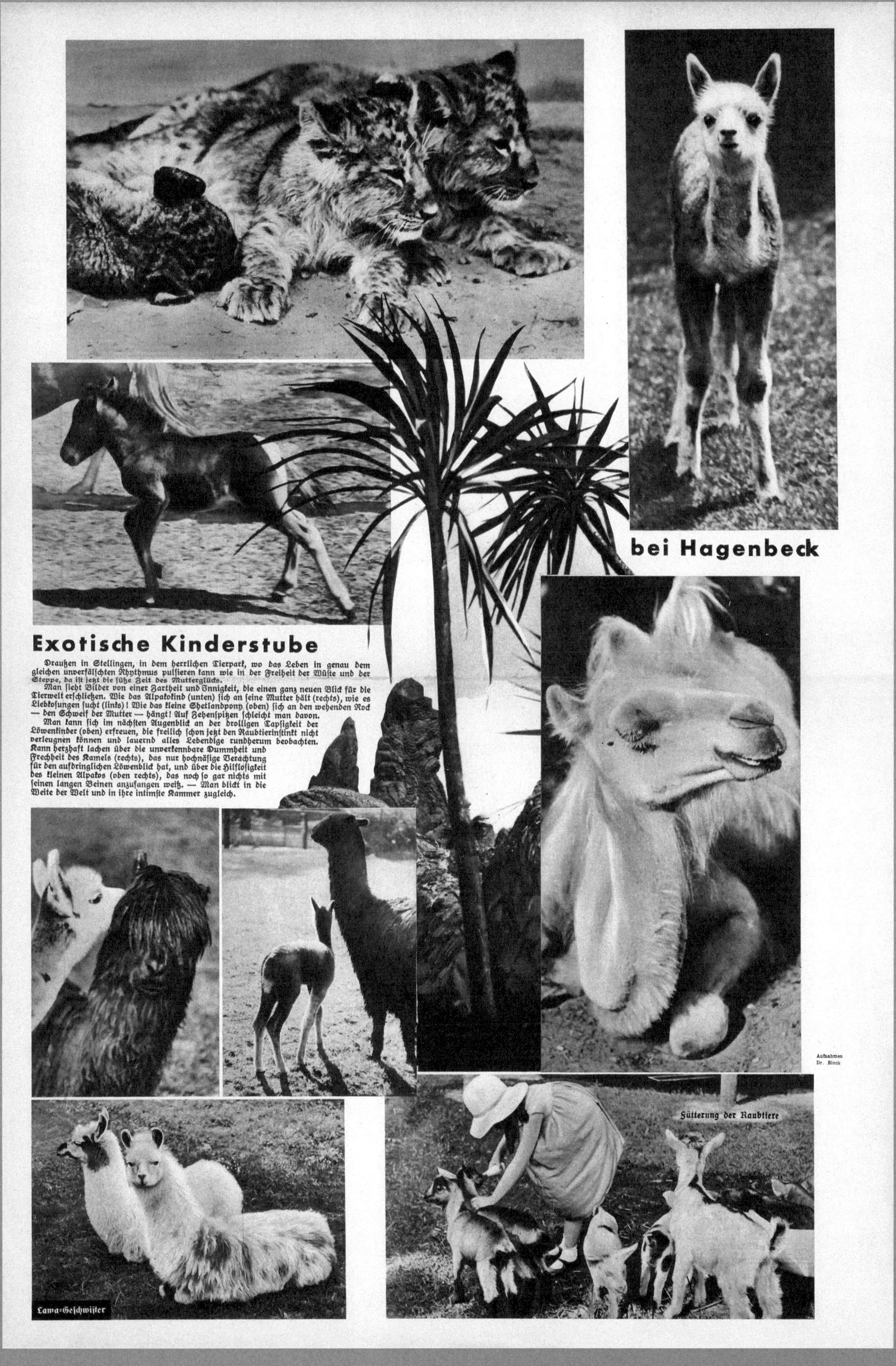

Exotische Kinderstube bei Hagenbeck

Draußen in Stellingen, in dem herrlichen Tierpark, wo das Leben in genau dem gleichen unverfälschten Rhythmus pulsieren kann wie in der Freiheit der Wüste und der Steppe, da ist jetzt die süße Zeit des Mutterglücks.

Man sieht Bilder von einer Zartheit und Innigkeit, die einen ganz neuen Blick für die Tierwelt erschließen. Wie das Alpakokind (unten) sich an seine Mutter hält (rechts), wie es Liebkosungen sucht (links)! Wie das kleine Shetlandpony (oben) sich an den wehenden Rock — den Schweif der Mutter — hängt! Auf Zehenspitzen schleicht man davon.

Man kann sich im nächsten Augenblick an der drolligen Tapsigkeit der Löwenkinder (oben) erfreuen, die freilich schon jetzt den Raubtierinstinkt nicht verleugnen können und lauernd alles Lebendige rundherum beobachten. Kann herzhaft lachen über die unverkennbare Dummheit und Frechheit des Kamels (rechts), das nur hochnäsige Verachtung für den aufdringlichen Löwenblick hat, und über die Hilflosigkeit des kleinen Alpakos (oben rechts), das noch so gar nichts mit seinen langen Beinen anzufangen weiß. — Man blickt in die Weite der Welt und in ihre intimste Kammer zugleich.

Aufnahmen Dr. Block

Fütterung der Raubtiere

Lama-Geschwister

"Exotic Nursery at Hagenbeck" (*Hamburger Anzeiger. Illustrierte Wochenbeilage*, no. 27, 1933)

Mesembryanthemum acinaciforme (Sour Fig), Hamburg, 1929

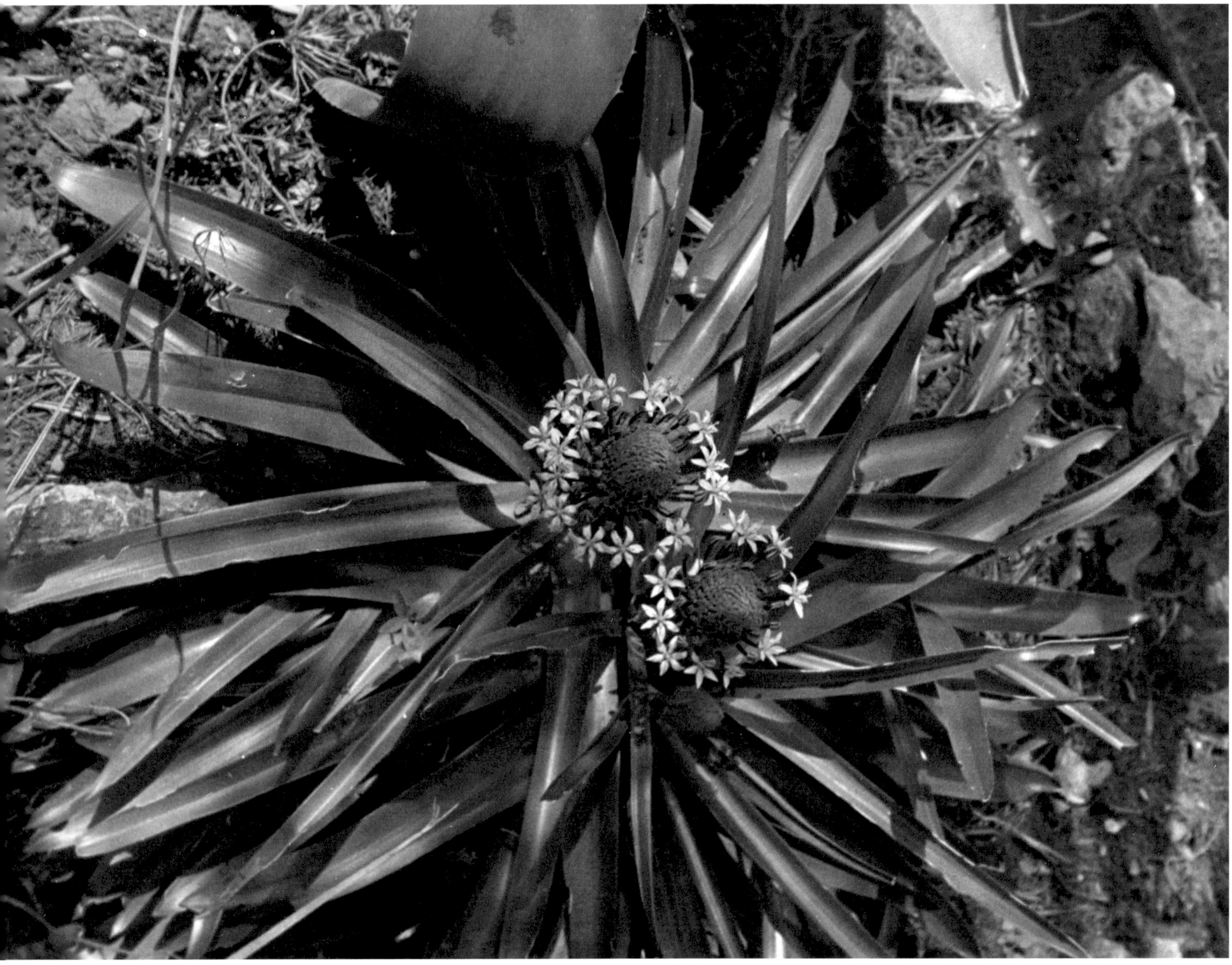

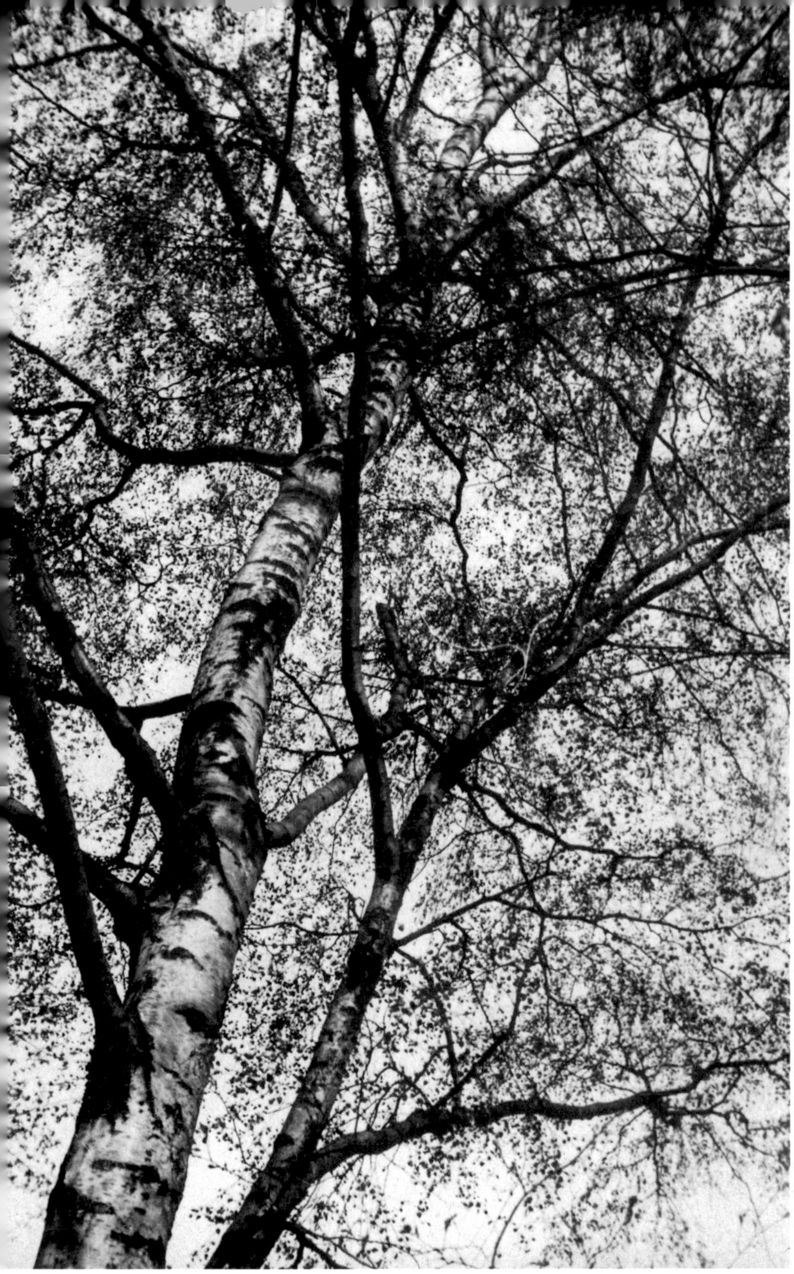

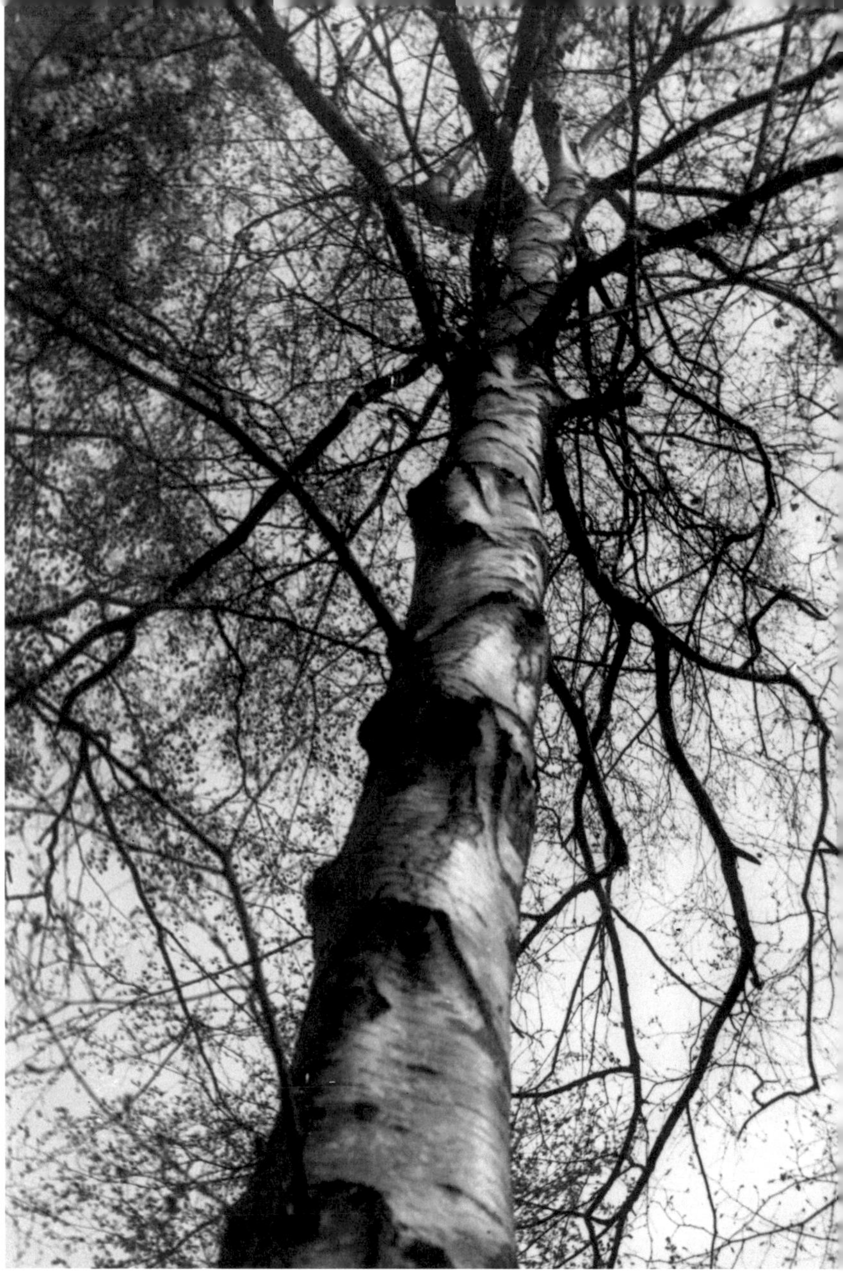

Studies of trees, Hamburg, 1929

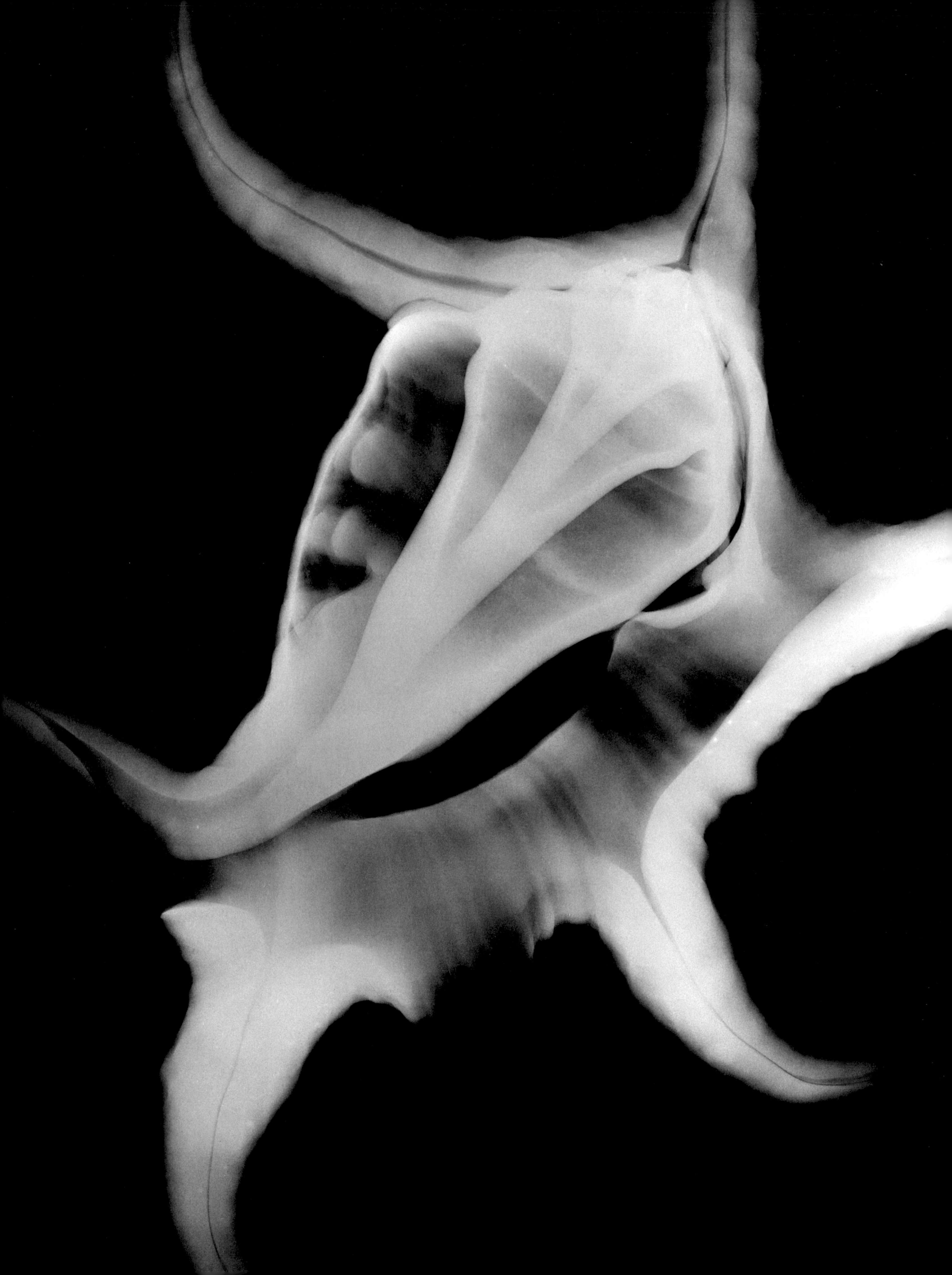

Studies of Building Forms in Nature

Photographs and X-rays of Shells

Among the photographs produced by Fritz Block in Hamburg, one group of images dating from 1931 has a special significance: still life photographs and X-rays of the shells of mollusks, specifically of mussels, snails, and cephalopods.[1] These two types of images exemplify different aspects of New Photography in Germany. Whereas the still life images draw from the documentation of scientific objects in the idiom of the New Objectivity, the abstracting tendencies of X-ray images illustrate how scientific photography influenced the New Vision. Particularly interesting is the extent to which Block approached these "builders of nature" with an architect's eye, exploring the diversity of their external forms as equally functional and aesthetic structures, while also making visible their inner principles of construction.

His unusually intense interest in this subject matter—inspired by personal motivation and not by any commission or opportunity to publish the images—resulted in over eighty different motifs, almost half of which are X-rays. Block thereby differs from other photographers of his era, who often produced only single photographs of mussels or snails. In the context of his oeuvre as a whole, the images are related to his nature studies of trees, grasses, and flowers, of which only a few examples have been preserved. At the same time, through their focus on forms, volumes, and structures, they also evince similarities with his photographs of technical installations. In a photo-historical context, Block's photographs are aligned with a general interest among photographers of the New Objectivity in the creations of nature, such as plants, fruits, crystals, or animals. The analytical gaze was considered related to and fully compatible with aesthetic fascination. Furthermore, Block's images draw on a longstanding tradition involving the depiction of shells, to which photographic representations and interpretations also belong.[2]

Pterocera chiragra (Chiragra Spider Conch), X-ray, 1931

Nature, Art, Science, and Photography

The human interest in seashells and snail shells dates back to the dawn of culture. Evidence of this has taken numerous forms throughout history, especially in the visual arts, ranging from still life paintings to handicrafts.[3] Early on, the pearly nautilus, or *Nautilus pompilius* played an important role due to its spiral-formed chambers. Shells also traditionally marked the threshold between nature and art. As collectors' items, they were preserved in curiosity cabinets, which included objects from nature and/or art objects, from which later scientific and museum collections evolved.[4] The zoological study of these objects led to the production of a large number of prints and books; their graphical illustrations not only conveyed a systematic order but also an aesthetic appeal, which was rooted in the diversity of shapes and colors found in the forms of nature.[5]

With the invention of photography in the second half of the nineteenth century developed a new medium of scientific documentation and artistic expression.[6] From the very beginning, shells were a preferred motif. Conchs were popular objects in still life photography and due to their sculptural forms also in stereophotography. The reasons for their popularity range from their ready availability and ease of use to their aesthetic and exotic appearance. Through the photographic illustration of zoological publications and manuals, which began in the 1850s but did not become widespread until the 1880s, these natural objects were also the subject of scientific photography. X-ray photography played a special role as of 1895 and provided new insights into the inner structure of the shells and mantles of mollusks.[7] As a specific area of scientific photography, X-ray photographs were soon featured in photographic publications and exhibitions, bringing about a dialogue with artistic photography.[8]

Photos of mollusks and snails not only served scientific purposes but—given Art Nouveau's orientation towards natural forms—also provided inspiration for artistic decorations and designs. For example, the portfolio *Formenwelt aus dem Naturreiche* (A World of Forms from Nature, 1902–04) by Martin Gerlach also has plates with photos of shells.[9] Par-

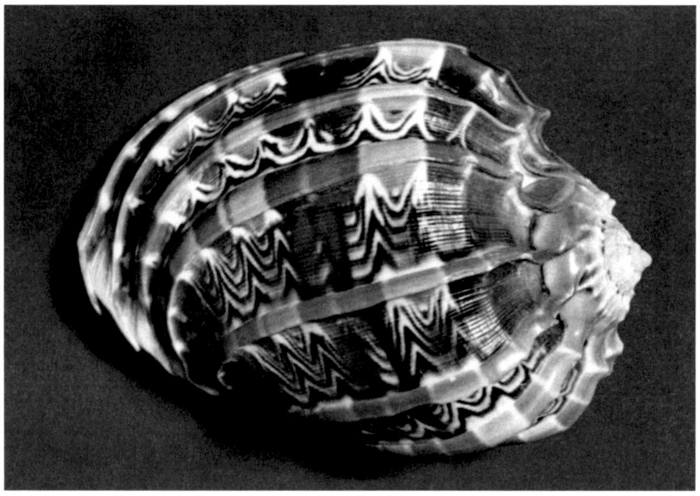

Harpa ventricosa (ventral harp shell), 1931

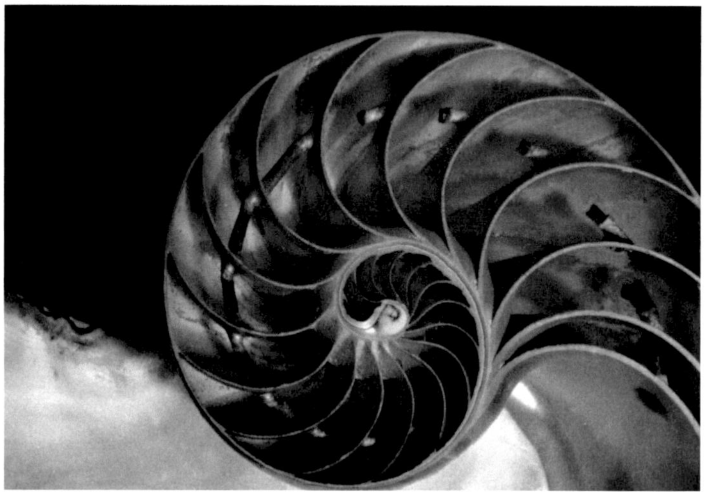

Nautilus pompilius (pearly nautilius), section, 1931

ticularly influential in this regard was the collection of plates *Kunstformen der Natur* (Art Forms in Nature, 1899–1904; second, abridged edition 1924) by Ernst Haeckel, which showed graphical illustrations of shells and snails, among other natural objects. Haeckel further addressed the creative and formative power of nature in his book *Die Natur als Künstlerin* (Nature as Artist, 1913), which was reprinted in 1924 and 1929—with photographic illustrations. A copy of the 1924 edition is included in Block's estate. The role of nature as an inspirational model for human technology is also addressed in the book *Die Pflanze als Erfinder* (The Plant as Inventor, 1920) by the biologist and popular scientific author Raoul Heinrich Francé, which particularly attracted the interest of architects. In addition to practical considerations, the theories of Natural Philosophy were of consistent relevance. This included the question whether an ideal aesthetic harmony was demonstrated in the order and structure of snails and shells, particularly in the case of the spiral-formed nautilus.[10]

In the 1920s the discussion surrounding the relationship between nature and art, or architecture, took a different turn. In a modern sense, the decorative appropriation of forms in nature was no longer of primary interest but instead the creative adaptation of its structural principles. This notion is also developed in the book *Wandlung der Form im XX. Jahrhundert* (Metamorphosis of Form in the Twentieth Century, 1926) by Ernst Kropp, which was published by the Deutscher Werkbund. As a member of the Werkbund, Block may have well been familiar with this publication. It includes anonymous photographs of seashells stuck upright into the sand like "buildings." These, however, were not intended "to inspire mimicry or use but to encourage a new form of looking and understanding that reveals to us the essence of form and enables us to gain a closer sense of the meaning and character of nature. It is not the task of humankind to build snail shells on a large scale [...]."[11]

Shells and New Photography

Not until the 1920s did seashells become a visual theme in a form of photography that was not merely documentary or illustrational but an artistic and autonomous medium. One early example is the photograph *The Spiral Shell* by Edward Steichen dating from 1921. Another pioneering milestone was the 1923 "Schelpennummer," the "shell issue" of the Dutch avant-garde journal *Wendingen* (series 5, nos. 8–9) [p. 89].[12] Photographs of these natural forms had never before been shown in such an extensive way and also in the context of art and architecture. Including text contributions by architect Hendricus Theodorus Wijdeveld and writer Roland Holst, the magazine addressed the (assumed) analogies between the structural principles of nature and architecture. To illustrate his text, Wijdeveld had commissioned photographs of conchs from the Zoological Museum of Amsterdam. The photographs of these objects stem from Dutch photographer Bernard F. Eilers (1878–1951), who was actually specialized in urban and architectural photography.[13]

The accompanying X-ray photographs were provided by the Amsterdam cardiologist and radiologist Joseph Bernhard (Rosenberg) Polak (1883–1942, murdered in Auschwitz). Primarily due to his images, the *Wendingen* "Schelpennummer" gained substantial international attention, both among architects like Le Corbusier, who himself had a collection of conchs,[14] and photographers such as László Moholy-Nagy.[15] In his Bauhaus book *Malerei, Photographie, Film* (Painting, Photography, Film, 1925, second edition 1927), a copy of which is included in Block's estate, Moholy-Nagy described X-ray images as "material transformed into light" and juxtaposed two images of Polak's with his own photograms as examples of scientific photographs that also have artistic merit.[16] The photo book *Urformen der Kunst* (Art Forms in Nature, 1928) by Karl Blossfeldt, including his no less influential photographs of plants, is something that Block may have also owned. That Blossfeldt's images were viewed in conjunction with the *Wendingen* magazine at the time is confirmed in a review in the *bauhaus* magazine: "since the special issue of the Dutch magazine *Wendingen* with the magnificent X-ray images based on shells, there has been no publication that has produced such a rich revelation of natural forms as this book [...]."[17]

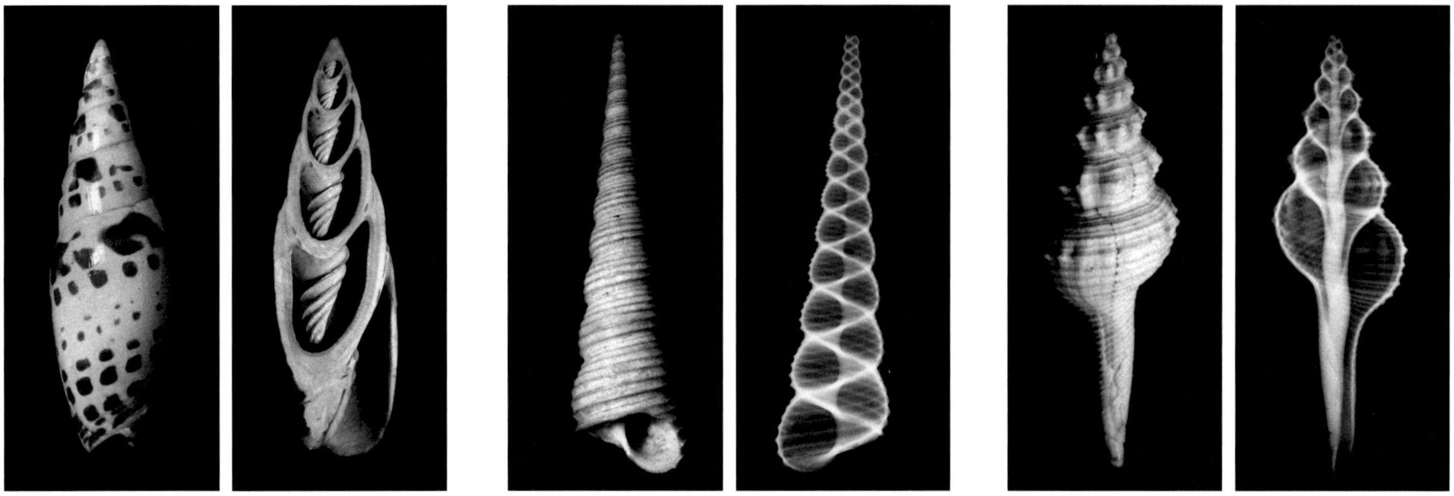

Mitra episcopalis (bishop mitra) – *Turritella imbricata* (auger shell) – *Fusus dupetit-thouarsii* (spindle shell), 1931

Block certainly must have seen the now iconic photograph of a pearly nautilus taken by Edward Weston in 1927, which was on view in the Deutscher Werkbund 1929 exhibition *Film und Foto,* presented first in Stuttgart and then in Berlin. Similar motifs by the German photographers Aenne Mosbacher and Aenne Biermann may well have been known to him through publications.[18] Shortly before Block, Arvid Gutschow, another Hamburg photographer of the New Objectivity, produced photographs of shells.[19] However, no evidence has been preserved that the two photographers personally discussed this visual theme.

Block was additionally inspired by X-ray photography, which was popularized through various books, among which are *Einführung in die Röntgen-Photographie* (An Introduction to X-ray Photography, 1922) by John Eggert, which had been reprinted five times by 1931. Moholy-Nagy published images from this volume in his Bauhaus book mentioned above. The book *Anleitung zur Röntgenphotographie* (Instructions for X-ray Photography, 1925) by Paul Knoche, published as part of the series *Photographische Bibliothek* (Photographic Library), describes the application of X-rays for medical purposes, in technological contexts, and in industry and science. One of the reproduced X-ray images shows a muricid shell. In the idiom of New Vision, photographers were primarily interested in furthering the artistic perspectives and means of expression enabled by X-ray photography. Having engaged in experiments with X-ray photography from an early phase onward, the Lette-Verein, a school for photography in Berlin, was prominently featured in the photographic yearbook *Das Deutsche Lichtbild* (1927–38) with multiple X-ray images, although not of shells. Examples of X-ray photography were included in exhibitions such as *Film und Foto* (1929) and *Das Lichtbild* (1930) and also in the photo book *foto-auge* (1929) by Franz Roh and Jan Tschichold. In the *Schaubücher* series of photo books, one volume, *Durchleuchtete Körper* (X-rayed Bodies, 1931), featured X-ray images of humans, animals, and plants, among which was a photograph by Polak from the magazine *Wendingen.*

Still Life, Section, and X-ray

Which of the examples named above was a direct influence on Block remains unclear—with one exception: the "Schelpennummer" issue of *Wendingen.* This provided a key source of inspiration for his still lifes and X-rays of shells and served as a reference. If not previously familiar with the magazine, he certainly must have come across it during his trip to the Netherlands in 1930 (a copy of the issue in question is preserved in his estate).

In Hamburg the conditions allowing Block to carry out this photographic project were favorable in two aspects. On the one hand, the Hanseatic city had a Zoological Museum (formerly known as the Natural History Museum) with a significant department dedicated to mollusks and an exhibition collection of shells that zoologist Eduard Degner worked to establish from 1927 onwards. It is likely, but not proven, that Block viewed this collection and gained inspiration from it. On the other hand, due to its international trade relationships, the harbor city of Hamburg had various shops that sold naturalia, where one could find shells from all over the world. A leading business in this field was Theodor Umlauff, Muschel Import–Export, which had been established in 1912 through the splitting of an older family firm. This company supplied museums and private collectors throughout Germany and beyond with shells, also for purely decorative purposes. Ordering through their catalogue, which was illustrated with line drawings and colored pictures, Block purchased a selection of objects for his own collection. He was apparently less interested in systematic, zoological considerations than in photographic effect. Nevertheless, a letter from Block's estate, sent from the Umlauff company on July 20, 1931 in response to an inquiry, confirms that Block was definitely interested in the correct nomenclature and the geographical origins of the snails and shells that he used for his still life and X-ray photographs.

His photographs, however, are only minimally labeled (usually with abbreviations and the number of the negative), so that the image captions used here largely resort to descriptions of the depicted objects.[20] In addition, a number of photographs reveal that as a self-taught photographer,

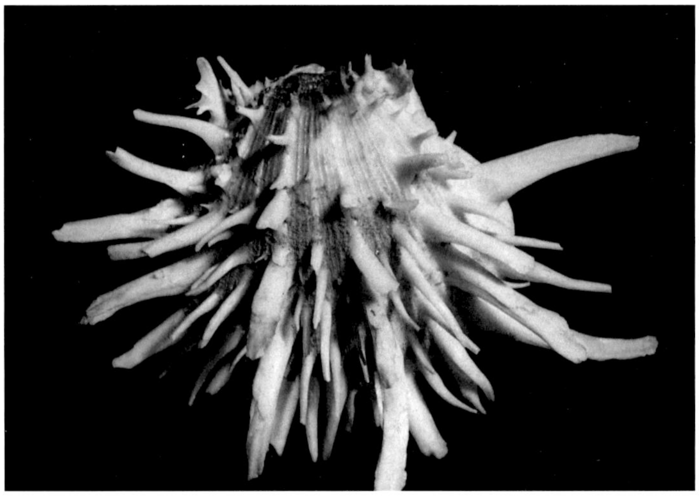

Madrepora sp. (deepwater stony coral), 1931

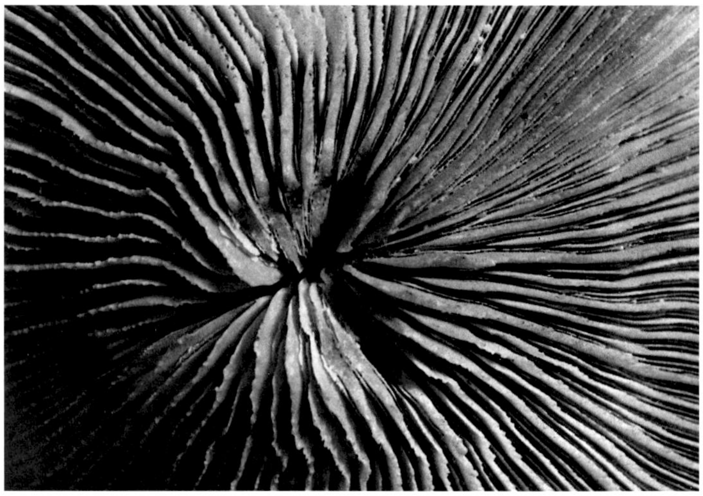

Fungia integra (mushroom coral), 1931

Block lacked certain skills in the field of object photography. Worthy of note is that Block used a Leica camera with 35-mm film, whereas Eilers, the photographer featured in *Wendingen* used an 18 × 24 cm large-format camera, which provided a greater sharpness of detail. It is not known who helped Block with his X-ray photographs, probably a friend who was a doctor. However, he did consider and describe these images as his own artistic works of photography. Block subsequently copied the large-format X-ray negatives onto 35-mm film, in order to be able to make prints more easily.

As in the images depicted in *Wendingen*, Block also took a three-step approach to his photographs: First he photographed the shells in a neutral, objective manner. Scientific documentation took precedent over artistic expression, and he therefore tended to avoid extreme close-ups or highly cropped views. The shells and snails (the latter predominating) were instead placed before a dark background and were photographed without dramatic lighting or arrangements. Block thereby accentuated the variety of forms, which ranged from decidedly technical, as in the pearly nautilus [p. 91] to the bizarre shapes of the branched murex [p. 97]. His photographs of the maple leaf triton, the wentletrap shell, and the sun carrier shell confirm this impression of diversity [p. 92], whereas his photo of the ventral harp shell highlights its surface pattern [p. 86]. Because they are shown in isolation, the relative dimensions of the objects, which actually differ substantially in size, are not conveyed, and a uniform monumentalization results that makes these natural objects seem like sculptural works of art. One deficit of this kind of photographic documentation was a lack of color, which was not an issue at the time, due to the lack of technical possibilities. Color would have been considered a decorative distraction from the intentions inherent to the photography of objects.

In a second step, Block photographed a number of shells that had been cut into vertical or horizontal sections, in order to illustrate their structure. Examples that he used in this context included the inevitable chambered or pearly nautilus [p. 86], the bishop mitra [p. 87], the grinning tun [p. 93], the Triton's trumpet [p. 94], and the horned helmet [p. 96] with their tapering convolutions. As an architect, Block was primarily interested in the organic repetition and variation of the same building components in the formation of a living structure. By penetrating the objects, his X-ray images offer a look into the detailed inner structure of shells, for example in his juxtaposition of photographs of the auger shell and the white trumpet spindle shell [p. 87]. This is particularly evident in photographs of a marble cone [p. 98], a Midas' ear cassidula [p. 99], and a common egg shell [p. 100]. Through the use of different ranges in focus and intensities of light, Block also achieved visual effects that make the forms appear—recalling the words of Moholy-Nagy—like abstract, schematic manifestations of light hovering in dark space. His X-rays of the Chiragra spider conch [p. 84], the short-clawed scorpion [p. 96], and the branched murex [p. 97] are striking examples. In addition to shells, Block photographed a number of coral samples, both as entire objects and as cropped close-ups [p. 88].

Functionality and Aesthetics

In his object photography and X-ray images, Block—an architect who tended to subscribe to rational functionalism—was not interested in organic shapes and forms as inspiration for architectural designs; instead he was concerned with a visual exploration of the structural laws of nature. First and foremost, he wished to use the shells to illustrate the thesis—which at the time was propagated simultaneously in the fields of modern architecture and technology—that functionality not only served utilitarian purposes but (for this very reason) also produced aesthetic qualities. He certainly was successful in conveying this with his body of photographs of mussels, snails, and other mollusks, which are impressive both in terms of number and range. However, his photos did not surpass the images already published by Eilers and Polak in *Wendingen* in 1923 in any groundbreaking way. At the same time, Block's photographs of shells can be considered a contribution to the photography of natural objects that is both unusual and typical of his era.

As with his other photographic work, Block provided his images to photo agencies, including Mauritius and Linden-Verlag, for sale to the illustrated press. Together with his wife Anna-Sophie he wrote an accompanying text "Small Creatures, Great Builders," which summarizes the most significant aspects of these photographs: "The world of forms [of snails and shells] is inexhaustible, from the simplest, clearest form of explicit objectivity to the most bizarre and romantic, resembling Chinese pagodas and baroque towers. [...] Many of the shells are so precise in form and of such technical precision, that one might think they had drawn inspiration from modern technology. [...] Particularly wondrous is the inspired, internal structure that is compiled from the same repeating fundamental components [...]. One can study these perfect formations extremely well through the exemplars that have been cut in half. But still much more beautiful than these sections and also much more revealing are the X-ray photographs, because they convey the relationship between the outer and the inner in such an interesting and astounding manner, providing such a beautiful insight into the meaningful development of these works of art and the carefully planned work of these lower life forms."[21]

Up until now, however, we have only been able to find a few examples of these photos by Block that were actually printed [p. 90]. In addition, they were only used to illustrate a given text and were not presented as unique works of artistic photography.[22] Block was not given the opportunity to produce a substantial publication of his photographs. Ten years later, Alfred Ehrhardt, another Hamburg photographer—who employed quite similar motifs—published his own photo book, *Muscheln und Schnecken* (Shells of Mussels and Snails, 1941). In contrast, for Block the visual theme of shells remained a brief but intensive episode from the year 1931. He subsequently did not produce any further photographs of objects or natural objects. Instead, he directed his camera towards the live animals in Hagenbeck's Tierpark, the Hamburg zoo. Not until later, in American exile, would Block once again return to photographing mussels and snails, this time in color. The shells that he photographed and that are reproduced here have not only survived as prints, but the original objects have also been preserved in his estate.

Only recently Block's photos served as a starting point for the conception of the exhibition "Nautilus. Snails, Mussels, and other Mollusks in Photography," the first ever comprehensive presentation on this subject. It was mounted early 2018 at the Alfred Ehrhardt Foundation, in Berlin.[23]

1 Roland Jaeger, "Baumeister der Natur. Conchylien in Objektaufnahmen und Röntgenbildern des Architekten und Fotografen Fritz Block von 1931," in *Nautilus. Schnecken, Muscheln und andere Mollusken in der Fotografie*, eds. Stefanie Odenthal and Christiane Stahl for the Alfred Ehrhardt Foundation (Petersberg, 2017), 17–23 and 54–55.
2 Christiane Stahl, "Die Conchylie als fotografische Kunstform," in *Nautilus* (see note 1), 25–110.
3 See also Dora Godan, *Mollusken. Ihre Bedeutung für Wissenschaft, Medizin, Handel und Kultur* (Berlin, 1996). – Ekhart Berckenhagen, "'Gift from the sea.' Zur Kulturgeschichte der Muschel," *Deutsches Schiffahrtsarchiv* 22 (1999), 361–400. – Ingrid Thomas, *The Shell. A World of Decoration and Ornament* (London, 2007).
4 Karin Leonhard, "Shell Collecting. On 17th-Century Conchology, Curiosity Cabinetts and Still Life Painting," in *Early Modern Zoology. The Construction of Animals in Science, Literature, and the Visual Arts*, eds. Paul J. Smith and Karl A. E. Enenkel (Leiden/Boston, 2007), 177–214.
5 Manfred Niekisch, "Die zoologische Buchillustration vom Holzschnitt bis zur Fotografie. Verknüpfung von Wissenschaft und Kunst," in *Imprimatur. Ein Jahrbuch für Bücherfreunde, N. F.* (2011), 37–62.
6 See Andreas Krase and Agnes Matthias, *Wahr-Zeichen. Fotografie und Wissenschaft* (Dresden, 2006).
7 Corey Keller, "Röntgenstrahlen," in *Fotografie und das Unsichtbare 1840–1900*, eds. Corey Keller, Monika Faber, and Maren Gröning (Vienna, 2009), n. p. – Vera Dünkel, "Röntgenblick und Schattenbild. Genese einer neuen Art von Bildern," (Emsdetten/Berlin, 2016. – René Harather, "Künstlerische Röntgenfotografie. Von den Anfängen bis zur Gegenwart," in *X-ray Art Photography*, ed. Werner Schuster (Munich, 2012), 8–45.
8 Hans Rooseboom, "Niks nieuws onder de zon. De röntgenfoto in het vocabulaire van de *Nieuwe Fotografie*," *Bulletin van het Rijksmuseum* 49, nos. 2–3 (2001), 247–257.
9 Astrid Lechner, "Martin Gerlachs 'Formenwelt aus dem Naturreiche.' Fotografien als Vorlage für Künstler um 1900," *Beiträge zur Geschichte der Fotografie in* Österreich 3 (Vienna, 2005).
10 See Rory Fonseca, "Shape and Order in Organic Nature: The Nautilus Pompilius," *Leonardo* 26, no. 3 (1993), 201–204. – Hans-Jörg Rheinberger, "Nautilus – Spiraltendenzen in Kultur und Natur," in *Nautilus* (see note 1), 9–15.
11 Ernst Kropp, *Wandlung der Form im XX. Jahrhundert, Bücher der Form* 5 (Berlin, 1926), plates 3–17; quotation, 43.
12 See Gerda Breuer, *Wendingen 1918–1931. Amsterdamer Expressionismus. Ein Architekturmagazin der 20er Jahre. Vom Städtebau zur Schriftgestaltung* (Darmstadt ,1992), 96–97. – Martijn F. Le Coultre, *Wendingen. A Journal for the Arts, 1918–1932* (New York/Blaricum, 2001), 138–39.
13 Anneke van Veen, *Bernard F. Eilers 1878–1951* (Haarlem, 2003), 46–47.
14 In a letter dated January 8, 1924, Le Corbusier thanked the editor for the outstanding issue of *Wendingen*, which reminded him of his own studies of conchs in a Paris museum collection twenty years ago (see *Bernard F. Eilers 1878–1951*, note 13, 45–46). In addition, the architect included an X-ray image of a nautilus by Polak in his book *Urbanisme* (1925, published in German in 1929 as *Städtebau*).
15 See Oliver A. I. Botar, "László Moholy-Nagy's 'New Vision' and the Aestheticization of Scientific Imagery in Weimar Germany," *Science in Context: Writing Modern Art and Science* 17, no. 4 (2004), 525–556.
16 Moholy-Nagy, L.[ászló]: *Malerei, Photographie* [1927: Fotografie], *Film*, vol. 8, *Bauhausbücher* (Munich, 1925), 62–63 and 64–65; 1927 (2nd edition), 68 and 70. – Moholy-Nagy mistakenly called the *Triton tritonis* and *Nautilus pompilius* the "shells," as commonly described. However, zoologically speaking these are respectively a snail and a cephalopod.
17 *bauhaus* 3, no. 1 (1929), 27.
18 For Aenne Mosbacher, see *Das Deutsche Lichtbild. Jahresschau 1931* (Berlin [1930]), 120. For Aenne Biermann, see Wilhelm Bölsche, *Der singende Baum* (Bad Pyrmont, 1931), 241 and facing 336.
19 G. Küster, "*Die Welt der Schnecken*," *Die Koralle* 7, no. 4 (Juli, 1931), 179–183. – [Eduard] Degner and Arvid Gutschow, "Schneckenschalen," *Atlantis* 7, no. 7 (1935), 413–416. – Stefanie Odenthal, ed. for Alfred Ehrhardt Foundation, *Arvid Gutschow* (Ostfildern, 2013), 87–96.
20 The descriptions follow the terms used in the catalogue of the Th. Umlauff company, which were noted by Block and based on the nomenclature of Linnaeus.
21 "Kleine Tiere, große Baumeister. (Zu den Muschelaufnahmen.)" (typed manuscript dated 1931 from the Fritz Block Estate Archive, Stockholm/Hamburg).
22 See the list of Block's photographic publications on p. 327.
23 See note 1. – The exhibition has been previously shown at the Landesmuseum für Kunst und Kulturgeschichte Oldenburg and the Kunsthalle Erfurt.

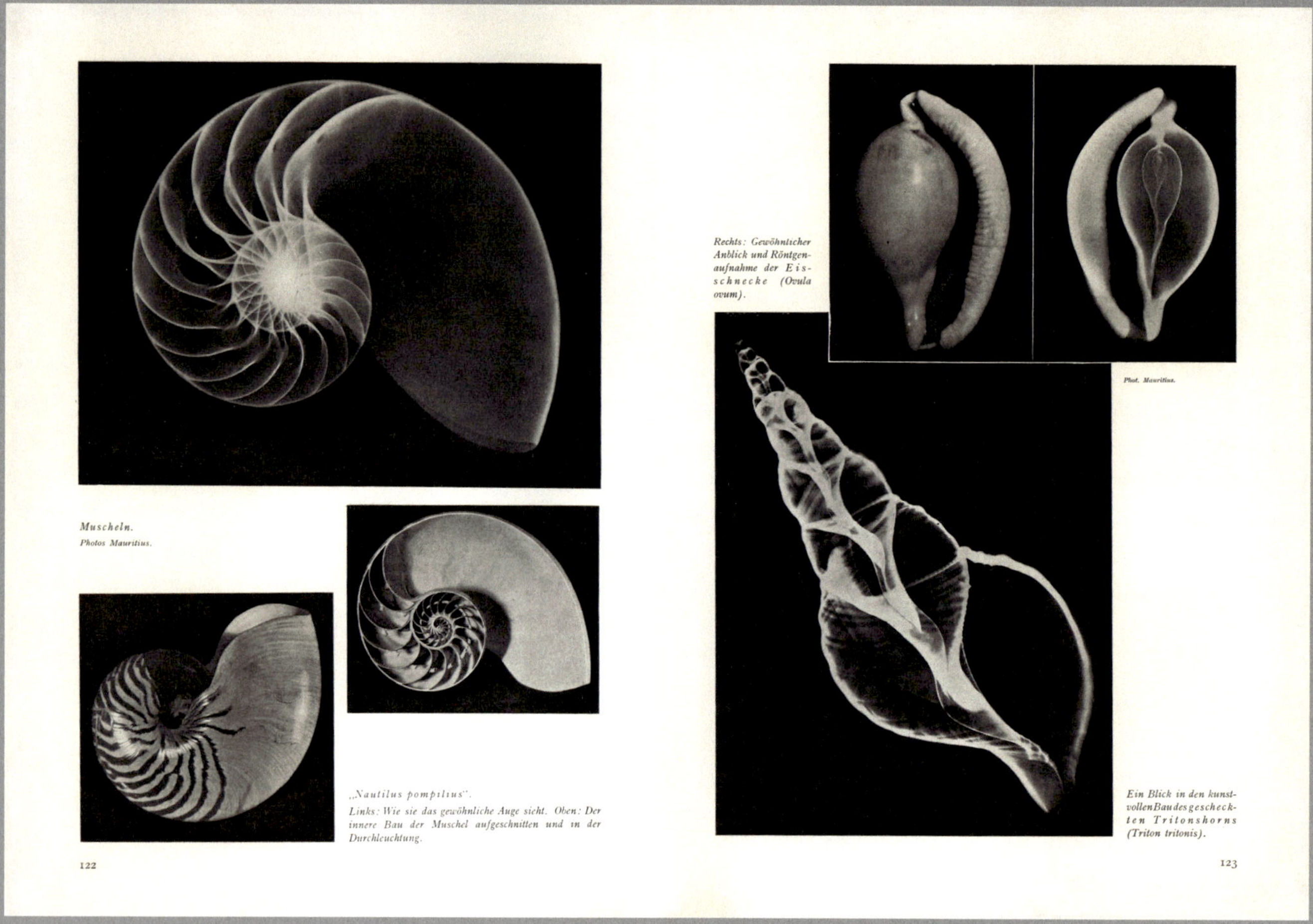

Muscheln.
Photos Mauritius.

„Nautilus pompilius".
Links: Wie sie das gewöhnliche Auge sieht. Oben: Der innere Bau der Muschel aufgeschnitten und in der Durchleuchtung.

122

Rechts: Gewöhnlicher Anblick und Röntgenaufnahme der Eisschnecke (Ovula ovum).

Phot. Mauritius.

Ein Blick in den kunstvollen Bau des gescheckten Tritonshorns (Triton tritonis).

123

"The Wonderful in Nature" (*Atlantis* 5, no. 2, 1933)

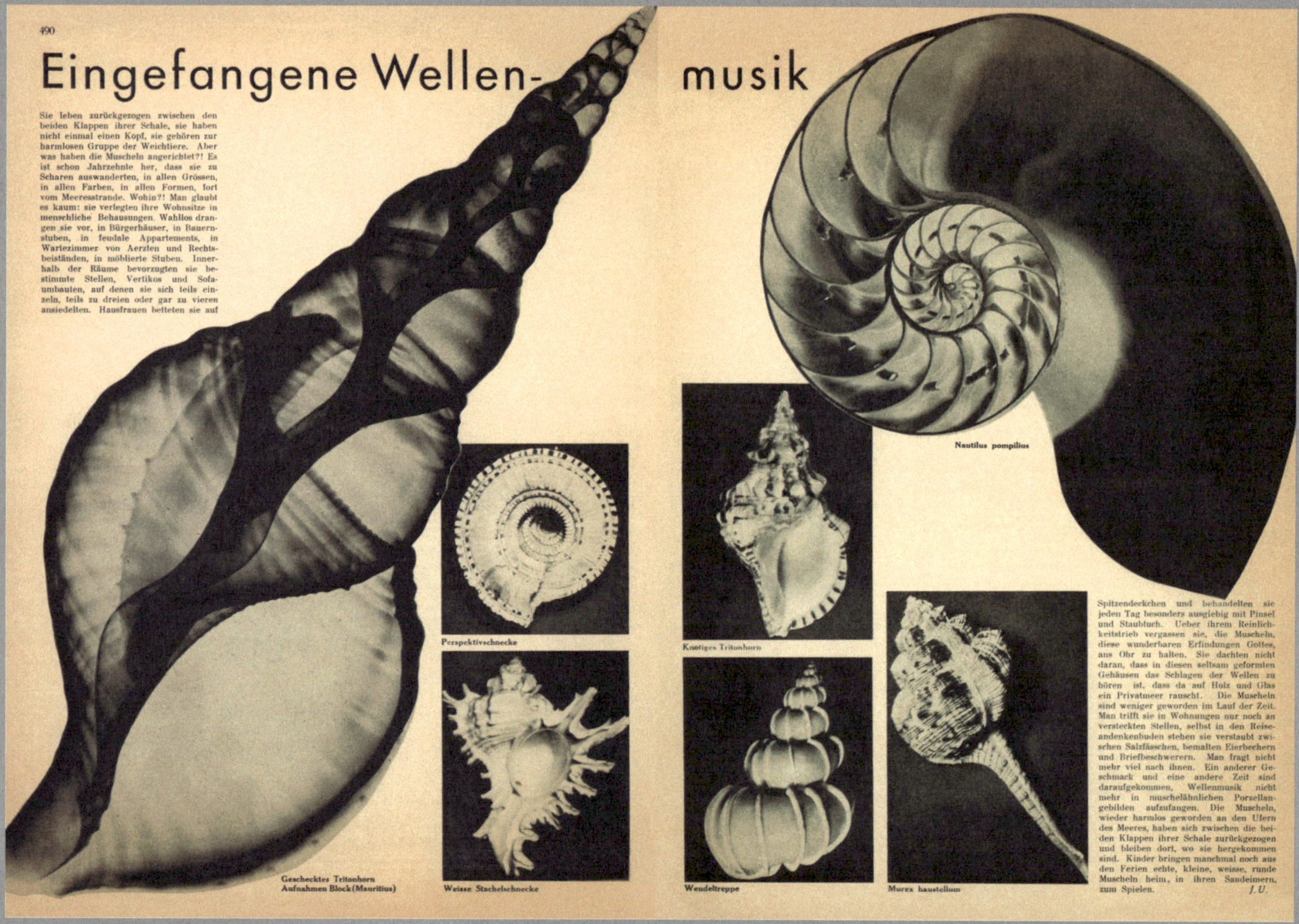

490

Eingefangene Wellen-musik

Sie leben zurückgezogen zwischen den beiden Klappen ihrer Schale, sie haben nicht einmal einen Kopf, sie gehören zur harmlosen Gruppe der Weichtiere. Aber was haben die Muscheln angerichtet?! Es ist schon Jahrzehnte her, dass sie zu Scharen auswanderten, in allen Grössen, in allen Farben, in allen Formen, fort vom Meeresstrande. Wohin?! Man glaubt es kaum: sie verlegten ihre Wohnsitze in menschliche Behausungen. Wahllos drangen sie vor, in Bürgerhäuser, in Bauernstuben, in feudale Appartements, in Wartezimmer von Aerzten und Rechtsbeiständen, in möblierte Stuben. Innerhalb der Räume bevorzugten sie bestimmte Stellen, Vertikos und Sofaumbauten, auf denen sie sich teils einzeln, teils zu dreien oder gar zu vieren ansiedelten. Hausfrauen betteten sie auf Spitzendeckchen und behandelten sie jeden Tag besonders ausgiebig mit Pinsel und Staubtuch. Ueber ihrem Reinlichkeitstrieb vergassen sie, die Muscheln, diese wunderbaren Erfindungen Gottes, ans Ohr zu halten. Sie dachten nicht daran, dass in diesen seltsam geformten Gehäusen das Schlagen der Wellen zu hören ist, dass da auf Holz und Glas ein Privatmeer rauscht. Die Muscheln sind weniger geworden im Lauf der Zeit. Man trifft sie in Wohnungen nur noch an versteckten Stellen, selbst in den Reiseandenkenbuden stehen sie verstaubt zwischen Salzfässchen, bemalten Eierbechern und Briefbeschwerern. Man fragt nicht mehr viel nach ihnen. Ein anderer Geschmack und eine andere Zeit sind daraufgekommen, Wellenmusik nicht mehr in muschelähnlichen Porzellangebilden aufzufangen. Die Muscheln, wieder harmlos geworden an den Ufern des Meeres, haben sich zwischen die beiden Klappen ihrer Schale zurückgezogen und bleiben dort, wo sie hergekommen sind. Kinder bringen manchmal noch aus den Ferien echte, kleine, weisse, runde Muscheln heim, in ihren Sandeimern, zum Spielen. *J. U.*

Geschecktes Tritonhorn
Aufnahmen Block (Mauritius)

Perspektivschnecke

Weisse Stachelschnecke

Knotiges Tritonhorn

Wendeltreppe

Nautilus pompilius

Murex haustellum

"Captured Music of the Waves" (*Haus, Hof, Garten*, no. 31, 1933)

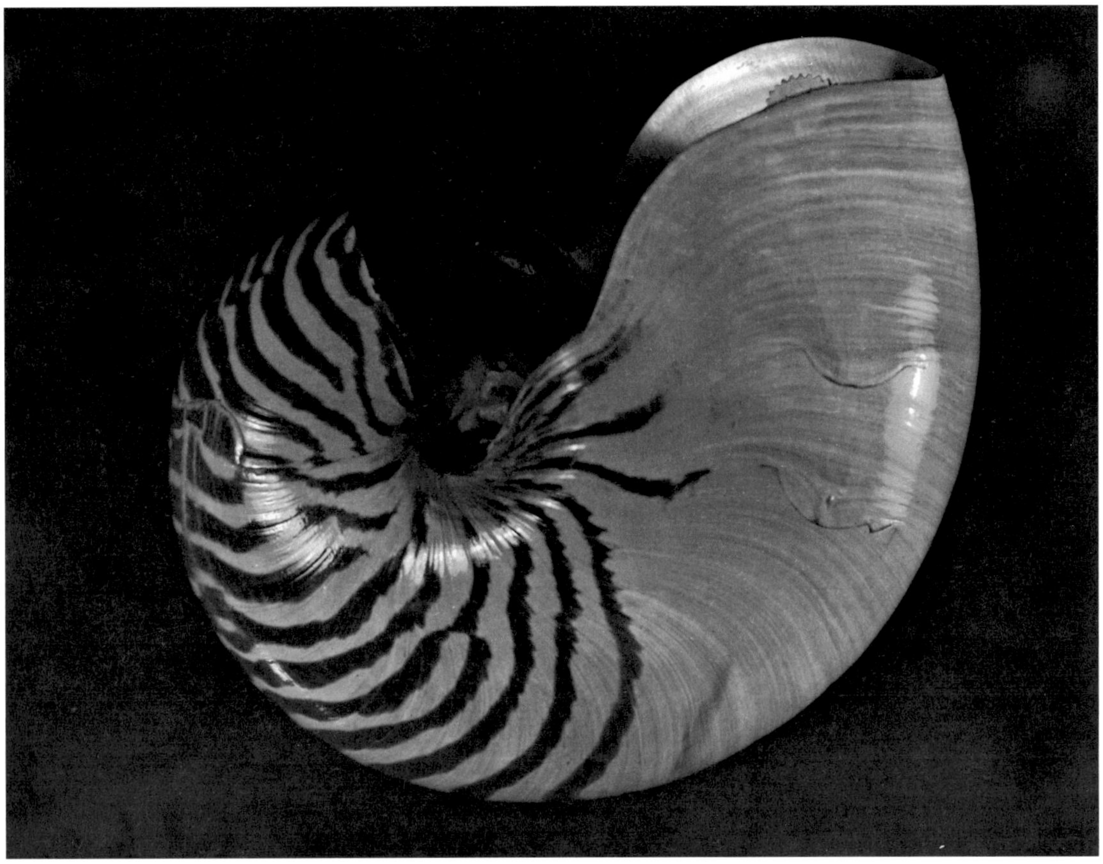

Nautilus pompilius (Pearly Nautilus), 1931

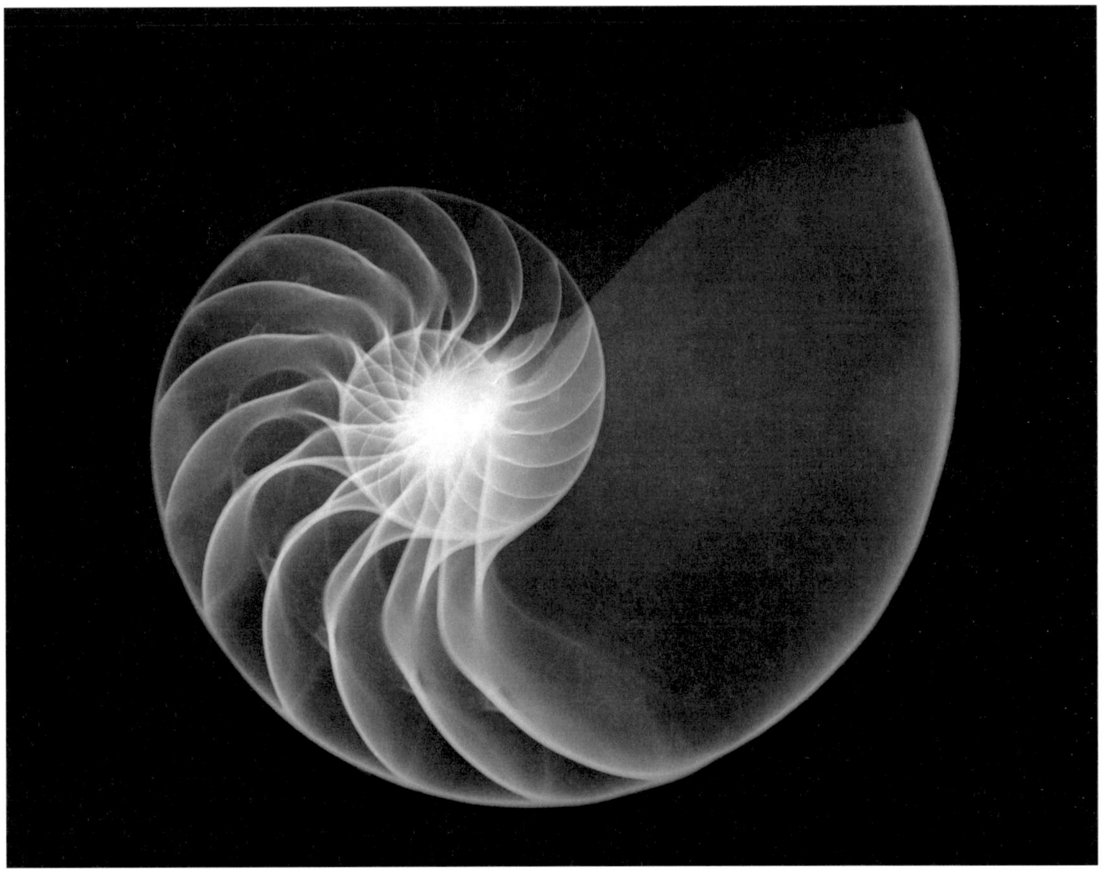

Nautilus pompilius (Pearly Nautilus), X-ray, 1931

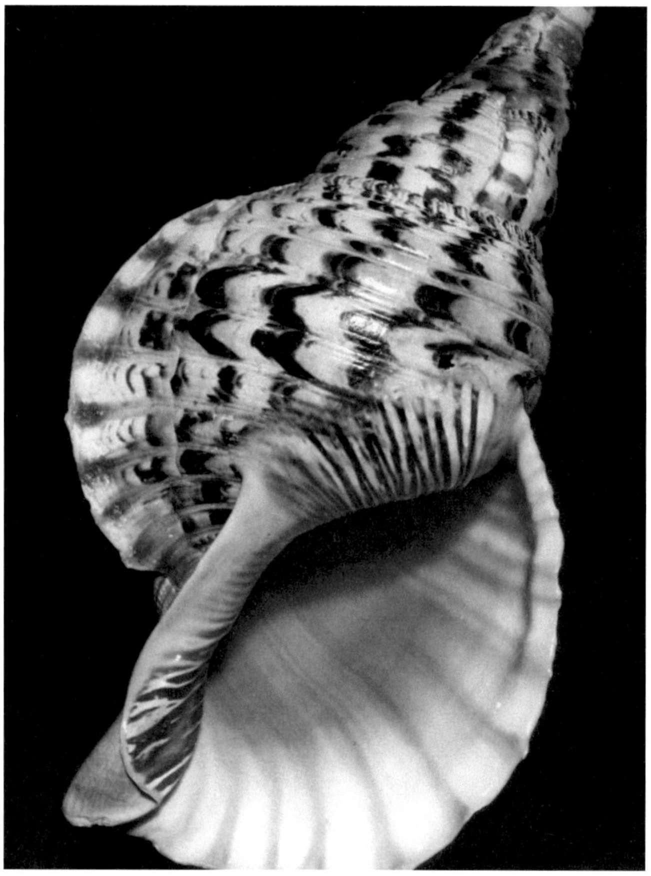

Triton tritonis (Triton's Trumpet), 1931

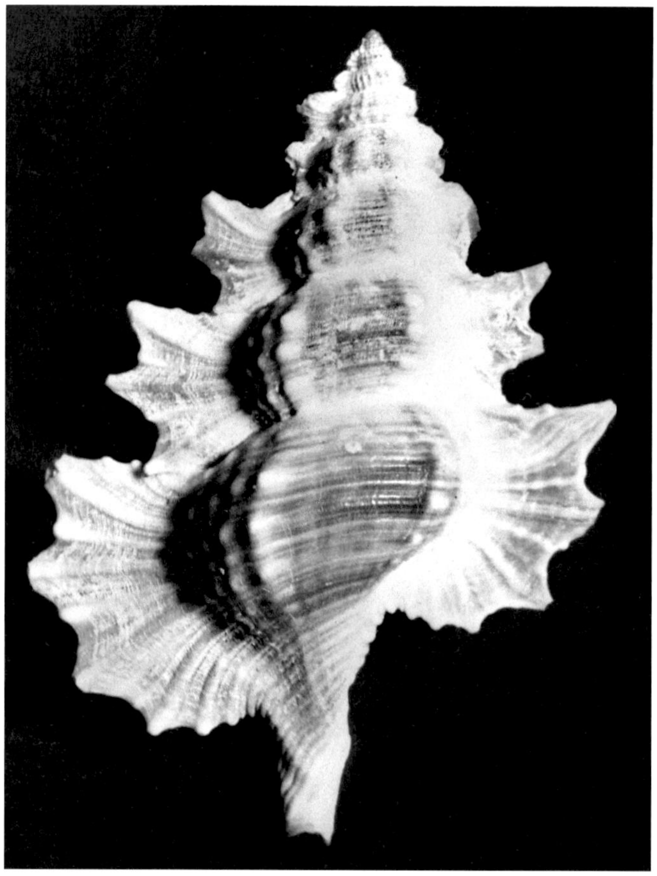

Ranella pulchra (Maple Leaf Triton), 1931

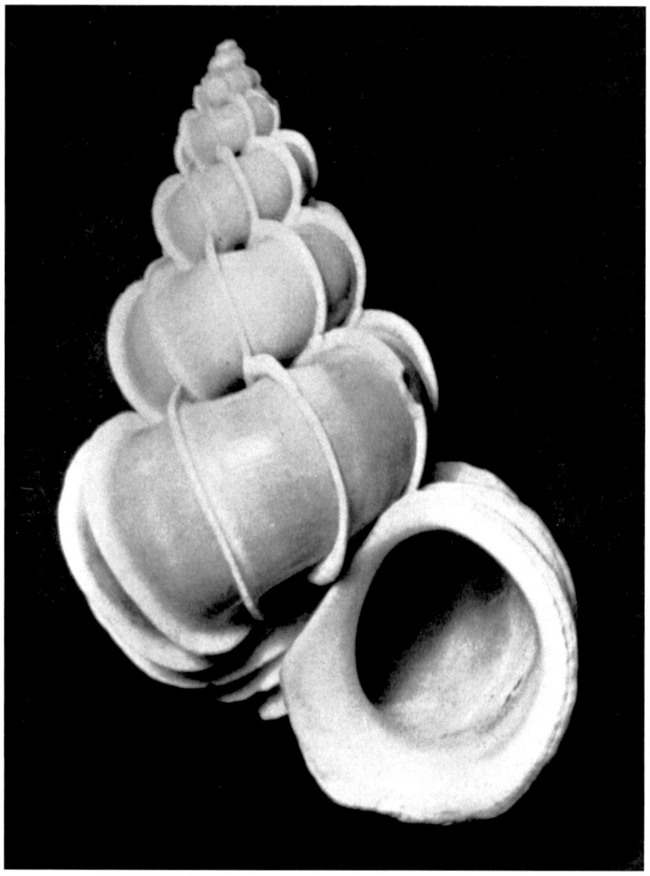

Scalaria preciosa (Wentletrap Shell), 1931

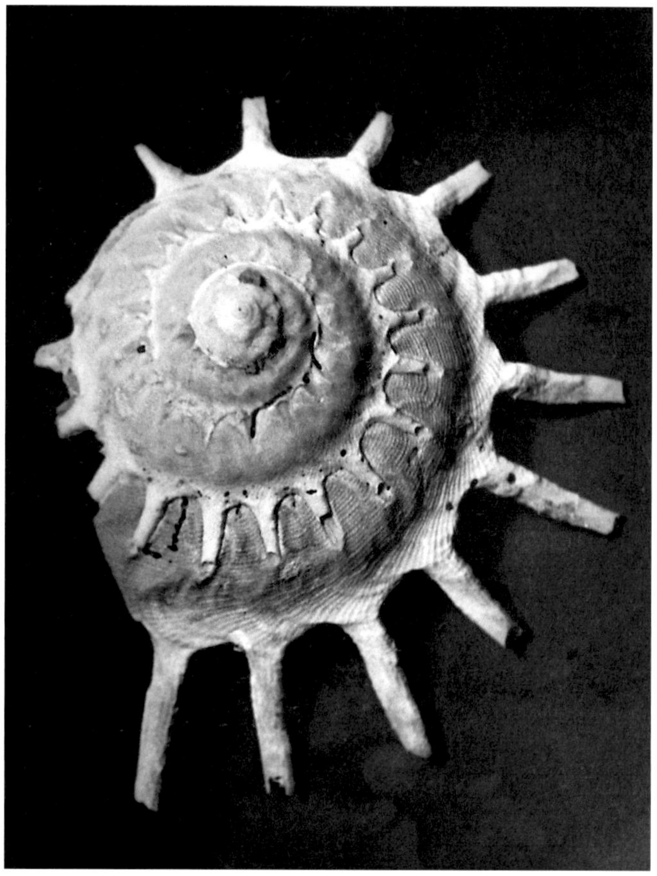

Stellaria solaris (Sun Carrier Shell), 1931

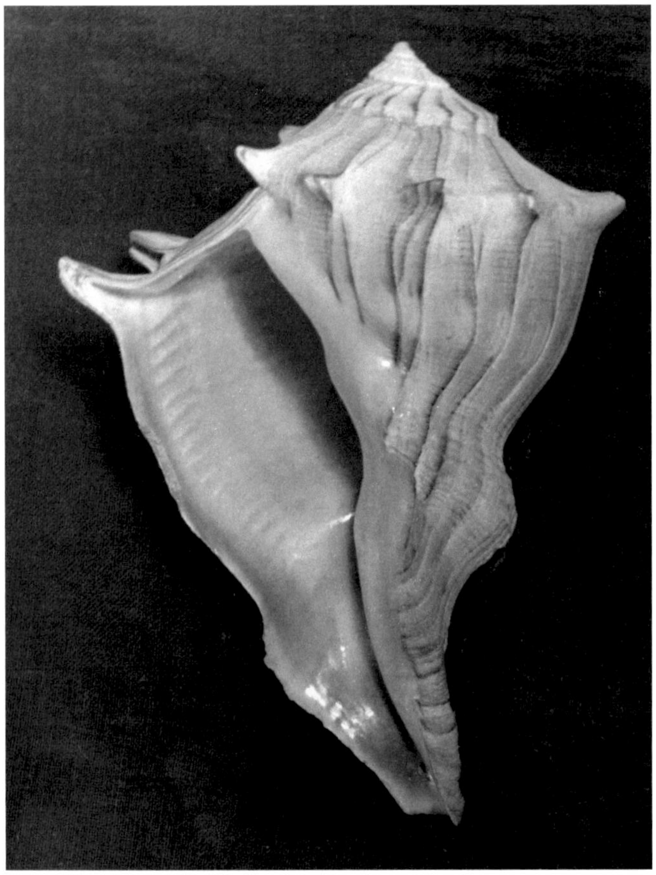

Busycon carica (Knobbed Whelk), 1931

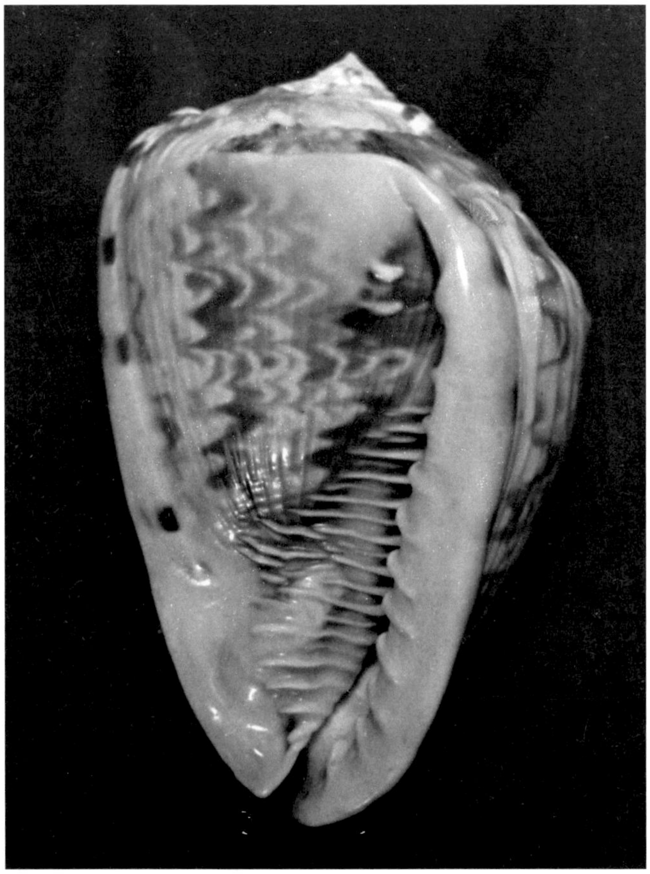

Cassis flammea (Flame Helmet), 1931

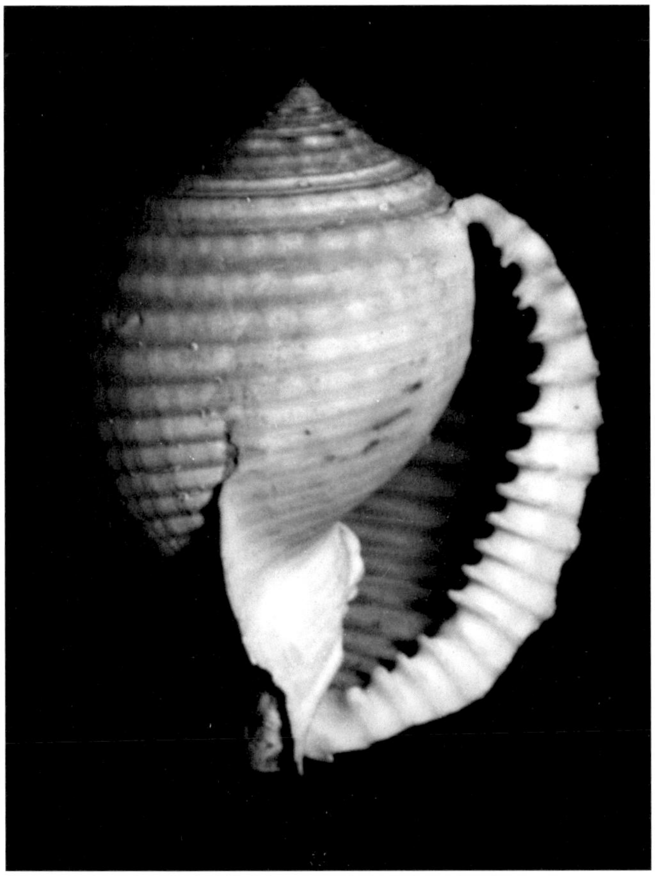

Malea ringens (Grinning Tun), 1931

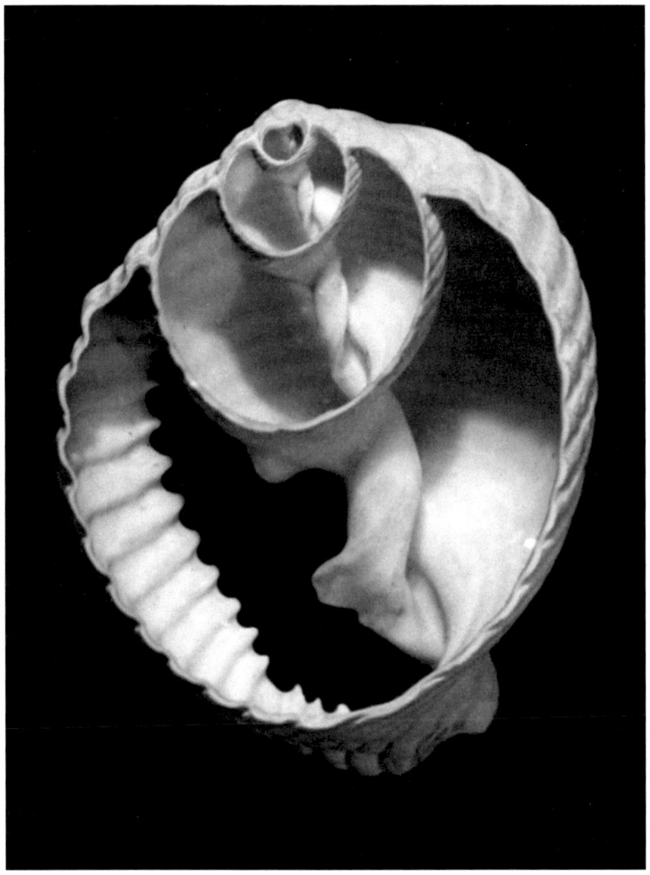

Malea ringens (Grinning Tun), section, 1931

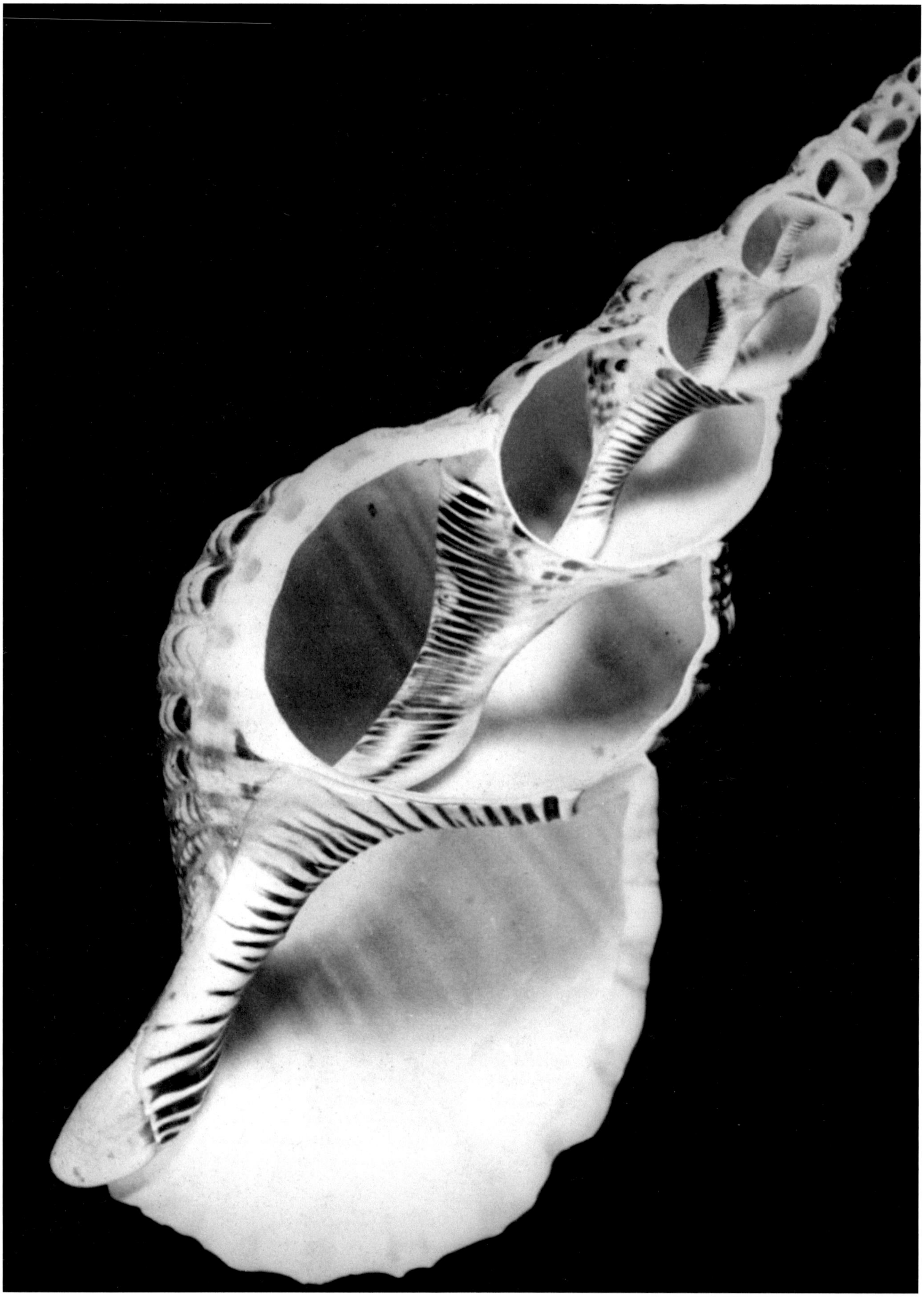

Triton tritonis (Triton's Trumpet), longitudinal section, 1931

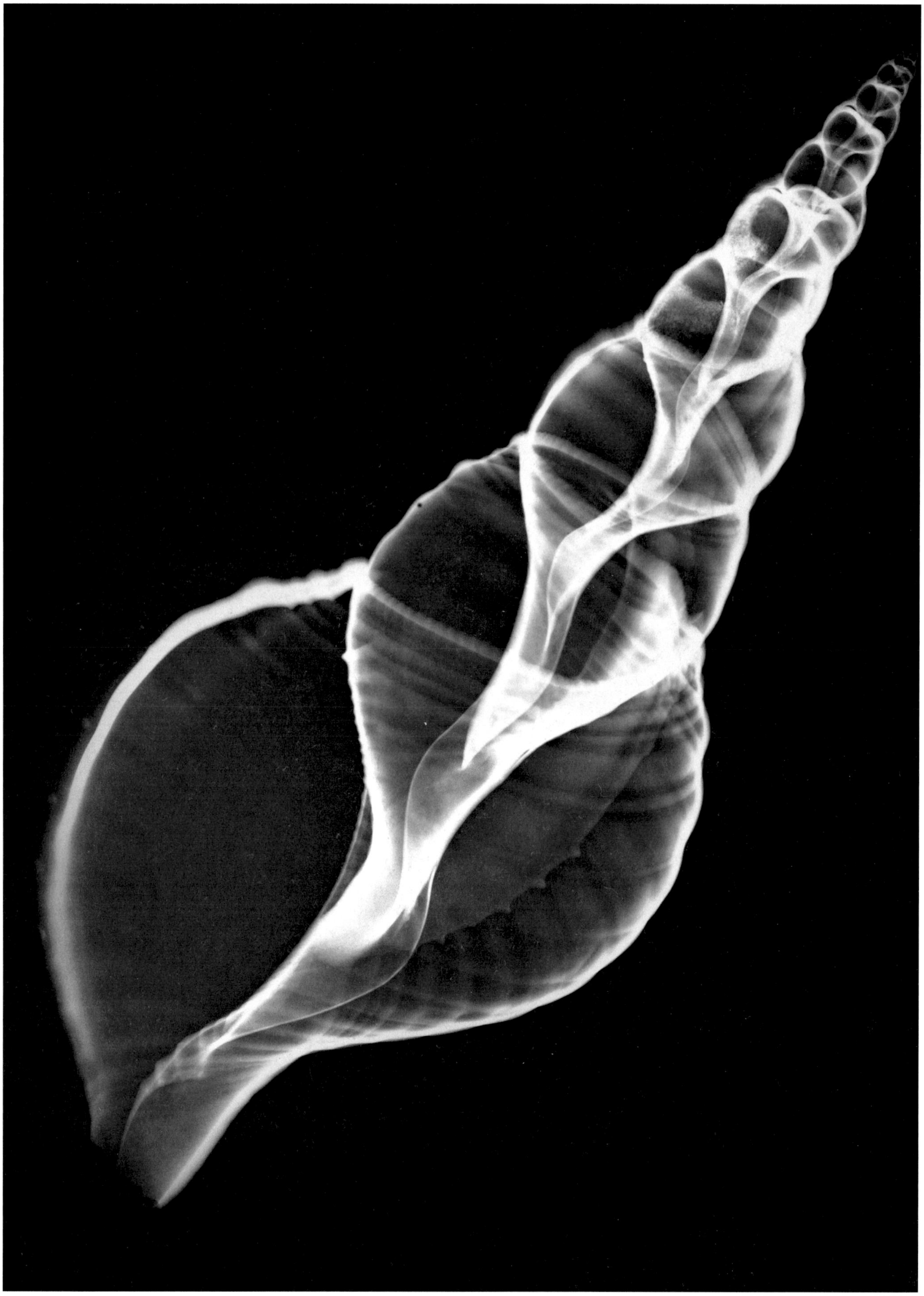

Triton tritonis (Triton's Trumpet), X-ray, 1931

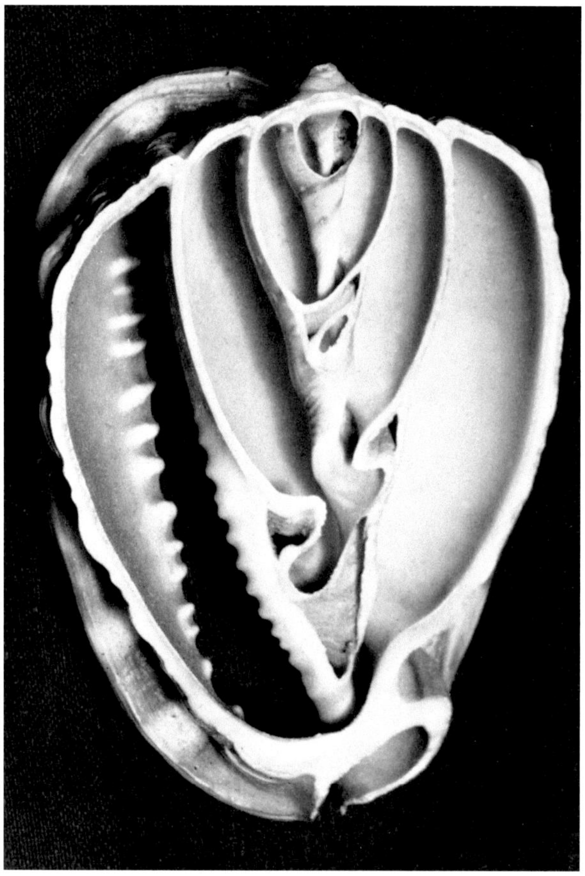

Cassis cornuta (Horned Helmet), section, 1931

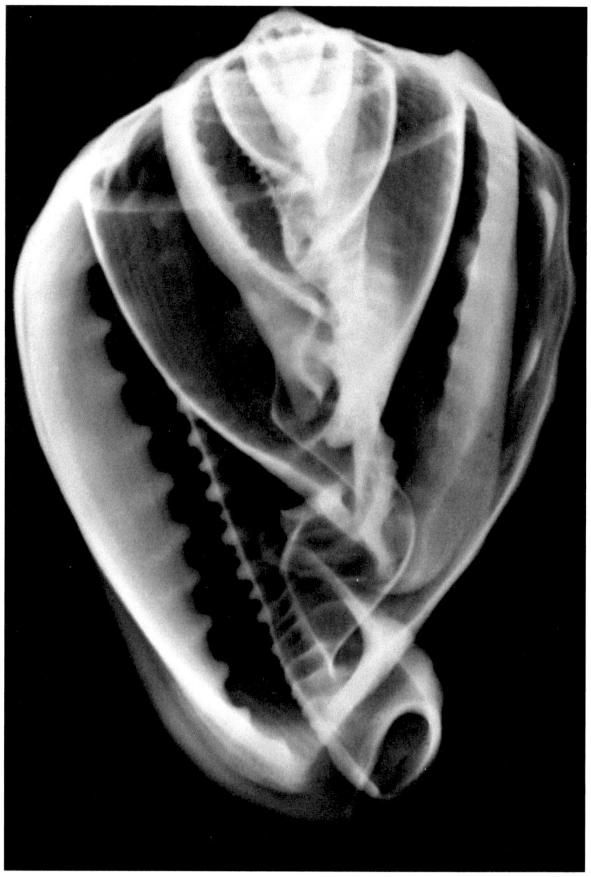

Cassis cornuta (Horned Helmet), X-ray, 1931

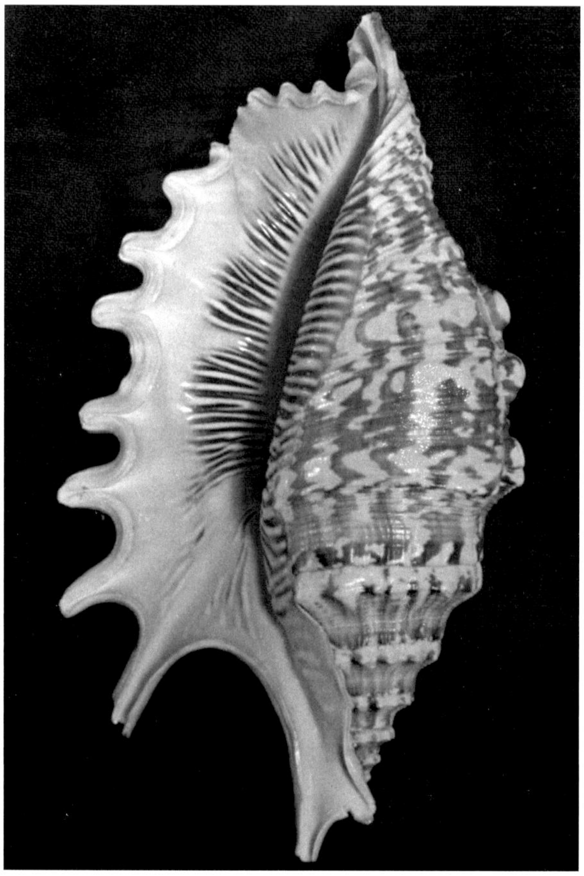

Pterocera elongata (Short-Clawed Scorpion), 1931

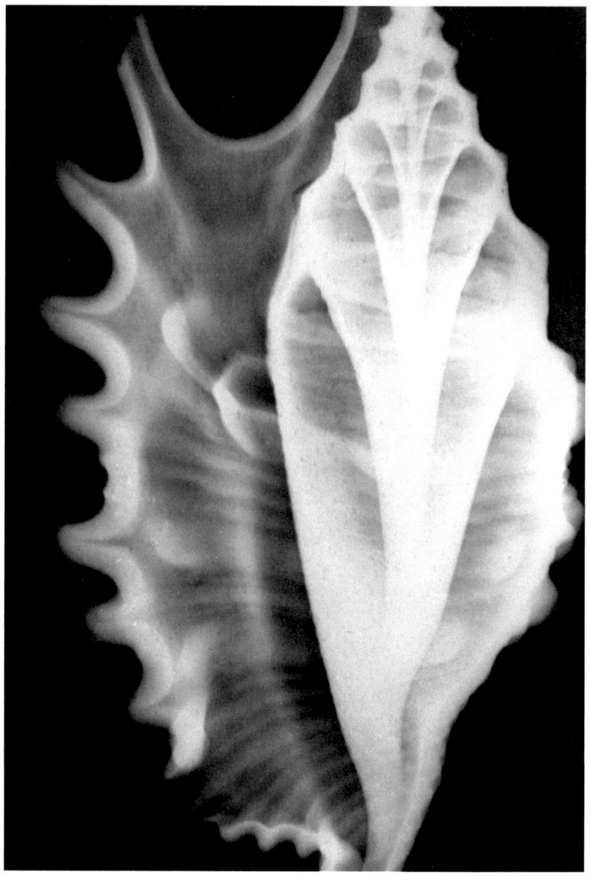

Pterocera elongata (Short-Clawed Scorpion), X-ray, 1931

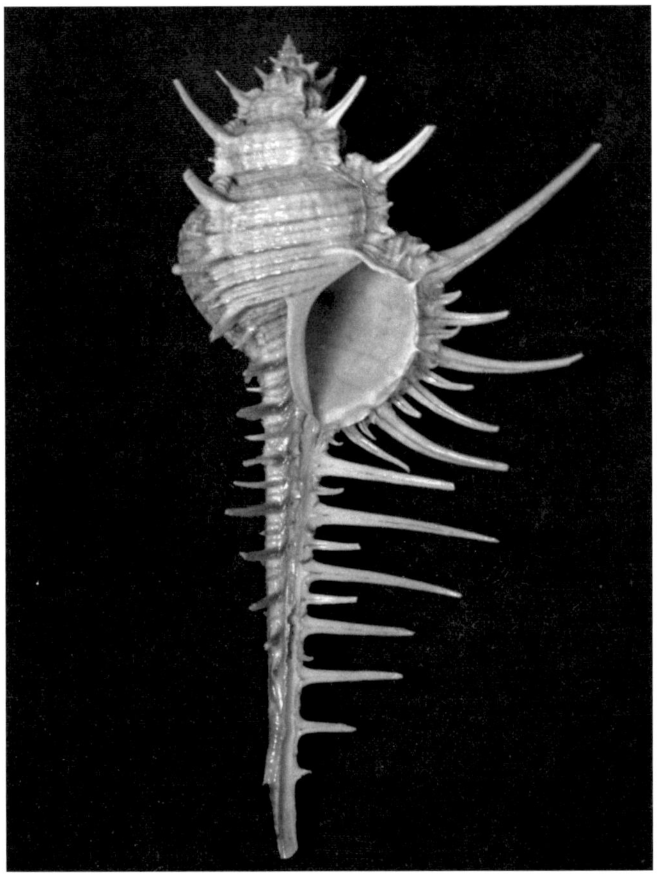

Murex troscheli (Troschel's Murex), 1931

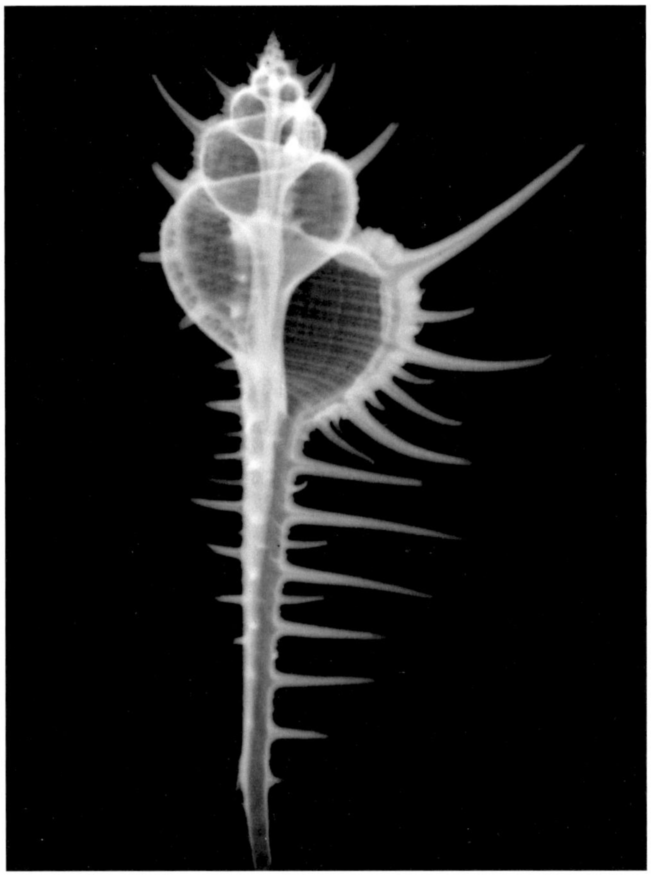

Murex troscheli (Troschel's Murex), X-ray, 1931

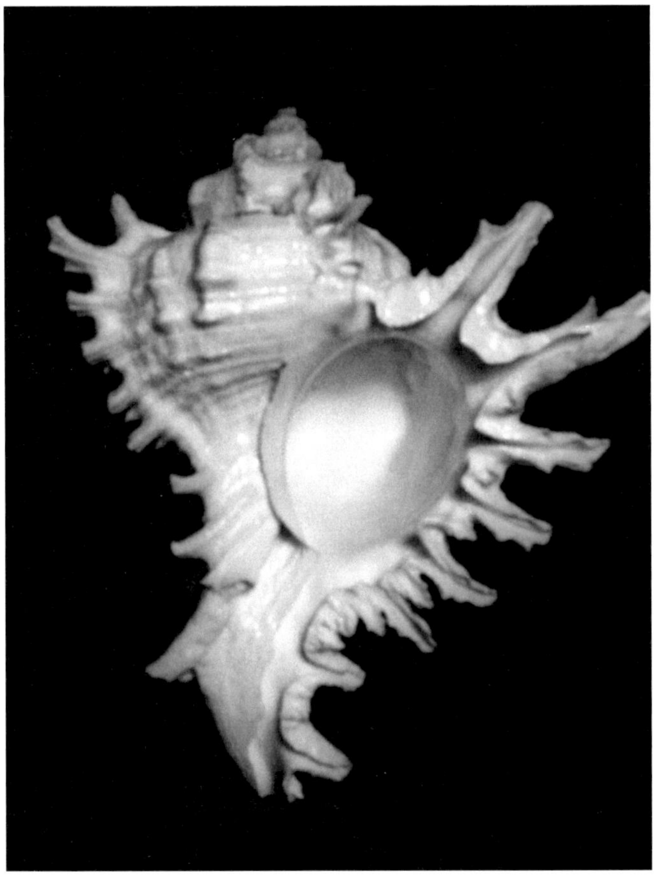

Murex inflatus (Branched Murex), 1931

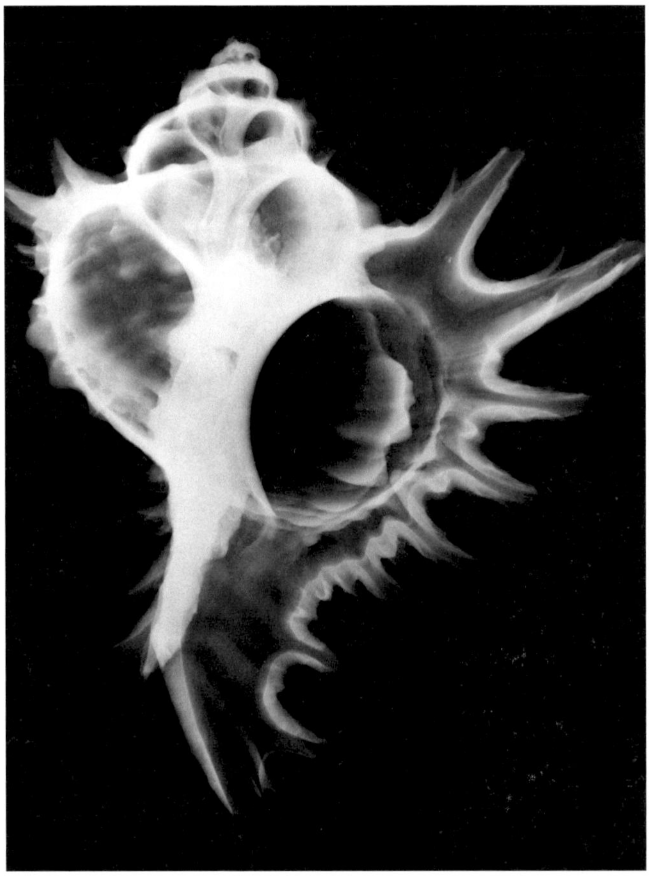

Murex inflatus (Branched Murex), X-ray, 1931

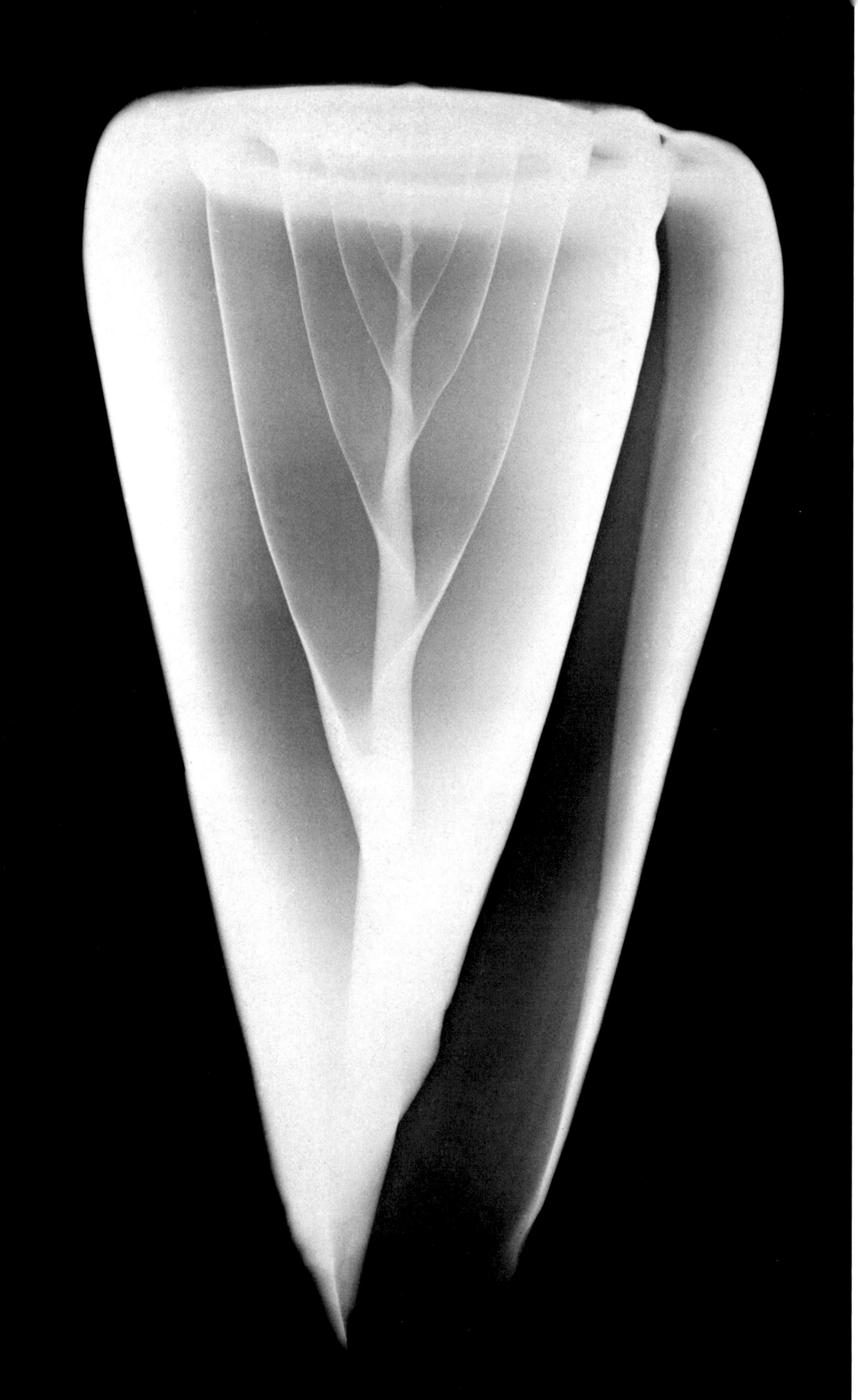

Conus marmoreus
(Marble Cone), X-ray, 1931

Ellobium aurismidae
(Midas' Ear Cassidula),
X-ray, 1931

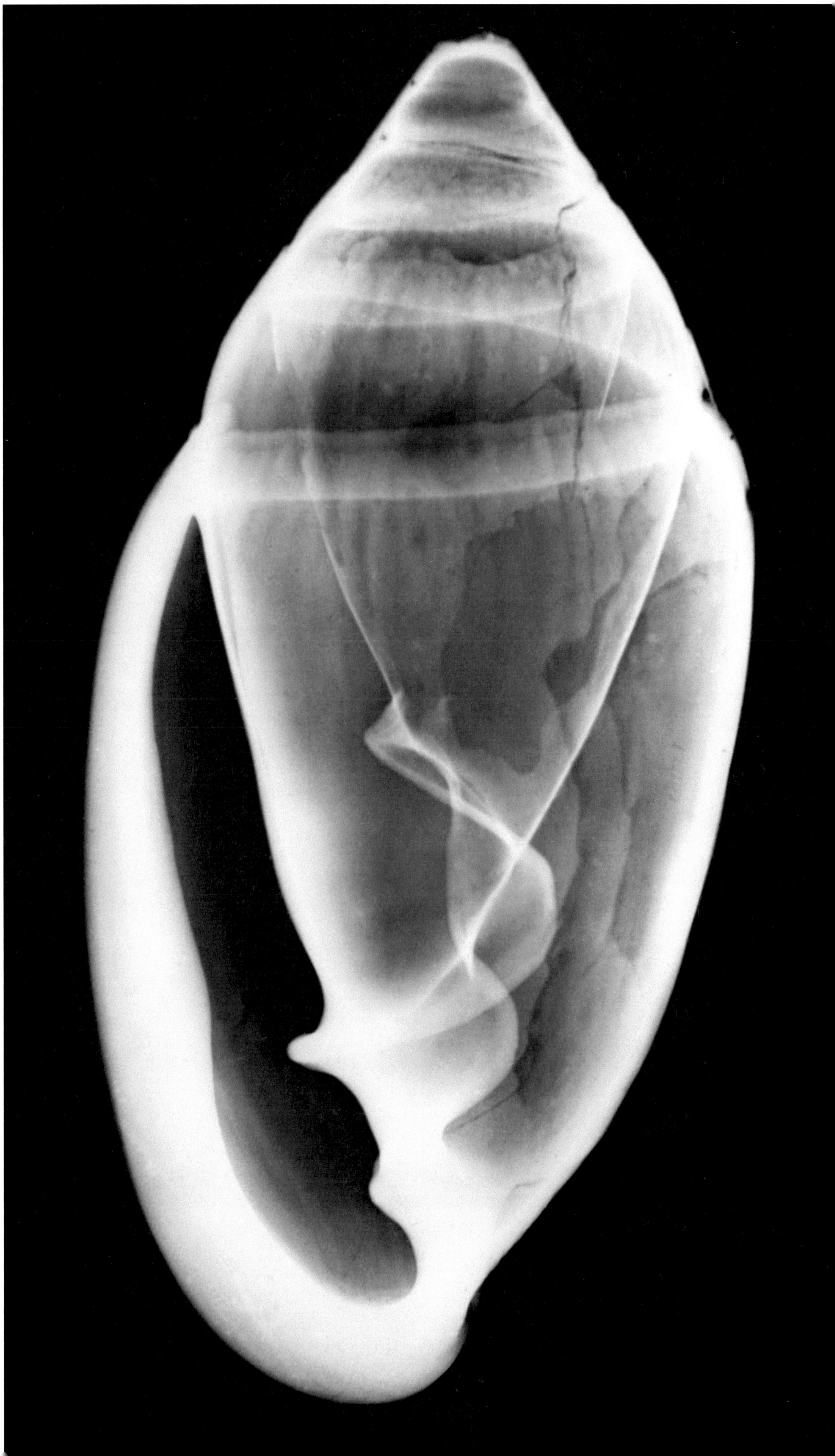

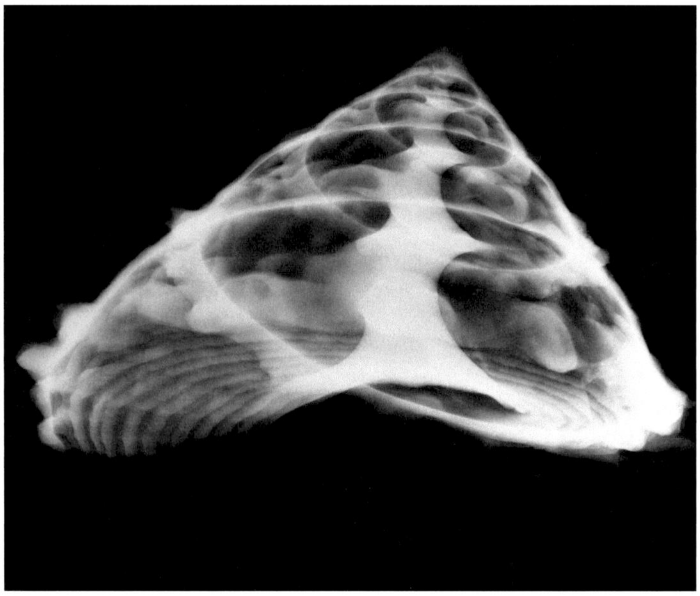

Trochus niloticus (Wavy Top Shell), X-ray, side view, 1931

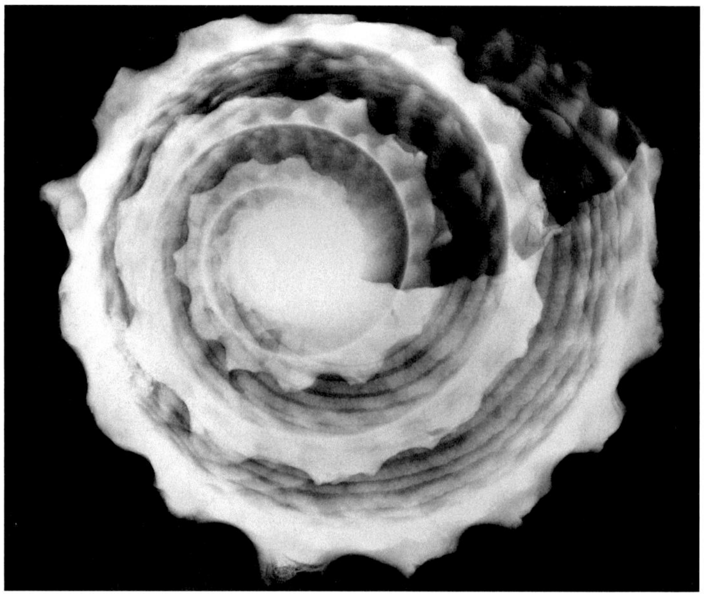

Trochus niloticus (Wavy Top Shell), X-ray, top view, 1931

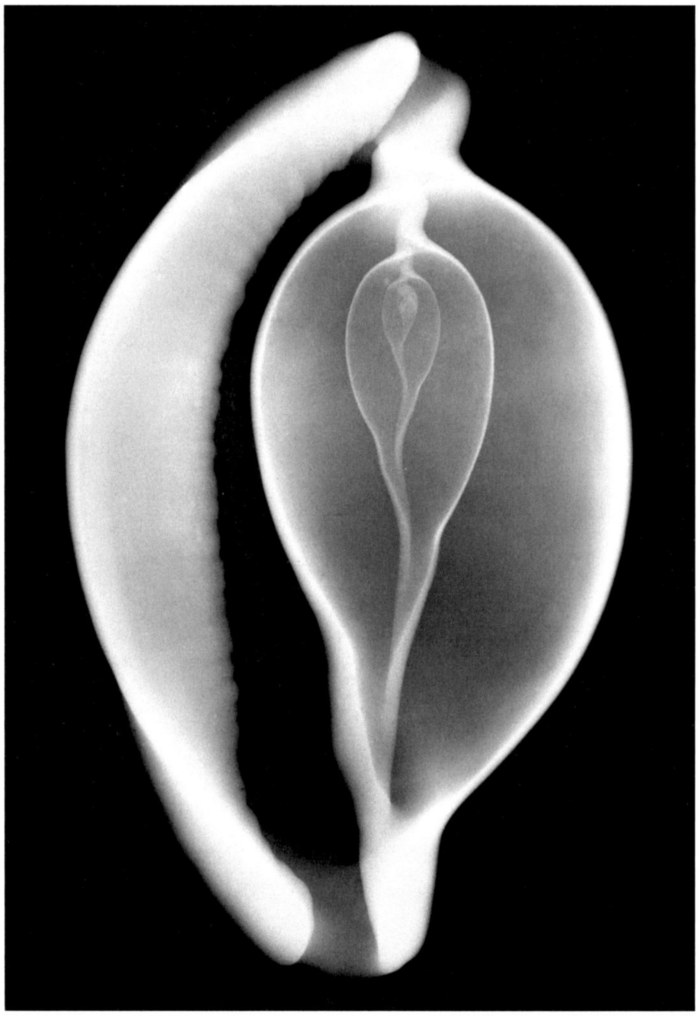

Ovula ovum (Common Egg Shell), X-ray, 1931

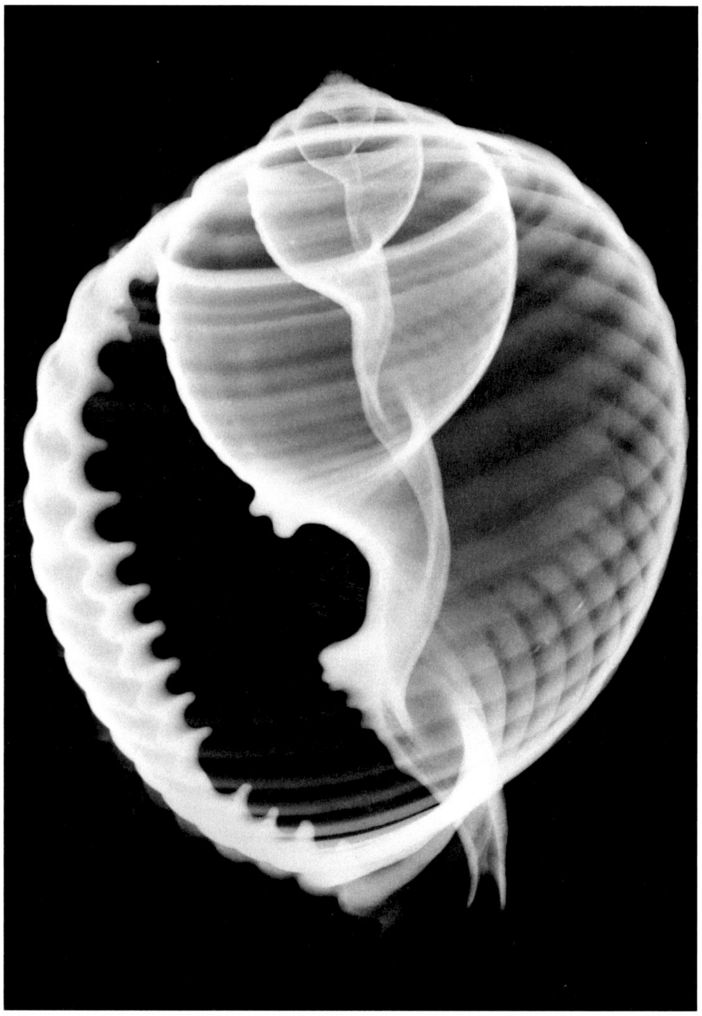

Malea ringens (Grinning Tun), X-ray, 1931

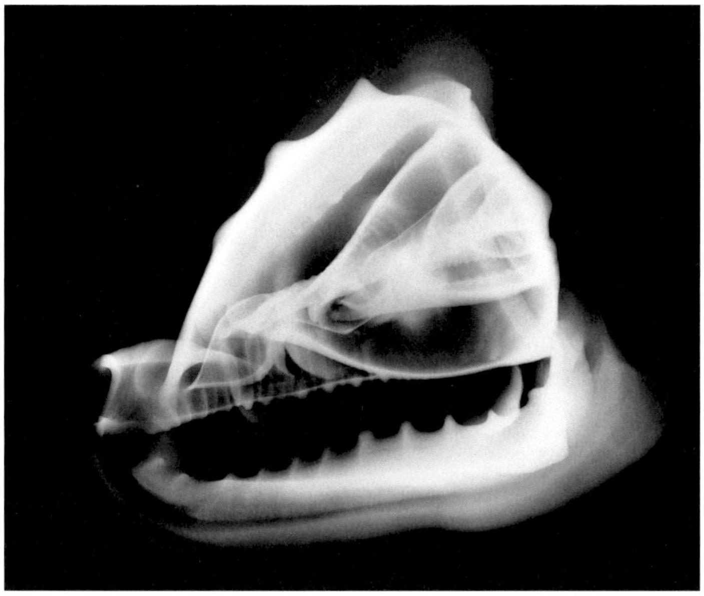

Cassis tuberosa (King Helmet), X-ray, 1931

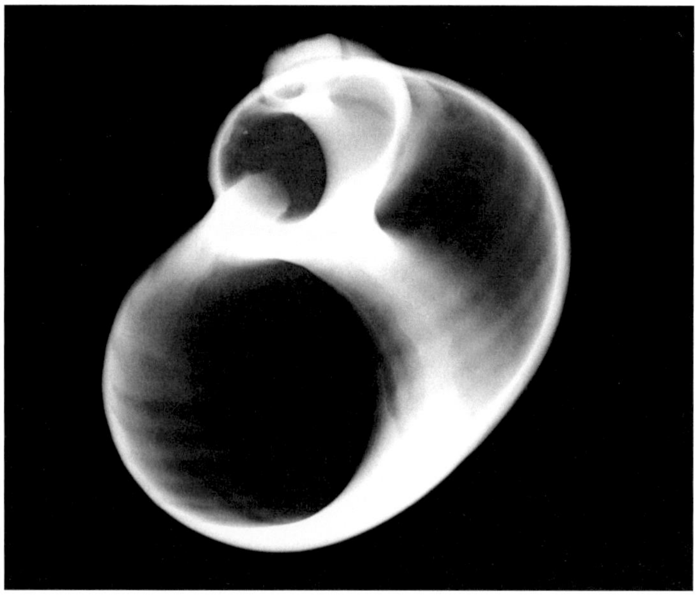

Turbo argryrostomus (Silver-Mouthed Turban), X-ray, 1931

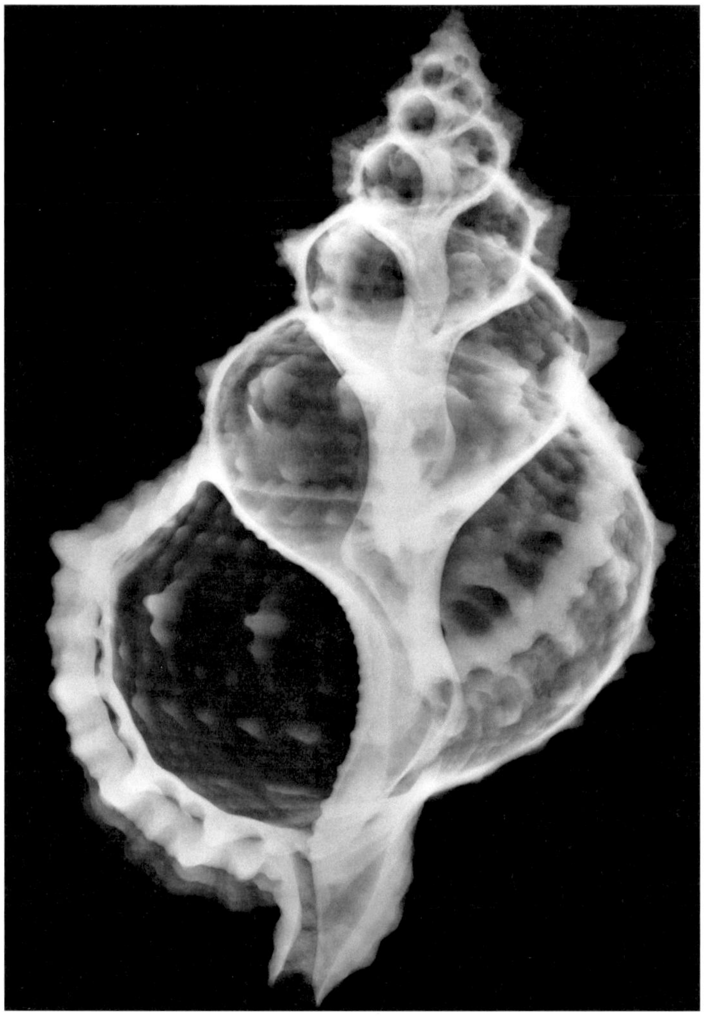

Triton lampas (Knobbed Triton), X-ray, 1931

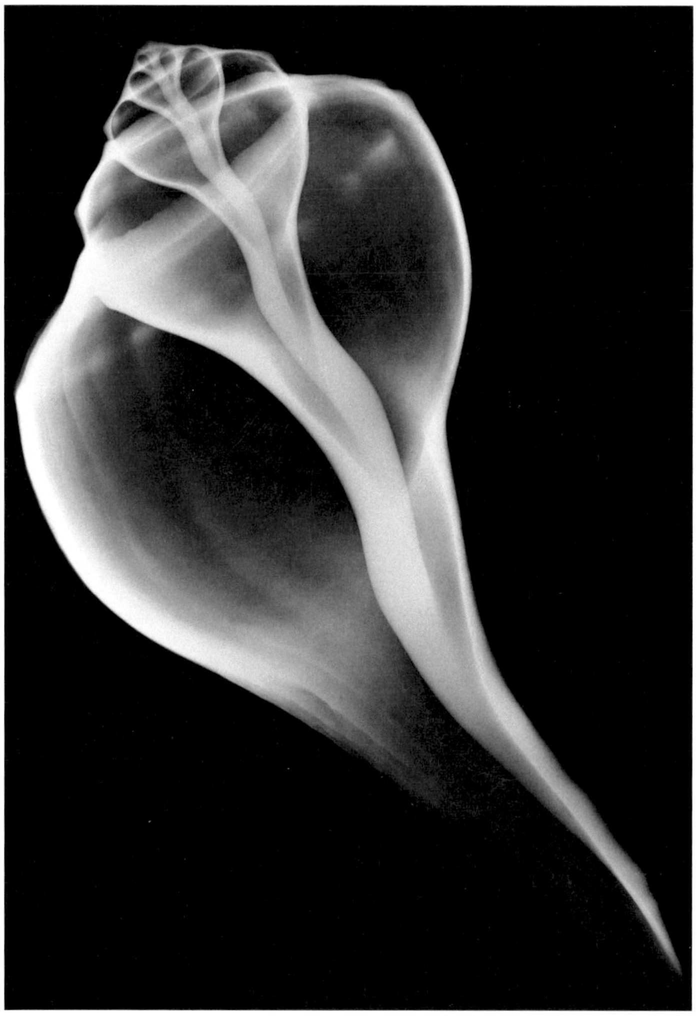

Busycon contrarium (Lightning Whelk), X-ray, 1931

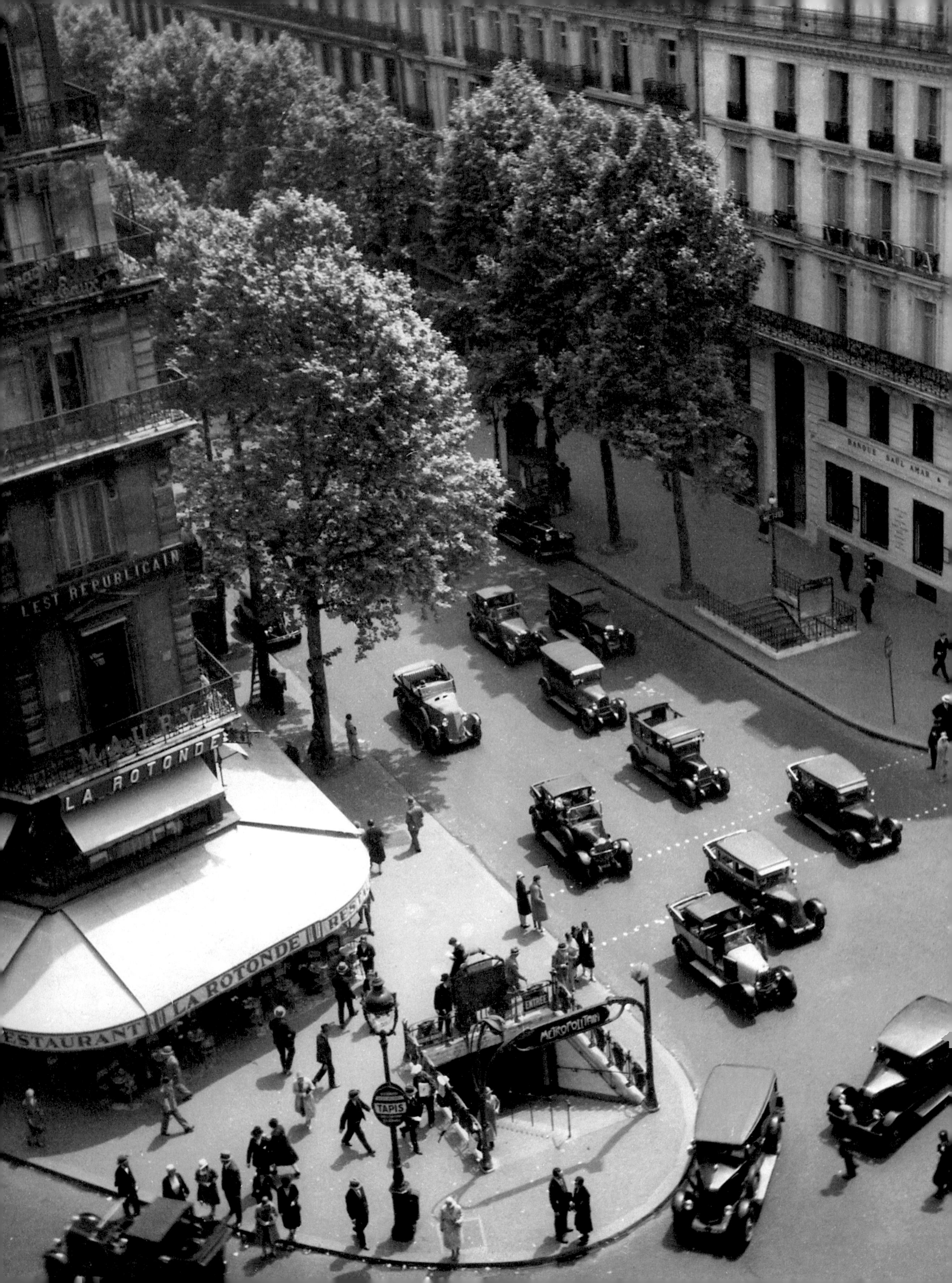
LEST REPUBLICAIN
MAURY
LA ROTONDE
LA ROTONDE
RESTAURANT
MÉTROPOLITAIN
ENTRÉE
TAPIS
BANQUE SAUL AMAR &

From Paris to Marseille and El Oued

Urban Images and Travel Photography around 1930

In addition to the city of Hamburg, another focal point of Fritz Block's photographic oeuvre was travel photography. Though based on his personal passion, such a focus was also typical for the time. A prerequisite was the global economic recovery following the First World War, which brought with it a boom in tourism and increased public interest in foreign cities and distant countries—and, therewith, a blossoming of urban and travel photography. But such photography no longer consisted simply of illustrative views; individual photographers rather sought to create an interpretation of the metropolis or landscape. This was aided, of course, by the proliferation of small-format cameras such as the Leica, which allowed for photojournalistic snapshots and reportages comprised of arrangements of single images.

Photographic travelogues played a prominent role in the illustrated press.[1] Moreover, the genre established itself on the book market as a special type of the photographic book form. One example is the series *Orbis Terrarum*, started in 1922 by the publishing house Ernst Wasmuth, in Berlin. The volumes were popular at the time and were also present in Block's library.[2] Similarly, the magazine *Atlantis* was founded in 1929, offering a forum for sophisticated travel photography. There were also book series such as *Das Gesicht der Städte*, *Orbis Urbium*, or *Die Reihe der Hundert*, which presented big cities from the point of view of individual photographers.[3] Such publications not only influenced Block's perceptions, they also encouraged him to create his own body of urban and travel photography.

For Block and his wife, Anna-Sophie, cultural experience was paramount to their travels—and from 1929 onward this experience was bound to photography. In contrast to professional press photographers, Block took photos for pleasure, without regard for a targeted publication. Still, his photographs are not "touristy" (there are but few pictures of his traveling-companion wife, for example); his visual concern was aesthetic. He did record his travel destinations, of course, but always through the lens of deliberately chosen image-themes. This is similar to his Hamburg photos, where two areas come repeatedly to the fore: structures resulting from constructions or the arrangement of objects, and people-watching, with an eye for scenes and moments. Once he returned to Hamburg, Block made prints of particularly poignant motifs and put them together for photo reportages, for which his wife most frequently authored accompanying text.

Block executed his travel reportage with photographic and cultural seriousness. About the required preparation, he wrote: "The photo reportage of foreign countries is one of the most interesting but also most difficult areas of photography, because the photo reportage of a country should lend a vivid picture of landscapes and urban planning, the manifestations of urban and rural areas; it should present the people in typical settings and convey a complete and substantial image to the viewer. [...] Since it is well known that one can only photograph well what one really knows and masters, reportage demands a profound involvement in the subject matter. [...] So, before you start a journey, you have to study in detail the maps, city layout, guides, and, above all, good literature. [...] This preliminary work, this working into the subject matter creates an unprecedented excitement; the future comparison of reality with the image one previously had is one of the strongest experiences of photo reporting and traveling."[4]

Paris

Like many culturally interested people, Block had a special affinity for the art capital Paris, which he first visited in 1914. His program then included the Eiffel Tower, Notre Dame, and The Louvre, Versailles, and Fontainebleau. The First World War and its aftermath pushed off his next Paris stay until the fall of 1925. The occasion was the exhibition *Exposition Internationale des Arts Décoratifs et Industriels Modernes*, which he visited in early October. Block also looked at examples of modern architecture in the burgeoning cityscape. He also pursued his interest in historical architecture, visited the Palace of Versailles again, and, on his return jour-

View from Galeries Lafayette department store onto Boulevard Haussmann, Paris, 1930

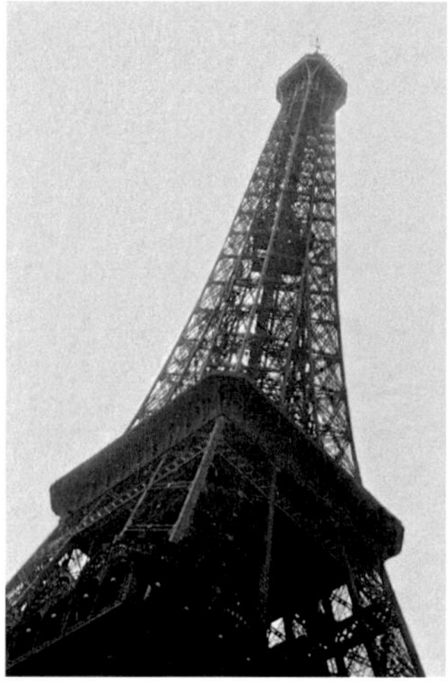

Eiffel Tower, Paris, 1930

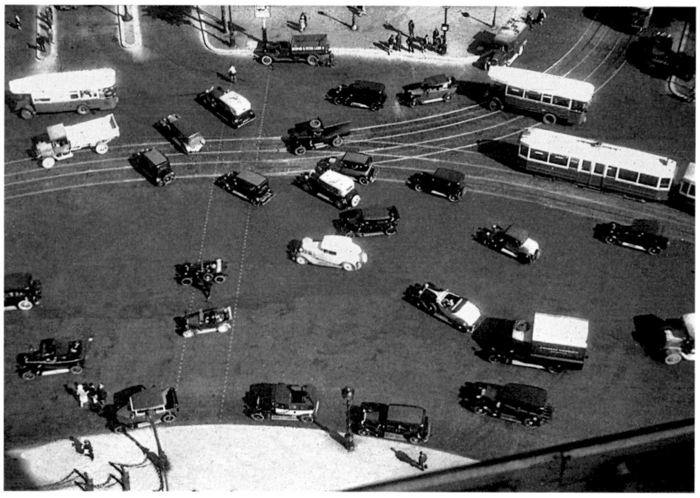

Downward view from the Arc de Triomphe de l'Étoile, Paris, 1930

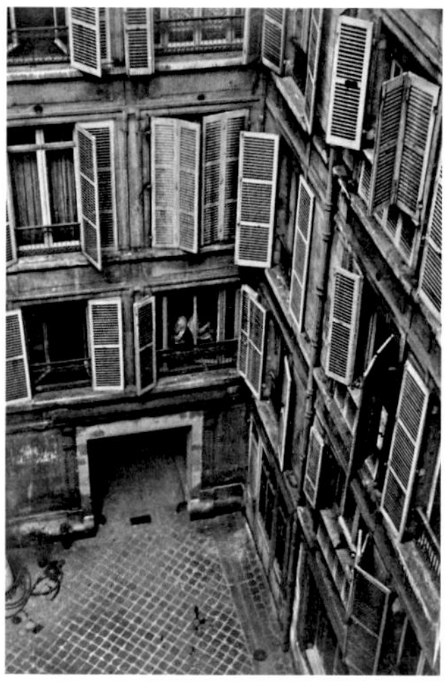

Back courtyard, Paris, 1930

ney, stopped at Chartres Cathedral. His architect's eye dominated the trip, that is—particularly as Block was not yet taking photographs.

Block was familiar with Paris not only from first-hand experience, but also from recent photographic literature in which the city played a prominent role.[5] Because of his interest in photography and because he prepared so thoroughly for his travels, it is safe to assume that Block owned books like the illustrated volume *Picturesque France. The Country, People, and Landscape* (1927), by Martin Hürlimann, from the series *Orbis Terrarum,* as well as the photo book *Paris* (1928), by Mario von Bucovich, from the series *Das Gesicht der Städte*, which also contains photographs by Germaine Krull. In addition, Block would have known Fritz Stahl's illustrated travel guide Paris. *Eine Stadt als Kunstwerk* (Paris. A City as a Work of Art, 1928), the book *100 x Paris* (1929), by Germaine Krull, from the series *Reihe der Hundert*, and Paul Cohen-Portheim's book *Paris* (1930), with photos by Sasha Stone.[6] The latter two contained more than the typical sights, and conveyed everyday insights into modern city life.

Block traveled to Paris twice in 1930, in June and September. Alongside his packed cultural agenda and avid photography, his abiding interest was in architecture. During his first stay, Block visited the exhibitions put on by the Deutscher Werkbund and the *Union des artistes modernes* (French Union of Modern Artists), and wrote about them for the architecture journal *Bauwelt*.[7] Subsequent to his second stay, Block published articles about modern architecture in France.[8] They were not accompanied by his own pictures, however; his articles were illustrated with photographs taken by professional architectural photographers.

Block took photos of the Eiffel Tower, of course, but not in a typically tourist manner of capturing the whole structure at once. Instead, he took extreme worm's-eye views [p. 104] and detail photos of the iron structure's various parts [pp. 112–113]. He concentrated on the kinds of technical details he had tested on the bridges, harbor cranes, and shipyards of Hamburg, and on Berlin's radio tower. But Block's perspectives were also common in the illustrated press of the time. He would have encountered Germaine Krull's similar photographs of the Eiffel Tower, published from 1928 onwards and also exhibited in the *Film und Foto* show.[9] We don't know, however, whether he also knew of Krull's portfolio *Métal* (1928). Block also photographed the cityscape from above, from the observation deck of the Eiffel Tower, for example, and from Notre Dame Cathedral. The structure and dynamism of the city are conveyed in his photographs taken from atop the Arc de Triomphe down to the roundabout of L'Étoile, with its radiating spokes of boulevards [p. 104]. The same applies to the view from the rooftop garden of the department store Galeries Lafayette [p. 102], on the corner of Boulevard Haussmann and Rue La Fayette, with the metro station Chaussée d'Antin and the restaurant La Rotonde[10], and the neighboring building's advertising façade [p. 114]. Photographer Marianne Breslauer had taken up the same vantage point during her studies in Paris, in 1929.[11] In such photographs, urban and travel photography incorporated the aesthetic principles of the New Vision.

Block was also interested in the expressions of modern cosmopolitanism in the French capital, which is why he captured many scenes of Parisian everyday life as symbols of the city's character. These included the second-hand booksellers on the banks of the Seine [p. 115], the cafes on the boulevards [pp. 116–117], and the Jardin du Luxembourg at lunch break [pp. 118–119], with children sending sailboats over the water basin [p. 121]. He also created images that evidence his special attention to the built structure as a means of composition. This can be seen in his photographs of workers erecting a fairground [p. 122] or trapeze acrobats at an outdoor circus [p. 123] in the Jardin d'Acclimatisation, on the northern edge of the Bois de Boulogne. When taking pictures of an airshow in the suburb of Vincennes, Block draws the viewer into the frame by photographing spectators from behind as they look at the aircraft above [p. 120].

He took a particularly compelling series of photos at the Parisian wholesale market Les Halles, portraying the market's characteristic people and traders [p. 124] as well as an impression of the flurry of activity. Here he discovered a variety of structured motifs: photographs of boxes and wooden barrels [pp. 126–127] and detailed studies of the

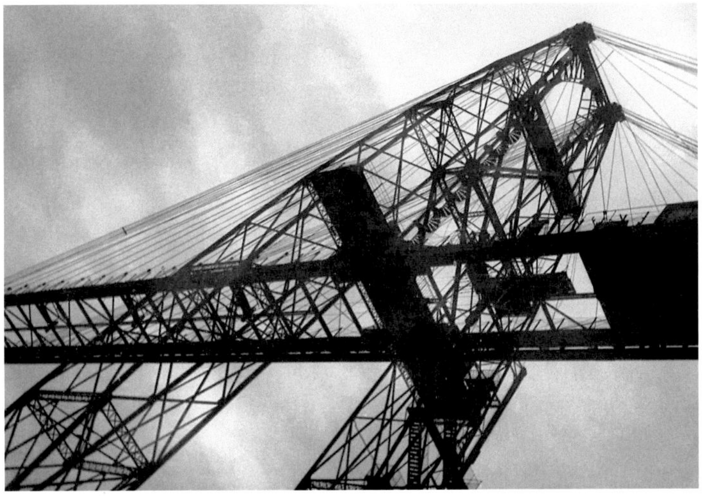

Pylon of the Pont Transbordeur, Marseille, 1930

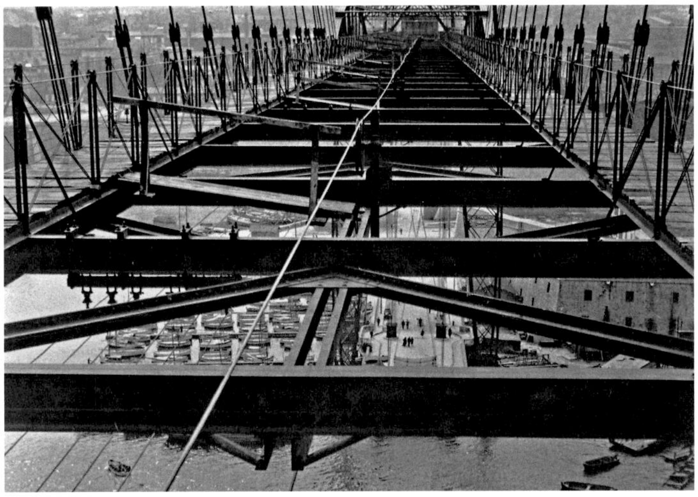

Girder of the Pont Transbordeur, Marseille, 1931

diversity of goods for sale [pp. 128–129]. Block also focused his photographic eye on less obvious aspects of urban life—whether they presented a formally attractive composition, such as a glimpse into a backyard [p. 104], or a subject that offered a view into the quotidian picture of big-city life: garbage removal [p. 130]. His photographs of a Gypsy trailer park at Porte de Choisy [p. 131]—already photographed by Eugène Atget—was framed as a work of social reportage. All in all, Block succeeded in creating a portrait of Paris that is, though by no means comprehensive, certainly multifaceted and individual. With this body of work, he ranks respectably among the more renowned photographers of this city.[12]

A Camera Discovers Paris

Back in Hamburg, Block evaluated and then published the photographic output of his Paris trips.[13] The first publication, "Pariser Leben", was printed in the illustrated weekly supplement of the *Hamburger Anzeiger* [pp. 110–111] at end of August 1930. Block's text reads: "Paris is, despite all the mechanization and technologization of modern life, the city of *joie de vivre* and life affirmation, a city full of excitement and romance. True, the city center echoes the pace of other world cities, but it maintains a tempo that allows life everywhere to unfold." Through the agency of the Linden-Verlag, in Munich, the illustrated newspaper supplement *Die Welt* published "*12 Uhr mittag in Paris*" [p. 119] (Noon in Paris), a page of photos with Block's impressions of a lunch break in the Jardin du Luxembourg in July 1931. In the middle of 1931, Block submitted a few of his Paris photographs to the competition *Das lebendige Bild*, sponsored by the photo magazine *Photofreund*. His image *Boulevard-Café in Paris*, which shows a man in an intimate conversation with a woman [p. 117], received first prize and was subsequently reprinted in *Photofreund Jahrbuch 1931/32* (1931). In early 1932, in the magazine *Die Leica,* it was printed as an example of a particularly successful snapshot.

At the end of 1931, Block planned to produce a book of photos about Paris, as he had done for Hamburg. He produced a dummy booklet with mounted photo prints, entitled *Eine Kamera entdeckt Paris* (A Camera Discovers Paris).[14] Directed at potential publishers, his proposal described the dummy as "a kind of script" to be illustrated by a few sample pages of imagery "that was not originally taken for this purpose," to demonstrate "what the general tone of the book should be." Block imagined a photographic travelogue in several languages: "If the book is commissioned, I would go back to Paris and take around 100 more photos. In part, I would re-take or supplement the photos in the book [...]." Finally, Block even proposed "to include other cities and areas that attract lots of tourists and are particularly suitable to this series." [15]

Block had already written a foreword to the book, in which he also expressed his view of modern photography: "[The Paris book] should show the life and bustle of the city, and teach us to see things of interest to people of our times. The excitement inherent here has something of the extraordinary to it, should be expressed in a different way: through the dynamics of the image, through juxtaposition, assembled as if in the cinema, rife with contrasts, rhythms, and frictions. The modern photo—if done right—is simply the most powerful expression of our time: clear, straightforward, and internationally intelligible [...]."[16] Block also set down clear ideas for the design and execution of the book. He envisioned a square format that "has become very popular in America for travel guides and brochures," with a flexible cover, so it can be folded and carried in a pocket: "For the cover, a photo montage is intended, or something similar with a cellophane wrapper, for protection. When folded, the whole should be held together by a rubber band, which is affixed to the book. This kind of presentation would also be something new. [...] Autotype would be an option for printing. Special attention should be given to typography."[17]

The book concept contained some innovative aspects, to be sure, but its positioning remains ambiguous: city guide or photo book? Its motifs would have also required additional, and technically better, images than Block had taken. It is not known, and also unlikely, that Block ever spoke to publishers. The number of existing photo books on Paris at the time, and, above all, the worsening world economic cri-

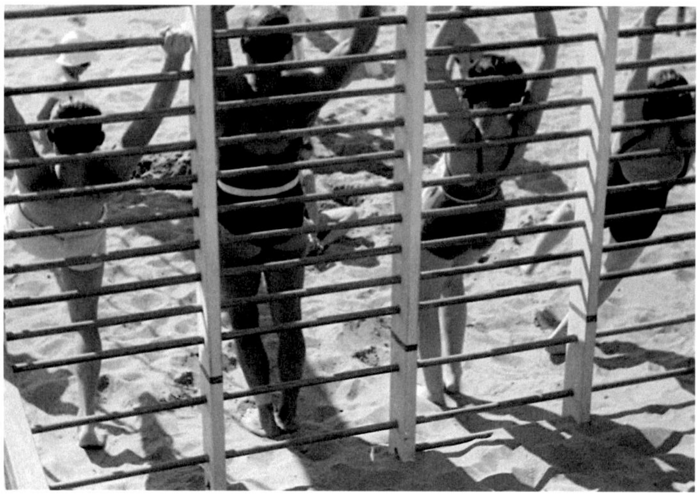
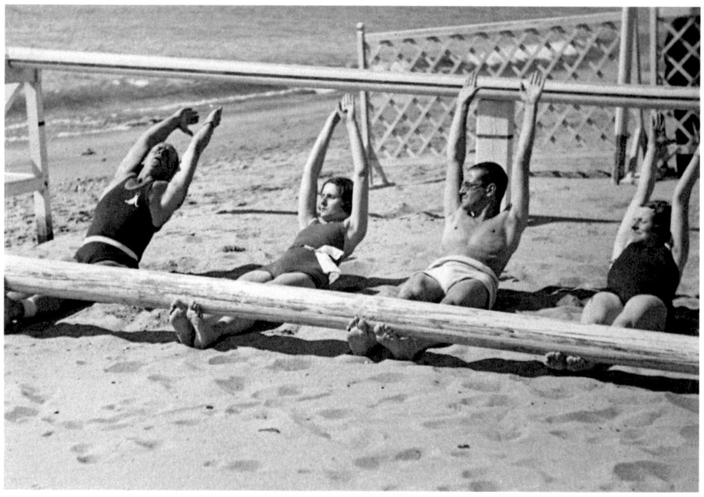

Workout at Juan-les-Pins beach, Côte d'Azur, 1931

sis, did not bode well for the project. In the end, Block's Paris book never happened.

However, Block did present his Paris photos in a lecture in February 1932, at the Kunstverein Hamburg's *Internationale Foto-Ausstellung*. Just prior to this, he presented his photos of New York from fall 1931. Accordingly, his lecture "Photo Reportage Paris" was based on a comparison of Paris and New York: "New York today, in everything the city of tomorrow, is the most modern metropolis. Paris of today, still a city of yesterday, is the least modern of all metropolises. New York: unprecedented pace and verve; Paris: a delicious quietness. [...] Both cities have in common their extraordinary contrasts [...]." In a manner typical of the time, and therefore also somewhat cliché, Block contrasts the mechanization of life in New York with the quality of life in Paris: "What distinguishes Paris from all other cities and what gives it its identity, is its distinct culture of humanity and individuality."[18]

Marseille and the Pont Transbordeur

At turn of the year 1928/29, Block and his wife spent their holidays on the Côte d'Azur. From Cap-d'Ail, near Monaco, they visited Monte Carlo, Menton, and Nice. On their return journey, in early January 1929, they spent two days in Marseille, where, according to his travel diary, Block saw and walked across the Pont Transbordeur (Transporter Bridge) for the first time. He did not take any photos. In early 1930, Block was on his way to and from Algeria (see below), in the city again—now equipped with a Leica. In the early summer of 1931, he traveled along the French Riviera and went to Marseille a third time and took more photos of the port city and the Transporter Bridge.

At the end of the 1920s, Marseille was a frequent pictorial theme in Germany's illustrated press; the unsavory reputation of the city's harbor district played a role. The main attraction, however, was the Transporter Bridge, a filigree bridge construction spanning the harbor basin on which a gondola ferry was pulled over the water. Two pedestrian walkways ran across the very top, which could be reached by stairs over the two pylons, atop of which observation decks were accessible via spiraling iron staircases. Built in 1905 and photographed countless times—albeit more conventionally—this monument, like the Eiffel Tower, became a destination and icon for the photographic avant-garde of the late 1920s. It offered an ideal motif for the New Objectivity's fascination with technology, and for the New Vision's interest in the bird's-eye view.[19] At the same time, the Transporter Bridge stood for the unity of technology and art, of functionality and aesthetics—one of the central demands of the modern age.

Art historian Sigfried Giedion played a major role in popularizing the monument, by publishing photographs of the Transporter Bridge he took in January 1927, in the art magazine *Der Cicerone*.[20] He also used some of the photos in his book *Bauen in Frankreich – Bauen in Eisen – Bauen in Eisenbeton* (Building in France – Building in Iron – Building in Ferroconcrete, 1928), a copy of which Block likely owned. Giedion's friend László Moholy-Nagy designed the dust jacket, with a high-contrast negative reproduction of the bridge, which illustrated its bold construction but also nearly transformed it into a photogram.[21] Moholy-Nagy went to Marseille in 1929 to make photos and films.[22] He, too, was fascinated by the structure and dynamics of the technical structure of the Transporter Bridge, and took advantage of it by shooting from the top, as he had from Berlin's radio tower.[23] As early as 1928, Herbert Bayer also took pictures of the Transporter Bridge. His photographs were shown in 1929, at the Deutschen Werkbund's exhibition *Film und Foto* in Stuttgart, which also exhibited Giedion's photos of the Eiffel Tower. That same year, Bayer's photographs were published with Germaine Krull's Marseille photos in the French magazine *VU*, among others.[24] Krull, however, took most of her photographs of the Transporter Bridge in June 1930.[25] It was around that time that Florence Henri, Tim Gidal, and a number of other photographers took shots of this bridge as well. Block saw this motif in the December 1930 issue of the Deutscher Werkbund journal *Die Form*—the issue in which his photos with texts about ship details appeared—in a photo series of the Transporter Bridge by film director and author Alex Strasser (1898–1974).[26]

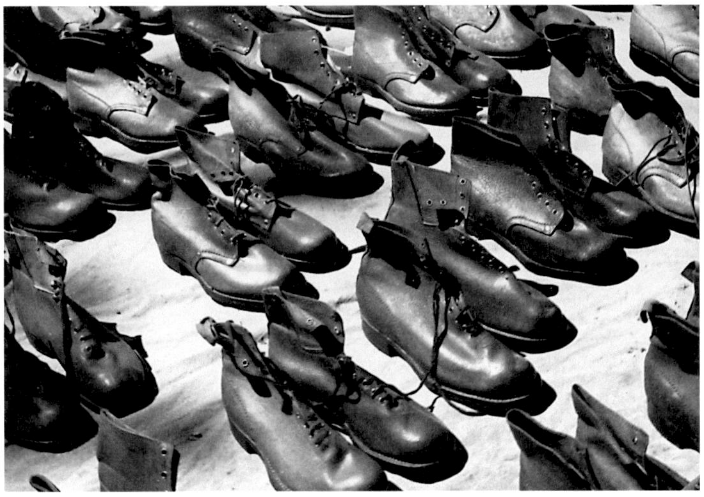

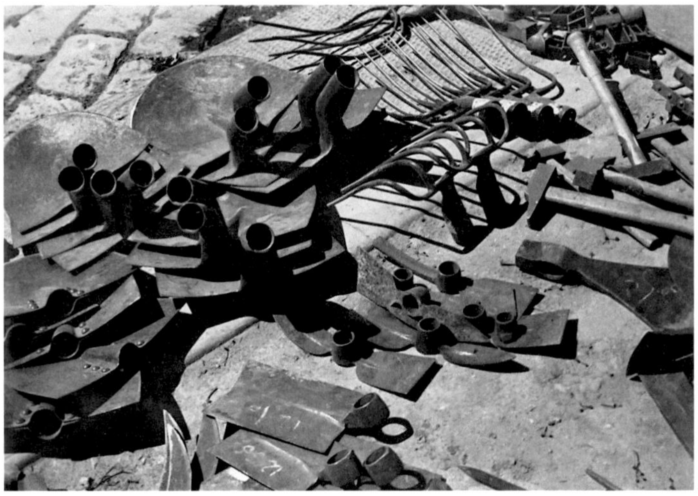

Shoes and working tools at a street market, Arles, 1931

On his two trips to Marseille, Block made around 70 photographs of the Transporter Bridge; 20 of them exist as prints of various sizes and quality [pp. 3, 105 and 134–139]. In 1930, he took photos primarily of the bridge construction, consisting of two pylons and the connecting bridge girder seen in partial views from below, and mainly backlit [pp. 105 and 134]. Block made better and more precise images in April 1931, when he photographed the pedestrian path spanning over the water [p. 3 and 105] as well as down at the foundations of the pylon resting in the water, with boats floating in front of them, and from above the steel-cable suspended gondola ferry [pp. 136–138]. These photos are similar to those by Bayer and Moholy-Nagy. Finally, Block added images of steel cables that fixated the pylons on the fortress-like building at the bank of the port basin, comparable to those by Germaine Krull. Among the photographers of the Transporter Bridge, Block, it seems, has been forgotten. This has in part to do with the incorrect attribution of one of his images: "Dr. Block" was erroneously ascribed as "D. R. Block".[27] As a result, the Hamburg photographer was still incorrectly identified in a 2006 exhibition catalogue at, of all places, the Hamburger Kunsthalle (Hamburg Art Museum) itself: courtesy was attributed to "D. R. Block, active around 1930. No other biographical information is known."[28]

In Marseille, Block was interested in a second subject: scenes of the harbor district, probably because of its similarities to Hamburg. A selection of these photographs was published in the September 1932 illustrated weekly supplement of the *Hamburger Anzeiger,* as a photo reportage from "Marseille—ein südlicher Welthafen" (Marseille—a Southern World Harbor) [pp. 132–133]. The accompanying text, by Anna-Sophie Block, reads: "Marseille has no significant art monuments. But as a landmark, in addition to the towering church Notre Dame de la Gare, it boasts a transporter bridge *le pont transbordeur* over the inland harbor. Its perfect technical execution is of great beauty—and also world famous."

Côte d'Azur and Provence

In the early summer of 1931, Block and his wife took a trip to the French Riviera—already a popular holiday destination, most frequently for the well-to-do, but also for tourists interested in modern art.[29] Their route led them from Antibes and Juan-les-Pins via Saint-Raphaël and Le Lavandou to Marseille, from there through the Camargue with Saintes-Maries-de-la-Mer, then through Provence to Aigues-Mortes, Arles, and Nîmes, to Pont du Gard and Orange. Block's photos of the trip are of a mix: some have the character of a travel protocol, including a few casual images, some of them incorrectly exposed; other photos have clear design effort behind them. The images that Block subsequently selected for prints underline this claim.

In Antibes, Block took detailed shots of plants—in the style of New Objectivity—in the botanical garden of the Villa Thuret, and he photographed scenes of the city and the port with boats and fishing nets. He was particularly interested in the posh Hôtel du Cap-Eden-Roc, with its rocky terrace, and in swimmers on Cap d'Antibes. He met with the architect Adolf Loos (1870–1933), who was residing at the seaside resort of Juan-les-Pins, for both recreation and a hotel construction project (alas, never completed). Apparently, Block's tour also included examples of modern architecture, including the house (Villa E-1027) by Eileen Gray and Jean Badovici in Roquebrune-Cap-Martin. In June 1931, Block published an article about the villa in the *Zentralblatt der Bauverwaltung*—though illustrated with photographs from another source.[30]

Modernity is not only characterized by technology, rationalization, and objectivity; it's also characterized by humans being liberated from social convention. This new attention to lifestyle and the body was expressed not least in sport, dance, and in recreational pleasure, including sunbathing and playing at the beach. These kinds of photos could be seen in the illustrated press each year during the summer months. Even representatives of the photographic avant-garde such as László Moholy-Nagy and Herbert Bayer captured beach scenes for the New Vision. Block's extensive photo series made on the Juan-les-Pins beach play to this fascination. These are not banal snapshots but rather well-planned images that combine spontaneity and composition, whether of people doing gymnastics [p. 106], beach beau-

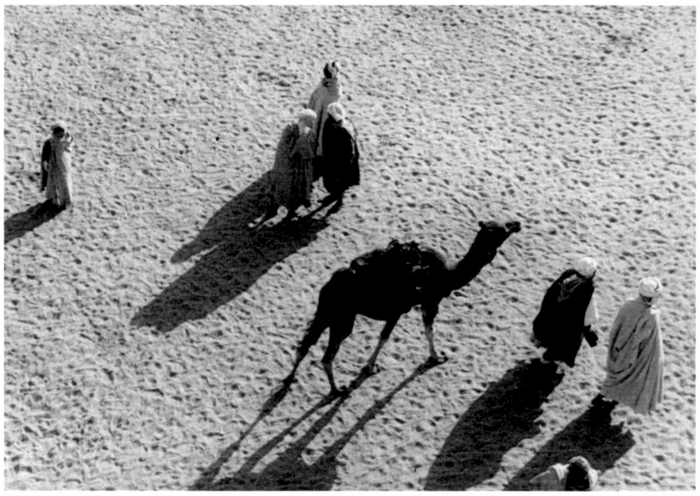

Near El Oued, Algeria, 1930

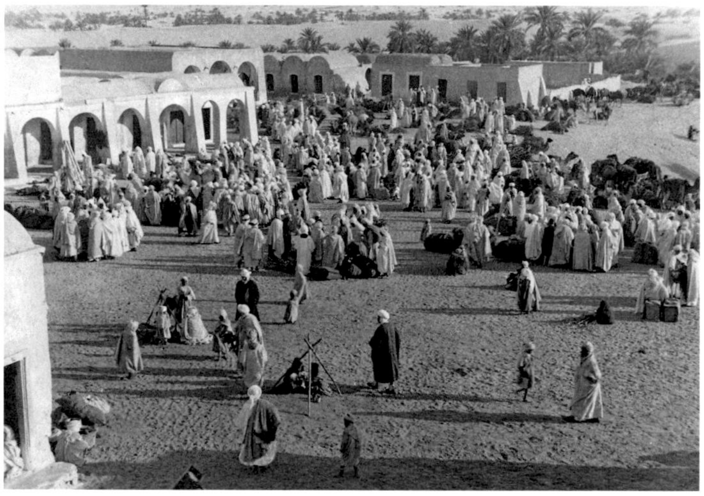

El Oued market, Algeria, 1930

ties, or children arranged in groups [p. 144]—sometimes seen from unusual perspectives: an image of a boy jumping out of the picture [p. 145] or, in the case of sunbathers, shot from above [pp. 146–147].

Of particular photographic interest for Block was a game played with a large gym ball, which provided him a variety of photographic situations, some of them comical [pp. 142–143]. One photo shows two rows of people sitting opposite each other on the beach moving a medicine ball down the row [p. 145]. The image is reminiscent of a photograph by Martin Munkácsi, which had been published on the cover of the *Berliner Illustrirte Zeitung* in the summer of 1929.[31] Block's image, of the same quality, was featured on the May 1931 cover of the *Hamburger Anzeiger* illustrated weekly supplement [p. 140]. In both cases, the ball cuts into the headline of the newspaper; however, as opposed to Block's image, in Munkácsi's cover the ball was collaged in. Block's beach photos clearly touched the zeitgeist: after appearing in the *Hamburger Anzeiger*, they were published in the magazine *Die Leica*, and then, in 1933, even the French magazine *Le Miroir du Monde* featured three of Block's beach motifs.

The landscape of the Camargue, however, provided Block with only a few subjects. He focused instead on the city wall of Aigues-Mortes, which offered charming views [p. 150]. Otherwise, he looked mostly for objects, such as those he found in the street market of Arles, where he captured an arrangement of shoes and tools [p. 107], or the detailed juxtaposition of motorcycles and wooden carts [pp. 148–149]. Block also concentrated on Roman architectural monuments, including the Nîmes Amphitheater, the aqueduct at Pont du Gard, and the Orange Theater [p. 151]. On the way back to Hamburg, he took photos of Strasbourg Cathedral.

Algeria and Tunisia

Another trip abroad led Block to North Africa, to Algeria and Tunisia—at the time were administered by the French. He probably travelled in early 1930, before he went to Paris and southern France. That this was his first photo trip is evident in the images' often-flawed exposures. The unfamiliar light and climate compounded the fact that Block also had to find his way in a world of motifs that were new to him; after all, this wasn't Hamburg. To prepare, he likely paged through the book *Nordafrika. Tripolis, Tunis, Algier, Marokko. Baukunst, Landschaft, Volksleben* (North Africa. Tripoli, Tunis, Algeria, Morocco. Architecture, Landscape, Life of the People, 1924) from the *Orbis Terrarum* series, featuring photographs by Lehnert & Landrock. This book of photos chronicles a round trip from Tunis via Algeria to Marrakesh in Morocco, with many pictures of sites that Block also visited and photographed. His own journey, however, took the opposite direction. From Marseille, Block and his wife took the ship to Algiers. Their other travel destinations were Timgad, El Kantara, Biskra and Sidi Okba, Touggourt, El Oued, Tozeur, El Kairouan, and finally, Tunis. From there, they went back to Marseille. Getting around in Algeria and Tunisia was done via minibus, as part of the tours organized by French and Algerian travel and transport companies for international tourists. Accompanying brochures and guides were sometimes even in German.

The surviving prints from this trip show Block's efforts not to lose himself in shots of the vast desert landscape. He concentrated on objects such as palms, camels, architecture, markets, and people, as well as formations of the sandy desert. The oasis city of El Oued offered him particularly suitable motifs: the hustle and bustle on the marketplace [p. 108] and views from the minaret over the roofscape of this "city of a thousand domes" [pp. 154–155]. In its fragmentary reproduction, the way the buildings are composed creates a unique expressiveness. Block was less interested in cultural travel impressions than in the photographic effects of shadows of people and camels cast by the setting sun [p. 108]. The clearest alignment with the perspective of the New Photography can be seen in Block's detailed studies of patterns and traces left by the wind or by camel caravans in the desert sand [p. 156–157].

Block assembled the footage from his North Africa trip into a photo reportage. It was published in July 1930, in the illustrated weekly supplement of the *Hamburger Anzeiger* under the title "Wunder der Wüste" [pp. 152–153]. He also submitted individual photos for publication in the photographic yearbook *Das Deutsche Lichtbild*. His photograph *El Oued (Die Stadt der tausend Kuppeln)* (The City of a Thousand Domes) was subsequently included into *Das Deutsche Lichtbild. Jahresschau 1931* (published at the end of 1930). Block also sent his pictures to the photo agency Linden-Verlag, in Munich, which led to the 1931 publication of some of his motifs in the Ullstein journal *Die Koralle* and in the volume *Ausgewählte Werke* (Selected Works, 1931), by the popular-science writer Wilhelm Bölsche.

Block's photographic endeavors in 1930 and 1931, in North Africa, Paris, and southern France encouraged him to embark on an extensive journey across the United States with his Leica.

1 See Robert Lebeck and Bodo von Dewitz, *Kiosk. Eine Geschichte der Bildreportage 1839–1973 / A History of Photojournalism* (Göttingen, 2001). – www.illustrierte-presse.de.

2 See Roland Jaeger, "Die Länder der Erde im Bild. Die Reihe *Orbis Terrarum* im Verlag Ernst Wasmuth, Berlin, und im Atlantis-Verlag, Berlin/Zürich," in *Autopsie. Deutschsprachige Fotobücher 1918 bis 1945. Vol. 1*, eds. Manfred Heiting and Roland Jaeger (Göttingen, 2012), 98–131.

3 Idem, "Ein Bilderkompendium aller Weltstädte. Die Reihe *Das Gesicht der Städte* im Albertus- Verlag, Berlin," in ibid., 202–217. – Idem, "Das billige Städtebuch von hoher Qualität. *Die Reihe der Hundert* im Verlag der Reihe, Berlin," in ibid., 218–223. – Idem, "Schöne Städte in schönen Bildern. Die Reihe *Orbis Urbium* im Verlag Dr. Hans Epstein, Wien," in ibid., *vol. 2* (Göttingen 2014), 218–225.

4 Fritz Block, "Photoreportage mit der Leica in Amerika," *Photofreund-Jahrbuch 1933*, ed. Fr. Willy Frerk (Berlin, 1932), 77–88; quotation, 77.

5 See Hans-Michael Koetzle, *Eyes on Paris. Paris im Fotobuch 1890 bis heute* (Munich, 2011). – Christian Bouqueret, *Paris. Les Livres de Photographie des Années 1920 aux Années 1950* (Paris, 2012).

6 See Birgit Hammers "*Sasha Stone sieht noch mehr". Ein Fotograf zwischen Kunst und Kommerz* (Petersberg, 2014), 97–104.

7 Fritz Block, "Deutsche Baukünstler in Paris," *Bauwelt* 21, no. 32 (1930), 999–1000.

8 Idem, "Studien des Pariser Architekten André Lurçat zum Kleinwohnungsbau," *Zentralblatt der Bauverwaltung* 51, no. 7 (1931), 101–107. – Idem, "Neue Baukunst in Frankreich," *Zeitschrift für Bauwesen* 81, no. 3 (1931), 53–65.

9 See Kim Sichel, *Germaine Krull. Photographer of Modernity* (Cambridge, MA, 1999) – Michel Frizot, Germaine Krull (Ostfildern, 2015).

10 This restaurant La Rotonde is not to be confused with the eponymous café La Rotonde, at the corner of Boulevard du Montparnasse and Boulevard Raspail, which became well known as a meeting place for artists and writers.

11 See *Marianne Breslauer. Fotografien*, eds. Kathrin Beer and Christina Feilchenfeldt (Wädenswil 2010) 21. Breslauer's photo dates from 1929, the print from 1930.

12 See, among others, Patrick Deedes-Vincke, *Paris. The City and its Photographers* (Boston/Toronto/ London, 1992). – *Voici Paris. Modernités photographiques, 1920–1950. La Collection Christian Bouqueret* (Paris, 2012).

13 See the list of Block's photo publications on page 327.

14 The dummy is in the Fritz Block papers, Architecture and Design Collection. Art, Design & Architecture Museum, University of California, Santa Barbara.

15 Fritz Block, *Zu dem Paris-Buch* (manuscript, 1931, Fritz Block papers, ibid.).

16 Fritz Block, *Zum Geleit* (manuscript, 1931, ibid., 9).

17 See note 15.

18 Fritz Block, *Foto-Reportage Paris* (manuscript, 1932, Fritz Block Estate Archive, Stockholm/Hamburg).

19 Karl J. Spurzem, "Le Pont Transbordeur," *mare. Die Zeitschrift der Meere* 11, no. 61 (2007), 90–100. – Kathrin Kohle, "Industrie und Technik," in *Ein neuer Blick. Architekturfotografie aus den Staatlichen Museen zu Berlin*, eds. Ludger Derenthal and Christine Kühn (Tübingen/Berlin, 2010), 53–56.

20 Sigfried Giedion, "Zur Situation der französischen Architektur II," Der Cicerone 19, 1927, no. 6 (1927), 174–189.

21 Arthur Rüegg, "Beziehung und Durchdringung – Eiffelturm und Pont Transbordeur," in *Sigfried Giedion und die Fotografie,* eds. Werner Oechslin and Gregor Harbusch (Zurich, 2010), 172–175.

22 See *Moholy Album*, ed. Jeannine Fiedler (Göttingen, forthcoming).

23 See François Bon, Olivier Lugon, and Philippe Simay, *Le pont transbordeur de Marseille. Moholy-Nagy* (Paris, 2013) (Collection Voir-Faire-Lire). – Olivier Lugon, "The Old Bridge, the Historian, and the New Photographer," in *Moholy-Nagy: Future Present*, eds. Matthew S. Witkovsky, Carol S. Eliel, and Karole P. B. Vail (New Haven / New York, 2016), 105–116.

24 Henri Danjou, "La porte du monde: Marseille," *VU* 2, no. 56 (1929), 276–278.

25 Pierre Mac Orlan, *Germaine Krull. Paris* (Paris, 1931) (Photographes Nouveaux), 55–56. – See also Germaine Krull (photos) and André Suarès (text), Marseille (Paris, 1935). – See also Sichel 1999 und Frizot 2015 (both note 9).

26 "Pont Transbordeur in Marseille. Fotos von Alex Strasser," *Die Form* 4, 1929, no. 23 (Dec. 1, 1929), 631–633.

27 Andreas Haus, "Charpente de la nouvelle vision. László Moholy-Nagy, Si[e]gfried Giedion et le pont transbordeur," in exh. cat. *Le Pont Transbordeur et la Vision Moderniste* (Marseille, 1991), 44–60. – Krisztina Passuth, "Moholy-Nagy. Marseille, Vieux-Port, 1929," in ibid., 63–71. – Bernard Millet, "Le pont transbordeur et la vision moderniste," in ibid., 73–82 (a photo by Block is on page 124).

28 Kathrin Simons, "Die Photographie der Avantgarde und Marseille: Der Pont Transbordeur," in exh. cat. *Im Licht des Südens. Marseille zu Gast* (Hamburg, 2006), 27–34. – Carolin Quermann, "Der Pont Transbordeur im Blick der Photographen," in ibid., 101–104 (illustrations thru 131; a photo by Block is on page 155); quotation, 133.

29 See Kenneth E. Silver, *Making Paradise. Art, Modernity, and the Myth of the French Riviera* (Cambridge, MA/London, 2001).

30 Fritz Block, "Neue Baukunst in Frankreich (Haus am Mittelmeer, Kap Martin, Roquebrune. Architekten: Eileen Gray und *Jean Badovici)," Zentralblatt der Bauverwaltung / Zeitschrift für Bauwesen* 51 (81), no. 25 (1931), 353–364.

31 *Berliner Illustrirte Zeitung* 38, no. 29 (July 21, 1929). – *Martin Munkacsi,* ed. F.C. Gundlach (Göttingen, 2006) 76–77. – *Die Erfindung der Pressefotografie aus der Sammlung Ullstein 1894–1945*, eds. Stiftung Deutsches Historisches Museum und ullstein bild / Axel Springer Syndication GmbH (Berlin, 2017), 123.

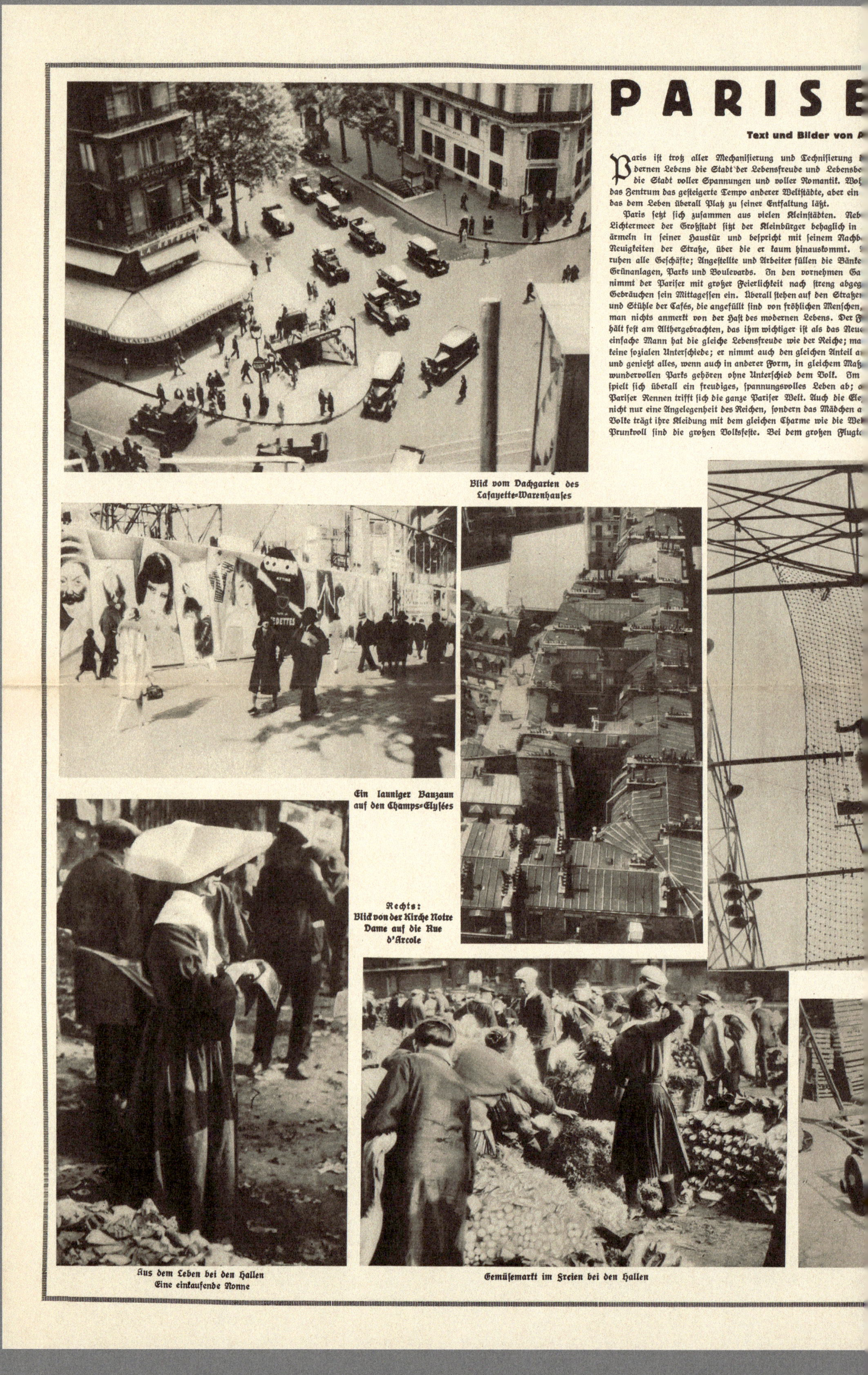

PARISE

Text und Bilder von A

Paris ist trotz aller Mechanisierung und Technisierung
dernen Lebens die Stadt der Lebensfreude und Lebensbe
die Stadt voller Spannungen und voller Romantik. Wo
das Zentrum das gesteigerte Tempo anderer Weltstädte, aber ein
das dem Leben überall Platz zu seiner Entfaltung läßt.

Paris setzt sich zusammen aus vielen Kleinstädten. Neb
Lichtermeer der Großstadt sitzt der Kleinbürger behaglich in
ärmeln in seiner Haustür und bespricht mit seinem Nachb
Neuigkeiten der Straße, über die er kaum hinauskommt.
ruhen alle Geschäfte; Angestellte und Arbeiter füllen die Bänke
Grünanlagen, Parks und Boulevards. In den vornehmen Ga
nimmt der Pariser mit großer Feierlichkeit nach streng abgeg
Gebräuchen sein Mittagessen ein. Überall stehen auf den Straße
und Stühle der Cafés, die angefüllt sind von fröhlichen Menschen,
man nichts anmerkt von der Hast des modernen Lebens. Der F
hält fest am Althergebrachten, das ihm wichtiger ist als das Neu
einfache Mann hat die gleiche Lebensfreude wie der Reiche; ma
keine sozialen Unterschiede; er nimmt auch den gleichen Anteil a
und genießt alles, wenn auch in anderer Form, in gleichem Maß
wundervollen Parks gehören ohne Unterschied dem Volk. Im
spielt sich überall ein freudiges, spannungsvolles Leben ab;
Pariser Rennen trifft sich die ganze Pariser Welt. Auch die Ele
nicht nur eine Angelegenheit des Reichen, sondern das Mädchen a
Volke trägt ihre Kleidung mit dem gleichen Charme wie die We
Prunkvoll sind die großen Volksfeste. Bei dem großen Flugt

Blick vom Dachgarten des Lafayette-Warenhauses

Ein launiger Bauzaun auf den Champs-Elysées

Rechts: Blick von der Kirche Notre Dame auf die Rue d'Arcole

Aus dem Leben bei den Hallen
Eine einkaufende Nonne

Gemüsemarkt im Freien bei den Hallen

"Life in Paris" (*Hamburger Anzeiger. Illustrierte Wochenbeilage*, no. 35, 1930)

LEBEN

r. Block, Hamburg

einige Bilder bringe, stiegen 300 Flieger zugleich auf. Die
sten Akrobatenstücke wurden ausgeführt; Flugzeuge aller
n waren zu sehen, und zum Schluß ritten 200 afrikanische Spahis
an eigens dafür aus den Kolonien hatte kommen lassen — bei
itergang eine glanzvolle Fantasia arabe. Dreihunderttausend
hatte dieses Volksfest nach der Vorstadt Vincennes gelockt.
ist auch das Leben im Bois de Boulogne, dem großen
wo für Unterhaltungen aller Art gesorgt ist. Ich bringe
ssantes Bild von einem Freiluftzirkus, der dort täglich seine
gen gibt.
ebenskraft dieser Stadt ist unverwüstlich und unverändert.
ge, was vielleicht Paris etwas von seinen Reizen und seiner
ichkeit nehmen könnte, ist der starke Einfluß des Fremden-
besonders des amerikanischen, dem in mancher Beziehung
nisse gemacht werden, die dem Ruf der Stadt nicht be-
ünstig sind; aber die Stätten, wo dies der Fall ist, meidet
er ängstlich. Auch der Fremde, der wirklich das Pariser Leben
nen und sich an ihm erfreuen will, wird ihnen fernbleiben,
wirkliche volle Leben ist nicht dort, wo man Fremden wider-
as bietet, was Paris niemals gehabt hat, was sie aber unter
tänden sehen wollen, sondern das lebendige Paris findet der
uf den Straßen und Plätzen, auf den großen Boulevards genau
den engsten Nebenstraßen, das findet er am frühen Morgen
Hallen, in den Cafés und Gaststätten mit echtem Pariser
in den Parks und auf den großen Volksfesten.

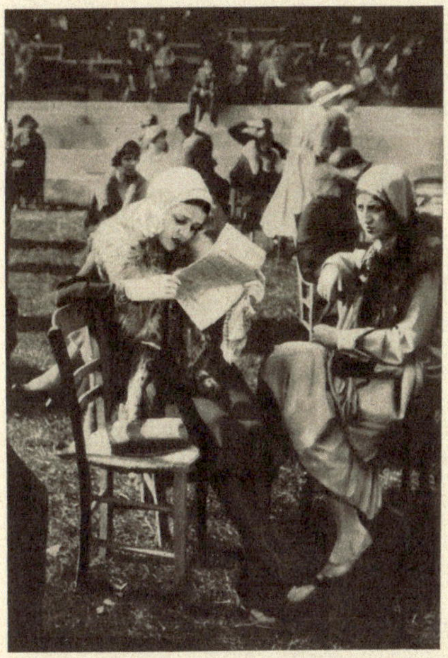

Auf dem Rennen

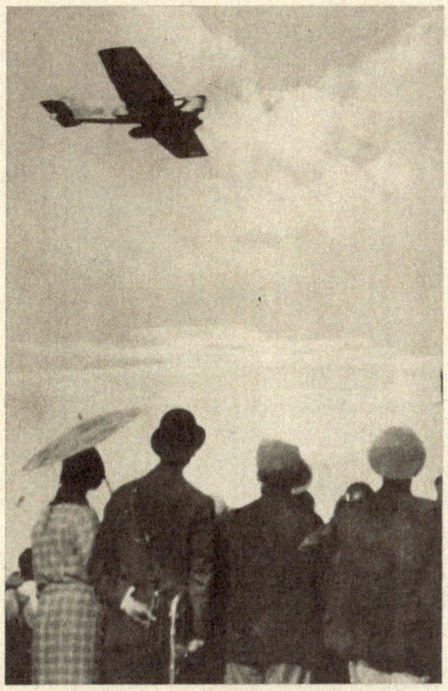

Flugtag

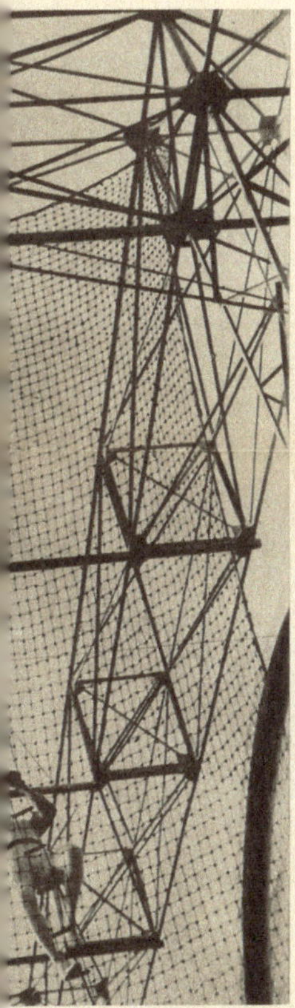

reien

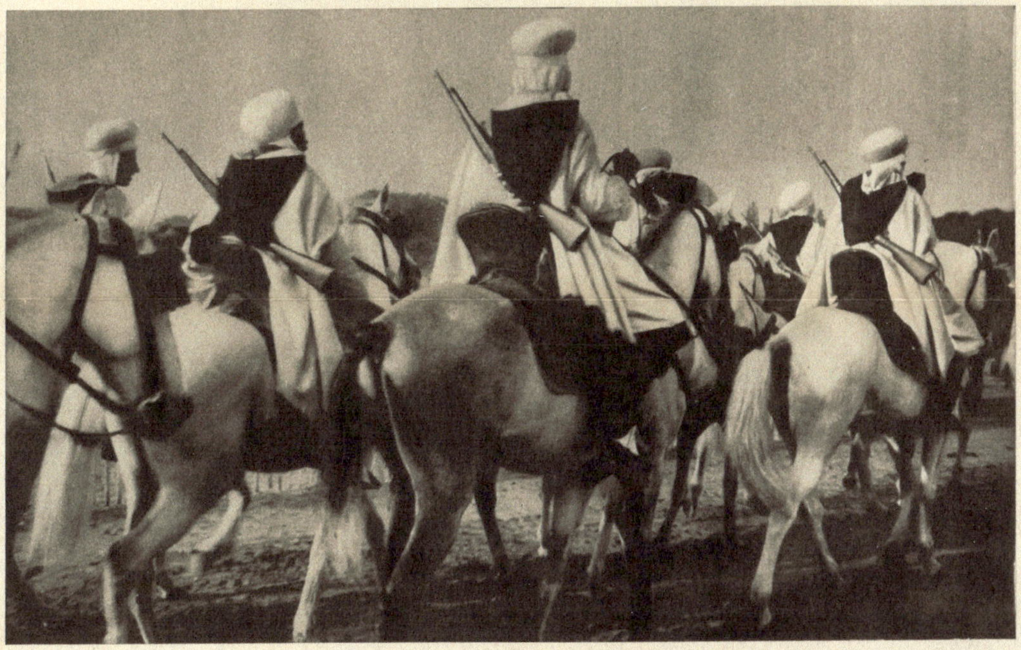

Auf dem Flugplatz von Vincennes reiten afrikanische Spahis eine Fantasia arabe

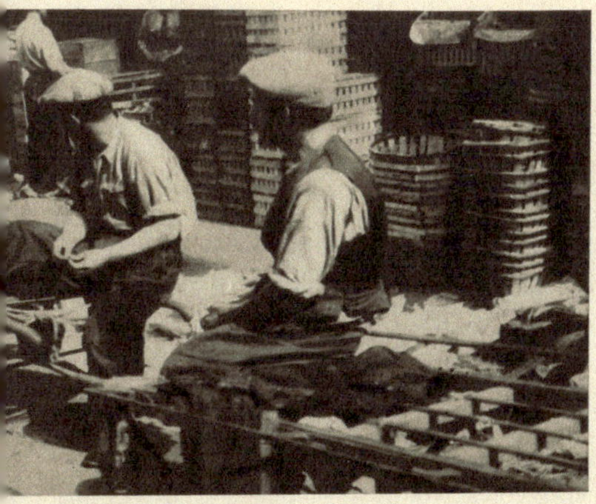

Frühmorgens vor den Hallen

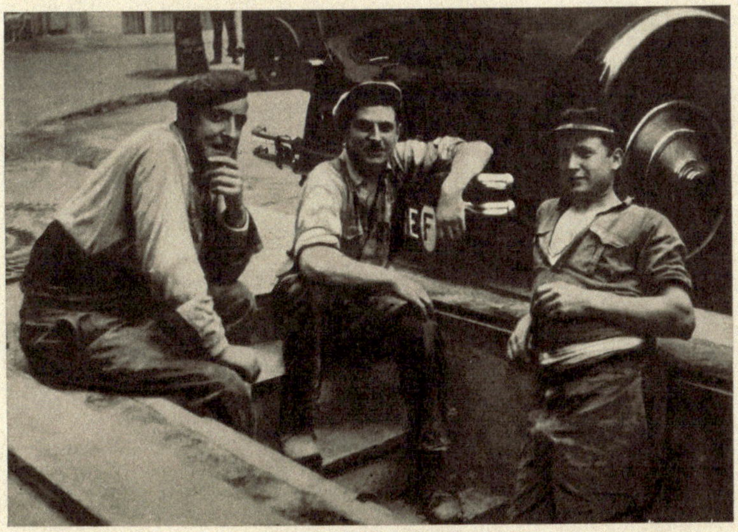

Paris, die Stadt der Gegensätze
Arbeiter während einer Pause vor der Madeleine

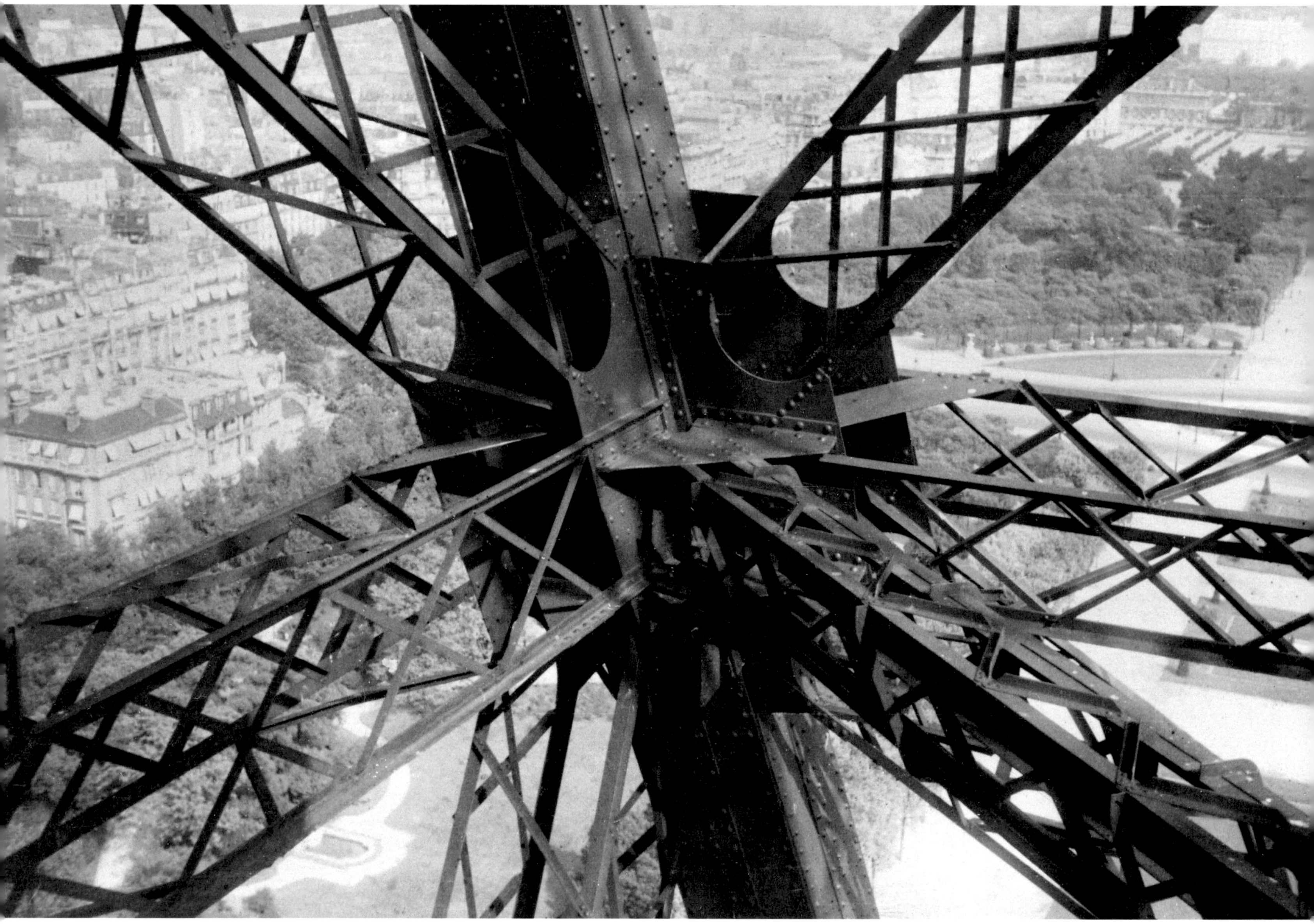

Construction detail of the Eiffel Tower, Paris, 1930

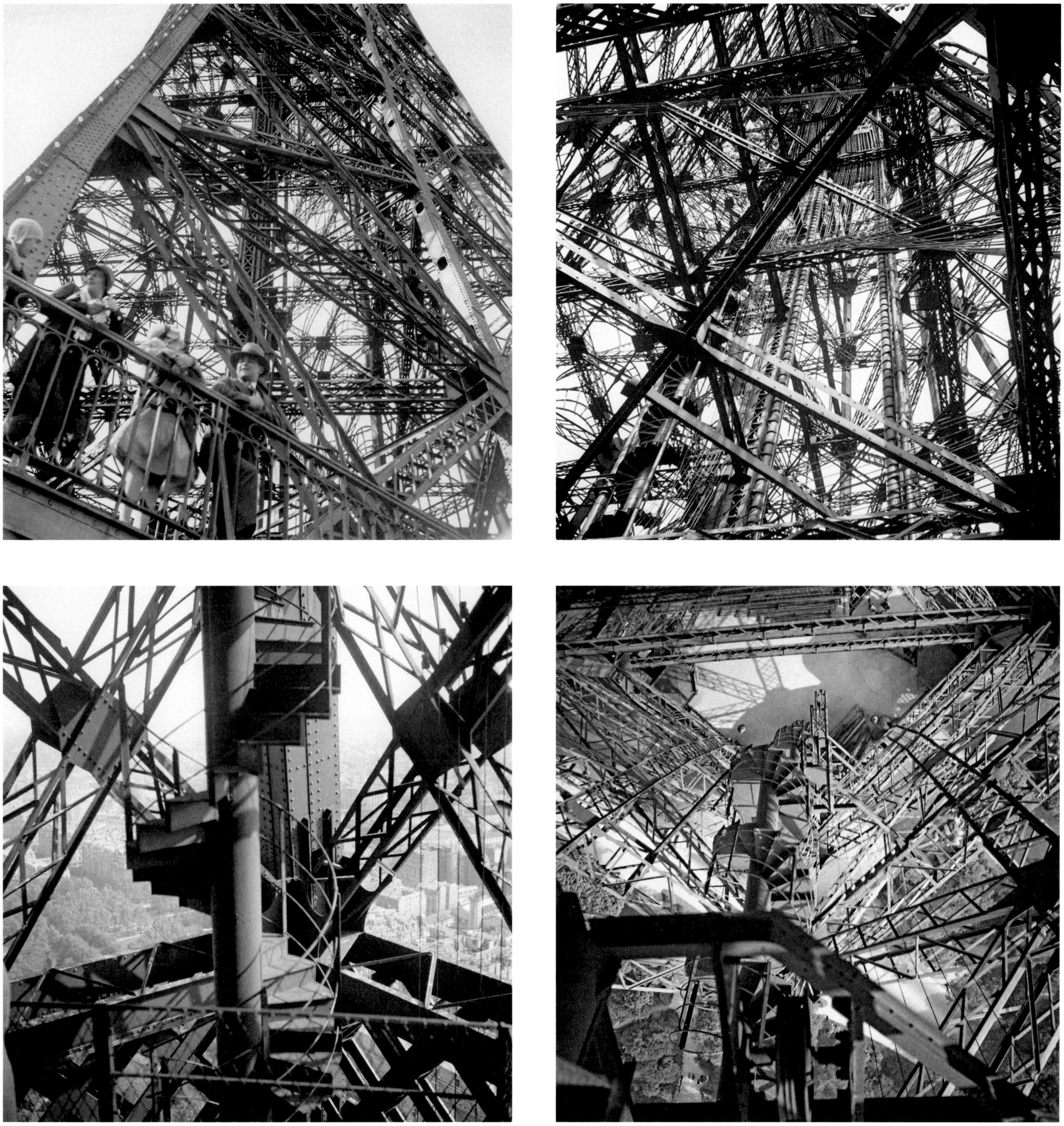

Construction details of the Eiffel Tower, Paris, 1930

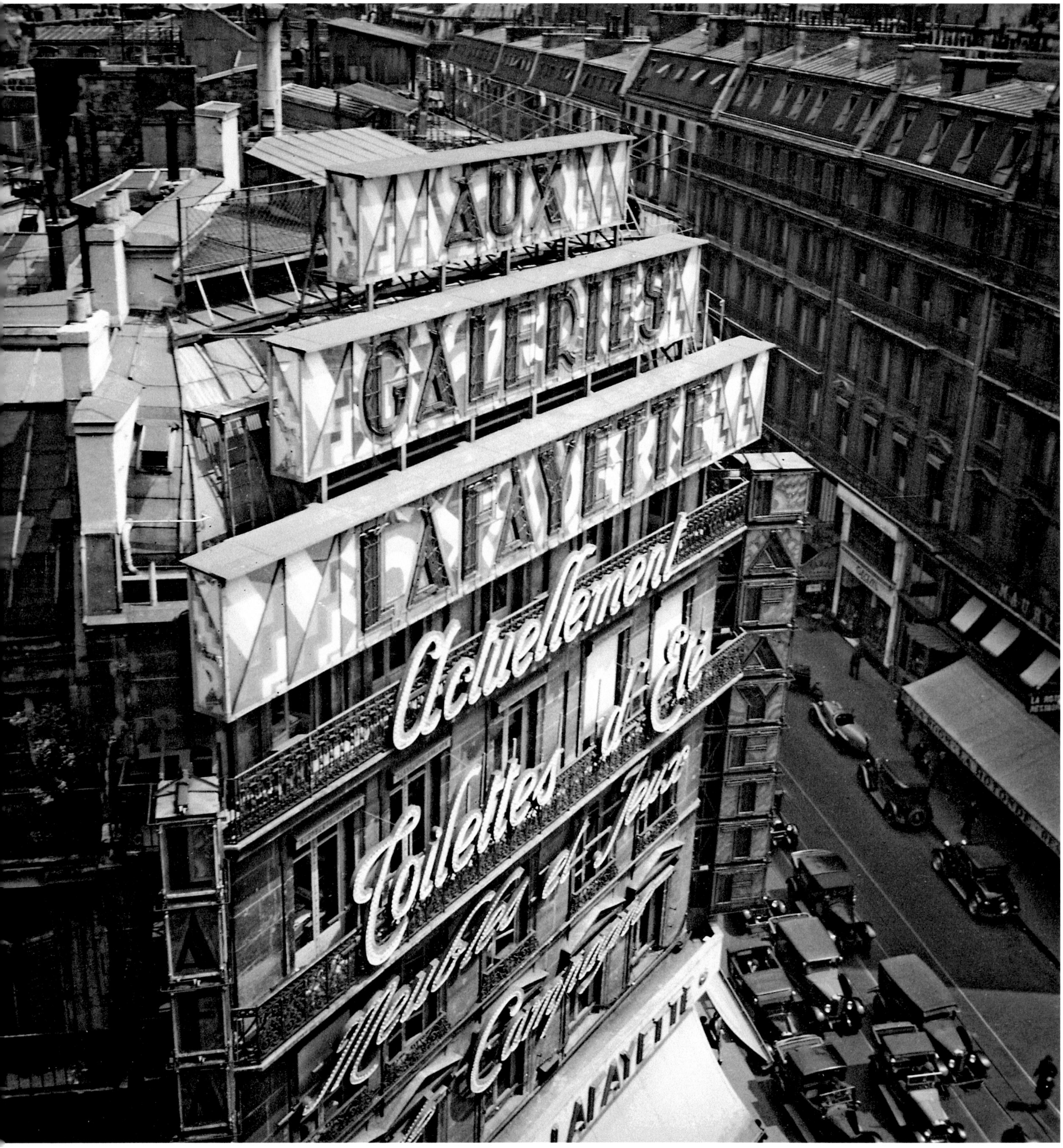

Façade lettering on the Galeries Lafayette department store, Paris, 1930

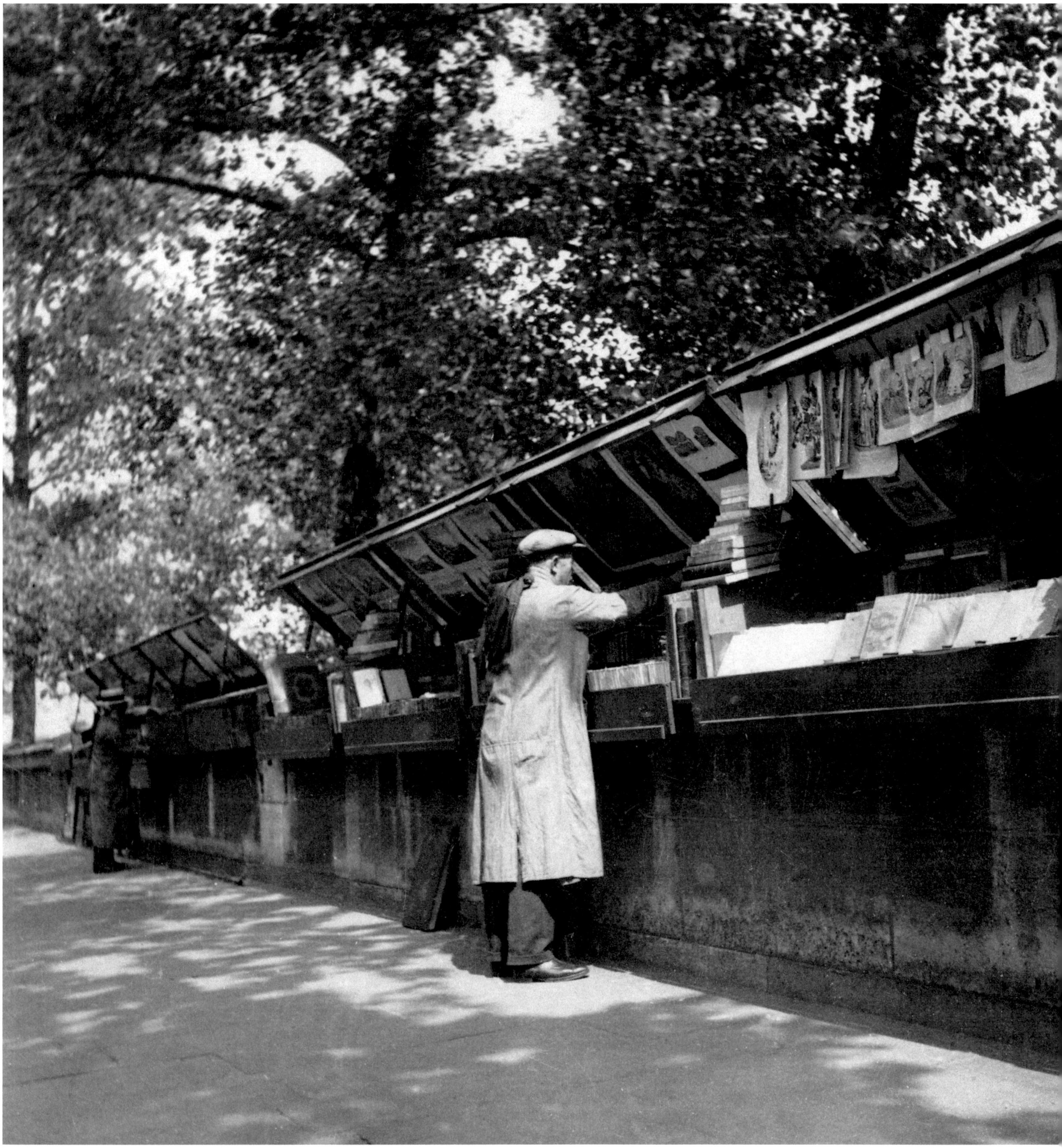

Bouquinistes along the banks of the river Seine, Paris, 1930

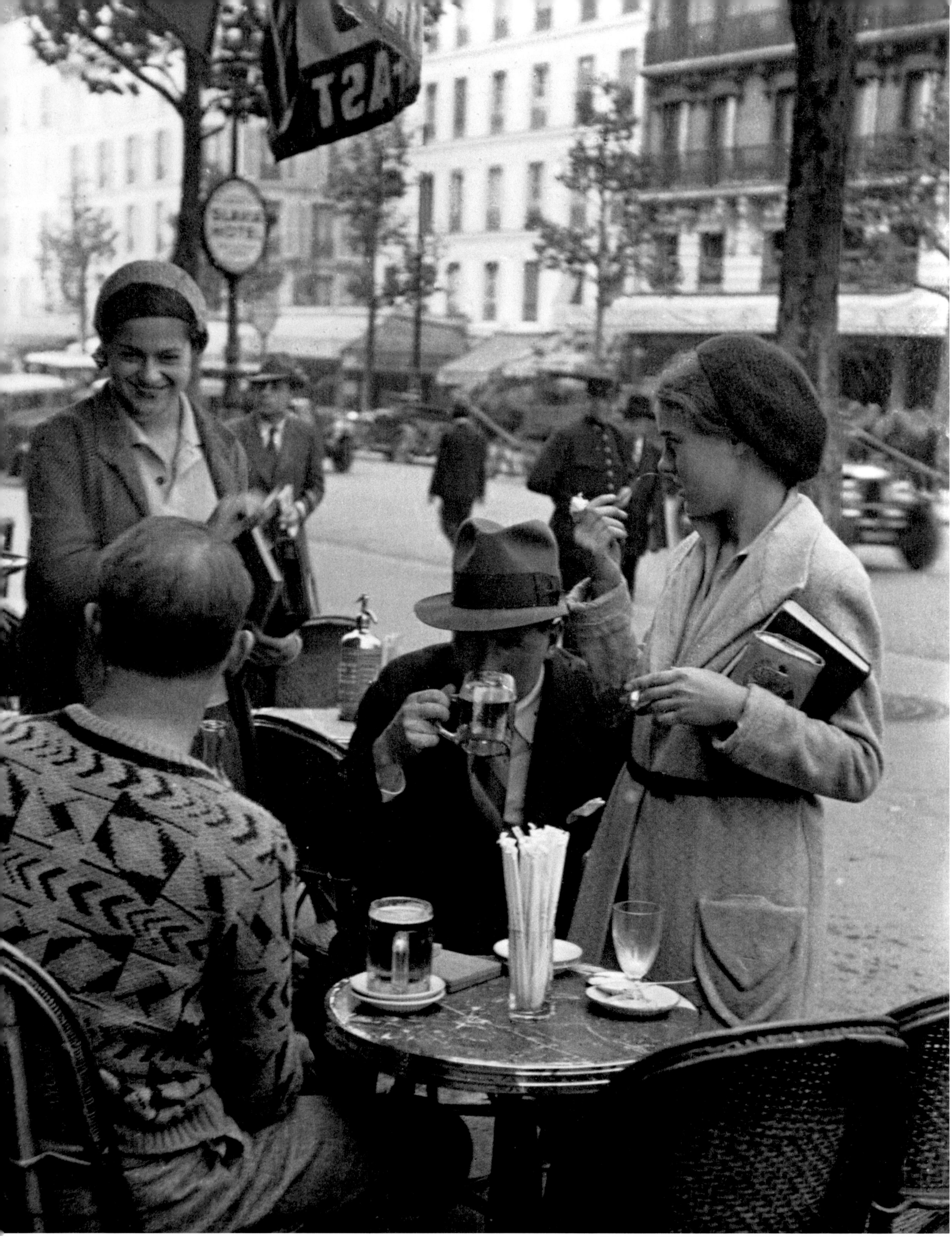
AST

At Boulevard cafés, Paris, 1930

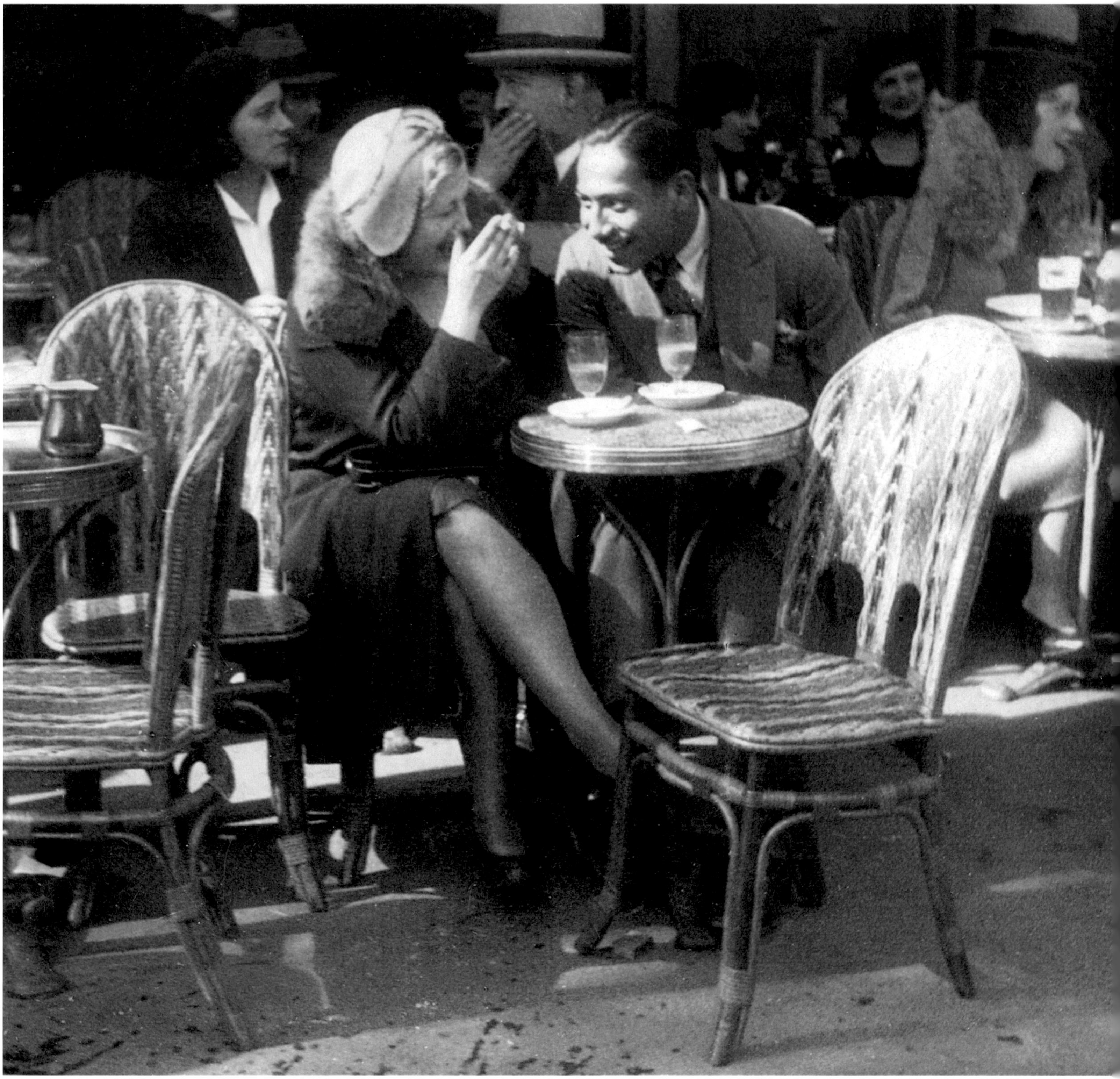

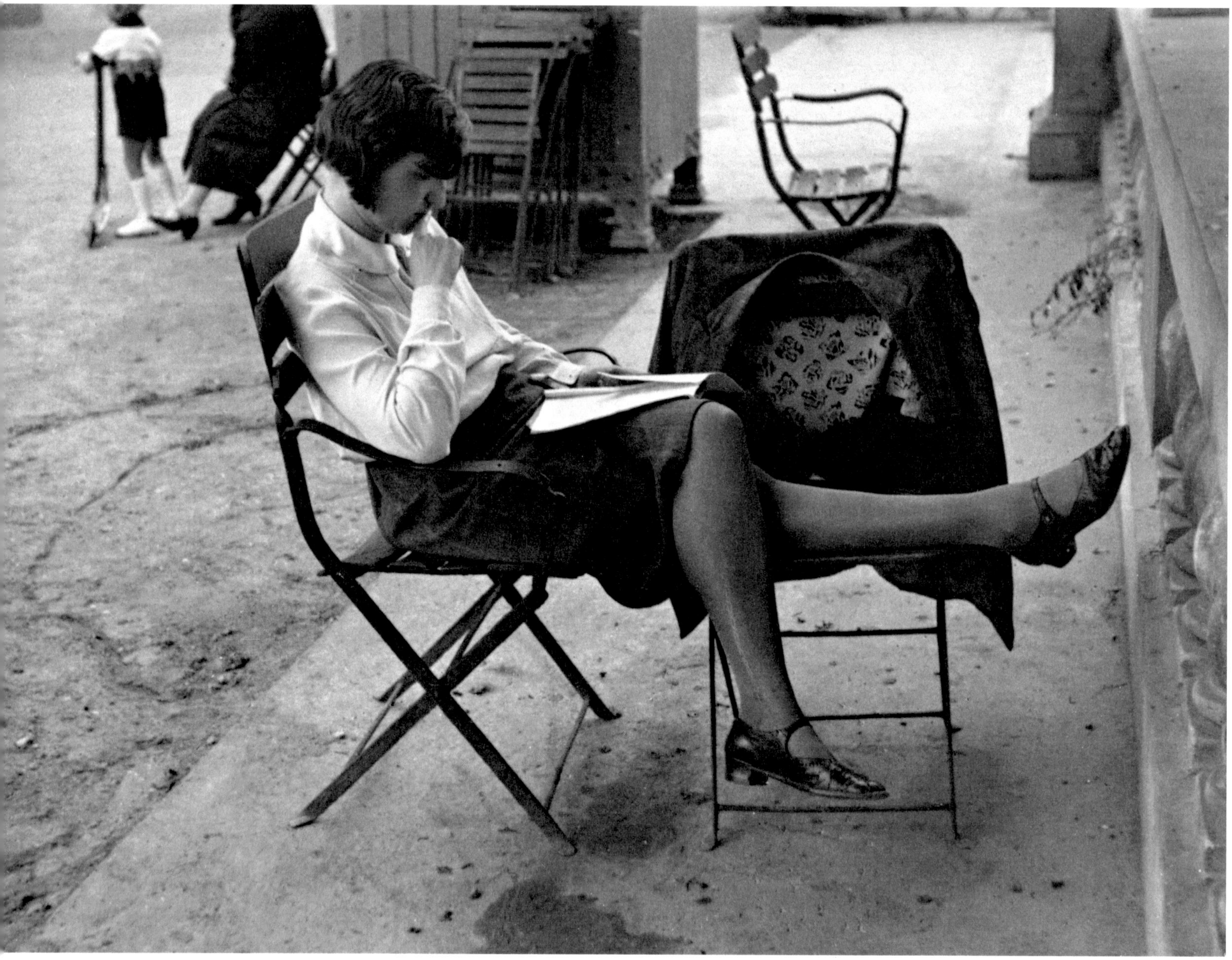

Student at the Jardin du Luxembourg, Paris, 1930

12 Uhr mittag in Paris

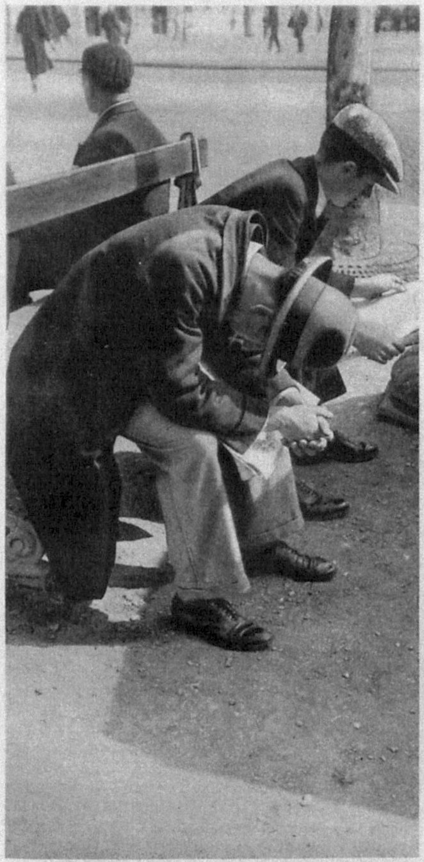

So bürgerlich hatten Sie sich Paris wohl nicht vorgestellt: Zeitung und ein Nickerchen.

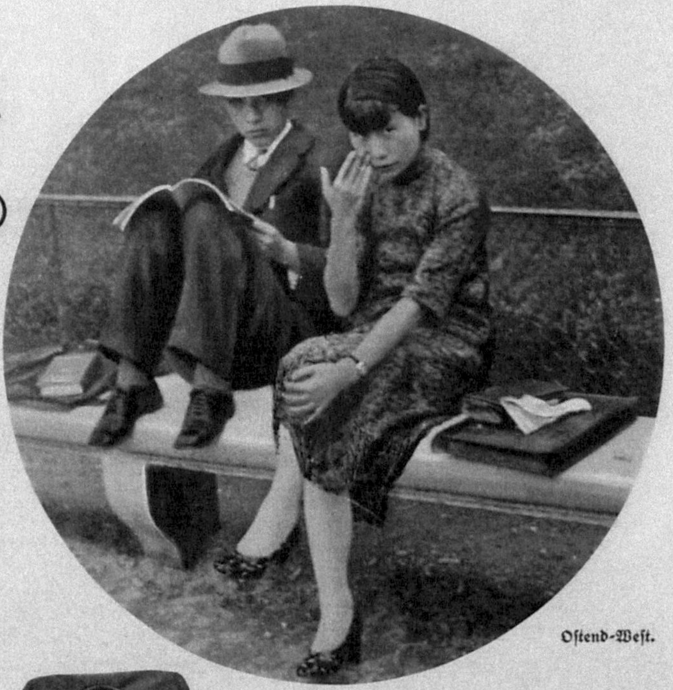

Ostend-West.

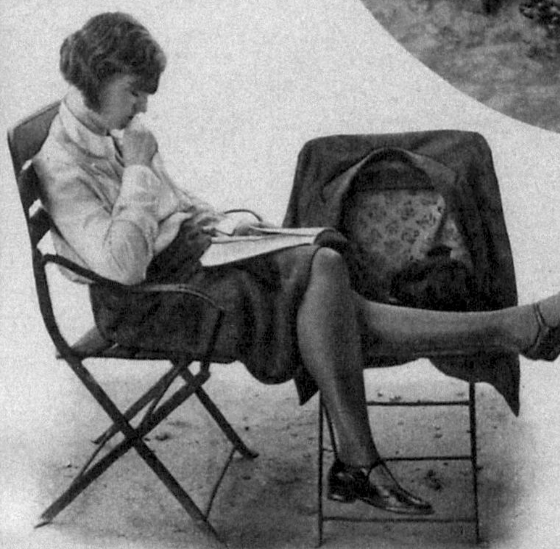

Man muß es sich bequem im Leben machen.

Gnädige Frau, seien Sie ehrlich! Haben Sie sich so Paris vorgestellt? Paris, die vornehmste unter den vornehmen Städten..., die Stadt der Freude, des Luxus, des Lichtes! Anmutiges Band der Seine, überspannt von vielen zierlichen Brücken, Parks mit dunklen, tausendjährigen, rauschenden Bäumen, Villenvororte, Boulevards, überall reiche, glückliche, sorgenfreie Menschen..., das ist Paris — das Trugbild von Paris, wie man es sich so gerne vorstellt... Ja, dieses Paris lebt nur in der Phantasie des allzu wirklichkeitsfernen Schwärmers. — Auch Paris hat seine Sorgen. Auch in Paris mußt du arbeiten, viel arbeiten, wenn du leben willst. Die fragwürdige „Romantik" der Boheme begeistert gewiß den Künstler nicht zu edlem Schaffen, wenn der Hunger in seinen Eingeweiden wühlt und kein Sou in der Tasche mehr vorhanden ist, mit dessen Hilfe er seinen brennenden Durst stillen könnte... — Zwölf Uhr mittags in Paris! Die jungen Arbeiter und Arbeiterinnen, die da die kurze Zeit der Mittagspause auf der Bank am Rande der Straße verbringen, haben gewiß nicht die Absicht, den Abend bei funkelndem Champagner in der Moulin-rouge zu durchschwärmen. Vielleicht sind sie froh, wenn das Verdiente ausreicht, um die Miete für das bescheidene Dachkämmerlein zu bezahlen, das man in einer wenig einladenden Straße des Armenviertels bewohnt! — Vielleicht sehnt sich der junge Student, der sich so freundlich mit seiner Kommilitonin aus dem Lande des Lächelns unterhält, nach einem bescheidenen Nebenverdienst, um sich ein dringend benötigtes Buch für die Vorlesung anschaffen zu können. Wer weiß? — Ob die jungen Mädchen die sichere Gewähr haben, daß das mühselige Werk ihrer Hände preiswert bezahlt wird? — Vielleicht täusche ich mich auch. Es ist möglich, daß es diesen jungen Menschen einigermaßen erträglich, ja sogar gut geht. Eines jedoch ist sicher: So glänzend geht es auch in Paris dem jungen Menschen von heute nicht, daß er sich auch nur einen Bruchteil jener kostspieligen Freuden leisten könnte, von denen wir Nichtpariser zu träumen versucht sind.

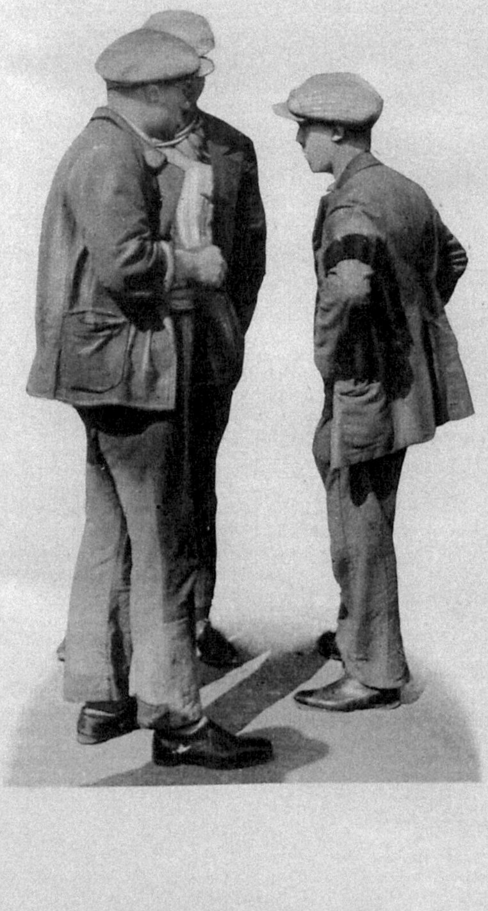

Bild links:

Pariser in typischer Arbeitskleidung zur Mittagszeit an irgend einem großen Boulevard.

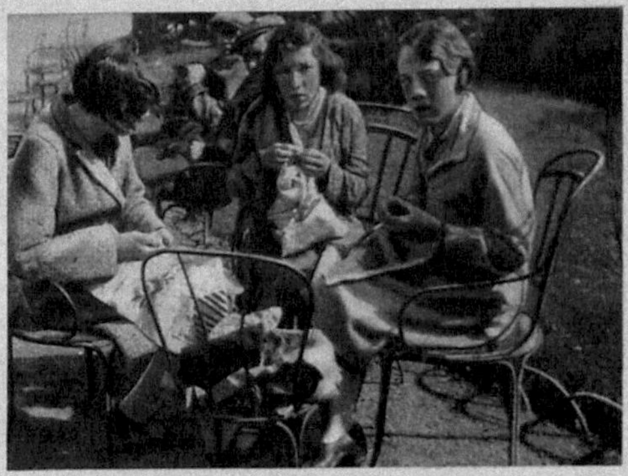

Häkeln und räkeln.

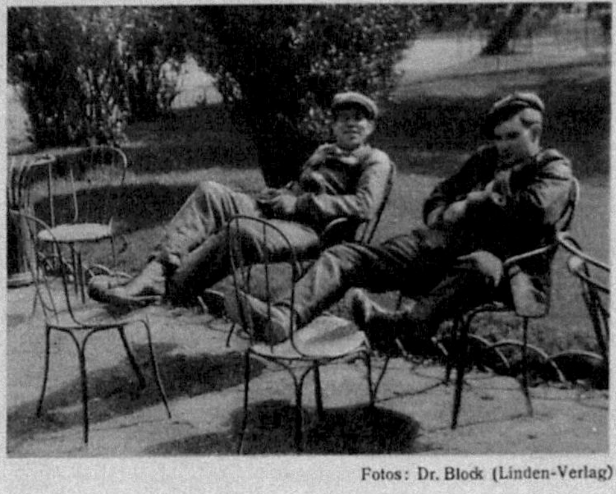

Angestellte und Arbeiter pflegen jede auf ihre Art der Ruhe.

Fotos: Dr. Block (Linden-Verlag)

"High Noon in Paris" (*Die Welt* 51, no. 29, 1931)

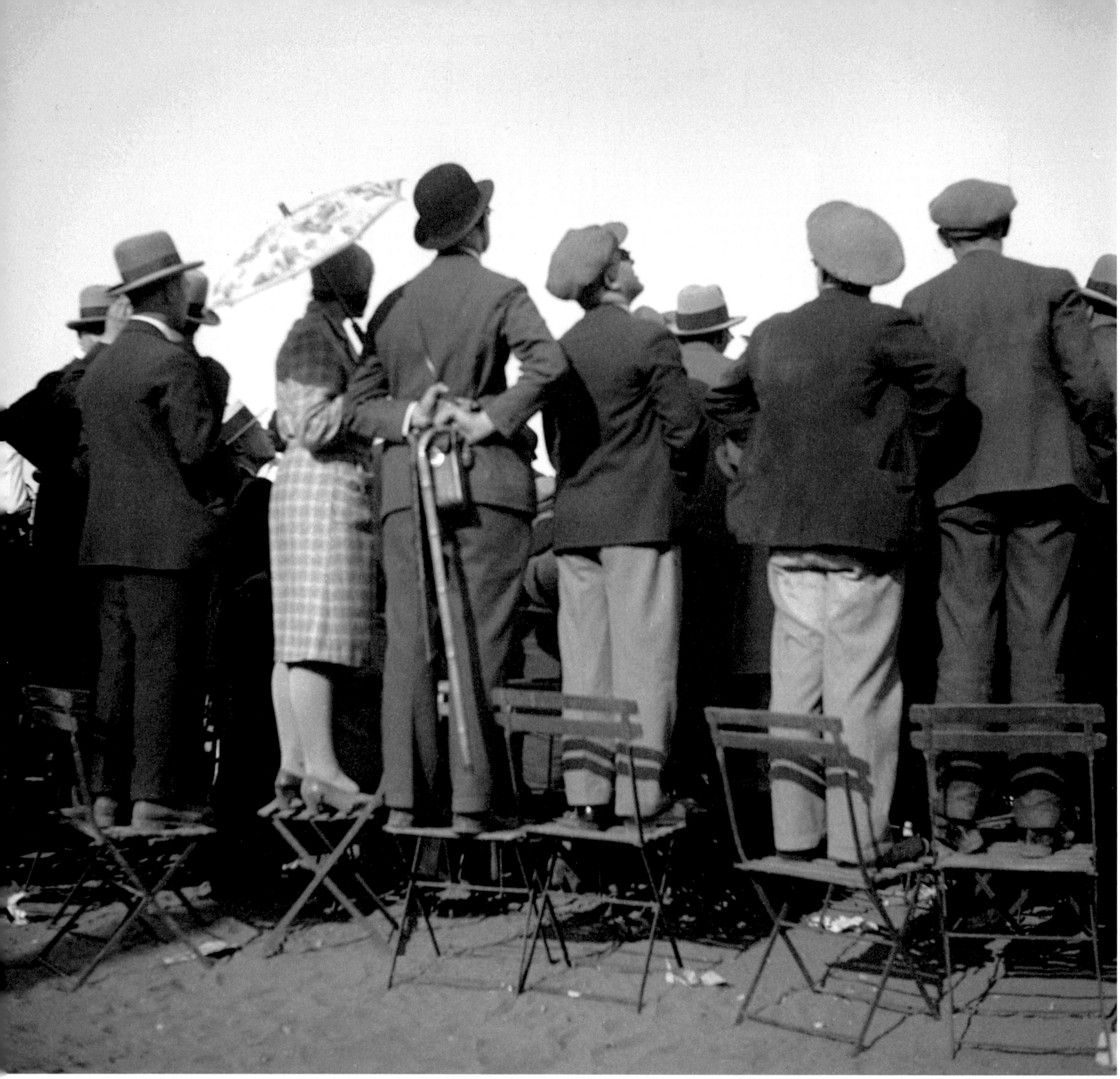

Spectators at a flight day, Vincennes near Paris, 1930

Boys at the pool of the Jardin du Luxembourg, Paris, 1930

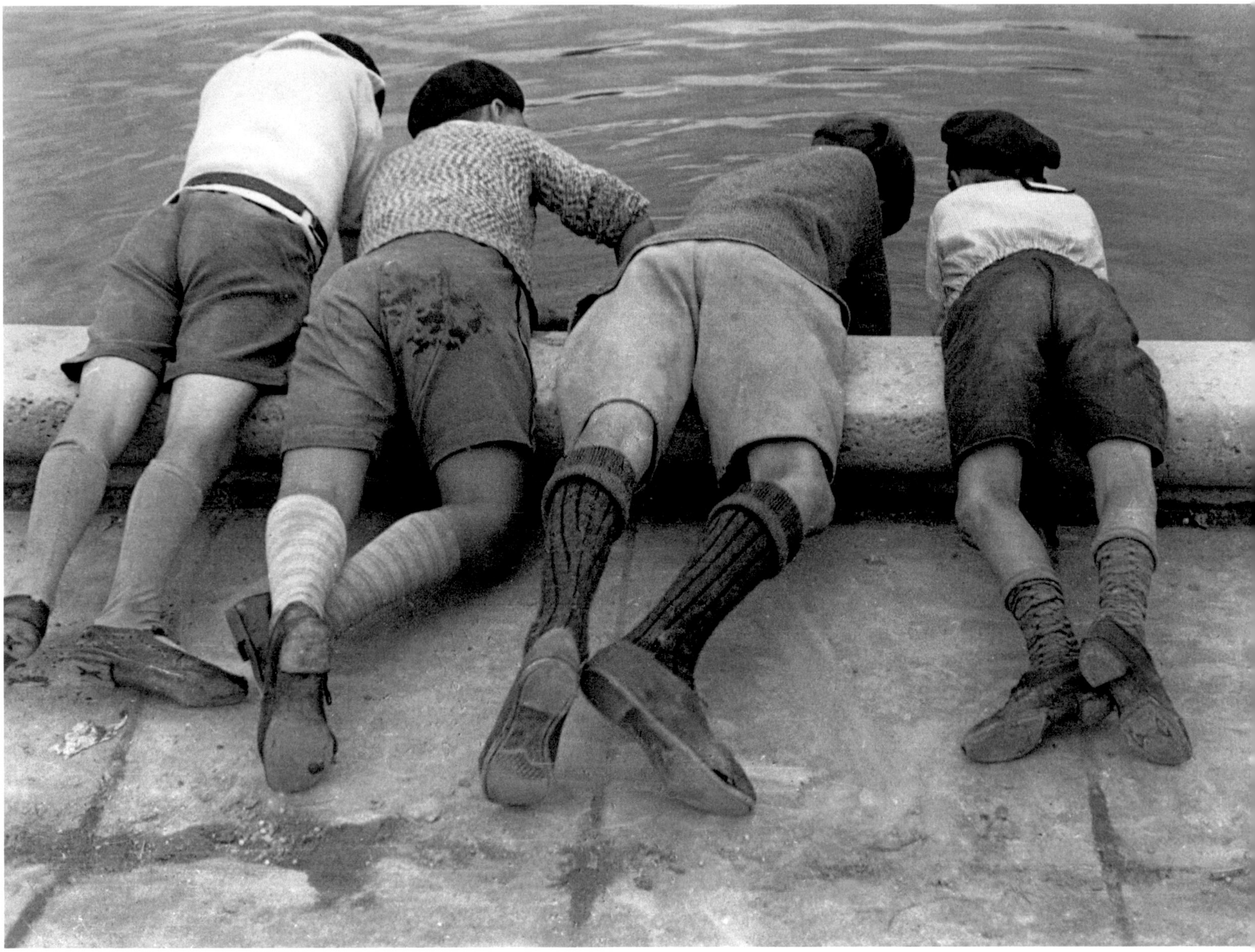

Construction work for a fair, Paris, 1930

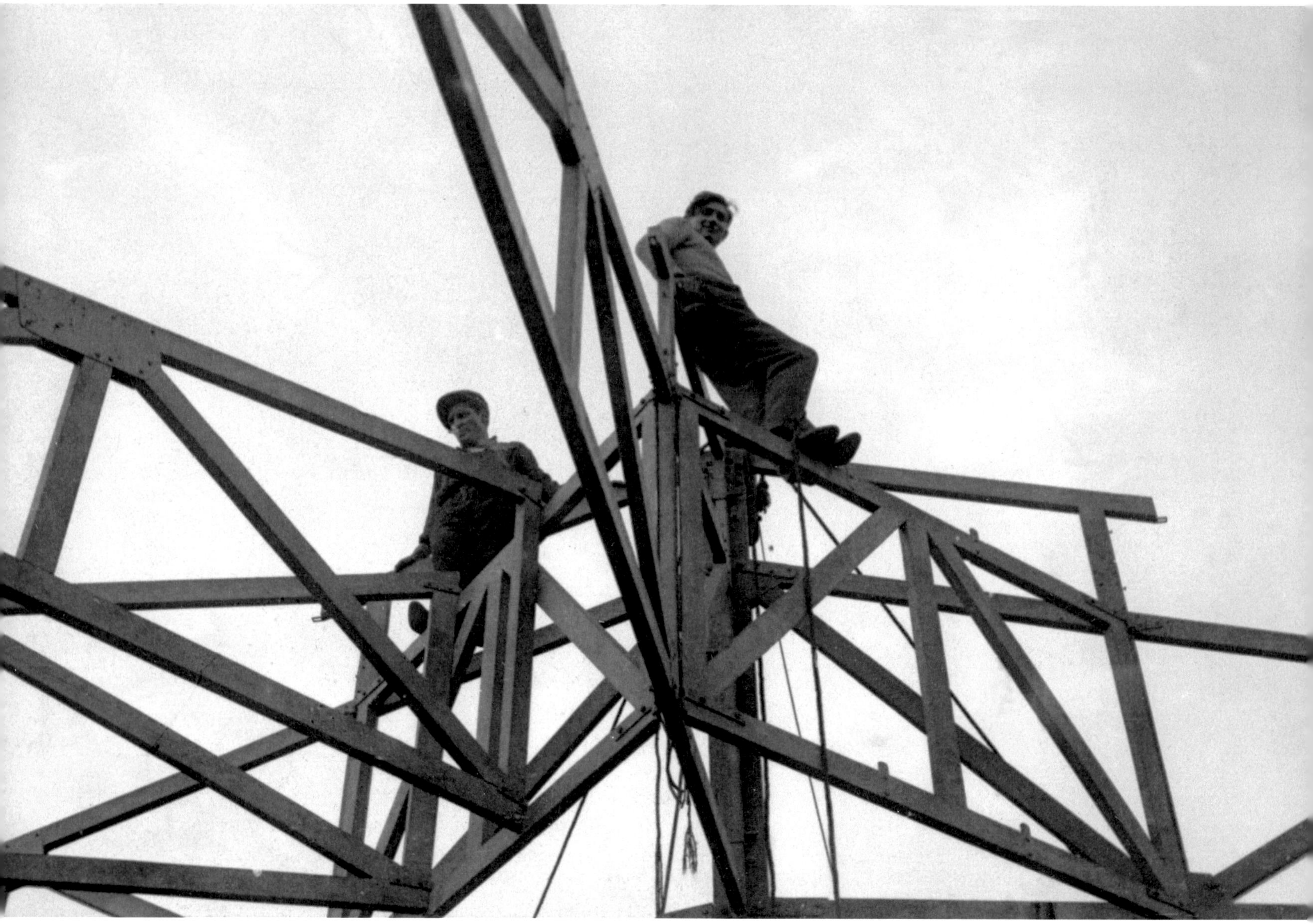

Aerialists of an open-air circus, Paris, 1930

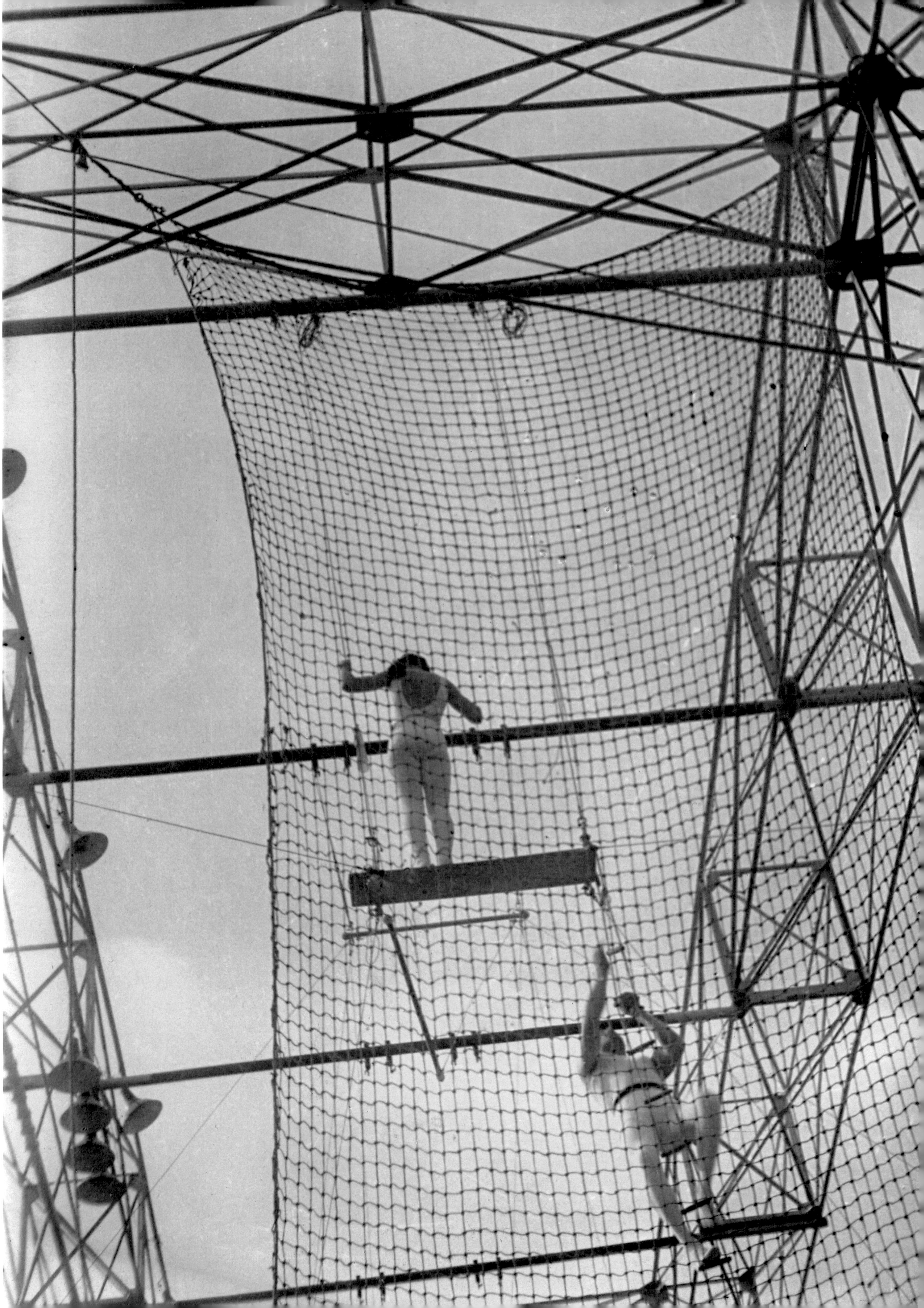

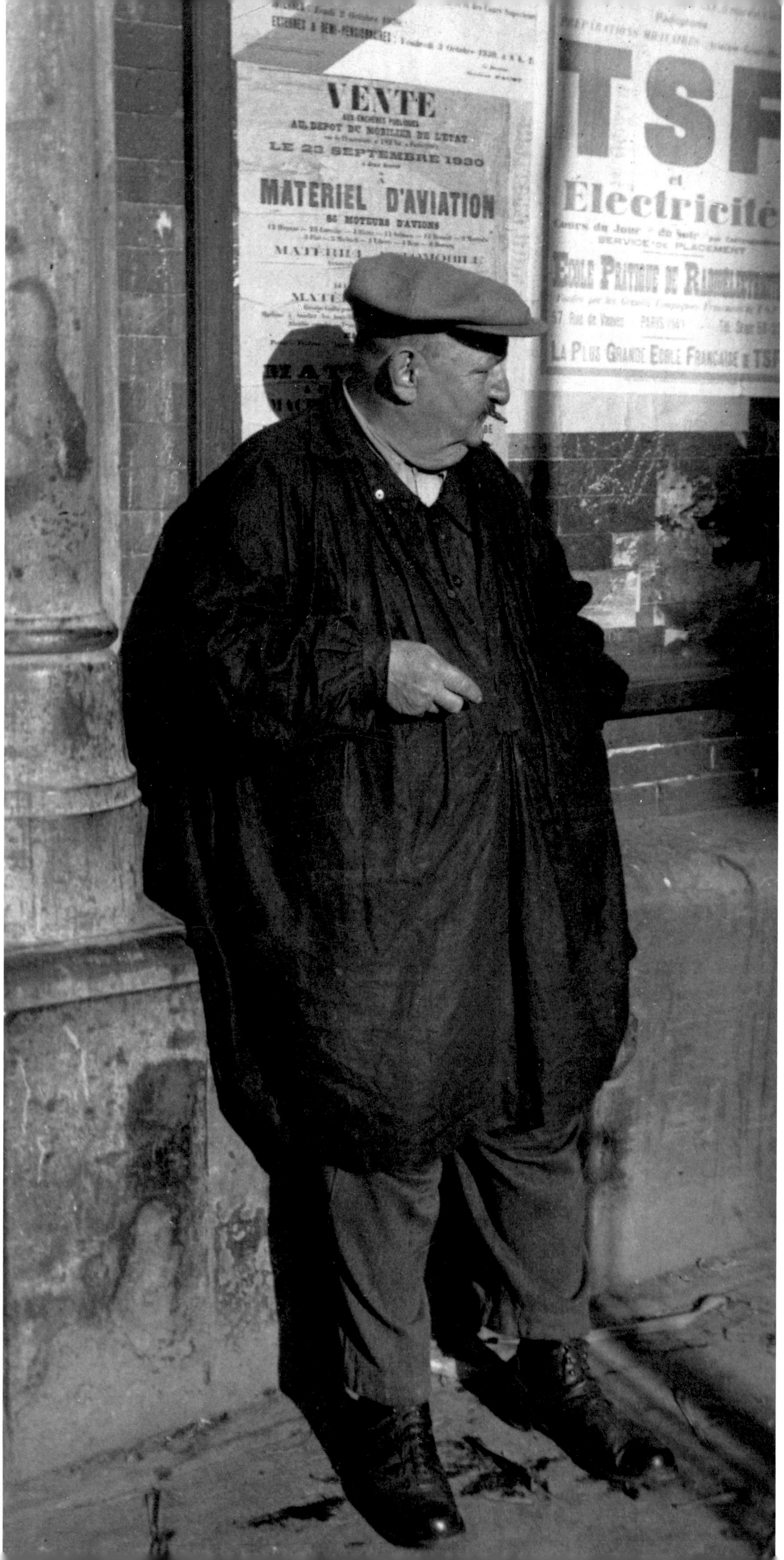

Figures of Les Halles
wholesale market,
Paris, 1930

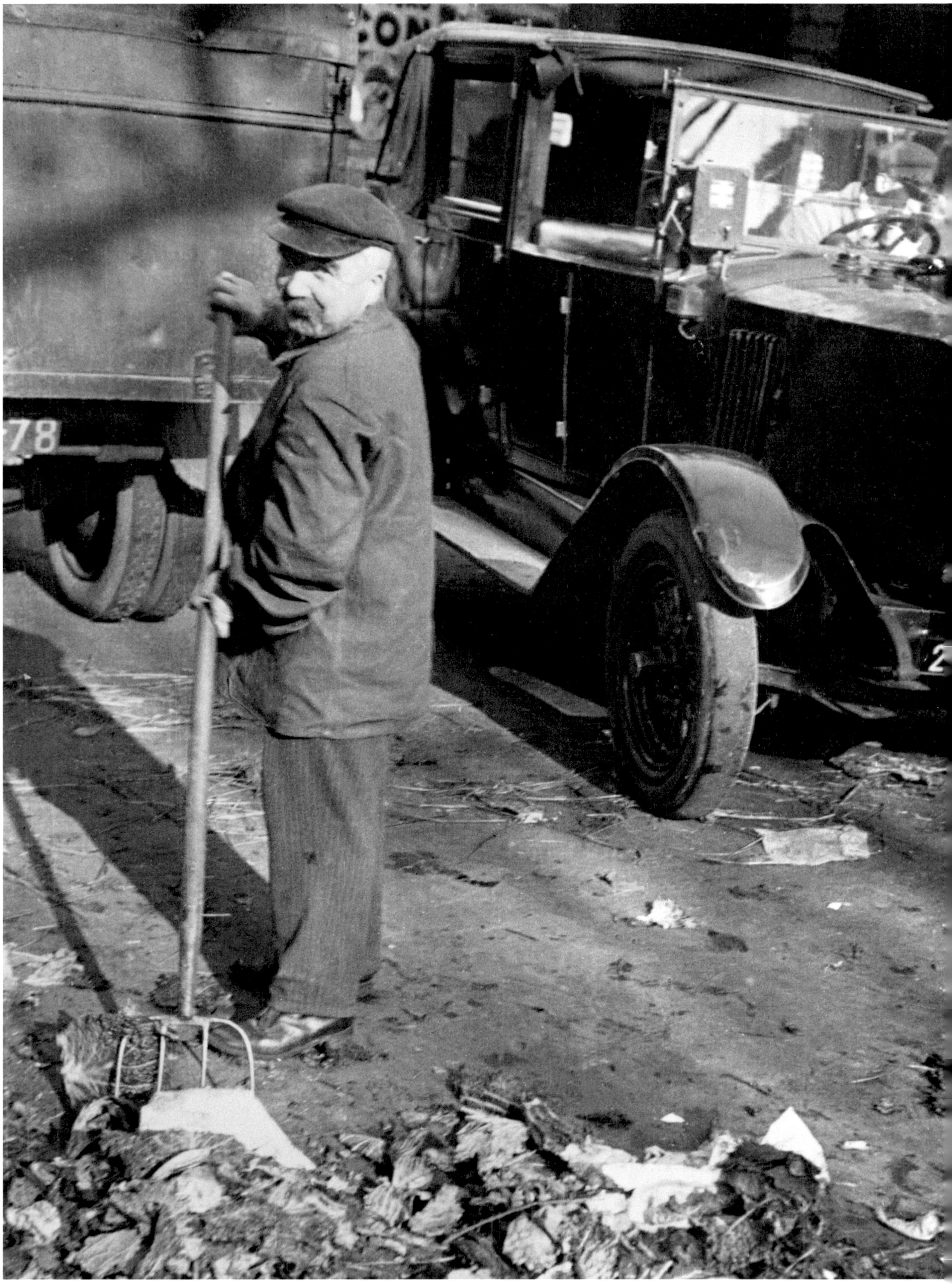

Merchandise containers at Les Halles wholesale market, Paris, 1930

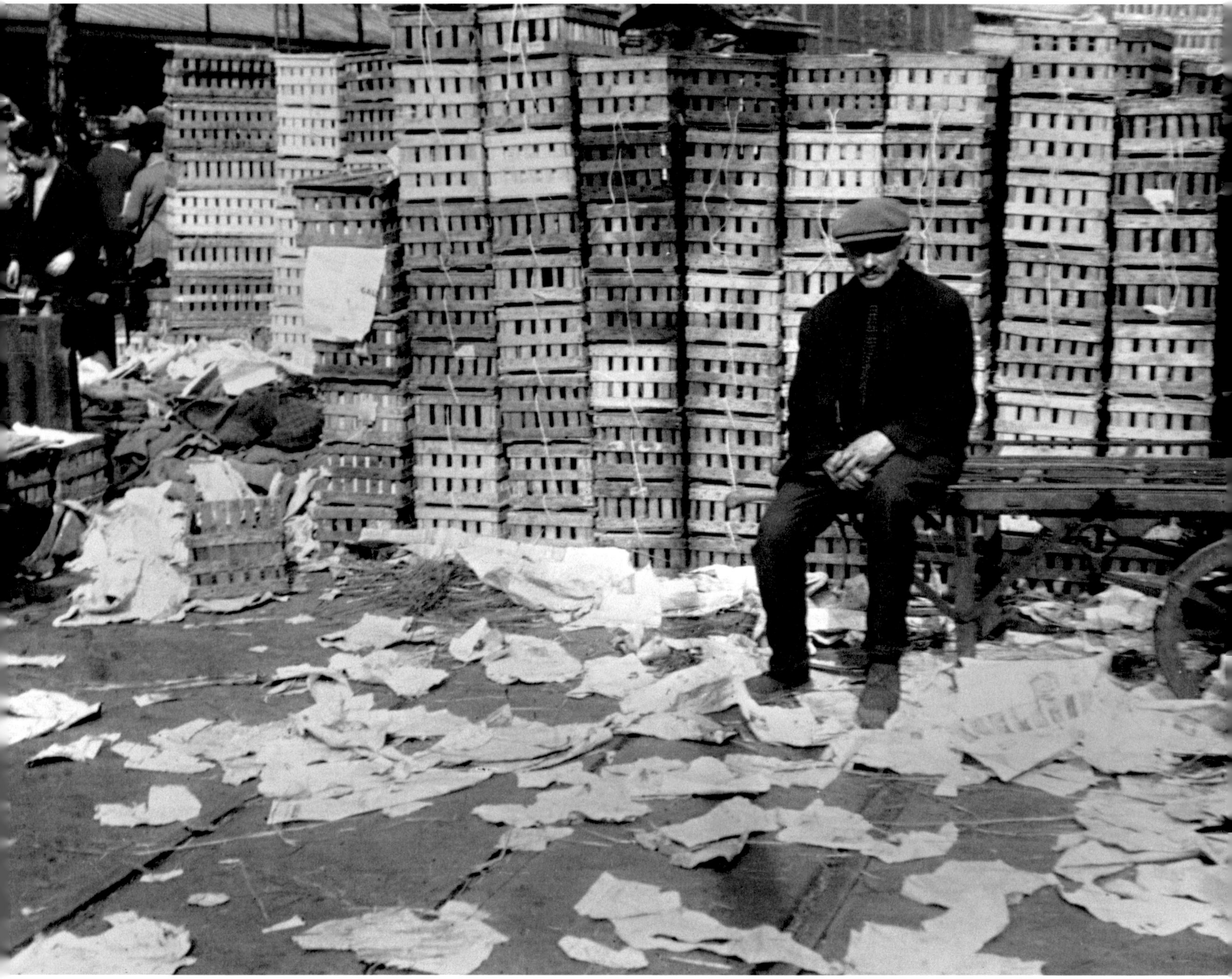

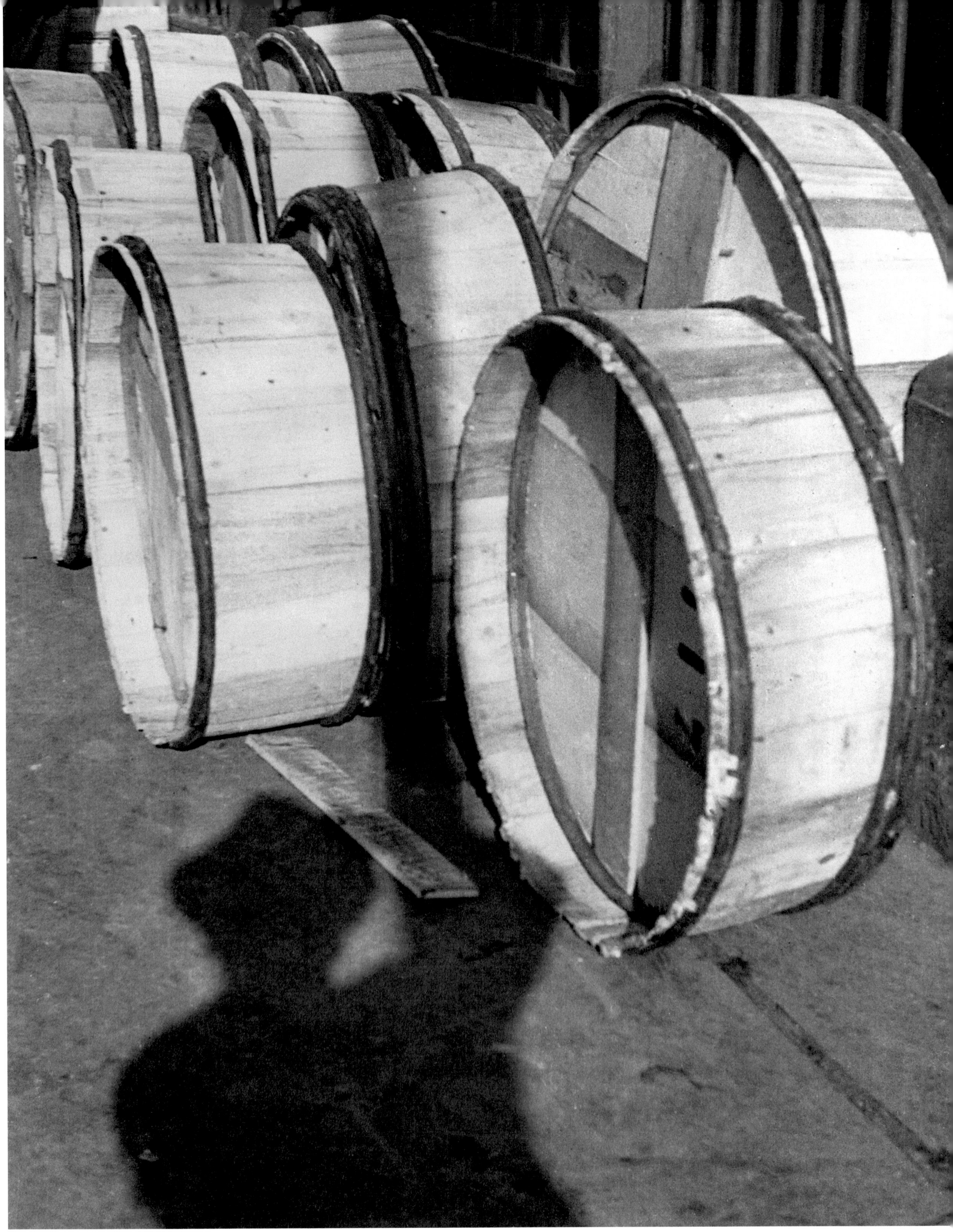

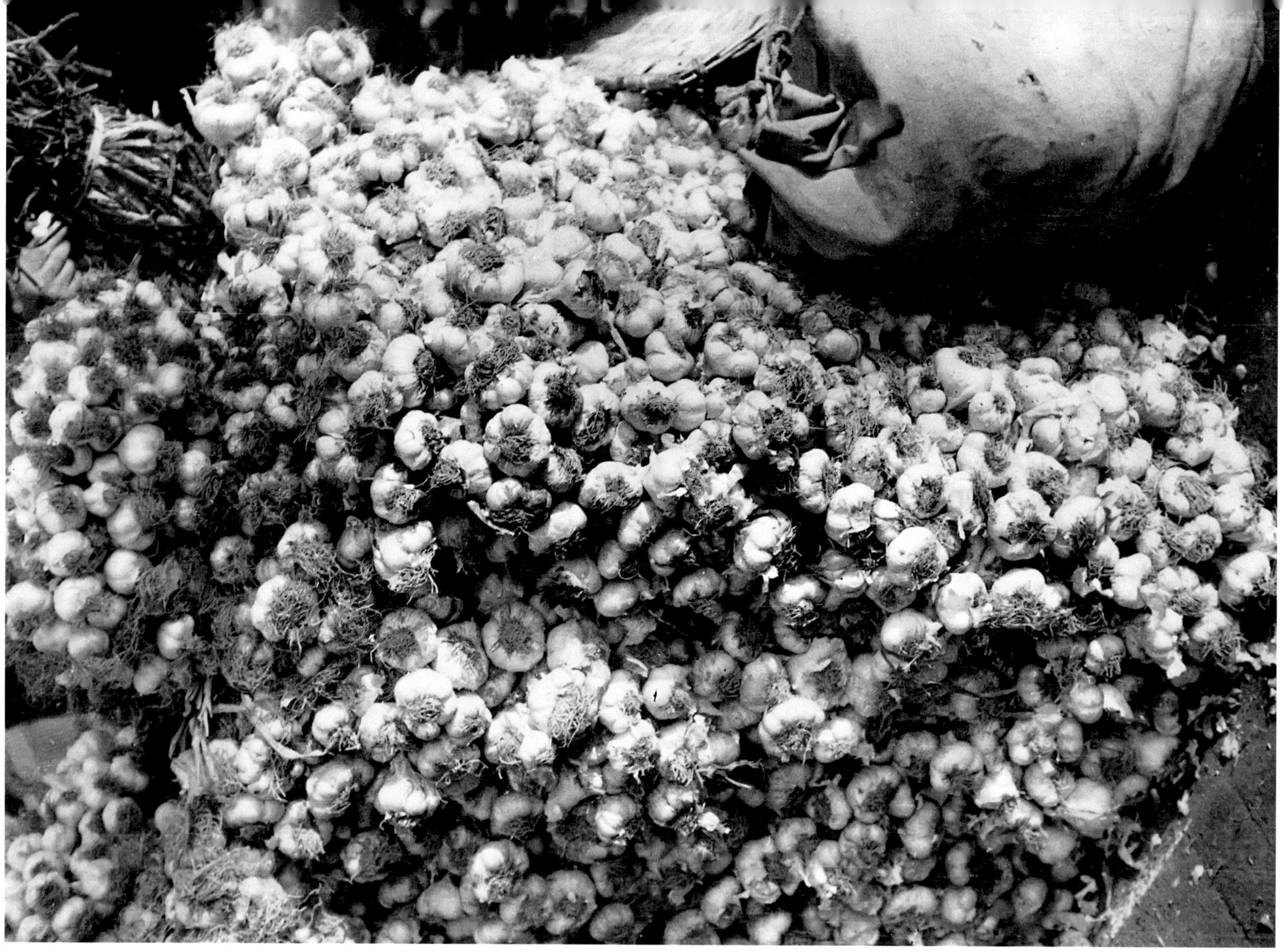

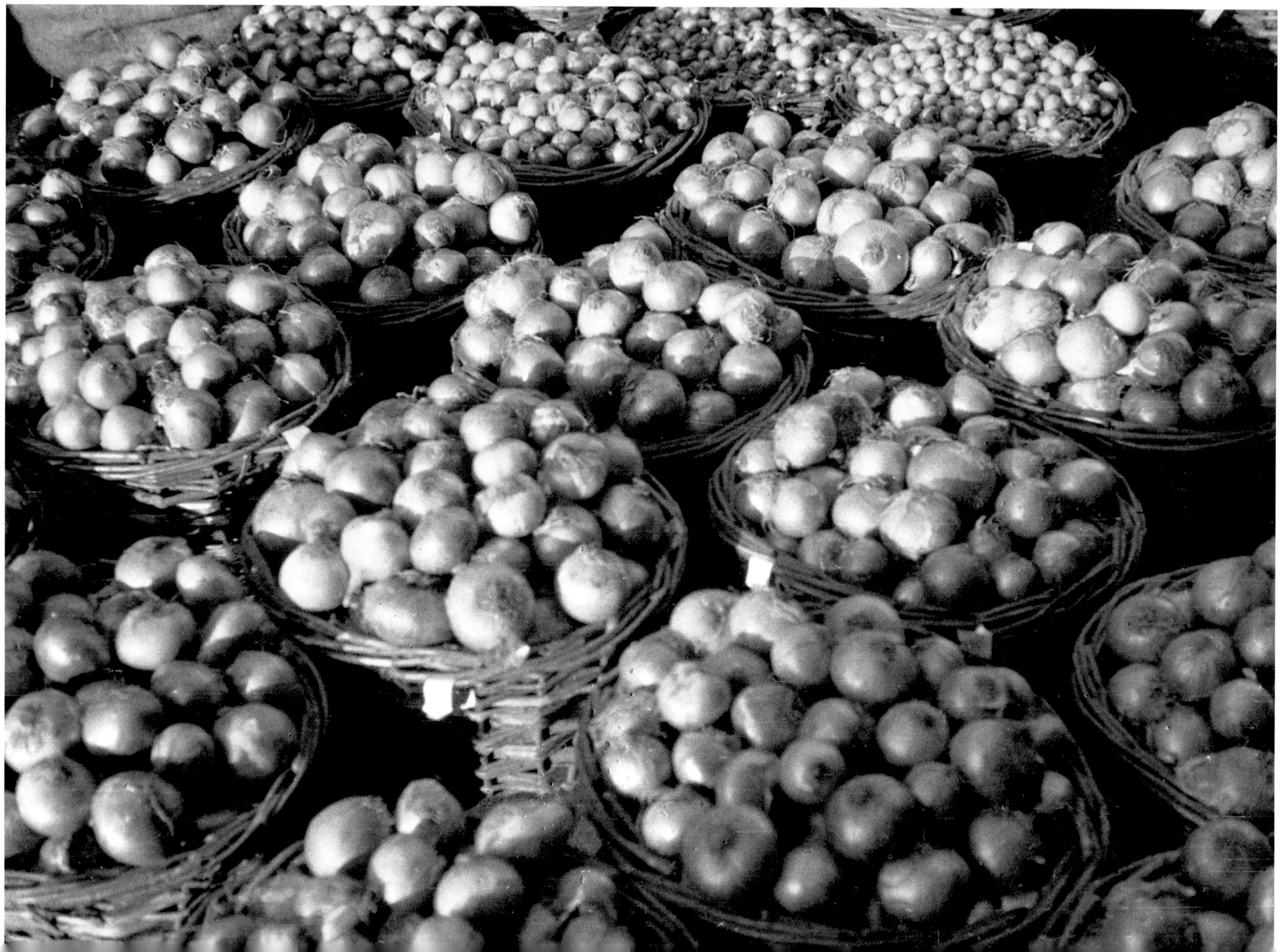

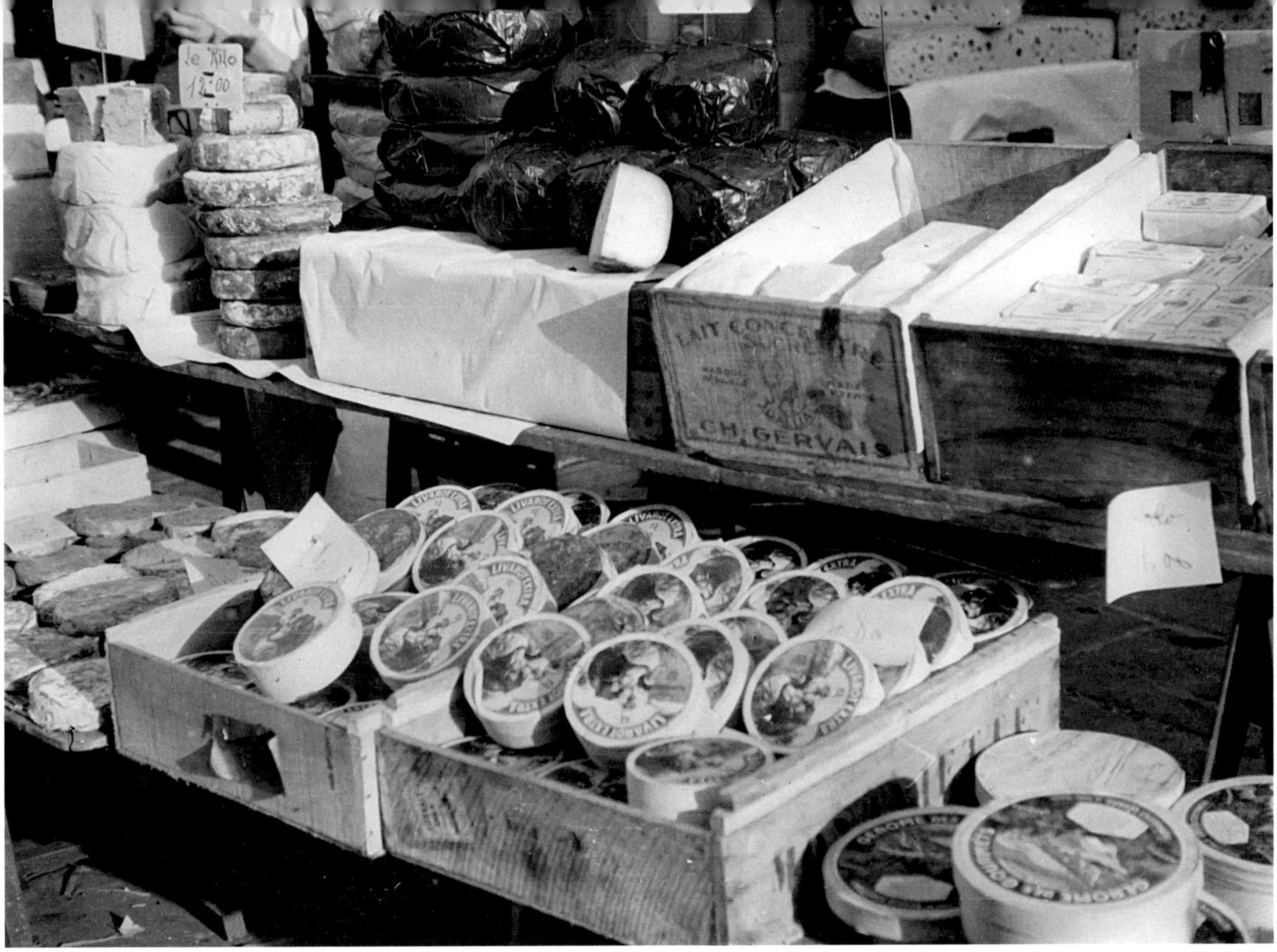

Display of foods at Les Halles wholesale market, Paris, 1930

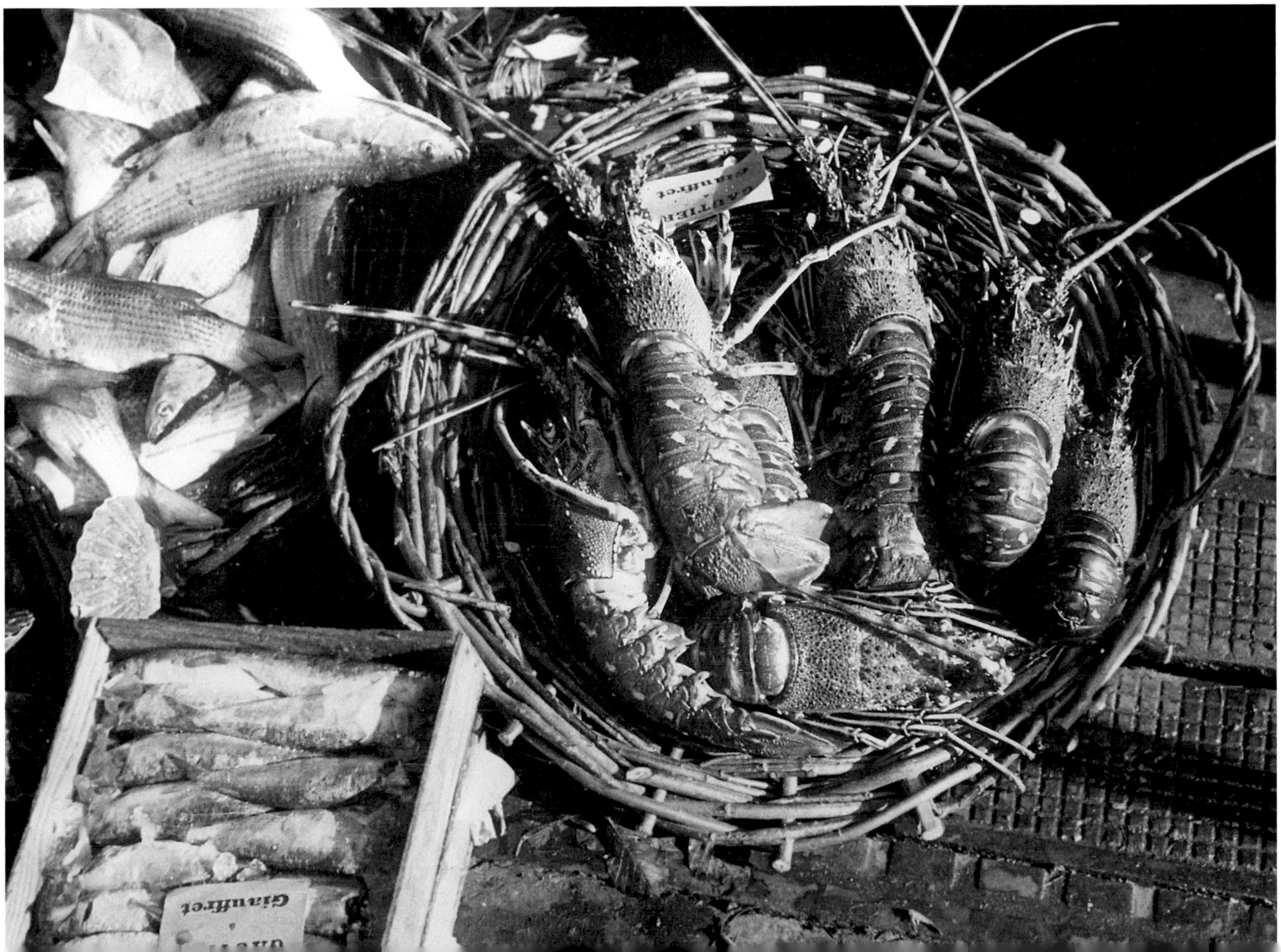

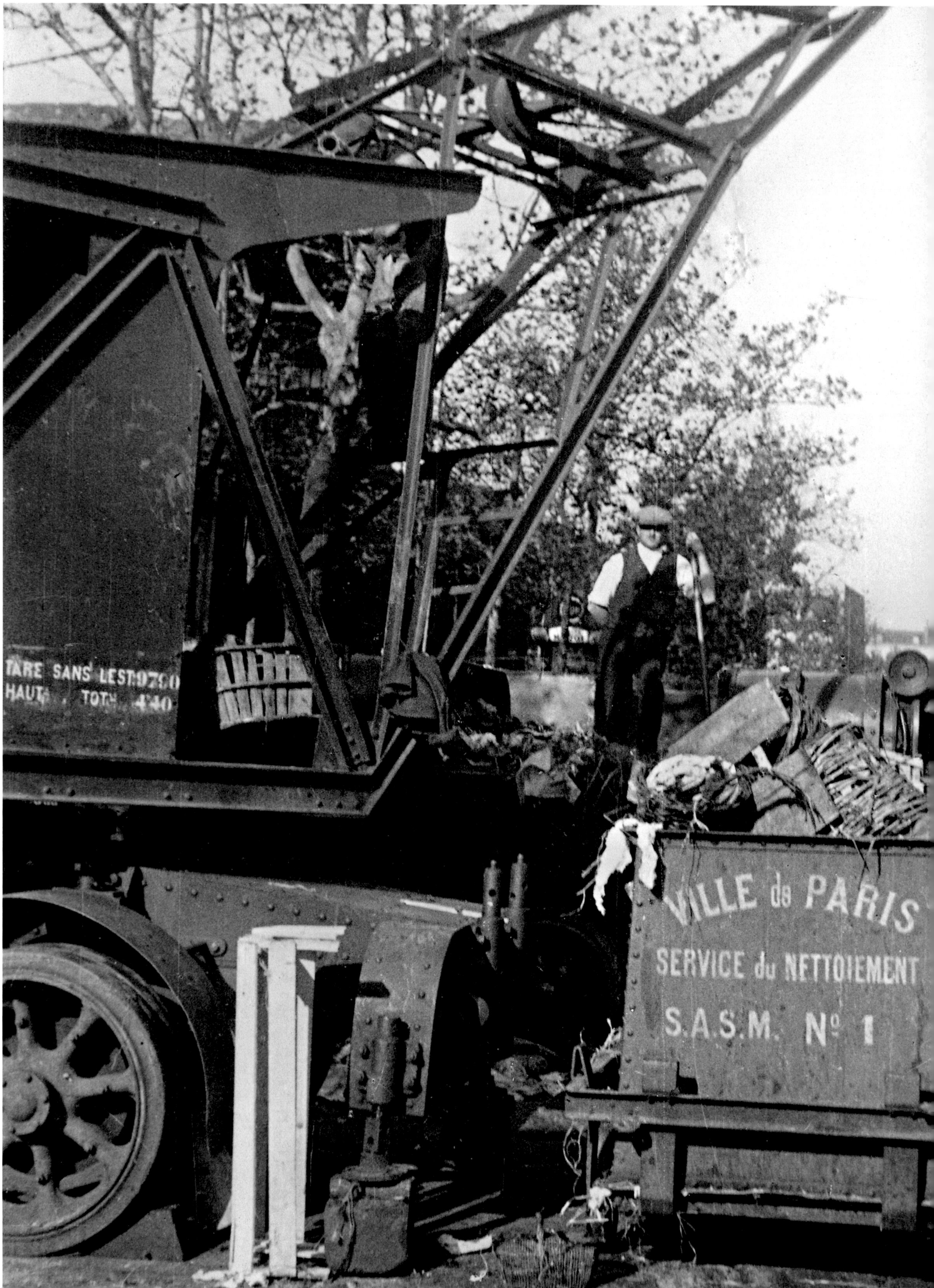
TARE SANS LEST
HAUT
VILLE de PARIS
SERVICE du NETTOIEMENT
S.A.S.M. N° 1

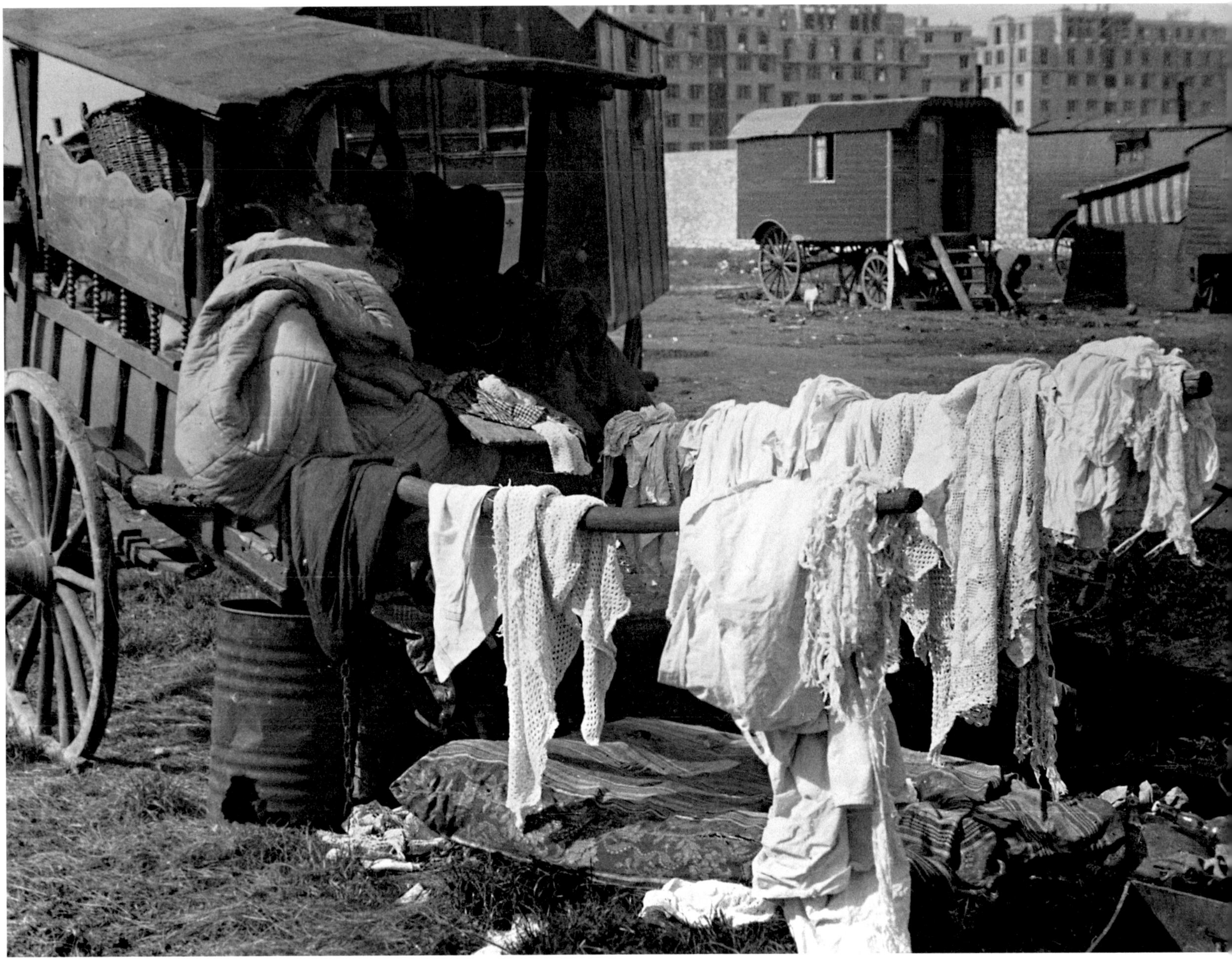

Gypsy wagons outside the Porte de Choisy, Paris, 1930

Municipal garbage collection, Paris, 1930

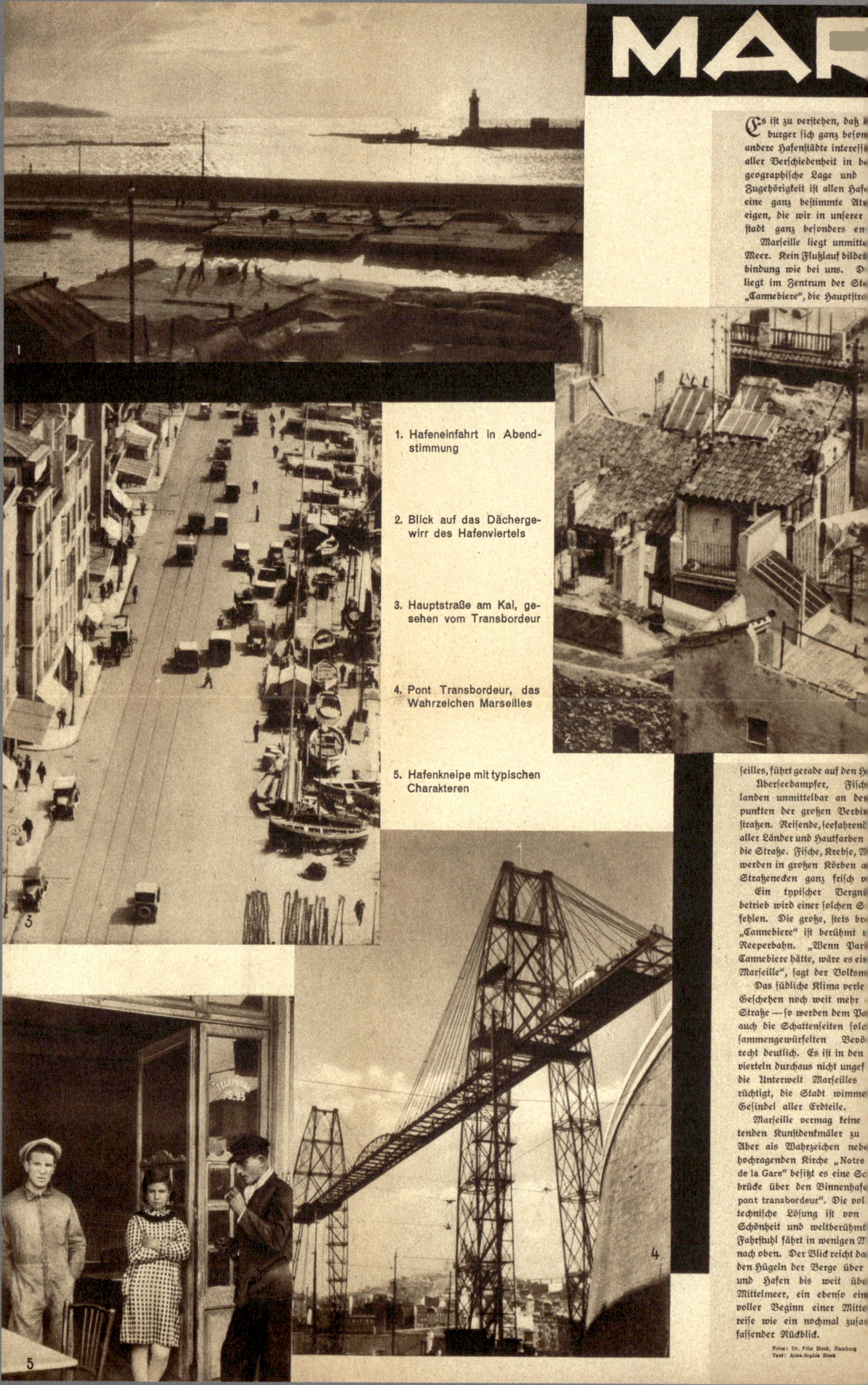

MAR

Es ist zu verstehen, daß
burger sich ganz beson
andere Hafenstädte interessi
aller Verschiedenheit in b
geographische Lage und
Zugehörigkeit ist allen Haf
eine ganz bestimmte At
eigen, die wir in unserer
stadt ganz besonders en
Marseille liegt unmitte
Meer. Kein Flußlauf bildet
bindung wie bei uns. D
liegt im Zentrum der St
„Cannebiere", die Hauptstr

1. Hafeneinfahrt in Abendstimmung

2. Blick auf das Dächergewirr des Hafenviertels

3. Hauptstraße am Kai, gesehen vom Transbordeur

4. Pont Transbordeur, das Wahrzeichen Marseilles

5. Hafenkneipe mit typischen Charakteren

seilles, führt gerade auf den H
Überseedampfer, Fisch
landen unmittelbar an de
punkten der großen Verbi
straßen. Reisende, seefahrend
aller Länder und Hautfarben
die Straße. Fische, Krebse, M
werden in großen Körben a
Straßenecken ganz frisch v
Ein typischer Vergnü
betrieb wird einer solchen S
fehlen. Die große, stets br
„Cannebiere" ist berühmt
Reeperbahn. „Wenn Pari
Cannebiere hätte, wäre es ei
Marseille", sagt der Volksm
Das südliche Klima verle
Geschehen noch weit mehr
Straße — so werden dem Pa
auch die Schattenseiten sol
sammengewürfelten Bevö
recht deutlich. Es ist in den
vierteln durchaus nicht ungef
die Unterwelt Marseilles
rüchtigt, die Stadt wimme
Gesindel aller Erdteile.
Marseille vermag keine
tenden Kunstdenkmäler zu
Aber als Wahrzeichen neb
hochragenden Kirche „Notre
de la Gare" besitzt es eine Sc
brücke über den Binnenhaf
pont transbordeur". Die vol
technische Lösung ist von
Schönheit und weltberühmt
Fahrstuhl fährt in wenigen M
nach oben. Der Blick reicht da
den Hügeln der Berge über
und Hafen bis weit übe
Mittelmeer, ein ebenso ein
voller Beginn einer Mitte
reise wie ein nochmal zusa
fassender Rückblick.

Fotos: Dr. Fritz Block, Hamburg
Text: Anna-Sophie Block

"Marseille, a Southern International Port" (*Hamburger Anzeiger. Illustrierte Wochenbeilage*, no. 36, 1932)

SEILLE IN ÜDLICHER WELTHAFEN

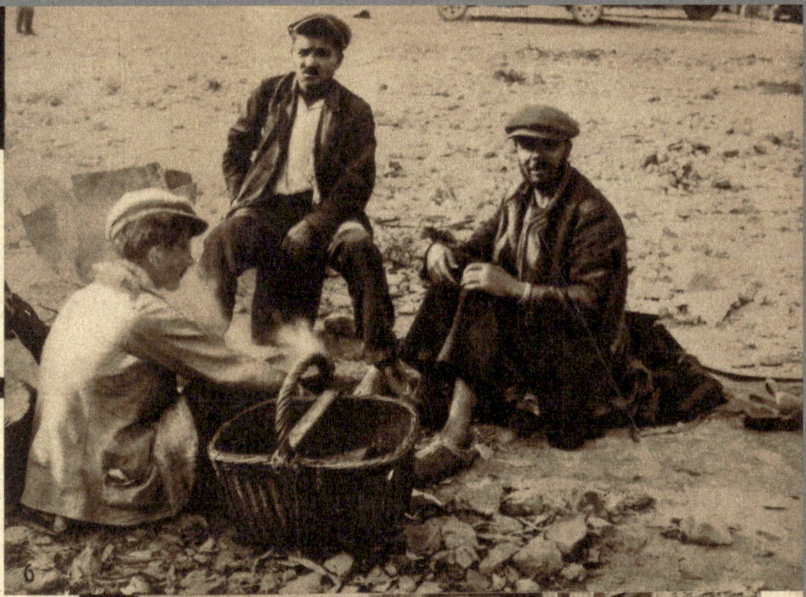

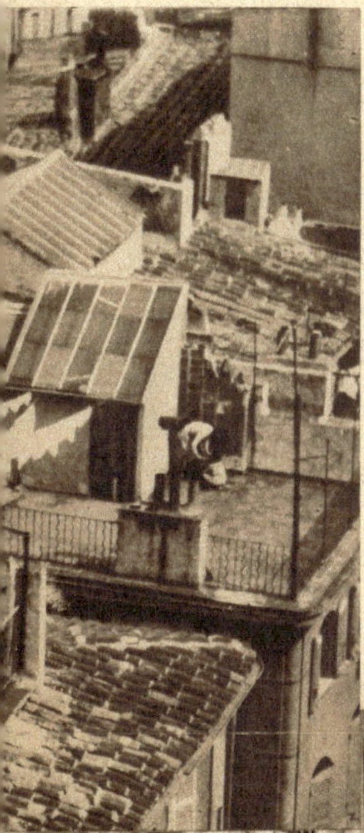

6. Asoziale Elemente: „Clochards" im Abbruchviertel

7. Marktszene im italienischen Viertel

8. Die „Elbstraße" am Mittelmeer

9. Der internationale Beruf des Schauermannes

10. Dreigespann am Feierabend

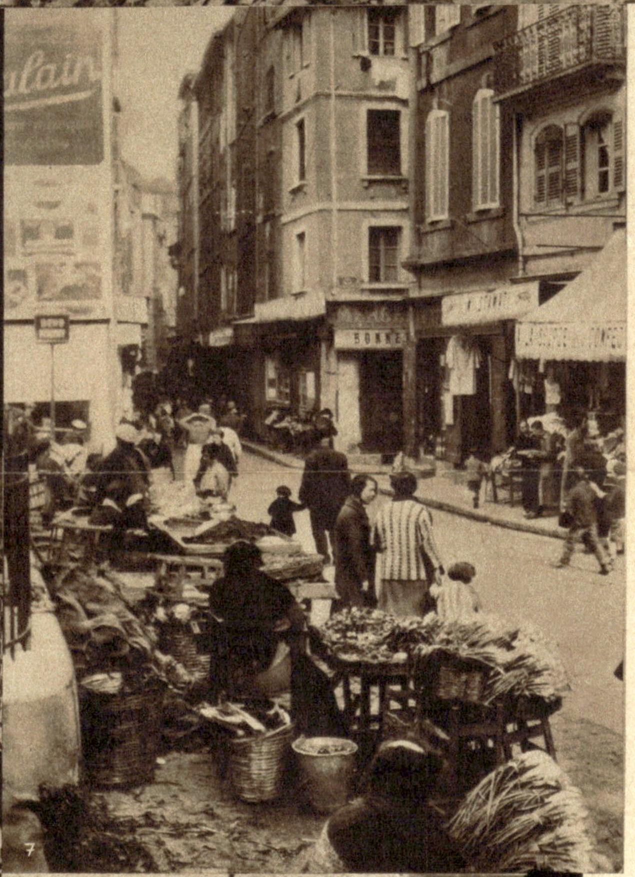

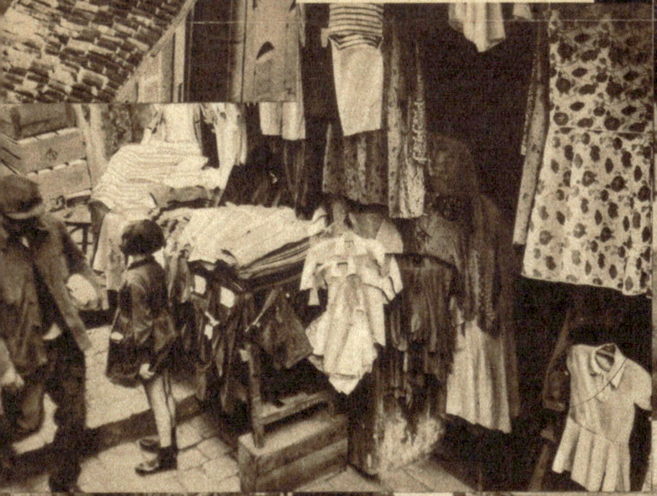

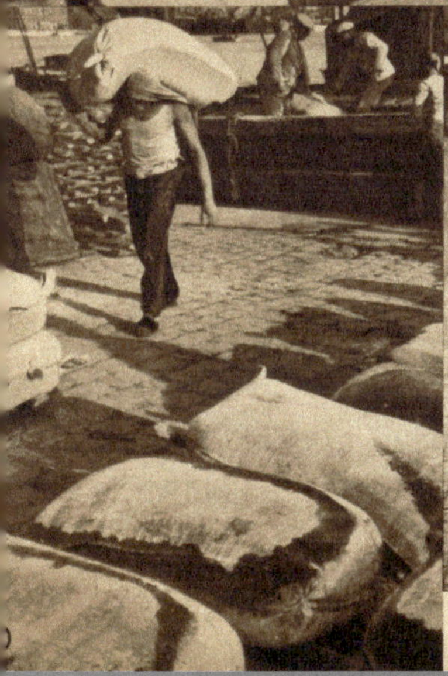

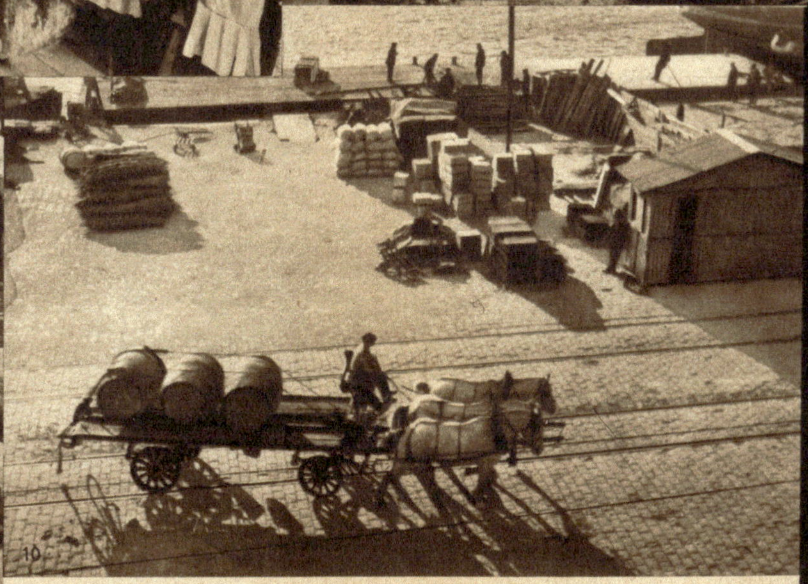

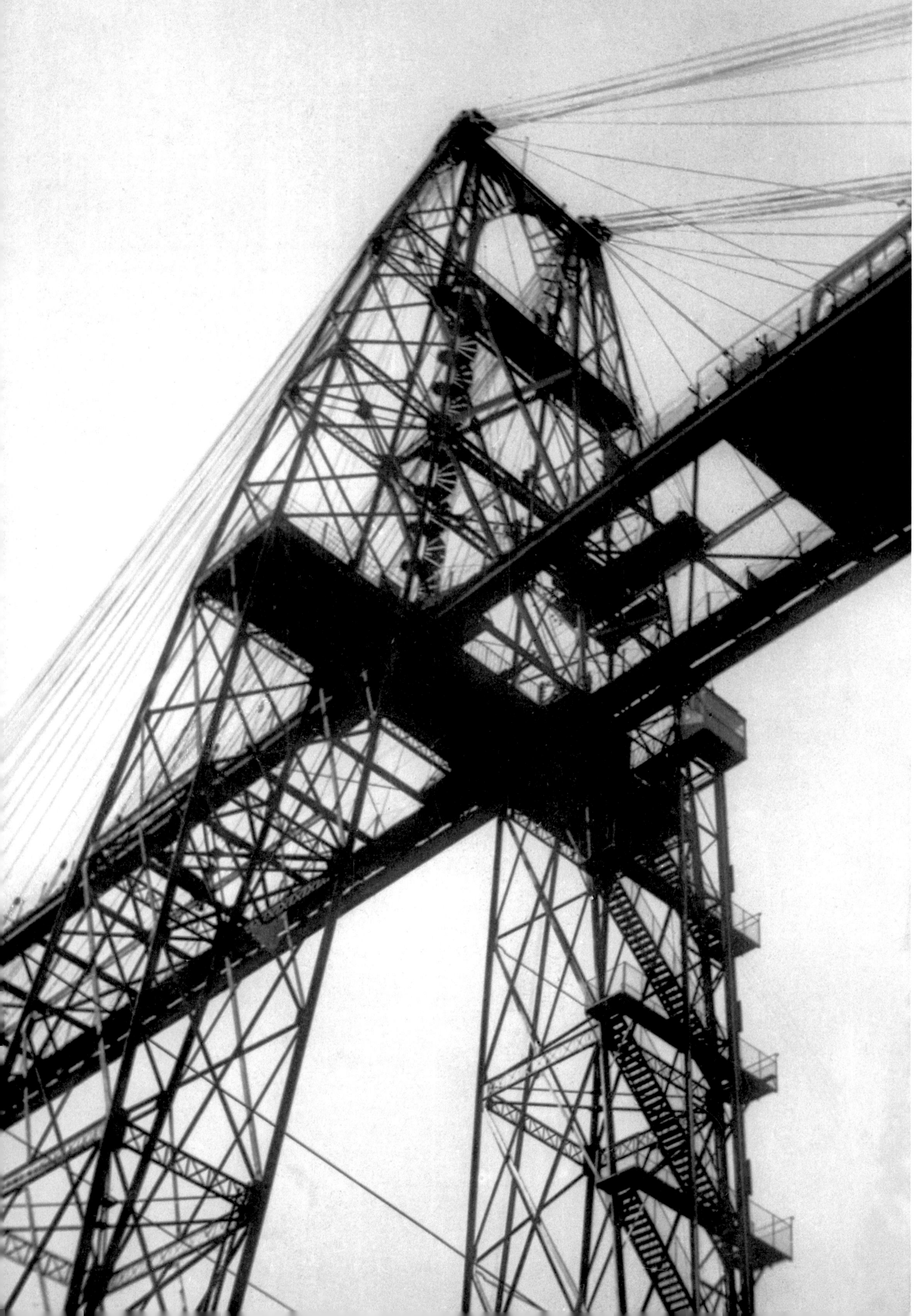

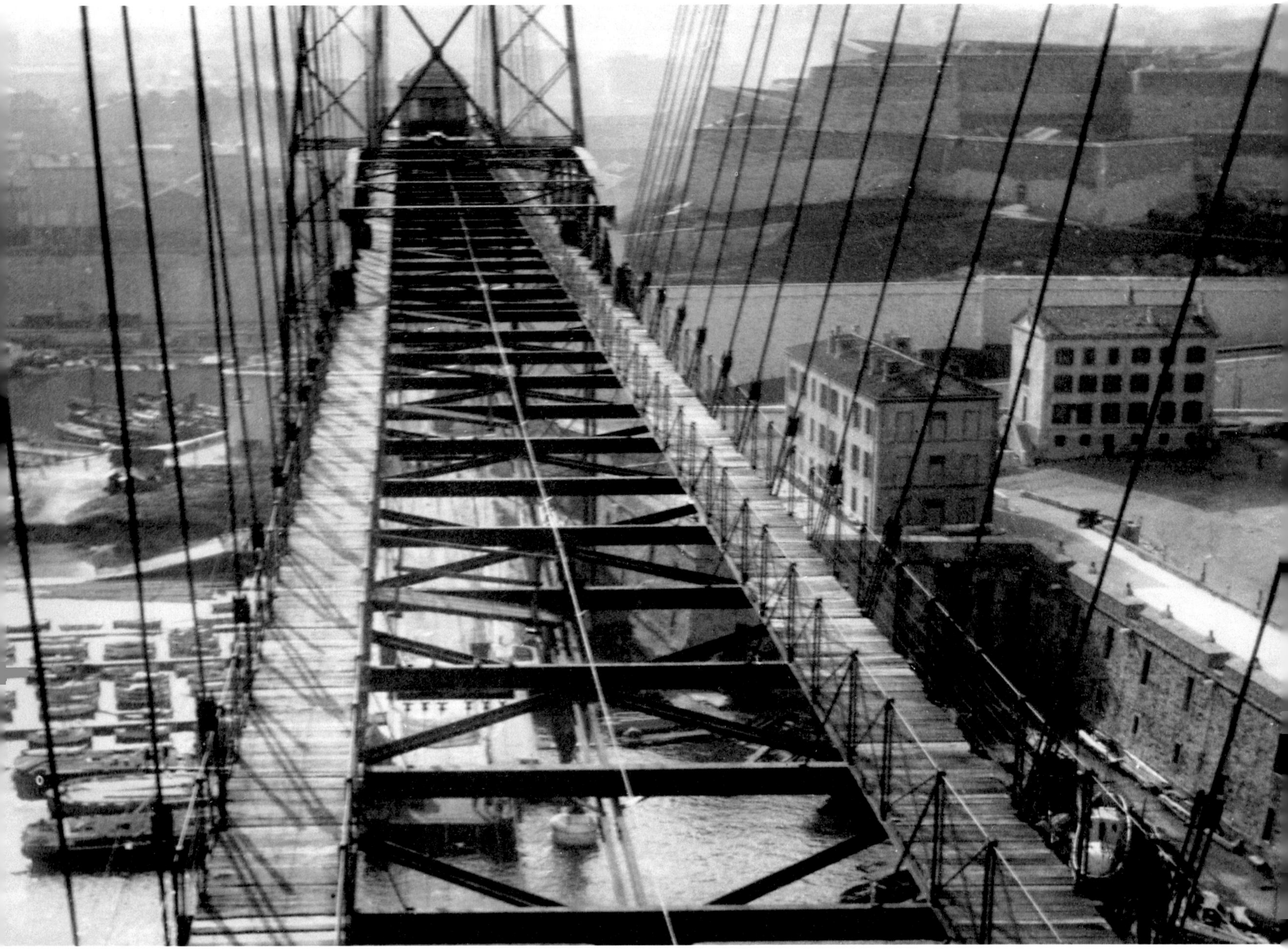

Bridge girder of the Pont Transbordeur (Transporter Bridge), Marseille, 1931
(also see page 3)

Pylon of the Pont Transbordeur (Transporter Bridge), Marseille, 1930

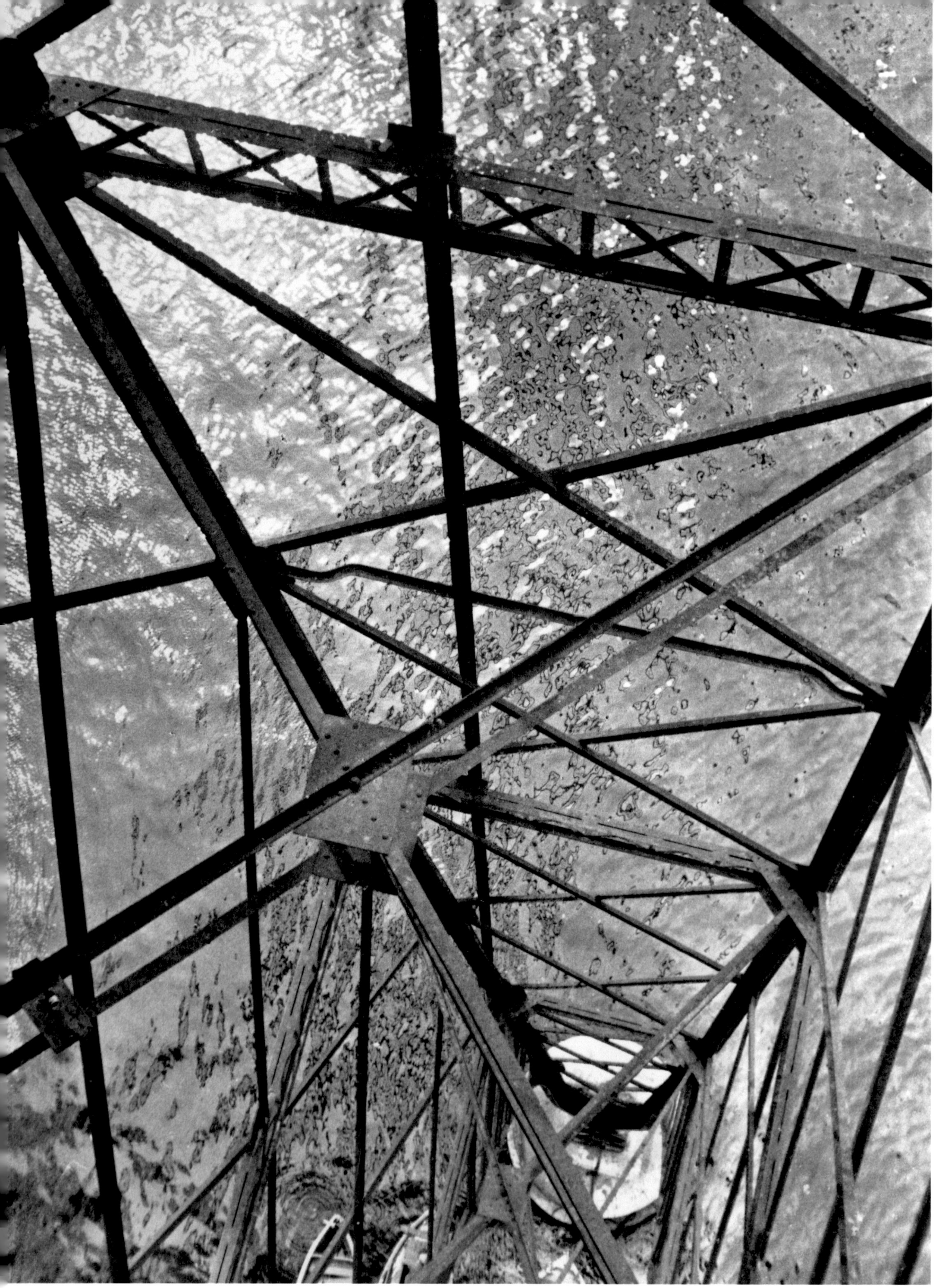

Downward view from the Pont Transbordeur (Transporter Bridge), Marseille, 1931

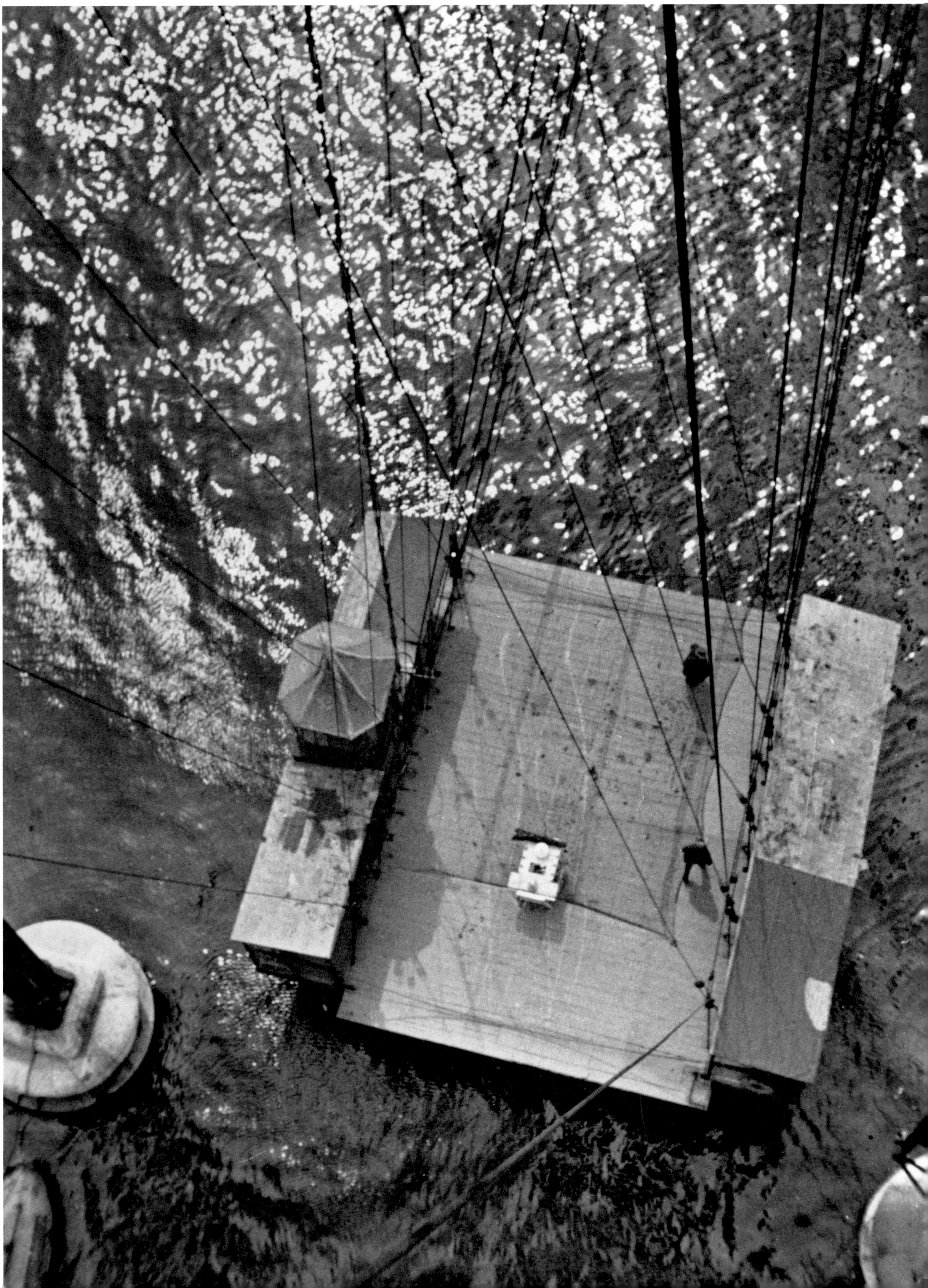

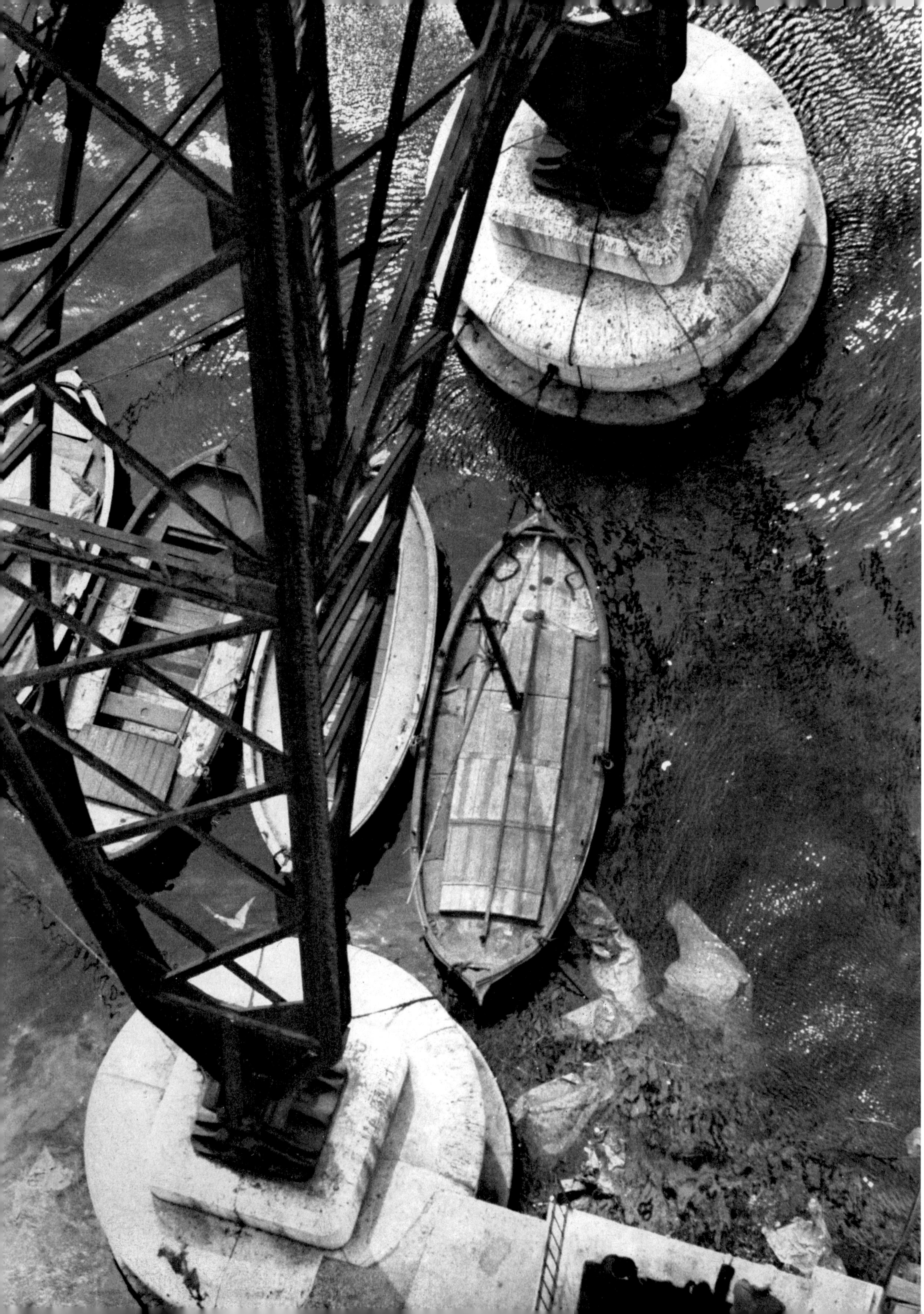

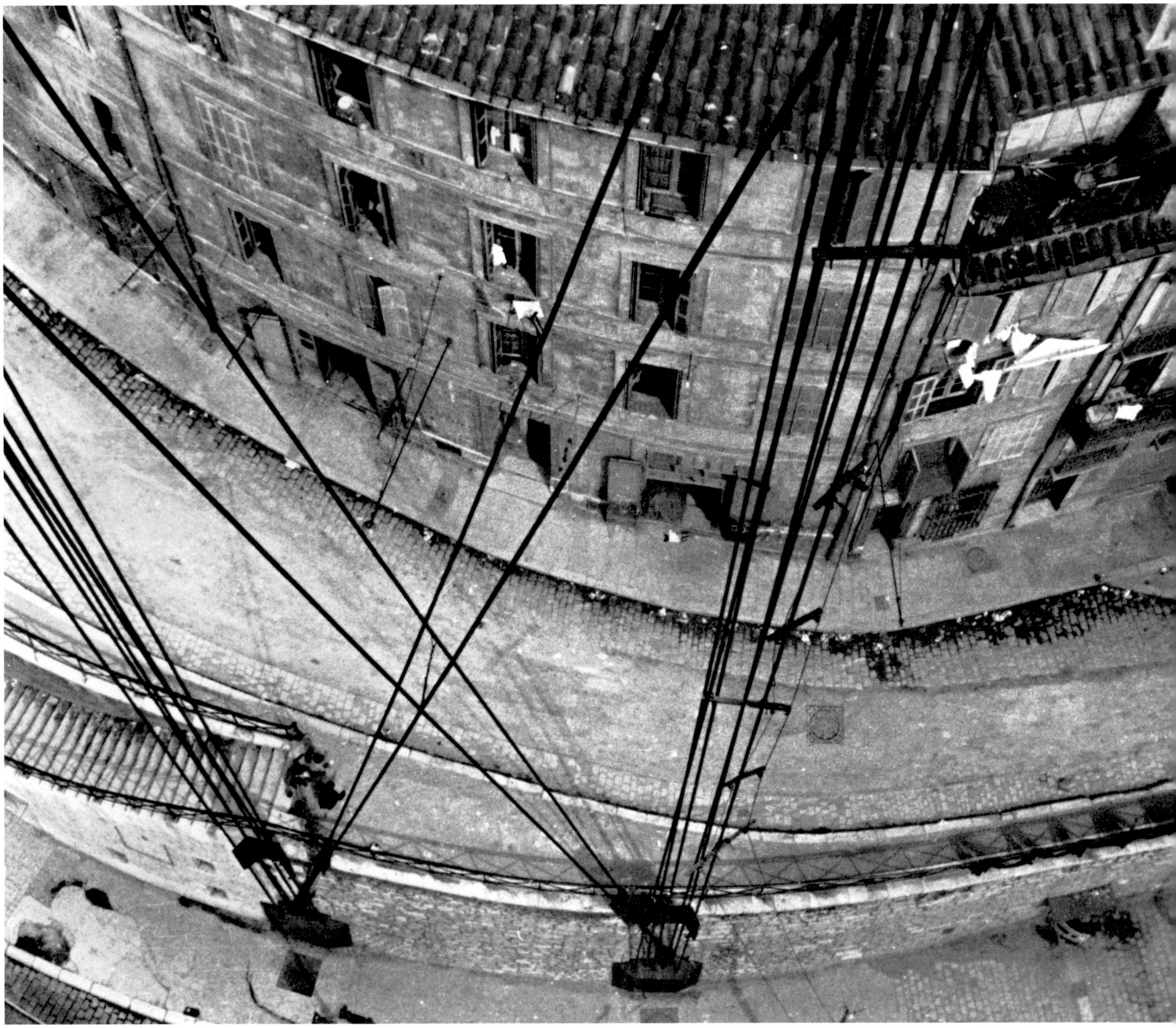

Downward view from the Pont Transbordeur (Transporter Bridge), Marseille, 1931

Nr. 22/1931 Sonnabend, den 30. Mai

Hamburger Anzeiger

vereinigt mit „Neue Hamburger Zeitung"

Illustrierte W … e in Kupfertiefdruck.

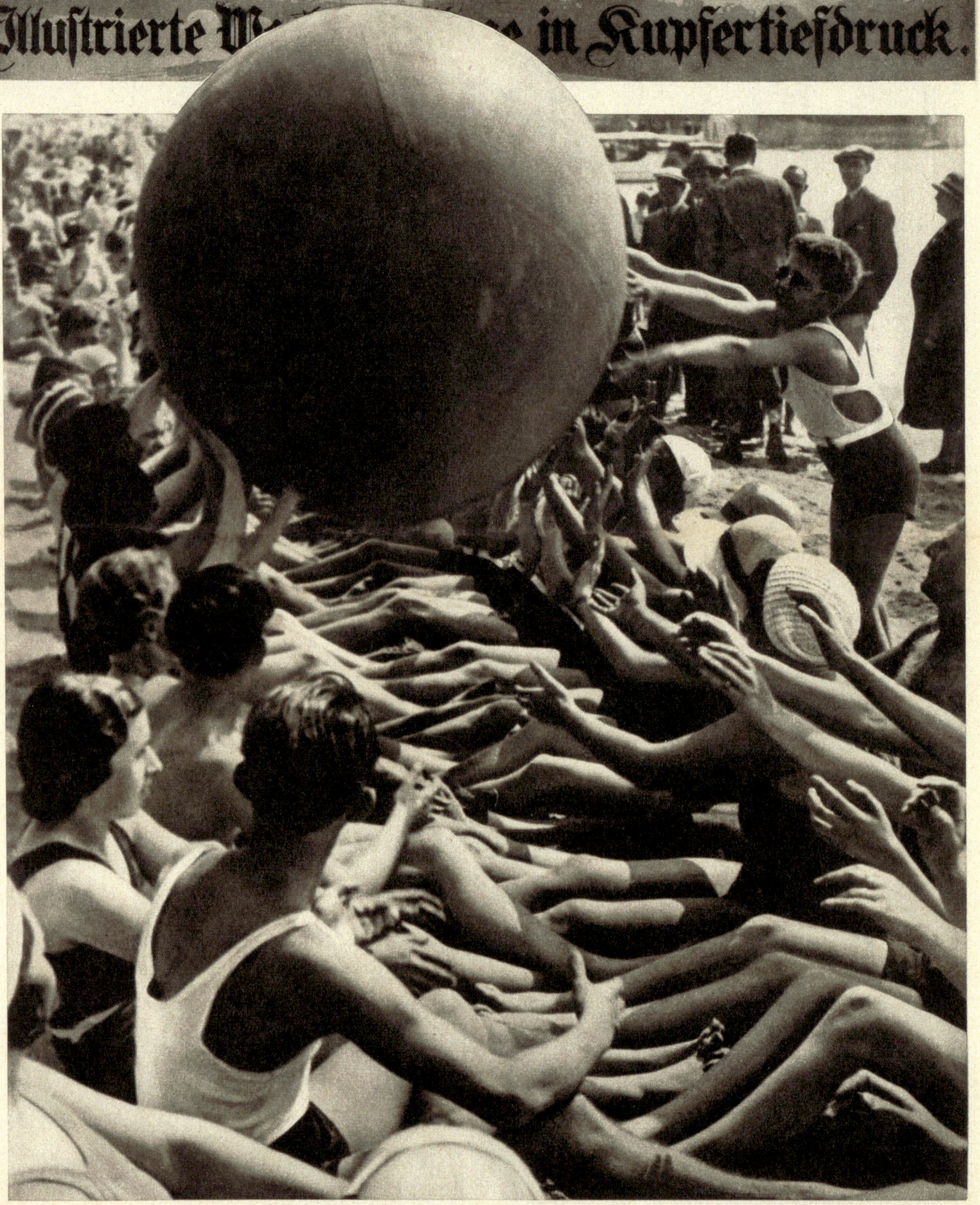

Ballspiel am Strande

Aufn. Dr. Block

"Ball Game on the Beach" (*Hamburger Anzeiger. Illustrierte Wochenbeilage*, no. 22, 1931)

Ball game on Juan-les-Pins beach, Côte d'Azur, 1931

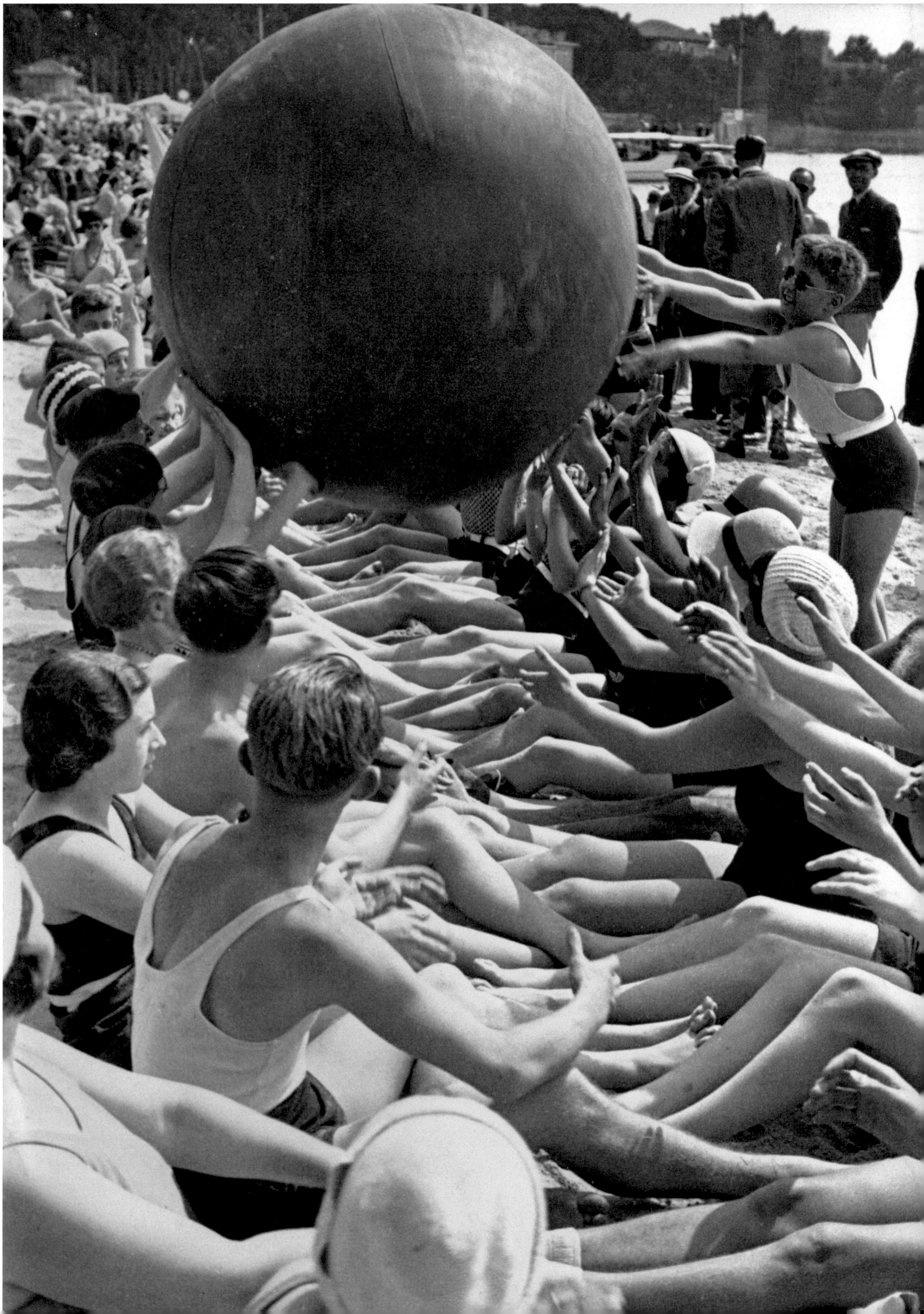

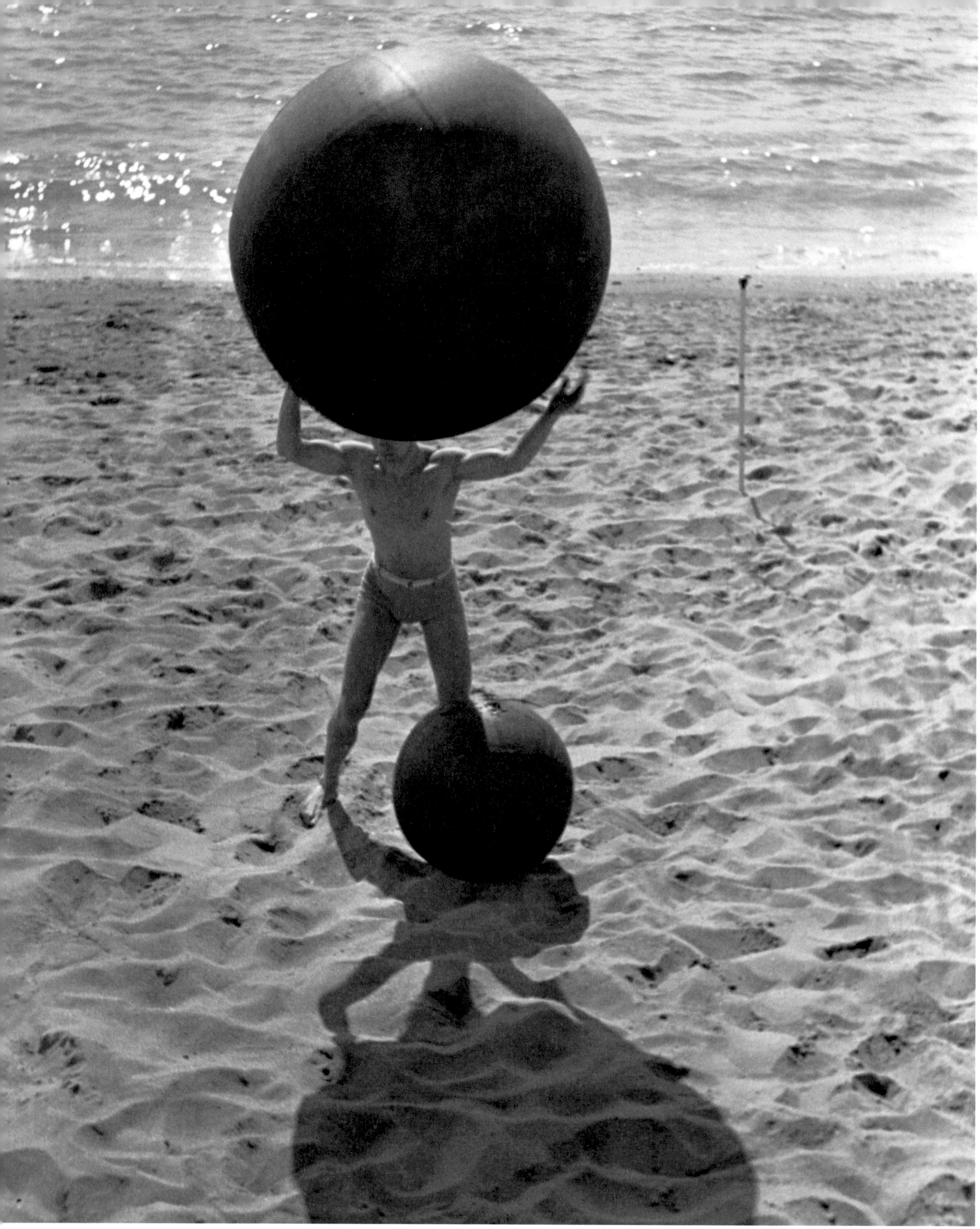

"Modern Atlas," Juan-les-Pins, Côte d'Azur, 1931

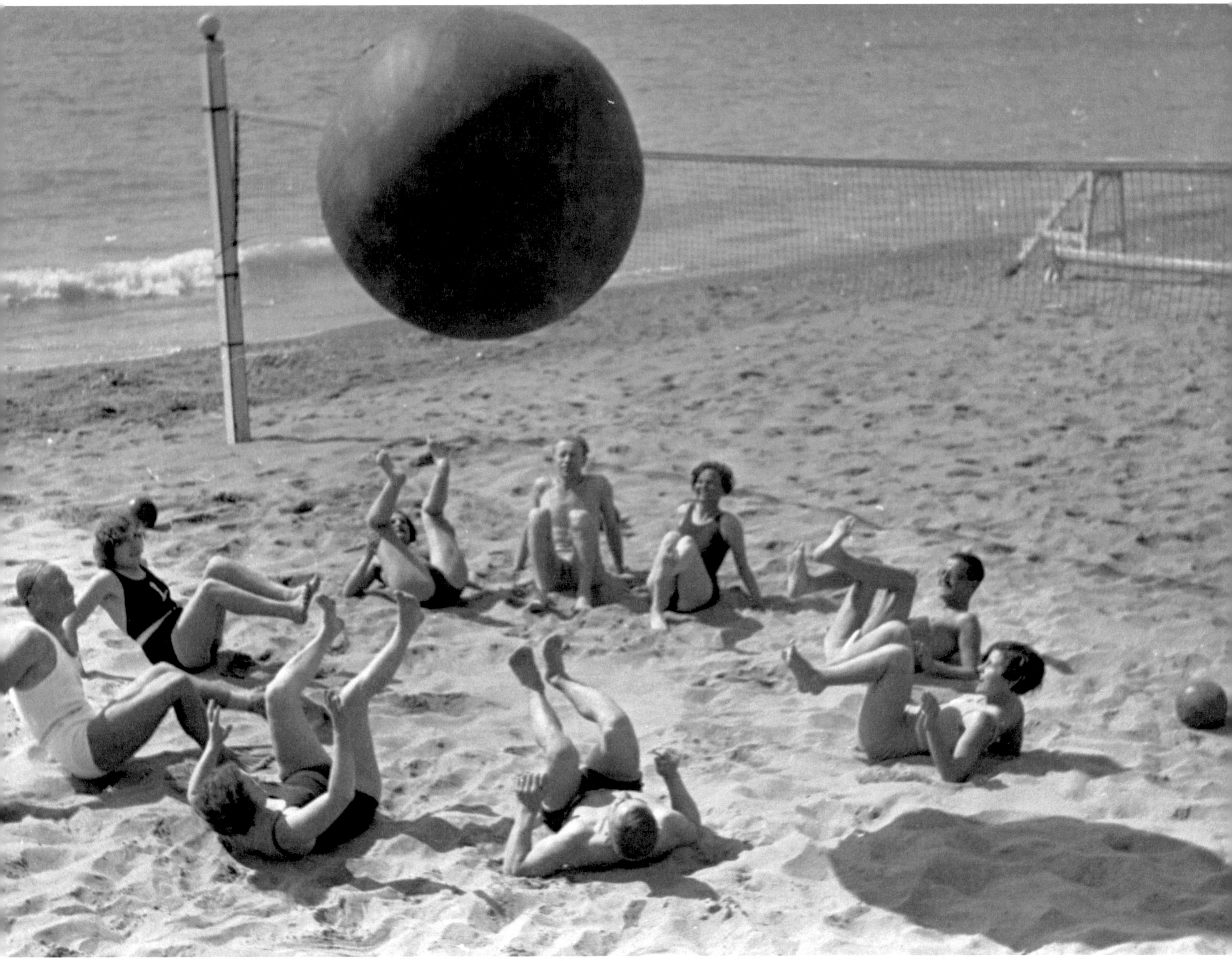

Medicine ball workout, Juan-les-Pins, Côte d'Azur, 1931

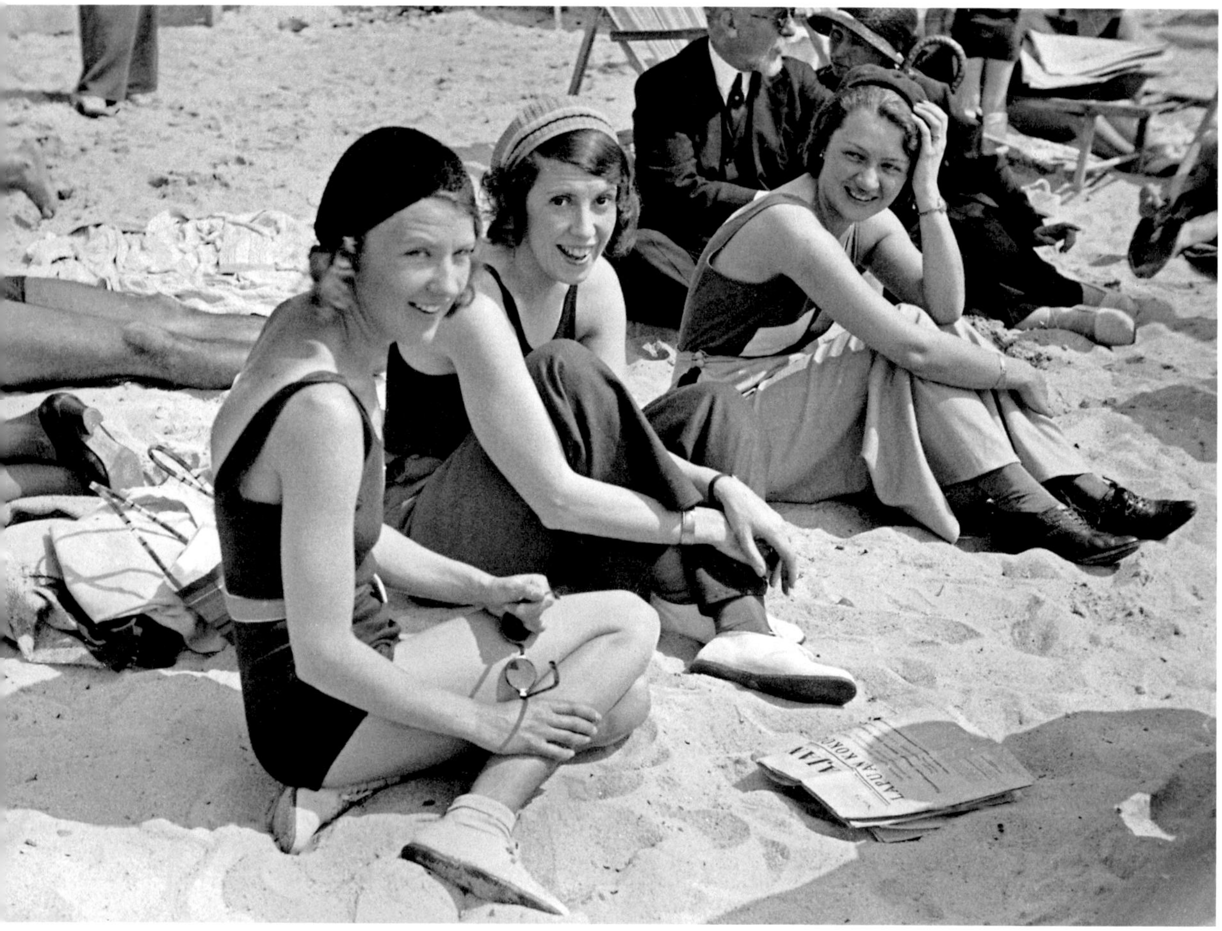

"Beach Beauties,"
Juan-les-Pins, Côte d'Azur,
1931

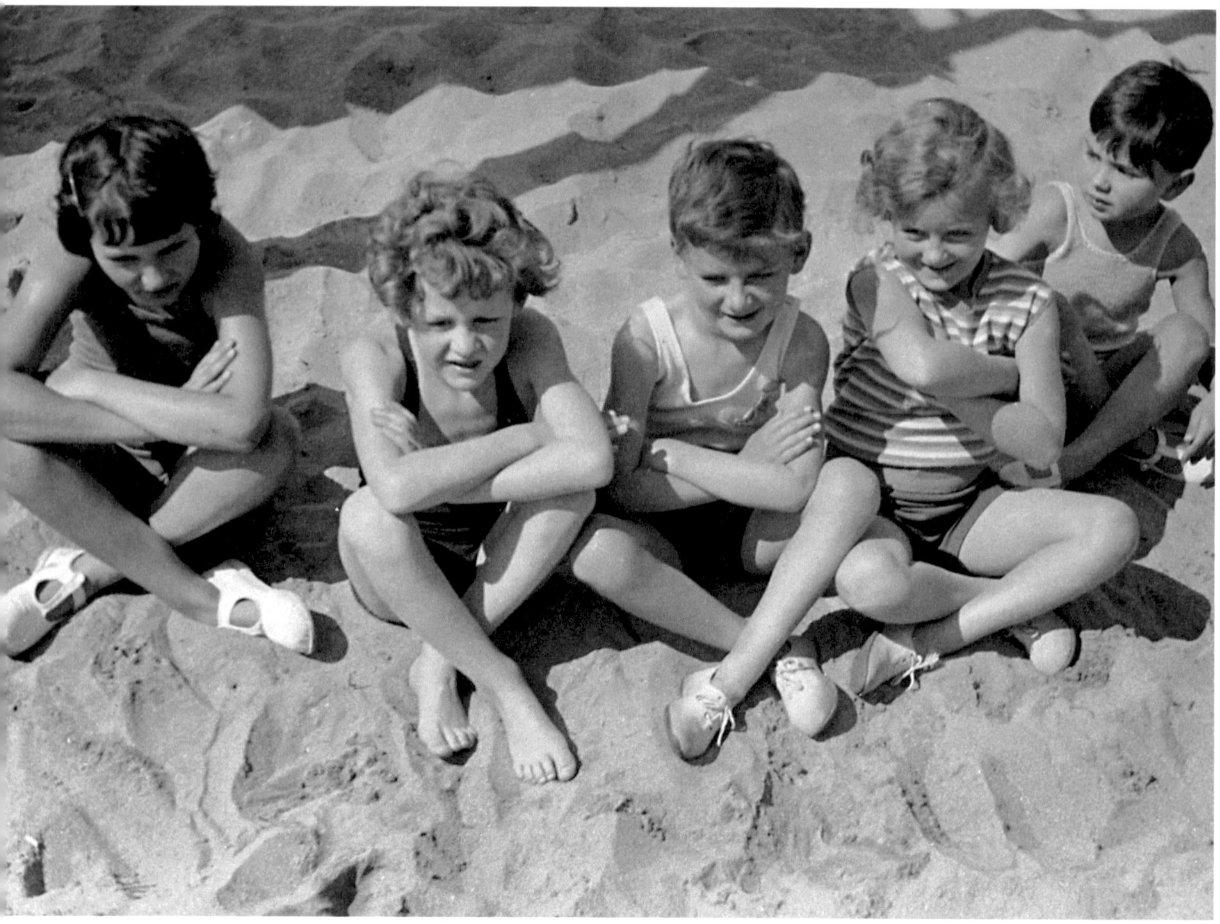

Children on the beach,
Juan-les-Pins, Côte d'Azur,
1931

"Jump!"
Juan-les-Pins, Côte
d'Azur, 1931

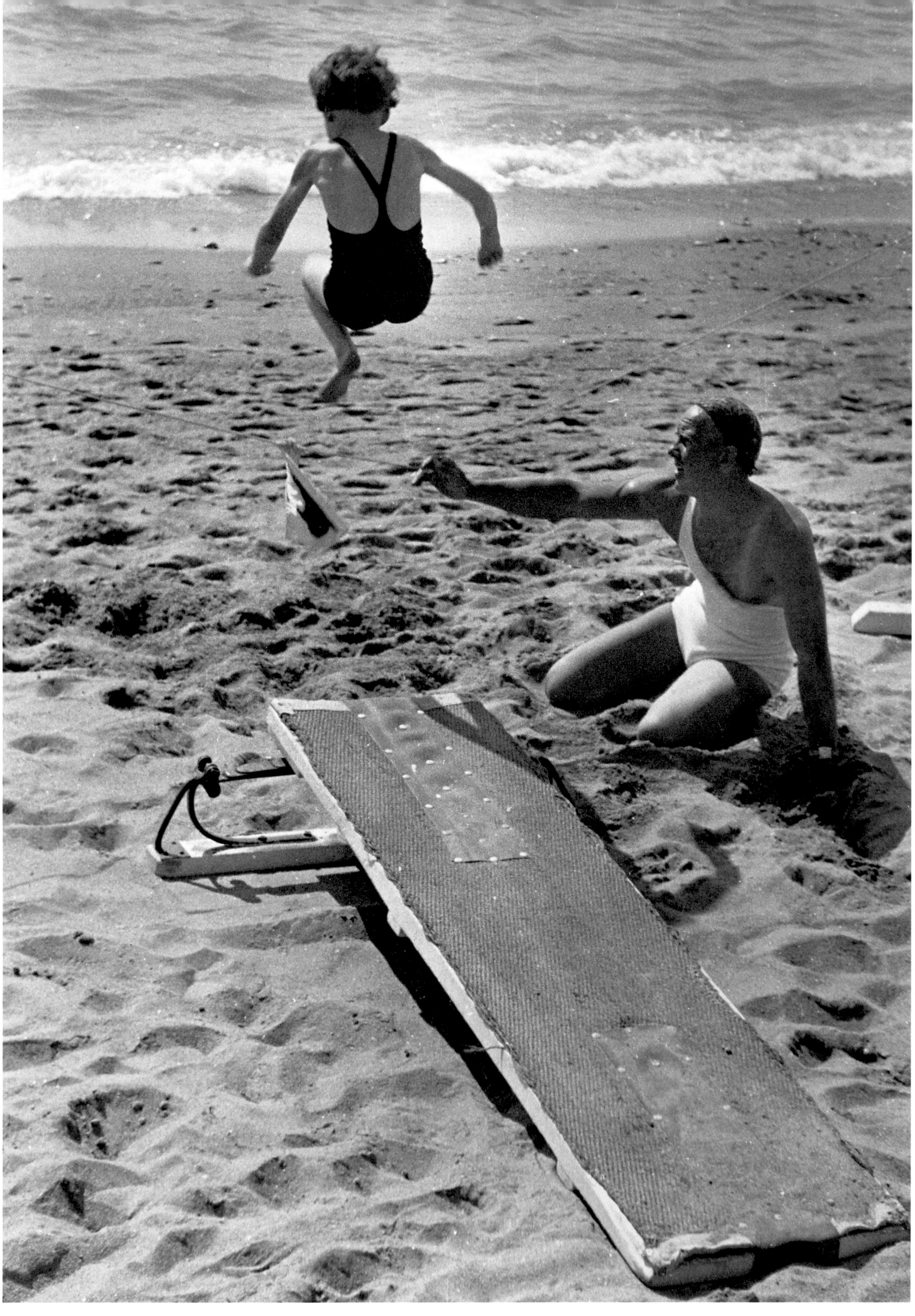

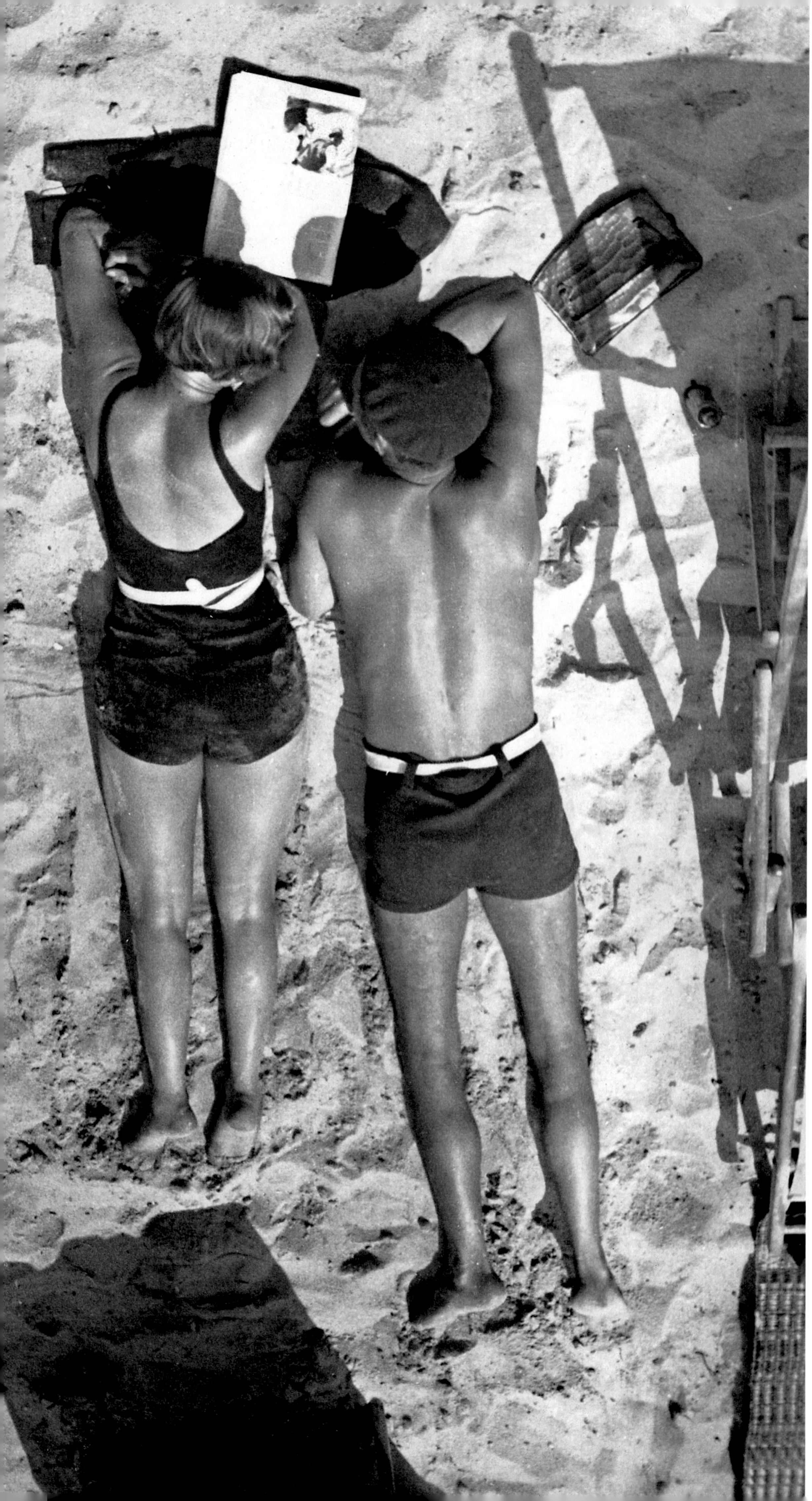

Sunbathing on the beach,
Juan-les-Pins, Côte d'Azur,
1931

"The Sportive Body," Juan-les-Pins, Côte d'Azur, 1931

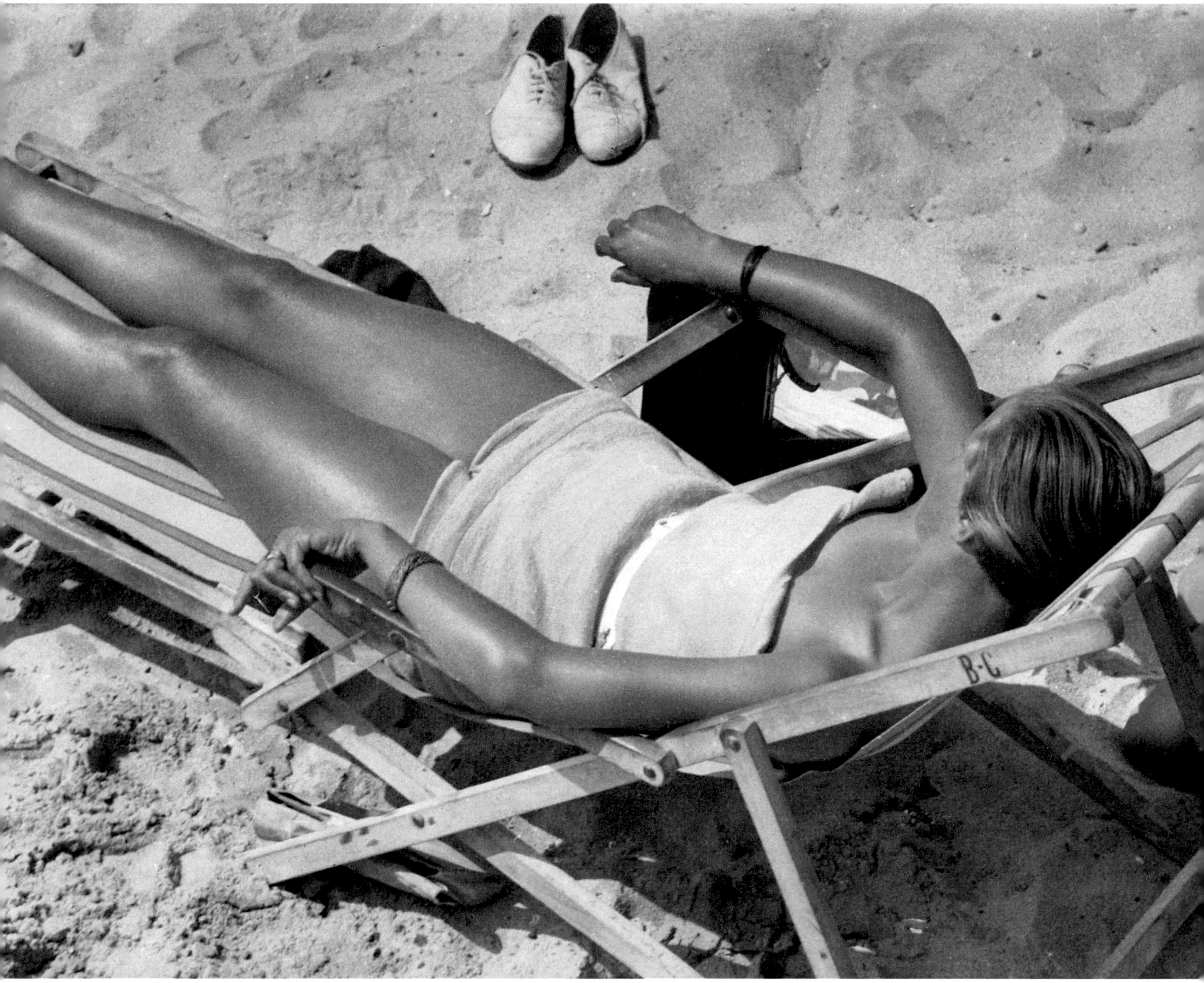

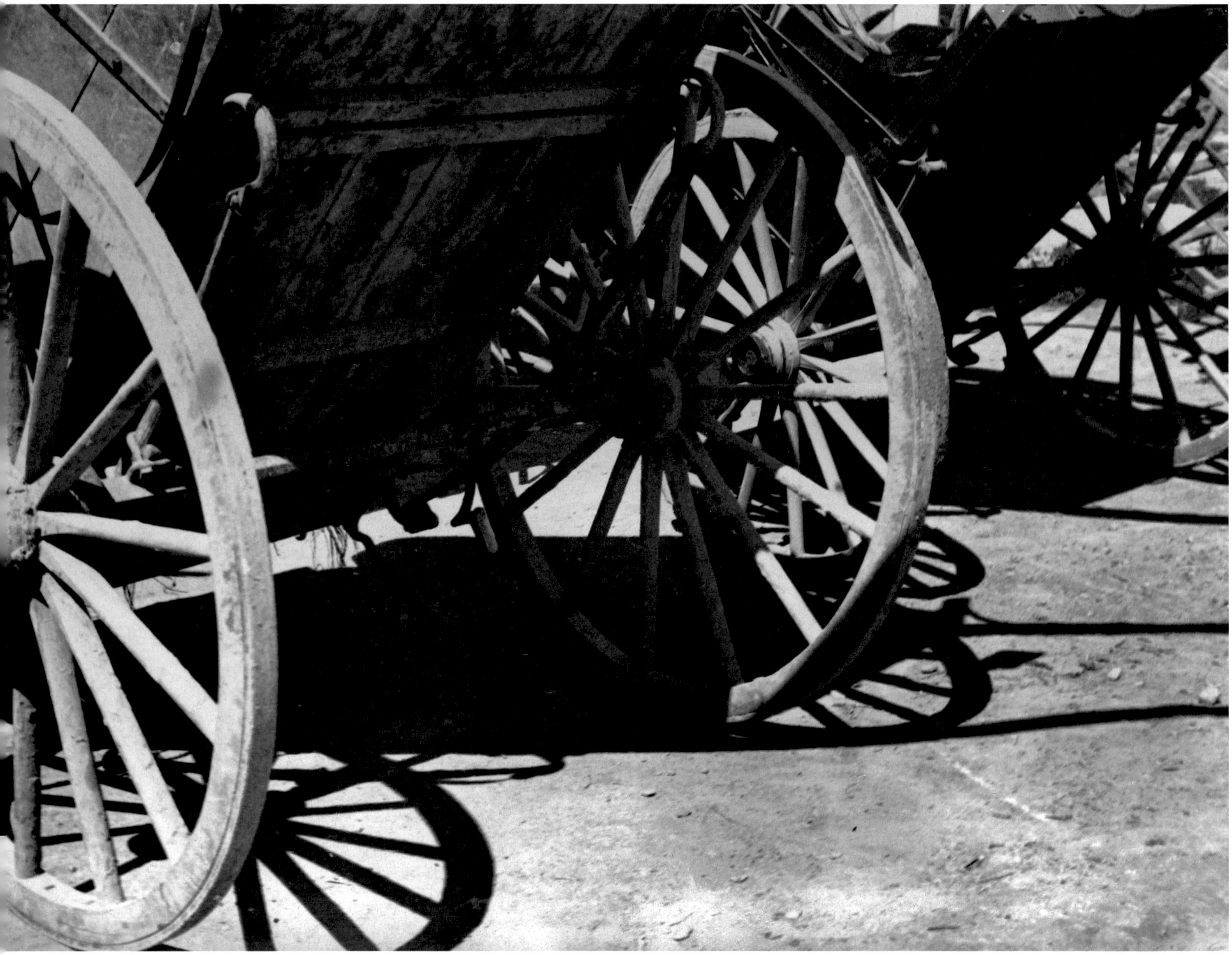

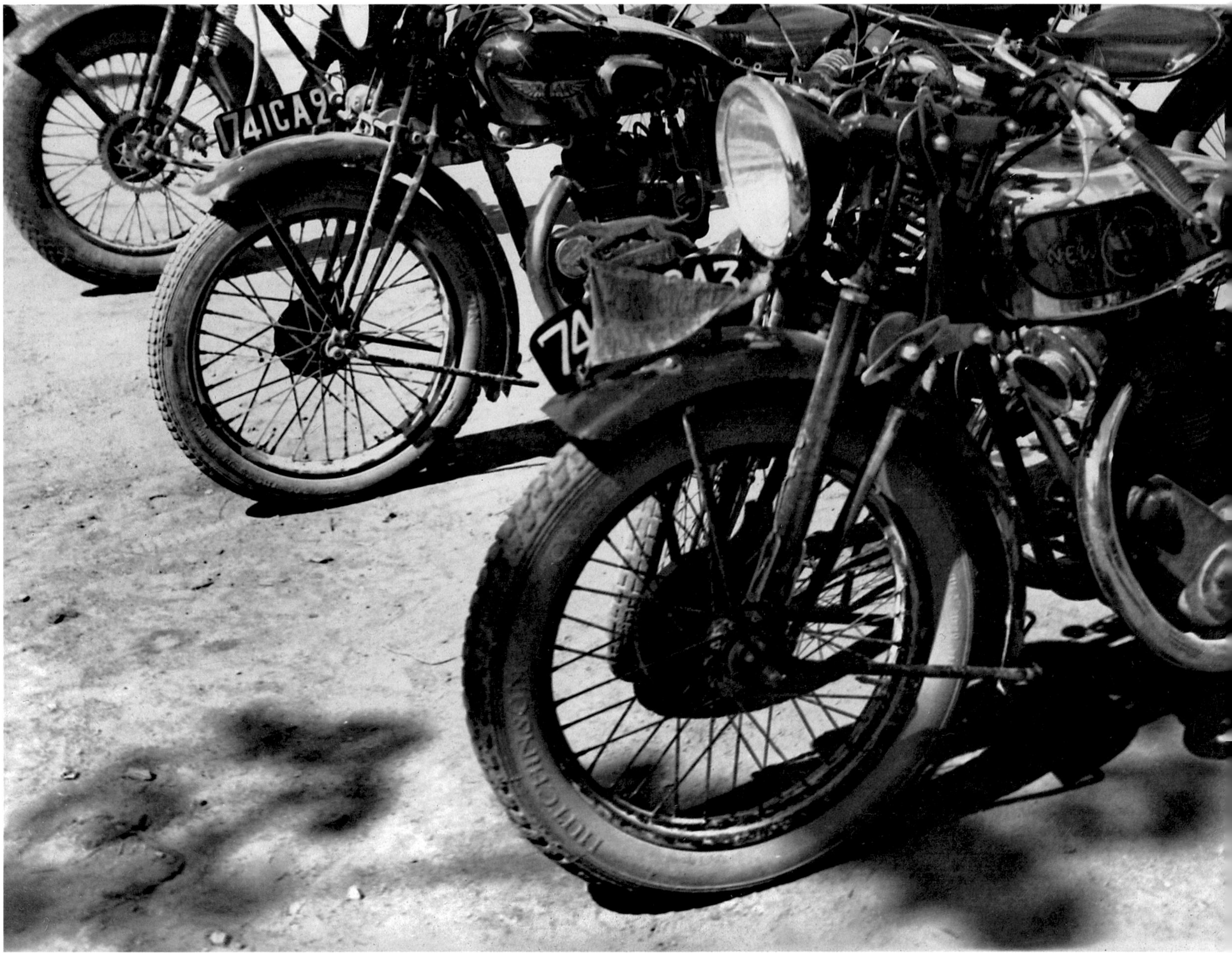

Carts and motorcycles, Arles, 1931

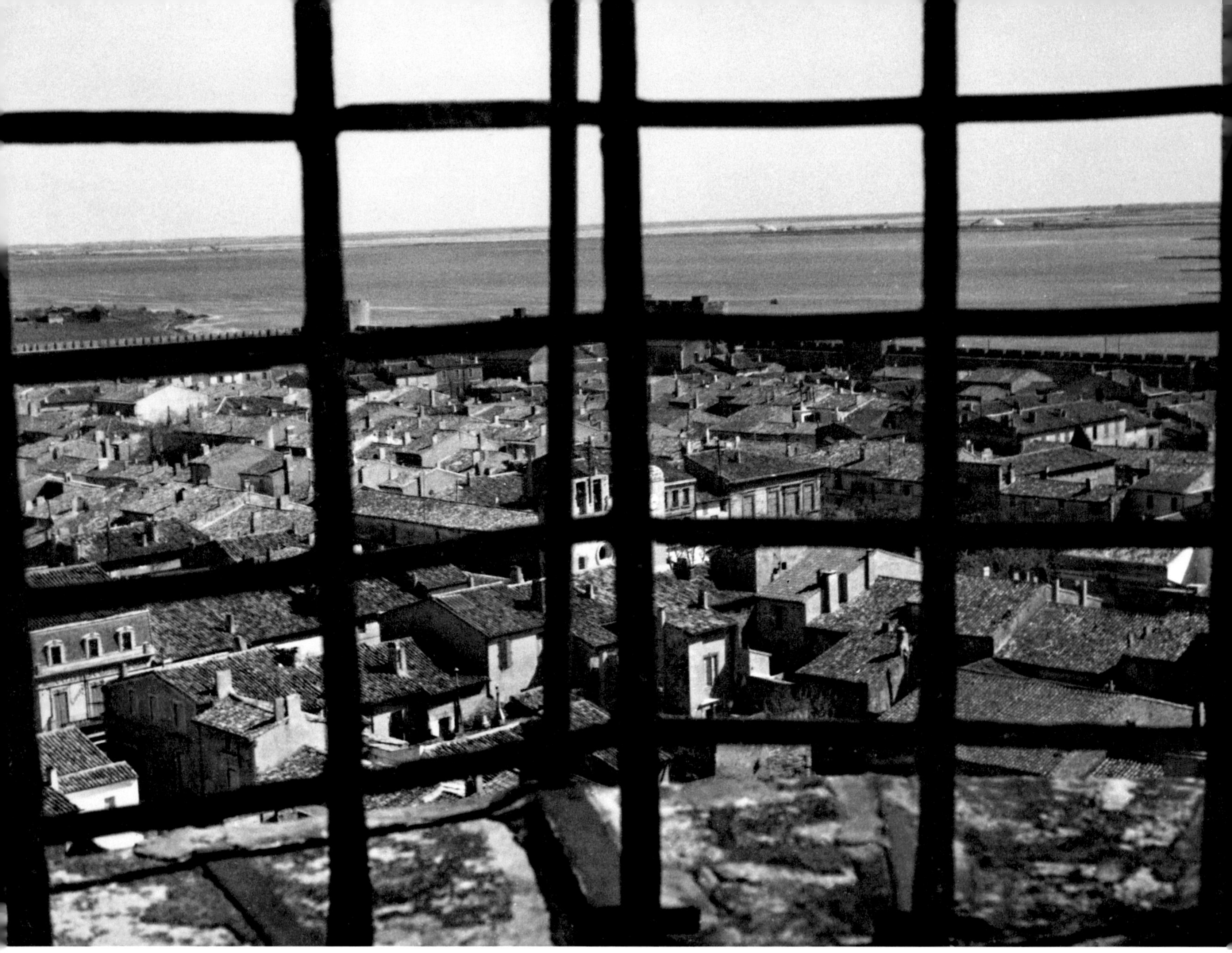

View onto Aigues-Mortes from a watchtower in the city wall, Provence, 1931

The Roman Theater of Orange, Provence, 1931

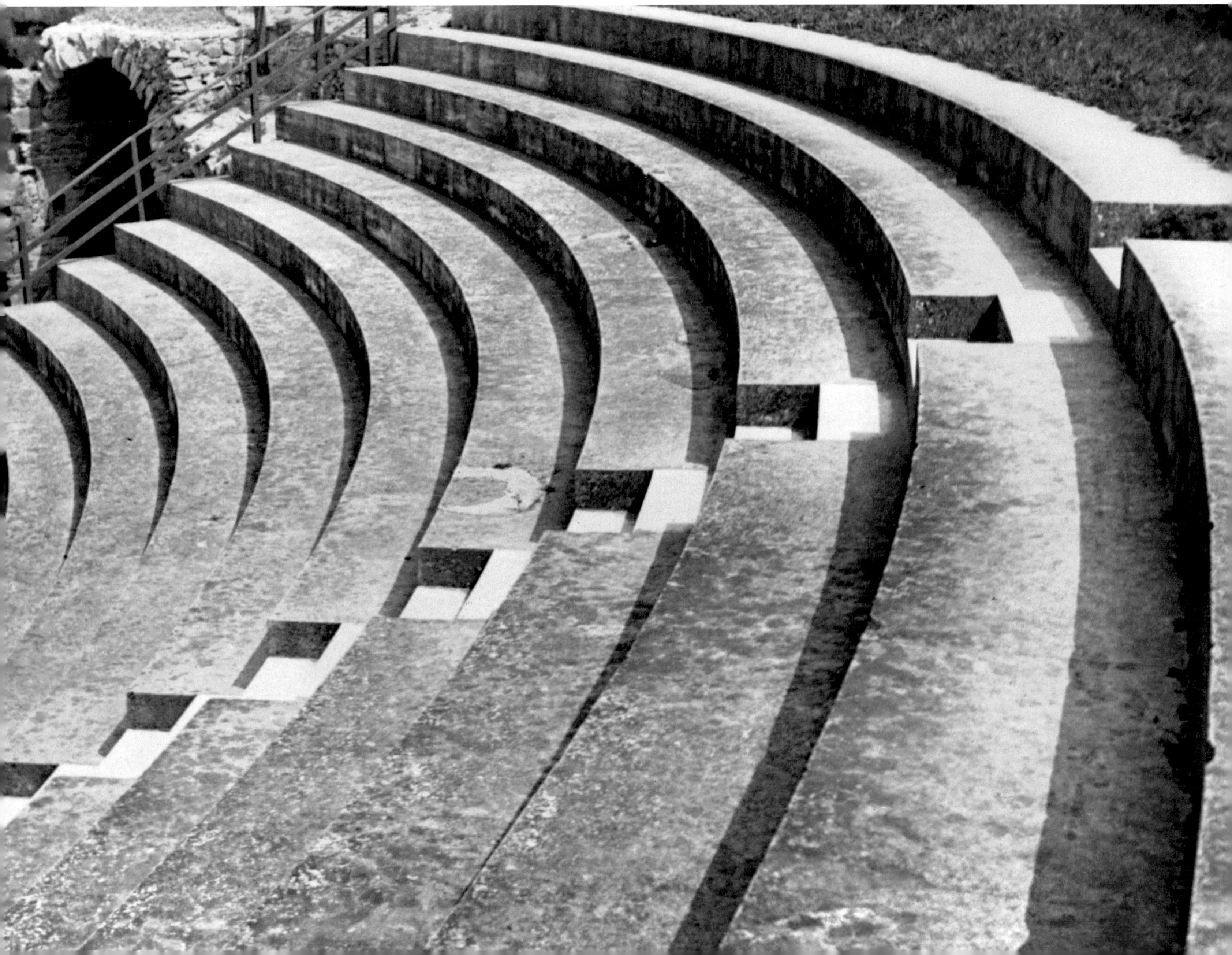

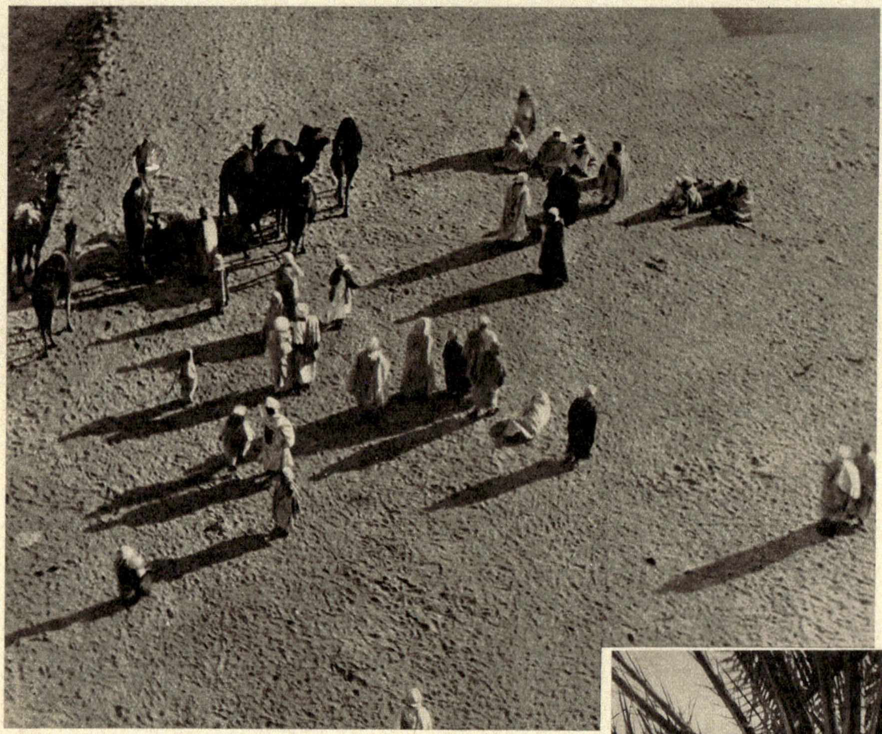

Aufbruch am Rande der Wüste

Wunder

Text von Universitätsprofessor Dr. Franz Wer

Fußwanderungen

Nach einigen Stunden unruhigen Schlafes wache ich 4 U
Bein durchzieht. Zähneklappernd schlürfe ich den heiße
trägt, wartet schon. Wir beide stapfen allein in die ein
Schatten der Morgendämmerung liegen, gerade auf die g
Djebel Melias, Taghla, Fenagha zu. Mit explosionsartiger
ist die ungeheure Wüste fühlbar erwärmt. Zusehends steig
den ungeheuern, schwarzen Felstrümmern anlangen, strömt
man nicht an ein Leben hier glauben kann. Und doch, in d
Hoch aufgerichtet sitzt auf einem Steinblock eine pracht
agame, die beim Herannahen des Fremden in rasender Ei
Steintrümmer hinweg ihr Heim aufsucht, die sandgelbe Hornvi
ihr Versteck, der Wüstenhase, dessen hell-isabellfarbiges Fell i
tritt, unsichtbar macht, alle wohnen in dieser schauerlichen
schwarzen Blätter und Zweige niedriger Pflanzen als Rest
übriggeblieben sind; und es ist kaum zu verstehen, wovon sie
das Mähnenschaf und das Stachelschwein, im Sommer ern
Immer höher steigt die Sonne, und um drei Uhr nachmit
Celsius. Die Luft zittert, so daß die Felswände sich zu bew
in einem Grade ausgetrocknet, daß man keinen Laut hervorbri
Luft bei windstillem Wetter das Befinden nicht schlecht; gib
heißen Sandmassen die unbedeckten Körperteile wie mit Tau
füllen sich bis zur Unerträglichkeit mit dem mehlfeinen Wüs
er zwischen die Lider.

Man muß bedürfn

Auf solchen Wüstenwanderungen lernt man es begreifen
außerordentlich bedürfnislos ist und ein Mann mit einer Han
Tag über nicht nur auskomm
denn das Nahrungsbedürfnis
wesentlich geringer, man em
kann man sich im Hochsomm
ich habe aber gefunden, daß
ganzen Tag im Freien verb
peratur an seinem Körper d
leidlich kühlen, dunkeln Raum
lähmend. Schon gegen 6 Uh
in den Häusern um diese Ze
Abendkühle im Freien ein u
türen, schwatzend und lachend
gleichen ertönt. Der dumpfe
wechselnden Rhythmus ist fü
pechschwarze Nächte mit unz

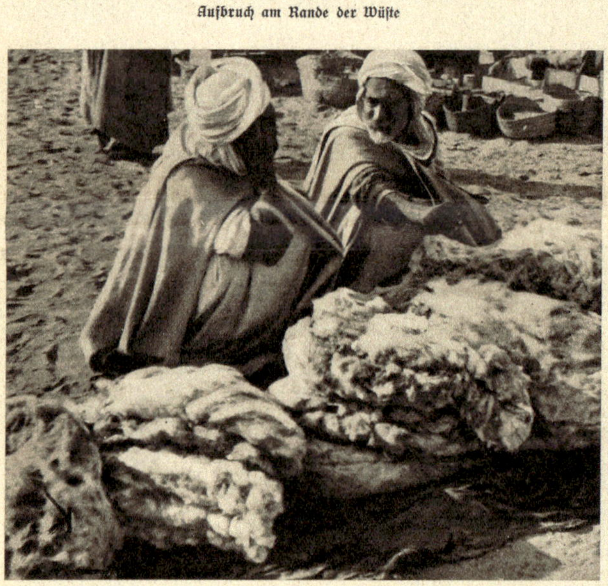

Rohe Wolle wird auf der Straße gehandelt

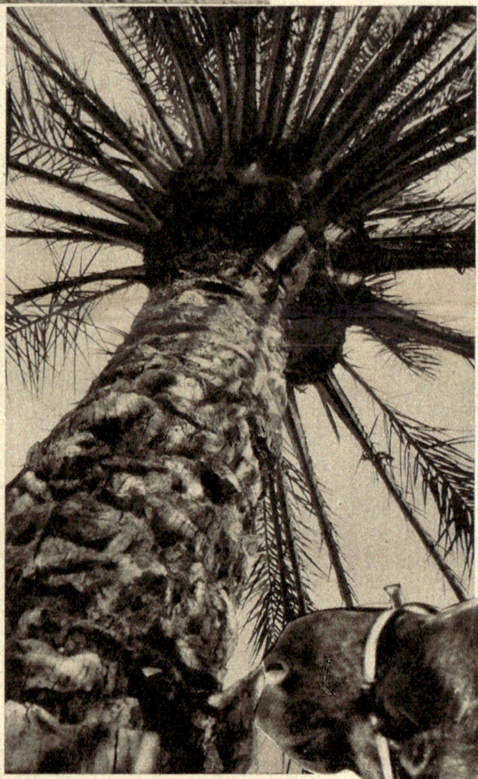

Phantastischer Blick zu einer Dattelpalme

Außerhalb

Man muß sich schon rech
Bereich von Cook and Son
gar nicht so schlimm ist, wi
gewandert, bis zum Mosesbr
hier so leben, wie sie wohl a
sammelnden Wüstensohn mit s
in ungemessene Zeiträume na

Diese Tage in völliger E
damals für mich von größte
erbeutete, ist seither meines
von mir selbst nicht mehr, als

Oft habe ich die roten, g
auf Kamelrücken; und es mu
wieder in diese grandiosen W
wandelbare Bläue etwas Erb
Sturm erstarrtes Meer in unz
lang bis über die Knöchel in
scheinbar schon ganz vom E

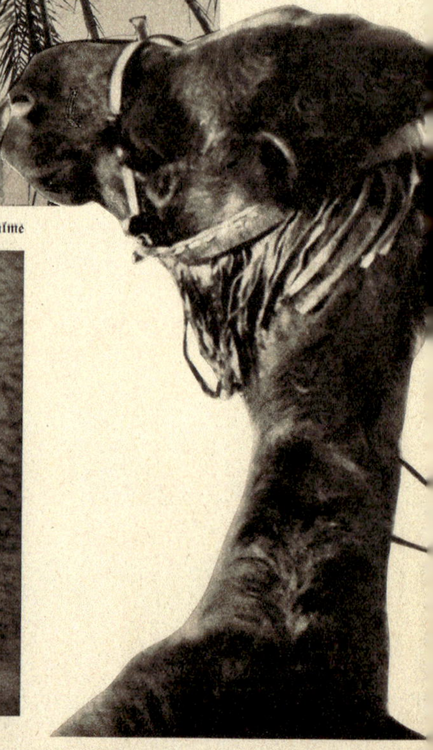

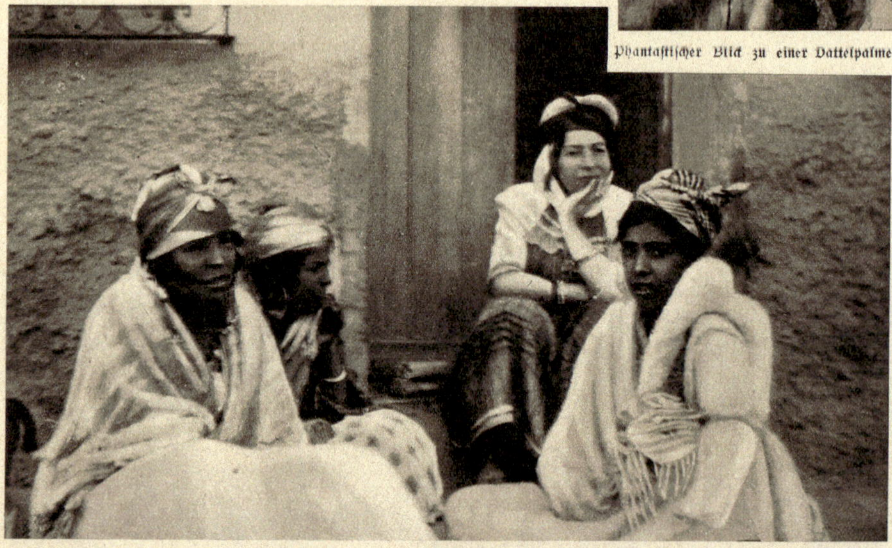

Ouled Nails, die sich durch Hetärendienste ihre Mitgift erwerben

"Wonders of the Desert" (*Hamburger Anzeiger. Illustrierte Wochenbeilage*, no. 28, 1930)

Wüste

r. Block, Hamburg

hara

ie Kühle (5 Grad) Mark und
unge, der den Tagesproviant
ste hinaus, über der noch die
marrokkanischen Grenzberge
onne auf, und in kurzer Zeit
gegen Mittag, wenn wir an
ne unendliche Hitze aus, daß
gen sich mannigfache Tiere.
nit gelbem Kopf, eine Atlos
weiten Sprüngen über die
ugsande zwischen den Blöcken
zenblick, da man fast auf ihn
von der Sonne verbrannten
Blütenpracht des Frühlings
entiere des saharischen Atlas,

meter im Schatten 56 Grad
Saumen und die Kehle sind
lge der vollkommen trockenen
dann peitschen die glühend-
Nasen- und Ohrenöffnungen
geschlossenen Augen dringt

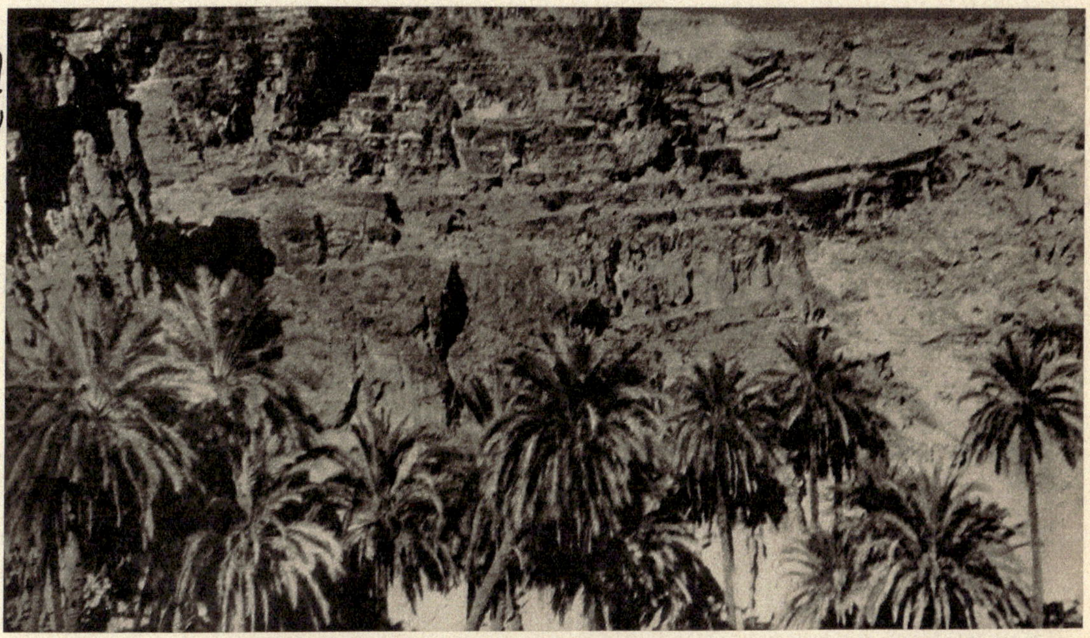

Felsen im Sand: Die Berg-
oase M'Chounêche
bei Biskra

den

Bevölkerung im allgemeinen
Käse und Datteln, den ganzen
nd und kräftig dabei bleibt;
r den Europäer mit der Zeit
Magen als Ballast. Weniger
von Flüssigkeiten gewöhnen;
shalten kann, wenn man den
nähliche Ansteigen der Tem-
wenn man etwa aus einem
h ins Freie kommt; in diesem Falle wirkt die Hitze geradezu
Hochsommer die Temperatur merkbar zu fallen. Während es
m Abschluß des Lichtes oft unerträglich warm ist, bringt die
ol mit sich. In den Oasenstädten hockt alles vor den Haus-
, und irgendein Instrument, eine Negertrommel oder der-
a weitverbreiteten Instruments, der Tarabuka, mit seinem
nit der Erinnerung an solche Abende verbunden, an die sich
Sternen anschließen.

eichs von Cook und Sohn

e oder arabische Wüste verziehen, um in Ägypten aus dem
n muß das Land auch im Sommer besuchen, was übrigens
nimmt. Tagelang sind wir in der Mokattamwüste herum-
es, salziges Wasser von den Beduinen geschöpft wird, die
Jahren gelebt haben; begegnet man so einem Heilkräuter
nsamen Steinwüste, dann glaubt man plötzlich einen Sprung
haben.

ben Sandmeer im Westen der Pyramiden verbracht, waren
s ich damals an merkwürdigen Eidechsen und Heuschrecken
Zoologen mehr wieder gefunden worden — allerdings auch
eimal, freilich im Winter, die betreffenden Stellen aufsuchte.

üstengebiete Nordafrikas durchstreift, zu Fuß, zu Pferd und
deren Konstitution zusammenhängen, daß es mich immer
getationslose Felsmassen in den Himmel ragen, dessen un-
hat, und wo anderseits ungeheure Sanddünen wie ein im
n endlose Ferne sich ausdehnen; und wenn man so, stunden-
ünen auf Dünen abwandert, bald in einem tiefen Tal,
wieder hoch oben auf einer scharfen, vom Wind aus-
Schneide, und wenn dazu die Sonne den müden Wanderer
er sicher ausdörrt, dann kann es vorkommen, daß man,
hinstolpernd, an kühle Wasser oder Biere denkt, die in
e winken. Und doch, immer lockt dieses Land, das
und furchtbar wie das Meer, mannigfaltig trotz seiner
rbig trotz seiner Eintönigkeit, die Heimat von Menschen,
edürfnisse leben und ohne viele Sorgen sterben.

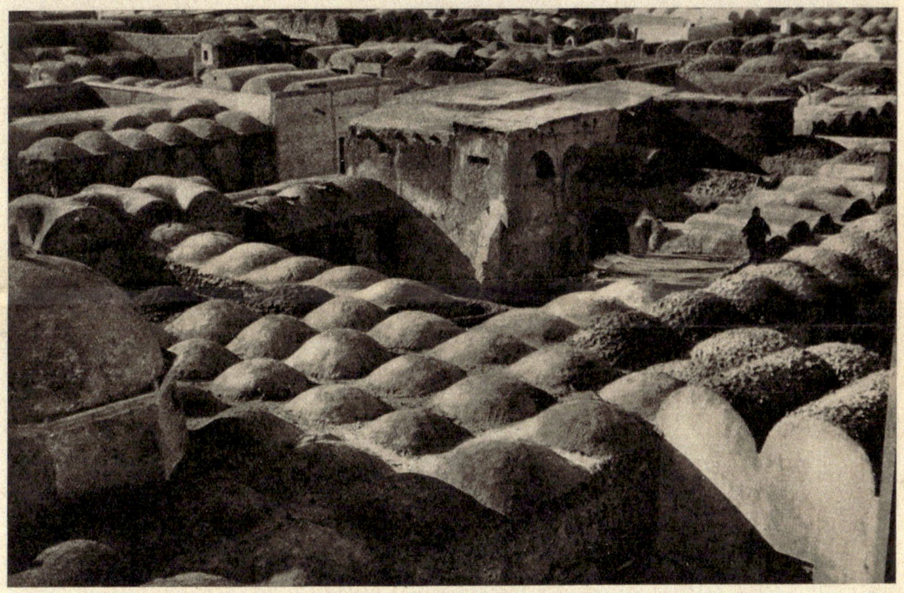

El Oued, die Stadt der tausend Kuppeln

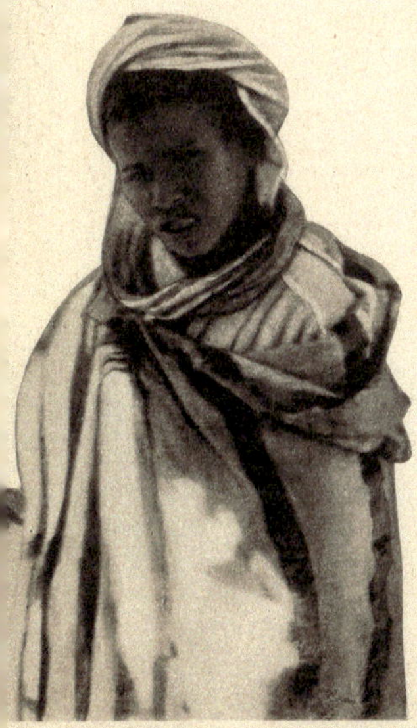

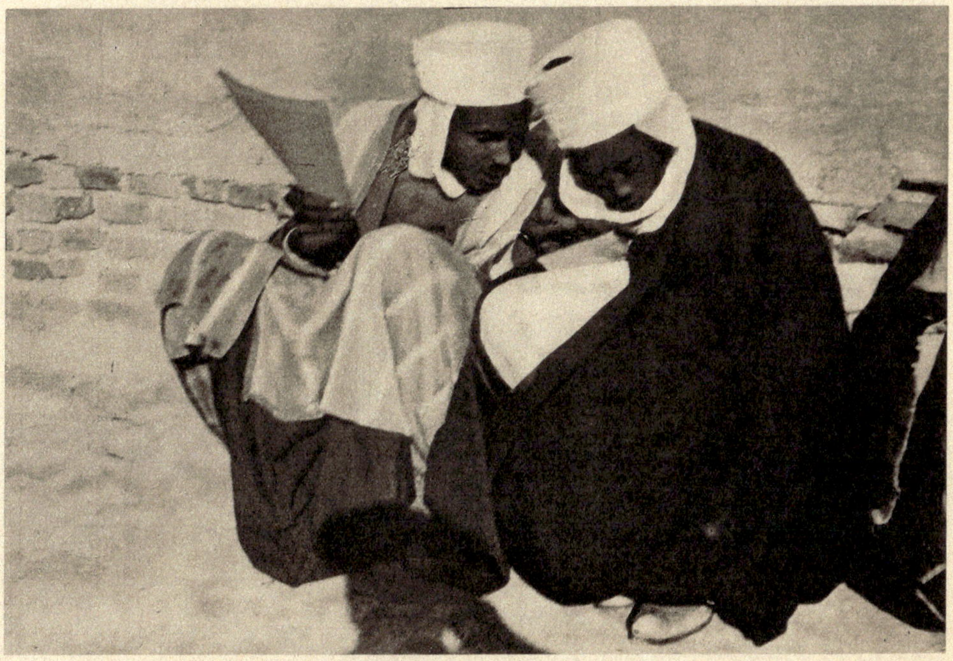

Koranschüler an der Mauer des Wüstenklosters Tamelhaat

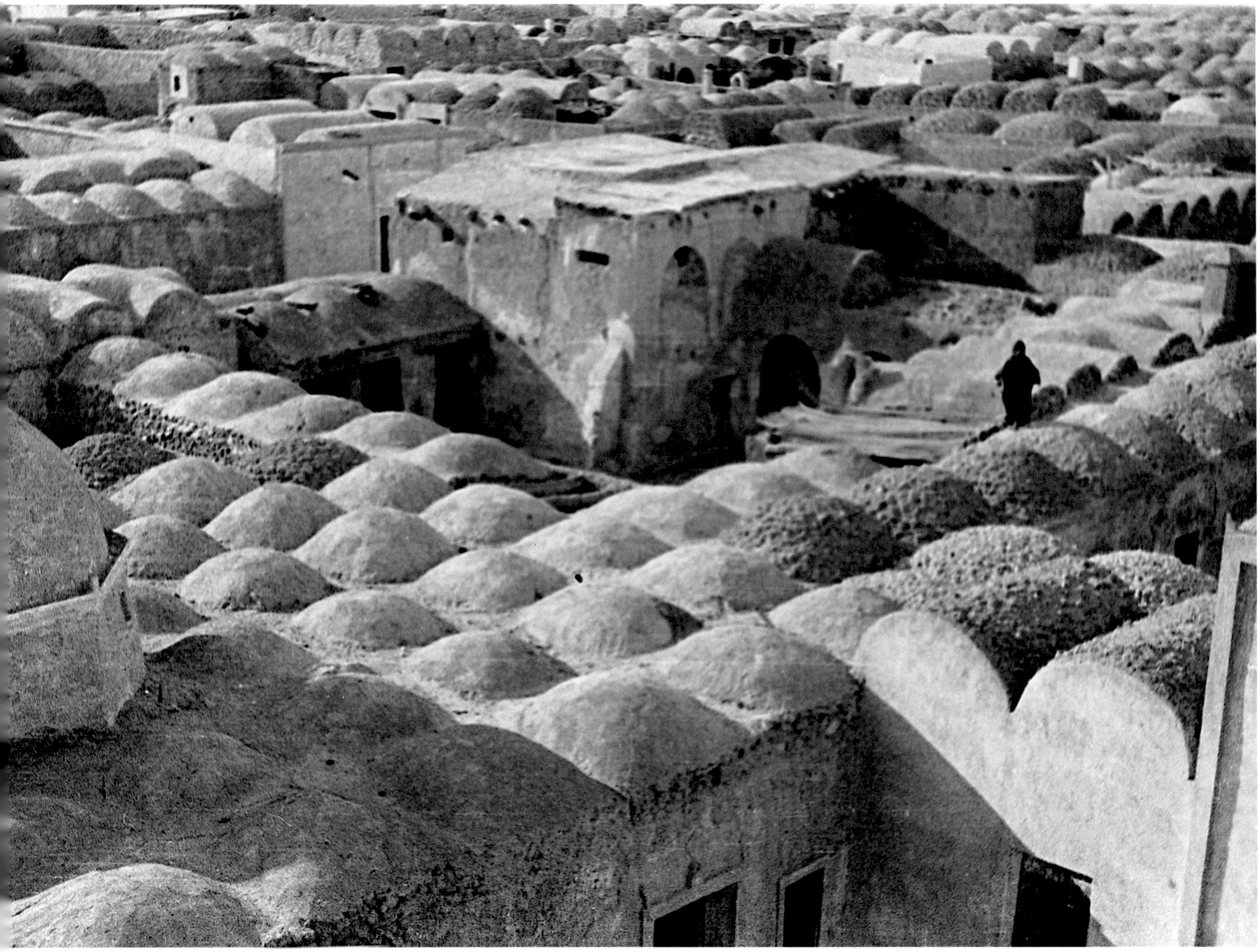

Roofs of El Oued, Algeria, 1930

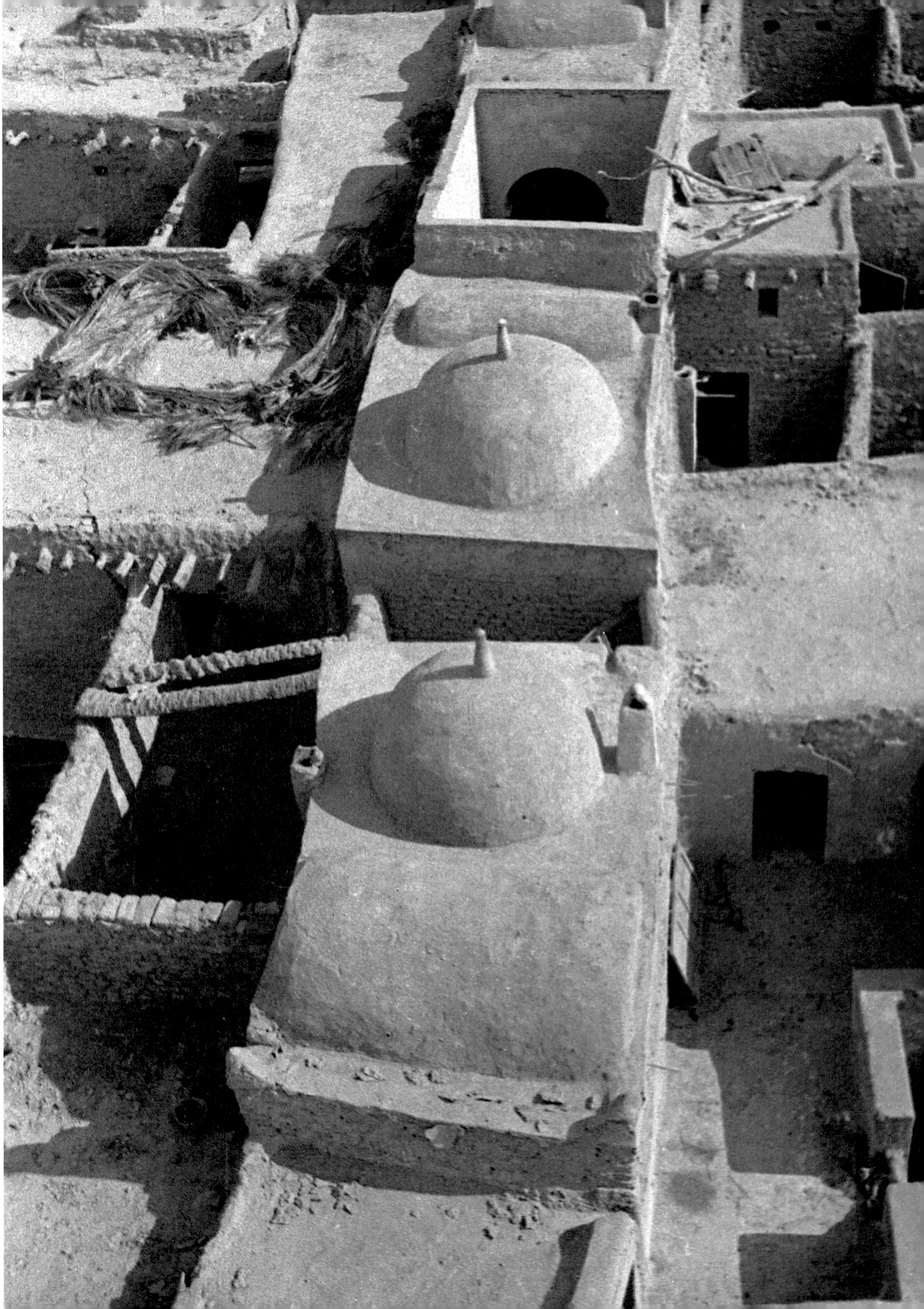

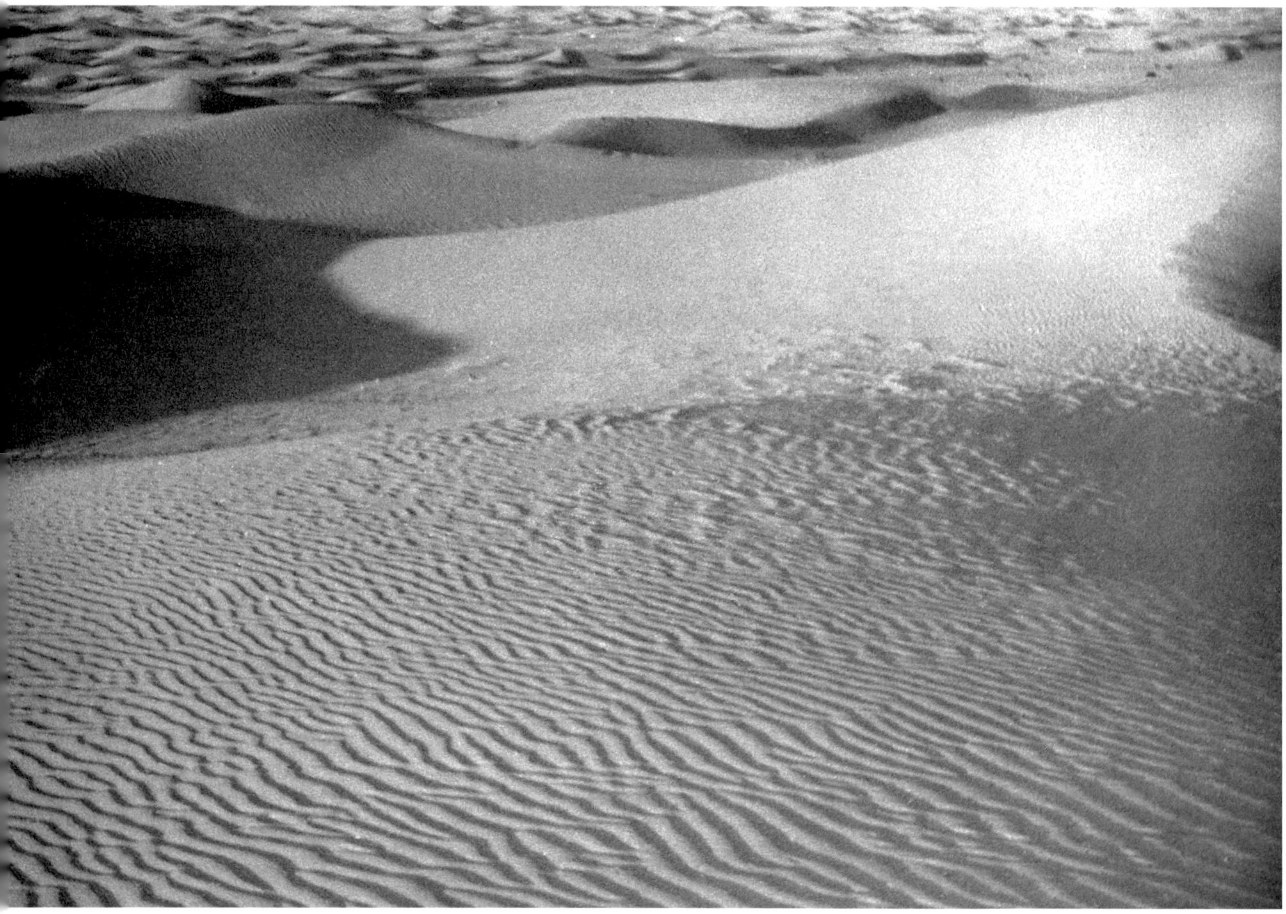

Sand dunes near El Oued, Algeria, 1930

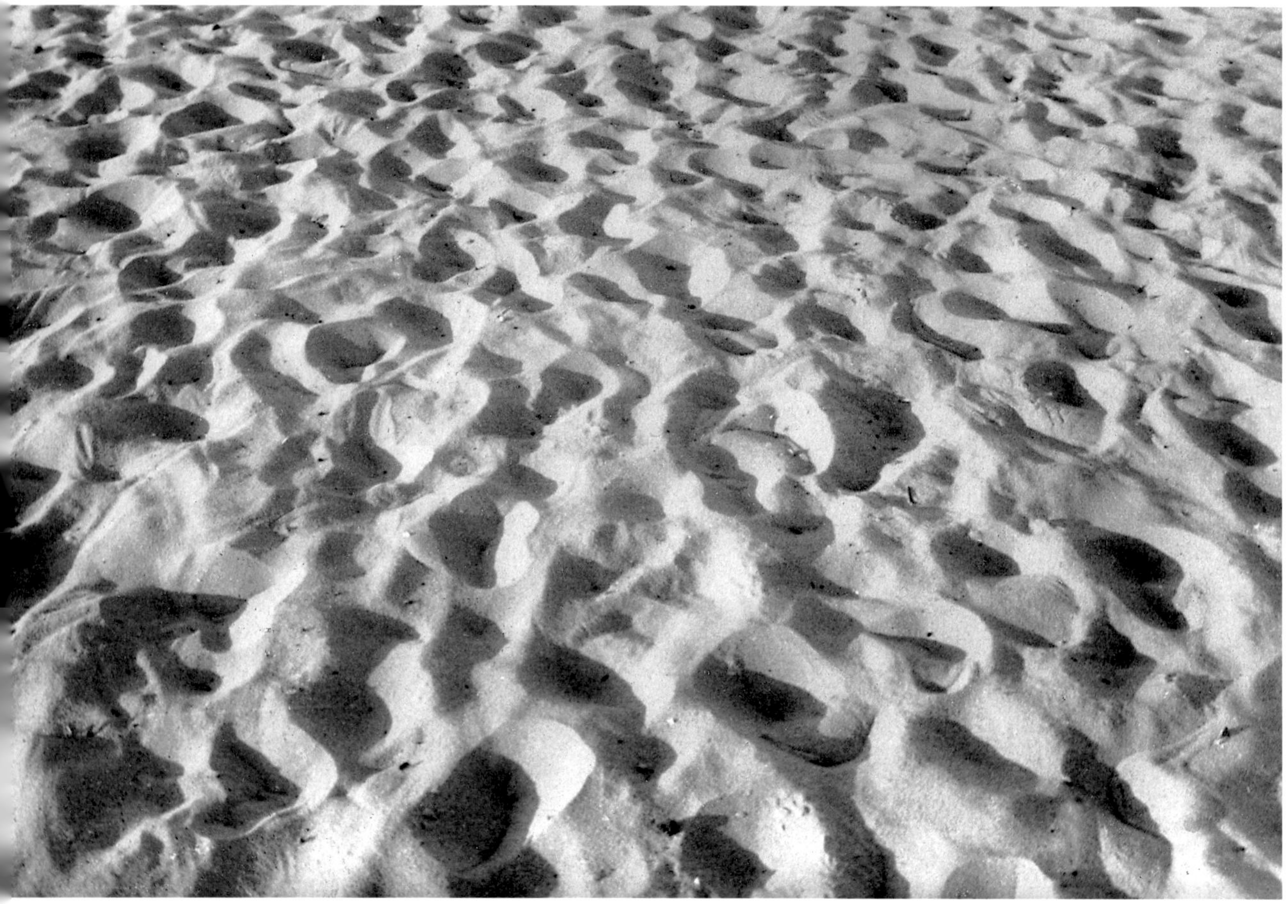

Footprints in
the desert sand,
Algeria, 1930

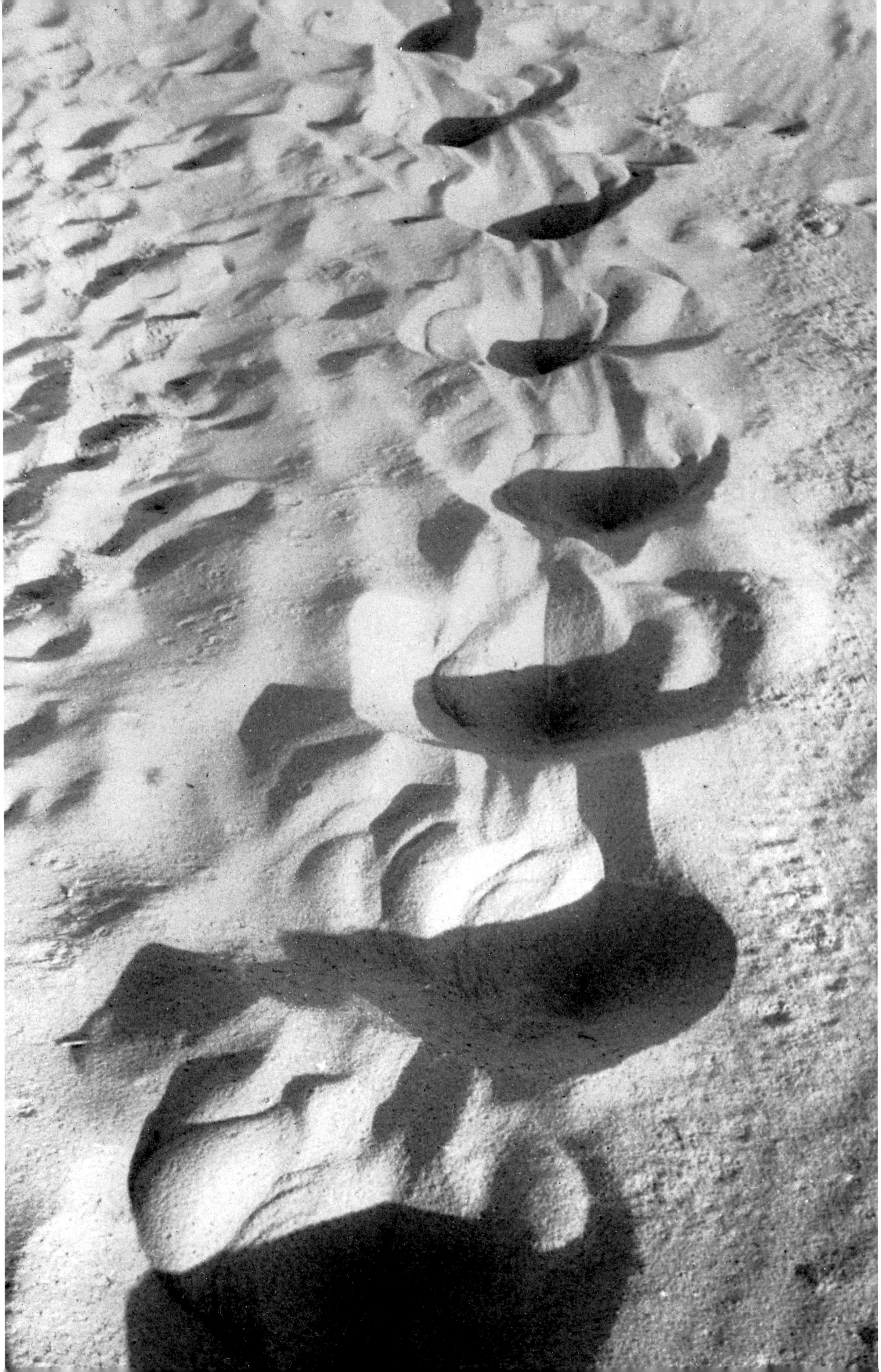

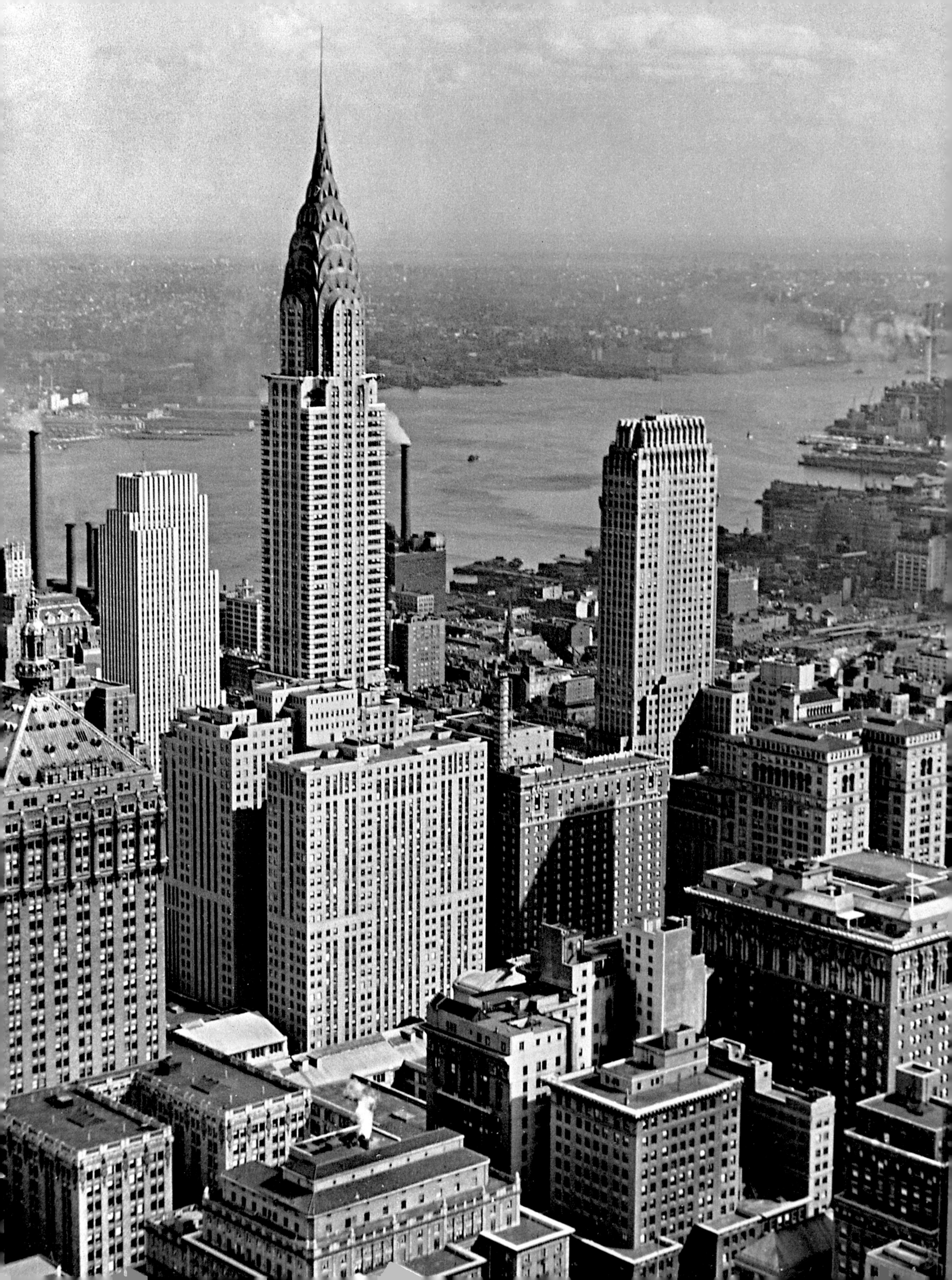

Traveling across America with a Leica

Photo reportages from the United States

In the fall of 1931, Fritz Block traveled across the United States of America— photographically his most prolific trip. His journey must be seen in light of the "Americanism" prevalent in Germany in the 1920s, which identified the United States with technical progress and economic prosperity—even resulting in a kind of social utopia. This enthusiasm—notwithstanding the variously pointed cultural and political critiques (particularly after the onset of the economic crisis in late 1929)—was articulated across the media landscape, and was continually a subject of the (photo-illustrated) press. This fascination was also reflected in the photography of New Objectivity, which shared with Americanism a similarly techno-rational worldview.[1] Another factor encouraging travel to the United States beginning in the mid-1920s was Germany's economic recovery. The port cities of Hamburg and Bremen, with their shipping companies Hamburg-America Line (Hapag) and North German Lloyd, played a key role, offering widely advertised tourist study and group trips to North America.

Architects Travel to America

Architects were an especially important business group to address for tourism. They traveled to America to visit cities, skyscrapers, and industrial plants, to study the rationalization of construction methods, and to inform themselves of developments in urban planning. Travel agencies and shipping companies put together suitable itineraries, often in connection with international conferences. The Bund Deutscher Architekten (Association of German Architects) encouraged its members to join such trips.

Friedrich Paulsen, editor of the high-circulation architecture journal *Bauwelt*, had traveled to the US in 1924 and subsequently published a multi-part series of articles in his magazine. Architects such as Max-Ernst Haefeli, Adolf Rading, and Wassili Luckhardt had reported, in words and pictures, on their professional travel impressions of the US,[2] while Walter Curt Behrendt, Paul Wolf, and Martin Wagner focused more on reporting on aspects of the urban planning they encountered.[3] The most prominent photo report, indeed the most photographically effective, was by Erich Mendelsohn, who spent most of his 1924 trip in New York. Titled *Amerika. Bilderbuch eines Architekten* (1926, 2nd edition 1928) (America. Picture Book of an Architect), it includes not only Mendelsohn's own photographs but also those by Danish architect Knud Lönberg-Holm (1895–1972), who had emigrated in 1923 from Altona, near Hamburg, through Holland, to the United States.[4] The Austrian architect Richard J. Neutra had also lived in the US since 1923; from there he reported for German architecture magazines. His photographs illustrate the pages of his books *Wie baut Amerika?* (1927) (How America Builds) and *Amerika. Die Stilbildung des neuen Bauens in den Vereinigten Staaten* (1930) (America. The Stylistic Development of New Building in the United States). The Hamburg architect Ernst Gerson (1890–1974) traveled to the United States in 1929, illustrating some of his articles with his own photographs.[5] In all likelihood, Block knew of some of these reports and publications.

As an architect, Block was a bit of a latecomer among America travelers. It was Walter Gropius who gave him the decisive impetus to go and experience the United States firsthand. After leaving his post as the director of the Bauhaus, Gropius and his wife, Ise, had traveled across the US, in the spring of 1928, visiting New York, Detroit, Chicago, Los Angeles, the Grand Canyon, and the Native American settlements in New Mexico and Arizona—the same journey Block would take.[6] He took photographs throughout, subsequently collating selected prints in three albums. The photos did not just include architectural motifs and high-rise constructions, they also documented travel scenes along the way. Naturally, some of these photos correspond subjects that Block photographed three years later, when he visited the same locations. Anna-Sophie Block recorded her own impressions in travelogues, as Ise Gropius had done before her. As for Walter Gropius, he did not, at the time, publish his private photos.

View of the Chrysler, Chanin, and Daily News Buildings from the Empire State Building, New York, 1931

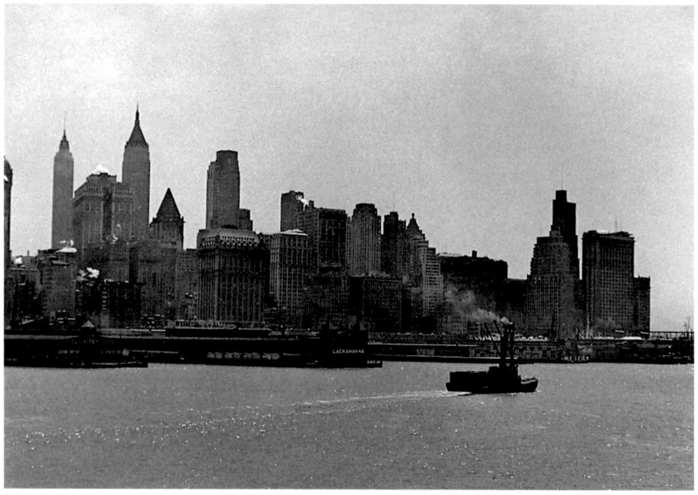

View of downtown Manhattan from the Hudson River, 1931

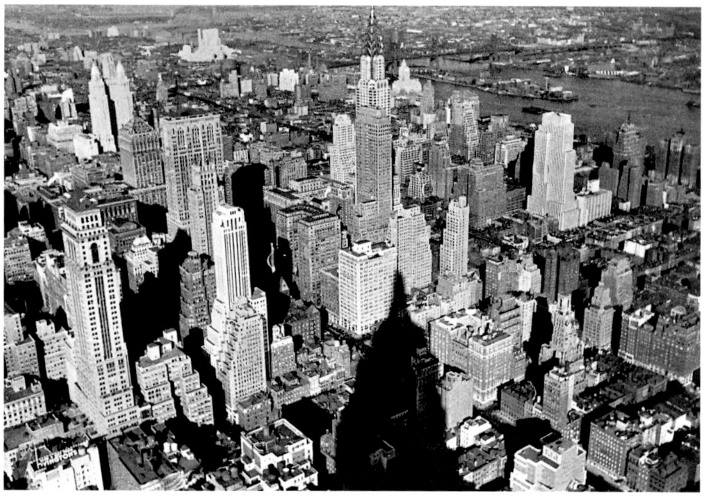

View of midtown Manhattan from the Empire State Building, 1931

Block knew Gropius through his work on the committees of the Deutscher Werkbund and, foremost, from the Bund Deutscher Architekten. In 1926, Block had traveled to Dessau for the opening of the Bauhaus building with a delegation of the Bund Deutscher Architekten. Moreover, Gropius was a member of the Research Committee for Contemporary Architecture of the Bund Deutscher Architekten, of which Block was managing secretary. Under the aegis of this organization, Gropius contributed an article to the volume *Probleme des Bauens* (The Problems of Building, 1928), which Block edited. According to his travel diary, Block was in Dessau again in August 1928, to visit the Masters' Houses. He met Gropius in Berlin shortly thereafter. One can safely assume they discussed Gropius's trip to America, and probably even skimmed through some photos. Block's wife later noted that Gropius advised her husband to go to North America if he wished to learn about the implications of rationalization on construction and building—although he would not like everything he might see.[7]

But Block's trip to America was less devoted to studying architecture and urban planning and more to the overall photographic experience of the country and its many contrasts. To prepare for the journey, he likely studied the illustrated book *Die Vereinigten Staaten. Das romantische Amerika. Baukunst, Landschaft und Volksleben* (Romantic America. Picturesque United States, 1927), by photographer Emil Otto Hoppé (1878–1972), who had traveled to the US in 1926.[8] The book contains some motifs Block took later, too, albeit in a less picturesque manner. According to his travel diary, Block visited Hoppé's photo exhibition *Das romantische Amerika* in Berlin in early November 1927. Inspiration for his stay in New York came from the city portrait *New York* (1930), by French travel writer Paul Morand. Although illustrated with only a few agency photos, the book deals with some places and topics that Block made the subject of his photo reportages.

For his America trip, Block was equipped with two Leica cameras and three lenses (wide-angle 35, standard 50, and telephoto 135 mm) as well as various filters and films.[9] According to the film numbers on the backs of the surviving prints, his route led from New York City to Niagara Falls, Detroit, and Chicago to San Francisco and Los Angeles. The return trip was via the Grand Canyon and New Mexico, and again to New York City. During his nine-week stay, Block shot more than 140 small-format film rolls, with a total of about 4,000 images, among which there were—as with any photographer—also many false exposures and insignificant shots. A considerable part of these images have been preserved in his estate as negatives, or, in reverse, as positives, as well as in a variety of prints, together representing Block's range of quality and thematic interest. Also in his estate are examples of the illustrated press with his United States photographs and photo reportages.

New York

On September 17, 1931, Block and his wife arrived in New York on the Hamburg-America Line's (Hapag) steamer *Reliance*. About the approach to the city, he later wrote: "The greatest impression of any American trip is the gateway to the New York City harbor. During the long sea voyage, you have seen nothing but water and horizon, and suddenly the silhouettes of the skyscrapers emerge from the long, narrow island of Manhattan. The closer you approach them, the more fantastic they appear [...]. Life intensifies in the air as well as on the water, at the same pace. When the sun goes down, all those giants emerge only in their outlines in wonderful pale pink tones, and then, gradually, the lights rise up on them and the structure of New York becomes increasingly surreal. Under the spell of this gigantism we stand as if glued to this image."[10] Block captured this impression in the dark [p. 170], as well as on a tour of the Hudson River around Manhattan [p. 160].

For Block, as for his contemporaries, New York embodied the modern metropolis: "New York, this archetype of a city, with the unprecedented dynamism of its masses of buildings, its skyscrapers, urban canyons, major engineering works, its incomparable location right at the water. In addition, the waves of traffic, which cannot be measured on European scale, this bustle of people of all races, which in no means overshadows their humanity. [...] Nowhere else are

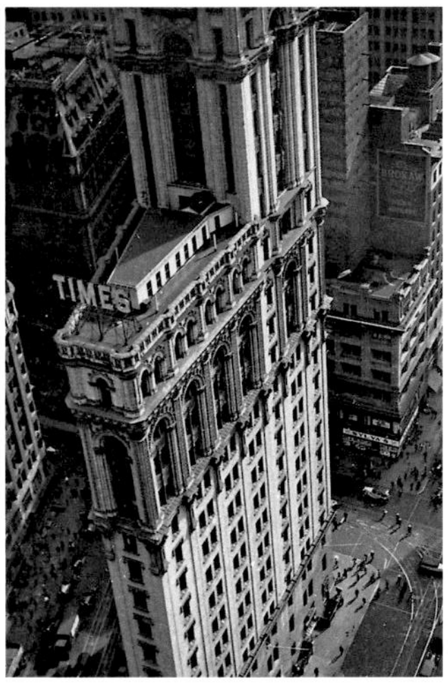 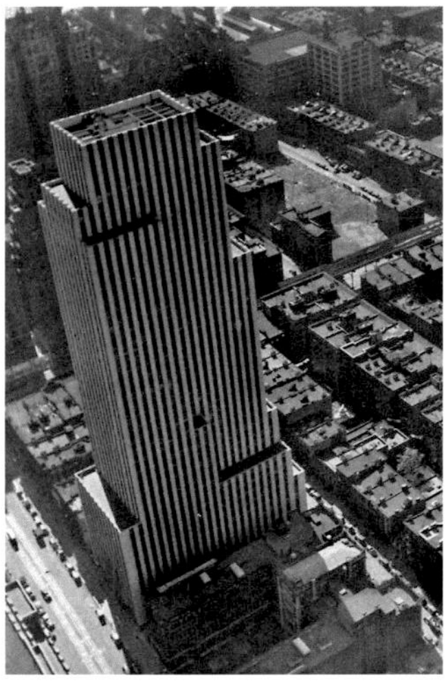 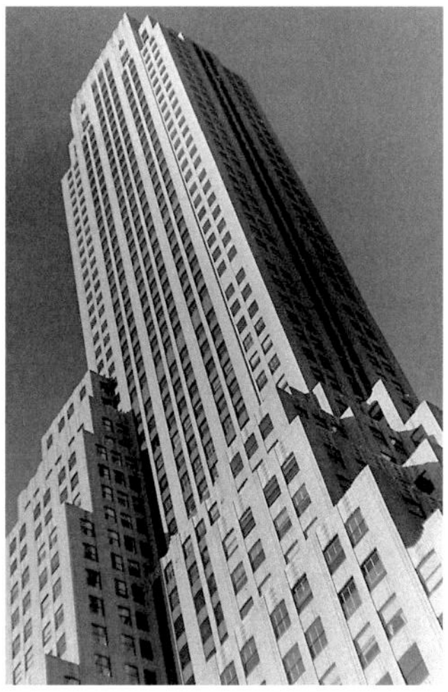 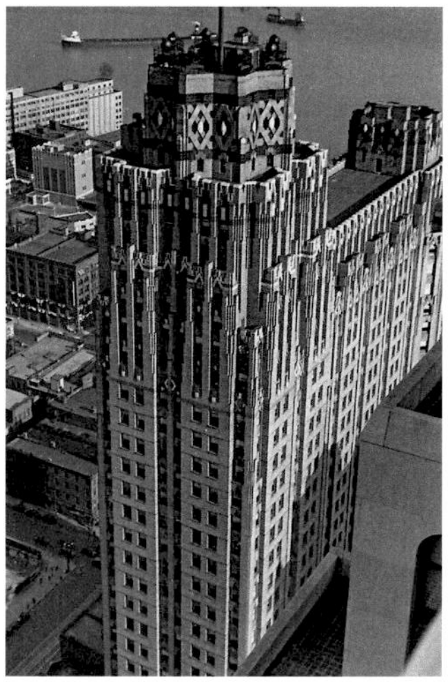

One Times Square (The Times Tower), Daily News Building, and 500 Fifth Avenue, New York, 1931 – Guardian Building, Detroit, 1931

the contrasts so unexpectedly juxtaposed, and no other city is equally full of excitement as this one. This city keeps you under its spell up to the moment you board the ship to leave. The experience of *the* big city is unique and, in this intensity, it has no equal in all the world [...]."[11]

It is in this spirit and with this feeling that Block approached New York City photographically. One of his first motifs was the Brooklyn Bridge, where he was able to apply his view of technical structures—trained on Hamburg's Elbe bridges and the Pont Transbordeur in Marseille. These included unconventional and fragmented views [pp. 172–173] as well as a view through the steel cables to the skyline of downtown Manhattan [p. 171]. The latter was not a new approach, however, but an obvious yet effective design tool that had been used by photographers such as Karl Struss (already in 1912) and Emil Otto Hoppé, as well as by Walter Gropius.

Block then took photos of the city's skyscrapers—in worm's-eye view from the street, and from on top of them: "You get the right impression of the city only from above, and the many skyscrapers scattered all over the city with their viewing terraces provide a convenient opportunity to study the city and its development."[12] Block looked down, for example, from the Chrysler Building (1928–30) [p. 158], onto the still art deco-style Chanin Building (1929) [p. 176] and the already more modern Daily News Building (1929–30) [p. 161]. Contrariwise, he directed his gaze up to the new skyscraper at 500 Fifth Avenue (1929–31) [pp. 161 and 179] and the Empire State Building, which was in the final stage of completion (1930–31) [p. 178] and already the tallest building in New York. From its observation deck, Block took a picture series of the stony sea of midtown Manhattan [pp. 160 and 174–175]. Then more top-down photos of buildings, including One Times Square (1903–05), the former *New York Times* publishing and commercial building [p. 161]. Images of the imposing portal of Pennsylvania Station Block took from his room in the Hotel Pennsylvania, across the street [p. 177].

Despite his enthusiasm, Block retained his criticism as an architect of American urban architecture: "I see that particularly in architecture and urban planning we are doing a lot of things much better in old Europe."[13] He found the eclectic or decorative style of many New York skyscrapers outdated: "Of course, we European architects specifically notice the buildings' luxurious execution. On one hand, this is tied to the high-quality execution of the building itself; but it also evidences, unfortunately, overly opulent, tasteless design, with all the excesses of a wildly proliferating formalism. There are only very few buildings in America that openly show the beauty of technical forms. It is hard to believe that some American architects—a number of who are or who work with ingenious builders—have such a fondness for poor decoration and architectural confections."[14]

Block was also attracted to motifs in which the objective world was transformed into an abstract composition of structures. For example, fire-escape stairways and the shadows they cast over the façade [p. 181], the water tanks on rooftops [p. 180], and the elevated train tracks and the shadow patterns they cast on the street below [p. 182]. Block showed the dynamics of the city's traffic with a photograph of a curving elevated train track [p. 183]. The aesthetic effect of technical design fascinated him as well at the Bayonne Bridge, which spans the Kill Van Kull, the waterway running between New Jersey and Staten Island. This steel arch bridge was not yet open for use, so Block was unable to take any close-ups. He instead made photos of its mighty arch from below during a boat trip around Manhattan [p. 184].

But above all, Block was excited about the openly visible construction and functional principles of the George Washington Bridge, crossing over the Hudson River: "In the case of the Washington Bridge, one of the greatest testimonials to technical beauty in the world, only a long and hard fight dissuaded the authorities of their intention to cover the pillars with Gothic architecture. A number of progressive-minded architects and engineers intervened to allow this magnificent structure to be shown in all its clarity."[15] The grand opening took place on October 24, 1931; it was open to traffic the next day. Block was therefore only able to take close-up shots of the bridge on his return trip, which he did, snapping a variety of views of the pylons and steel

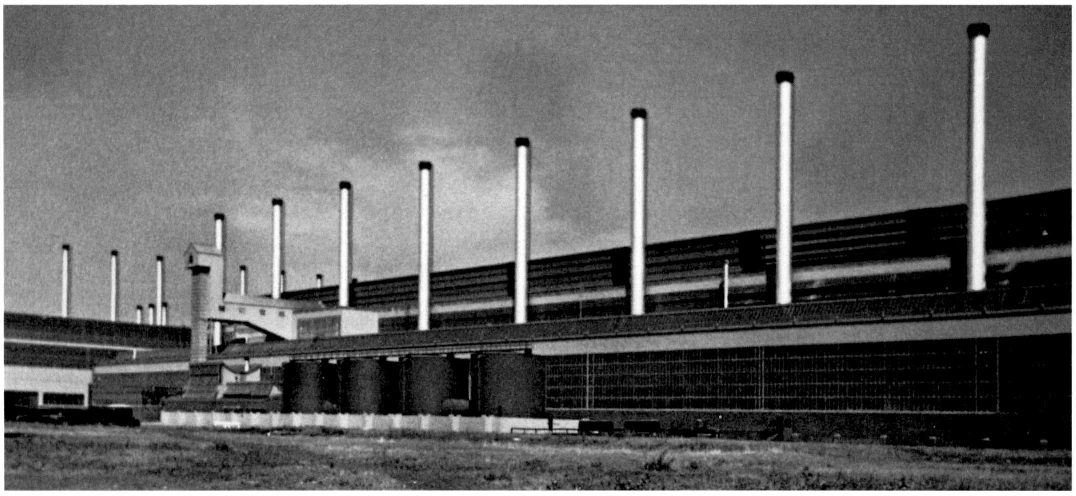 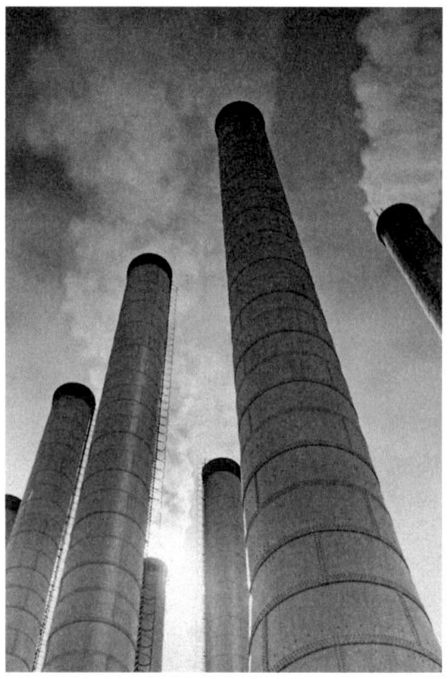

Open-hearth furnace and smokestacks of the Ford Factory in Dearborn, Detroit, 1931

cables [pp. 4 and 185–186]. In contrast to images of the bridge made at the same time by Edward Steichen (1879–1973), Block took the principles of the New Vision a step further, by photographing only details of the steel cables against the sky, reducing them to an abstract composition of lines [p. 187].

The next day, Block took up the role of a photojournalist, riding up Fifth Avenue by bus and taking photos from the viewing deck [pp. 190–191]. This idea was not new: as early as in 1929 a series of articles entitled "*Dichterstafette auf dem Autobus*" was published in the *Berliner Tageblatt*, portraying a large metropolis from this perspective. In New York, Block captured lively scenes of bustling traffic and the random encounters of pedestrians on the sidewalks [pp. 188–189]. His wife Anna-Sophie later wrote: "These snapshots, taken completely discreetly from the top of a bus, convey a vivid picture of the American people, their casualness, agility, amicability, and carefreeness. These photos offer an impression of street life, of tempo, and of the traffic's pulsing dynamism that a picture from below could never convey so insistently and memorably."[16]

Block had to deal simultaneously with both the artistic demands and technical challenges of photography. These were fused when he tried to capture Broadway's luminous advertising lights at night. At the beginning of his stay, he was unable to properly capture such scenes because the film available to him was not sufficiently light sensitive. But during the few days he spent in New York on his return trip, he had more luck. On November 9, 1931, Times Square was illuminated with flak spotlights for the film premiere of *The Champ* at Astor Theatre. This provided the necessary illumination for a photo series [pp. 192–197], which Block shot with the new Kodak SS film: "New York at night is a special experience [...]. This jumble of advertising, glamor, and lights reaches a climax on Broadway between Herald Square and Columbus Circle, [...] New York's main entertainment district. [...] Its explosive spectacle of advertising is hard to beat."[17]

Block's interest also included everyday urban life and groups in American society. He created photo series about restaurants, and about Americans' enthusiasm for sports, especially baseball. He made photo reportages of women of various social classes and children of different races [pp. 198–199]. The economic realities did not escape him: he photographed scenes of unemployment across the cityscape: "After the end of prosperity, in 1929, a crisis—one larger than the country has ever seen—also found its way here. Though one would like to believe appearances—that life is much better because it seems to carry on as usual—appearances can be deceptive. [...] There is no state unemployment benefit; only private charities take care of people in need. [...] The unemployed sit around in parks and public squares. America, the land of breathless tempo, has changed its tune." Accompanying texts on these subjects have been preserved, but only few prints.[18]

Many of Block's New York images are examples of modern street photography, quickly captured snapshots taken in public space of anonymous passersby, groups or individuals, or of seemingly casual scenes, which offer an authentic impression of place, events, and atmosphere.[19] This is particularly true for photos that Block made in Manhattan's ethnically diverse neighborhoods: "The inexhaustible trove of New York's immigrant districts: Chinese, Jewish, Syrian, Italian, and Negro neighborhoods, and the marvelous New Yorkers with their ease and carefree way."[20] Block met Wall Street bank employees at lunchtime [p. 200], and encountered a still orthodox world in the Jewish quarter [p. 201]. In Little Italy, he observed both sinister and friendly types [p. 202], street sellers at work [p. 203], and the eagerness of shoeshine boys [p. 203]. He was able to create particularly expressive shots in Harlem, where he took pictures mostly of children and adolescents on the streets [pp. 206–209], but also of other everyday scenes [pp. 204–205]. In the text for this photo reportage, Anna-Sophie Block addressed American racial segregation, but also herself deployed the "negro" clichés of the time.

A day trip finally brought Block to Coney Island, where the hustle and bustle of showmen offered a variety of motifs.[21] Already in some of his Hamburg photo reportages, Block had shown a special fondness for the circus and other

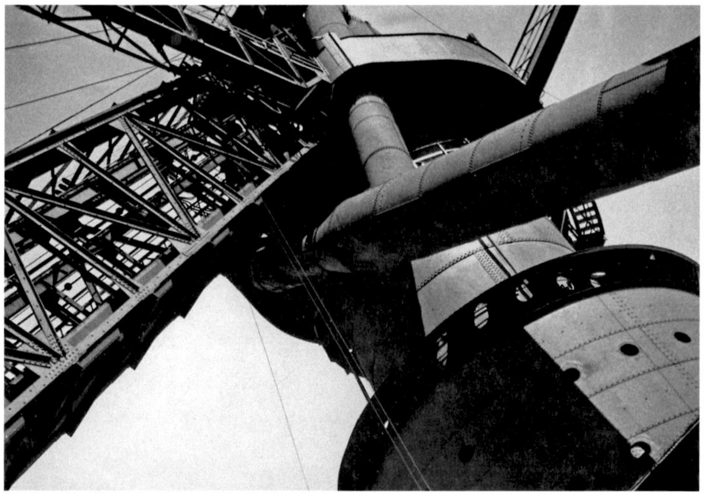
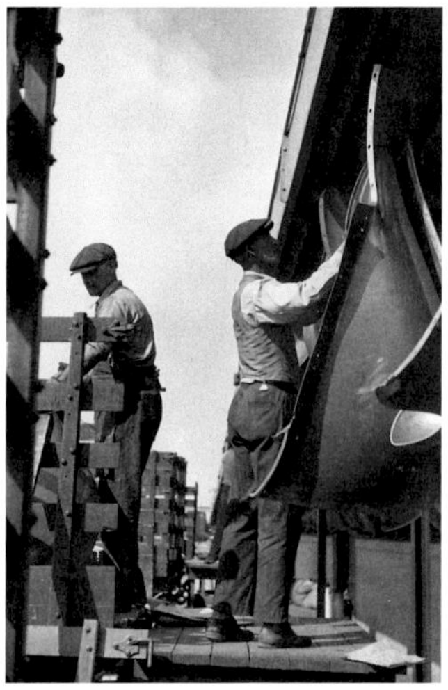
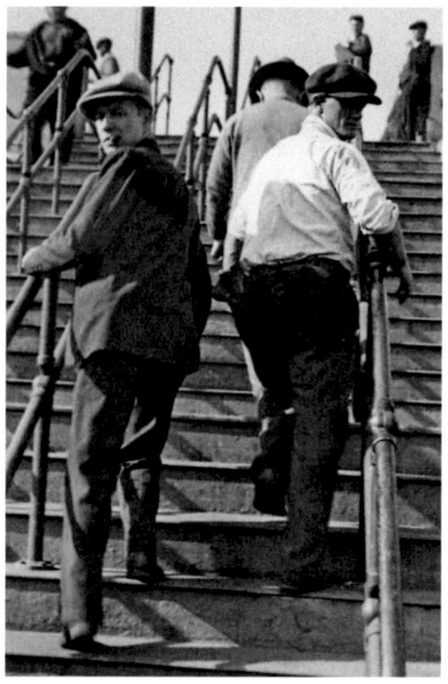

Blast furnace charging platform, workers at the loading ramp, and shift change, Ford Factory in Dearborn, Detroit, 1931

forms of popular entertainment. At Coney Island, he took photos of carousels, show booths, and the barkers soliciting audiences for them [p. 211] as well as of the boardwalk and posters advertising stage performances [p. 213]. The Ferris wheel, here called the Wonder Wheel [p. 212], spoke, of course, to Block's photographic focus on the aesthetic structures within industrial constructions and their graphic effects, of which he took only detailed shots.

In total, Block's New York photographs offer a multi-faceted body of work that combine the visual strategies of New Objectivity and New Vision, street photography, and photo reportage. If Block would have been able to expand his pictorial material and publish it as a book at that time, it would have been perhaps the first modern photo book by a single photographer-author about New York, even before Edward M. Weyer's *Metropolis. An American City in Photographs* (1934) and Mario (von) Bucovich's *Manhattan Magic* (1937).[22] Now, at least in retrospect, it is apparent that Block made a remarkable contribution to the photographic history of New York, characteristic for the period of the years surrounding 1930.

Detroit, Chicago, and Los Angeles

"But New York is not America," Block correctly stated.[23] The next stop on his itinerary was Niagara Falls. Here, Block took the obligatory photos of the impressive natural spectacle, but he was more interested in the nearby power stations, with their technical offerings of cable towers, control centers, and insulators [pp. 164 and 214–215], which he photographed in detail and from unusual perspectives. Parallels to motifs by Albert Renger-Patzsch and other German representatives of the New Objectivity are obvious, though Block mainly chose angles that transitioned from the mere technical-documentary to the principles of New Vision.

Block's next stop was Detroit. The few photos he took included the Guardian Tower (1929), which is comparable to New York's art deco skyscrapers [p. 161]. A theme of the era Block had repeatedly dealt with, also as an architect, was the rationalization of life derived from technology and economics. Block visited the Ford Factory in Dearborn, near Detroit, which was considered the epitome of modern production at the time, along with New York's skyscrapers, and was an integral part of any American trip taken by architects and photographers: "When we speak of the mechanization of work today—rationalization, conveyor belts—we involuntarily think of Ford, his company, and his theories. The opponents of these developments see Ford as the chief culprit for the excesses caused by failed or misguided rationalization in the aftermath of the economic crisis. [...] Certainly, however, the new Ford Factory, the River Rouge factory, is the symbol of a modern production plant, a symbol and a document for everything that is linked to the terms *rationalization, mechanization,* and *technical beauty*. That's why visiting this factory is one of the strongest impressions America has to offer [...]."[24]

Emil Otto Hoppé had already photographed the Ford Factory during his trip to the United States, in 1926, and he incorporated some of these pictures in his photo book *Romantic America. Picturesque United States* (1927), including the distinctive smokestacks of the power station—symbols of modernity and prosperity. The new River Rouge factory, built by German-born architect Albert Kahn, was not completed until 1927, and thus not included in Hoppé's volume. More influential in photographic history were the shots taken by artist and photographer Charles Sheeler (1883–1965), which he made on behalf of Ford in fall 1927, as part of an advertising campaign for the new Model A.[25] Sheeler did not photograph the product itself but rather the factory's architecture and production lines where the cars were made. He rarely included people—neither to show scale nor as workers. Over a six-week period, he chose around 30 motifs, the most famous of which is the *Criss-Crossed Conveyors*, which shows crossing conveyor belts in front of rising smokestacks in a combination of constructive objectivity and technical pathos. Sheeler's photographs were presented in Germany as an example of modern industrial photography, at the 1929 Werkbund exhibition *Film und Foto*, where Block would have seen them. Block's photo reportage of the Ford Factory, which he probably concluded in just a few days or even a single visit, shares some similari-

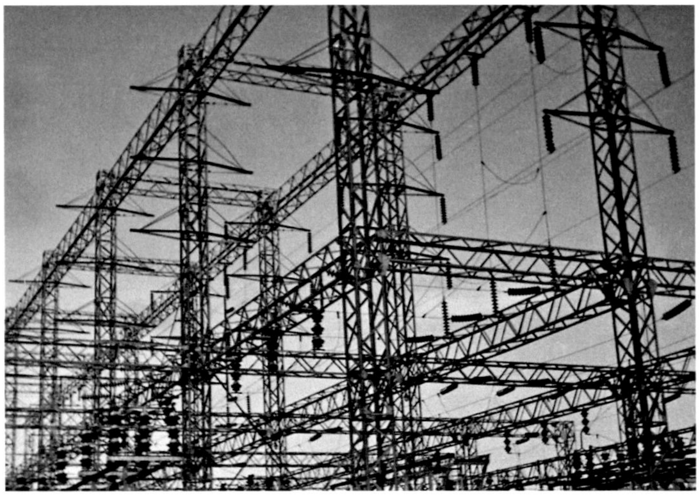

Cable suspensions of a transformer station, Niagara Falls, 1931

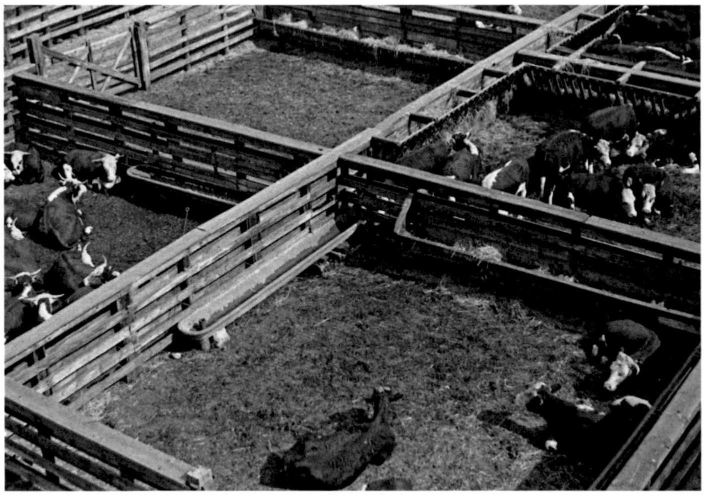

Cattle enclosures at a slaughterhouse complex, Chicago, 1931

ties with Sheeler's images, but the spectrum of his subject matter is more varied and focused on details.

Block also photographed the entire car plant and factory architecture as part of an industrial landscape [p. 162 and 220]. Then he approached the factory's power station and water tower, smokestacks, and conveyor belts [pp. 216–217 and 221]. He devoted a whole series of extreme worm-eyed images to the shiny metallic ensemble of towering smokestacks [pp. 5, 162 and 223]. In deliberate contrast, he portrayed the mighty blast furnaces as rusty, monstrous, large-scale sculptures in effectively composed details [pp. 163 and 224–225]. Alongside the physical industrial facilities, Block was also interested in the manufacturing process, especially the assembly line [p. 227]. He took photos of workers in the production process [pp. 163 and 226], the shift change [p. 163], and the parking lot with employees' cars [p. 229]. Block's Detroit images thus linked industrial photography with aspects of social reportage. He also took photos of the factory's car cemetery, with junk Model-Ts ready for scrapping [p. 228]. Finally, like Sheeler, Block took pictures of Ford aircraft and aircraft engines, which the company custom produced. His close-ups introduced propeller motors as simultaneously functional and aesthetic objects of the machine age [pp. 230–231].

Only a few of Block's Chicago motifs have survived. Among them are a rigorously composed photograph of the footbridge of the two-story West Lake Street bascule bridge, spanning the Chicago River, and a view through its steel construction across the river to the city [pp. 165 and 234]. Block also visited a slaughterhouse, considered a locus of advanced rationalization, where he photographed the geometric grid of cattle enclosures [pp. 164 and 235] as well as, in more drastic images, the slaughtering and disassembling process. It is not known if Block visited and photographed the Chicago Tribune Tower, Frank Lloyd Wright's buildings in Oak Park, or the city's grain silos, as Walter Gropius had. His visit of the city was probably too short.

Block and his wife continued their journey from Chicago to San Francisco, where Block did not take many photographs. Their focus was more on visiting relatives in San Mateo than on extensive photo excursions into the city. The few surviving motifs are from Chinatown. The Blocks spent noticeably more time in Los Angeles, which had garnered intense international interest in the run-up to the 1932 summer Olympics [pp. 236–237]. "Los Angeles itself is ugly," wrote Anna-Sophie Block about the city that would later become her exile home for nearly fifty years. Block's judgment was more differentiated, from a photographic point of view: "Los Angeles is interesting because of its tremendous expansion and rapid growth, the juxtaposition of mansions and oil towers on the same street, not to mention the Hollywood suburbs, in which, however, you will search in vain for any film romance [...]. But the Los Angeles area is filled with beauties and wonders: sea, coast, miles of fruit and flower plantations, lush tropical landscape, and desert. The dimensions of everything in America are huge, including nature [...]."[26]

Downtown, Block took images only of the Eastern Building (1930), another art deco-style high-rise [p. 165]. Unlike Gropius, Block did not visit the Lovell Health House (1927–29), by Richard J. Neutra, which was more in line with his own conception of architecture (he would document it twelve years later, in color; see page 311). Block looked rather for motifs in the historic district of Olvera Street, in which since 1930 the city had commemorated its Mexican heritage [p. 238]. And as in New York, he took some street photography: passers-by in the entertainment district [p. 239], and portraits of newspaper boys [p. 239]. Incidentally, for Block—as for many photographers—Los Angeles was difficult to grasp; even Hollywood, for which he had high hopes, had little to offer. He focused his attention instead, and again, on technical structures: the masts and cables of power and telephone lines [p. 240]. At the Alameda power plant, in San Pedro, he found similar subjects [pp. 242–243], among them a composition of smokestacks and metal struts [p. 241], which had been shot by a young Brett Weston (1911–1993) in late 1927 and was reproduced in Richard J. Neutra's book *America* (1930), and used by El Lissitzky for the design of the book's dust jacket. Finally, Block's studies of technical structures included the bizarre accumulations of oil

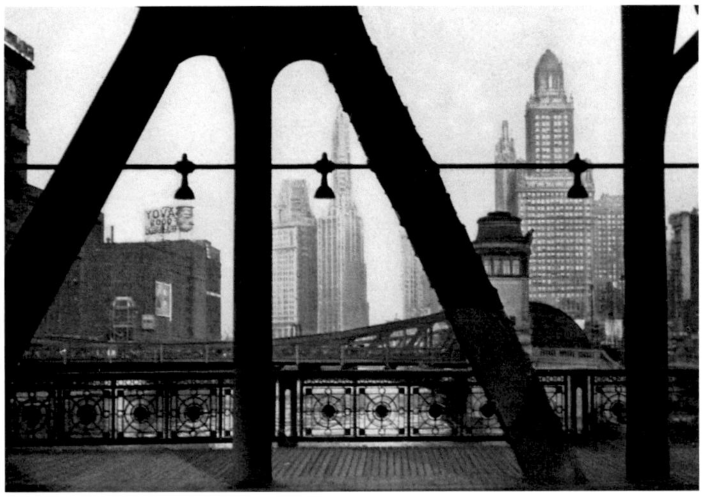

West Lake Street Bridge, Chicago, 1931

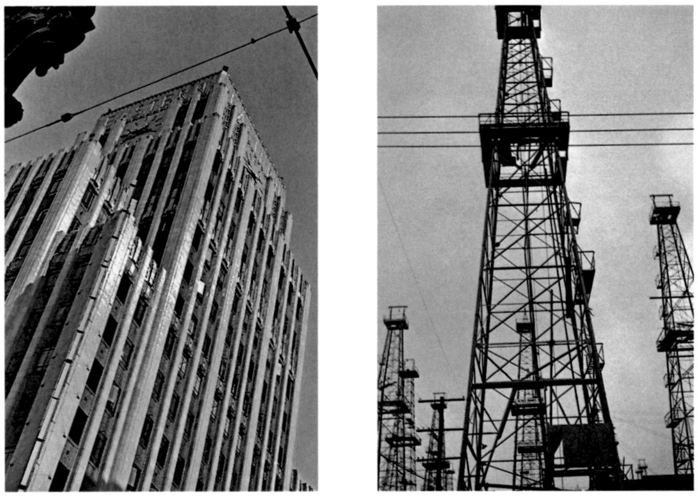

Eastern Building and oil rigs, Los Angeles, 1931

derricks, which he shot both at Signal Hill [pp. 165 and 244] and along the coast near Santa Barbara [p. 245].

Block was also interested in compositions of natural forms, and he recorded California flora at the Huntington Botanical Gardens [p. 246]. His detailed close-ups of cacti and agaves are tied to the photographic tradition of New Objectivity in Germany. Photos of California fan-palms, in Palm Canyon, near Palm Springs [p. 247], mark a transition to landscape photography, which he continued at the Grand Canyon. With his 35-mm Leica, Block managed to take some astonishing panoramic shots of the Canyon's stone formations [pp. 166 and 248–249]. Trips to Native American reservations were part of every visit to the American West. In New Mexico, Block first toured the ruins of the abandoned cliff dwellings of the Puyé Indians, north of Santa Fe [p. 252]. He then drove to Taos Pueblo, the settlement of the Taos Indians [p. 250], which Hoppé had also earlier photographed. Block took photos of the adobe-brick dwellings, their cubic structures related in some ways to European architectural modernism. He also captured scenes of everyday life in the settlement, including an Indian dance—aware, of course, that it was staged for tourists. Block's photos of Native American elders in Taos proved once again his sensitivity for creating expressive portraits [pp. 166 and 254–255].

Block later reported how these pictures came about: "You are permitted to take photos at Indian reservations, but for a fee of one dollar for the village and 25 cents to each of the individuals. In exchange, the Indian subject will stand nicely for a photo, but look stiff. To get them to relax a bit, I would usually tell them it would take a while until the camera was set up. So I talked to them and made jokes; during these conversations I took my close-up headshots. When the person finally posed for the photos, the images I wanted had already been made. [...] Because my equipment consisted of three different lenses and two camera bodies with sockets for changing lenses, I could easily work with two different films and lenses. [...] At one of the most beautiful Indian reservations in New Mexico, I had arrived in the evening, about half an hour before nightfall. Time was precious. I wanted to take pictures of the village, landscape, and houses, and as many close-ups of these impressive faces as I could. Of course, these motifs appeared in front of my camera at random. But since I had the telephoto and standard lens both at the ready, I could make full use of the short time left to take some sixty photographs. And if you have bad luck with one camera body, there's still the second one—so I would strongly recommend taking two camera bodies when you go on longer trips."[27]

The Blocks returned to New York by train, where he took the aforementioned shots of Broadway by night [pp. 192–197] and of the now-passable George Washington Bridge [pp. 185–187]. Back in Hamburg, he spent the following months evaluating of the photographic output of his journey. His conclusion: "For a photographer, America is a rich bounty."

Photos in Exhibition and Press

The *Internationale Foto-Ausstellung*, at the Kunstverein Hamburg in January and February 1932, offered Block the opportunity to present his America photos (see page 19). It was based on the private collection of the Dresden industrialist Kurt Kirchbach, and complemented by works of Hamburg photographers. Block's photos were mainly of New York, which he displayed less as individual works and more as the motifs of photo reportage. The art historian Carl Georg Heise, an early supporter of modern photography generally, and specifically of Albert Renger-Patzsch, emphasized Block's contribution in his review of the show: "It is exhilarating to see how slowly but surely a new spirit enters one of the most common and seemingly most banal places for photography: the reportage [...]. Dr. Block's America reportage is more exciting and memorable than many thick books on the subject."[28]

To accompany the exhibition, Block delivered a slide lecture on New York,[29] in which he expressed a confidence in the medium of photography typical for the times: "I will document New York the way it is, in images seen through the completely objective eye of the camera, in the generally intelligible language of photography."[30] According to a review of the lecture, "the distinguished photographer

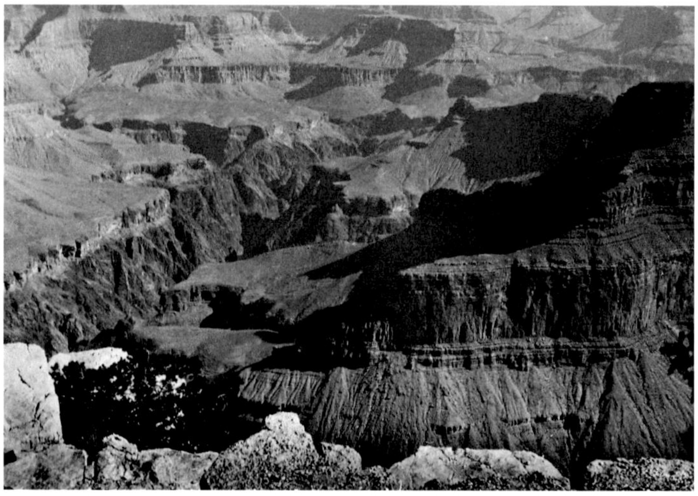

Grand Canyon, view of the North Rim, Arizona, 1931

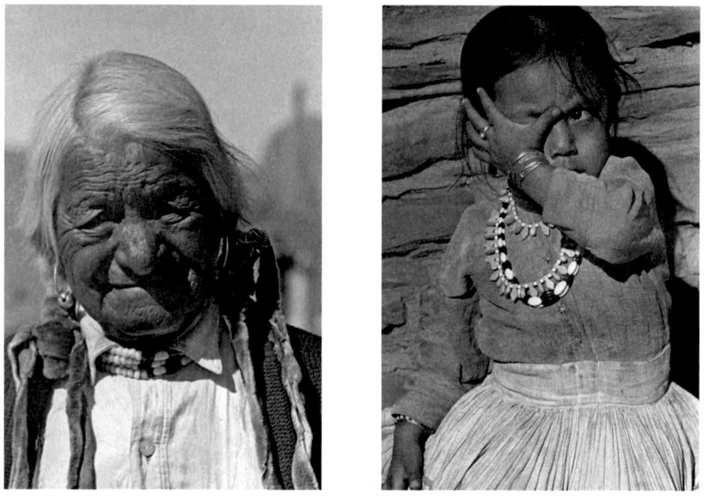

Old Native American and Native American child, New Mexico, 1931

presented about 200 slides he took, along with several uncut Leica films, unique studies that are more distinct than any extensive folio in capturing the essence, tempo, rhythm, and way of life of this fantastic, incomparable city."[31] In April 1932, Block repeated his New York photo lecture in Hamburg for the Society of Friends of the United States, whose members were obviously impressed: "[Block's] photographic journey through New York electrifies, this strange passage into vertically growing masses of building, the mountains of New York at night, steep-angle points-of-view onto the giants, bridges, dizzying iron-constructions of grandiose formats. Dr. Block [...] received a lively applause."[32]

Following the Hamburg exhibition, a selection of Block's America photos was acquired for Kurt Kirchbach's collection. In 1997, a part of this collection was auctioned at Sotheby's in London as the alleged "Helene Anderson Collection," with a fabricated provenance.[33] Among the images were five New York photos by Block.[34] In 2005, another, smaller part of the former Kirchbach Collection was auctioned at Villa Grisebach in Berlin, this time with the correct provenance. Block was represented by his image *Zwei Negerjungen aus Harlem* (*Two Negro Boys from Harlem*) [p. 206].[35] The mounts of the prints all still bore the Hamburg exhibition numbering (the abbreviation "H. A." referred to the "Hamburg Ausstellung", not a "Helene Anderson"!). The numbers of Block's photos from the Kirchbach collection range from 397 to 414, so we know that at least eighteen photos were shown at the Hamburg exhibition.

Block compiled his America photographs for thematic photo reportages for the illustrated press, for which Anna-Sophie wrote short texts. Given the journalistic interest in the topic of America, there were a considerable number of publications[36]. Block's photo reportage on Detroit came out in February 1932, as a cover story in the illustrated supplement of the *Hamburger Anzeiger* [pp. 216 and 218–219].[37] This was followed by publications, some double-page spreads, of his Coney Island photos [p. 210], American women and children of various races [pp. 198–199], Los Angeles [pp. 236–237], and Native Americans [pp. 250–251]. Other papers, including the *Hamburger Illustrierte*, printed Block's photo reports on Harlem [pp. 204–205]. The *Schweizer Illustrierte Zeitung* published his photo reportage from a bus ride on Fifth Avenue [pp. 188–189]. In May 1932, Block published "Fotoreportage New York" accompanied by his own text, in the architectural journal *Baugilde* [pp. 168–169], which also contained images of the Ford Factory in Detroit. A richly illustrated cover story on the Ford Factory, also accompanied by his text, appeared in September 1932, in the Werkbund magazine *Die Form* [pp. 232–233].

Finally, Block published a photographic record of his North America trip in the *Photofreund-Jahrbuch* 1933, in the fall of 1932, and he included photo-technical information. In addition, he reported on the particular challenges of his Broadway night shots and the general problems of photography in large American cities: "It is completely impossible to stand quietly, not to mention to set up a tripod and make any lengthy preparations amidst the bustle of the city. The skyscrapers are usually lined by very narrow streets, so you have to take your shots hastily as you pass by as part of the crowd [...]."[38] Block emphasized that the Leica's ease of use and inconspicuousness had been particularly helpful. With certain filters he was able to "overcome the atmospheric difficulties, especially in New York, with its air polluted with dust, soot, and humidity—the reason why one sees so few totally clear images of New York. [...] In any case, the architectural photographs I made in America have found special recognition because of their sharpness and clarity. Even photo agencies in New York told me that there were few New York cityscapes of such clarity and that were able to surmount the fog and humidity of New York."[39] The North German Lloyd shipping company in Bremen printed Block's photos in its brochure *Lloyd-Reisen nach U.S.A.* (1932) to promote cruises to North America.

The magazine *Der Querschnitt* included a photo of Fifth Avenue by Block in its special issue *Amerika heute,* at the end of August 1932. The issue also featured images by the photographer Hans Casparius (1900–1985), who had spent that same September 1931 week as Block in New York shooting similar subjects.[40] In December 1935, *Der Querschnitt* published three more of Block's New York photos, in yet another America issue; and in February 1936 they published one of his Chicago photos—in both instances with Block named in the credits. Recall that by this time Block, as a Jew, was not permitted to publish in the German press. Crediting him can only be explained by photo editors using pictures from a photo agency. More bleakly, just three years earlier, at the beginning of 1933, photos by Block had been published by the National Socialist journal *Illustrierter Beobachter,* to accompany an article on "Harlem, the Negro City of New York," about the "racial problems" in America, criticizing the concept of the "melting pot".

In Germany, the racist ideology of the National Socialists was directed foremost against Jews, and thus against Fritz and Anna-Sophie Block. Their living conditions in Hamburg deteriorated gradually beginning in 1933, the year the Nazis came to power. By the end of 1938, the Blocks would return to the United States, this time as émigrés—and for good.

1 Herbert Molderings, "'Amerikanismus' in der deutschen Fotografie der zwanziger Jahre," in *Camera Austria*, 1987, Nr. 22, 25–38. – Idem, "Amerikanismus und Neue Sachlichkeit in der deutschen Fotografie der zwanziger Jahre," in idem, *Die Moderne der Fotografie* (Hamburg, 2008), 71–91.
2 See Max-Ernst Haefeli, "Reiseeindrücke eines Architekten in Nordamerika," in *Die Baugilde* 6, 1924, no. 11, 153–157, and no. 16, 302–305. – Adolf Rading, "Reise nach den Vereinigten Staaten," in *Der Neubau* 7, 1925, no. 3, 29–33, and no. 5, 57–60. – Idem, "Amerika," in *Die Baugilde* 9, 1927, no. 17, 1026–1027. – W.[assili] Luckhardt, "Stand der modernen Baugesinnung in Amerika," in *Bauwelt* 20, 1929, no. 46, 1118–1134.
3 Walter Curt Behrendt, *Städtebau und Wohnungswesen in den Vereinigten Staaten. Bericht über eine Studienreise* (Berlin, 1926). – Paul Wolf, "Städtebauliche Reiseeindrücke in den Vereinigten Staaten von Amerika," in *Deutsche Bauzeitung* 62, 1928, no. 102/103, 861–880, and no. 104, 881–886. – Martin Wagner, *Städtebauliche Probleme in amerikanischen Städten und ihre Rückwirkung auf den deutschen Städtebau* (Berlin, 1929).
4 Herbert Molderings, "Mendelsohn, Amerika und der ›Amerikanismus‹," in *Reprint of Erich Mendelsohn: Amerika* (Basel, 1991) 83–92. – Roland Jaeger, "Bilderbücher eines Architekten. Erich Mendelsohn im Rudolf Mosse Buchverlag," in *Autopsie. Deutschsprachige Fotobücher 1918 bis 1945. vol. 1*, Manfred Heiting and Roland Jaeger, eds. (Göttingen, 2012), 174–187.
5 Ernst Gerson, "Reise-Eindrücke in Nordamerika," in *Der Städtebau* 24, 1929, no. 11, 293–300. – Idem, "Amerikanische Geschäftsbauten und Wohnhäuser," in *Wasmuths Monatshefte für Baukunst*, 14, 1930, no. 1, 22–34.
6 *Walter Gropius. Amerika Reise 1928 / Walter Gropius. American Journey 1928*, Gerda Breuer and Annemarie Jaeggi, eds. (Wuppertal/Berlin, 2009).
7 Anna-Sophie Block, *(oral history interview). Los Angeles 1979* (Fritz Block Estate Archive, Stockholm/Hamburg).
8 See Philip Prodger, *E.O. Hoppé's Amerika. Modernist Photographs from the 1920s* (New York, 2007). – Roland Jaeger, "Unterwegs zur Moderne. Die deutschsprachigen Fotobücher von Emil Otto Hoppé," in Heiting/Jaeger 2012 (note 4), 224–247, esp. 228–231.
9 Fritz Block, "Fotoreportage mit der Leica in Amerika," in *Photofreund-Jahrbuch 1933*, Fr. Willy Frerk, ed. (Berlin, 1932) 72–88; quotation, 83.
10 Fritz Block, "Fotoreportage New York," in *Baugilde* 14, 1932, no. 9, 437–444, quote 437.
11 Block 1932 (note 9), 77.
12 Block 1932 (note 10), 438/440.
13 Fritz Block: Fotoreportage New York. Mss. Hamburg 1932 (Fritz Block Estate Archive, Stockholm/Hamburg), 2.
14 Ibid.
15 Block 1932 (note 10), 443.
16 Anna-Sophie Block, "Der Fotograf fährt auf dem Dach des Bus durch die Fifth (V.) Avenue," typoscript 1931/32 (Fritz Block Estate Archive, Stockholm/Hamburg).
17 Block 1932 (note 13).
18 See the list of typescripts on pages 327–328.
19 Wolfgang Brückle, "Straßenfotografie in New York 1890–1950," in *New York Photography 1890–1950. Von Stieglitz bis Man Ray*, Ortrud Westheider, ed. (Hamburg, 2012) 28–41.
20 Block 1932 (note 9), 78.
21 Vgl. Robin Jaffee Frank, *Coney Island. Visions of an American Dreamland 1861–2008* (New Haven/London, 2015).
22 See *New York in Photobooks*, Horacio Fernández, ed. (Barcelona, 2016).
23 Block 1932 (note 9), 78.
24 Fritz Block, "Die neue Ford-Fabrik. Das River Rougewerk in Dearborn bei Detroit," in *Die Form* 7, 1932, no. 9, 268–275, quote 268.
25 See Terry Smith, *Making the Modern. Industry, Art, and Design in America* (Chicago/London, 1999), 112–135. – Theodore E. Stebbins, Gilles Mora, Karen E. Haas, *The Photography of Charles Sheeler* (Boston/New York/London, 2002).
26 Block 1932 (note 9), 79.
27 Ibid., 82 and 85.
28 Carl Georg Heise, "Photographie und kein Ende," in *Hamburger Fremdenblatt*, Jan. 21, 1932.
29 *Hamburgischer Correspondent*, no. 39, Jan. 24, 1932.
30 Block 1932 (note 13), 1.
31 -es., "Foto-Reportage Neuyork," in *Hamburger Fremdenblatt*, ca. Jan. 20, 1932 – See also Hamburger Nachrichten, no. 47, Jan. 20, 1932.
32 Mg.,"Photo-Reportage New York. Ein Architekt wird zum Kameramann," in *Hamburgischer Correspondent*, no. 199, April, 29,1932.
33 See Herbert Molderings, "Die internationale Foto-Sammlung Kurt Kirchbach, Dresden. Eine Pioniersammlung der modernen Fotografie," in idem 2008 (note 1), 273–284.
34 Sotheby's, *Important Avant-Garde Photographs of the 1920s & 1930s. The Helene Anderson Collection. Sale LN7267* (London, 1997) 14, no. 6–10.
35 Villa Grisebach, *Auktion Nr. 129 Photographie* (Berlin, 2005) no. 1137.
36 See the list of photo publications on pages 327–328.
37 See Bodo von Dewitz and Robert Lebeck, *Kiosk. Eine Geschichte der Fotoreportage 1839–1973 / A History of Photojournalism.* (Göttingen, 2001), 148.
38 Block 1932 (note 9), 79.
39 Ibid., 84.
40 See *Arnold Höllriegel. Amerika-Bilderbuch. Mit Fotografien von Hans G. Casparius*, Michael Grisko, ed. (Göttingen, 2012).

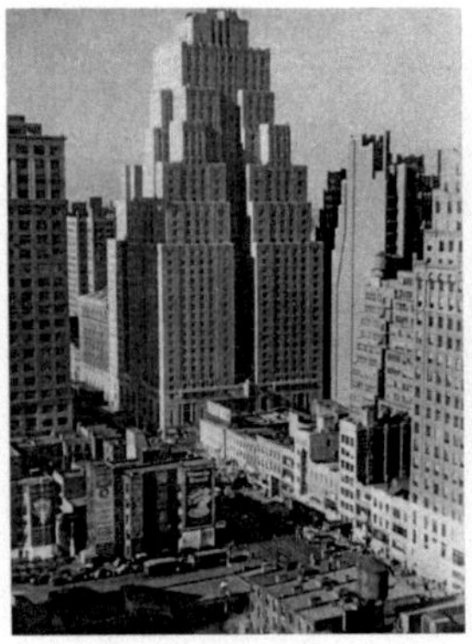

Hotel New-Yorker vom Pennsylvania Hotel aus gesehen. Ein besonders gutes Beispiel für die vom Zonengesetz geforderte Abtreppung.

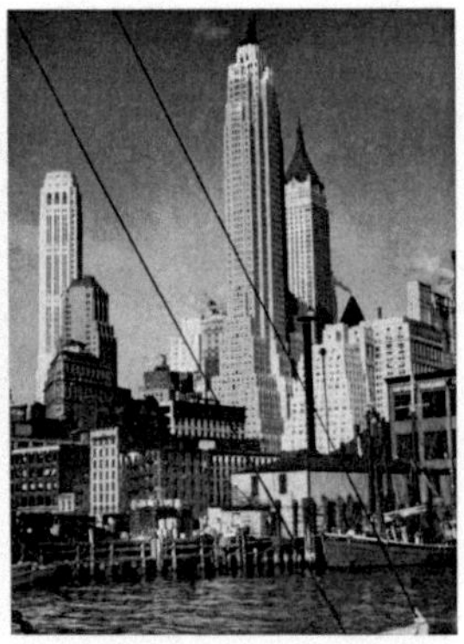

Blick vom Fischmarkt an der Fultonstreet auf das Bank- und Börsenviertel in Süd-Manhattan.

FOTOREPORTAGE NEW YORK

Text und Foto von Dr. Ing. Fritz Block, Architekt BDA, Hamburg

Der stärkste Eindruck einer Amerikareise ist die Einfahrt in den New-Yorker Hafen. Während der langen Seefahrt hat man nichts als Wasser und Horizont gesehen, und nun tauchen mit einem Male gigantisch im Nebel die Silhouetten der Wolkenkratzer empor aus der langen, schmalen Insel Manhattan. Je mehr man sich ihnen nähert, um so phantastischer wird das Bild; das ist mit europäischem Maßstab nicht mehr zu messen. In der Luft und auf dem Wasser ist die gleiche Steigerung des Lebens, das gleiche Tempo. Wenn dann die Sonne untergeht, all diese Giganten nur noch in ihren Umrissen erscheinen in wundervollen blassrosa Tönen und nun allmählich die Lichter an ihnen emporklettern, dann wird das Gebilde New York immer unwahrscheinlicher. Man ist so im Banne dieser Gigantik, dass man wie festgenagelt vor diesem Bilde steht. Wenn man dann am nächsten Morgen aus einem Fenster irgendwo hochoben in einem Hotelriesen auf das Gewimmel der Menschen und das mit wüstem Lärm sich vollziehende Erwachen der Stadt schaut, stürzt man sich mit ungestümer Eile mitten in das Getümmel. Das ist „die" grosse Stadt, tausendfach gesteigert in all ihren Ausdrucksformen und Funktionen, wild und packend zugleich.

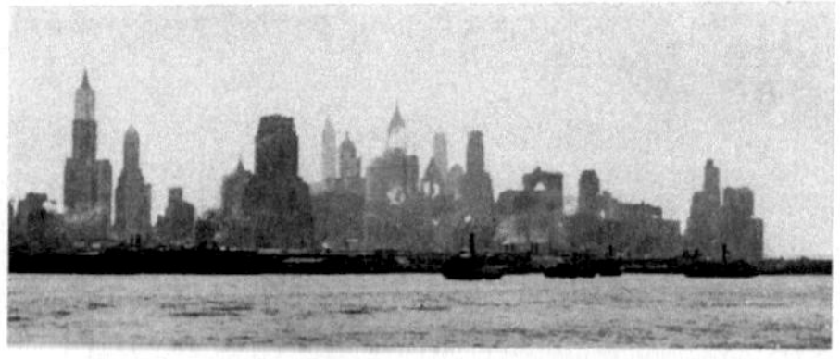

Einfahrt in New York. Die Südspitze Manhattans vom Hudson aus, ein Bild, wie es sich bei der Einfahrt in den New-Yorker Hafen darbietet.

1

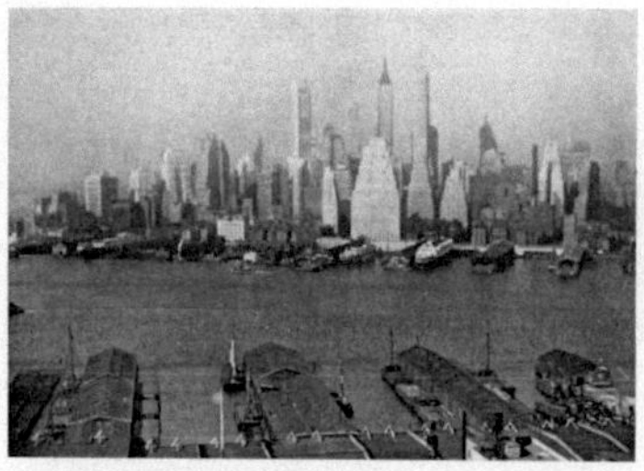

2

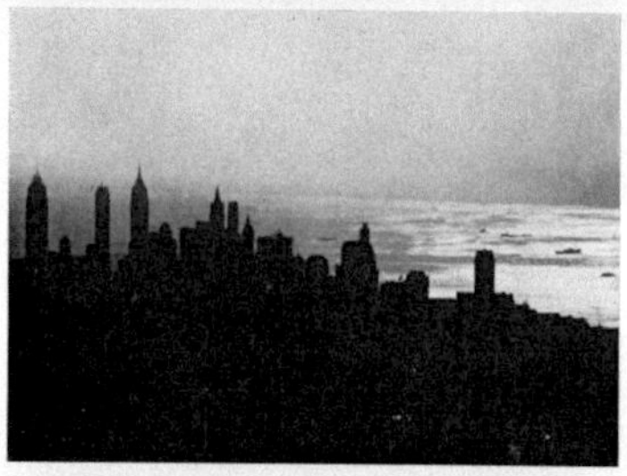

3

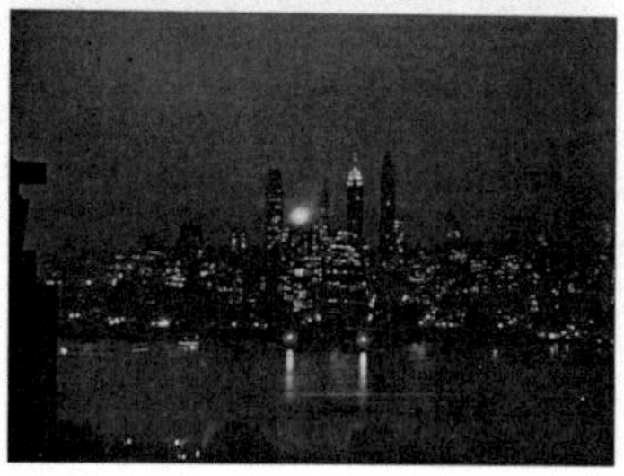

Betritt man die Strassenschluchten an einem trüben Tage, an dem die Luft voller Kohlenstaub und Dunst ist, könnte man glauben, es gäbe nichts Trostloseres auf dieser Welt. Hat man aber das Glück, einen schönen, klaren Tag zu erwischen, dann geniesst man die Schattenwirkung in dieser brennenden Steinwüste. Was man eben noch als öde empfand, ist jetzt Oase. Langsam gleitet die Sonne von der Spitze dieser Riesen die Hauswände hinab, und trifft sich mit den Schatten der gegenüberstehenden. Dumpf und benommen wandert man die Schluchten entlang, dorthin, wo helles Licht ihr Ende anzeigt. Man gelangt auf irgendeinen Platz, aber nicht Platz nach europäischen Begriffen: einen Raum im Freien, einen Ruhepunkt, sondern vielfach ist es das volle Gegenteil. Es sind meistens mehr Inseln der Reklame, als der Ruhe. Die Häuser steigen noch höher empor, ungegliedert, da das Zonengesetz hier keinerlei Beschränkung auferlegt, aber meistens über und über beladen mit Reklame, die bei dem grossen Abstand um so besser zur Wirkung kommt. Wirklich schöne Plätze gibt es kaum in New York; noch weniger ruhige, aber die Menschen haben sich an den Lärm gewöhnt und sie geniessen mit grosser Wonne die Sonne in ihren Ruhestunden oder Minuten auf den Bänken hier im Grünen. Besonders die Wasserfront mit frischer Brise von der See her erfreut sich grosser Beliebtheit, und da wieder am meisten die Battery, der freie Platz an der Südspitze Manhattans, die Stelle, von der die bauliche Entwicklung New Yorks ihren Anfang genommen hat. Absolut wirksam wird das steinerne Manhattan nur an einer Stelle unterbrochen, im Centralpark, der den Raum zwischen V. Avenue und VIII. Avenue in der Breite, und zwischen 59. und 110. Strasse in der Länge einnimmt. Das ist die Lunge des Riesenmenschen New York. Grosse Wiesen wechseln ab mit künstlichen Felspartien und Seen. Ein kleiner Zoo, Spiel- und Sportplätze sorgen für Unterhaltung und Zerstreuung, und das Ganze wird von breiten Betonstrassen durchzogen und von Wolkenkratzern eingefasst.

Aber den rechten Eindruck der Stadt bekommt man erst von oben, und die vielen in allen Stadtteilen zerstreuten Hochhäuser mit ihren Aussichtsterrassen bieten eine bequeme Gelegenheit, in Ruhe die Stadt und ihre Entwicklung zu studieren. Da ist zunächst das Woolworth-Hochhaus am unteren Broadway, von dem man einen weiten Ueberblick über das südliche Manhattan und seine Wasserfronten hat, bis hinüber nach Brooklyn, der Wohnstube von New York, der Wohnstadt des Arbeiters und Mittelstandes auf der einen, bis New Yersey — der Fabrikstadt — und bis Staten Island auf der anderen Seite. Ferner übersieht man hier das Wasser zwischen New York und den Narrows, der Einfahrt in die New-Yorker Bucht, mit den vielen Inseln, lebendigen Ufern und dem riesen-

1 Südspitze Manhattans vom Dachgarten des Hotels St. George in Brooklyn aus. In der Mitte des Bildes das Bank- und Börsenviertel.

2 Silhouette der Südspitze Manhattans bei Sonnenuntergang, gesehen vom Empire State Building aus.

3 Blick auf die Südspitze Manhattans vom Dachgarten des Hotels St. George in Brooklyn bei Nacht.

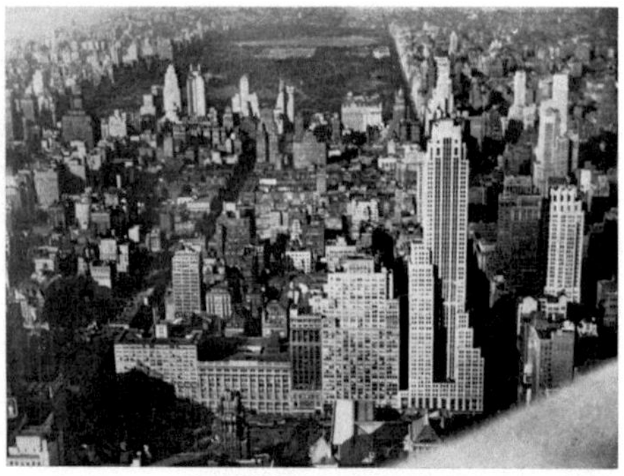

Mittelmanhattan vom Empire State Building aus. Vorn rechts im Bilde das Hochhaus V. Avenue 500 an der Kreuzung von V. Avenue und 42. Strasse, erbaut von den Architekten des Empire State Building Shreve, Lamb und Harmon. Oben im Bild der Centralpark, in der Mitte die VI. Vvenue, auf den Centralpark zuführend.

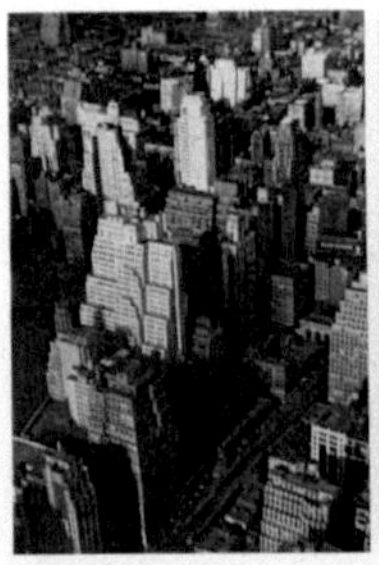

Hochhäuser in Mittelmanhattan, vorn rechts die Hochbahn.

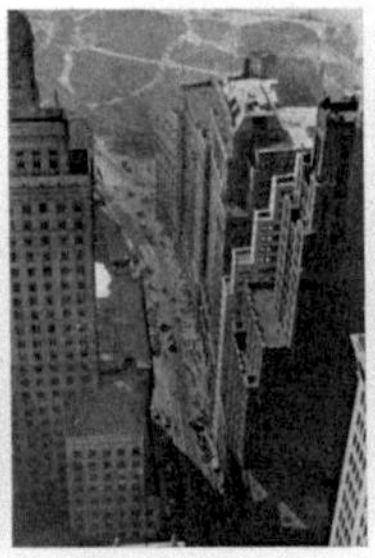

Blick vom Hochhaus Wallstreet one auf den unteren Broadway mit der Einmündung in die Battery.

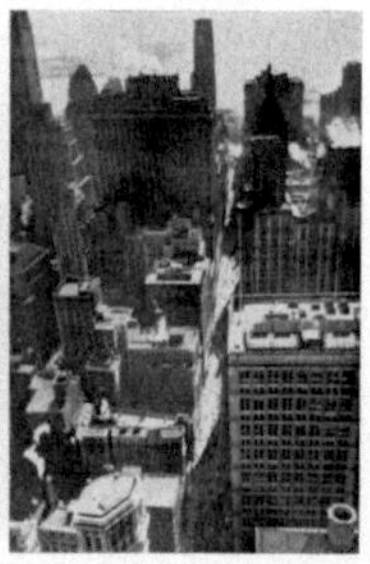

Blick vom Woolworth-Gebäude nach Süden: Untermanhattan, zu beiden Seiten des Broadway.

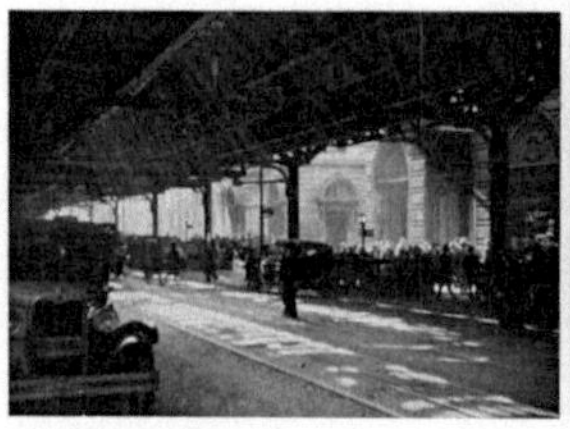

Unter den Geleisen der Hochbahn in Südmanhattan.

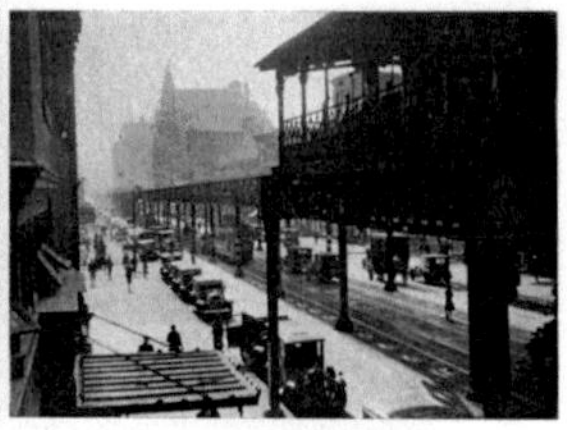

Geleise und Freiluftbahnsteig der Hochbahn im Strassenbilde.

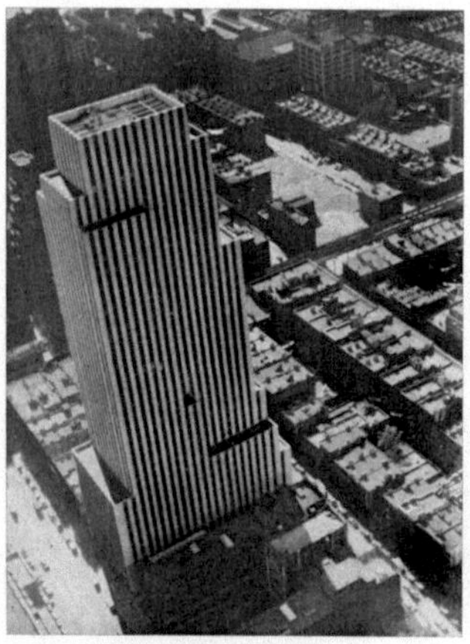

Das Gebäude der Zeitung Daily News, 42. Strasse und 3. Avenue, vom Chrysler aus gesehen. So sieht das Stadtbild aus, wenn innerhalb normaler Bebauung plötzlich ein Wolkenkratzer emportaucht.

haften Schiffsverkehr. Von hier sieht man hinein in den unteren Broadway mit seinen Hochhäusern und in das Banken-Viertel, dem hässlichsten und ungeordnetsten Teil von New York, mit vorwiegend alten, aber auch einigen neuen architektonisch besseren Hochhäusern: ein ungeregeltes wüstes Chaos. Einige Kirchen, einst die Wahrzeichen und höchsten Punkte New Yorks, vertreten das historische Moment und wirken wie Kinderspielzeug in der Umgebung der Wolkenkratzer. Als der kostbare Boden hier rings um Wallstreet, das Börsenviertel, bebaut oder besser überbaut war, drangen die Wolkenkratzer immer weiter und weiter nach Norden vor und ein zweites Centrum, eine zweite City entstand weiter nördlich in Mittel-Manhattan; sehr viel bewusster und klarer angelegt und sehr viel erfreulicher in architektonischer Beziehung. Wenn man gerecht urteilen will, muss man sagen, dass der Fortschritt in den letzten 10—20 Jahren hier sicherlich ebensogross ist wie nur in irgend einer Großstadt der Welt, wenngleich auf der anderen Seite auch die neuesten Bauten noch recht viel zu wünschen übrig lassen und man wünschen möchte, dass diese grössten Aufgaben mehr in Hände wirklich Berufener auch in architektonischer Beziehung kämen, denn in organisatorischer und technischer Beziehung sind sie zweifellos Höchstleistungen.

In dieses städtebauliche Gebilde Mittel-Manhattan hat man besonders eindringliche Blicke von den Hochhäusern aus, dem augenblicklich höchsten Gebäude der Welt — dem Empire State —, dem Chrysler — Daily News — und Paramountgebäude. Besonders grotesk ist die Erscheinung des Stadtviertels dort, wo plötzlich in ein jungfräuliches Gelände vereinzelte Wolkenkratzer vordringen, wie z. B. das Daily News Haus. Unerhört ist der Eindruck, wo sich unmittelbar solche Riesen gegenüberstehen und man von der Spitze des einen auf den anderen herunterblickt. Aber auch der Blick auf das ganze Hochhaus-Viertel, in die Hauptverkehrsadern hin-

"Photo Reportage New York (and Detroit)" (Baugilde 14, no. 9, 1932)

ein (Broadway, V. Avenue) ist überwältigend. Nun einiges zu den Hochhäusern selbst. Dass sie technisch mit allen Errungenschaften unserer Zeit ausgestattet sind, erwähnte ich schon. Hierüber ist in Fachzeitschriften so viel geschrieben, dass ich mir ersparen kann, es nochmals zu bringen, desgleichen über die Konstruktion, die fast immer aus Eisen besteht, weil in Beton die Pfeiler bei der gewaltigen Höhe zu grosse Dimensionen bekämen, ferner das Eisen, das in Amerika bei Tage gefördert wird, etwa die Hälfte kostet als bei uns, weil die Konstruktion in der Werkstatt sehr weit vorgearbeitet wird, wo die Arbeit besser eingeteilt und Maschinen in hohem Masse eingesetzt werden können, und vor allem, weil der Arbeitslohn sehr viel höher ist als bei uns. Diese Vorbedingungen für den Eisenbau sind eben völlig andere als bei uns; daher die fast ausschliessliche Verwendung von Eisen beim Hochbau. Grundrisslich hat sich gewissermassen ein Standard herausgebildet, der durch zwei Faktoren bestimmt wird, die viel zu wenig betont werden, und auf Grund deren bei uns auch automatisch diese Grundrisse als Vorbilder ausschalten. Diese beiden Faktoren sind künstliche Belüftung und künstliche Belichtung. Infolgedessen kennt man in Amerika keine Luftschächte und Lichthöfe, sondern die ganze Grundfläche wird bebaut. Bei den geradezu phantastischen Bodenpreisen spielen die hohen Kosten für künstliche Belichtung und Belüftung keine Rolle. Die Kostbarkeit der Ausführung

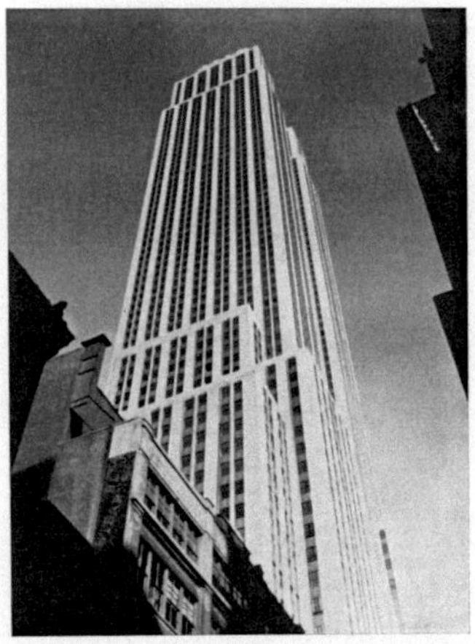

Empire State Building, mit 102 Stockwerken „augenblicklich" das höchste Gebäude der Welt. (Vgl. „Empire State Building — Der Werdegang des höchsten Hauses der Gegenwwart", Verlag W. & S. Loewenthal, Abteilung Baugilde, Berlin. — RM. 0,75 inkl. Porto.)

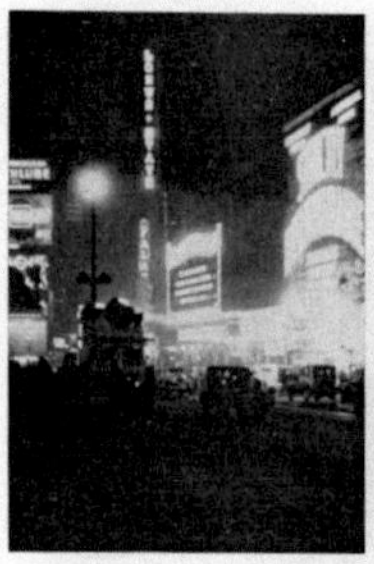

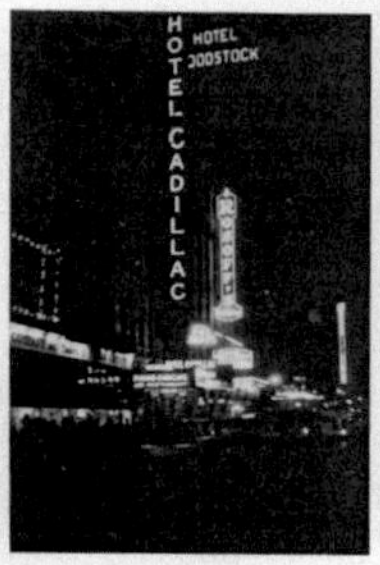

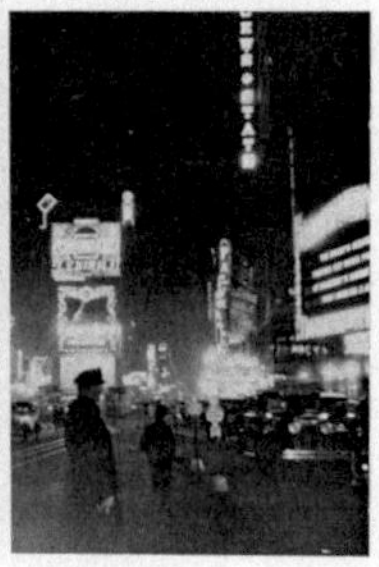

„Der grosse weisse Weg", der mittlere Broadway, das Hauptvergnügungsviertel von New York, im Lichtmeer bei Nacht.

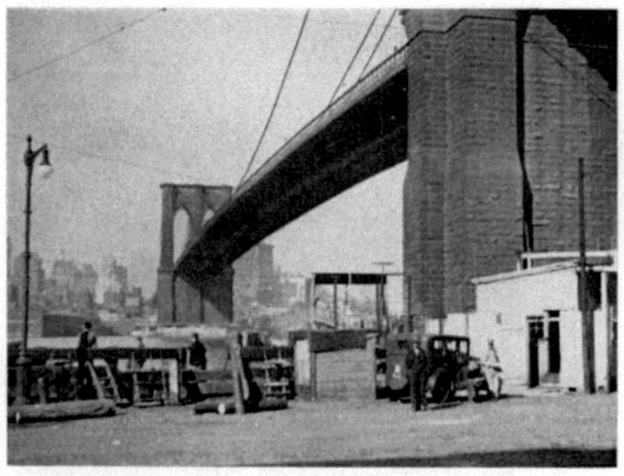

Die Brooklynbrücke von der Brooklyner Seite aus gesehen.

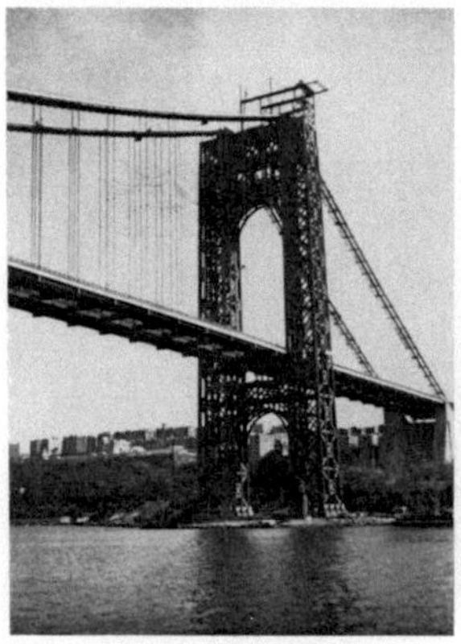

Die neue Washingtonbrücke, die in der Höhe der 179. Strasse den Hudson überbrückt.

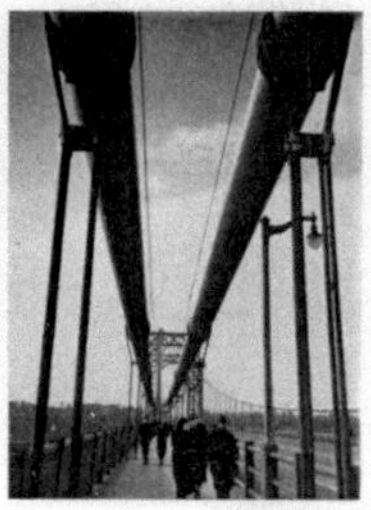

fällt uns europäischen Architekten natürlich besonders auf. Diese Tatsache bringt einmal eine ganz hochwertige Ausführung der Bauten mit sich, auf der anderen Seite aber leider auch eine sehr üppige und geschmacklose Formengebung mit allen Auswüchsen eines wüst wuchernden Formalismus. Es gibt nur ganz wenige Bauten in Amerika, die unverhohlen die Schönheit der technischen Formen zeigen. Den amerikanischen Architekten, die zum Teil selbst sehr geniale Konstrukteure sind oder doch mit solchen zusammenarbeiten, sollte man eine solche Vorliebe für schlechte Dekoration und Konfektion in der Architektur eigentlich nicht zutrauen. Ja, diese Vorliebe für Dekoration macht selbst bei Ingenieurbauten nicht Halt.

Bei der Ende vorigen Jahres eingeweihten Washingtonbrücke, einem der grossartigsten Zeugnisse technischer Schönheit auf der ganzen Welt, hat es schwere Kämpfe gekostet, die Behörde von ihrer Absicht, die Brückenpfeiler mit gotischer Architektur zu bekleiden, abzubringen. Nur dem Eingreifen einer Anzahl fortschrittlich gesinnter Architekten und Ingenieure gelang es durchzusetzen, dass diese herrliche Konstruktion in ihrer Klarheit gezeigt wurde. Ein weiteres schönes Beispiel einer neuen Brücke, besonders kühn in der Konstruktion, ist die Kill van Kull Brücke. Auch sonst bietet New York eine reiche Auswahl technischer Grosswerke, die durch ihre Schönheit und unerhörte Kühnheit fesseln, angefangen von der bereits vor etwa 50 Jahren errichteten Brooklyn-Brücke bis zu den vielen Kai-Anlagen, Speichern, Kraftwerken und Fabriken an der Wasserfront. In diesen Ingenieurbauten finden wir Architekten ganz besonders wertvolle Anregungen.

Ein besonderes Erlebnis ist zuletzt noch New York bei Nacht. Da erreicht dieses Durcheinander von Reklame, Glanz, Lichtfülle einen Höhe-

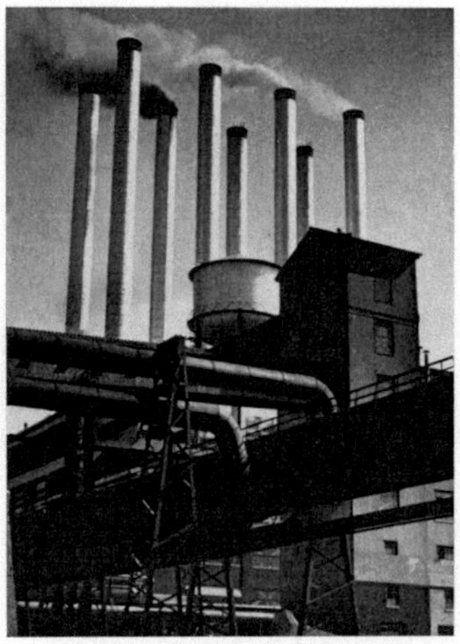

Kraftzentrale mit Gichtgaszuleitung im River Rouge Werk von Ford, Detroit.

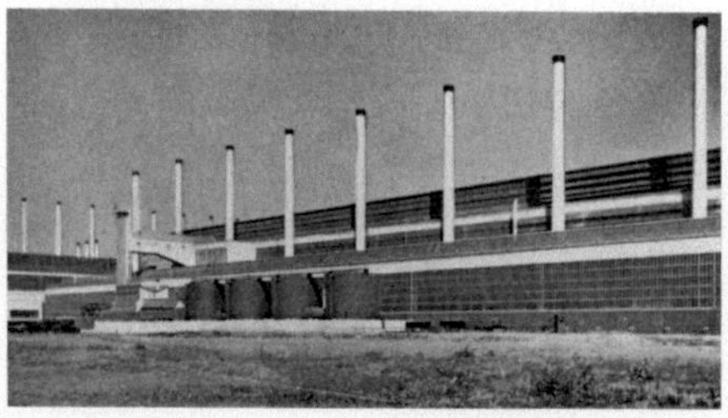

Neues Fabrikgebäude im River Rouge Werk, Architekt: Kahn, Detroit.

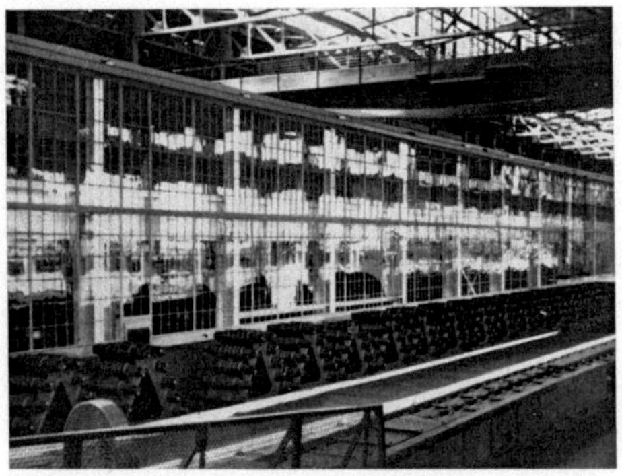

Neues Fabrikgebäude im River Rouge Werk von Ford. Innenansicht. Architekt: Kahn, Detroit.

punkt auf dem Broadway zwischen Harald Square und Columbus Circle, dem „grossen weissen Weg", dem Hauptvergnügungsviertel von New York. Hier geht diese grosse, in ihren kulturellen Ansprüchen äusserst bescheidene Menschenmenge billigen Vergnügungen nach.

Was hier an sich selbst überbietender Reklame und Lichtfülle geboten wird, ist kaum noch zu übertreffen. Wenig sympathisch in seinem Untergrund, aber doch imponierend und gewaltig in der Wirkung. Der Franzose Duhamel, dem in seiner stockfranzösischen Einstellung alles Amerikanische verhasst ist und der infolgedessen auch vielfach falsch und zu pessimistisch urteilt, nennt das die „gewerbsmässige Unzucht des Lichtes".

Für fotografisch Interessierte! Die Aufnahmen sind sämtlich mit der Leica gemacht, und zwar mit drei verschiedenen Objektiven: dem Standard Objektiv von 50 mm Brennweite, dem Weitwinkel von 35 mm und dem Teleobjektiv von 135 mm Brennweite. Die Aufnahmen vom nächtlichen Broadway sind als Momentaufnahmen auf dem panchromatischen S. S. Film von Kodak mit der Oeffnung 3,5 gemacht worden.

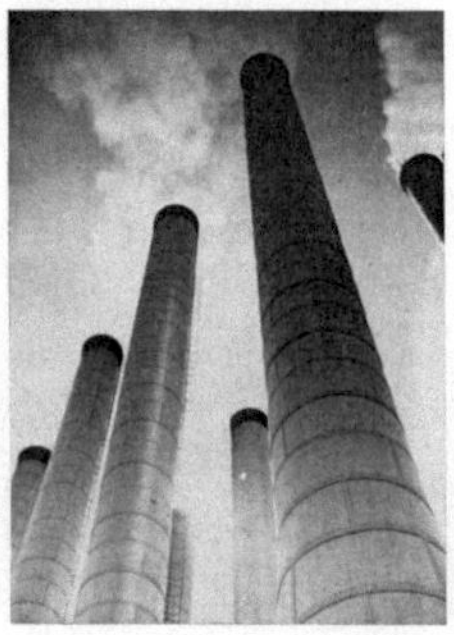

Metallschornsteine vom Kraftwerk River Rouge (Ford).

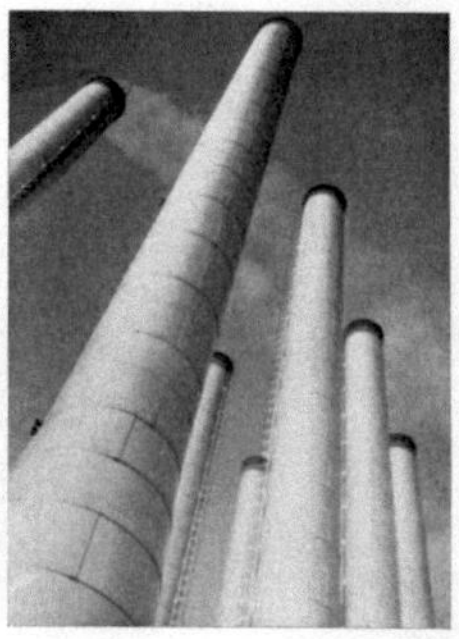

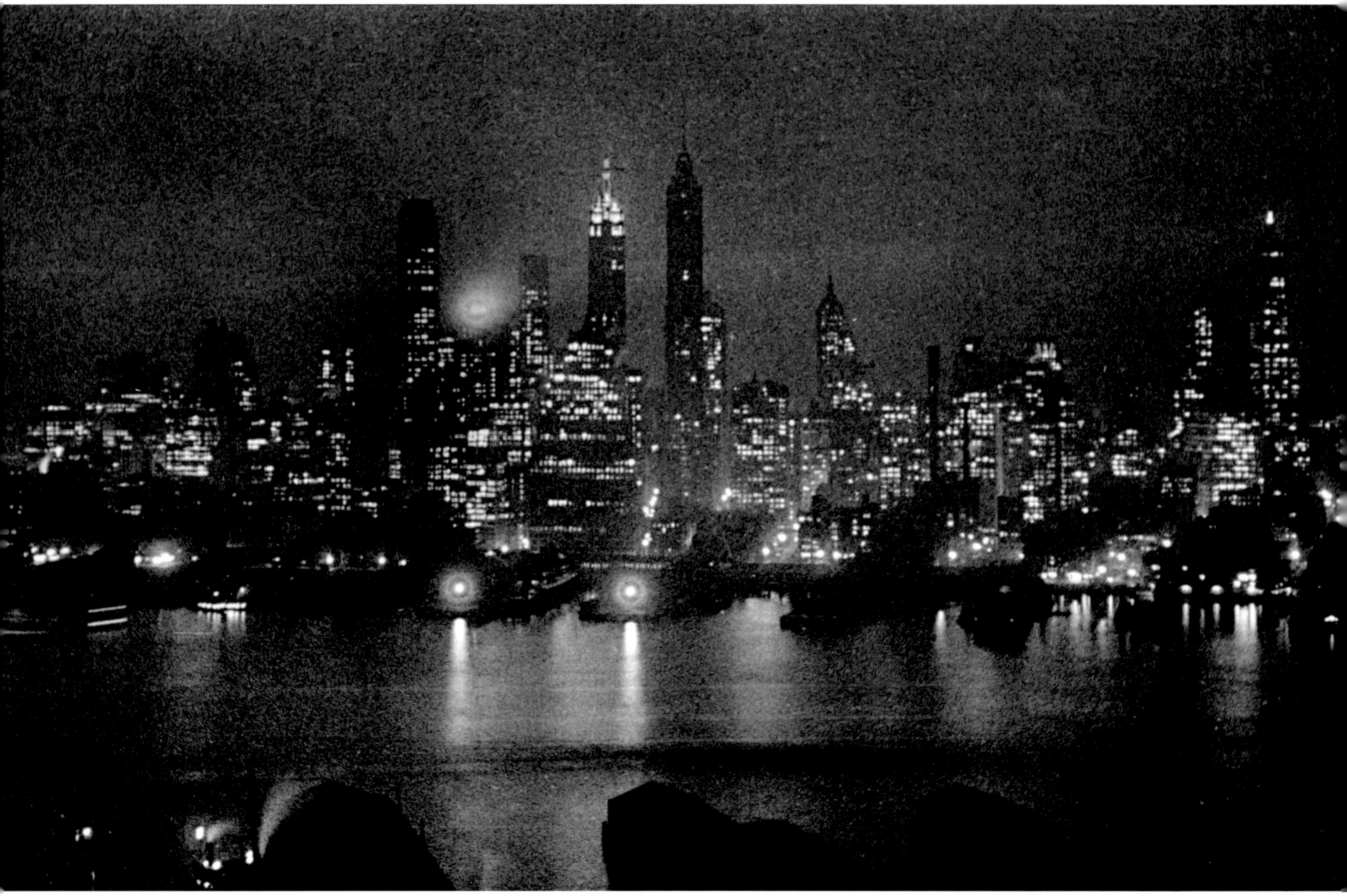

View of Lower Manhattan at night, New York, 1931

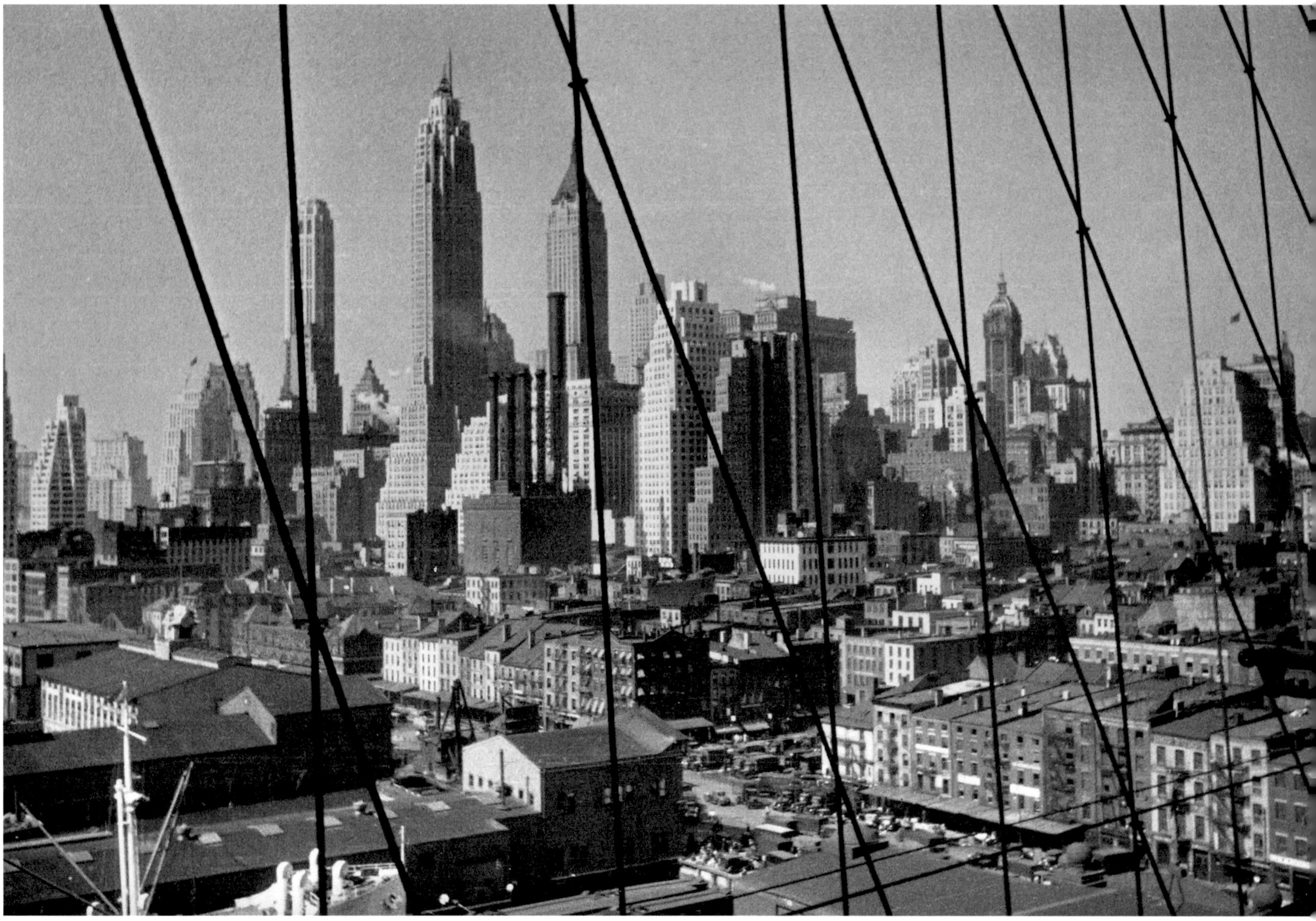

View of Lower Manhattan from the Brooklyn Bridge, New York, 1931

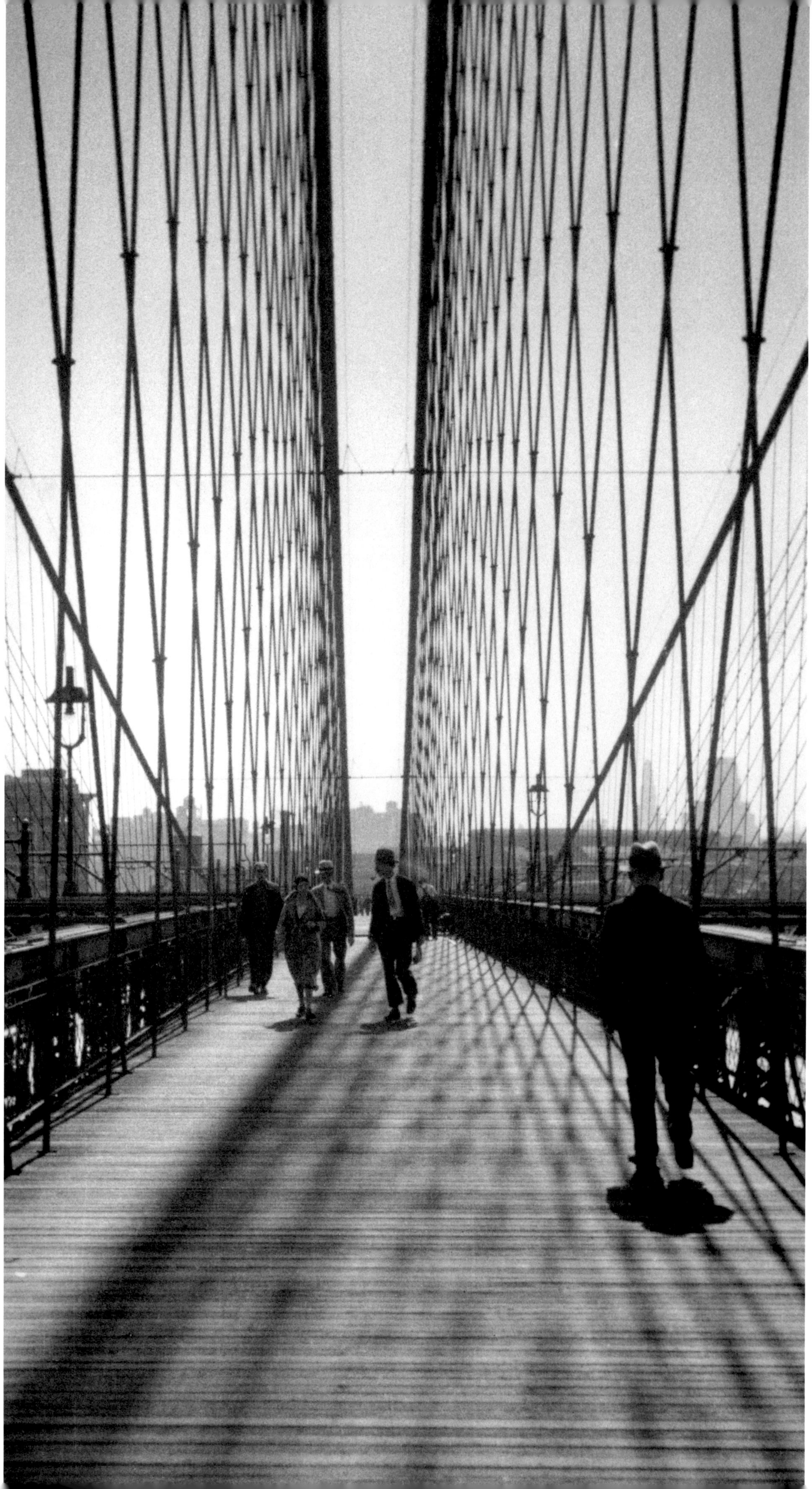

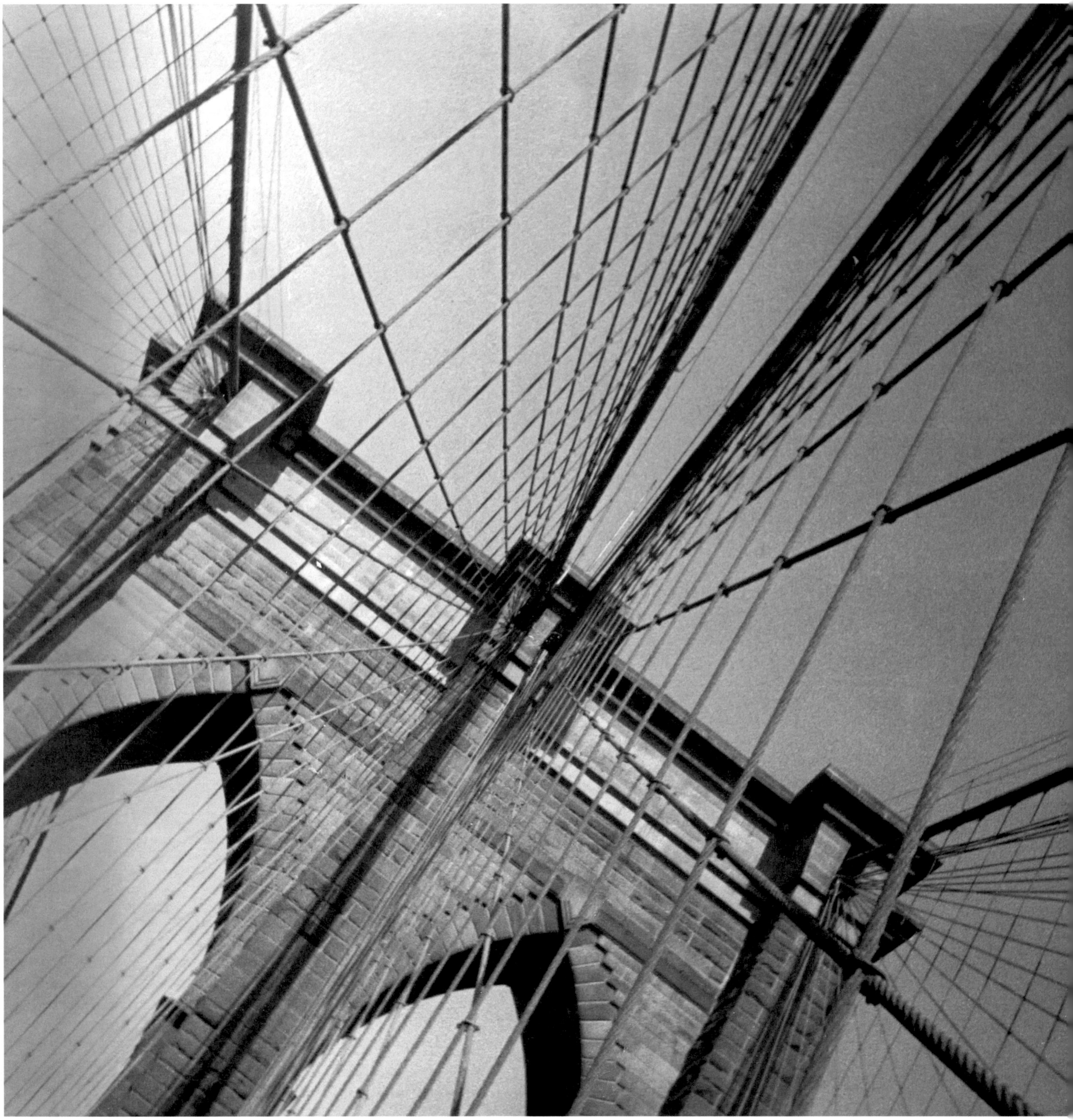

Brooklyn Bridge, New York, 1931

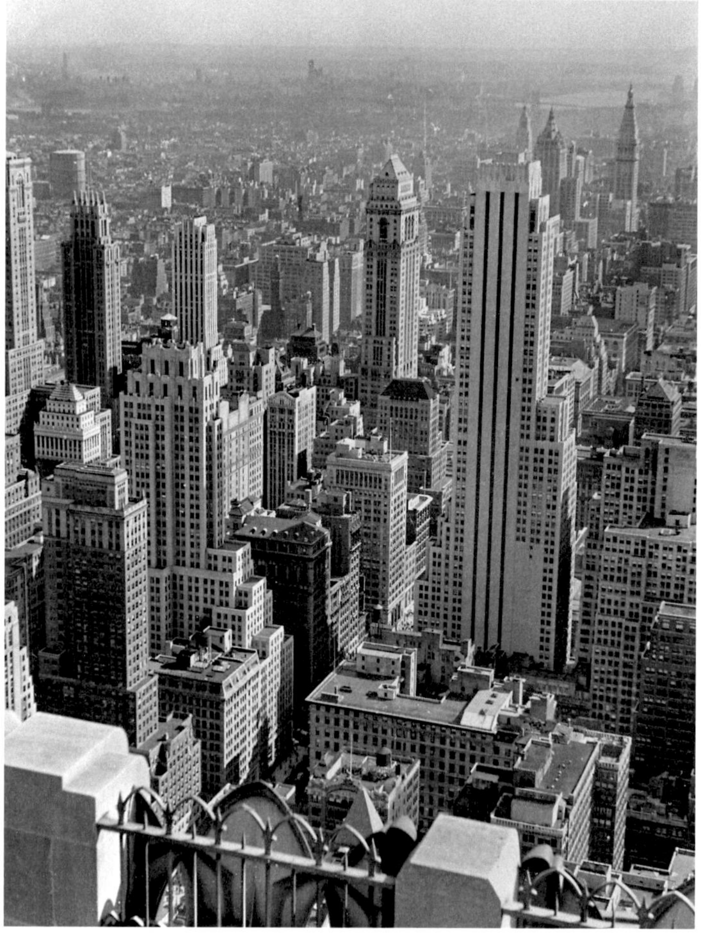
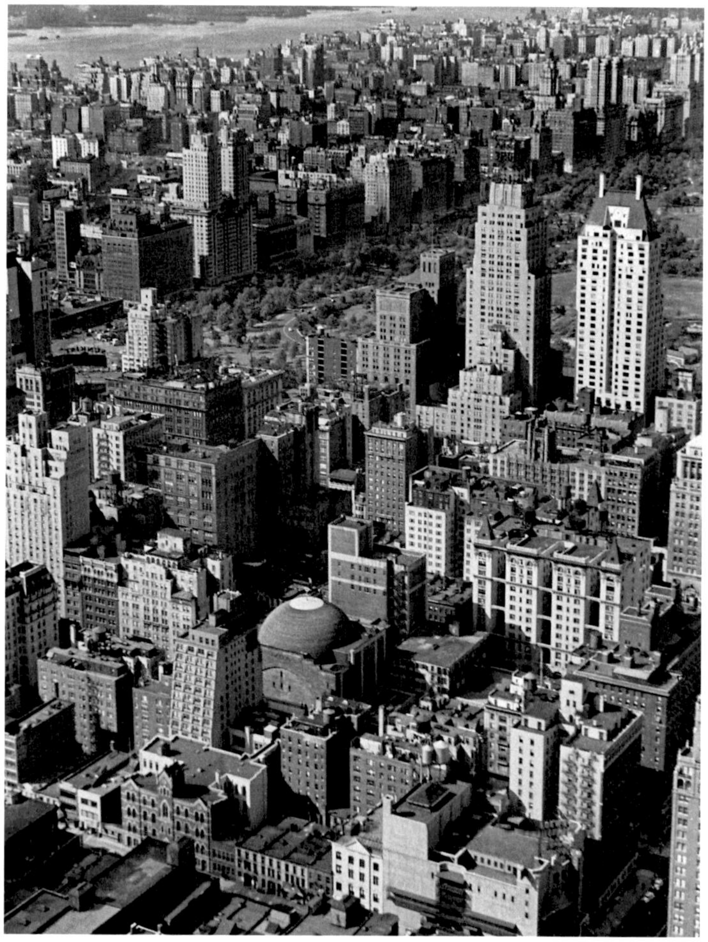
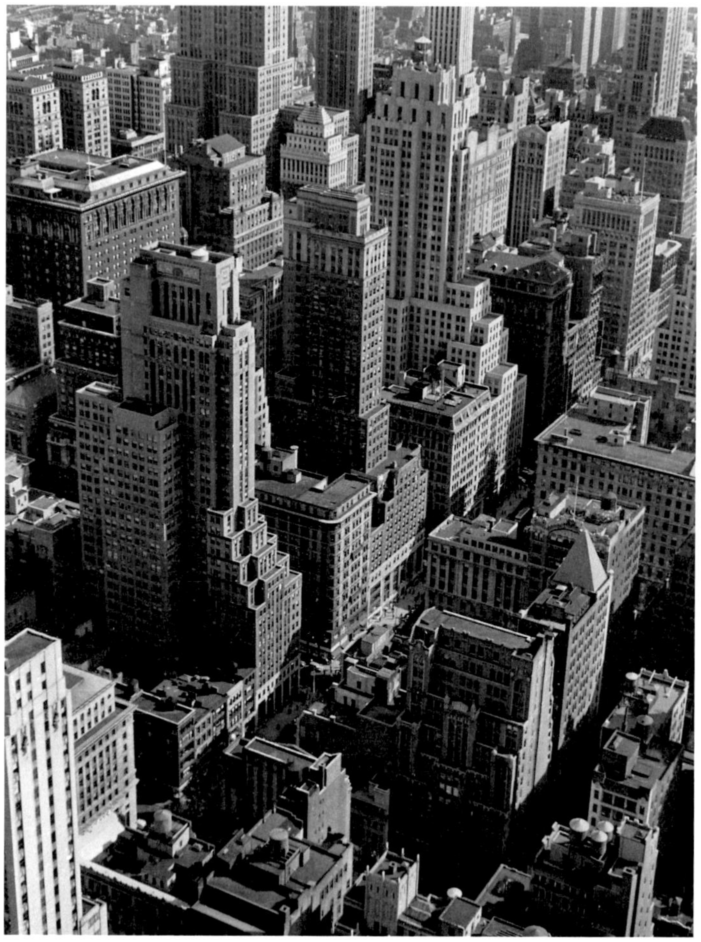
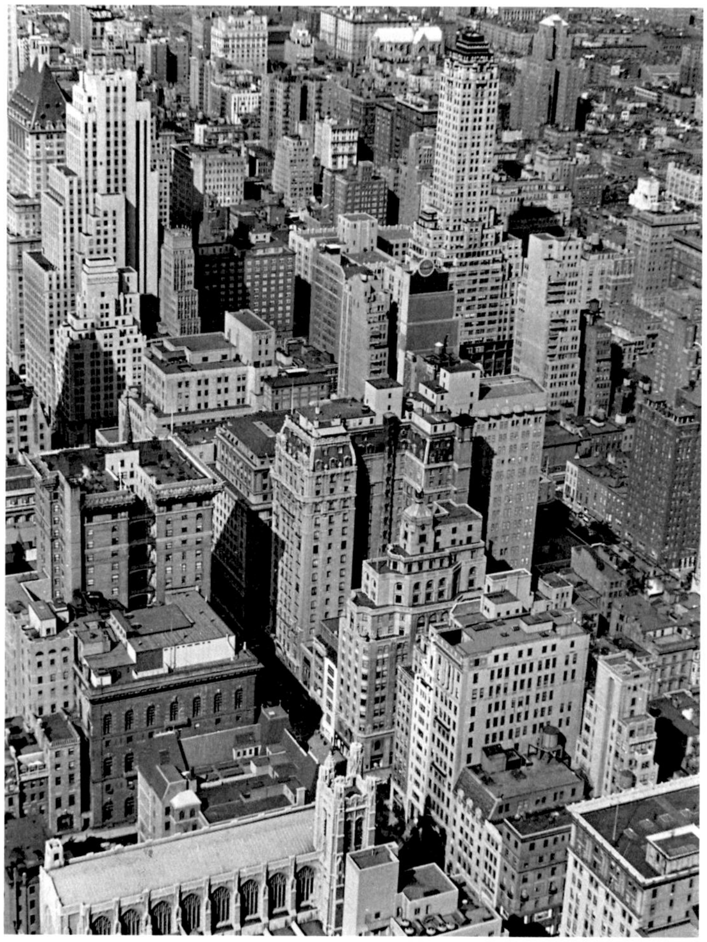

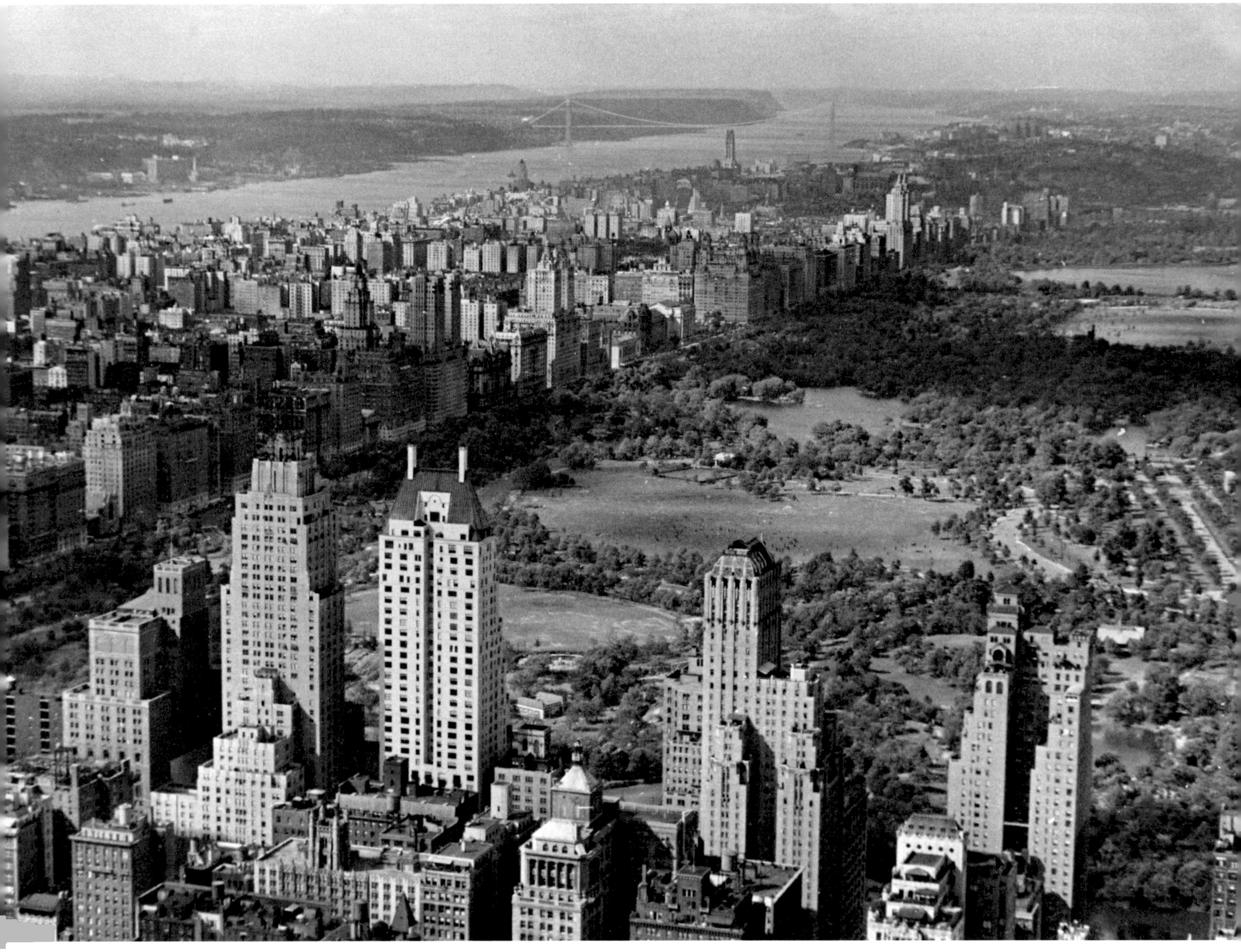

Views of Manhattan from the Empire State Building, New York, 1931

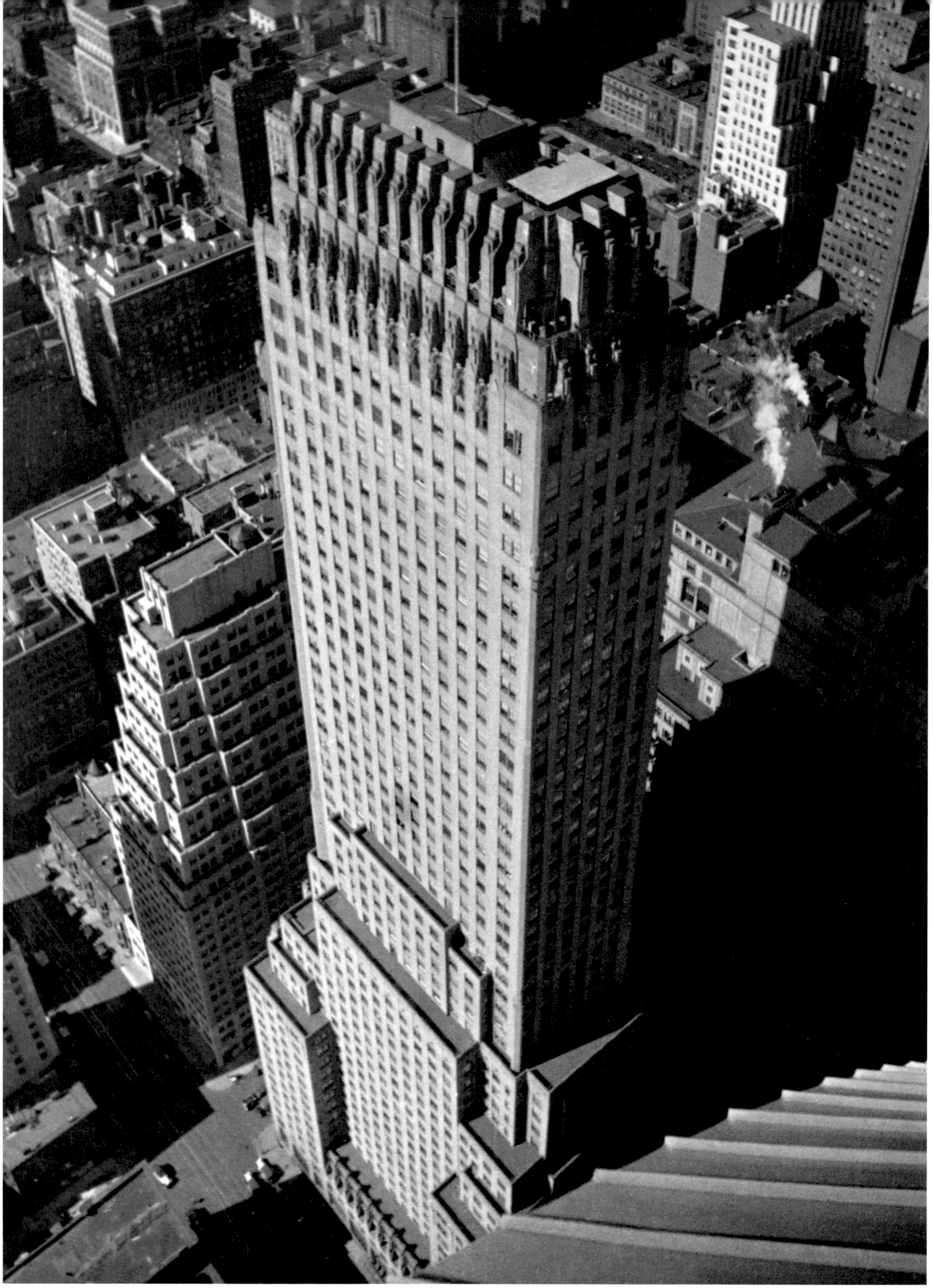

View onto the Chanin Building from the Chrysler Building, New York, 1931

View of Pennsylvania Station from Hotel Pennsylvania, New York, 1931

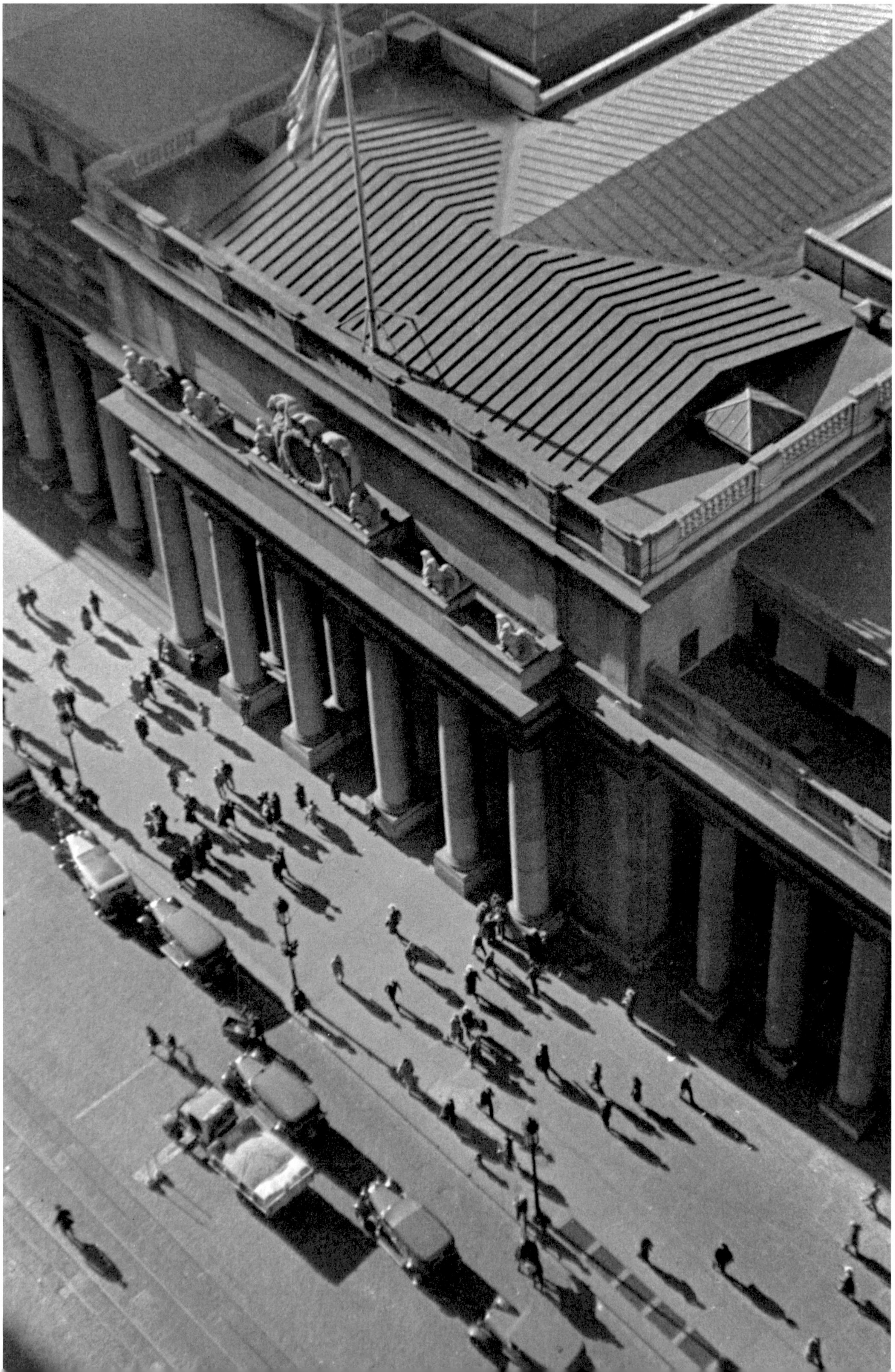

Empire State Building, New York, 1931

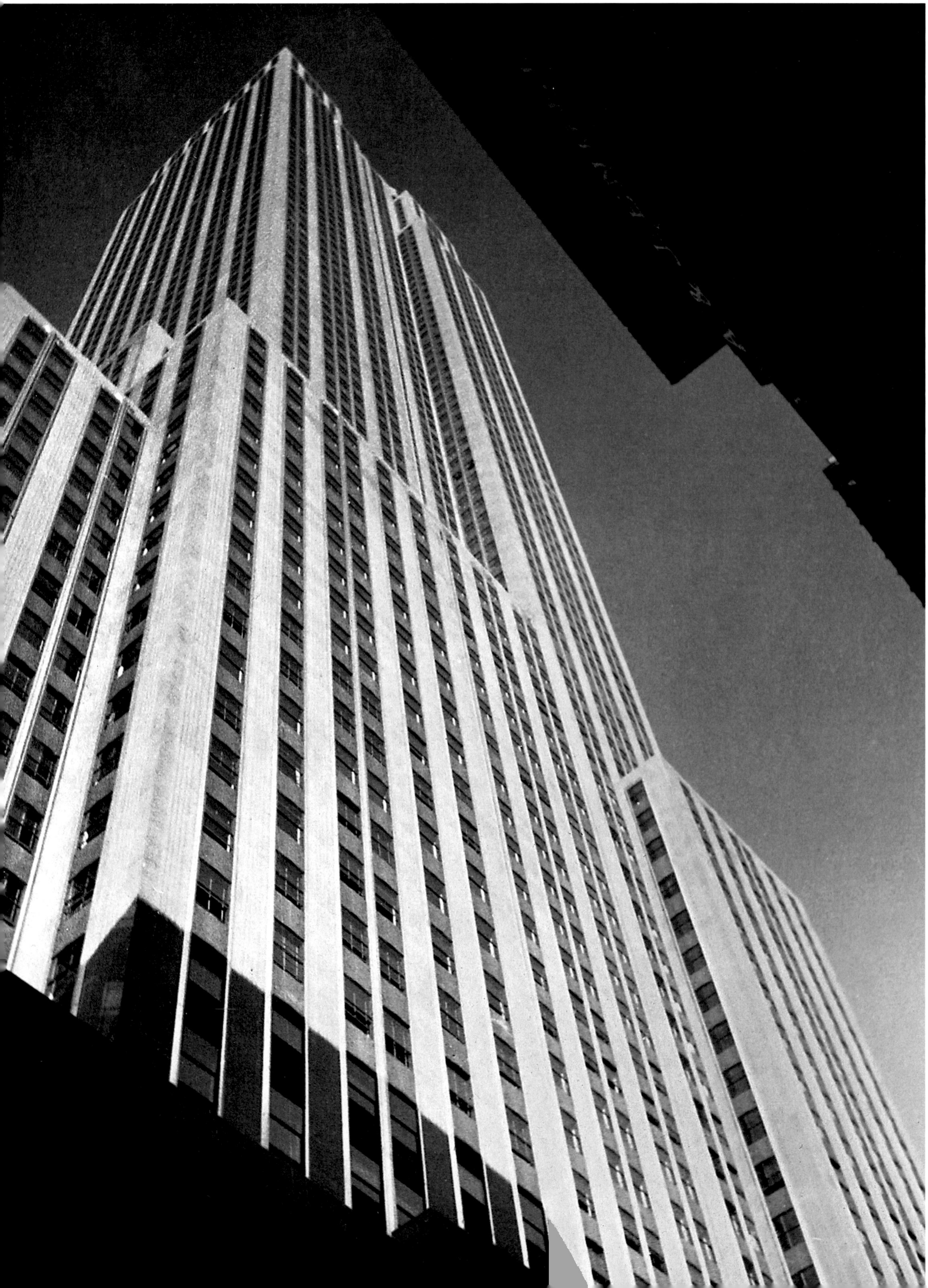

500 Fifth Avenue, New York, 1931

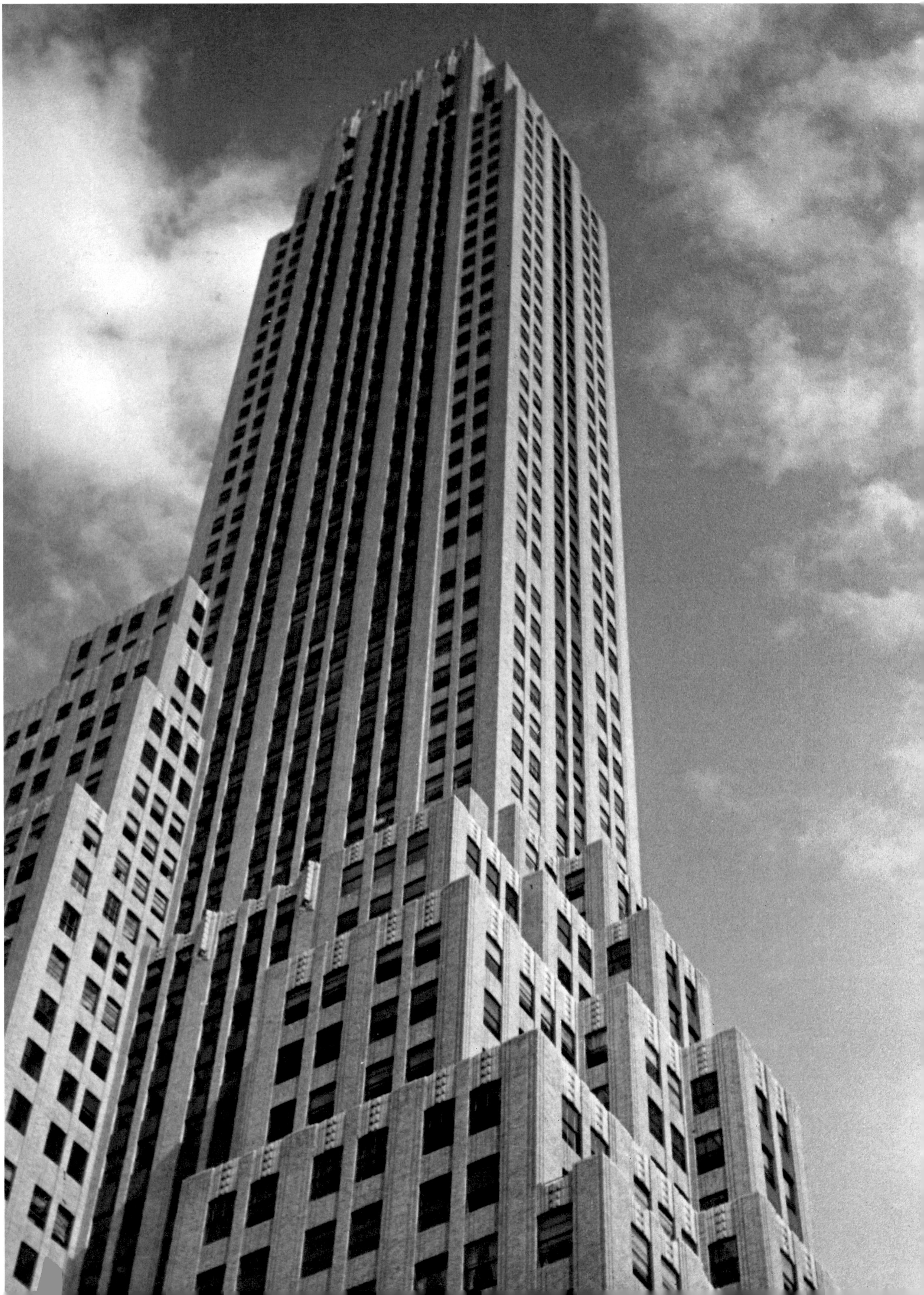

Rooftops with water tank, New York, 1931

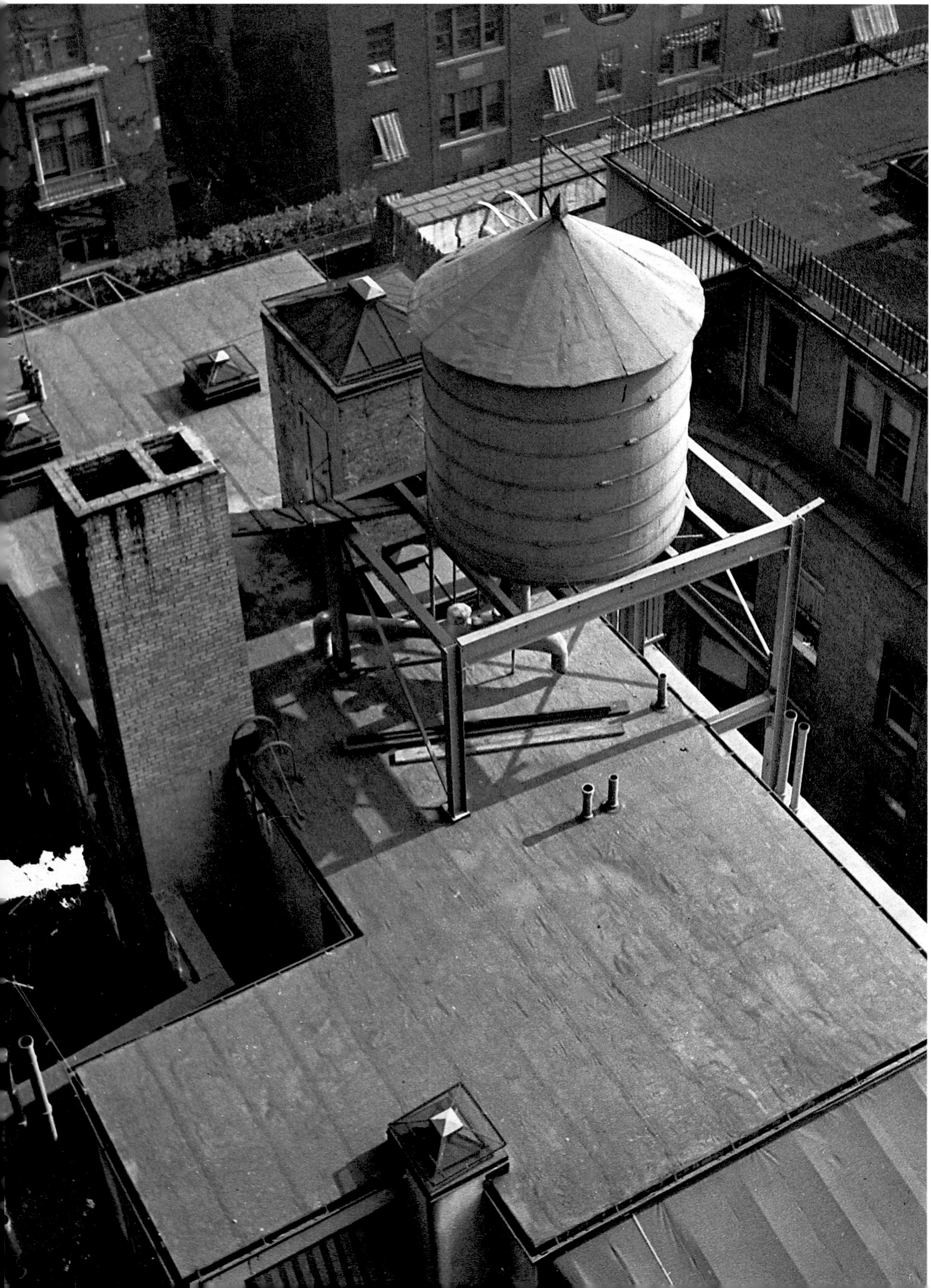

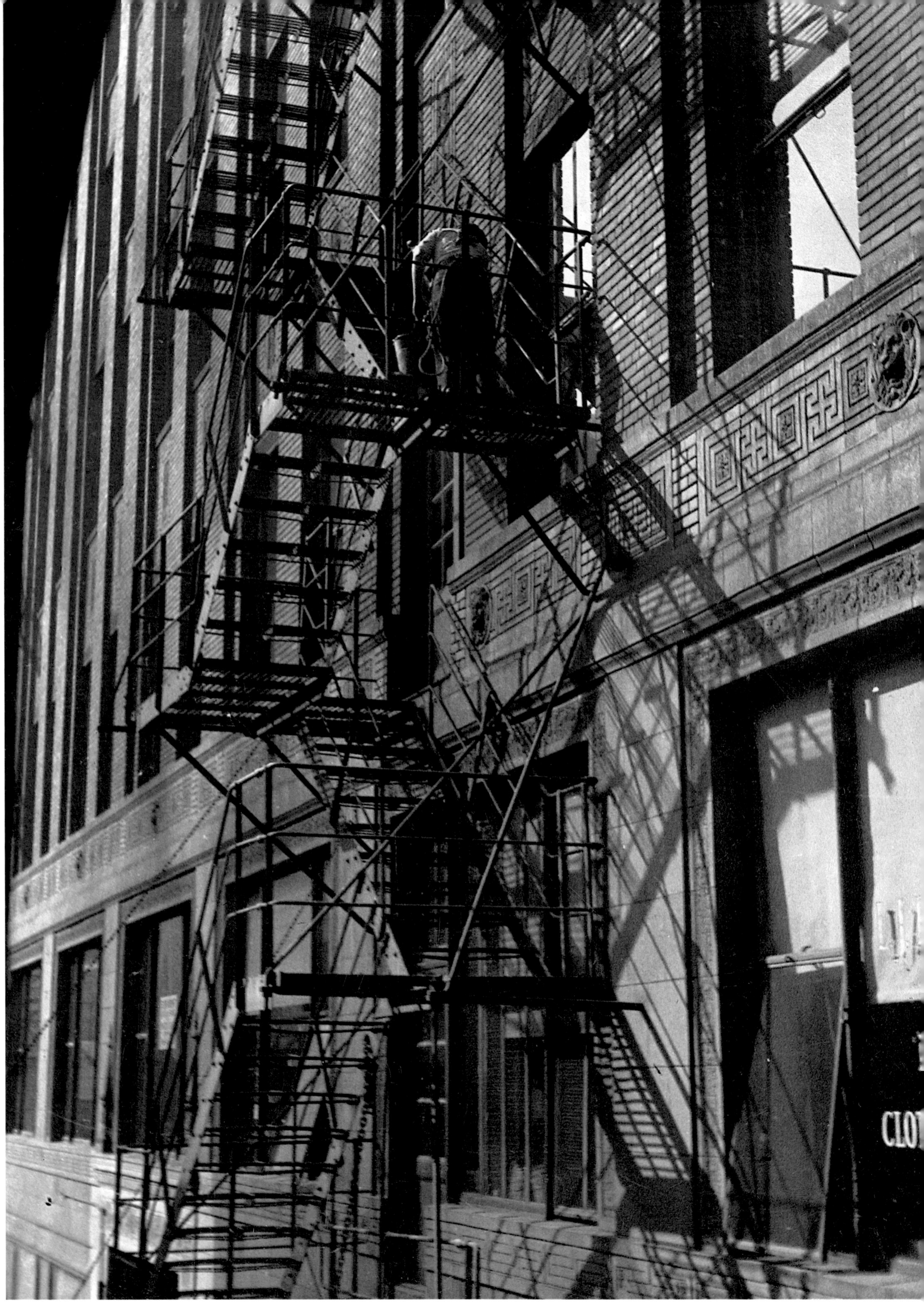

Façade with fire escape ladder, New York, 1931

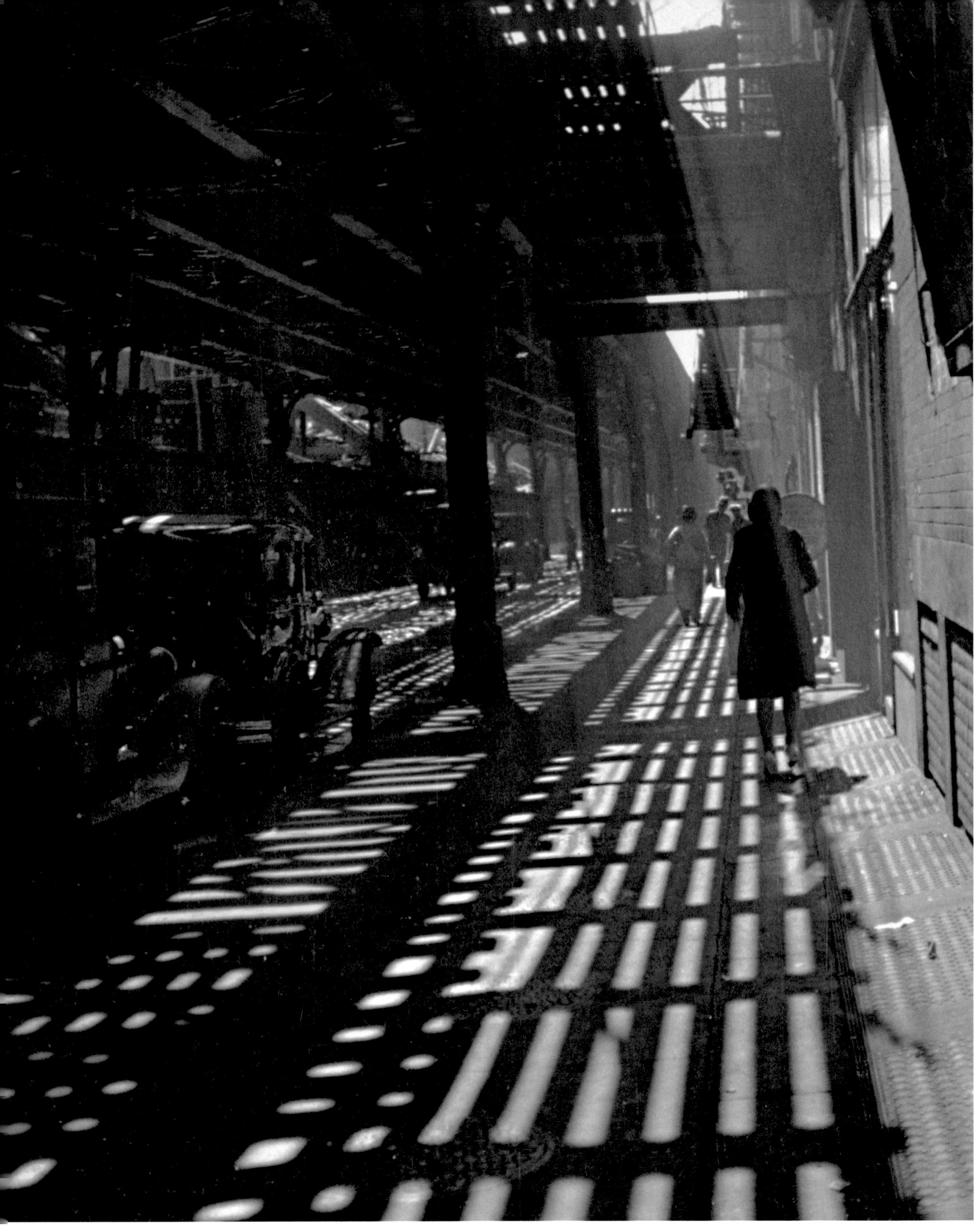

Under the “Elevated,” New York, 1931

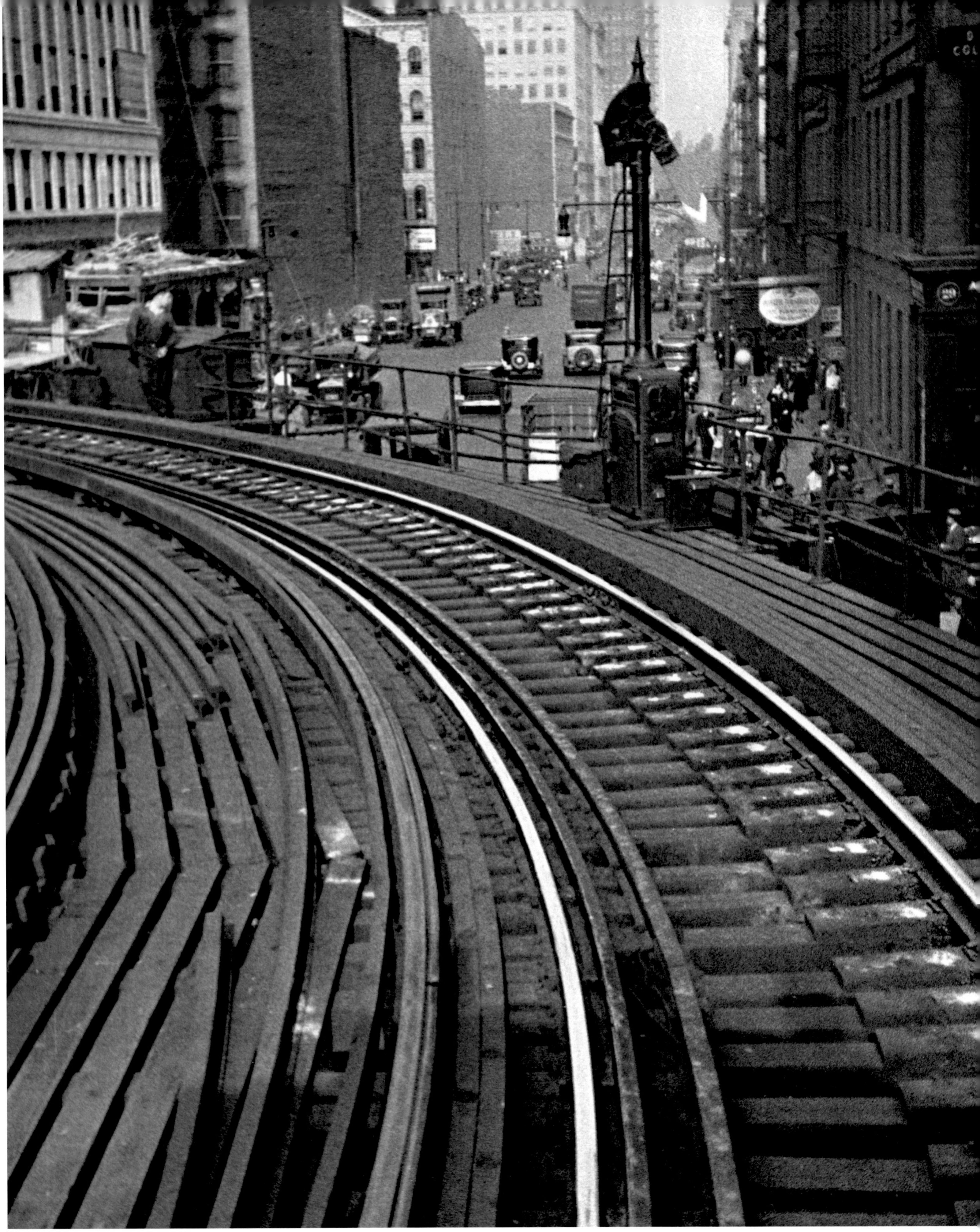

Curved tracks of the “Elevated,” New York, 1931

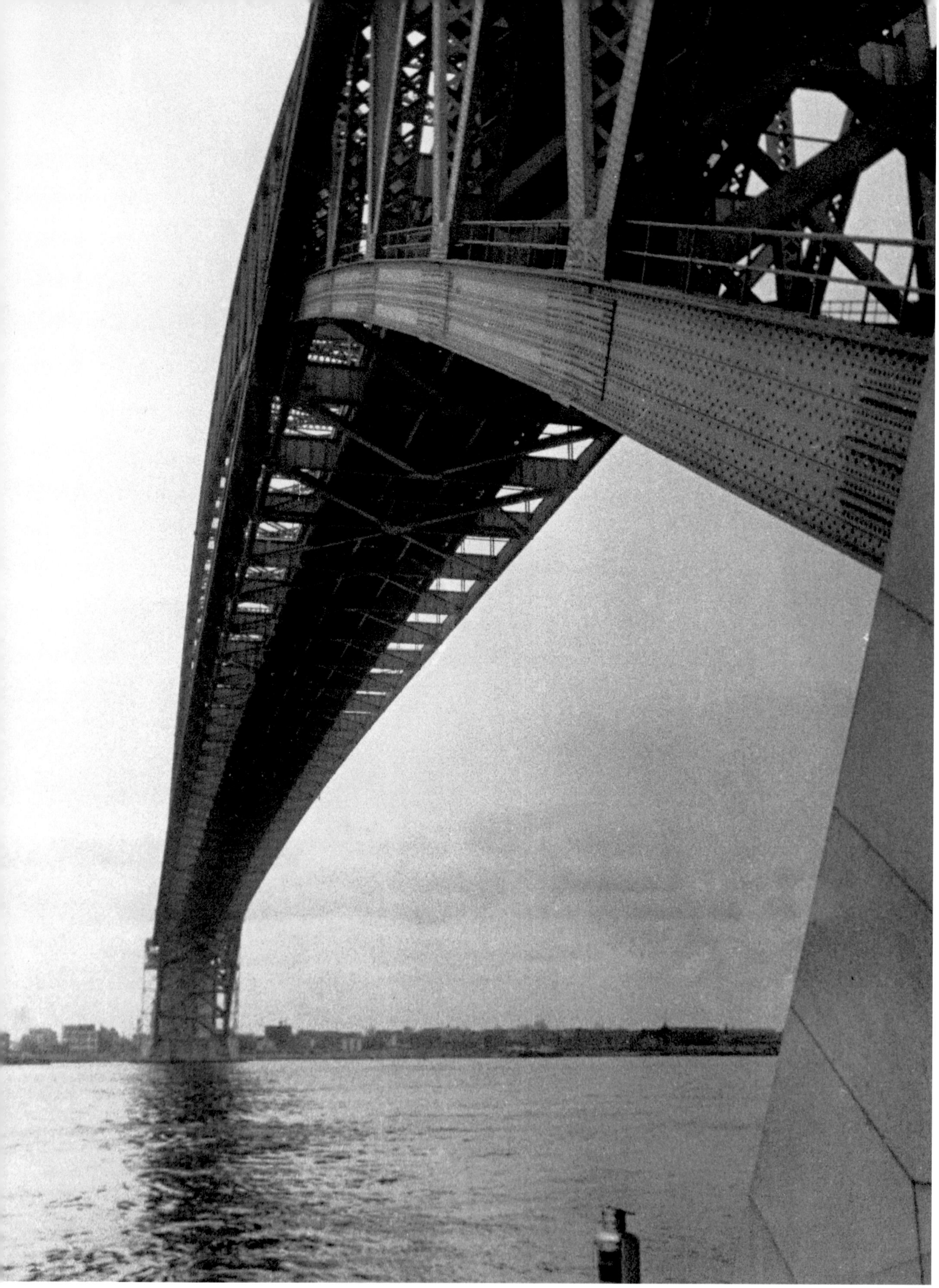

Bayonne Bridge, New Jersey to Staten Island, New York, 1931

George Washington Bridge, New York, 1931
(also see page 4)

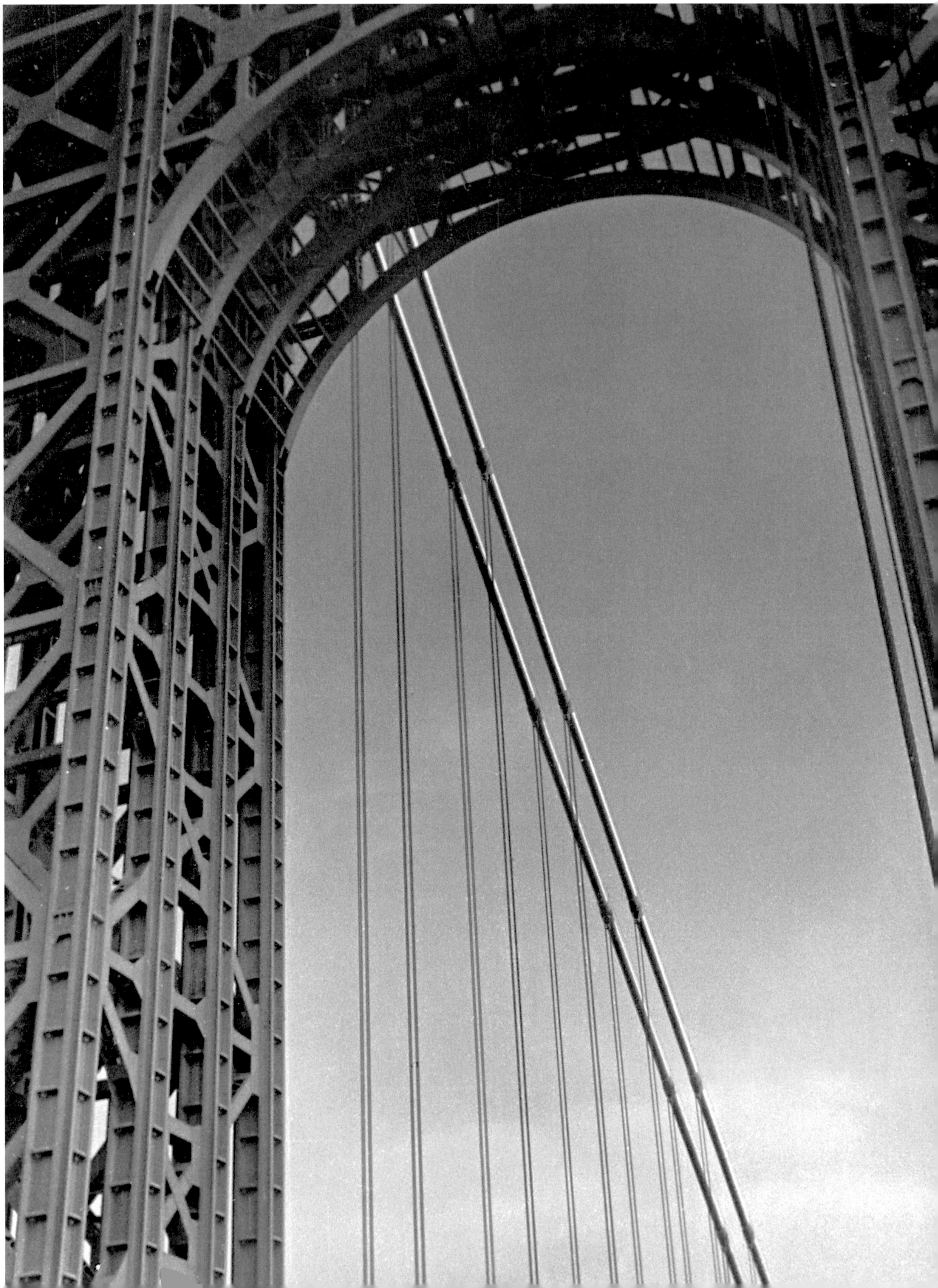

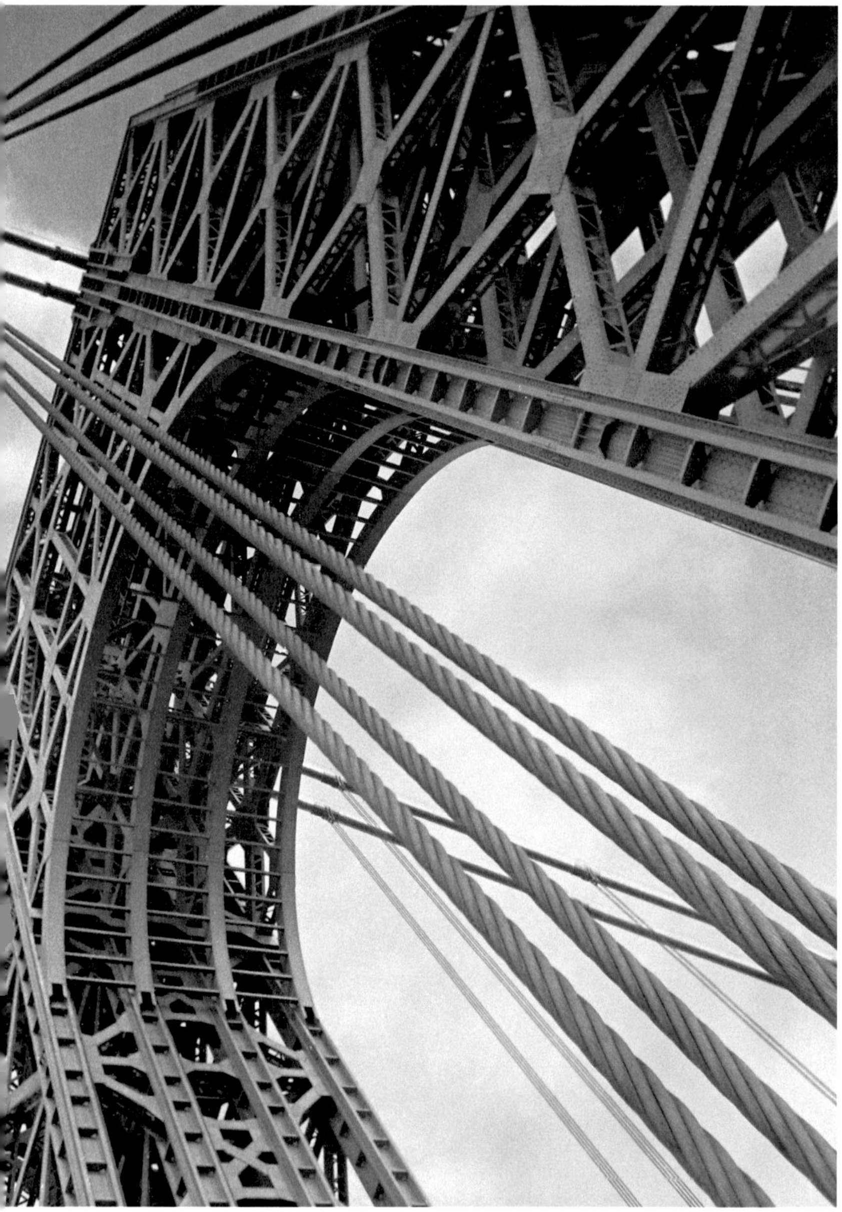

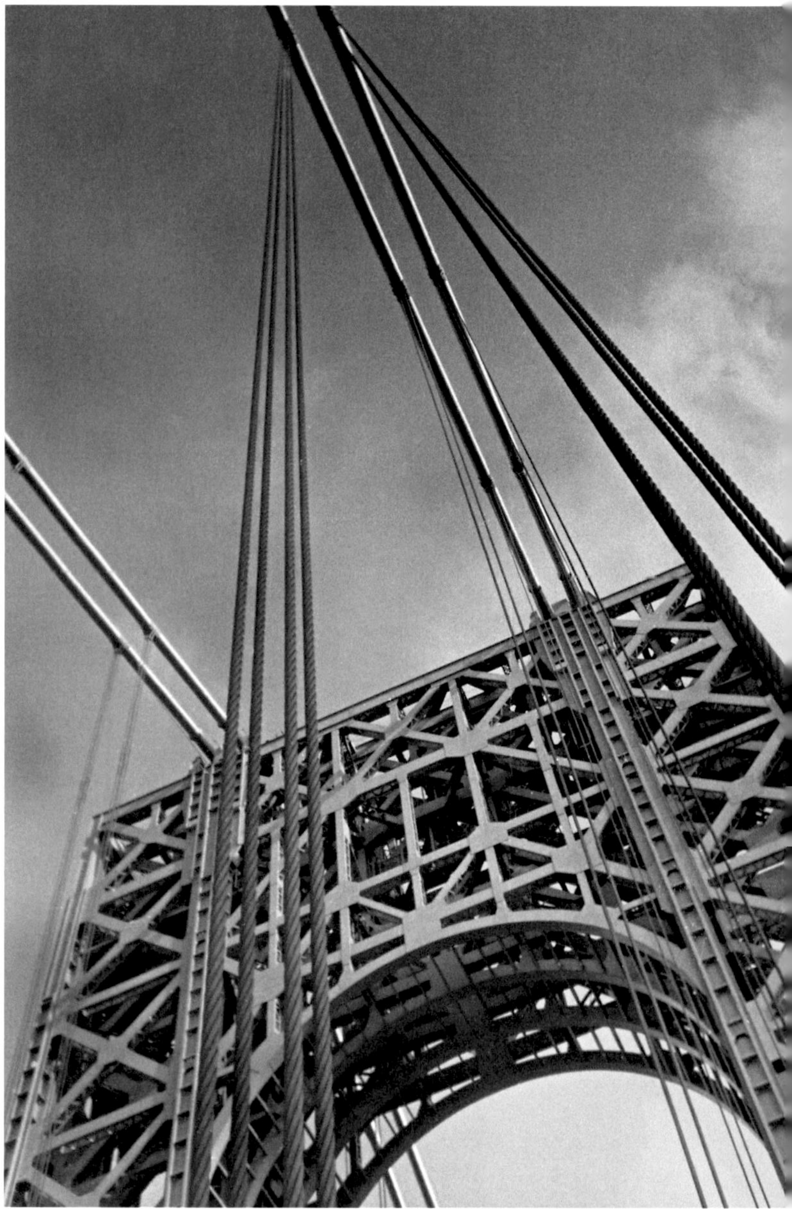

George Washington Bridge, New York, 1931

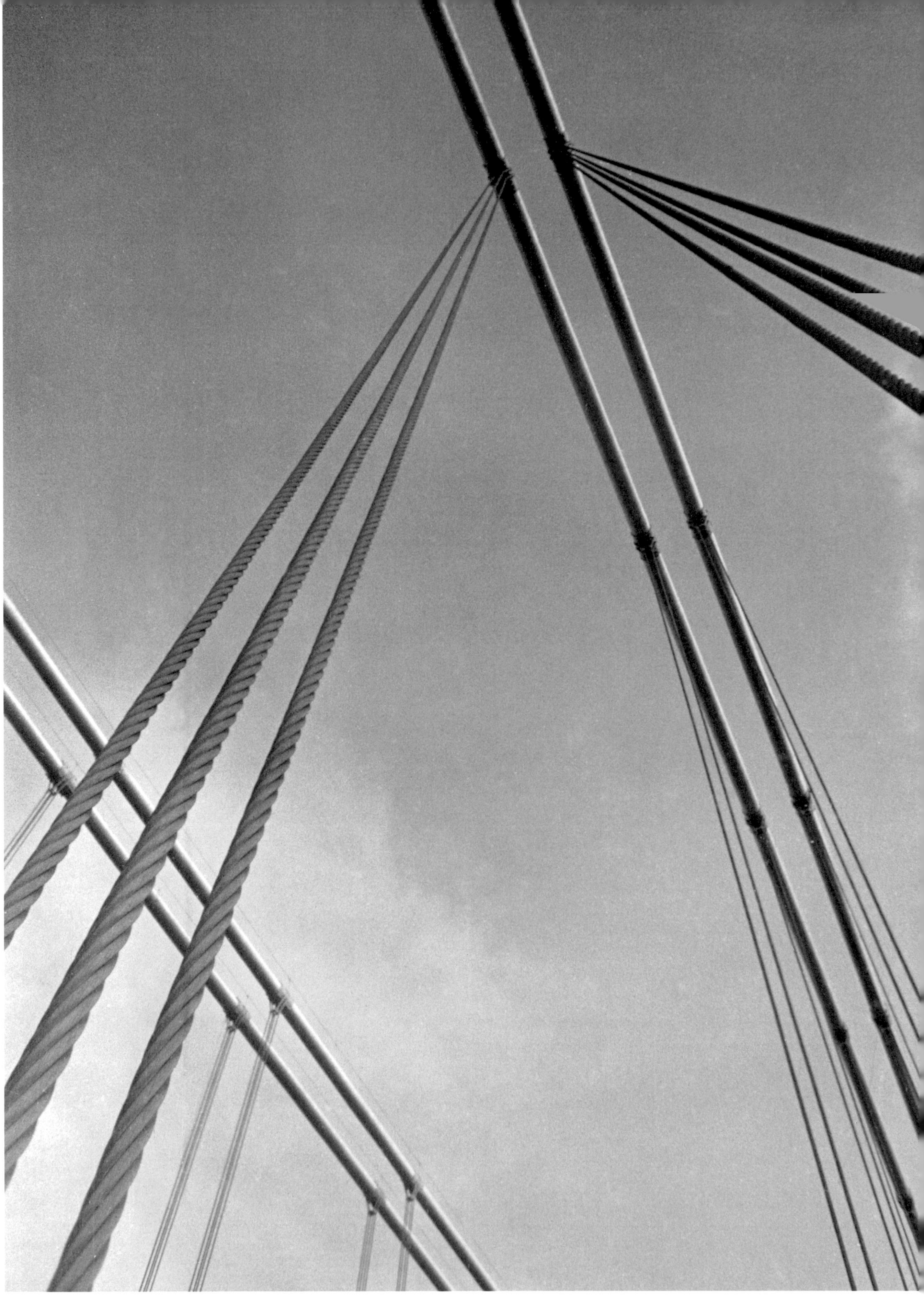

Steel cables of the George Washington Bridge, New York, 1931

Wenn Sie von den Straßen Neuyorks hörten, die den südlichen Stadtteil, Manhattan, durchziehen, ist Ihnen sicher ein Name im Gedächtnis geblieben; der *Broadway*. An der Bezeichnung der ersten, dritten, fünften, siebenten usw. Straße sind Sie aber sicher achtlos vorbeigegangen. Und doch ist gerade die fünfte Straße, die *Fifth Avenue*, die in Süd-Nord-Richtung mitten durch das Herz Neuyorks zieht und vom *Washington Square* aus in endloser schnurgerader Richtung am Zentralpark vorbei bis zum *Harlem River* führt, die eleganteste Wohnstraße und

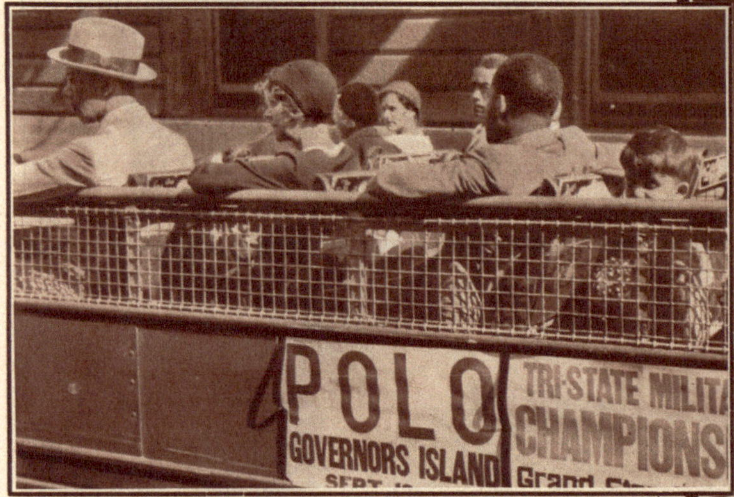

Vom Dache des Bus aus genießt man einen prächtigen Blick auf den lebhaften Straßenverkehr.

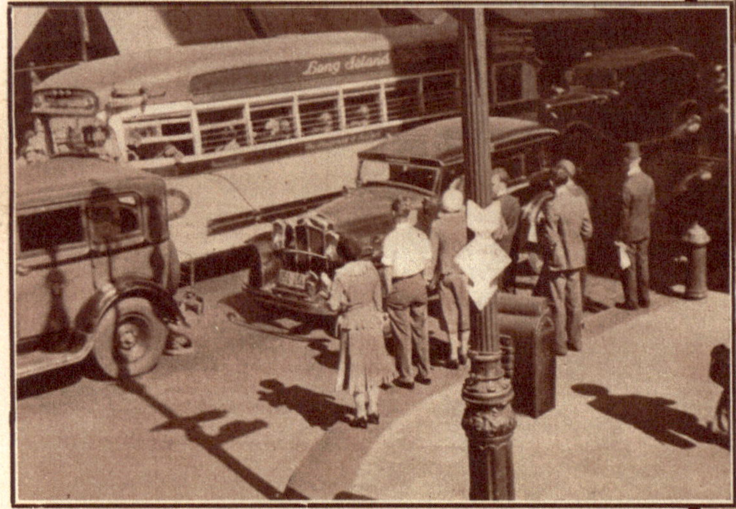

Auto an Auto. Der Fußgänger wartet geduldig, bis der Straßenübergang freigegeben wird.

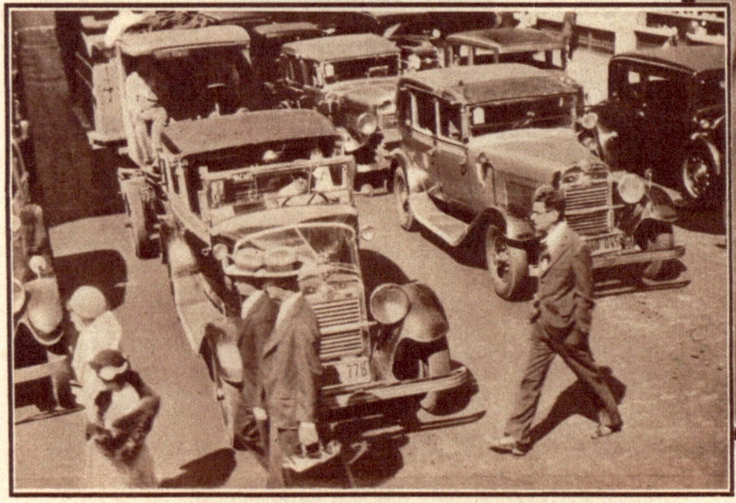

Ist der Moment gekommen, wo der Durchgang frei ist, stoppen die Autoschlangen und warten, bis das Zeichen zur Weiterfahrt erfolgt.

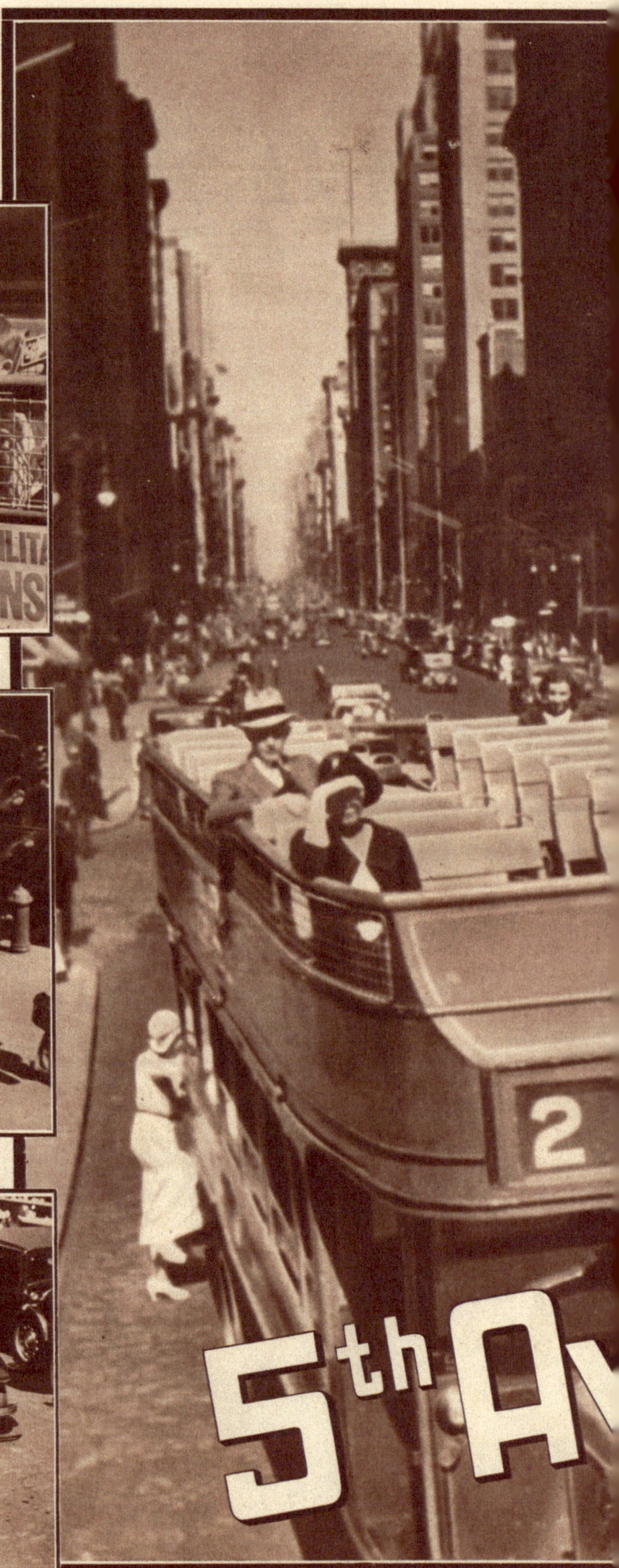

Links und rechts der Straße türmen sich riesige Gebäude auf. Man fähr eine regelrechte Häuserschlucht, deren Tiefe im Schatten liegt.
(Photos Dr. Block.)

"Fifth Avenue in New York" (*Schweizer Illustrierte Zeitung* 21, no. 23, 1932)

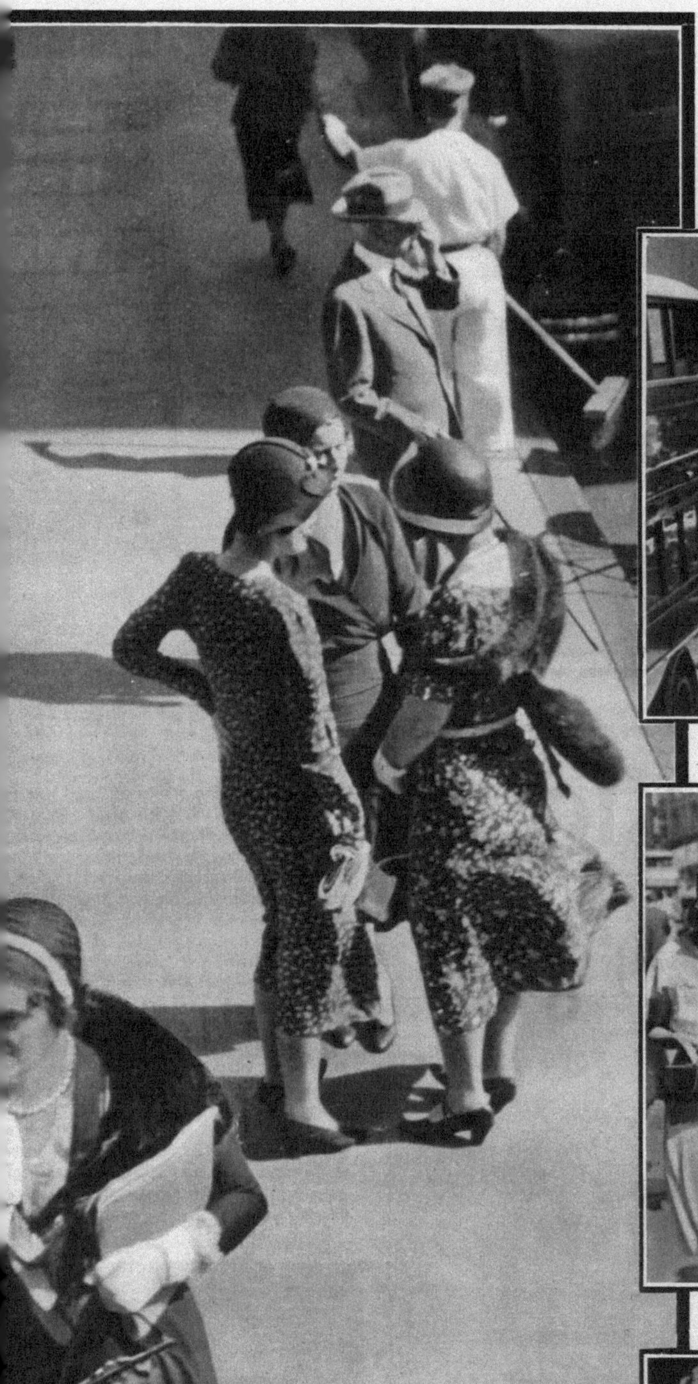

engebrumm, Hupen, Straßenlärm der endlos zirkulierenden Autos. Aber ndert die Damen der *Fifth Avenue* ebensowenig wie anderswo daran, am oirrand ihren «*Cozy chat*» — eine gemütliche Plauderei — abzuhalten, ein Bild der Ruhe im ringsum tobenden Sturm.

die Hauptverkehrsader der Neuyorker Geldaristokratie. Hier sind die vornehmsten Hotels und Restaurants vom Range eines Waldorf-Astoria, hier finden wir die prächtigsten Klubhäuser, die Milliardärspaläste der Vanderbilts usw., die schönsten Kirchen, und eine Anzahl hervorragender öffentlicher Bauten, wie die berühmte *Metropolitan Opera*, die *Carnegie Hall*, Bibliotheken, Museen, die umfangreichen Bauten der *Columbia University*, und noch hunderterlei Gebäude von Namen und Rang. Und dementsprechend ist auch das Leben und der Verkehr in der *Fifth Avenue*, worüber unsere Bilderserie anschaulich zu erzählen weiß.

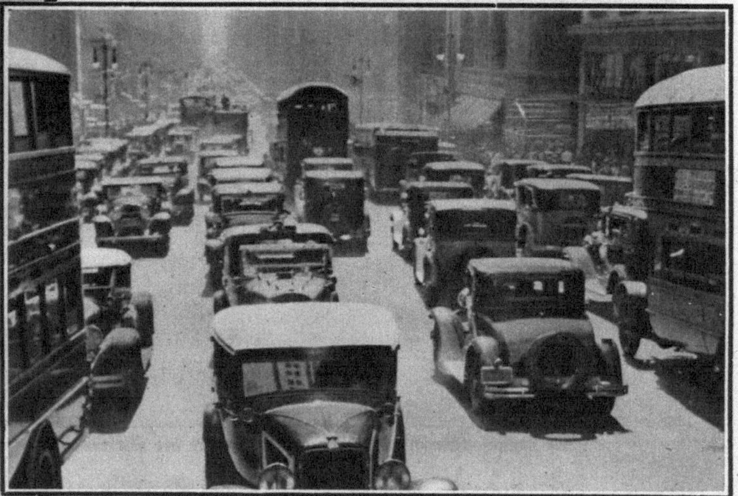

Ein scheinbar beängstigendes Durcheinander von Autos. Aber der Neuyorker Fahrer ist so diszipliniert, daß Verkehrsunfälle verhältnismäßig selten vorkommen.

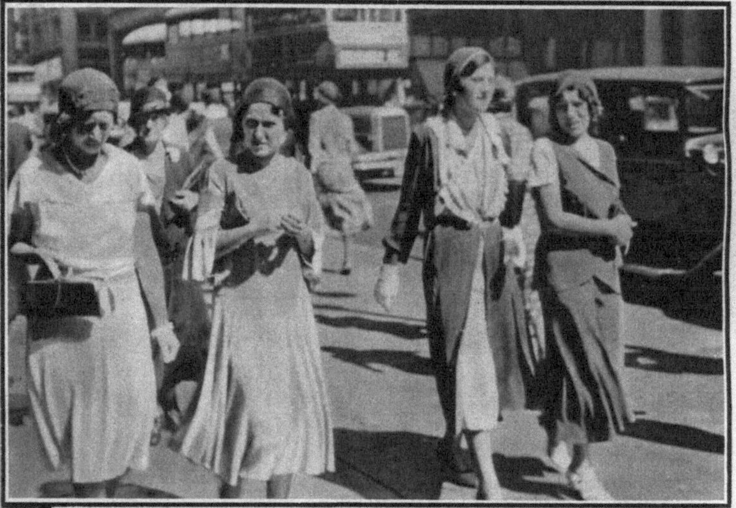

Warum nur lauter Damen auf der Straße? Die Herren haben hier keine Zeit, spazieren zu gehen, die sitzen im Geschäft oder eilen im Auto davon.

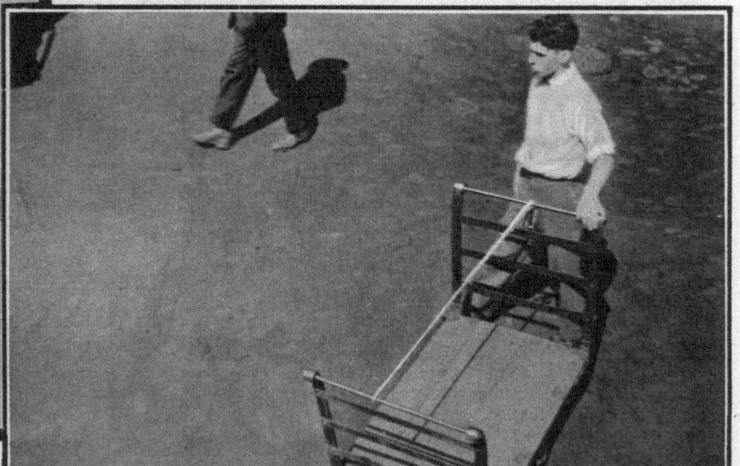

Ein Bild, das gar nicht in den Autoverkehr der *Fifth Avenue* gehört und das doch dort aufgenommen wurde.

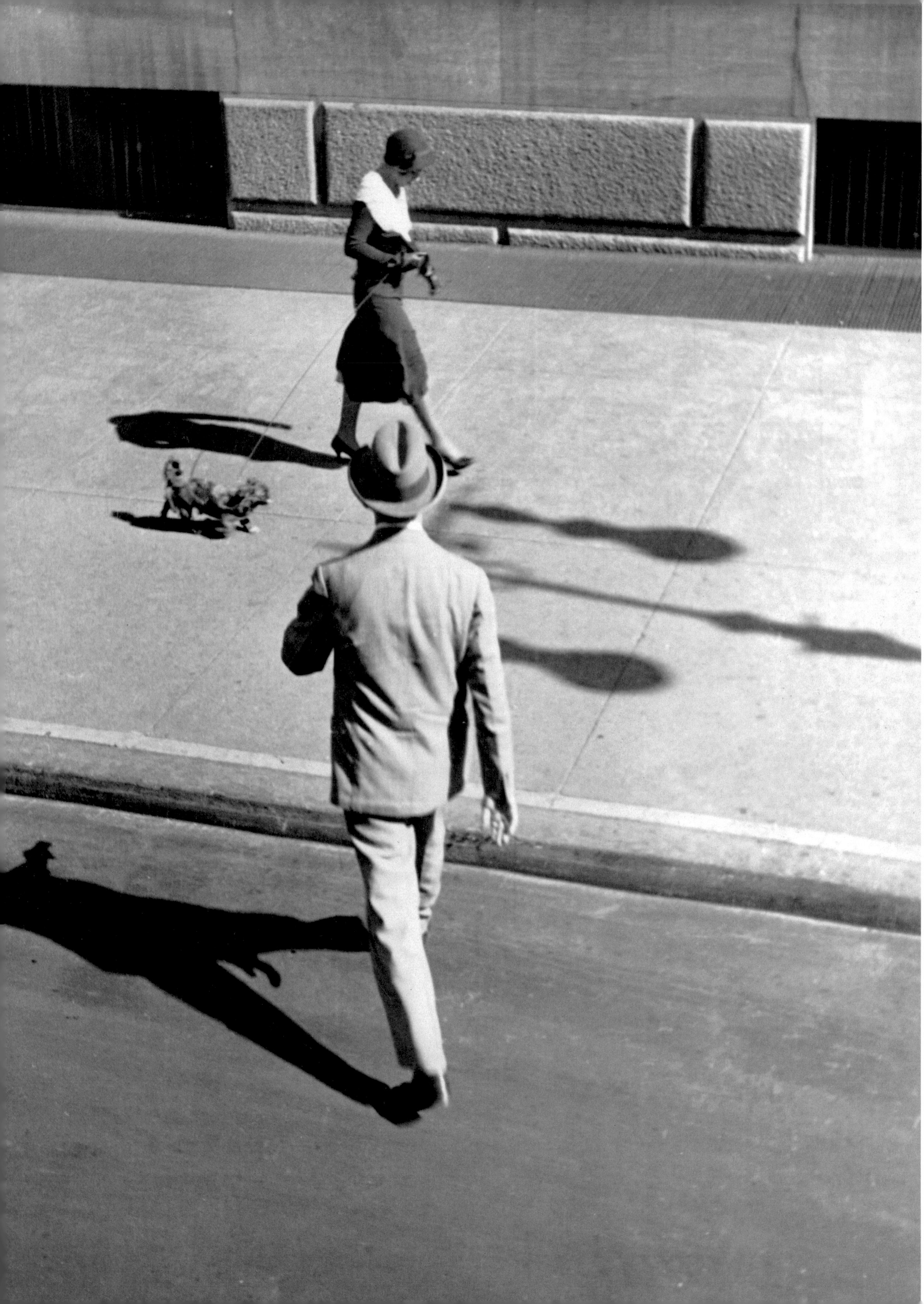

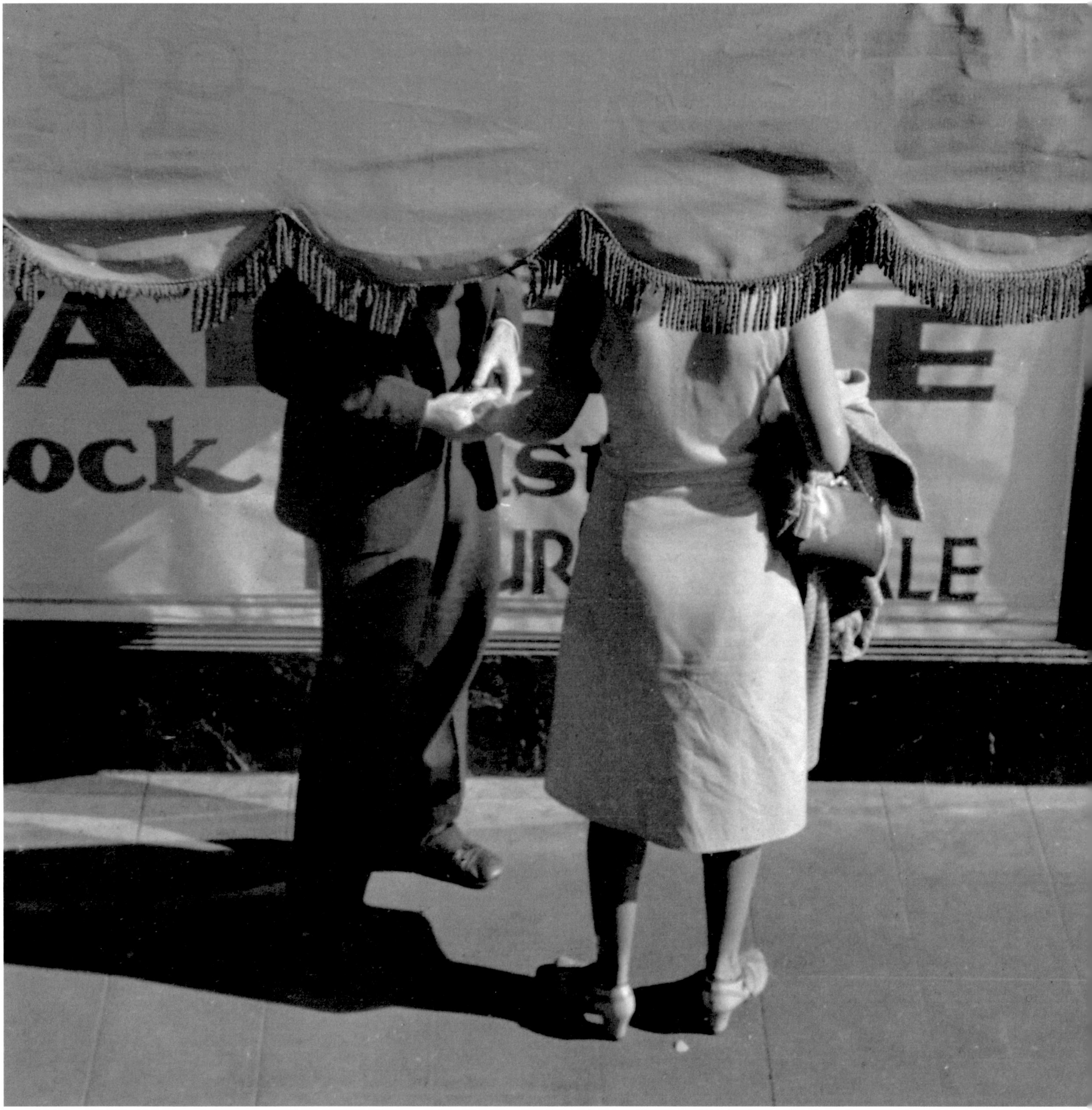

Encounters on Fifth Avenue, New York, 1931

Broadway at night (Loewe's State Theatre), New York, 1931

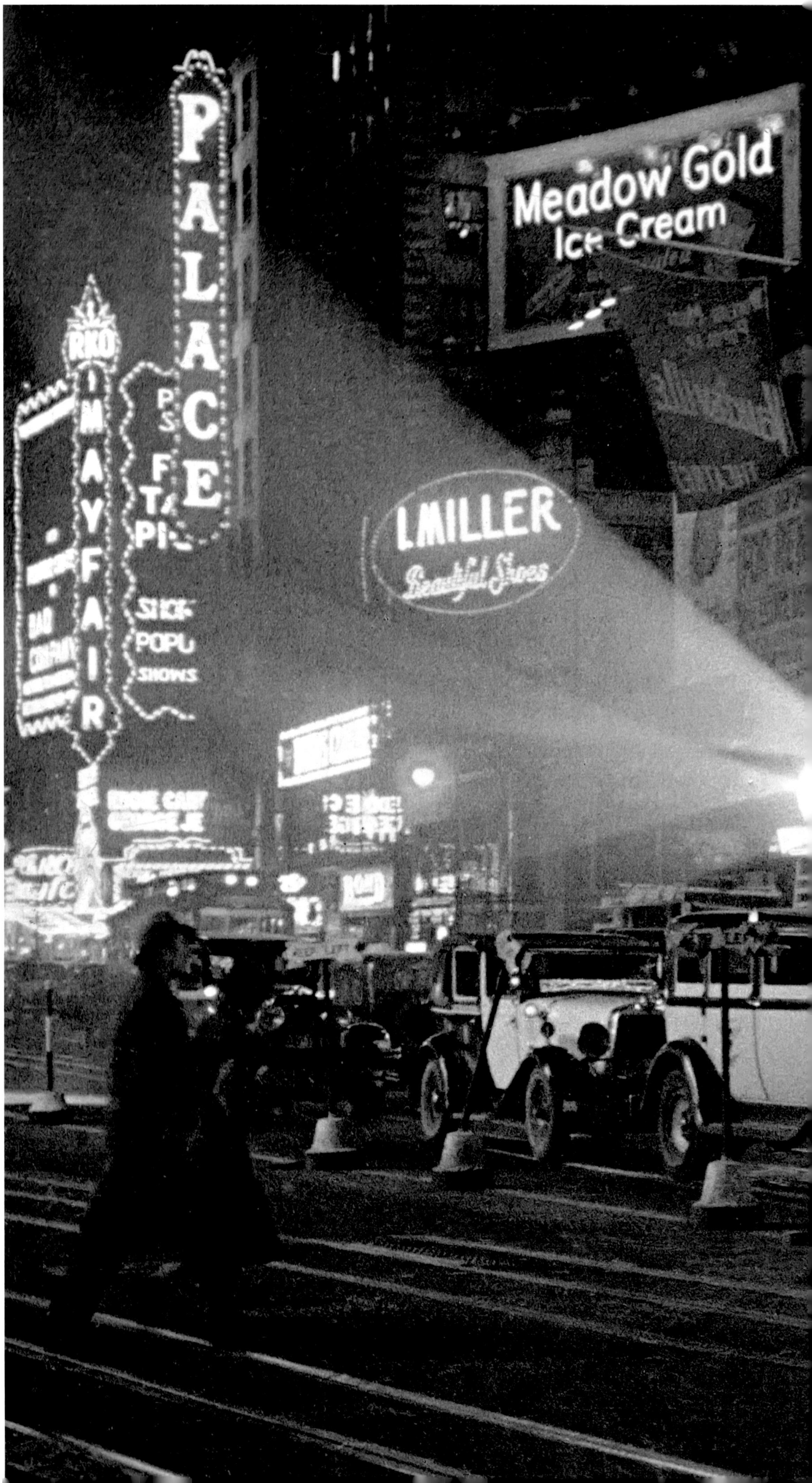

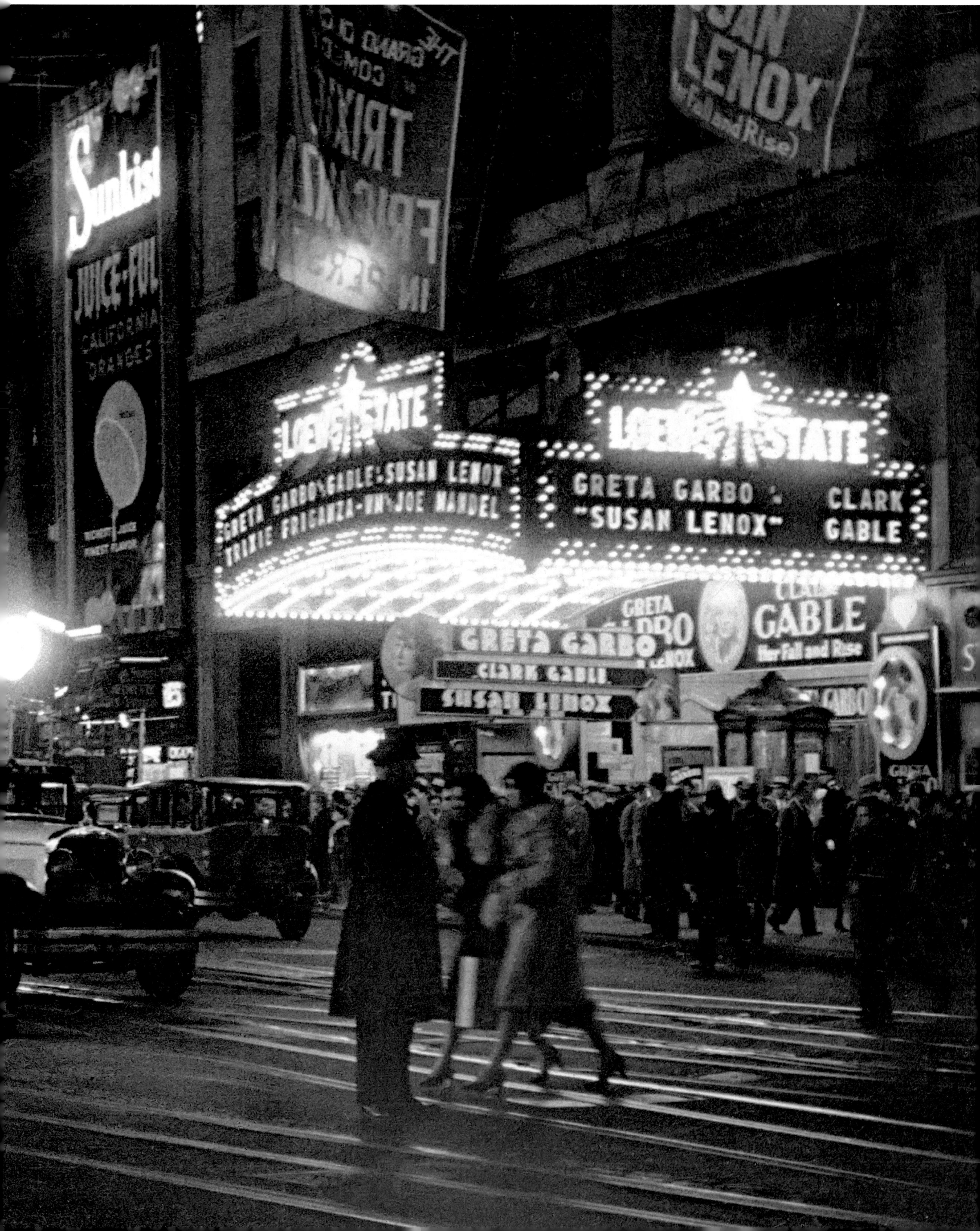
Sunkist
JUICE-FUL
CALIFORNIA ORANGES
LOEWS STATE
GRETA GARBO & GABLE · SUSAN LENOX
TRIXIE FRIGANZA · WM. JOE MANDEL
LOEWS STATE
GRETA GARBO & CLARK GABLE
"SUSAN LENOX"
LENOX
(Her Fall and Rise)
GRETA GARBO
CLARK GABLE
SUSAN LENOX
GABLE
Her Fall and Rise

Broadway at night (Times Square and Palace Theatre), New York, 1931

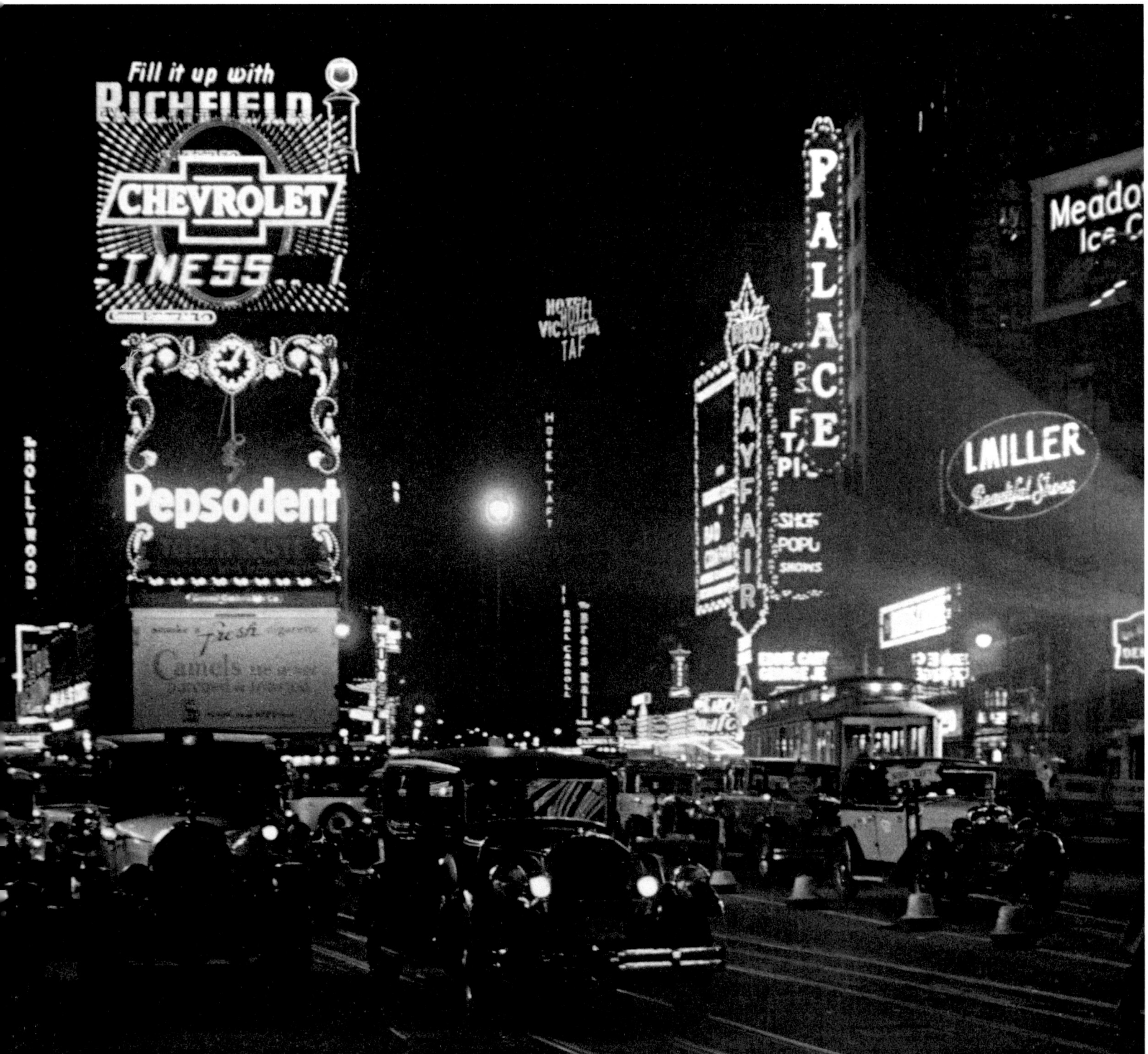

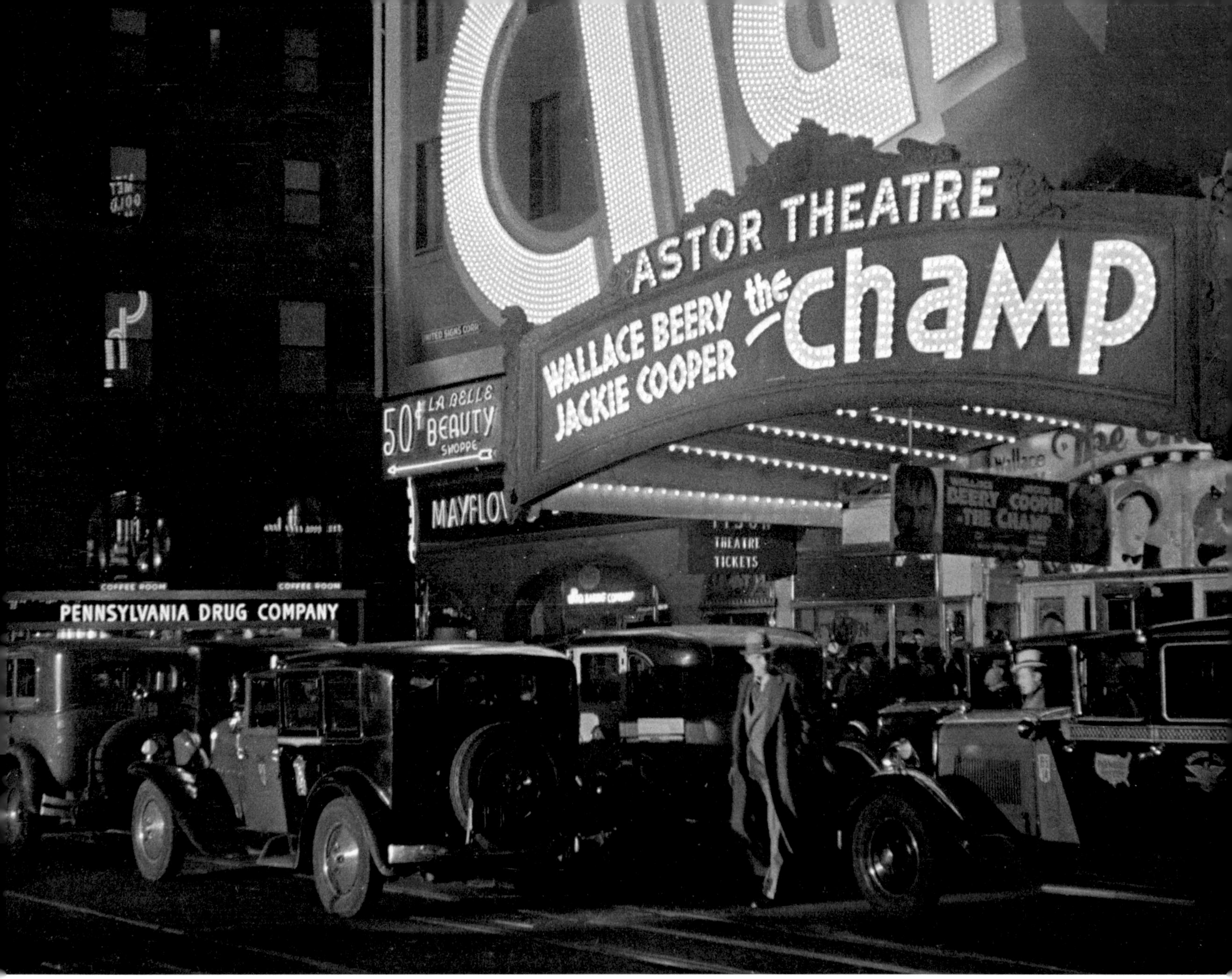

Broadway at night (Premiere of "The Champ" at Astor Theatre), New York, 1931

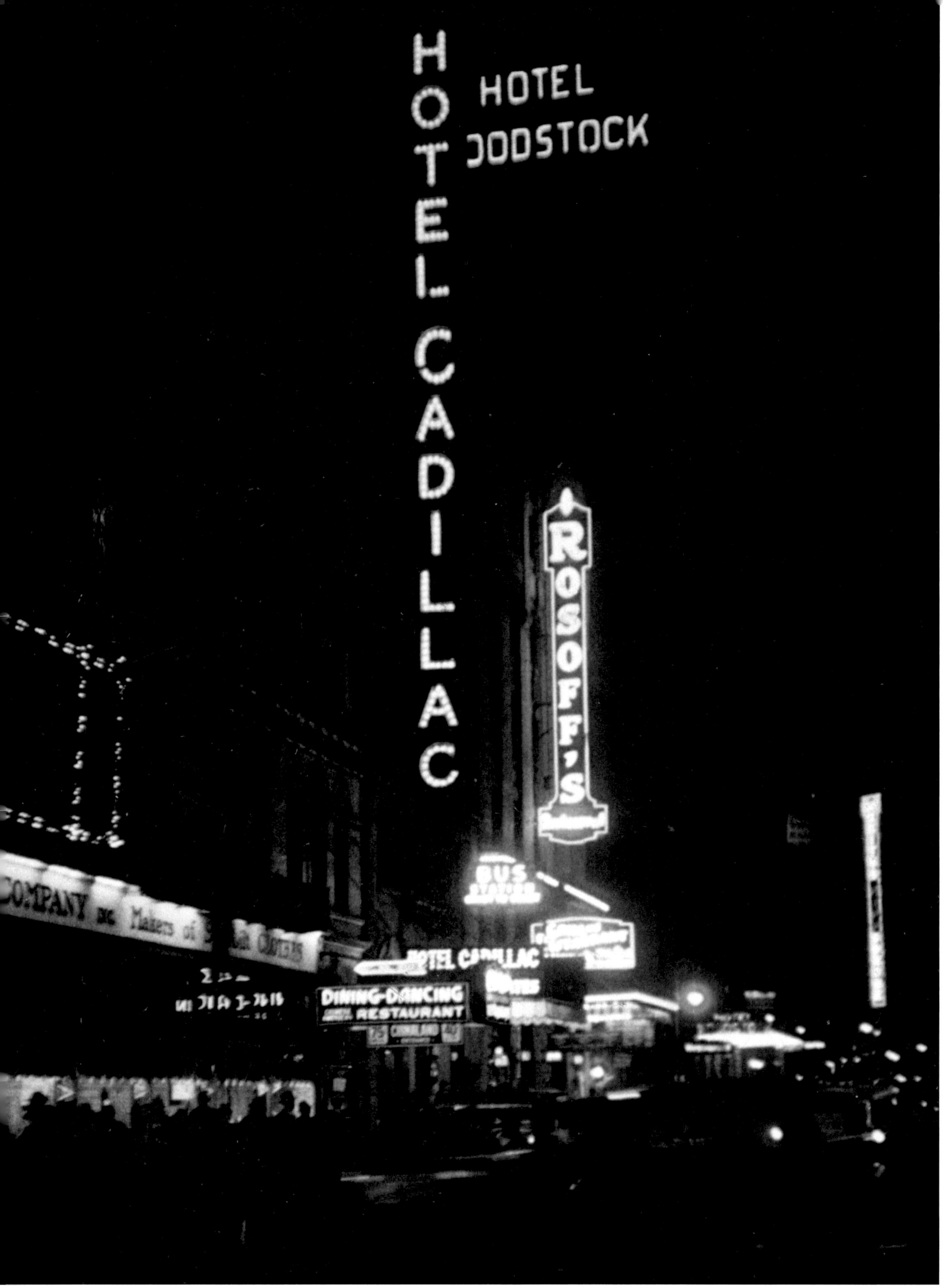

Broadway at night (Hotel Cadillac and Rosoff's Restaurant), New York, 1931

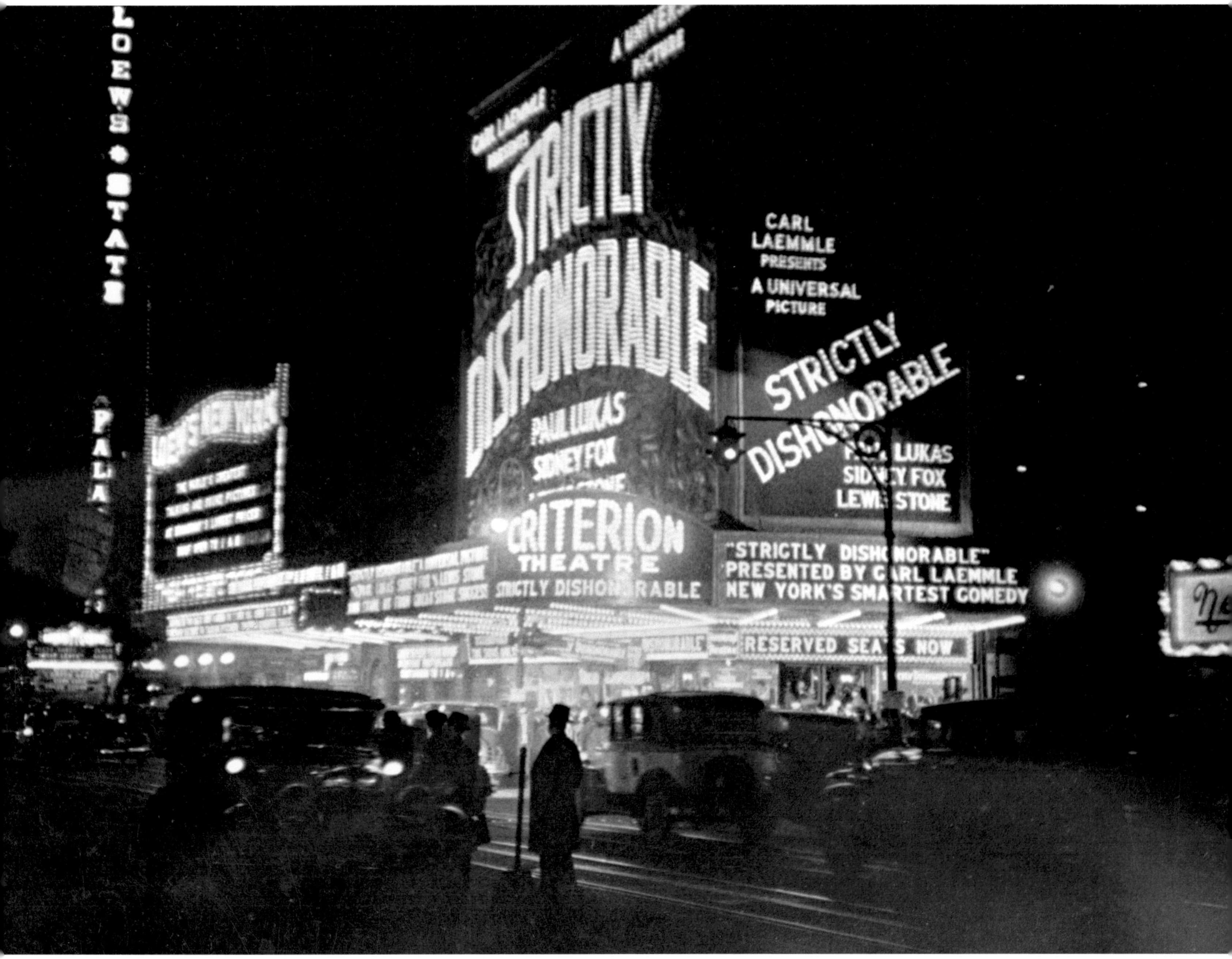

Broadway at night (Criterion Theatre), New York, 1931

Amerikanerinne

Über die Amerikanerinnen ist viel geschrieben worden. deutsche Frau interessiert sich sehr für ihre Geschlec jenseits des Ozeans, hört sie doch stets von ihrer Son Verwöhntheit, Gepflegtheit sowie von ihrer beruflichen und Unabhängigkeit.

Es ist der amerikanischen Frau tatsächlich gelungen, Maße fast widersprechende Eigenschaften zu vereinen. ratete Frau des reichen Mannes mag sie verwöhnt sein, stehen ihr in dieser Situation außer den gesellschaftlichen g Pflichten, denen sie sich nicht nur mit Geldopfern, sonder Einsetzung ihrer persönlichen Zeit und Arbeitskraft unter Pflege aller kulturellen Dinge obliegt fast ausschließlich da der Mann neben seinem aufreibenden Beruf dafür erübrigen kann.

Nur ein kleiner Prozentsatz der Amerikanerinnen ist n auf der Welt in Überfluß gebettet. Die große Zahl der besorgt die zwar kleine und bequeme Wohnung ohne H Dienstboten sind unerschwinglich teuer. Nur für Wäsche stundenweise die Negerin zur Verfügung. Gerade diese stimmt ja das Stadt- und Straßenbild. Ihre Fähigkeit, na Arbeit am Leben außer dem Haus teilzunehmen in nicht te modischer Kleidung, guter Frisur, gepflegtem Gesicht un läßt uns eine recht gute Tageseinteilung vermuten. vielen Haushaltungen greift der Mann, ohne seine Würde zu helfend zu, eine Form des Verwöhnens, die nichts koste spart. Viele Frauen aus kinderlosen Ehen sind beruf werden ihrer Doppelaufgabe gut gerecht.

Die beruflich tätige alleinstehende Frau belastet sich nicht mit Hausfrauensorgen. Sie wohnt im Junggese Boardinghouse, auch im möblierten Zimmer. Sie ist se angewiesen, nicht schön, sondern gut und gepflegt auszuse den Büros, in den Restaurants sieht man erstaunlich vie jugendliche Mädchen, denen kein Alter anzusehen ist. Ih zur Liebenswürdigkeit mag die Glätte der Gesichter erhal

Die amerikanische Frau ist eine gute Sportlerin. fahrerin ist sie sicher und rücksichtsvoll auch im Großst ihre Erfolge im Golf, Hockey, Tennis, Schwimmen u veröffentlichen die Zeitungen mit Bildern.

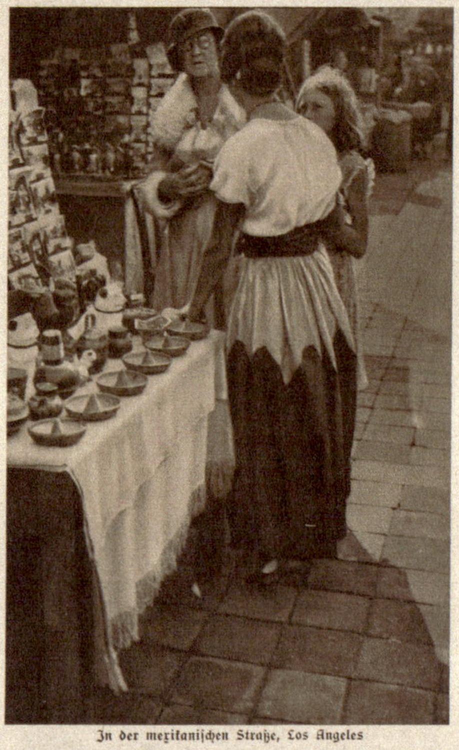
In der mexikanischen Straße, Los Angeles

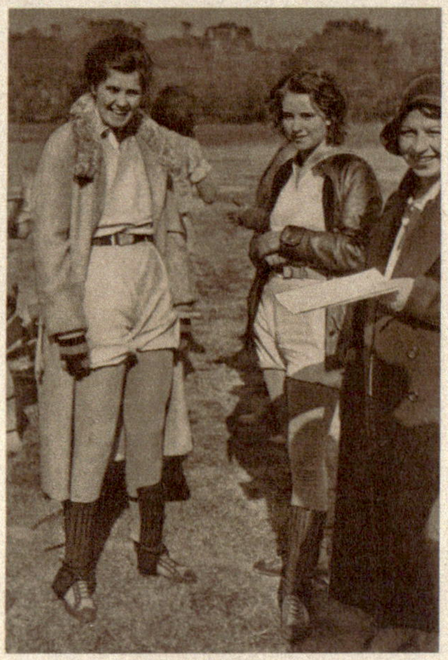
Hockeyspielerinnen

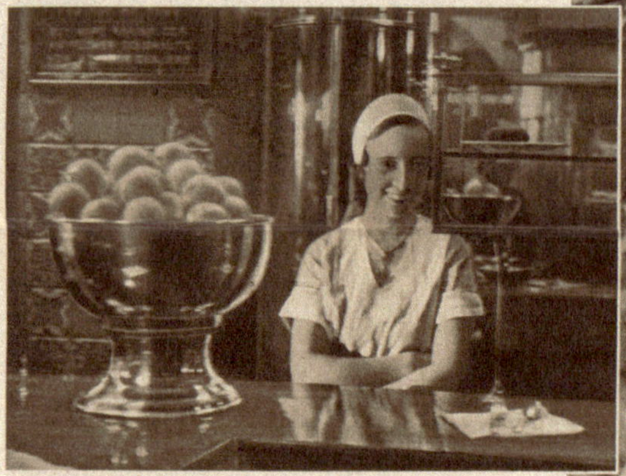
Kellnerin in einem Broadway-Restaurant, Neuyork

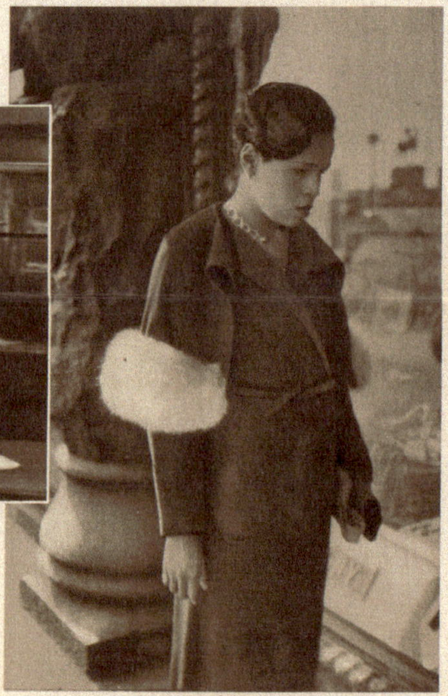
Negerschönheit

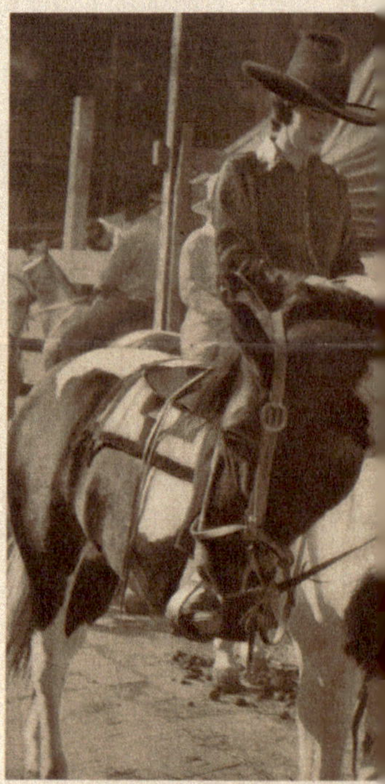
Cowgirl, Kalifornie

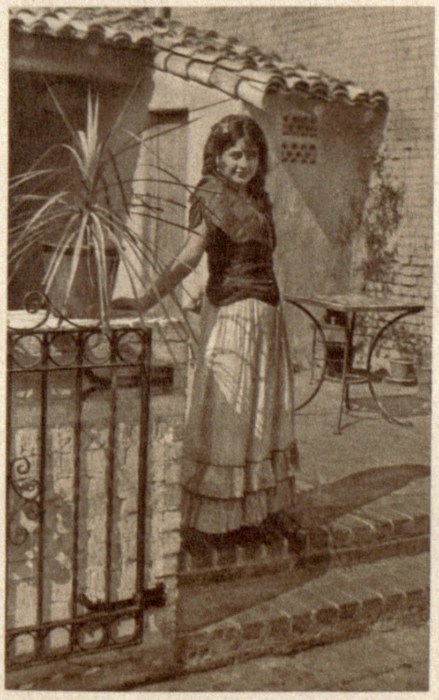
Mexikanerin, Los Angeles

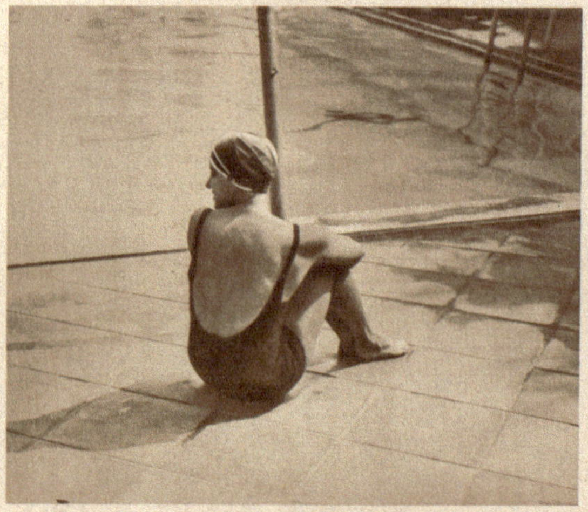
Die sportliche Frau. Schwimmbad im Hotel Ambassador, Los Angeles

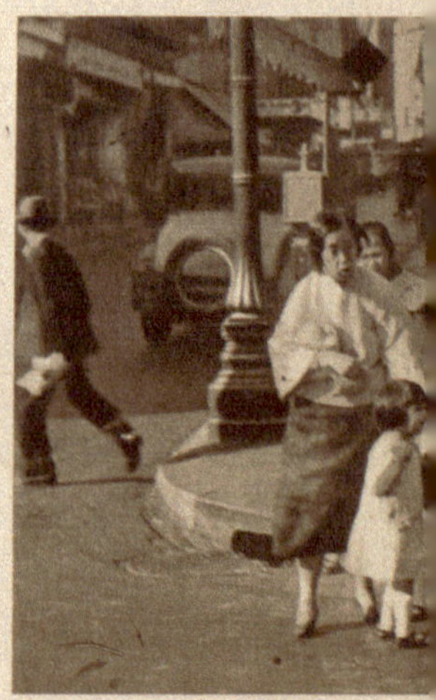
Chinesinnen im

"American Women and Children of all Races" (*Hamburger Anzeiger. Illustrierte Wochenbeilage*, no. 19, 1932)

amerikanische Kinder aller Rassen

ganz andere Note bringt die farbige Frau in das Bild
te. Die Negerin von der Karikatur der aufgeschwemmten
Matrone bis zur eleganten Mondänen, im Westen die
Tracht gehende Chinesin, die europäisch gekleidete zierliche
ı, reizende Kinder an der Hand, ziehen anziehend die
sich. Der Indianerin begegnet man in den Reservationen;
ı Städten sein mögen, verschwinden in der Menge.
auch durch das junge Frauenwahlrecht die politische
r Frau heute offiziell anerkannt ist, so kann man wohl
ı, daß auch ohne dies der Wille des weiblichen Geschlechtes
ntlichen Leben schon immer seinen Stempel aufgedrückt
s Erzieherin der Jugend (überwiegend weibliche Lehrer
nar school, high school and college), als erste Instanz in
gen der Wohlfahrt und des kulturellen Lebens hat die
elt es verstanden, ihre Ansichten und Wünsche bis in die
ung (z. B. Prohibition) durchzusetzen. Vor Gericht ist
age schwerwiegend. In Eheprozessen gelingt es ihr leicht,
iges Urteil für sich zu erringen. Jede Frau gilt als Dame,
dem Herrn das Zeichen zum Gruß, eine Belästigung kann
zeiliche Folgen haben.
Bewunderung muß man feststellen, wie die Frauen es
sich die aus der früheren Kolonialzeit des Frauenmangels
ıde Sonderstellung zu erhalten.
den Europäer, der amerikanische Städte bereist, ist allein
Studium der Menschen lohnend, dieses Gewimmel aller
nd Schattierungen, das besonders unverfälscht in der bunt
ngewürfelten Kinderwelt hervortritt.
en langgedehnten, öden, teilweise trostlosen Wohnquartieren
n Städte Nordamerikas kann man die Kinder aller Rassen
n. Vom schlafenden Baby im Wagen, von der Mutter
schwarzen Kindermädchen in den Park gefahren, bis zum
, das selbständig seine Wege geht.
leine Negerkind nennt der Amerikaner „pickaninny“. Es ist
sehr hübsch mit den leuchtenden dunkeln Augen und dem
, spaßig anzusehen in der grotesken bunten Kleidung mit
gabten, neckischen Bewegungen.
besonders reizend sind die Kinder der Asiaten. Die
kleiden sich europäisch, hingegen erhält sich der Chinese sehr hartnäckig seine schöne heimische Tracht. Er wohnt in eigenen Quartieren, hat eigene Theater, in die die bildhübschen Kinder mitgenommen werden.

Die Kinder der Indianer sieht man nur in den Reservationen, den großen Gebieten, die den Indianern von der Regierung zum Wohnen, sei es als Nomaden oder in seßhafter Form, bereitgestellt sind. Die Rasse erinnert an den Typ der Eskimos. Glatte schwarze Haare werden von beiden Geschlechtern lang getragen. Seit kurzem trägt das kleine Indianermädchen den sieghaften Bubikopf, die Ponys weit in die Stirn fallend.

Die Kinder der gänzlich ins Proletariat abgesunkenen Rasse sind auf Fremdenindustrie gedrillt, doch sind sie nicht ohne sympathische Scheu und laufen mit der erbeuteten Gabe eilig davon. Bei all der Zivilisierung und Mechanisierung in diesem Lande erfreuen den Beschauer stets die Züge der jugendlichen Frische und Unverdrossenheit, die aus dem kindlichen Tun und Treiben abzulesen sind.

Anna Sophie Block.

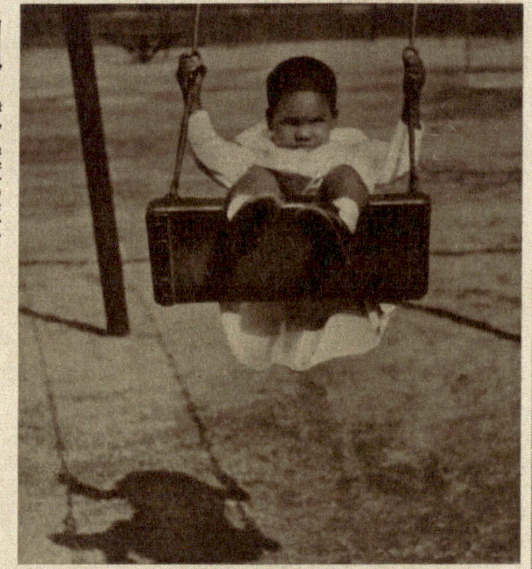

Schaukelndes Negerkind, Harlem

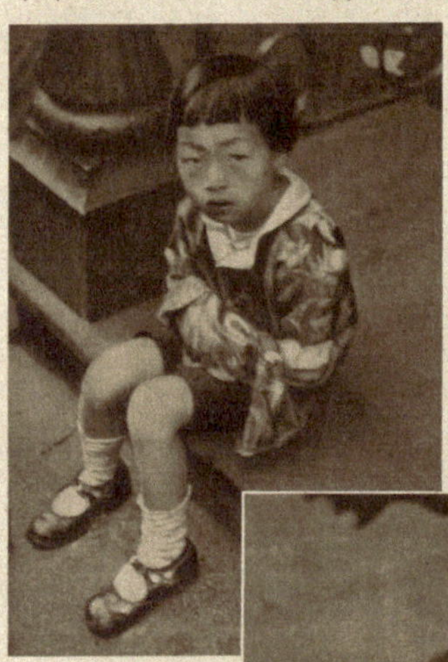

Chinesenkind

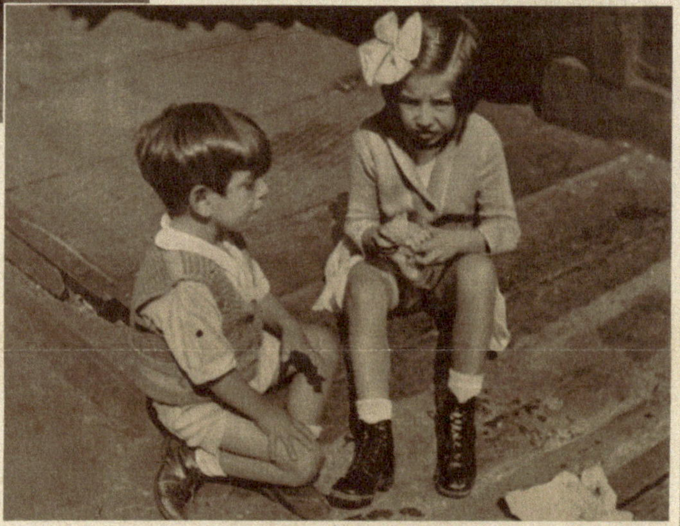

Kinder im italienischen Viertel, Neuyork

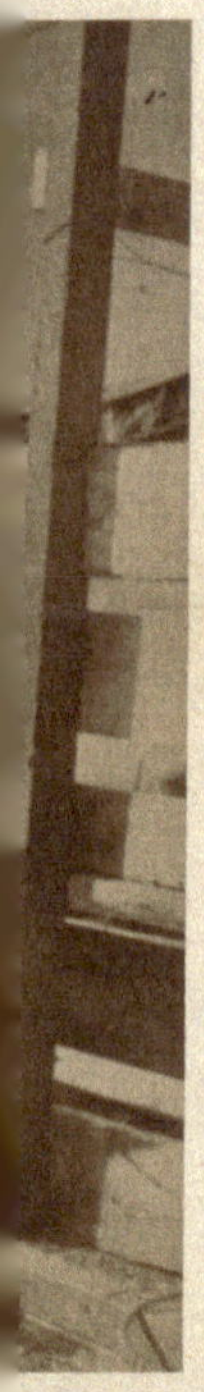

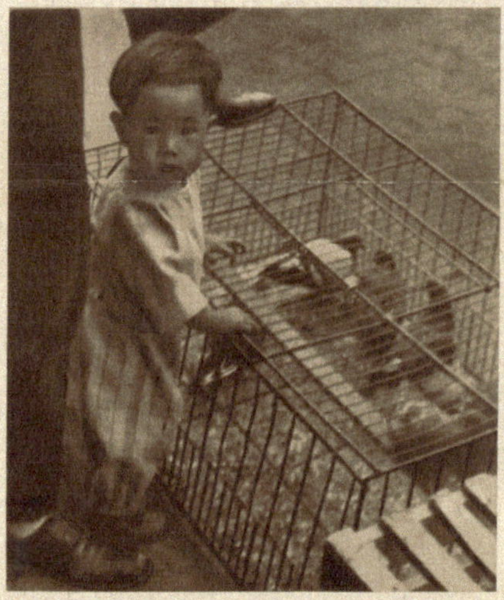

Chinesenkind

Aufnahmen Dr. Block

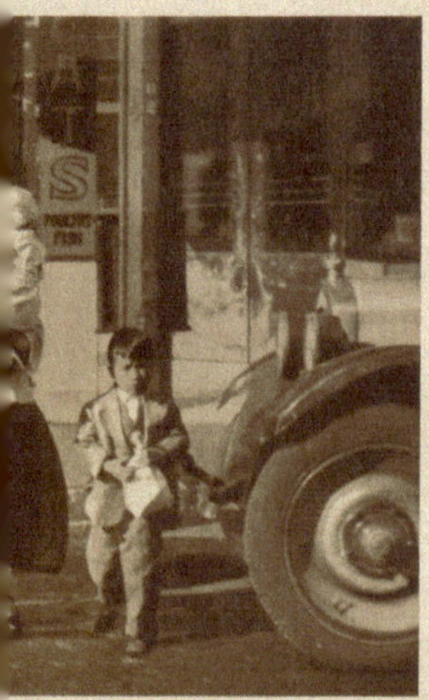

San Franzisko

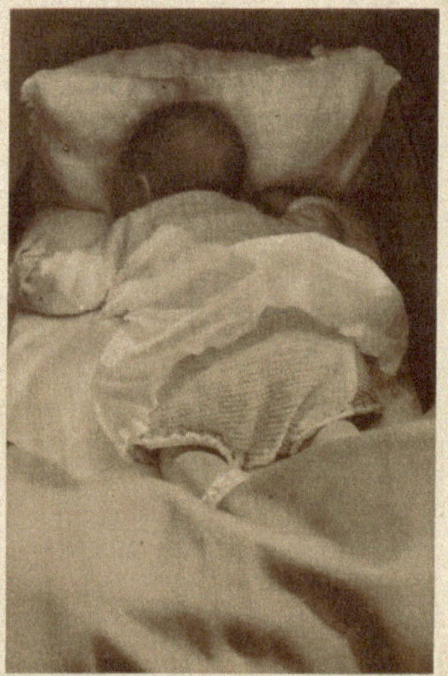

Baby im Freien

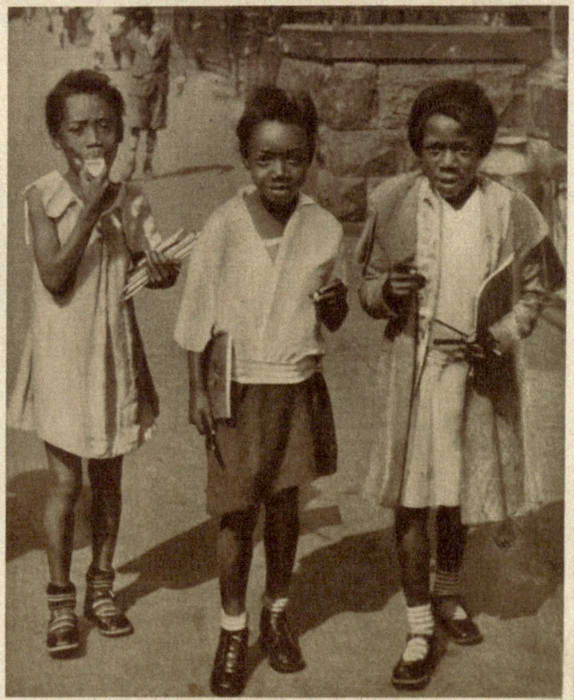

Negermädchen auf dem Schulweg

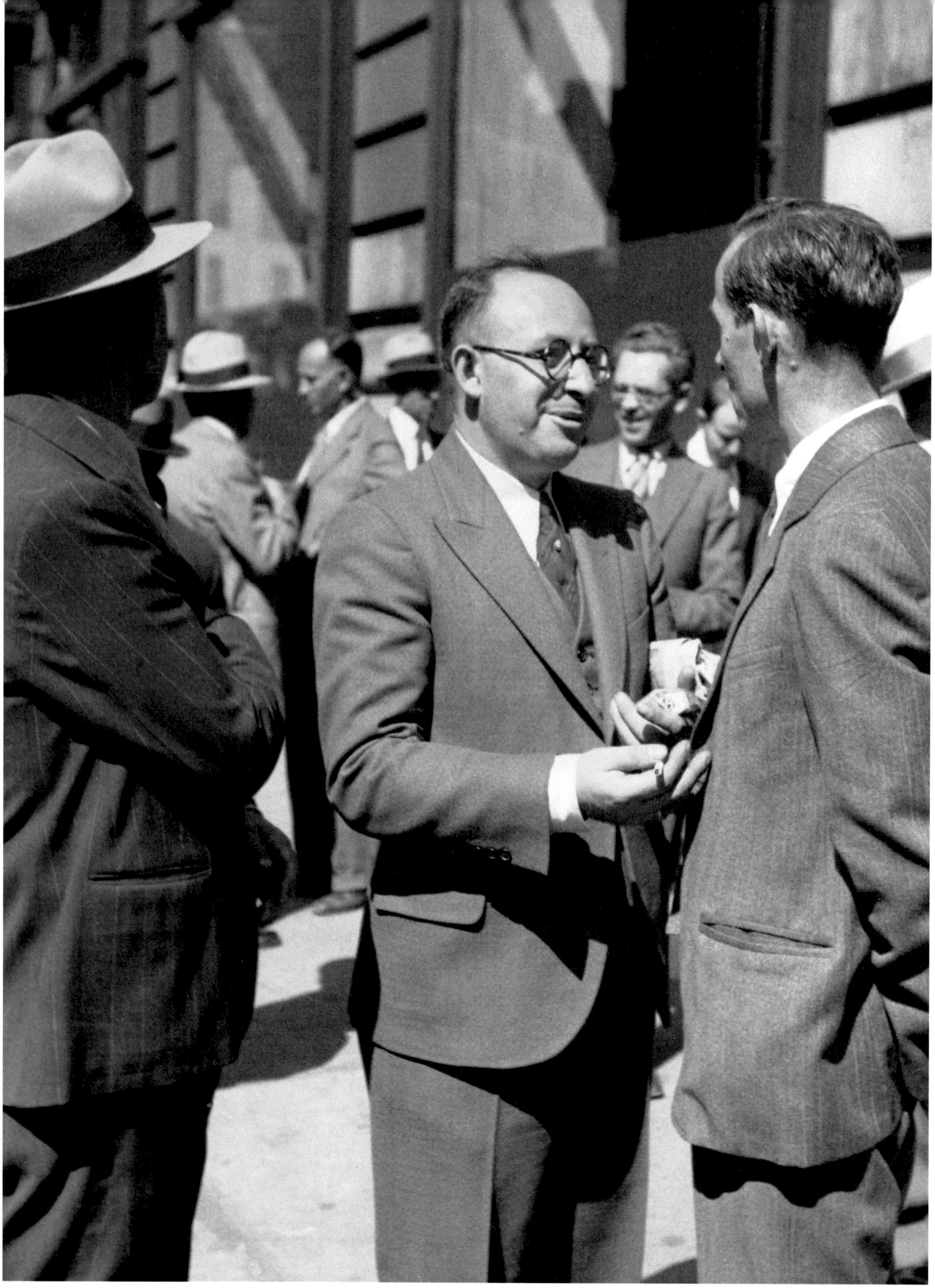

Lunch break on Wall Street, New York, 1931

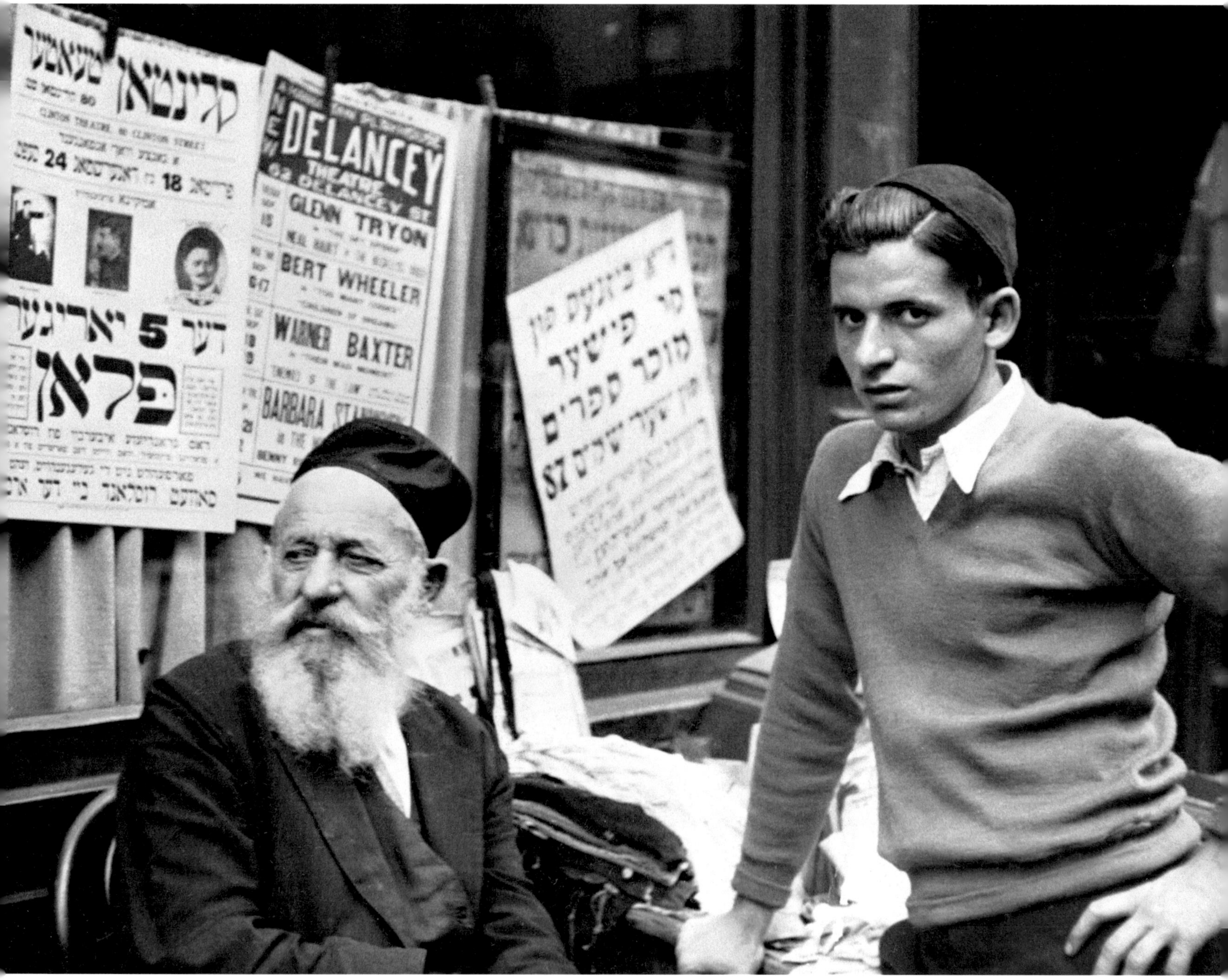

In the Jewish Quarter of the Lower East Side, New York, 1931

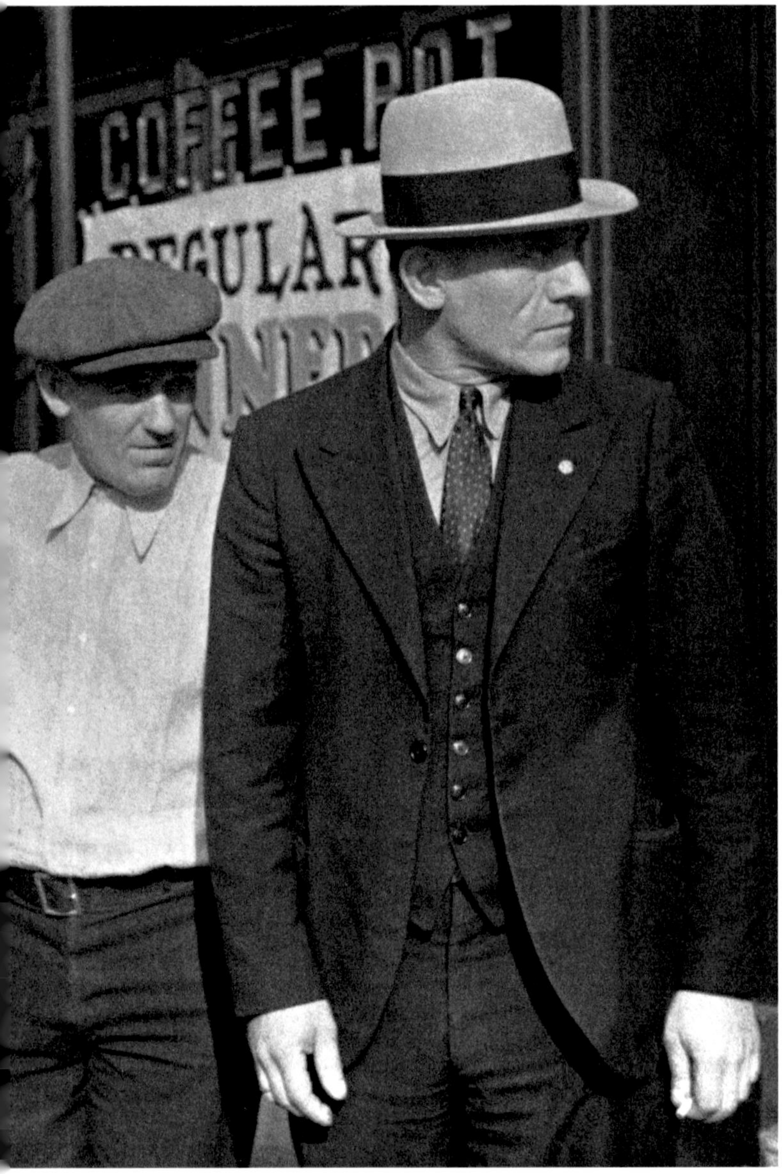

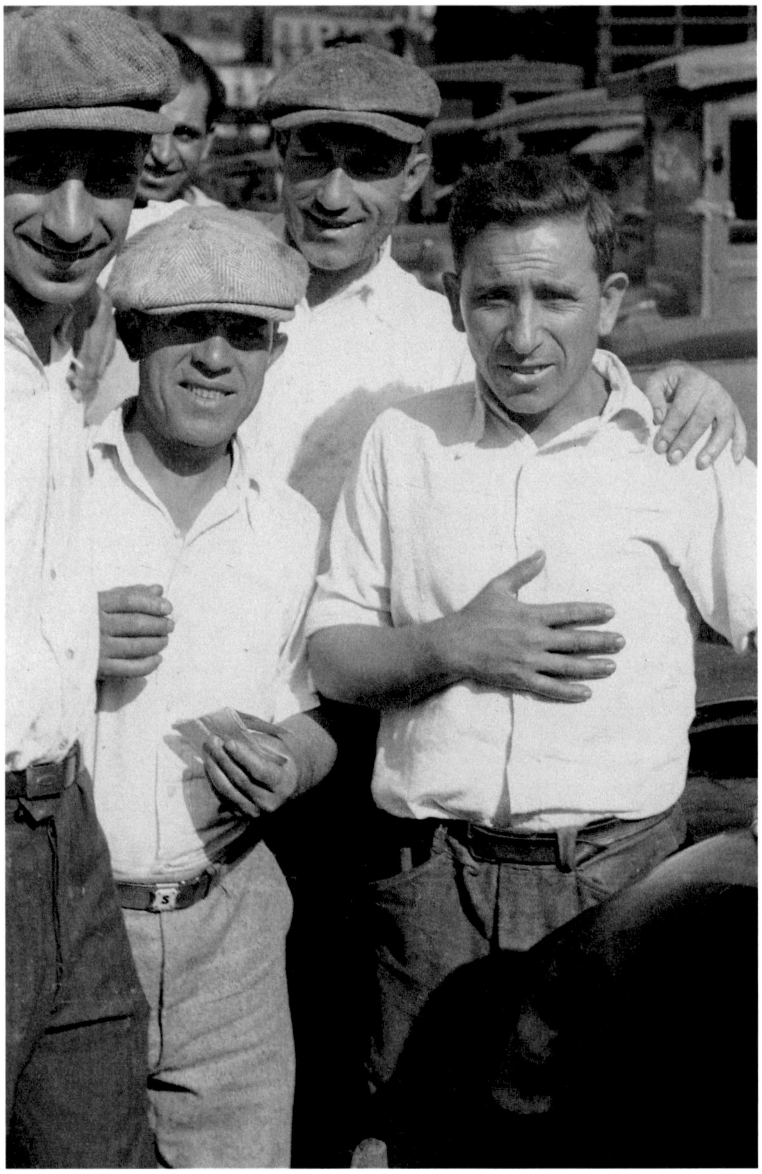

People on the street, New York, 1931

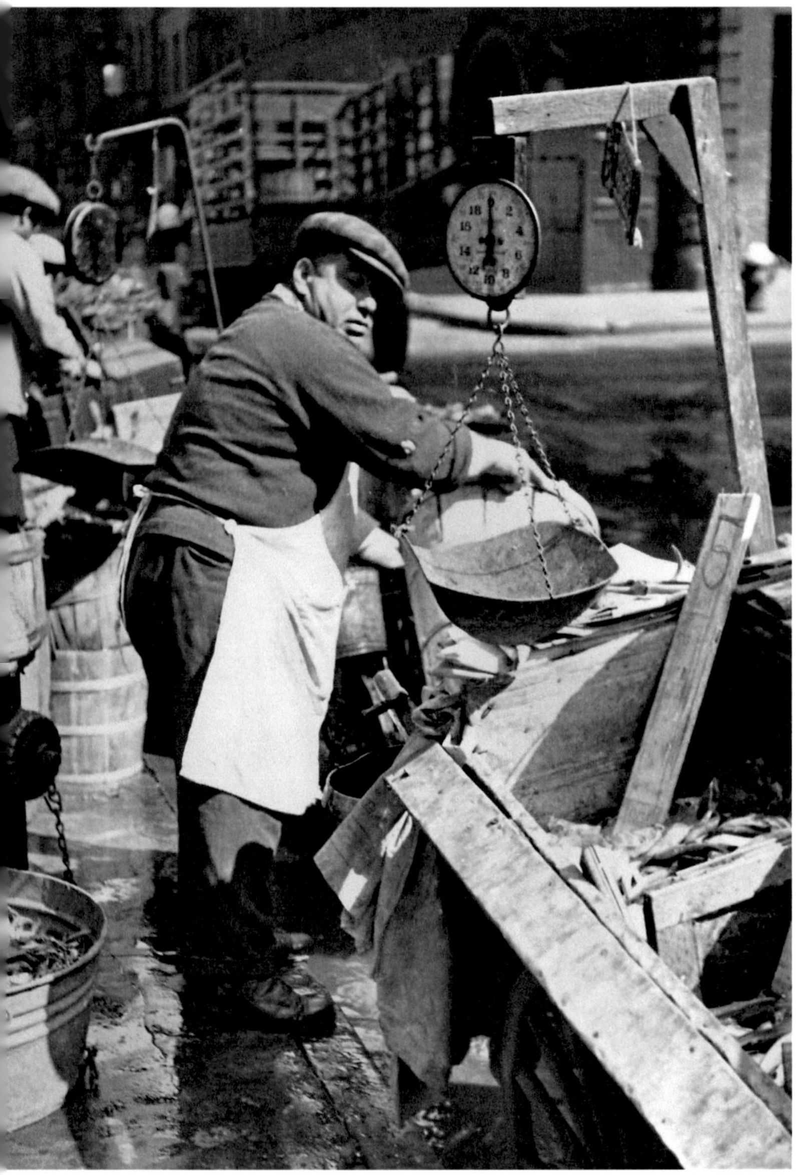

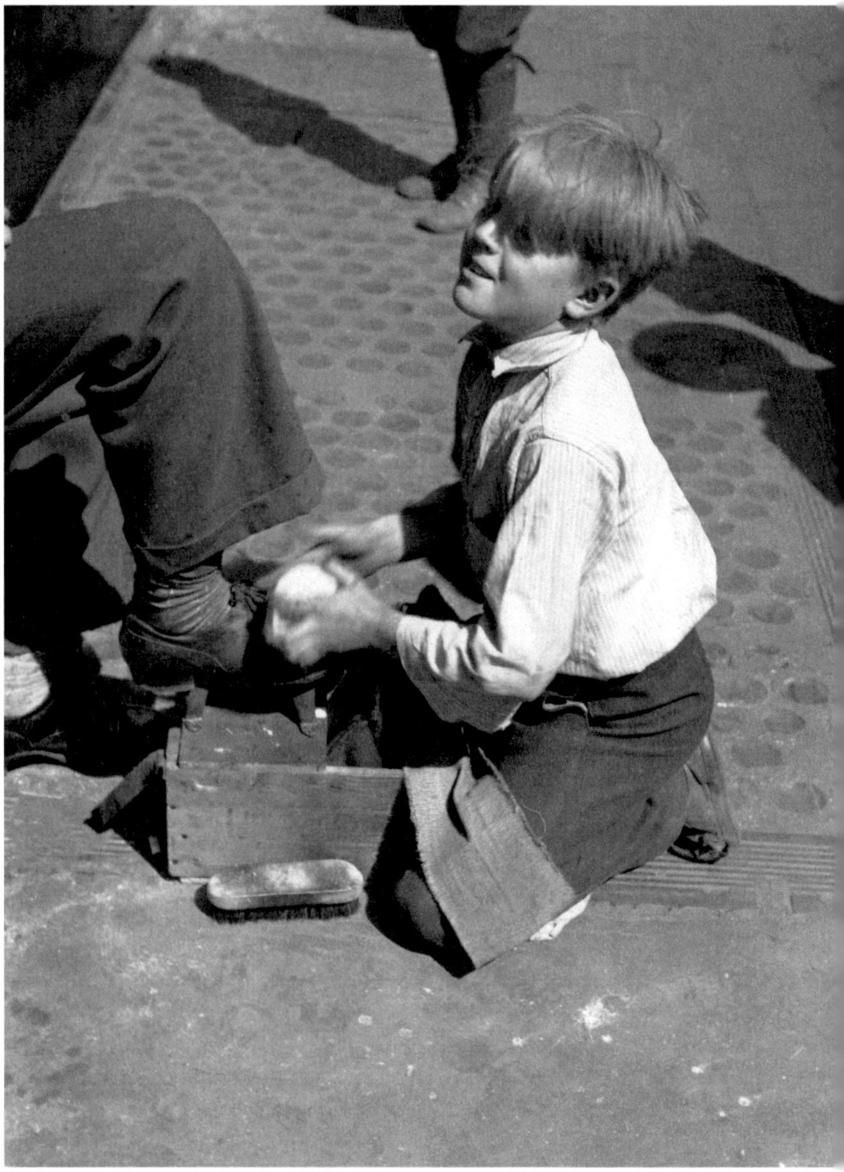

Street merchant in Little Italy, New York, 1931

Shoeshine boy, New York, 1931

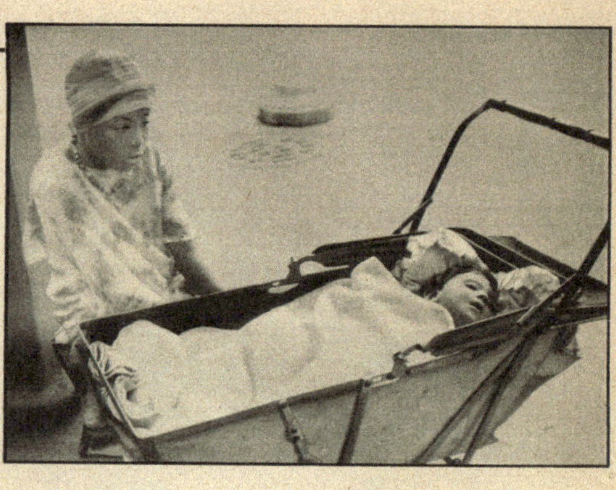

Aunt Lu werde ich so leicht nicht vergessen. Sie war meine Haushälterin in meinen Neuyorker Jahren. Wie viele Leute in Amerika, die auf gutes Essen Wert legen, ließ ich mir meine Küche durch eine waschechte farbige Südstaatlerin besorgen. Ein Truthahn à la Maryland zur Weihnachtszeit mundet nämlich ebenso köstlich wie unsere gute alte Festgans, und Aunt Lu verstand ihren Truthahn zu bereiten wie nur irgendeine von den hunderttausend Negerköchinnen, die südlich des Potomac in jeder amerikanischen Familie, die etwas auf sich hält, anzutreffen sind.

Sie war kohlrabenschwarz, und trotz ihrer dreiundsiebzig Jahre hatte sie die fatale Gewohnheit, sich wie ein Broadway-Flapper herauszuputzen und Schminke auf ihre Wangen zu legen, so daß sie in allen Farben des Regenbogens leuchteten. Auf ihren breiten Schultern trug sie ein Stück amerikanischen Schicksals, und wenn sie gut aufgelegt war, mußte sie mir aus

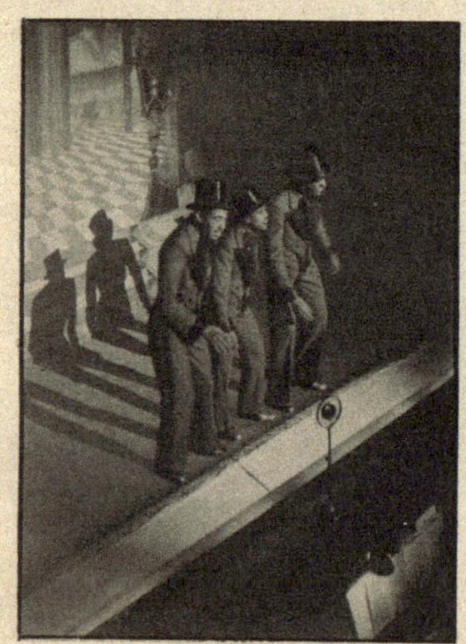

Stepptänzer in einem Negertheater

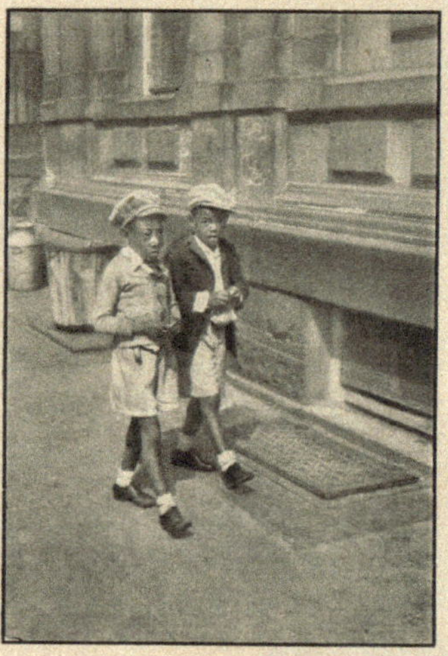

Zwei kleine Negerlein

HA

Text von Dr. A. Halfeld

nischen Schicksals, und wenn sie gut aufgelegt war, mußte sie mir aus Kindheit erzählen — aus ihrer virginischen Heimat, in der sie noch als Skl baby das Licht der Welt erblickt hatte. Aber als aufrechte Frau war sie sch und recht durchs Leben gegangen, und in ihren alten Tagen war es ihr schö Glück, von ihren Töchtern besucht zu werden, die bereits Mischlinge waren, Kellerexistenz wie ihre Mutter führten und eine durchaus passable Wohnun

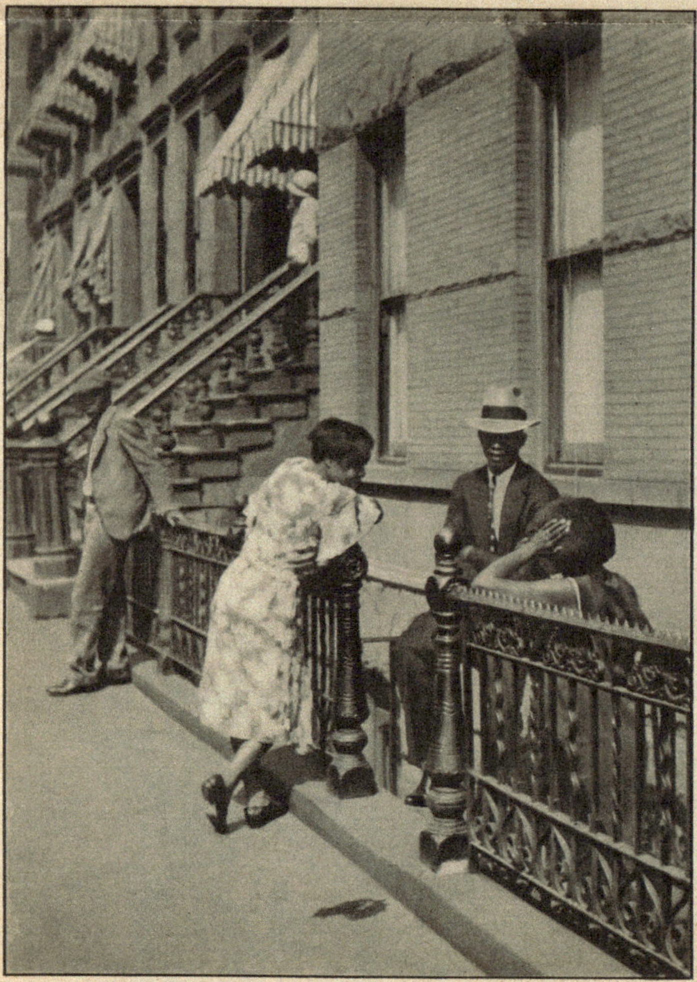

Auch in Harlem hat man Zeit

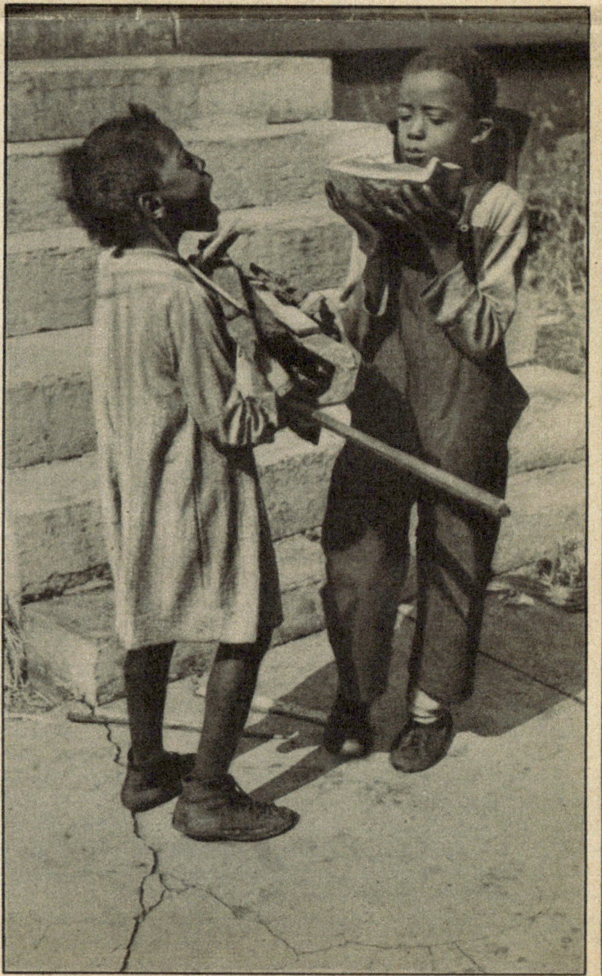

„Einen Happs, bitte!"

"Harlem" (*Hamburger Illustrierte* 14, no. 16, 1932)

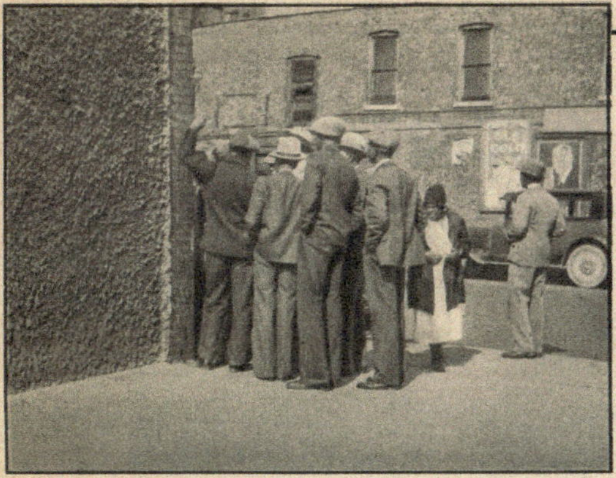

.EM

Photos von Dr. Block

, dem Neuyorker Negerviertel, ihr eigen nannten. — Wie die Kletten die Neger zusammen. Wo sie unter Weißen leben, da ballen sie sich zu Haufen. Harlem ist solch eine Ballung von 250000 farbigen Menschen, Fluch ihrer Rasse strengstens vom übrigen Neuyork scheidet. In Manhattan Schuhputzer, Gepäckträger, Hafenarbeiter oder Straßenkehrer, aber die rants, die Kirchen, die Theater und die Kinos bleiben ihnen dort verschlossen.

Erst in Harlem können sie Menschen sein, wie die anderen sich vergnügen und endlich einmal — sei es auch nur auf Stunden — das Gefühl loswerden, Auswurf der Menschheit zu sein.

Gleich wo der Zentralpark im Norden Manhattans endet, zwischen Fünfter und Siebenter Avenue, streckt sich Harlem über fünfzig oder sechzig Straßenzüge aus. Mit seinen recht prunkvollen Wohnbauten, seinen Kirchen und Theatern hat es sich an seiner Wiege nicht träumen lassen, daß es einmal die Zuflucht der Neger aus den amerikanischen Südstaaten, aus Afrika und Westindien werden würde. Ganz im Gegenteil, es sollte ein neues Residenzviertel für wohlhabende Neuyorker Bürger sein. Aber plötzlich kam der Krieg und kamen die Kriegsschieber und die turmhohen Arbeiterlöhne. Selbst die Neger waren

Fortsetzung auf Seite 14

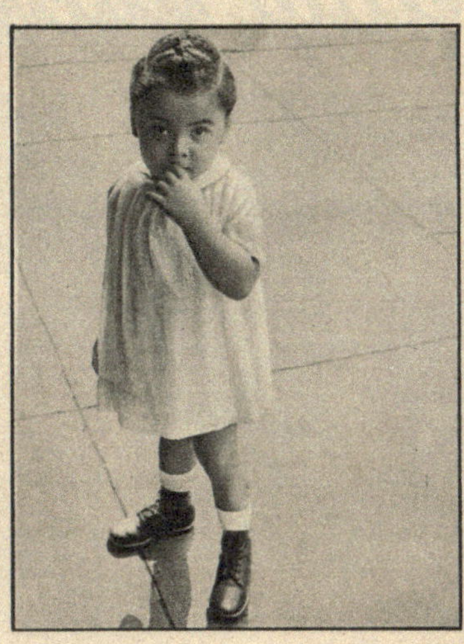

Ob weiß, ob schwarz — Kinder sind Kinder

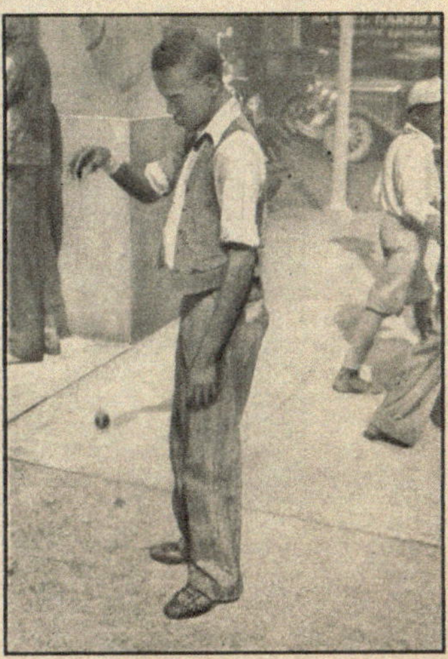

Ernsthaftes Spiel

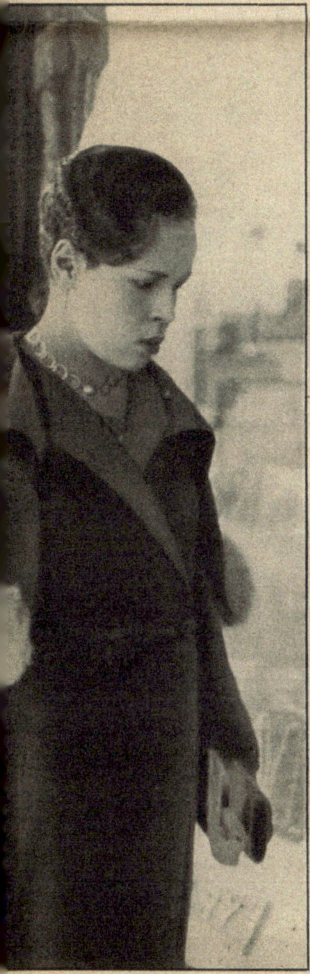

Die Elegante

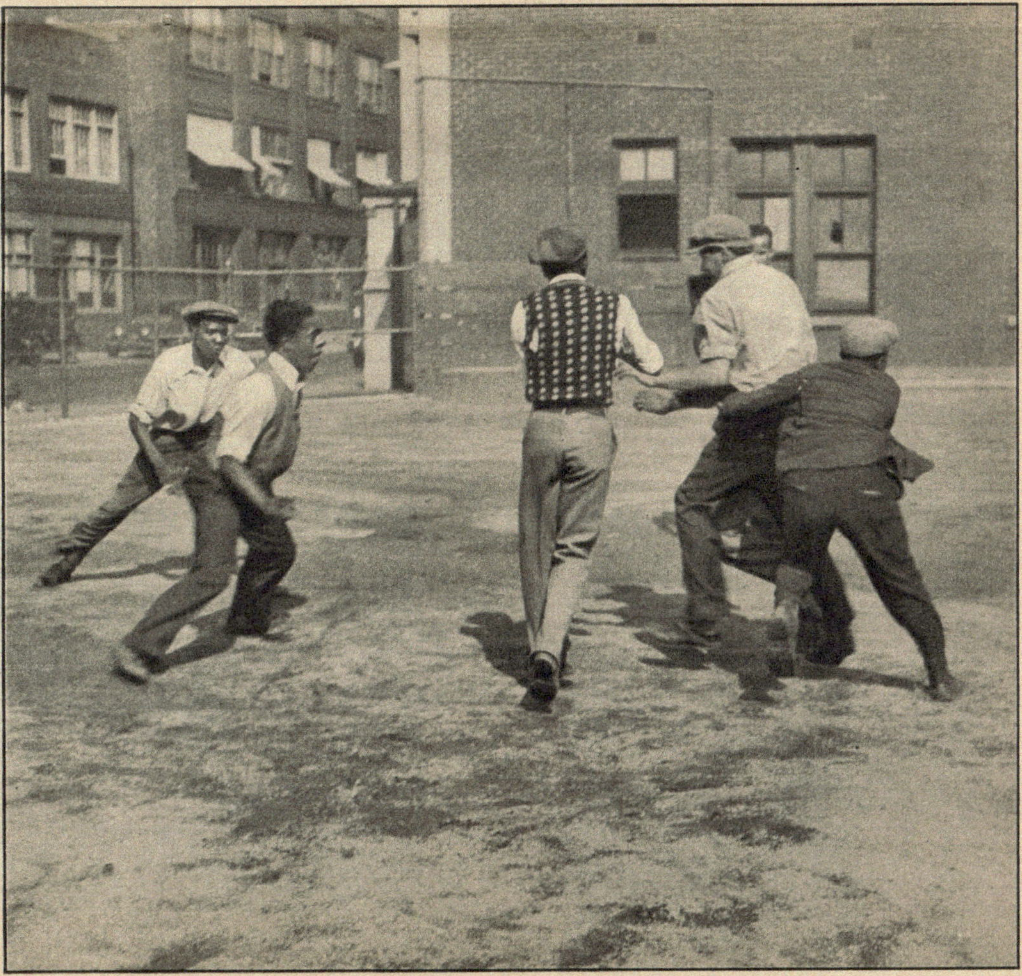

Fußball zwischen den Häusern

"Two Negro Boys," Harlem, New York, 1931

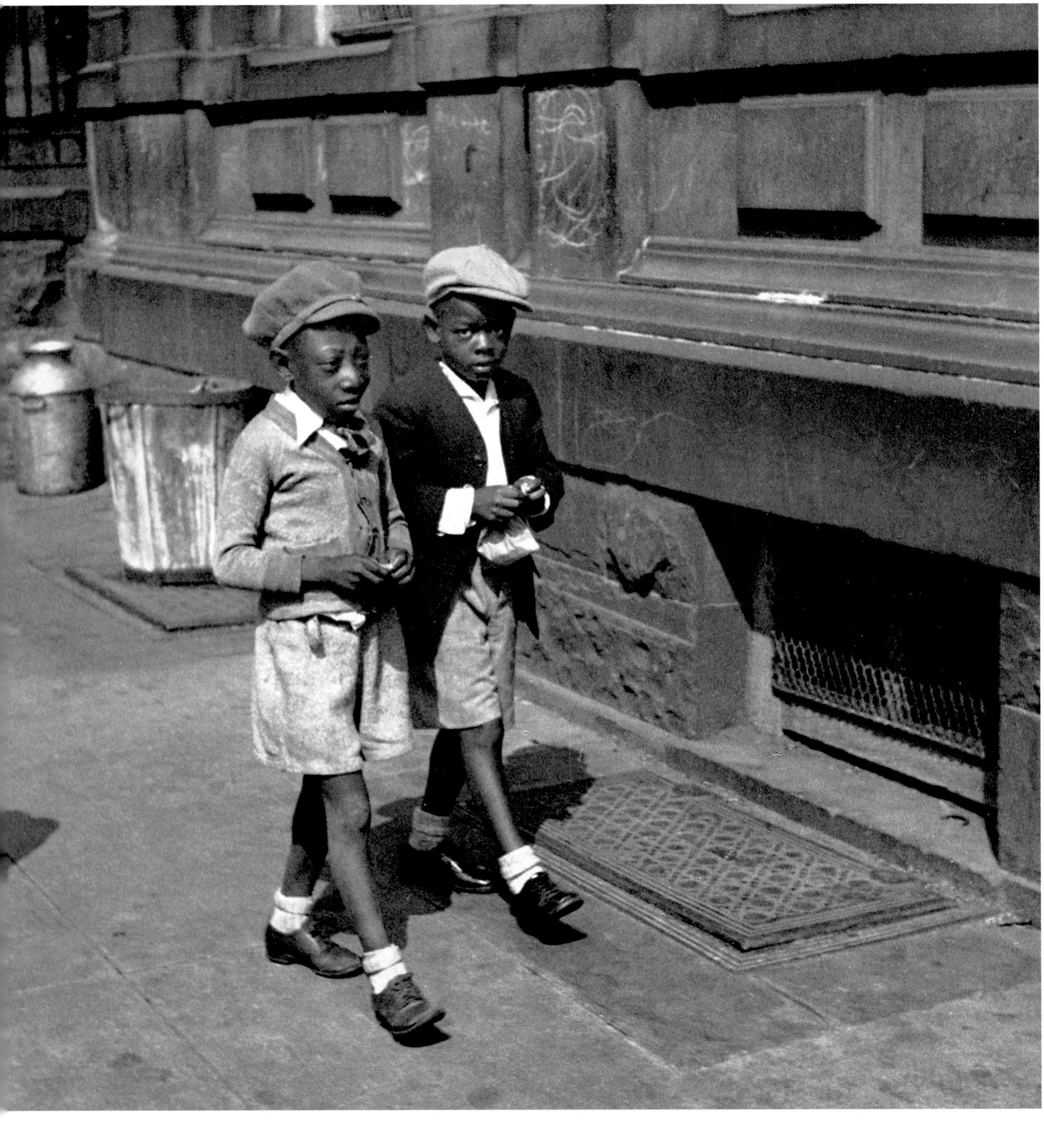

"School Children," Harlem, New York, 1931

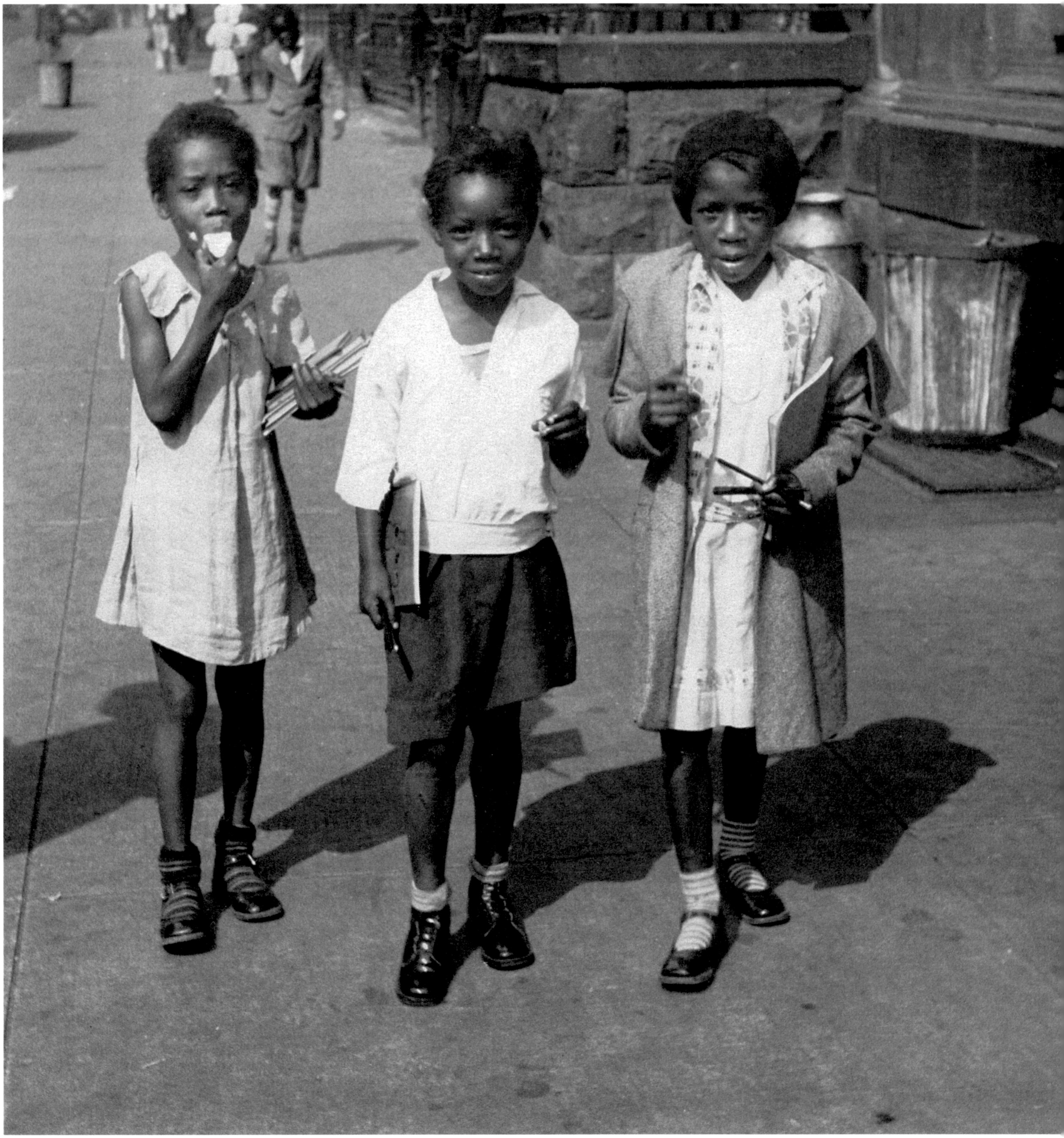

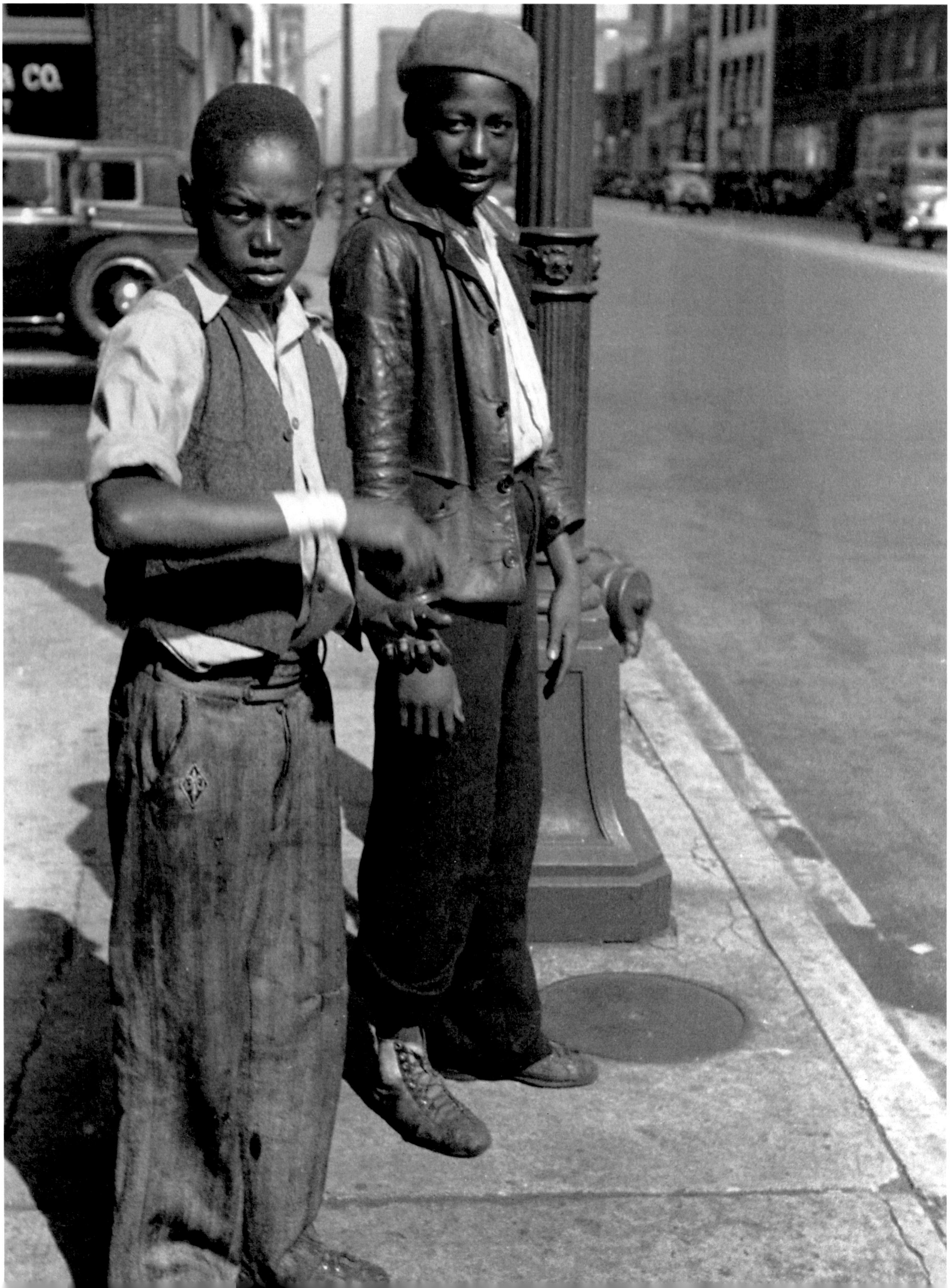
CO.

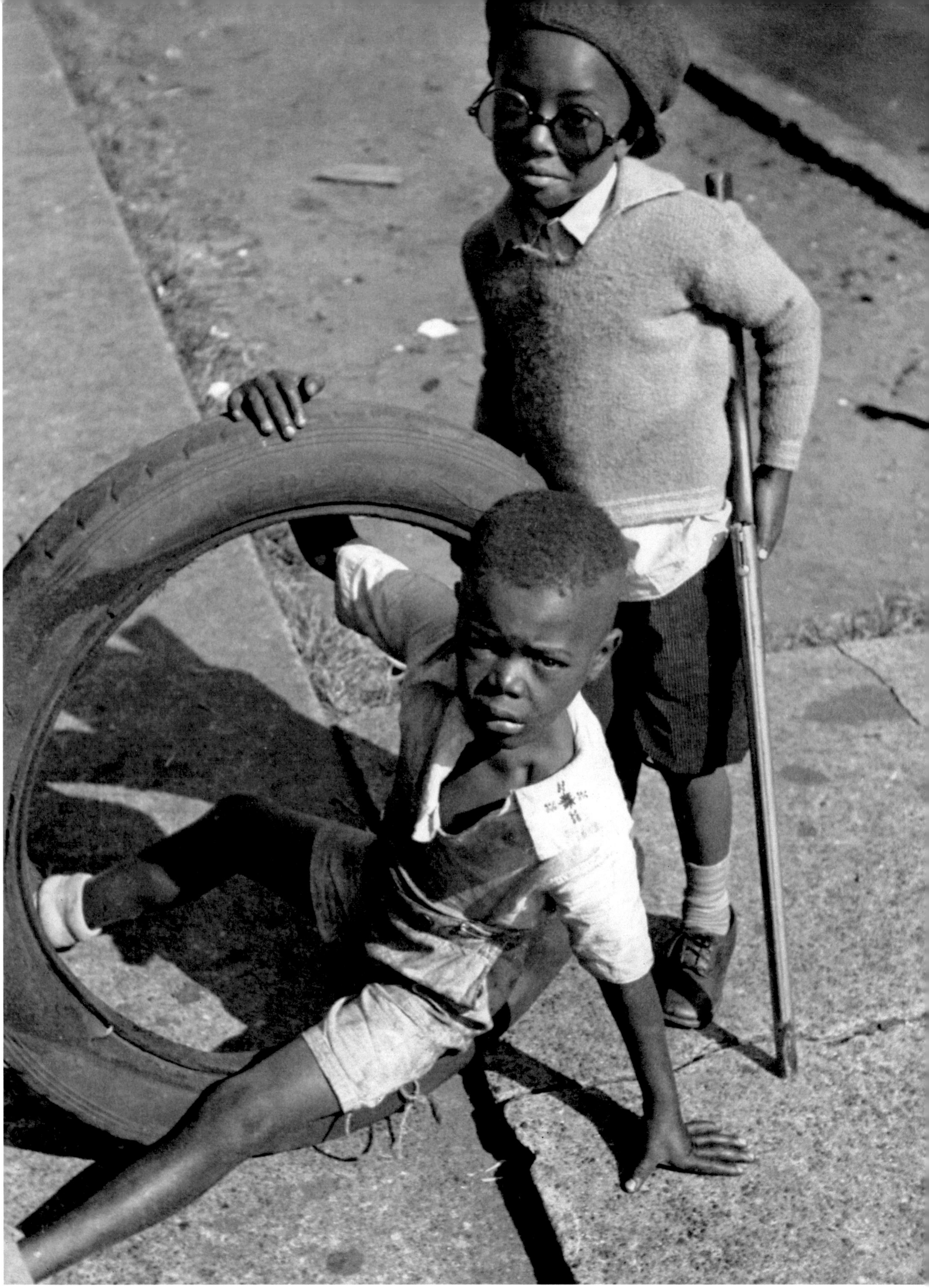

"Negro Boys," Harlem, New York, 1931

Nr. 32/1932 Sonnabend, den 6. August

Hamburger Anzeiger

vereinigt mit „Neue Hamburger Zeitung"

Illustrierte Wochenbeilage in Kupfertiefdruck.

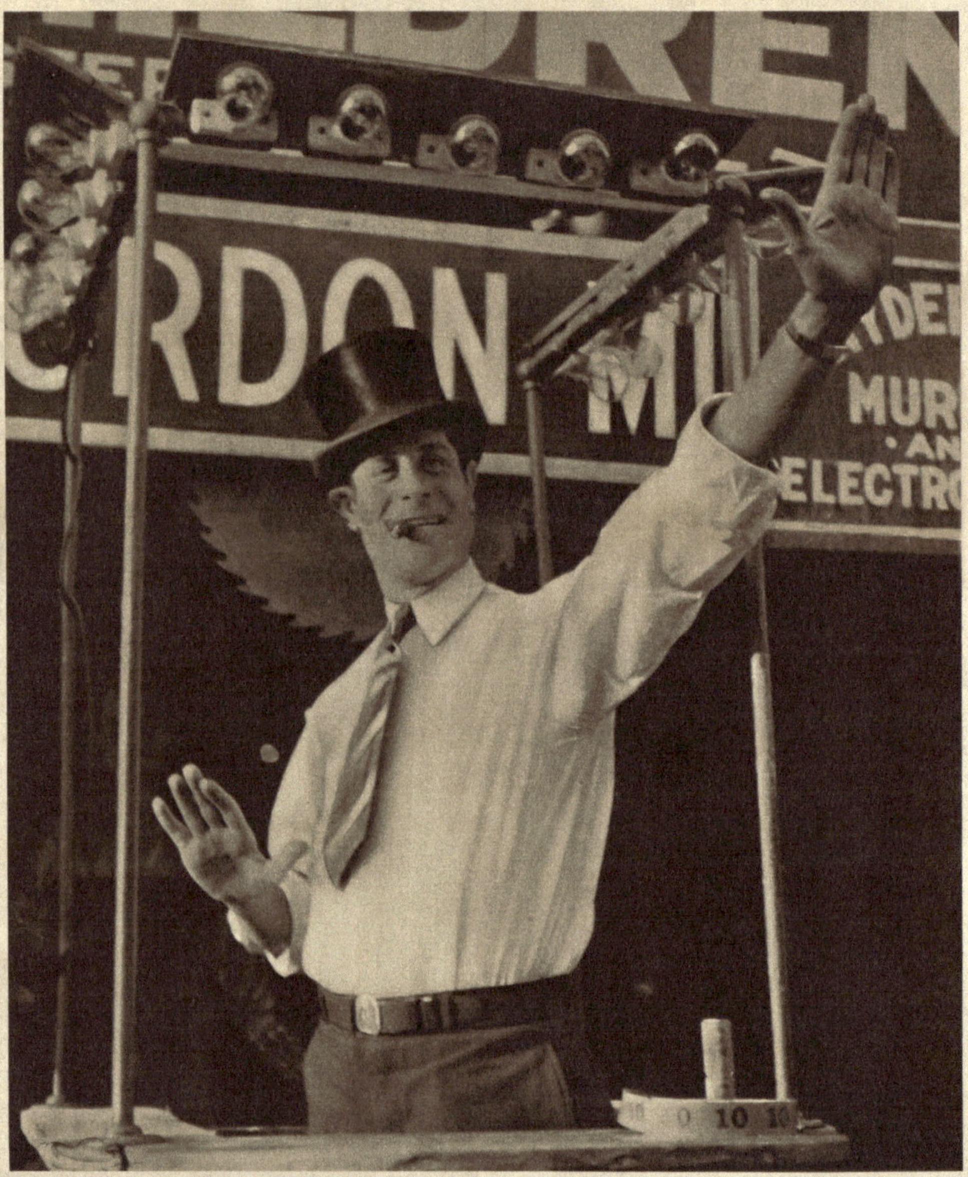

Aufn. Dr. Block

Ladies and Gentlemen...

beachten Sie die Doppelseite dieser Beilage! Sie zeigt Ihnen Bilder von Coney Island, dem Badestrand und Rummelplatz New Yorks, der neulich beinahe ganz abbrannte

"Barker at Coney Island, New York, 1931" (*Hamburger Anzeiger. Illustrierte Wochenbeilage*, no. 32, 1932)

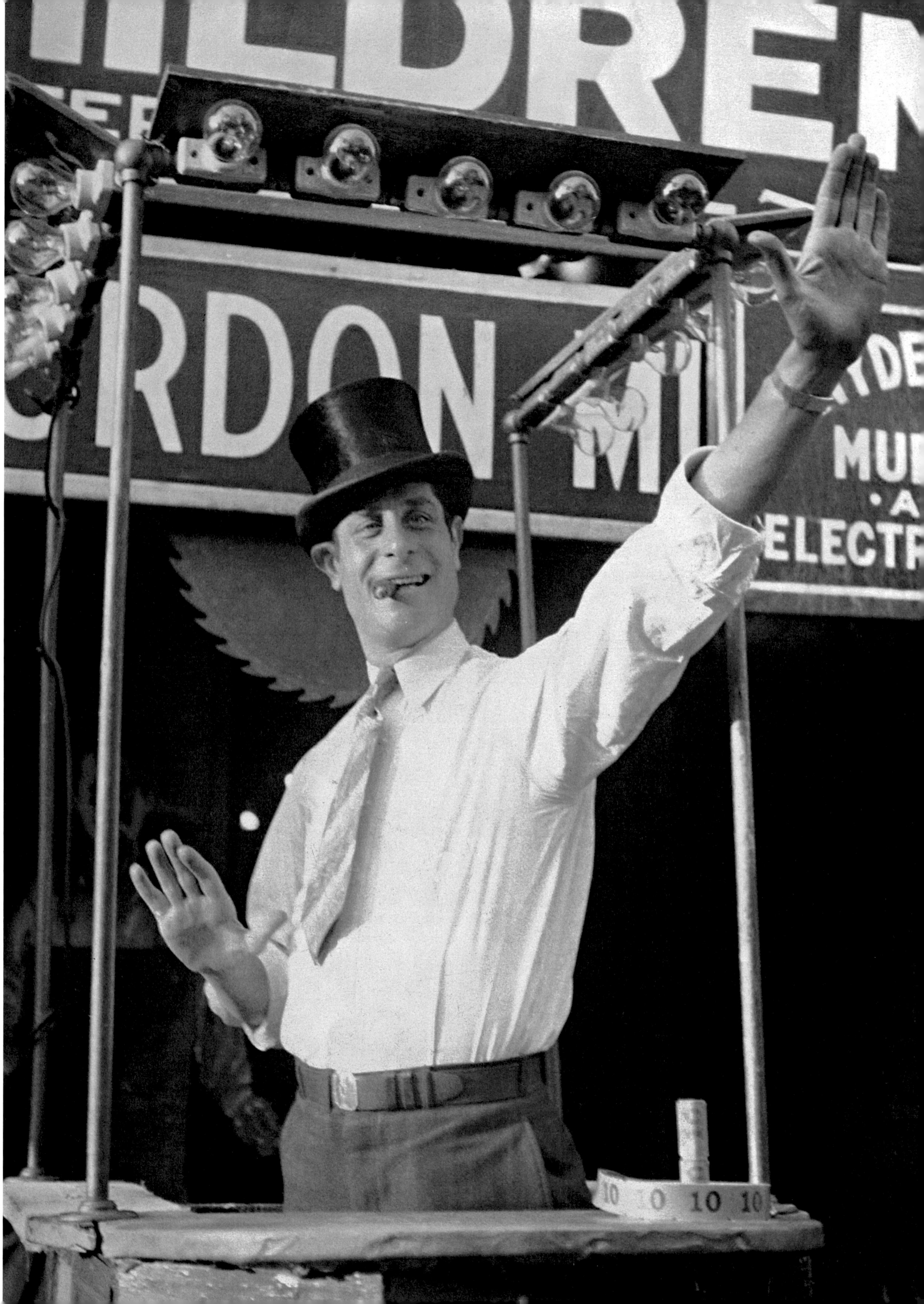
ILDREN
RDON MI
RDE
MU
A
ELECTR
10 10 10 10

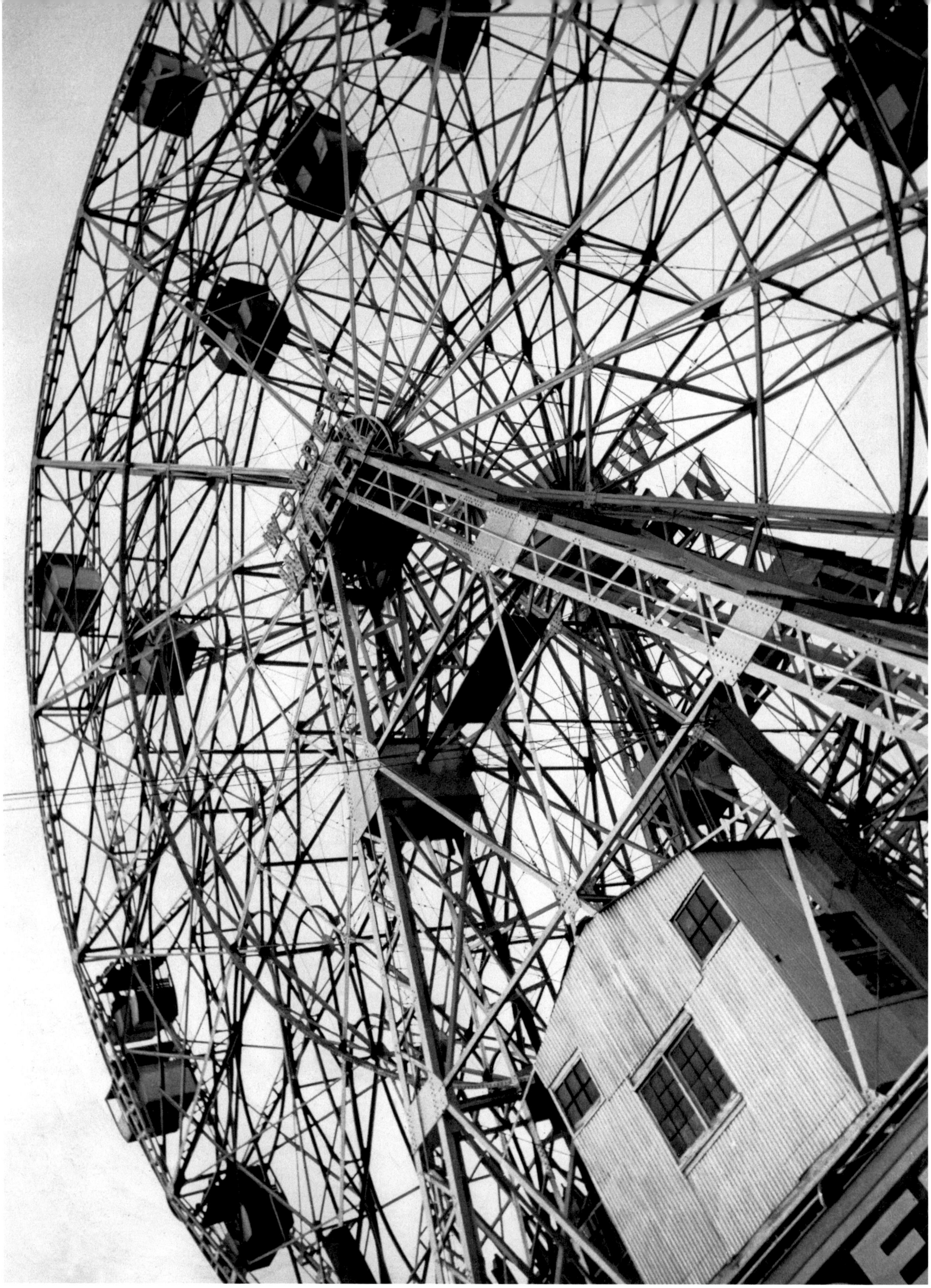

Wonder Wheel at Coney Island, New York, 1931

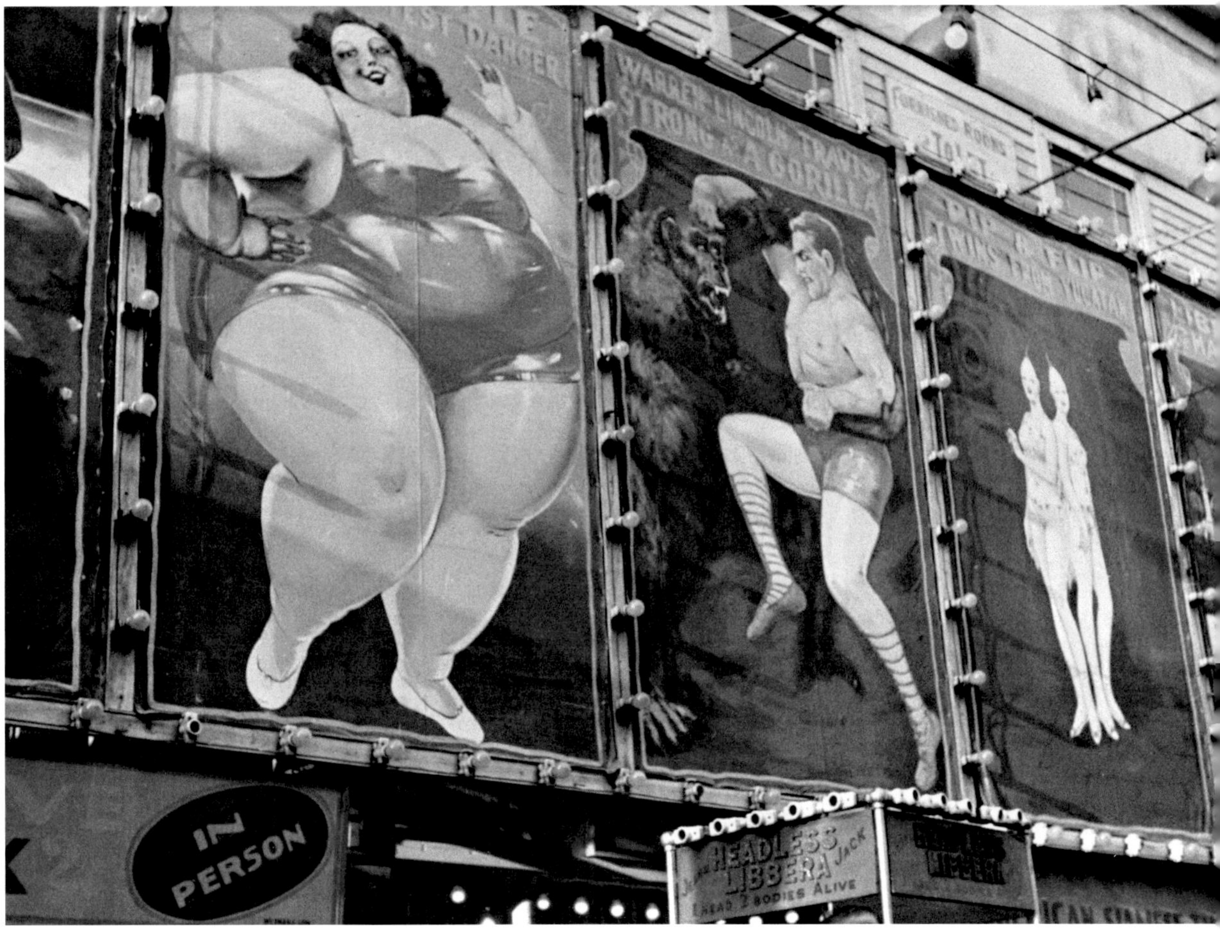

Show posters at Coney Island,
New York, 1931

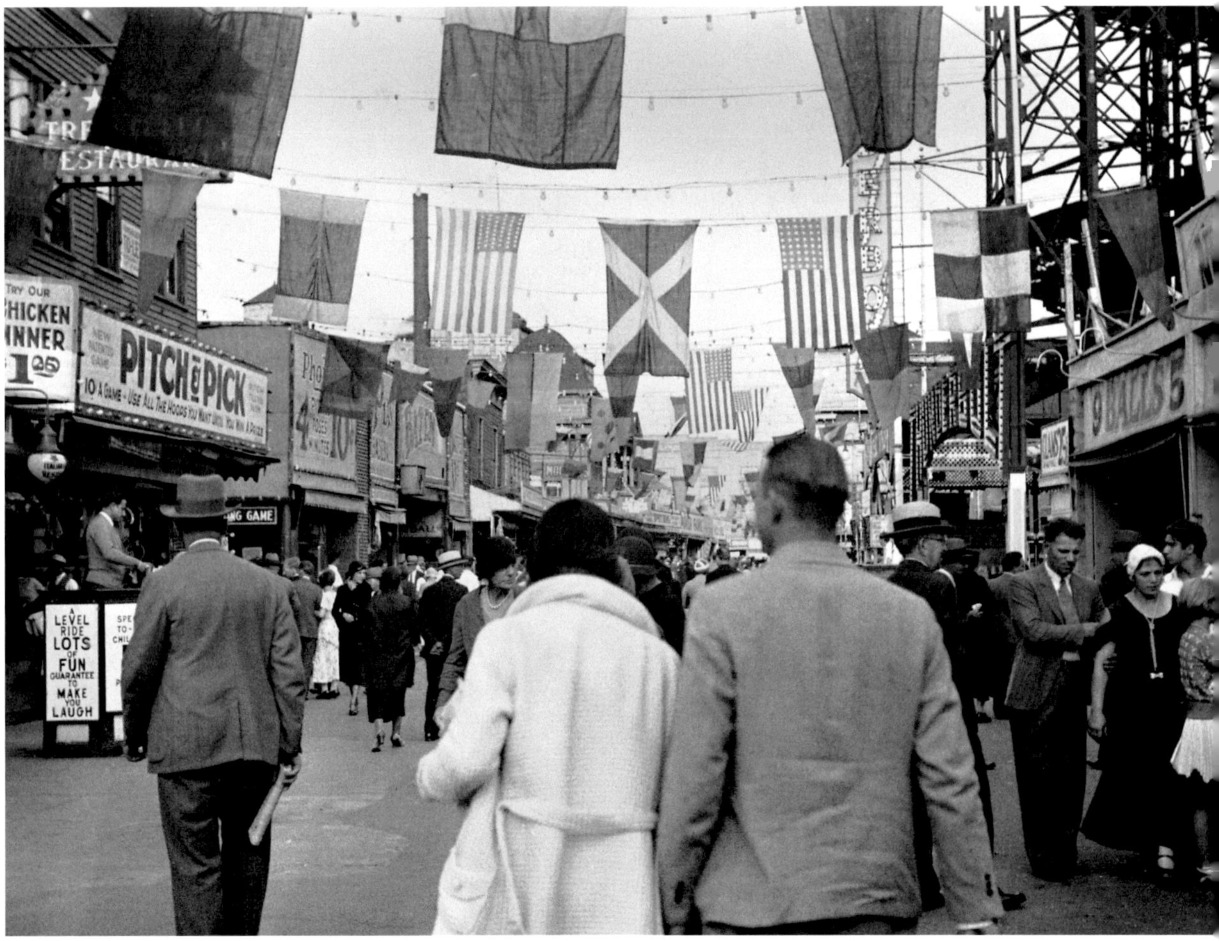

Boardwalk on Coney Island,
New York, 1931

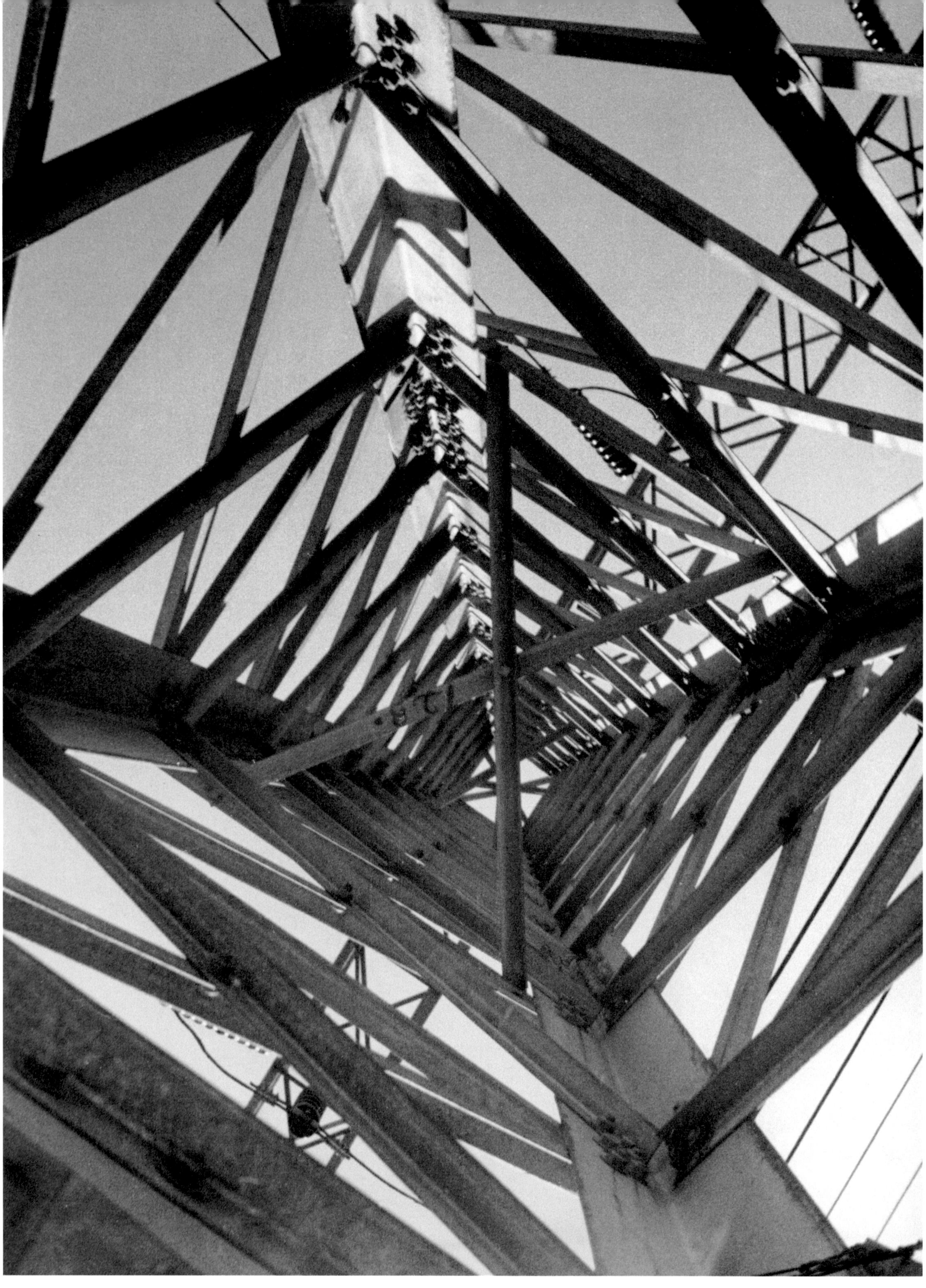

High-voltage pole, Niagara Falls, 1931

Switching station, Niagara Falls, 1931

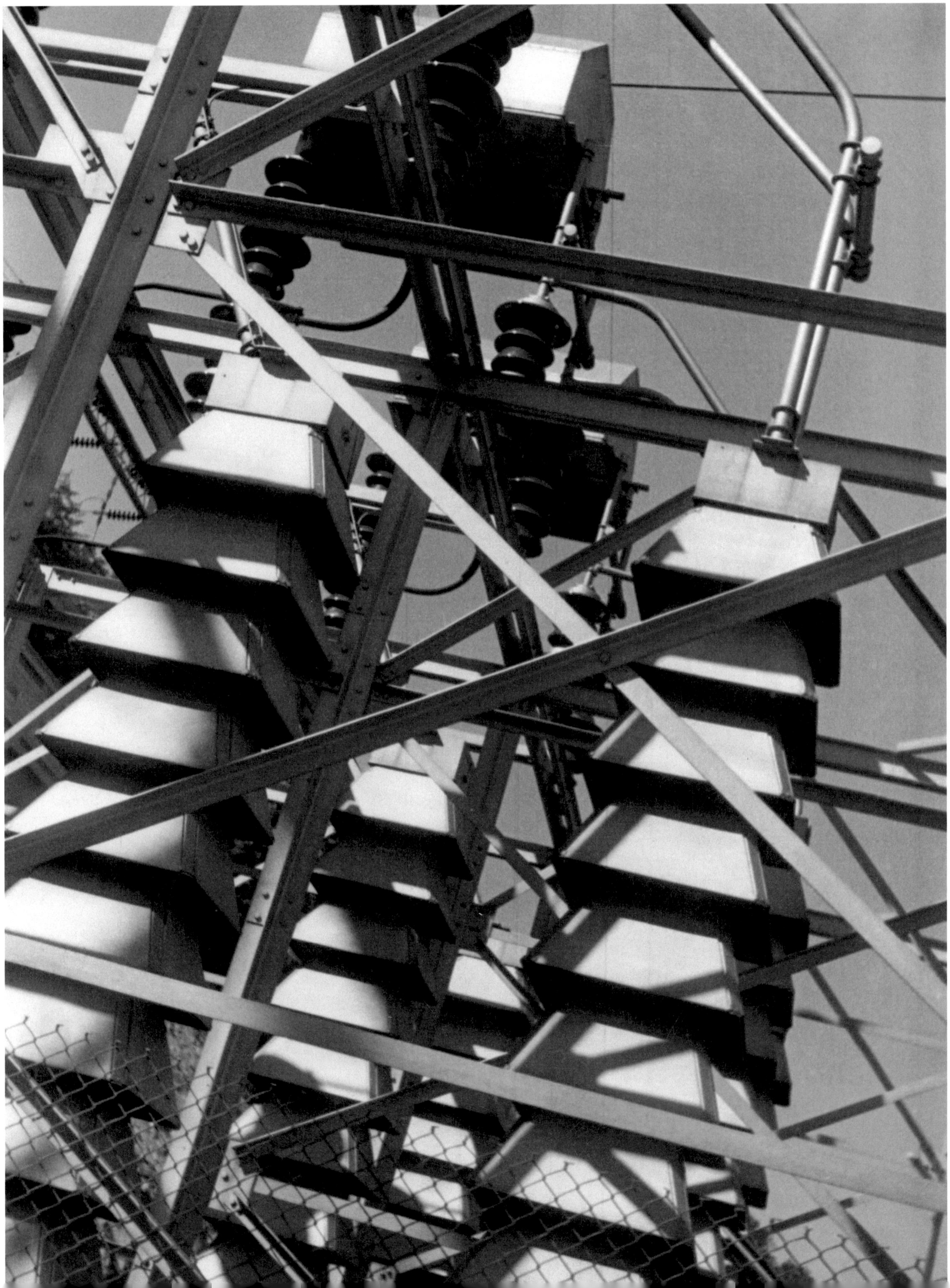

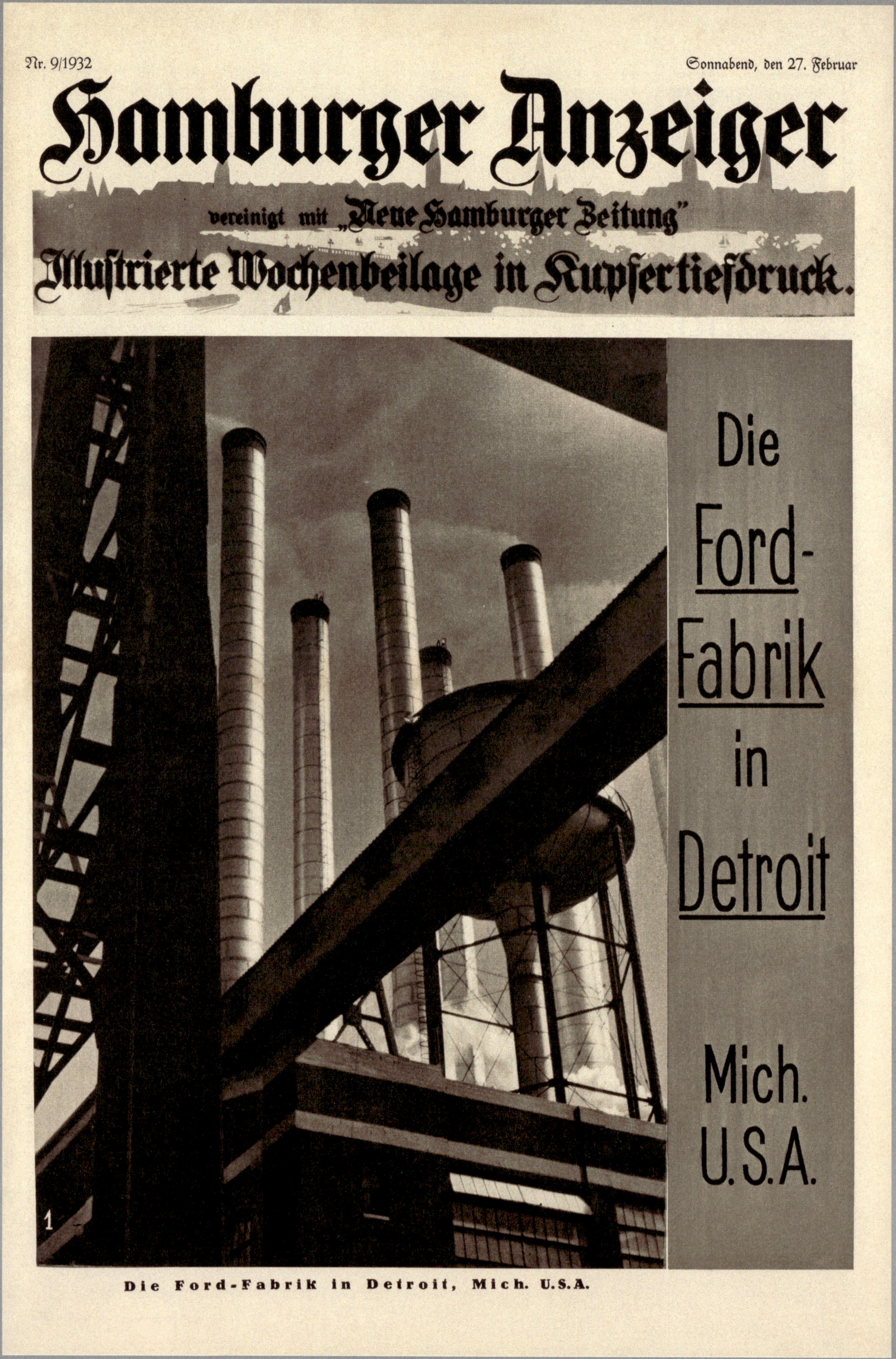

Nr. 9/1932 Sonnabend, den 27. Februar

Hamburger Anzeiger

vereinigt mit „Neue Hamburger Zeitung"

Illustrierte Wochenbeilage in Kupfertiefdruck.

Die Ford-Fabrik in Detroit, Mich. U.S.A.

"The Ford Factory in Detroit, Mich. U.S.A." *(Hamburger Anzeiger. Illustrierte Wochenbeilage, no. 9, 1932)*

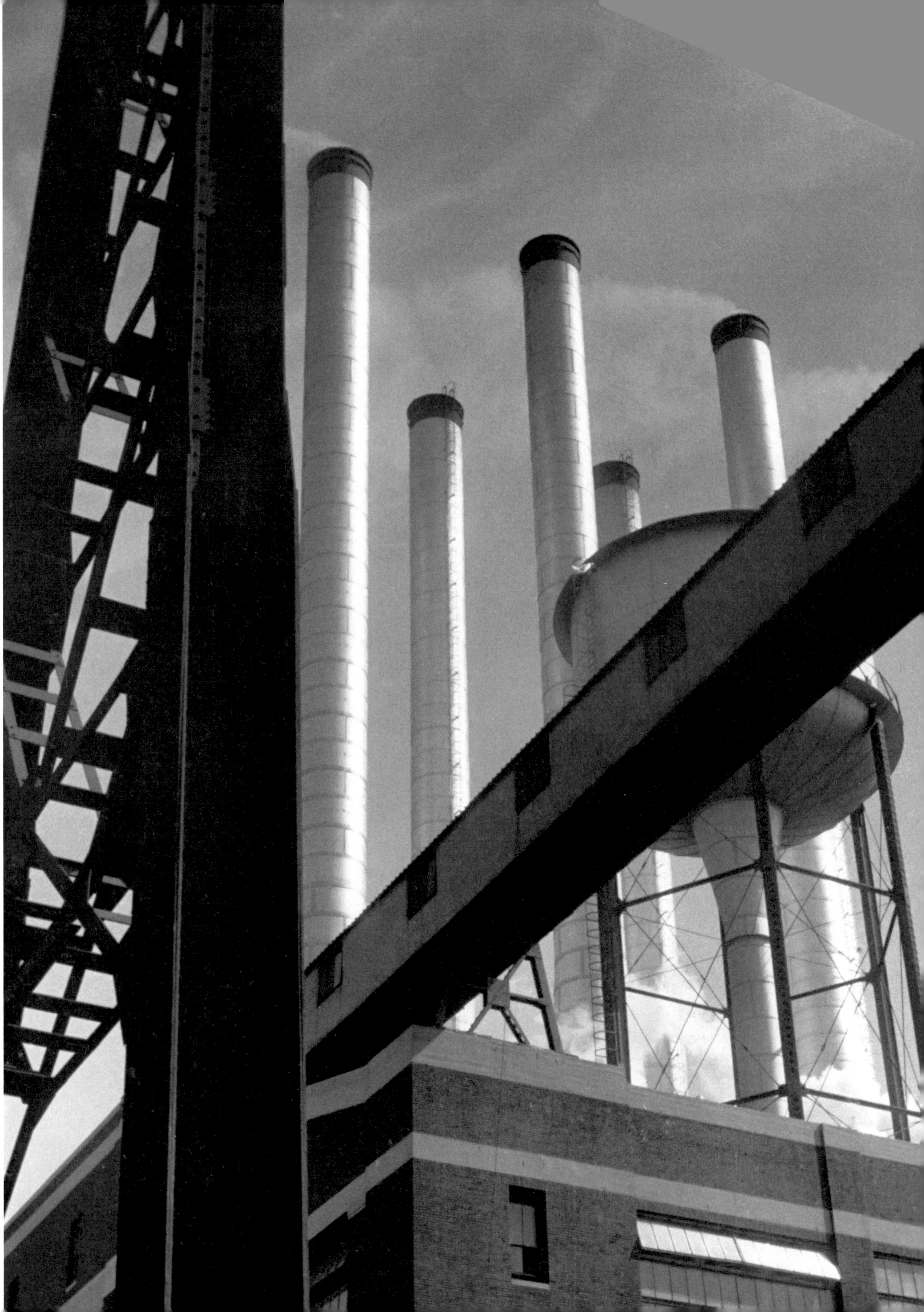

Die Ford

Der Name Ford bedeutet ein Programm. Auf der ganzen Welt sieht man in ihm den Bahnbrecher des Rationalisierungsgedankens. Ford und laufendes Band sind unzertrennbare Begriffe. So gehört der Besuch der Fordfabrik in Detroit zu den eindrucksvollsten Erlebnissen einer Amerikareise. Fords Lebenswerk ist die Schaffung des Autos für jedermann; des Autos als durchaus notwendigen Gebrauchsgegenstandes.

Im ganzen Lande spürt man die Auswirkungen der Einführung des billigen Kleinwagens. Wegebau, Touristik, die Wochenendbewegung wären ohne den billigen Ford und seine Nachahmer in heutiger Form undenkbar. Noch unmöglicher wäre die große Ausdehnung vieler amerikanischer Städte, wie Los Angeles, Detroit, Pittsburg, die trotz der phantastisch weiten Ausdehnung kein öffentliches Beförderungsmittel, Hoch- und Untergrundbahn, besitzen — die elektrische Bahn hat in Amerika kaum noch Beförderungswert, außer für ganz kurze Strecken —.

Nicht nur das „Was“ interessiert auf dem Fabrikgelände, sondern vor allem das „Wie“. Vom Transport der Materialien, vom Zusammenströmen der Arbeitermassen, durch den ganzen Arbeitsvorgang bis zum Versand und zur Verwaltung entgeht keine Phase der ständigen Beobachtung in bezug auf größte Ausnutzung an Material und Zeit. Berühmt ist der ganze Betrieb durch die größtmögliche, peinlichste Sauberkeit. Wie Wahrzeichen stehen die silberbronzierten Schornsteine (1, Titelbild) gegen den Himmel. Die für eine Fabrik erstaunliche Helligkeit wird durch die Auflösung der Wände in Glas erreicht (2). Soweit wie möglich wird hygienischen Forderungen Rechnung getragen. Gesundheitlich Schwachen wird die Möglichkeit gegeben, im Freien zu arbeiten (3). Das laufende Band (4) ist im Tempo zu regeln, erspart Wege, Bücken und schweres Tragen. Eine Versetzung des Arbeiters, um der Eintönigkeit zu entgehen, ist auf Wunsch möglich. Dadurch, daß jeder Arbeiter immer nur einen bestimmten Handgriff in dem großen Prozeß macht, braucht man keine gelernten Arbeiter; eine Ausbildungszeit von 3 bis 4 Tagen genügt.

Die Belegschaft war im Herbst 1931 1/3 der Kapazität. Auch dann noch vollzieht sich der Schichtwechsel (5) alle 15 Minuten, um die Verstopfung der Zu- und Abfahrtstraßen zu vermeiden.

Die Wagen der auf dem Werk Beschäftigten sammeln sich auf großen Parkplätzen (6). Vier bis sechs Arbeiter benutzen zusammen einen Wagen; Luxuswagen sind es gerade nicht.

Was nach jahrelangem Gebrauch aus den Autos wird, sieht man an den zum Einschmelzen von Ford seit einigen Monaten aufgekauften Autoleichen (7). Auf diese Weise wird Detroit und Umgebung jetzt von ihnen befreit.

Aufnahmen Dr. Block

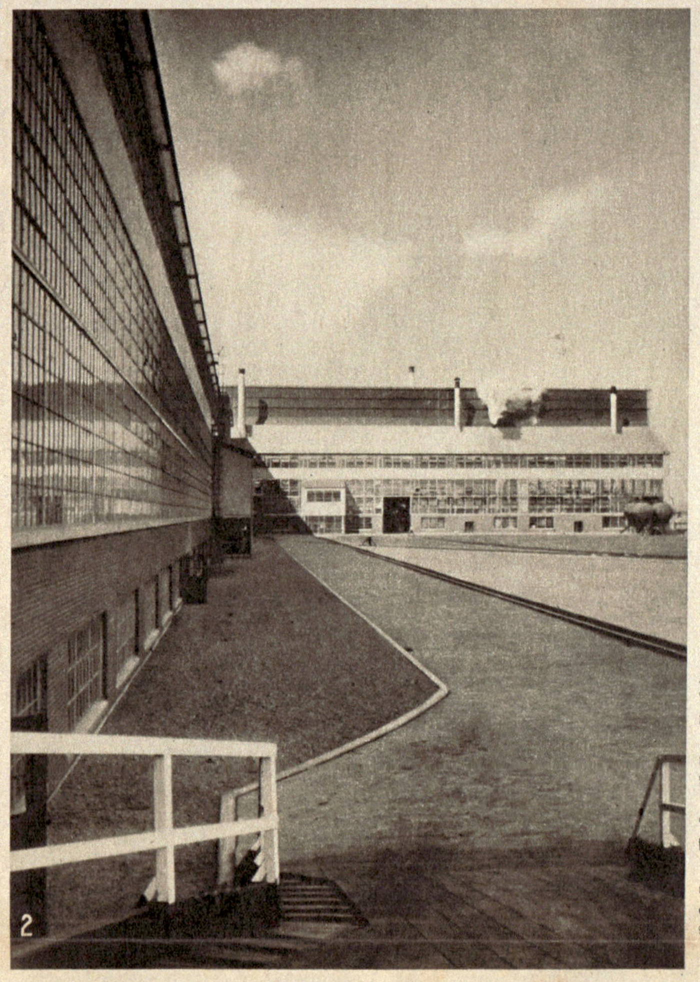

2

Ford-Fabrik
Ansicht eines der architektonisch mustergültigen Fabrikgebäude

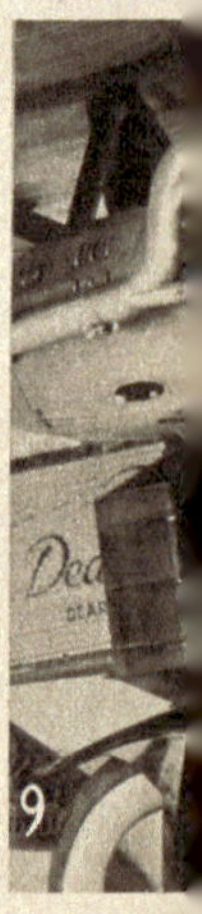

9

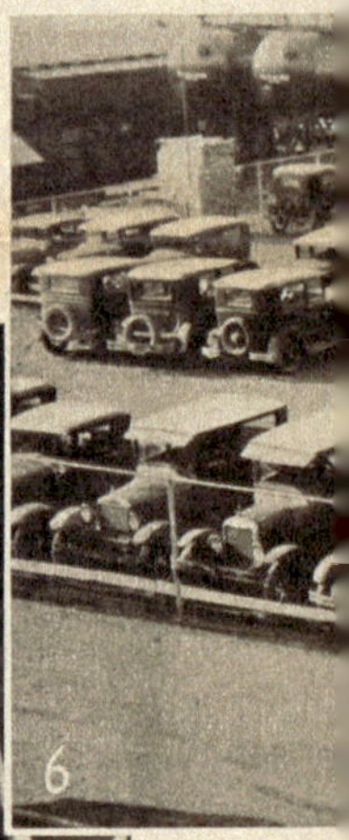

6

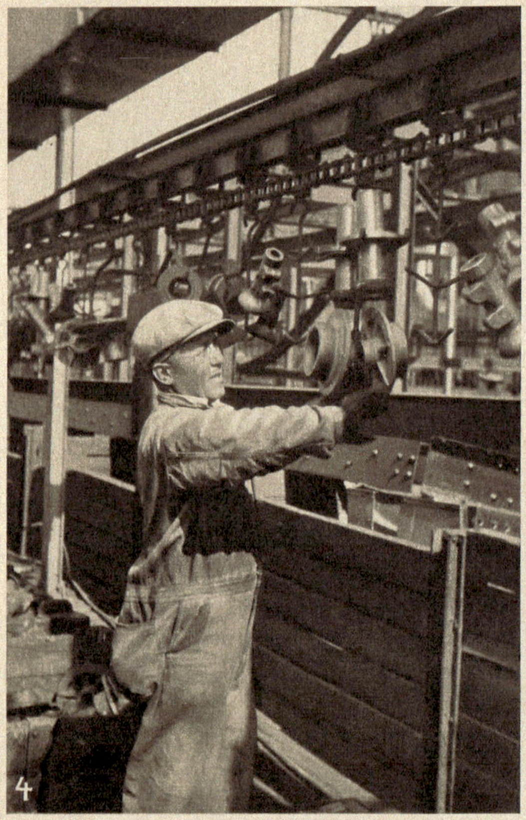

4

Arbeiter am laufenden Band

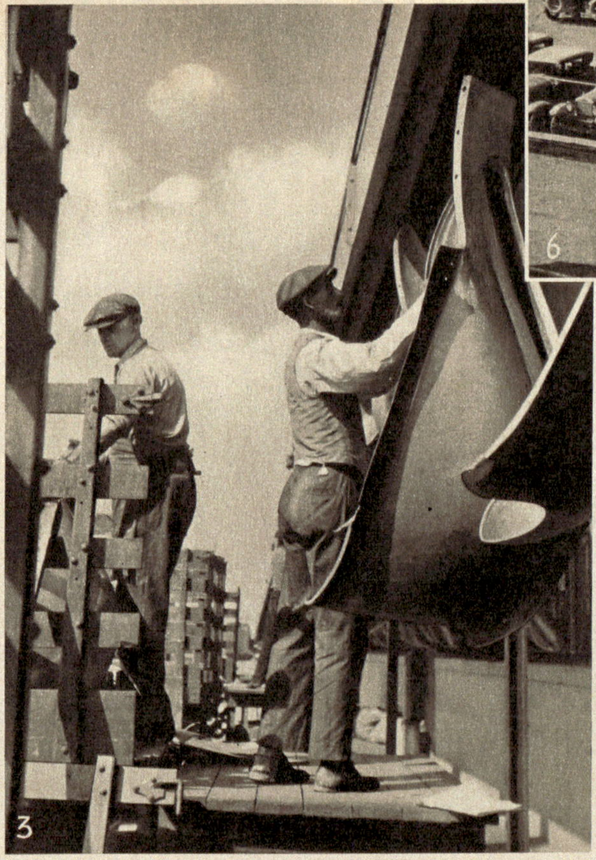

3

Am laufenden Band im Freien

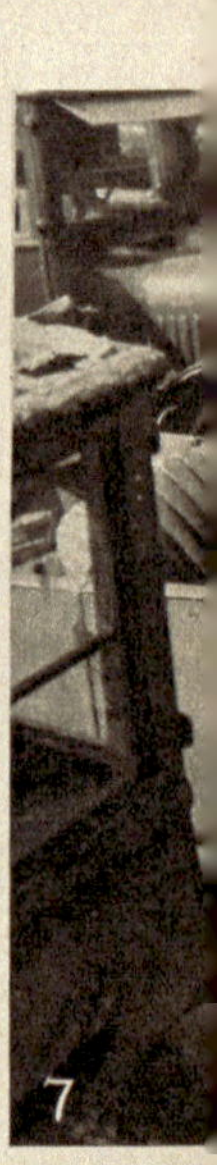

7

"The Ford Factory" (*Hamburger Anzeiger. Illustrierte Wochenbeilage*, no. 9, 1932)

Fabrik

en Band fertig herunterkommenden Wagen (8) sind alle verkauft. Auf
rbeitet. Die Möglichkeit, fristlos zu kündigen, erlaubt dieses Prinzip.
heuer erscheinenden Härte rechnet in Amerika jeder Angestellte. Bis-
terkommen in anderen Fabriken oder auch anderen Berufen im Bereich
ite, seit der für Amerika in so krasser Form erstmaligen Arbeitslosigkeit
stimmungen zur Katastrophe aus. Der Mindestlohn des ungelernten
Herbst 1931 sechs Dollar den Tag. Versicherungen und Unterstützungen
nicht. Der Flugzeugbau (9) beschränkt sich auf in Auftrag
stellung. Ein großer Flugplatz, ein Hotel verdanken ebenfalls ihr
aft des berühmten Industriellen.

Anna Sophie Block.

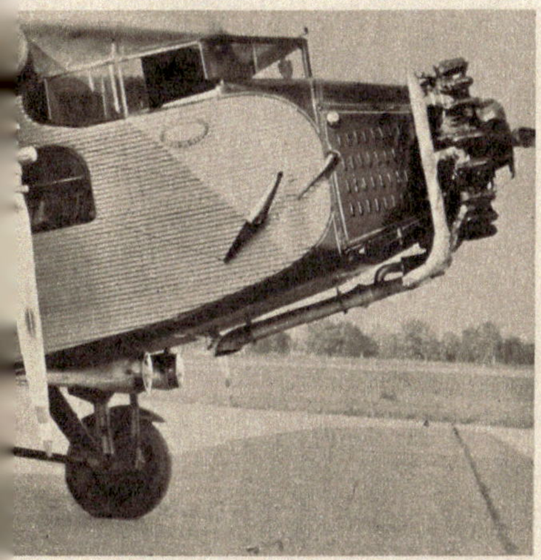

Flugzeug. Auffallend die schöne Form

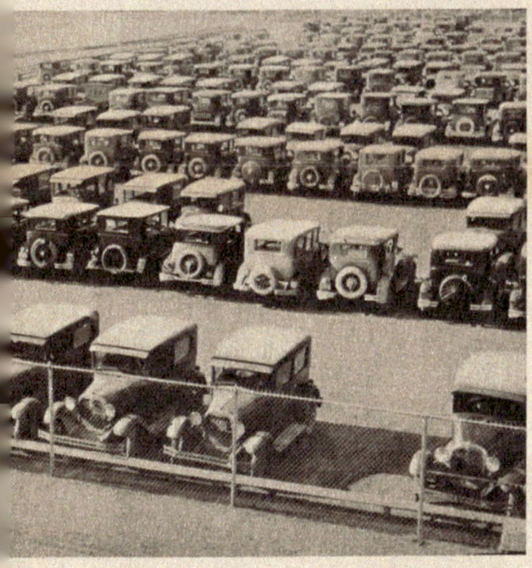

Der Wagenpark der Arbeiter

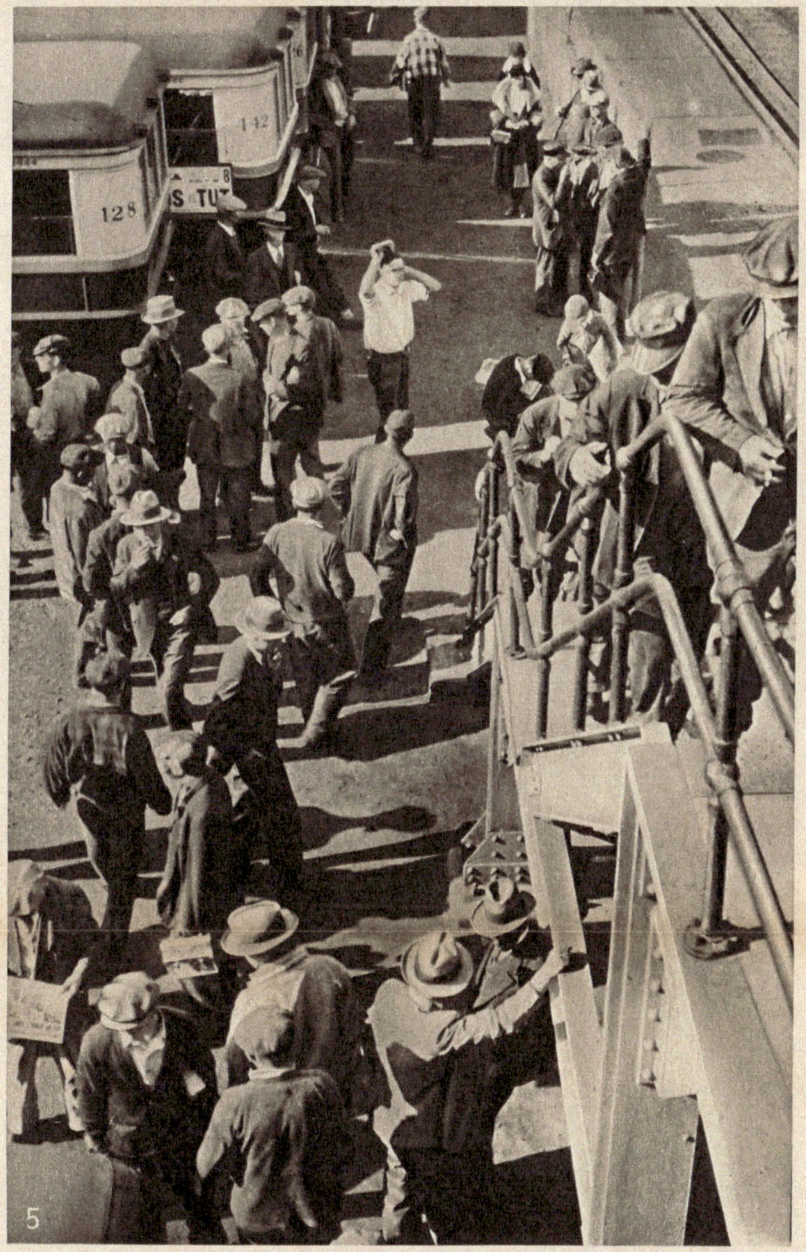

Schichtwechsel

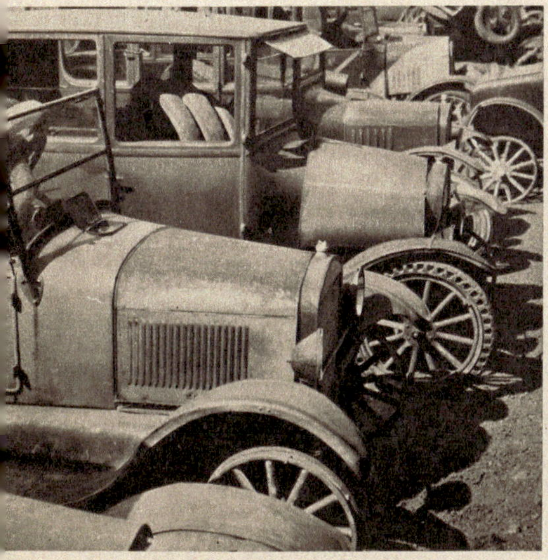

Von Ford aufgekaufte Autoleichen

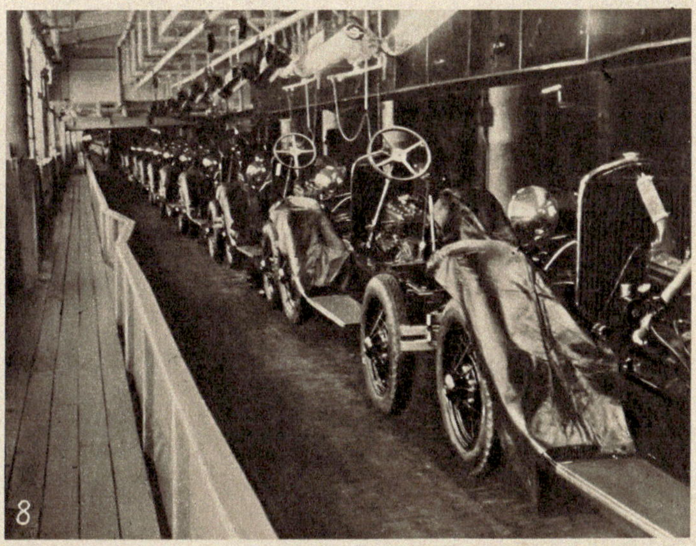

Laufendes Band mit halbfertigen Wagen

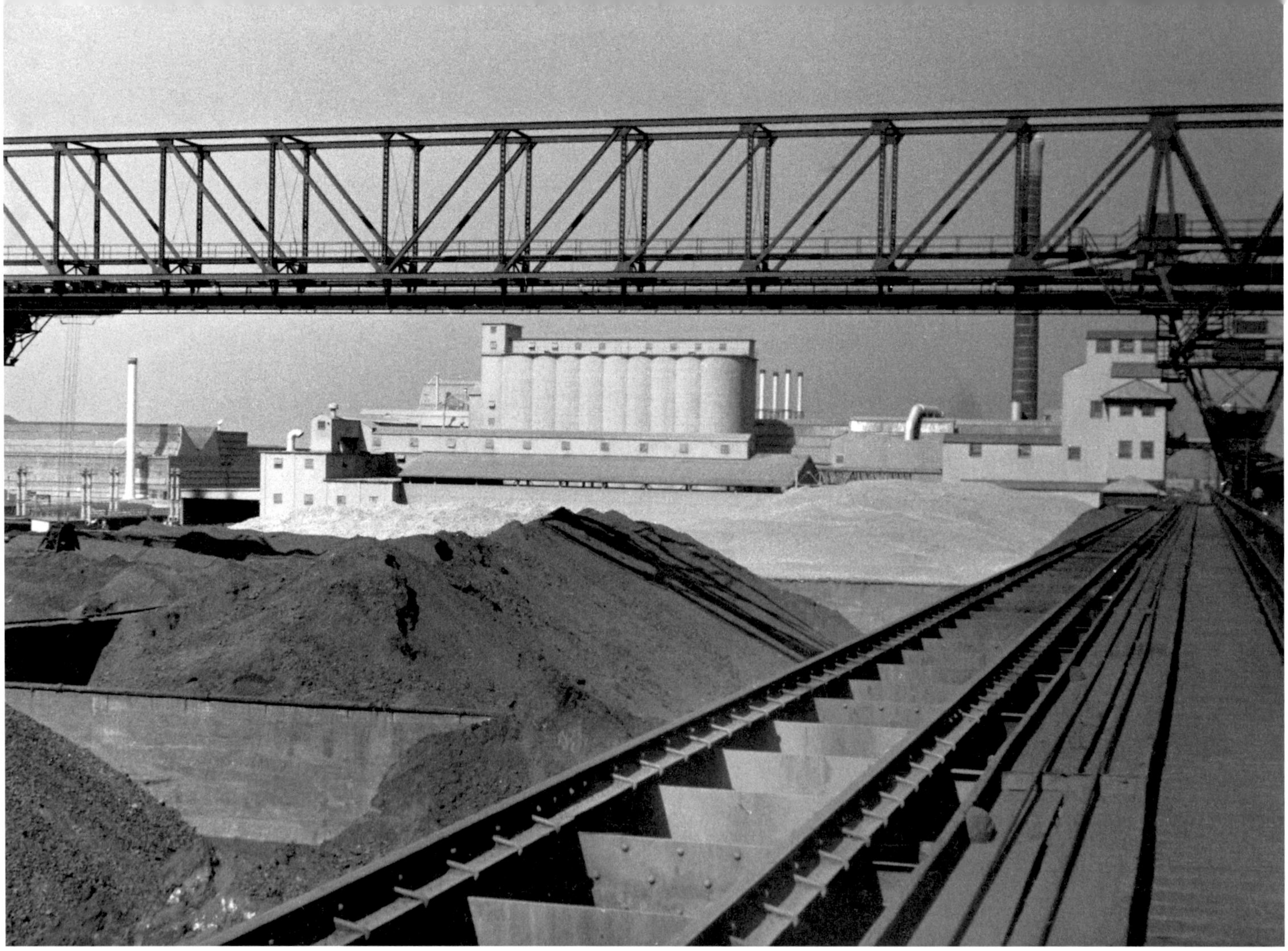

Coal and ore bunker of the Ford Factory in Dearborn, Detroit, 1931

Open hearth building of the Ford Factory in Dearborn, Detroit, 1931

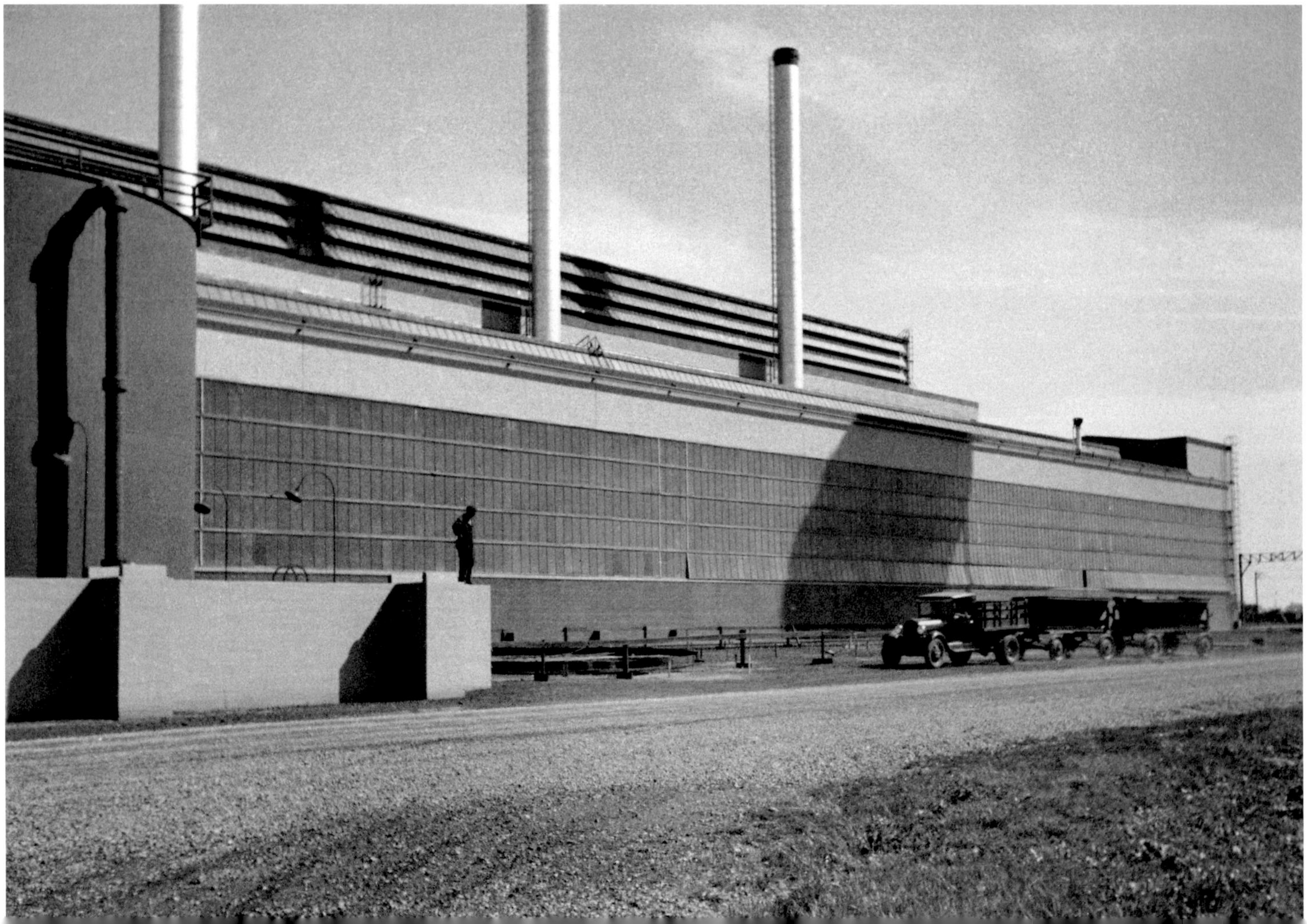

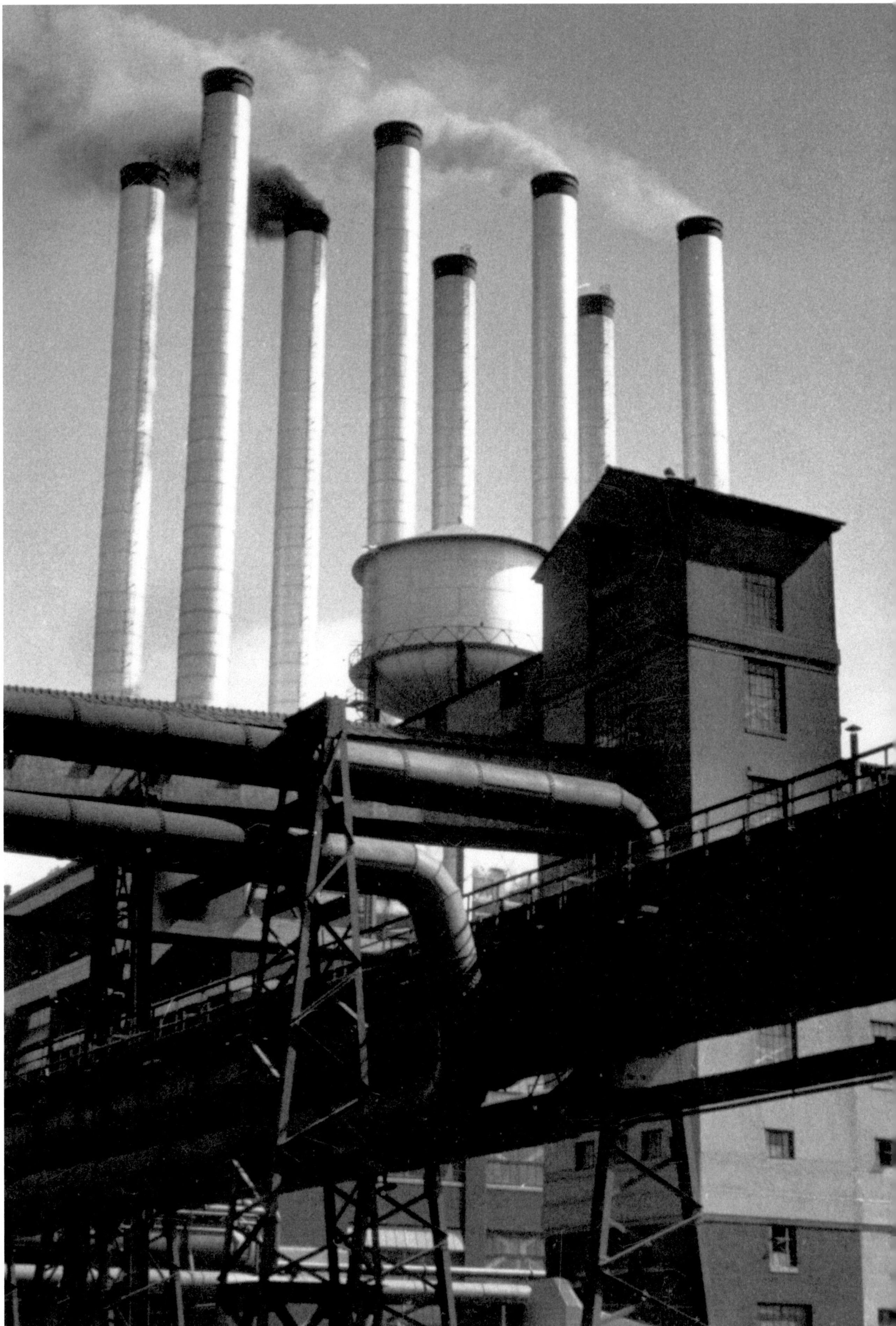

Power station of
the Ford Factory in
Dearborn, Detroit, 1931

Water tower of the Ford Factory in Dearborn, Detroit, 1931

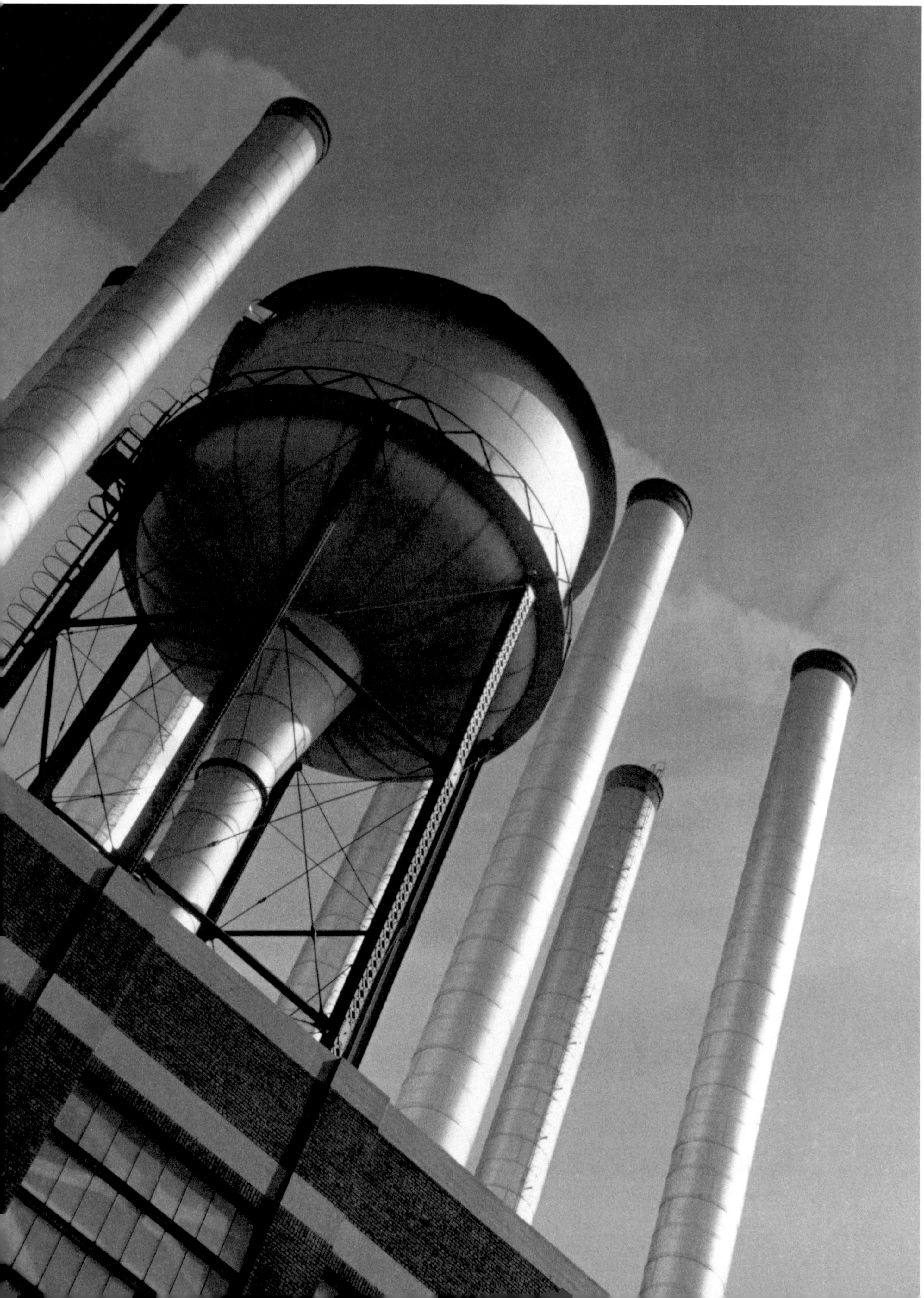

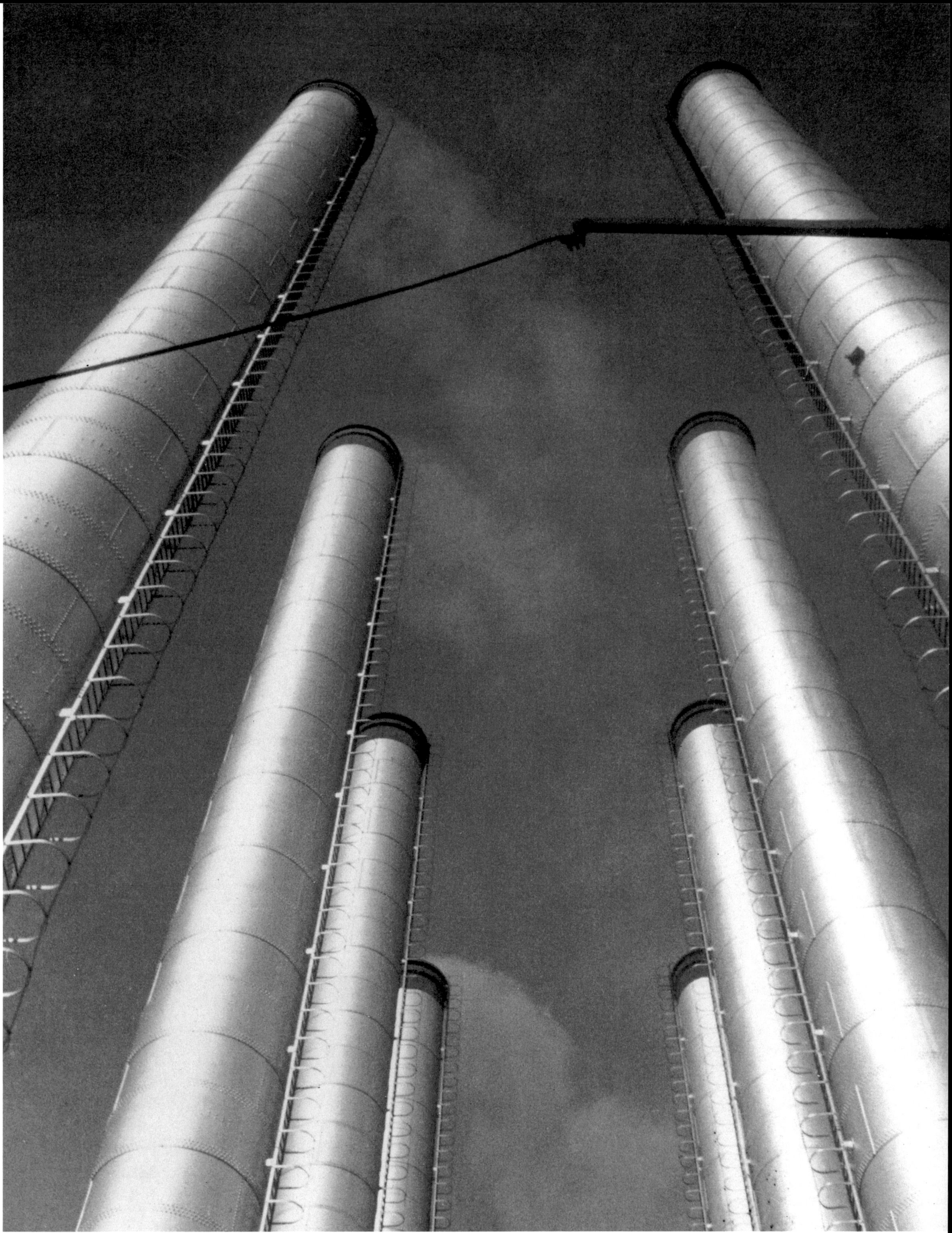

Smokestacks of the Ford Factory in Dearborn, Detroit, 1931
(also see page 5)

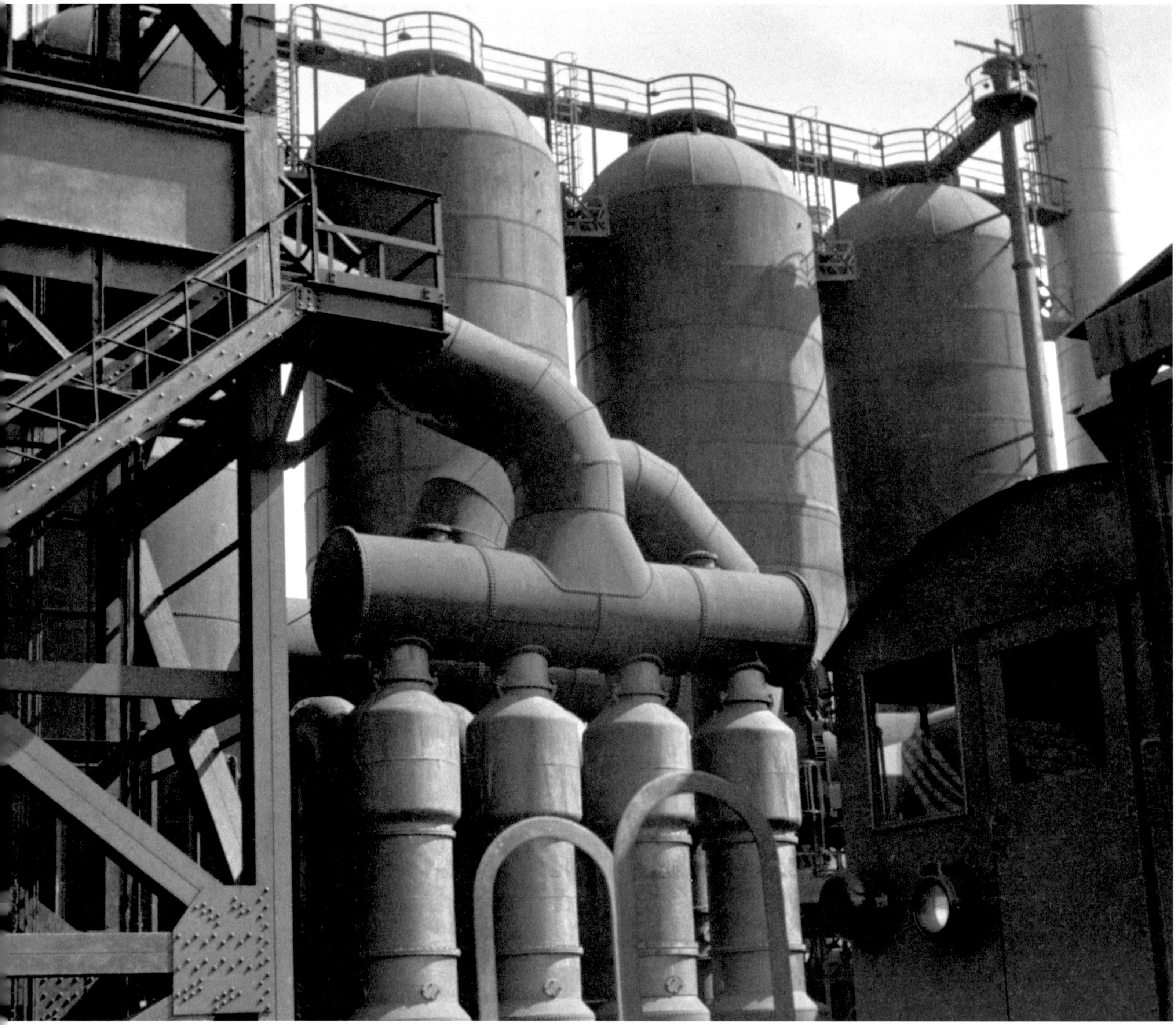

Blast furnace of the Ford Factory in Dearborn, Detroit, 1931

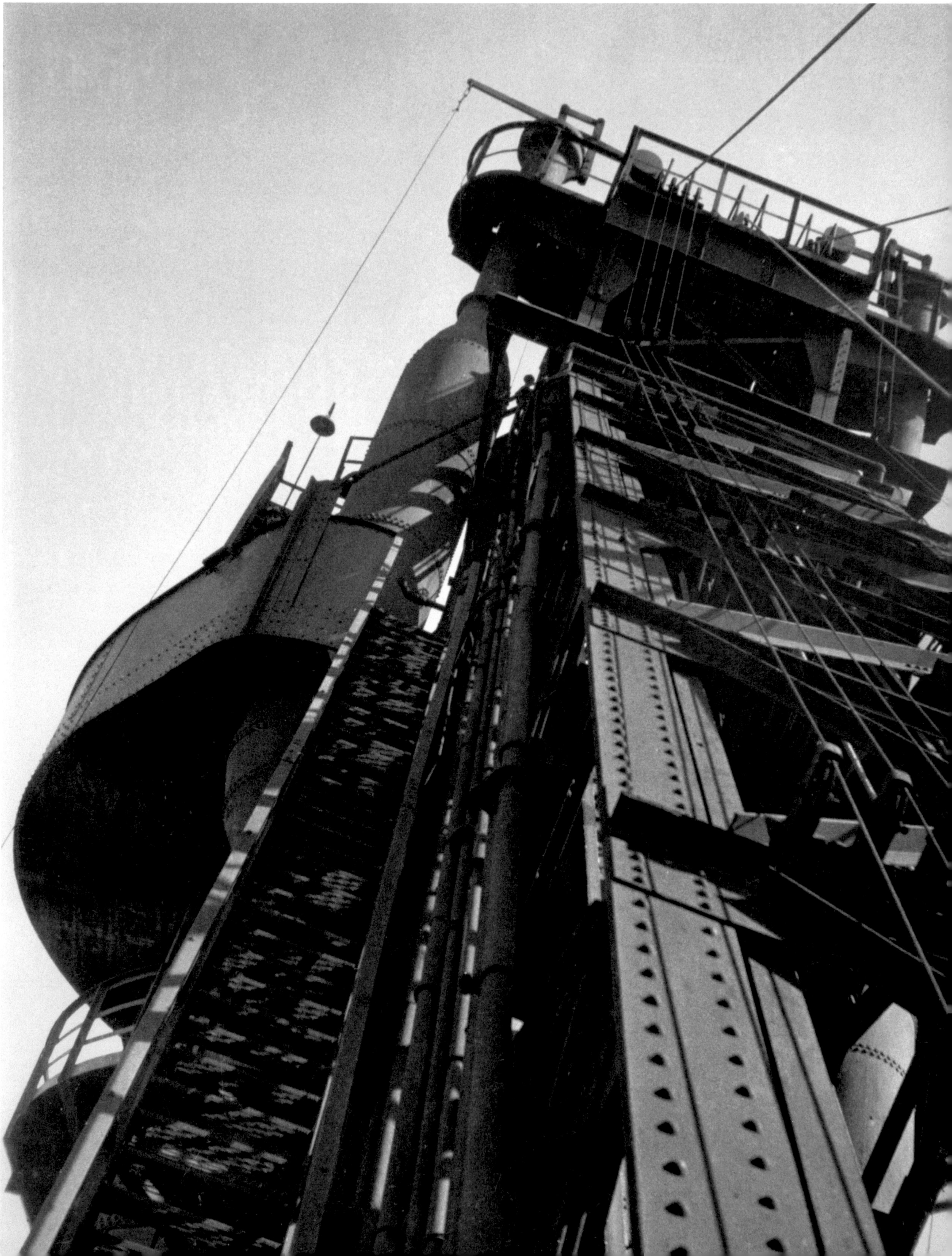

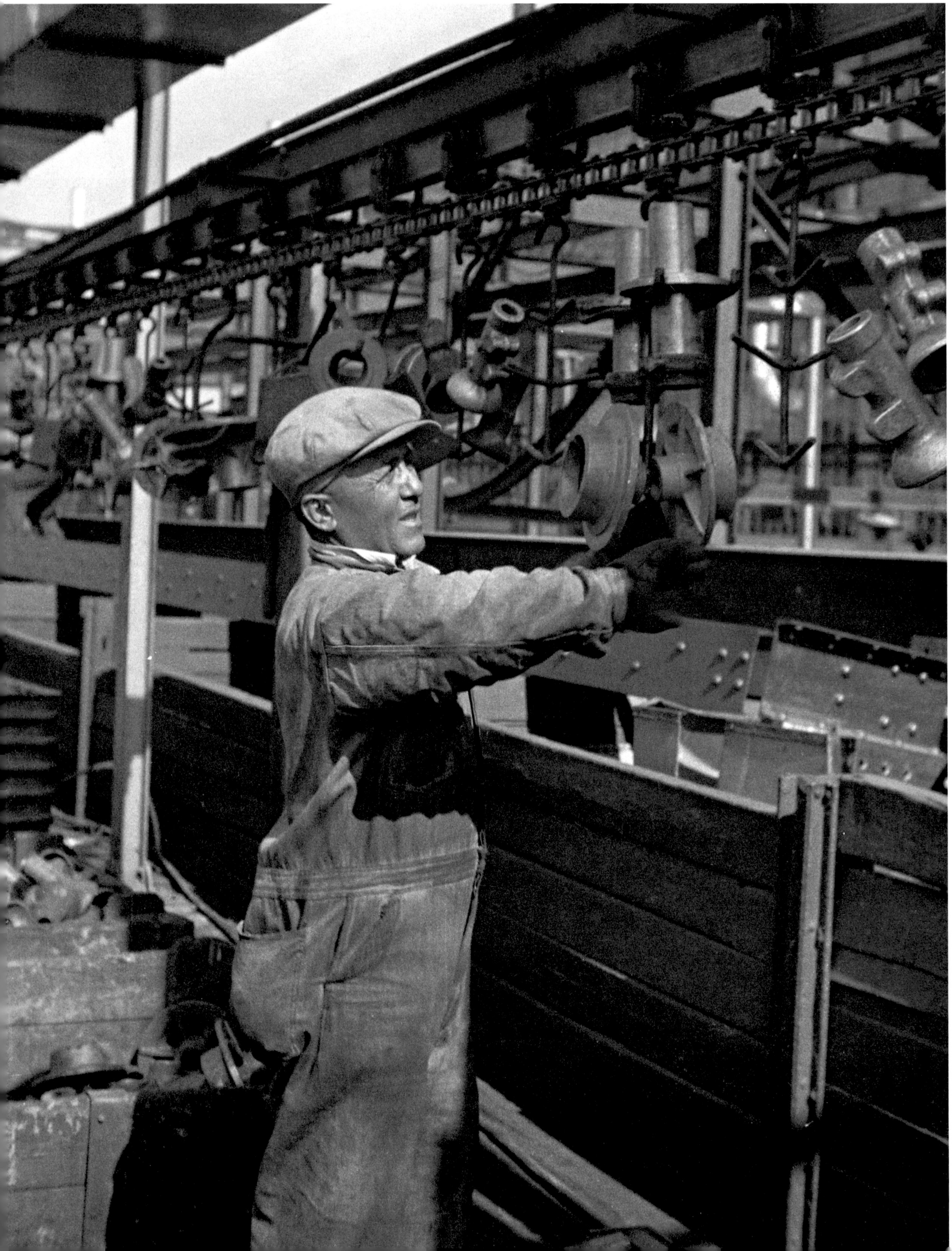

Worker at raw material conveyor of
the Ford Factory in Dearborn, Detroit, 1931

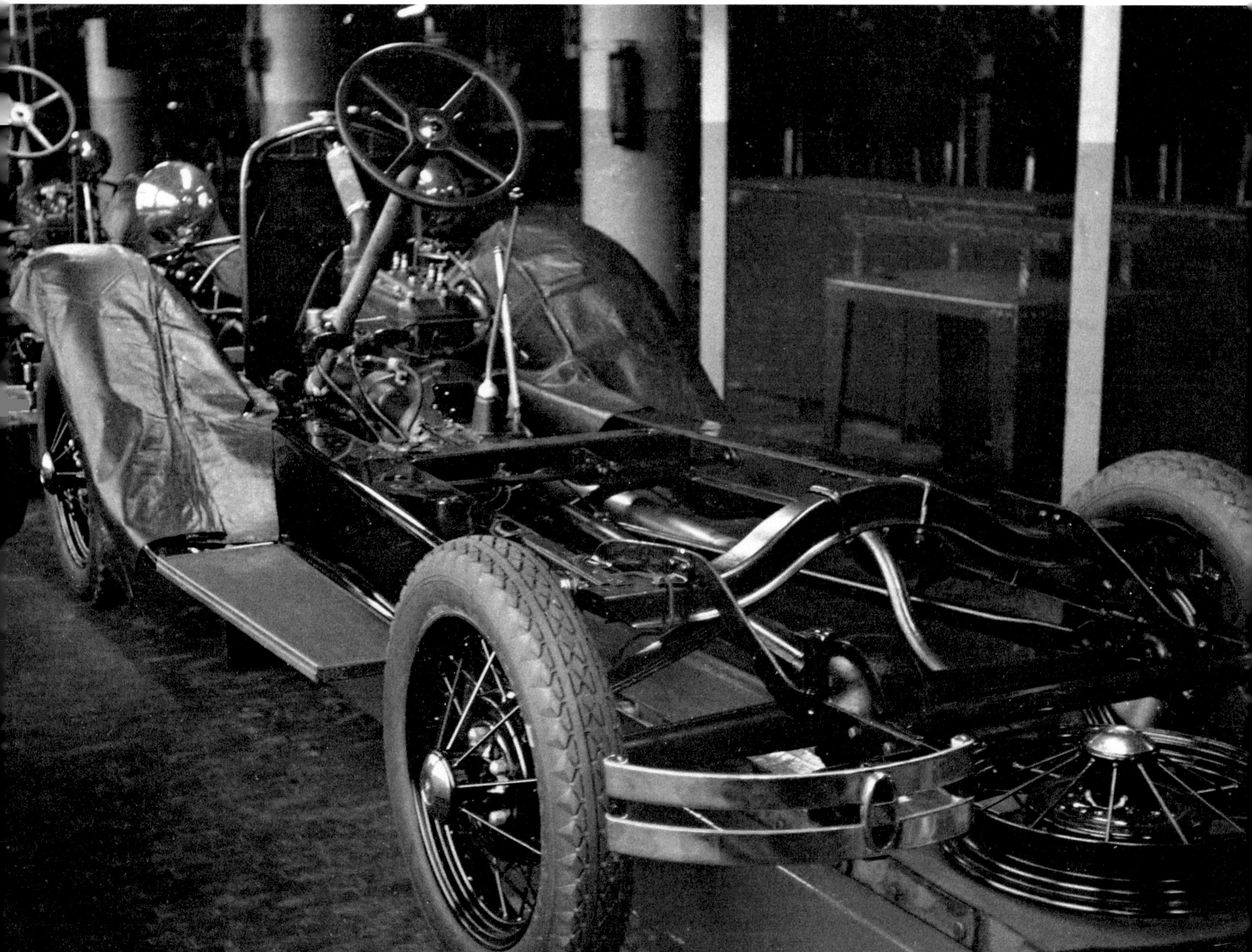

Final assembly of the Ford Factory in Dearborn, Detroit, 1931

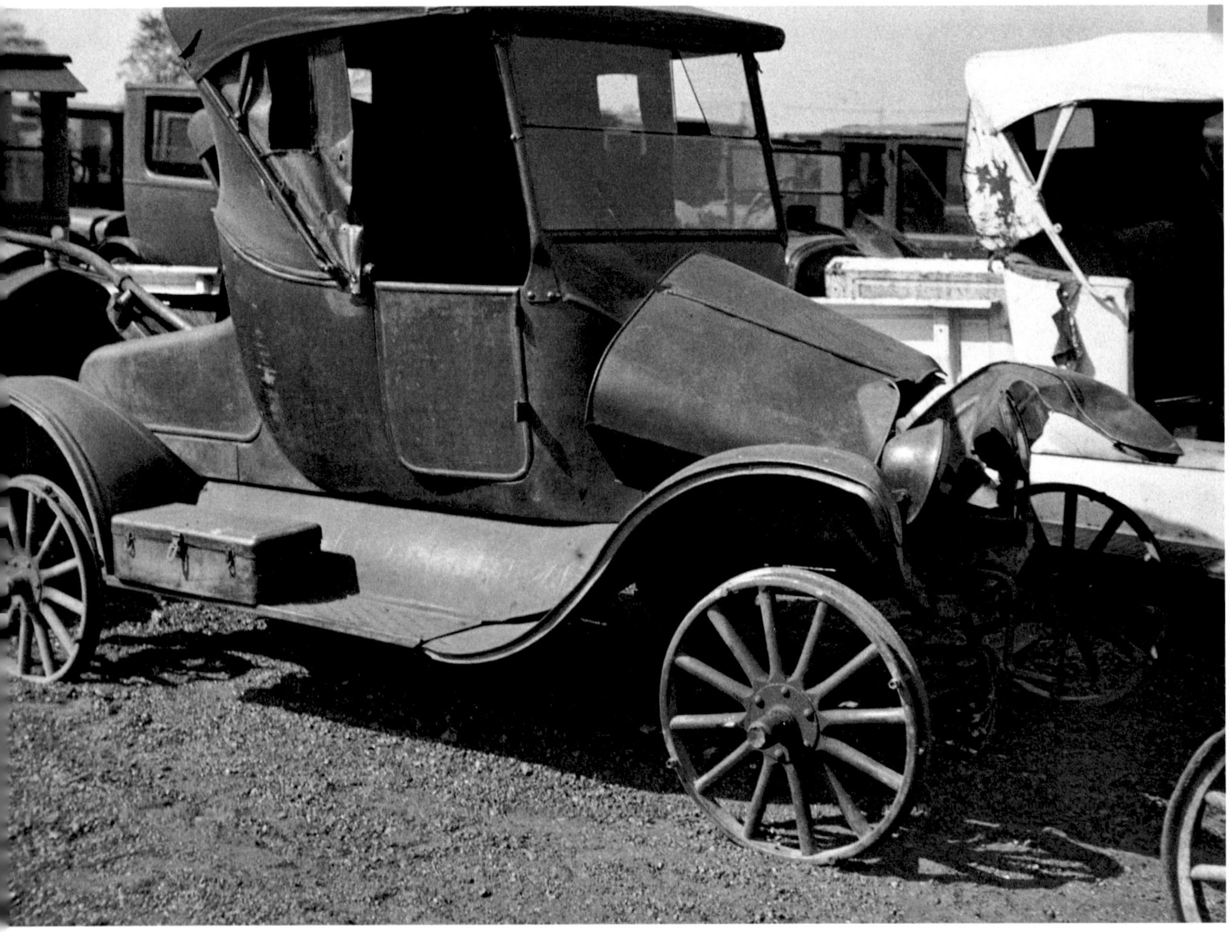

Old Ford model "T" at the Ford Factory in Dearborn, Detroit, 1931

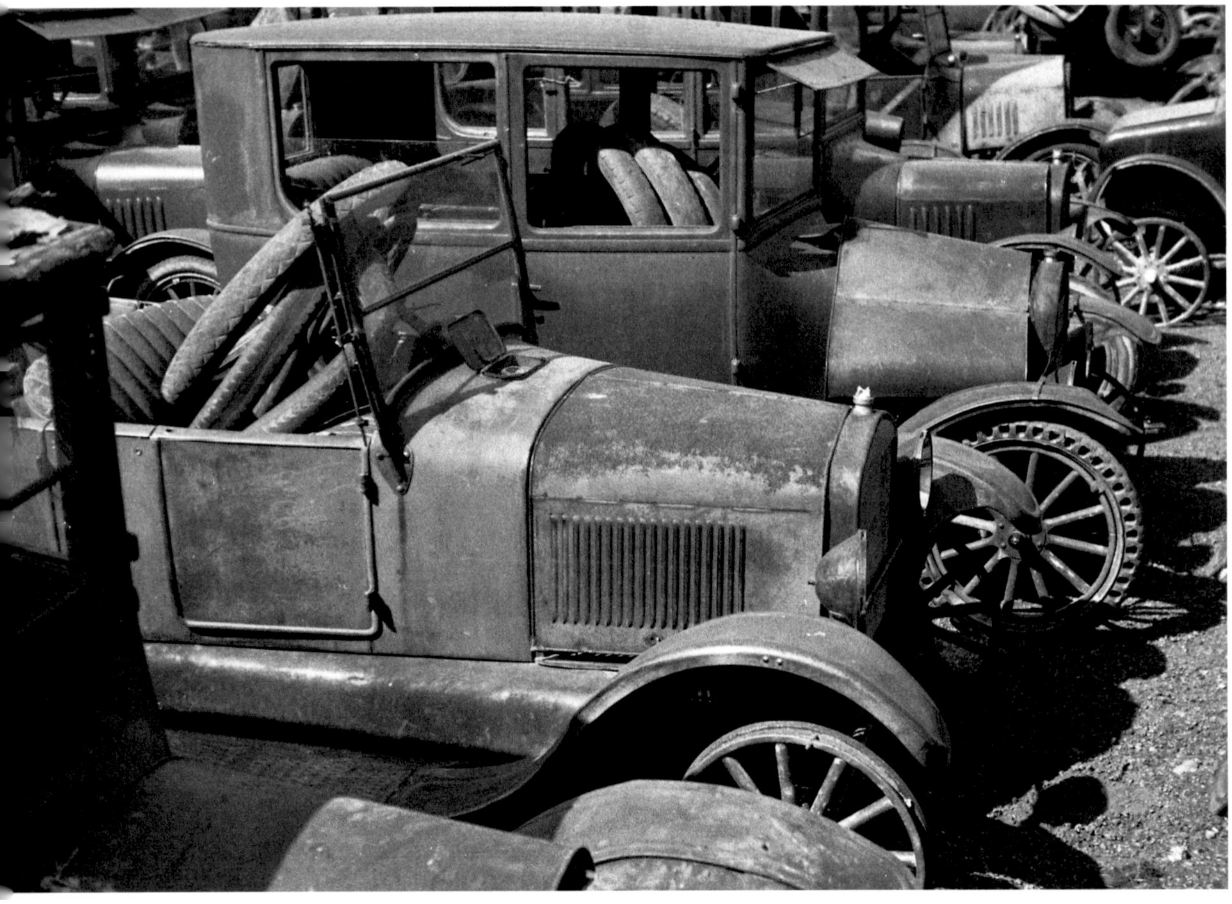

"Car Corpses" at the Ford Factory in Dearborn, Detroit, 1931

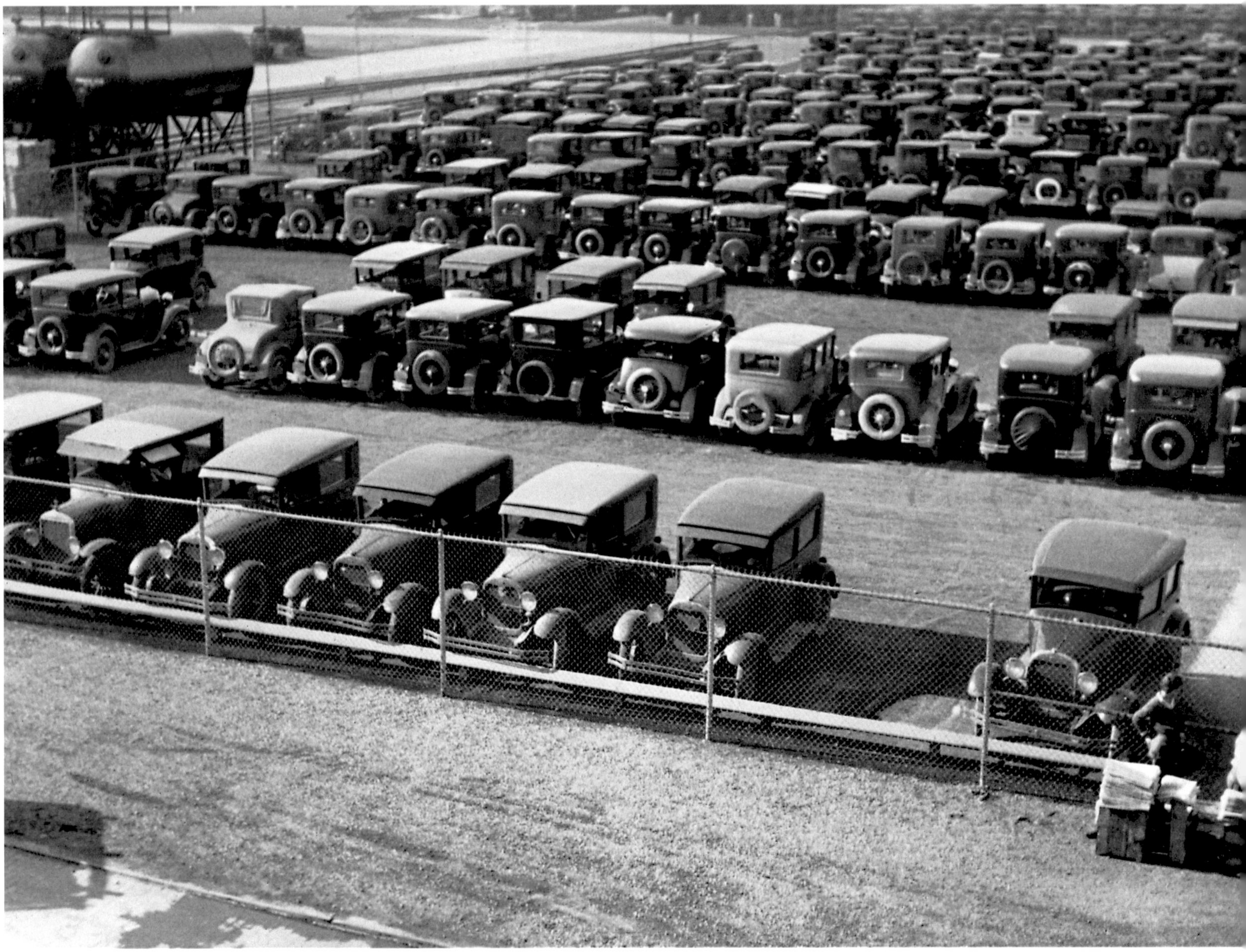

Factory employee parking lot at the Ford Factory in Dearborn, Detroit, 1931

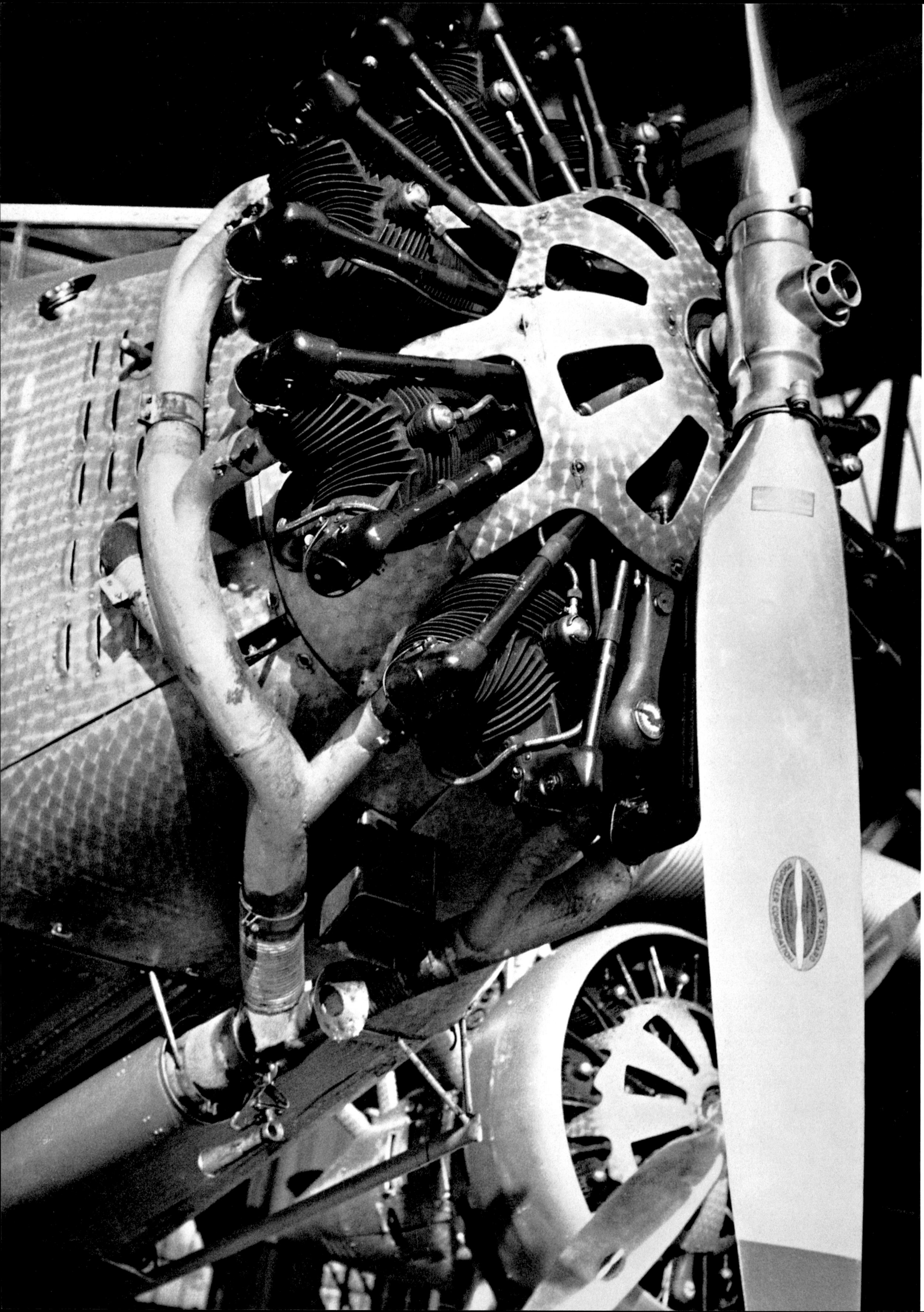
HAMILTON STANDARD
PROPELLER CORPORATION

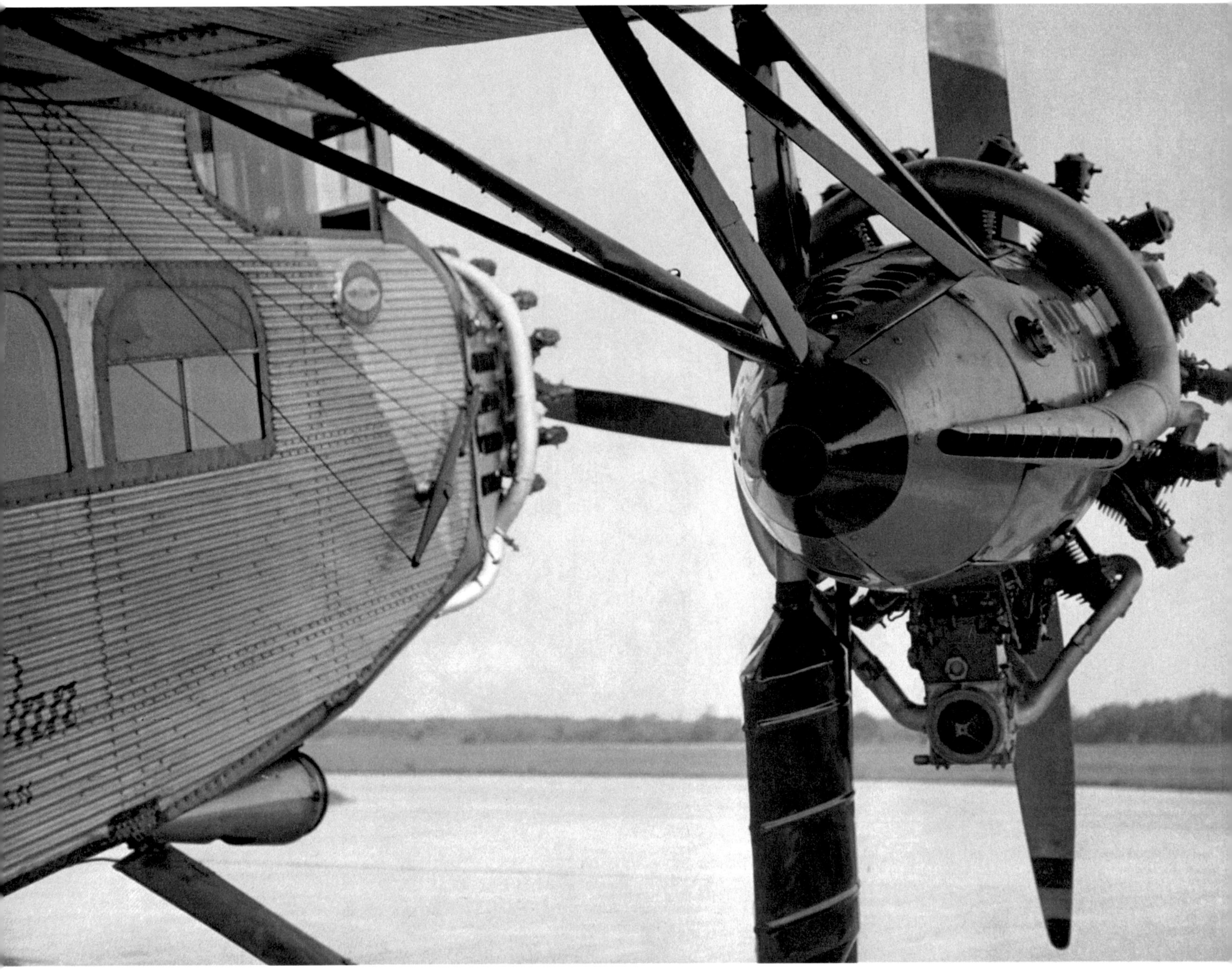

Radial engine and engine suspension of a Ford Trimotor aircraft
at the Ford Factory in Dearborn, Detroit, 1931

DIE FORM

ZEITSCHRIFT FÜR GESTALTENDE ARBEIT

7. JAHR MIT BEILAGE „DAS KUNSTBLATT"

HEFT 9

15. SEPTEMBER 1932

VERLAG HERMANN RECKENDORF G.M.B.H. BERLIN SW 68

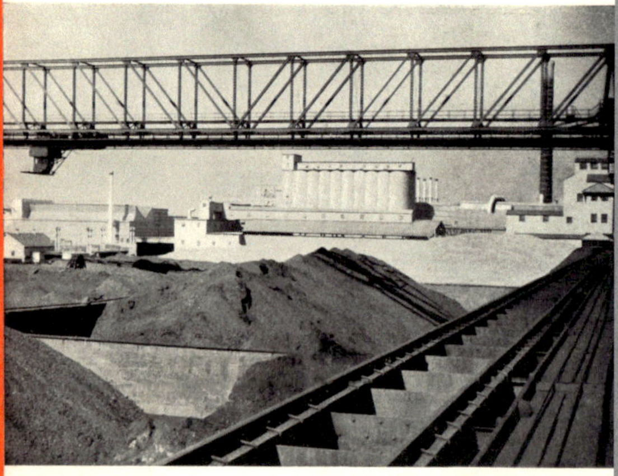

wesen, und niemand kann behaupten, das Wichtigste über die Geistigkeit jener Zeit zu wissen, der nicht das innere Wesen dieses Werks sich zu eigen gemacht hat. Und das gilt für die Kunst aller Grade und Zeiten. Deshalb ist es sinnlos, wenn die Soziologie versucht, der Kunstwissenschaft ihren Stoff zu entreißen. Sie kann damit nichts beginnen. Wohl aber kann sie das, was eine wirklich in die Tiefe des Wesens dringende Kunstwissenschaft von sich aus ermittelt hat, für ihre Zwecke gebrauchen, wie es umgekehrt für die Kunstwissenschaft nur heilsam sein kann, wenn sie von Zeit zu Zeit auch einmal den Blick vom Kunstwerk weg auf die Zeit richtet, in der es entstanden ist.

Die neue Ford-Fabrik

das River Rougewerk in Dearborn bei Detroit

Text und Aufnahmen: Dr.-Ing. FRITZ BLOCK

Im Jahre 1928 verlegte Ford einen großen Teil seines Betriebes in das neu angelegte River Rougewerk in Dearborn westlich von Detroit, in dem in normalen Zeiten 120 000 Mann beschäftigt werden. Ford und sein Werk sind heiß umstritten. Wenn man heute von Mechanisierung des Arbeitsprozesses, Rationalisierung, laufendem Band spricht, so denkt man dabei unwillkürlich an Ford, sein Werk und seine Theorien, und die Gegner dieser Dinge sehen in ihm auch den Hauptschuldigen für die Auswüchse, die eine fehlgeschlagene oder fehlgeleitete Rationalisierung im Gefolge der Wirtschaftskrise gehabt hat. Es ist hier nicht die Stelle, sich mit diesen Dingen auseinanderzusetzen, sicher aber ist die neue Ford-Fabrik, das River Rougewerk, das Sinnbild der modernen Fabrik, ein Symbol und Dokument für alles, das mit den Begriffen Rationalisierung, Mechanisierung, technischer Schönheit irgendwie im Zusammenhang steht. Deshalb gehört der Besuch dieses Werkes mit zu den stärksten Eindrücken, die Amerika überhaupt zu bieten hat; und wer unbefangen urteilt, kann sich an diesem Dokument restlos und objektiv mit vielen Dingen auseinandersetzen. Fords produktiver Gedanke war, Schaffung des Autos für jedermann, und kein anderes Ereignis hat so auf die Entwicklung des Landes, seinen Städtebau, seine Wohn- und Lebensgewohnheiten, Straßenbau, die Erschließung weiter Landstrecken eingewirkt. Das Kleinauto hat die amerikanische Welt umgestaltet. Es gibt schlechthin keinen Zweig des Lebens, dessen Grundlagen nicht auf der Einführung der Kleinautos beruhen. Ihm verdankt eine neue Welt ihre Erscheinungsformen.

Die Fordfabrik ist die Welt eines großen Mannes, er-

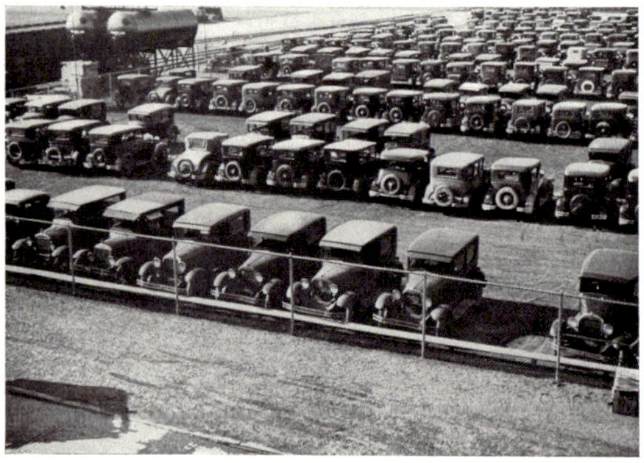

Parkplatz für Arbeiter-Automobile
Les autos des ouvriers stationnant au parc
Parking-place for workers automobiles

Foto: Dr. Block

baut in seinem Geiste, beherrscht von seinen vielfach neuen und umstürzenden Gedanken. Als Architekt stand ihm ein geborener Deutscher, Albert Kahn, zur Seite, dessen Fabrikbauten eine ausgezeichnete Leistung darstellen. Der erste Eindruck, den man schon von weitem von der Fordfabrik hat, ist Einfachheit und Klarheit bis zum Äußersten, Ordnung und ein Kult der Sauberkeit und Helligkeit. Bemerkenswertes Sinnbild: die aluminiumfarbenen Schornsteine.

Die Architektur hat die hohe Schönheit, Klarheit und Knappheit der Form eines Fordwagens, eines Fordmotors. Funktion und Form sind überall eins und nicht voneinander zu trennen. Klarheit, Bewußtheit, Sparsamkeit aller Mittel, ein starker Glaube an alles Technische ist dem Werk und den Menschen, die dort arbeiten, eigen und teilt sich dem Besucher, auch dem — der sonst den Dingen fernstehen mag — mit. Es ist das große Wunder der Technik unserer Zeit. Wie hier alles selbstverständlich und auf den letzten Ausdruck gebracht ist, wurde mir erst klar, als ich einige Tage später eine Konkurrenzfabrik in der gleichen Stadt mit einer ähnlichen Erzeugung besichtigen konnte. In der Fordfabrik ist eine in ihren Ausmaßen einzige vertikale Organisation aufgebaut. Die Fabrikation beginnt in den eigenen Kohle- und Erzgruben und endet mit dem fertigen

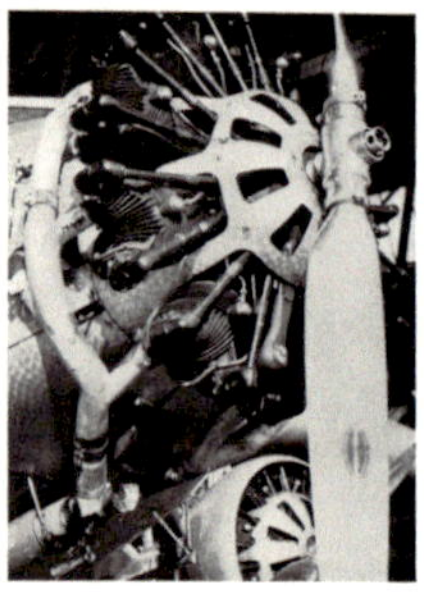

Flugzeugmotor
Moteur d'avion
Aeroplane-motor

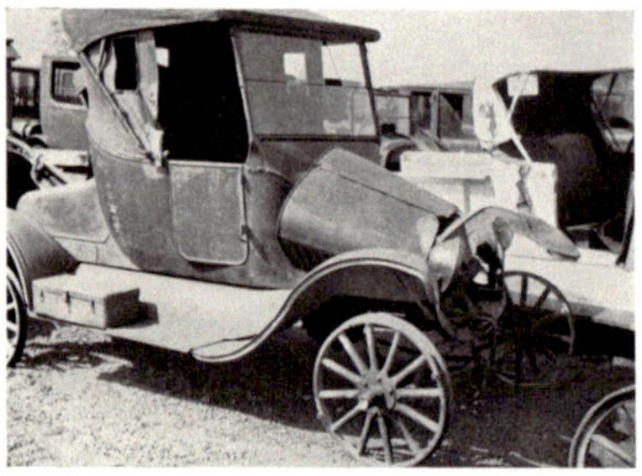

Altes Modell „T"
Un exemplaire de l'ancien modèle „T"
Old Model „T"

Fotos: Dr. Block

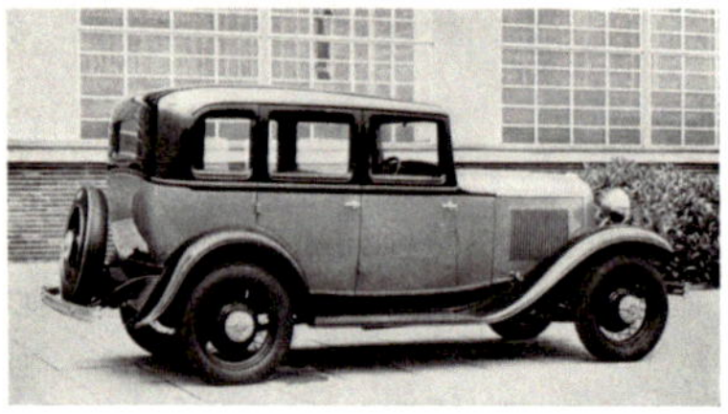

Der neue „Fordor" 8 Cylinder 14/65 PS
La nouvelle „Fordor"
The new „Fordor"

Foto: Motor Company GmbH., Altona

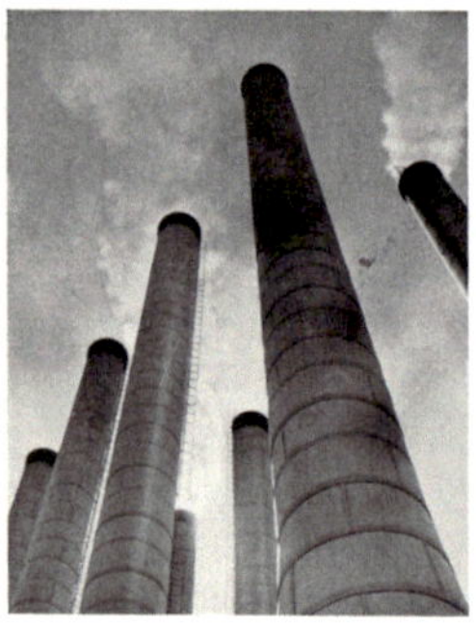

Fordwerk Riverrouge, Schornsteine des Kraftwerks
Les Usines Ford à Riverrouge. — Les cheminées de la centrale électrique
Ford plant Riverrouge, chimneys of the power-plant

Wagen, so wie er in die Hand des Kunden kommt. Ausgeschlossen ist nur die Verarbeitung von Gummi. Die Ford-Motor Company hat eigene Hochöfen, Koksöfen, Gießerei, Maschinen-Werkstätten, Karosserie-Abteilung, Glasschmelzerei, Glasfabrik, Zementfabrik, Papierfabrik, ein eigenes Stahlwerk, eine Nebenproduktenfabrik — nichts wird hier vergeudet oder bleibt unverwendet — eine Lokomotivreparatur-Werkstatt und ein eigenes Kraftwerk. Das River Rougewerk hat Lagerhäuser und Silos mit einer Fassungskraft von 2 Millionen tons. Erze und Kohle werden auf eigenen Schiffen an das Werk herangebracht. Alles, was zur Fabrikation gebraucht wird, erzeugt das Werk selbst, so daß sich der Preis des Wagens fast völlig aus Arbeitslöhnen zusammensetzt. Alle Arbeitsvorgänge sind weitmöglichst mechanisiert und die menschliche Arbeitskraft weitgehend durch mechanische ersetzt. Alle Werkzeuge sind auf den letzten Grad der Vervollkommnung gebracht. Die Anfertigung jedes Einzelstückes wird so weit wie möglich in Einzeloperationen zerlegt und jede von ihnen in einem Minimum an Zeit vollbracht von einem Arbeiter, der nur diesen einen Handgriff ausübt und es dabei zu erstaunlichen Leistungen bringt. Es werden von Menschenhand nur Arbeiten verrichtet, die maschinell nicht geleistet werden können. Mensch und Maschine arbeiten mit einer Präzision zusammen, daß keinerlei Leerlauf möglich ist. Die Handgriffe sind so ausgeklügelt, daß der Arbeiter seinen Standort nicht zu verlassen braucht. Anordnung

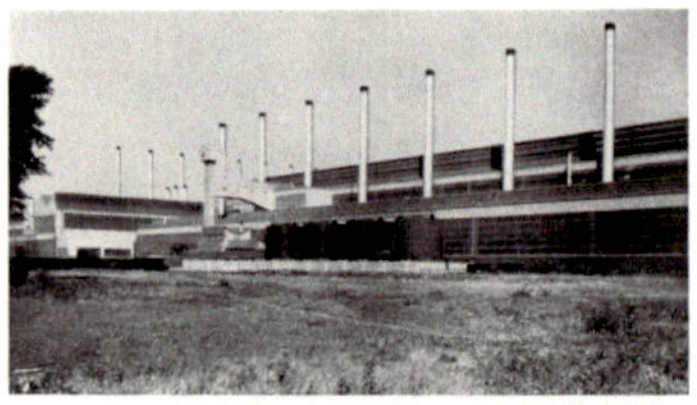

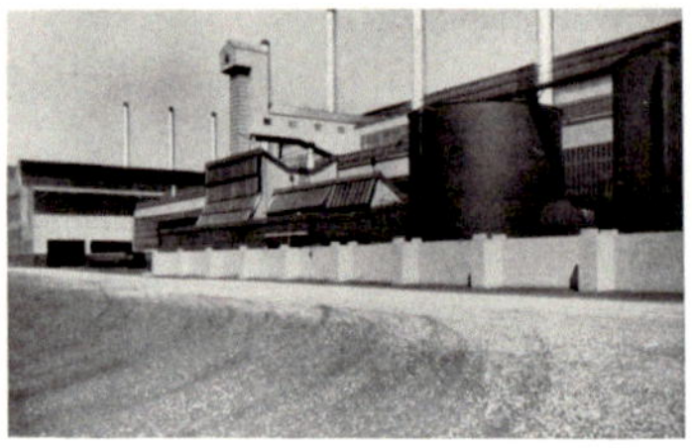

Gebäude der Siemens-Martin-Ofen
La hall des fours Siemens-Martin
Building of Siemens-Martin-furnaces

Fotos: Dr. Block

"The New Ford Factory" (*Die Form* 7, no. 9, 1932)

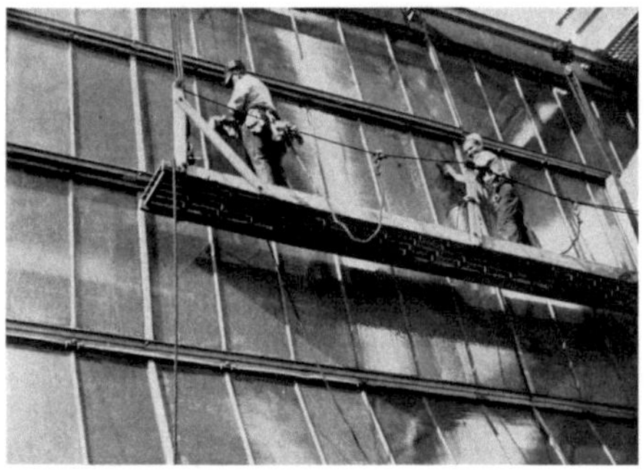

Fensterputzen

Nettoyage des vitres

Window-cleaning

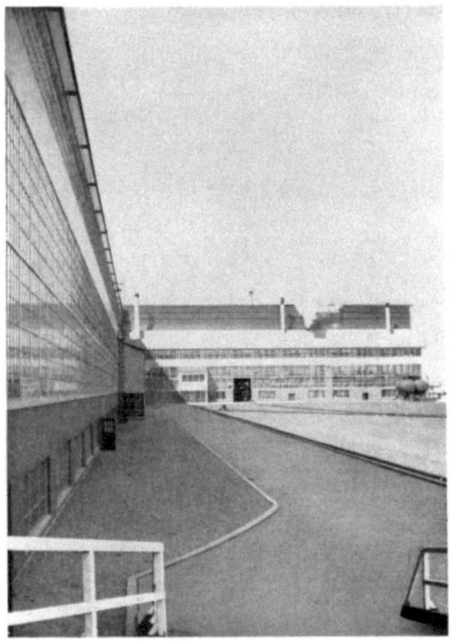

Stahlwalzwerk. Seitenansicht

L'aciérie vue de la cour

Steel-rolling-mill. Side view

Fotos: Dr. Block

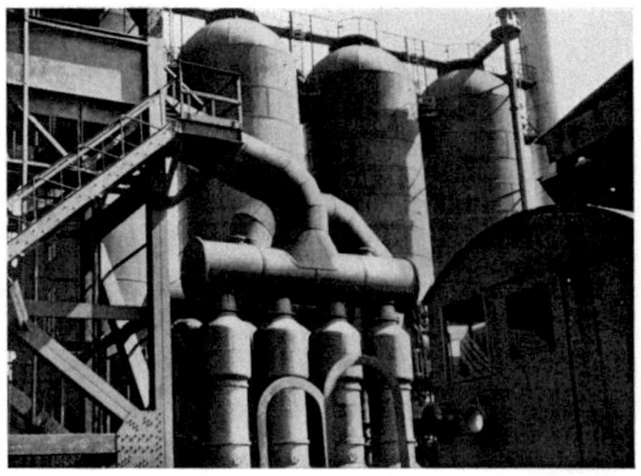

Teil des Hochofens (Wind-Erhitzer)

Une partie de l'installation des hauts-fourneaux (les récupérateurs)

Part of blast-furnace (Heating-furnace)

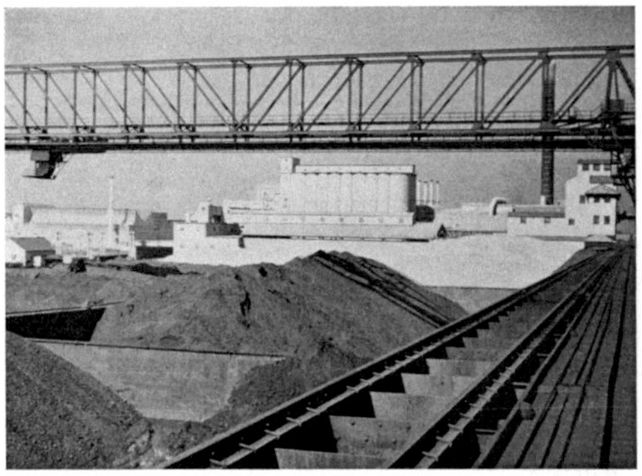

Kohle- und Erzbunker

Parc à charbon et soutes à minerai

Coal- and ore-bunker

Fotos: Dr. Block

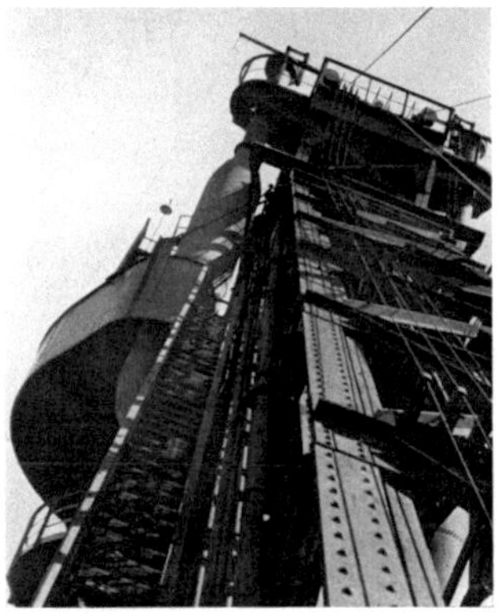

Teil des Hochofens

Une partie du haut-fourneau

Part of blast-furnace

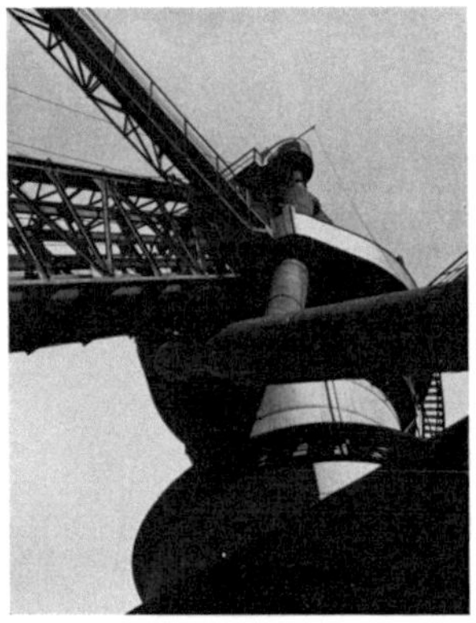

Ladebühne des Hochofens

Chargeur de haut-fourneau

Loading-bridge of blast-furnace

Fotos: Dr. Block

der Räume, Maschinen und Transportwege entspricht genau dem Arbeitsgange. Zubringung und Abtransport geschehen einzig durch das laufende Band, oder vielmehr ein System von laufenden Bändern, die Tempo und Rhythmus der Arbeit regeln und gewissermaßen wie die Aluminiumschornsteine ein Symbol der Fordfabrik bedeuten; für den einen das Symbol der Präzision und planmäßigen Arbeitens, für den anderen das der Versklavung und Abstumpfung des arbeitenden Menschen.

Ich habe in allen Werkstätten die Arbeit am laufenden Band verfolgt, um mir in dieser Hinsicht ein eigenes, unbefangenes Urteil zu bilden, und bin zu der Überzeugung gekommen, daß die Arbeitskräfte wohl gut ausgenutzt, aber nicht ausgesaugt werden. Die Verrichtungen sind sehr ausgeklügelt, aber die Arbeiter können sie im allgemeinen gut in der zur Verfügung stehenden Zeit verrichten. Nur verhältnismäßig selten kommt es vor, daß sich zwei oder mehr Arbeitsstücke stauen. Was aber sonst für den arbeitenden Menschen getan wird, abgesehen von dem sehr hohen Reallohn, ist mustergültig.

Alle Hallen sind strahlend hell, ausgezeichnet gelüftet und kühl; es herrscht ein Kult der Sauberkeit in allen Betrieben. Die Bekleidung der Arbeiter hängt in den Arbeits-

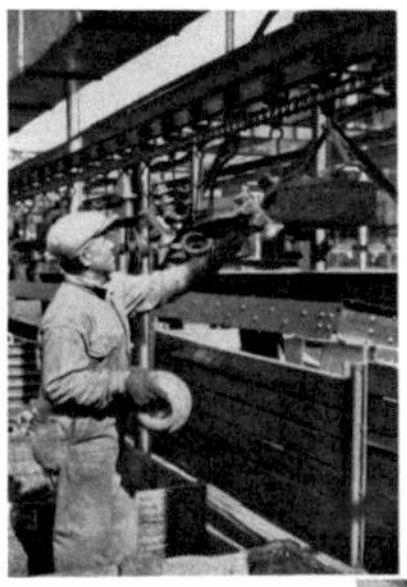

Rohmaterial-Transportband im Freien

Transport du matériel brut au convoyeur

Conveyor for raw materials in the open

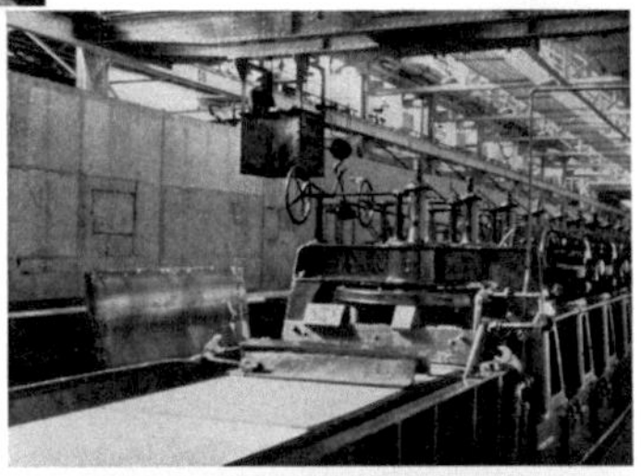

Glasschleiferei

Polissage des glaces

Glas-grinding

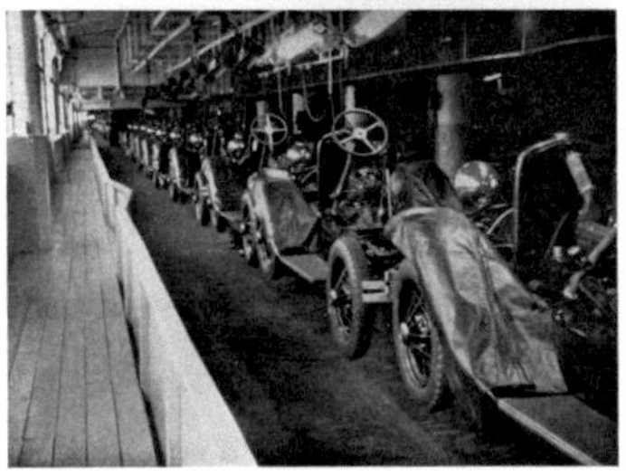

Laufendes Band mit halbfertigen Wagen

Une série de voitures semi-finies sur la table roulante

Conveyor with half-finished cars

Fotos: Dr. Block

West Lake Street Bridge over the Chicago River, Chicago, 1931

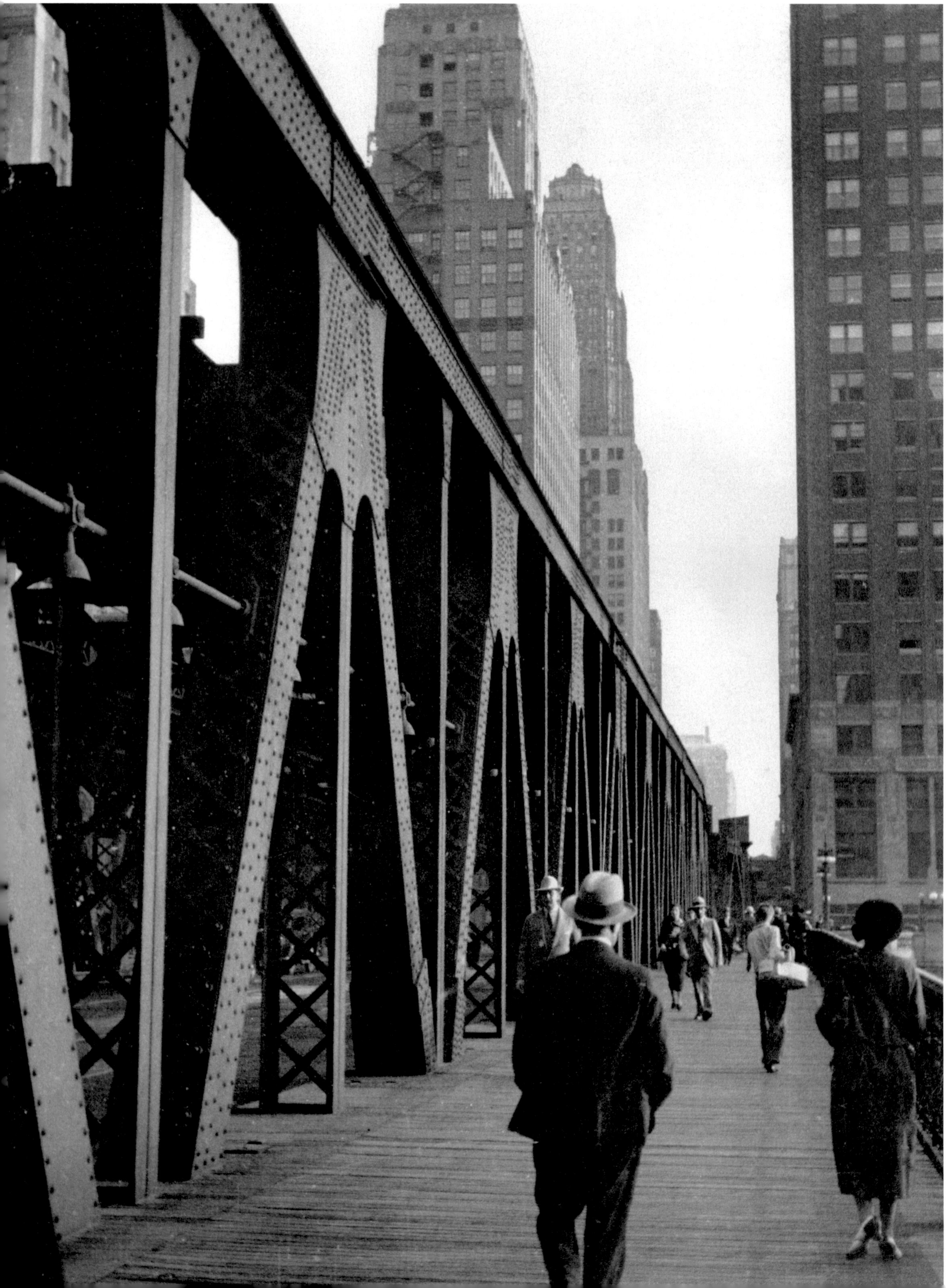

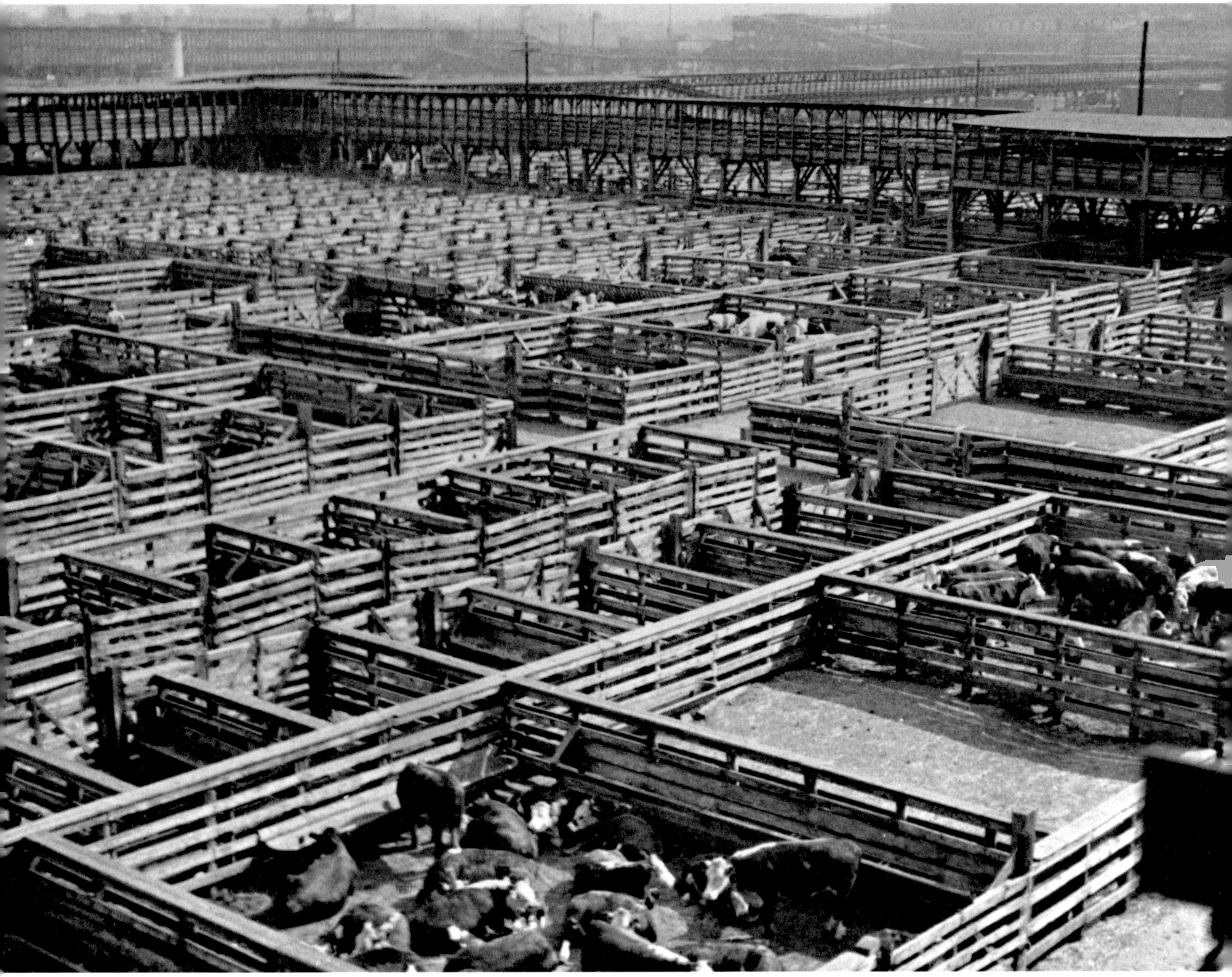

Cattle in slaughterhouse enclosures, Chicago, 1931

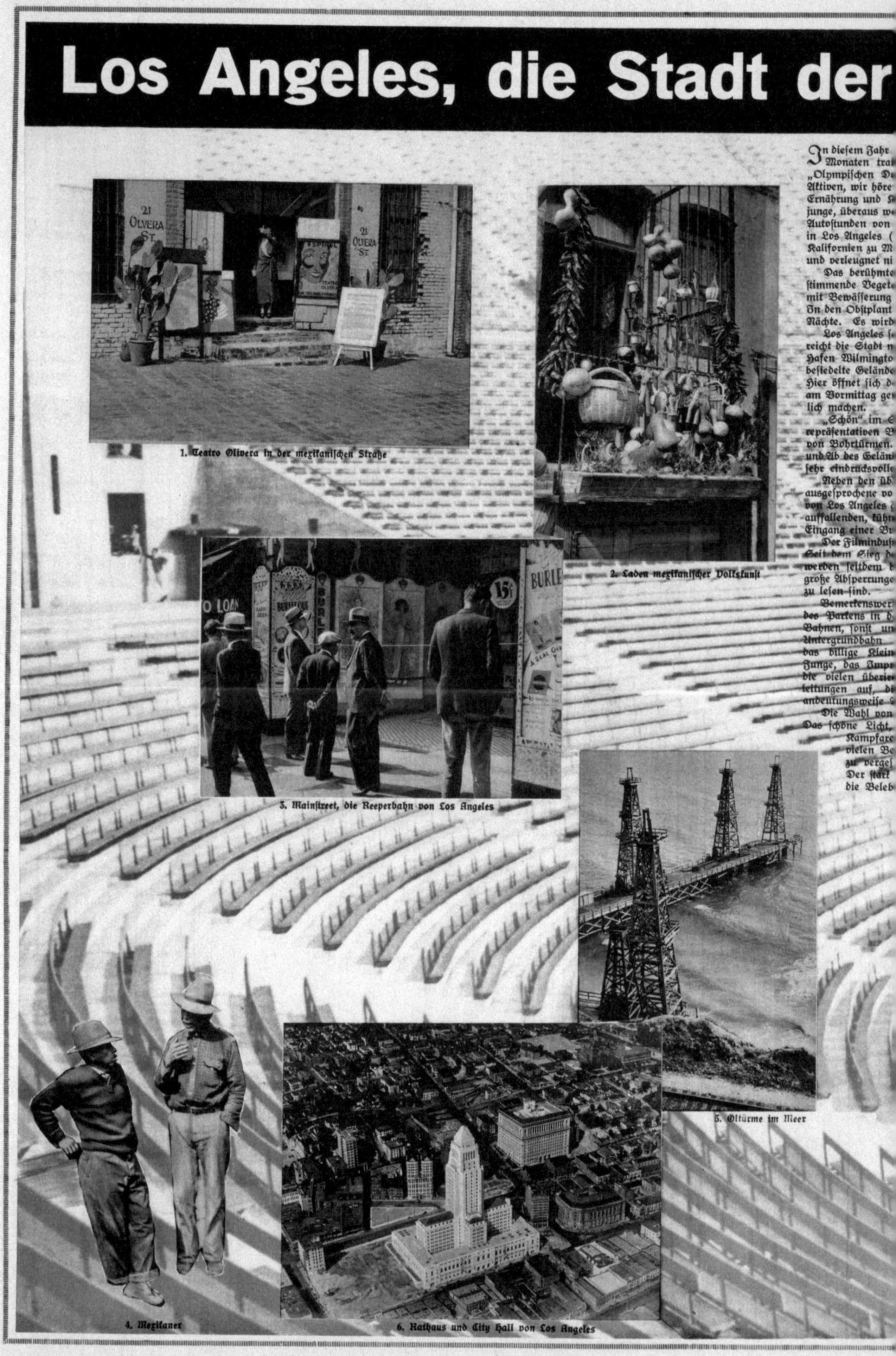
Los Angeles, die Stadt der

In diesem Jahr
Monaten tra
„Olympischen D
Aktiven, wir höre
Ernährung und K
junge, überaus w
Autostunden von
in Los Angeles (
Kalifornien zu M
und verleugnet ni
Das berühmte
stimmende Veget
mit Bewässerung
In den Obstplant
Nächte. Es wird
Los Angeles s
reicht die Stadt n
Hafen Wilmingto
besiedelte Geländ
Hier öffnet sich d
am Vormittag ge
lich machen.
„Schön" im E
repräsentativen V
von Bohrtürmen.
und Ab des Gelän
sehr eindrucksvoll
Neben den üb
ausgesprochene vo
von Los Angeles
auffallenden, kühn
Eingang einer Br
Der Filmindus
Seit dem Sieg d
werden seitdem
große Absperrunge
zu lesen sind.
Bemerkenswer
des Parkens in d
Bahnen, sonst un
Untergrundbahn
das billige Klein
Junge, das Impr
die vielen überir
leitungen auf, di
andeutungsweise
Die Wahl von
Das schöne Licht,
Kampfare
vielen Be
zu verges
Der stark
die Beleb

1. Teatro Olivera in der mexikanischen Straße

2. Laden mexikanischer Volkskunst

3. Mainstreet, die Reeperbahn von Los Angeles

4. Mexikaner

5. Öltürme im Meer

6. Rathaus und City Hall von Los Angeles

"Los Angeles, City of the 1932 Summer Olympics" (*Hamburger Anzeiger. Illustrierte Wochenbeilage*, no. 26, 1932)

lympischen Spiele von 1932

m Brennpunkt stärksten Interesses. Schon seit
leute, berichtet die Presse. Wir hören vom
ndenen Bungalows zur Unterbringung der
er die Fragen der Eingewöhnung in bezug auf
näher, als über Los Angeles zu berichten. Die
adt liegt im südlichen Kalifornien, nur wenige
Grenze entfernt. Eine mexikanische Straße
den nahen Einfluß am besten, gehörte doch
durch die Vereinigten Staaten im Jahre 1846
he Kultivierung durch spanisches Abkommen.
isch, also regenarm. Die die Landschaft be-
eschaffen. Ohne Bewässerung gedeiht nichts,
ische Gärten, Parke, Anlagen (Abb. 7 u. 8).
Öfen zur Überwindung von Frostschäden kalter
it geerntet.
b. 11 u. 12). Fast ganz ohne Bodenbewegung
nstädten Santo Monica, Long Beach und dem
heran. Langsam steigt das ungeheure, flach
Hollywood, Pasadena und Beverly Hills über.
die Kalifornischen Berge, die im Winter nach
den Skilauf nach 2 Stunden Autofahrt mög-

derner Betrachtungsweise sind, außer einigen
e Stadtteile der Ölfelder mit ihren Wäldern
wie im Gebiet des „Telegraph Hills", ein Auf
5 zeigt) das Am und Im Meer hinzu, entstehen
Überschneidungen.
eganten Läden und Hotels hat die Stadt sehr
den. Die „Mainstreet" könnte die Reeperbahn
Zum Beispiel zeigt Abb. 3 den mit für Amerika
cht mißzuverstehenden Vorführungen lockenden

nur in seltenen Fällen auf der Straße (Abb. 10).
eder viel Arbeit in die Studios verlegt; auch
nmen, um störende Geräusche zu vermeiden,
n dann in den Zeitungen sensationelle Berichte

der Autos mit dem schwierigen Problem
Beach und nach Pasadena gehen elektrische
uslinien den Verkehr. Keine Hoch-, keine
eit auseinanderliegenden Stadtteile. Nur
Wachstum der Stadt ermöglichen. Das
fornischen Städte fällt dem Europäer durch
isorischen Telephon-, Telegraph- und Licht-
sten durch Stadt und Land ziehen (z. B.

„Olympischen" Stadt ist wohl recht glücklich.
Nächte, die sicher dann virtuos beleuchteten
abendlichen Konzerte im Freien werden die
Im Umkreis locken See, Gebirge und nicht
zu Fahrten auf wunderbaren Autostraßen.
ion leidenden Stadt (Film, Ölpreise) kommt
mmenden Wochen sehr zustatten.

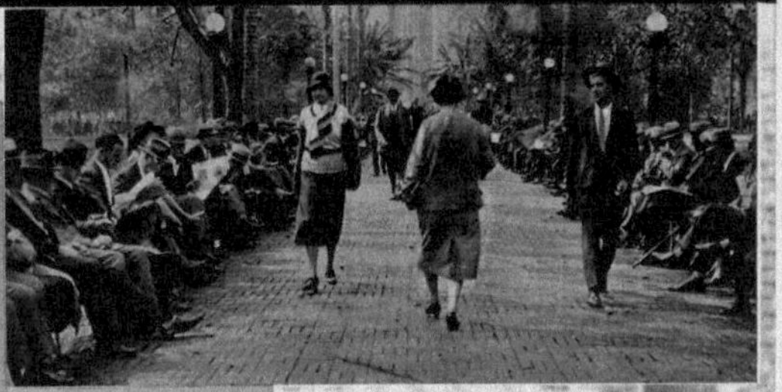

8. Erwerbslose im öffentlichen Park

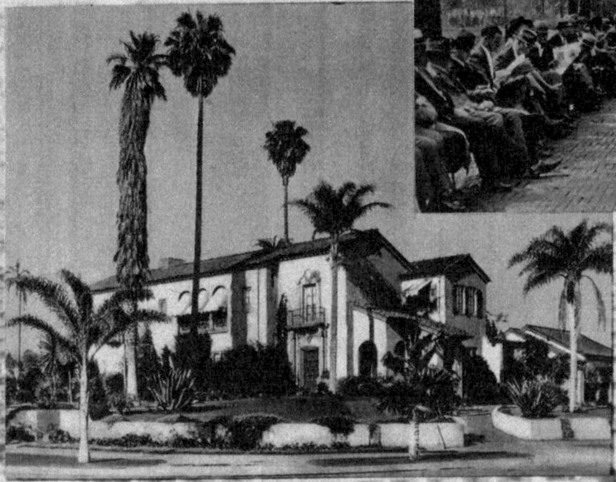

7. Typisches Landhaus

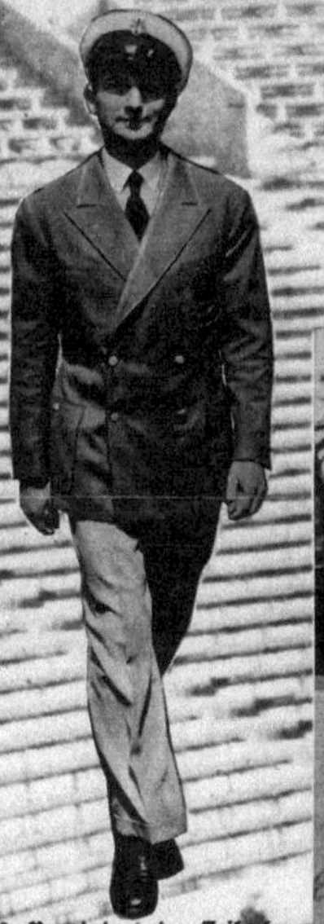

9. Paradedreß der Teilnehmer

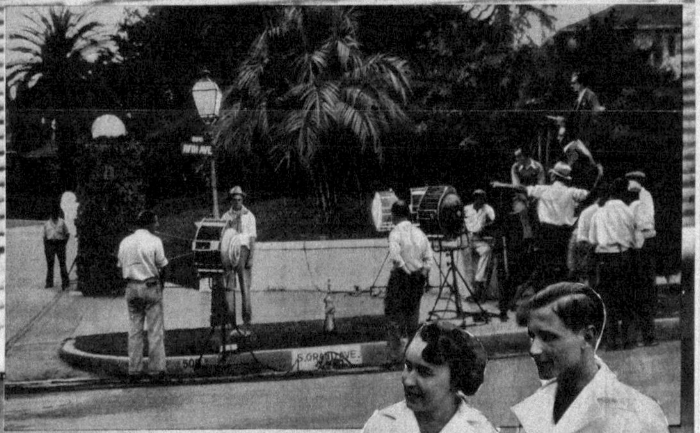

10. Filmaufnahme in Pasadena

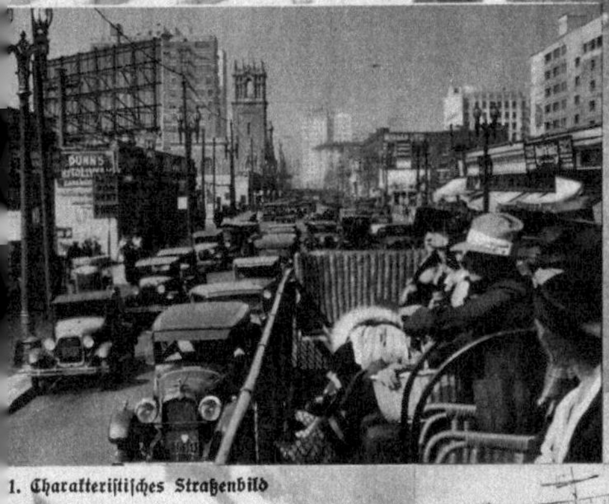

1. Charakteristisches Straßenbild

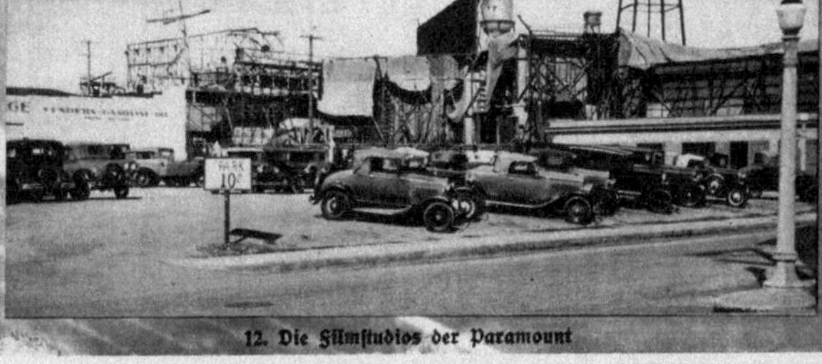

12. Die Filmstudios der Paramount

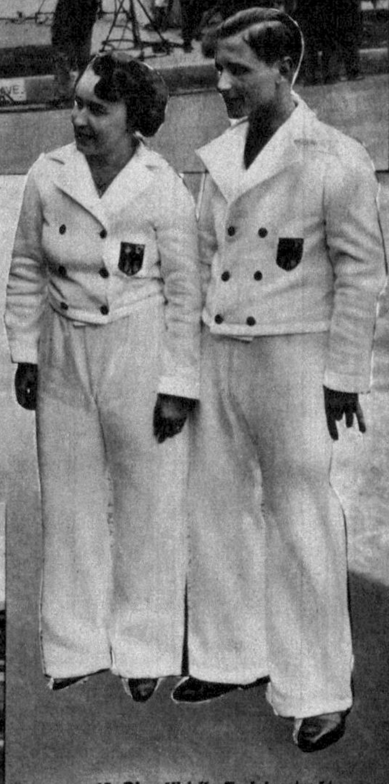

13. Die offizielle Trainingstracht

Aufnahmen Dr. Block und Wide World
Text Anna Sophie Block

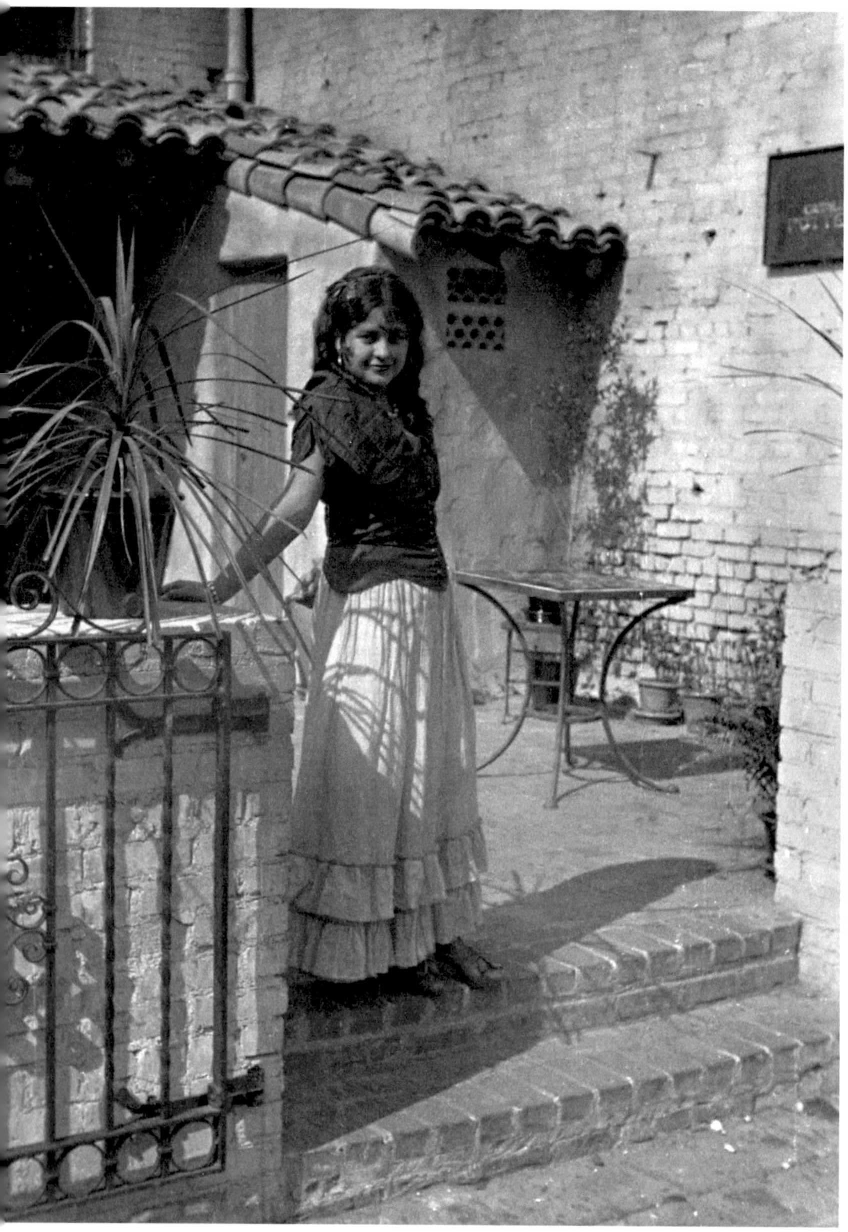

Mexican girl,
Olvera Street, Los Angeles, 1931

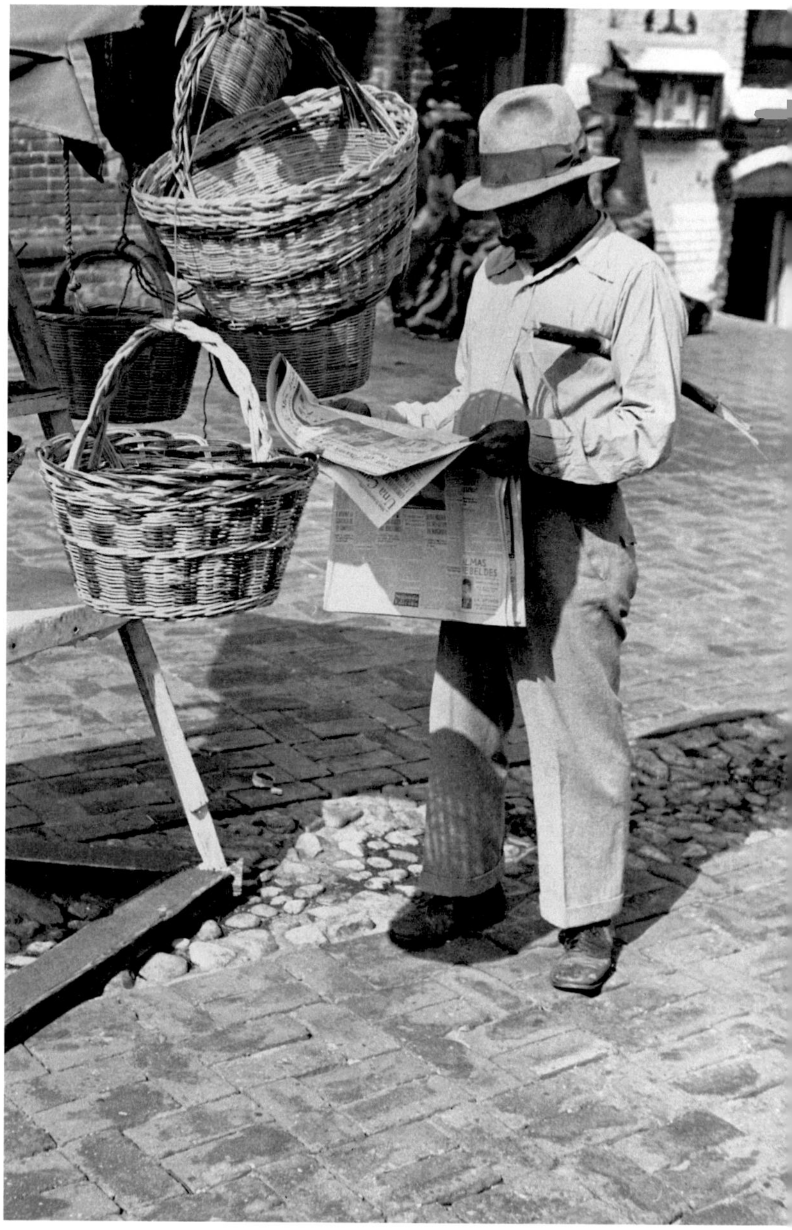

Mexican street peddler,
Olvera Street, Los Angeles, 1931

"District of temptations,"
Los Angeles, 1931

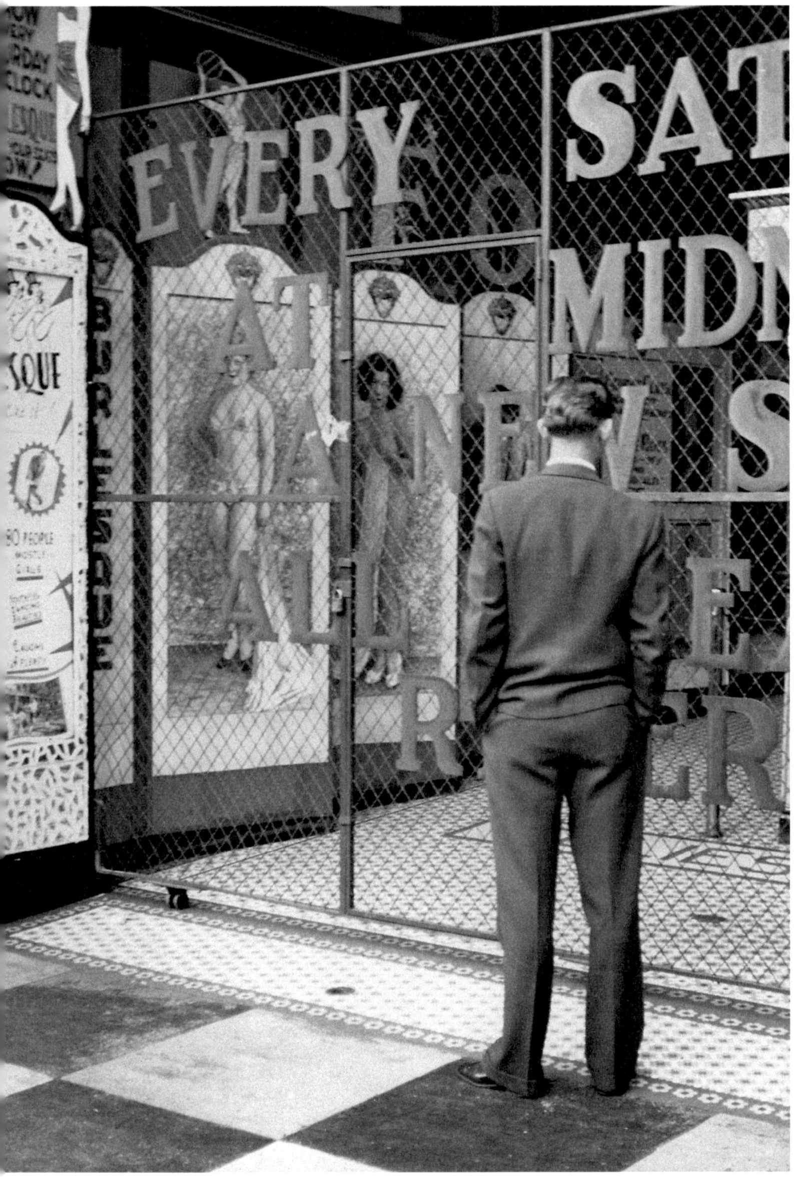

Newsboy,
Los Angeles, 1931

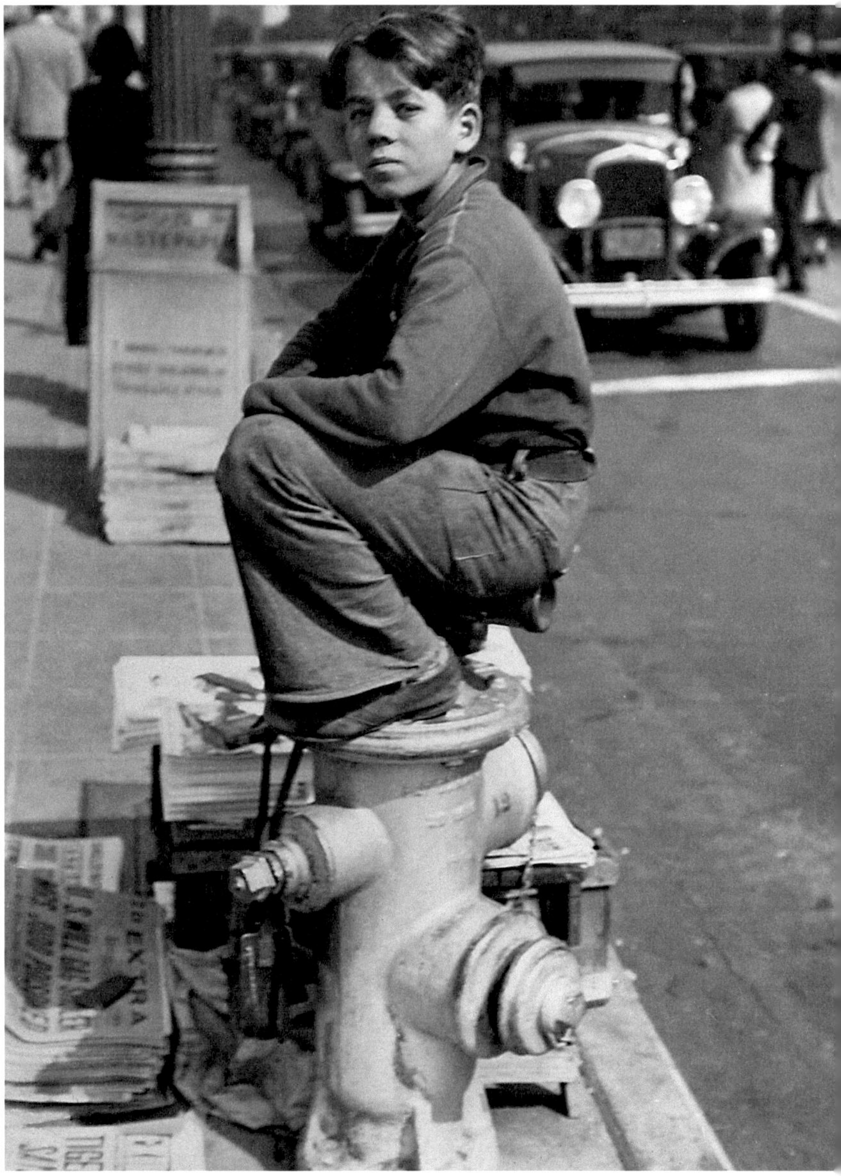

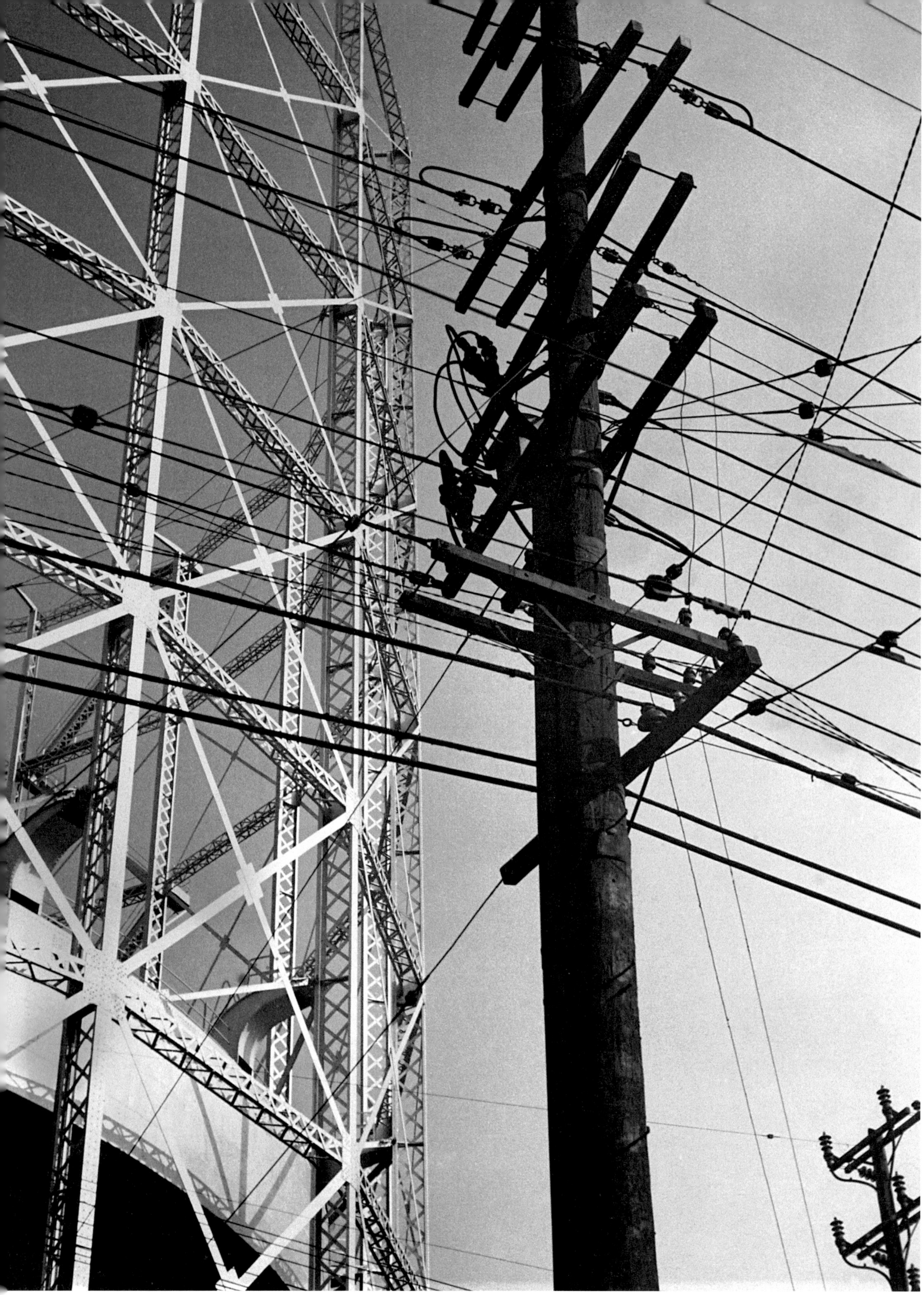

Gas and electricity, Los Angeles, 1931

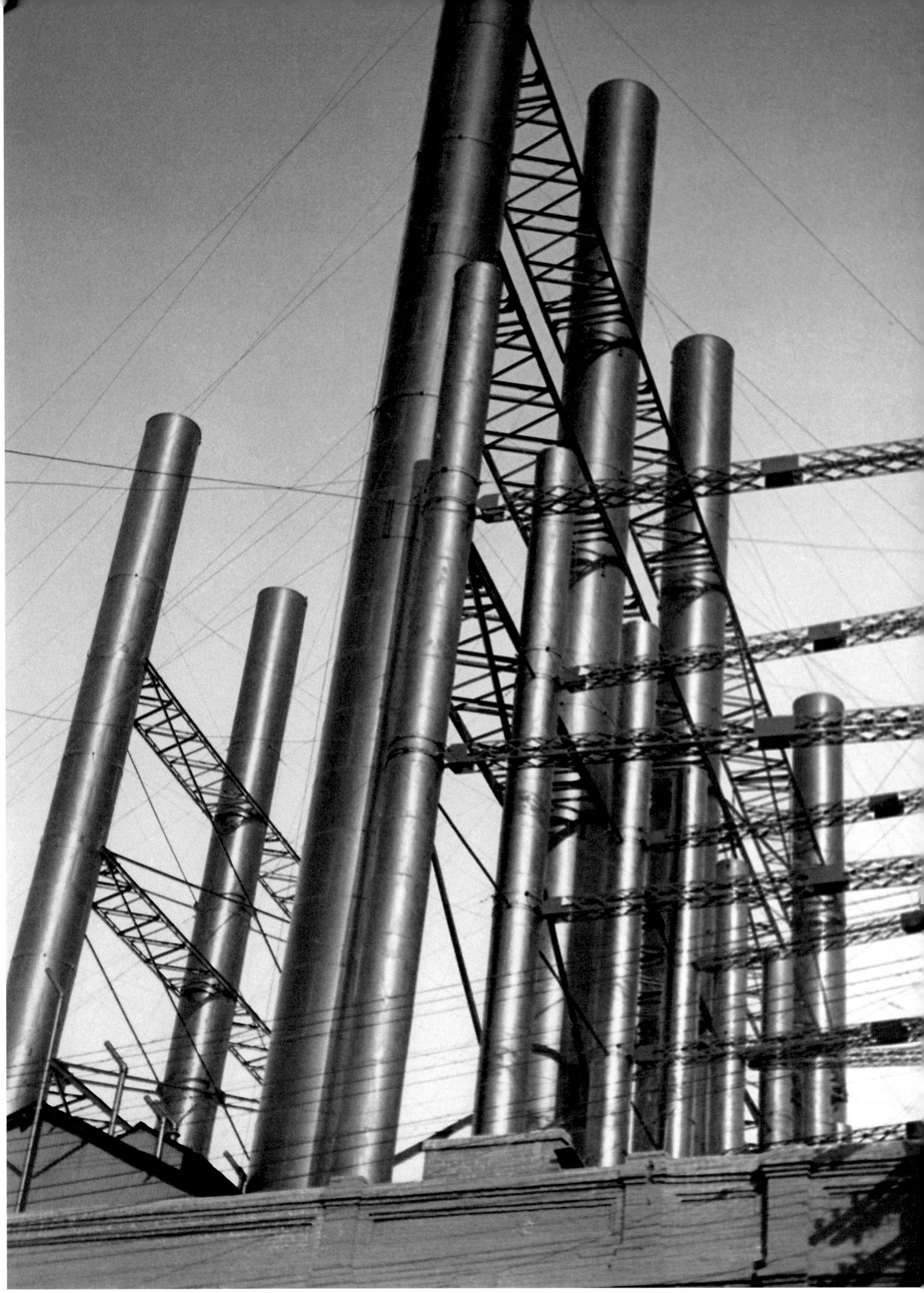

Smokestacks (Alameda Steam Generating Plant), Los Angeles, 1931

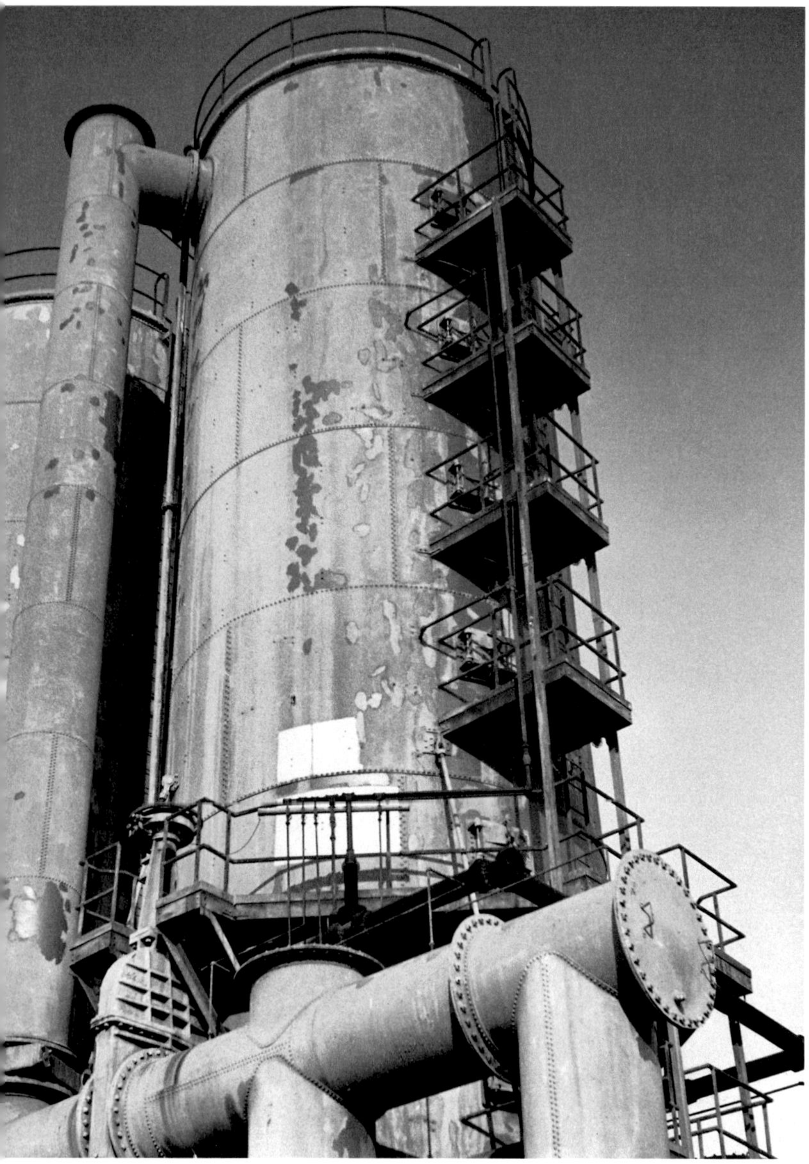

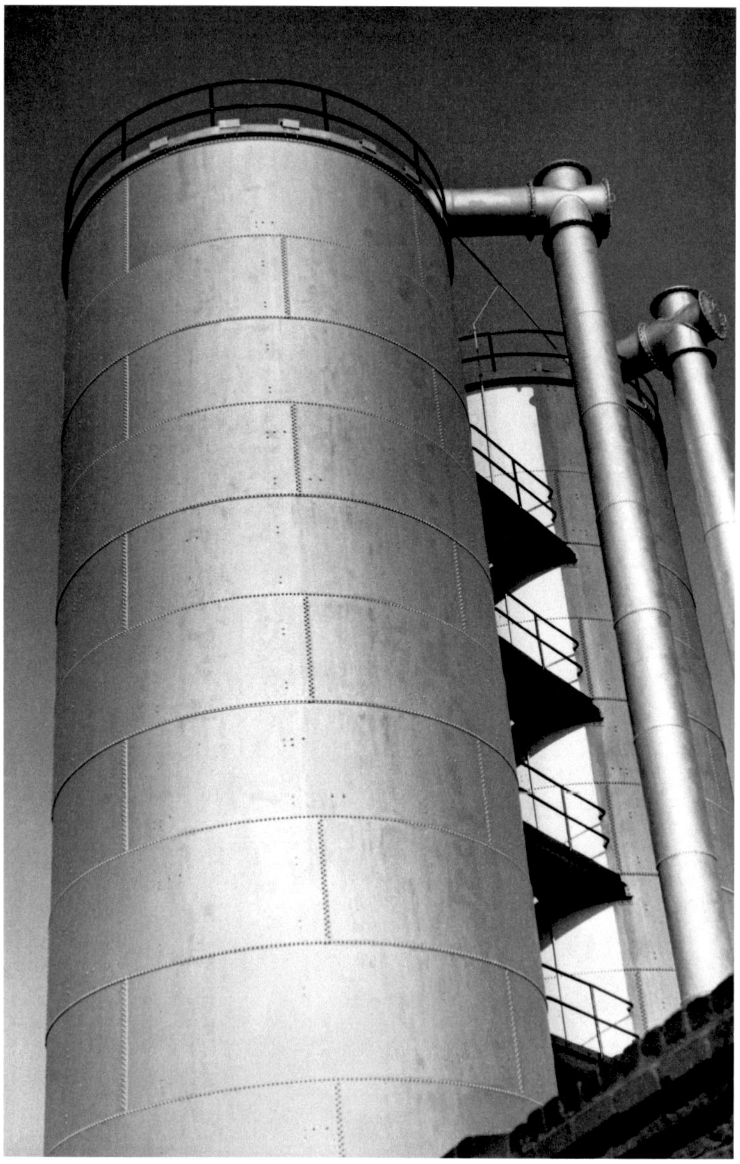

Public Works, Los Angeles, 1931

Public Works, Los Angeles, 1931

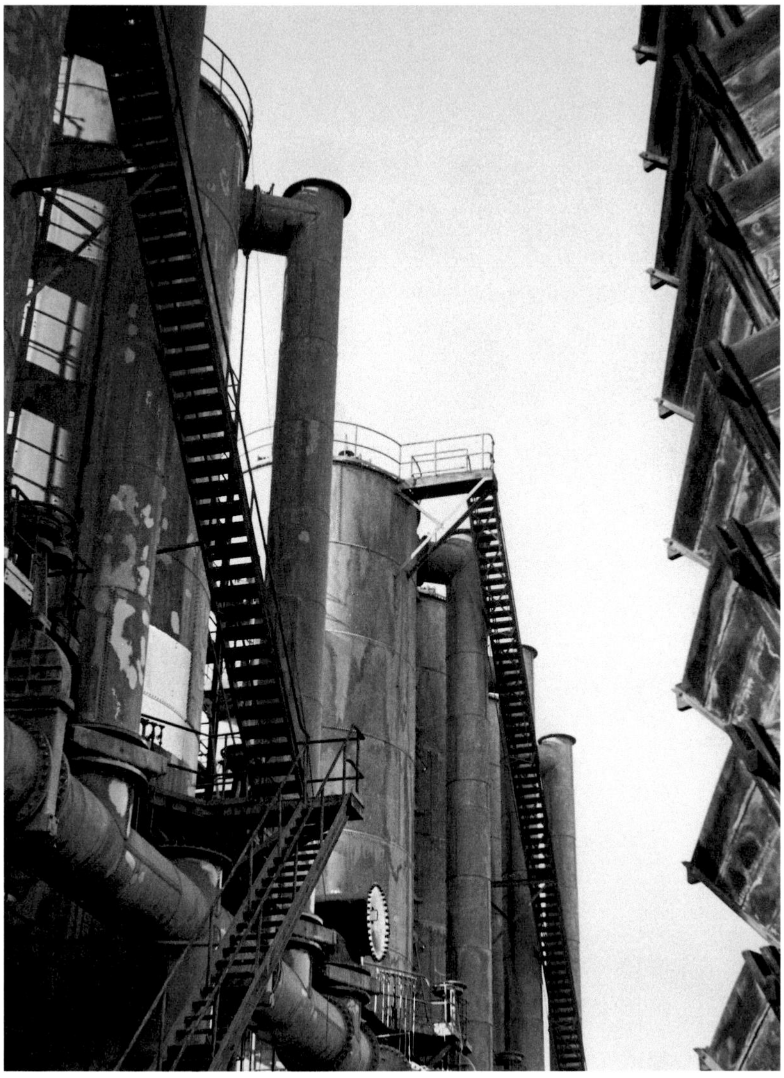

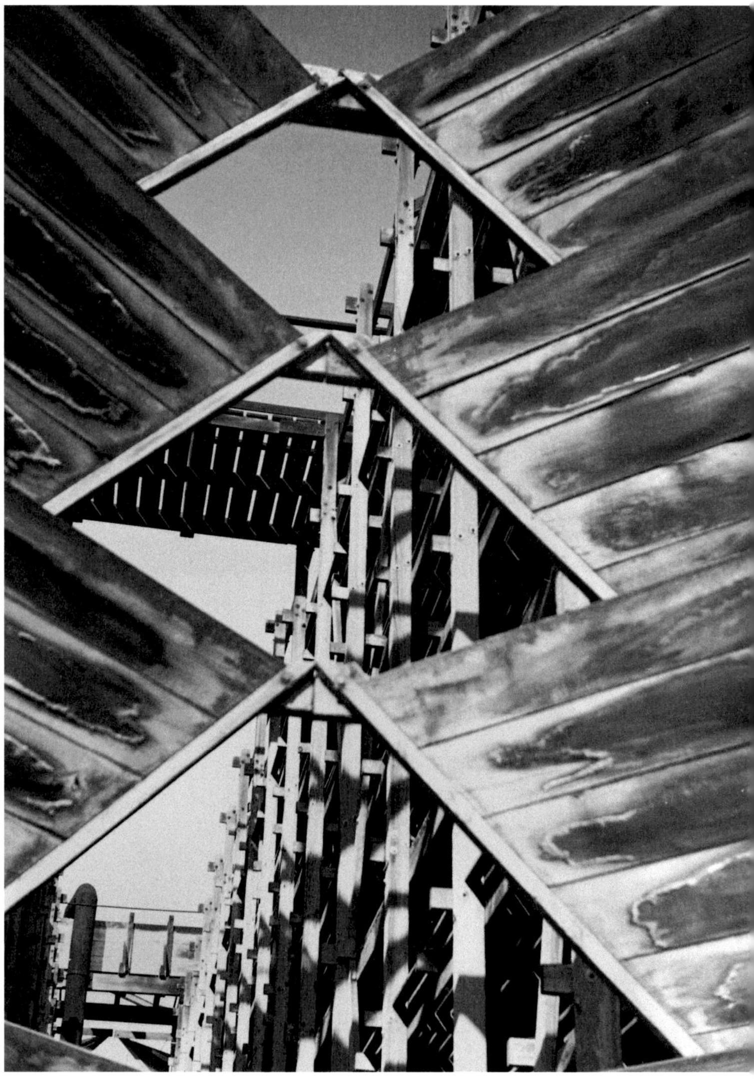

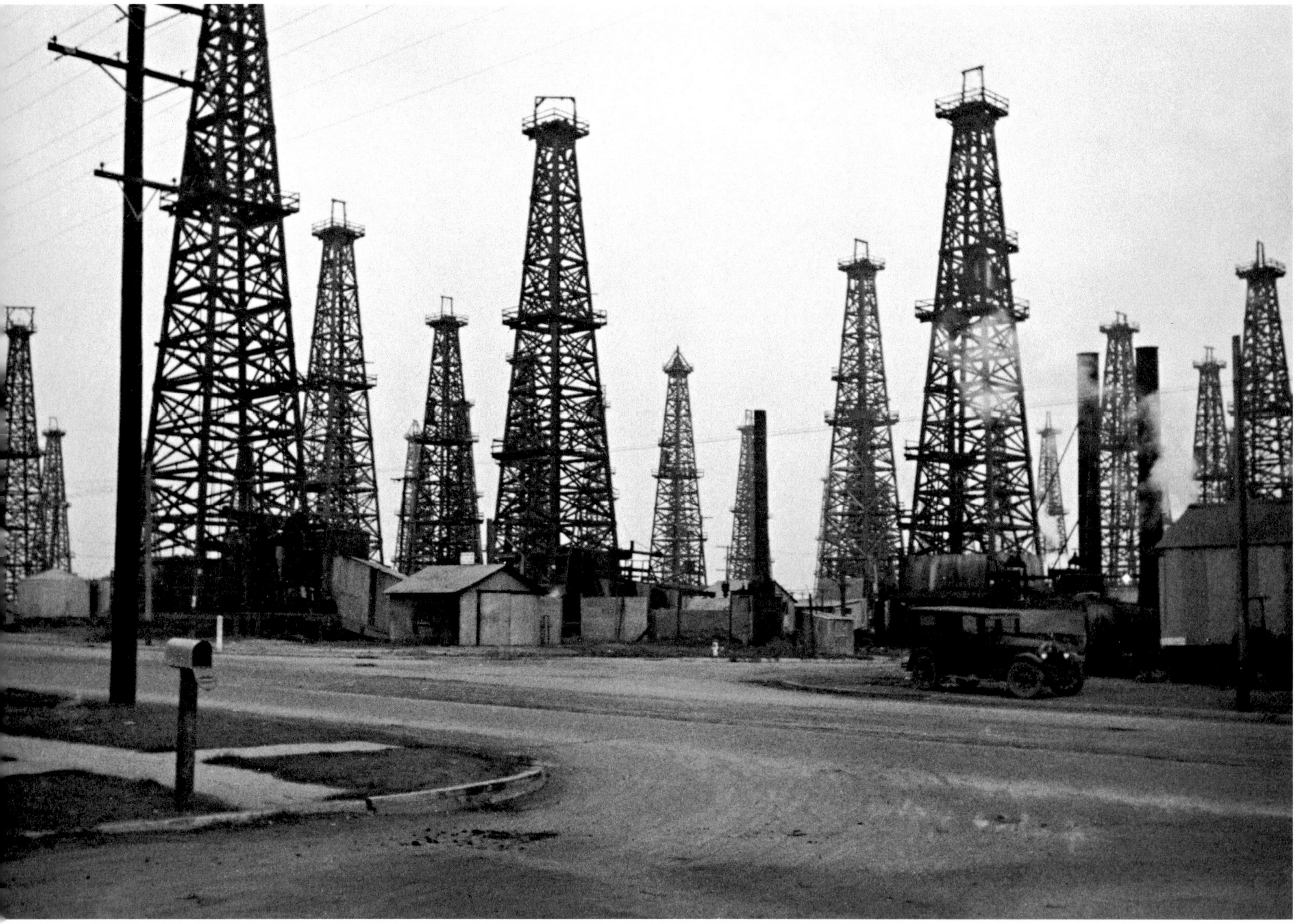

Oil Towers on Signal Hill at Long Beach, 1931

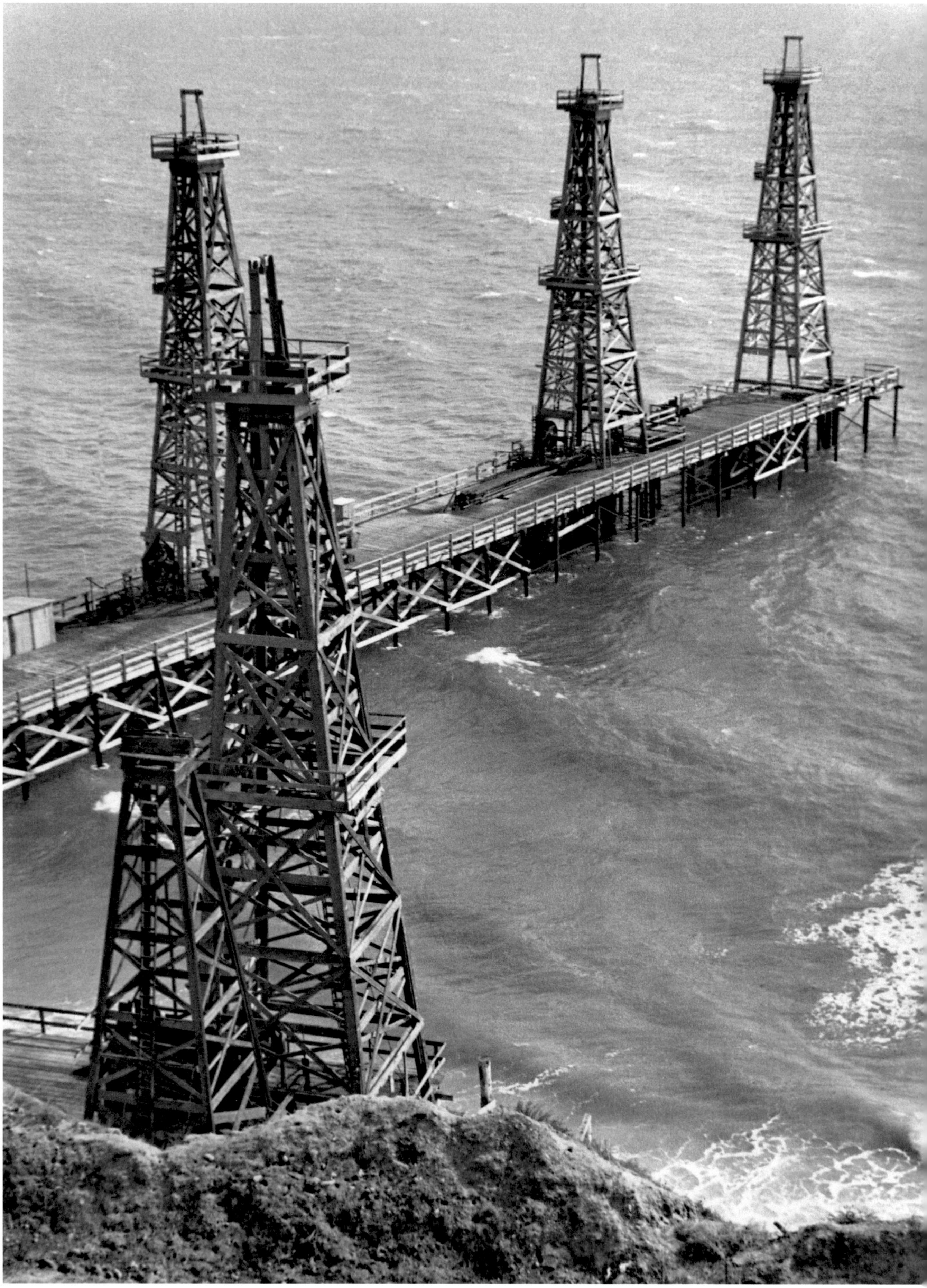

Oil Towers on the Coast at Santa Barbara, 1931

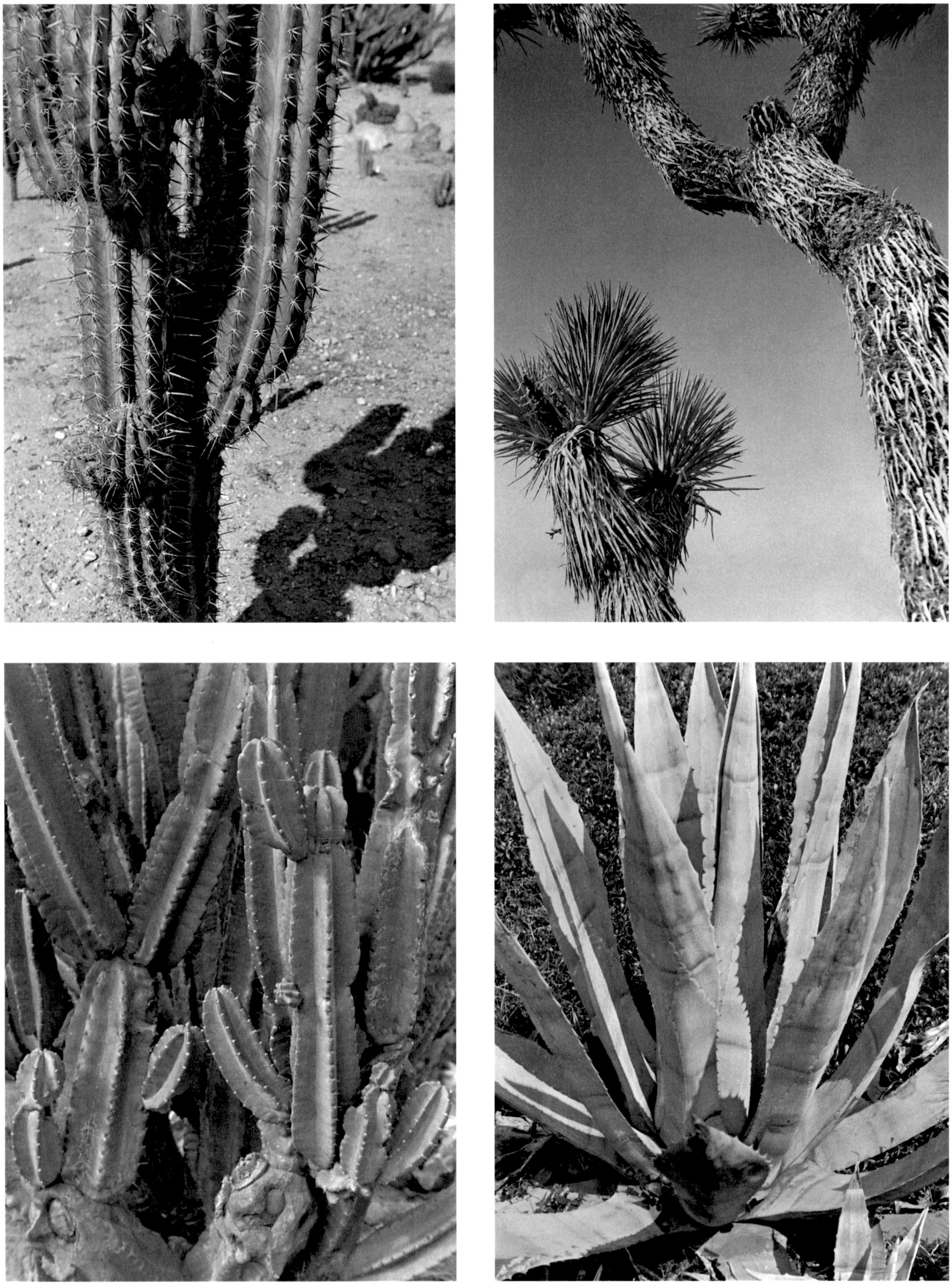

California plants in the Huntington Botanical Gardens, Los Angeles, 1931

Palm Canyon at
Palm Springs, 1931

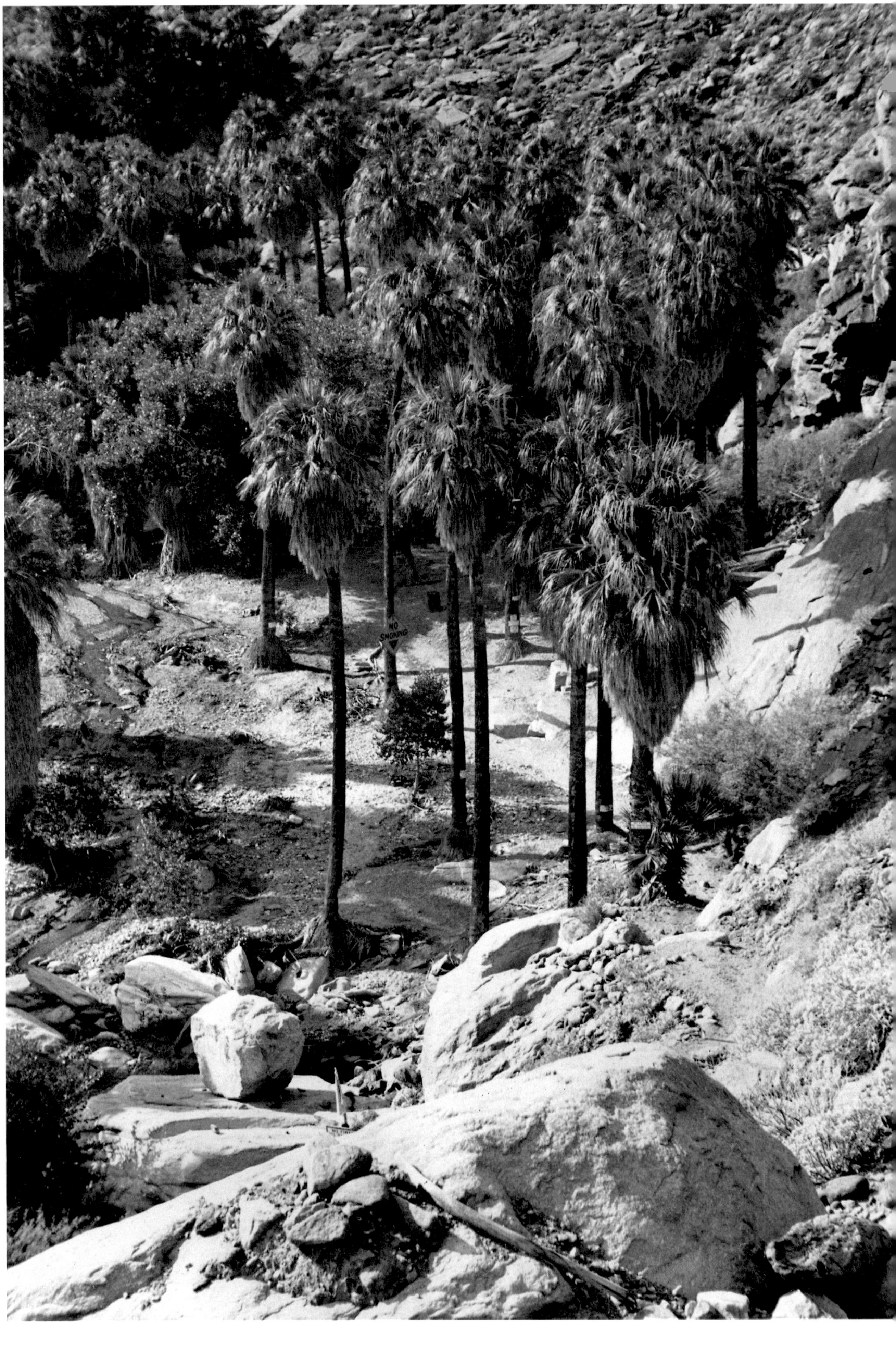

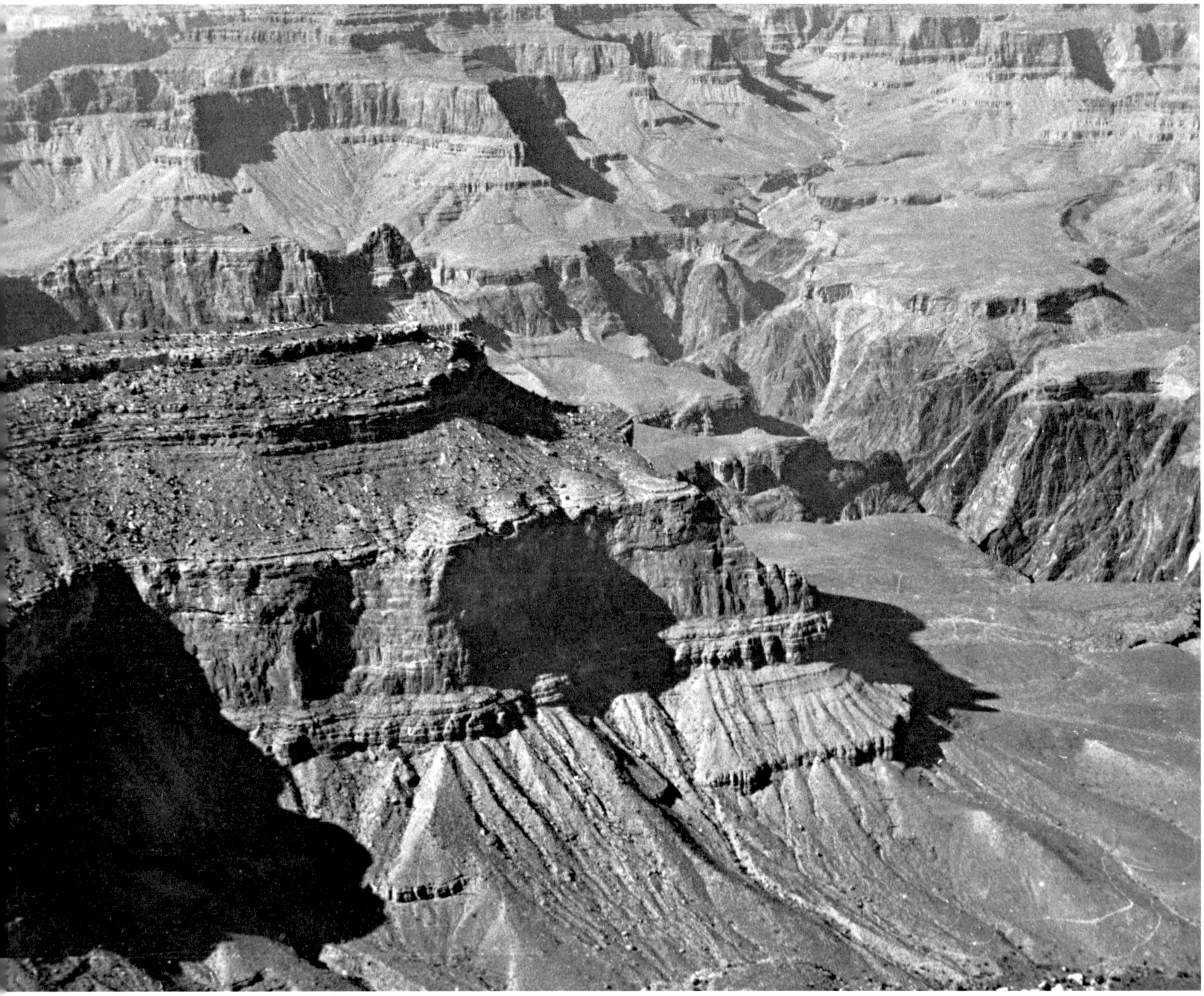

Grand Canyon, Arizona, 1931

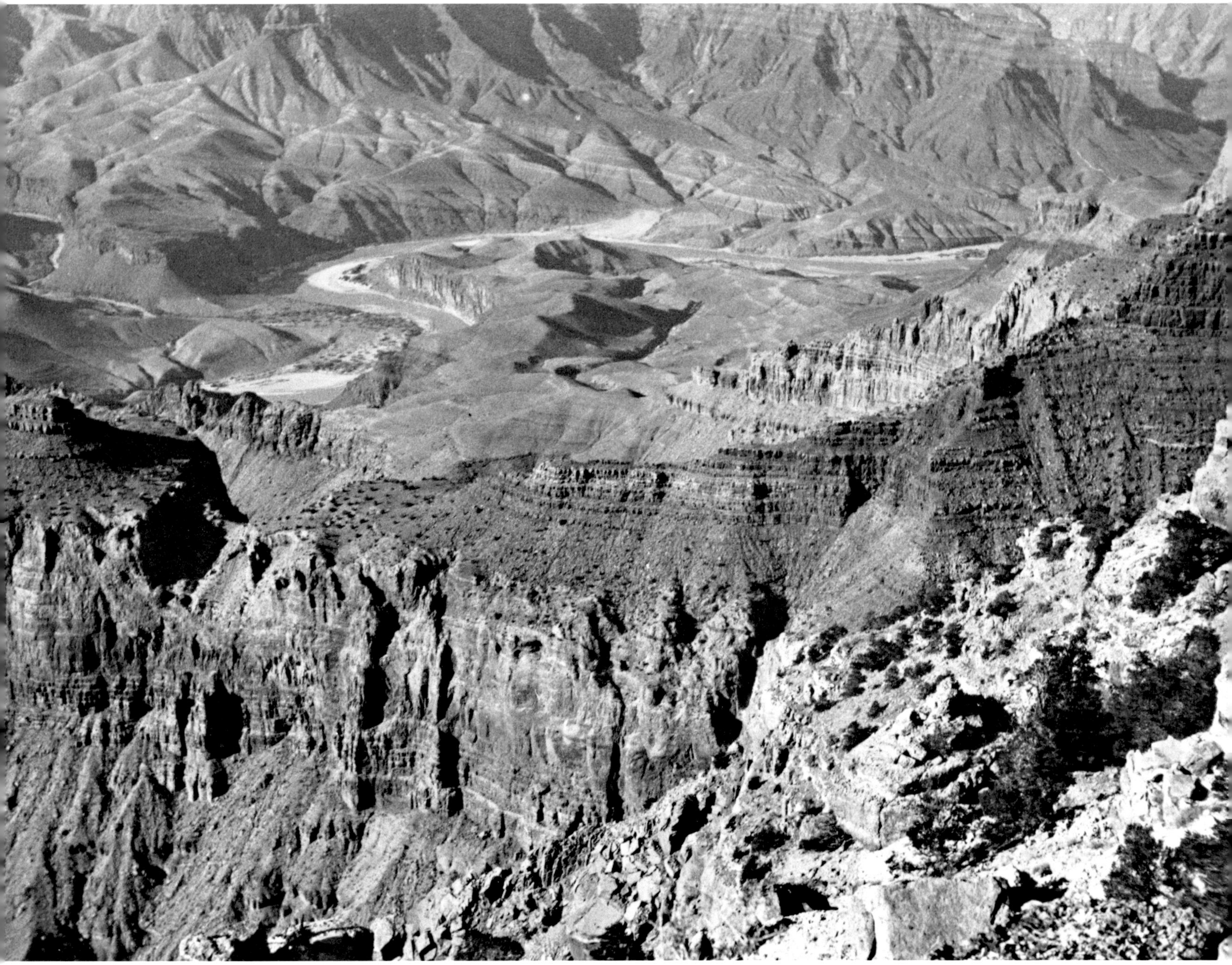

Grand Canyon with Colorado River, Arizona, 1931

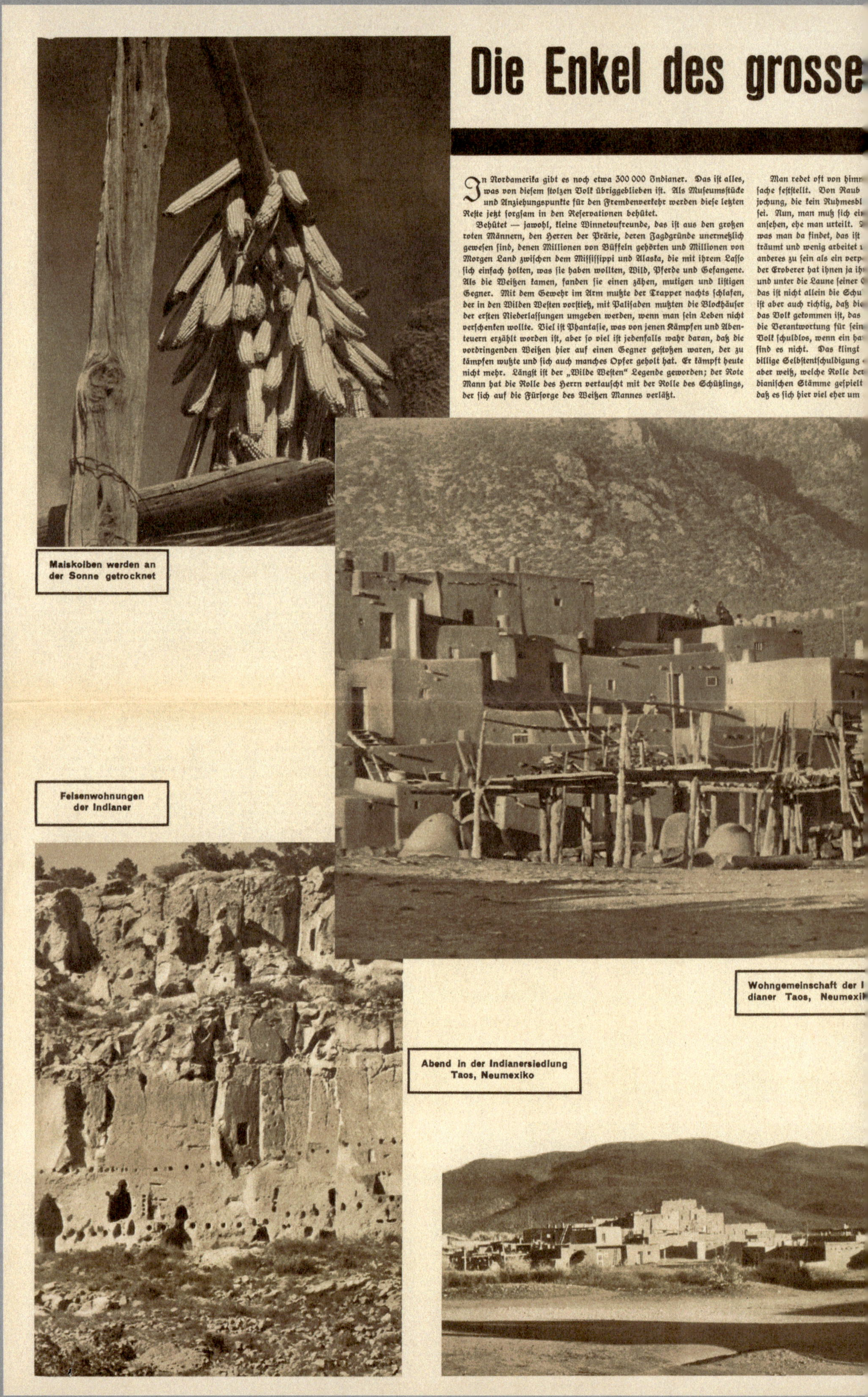

Die Enkel des grosse

In Nordamerika gibt es noch etwa 300 000 Indianer. Das ist alles, was von diesem stolzen Volk übriggeblieben ist. Als Museumsstücke und Anziehungspunkte für den Fremdenverkehr werden diese letzten Reste jetzt sorgsam in den Reservationen behütet.

Behütet — jawohl, kleine Winnetoufreunde, das ist aus den großen roten Männern, den Herren der Prärie, deren Jagdgründe unermeßlich gewesen sind, denen Millionen von Büffeln gehörten und Millionen von Morgen Land zwischen dem Mississippi und Alaska, die mit ihrem Lasso sich einfach holten, was sie haben wollten, Wild, Pferde und Gefangene. Als die Weißen kamen, fanden sie einen zähen, mutigen und listigen Gegner. Mit dem Gewehr im Arm mußte der Trapper nachts schlafen, der in den Wilden Westen vorstieß, mit Palisaden mußten die Blockhäuser der ersten Niederlassungen umgeben werden, wenn man sein Leben nicht verschenken wollte. Viel ist Phantasie, was von jenen Kämpfen und Abenteuern erzählt worden ist, aber so viel ist jedenfalls wahr daran, daß die vordringenden Weißen hier auf einen Gegner gestoßen waren, der zu kämpfen wußte und sich auch manches Opfer geholt hat. Er kämpft heute nicht mehr. Längst ist der „Wilde Westen" Legende geworden; der Rote Mann hat die Rolle des Herrn vertauscht mit der Rolle des Schützlings, der sich auf die Fürsorge des Weißen Mannes verläßt.

Man redet oft von himm
sache feststellt. Von Raub
jochung, die kein Ruhmesbl
sei. Nun, man muß sich ei
ansehen, ehe man urteilt.
was man da findet, das ist
träumt und wenig arbeitet
anderes zu sein als ein verp
der Eroberer hat ihnen ja ih
und unter die Laune seiner
das ist nicht allein die Schu
ist aber auch richtig, daß di
das Volk gekommen ist, das
die Verantwortung für sein
Volk schuldlos, wenn ein ha
sind es nicht. Das klingt
billige Selbstentschuldigung
aber weiß, welche Rolle der
dianischen Stämme gespielt
daß es sich hier viel eher um

Maiskolben werden an der Sonne getrocknet

Felsenwohnungen der Indianer

Wohngemeinschaft der I
dianer Taos, Neumexik

Abend in der Indianersiedlung Taos, Neumexiko

"Grandchildren of Big Winnetou" (*Hamburger Anzeiger. Illustrierte Wochenbeilage*, no. 21, 1933)

innetou

Indianerin, von der Feldarbeit heimkehrend

t, wenn man diese Tat-
terdrückung und Unter-
der weißen Zivilisation
von heute aus der Nähe
s anders denken. Denn
te Rasse, die trinkt und
den Ehrgeiz hat, etwas
emdenindustrie. Gewiß,
ommen, sie unterworfen
agenschaft erschlafft, und
Das ist alles richtig. Es
ht als ein Schicksal über
iemals wird einem Volk
en; niemals ist also ein
hat. Auch die Indianer
ophiererei oder wie die
ißen Rasse. Wenn man
Niederwerfung der in-
schon zugeben müssen,
um eine Niederwerfung

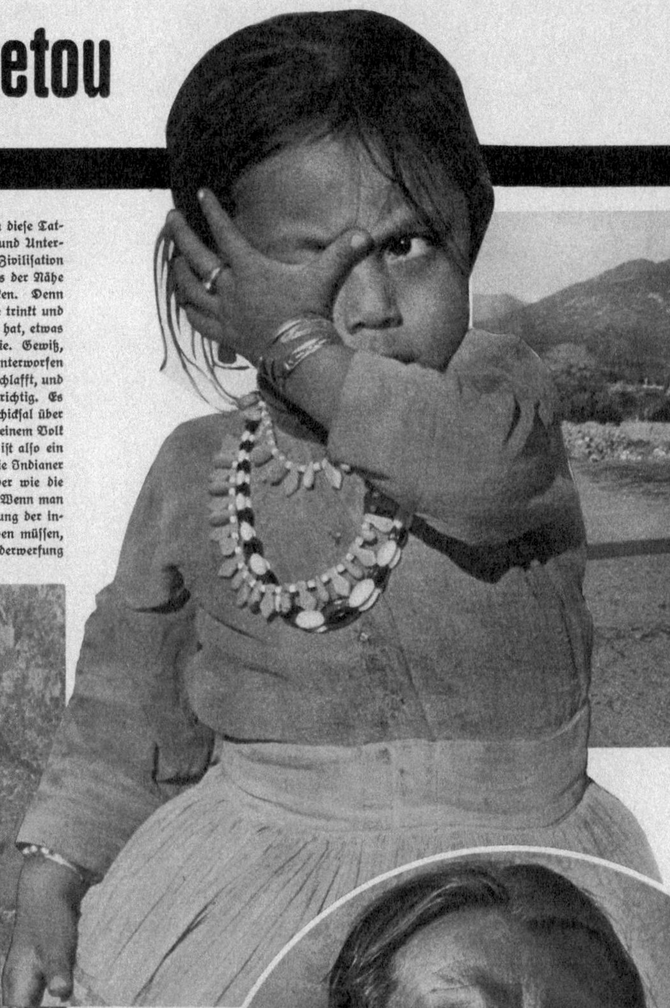

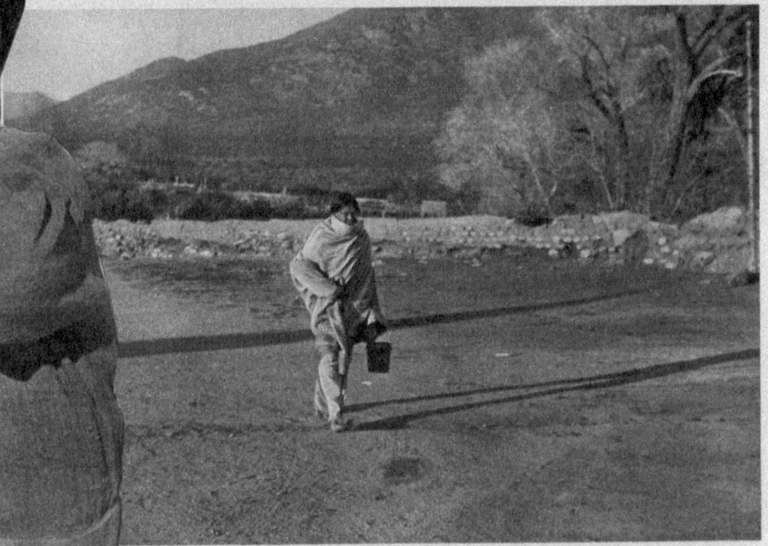

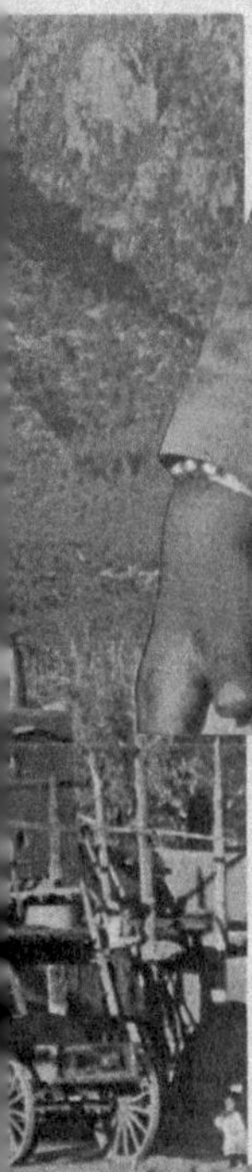

handelt. Die großen roten Männer sind eben einer betäubenden Versuchung unterlegen. Und ihre Gefangenschaft ist eine Folge ihrer Schlappheit, nicht umgekehrt ist die Schlappheit eine Folge der Gefangenschaft...

Jetzt leben die Rothäute also fast ausschließlich in den von der Regierung zur Verfügung gestellten Bezirken, zum Teil noch als Nomaden, die meisten sind aber seßhaft. Faul und wenig zu ständiger Arbeit geeignet, leben sie von Zuwendungen des Staates. Ackerbau und Viehzucht werden in primitiver, kümmerlicher Form betrieben. Hier und da haben Petroleumfunde auf dem Grundbesitz einzelnen zu Wohlstand verholfen, im übrigen aber sorgt der Staat. Er tut es nicht schlecht. In den für die Indianer eingerichteten Schulen wird die Jugend für das praktische Leben und für den Erzieherberuf vorbereitet, so daß den Stämmen sogar eigene Lehrer zur Verfügung stehen. Die Indianer sind Christen aller Konfessionen und Sekten, doch behalten sie in ihrer Unbekümmertheit durchweg ihre alten religiösen Vorstellungen, insbesondere ihre Feste und Tänze nebenher bei. Gerade in diesen Festen und Tänzen haben sie viel Ursprüngliches in die heutige Zeit hinübergerettet.

Die Aufnahmen sind aus den Dörfern der Puebloindianer in Neumexiko, vereinzelt auch aus Arizona. Die Alten mit den herrlich durchgearbeiteten Köpfen (auch der Mann trägt Zöpfe) bieten dankbare Bilder.

Wo diese Indianerreservationen in der Nähe großer Eisenbahnlinien liegen oder durch das Auto einigermaßen bequem zu erreichen sind, hat sich die Fremdenindustrie ihrer bemächtigt. Sie kommt der naiven Sucht des Amerikaners nach Reiseromantik nach Kräften entgegen. Da müssen diese letzten Reste eines stolzen Volkes täglich zu bestimmten Stunden neugierigen Reisenden religiöse Gebräuche und Tänze vorführen...

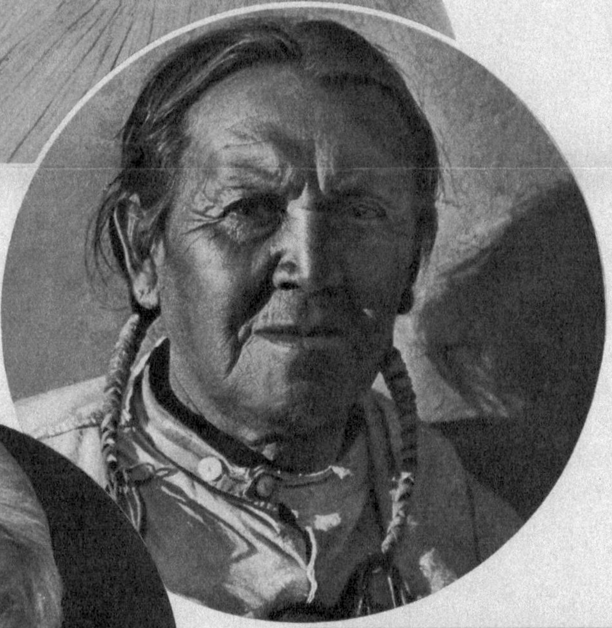

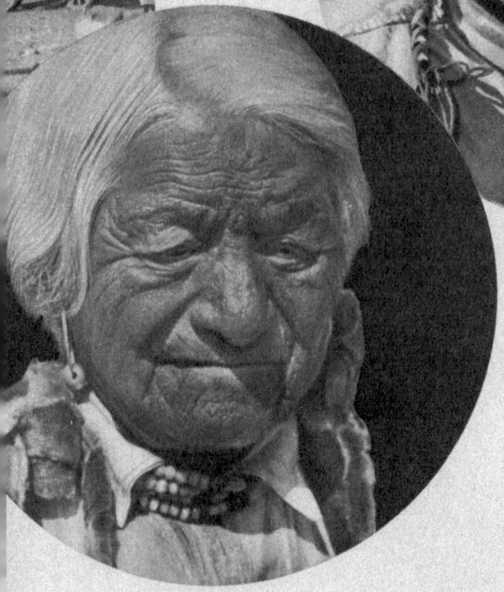

In den Kreisen :
Indianer-Squaws

Indianertanz
(Eingeborenenzeichnung)

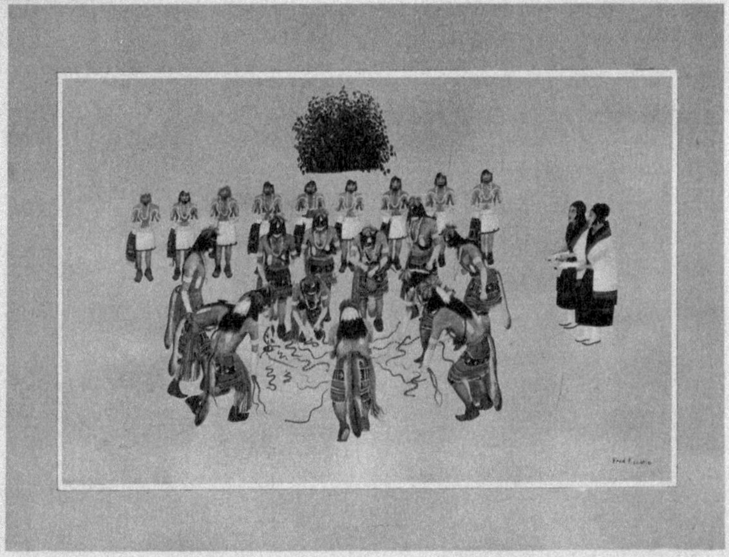

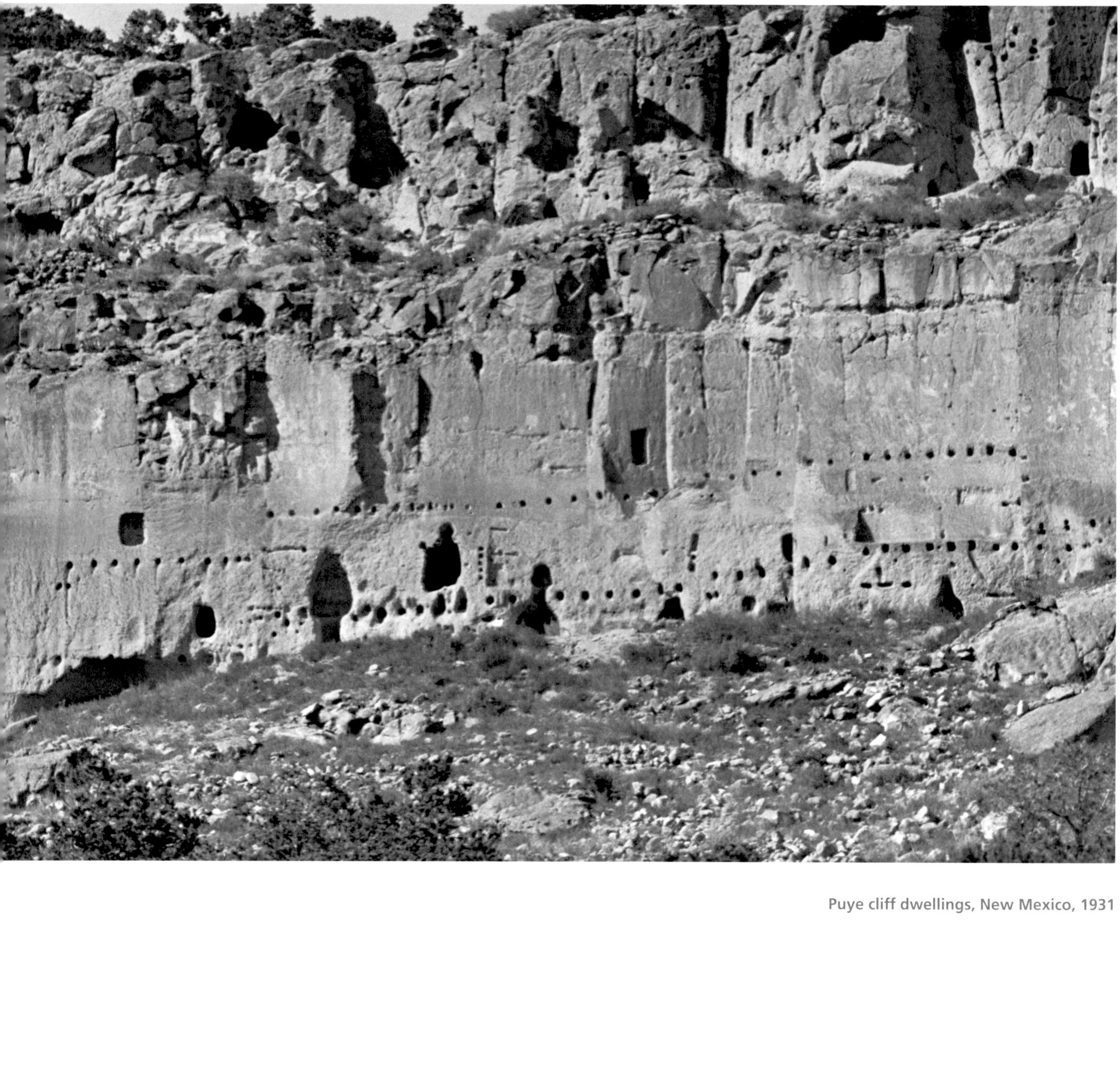

Puye cliff dwellings, New Mexico, 1931

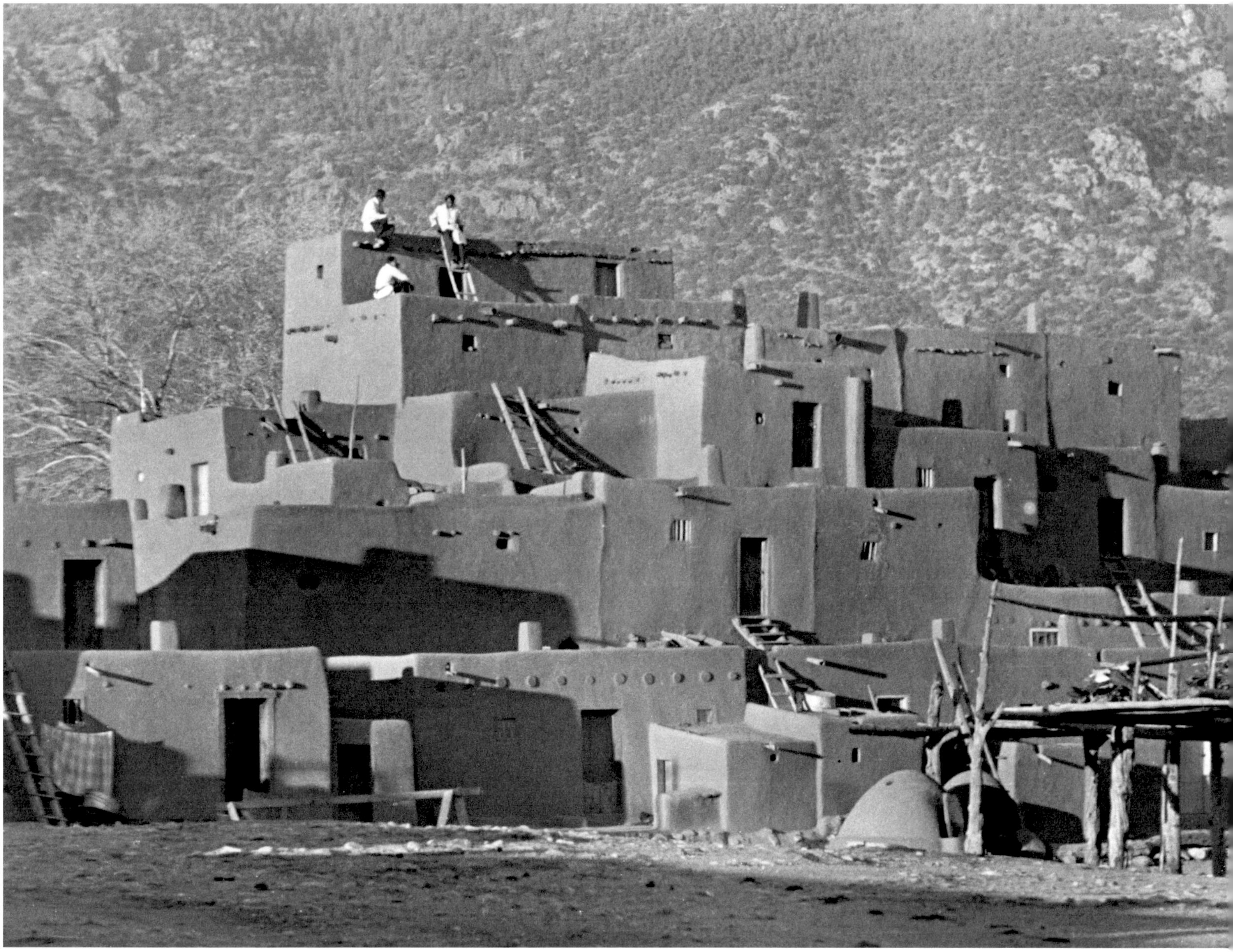

Native American dwellings in Taos Pueblo, New Mexico, 1931

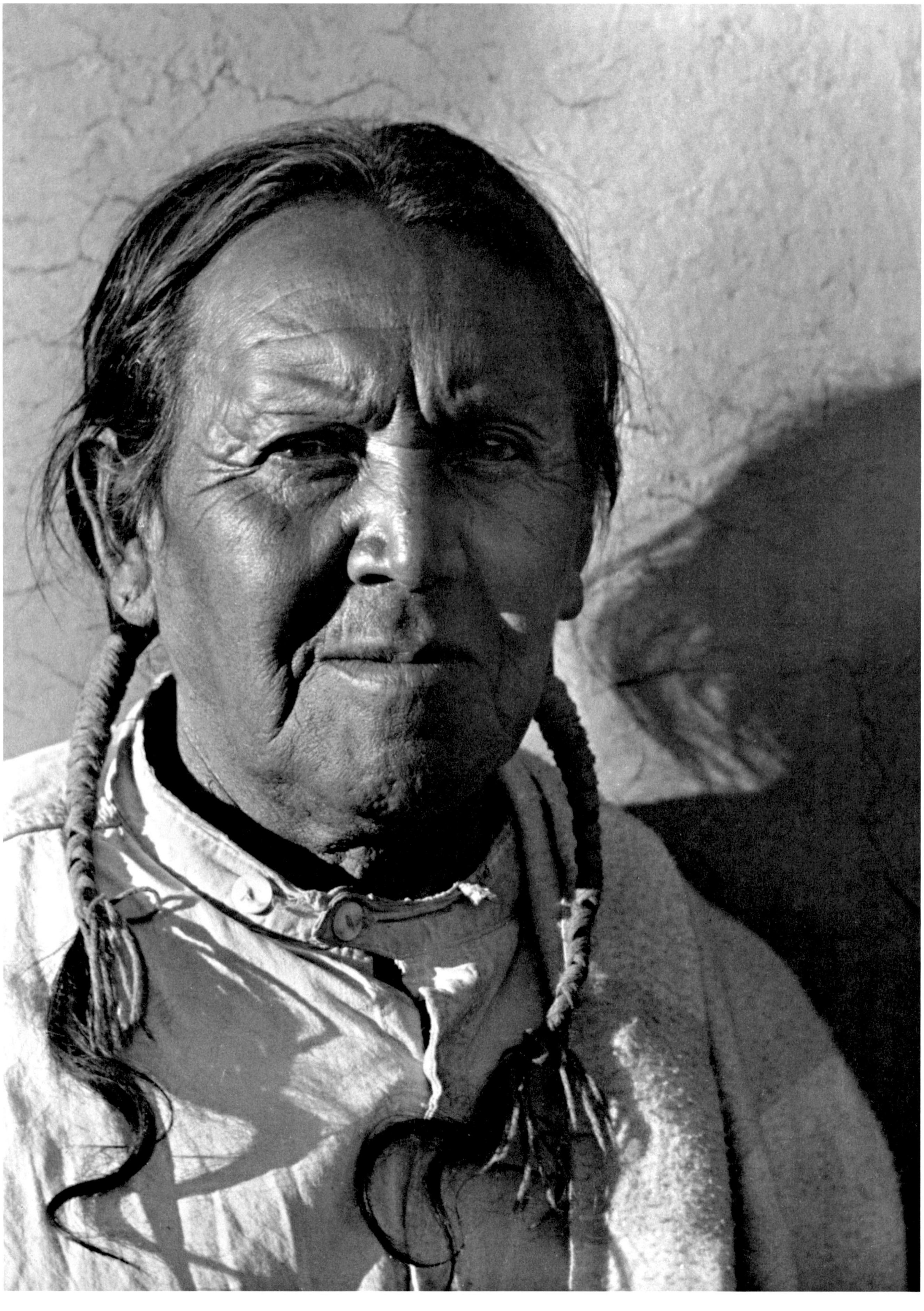

Old Native American in Taos Pueblo, New Mexico, 1931

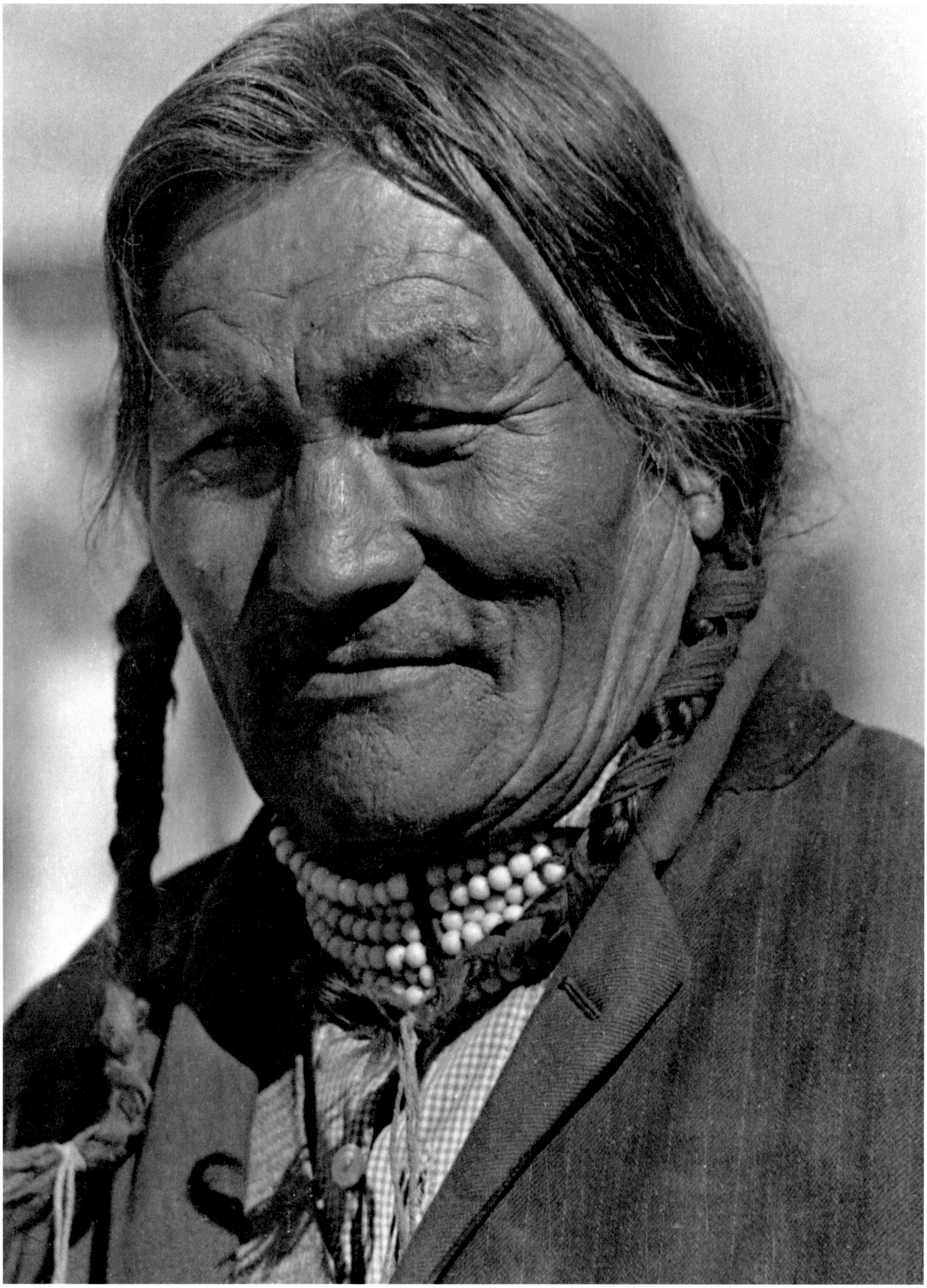

Old Native American in Taos Pueblo, New Mexico, 1931

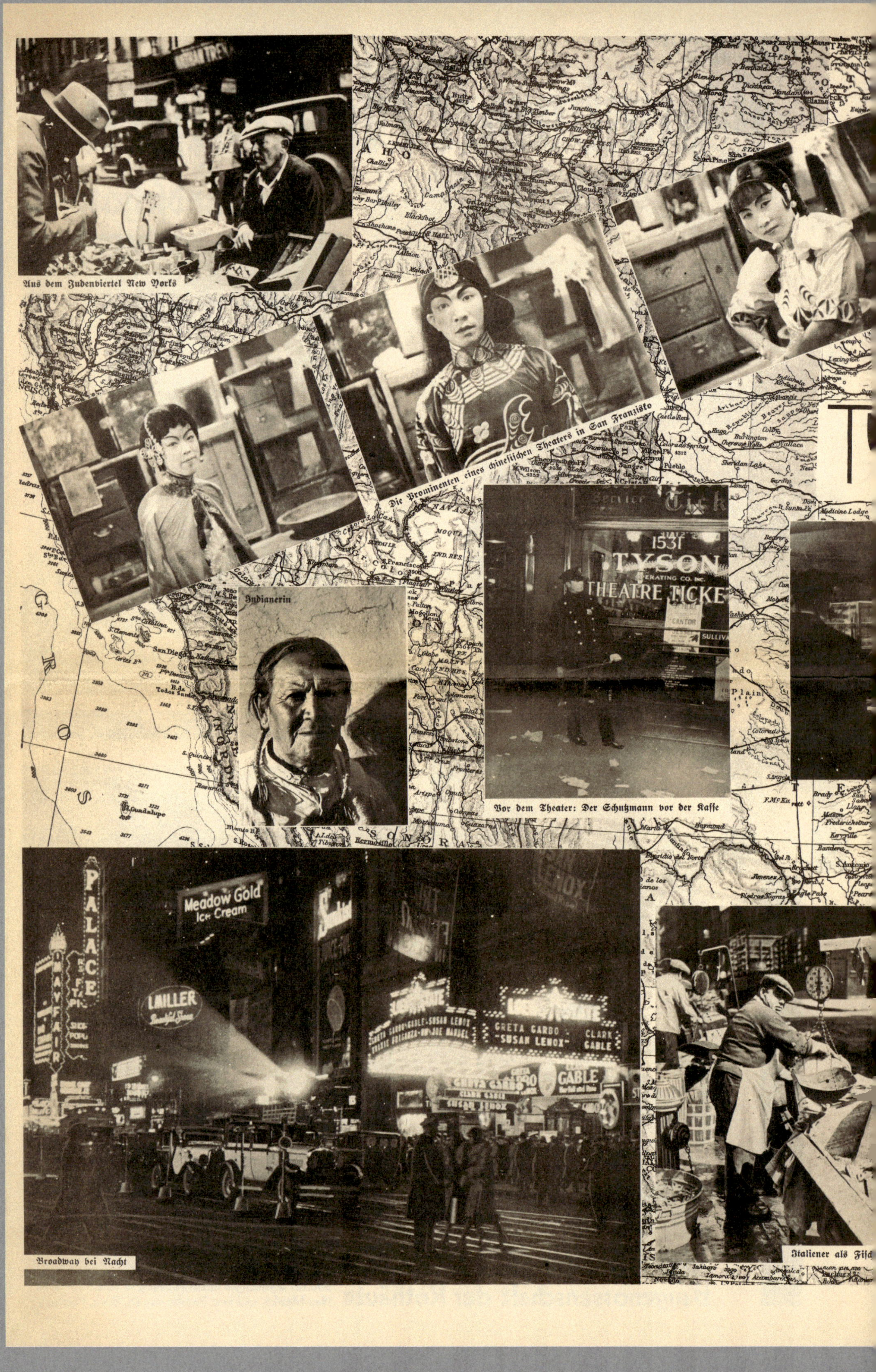

"Types of People in the US" (*Hamburger Nachrichten. Bilderrundschau*, no. 16, 1932)

…EN in U.S.A.

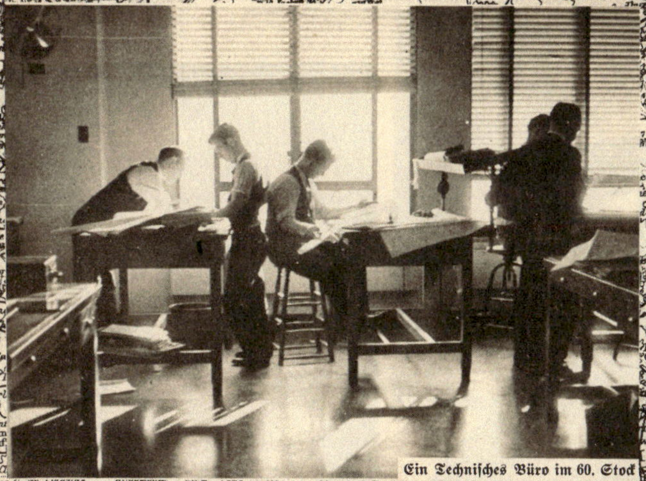

Ein Technisches Büro im 60. Stock

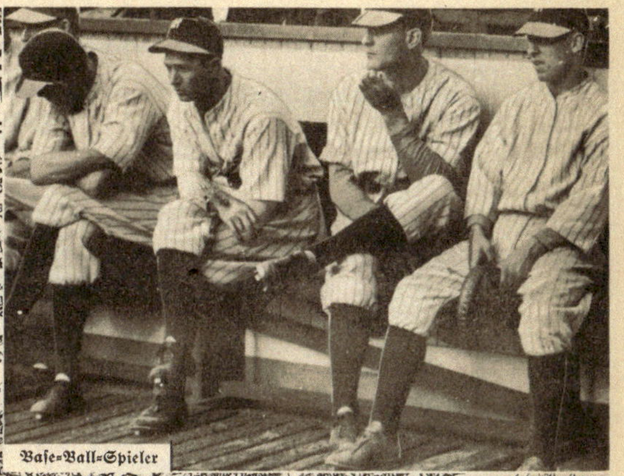

Base-Ball-Spieler

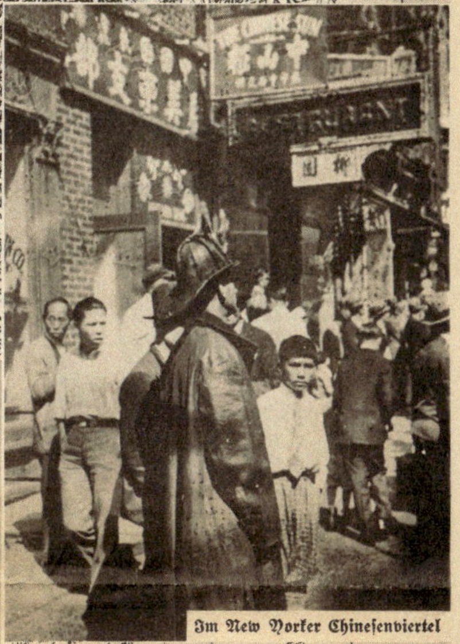

Im New Yorker Chinesenviertel

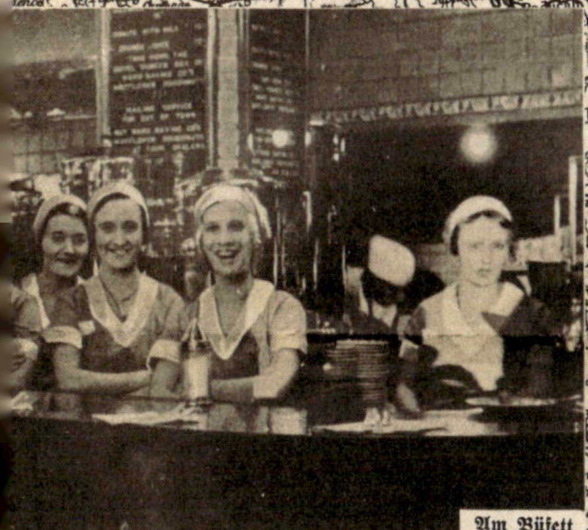

Am Büfett

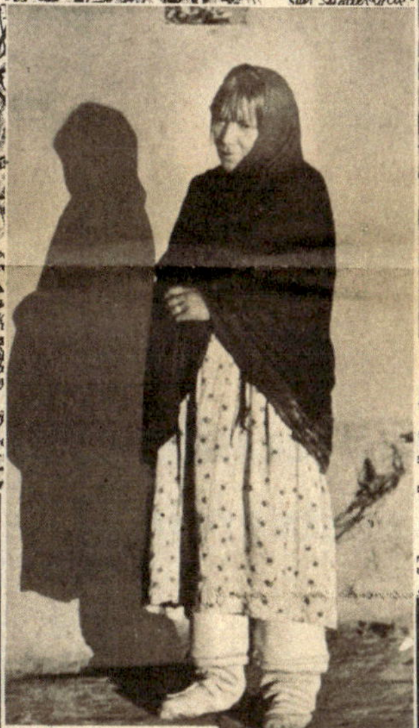

Indianerin von Taos

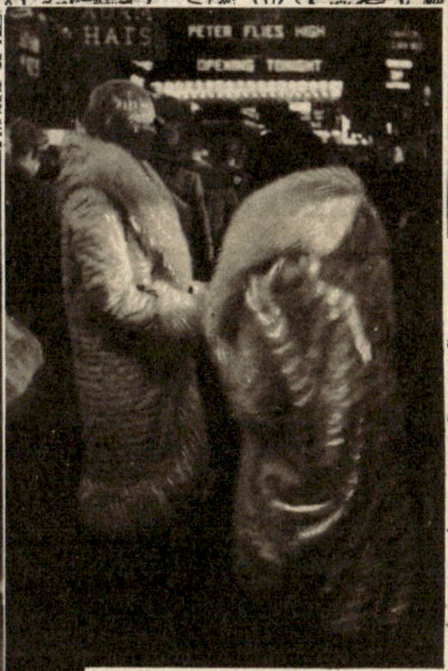

Vor dem Theater: Zierden der Loge

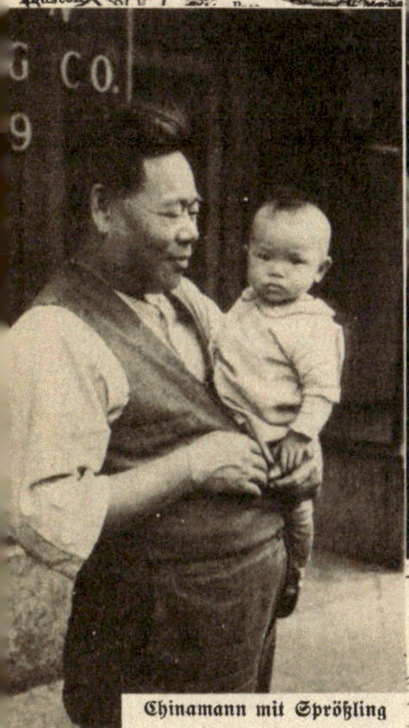

Chinamann mit Sprößling

(Aufnahmen von Dr. Block, Hamburg)

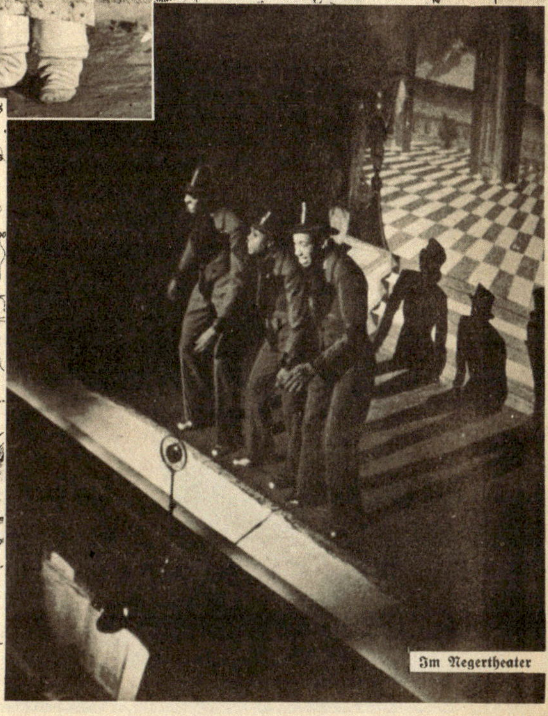

Im Negertheater

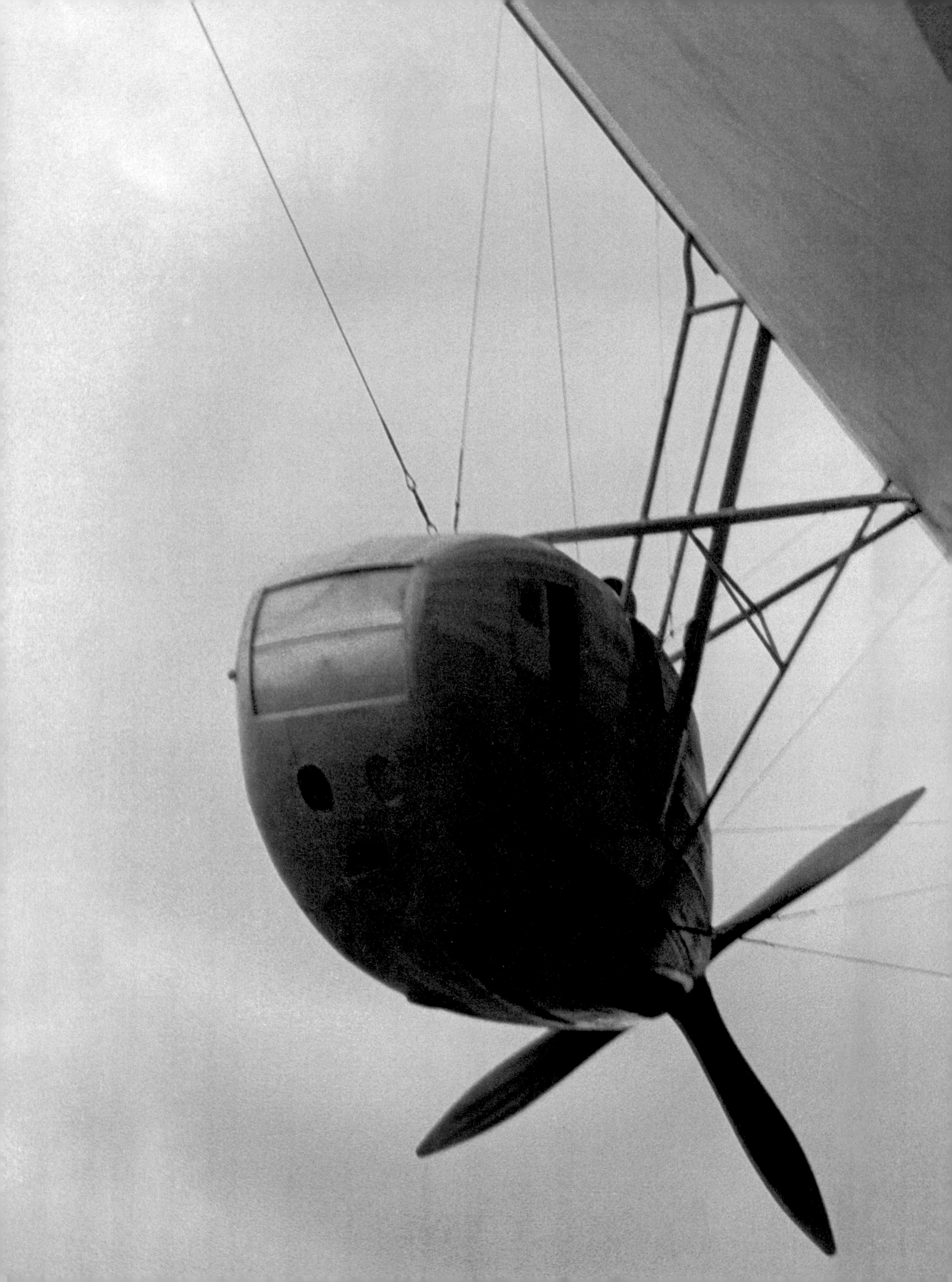

A Zeppelin Flight and a World Cruise

Travel Impressions from the 1930s

In the further course of the 1930s, Fritz Block devoted himself entirely to travel photography. As his interest in the subjects of technology and the big city receded—a trend typical of the time—he focused increasingly on people, cultural monuments, and landscapes. Nevertheless, the principles of New Photography continued in his work, but since Block's images are so strongly determined by his respective travel destinations, it's difficult to make generalizing statements; the images rather give the impression of being comprised of a wide range of photographic subjects. It is worth noting, however, that from the middle of 1933, Block no longer photographed in Germany, but only on his trips abroad. As a Jew, he could no longer publish his photographs in the German press.

Austria and Hungary

In the fall of 1932, Block and his wife, Anna-Sophie, went on a trip through Austria and Hungary, with city stops in Vienna, Salzburg, and Budapest. Only a few photos of Salzburg are preserved; no photos of Vienna survived. Records in Block's estate, however, evidence that he gathered photographic material of these locations for photo reportages. The accompanying text to Vienna suggests that there were views from St. Stephen's Cathedral onto the city, but also more atmospheric motifs, such as Heuriger wine taverns, city strolls, visits to cafe houses, and Fiacer horse-drawn carriages. The basic message of the images was that the city had more of a traditional than modern character: "Up and down its main avenues, which display a metropolitan character, Vienna has nevertheless retained a light spirit of a previous century's operetta."[1]

In the "festival city" of Salzburg, Block seems not to have found very inspiring subjects. Naturally, he took shots of the usual views of the city: up to Salzburg Castle and down from Mönchsberg plateau, as well as churches and Baroque buildings—all of the images rather conventional [p. 264]. His photographic sensibility is better evidenced in the close-up, worm's-eye-view photographs of sculptural details in the Mirabell Palace Gardens or city fountains. [p. 265]. Texts for the Vienna and Salzburg photo reportages were written by Block's wife, but not until early summer 1933, when it became clear that Block would no longer be able to publish in the German press. Accordingly, no printed documents have been found.

More productive photographically for Block was his stay in Budapest. In two photo reportages, he exemplarily captured the social and economic differences of the Hungarian capital. First, in pictures made at the legendary Gellért Thermal Bath, which since 1927 had featured an outdoor swimming area with a wave pool. During the worldwide economic depression, the location was known as a meeting place for privileged clientele, and as a catwalk for beauties and the fashion-conscious. The scenes Block observed confirm the impression of a sophisticated spa culture [pp. 267–269]. Via the Parisian photo agency Nord-Sud, one of his photos made it onto the August 1933 cover of the French photo magazine *Photomonde* [p. 266]. In deliberate contrast stands Block's reportage of the fruit and vegetable market on the banks of the Danube. His photographs show peasant women, young and old, mostly of German descent, in traditional costume [p. 260].[2] The photos convey respect and empathy for the women's modesty and appearance.

Publication Ban

When the National Socialists assumed power, at the end of January 1933, living conditions for Jews in Germany began to worsen incrementally. As totalitarian control descended upon the German press, Block lost the opportunity to publish his photos there. In August 1933, he was listed in the extreme right-wing, anti-Semitic newspaper *Deutsche Nachrichten* among the "Jews and foreigners" no longer to be employed by German newspapers and magazines, alongside Martin Munkácsi, Alfred Eisenstaedt, and others.[3]

Block's photos were still used up until 1936, however—albeit in rare cases—owing either to editorial negligence or

Engine nacelle of a Zeppelin airship, Friedrichshafen, Germany, 1933

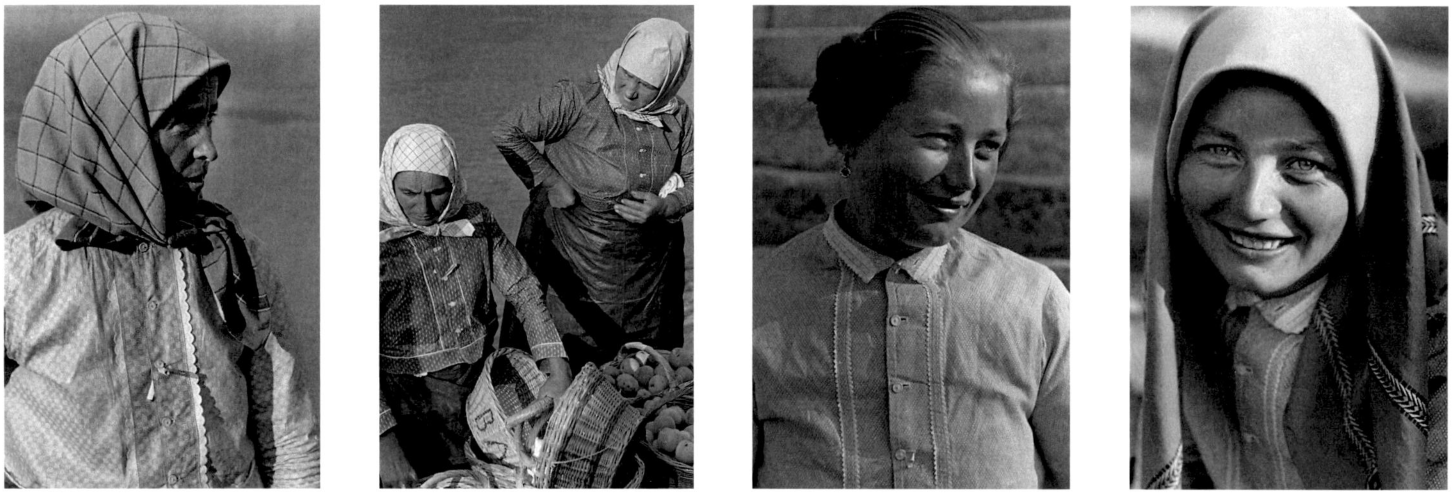

Old and young country women at the farmers market on the banks of the Danube, Budapest, Hungary, 1932

to their transmission via photo agencies. Such was the case with Block's striking underside shot of the turbine steamship *Europa,* in the floating dock of the Hamburg shipyard Blohm & Voss [p. 1]. It was reprinted, as a symbol of German industrial pride, in the National Socialist propaganda books *Deutschland zwischen Nacht und Tag* (Germany between Night and Day, 1934), by Friedrich Heiss, and *Deutsches Schaffen – Deutsches Land* (German Production – German Nation, 1934), by Hans Thierbach—both courtesy of "Dr. Block (Mauritius)." Since neither negative nor print of this shot has been preserved, these instances are also the only proof of its existence. Block partially reclaimed and then received his prints back from photo agencies. In his estate are numerous photos with stamps, stickers, and notes of agencies on the backs of them.

Block was affected by the political changes in Germany, particularly in his primary profession as an architect. The firm Dr. Block & Hochfeld was no longer able to work as self-employed architects for new buildings in Hamburg. Their activities were limited to renovating and subdividing apartments, mostly those belonging to Jewish owners.[4] In October 1933, Fritz Block and Ernst Hochfeld were themselves expelled, for being Jewish, from the Bund Deutscher Architekten (Association of German Architects), for whom Block had volunteered for many years. In November, they were also excluded from the Deutscher Werkbund (German Association of Craftsmen).

Zeppelin Flight to Brazil

In order to distance themselves from the events transpiring in Germany, Block and his wife undertook a zeppelin journey in August and September 1933, which took them from Friedrichshafen, on Lake Constance, via Pernambuco (now Recife), to Rio de Janeiro, and then back to Seville, Spain. The occasion was to visit friends from Hamburg who had immigrated to Brazil for professional reasons. Zeppelin travel was considered the ultimate travel experience. Beginning in 1930 (up until 1937), there was regular airship transportation between Germany and Brazil. The airship *LZ 127 Graf Zeppelin* could carry up to 25 paying passengers. Journalists and photographers were often taken along, which subsequently provided advertising coverage.

The "zeppelin" topic was particularly felt in Hamburg, since the agency representing zeppelin trips to South America fell under the aegis of the Hamburg-America Line. In April 1932, for example, the *Hamburger Illustrierte* ran a report on a zeppelin flight from Friedrichshafen to Pernambuco.[5] A visit of the airship *LZ 127 Graf Zeppelin* to Hamburg in June 1932 also attracted attention. Overall, zeppelin flights were the subject of many articles in the illustrated press and in (photo) books, which Block would also have noticed.[6]

From a photographic point of view, a zeppelin trip was attractive in two ways: on the one hand, technical fascination with the airship itself and, on the other, a comfortable view from far above, in the passenger gondola. Here are joined two forms of the New Photography: technical imagery of New Objectivity, and aerial photography as a form of expression in the New Vision movement. Accordingly, Block also made detail shots of the airship before taking off from Friedrichshafen, in order to highlight its impressive dimensions and technical complexity [pp. 258 and 272–273]. Block apparently lacked an incentive to undertake a more intense study of the subject, however, since many high-quality corporate photos of the zeppelin airships already existed and were made available to travelers.

Block's wife kept a diary of their Brazil trip, illustrated with corporate photos but also with many of her husband's photographs.[7] She reports that, among other things, "8 Leicas were on board." The Blocks' traveling companions included photographer Alfred Eisenstaedt (1898–1995), with whom Block had an extensive exchange about photography. On this trip, Eisenstaedt made one of his most well known photos: two mechanics repairing the outside of the zeppelin in flight. The journalist and travel writer Arthur Rehbein was also on board. An account of his zeppelin flight appeared in the book *Über Schwellen und Wellen und Wolken* (Over Swells and Waves and Clouds, 1935), which includes a photo of him and the Block couple comfortably breakfasting in the gondola.[8] (Communication between the Blocks and Rehbein

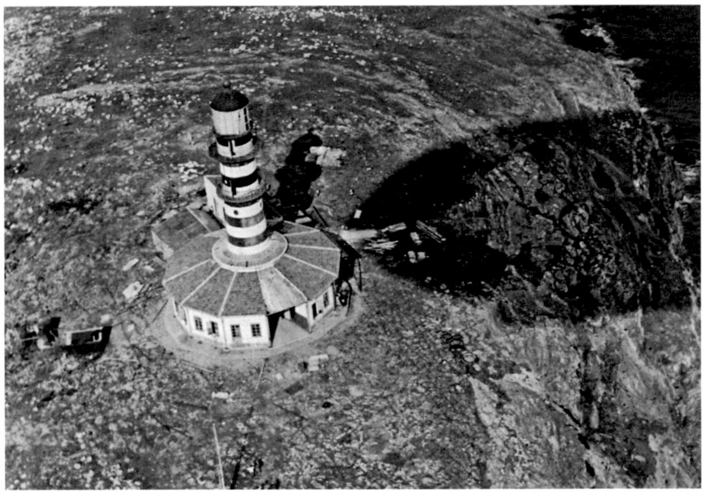

Zeppelin over the Abrolhos Lighthouse, Brazil, 1933

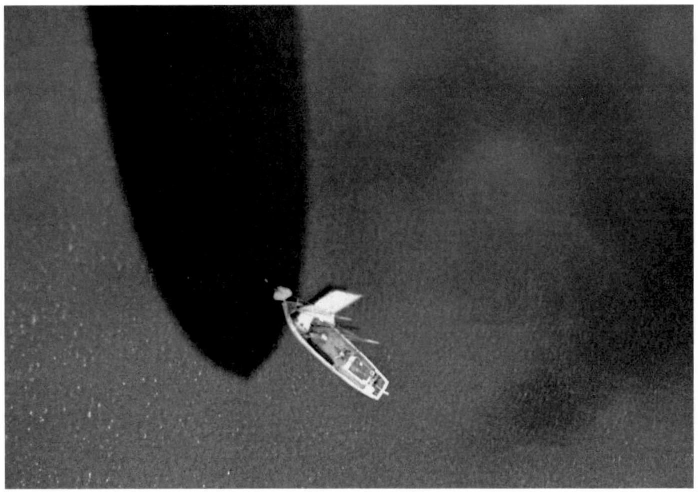

Zeppelin over a boat off the Brazilian coast, 1931

was likely not unproblematic, since Rehbein was a staunch National Socialist.) Other traveling companions were the cinematographer Harry Ringger and film producer Hubert Schonger, who during this flight shot the documentary *Nach Südamerika in drei Tagen* (To South America in Three Days, 1934).

For Block, taking photos from the zeppelin proved to be less productive than expected, since visibility was often limited by dense air and inclement weather. Nevertheless, he did get some shots of cloud formations and the rather shapeless ocean from above. Better photo opportunities were offered when the airship flew over ships [p. 275], or of the zeppelin's shadow thrown onto the objects below—various boats or the lighthouse of Abrolhos Island [p. 261]. Above all, Block documented the transition from ocean to land along the coast of Brazil [p. 274], where variegated manifestations of nature could be captured in one picture. One of the few shots over land is his view of the pilgrimage church Bonfin, in Salvador da Bahia [p. 275].

While Alfred Eisenstaedt immediately took the return flight to Europe, the Blocks stayed a full month in Rio de Janeiro. Although Block photographed the vegetation, the beach at Copacabana, and a visit to a snake farm, he seemed unconvinced of the results; only later did he select a few of these motifs for prints. The encounter with Hans August Reyersbach (1898–1977) was recorded in private photographs. He had gone to school in Hamburg with the brother of Anna-Sophie Block (née Levy), and had become part of the Levy's circle of friends. Reyersbach's sister was married to a son of the Hamburg merchant family Magnus, who immigrated for professional reasons with her to Brazil and ran an import-export company in Rio.

Previously, Reyersbach had worked as a commercial artist in Hamburg. At the end of 1923, he relocated to Rio de Janeiro to work at Magnus because of the poor economic situation in Germany and his lack of clear professional goals. In 1935, he married his Hamburg childhood friend Margret Waldstein, who visited him in Rio. In early 1936, they returned to Europe together. After years of exile in Paris, the couple immigrated to New York in 1940. In the United States, Reyersbach became known under the name "H. A. Rey," the creator and illustrator of the extremely successful children's book series *Curious George*.[9] He stayed in touch with the Blocks.

Although Block and his wife had booked a passage on the steamer *Cap Arcona* for their return trip, they exchanged it for the uniqueness of a zeppelin flight. Alas, for a photographer, the return flight was also not advantageous. In her travel diary, Anna-Sophie Block notes: "On the return journey […] more stringent regulations had come into force. Only photography over water was permitted. So Fritz's camera missed a few Brazilian coastal towns and, unfortunately, the southern part of Andalusia before landing in Spain." Block still photographed in Seville, including the bullfight arena [pp. 276–277], but only a few images from this series survived.

Switzerland, London, and Dalmatia

Between 1933 and 1935, the Blocks traveled several times to Switzerland, including for winter holidays in the Upper Engadine valley. This stay offered Block the opportunity for landscape photography in the mountains, a genre of which he was not especially fond—and so did not produce any extraordinary results [p. 262]. He had more success with images taken under the principles of the New Photography, including close-ups of branches breaking through snow cover, or studies of ski traces in the snow [p. 271]. In St. Moritz, Block also captured the momentum of ice skaters' movements in an almost cinematic sequence of individual shots [p. 270]. However, these were not new types of images: Swiss photographers such as Albert Steiner or Emil Meerkämper had often photographed and published similar motifs.

In the mid-1930s, Block made additional trips to France, Italy, and Denmark, but no photos survived. In his estate is a series of 20 photographs of the Petticoat Lane Market [pp. 278–281], which may have originated during his stay in London in late fall of 1935. This motif is linked to photo reportages Block made at Hamburg's St. Pauli fish market, and at Les Halles wholesale food market, in Paris. The photos provide an atmospherically dense image of market activ-

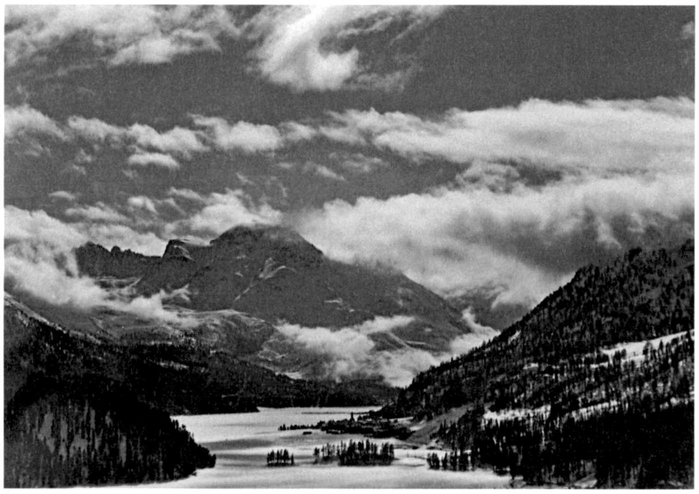

View of the Upper Engadine valley, Switzerland, ca. 1933

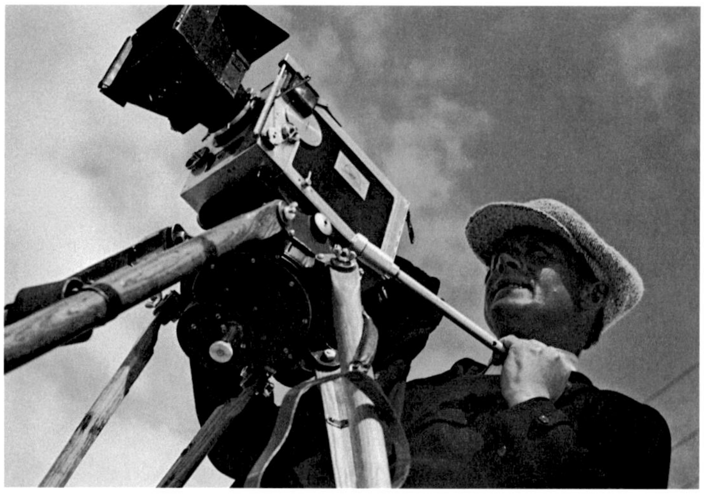

Sepp Allgeier filming in the Upper Engadine, Switzerland, ca. 1933

ity and its actors. At the same time, they show an affinity to László Moholy-Nagy's Leica photographs, made at the same time from various street markets in London and published in *The Street Markets of London* (1936), by Mary Benedetta. Moholy-Nagy states in the preface that these types of photos are not about image composition but rather about the image's close approximation to reality. This applies as well to Block's photos, which combine photo journalistic reportage with social documentation.

In the spring of 1937, Block and his wife traveled via Venice to Dalmatia, the coastal region of Croatia in (former) Yugoslavia. They visited the cities of Split and Dubrovnik, among others, as well as the island of Hvar. The resulting images, mainly of landscapes and monuments, were examples of the kinds of travel photography published in the 1930s in the cultural magazine *Atlantis*. But Block selected only a few motifs for prints, including views over the roofscape of the old town of Dubrovnik or impressions of traditional wooden shipbuilding on the Dalmatian coast [pp. 282–283]. In both cases, albeit in different ways, his eye for the image-effect of constructed structures is patently visible.

Cruise Around the World

As life for Jews in Germany continued to worsen, at the end of 1937 Block and his wife decided to undertake a longer journey: around the world by ship. This served several purposes: temporarily escaping the Nazi regime, with the vague hope for an improvement of the situation during their absence. But they were also searching for potential places of exile. Moreover, an expensive cruise was one of the few options left for Jews in Germany to spend larger amounts of money as they wished. Should they emigrate, a Reich Flight Tax and other fees would have a significant impact on their funds. Given the dire circumstances of this journey, photography for Block played a decidedly subordinate role. He was also now in possession of a 16-mm film camera, which he tried out during the journey.

The trip around the world, on the Canadian ship *Empress of Britain,* started in mid-January 1938 and led the Blocks from the Mediterranean Sea across Southeast Asia, and then from the South Pacific to the American West Coast, where they arrived in late April 1938. Anna-Sophie Block's travel description offers information about the stations and the route.[10] The trip began in Naples and led from Greece to Palestine, where Block met with a friend, the architect Adolf Rading, who had emigrated here. Block, however, did not consider the country as a place for exile. In his opinion, it was more for young people; he felt too old for building a country anew. He was also disturbed by the uncertain political situation. Unfortunately, Block neither photographed nor filmed while in Palestine.

The Blocks continued to Cairo by train. Through Suez, they took a ship to North India and Ceylon (now Sri Lanka). The next destinations were Singapore, Bangkok, Hong Kong, and Manila, then Java and Bali, and, finally, Australia (Sydney and Melbourne) and New Zealand. For Block, Australia did not qualify as exile because its level of civilization was not as developed as he was accustomed. Passing the Fiji Islands, the Blocks reached Hawaii, where a letter from German friends awaited them with the urgent advice that "a change of domicile" was advisable. In the meantime, Hitler's power had expanded because of the Austrian "Anschluss" (annexation of Austria). In San Francisco, the Blocks decided to make California their exile home. But first, they began their return journey, via New York. From there, they commissioned Anna-Sophie Block's brother to start selling their assets and real estate in Hamburg.

Despite the oppressive circumstances of the cruise, Block took countless pictures and shot a few 16-mm films. But the dashing through countries and scattered impressions did not give him the appropriate access to certain subjects, especially as he was never interested in mere "tourist" motifs. Above all, his photographs of characteristic markers of the countries visited are photographically convincing, in particular those from northern India. Block was able to capture intense portraits of children, women, and men in regional dress [pp. 284–287]. It seems reasonable to suppose that the photographer, who was racially persecuted in Germany, wanted to create a document of the ethnic diversity of humanity and, simultaneously, of individual dignity.

Emigration to the USA

Contrary to all warnings, Block and his wife returned to Hamburg in June 1938, to say goodbye to family and friends, to prepare their emigration in an orderly manner, and to dissolve the architectural firm Dr. Block & Hochfeld. Farsightedly, they exchanged their Mercedes-Benz for a Ford, and sold their real estate. But it took another three months until the Blocks received their "Quota Immigration Visa," their entry visa for the US, in early October. Relatives of the Block's in New York issued an affidavit. While boxing up household goods, loyal carpenters built small compartments in the furniture to hide valuables. Block's emigration thus took place under a forced relinquishment of numerous assets—but excluding a portion of their personal property, not least, his photographic archive. Thanks to this circumstance, his photographic oeuvre can be presented in this book.

In November 1938, the situation in Germany became more dangerous. On the night from November 9 to 10, there were pogrom-like attacks on Jews, including the destruction of synagogues, also in Hamburg. On November 10, the day after what the National Socialists cynically called the "Night of Broken Glass," the Blocks rushed to the British Consulate to secure their transit visa for ship passage to America. Since Block was particularly endangered, he wanted to fly ahead to London on November 11, to start the booked passage in Southampton. He was arrested at the Hamburg airport. The pretext was an English-pound note he was carrying with him, interpreted as a violation of foreign-exchange regulations.[11] Block was detained for three days at Sachsenhausen Concentration Camp near Oranienburg. His wife's decisive intervention succeeded in freeing Block and reclaiming their confiscated passports. Nevertheless, the detention left traces on Block's health, as his wife later recalled: "The rough treatment and the stress of those days had serious effects on his health, from which a full recovery has never occurred."[12] The passport stamp reading "Hafen Hamburg, ausgereist am 16. November 1938" (Hamburg Habour, left the country on 16 November 1938) was the final seal on Fritz and Anna-Sophie Block's former life in Germany.

Their passage with the *SS Manhattan*, a ship belonging to the United States Lines, sailed over Boulogne and Southampton to New York. There, the Blocks had deposited enough cash at the end of their world trip to finance their first period of exile. From New York, they took a Greyhound bus to Los Angeles, where later the moving van arrived with their household goods and car. The Blocks would now begin to build a new life—one in which photography would play a central role.

1 Anna-Sophie Block, *Wien* (typescript, June 3, 1933, Fritz Block Estate Archive, Stockholm/Hamburg).
2 Idem, "Budapest an der Donau," in *Hamburger Anzeiger. Illustrierte Wochenbeilage*, 1933, no. 18 (Jan. 21).
3 "Deutsche Bilder in der Presse. Verzeichnis deutscher Pressephotographen / Liste der Juden und Ausländer," in *Deutsche Nachrichten* 1933, no. 32 (first issue in August), 3–4. See Diethart Kerbs, "Die Epoche der Bildagenturen. Zur Geschichte der Pressefotografie in Berlin von 1900 bis 1933," in *Die Gleichschaltung der Bilder. Zur Geschichte der Pressefotografie 1930–36*, eds. Diethart Kerbs, et al. (Berlin 1983), 32–73 (on page 65 the date of the source for the list is not correct).
4 See Roland Jaeger, *Block & Hochfeld. Die Architekten des Deutschlandhauses. Bauten und Projekte in Hamburg 1921–1938. Exil in Los Angeles* (Berlin, 1996), 15–16.
5 *Hamburger Illustrierte*, 1933, no. 14 (April 2).
6 See, for example, Max Geisenheyner, *Mit "Graf Zeppelin" um die Welt. Ein Bild-Buch* (Frankfurt, 1929). – Hans von Schiller (introd.), *Im Zeppelin über der Schweiz* (Zürich/Leipzig 1930, *Schaubücher*, vol. 36). – Albert Sonntag, *Mit Graf Zeppelin und Kondor-Flugzeugen Europa–Brasilien* (Bonn, 1932).
7 The 32-page travel diary contains 130 small-format photographs, nearly half of them by Block (Fritz Block Estate Archive, Stockholm/Hamburg).
8 Arthur Rehbein, *Über Schwellen und Wellen und Wolken. Besonnte und besinnliche Reisen* (Berlin, 1935), 214–242. Information kindly provided by Sylk Schneider, Weimar.
9 Roland Jaeger, "Der Schöpfer von 'Curious George': Kinderbuch-Illustrator H. A. Rey," in *Aus dem Antiquariat*, 1997, no. 10, A543–A551. – Idem, "H. A. und Margret Rey," in *Deutschsprachige Exilliteratur seit 1933, vol. 3, USA, part 2*, eds. John M. Spalek, Konrad Feilchenfeldt, and Sandra H. Hawrylchak (Bern/München, 2000) 351–360. – Uwe Franzen and Wilfried Weinke, "Wo man *Bücher verbrennt... .*" *Verbrannte Bücher, verbannte und ermordete Autoren Hamburgs* (Hamburg, 2017), 278–293.
10 Anna-Sophie Block, *Unsere Reise um die Welt im Jahre 1938 mit dem Dampfer* Empress of Britain *der Canadian Pacific, zusammengestellt aus Briefen und Berichten von der Reise* (typescript, Fritz Block Estate Archive, Stockholm/Hamburg). Block's 16mm films are also part of the archive.
11 Staatsarchiv Hamburg, Signatur: 213-11_03138/39 (Landgericht). Block, Dr. Fritz wg. Devisenvergehen.
12 Staatsarchiv Hamburg, Signatur: 351-11_17884 (Amt für Wiedergutmachung). Wiedergutmachungsakte Anna-Sophie Block, Antrag 1955, 3.

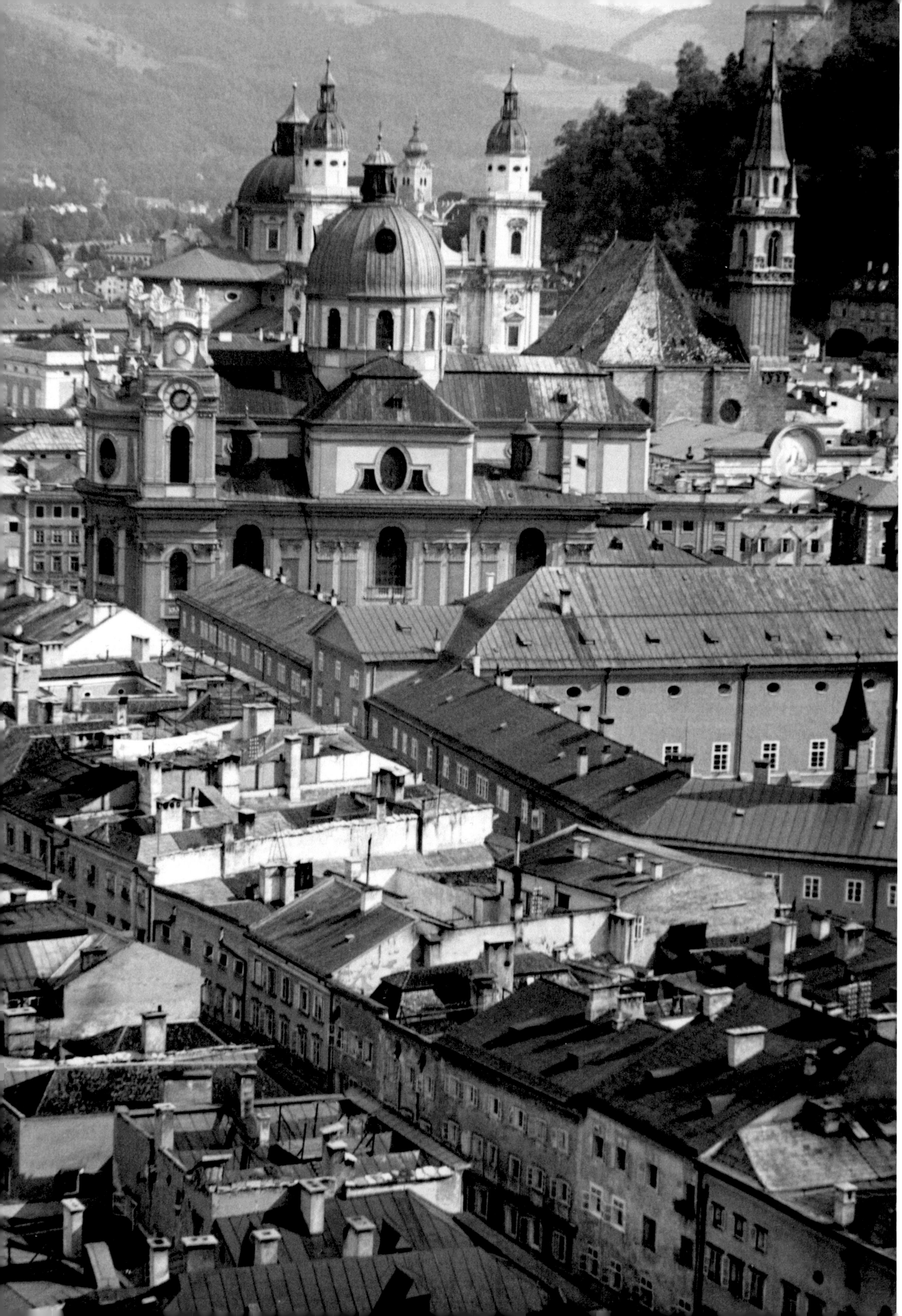

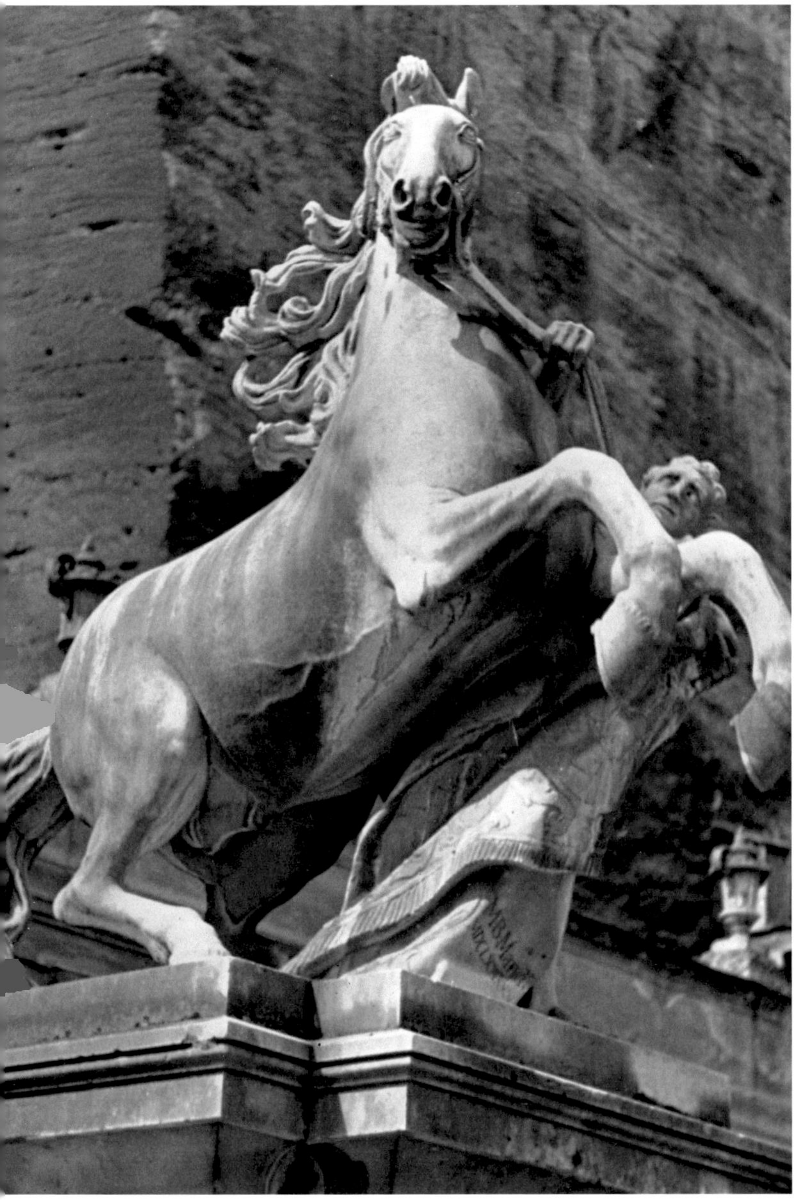

"Horse Tamer" statue at the Horse Pond,
Salzburg, Austria, 1932

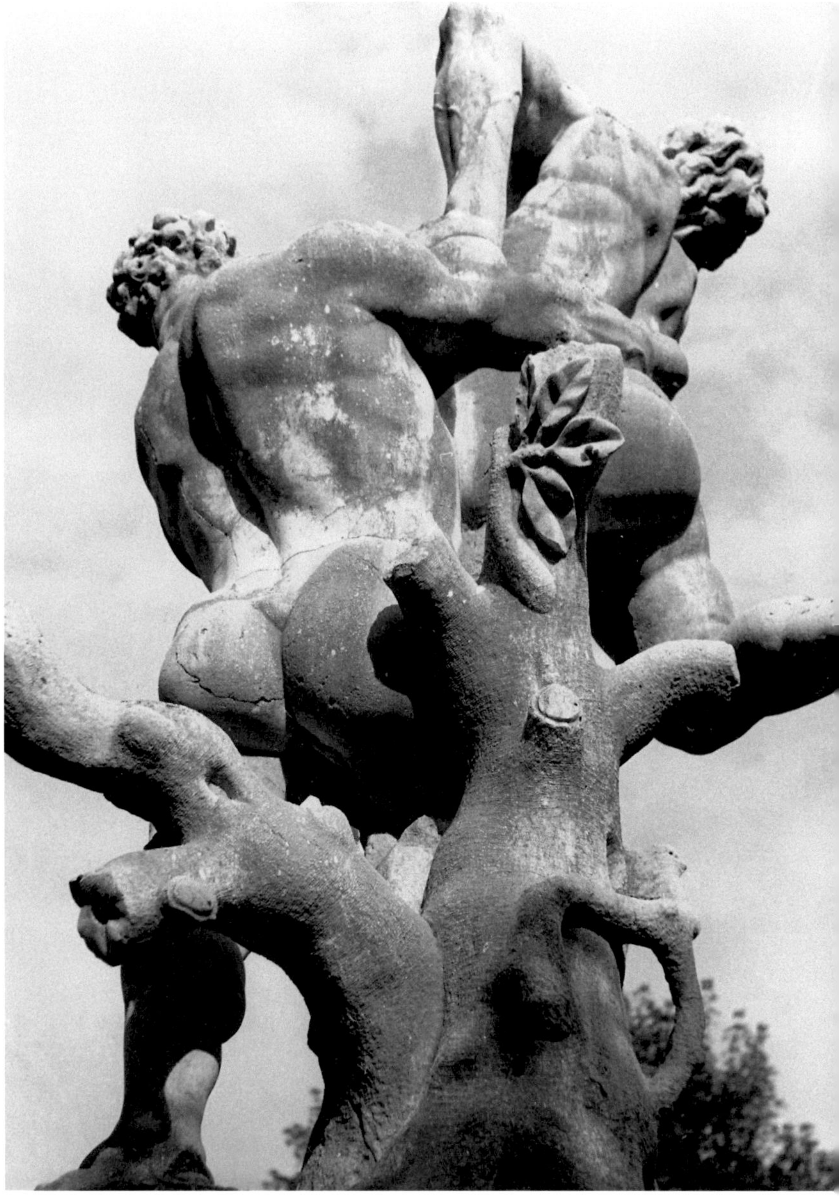

Sculpture in the Mirabell Gardens,
Salzburg, Austria, 1932

View over Salzburg, Austria, 1932

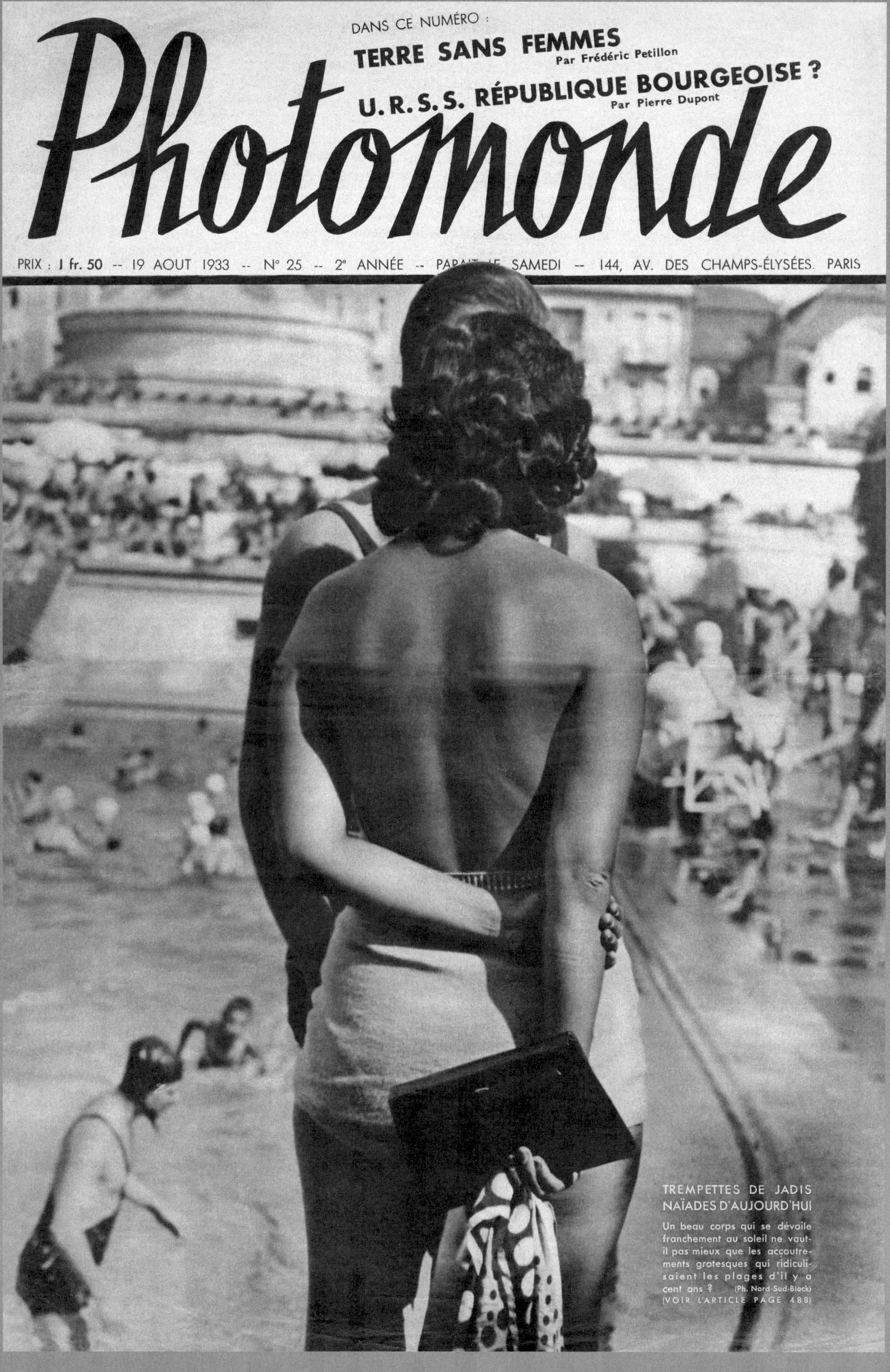
DANS CE NUMÉRO :

TERRE SANS FEMMES
Par Frédéric Petillon

U.R.S.S. RÉPUBLIQUE BOURGEOISE ?
Par Pierre Dupont

Photomonde

PRIX : 1 fr. 50 -- 19 AOUT 1933 -- N° 25 -- 2e ANNÉE -- PARAIT LE SAMEDI -- 144, AV. DES CHAMPS-ÉLYSÉES. PARIS

TREMPETTES DE JADIS
NAÏADES D'AUJOURD'HUI

Un beau corps qui se dévoile franchement au soleil ne vaut-il pas mieux que les accoutrements grotesques qui ridiculisaient les plages d'il y a cent ans ? (Ph. Nord-Sud-Block)
(VOIR L'ARTICLE PAGE 488)

"In the Gellért Bath" (*Photomonde* 2, no. 25, 1933)

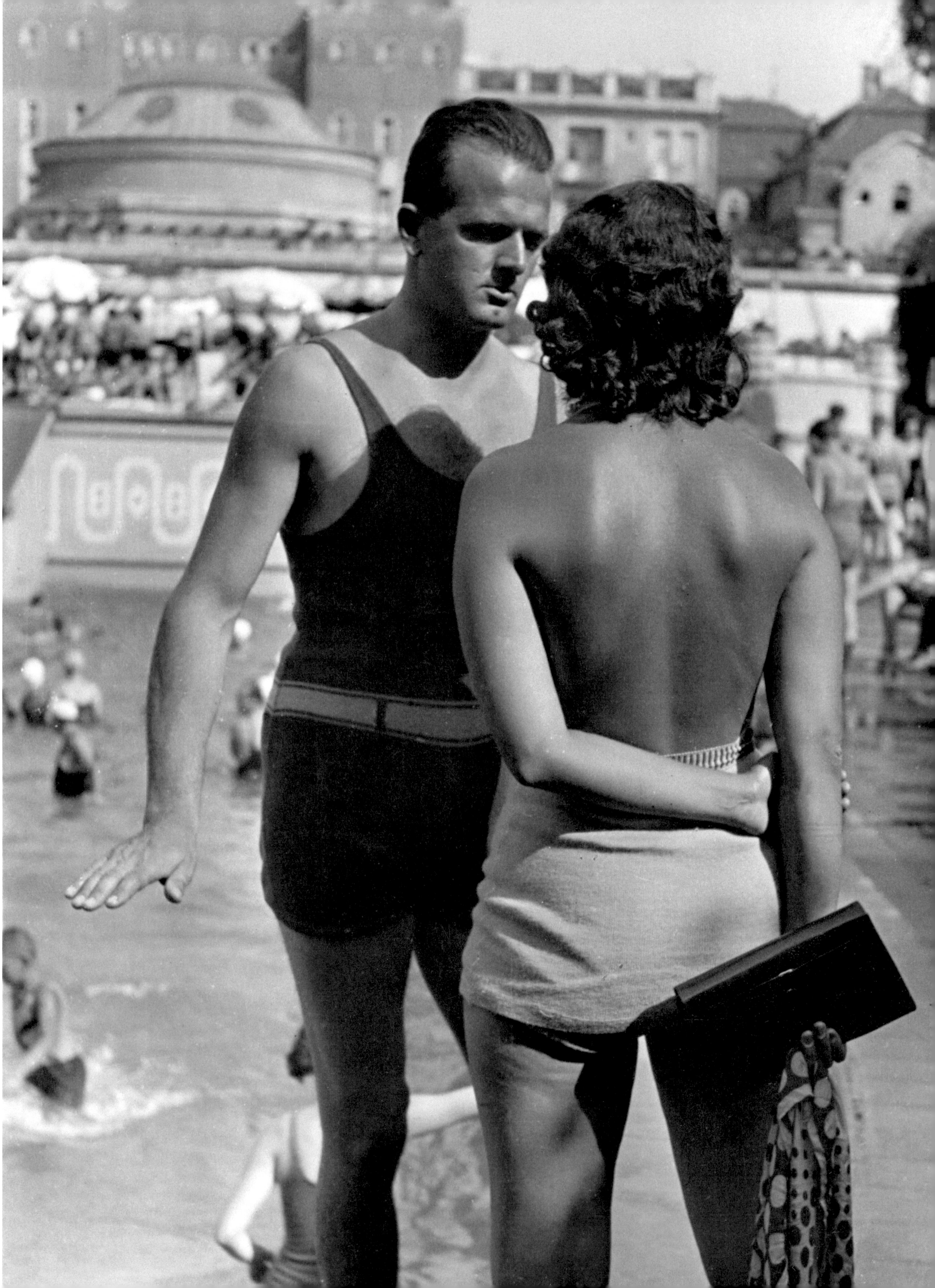

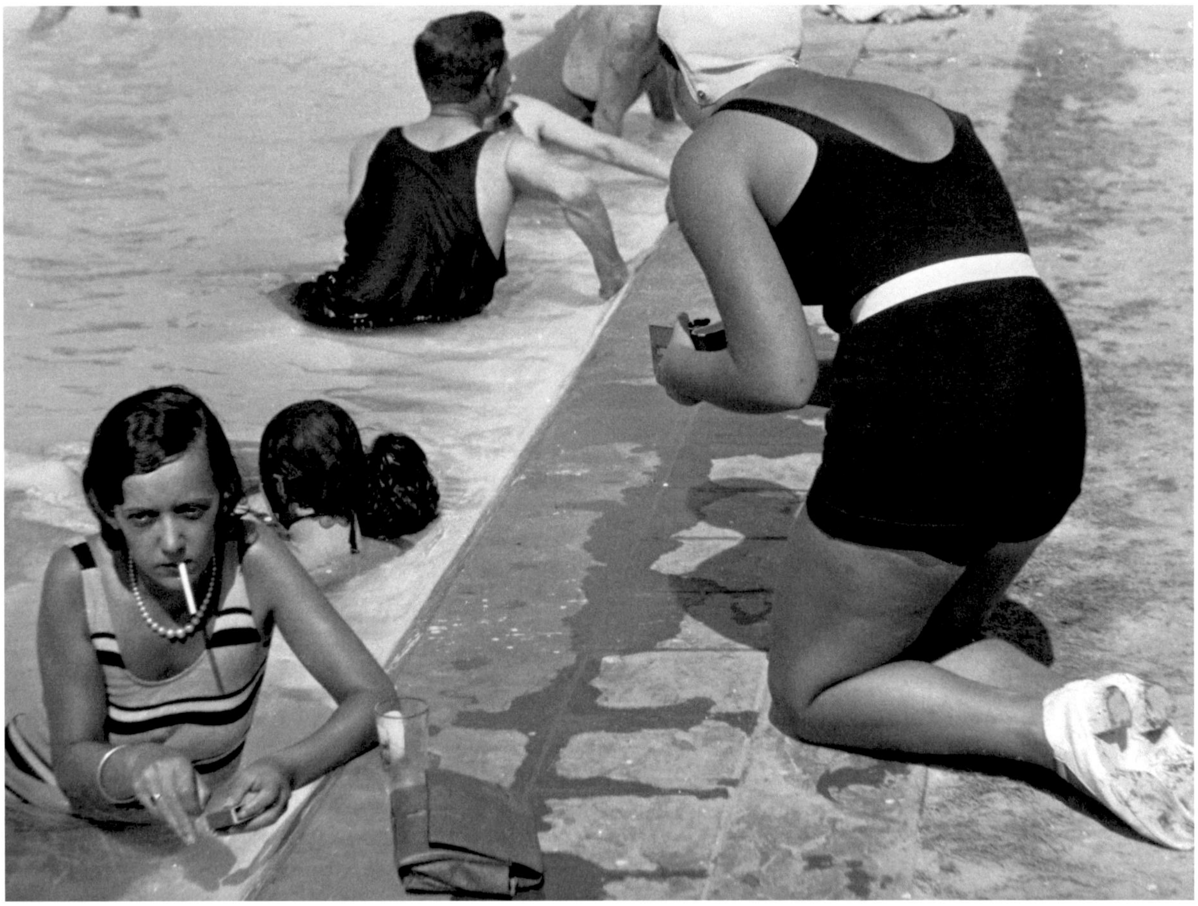

In the Gellért Bath, Budapest, Hungary, 1932

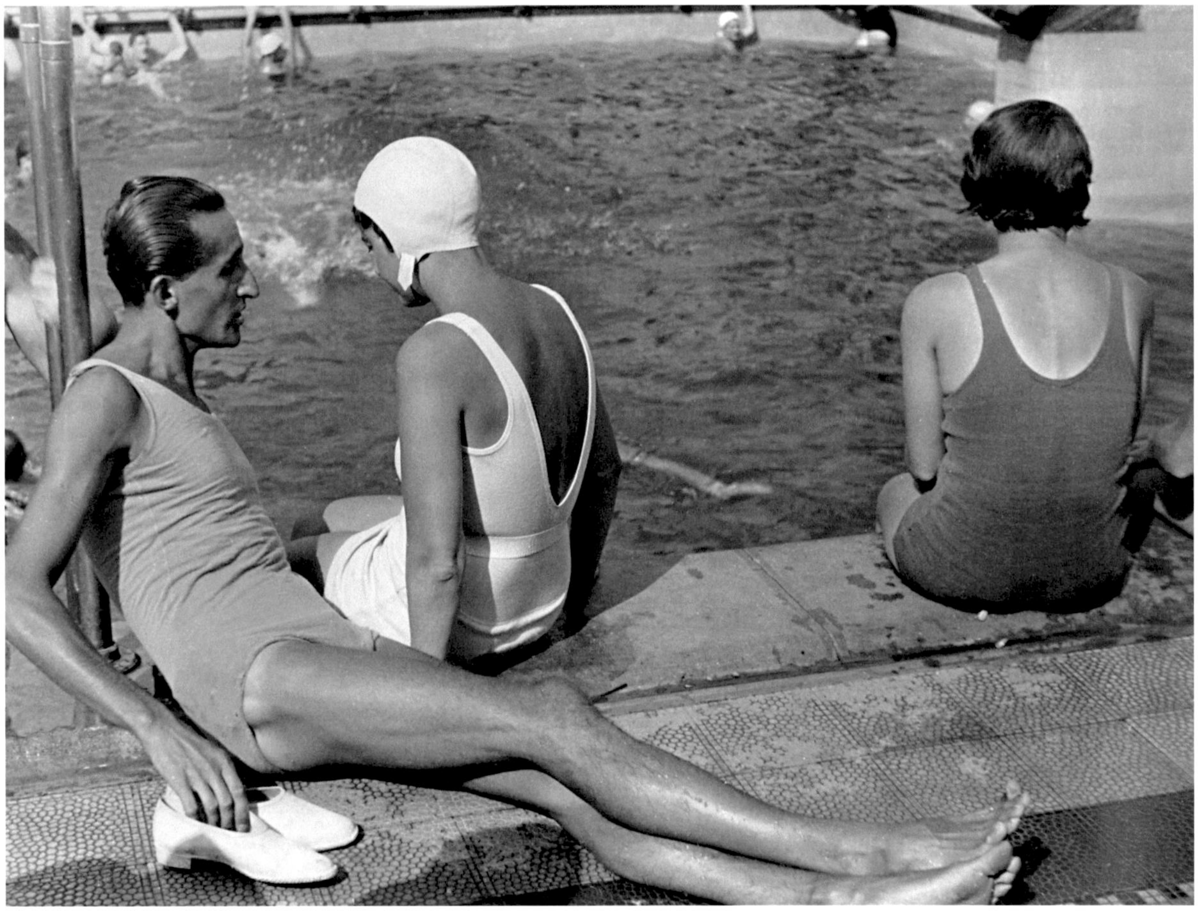

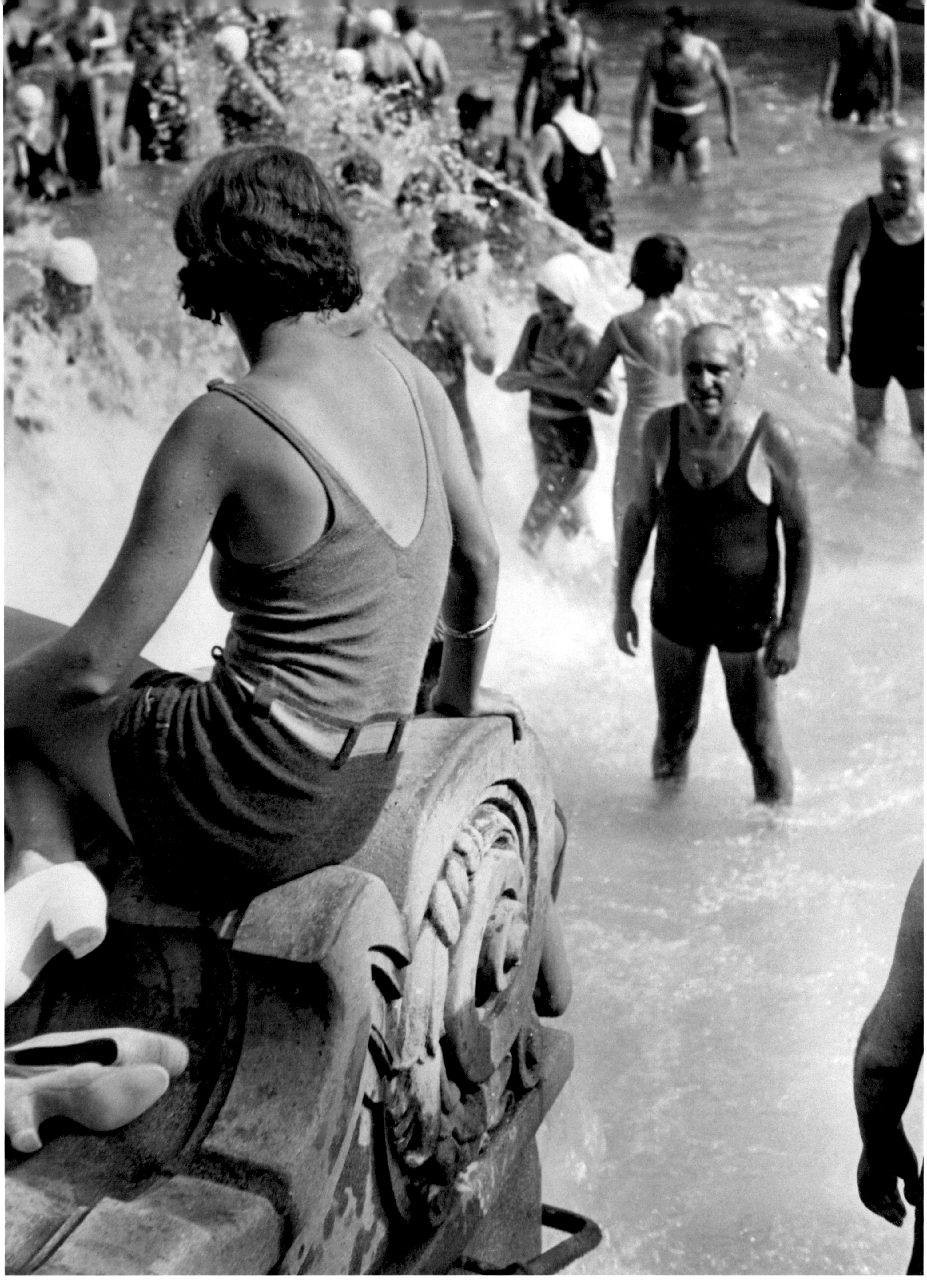

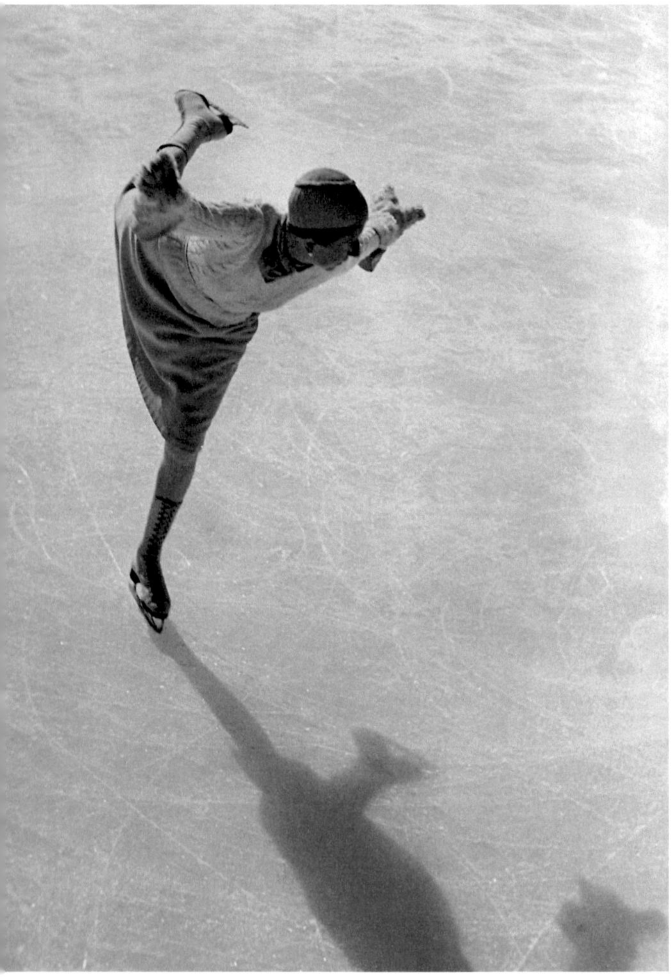

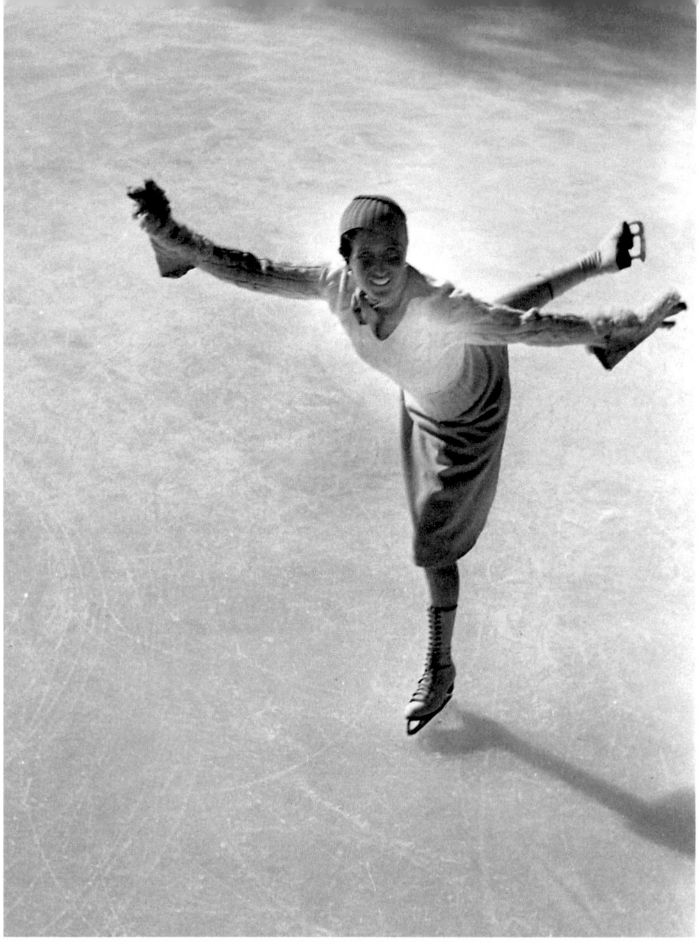

Figure skater Thea Frenssen and partner
in St. Moritz, Switzerland, ca. 1933

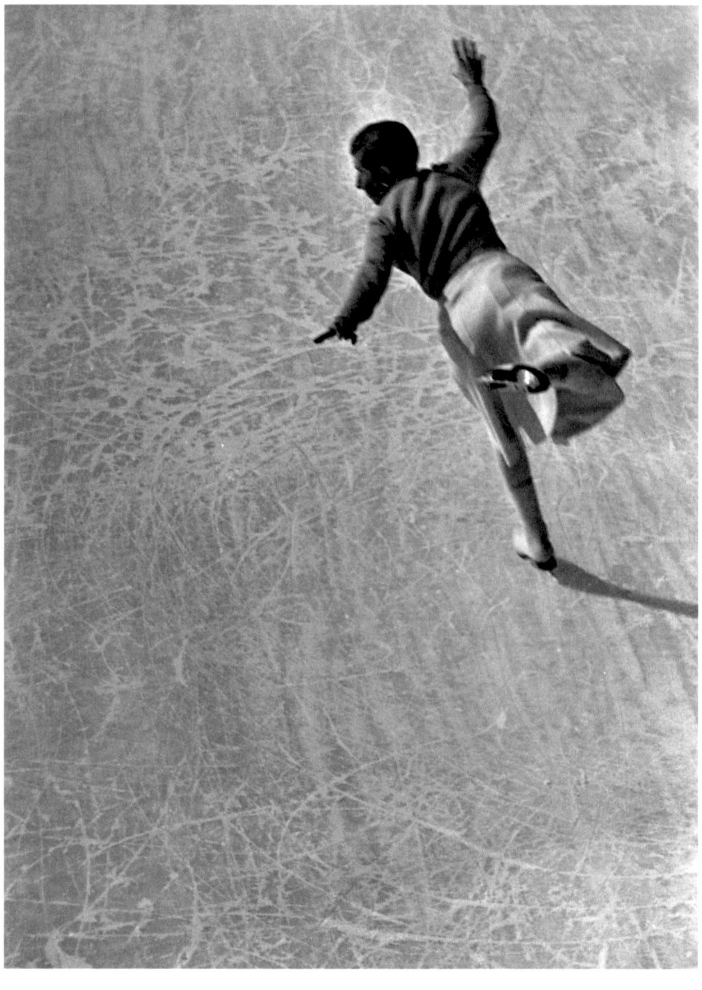

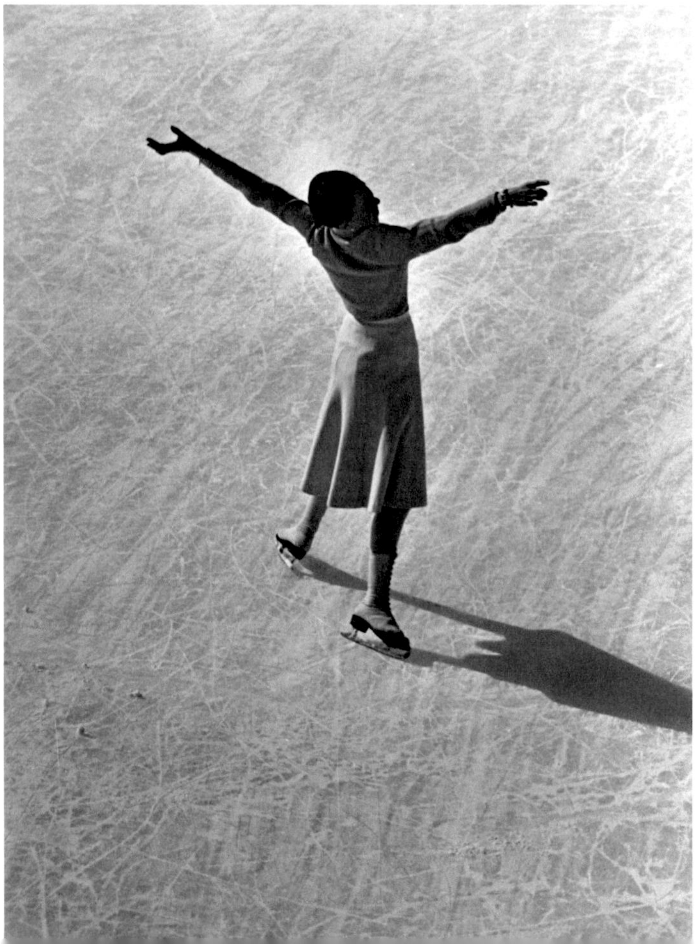

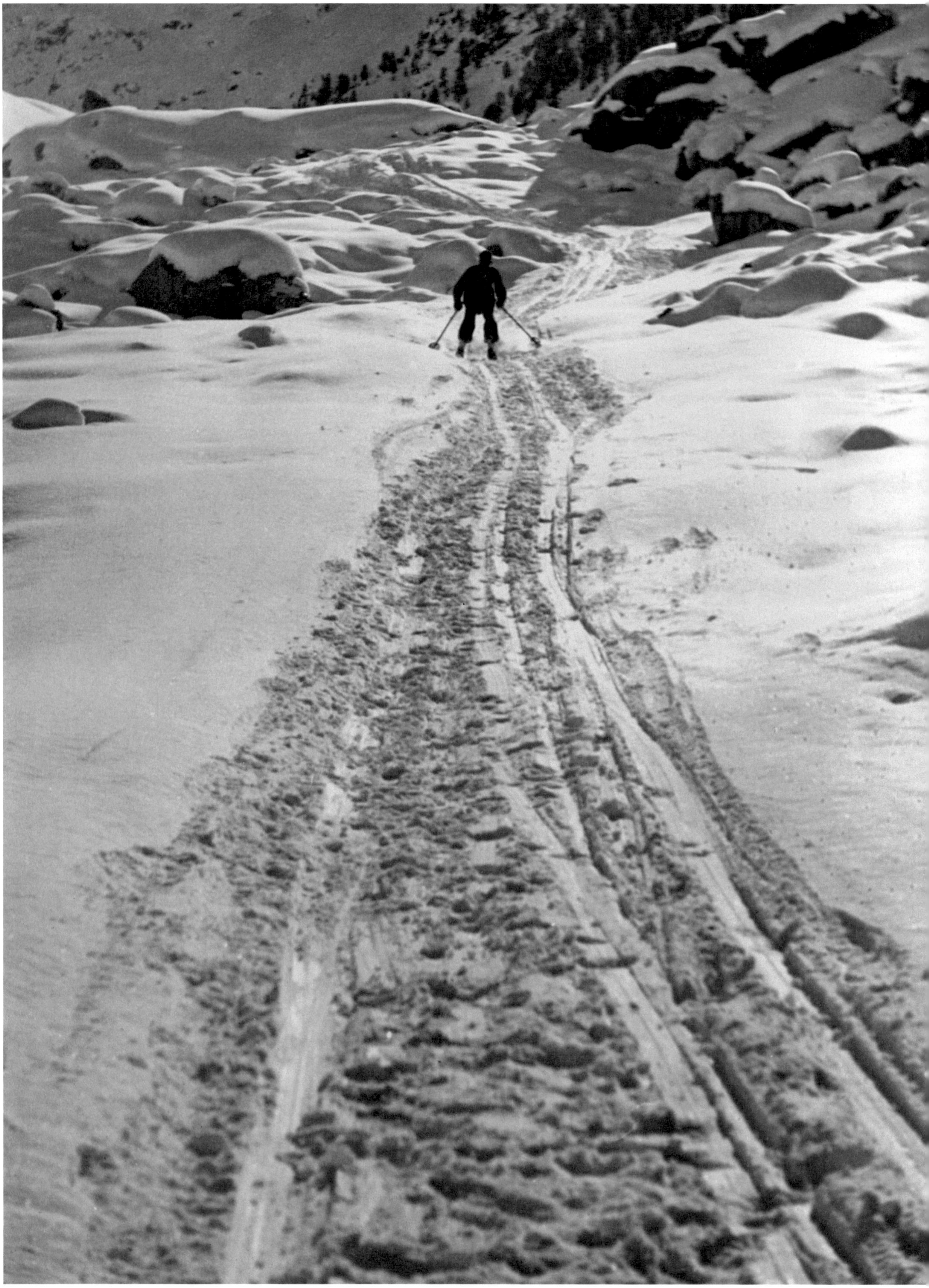

Skiing in the
Upper Engadine,
Switzerland,
ca. 1933

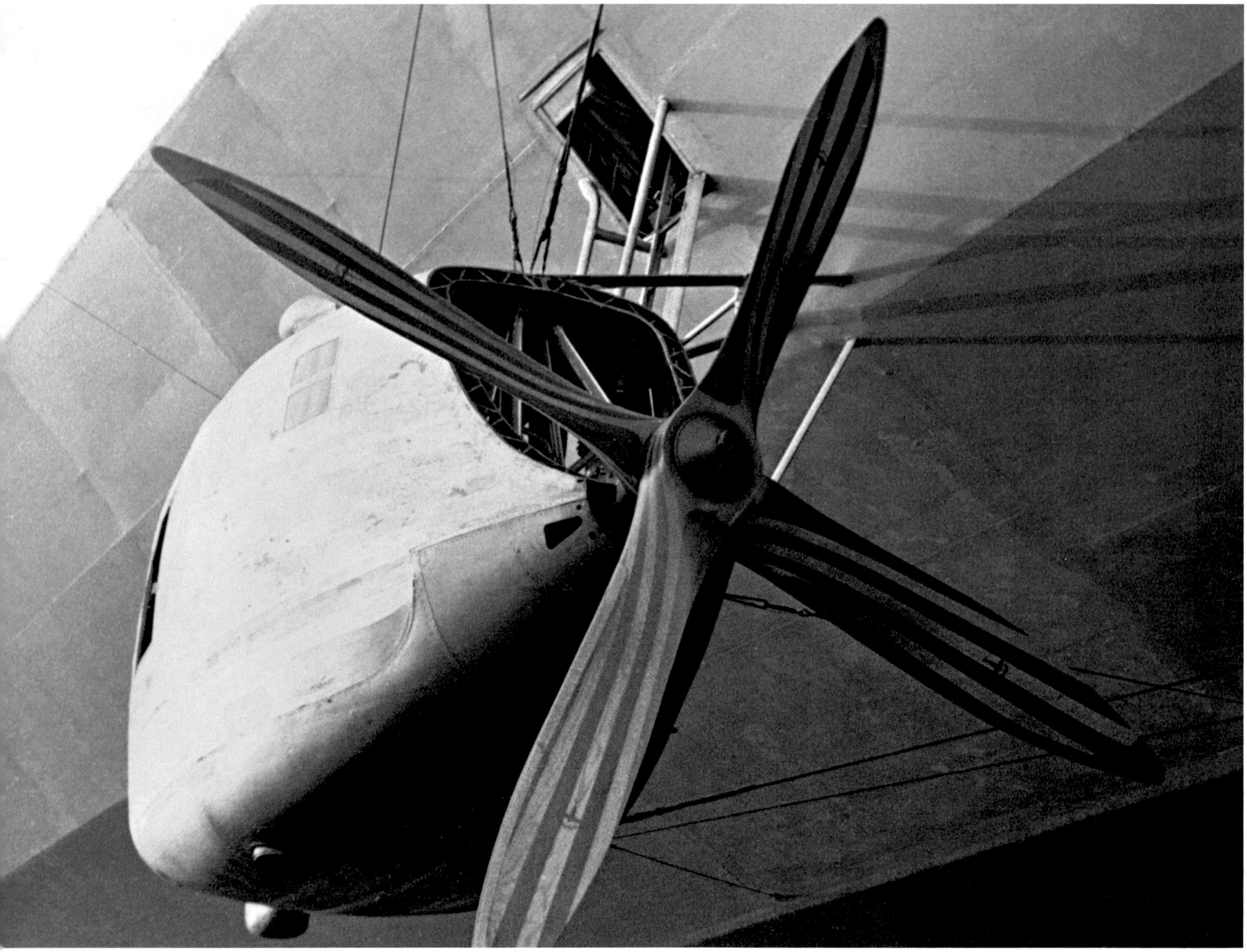

Engine of a Zeppelin airship, Friedrichshafen, Germany, 1933

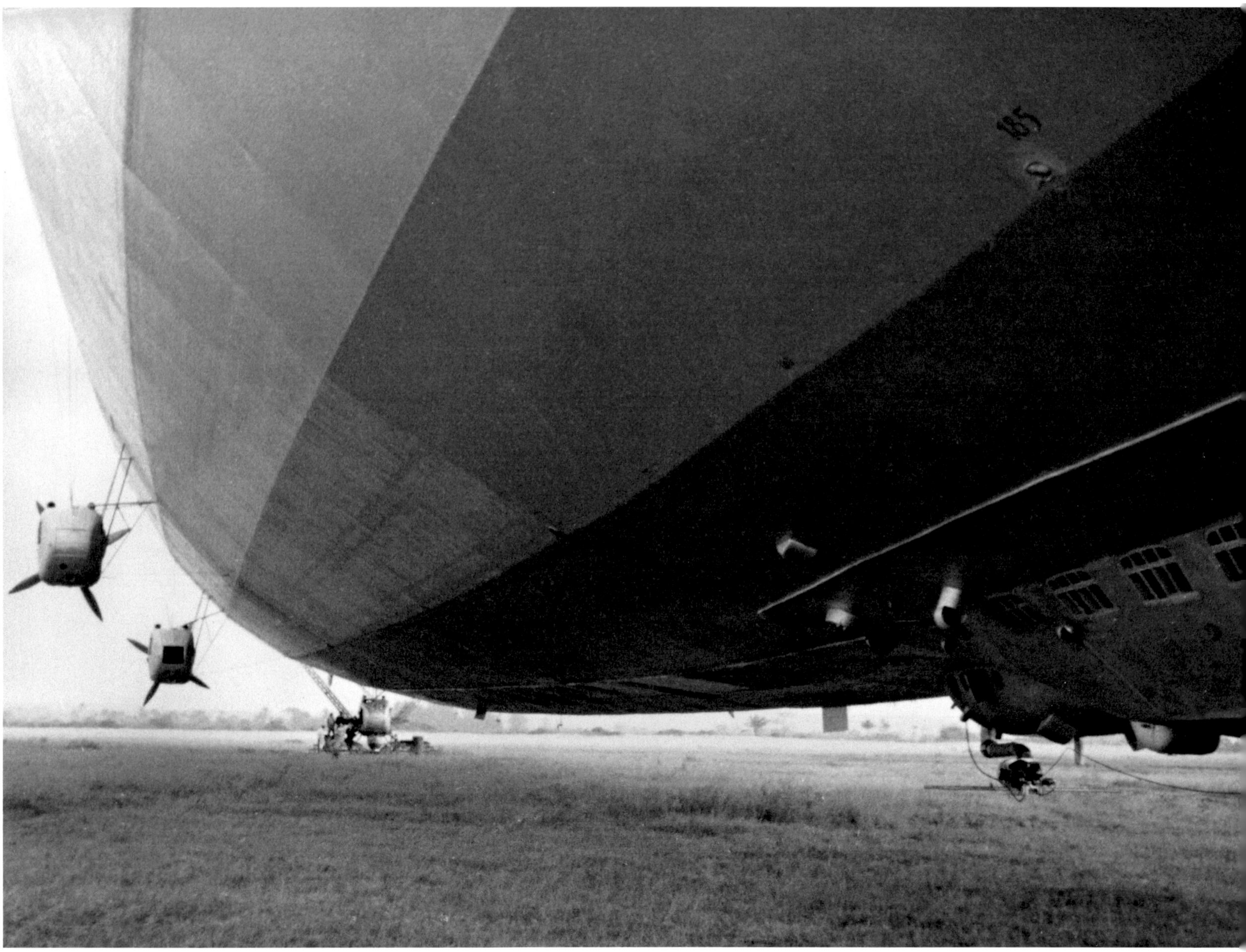

Zeppelin airship, Friedrichshafen, Germany, 1933

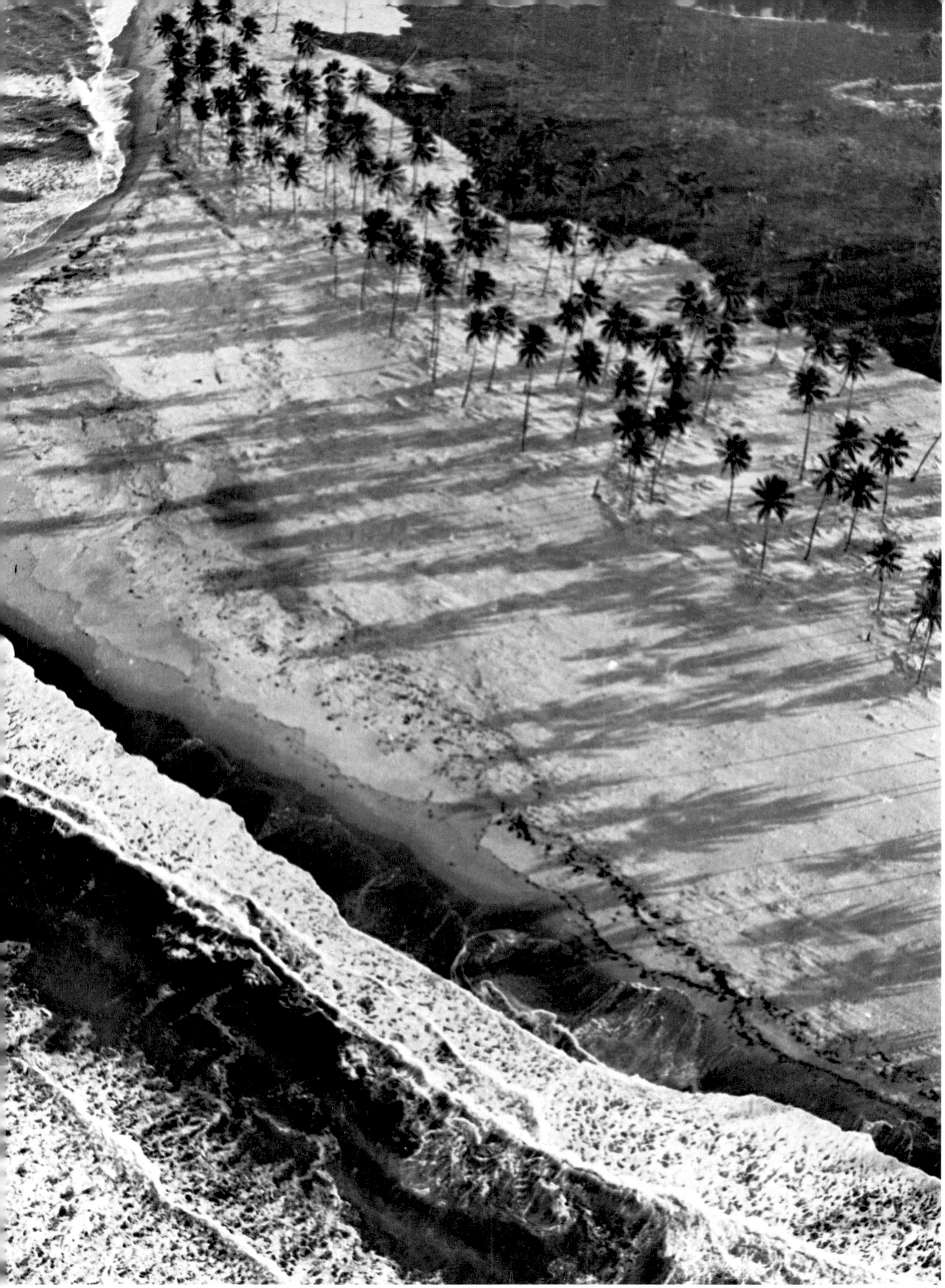

Aerial view from a Zeppelin airship onto Brazil's Coastline, 1933

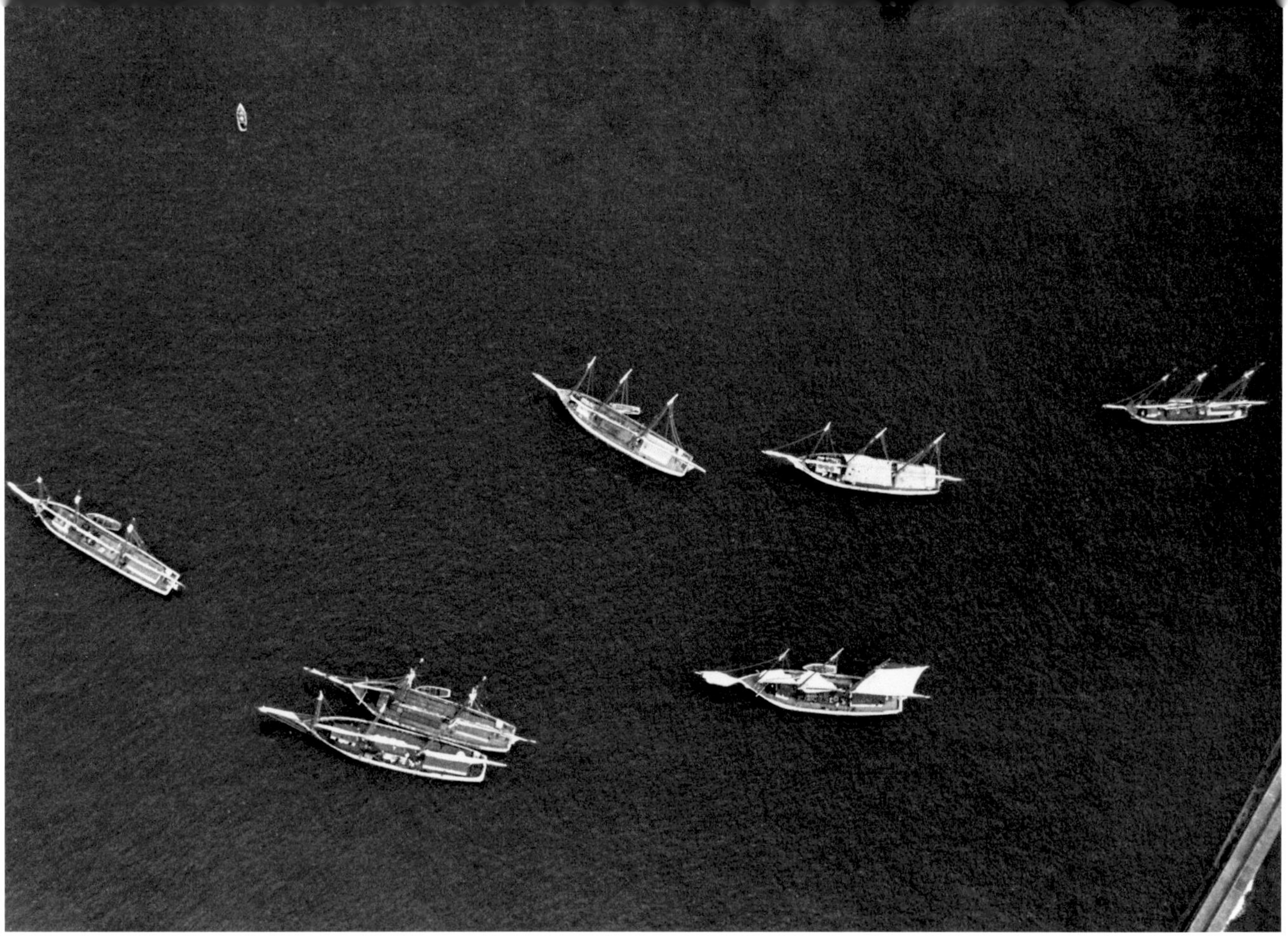

Aerial view from a Zeppelin airship onto sailing boats off the Coast of Brazil, 1933

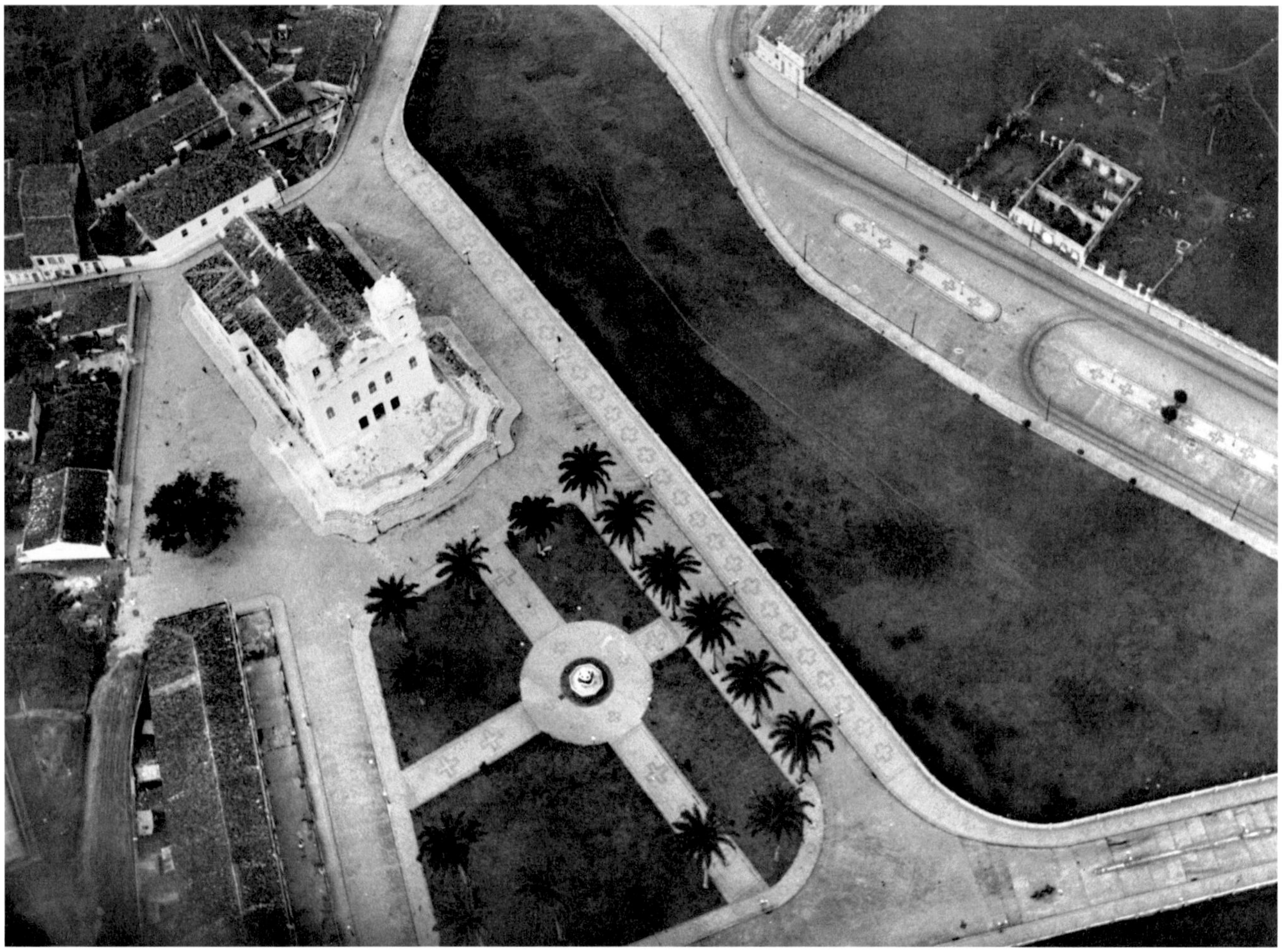

Aerial view from a Zeppelin airship onto the pilgrimage church Bonfim in Salvador da Bahia, Brazil, 1933

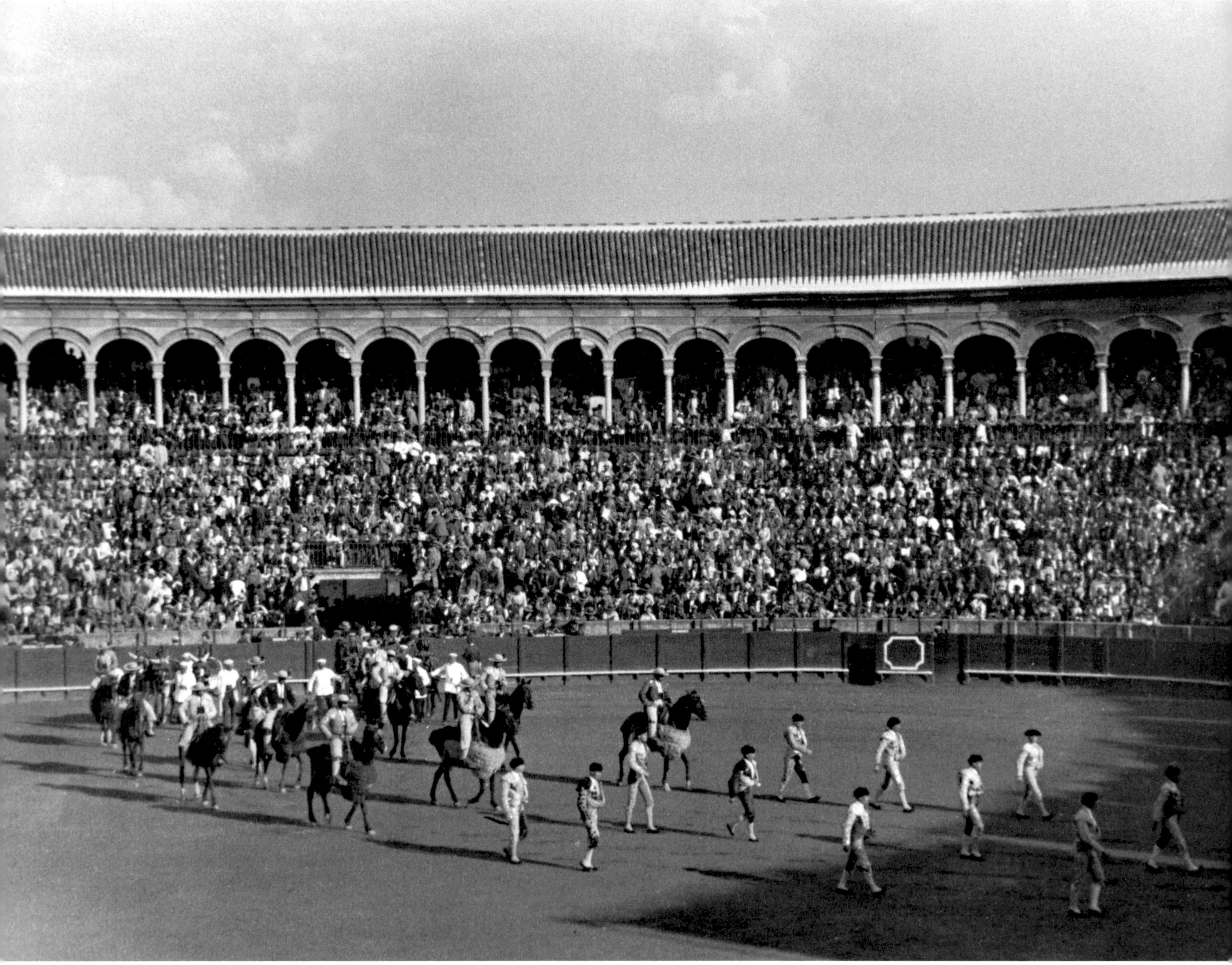

Bullring, Seville, Spain, 1933

Bullfight, Seville, Spain, 1933

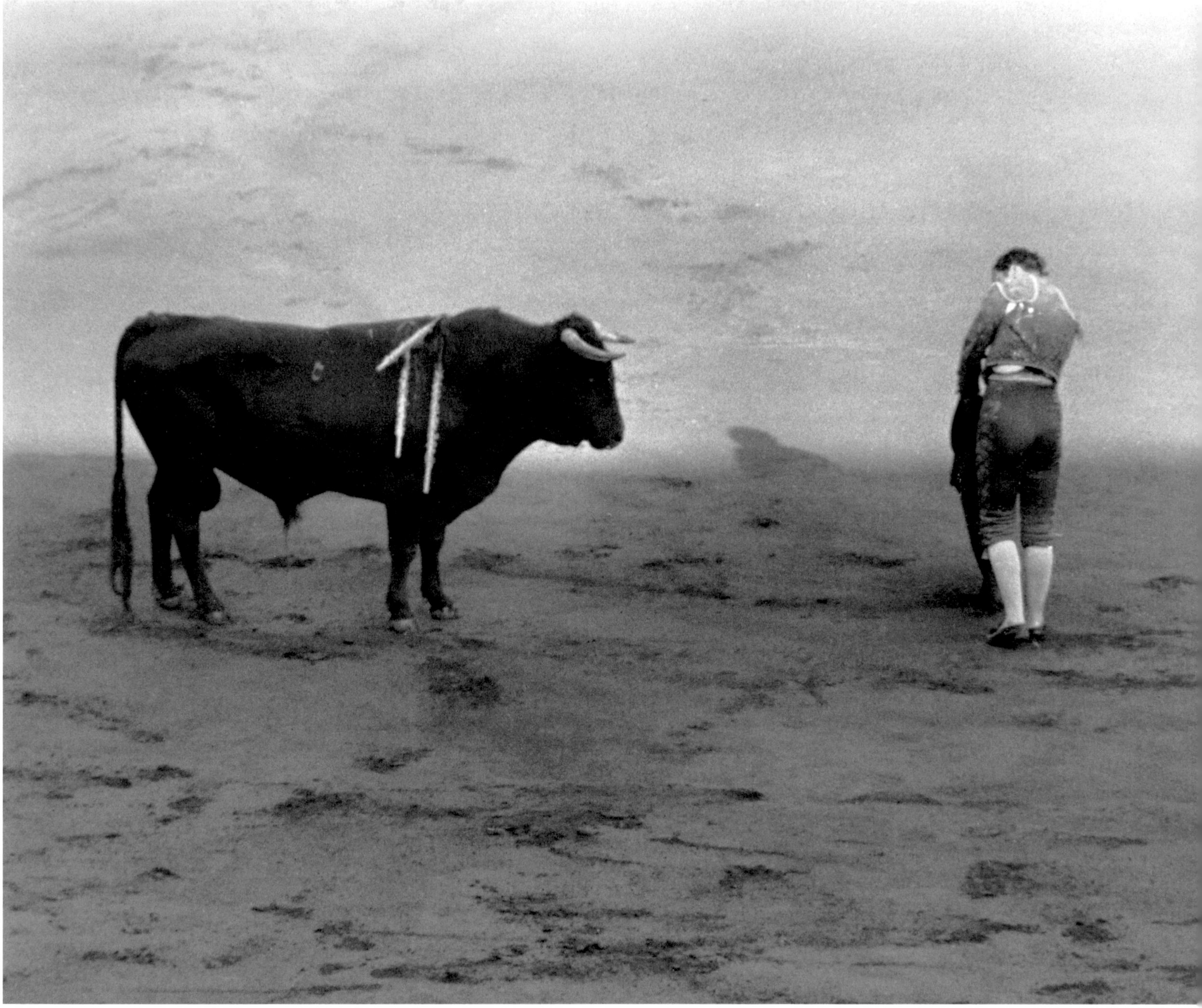

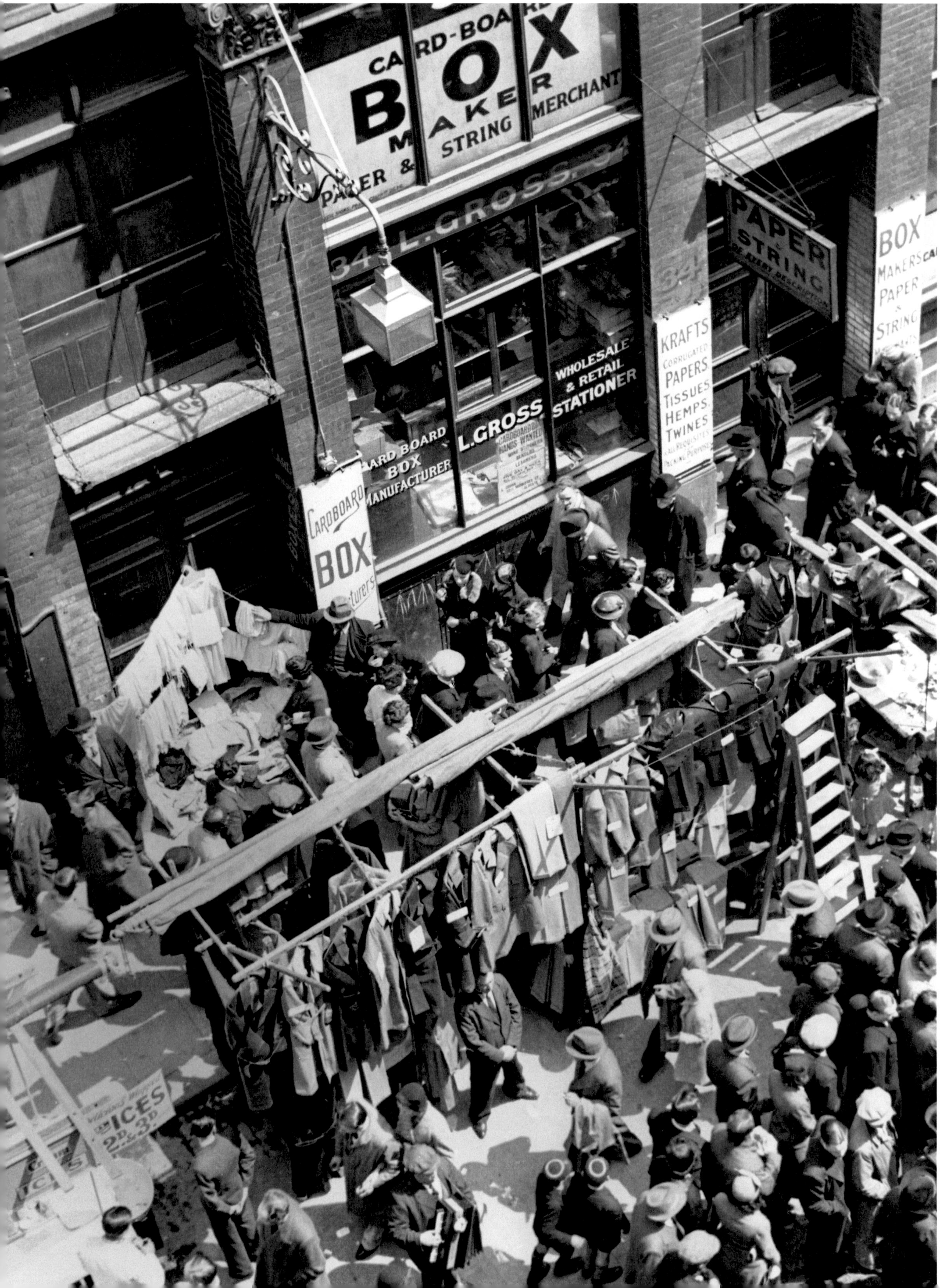
BOX
MAKER
STRING
MERCHANT
L.GROSS
WHOLESALE & RETAIL STATIONER
L.GROSS
BOX
MANUFACTURER
BOX
PAPER & STRING
KRAFTS
CORRUGATED
PAPERS
TISSUES
HEMPS
TWINES
BOX
MAKERS
PAPER
&
STRING
ICES
2D & 3D

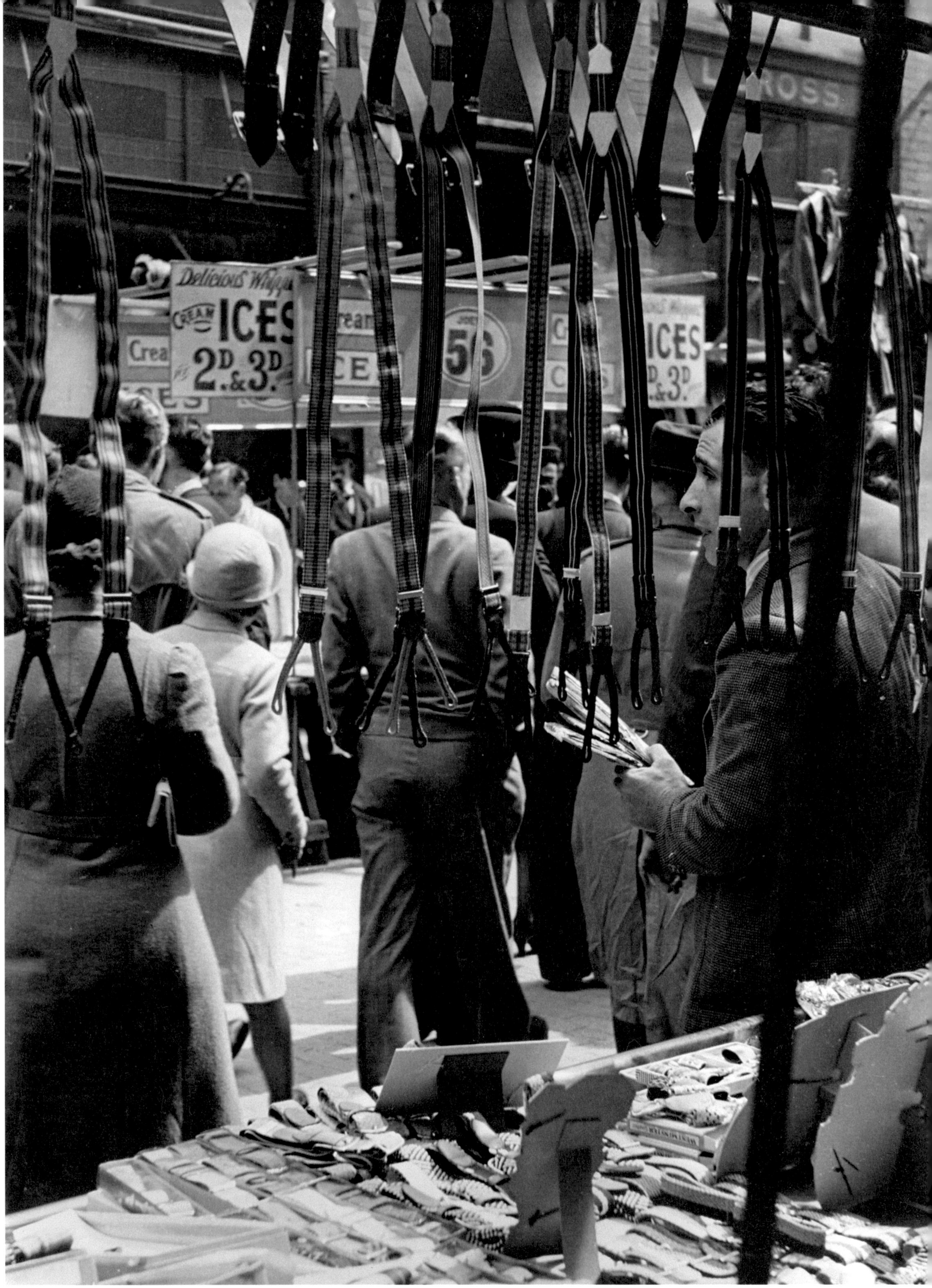

Petticoat Lane Market, London, Great Britain, 1935

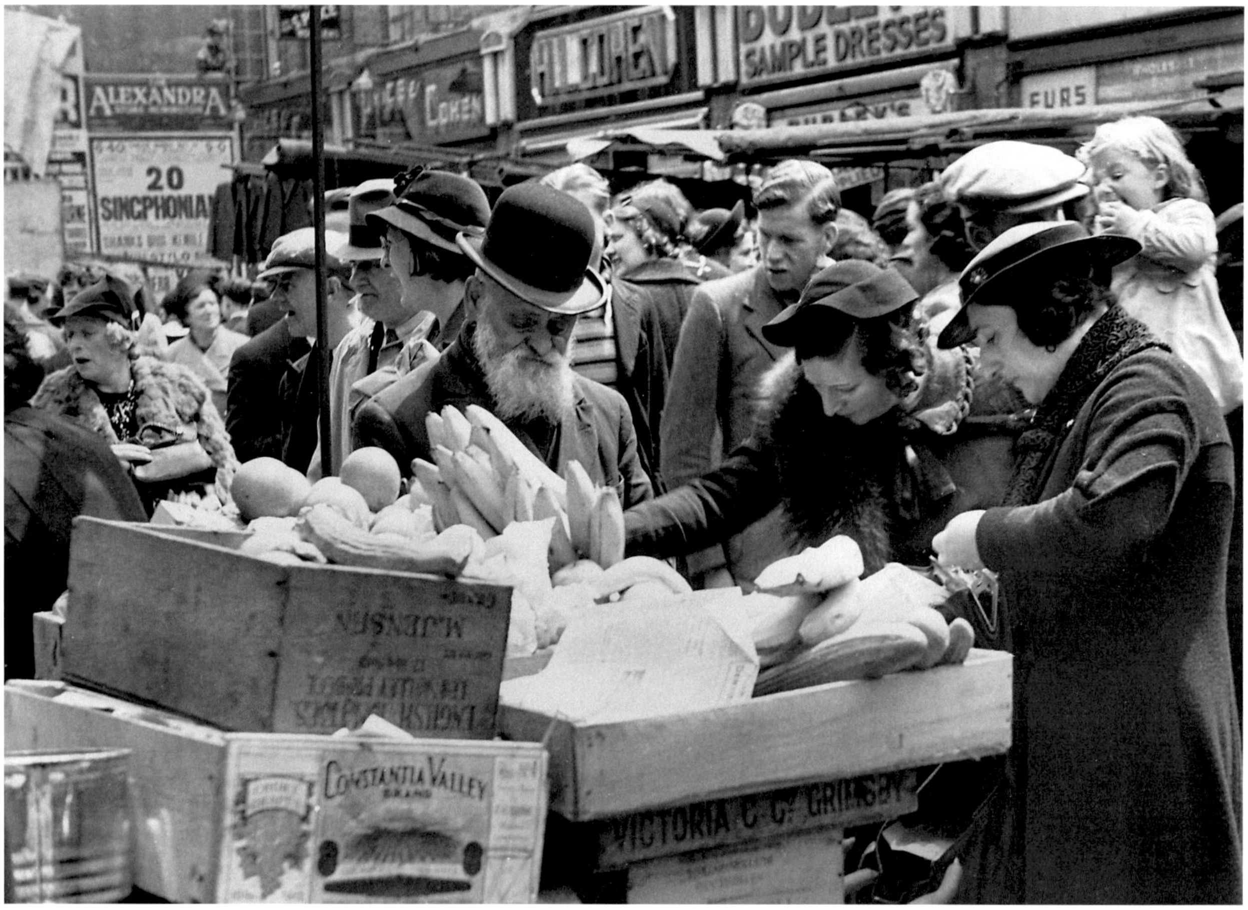

Petticoat Lane Market, London, Great Britain, 1935

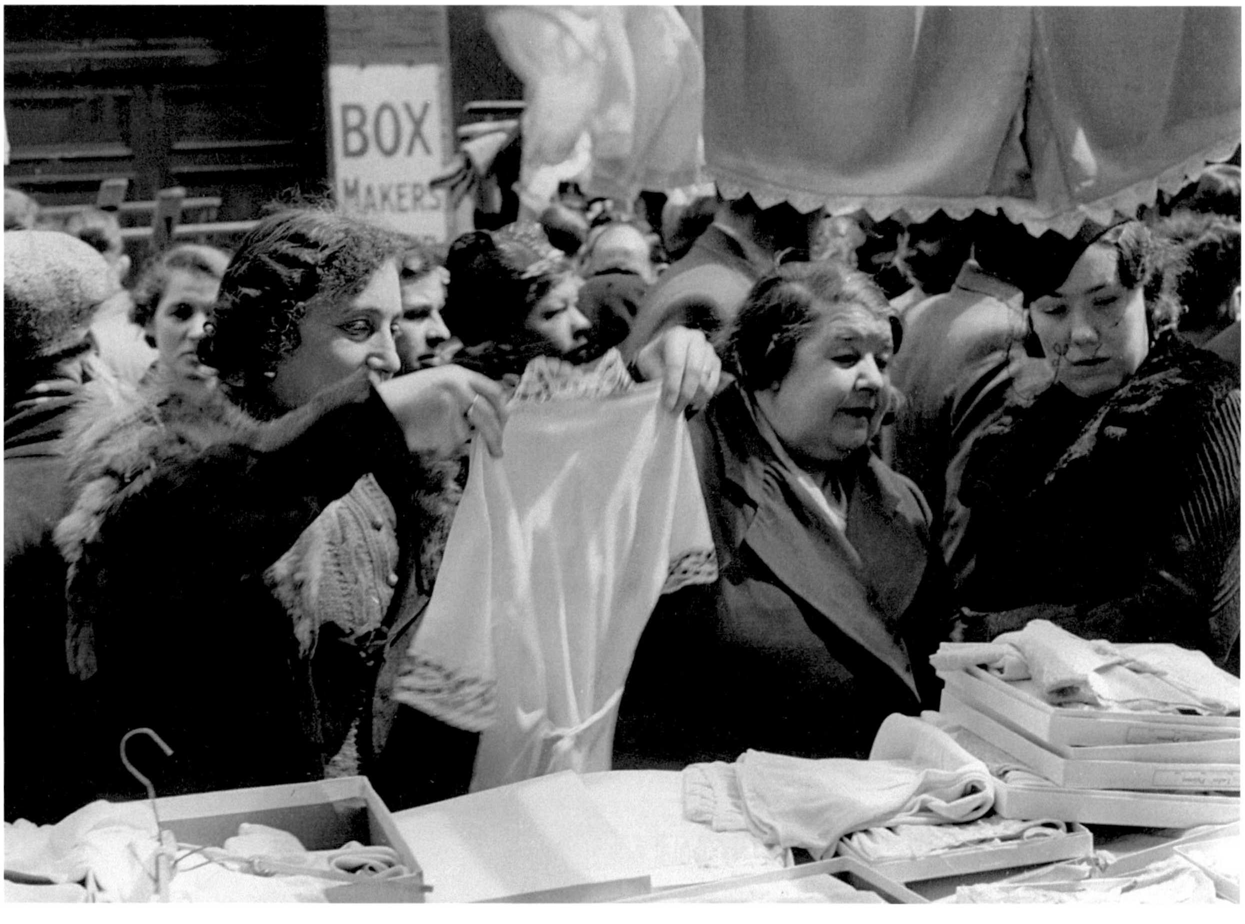

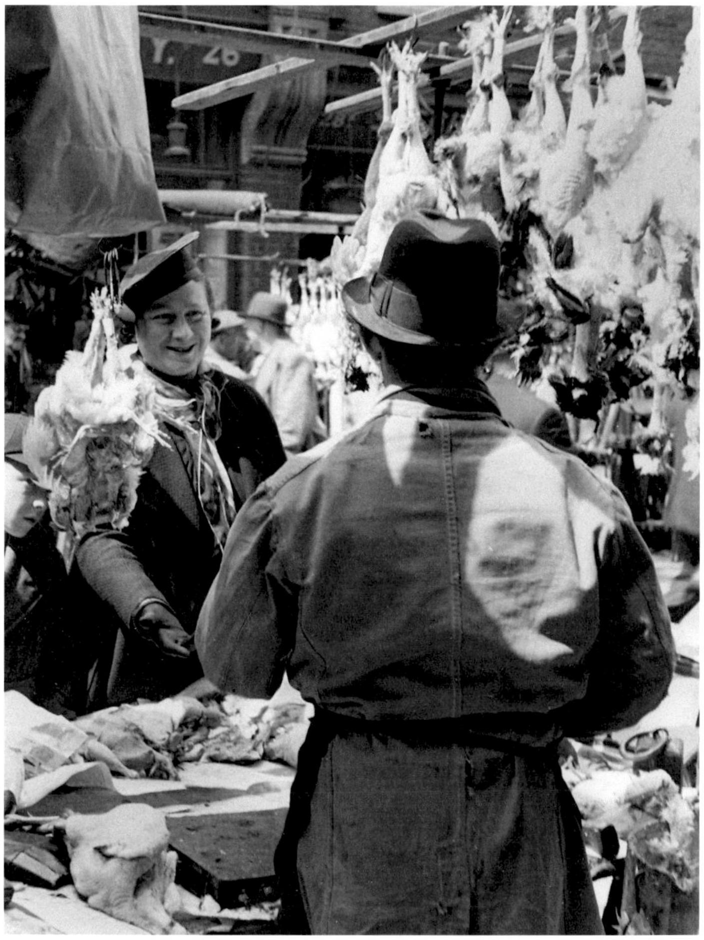

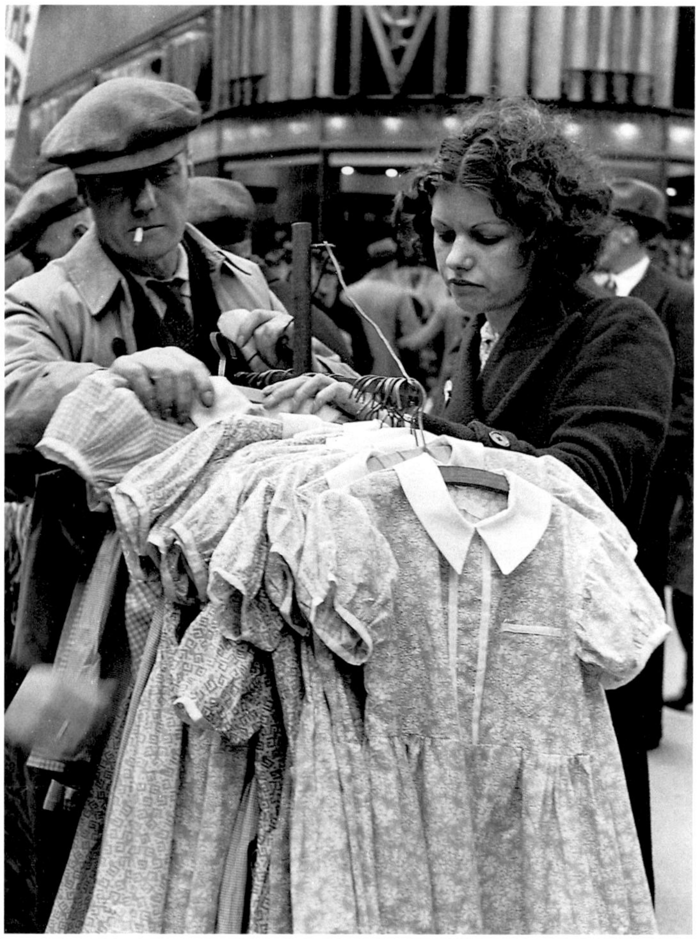

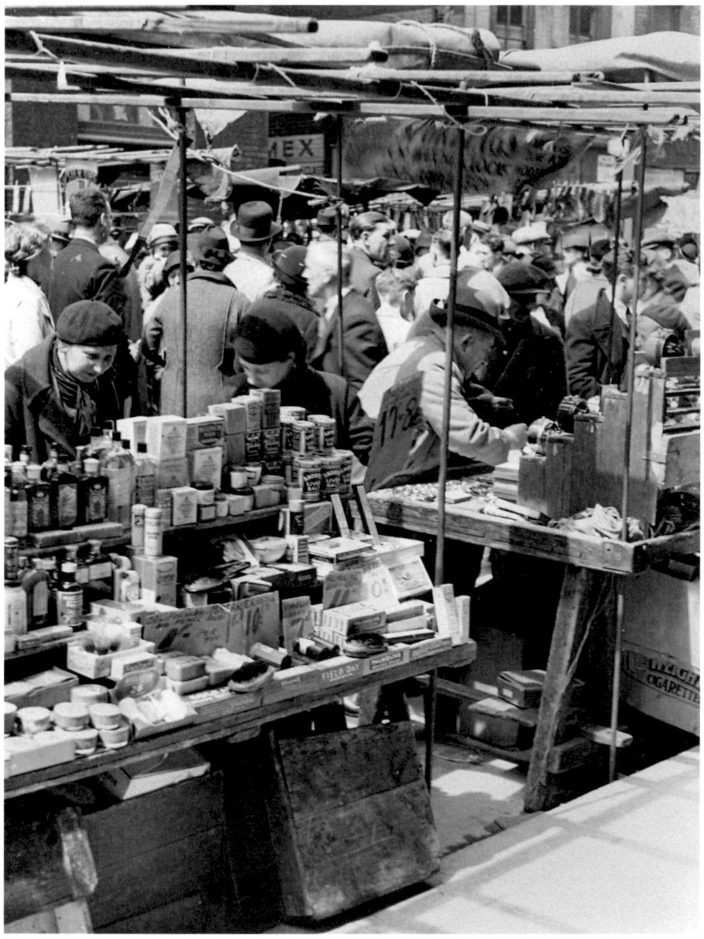

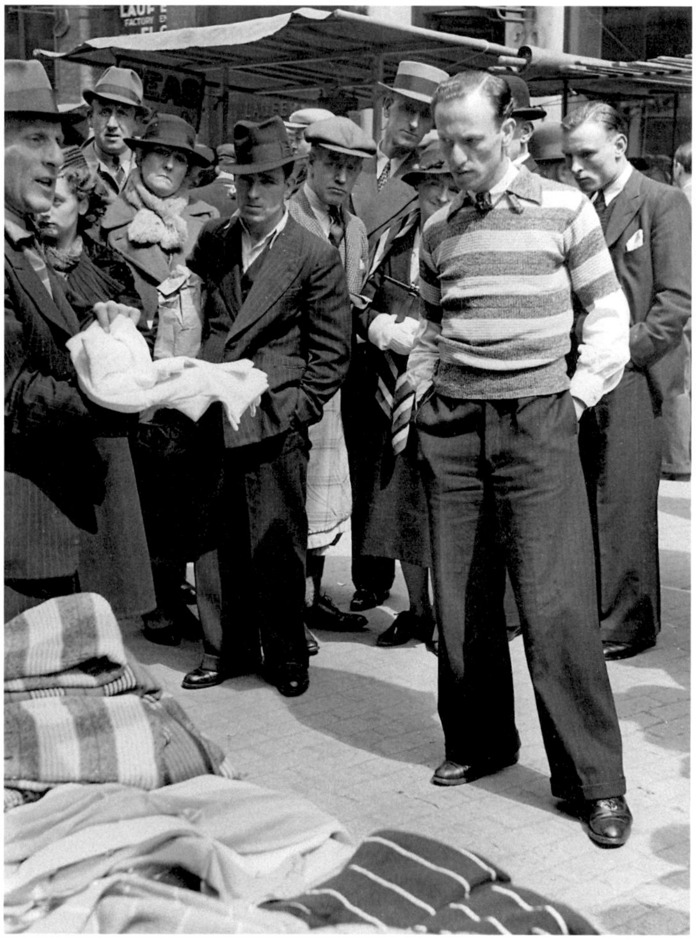

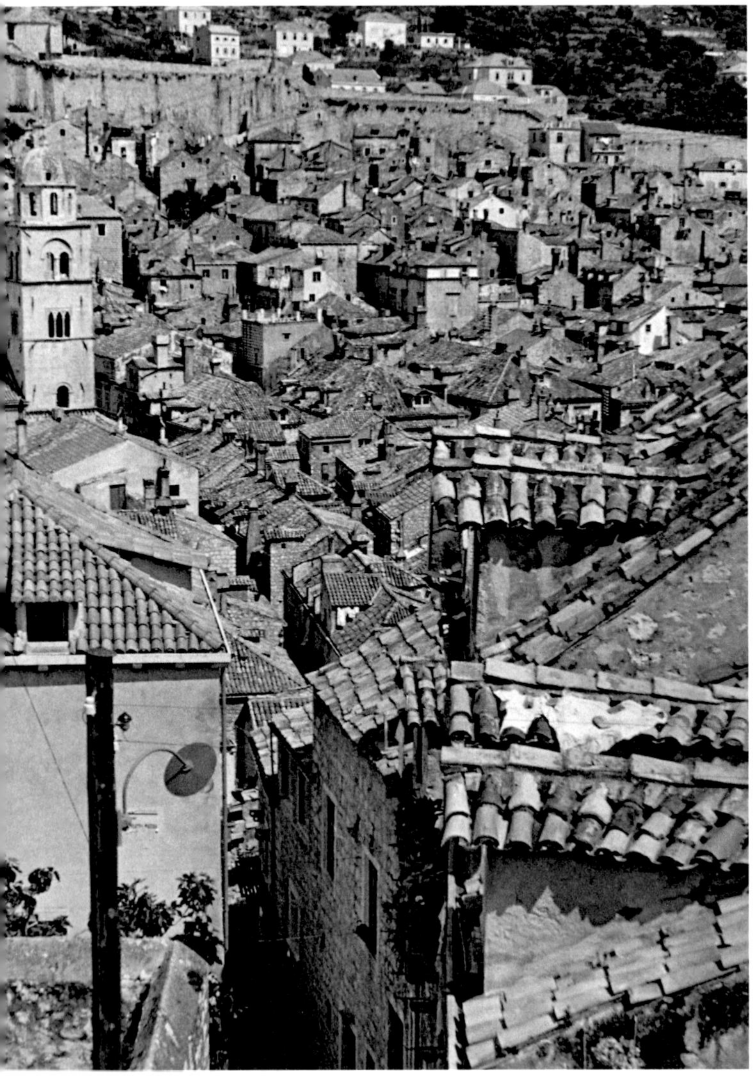

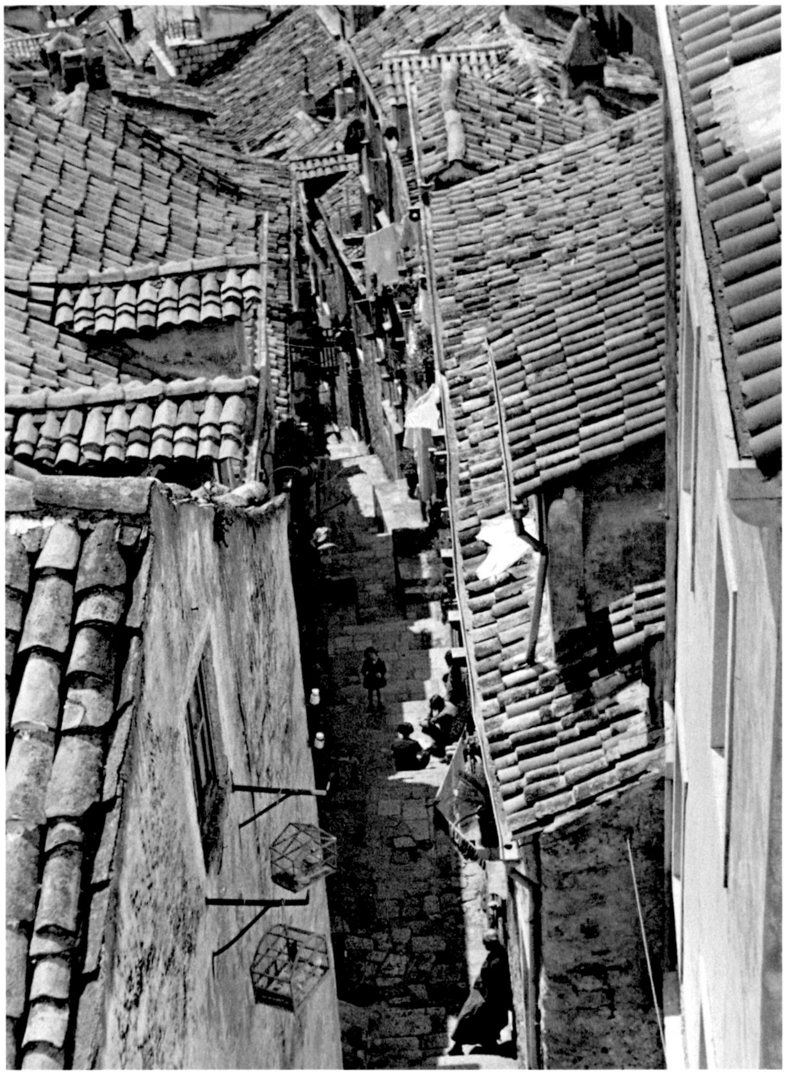

View over the roofs of Dubrovnik, Dalmatia, Yugoslavia, 1937

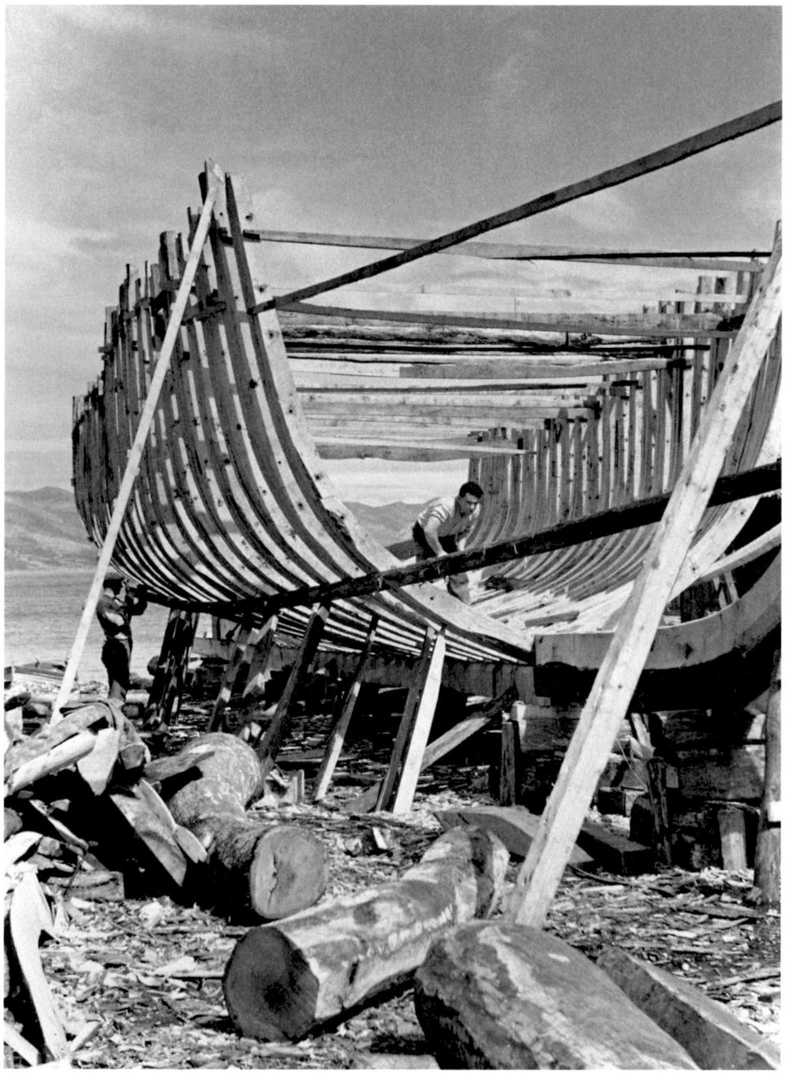

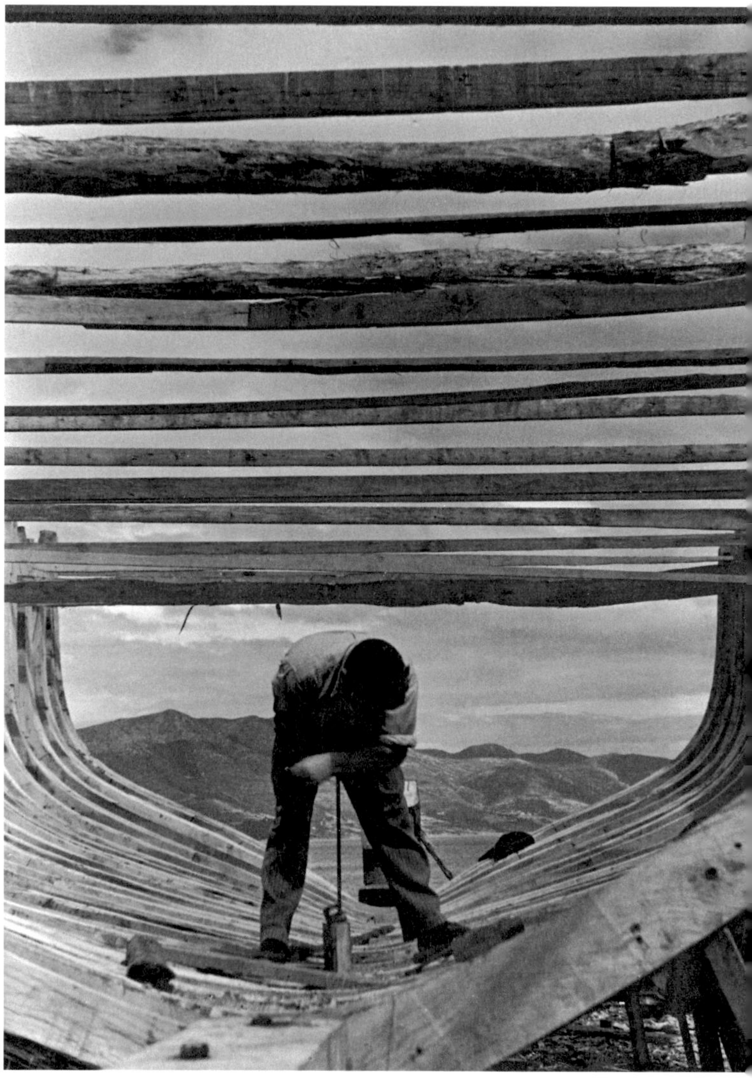

Ship building on the Adriatic Sea, Dalmatia, Yugoslavia, 1937

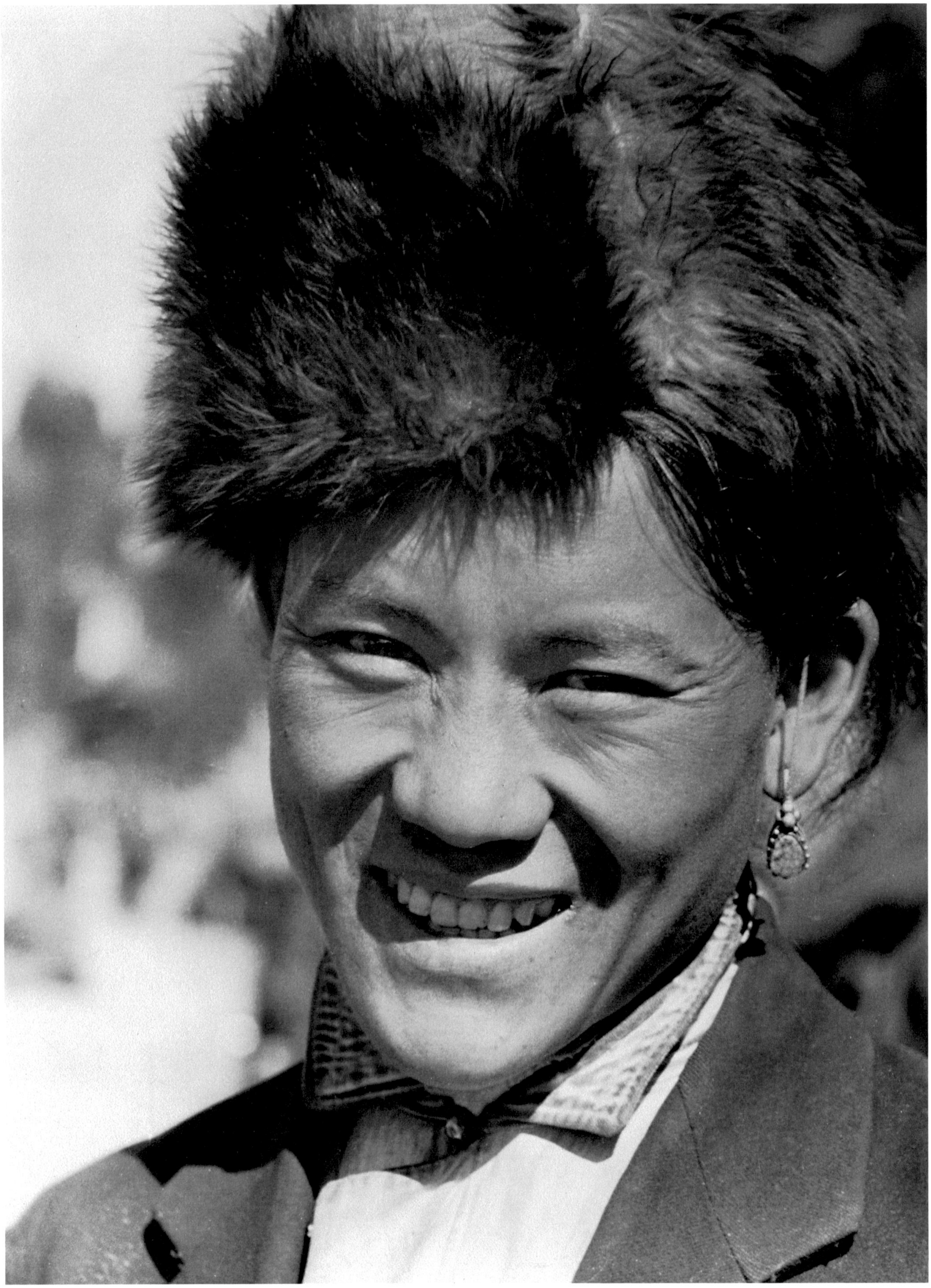

Boy from Northern India, 1938

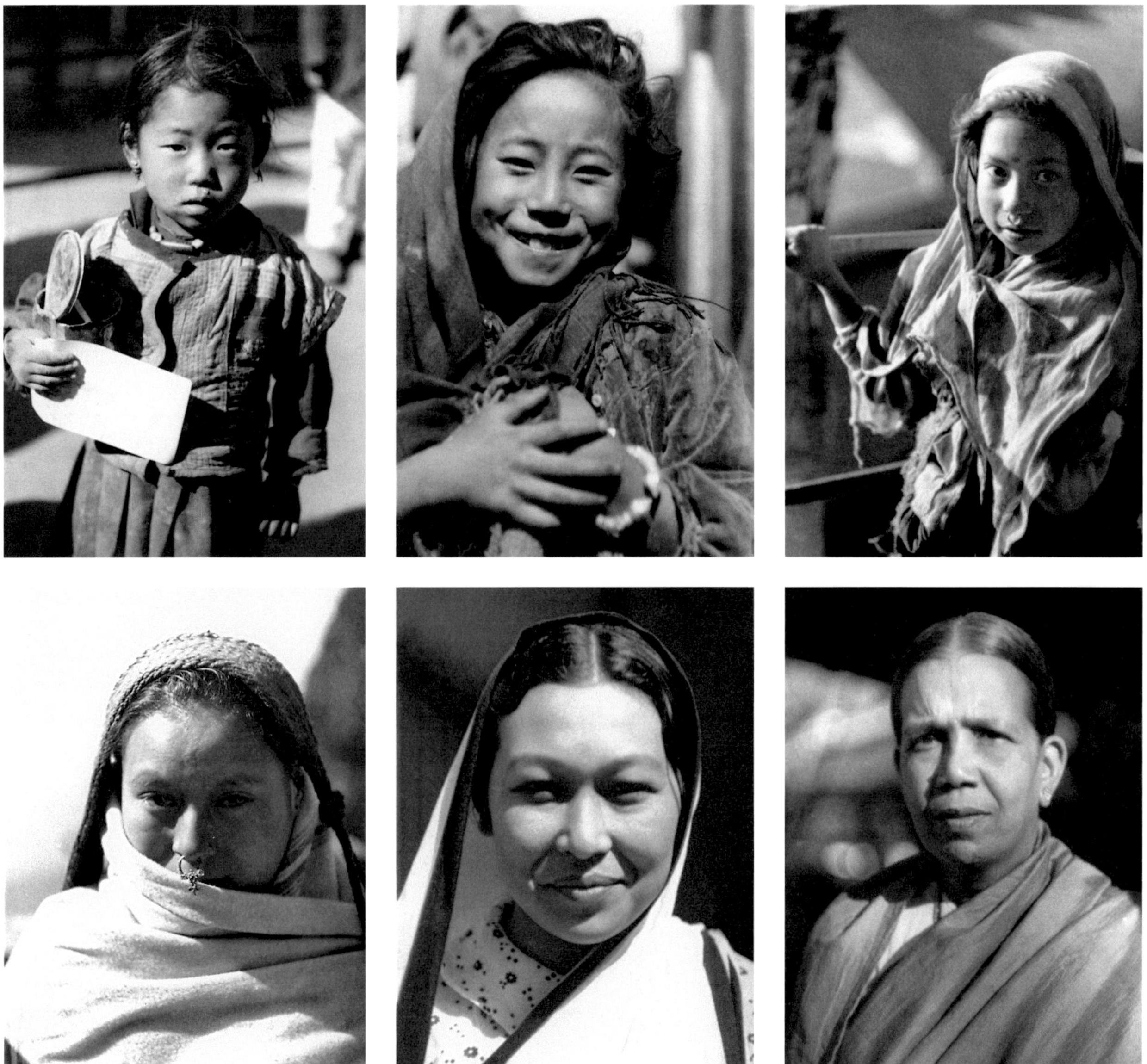

Children, women, and men from Northern India, 1938

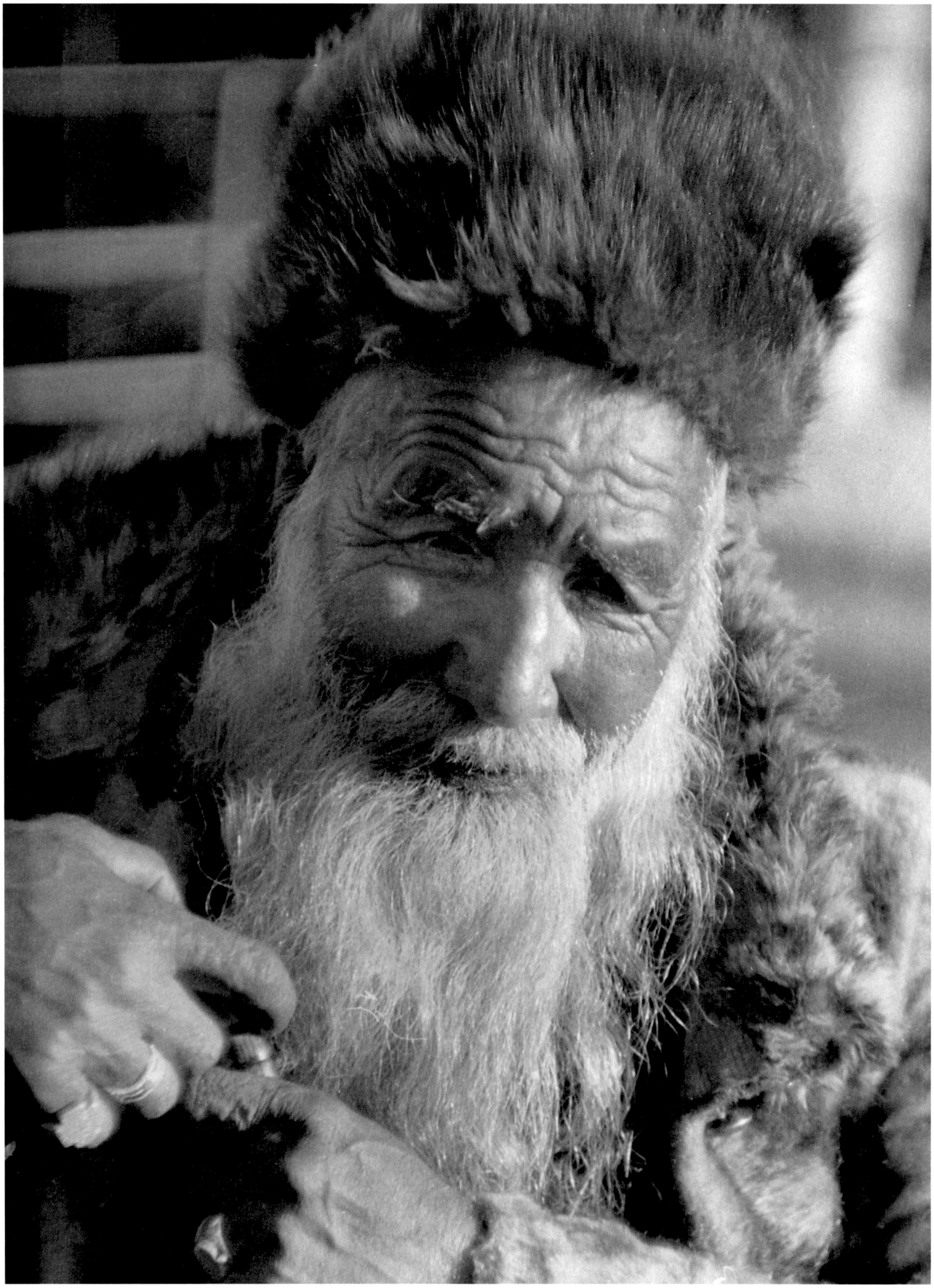

Old man from Northern India, 1938

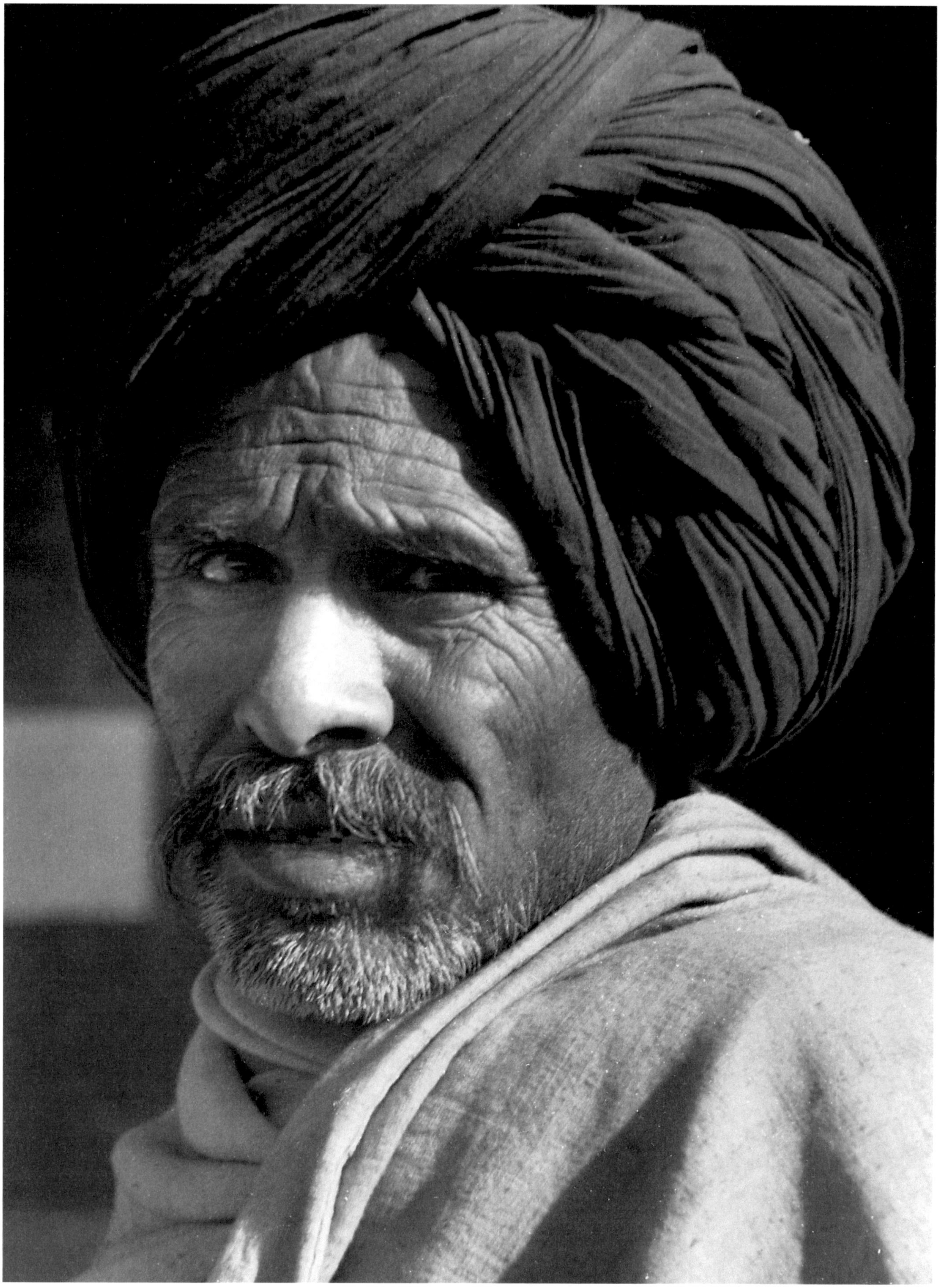

Man from Northern India, 1938

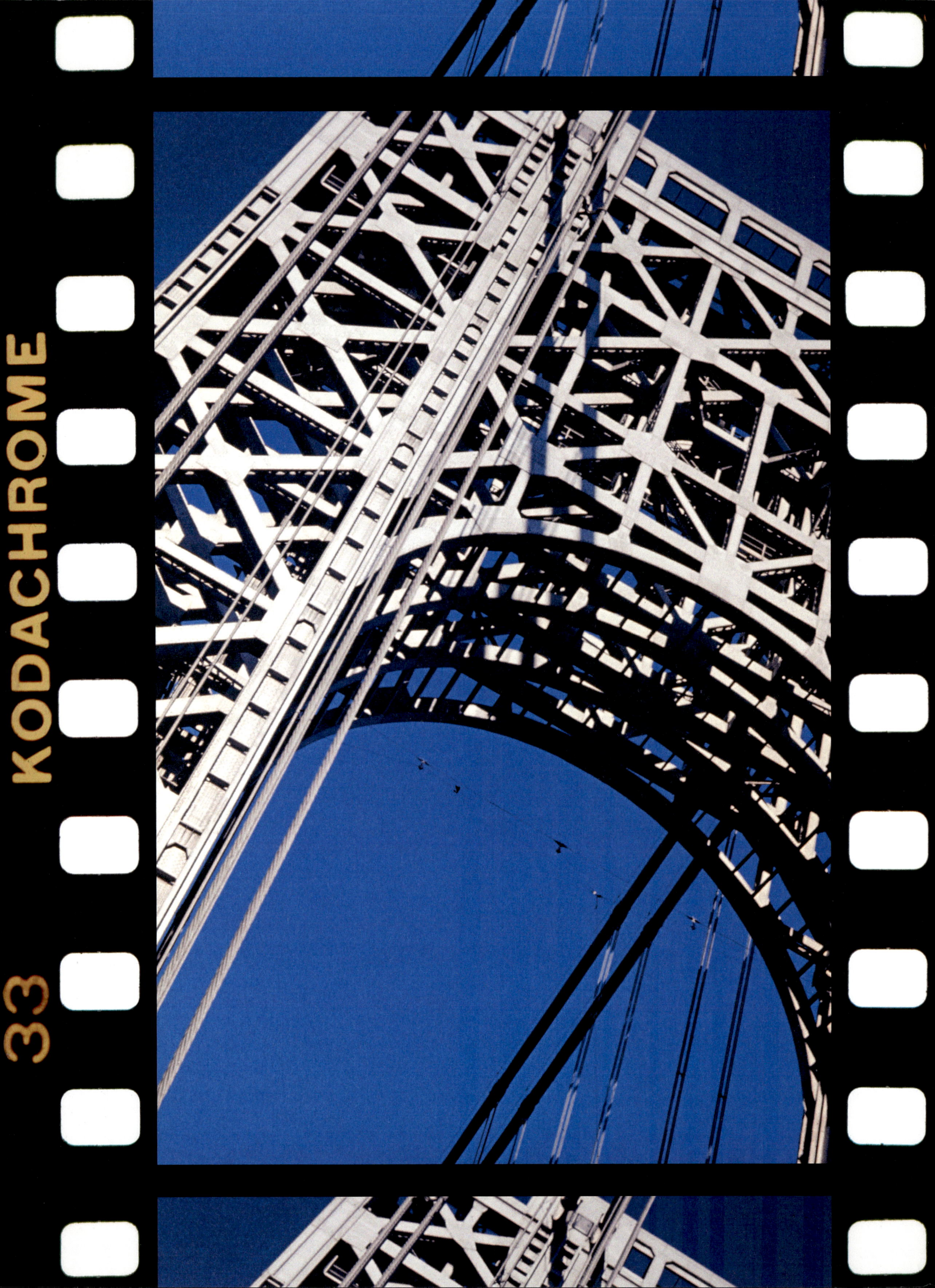
KODACHROME
33

The School of Seeing in Kodachrome

Color Slides of Architecture, Art, and Technology

Preserved in the estate of Fritz Block are several thousand 35-mm slides, which the photographer produced from 1940 onward, while living in exile in America.[1] Some show different aspects of everyday life in Los Angeles. Others are thematic series: on modern architecture in California, forms found in nature and in technology, industrial design, modern sculpture, and art and artifacts from various cultures. The significance of this body of work within the history of photography lies not such much in the artistic quality of individual motifs as in the underlying concept of creating an "educational color library" for progressive art education and correspondingly for training a sense for color among young people. Often these images were early or even the first color photographs of the given object. Block's color slide production added yet another dimension of photographic expression to his already multi-faceted work in black and white. Furthermore, his slide work represents an unusual contribution to the history of color photography and a remarkable individual achievement within the context of exile photography.[2] Also significant is the way in which Block's color slide production exemplifies the cultural transfer that emigrants from Europe brought to America—drawing on the photographic vision, concepts of art education, and universalist understanding of modernism that had emerged in the 1920s in Germany.

Color Photographer

In Los Angeles, Block soon realized that he would not be able to continue his work as an architect, lacking an American license and the corresponding language skills and specialized knowledge. Given the predominant construction methods in California at the time, he also was not overly interested in pursuing this course. After years of working for himself, he did not wish to consider working for someone else, and his hearing impairment was a handicap. Block therefore looked for meaningful work that would also provide him with an income. In the spring of 1939, the *Hollywood Citizen-Examiner* published an article with the headline "German Architect Here to Start Life Anew," in which Block explained his future plans: "I think I make photography a profession now."[3] In fact, he did ultimately decide to make photography, which had previously been more or less a hobby, his main career. First, he set about reassessing the photo archive that he had brought with him. He made new prints from black-and-white slide films, and attached English labels to the back of these as well as older prints, in order to sell them to photo agencies in the United States. He also compiled portfolio albums with a representative selection of his photographs.[4]

However, black-and-white photography did not prove to be a promising endeavor for Block, since he lacked the connections to the American press necessary for selling his images, and there was no demand for his existing photos, since the content was no longer current. Out of necessity and curiosity, Block, who was meanwhile fifty years old, turned to color photography in the new format of color slides. Kodak and Agfa, the leading film companies in the US and Germany respectively, had introduced new multi-layer films for 35-mm color slides (Kodachrome and Agfacolor) with great marketing fanfare in the second half of the 1930s—and thereby helped to establish color photography.[5] Now also amateurs could take color photographs in an easy and economical manner. Initially Block had taken a skeptical and negative stance towards photographers who had embraced this development: "In the thirties, at the time when our present color material, Kodachrome and Agfacolor came up, I was one of its most passionate enemies. I was disgusted with its naturalism, with the crying colors and the terrible manner in which this material was prostituted. However, after some time I recognized the inherent artistic possibilities of the material, which so far had not been exploited."[6] On his 1942 registration card, required by the Defense Security Service, he already listed his profession as "color photographer." In the US he maintained the use of his academic title, in order to underscore the didactic aim of his work. Nevertheless, he americanized his first name to

George Washington Bridge, New York, ca. 1950

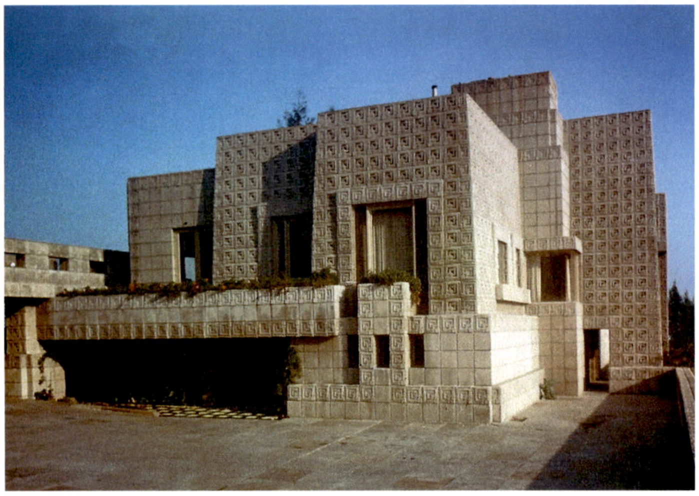

Frank Lloyd Wright, Ennis Residence (1923), Hollywood, 1943

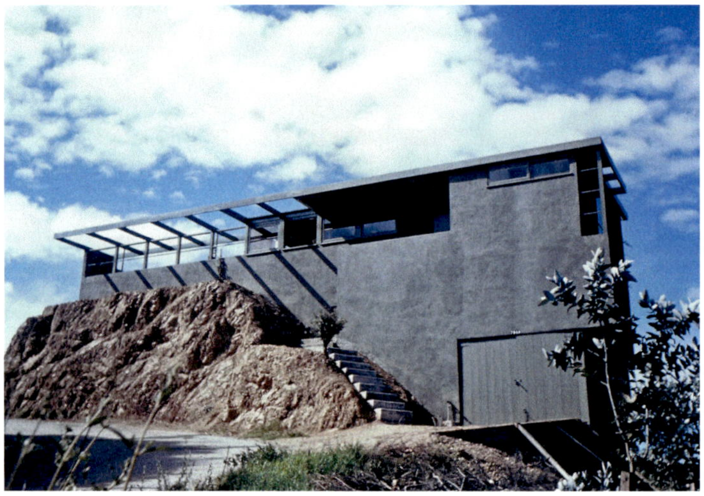

Rudolph M. Schindler, Harris Residence (1942), Los Angeles, 1943

"Fred," since "Fritz" sounded too German. From then on he pursued photography under the name "Dr. Fred Block."

Educational Color Photography

Block's main aim was not to produce color photography of artistic quality, but instead to make color slides for progressive visual education. The development of slide film had led to a range of innovations in this field. Schools, colleges, and universities purchased projectors and set up slide libraries. Block realized that there was a lack of contemporary motifs for this purpose. Commonly widespread were images of paintings or architectural monuments.[7] He was first commissioned by the Board of Education in Los Angeles to produce color slides on general topics with series titles such as *Animals*, *Vegetables and Fruits*, *Garden Flowers*, *Flowering Trees*, *Palm Trees*, *Parks*, *Clouds*, *Farming*, *Making Bread*, *Circus*, *The Zoo*, *California Beach*, *Railways*, and *Harbors*. Between 1940 and 1945 Block produced over twenty such series, each with some forty motifs. This work provided him with income and also helped him gain practical experience in the production and duplication of color slides. It also aligned with his modernist concept of art, in which aesthetic education should take place as part of everyday experience and should start at a young age.

Given their purpose, Block's photographs for these series were illustrative and did not convey high artistic ambitions. The motifs that are most interesting from today's perspective are those that give a color impression of the early 1940s in Los Angeles. One example is the series *Who Comes to Your Home*, which was intended to explain to young people which type of services and trades are needed for the home and which cars the different workmen and delivery men drove [p. 300]. His series *Trucks* had a similar orientation, showing different types of commercial trucks and their functions [p. 301]. However, Block photographed the city of Los Angeles exclusively for his series, not from the perspective of a reporter. His images of the beach at Santa Monica and the oil rigs off the coast at Santa Barbara were taken for his series *California Beach* [p. 320], and those at MacArthur Park for his series *Parks* [p. 321]. The few slides that he made which are relevant to events at the time are the photos that Block took on August 14, 1945 after the parade in downtown Los Angeles to celebrate V-J Day, the end of World War II in the Pacific [p. 321].

Walter C. Arensberg

As he was establishing his new business as a photographer, Block received support from various sources. One important patron from 1941 onward was Walter C. Arensberg (1878–1954), an eminent collector of pre-Columbian and modern art in Los Angeles. Arensberg also helped Block, who was classified as an "enemy alien" upon the entry of the US into World War II. For this reason, he was supposed to surrender his camera in 1942. Arensberg then wrote to United States Attorney, Southern District of California, "Dr. Block is a professional photographer and without his camera he is deprived of the means of making a living. I have known Dr. Block for more than one year, and, as a citizen of the United States, I can give you my complete assurance of his loyalty to the United States, and I am willing to assume the responsibility that Dr. Block would not make use of his camera in any way harmful to the United States of America." [8] Arensberg also served as the official sponsor of Block and his wife for their application of US citizenship in 1943, which they received in April 1944.

Walter C. and Louise Arensberg had transformed their home in Hollywood into a private museum, which could be visited by appointment. In 1933 an extension had been built onto the house by architects Richard J. Neutra and his assistant Gregory Ain, which created an extra room to house a number of key works in the collection, including *Nude Descending a Staircase, No. 2* (1912) by Marcel Duchamp and *Soft Construction with Boiled Beans (Premonition of Civil War)* (1936) by Salvador Dalí. The only known color photographs of this gallery space [p. 290] stem from Block.[9] According to their numbering, they were apparently produced for the color slide series *Modern Architecture I* (1943) but were removed from the series around 1950. Probably some years later, Block also photographed the collection of modern sculpture in the Arensberg's house, which included import-

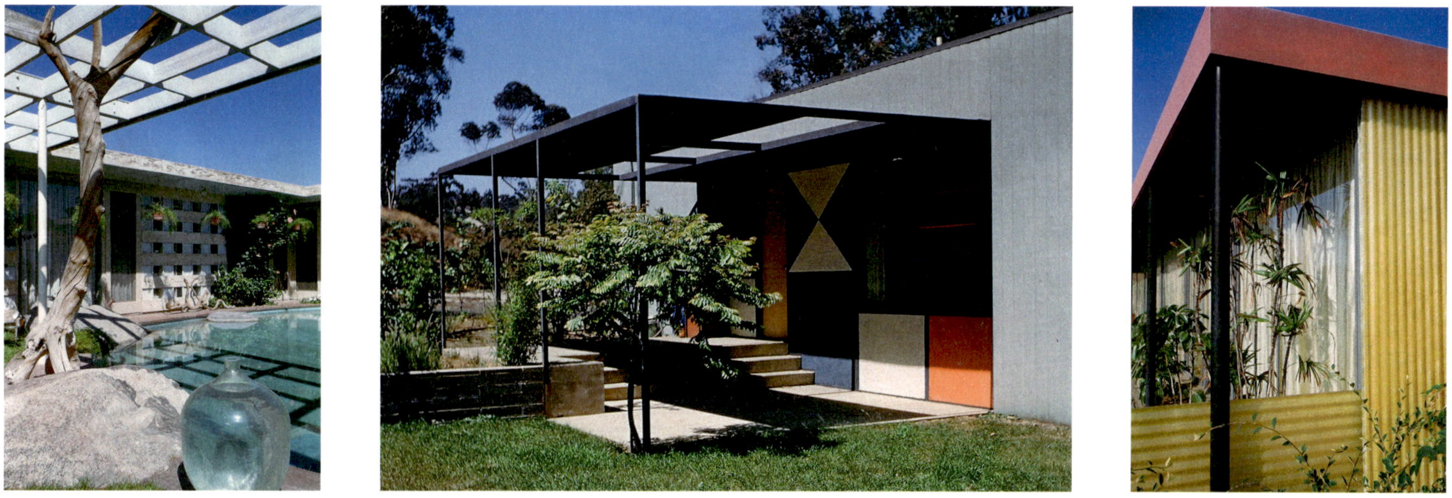

Raymond Loewy, Loewy House (1946), Palms Springs – Charles Eames / Eero Saarinen, Entenza House (1949), Santa Monica – Raphael S. Soriano, Case Study House (1950), ca. 1950

ant works by Constantin Brâncuși such as *The Princess* (1915/16) [p. 304], and he subsequently integrated these images into his color slide series *Modern Sculpture* (1949).

Neutra, Gropius, and Wright

Although Block had given up his work as an architect, he had by no means lost interest in architecture. He intensively studied the modern architecture of southern California and developed a corresponding color slide series that was new in such a form. For this purpose he closely examined architectural journals and corresponded with architects.[10] His exchange with Richard J. Neutra was particularly fruitful, and Block took numerous photographs of his buildings in Los Angeles and its surrounding areas. However, for the publication of his works, Neutra did not use Block's images, but preferred the technically superior and even spectacular architectural photographs of Julius Shulman (1910–2009), with whom he had already been working for an extended period of time. But in the early 1940s Shulman was still predominantly employing black and white, since there were very few possibilities for publishing color images.

In order to gather suggestions about where he might be able to sell his architectural color slides, Block contacted Walter Gropius in 1943, also a German architect and émigré, who had meanwhile assumed the position as head of the Architecture Department at Harvard University. Gropius expressed an interest in helping Block: "I am glad to have heard from you at last and to see that you have been very busy developing something of your own here in your country. Of course, I am very interested in the photographs you are making [...]."[11] Block thereupon send him image materials: "I believe that this new medium of color slides could become a superb medium of propaganda for modern architecture, since this country is very open to it. [...] From the initial responses, the interest among universities and colleges is happily quite substantial, and there is such great enthusiasm for my slides, that I plan to fully dedicate myself to this field of modern art."[12] Gropius gave Block the name of someone at Harvard, and also at the Museum of Modern Art in New York: "Mrs. [Elizabeth] Mock, who has charge of the Department of Architecture and is a very understanding person [...] is just now preparing a collection of the best modern architecture [...] in the United States."[13] In the letter accompanying the return of color slides back to Block in November 1943, Gropius wrote: "I have shown them to quite a lot of people around here. [...] I admire your initiative in going into this field and making a business out of it."

By corresponding with American architectural and art historians, Block sought further suggestions for his architecture series. In July 1943, he was encouraged by Walter W. Horn (1908–1995)—an art historian who had fled from Nazi Germany the US via Florence and was working in the Art Department of the University of California, Berkeley—to expand his series with additional images of Frank Lloyd Wright's buildings: "The collection in its present stage is too restricted to Los Angeles. To have a few outstanding non-Californian examples would be a better selling point."[14] Block then wrote to Wright in July, 1943: "Being a veteran in appreciating the ingenuity of your work, I have in mind to render the entire work of your life in color slides and in adequate quality [...]. I hope my material will help to make modern architecture more popular in this country."[15]

Wright selected a number of color slides from the samples of his buildings sent by Block for his own collection.[16] However, these images were never used in publications on the architect, or at least they were never labeled as such. Around 1950 Block traveled to visit Wright in Taliesin West, Arizona, in order to photograph the architect's winter home and studio and to show him not only his architectural photographs but also his color slide series *Beauty in Nature* and *Expressive Forms in Nature*. These series were tellingly of particular interest to Wright, as Block happily then reported: "I am delighted to tell that Frank Lloyd Wright showed much interest in just this material. He gave acknowledging and wise comments [...]. I am proud to say that this material, created for children and budding artists, induced our country's greatest artistic genius to add these series besides others to his own slide collection."[17]

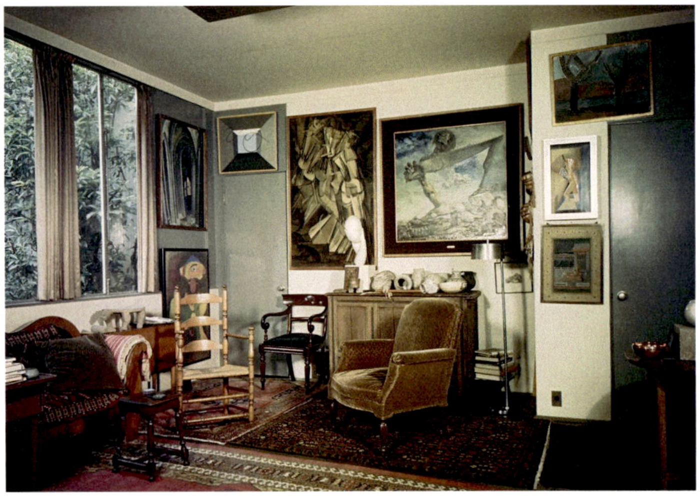

Richard J. Neutra / Gregory Ain, Arensberg Residence, gallery room (1933), Hollywood, 1943

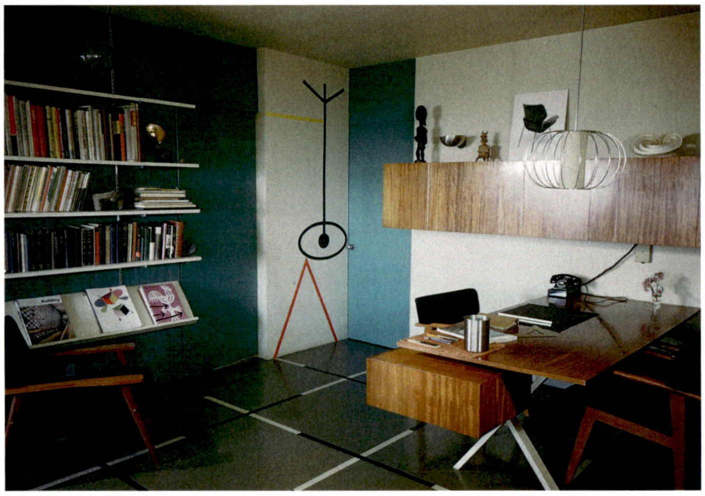

Alvin Lustig, office and studio of the designer (1947), Los Angeles, ca. 1950

Museum of Modern Art, New York

Block received particular recognition and support from the Museum of Modern Art in New York. Following Gropius' recommendation, he contacted Elizabeth (Bauer) Mock (1911–1998), who was head of the Department of Architecture and Design at the museum from 1942 to 1946. She was considered an influential supporter of modern architecture in the US, and at the time she was preparing the exhibition *Built in the U.S.A. 1932–1944* (1944). In late August of 1943 she answered in response to Block sending a collection of color slides: "The slides are extremely handsome—carefully selected, well-composed and, for the most part, excellent in color."[18] She gave Block information on additional buildings of modern architecture in California that he could take into consideration and also gave him the addresses of progressive schools and boards of education. In addition, she suggested that his slide series should be made available in New York, as material available for loan through the museum's library.[19]

The Museum of Modern Art thus became one of Block's most important sales partners. Bernard Karpel (1911–1986), initially the deputy director and later the director of the library, made sure that Block's color slides could not only be viewed on site but also loaned out (not until the mid 1950s did the museum discontinue this service). In addition, as part of its educational program "Pictures at Work!" the museum library sent information about their learning materials to educational institutions throughout the country—and included Block's catalogue of color slides.[20] Out of thanks for their experienced help, Block donated a selection of his color slides on architecture to the museum.[21]

Dr. Block Color Productions

Encouraged by the positive response to his architecture series, Block expanded his color slide service to the one-person company Dr. Block Color Productions in 1943. Until his death in 1955, he produced twenty-seven thematic series, which encompassed some 3,300 motifs. The topics were guided by Block's practical limitations, since the objects had to be accessible to him either in the city, in private collections, or in museum exhibitions. At the same time, his series covered a broad range of themes, since his own cultural interests were very broad. The leitmotifs running throughout Block's work remained his commitment to modern design, a universal concept of art that transcended specific eras and cultural spheres, and an understanding of contemporary art: "The selection of the material is based exclusively on its importance for the creative artist and the degree of inspiration it may give him for his own work. There are no historic or intellectual considerations of any kind. The affinity to contemporary movements is decisive."[22]

Block developed the series, took the photographs, and duplicated the slides in a process that he himself developed. His offerings were flexible and reasonable in price; one could purchase entire series, a selection of images, or individual slides. The slides were delivered in stamped (i.e. with "Dr. Block Color") cardboard mounts, which were numbered by hand. Over the years, certain motifs were exchanged within or added to certain series, which explains the slight differences between the series that have been preserved. Every series was accompanied by a copied brochure with a short text that not only explained the given topic but also served to advertise Block's products. Also included was a detailed list of the given motifs, which for works of art was accompanied by information about the museum or private collection where they were found. In addition to sending out order sheets [p. 329], Block advertised through references in specialized magazines and listings in catalogues of educational materials. Although Block's earnings from his color slide production were modest, they did provide him with an independent income in exile. There were even periods when he was able to hire an assistant to duplicate slides. Block's wife, Anna-Sophie, also provided essential support, by drawing up lists, performing the administrative work for the business, and driving him to photo shoots with the car.

Architecture

Encompassing some 800 motifs, the architecture series were a focus of Block's color slide production: "Buildings cannot be moved or sent to exhibits. Therefore it seems most

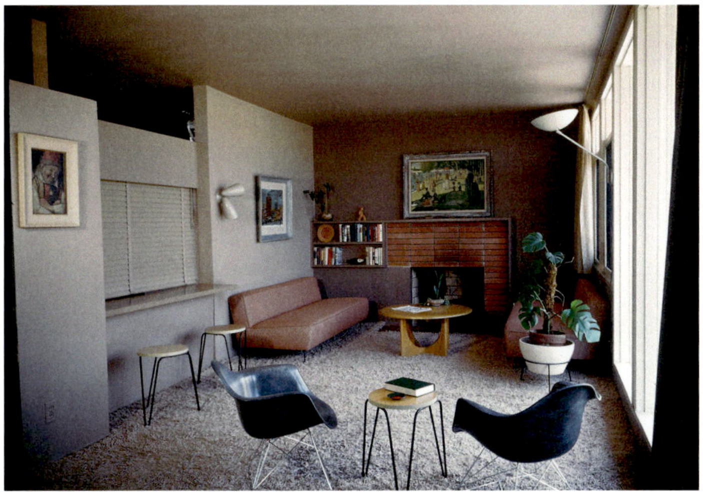

Gregory Ain et al., Mar Vista Housing Group (1948), living room, Mar Vista, ca. 1950

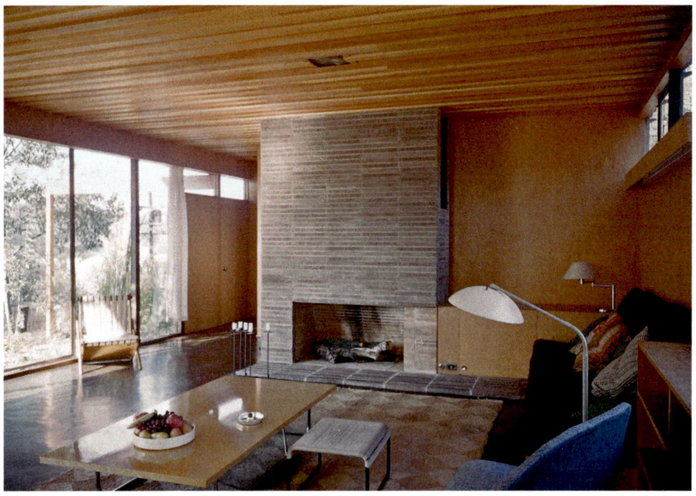

Richard J. Neutra, Reunion House (1951), living room, Los Angeles, 1952

important that we have good photos, which interpret them adequately for us and posterity."[23] But Block's architecture photos are not professionally composed photographs of the kind that Julius Shulman produced in southern California. Block worked exclusively with a 35-mm camera, often without a tripod and without any complex lighting for interior spaces. He instead showed the buildings and interior settings from the authentic perspective of the average passer-by or normal visitor. Furthermore, he was primarily interested in illustrating functional aspects of the architecture, its integration into its natural setting, and the structure and furnishings of the individual rooms. Primarily due to their color, the photographs convey a lively impression of the fresh, new architectural ideas that were manifested among the palms and beneath the blue sky.

The first series, *Modern Architecture I* (1943), which contained 333 color slides of exteriors and interiors, is organized by architect and year of construction. The spectrum spans the period from Frank Lloyd Wright's Barnsdall Residence (1920) and his Ennis Residence (1923) [p. 290] in Hollywood to Richard J. Neutra's Channel Heights Housing Project (1943) [p. 294] in San Pedro; but most buildings stem from the period around 1940. The series begins with Wright, who is represented in some fifty slides, which also include his Sturges Residence (1938) [p. 310] in Brentwood Heights. Neutra follows with over 120 images, among them his Dr. Lovell Health House (1928) [p. 311], the Grace Lewis Miller Residence (1937) in Palm Springs [p. 312], and Ralph Waldo Emerson High School in Westwood (1937) [p. 314]. Introduced as additional representatives of southern Californian modernism are: William Lescaze with his CBS Building (1938) [p. 318] in Hollywood; Harwell Hamilton Harris with the Byron Pumphrey Residence (1939) [p. 317]; Rudolph M. Schindler with the Buck Residence (1934) [p. 313] and the Harris Residence [p. 290]; Edward R. Lind with the Douglas Kennedy Residence (1939) [p. 313]; and Julius R. Davidson with the Drucker Apartments (1940) [p. 313].

Around 1945, Block drew on this image material for a special series produced for US governmental organizations, *Modern Architecture in the U.S.A.*[24] His accompanying text documents the view of an immigrant architect from Europe on modern American architecture. Block talks about the exchange between Europe and America and emphasizes the particular significance of Frank Lloyd Wright as a mediator between the two. He also underscores the pioneering role played by southern California within modern architecture, not least due to the influence of architects from Europe who settled there.

An updated continuation of this series was *The New Concept of Space* (1952), also titled *Modern Architecture II,* with 468 photographs largely dating from the postwar era. In addition to architectural magazines, Block garnered information from different sources, including an issue of the *Museum of Modern Art Bulletin* about a symposium that had taken place at the museum "What is Happening to Modern Architecture?" (Spring 1948, vol. XV, no. 3). He additionally drew inspiration from the exhibition *Domestic Architecture of the San Francisco Bay Region* at the San Francisco Museum of Art in the fall of 1949 and its accompanying catalogue. He also made use of the innovative architectural guide, *A Guide to Contemporary Architecture in Southern California* (1951), which was designed by Alvin Lustig and illustrated with black-and-white photographs by Julius Shulman.

The core of this second architecture series consisted of thirty-six exterior and interior photographs of Frank Lloyd Wright's Taliesin West (1938–42) [p. 310], the architect's winter quarters and studio near Scottsdale, Arizona, which Block had visited around 1950. The second emphasis, including some fifty images, was once again the buildings of Richard J. Neutra, including the Tremaine Residence (1949) [p. 311] in Santa Barbara along with buildings built for Aloe Hospital Equipment Company (1949) [p. 316] and Northwestern Mutual Fire Insurance (1951) [p. 315] in Los Angeles. In addition, it presented, in alphabetical order, the works of further architects largely from southern California, among them the Loewy Residence (1946) [p. 312] and the addition to the Frey House (1948) [pp. 291 and 313] in Palm Springs by John Porter Clark and Albert Frey; the Hermann Miller showroom (1949) in Los Angeles with furnishings by Charles

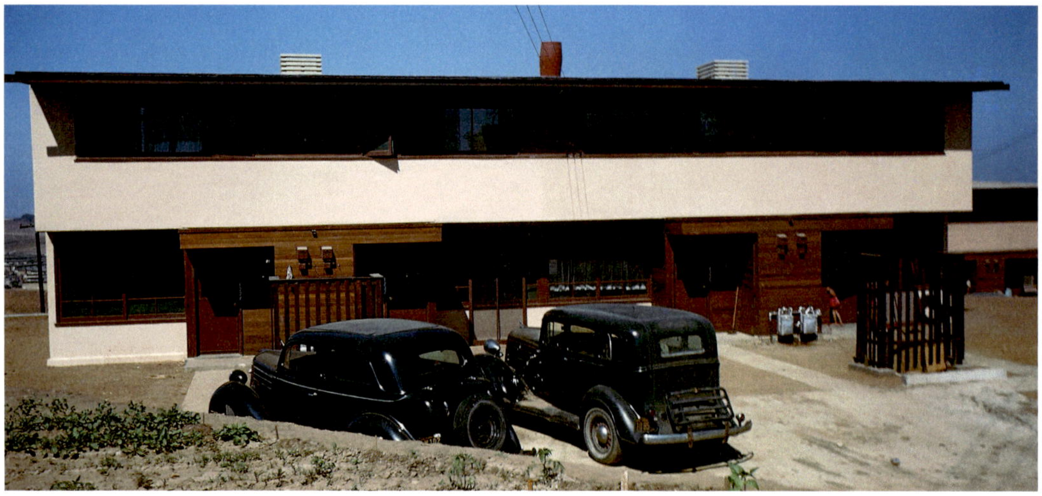

Richard J. Neutra, Channel Heights Housing Project (1943), two-story unit, San Pedro, 1943

Eames; the Foster House (1950) [p. 313] in Sherman Oaks by John Lautner; the studio (1947) [p. 292] of graphic designer Alvin Lustig; the Robinson's Beverly department store by Pereira & Luckman (1952) [p. 315] along with its parking level [p. 295]; Palm Springs High School (1948/49) [p. 314] by Williams, Williams and Williams; and the Prudential Building (1949) [p. 319] by Walter Wurdeman and Welton Becket. Some of the Case Study Houses were also included: the Entenza House (1949) by Charles Eames and Eero Saarinen and the Case Study House (1950) by Raphael S. Soriano [p. 291].

Block's third architectural series, *Home Making for Moderns* (1952), is based on a selection of eighty two slides from the previous series and added motifs. These only show interiors, which are not organized by architect but by the type and function of the rooms. In the accompanying text Block emphasizes three characteristics of contemporary modern architecture: first "the Outside, relations between house and site, the house as the three-dimensional expression of the free plan"; then "the Inside, the free plan, new constructions methods and the liberated wall permit full spatial freedom"; and finally "the Materials, a new awareness of the nature of the materials—old and new—is influencing form and spatial design." His self-advertising in the brochure reads: "Photographed by a master technician who has developed an educational series unmatched by anything available in either America or Europe, Dr. Block's color slides on American Architecture [...] demonstrate his experience as an architect and his insight as a photographer."

Design

Block applied his understanding of modern design, garnered from architecture, to design and crafted objects. This is exemplified in the one hundred photographs of his series *Modern Industrial Design* (1949) [pp. 297 and 305]. It is largely based on objects in the Industrial Design Collection of the Museum of Modern Art in New York, which Block photographed on site. The motifs range from chairs by Alvar Aalto, Marcel Breuer, Ludwig Mies van der Rohe, Charles Eames, and others to applied design by the Bauhaus, design products by Raymond Loewy, and kitchen appliances and household items. In addition, Block juxtaposed industrial design products (largely designs by Charles Eames) with samples of hand-made ceramics (by Glen Lukens, Marguerite Wildenhain, and Beatrice Wood) and hand-woven textiles (by Dorothy Liebes and Anni Albers). The accompanying text comments on these the latter objects: "Those examples show that craftsmanship has its place and undiminished merits in the modern machine age."

Block further illustrated these thoughts in two additional series, *Modern Ceramic Arts* (1946) offers an overview of works by different ceramicists in southern California. *The Potter's Workshop* (1949) was photographed in the workshop of the German-British ceramicist Marguerite (Friedlaender-)Wildenhain, who emigrated to the US in 1940. It shows her simple studio in Guerneville, California and also follows the development of a pitcher from the raw material of the clay to the decoration of the finished work.

Characteristic of Block's functional understanding of art are the 182 motifs of the series *Materials and their Creative Use* (1953), which traces forms created by nature, humankind, and artists—organized by material (stone, glass, plastic, etc.). The range of examples extends from natural objects to industrial products, and works of art from museums, private collections, and artists' studios. The brochure for the series emphasizes the particular capability of color photography to demonstrate the quality and effects of different materials: "The extraordinary capacity of color photography for rendering texture makes this medium particularly suited to this series. [...] Designed to fill a gap in visual materials for education, this integrated set of colorslides glorifies the manual dexterity of man and illuminates his profound convictions about the creative use of materials." In contrast, a more documentary commission was the series *California Artists: Visual Statements* (1952) with photographs of an exhibition at the Los Angeles Pacific Arts Association.[25]

Nature and Technology

Inspired by the idea of a foundation course or school of seeing, Block wished to cultivate an awareness for aesthetics in

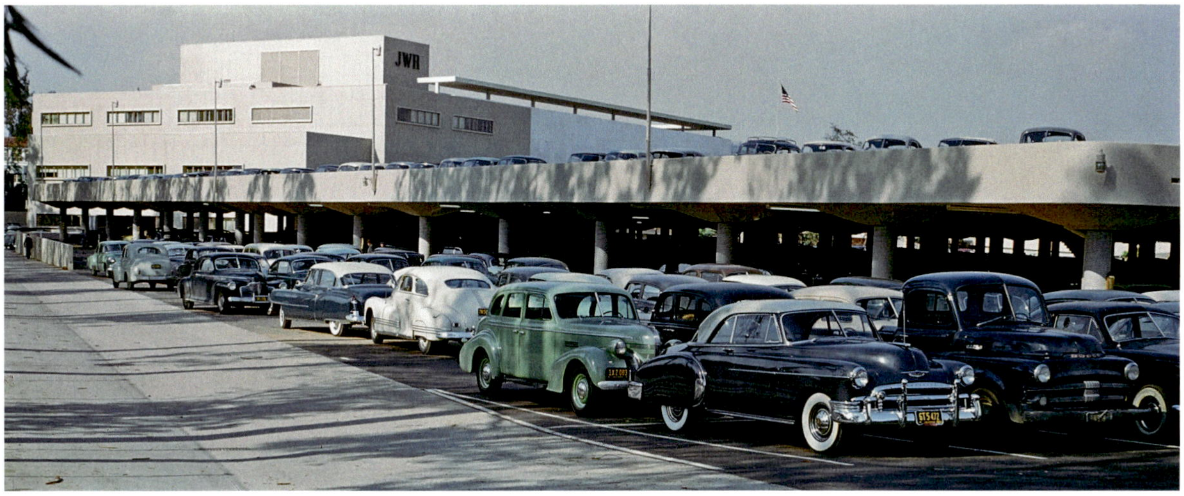

Pereira & Luckman, "Robinson's Beverly" Department Store (1952), parking levels, Beverly Hills, 1952

everyday life through additional color slide series. For this purpose, he drew on his photographic explorations of forms found in nature and technology from the period around 1930 in Germany. His series *Revelation of Beauty in Nature* (1946) [p. 302] showed 120 examples of how functionality had produced beauty in animals, plants, minerals, and crystals as well as geological formations from the National Parks of western America: "Our color slides emphasize the satisfaction of dramatic selection in looking at creation. Nature is a form builder, yet is too protean to be functional alone. Happily for us, and for the senses that seem least constraint in childhood, nature manifests beauty for its own sake."

The related series *Expressive Forms in Nature* (1949) contains one hundred photographs of different natural forms found in nature [p. 303] that served as inspiration and models for modern artistic design: "Forever, nature constitutes the inexhaustible and basic raw material of the artist. [...] Rather than natural subjects en masse, viewed grossly and without sensitivity, we have presented those parts and such aspects as have a direct relation to form." The motifs are organized in a typological manner, according to forms and structures in anorganic materials (geometric, tectonic, spiral, etc.) and in the organic world (circular, branching, bizarre, etc.). The series was accompanied by a text written by German art historian Alois J. Schardt (1889–1955), who had also immigrated to Los Angeles in 1939.

In order to illustrate the creative potential and power of nature to shape form, Block included images of shells in both series. For this purpose he photographed items from in his seashell collection that he had brought with him to Los Angeles from Hamburg, this time in color [p. 296]. This crossover between nature and art is also relevant to his series *Animals in Art* (ca. 1950), which presents examples of animals represented in art, from early cultures to Expressionism and contemporary art: "Primitive and modern art are very close in their power of giving life to the animal concept."

Complementing his natural motifs, Block's color slide series *Technical Beauty* (1949) included forty photographs which trace the shift in the aesthetic perception of construction and design in modern technology: "Not very long ago purely technical works and constructions were considered ungainly and ugly, but our time has discovered their beauty. They are the finest expression of the will and feeling for life of our time. Their beauty is the beauty of pure form derived exclusively from function and design." Block was convinced that this process had also influenced the development of modern art and architecture. Through his color slides, young people were to gain awareness and understanding for this field in their everyday environment as an expression of functional aims and thoughtful design. These photographs include the forms of ships, airplanes, trains, bridges, industrial complexes, oil tanks, smelting furnaces, and chimneys, which are usually shown in cropped compositions emphasizing dynamism, strength, and elegance [pp. 288, 296, 306–309 and 331–335].

Modern Sculpture

With works of art, Block intentionally avoided reproducing paintings, since there were already enough offerings of this kind on the market. Instead, he concentrated on photographing sculptures, which, as three-dimensional objects, provided more options in terms of composition. As with southern Californian architecture, also in this area he often produced the first color photographs of the depicted works. His series *The Work of Henry Moore* (1949) was based on the major retrospective of the artist's sculptures and drawings in 1946/47, which was organized by the Museum of Modern Art in New York and traveled to The Art Institute of Chicago and then to the San Francisco Museum of Modern Art, where Block visited the exhibition twice [p. 304]. In the accompanying brochure for this series, he proudly cites a letter from Henry Moore: "[The slides] are surprisingly good and I am glad that you intend to distribute them for visual education. They give a remarkable sense of the texture and of the material and a remarkable sense of spaciousness."

The series *Modern Sculpture* (1949) had a broader scope. Based on the works in the sculpture collection of the Museum of Modern Art, New York, including a work by Jacques Lipchitz [p. 297], it was supplemented by sculptures shown in the special exhibition *Naum Gabo – Antoine Pevs-*

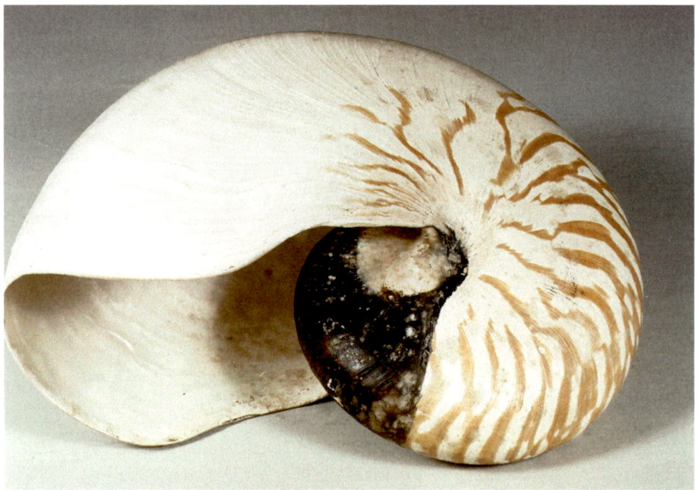
Chambered Nautilus, 1948

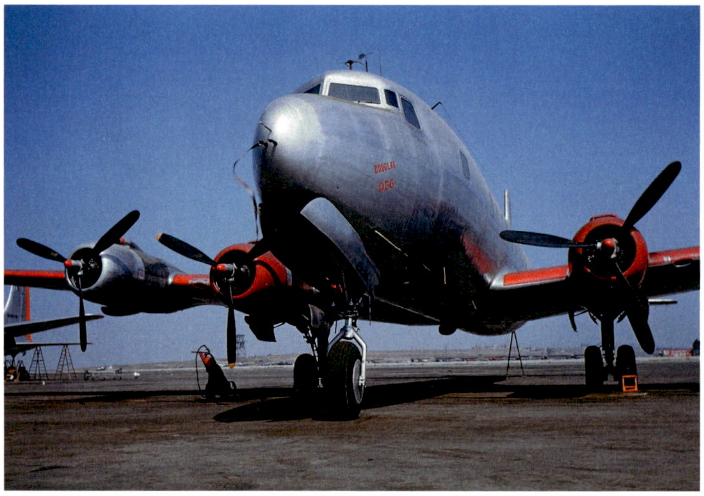
Airplane, 1948

ner (1948) [p. 304]. Also included were exemplars from the collection of Walter C. and Louise Arensberg, largely works by Constantin Brâncuși [p. 304]. For his third series *Sculpture of Our Century* (1953), Block photographed works from the major traveling exhibition *Sculpture of the Twentieth Century,* which was shown in 1952/53 in Philadelphia, Chicago, and New York. The accompanying catalogue, *Sculpture of the Twentieth Century* (1952), included only black-and-white illustrations—thereby indirectly affirming the novelty and additional expressive impact of Block's color photographs. When assessing the photographic quality of his images, it must be taken into consideration that he had to improvise when photographing on site, for example in terms of the lighting or by using rolls of paper that he brought with him in order to produce a uniform background. In addition, Block was not concerned with artistic compositions but with documenting works appropriately.

American Art

In keeping with his universalist understanding of art, Block consciously included works and artifacts from various regions and peoples in his slide productions. These series are merely summarized here (and are not depicted), because these are purely documentations of different objects. The image material is primarily of interest within relevant disciplines, although it does provide insights into the holdings of private and museum collections and what was shown in exhibitions. In addition, these series bear witness to the fact that Block also engaged with the cultural history of his country of exile, which was not necessary a given among emigrants.

In 1949 he traveled to the Denver Art Museum, the Museum of New Mexico in Santa Fee, and the Taylor Museum of the Colorado Springs Fine Arts Center, in order to photograph examples of carved, religious *Santos* figures from the Spanish colonial period and works of Native American art. A daily newspaper from Colorado Springs reported on the visit by the enthusiastic photographer: "Dr. Block is an ex-architect who put his photography vocation into his professional category when he came to the United States. Now a resident of Hollywood, Calif., he goes about the country photographing the great art collections [...]. As for the Santos collection he literally jumped up and down in his enthusiasm [...]. Bustling about his photo-floods, squinting thru the camera's focusing apparatus he said 'the United States only religious art is in the Southwest, and this is it.'"[26] This project produced the series *Santos: Our Religious Folk Art* (1950): "These sculptures and painted panels, vividly colored, represent a genuine folk art, the true expressionistic art of America."

Supplemented by collections of additional museums, three remarkable series followed as of 1950; the multi-part series *North American Indian Art* encompassed some six hundred images. It included *Part I: The Southwestern Area*, *Part II: The Northwest Coast,* and *Part III: The Western-Plains and Eastern Indian Tribes*. In addition to providing an anthropologically oriented documentation of these works, Block was simultaneously interested in their parallels to modern art and design: "Indian art of this continent embodies what we today consider basic in contemporary art and design. Its vigor of expression demonstrates its relevance to the art of our time; its simplicity of vision makes it a perennial source of inspiration." In the accompanying brochure the text confidently points to the importance of this image material for cultural history: "The collection of 625 slides[...] represents material of anthropological, historical, and artistic significance which, in respect to the quality of object and scale of presentation, is unsurpassed." Naturally Block was also interested in forms of Native American architecture [p. 298].

Other Cultures

The common idea running through his interest in including foreign cultures was to recognize their cultural achievements and their influence on contemporary art. The series *Bushman Paintings* (1949) was an exception within these series, simply because it portrayed reproductions out of correspondingly illustrated books. In contrast, the series *African Negro Art* (1949) consisted of original photographs, as in all of Block's other series. Through these images Block wished to underscore the seminal nature of African art and the inspiration it gave to modern art. The works predominantly

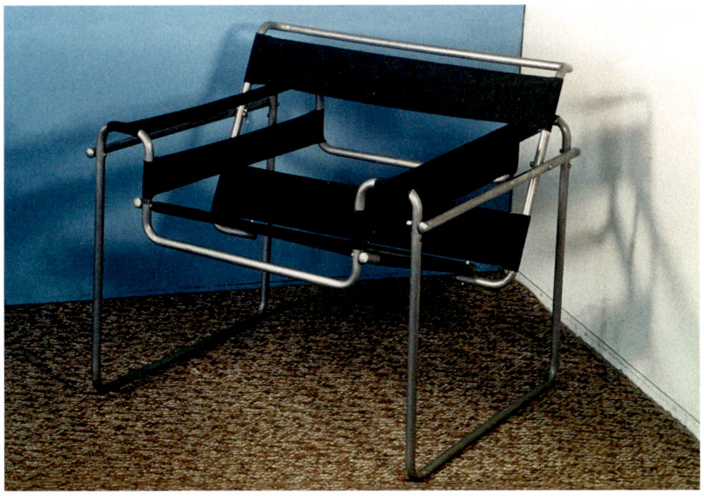

Marcel Breuer, *Wassily Chair* (1925), 1948

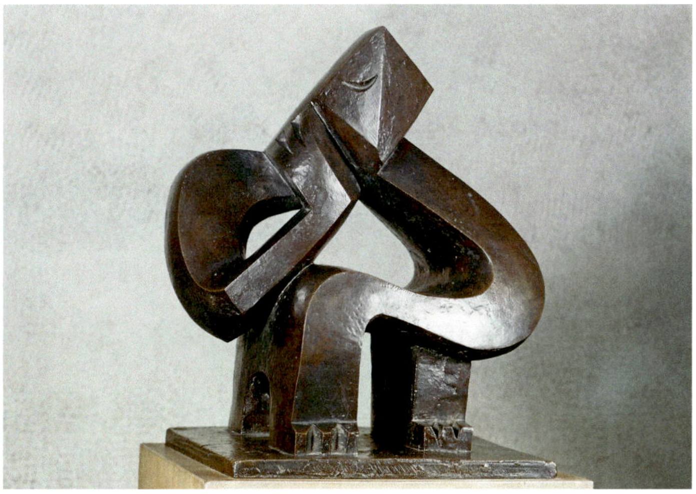

Jacques Lipchitz, *Seated Man* (1925), 1948

stemmed from the Brooklyn Museum, New York, the Peabody Museum of Archaeology and Ethnology at Harvard University, and the Buffalo Museum of Science, and from numerous, largely southern Californian, private collections. Furthermore, Block also included examples from the exhibition *African Negro Sculpture* (1948) mounted by the M. H. de Young Memorial Museum in San Francisco. Here too, he was aware of the pioneering nature of his work: "For the first time, an extensive selection of color slides on African Art is offered to the teacher, scientist, and student of design."

The series *Art of the South Pacific* (1949) was also based on new visual material. The photographs stem from the exhibition *Arts of the South Seas* (1946) in the Museum of Modern Art, New York, and works from additional museums and private collections. For his series *The Art of Ancient Peru* (1954) Block photographed items in the traveling exhibition *Ancient Art of the Andes* (1954) at the Museum of Modern Art, New York. In this context he criticizes the fact that a recently published book, *The Art of Ancient Peru* (1954), "unfortunately omits the element of color, so essential to an understanding of these bygone craftsmen." In the early 1950s Block produced four series on the art of the East, also drawing on various museum and private collections to compile *Chinese Art*, *Art of India, Persian Art,* and *Japanese Art*. In the supplementary brochure to the particularly extensive series on Chinese art, with 257 motifs, he described what applied to most of his color slides of artworks: "Many of these beautiful Chinese objects are available here in color for the first time; others are presented anew through the eyes of a skilled and sensitive photographer."

Color Photography and Art Education

In late 1948 George W. Eggers (1883–1958), whose final position was the head of the Department of Art at City College in New York, wrote an extensive positive critique of "Dr. Fred Block's Sets of Color Slides" in the *College Art Journal*: "To bring together a corpus of the headiest and most sparkling stuff there is for the human eye to imbibe has been the quest of Dr. Fred Block. [...] The result is a series of coherent groups of some thousand Kodachrome slides. These are taken from many phases of nature and from almost every field of human endeavor—excepting that of painting. [...] The collection aims at universality. The subjects include natural materials, animal, vegetable and mineral; works of primitive art of all kinds, modern sculpture and architecture [...]. Every slide is composed with fastidious precision as to background, lightning, photography, and total effect [...]. Each subject is arranged, photographed, and carried through to completion by the author himself—true product of the artist-craftsman's own meticulous attention. [...] Dr. Block is well qualified for the task he has undertaken. A rewarding career as a progressive architect in Germany and long practice in the craft of designing has sharpened his feeling for style and distinction in visual things."[27] The magazine *Everyday Art* also featured Block's work enthusiastically in 1951, even if the praise of his color slide production tends to go a bit far: "Dr. Fred Block is today probably one of the greatest experts in color photography in the United States. Not only is his work outstanding in technical perfection but his unusual approach to nature, and the high creative spirit of the subject matter in his slides make his effort absolutely unique."[28]

Block also explored the theory behind the function of his photographs as training young people in their sense of color. In a text that he wrote in 1951 but never published, "Color-Photography and Art Education," he explained the concept and technique of his work. In another German-speaking manuscript on "Color Photography als Erzieher zum Farbsehen" (1950) Block additionally explored the physiology and psychology of perception in relation to color photography and decried the lack of awareness for quality: "For this reason, educational color libraries should only be established with the best color photographs [...]. A library of first-class color slides encompassing all spheres of American life [...]. With the interest shown by young people in such works, they could take on an educational value equal to that of our museums [...]."[29] However, his fascination for color slides was imbued with an overestimation of the aesthetic potential of the medium that was typical of the era.

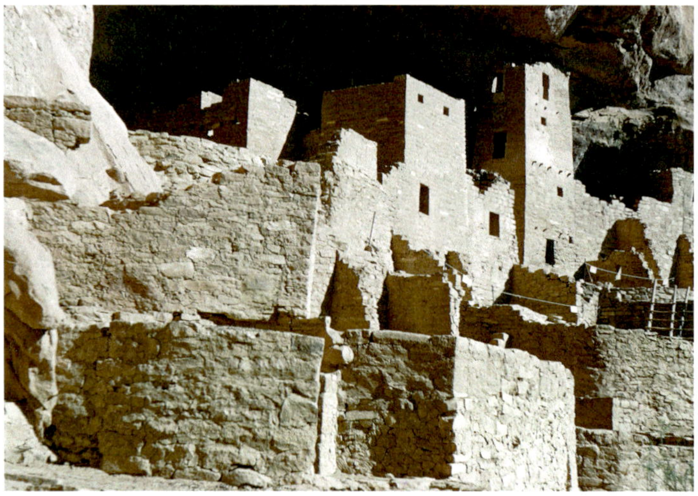
Mesa Verde, Cliff Palace, Colorado, ca. 1950

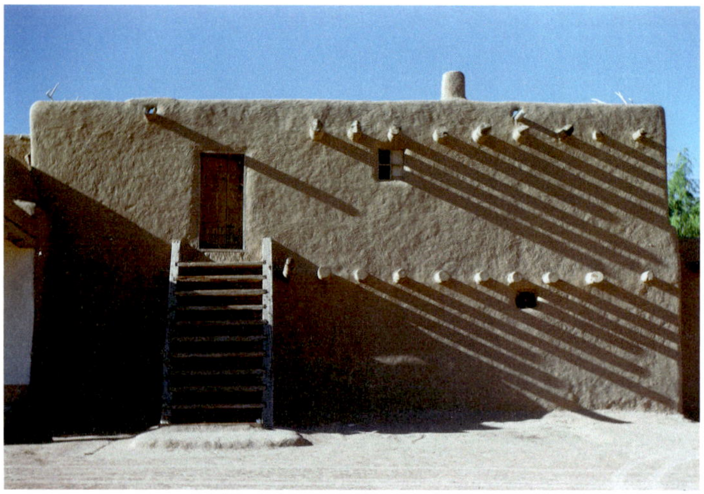
San Ildefonso Pueblo, New Mexico, ca. 1950

Color Photography Exhibition

Block was given unique recognition through the inclusion of his color slides in the *Color Photography Exhibition* at the Museum of Modern Art, New York in early summer 1950, the first exhibition ever on color photography mounted by this museum. On view were color photographs and "color transparencies," that is color slides, by over seventy-five photographers, including Ansel Adams, Richard Avedon, Robert Capa, Henri Cartier-Bresson, Walker Evans, Elliot Erwitt, Andreas Feininger, Paul Outerbridge, Irving Penn, Paul Strand, Charles Sheeler, Edward Weston. Although Block's works in the exhibition represented a supplementary aspect of color photography, it was a particular honor for him to be included in this circle of well-known photographers. As with his black-and-white photography shown in the 1932 *Internationale Foto-Ausstellung* in Hamburg, also in America he had managed to affiliate himself with the avant-garde.

The list of works shown includes some forty images under Block's name. However, these were not shown as projections but as sequential strips of color prints (Pavelle color / Ansco printon). It is unknown precisely which motifs these were, but it must have been a cross section of his production, probably also including images from objects in the museum. In the exhibition press release, the museum librarian Bernard Karpel wrote: "Dr. Fred Block has devoted the past ten years to the perfection of an intensive and poetic technique. Its objective is the colorful inventory of the most significant artifacts of primitive and modern times, its method is the fullest realization of essential forms and textures. Committed to the medium of the educational color slide, his vision recalls the perennial wonder with which we face the phenomena of man and nature made manifest as artist."[30]

Block visited the exhibition personally, also from the aspect of following the progress that was being made in terms of producing quality slide film, which not only was leading to satisfactory color prints but also making it possible to use color images in books that were of better quality and less expensive: "The inexpensive printing processes on three-layer materials are making remarkable progress [...]. For the last years the use of color photography for book illustrations has also improved definitely. Books with color illustrations will soon be possible for short press runs, and they are going to become better and cheaper. I had often requests for my material in portfolio or book form for teaching purposes, and I hope for such editions in the future."[31] However, his color photographs were never published in book form.

In order to take photographs at the Museum of Modern Art, Block made multiple stays in New York between 1948 and 1952. During these times he took the opportunity to photograph the city. He largely retook scenes that he had photographed in black and white in 1931—such as the George Washington Bridge [pp. 288 and 336], the view of Manhattan through the cables of the Brooklyn Bridge, and the shadows cast by the "Elevated" [p. 323]. He added new individual motifs, such as Rockefeller Center [p. 322] and social housing projects, but he did not manage to create a comprehensive color portrait of New York.

Digitally Accessible

For his color slide production, Block undertook various trips to exhibitions, museums, and collections in the US, but he never returned to Germany. From the mid 1940s onward his health was compromised by diabetes (and cigar smoking), and in the 1950s he suffered a series of minor strokes. On January 23, 1955 Fritz (Fred) Block died at the age of sixty-five in Los Angeles. His wife Anna-Sophie continued the business of "Dr. Block Color Productions." Around 1980 a number of slide series were taken over by the company Kaidib Films International, which was based in Glendale outside of Los Angeles and had also been selling color slides for art education since 1961. Block's series on modern architecture and sculpture remained available, but they were naturally no longer current. Some of his image material was therefore arranged in new thematic groupings, for example a selection from Block's architectural series for a series on *Frank Lloyd Wright in the Southwest*,[32] encompassing fifty-six slides. Images from his *Modern Industrial Design* series were also regrouped in two series under the bold title *Bauhaus Design*, each containing eighty motifs. Given the steep decline in demand, the sale of "Dr. Block's Color Slides" ended in 1992.

Block's color slide productions subsequently were forgotten. Although the series are still extant at a number of American educational institutions, they were not archived as works of photography, and due to changes in media they are no longer in use. Particularly Block's early color photographs of the buildings and interiors of Californian modernist architecture have long been overlooked as source material of architectural historical value.[33] Although mentioned in a 1996 monograph on the architectural firm of Dr. Block & Hochfeld,[34] interest in these images has returned only gradually.[35] The University of Southern California Digital Library (USCDL), Los Angeles has meanwhile digitalized Block's color slide series on architecture (although duplicates were used, the quality of which does not compare to the master slides preserved in the estate—with their surprisingly fresh color), and in 2016 they made them available online as part of their Architectural Teaching Slide Collection.[36]

Block's color slide production shared the fate of early Kodachrome images, which have been preserved as color slides but due to a lack of contemporary prints or use in publications have never received much attention. The possibility of digitalizing the motifs makes this segment of photographic history—and ultimately also this color phase of Fritz (Fred) Block's work—more readily visible today.

In late 1985 his widow Anna-Sophie wrote in a letter shortly before her 90th birthday: "I plan to substantially reduce the number of my belongings. So many photos, negatives and prints, from Fred's production. I will not hold back in throwing things away." Luckily she was not able to implement these plans on a large scale. After her death in 1986 what was left of Fritz Block's photographic materials remained in the possession of the family. The first overview of the Fritz Block Estate Archive, Stockholm/Hamburg, was shown in 2017 in the exhibition "Fritz Block. New Photography – Modern Color Slides" at the Alfred Ehrhardt Foundation, Berlin.[37]

1 Documents with no indication of source are found in the Fritz Block Estate Archive, Stockholm/Hamburg. The quotations on the color slide series are taken from the brochures that accompanied individual slide series. – It is not always possible to determine the exact date of individual photographs, since Block sometimes developed his color slide series over a long period of time. The dates listed here are based on plausible attributions or refer to the year in which the series was released.
2 However, Block is missing in Klaus Honnef and Frank Weyres, *Und sie haben Deutschland verlassen...müssen. Fotografen und ihre Bilder 1928–1997* (Bonn, 1997).
3 *Hollywood Citizen-Examiner*, March 24, 1939.
4 One album is in the Fritz Block Estate Archive, Stockholm/Hamburg; two others are in the Fritz Block papers, Architecture and Design Collection of the Art, Design & Architecture Museum, University of California, Santa Barbara.
5 See Els Rijper, *Kodachrome. The American Invention of Our World, 1939–1959* (New York, 2002).
6 Fred Block, *Color-Photography and Art Education* [manuscript] (Los Angeles, 1951), 6.
7 The figure best comparable to Block is Julius Rosenthal, who emigrated from Germany to Chicago in 1936, where he ran a reproduction service for the Art Institute of Chicago and starting in 1940 also set up a business selling slides, initially with black-and-white photographs and later with color photographs, largely of the museum's collection. See Benjamin Kessler, "Julius and John Rosenthal and Rosenthal Art Slides," *Visual Resources. An International Journal on Images and Their Uses* 22, no. 3 (2006), 265–272.
8 Arensberg to the United States Attorney, Southern District of California, January 23, 1942. See the correspondence between Arensberg and Block in the Philadelphia Museum of Art, Archives, Arensberg Archives, Correspondence, A. General Correspondence, box 3, folders 25–27.
9 See Mark Nelson and William H. Sherman, *Hollywood Arensberg* (in preparation). Mark Nelson, New York, reconstructed the presentation of Walter C. and Louise Arensberg's art collection in their house through historical photographs, including the only known color photographs taken by Block.
10 See the correspondence in the Fritz Block papers (see note 4).
11 Gropius to Block, May 17, 1943.
12 Block to Gropius, July 23, 1943.
13 Gropius to Block, August 26, 1943.
14 Horn to Block, July 1943, quoted in the letter from Block to Frank Lloyd Wright (see note 15).
15 Block to Frank Lloyd Wright, July 17, 1943.
16 Eugene Masselink, Frank Lloyd Wright's secretary, to Block, October 14, 1943 and January 19, 1944.
17 Block 1951 (see note 6), 3.
18 Mock to Block, August 27, 1943, Fritz Block papers (see note 4).
19 Mock to Block, September 29, 1943, ibid.
20 Bernard Karpel, "The Public and the Library," *The Bulletin of the Museum of Modern Art* 11, no. 3 (January 1944), 3–9, quoting 6.
21 *Ibid.*, no. 2 (October/November 1943), 26.
22 Block 1951 (see note 6), 5.
23 Ibid., 8.
24 Fritz Block papers (see note 4).
25 J.[ohn] W. O.[lsen], "Pacific Arts Produces. Visual Statements are Issued," *Art Education* 6, no. 1 (1953), 10–11.
26 *Colorado Springs Gazette Telegraph*, May 5, 1949.
27 George W.[illiam] Eggers, "Dr. Fred Block's set of color slides," *College Art Journal* 8, no. 2 (Winter 1948–49), 95–100; quotation, 96.
28 "Color Photography as Created by Dr. Fred Block," *Everyday Art* 30, 1951, no. 2 (November/December), 10.
29 Fred Block, "Color Photography als Erzieher zum Farbsehen" [manuscript], (Los Angeles, ca. 1950), 10.
30 The Museum of Modern Art Archives, NY, MoMA Exhs., series 445, folder 3.
31 Block 1951 (see note 6), 12–13.
32 Thos. G. Dibble (ed.), *Frank Lloyd Wright in the Southwest. Photographed by Dr. Fred Block* (Glendale n. d., c. 1982). – Idem, *Bauhaus Design. Photographed by Dr. Fred Block* (Glendale, 1982). – Idem, *Bauhaus Part II. Photographed by Dr. Fred Block* (Glendale, 1986).
33 For example, Block's color slides were not mentioned in Wendy Kaplan, *Living in a Modern Way. California Design 1930–1965* (Los Angeles / Cambridge, MA, and London, 2011).
34 Roland Jaeger, *Block & Hochfeld. Die Architekten des Deutschlandhauses. Bauten und Projekte in Hamburg 1921–1938. Exil in Los Angeles* (Berlin, 1996), esp. 232–239.
35 Susan Morgan, "Almost Lost, then Found," *Modern Magazine* (Winter 2017) (http://modernmag.com/almost-lost-then-found/) (last accessed February 12, 2018).
36 http://digitallibrary.usc.edu/cdm/landingpage/collection/p15799coll42 (last accessed February 12, 2018).
37 See the accompanying brochure Roland Jaeger, *Photo-Eye Fritz Block. New Photography – Modern Color Slides* (Berlin, 2017).

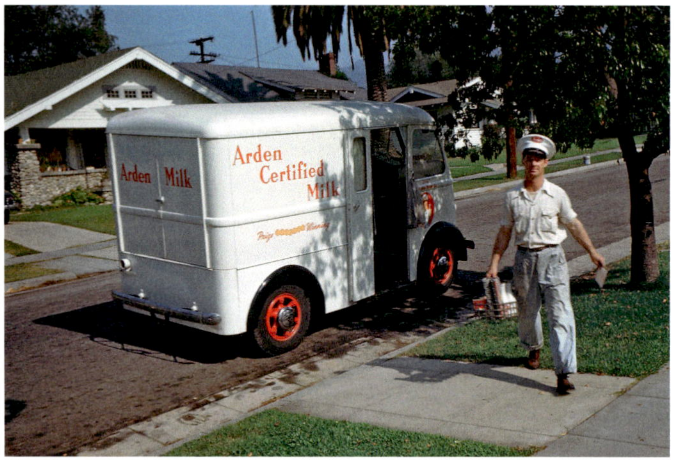

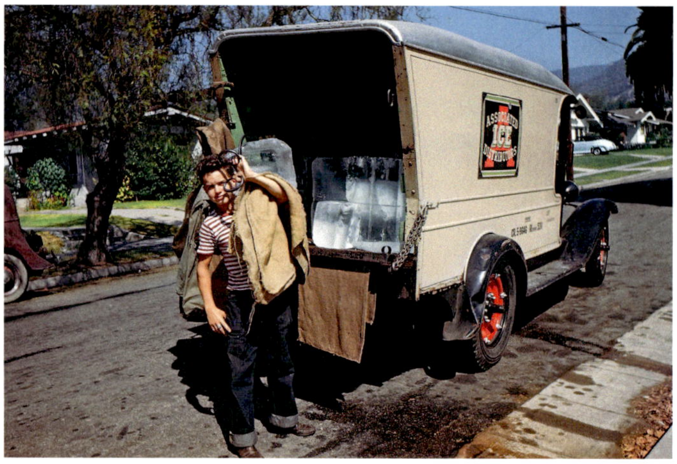

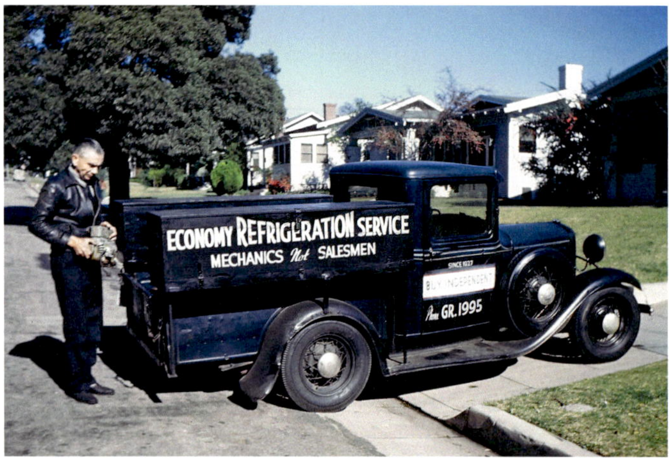

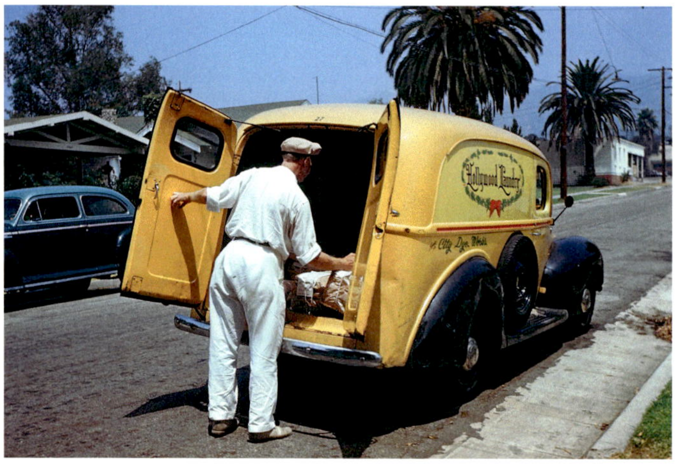

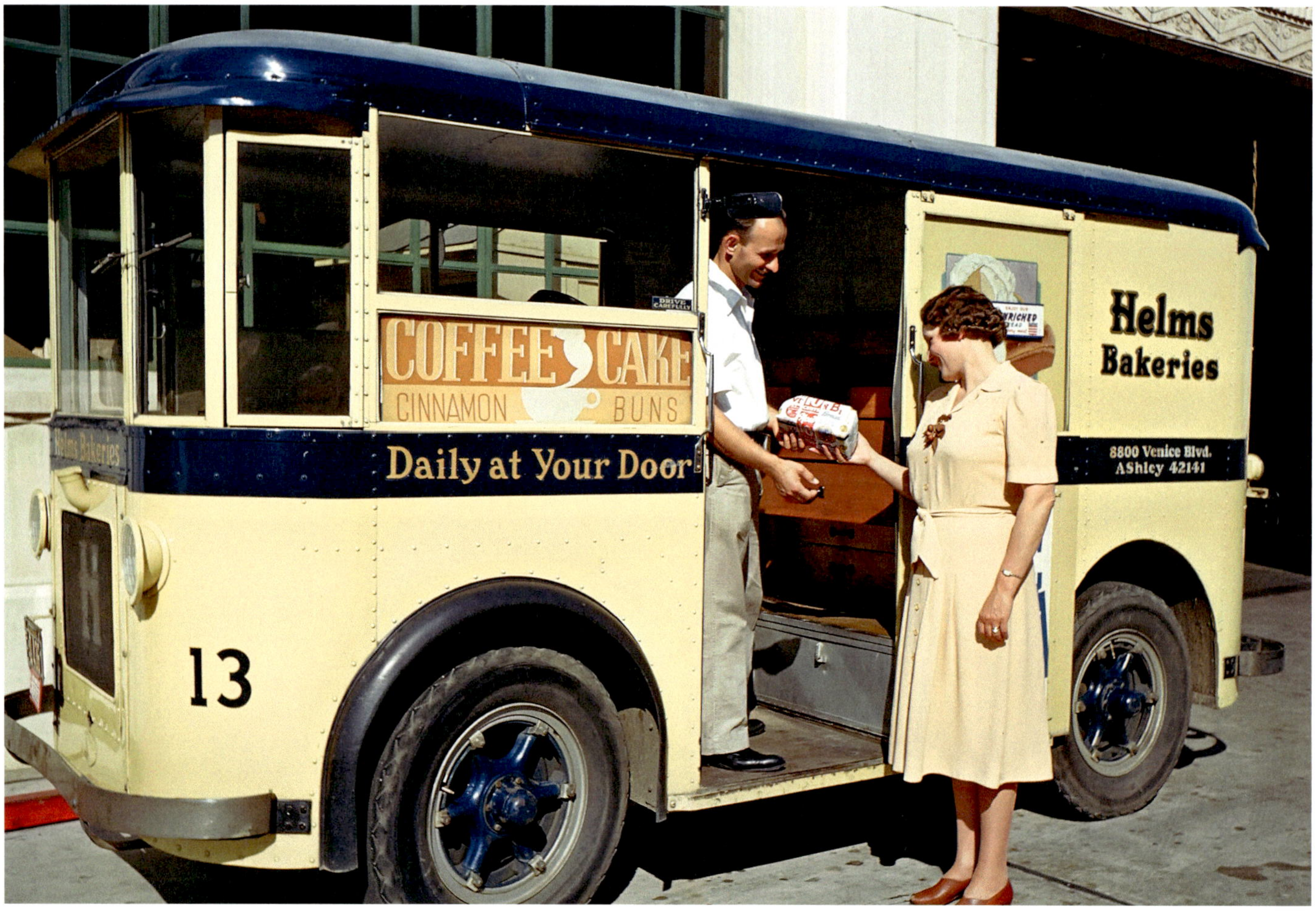

From the color slide series *Who Comes to Your Home*, ca. 1942: Milk Man – Ice Man –Mechanic – Laundry Man – Bread Man

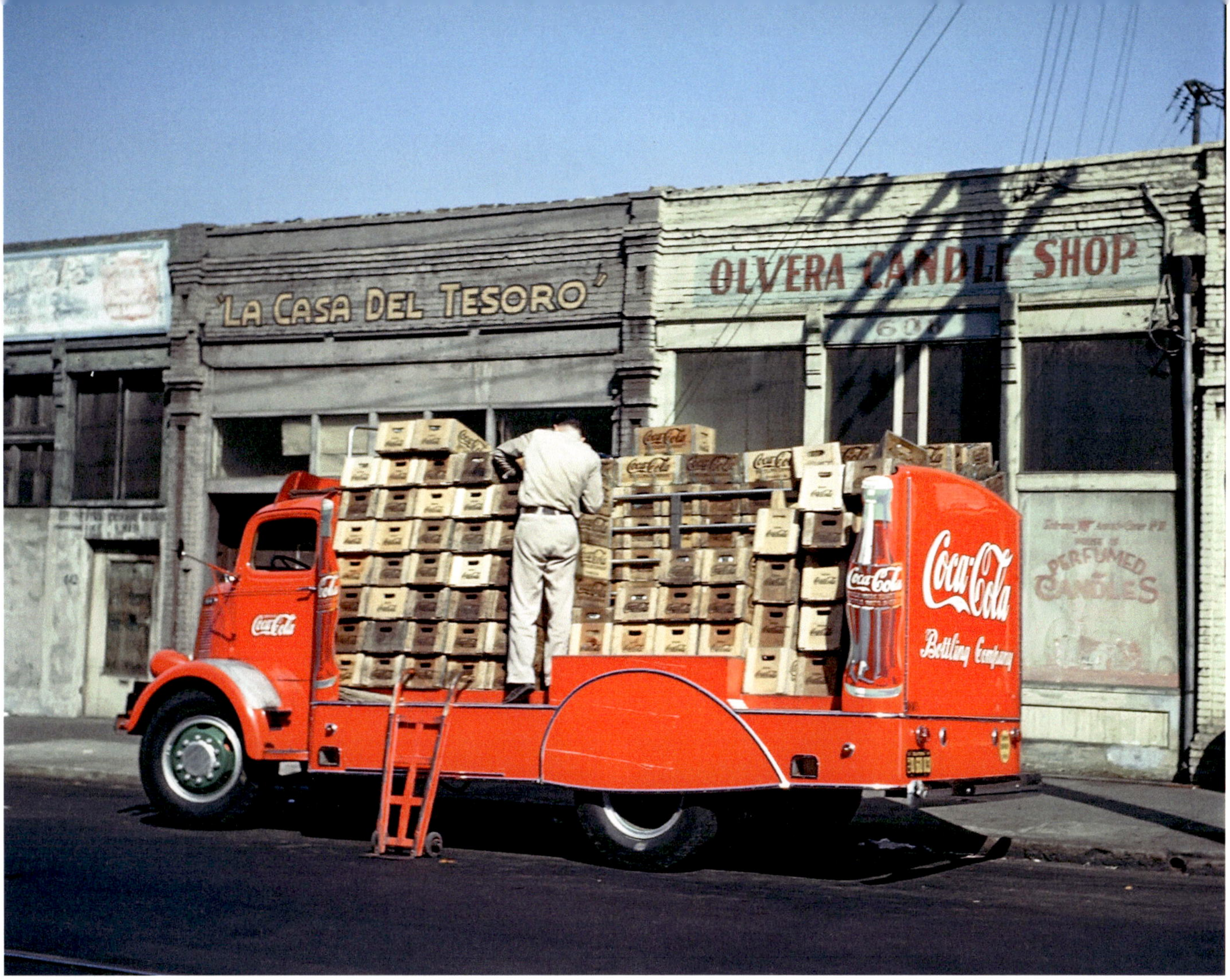

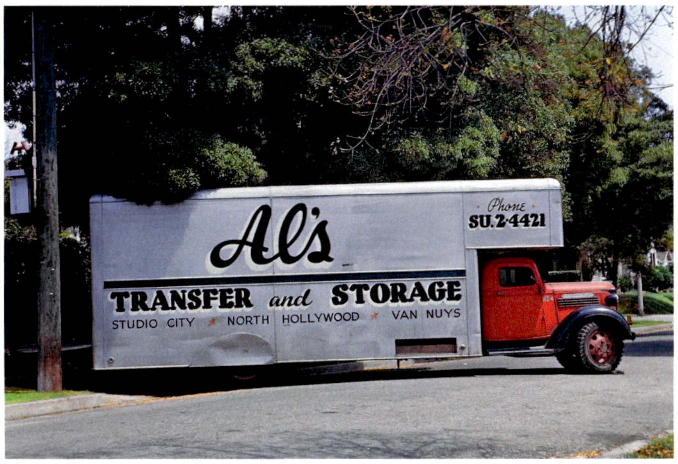

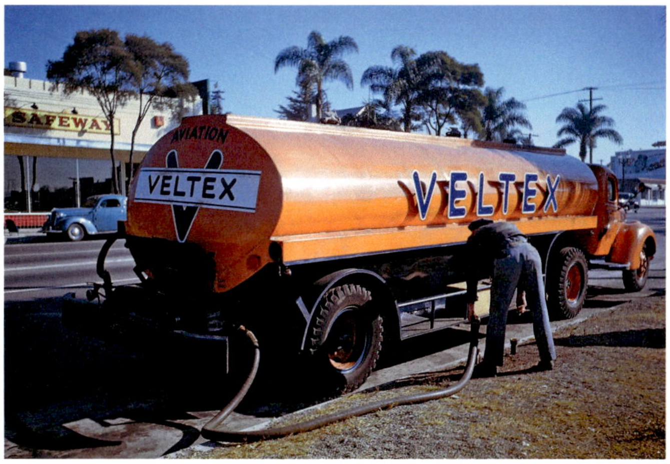

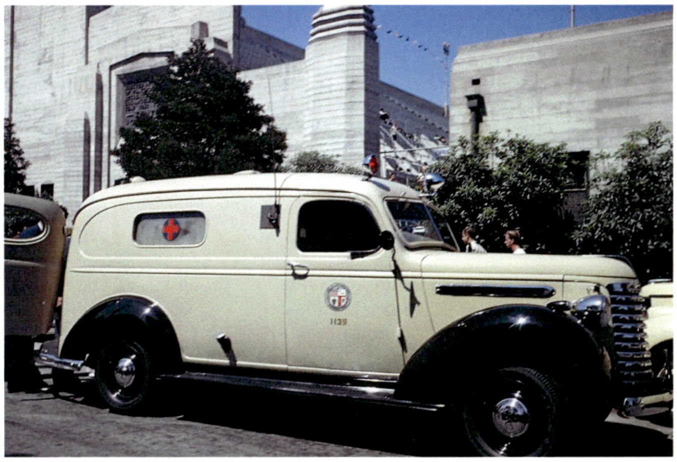

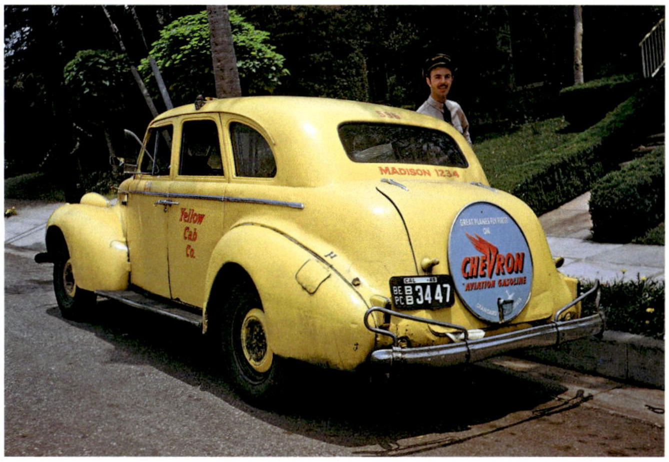

From the color slide series *Trucks*, ca. 1942: Beverage Truck – Moving Van – Fuel Truck – Ambulance – Taxicab

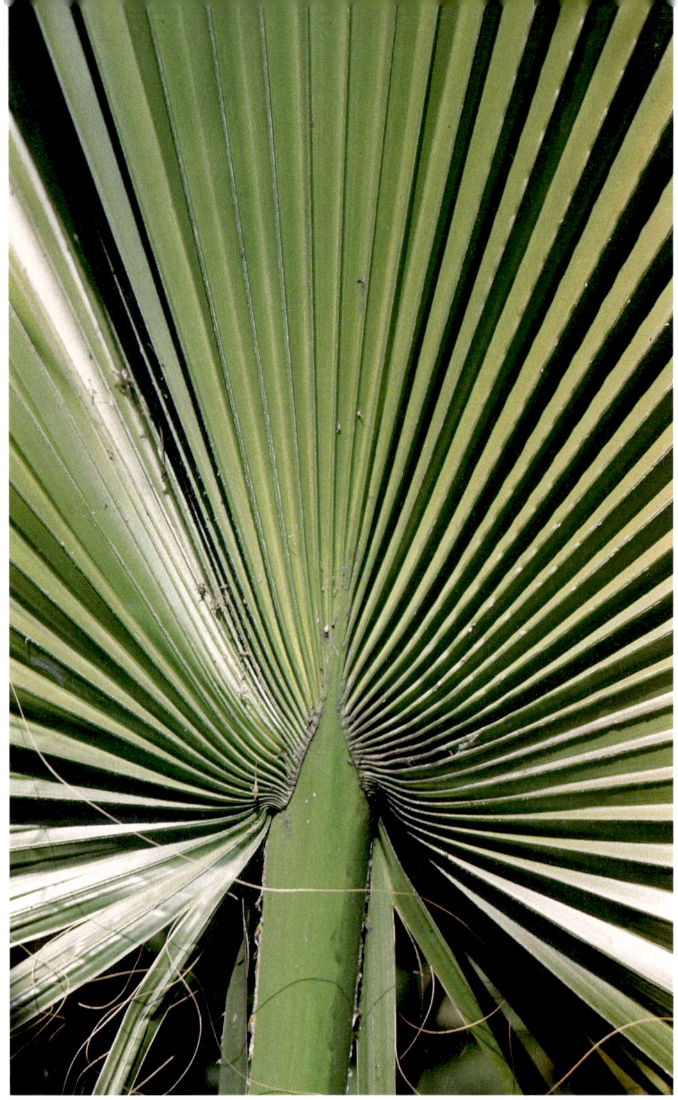

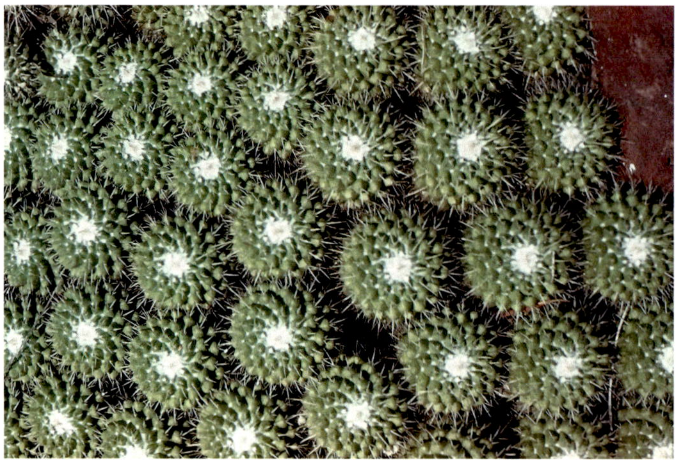

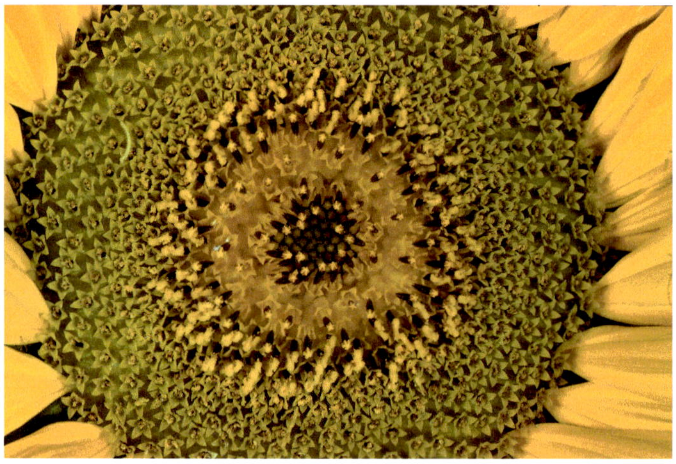

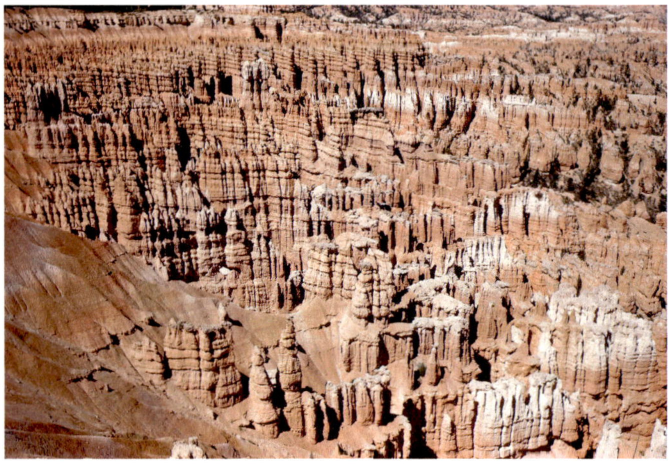

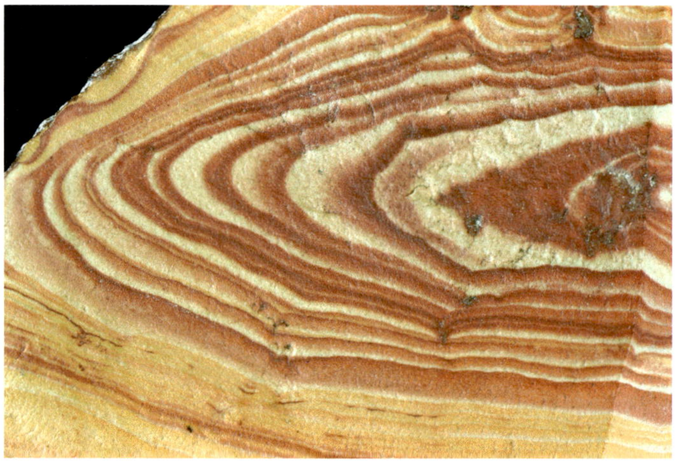

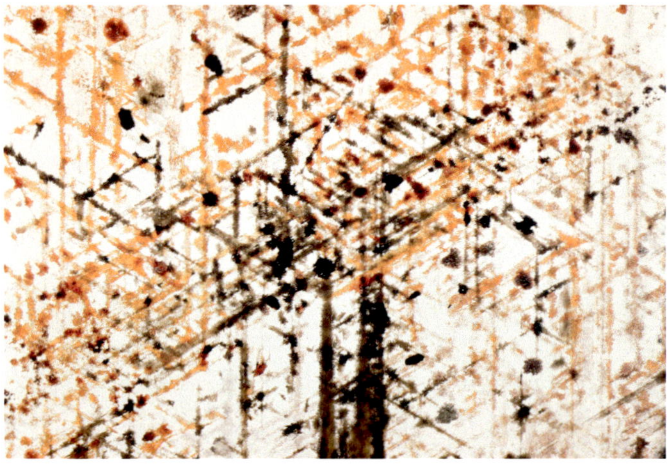

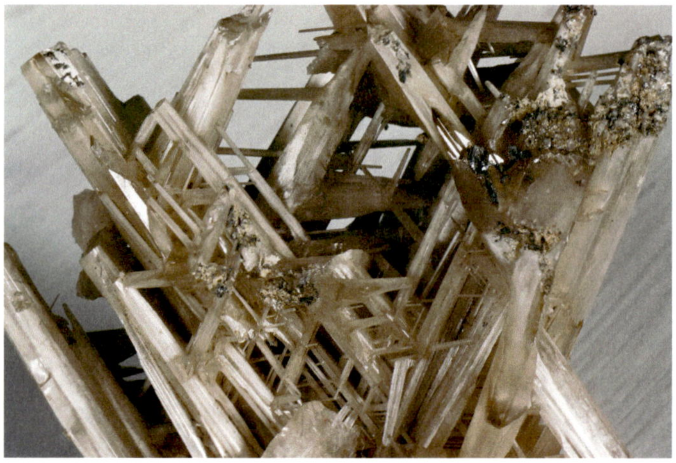

From the color slide series *Revelation of Beauty in Nature*, ca. 1946: Palm Leaf – Pincushion Cactus – Sunflower – Bryce Canyon – Wonderstone Rhyolite – Magnetite and Hematite – Cerussite Crystals

From the color slide series *Expressive Forms in Nature*, 1949: Sunset Moth – Peacock Making Tail – Chambered Nautilus – Sundial Shell – Branches of Dying Tree – Cactus Blossoms – Giant Cactus

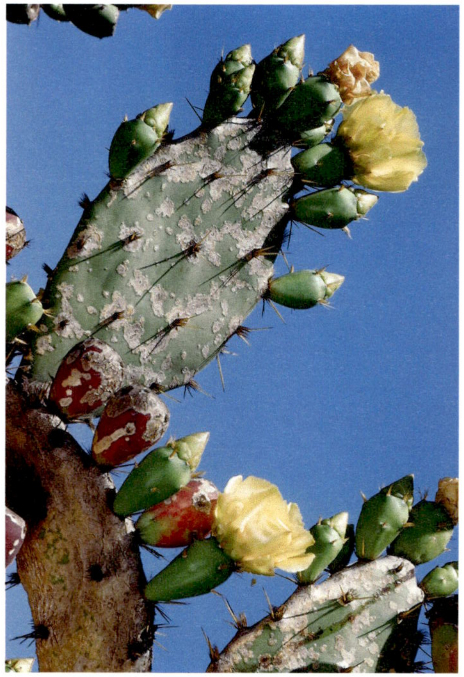
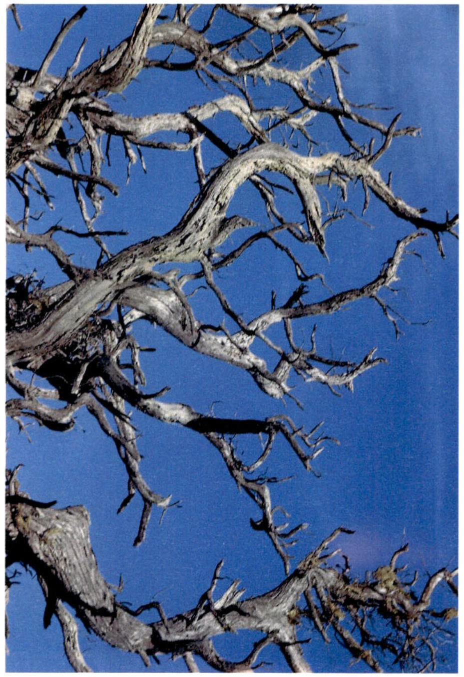
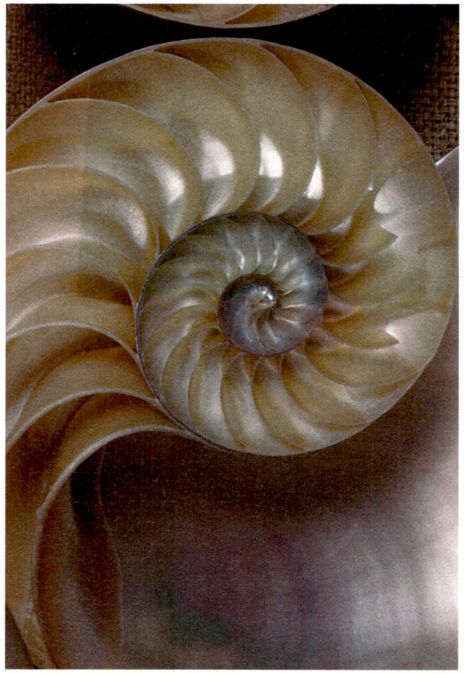
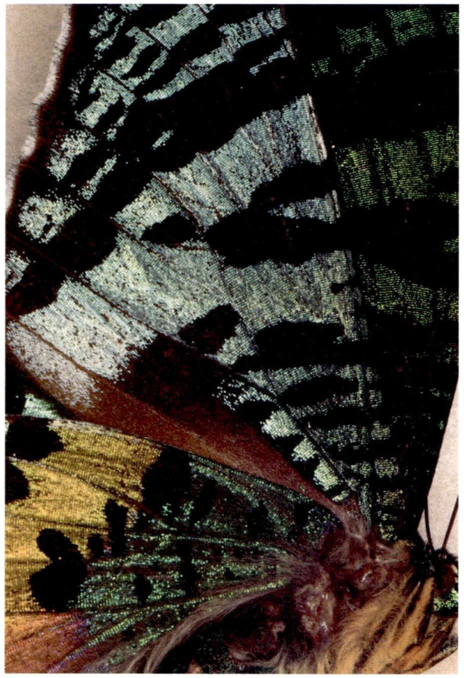
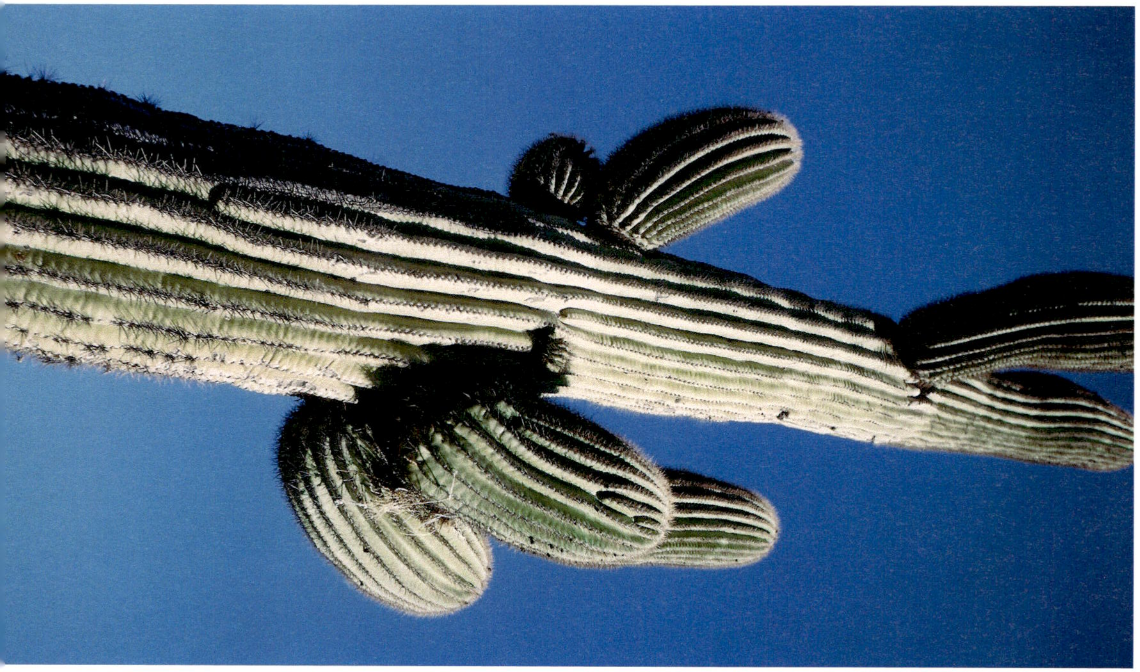
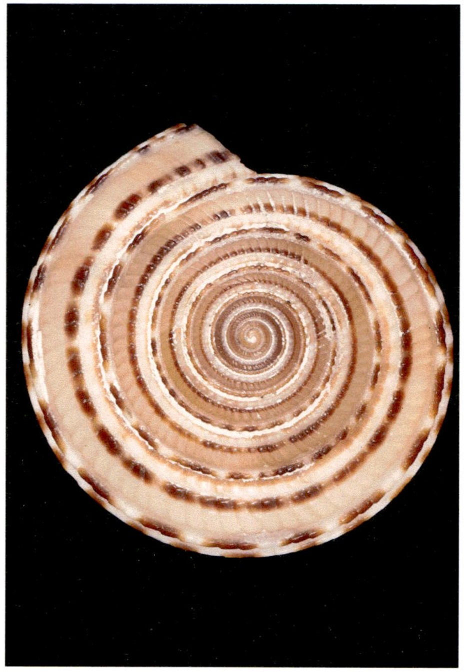
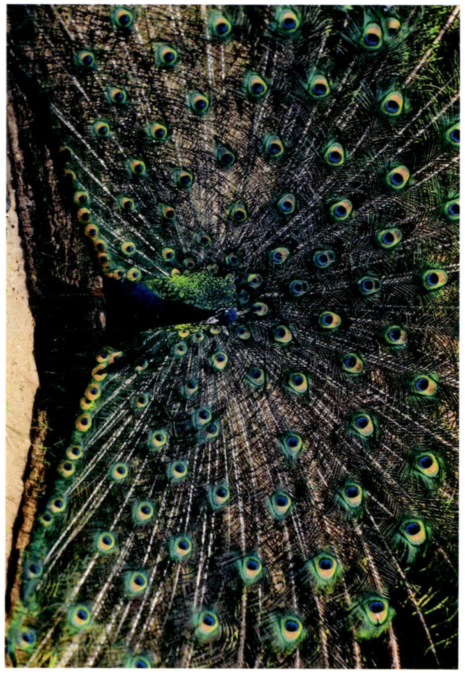

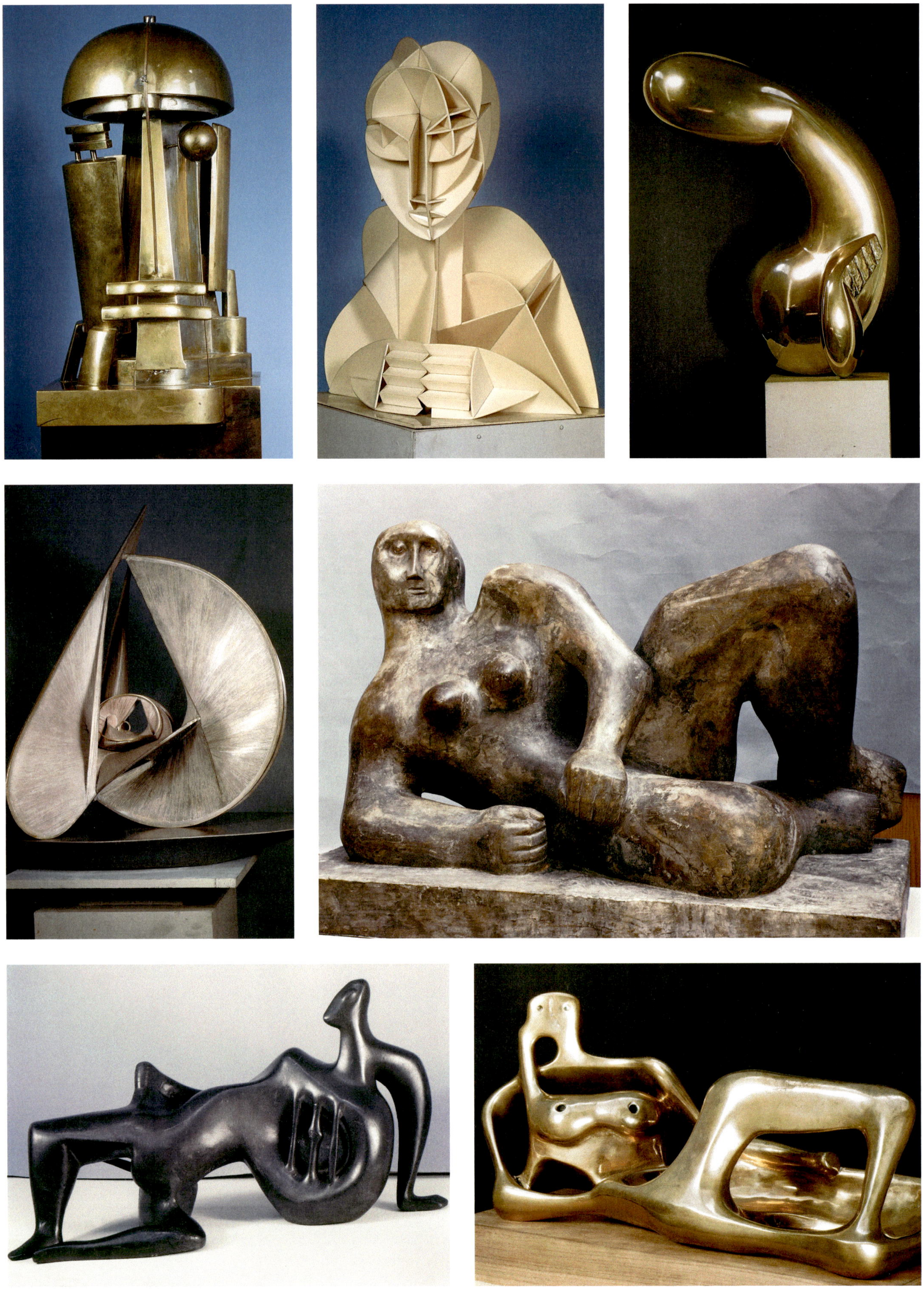

From the color slide series *Modern Sculpture*, 1949, and *The Work of Henry Moore*, 1949: Rudolf Belling, *Head*, 1924 – Naum Gabo, *Bust (Constructed Head No. 2)*, 1916 – Constantin Brâncuși, *The Princess*, 1916 – Antoine Pevsner, *World Construction*, 1947 – Henry Moore, *Reclining Figure*, 1932, 1931, and 1945

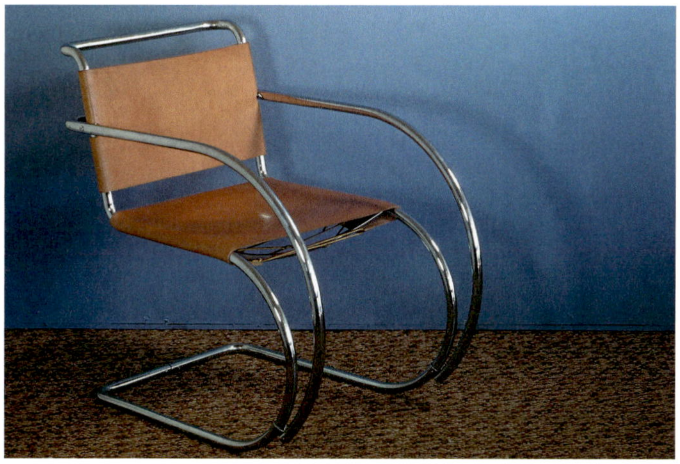

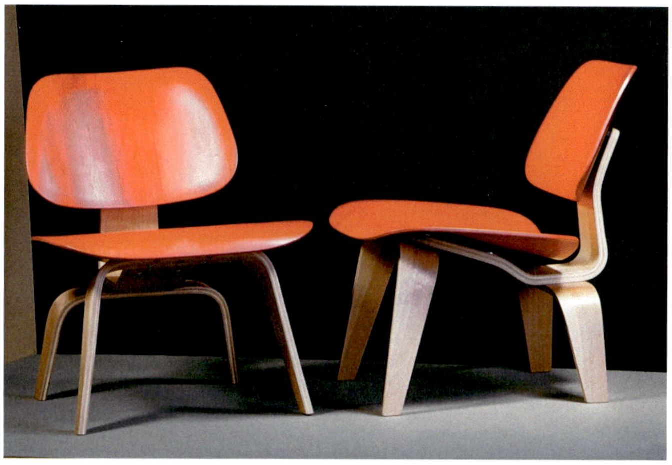

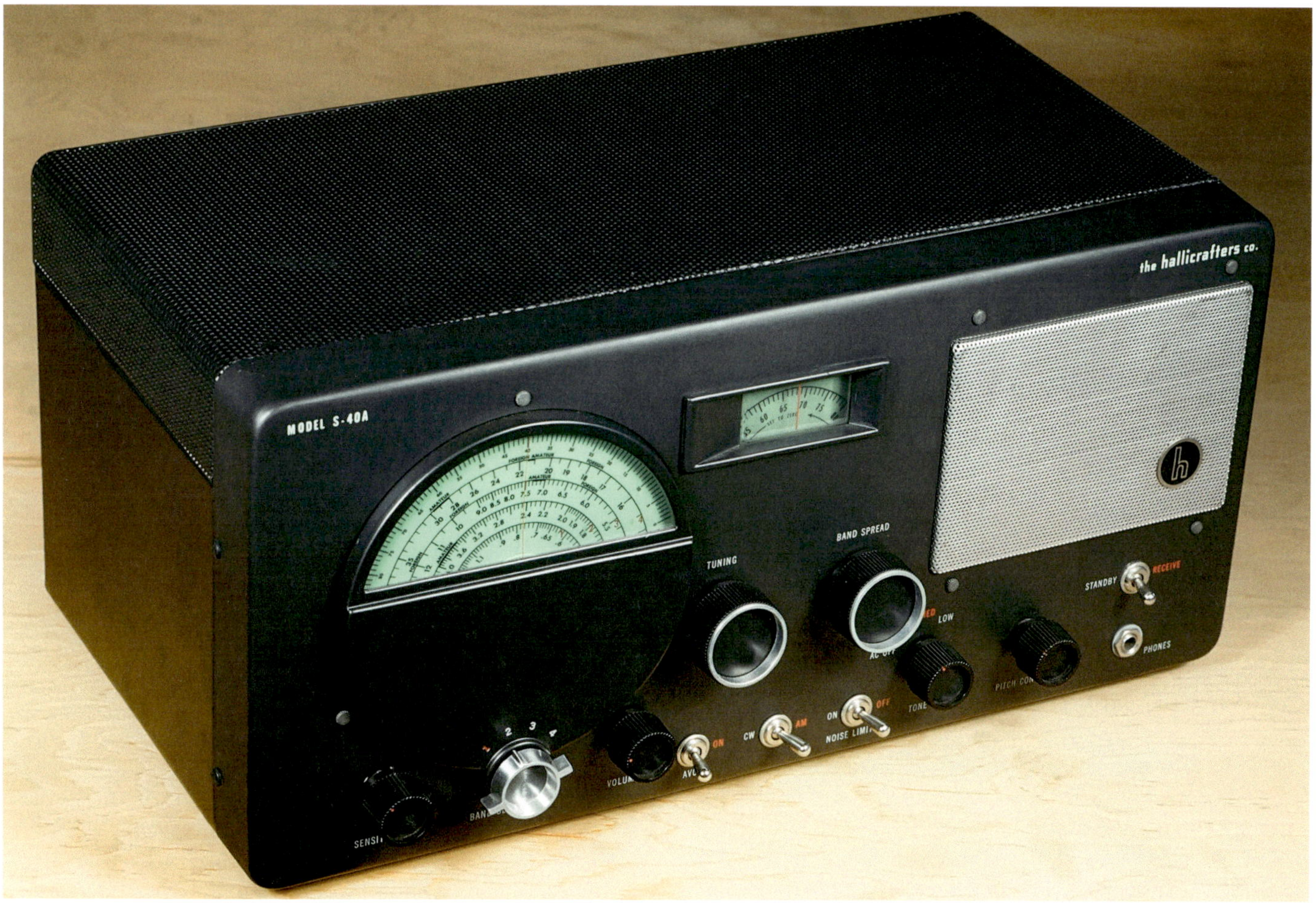

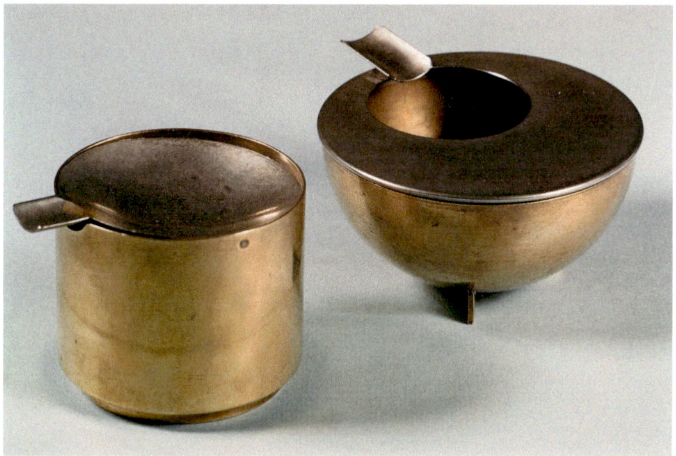

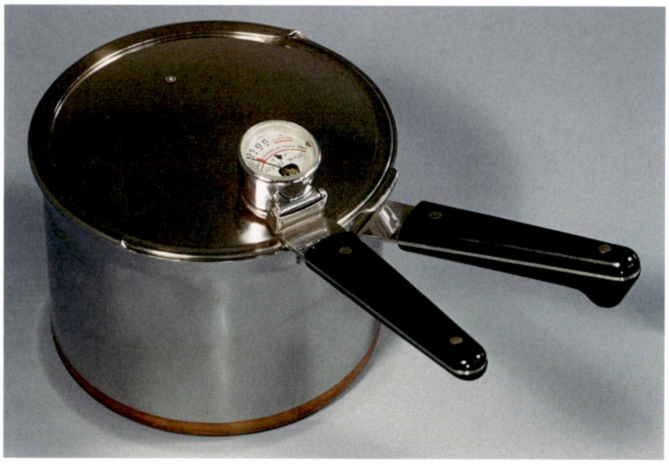

From the color slide series *Modern Industrial Design*, 1949: Ludwig Mies van der Rohe, Tubular Steel Cantilever Chair, 1927 – Charles Eames, Lounge Chairs, 1945 – Raymond Loewy Assoc., Radio Receiver, 1946 – Marianne Brandt, Ashtrays, 1924 – Archibald Welden, Pressure Cooker, 1947

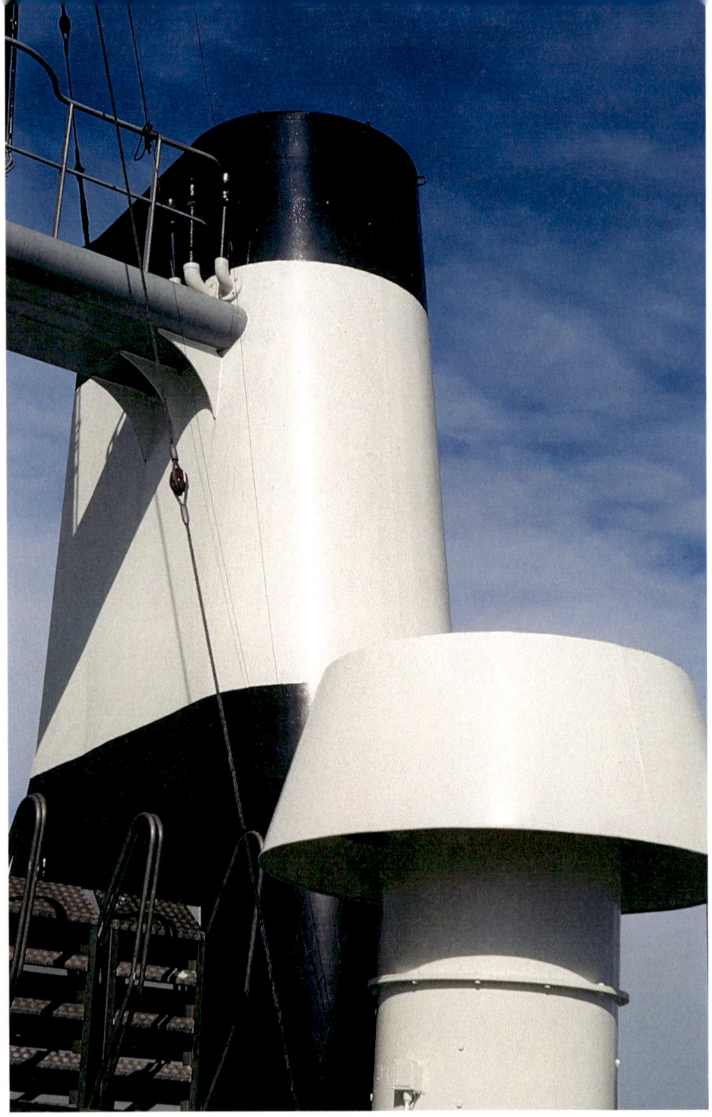

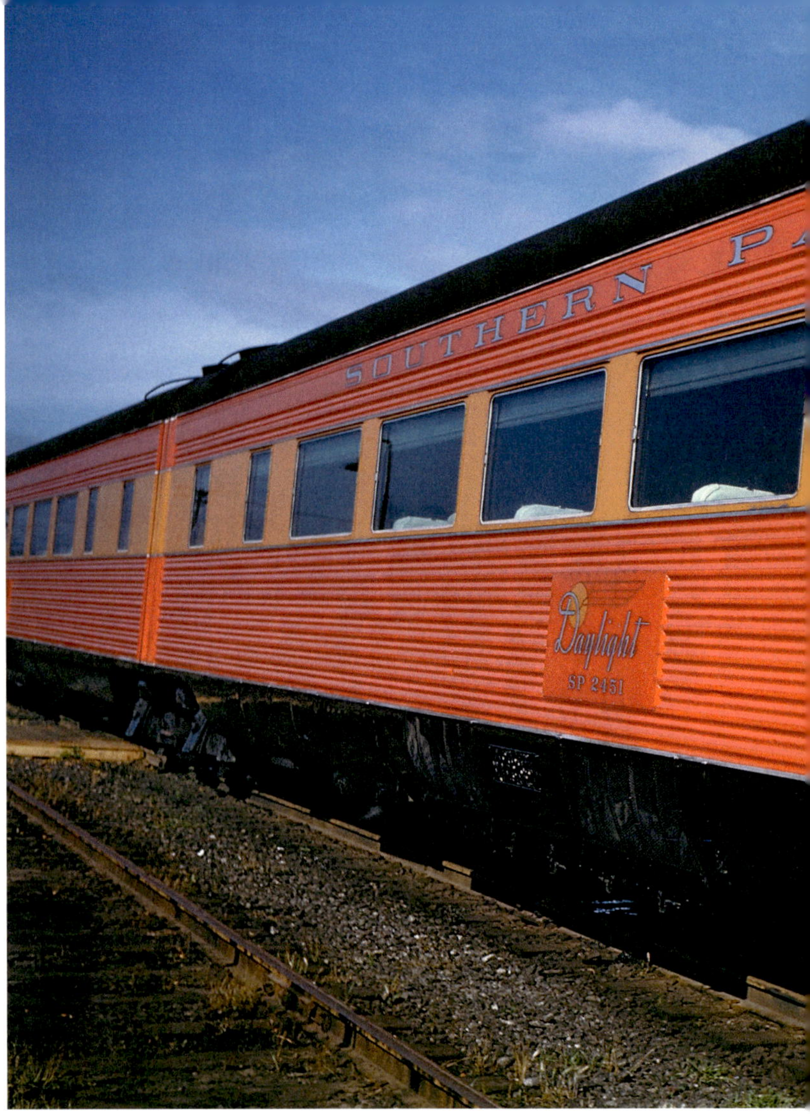

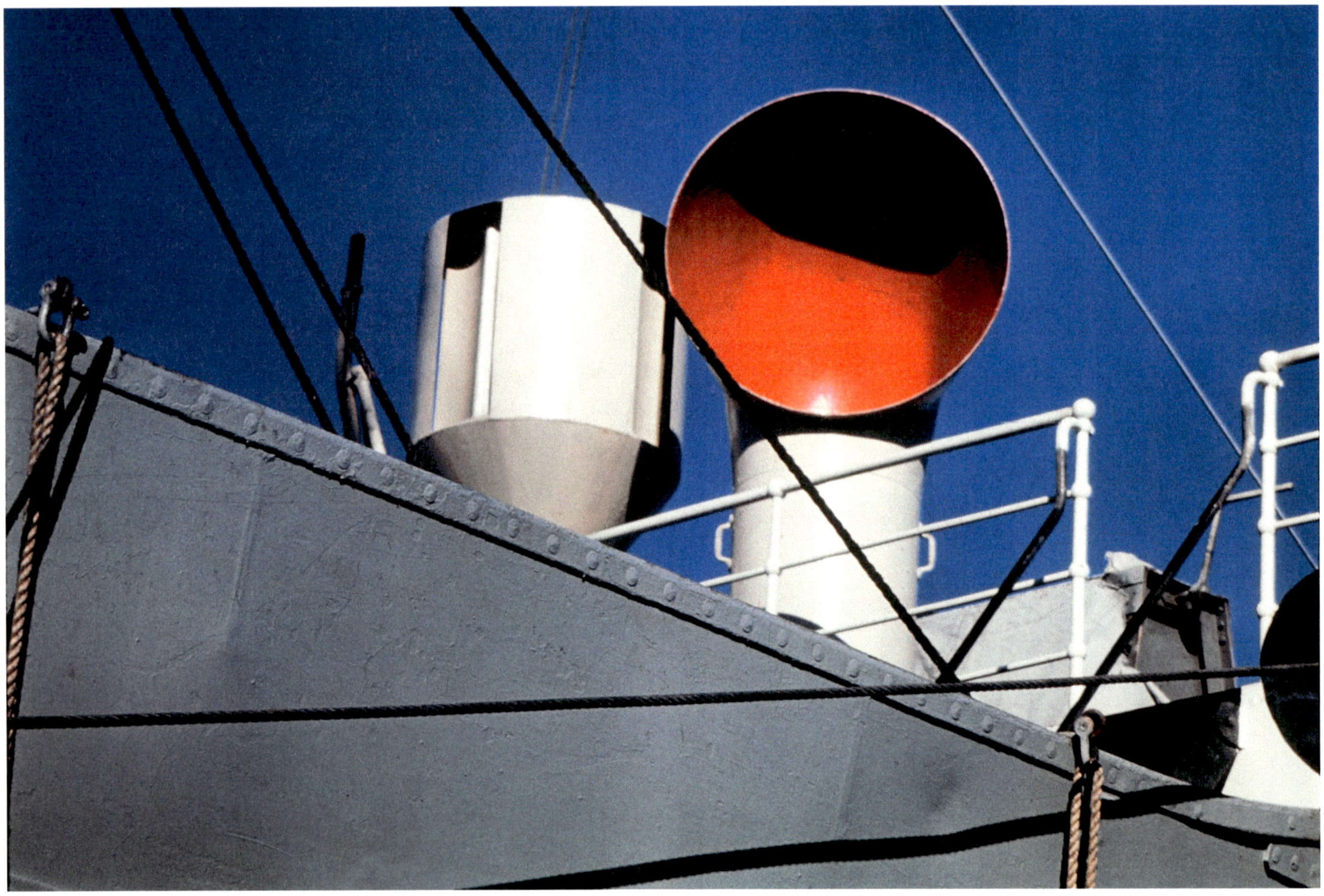

From the color slide series *Technical Beauty*, 1949: Ship's Funnel – Railway Wagon – Ship's Hull, Deck Rail, and Ventilators – Locomotive – Airliner

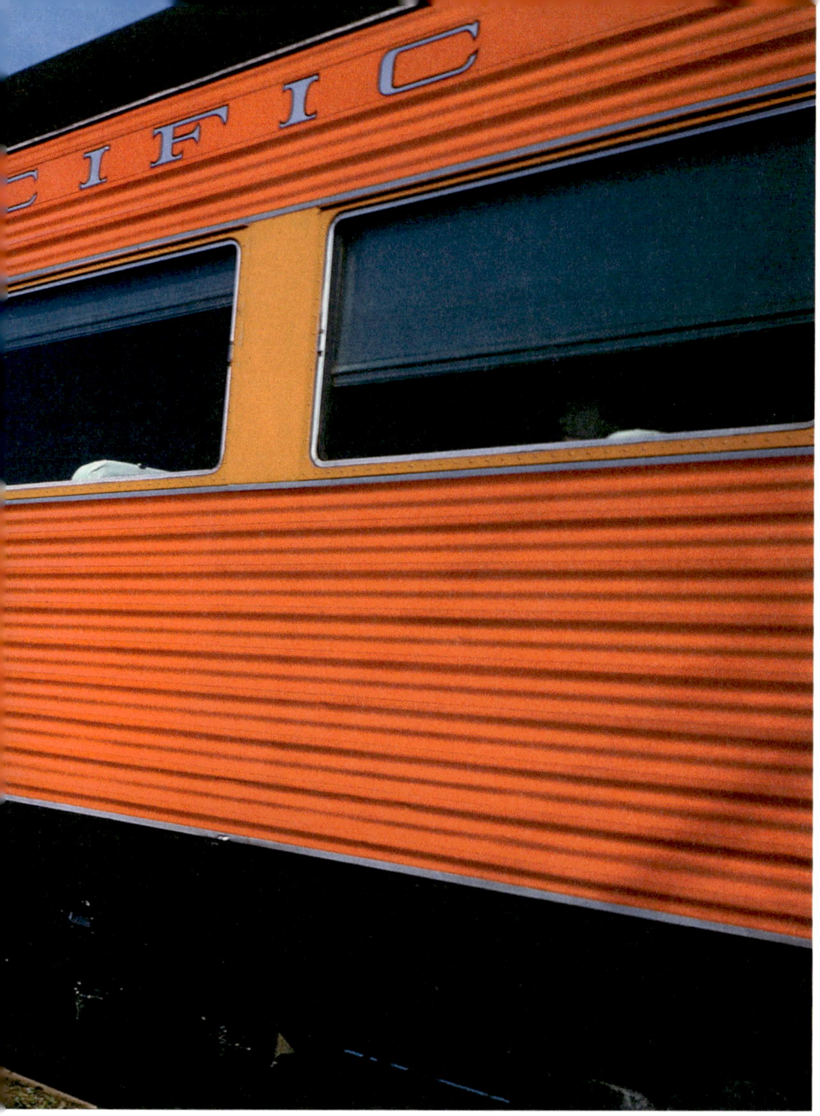
CIFIC

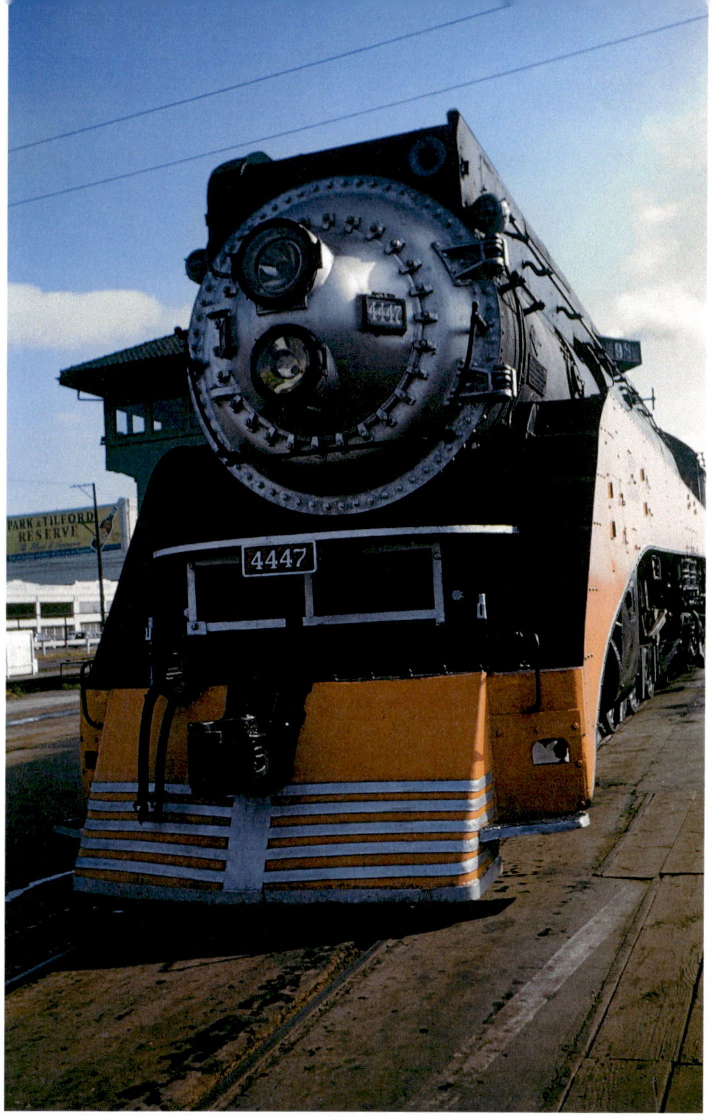
4447
PARK & TILFORD
RESERVE

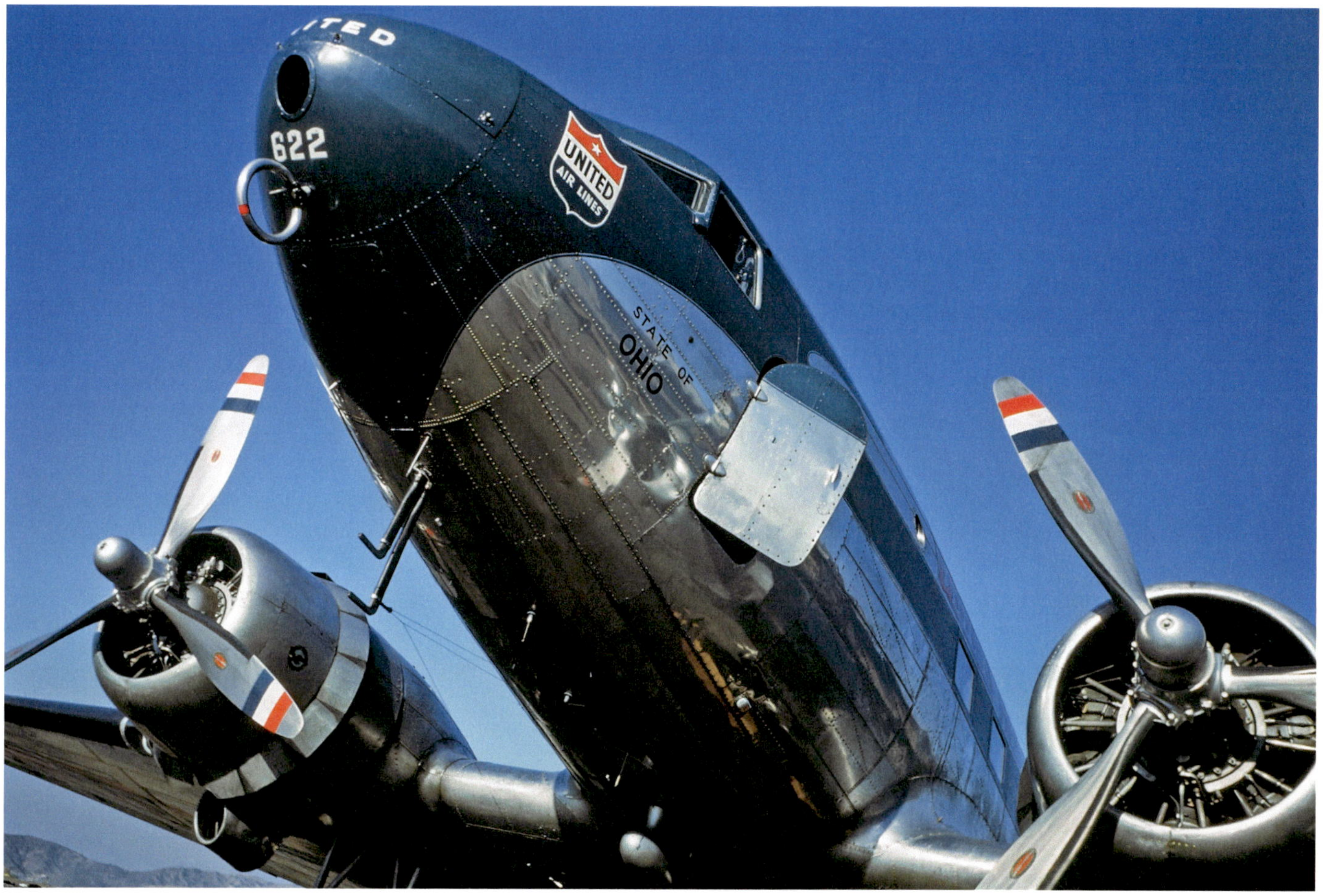
622
UNITED
AIR LINES
STATE OF
OHIO

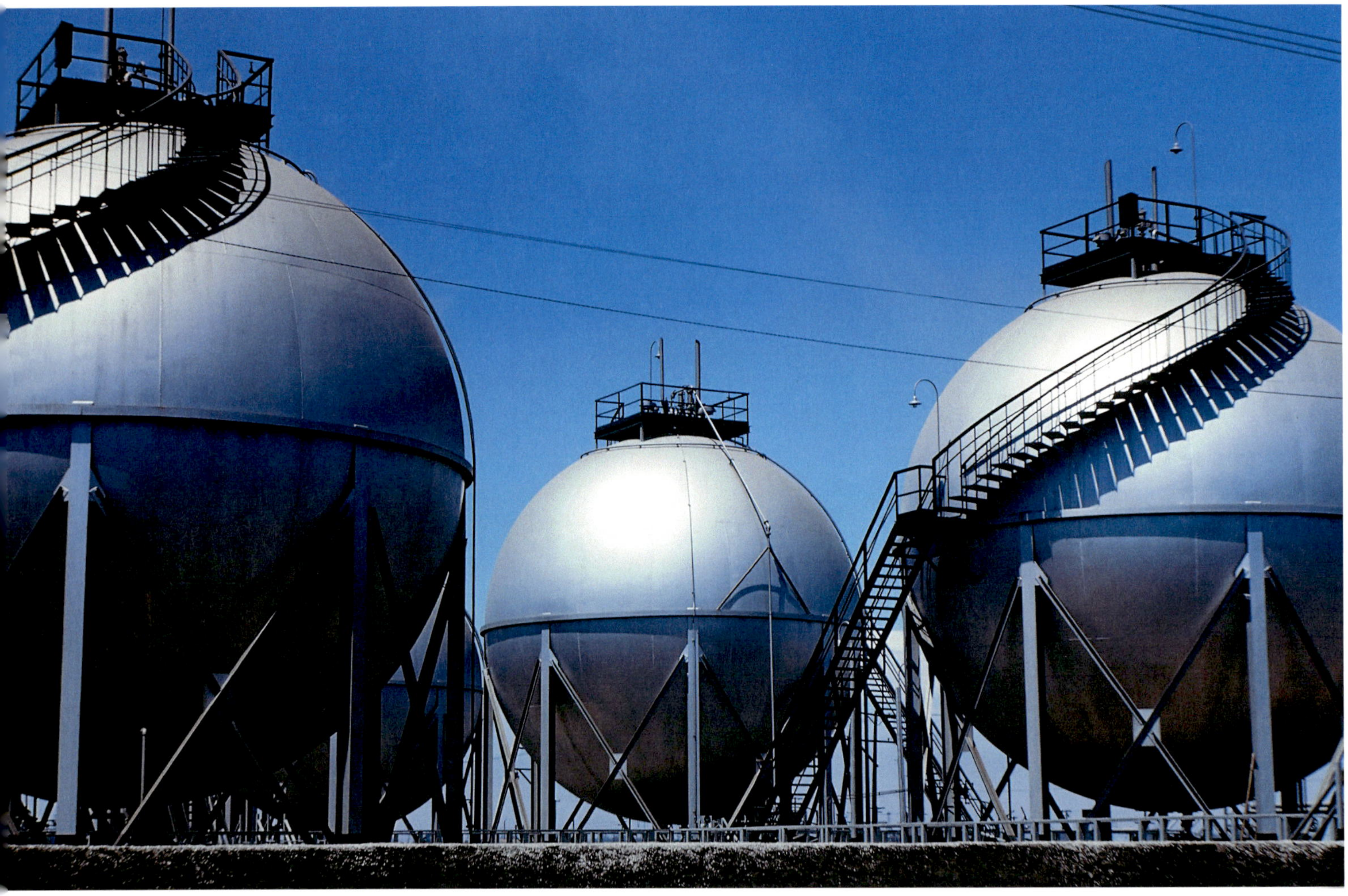

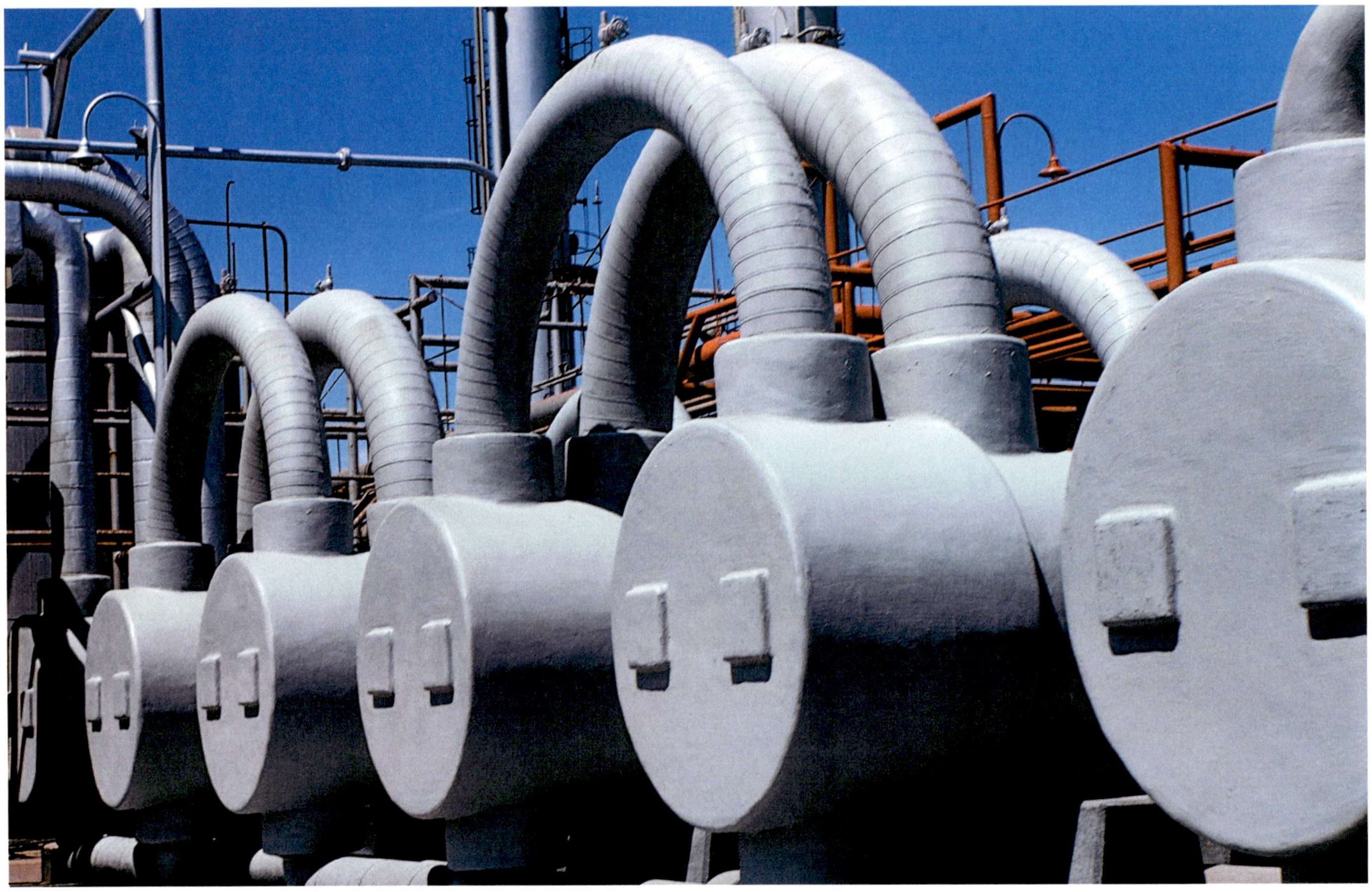

From the color slide series *Technical Beauty*, 1949: Spherical Butadiene Containers – Tanks and Pipes

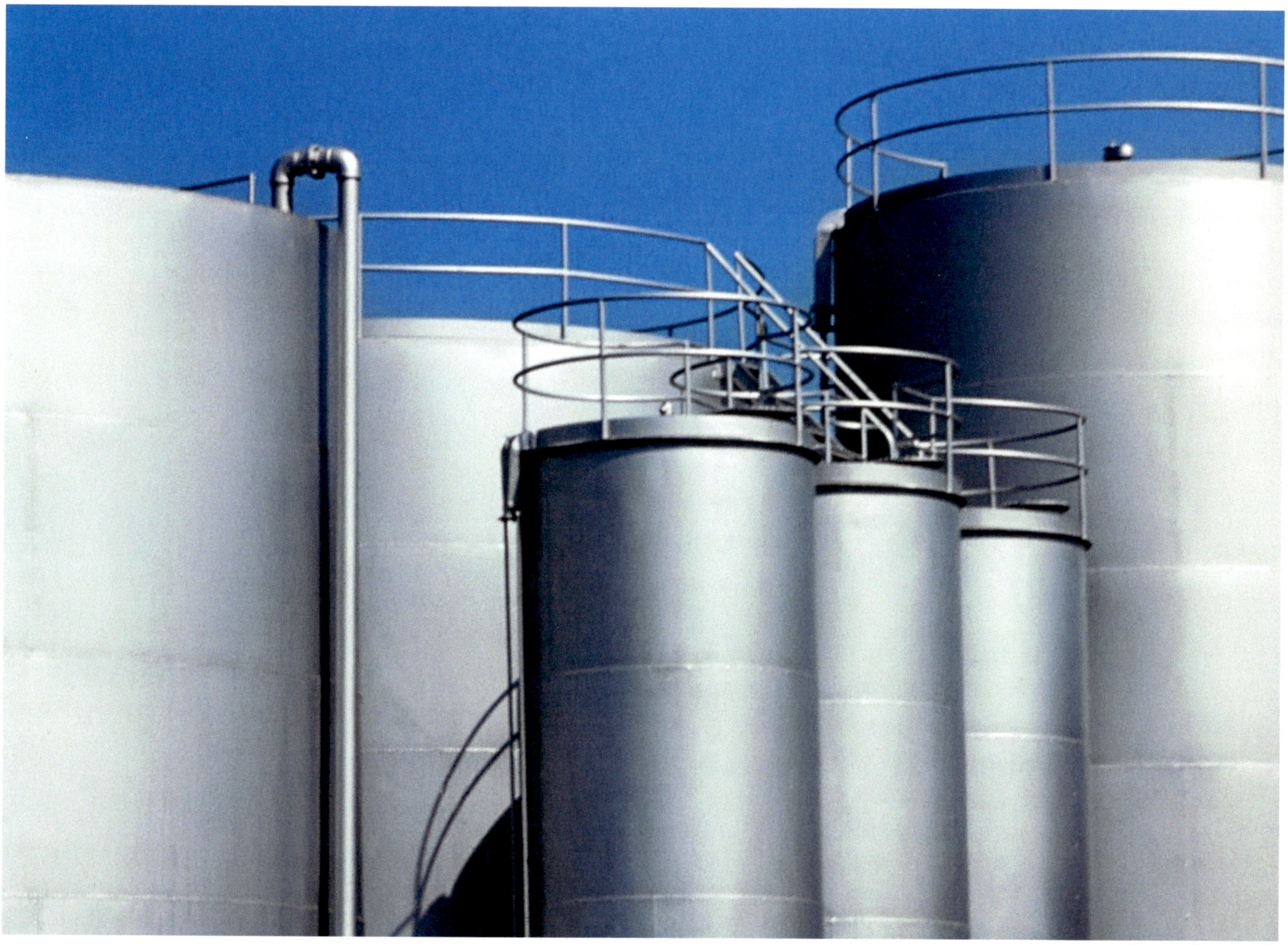

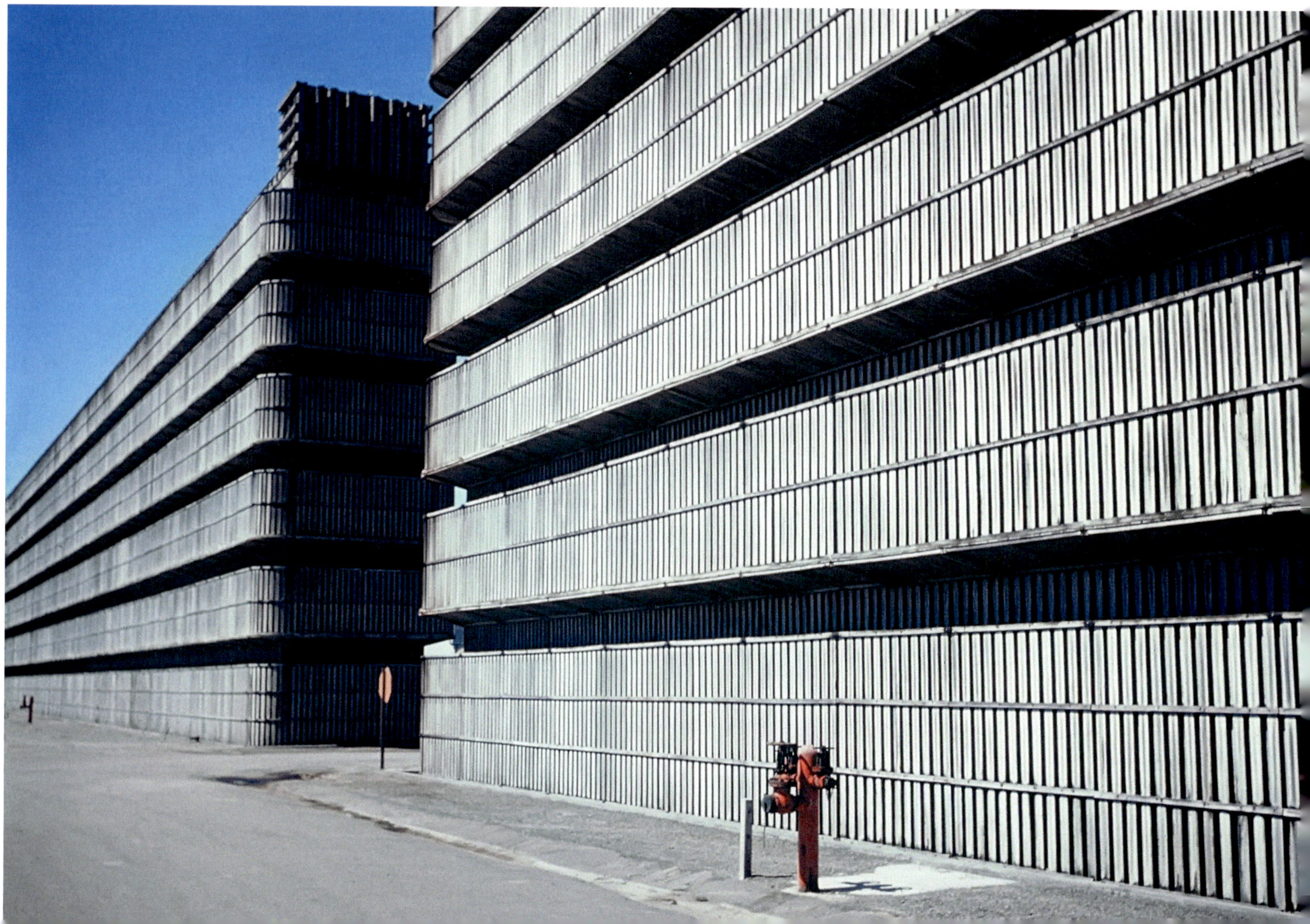

From the color slide series *Technical Beauty*, 1949: Tanks of an Oil Refinery – Row of Water Coolers

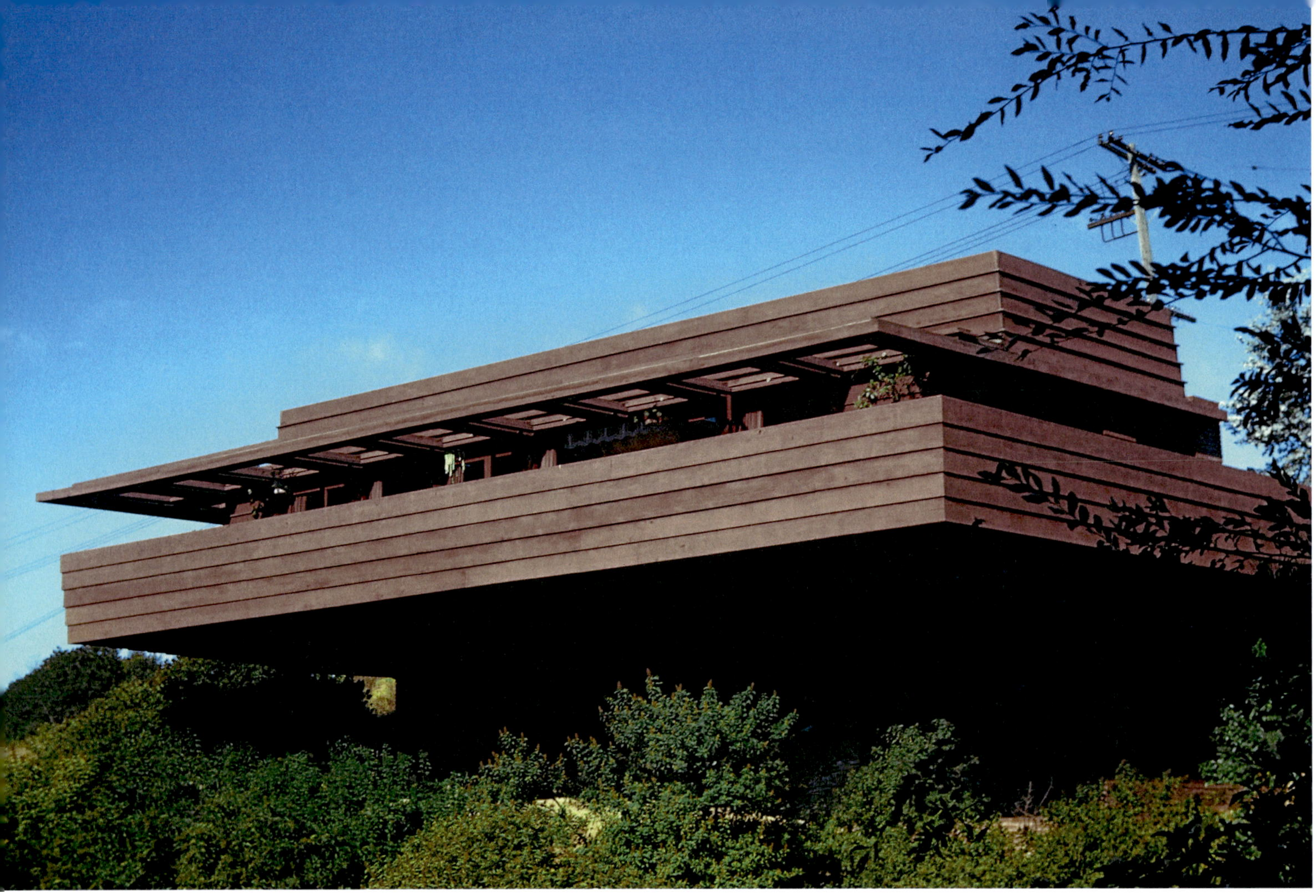

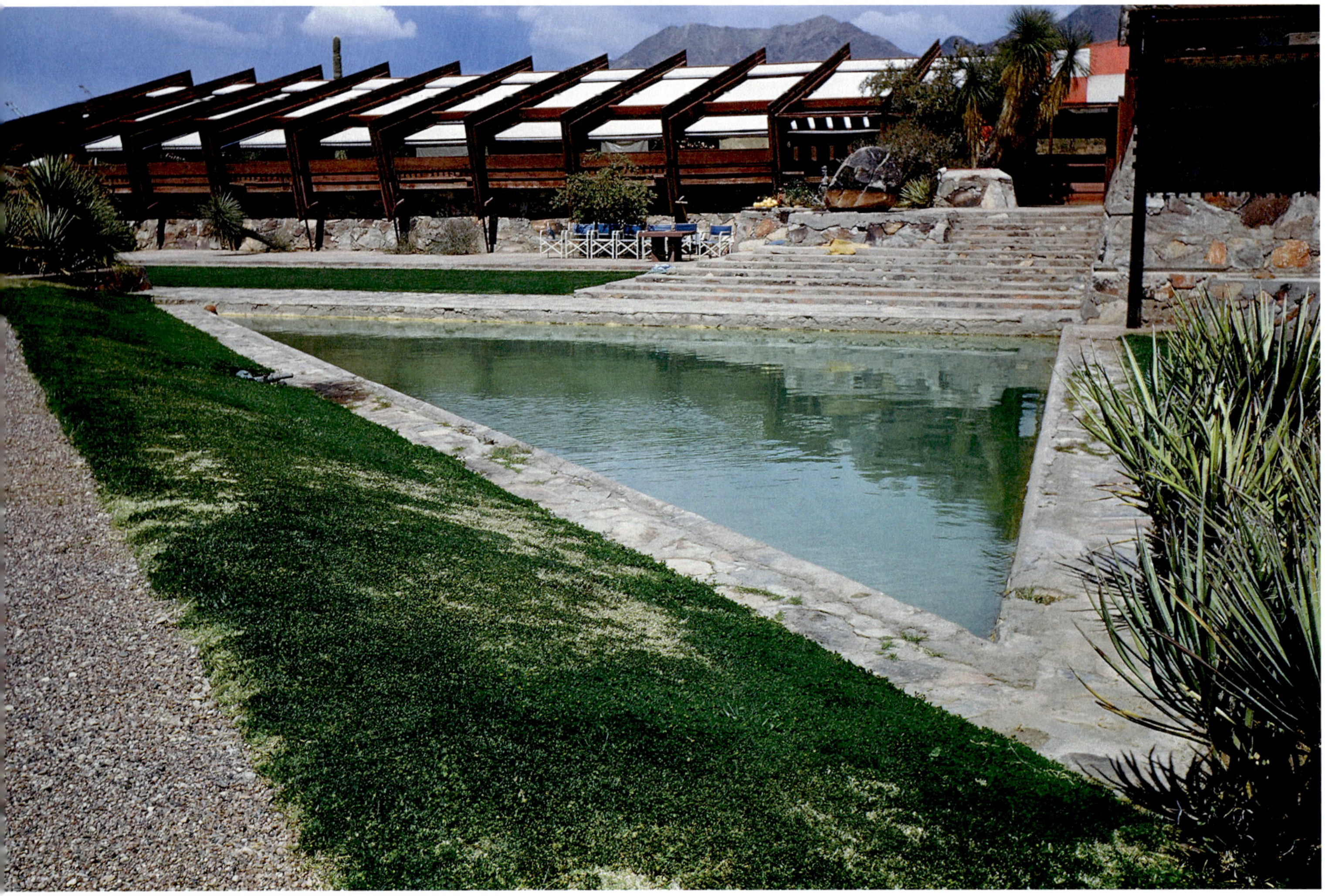

From the color slide series *Modern Architecture I* and *II*, 1943 and 1952:
Frank Lloyd Wright, Sturges Residence, Brentwood, Los Angeles, 1938 – Frank Lloyd Wright, Taliesin West, Water Basin, Arizona, 1938–42

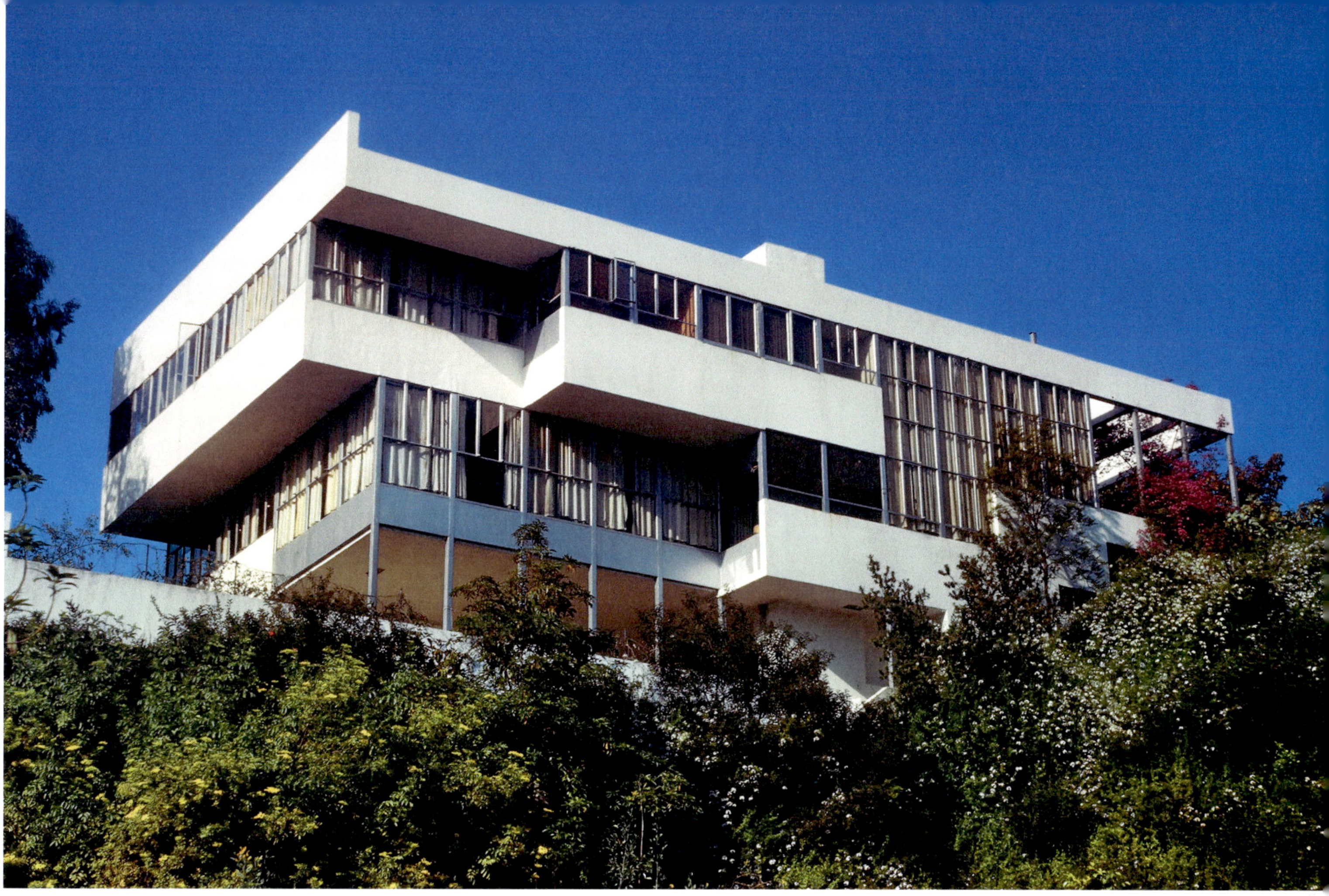

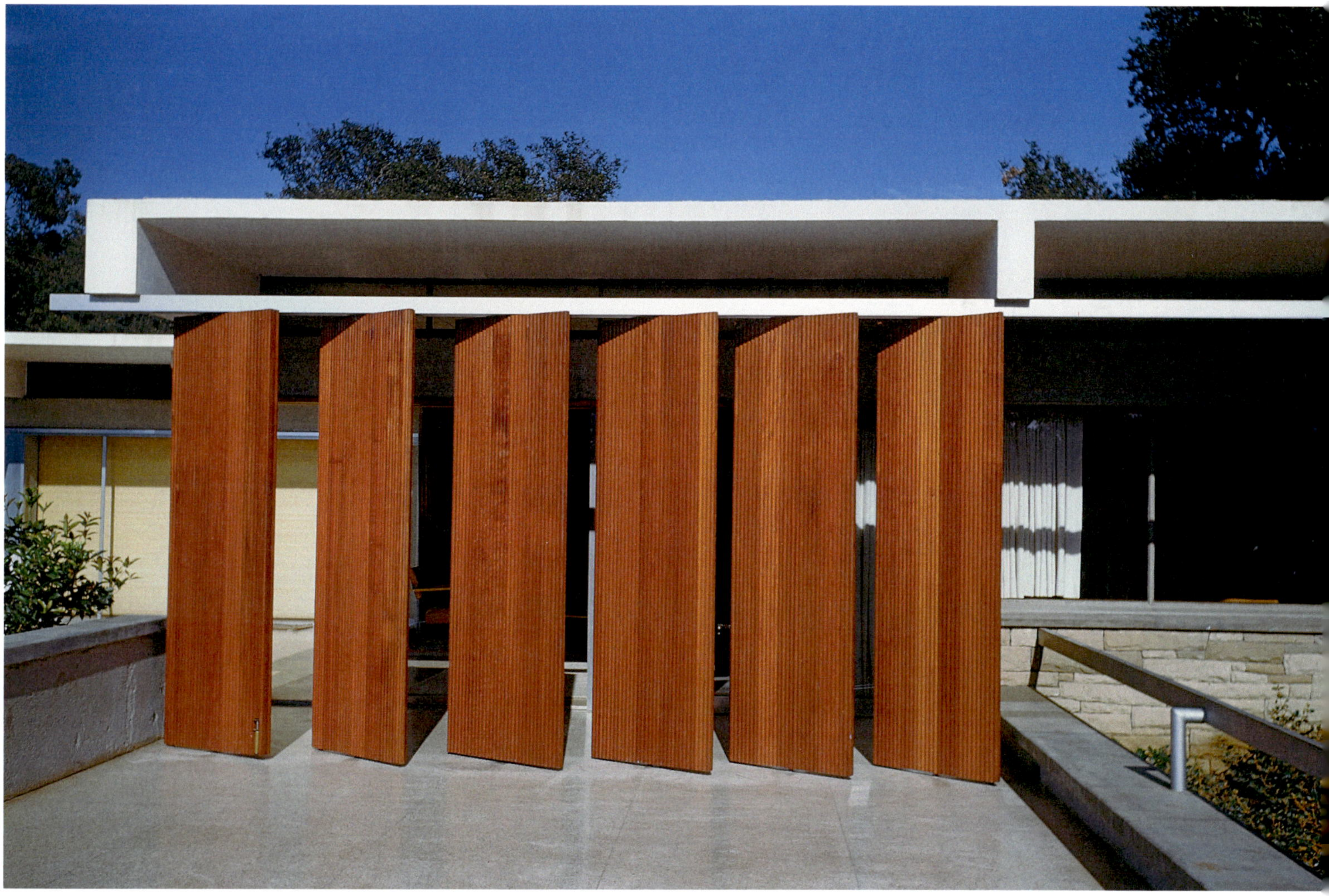

From the color slide series *Modern Architecture I* and *II*, 1943 and 1952:
Richard J. Neutra, Health House (Lovell Residence), Los Angeles, 1928 – Richard J. Neutra, Tremaine Residence, Montecito, 1949

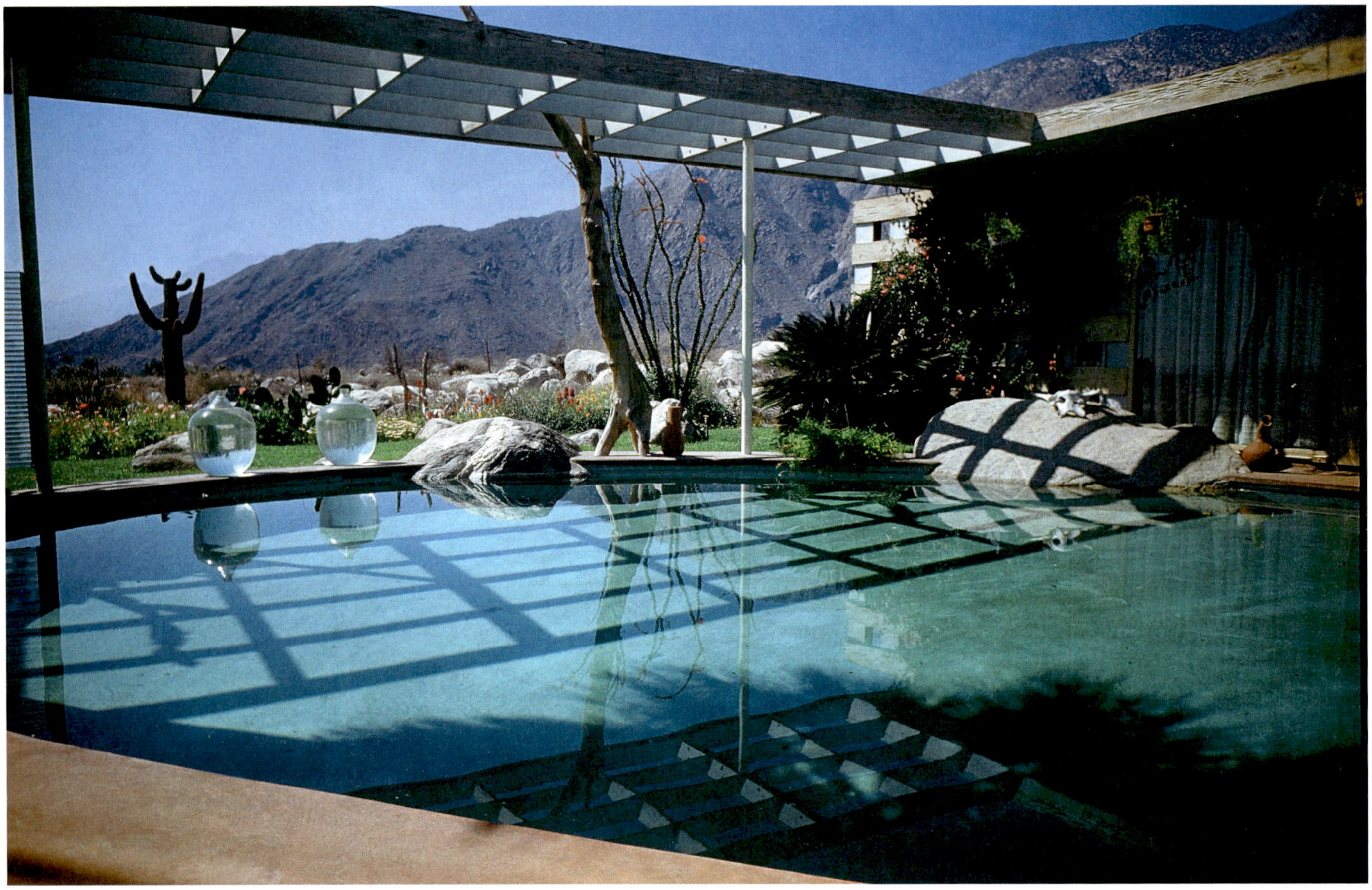

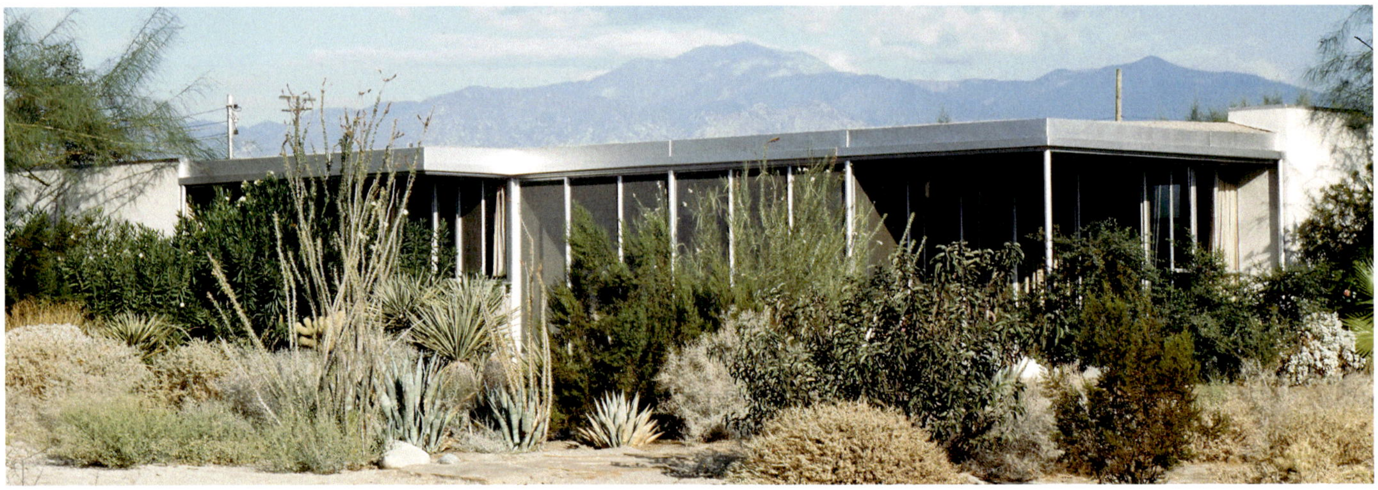

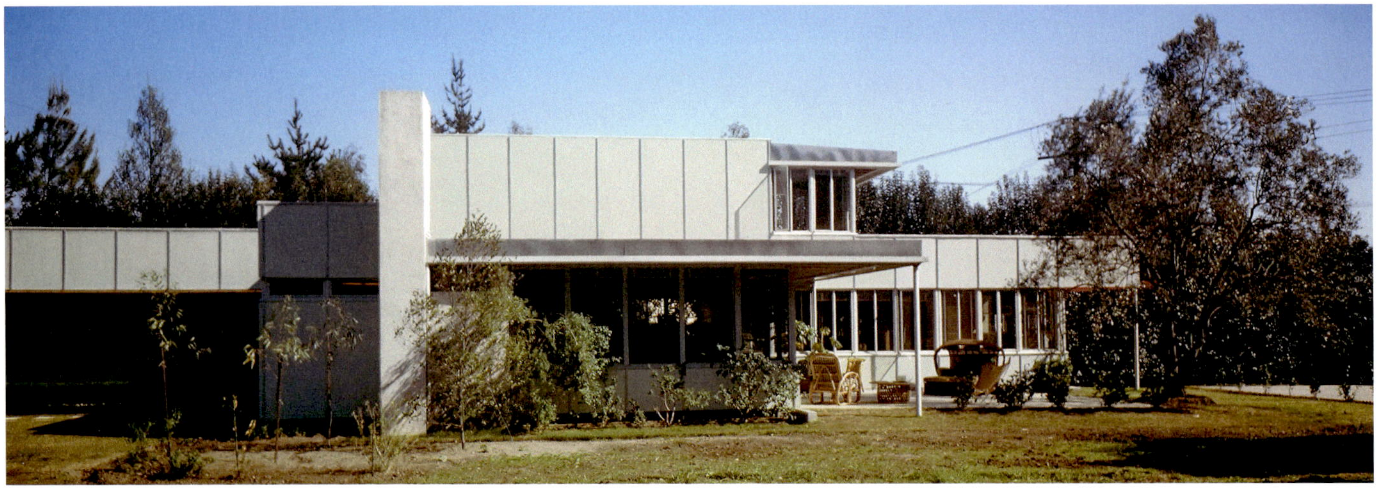

From the color slide series *Modern Architecture I* and *II*, 1943 and 1952: John Porter Clark and Albert Frey, Loewy Residence, Palm Springs, 1946 – Richard J. Neutra, Miller Residence, Palm Springs, 1937 – Richard J. Neutra, Plywood House, Brentwood Glen, Los Angeles, 1943 (designed 1936)

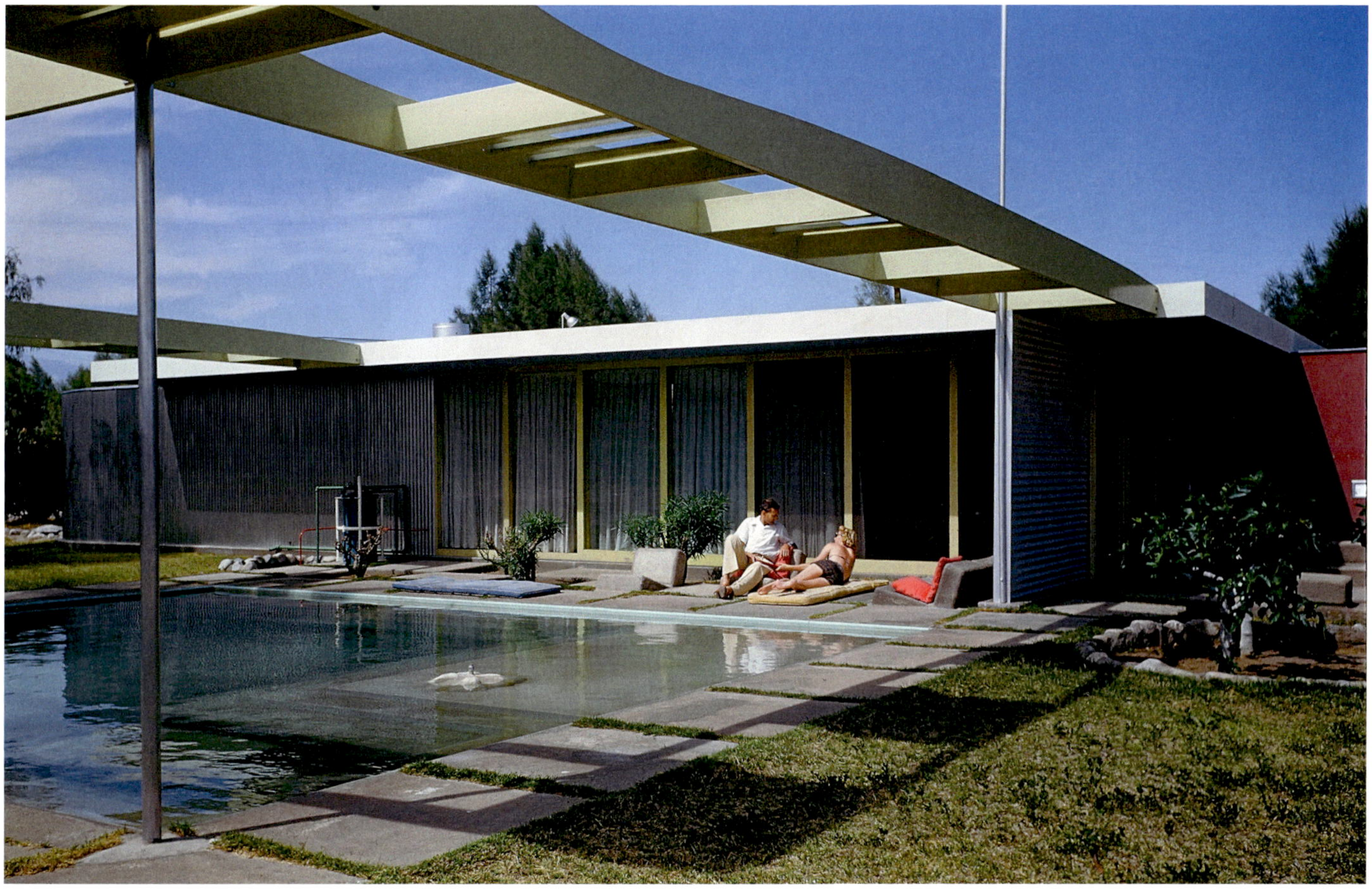

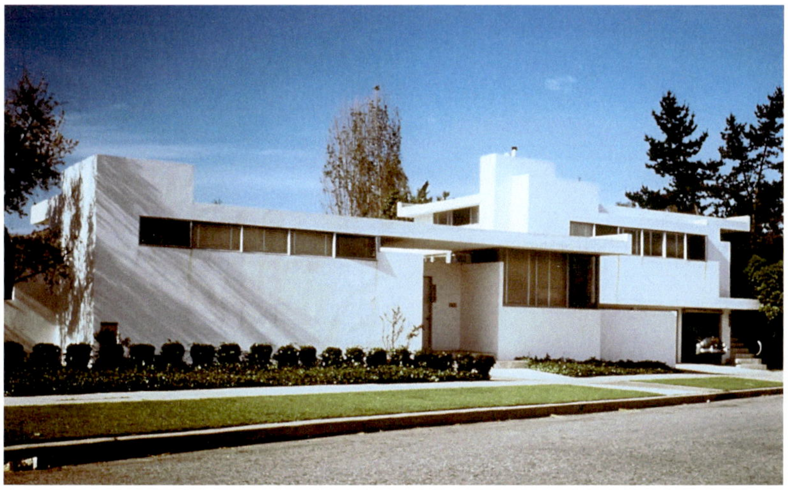

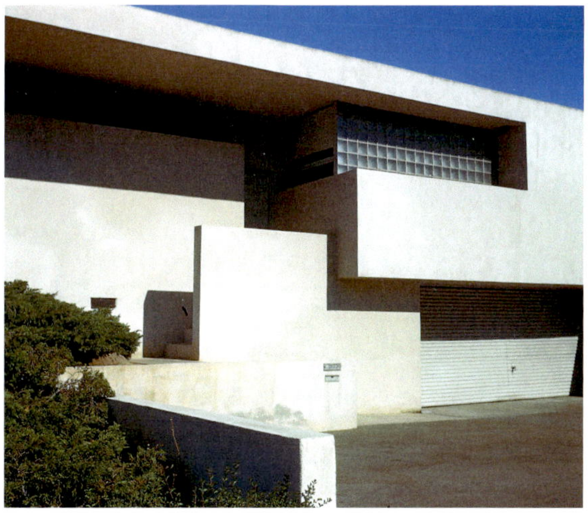

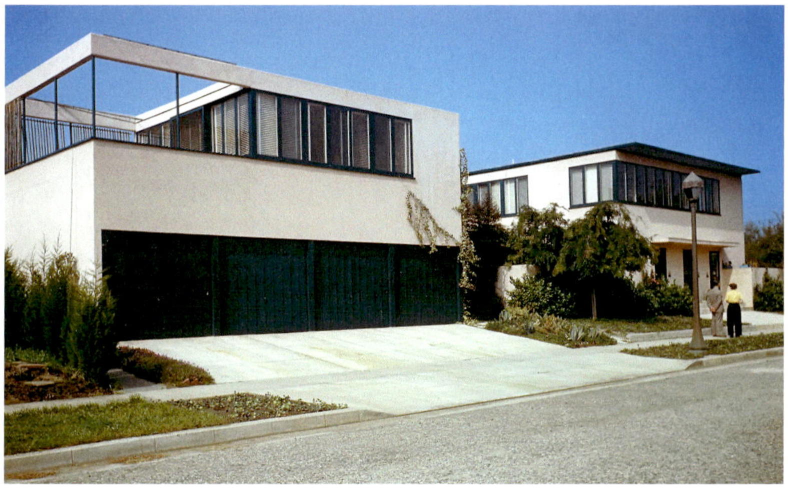

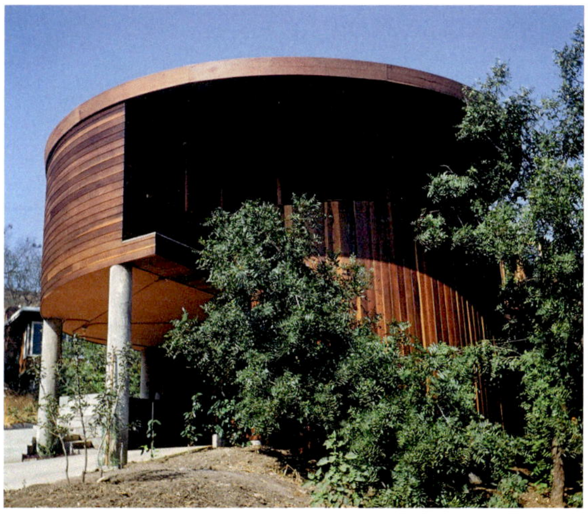

John Porter Clark and Albert Frey, Frey Residence, Palm Springs, 1948 – Rudolph M. Schindler, John J. Buck Residence, North Hollywood, 1934 – Edward R. Lind, Douglas Kennedy Residence, Hollywood, 1939 – Julius R. Davidson, Drucker Apartments, Los Angeles, 1940 – John Lautner, Foster Residence, Sherman Oaks, Los Angeles, 1950

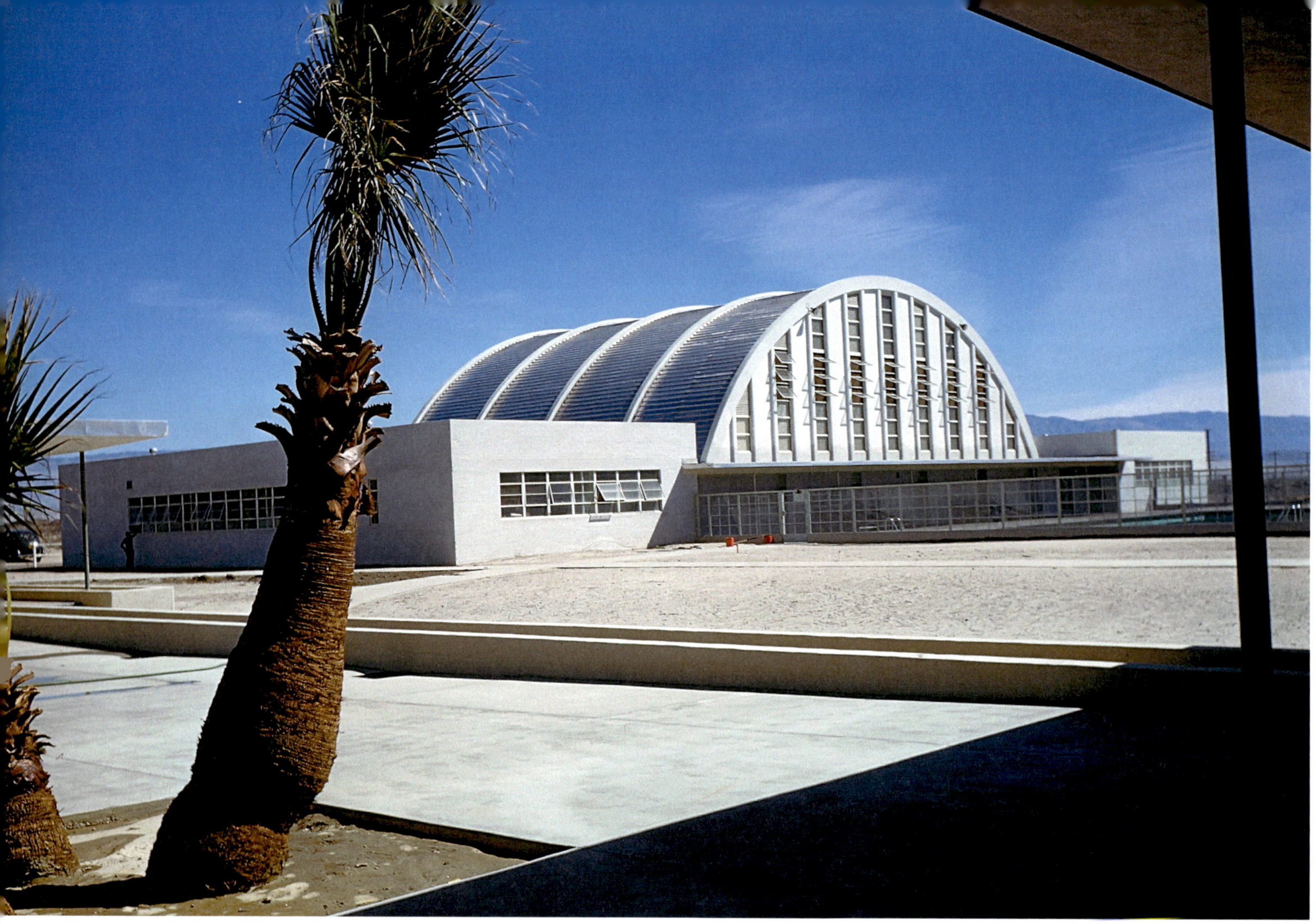

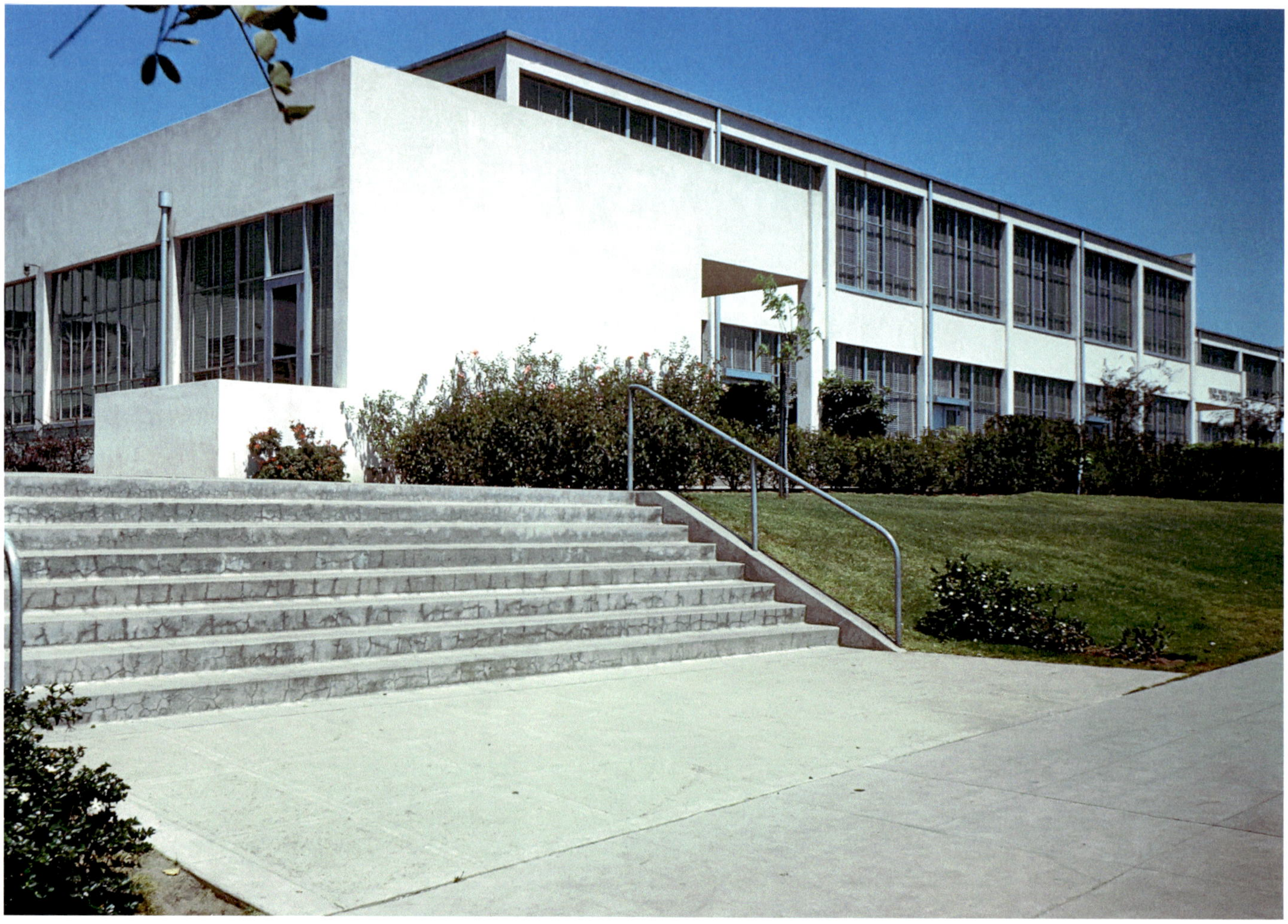

From the color slide series *Modern Architecture II*, 1943 and 1952: Williams, Williams and Williams, Palm Springs High School, Palm Springs, 1948/49 – Richard J. Neutra, Ralph Waldo Emerson High School, Westwood, 1937

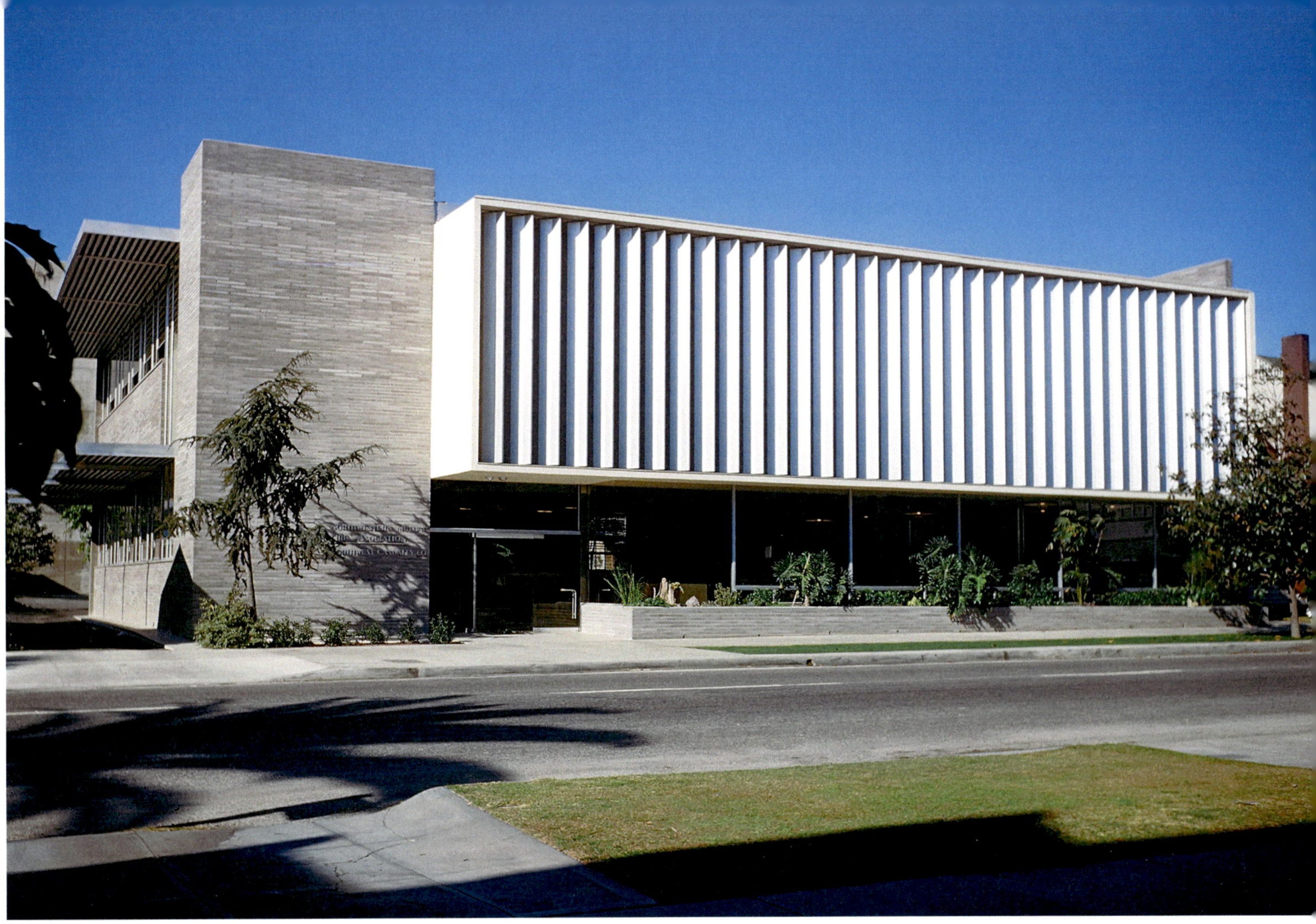

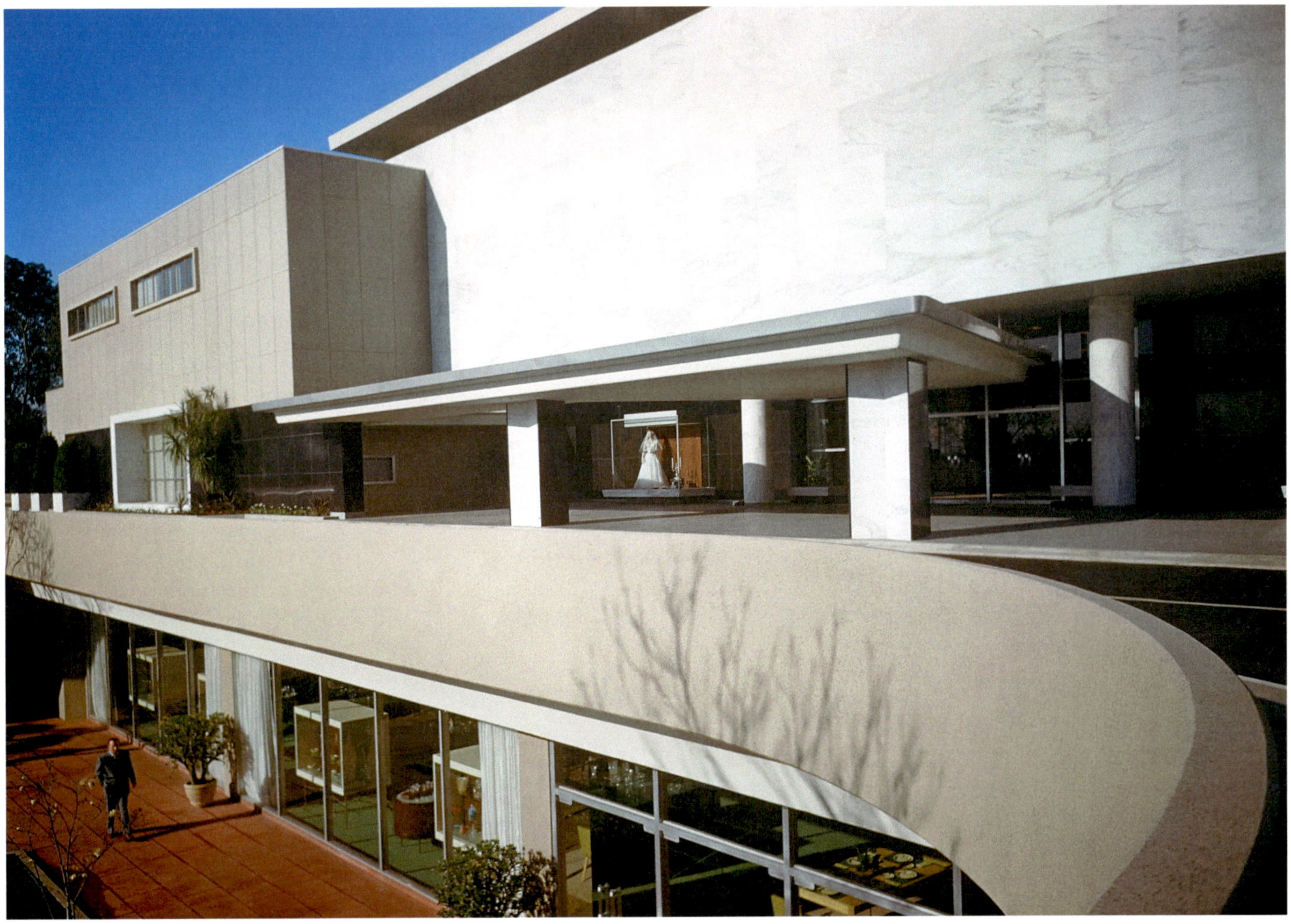

From the color slide series *Modern Architecture II*, 1952: Richard J. Neutra, Northwestern Mutual Fire Insurance Building, Los Angeles, 1951 – William Pereira & Charles Luckman with Charles Matcham, Robinson's Department Store, Beverly Hills, 1952

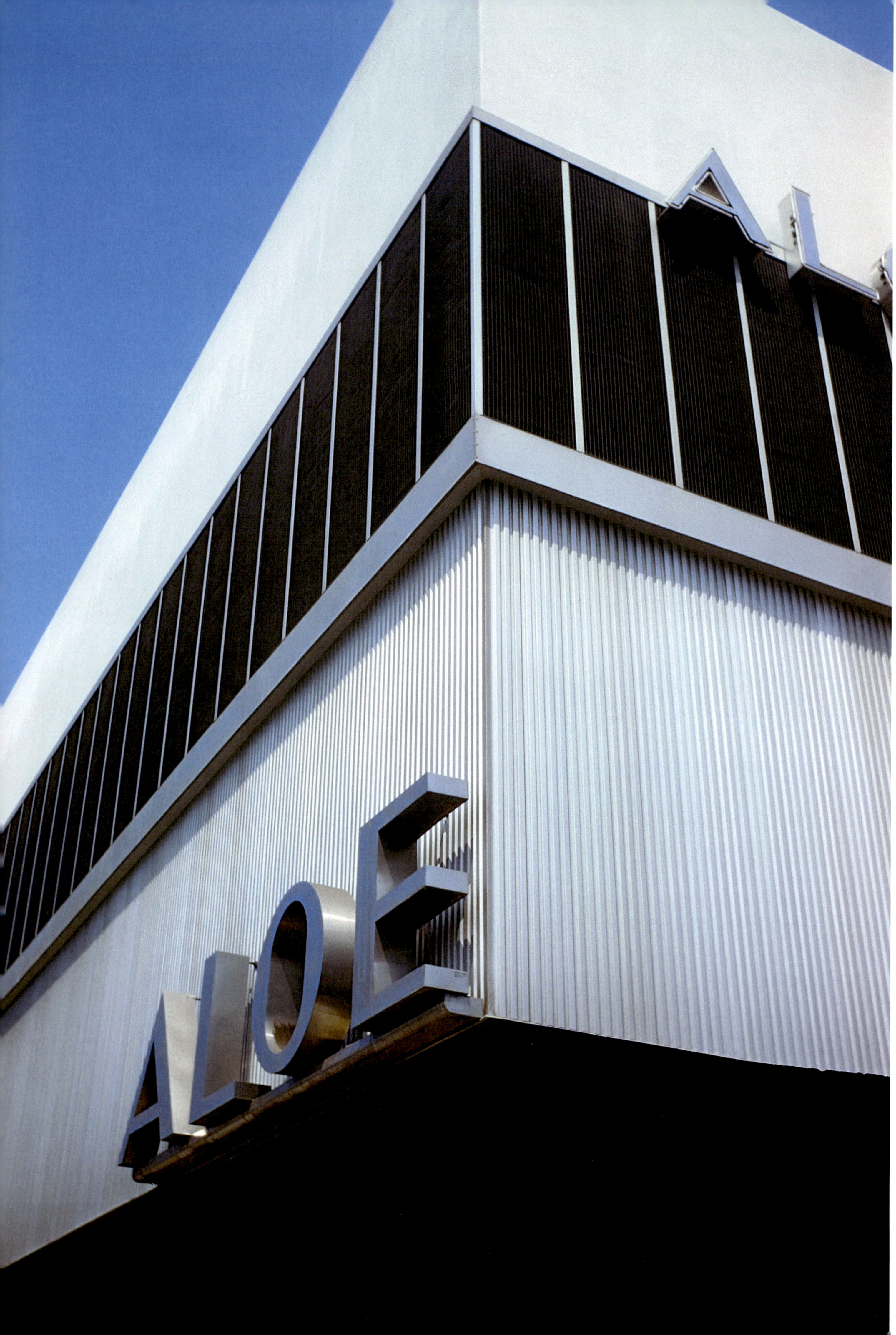

From the color slide series *Modern Architecture II*, 1952: Richard J. Neutra, Aloe Hospital Equipment Company, Los Angeles, 1949

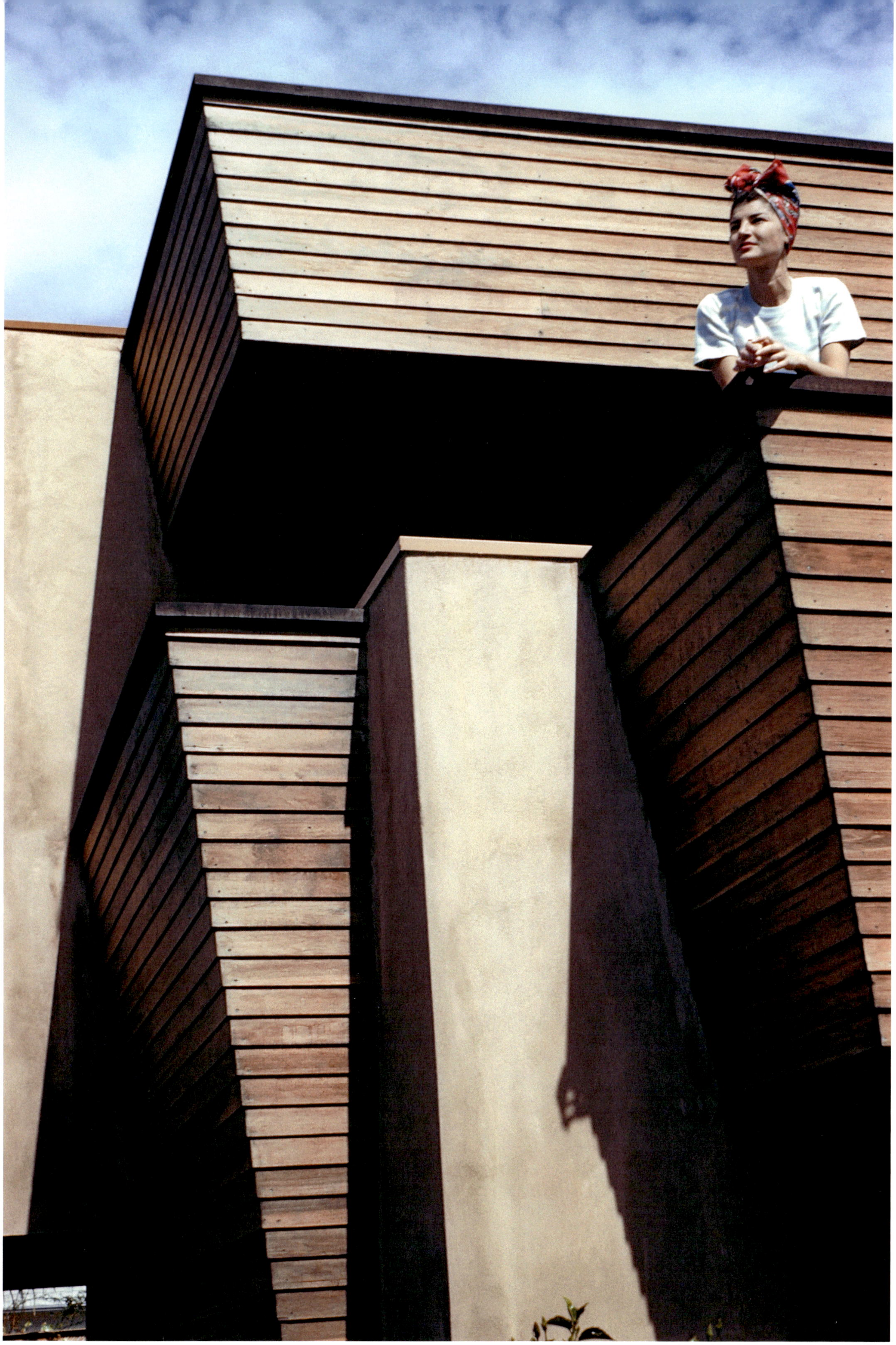

From the color slide series *Modern Architecture I*, 1943: Harwell Hamilton Harris, Byron Pumphrey Residence, Los Angeles, 1939

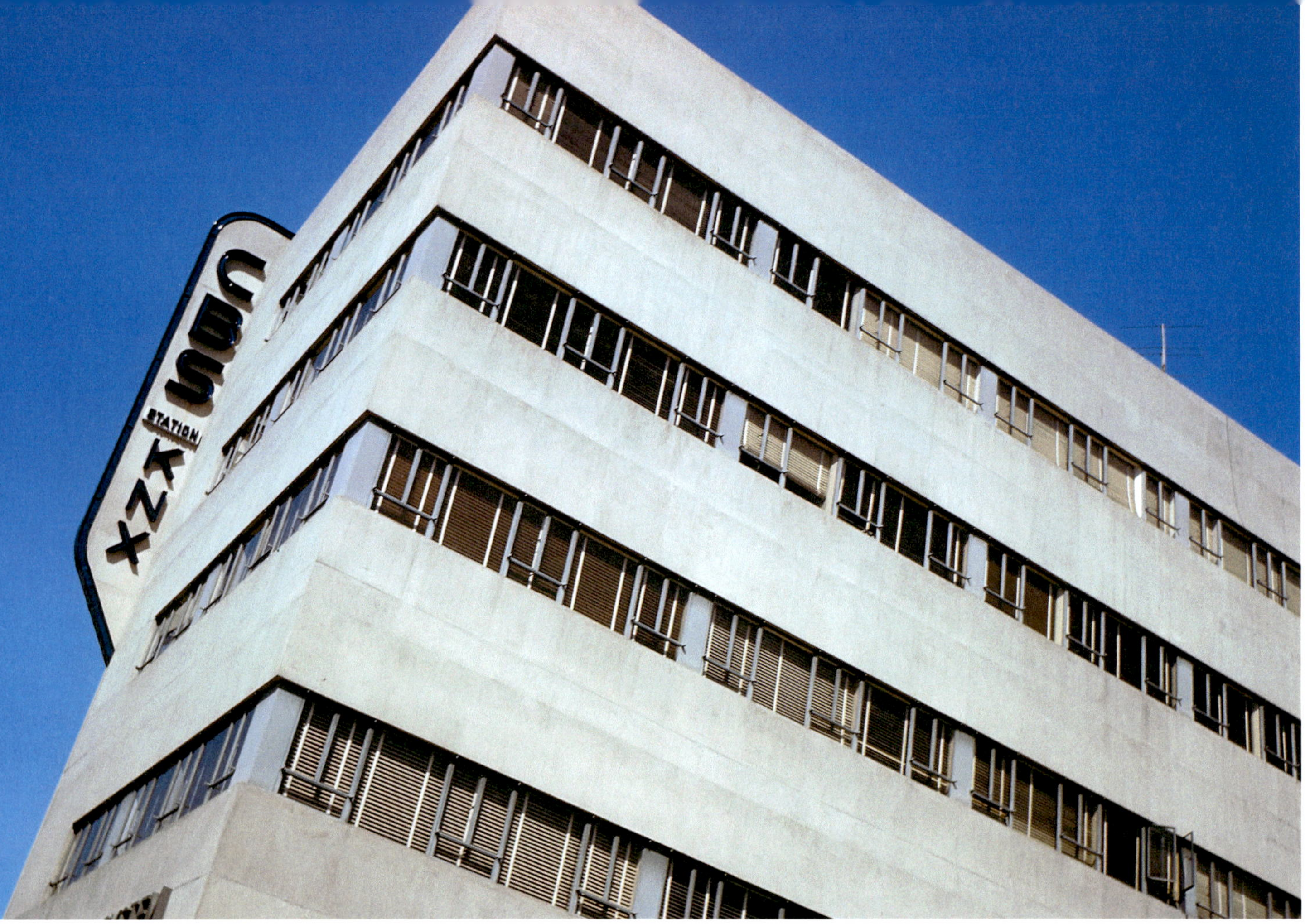

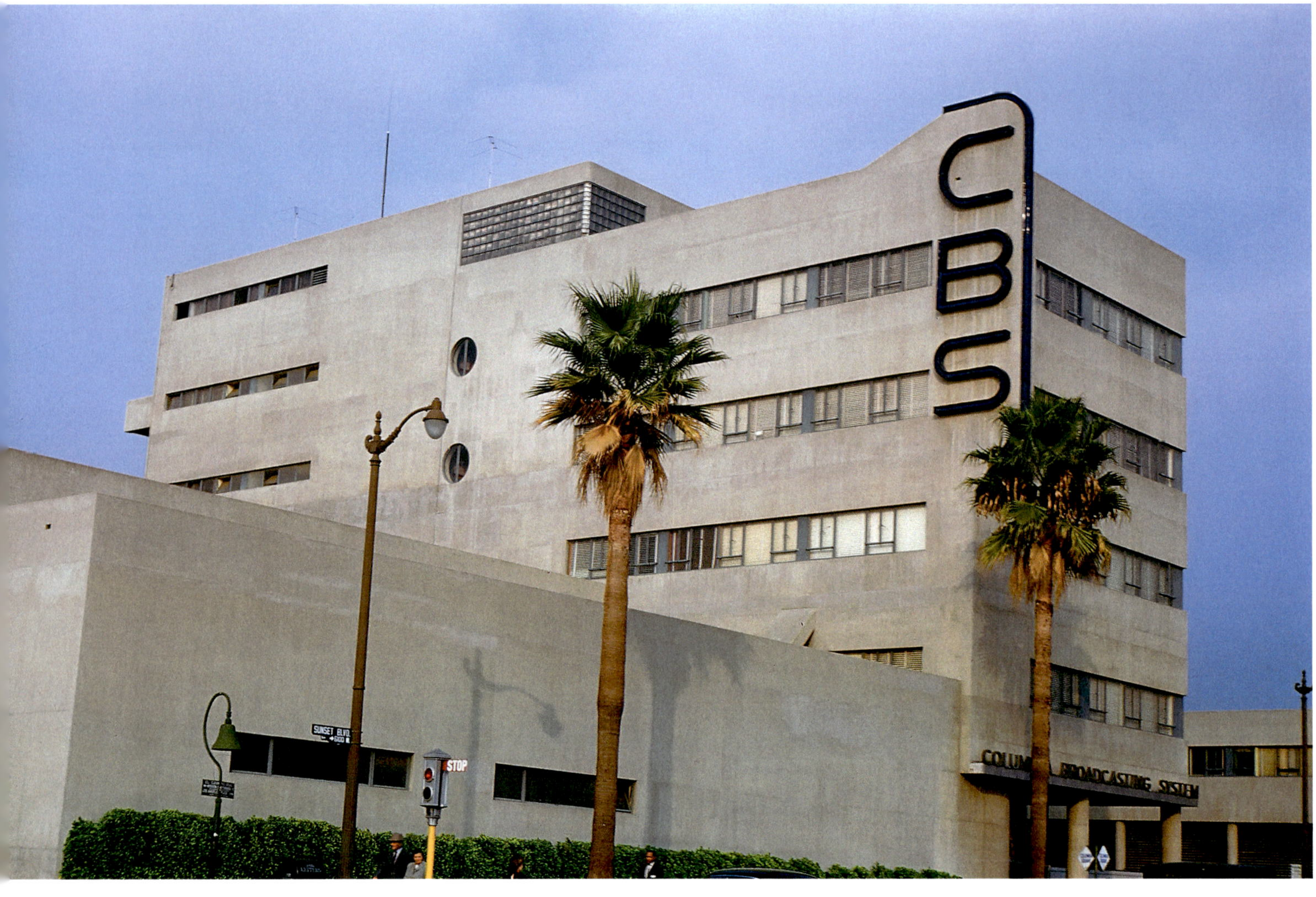

From the color slide series *Modern Architecture I*, 1943: William Lescaze, Columbia Broadcasting System Headquarters, Hollywood, 1938

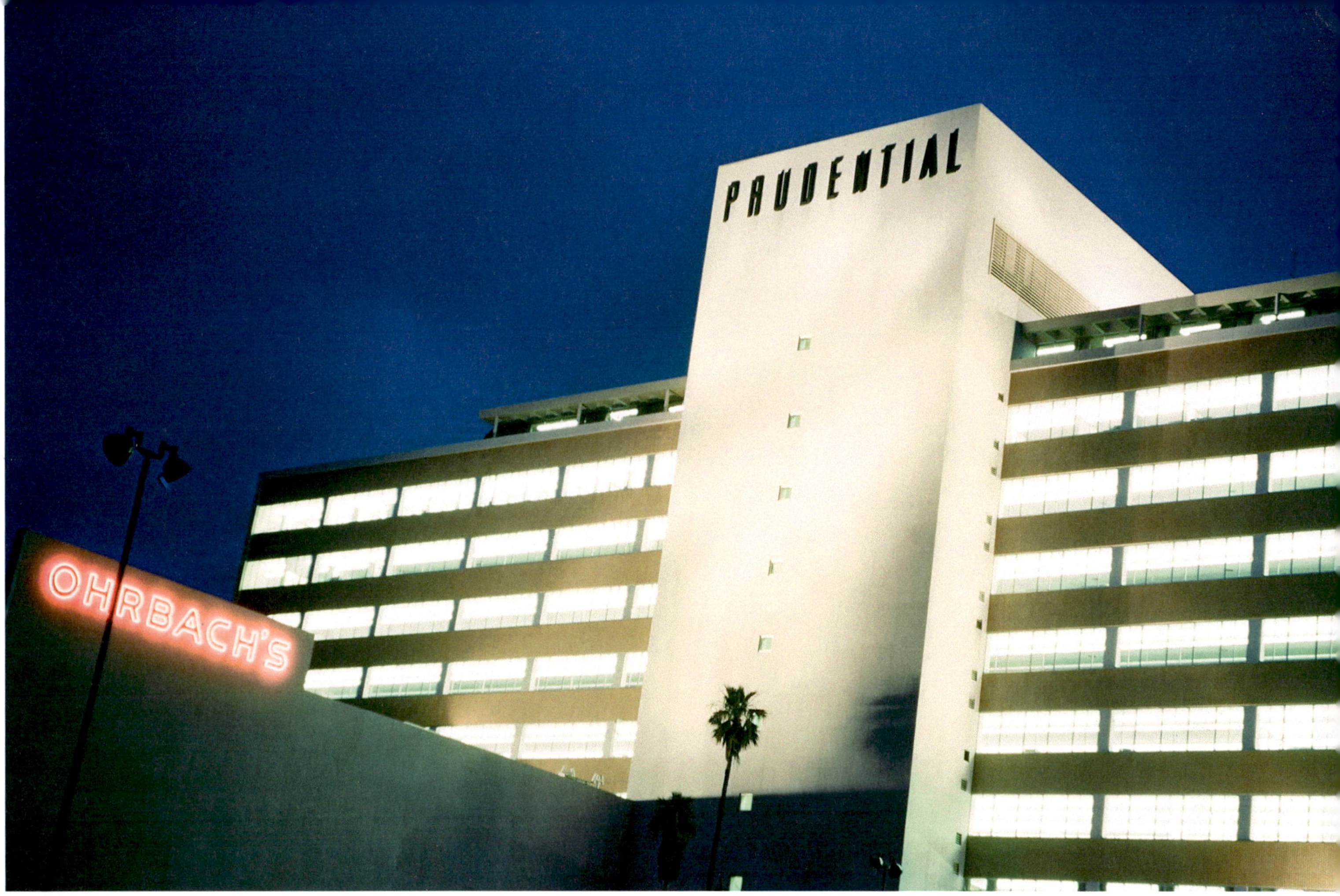

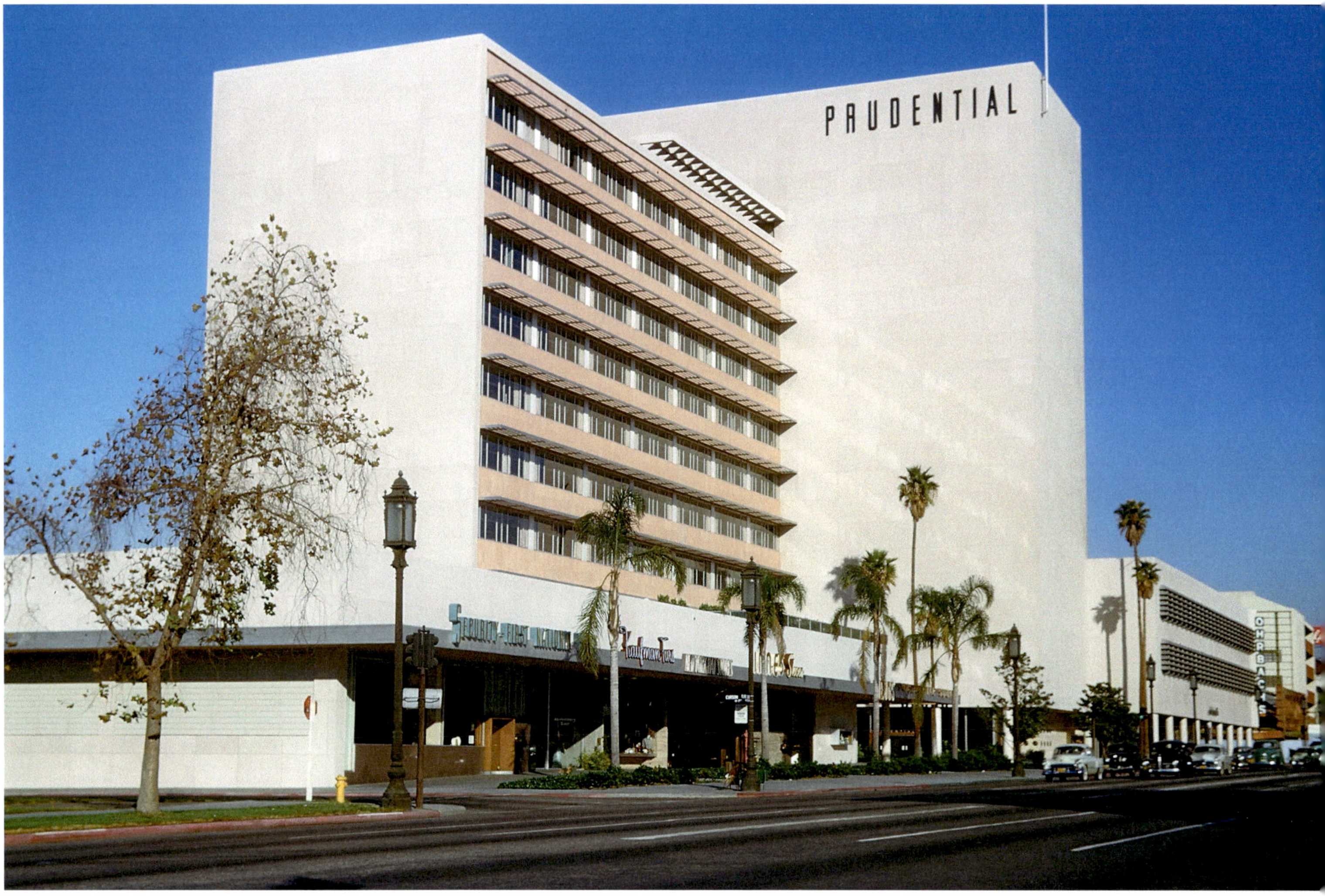

From the color slide series *Modern Architecture II*, 1952: Walter Wurdeman and Welton Becket, The Prudential Insurance Company Building, Los Angeles, 1949

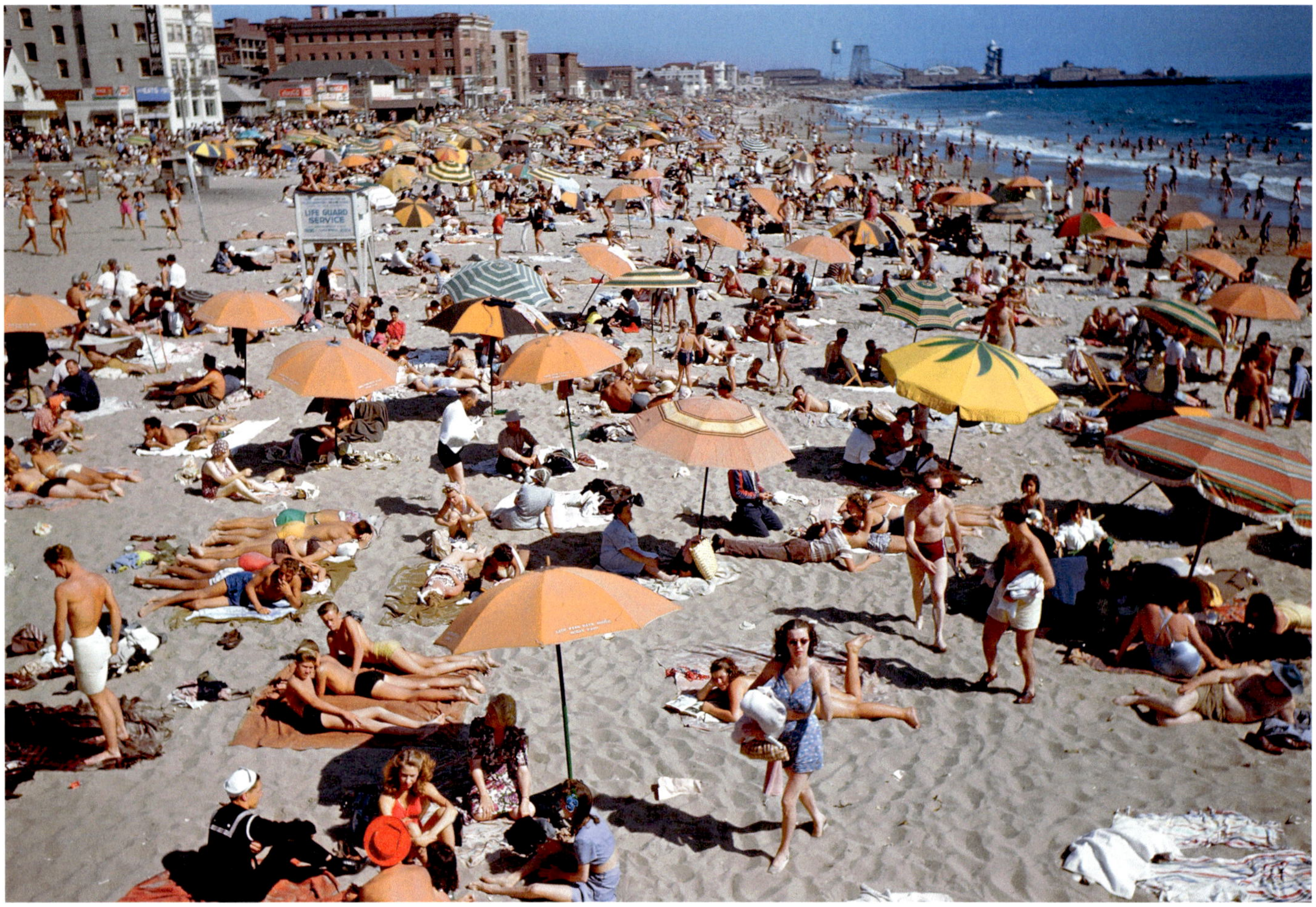

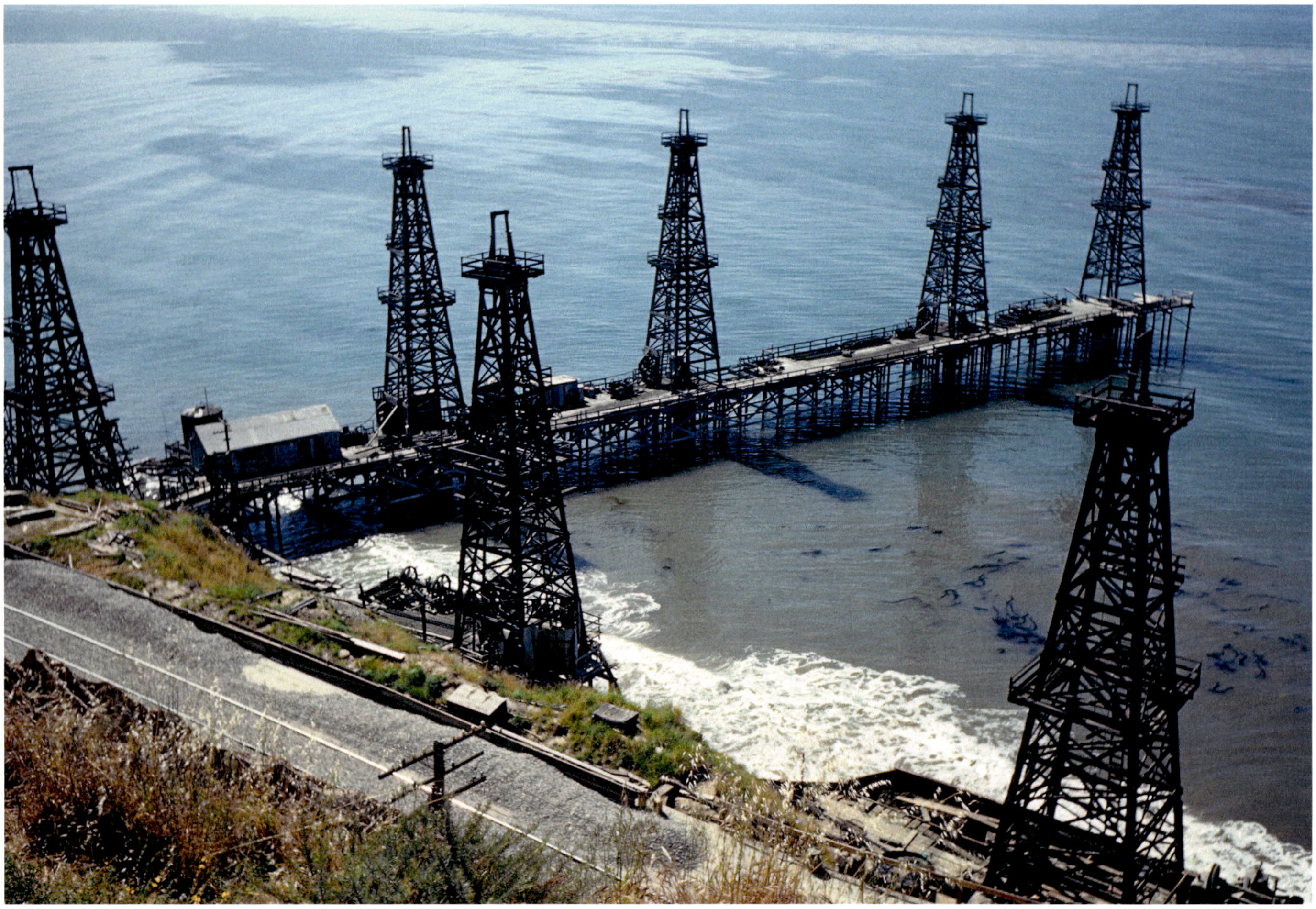

Santa Monica Beach, ca. 1945 – Oil Towers on the Coast near St. Barbara, ca. 1945

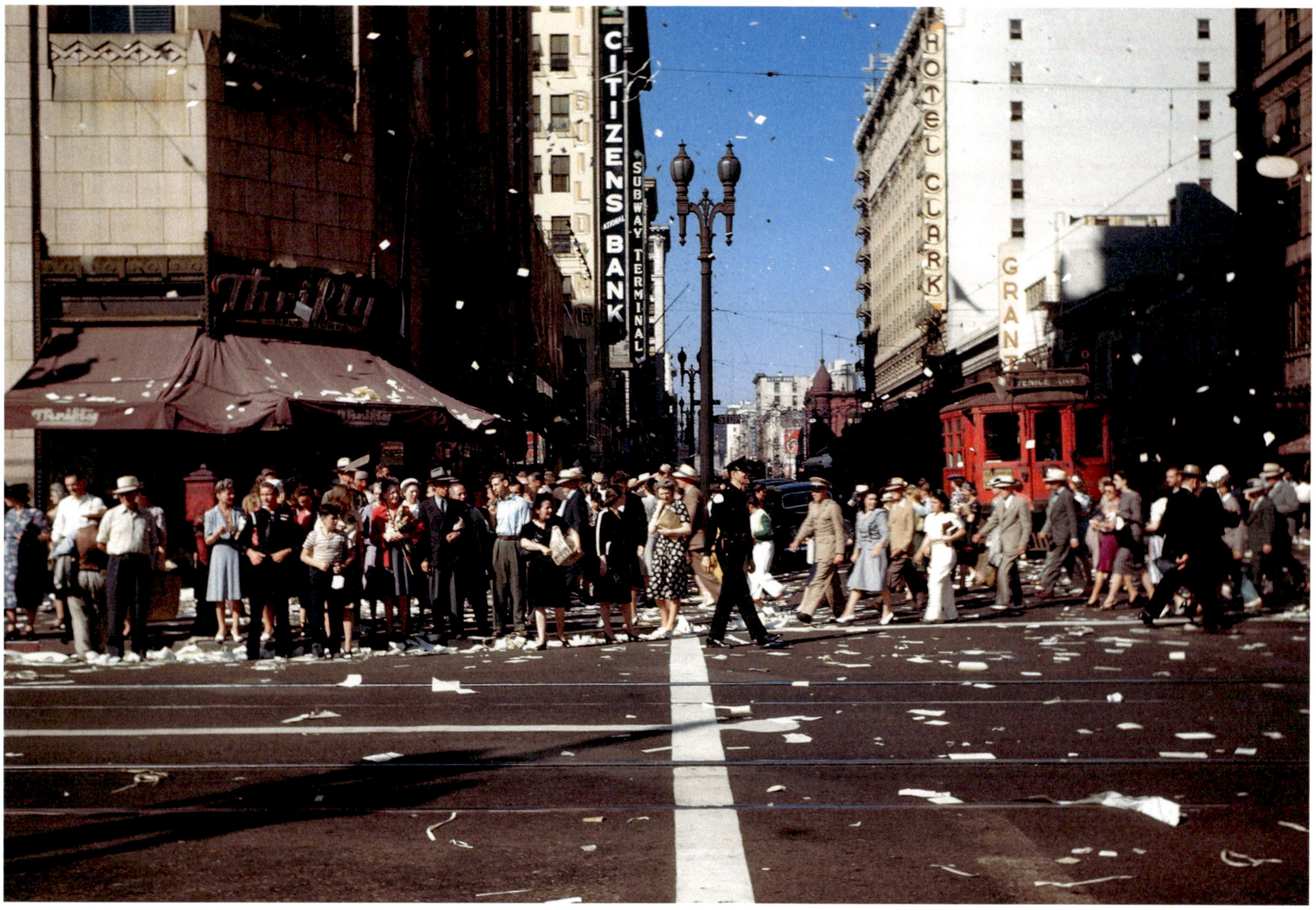

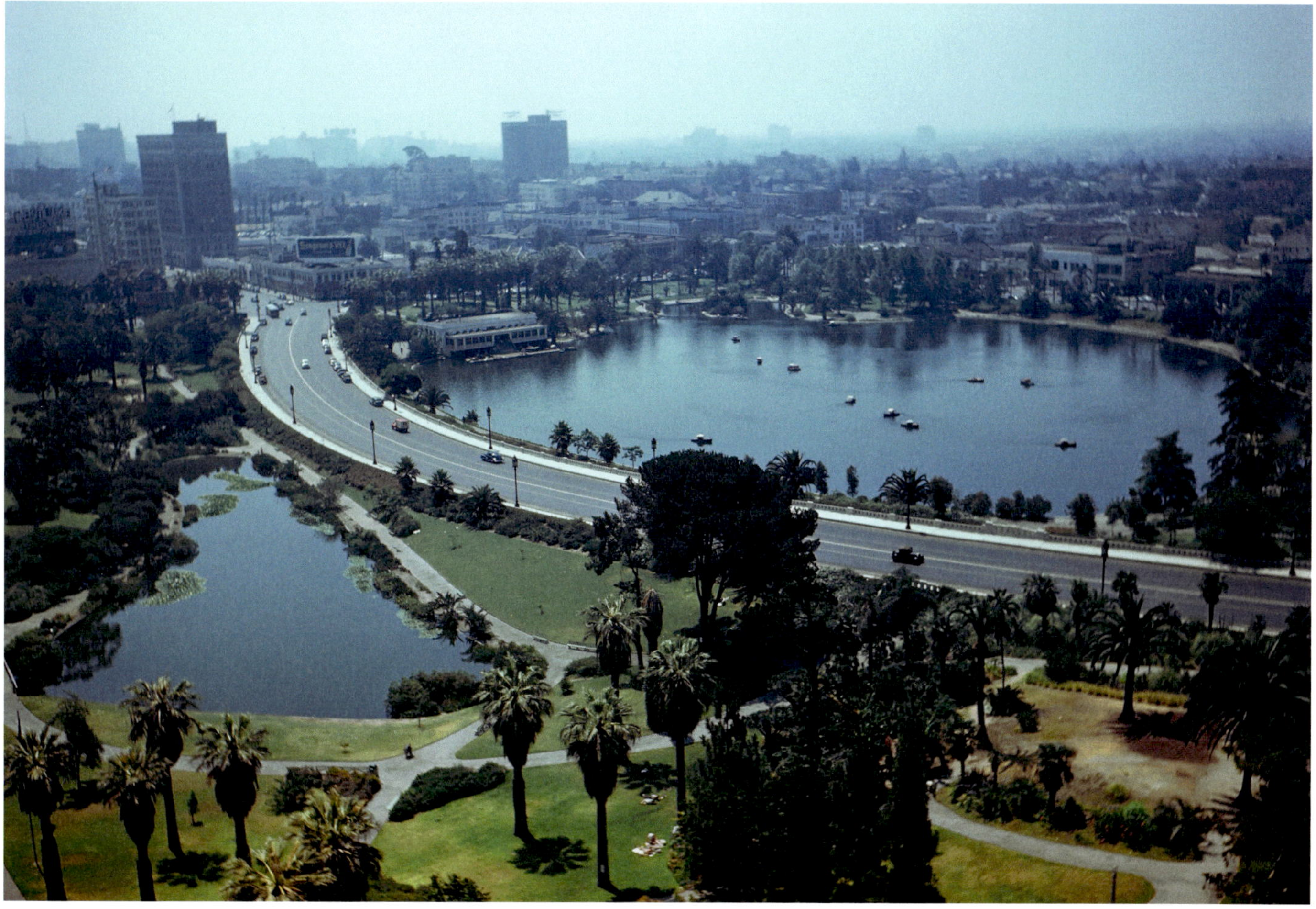

V-J Day, Downtown Los Angeles (Hill Street and Fifth Street), August 14, 1945 – MacArthur Park and Wilshire Boulevard, Los Angeles, ca. 1945

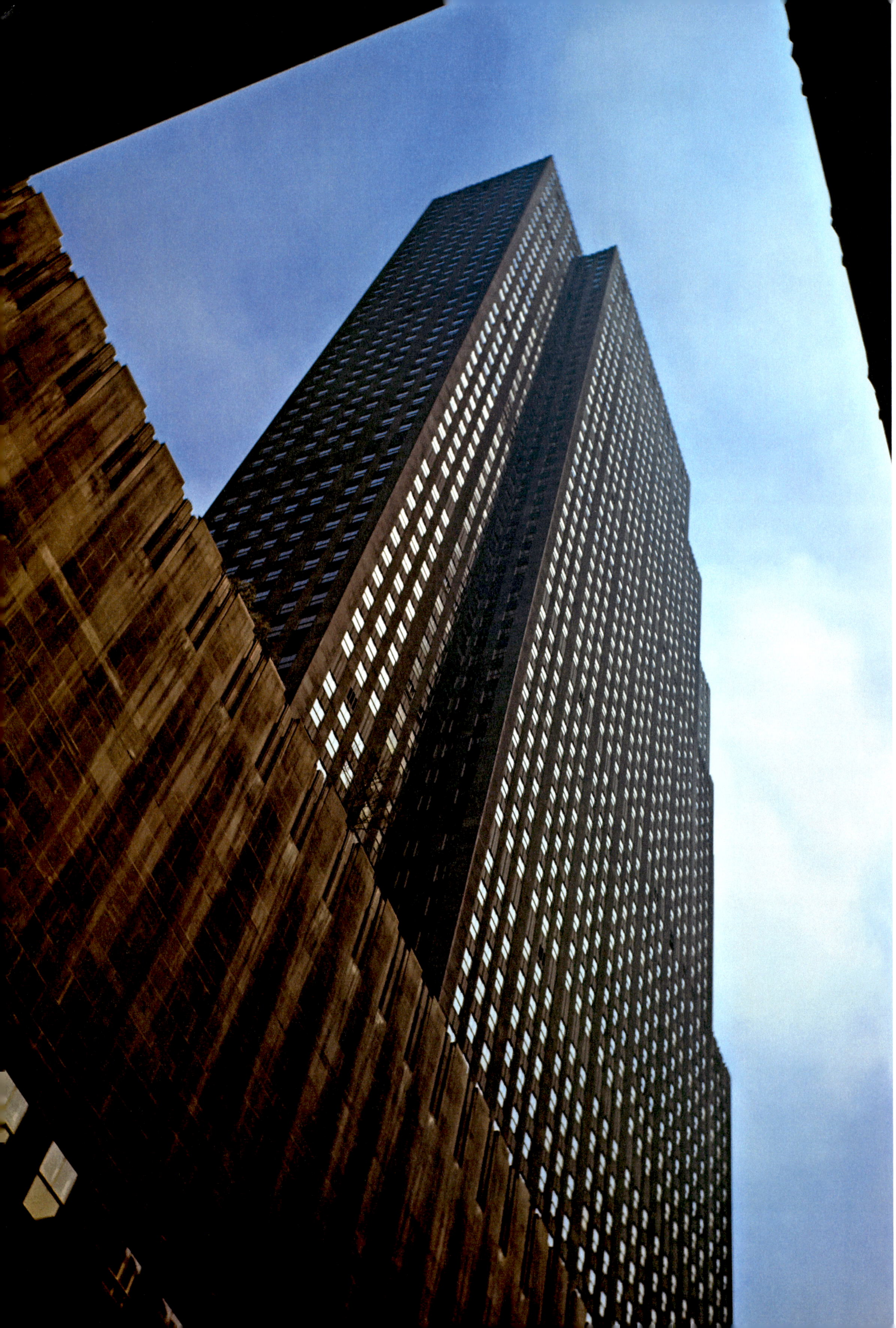

RCA Building, Rockefeller Center, New York, ca. 1950

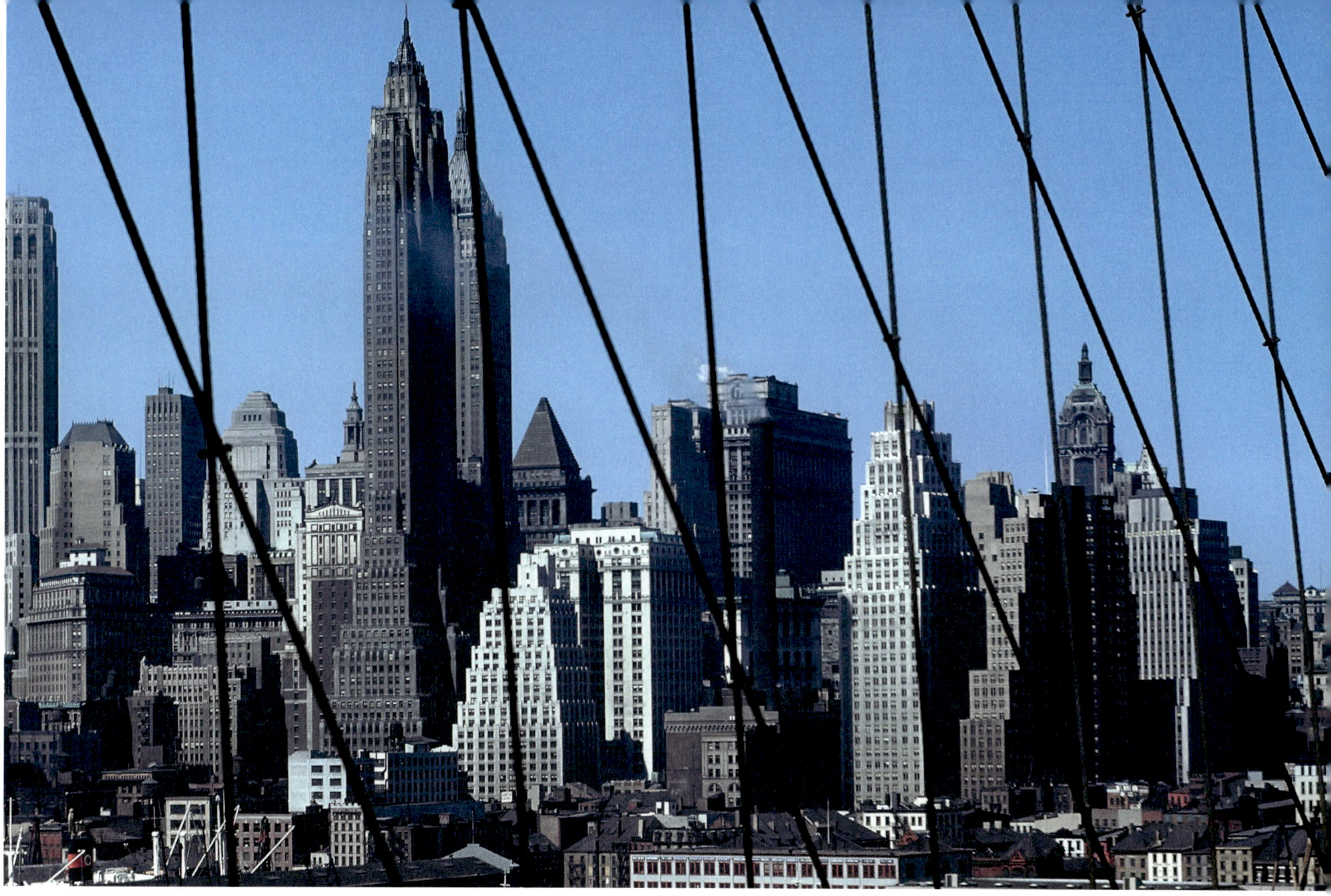

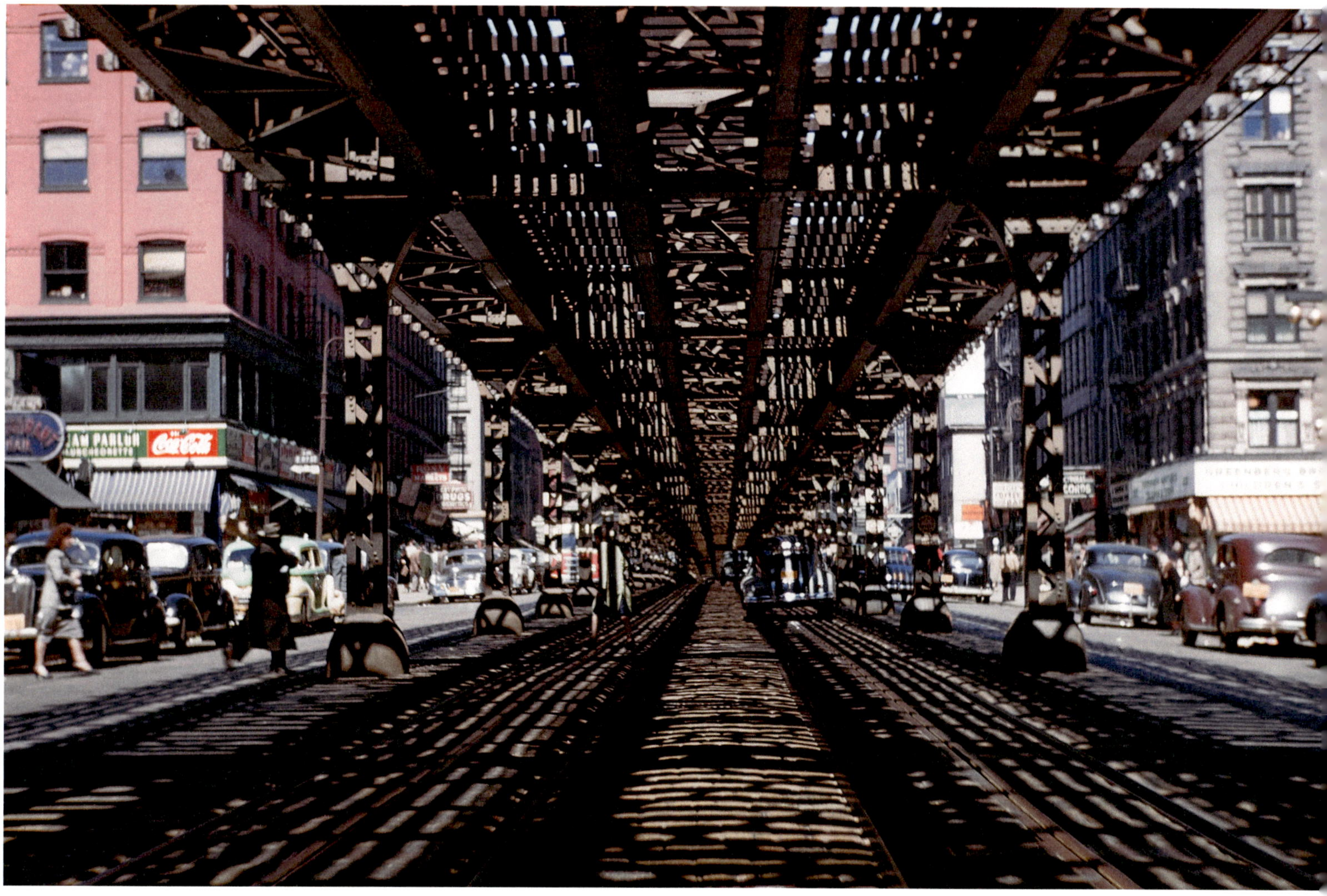

View of Manhattan from the Brooklyn Bridge, New York, ca. 1950 – Under the "Elevated" at Third Street, New York, ca. 1950

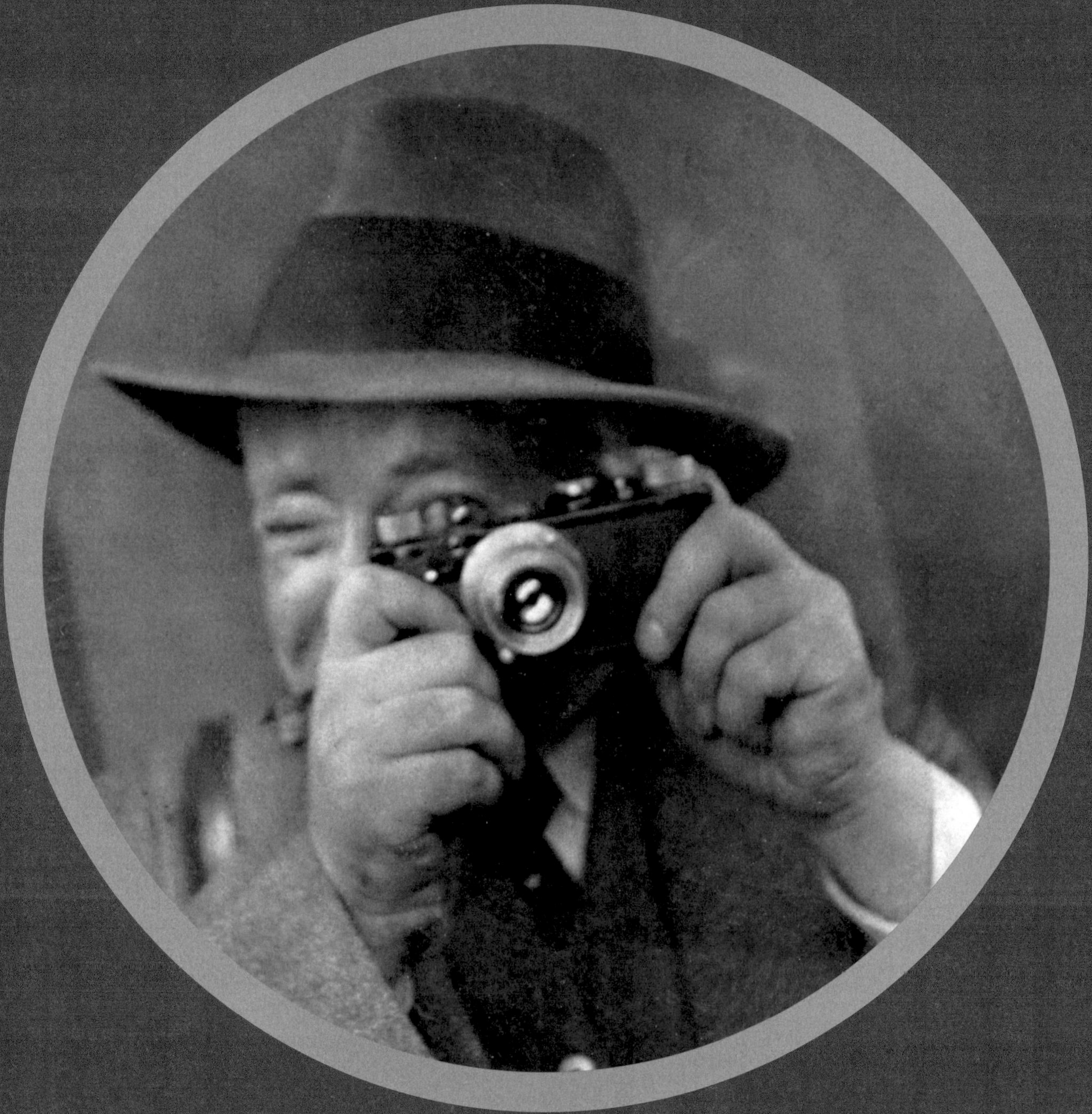

Appendix

Biography – Writings – Photo Publications and Color Slide Series

Biography

1889 Fritz Block is born on January 13, in Warburg, Westphalia

1908–13 Studies architecture at the technical universities of Karlsruhe, München, Darmstadt, and Dresden

1913 Receives diploma at Dresden; study trip to southern France

1915 Receives doctorate in engineering (Dr. Ing.) at the Technical University of Dresden

1916–18 Exempted from military service due to congenital deafness; works in the department of Planning and Construction of Königsberg, Prussia

1918 Receives Schinkelpreis from the Architekten-Verein zu Berlin (National Award for Architecture by the Berlin Association of Architects)

1921 Moves to Hamburg

1921–38 Founds the architectural firm Dr. Block & Hochfeld with Ernst Hochfeld (1890–1985) in Hamburg; designs residences, apartment buildings, commercial buildings, interiors, and furniture

1922–33 Joins the Bund Deutscher Architekten

1924–33 Joins the Deutscher Werkbund

1925 Marries Anna-Sophie Levy (1895–1986); travels to Italy

1925 Monograph on the architectural firm Dr. Block & Hochfeld appears in the series *Neue Baukunst*

1926 Trip to Holland and Belgium in April; to Switzerland and Sicily in the fall

1926 Participates in the architecture exhibitions *Typen neuer Baukunst* of the Städtische Kunsthalle Mannheim and *Neuzeitlicher Volkswohnungsbau im In- und Auslande* in Hamburg

1927–29 Joins the editorial board of architecture at the cultural magazine *Der Kreis*, in Hamburg

Self-portrait of Fritz Block, New York, 1931

1927 Reports on the Deutscher Werkbund exhibition *Die Wohnung* and the Weissenhofsiedlung, Stuttgart, in *Der Kreis*

1925–33 Becomes managing secretary of the *Studienausschuss des Bundes Deutscher Architekten für zeitgemäßes Bauen* (Research Committee of the Association of German Architects for Contemporary Architecture)

1927–33 Joins the architectural committee within the Deutscher Werkbund

1927 Edits the book *Probleme des Bauens. Der Wohnbau* in co-operation with the *Studienausschuss des Bundes Deutscher Architekten für zeitgemäßes Bauen*

1928 Travels to Venice and Egypt in January

1928–31 Joins the expert council of the *Reichsforschungs-Gesellschaft für Wirtschaftlichkeit im Bau- und Wohnungswesen* (Imperial Research Society for Economic Efficiency in Building and Housing)

1928/29 Receives a major commission: the Deutschlandhaus, a business and cinema building in Hamburg

1929 Begins photographic activity

1929 Participates in the photography section at the *Kunst-Ausstellung Altona* in August; presents construction photos of the Deutschlandhaus at the *Deutscher Architekten- und Ingenieurtag* (German Architects' and Engineers' Convention), Hamburg, in September; publishes ship photos in *Die Form* in December; reports on modern Dutch architecture in *Bauwelt*

1929–31 Publishes photo reportages on the Deutschlandhaus in German architecture magazines; takes photos of the Hamburg harbor and Blohm & Voss shipyard

1930 Travels to Marseille, Algeria, and Tunisia; travels to Paris; reports for the *Bauwelt* on the Deutscher Werkbund exhibition in Paris; participates in the *Internationale Ausstellung "Das Lichtbild,"* München

1930–33 Membership in the Akademie für Städtebau, Abt. Niedersachsen (Academy for Urban Design, Lower Saxony Section); publishes photo reportages in the weekly supplement of the daily paper *Hamburger Anzeiger* as well as in other illustrated newspapers and magazines

1931–33 Joins the Hamburg Leica-Club; publishes photos in the journal *Die Leica* and in promotional brochures of the Ernst Leitz Company, Wetzlar

1931 Makes photos and X-rays of shells, snails, and other mollusks; travels to southern France in early summer; reports on modern architecture in France for *Zentralblatt der Bauverwaltung*; travels through the USA (New York, Niagara, Detroit, Chicago, San Francisco, Los Angeles, Grand Canyon, New Mexico, New York) in September-October (total output of ca. 4,000 photos)

1931/32 As a consequence of the world economic crisis, Dr. Block & Hochfeld specialize in residential apartment subdivisions

1932 Participates in the Kunstverein Hamburg's *Internationale Foto-Ausstellung* in January; publishes "Fotoreportage New York" in *Baugilde*, and "Photoreportage mit der Leica in Amerika" in *Photofreund-Jahrbuch 1933* and "Die neue Ford-Fabrik" in *Die Form;* trip through Austria and Hungary in September

1933 Forced to cease both photojournalism and architecture in Germany as a result of the National Socialists seizure of power; Zeppelin flight from Friedrichshafen, Germany, to Rio de Janeiro, Brazil, and back to Seville, Spain, in August-September; excluded from Bund Deutscher Architekten in October; henceforth restricted architectural activity on apartment subdivisions

1933–35 Travels to Switzerland

1935 Travels to London

1937 Travels to Dalmatia (Croatia) in early summer; participates in the modification of the community house of the Jewish Cultural League Hamburg

1938 Takes a world cruise from Venice to Palestine, and to Ceylon (Sri Lanka), India, Java, and Bali, Australia, and New Zealand, Fiji, and Hawaii to San Francisco. Return journey via New York and London, from January to the beginning of June. Liquidates architectural firm in Hamburg; on November 11, temporary detention in the Oranienburg concentration camp; released on November 16; emigration to the US; arrives in Los Angeles

1939 In Los Angeles, works on his own archive of black-and-white negatives and photo prints

1940 Switches to color photography with color slides (Kodachrome); produces thematic color slide series for progressive art education

1943 Completes the first color slide series on Californian architectural modernism; begins to cooperate with the Museum of Modern Art, New York

1943–54 Establishes Dr. Block Color Productions; creates and distributes 27 color slide series on architecture, art, sculpture, design, technology, and nature

1944 Receives American citizenship

1948 Article on Dr. Block Color Productions appears in *College Art Journal*

1950 Participates in the *Color Photography Exhibition*, Museum of Modern Art, New York

1952 Completes a second color slide series on California's architectural modernity

1955 Fritz (Fred) Block dies on January 23, in Los Angeles; Anna-Sophie Block continues Dr. Block Color Productions

1980 Kaidib, in Glendale, California, acquires Dr. Block Color Productions. Distribution of individual color slide series continues until 1992

1986 Anna-Sophie Block dies in Los Angeles

1986 The heirs of Anna-Sophie Block donate Fritz Block's architectural estate to the Architecture and Design Collection of the Art, Design & Architecture Museum at the University of California, Santa Barbara; photographic material remains in the Fritz Block Estate Archive, Stockholm/Hamburg

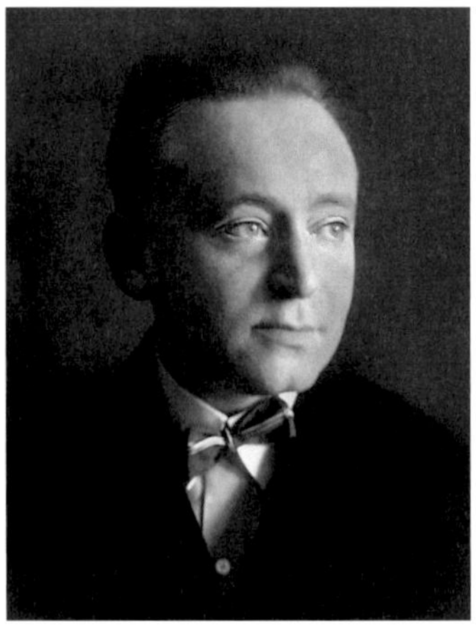

◁ Fritz Block, ca. 1920

▷ Fritz and Anna-Sophie Block (automat photos), ca. 1928

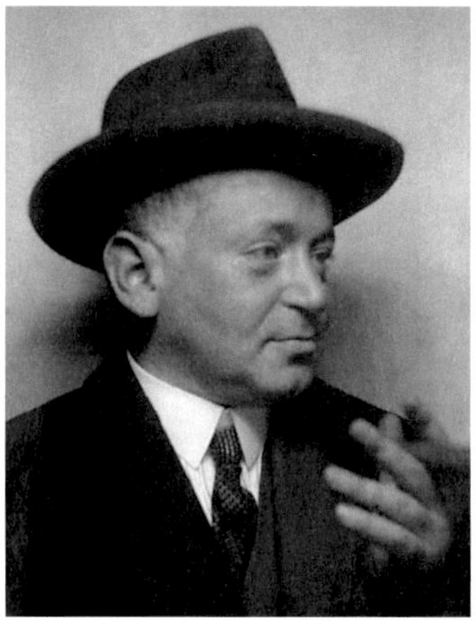

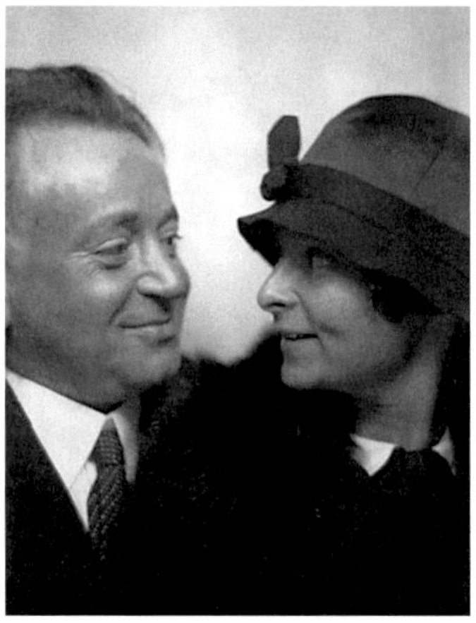

Writings on Architecture

"Das Königsberger Bürgerhaus," *Der Profanbau* 13, no. 3/4 (1917), 25–44, and no. 5/6, 45–60 (also as special edition)

"Die kirchliche Baukunst im alten Bistum Comminges (Pyrenäen)," *Zeitschrift für Bauwesen* 67 (1917), col. 295–339 and 443–478, illustr. on plate 20 in the atlas (also as special edition, 1–42)

"Die Pläne für die Stadterweiterung und Hafenanlagen der Stadt Königsberg i. Pr.," *Neudeutsche Bauzeitung* 14 (1918), 55–61 and 65–71

"Denkmäler frühgermanischer Baukunst in den Pyrenäen," *Zentralblatt der Bauverwaltung* 38 (1918), no. 23/24, 109–112

The Jewish Hospital. Illustrations of the plans of a Jewish hospital at Königsberg i. Prussia. Project by Dr.-Ing. Fritz Block, architect D.W.B. (Königsberg, 1920)

"Von der Einkehr und Besinnung," *Innendekoration* 35, no. 1 (1924), 35–37 (illustr. thru 41)

"Über Volkswohnungsbau," in *Internationale Architektur-Ausstellung ›Typen neuer Baukunst‹. Wander-Ausstellung der Städt. Kunsthalle Mannheim. Sonder-Ausstellung des B.D.A.: Neuzeitlicher Volkswohnungsbau im In- und Auslande*, ed. Bund Deutscher Architekten / Landesbezirk Nord (Hamburg, 1926), 11–16

"Die Normungs- und Typisierungsbestrebungen und der BDA," *Die Baugilde* 8, no. 24 (1926), 1309–1312 (also as special edition: *Neues Bauen und Neues Wohnen*, ed. Arbeitsgemeinschaft für Rationalisierung im Bauwesen (Berlin n. d. [1927]), 1–13)

"Der Hamburger Wettbewerb für ein Groß-Wohnhaus-Viertel an der Jarrestraße," *Die Baugilde* 9, no. 2 (Jan. 27, 1927), 71–73

"Wohnform und Wandlungsfähigkeit," *Die Form* 2, no. 2 (1927), 40–46 (also in: *Stein – Holz – Eisen* 41, no. 23 (June 9, 1927), 505–508 (illustr. thru 509)

"Neues Wohnen. Zur Ausstellung ›Neues Wohnen‹ in der Stadthalle," *Hamburger Nachrichten,* Sept. 16, 1927

"Rationalisierung im Bauwesen. Grundsätzliche Fragen," *Hamburger 8 Uhr Abendblatt,* Sept. 13, 1927

"Die neue Wohnung (Zur Stuttgarter Ausstellung)," *Der Kreis. Zeitschrift für künstlerische Kultur* 4, no. 10 (1927), 565–572

"Vorwort," *Probleme des Bauens. Band 1. Der Wohnbau,* ed. Fritz Block in collaboration with the Studienausschuss des Bundes Deutscher Architekten für zeitgemäßes Bauen (Potsdam: Müller & Kiepenheuer, 1928 [1927]), 7

"Haus und Wohnung des modernen Menschen (Funktion und Form)," *ibid.*, 87–115

"Haus und Wohnung des modernen Menschen (Funktion und Form)," *Das ideale Heim* 2, no. 11 (1928), 546–550

"Kleinwohnung und Bestform" (1928) [typescript]

"Bauwirtschaft und Bauforschung," *Der Baukurier,* April 16, 1929

"Die Weiterentwicklung der holländischen Architektur," *Bauwelt* 20, no. 9 (Feb. 28, 1929,), suppl. 9–16 (= 197–204)

"Fabrik van Nelle in Rotterdam," *Bauwelt* 20, no. 29 (July 18, 1929), suppl. 1–4 (= 667–670)

Technische Tagung in Berlin / 15. bis 17. April 1929, ed. Städtebau und Wohnungsbau, Reichsforschungsgesellschaft für Wirtschaftlichkeit im Bau- und Wohnungswesen e.V. (Berlin, 1929), 1–11

"Grundsätzliches zum Siedlungsbau," *Zentralblatt der Bauverwaltung* 50, no. 17 (April 30, 1930), 313–316, and no. 16 (May 7, 1930), 333–335

"Deutsche Baukünstler in Paris," *Bauwelt* 21, no. 32 (Aug. 7, 1930), 999–1000 (with illustr. in suppl. 1–16 = 1001–1016, also in no. 24, suppl. 1–8 = 757–764)

"Studien des Pariser Architekten André Lurçat zum Kleinwohnungsbau," *Zentralblatt der Bauverwaltung* 51, no. 7 (Feb. 18, 1931), 101–107

"Neue Baukunst in Frankreich," *Zeitschrift für Bauwesen* 81, no. 3 (March, 1931), 53–65

"Neue Baukunst in Frankreich (Haus am Mittelmeer, Kap Martin, Roquebrune. Architekten: Eileen Gray und Jean Badovici)," *Zentralblatt der Bauverwaltung / Zeitschrift für Bauwesen* 51 (81.), no. 25 (June 20, 1931), 353–364

"Die Bau-Ausstellung Hamburg," *Baugilde* 14, no. 9 (1932), 445–454

"1. Bauabschnitt der Stadtrandsiedlung Hamburg," *Baugilde* 15, no. 4 (Feb. 25, 1933), 167–168 (illustr. thru 183)

Photo Publications

All of Fritz Block's known photos and photo reportages in print are listed according to subject, with the quantity of his photos in square brackets. Preceding these is information about the typescripts, mainly by Anna-Sophie Block, for the photo reportages preserved in the estate. In addition, there are newspaper clippings with individual photos by Block, without reference. These are archived as part of the Fritz Block papers at the Architecture and Design Collection of the Art, Design & Architecture Museum at the University of California, Santa Barbara.

Deutschlandhaus

Fritz Block, "Bildbericht über einen Großbau," *Deutsches Bauwesen* 5, no. 9 (1929), 226–228 [10 of 11]

Fritz Block, "Der Bau des Deutschlandhauses in Hamburg," *Die Form* 5, no. 5 (March 1, 1930), 118–120 [12]

N. A., "Architekten Dr. Block u. Hochfeld, Hamburg. Deutschlandhaus in Hamburg," *Bauwelt* 21, no. 21 (May 21, 1931), suppl. 1–8 (= 711–718) [probably 13 of 20]

N. A., "Das Deutschlandhaus in Hamburg, seine Konstruktionen und technischen Anlagen," *Zentralblatt der Bauverwaltung / Zeitschrift für Bauwesen* 51, No. 21 (May 27, 1931), 301–306 [7 of 13]

Hamburg

N. A., "Rund um den Fischmarkt. Typen, die nicht jeder kennt," *Hamburger Anzeiger. Illustrierte Wochenbeilage*, no. 42 (Oct. 17, 1931), n. p. [probably 2 of 16]

N. A., "Hamburger Karneval," *Hamburger Illustrierte* 14, no. 6 (1932), 20–21 and 24 [3 of 7]

Bauausstellung [photo], *Hamburger Anzeiger. Illustrierte Wochenbeilage*, no. 14 (April 2, 1932,), n. p. [1]

Ships and ship building

Franz Kollmann, "Versuche zur technischen Formanalyse," *Die Form* 4, no. 23 (Dec. 1, 1929), 625–630 [cover photo and 10]

Spectator, "Hamburger Werftarbeit," *Hamburger Anzeiger. Illustrierte Wochenbeilage*, no. 5 (Jan. 31, 1931), n. p. [probably 5 of 11]

Beginn der Mittagspause [photo], *B[lohm] & V[oss] Werft-Zeitung* 2, no. 5 (Feb. 27, 1931) [cover photo]

N. A., "Ein Schiff wird gebaut," unidentified illustrated newspaper, 1933, 436–437 [9]

Raft der Werft von Blohm & Voss [photo], *Thierbach, Hans: Deutsches Schaffen – Deutsches Land* (Berlin: R. C. Schmidt & Co., 1934), 217 [1]

[Die ›Europa‹ im Schwimmdock von Blohm & Voss] [photo], Friedrich Heiss, *Deutschland zwischen Nacht und Tag* (Berlin: Volk und Reich, 1934, first printing), 261 [1]

Geformter Stahl [photo], [see the article "Schönheit der Technik" von Albert Werner, 2–5] *Das Echo. Zeitschrift der Deutschen im Ausland* 54, no. 2518 (second issue in May 1935), 5 [1]

Circus

Menschen im Zirkus (Sarrasani Hamburg) Wanderzirkus. Kleinstadtromantik in der Grossstadt [typescripts]

N. A., "Wanderzirkus. Kleinstadtromantik in der Großstadt Hamburg," *Hamburger Anzeiger. Illustrierte Wochenbeilage*, no. 35 (Aug. 29, 1931), n. p. [12]

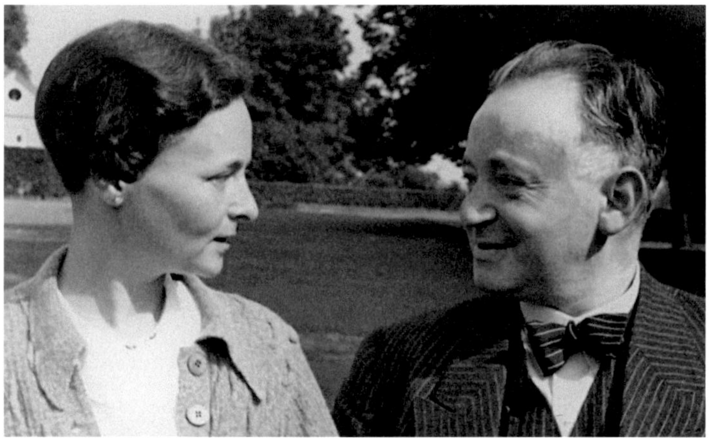

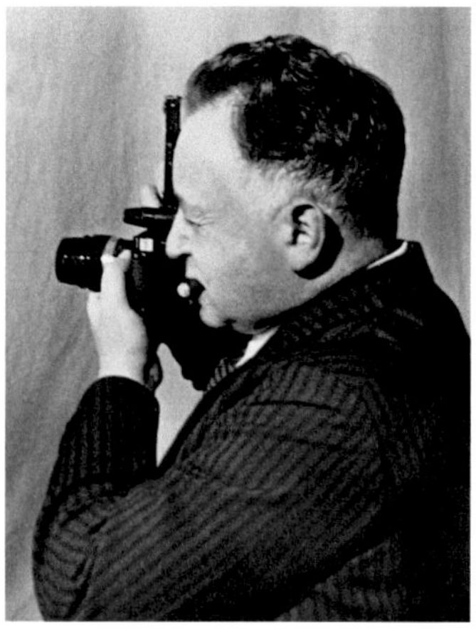

◁ Fritz and Anna-Sophie Block, ca. 1930

▷ Fritz Block, ca. 1932

"Erro, Menschen im Zirkus," *Das Echo der Woche*, no. 21 (June 19, 1932), n. p. [7]

N. A., "Der Zirkus kommt!," *Basler Illustrierte Zeitung* 1, no. 42 (1932), 1013–1015 [4]

Die Clowns François und Etté [photo], *NORAG. Das offizielle Organ der Nordischen Rundfunk AG (Ausgabe B)* 9, no. 28 (July 10, 1932) [cover photo]

"Proben moderner Porträtphotographie," *Hamburger Anzeiger. Illustrierte Wochenbeilage*, no. 50 (Dec. 10, 1932), n. p. [2 of 5]

N. A., "Clowns. Das Geheimnis der Spaßmacher," *Das Echo der Woche*, no. 45 (Dec. 4, 1932), n. p. [4]

Animals

"Tierkinderschau in Hagenbecks Tierpark Stellingen" [typescript]

"Lustige Beobachtungen aus der Tierwelt," *Münchner Illustrierte Presse*, no. 6 (Feb. 8, 1931), 187 [1]

Schwäne [photo], *Deutscher Kamera-Almanach 1932,* ed. Karl Weiss (Berlin: Union, [1931]), 129 [1]

N. A., "Exotische Kinderstube bei Hagenbeck," *Hamburger Anzeiger. Illustrierte Wochenbeilage*, no. 27 (July 8, 1933), n. p. [9]

Trees

Hängende Äste [photo], Wilhelm Bölsche, *Auf dem Menschenstern* (Leipzig: E. Haberland, 1930; also Bad Pyrmont: Friedrich Gersbach, n. d. [1931]) (Ausgewählte Werke, vol. 5), facing 241 [1]

Shells

"Kleine Tiere, große Baumeister (Zu den Muschelaufnahmen.)" [typescript]

J. U., "Eingefangene Wellenmusik," *Haus, Hof und Garten. Illustrierte Wochenschrift des Berliner Tageblatts* [also a suppl. of *Hamburger Anzeiger*], no. 31 (1933), 490–491 [7]

Dolf Sternberger "Das Wunderbare in der Natur," Atlantis 5, no. 2 (1933, Feb.), 122–123. (text) and 124–126 (illustr.) [6]

Germany

"Thomaswerk. Aufnahmen an der Kruppschen Friedrich Alfred Hütte in Rheinhausen," "Oktoberfest" [typescripts]

No proofs located.

North Africa

Bildserie Sahara [typescript]

Franz Werner, "Wunder der Wüste," *Hamburger Anzeiger. Illustrierte Wochenbeilage*, no. 28 (July 12, 1930), n. p. [8]

El Oued. Die Stadt der tausend Kuppeln [photo], *Das Deutsche Lichtbild. Jahresschau 1931* (Berlin: Robert und Bruno Schultz, [1930]), 140 [1]

Karl Haushofer, "Erzieher des Menschengeschlechts. Steppen und Wüsten," *Die Koralle* 7, no. 6 (Sept. 1931), 246–250 [4]

Nomadenkind [photo], Wilhelm Bölsche: *Die Eroberung des Menschen* (Leipzig: E. Haberland, 1930; Bad Pyrmont: Friedrich Gersbach, n. d. [1931]) (Ausgewählte Werke, vol. 1), facing 192 [1]

Wüstenstadt [El Oued] [photo], idem, *Aus der Schneegrube*, ibid., vol. 3, facing 193 [1]

Wüstenstadt [El Oued] [photo], idem, *Weltblick*, ibid., vol. 4, facing 128 [1]

Sand [photo], idem, *Die Schöpfungstage / Aus Urtagen der Tierwelt*, ibid., vol. 6, facing 65 [1]

Paris

Fritz Block, "Foto-Reportage Paris," idem, "Zu dem Paris-Buch" [typescripts]

Fritz Block, "Pariser Leben," *Hamburger Anzeiger. Illustrierte Wochenbeilage*, no. 35 (Aug. 30, 1930) [11]

N. A., "12 Uhr mittag in Paris," *Die Welt*, no. 29 (July 19, 1931), 485 [6]

›Weltstadt [Paris]‹. Wilhelm Bölsche, *Aus der Schneegrube* (Leipzig: E. Haberland, 1930; Bad Pyrmont: Friedrich Gersbach, n. d. [1931]) (Ausgewählte Werke, vol. 3), facing 305 [1]

Boulevard-Café in Paris [photo], *Photofreund* 11, no. 18 (Sept. 20, 1931), 328 [1]

Boulevard-Café in Paris [photo], *Photofreund Jahrbuch 1931/32,* ed. Fr. Willy Frerk (Berlin: Photokino-Verlag, 1931), 45 [1]

Boulevard-Café in Paris [photo], *Die Leica. Hefte für Kleinfilm-Photographie und -Projektion* 1, no. 5 (Jan.–Feb. 1932), VIII [1]

Marseille and Côte d'Azur

"Marseille" [typescript]

Anna-Sophie Block, "Marseille – ein südlicher Welthafen," *Hamburger Anzeiger. Illustrierte Wochenbeilage*, no. 36 (Sept. 3, 1932), n. p. [10]

Ballspiel am Strande [photo], *Hamburger Anzeiger. Illustrierte Wochenbeilage*, no. 22 (May 30, 1931) [cover photo]

Im weichen Sand [photo], *Die Leica. Hefte für Kleinfilm-Photographie und -Projektion* 1, no. 2 (July–Aug. 1931), I [1]

[Ballspiel am Strande], *ibid.*, VII [1]

›So wird man braun,‹ *ibid.*, 49 [1]

Marcel Berger, "Marins," *Le Miroir du Monde* 4, no. 177 (July 22, 1933), 103–104 [probably 3 of 9]

Lustiges Spiel mit dem Ballungeheuer [photo], *Für die Familie* 30, no. 20 (1935), 1 [cover photo]

Auf zum Wannsee [photo], *Berliner Bär* 4, no. 25 (1936), 4 (›Moderner Atlas‹) [1]

USA

"Amerikanerinnen," "Amerikanische Kinder aller Rassen," "Amerikanische Restaurants," "Studenten in U.S.A.," "Arbeitslose in Amerika," "Amerikanische Sportbegeisterung" [typescripts]

N. A., "Auf Arbeitssuche in New York," unidentified magazine (April 4, 1932), n. p. [probably 3 of 6]

Anna-Sophie Block, "Amerikanerinnen und amerikanische Kinder aller Rassen," *Hamburger Anzeiger. Illustrierte Wochenbeilage*, no. 19 (May 7, 1932), n. p. [14]

"Das Gesicht des Sports," *Das Leben* 11, no. 11 (May 1934), 6–13 [2, on p. 10 and 11]

N. A., "Typen in USA," *Hamburger Nachrichten, Bilderrundschau*, no. 16 (April 16, 1932,), n. p. [16]

New York

Fritz Block, "Fotoreportage New York" [typescript for a slide lecture]

Fritz Block, "Fotoreportage mit der Leica in Amerika" [typescript of his essay in *Photofreund-Jahrbuch 1933*]

"Der Fotograf fährt auf dem Dach des Bus durch die Fifth [V.] Avenue," "Coney Island, der Rummelplatz von New York," "New York ohne Tempo," "Der Zentralpark, die Lunge von New York," "Der Broadway, das Hauptvergnügungsviertel von New York" [typescripts]

Fifth Avenue [photo], *Der Querschnitt* 12, no. 8 (1932), facing 541 [1]

Fritz Block, "Fotoreportage New York [incl. Detroit]," *Baugilde* 14, no. 9 (May 10, 1932), 437–444 [25]

New York, Kino-Premiere [photo], *Die Leica. Hefte für Kleinfilm-Photographie und -Projektion* 2, no. 4 (Nov.–Dec. 1932), 108 [1]

New York: Der nächtliche Broadway [photo], *ibid.*, 123 [1]

Brooklynbrücke in New-York [photo], *Das Foto-Jahr 1934* (Halle [Saale]: Wilhelm Knapp, 1933), 84 [1]

N. A., "Strassentypen in New York," *Der Sonntag* (suppl. of *Hamburger Anzeiger*), no. 36 (1932), 985 [5]

Ralf Anders, "Querschnitt durch New York," unidentified illustrated magazine, probably 1932, 1253–1255 [9]

N. A., "5th Avenue in New York," *Schweizer Illustrierte Zeitung* 21, no. 23 (June 1, 1932,), 774–775 [8]

N. A., "Mittag in Neuyork," *Schweizer Illustrierte Zeitung* 21, no. 33 (Aug. 10, 1932), 1141 [3], see text "Die Mittagsstunde in Neuyork ... ", 1140

Ladies and Gentleman ... [photo], *Hamburger Anzeiger. Illustrierte Wochenbeilage*, no. 32 (Aug. 6, 1932) [cover photo]

N. A., "Coney Island," *ibid.*, n. p. [probably 1 of 9]

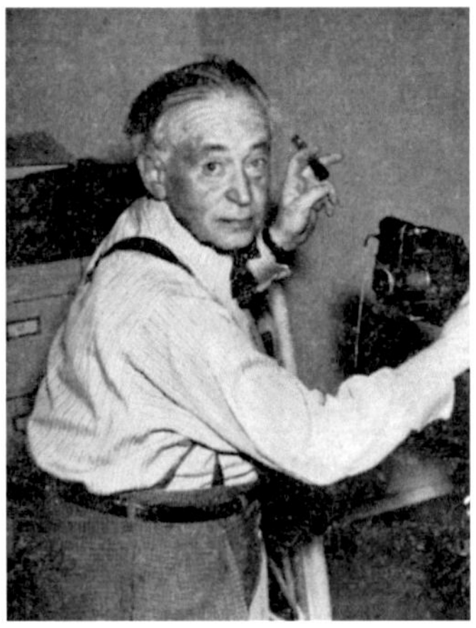

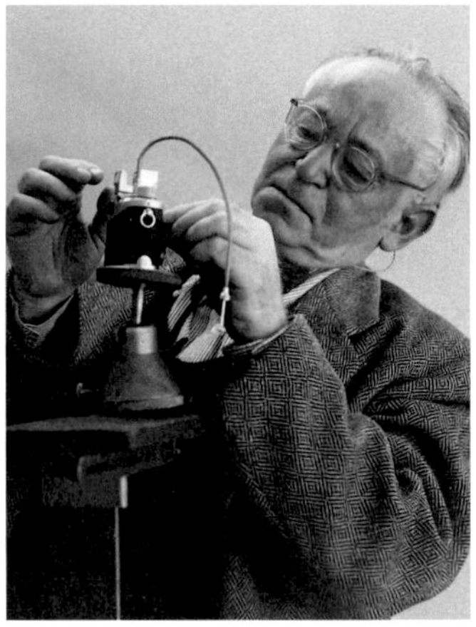

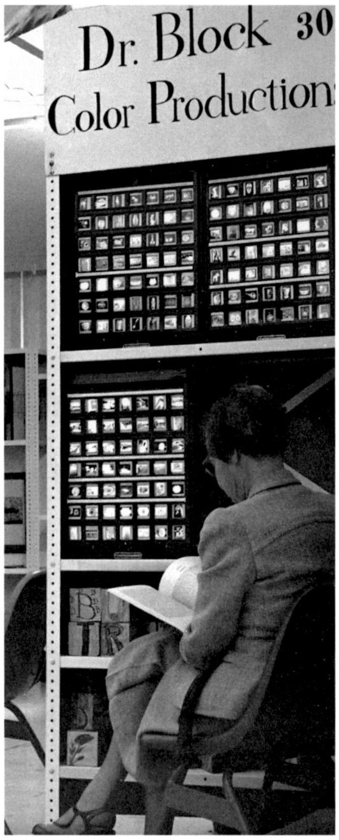

◁ Fritz Block (newspaper photo), 1949

Fritz Block, ca. 1954

▷ Presentation stand for "Dr. Block Color Productions" in Los Angeles, 1957

Fritz Block, "Photoreportage mit der Leica in Amerika,", *Photofreund-Jahrbuch 1933*, ed. Fr. Willy Frerk (Berlin: Photokino-Verlag, 1932), 77– 88 (illustr. beginning 72) [20]

Broadway bei Nacht [photo], *Der Querschnitt* 15, no. 12 (1935), facing 550 [1]

Brooklyn Bridge [photo], *ibid.*, facing 550 [1]

5th Avenue [photo], *ibid.*, facing 558 [1]

Harlem

"Harlem, die Negerstadt New Yorks," "Bilder aus Harlem, dem Negerviertel New Yorks" [typescripts]

A.[dolf] Halfeld, "Harlem," *Hamburger Illustrierte* 14, no. 16 (April 16, 1932), 6–7 and 14 [10]

N. A., "Die Neger von New York," *Echo der Woche. Illustriertes Blatt der Wasserkante*, no. 20 (June 12, 1932), n. p. [5]

N. A., "Bilder aus Harlem, dem Negerviertel New Yorks," *Hamburger Anzeiger. Illustrierte Wochenbeilage*, no. 35 (Aug. 27, 1932), n. p. [7]

N. A., "Harlem, die Negerstadt New Yorks," *Altonaer Nachrichten Illustrierte*, Oct. 15, 1932, 15 [5]

Philippe Soupault, "Le Problème Nègre aux États-Unis. Croissance d'une race-enfant," *Le Miroir du Monde*, vol. 4, no. 170 (June 3, 1933), 579–580 [2 of 5]

N. A., [Anna-Sophie Block], "Harlem, die Negerstadt Neuyorks," *Der HiA im Bilde. Beilage zum Handelsstand im Auslande. Zeitschrift des GDA*, 1933, no. 3, 33–35 [4]

N. A., "USA melting pot? Rassenprobleme in Amerika," *Illustrierter Beobachter* 8, series 5 (Feb. 4, 1933), 194–195 [6]

Detroit and Chicago

Fritz Block, "Die neue Ford-Fabrik, das River Rougewerk. Fotoreportage, Hamburg" [typescript]

Die Ford-Fabrik in Detroit, Mich. U.S.A. [photo], *Hamburger Anzeiger. Illustrierte Wochenbeilage*, no. 9 (Feb. 27, 1932) [cover photo]

Anna-Sophie Block, "Die Ford-Fabrik," *ibid.*, n. p. [8]

Fritz Block, "Die neue Ford-Fabrik. Das River Rougewerk in Dearborn bei Detroit," *Die Form* 7, no. 9 (Sept. 15, 1932), 268–275 [cover photo, 15]

Fritz Block, "Fotoreportage New York," *Baugilde* 14, no. 9 (May 10, 1932), 437–444, see for Detroit 442–444 [5]

Schornsteine [photo], *Die Leica. Hefte für Kleinfilm-Photographie und -Projektion* 2, no. 3 (Sept.–Oct. 1932), V [1]

Schornsteine Ford-Detroit [photo], *Allgemeine Automobil Zeitung* 35, no. 16 (April 21, 1934), 11 [1]

Blick auf Chicago [photo], *Der Querschnitt* 16, no. 2 (1936), facing 96 [1]

Los Angeles

"Los Angeles, die Stadt der Olympischen Spiele von 1932" [typescript]

Anna-Sophie Block, "Los Angeles, die Stadt der Olympischen Spiele von 1932," *Hamburger Anzeiger. Illustrierte Wochenbeilage*, no. 26 (June 25, 1932), n. p. [ca. 10 out of 13]

New Mexico

"Grand Canyon," "Bei den Indianern in Neu-Mexiko" [typescripts]

N. A., "Die Enkel des großen Winnetou," *Hamburger Anzeiger. Illustrierte Wochenbeilage*, no. 21 (May 27, 1933), n. p. [9]

N. A., "Indianer Neu-Mexiko," *Hamburger Illustrierte* 14, no. 31 (July 30, 1932), 21 [6]

›Baugenossenschaft der Rothäute,‹ *Hamburger Nachrichten. Bilderrundschau*, no. 16 (April 16, 1932,) [3 cover photos]

H. W. Stein, "Bei den Indianern Neumexikos," *Durch alle Welt*, 1934, no. 1, 25–26 [5]

Austria and Hungary

"Die Festspielstadt Salzburg," "Wien," "Budapest als Bäderstadt," "An der Donau in Budapest" [typescripts]

Trempettes de jadis – Naïades d'aujourd'hui [photo], *Photomonde* 2, no. 25 (Aug. 19, 1933) [cover photo]

Anna-Sophie Block, "Budapest an der Donau," *Hamburger Anzeiger. Illustrierte Wochenbeilage*, no. 18 (Jan. 21, 1933), n. p. [4]

New Publications

Roland Jaeger, "Der Architekt Fritz Block als Photograph," in idem *Block & Hochfeld. Die Architekten des Deutschlandhauses. Bauten und Projekte in Hamburg 1921–1938. Exil in Los Angeles* (Berlin: Gebr. Mann, 1996), 223–241 [16]

Roland Jaeger, "Fritz Block. Mit der Leica um die Welt. Teil 1: Europa / Fritz Block. Around the World with Leica. Part 1: Europe," *Leica Fotografie International*, 2005, no. 4 (May), 6–17 [20]; "Teil 2 / part 2: Amerika / America," *ibid.*, no. 5 (June/July), 14–25 [20]

Roland Jaeger, *Foto-Auge Fritz Block. Neue Fotografie. Moderne Farbdias / Photo-Eye Fritz Block. New Photography. Modern Color Slides* (Berlin: Alfred Ehrhardt Stiftung, 2017) [15]

Color Slide Series

Between 1943 and 1954 Dr. Block Color Productions produced a total of 27 thematic color slide series. The following numbering of the undated series is based on the order form used in the mid-1950s, while the approximate dating of publishing of theses series is added in parentheses. Each series was accompanied by a copied list of motifs with a short introductory text. The quantity of color slides is indicated in square brackets.

1 African Negro Art (1949) [110]
2 Art of the South Pacific (1949) [107]
3 Bushman Paintings (1949) [22]
4 Santos: Our Religious Folk Art (1950) [70]
5 Revelation of Beauty in Nature (1946) [120]
6 Expressive Forms in Nature (1949) [100]
7 Modern Sculpture (1949) [83]
8 The Work of Henry Moore (1949) [77]
9 Modern Industrial Design (1949) [100]
10 Modern Ceramic Arts (1946) [74]
11 The Potter's Workshop (1949) [34]
12 Technical Beauty (1949) [40]
13 Modern Architecture I (1943) [256]
14 Home Making for Moderns (1952) [82]
15 Modern Architecture II. The New Concept of Space (1952) [468]
16 North American Indian Art. Part I: Southwestern Area (1950) [288]
17 North American Indian Art. Part II: Northwest Coast (ca. 1950) [201]
18 California Artists: Visual Statements (1952) [40]
19 Sculpture of Our Century (1953) [77]
20 North American Indian Art. Part III: The West-Plains and Eastern Tribes (ca. 1950) [136]
21 The Art of Ancient Peru (1954) [137]
22 Animals in Art (ca. 1950) [141]
23 Materials and Their Creative Use (1953) [182]
24 Chinese Art (ca. 1952) [257]
25 Persian Art (ca. 1952) [69]
26 Japanese Art (ca. 1952) [107]
27 Art of India (ca. 1952) [60]

In addition, typescripts about his color slide production written by Fritz (Fred) Block, but not published:

Modern Architecture (ca. 1945)
Color Photography As an Educator of Color Vision (ca. 1950) Color-Photography and Art Education (1951)

R E Q U E S T   S H E E T

For detailed lists of Dr. Block Color Slide Series.

Please mark series in which you are interested and mail this sheet to:

The Museum of Modern Art--Library
11 West 53rd Street
New York, N. Y. 10019

/OR/

Dr. Block Color Productions
1309 North Genesee Avenue
Hollywood, California 90046

Please send purchase orders to
Block Color Productions only.

				No. of Slides	
No.	1	(AF)	African Negro Art	110	$ 82.50
No.	2	(SP)	Art of the South Pacific	107	80.25
No.	3	(BP)	Bushman Paintings	22	16.50
No.	4	(SA)	Santos: Our Religious Folk Art	70	52.50
No.	5	(BN)	Revelation of Beauty in Nature	120	90.00
No.	6	(EX)	Expressive Forms in Nature	100	75.00
No.	7	(SC)	Modern Sculpture	83	62.25
No.	8	(HM)	The Work of Henry Moore	77	57.75
No.	9	(ID)	Modern Industrial Design	100	75.00
No.	10	(CA)	Modern Ceramic Arts	74	55.50
No.	11	(PO)	The Potter's Workshop	34	22.50
No.	12	(TB)	Technical Beauty	40	30.00
No.	13	(MA)	Modern Architecture I	256	192.00
No.	14	(HO)	Home Making for Moderns	82	61.50
No.	15	(MA)	Modern Architecture II The New Concept of Space	468	351.00
No.	16	(IA)	North American Indian Art Part I: The Southwestern Area	288	216.00
No.	17	(IA)	North American Indian Art Part II: The Northwest Coast	201	150.75
No.	19	(XX)	Sculpture of Our Century	77	57.75
No.	20	(IA)	North American Indian Art Part III: The West-Plains and Eastern Indian Tribes	136	102.00
No.	21	(PE)	The Art of Ancient Peru	137	102.75
No.	22	(AA)	Animals in Art	141	105.75
No.	23	(CM)	Materials and Their Creative Use	182	136.50
No.	24	(CH)	Chinese Art	257	192.75
No.	25	(PER)	Persian Art	69	51.75
No.	26	(JA)	Japanese Art	107	80.25
No.	27	(AI)	Art of India	60	45.00

Single slides	$ 1.00
In lots of 25 or more, each	.90

Your name____________________ Date____________

Position or Function__________________________

Street City State Zip Code

PHOTO-EYE FRITZ BLOCK
New Photography –
Modern Color Slides

Concept, Image Selection, and Text
Roland Jaeger, Hamburg

Photos
Fritz Block Estate Archive, Stockholm/Hamburg. – Fritz Block papers, Architecture and Design Collection. Art, Design & Architecture Museum, University of California, Santa Barbara (pp. 113–114, 120). – Dietmar Katz, Berlin (pp. 8–9)

Print Documents
Sammlung Roland Jaeger, Hamburg. – Architecture and Design Collection. Art, Design & Architecture Museum, University of California, Santa Barbara (pp. 44–45, 52–53, 68, 77, 204–205, 256–257, 266)

Scans
Dietmar Katz, Berlin (photos, color slides, print documents). – Fotolabor Jan Kopp, Hamburg (color slides). – Roland Jaeger, Hamburg (photos, print documents). – Architecture and Design Collection. Art, Design & Architecture Museum, University of California, Santa Barbara, (photos, print documents)

Proofreading
Hartmut Schönfuß, Berlin

Translation from German
Maka / Magill Translations, Berlin
Laura Schleussner, Berlin

Book Design, Typography, and Layout
Peter Nils Dorén Grafikdesign, Berlin, and Roland Jaeger, Hamburg

Typeface
Frutiger

Image Editing and Separations
Bild1Druck, Berlin

Paper
LuxoArt Samt 150g

Printing and Binding
DZA Druckerei zu Altenburg GmbH, Altenburg

Publisher
Scheidegger & Spiess AG, Zürich
www.scheidegger-spiess.ch

German Edition
Roland Jaeger
FOTO-AUGE FRITZ BLOCK
Neue Fotografie – Moderne Farbdias
ISBN 978-3-85881-531-6

English Edition
ISBN 978-3-85881-789-1

Acknowledgements
Scheidegger & Spiess is being supported by the Federal Office of Culture with a general subsidy for the years 2016–2020.

The translation for the English edition was made possible by the Hamburger Stiftung zur Förderung von Wissenschaft und Kultur.

The presentation of the Californian modernist architecture was made possible by the Villa Aurora & Thomas Mann House e.V.

VA·
TMH
VILLA AURORA
THOMAS MANN HOUSE

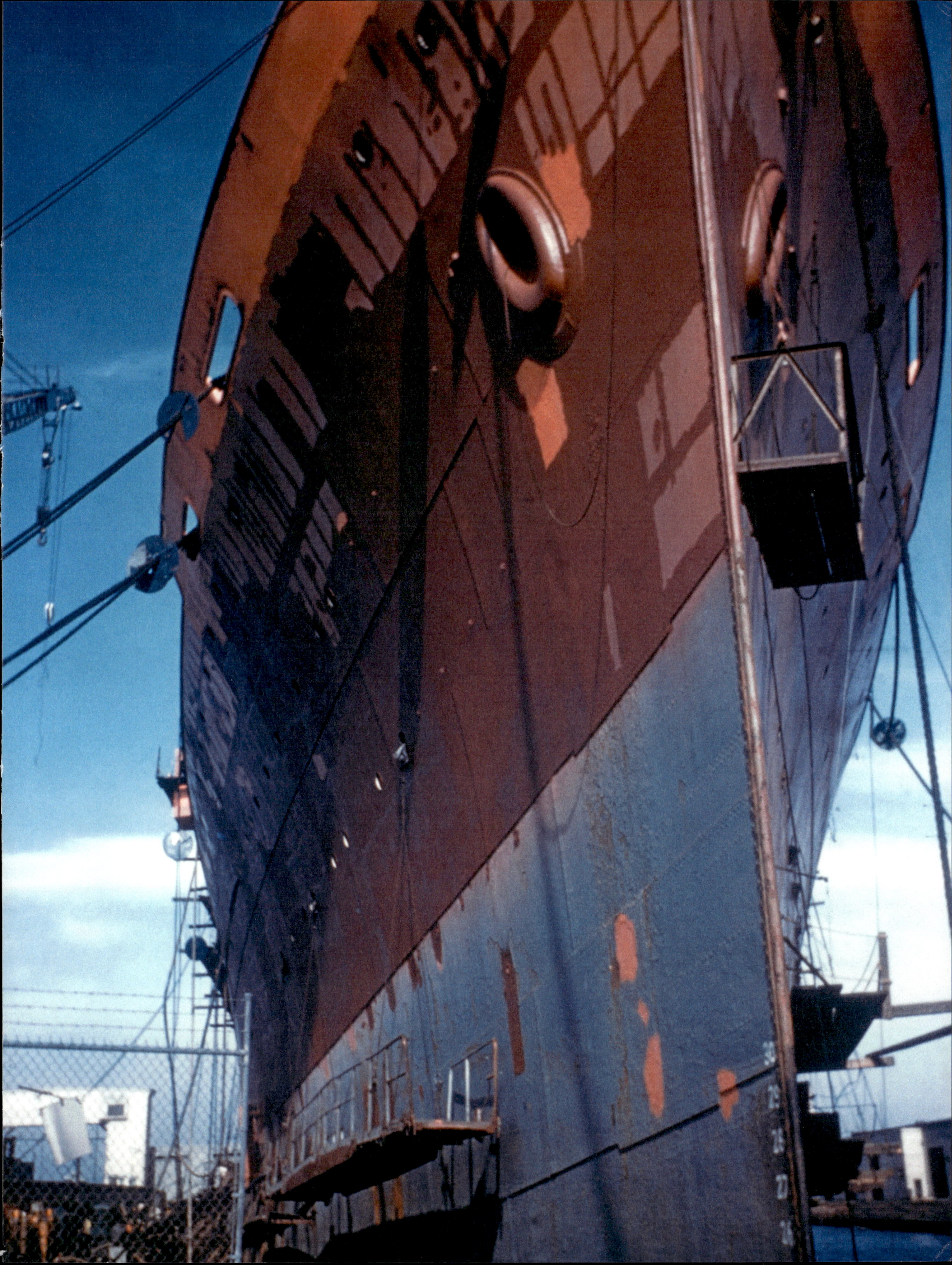

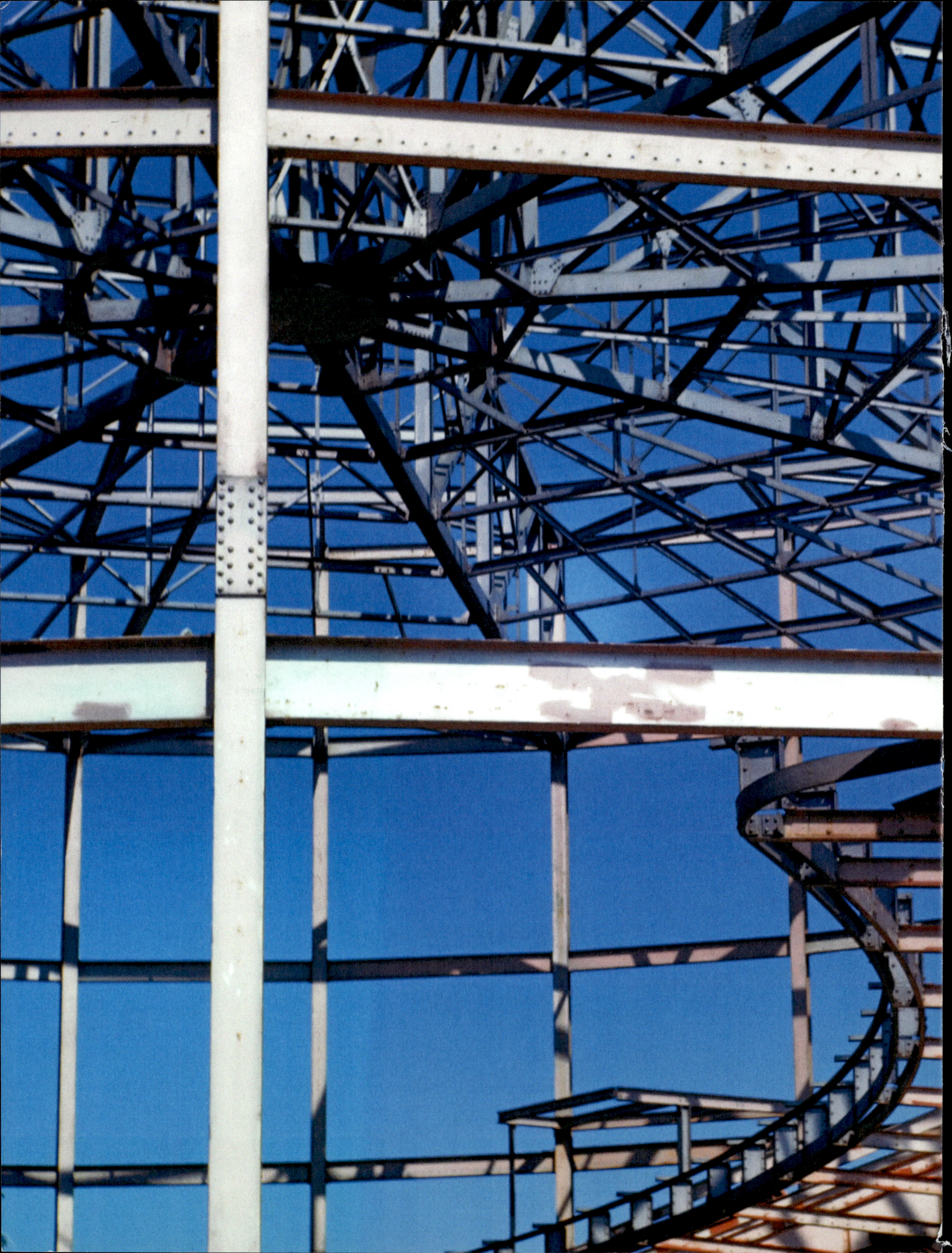

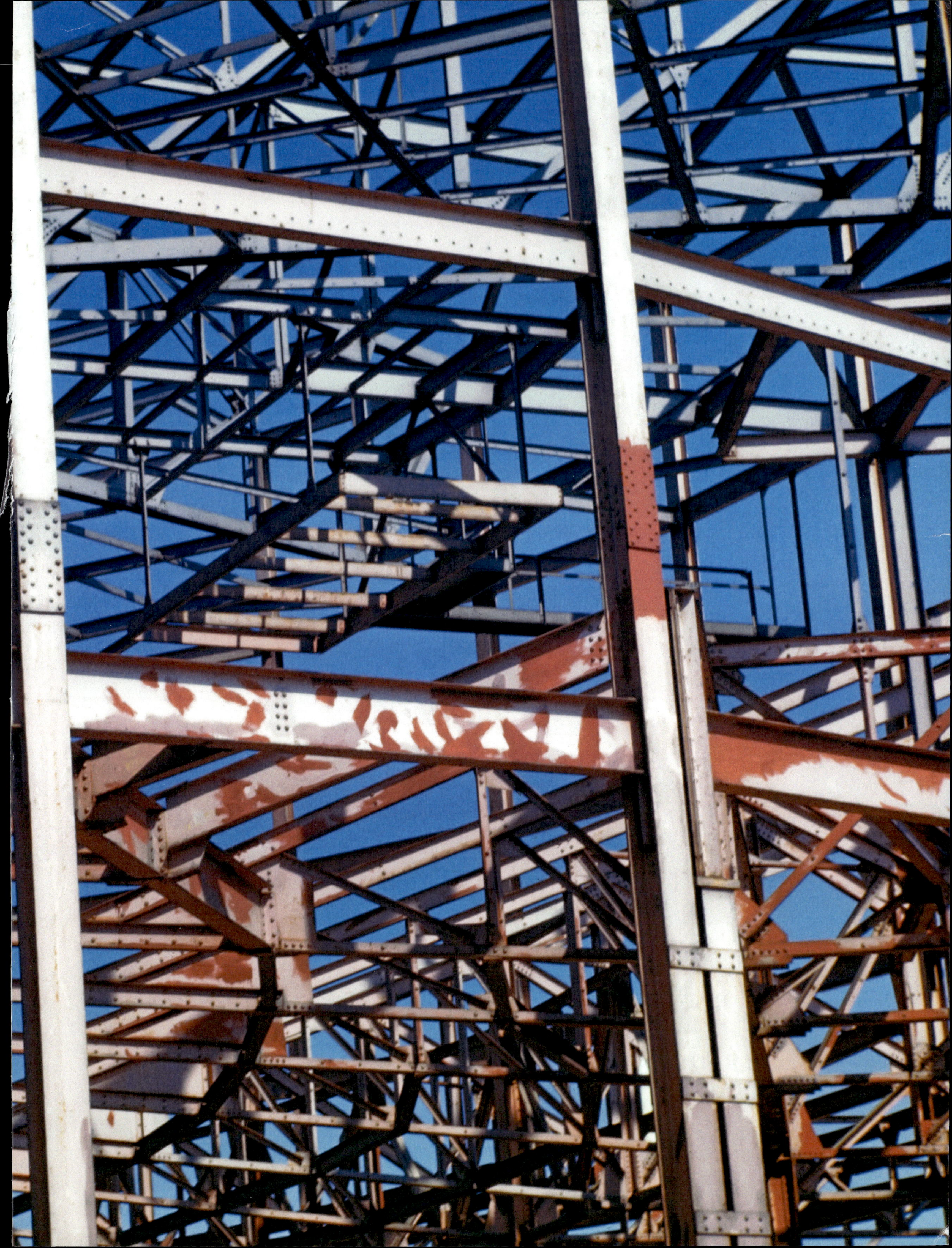

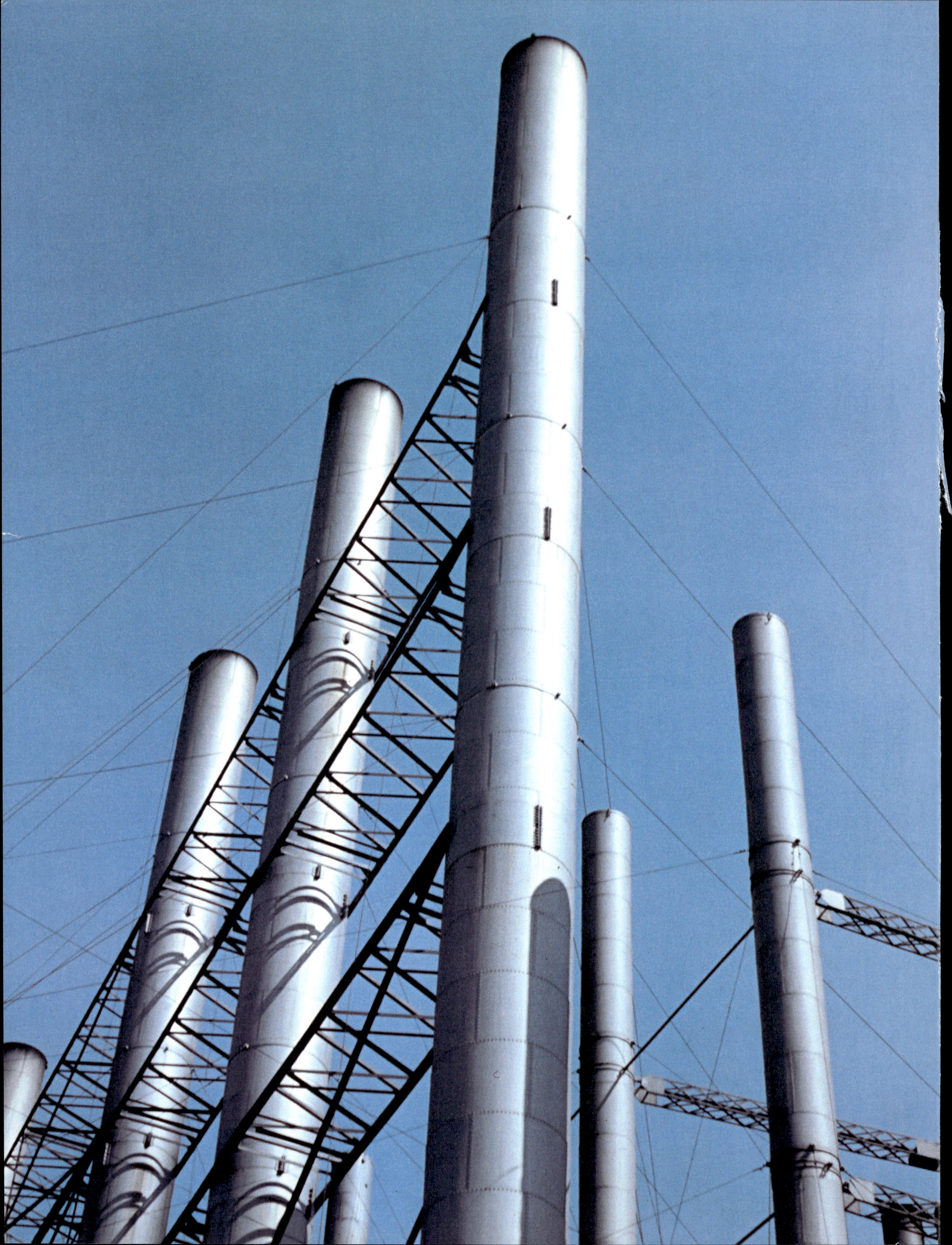

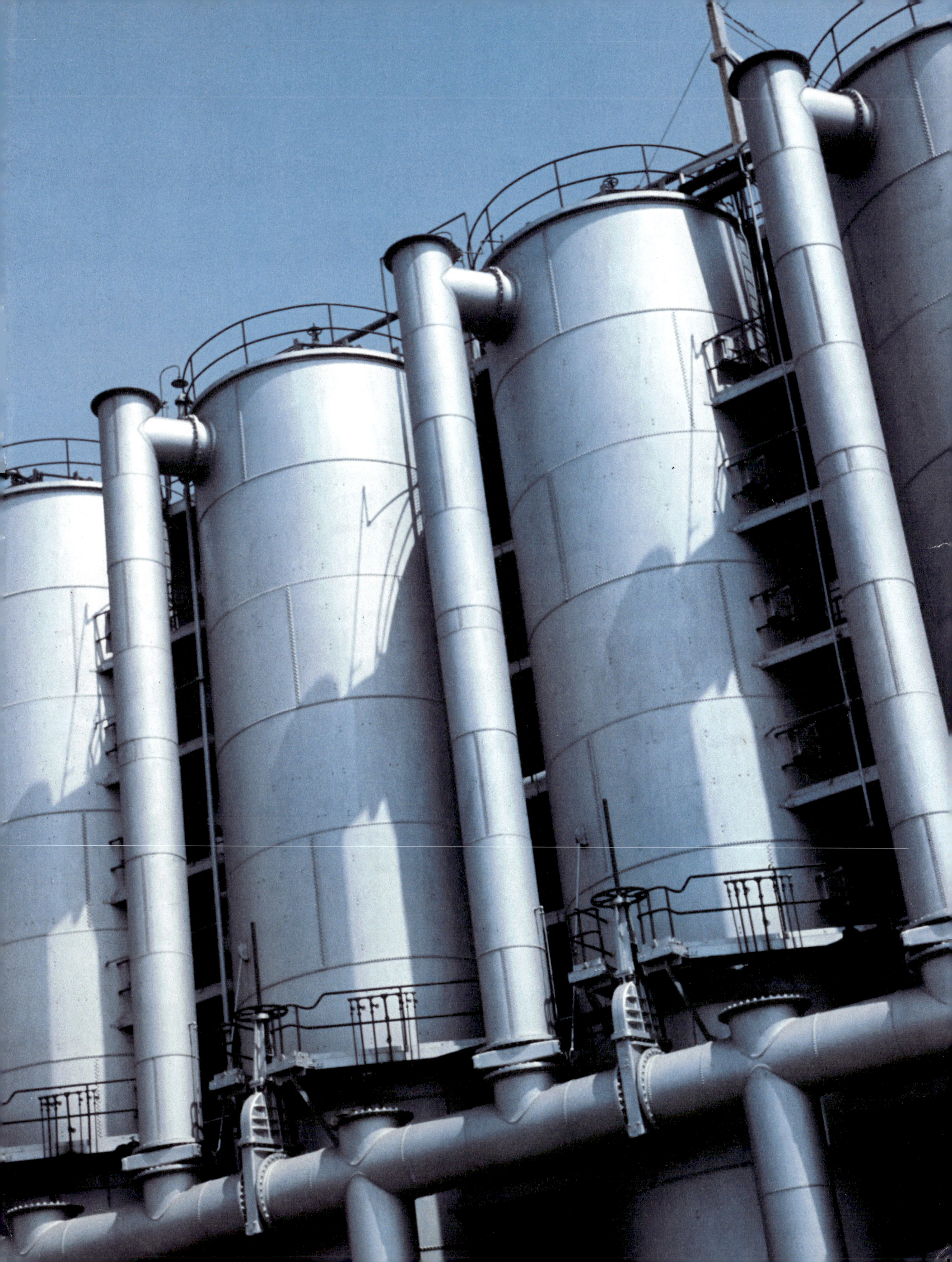

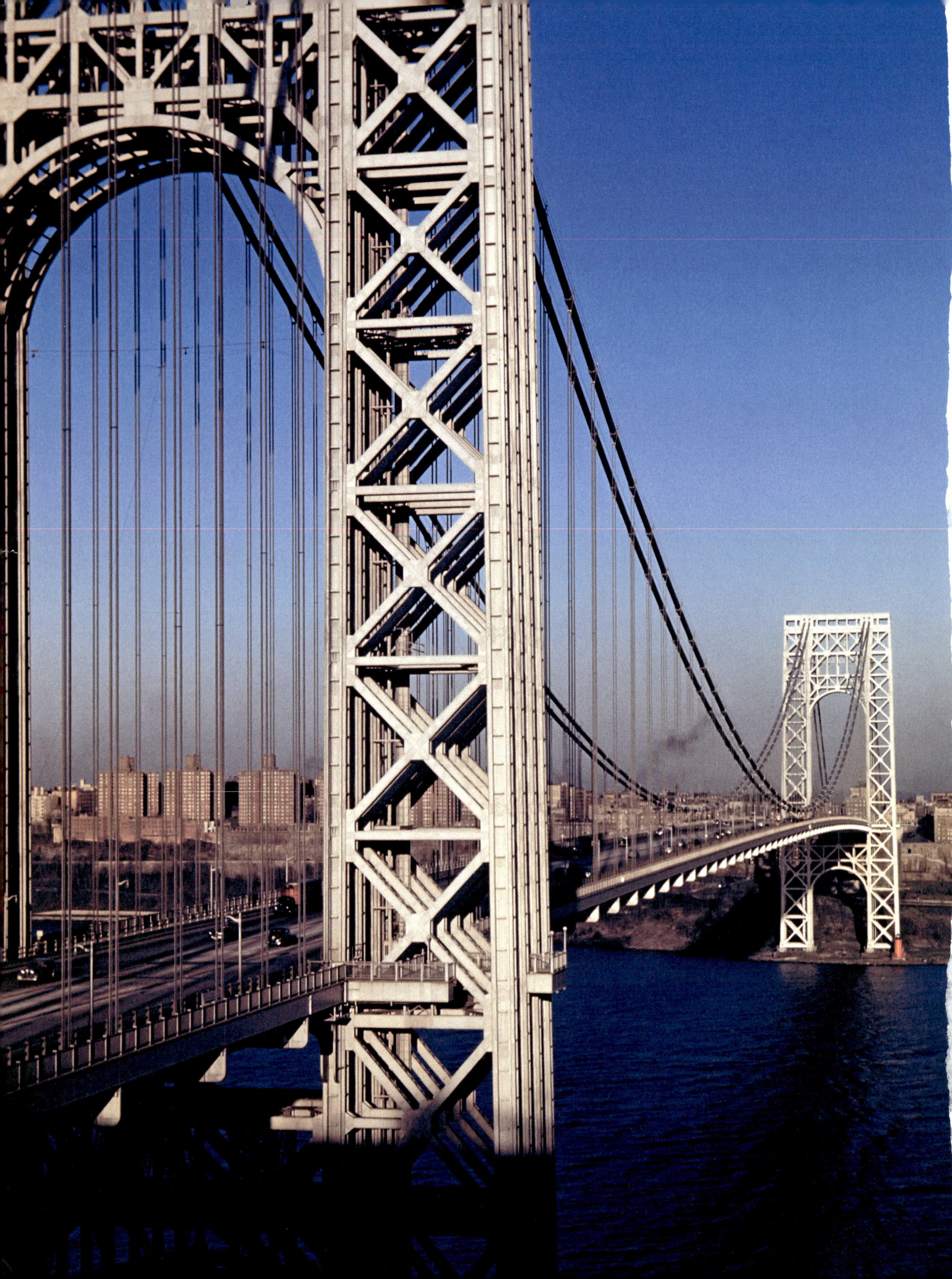

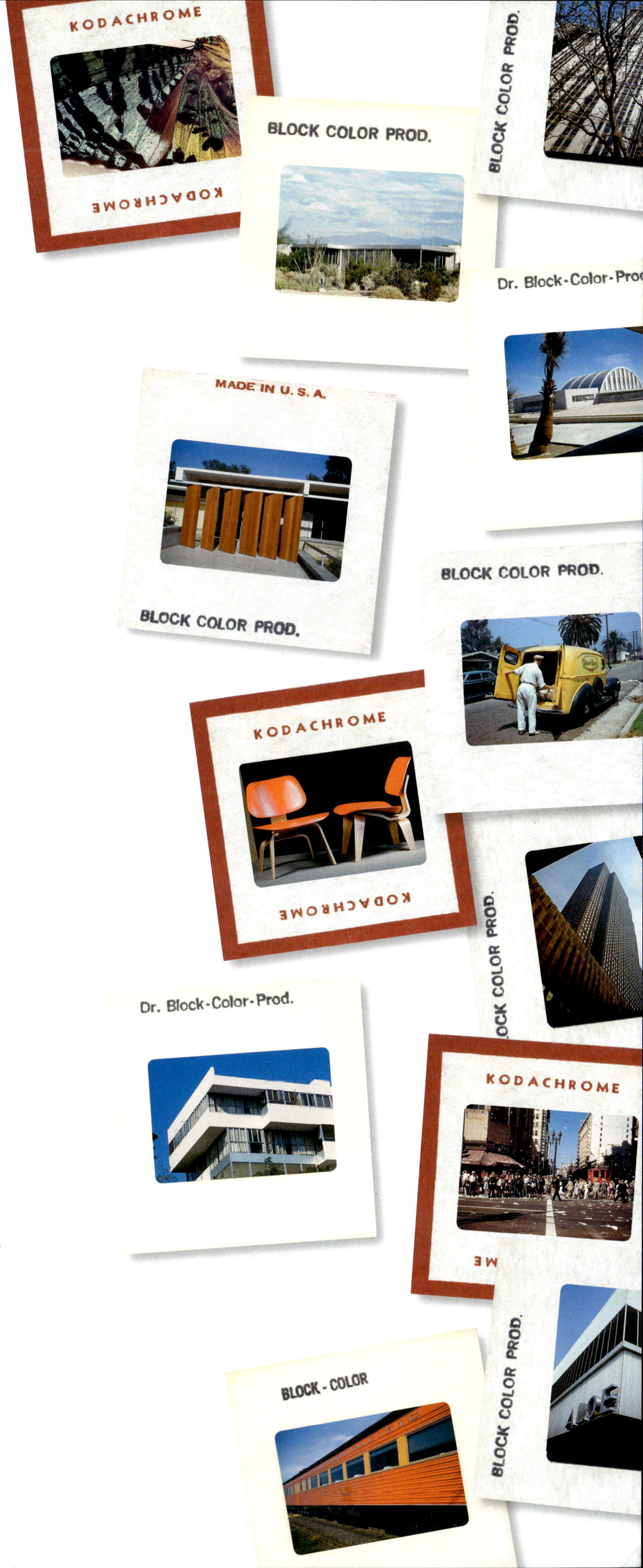

page 331
Ship's prow, Long Beach, 1948

page 332 / 333
Steel construction for an auditorium ceiling, Los Angeles, 1948

page 334
Smokestacks with steel struts, Los Angeles, 1948

page 335
Tanks, Los Angeles, 1948

page 336
George Washington Bridge, New York, ca. 1950

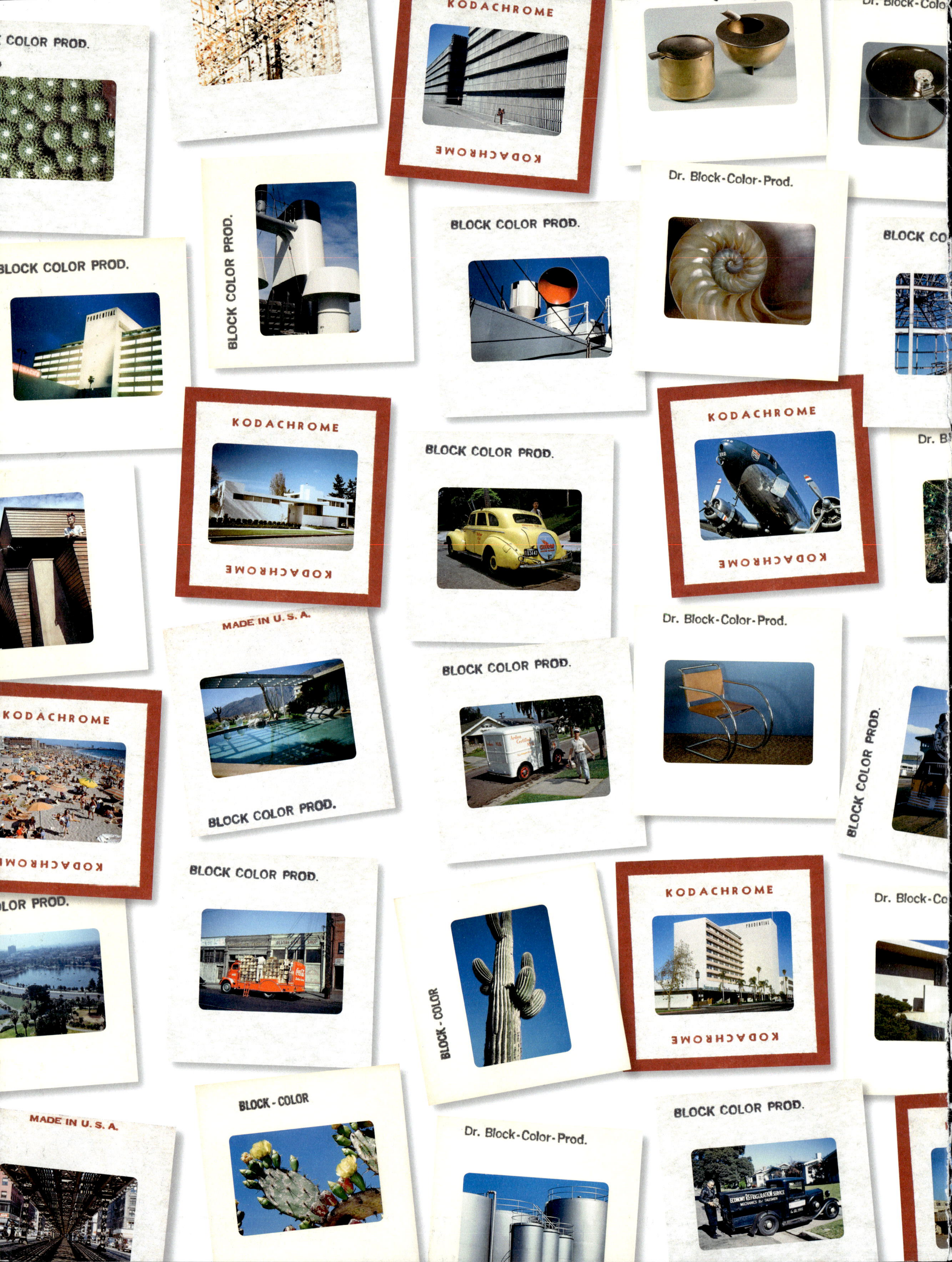
COLOR PROD.
KODACHROME
KODACHROME
Dr. Block-Colo
BLOCK COLOR PROD.
Dr. Block-Color-Prod.
BLOCK COLOR PROD.
BLOCK CO
BLOCK COLOR PROD.
KODACHROME
KODACHROME
BLOCK COLOR PROD.
KODACHROME
KODACHROME
Dr. Bl
MADE IN U.S.A.
Dr. Block-Color-Prod.
BLOCK COLOR PROD.
KODACHROME
KODACHROME
BLOCK COLOR PROD.
BLOCK COLOR PROD.
BLOCK COLOR PROD.
LOR PROD.
KODACHROME
KODACHROME
BLOCK-COLOR
Dr. Block-Co
MADE IN U.S.A.
BLOCK-COLOR
Dr. Block-Color-Prod.
BLOCK COLOR PROD.